Handbook of Social Work Practice
with Vulnerable and Resilient Populations

Handbook of Social Work Practice with Vulnerable and Resilient Populations

Alex Gitterman, editor

SECOND EDITION

COLUMBIA UNIVERSITY PRESS
New York

Columbia University Press
Publishers Since 1893
New York   Chichester, West Sussex

Second Edition, 2001

Library of Congress Cataloging-in-Publication Data

Handbook of social work practice with vulnerable and resilient
populations / Alex Gitterman, editor
        p.   cm.
  Includes bibliographical references and index.
  ISBN 978-0-231-11396-0(cloth : alk. paper)
      1. Social service—United States.   2. Social work with the
  socially handicapped—United States.   I. Gitterman, Alex

HV91 H265 2001
361.3'2—dc21
                                                      00-060144

Casebound editions of Columbia University Press books are
printed on permanent and durable acid-free paper.

Printed in the United States of America
c 10 9 8 7 6

*In memory of my dear friends and colleagues
Professors Sherman Barr, Carel B. Germain,
Mary Funnyé Goldson, Charles Grosser,
Melvin Herman, William Schwartz
and Hyman Weiner.*

*All were dedicated educators with profound
social vision.*

and

*In memory of Lisa S. Steinberg,
the daughter of close friends and colleagues,
an effervescent young woman,
whose genuine warmth, kindness, and zest for life
lives on in our hearts.*

TABLE OF CONTENTS

ACKNOWLEDGMENTS

I wish to express my deep appreciation to the contributors for their willingness to prepare a chapter for the *Handbook.* They accepted and carried out a difficult and comprehensive assignment.

I am very appreciative for their conscientiousness in following a demanding outline, their openness to editorial suggestions, their willingness to rewrite drafts, and their good spirit about my constant e-mailing and calling to "inquire" about their progress. I hope you will be as pleased as I am with their significant accomplishments and contributions to the profession's literature.

I also would like to thank John Michel, Senior Executive Editor, Columbia University Press, for his interest in and commitment to this project.

Finally, I am most grateful to my family and friends for their ongoing love and support.

A.G.

CONTRIBUTORS

Sheila H. Akabas, Ph.D.
Director, The Workplace Center,
Columbia University School of Social
Work

Bruce Armstrong, D.S.W.
Associate Clinical Professor,
Columbia University School of
Public Health, Center for Population
and Family Health

Toby Berman-Rossi, D.S.W.
Professor, Barry University School of
Social Work

Lori Bikson, J.D.
Ph.D. Candidate, Columbia
University School of Social Work

Ellen B. Bogolub, Ph.D.
Associate Professor, Adelphi
University School of Social Work

Susan Braiman, M.S.W.
Social Worker in Private Practice

Barbara von Bulow, Ph.D.
Associate Director, Columbia
Psychiatric Associates

Jay Callahan, Ph.D.
Director of Programs, National
Patient Safety Foundation

Bonnie E. Carlson, Ph.D.
Professor, School of Social Welfare,
Nelson A. Rockefeller College of
Public Affairs and Policy, The
University at Albany, State
University of New York

Deborah Choi, M.S.W.
Ph.D. Candidate, School of Social
Welfare, Nelson A. Rockefeller
College of Public Affairs and Policy,
The University at Albany, State
University of New York

Grace H. Christ, D.S.W.
Associate Professor, Columbia
University School of Social Work

Marcia B. Cohen, Ph.D.
Associate Professor, University of
New England School of Social Work

Jacqueline Corcoran, Ph.D.
Assistant Professor, University of
Texas School of Social Work,
Arlington

Barbara Oberhofer Dane, Ph.D.
Associate Professor, New York
University Shirley M. Ehrenkranz
School of Social Work

Diane Drachman, Ph.D.
Associate Professor, University
Connecticut School of Social Work

Prudence Fisher, M.S.
Research Scientist, New York State
Psychiatric Institute, Columbia
University College of Physicians and
Surgeons

Richard B. Francoeur, Ph.D.
Assistant Professor, Columbia
University School of Social Work

George S. Getzel, D.S.W.
Professor, Hunter College School of
Social Work

Alex Gitterman, Ed.D.
Professor, University of Connecticut
School of Social Work

Naomi Pines Gitterman, M.S.W.
Director, Social Work Program,
Mercy College

Joanne Gumpert, D.S.W.
Associate Professor, Marywood
University School of Social Work

Lorraine Gutiérrez, Ph.D.
Associate Professor, University of
Michigan School of Social Work

Meredith Hanson, D.S.W.
Associate Professor, Fordham
University, Graduate School of Social
Service

Nina Rovinelli Heller, Ph.D.
Associate Professor, University of
Connecticut School of Social Work

André Ivanoff, Ph.D.
Associate Professor, Columbia
University School of Social Work

Aurora P. Jackson, Ph.D.
Associate Professor, Pittsburgh
University School of Social Work

Harriette C. Johnson, Ph.D.
Professor, University of Connecticut
School of Social Work

Edith Lewis, Ph.D.
Associate Professor, University of
Michigan School of Social Work

Ellen Lukens, Ph.D.
Assistant Professor, Columbia
University School of Social Work

Michael Mancini, M.S.W.
Ph.D. Candidate, School of Social
Welfare, Nelson A. Rockefeller
College of Public Affairs and Policy,
The University at Albany, State
University of New York

Philip McCallion, Ph.D.
Assistant Professor, School of Social
Welfare, Nelson A. Rockefeller
College of Public Affairs and Policy,
The University at Albany, State
University of New York

Brenda G. McGowan, D.S.W.
Professor, Columbia University
School of Social Work

C. Aaron McNeece, Ph.D.
Professor, Florida State University
School of Social Work

Claudia L. Moreno, Ph.D.
Assistant Professor, Columbia
University School of Social Work

Albert R. Roberts, Ph.D.
Professor, Rutgers University

Angela Shen Ryan, Ph.D.
Professor, Hunter College School of
Social Work

Izumi Sakamoto, M.S.W.
  Ph.D. Candidate, University of
  Michigan School of Social Work

Joan E. Saltman, Ph.D.
  Assistant Professor, West Virginia
  University School of Social Work

Gregory C. Smith, Ed.D.
  Associate Professor, Department of
  Human Development, University of
  Maryland

Mary Sormanti, Ph.D.
  Assistant Professor, Columbia
  University School of Social Work

Ronald W. Toseland, Ph.D.
  Director, Rengel Institute of
  Gerontology, School of Social
  Welfare, Nelson A. Rockefeller
  College of Public Affairs and Policy,
  The University at Albany, State
  University of New York

Carol T. Tully, Ph.D.
  Associate Dean, Raymond A. Kent
  School of Social Work, University of
  Louisville

Joanne E. Turnbull, Ph.D.
  Executive Director, National Patient
  Safety Foundation

Ernst O. VanBergeijk, Ph.D.
  Assistant Professor, Fordham
  University Graduate School of Social
  Services

Lynn Videka-Sherman, Ph.D.
  Professor, School of Social Welfare,
  Nelson A. Rockefeller College of
  Public Affairs and Policy, The
  University at Albany, State
  University of New York

Nancy Boyd Webb, D.S.W.
  Professor, Fordham University
  Graduate School of Social Services

Stephen W. Willroth, M.S.W.
  Social Worker, New York
  Presbyterian Chelsea Center for
  Special Studies

PREFACE

The Handbook of Social Work Practice with Vulnerable Populations, published in 1991, focused on the debilitating circumstances and suffering faced by large sectors of our client population. Wherever social workers practice, they deal with people who are overwhelmed or burdened by stressful life conditions, circumstances, and events. The problems are stressful because they are either chronic and persistent, or they are acute and unexpected. They are frequently exacerbated by an individual's lack of internal resources or external supports or both. When these factors are present, social workers help people at risk of physical, cognitive, emotional, and social deterioration.

To respond to contemporary social realities and conditions, most social work schools have assumed a broad ecosystems perspective to reflect the complex relations between people and their environments. This perspective provides the bases for conceptualizing and teaching various professional methods (e.g., advocating, mediating) and integrated and generalist practice (e.g., individual, family, group, community). Several widely used social work texts conceptualize and illustrate this perspective. Though providing generic and generalist knowledge and skills, they waver in the specialized knowledge required to help the most severely vulnerable and powerless populations.

The *Handbook* met a significant need by providing specialized knowledge, methods, and skills. It was positively reviewed and adopted by advanced clinical and generalist programs. After the book's publication, I had a serious concern. Namely, the *Handbook* did not describe how people survive and cope with such debilitating problems as hunger, homelessness, AIDS, family and community violence, and traumatic losses or vulnerabilities such as the consequences of mental illness, developmental difficulties, imprisonment, or job loss. Since many of our theoretical approaches focus on individual pathology, other dimensions of the human experience such as resourcefulness, strengths, coping, courage, and recovery remain unrecognized. This unbalanced perspective may further marginalize and oppress our clients.

In the new edition, the focus is expanded to include resiliency and protective factors, the positive poles of the human experience, in order to examine such questions as: Why do some people collapse under certain life conditions and circumstances while others remain relatively unscathed? What accounts for the marked individual variations in people's responses to stress and adversity? What accounts for the surprisingly large number of people who somehow, at times miraculously, manage their adversities? How do people adapt, cope, overcome, and meet the challenges of physical and mental conditions, severe losses and traumas, and chronic discrimination and oppression? Why do some people thrive and not simply survive in the face of life's inhumanities and tragedies?

Webster's dictionary defines *resilience* as "the tendency to rebound or recoil, to return to prior state, to spring back." The process of regaining functioning following on the footsteps of adversity does not suggest that one is incapable of being wounded or injured. Rather, a person can bend, lose some of his or her power and capability, yet recover and return to prior level of adaptation. Thus, one important element in the study of resilience lies in the power of recovery and the protective factors that cushion the blows. Other elements include the person:environment processes that help people to overcome severe obstacles and function competently. This knowledge is essential to social work practice.

Social workers who develop knowledge and curiosity about the positive as well as the negative poles of people's lives are more likely to formulate balanced assessments and responsive interventions. People's life stories, for example, represent their search to find meaning and coherence in their own lives. By inviting and attentively listening to people's life stories rather than fitting their behaviors into diagnostic schema and labels, we are more likely to discover how people have managed to survive in stressful or traumatic circumstances. And their strengths provide the foundation and motivation for further mastery (De Jong and Miller 1995; Germain and Gitterman 1996; Hurd, Moore, and Rogers 1995; Saleebey 1997).

Children dealing with parental alcoholism or divorce, for example, find ways to disengage and to develop psychological distance from daily conflicts and hassles. The social worker must assess the potential functional and dysfunctional dimensions of the emotional distancing. Adaptive distancing requires the ability to disengage internally while pursuing and sustaining external connections. The combination of internal distancing and external reaching out represent significant protective factors and processes. In contrast, a flight into social as well as emotional isolation symbolizes risk factors and processes. For another example, in helping a disheveled, odorous, homeless woman, the social worker must understand the function that smelling and unattractiveness have in coping with sexual vulnerability and potential violence as well as the dysfunctional aspects of alienating potential support networks.

Research studies identify various protective factors that mediate, moderate, or ameliorate risk of maladaptive outcomes. They include individual factors such as temperament and self-esteem; family factors such as attachment to at least one person and consistent parenting; and external supports such as responsiveness of relatives, peer group, and social and community institutions. A configuration of these factors creates processes that either increase the protective cushions and opportunities provided by the social environment and/or dissipate the impact of risk factors by modifying the risk or people's exposure to it, or decreasing the potential negative chain reaction (Smith and Carlson 1997). In the new edition, significant content is added in each chapter on resilience and protective factors and their relevance for assessment and interventions. To reflect this reconceptualization, the book's title is changed to: *The Handbook of Social Work Practice with Vulnerable and Resilient Populations.*[1]

What does the social worker need *to know* and be able *to do* to provide resourceful programmatic and clinical services to such populations? The *Handbook* explores these questions, according to two distinctive sets of issues. Part I, "Life Conditions," examines social work practice with vulnerable and resilient populations who essentially have to cope with chronic life conditions that have dynamic genetic, biochemical, and physiological bases. Chapters on AIDS, alcoholism and other drug addictions, borderline personality, chronic physical illness and disability, depression, developmental disabilities, eating problems, learning disabilities, and schizophrenia, all explore the theoretical, empirical, demographic, programmatic, and clinical issues with which social workers need to be familiar to provide relevant and empowering services.

Part II, "Life Circumstances and Events," examines social work practice with populations that often confront desperate life circumstances such as homelessness and very stressful life events such as the death of a child. Why do some people collapse under relatively minor life strains while others remain relatively unscathed by traumatic experiences such as extreme poverty, racism, homophobia, family violence, sexual and other forms of abuse, or loss of a loved one? Why do some people emotionally survive catastrophe while others become bitter, jaded, and less of a person than they were previously? How do some people forge ahead when life seems unbearable—when trust and hope might have been taken away—yet others are so emotionally vulnerable that seemingly minor losses and rebuffs can be devastating? Chapters on adolescent pregnancy, child abuse and neglect, children in foster care, crime victims, death of a child, death of a parent, divorce, families in sparsely populated areas, family caregivers of the frail elderly, gay and lesbian persons, homelessness, immigrants and refugees, imprisonment and community corrections, intimate partner abuse, older persons in need of long-term care, single parenthood, suicide, women of color, and workers in job jeopardy similarly explore the theoretical, empirical, demographic, programmatic, and clinical issues.

A common chapter outline integrates the chapters as each contributor begins with a theoretical, empirical, and political examination of the subject. This discussion is followed by a demographic exploration of the specific population and its subpopulations. For example, in a discussion of homelessness, the problems and needs of those who are mentally ill are differentiated from those who became homeless because of job loss and eviction. Each chapter examines the respective population's and subpopulations' vulnerabilities and risk factors as well as resilience and protective factors. Each chapter also describes programs and social work contributions and discusses how the social worker assesses the client's (individual, family, group, community) life stresses, their internal resources and limitations, apparent obstacles and available environmental supports, and how the social worker intervenes depending on her or his understanding of the condition, circumstance, and event. Distinctive practice principles and skills are highlighted. Finally, each chapter concludes with the presentation of an illustration according to two foci: (1) an erudition in microcosm of the particular life issue and (2) an identification and analysis of the particular aspects of assessment and interventions generalizable from the particular illustration.[2]

While, historically, the profession of social work has assumed the task of providing social services to disadvantaged and vulnerable populations, this task has become significantly more difficult to fulfill. For the stubborn truth is that problems have been increasing, while resources to mitigate them decrease. Those with less get less! The societal response to the needs of these populations has become increasingly punitive and rejecting. Given these bitter realities, resilience and heroism are required not only from the client population but from the social work community as well. And this has been actually the case among many social workers in their efforts to provide meaningful services. Through descriptions of responsive social programs and social work's contributions to them and presentation and discussion of practice illustrations, this book attempts to capture the profession's resilience and creativity.

Alex Gitterman

Notes

1. Caveat: A *New Yorker* magazine cartoon shows a man drowning and a lifeguard taking his eyes from a magazine to inform concerned bathers: "We're encouraging people to become involved in their own rescue." I am concerned about the current popularity of concepts like resilience and empowerment. In desperate times, the profession's language is becoming more romantic and flowery. We want to make explicit that by resilience we are not promoting the myth that any person can succeed if he or she simply works hard enough.
2. In the new edition, the authors were encouraged to illustrate family, group, community, and programming practice as well as individual practice.

References

De Jong, P. and S. D. Miller. 1995. "How to Interview for Client's Strengths." *Social Work* 40(6):729–36.

Germain, C. B. and A. Gitterman. 1996. *The Life Model of Social Work Practice: Advances in Knowledge and Practice.* New York: Columbia University Press.

Hurd, E. P., C. Moore, and R. Rogers. 1995. "Quiet Success: Parenting Strengths Among African Americans." *Families in Society* 76(September):434–42.

Saleebey, D., ed. 1997. *The Strengths Perspective in Social Work Practice.* New York: Longman.

Smith, C. and B. Carlson. 1997. "Stress, Coping, and Resilience in Children and Youth." *Social Service Review* 71(2):231–56.

Handbook of Social Work Practice
with Vulnerable and Resilient Populations

1

Social Work Practice with Vulnerable and Resilient Populations

Alex Gitterman

Through my teaching and practice experiences, I have become distressed by the increasing degradation and distress faced by large sectors of the client population served by social workers. Students and professionals confront daily the crushing impact of such problems as mental illness, substance abuse, disability and death, teenage pregnancy, and child neglect and physical and sexual abuse. Clients suffer from the debilitating effects of such life circumstances as homelessness, violence, family disintegration, and unemployment. The miseries and human suffering encountered by social workers in the new millennium are different in degree and kind from those encountered in the 1960s, 1970s, 1980s, and 1990s. The dismantling of the welfare state and the consequences of welfare "reform" are examples of newly devastating social phenomena.

Social workers in practice today deal with profoundly vulnerable populations, overwhelmed by oppressive lives, and circumstances and events they are powerless to control. The problems are often intractable because they are chronic and persistent, or acute and unexpected. When community and family supports are weak or unavailable and when internal resources are impaired, these populations are very vulnerable to physical, cognitive, emotional, and social deterioration. Yet, in spite of numerous risk factors and vulnerabilities, a surprisingly large number of children, for example, mature into normal, happy adults. Why do some people remain relatively unscathed and somehow, at times, miraculously manage their adversities? Why do some thrive and not simply survive in the face of life's inhumanities and tragedies? To more fully understand the human experience, this book examines both vulnerability and risk factors as well as resilience and protective factors.

DEFINING AND EXPLAINING LIFE CONDITIONS, CIRCUMSTANCES, AND EVENTS

After a brief introduction about the respective population, contributors analyze the definitions of the life condition, circumstance, or event. What are the different political and theoretical definitions and explanations of the condition, circumstance, or event? What are the effects of the definitions and explanations on the larger community, service providers, and service users? With certain "personality conditions" such as chronic depression, schizophrenia, and borderline personality, and with certain addictions such as alcoholism, growing evidence suggests potent predisposing genetic, biochemical factors. Researchers' studies have, for example, analyzed the life careers of identical twins separated at birth and have used other tracking designs to find significant genetic linkages to alcoholism (Cloninger 1983, 1987; Cloninger, Bohman, and Sigvardsson 1981; Cloninger, Sigvardsson, and Bohman 1988; Goodwin et al. 1973), borderline personality (Andrulonis et al. 1981), depression (Gershon 1983; Mendlewicz and Rainer 1977; Wender et al. 1986), and schizophrenia (Feldman, Stiffman, and Jung 1987; Kety 1988).

These conditions have in common certain genetic and neurochemical predisposition. With alcoholism, for example, serotonin, a synthesized molecule in the brain, has been associated with depression. Experiments with rats have shown that when levels of serotonin have been decreased, the result was a marked increase in alcohol consumption. In contrast, raising the levels of serotonin resulted in a pronounced reduction of alcohol intake (Zhukov, Varkof, and Burov 1987). Based on a review of research, Wallace (1989) identified different types of alcoholics: (1) the "hyper-aroused," who may suffer from too high a level of serotonin and seek out alcohol to sedate and blot out stimulation overload; and (2) the "anhedonic," who may suffer from a too low level of serotonin and seek alcohol to excite and arouse and compensate for stimulation underload. The brain also manufactures natural substances that have pain-killing properties. Blum and Topel (1986) found the less this substance was present in mice, the more they consumed alcohol. Thus, genetically induced chemical imbalances appear to be associated with various life conditions.

With AIDS, our vulnerability to parasitic relations with microorganisms from within and without is ominous. AIDS has become the leading cause of death among all Americans aged 25 to 44. The biological reality of AIDS demonstrates how defenseless our immune systems can be to parasitic and toxic environments. With other life conditions such as anorexia and bulimia, the genetic linkages have not yet been discovered. Thus far, personality and family dynamic explanations are most frequently offered to explain these conditions. We should not, however, be surprised if in the near future genetic and biochemical predisposing conditions are discovered. With obesity, however, there is clear evidence of genetic influence (Foch and McClearn 1980).

Chronic physical illnesses and disabilities and learning and developmental disabilities reflect problematic physiological and neurological functions. Developmental disability often has genetic determinants (Abuelo 1983; Dickerson 1981). Similarly, a possible genetic basis for the condition of Alzheimer's disease (Schmeck 1987a) and cancer has also been identified (Schmeck 1987b, 1987c). Even though many of the presented life conditions have genetic determinants, they may not be inherited. Certain toxic environmental agents can damage and disrupt normal genetic processes. A mother abusing alcohol, for example, may give birth to an infant with fetal alcohol syndrome, which is often characterized by developmental disability, facial deformity, etc. Radiation can cause infertility and birth defects (Rauch 1988). Whatever the cause, physiological and cognitive impairments severely curtail human activities. People with these life conditions often suffer for protracted and indefinite time periods. Their neurological and physiological disabilities create limitations and burdens of varying severity.

Genetic, biochemical, neurological loading, and predisposition to a condition does not imply, however, that a person will necessarily acquire the condition or, if the person does acquire it, will be debilitated by the condition. The resources and the limitations in the person's environment, i.e., family, relatives, friends, workmates, neighbors, community, organizations, and spiritual life, all transact with individual constitutional resources and limits. On one end of the continuum, high genetic and organic loading may push certain people toward alcoholism, depression, borderline personality, or schizophrenia regardless of how protective and supportive the environment (albeit a supportive environment can certainly cushion its consequences). Similarly, a youngster born developmentally disabled or severely physically disabled has to function within the constraints of these neurophysiological impairments. Although supportive environments can provide essential instrumental and expressive resources, they cannot eliminate the disability itself. On the other end of the continuum, severely impoverished and invalidating environments may push certain people toward alcoholism or depression no matter how well they are constitutionally endowed. A youngster repeatedly exposed to malnourishment and physical and emotional abuse may succumb to these harsh environmental assaults by alcoholism or depression with limited, or even without, genetic predisposition. Studies of psychiatric epidemiology have demonstrated that the lower the social class, the higher the rates of mental illness and the greater the severity of the mental illness (Dohrenwend and Dohrenwend 1981; Hollingshead and Redlich 1958).

Family, community, and society dysfunctions provide the most frequent theoretical explanations for the distressing life circumstances and events presented in this book. Unplanned pregnancies, for example, are associated with poverty, repeated academic failures, and pervasive lack of opportunities with consequent hopelessness and despair. Community and family norms reinforce or mitigate the personal impact of poverty. In intimate partner violence, the female as victim of her male partner is the principal problem. A pattern of control over the female maintained by physical, emotional, and sexual abuse is associated with violence and battering. On a more general level, sexism and sex-role socialization surely contribute to, if not induce, intimate partner violence. Boys observing their fathers abuse their mothers are more likely than otherwise to be violent toward their own wives (Gelles and Straus 1988). Clearly, intimate partner violence is learned behavior that has to be unlearned.

No citizen, regardless of class or social status, is safe from crime. Women, children, and the elderly, especially those living in poor communities, are at highest risk of victimization by crime. They simply are easier prey! Perpetrators tend to be caught in a cycle of family poverty, illiteracy, drugs, racism, child abuse, and family violence. When they are incarcerated, they usually return to their community further damaged, hardened, and embittered. They often become socialized to a lifetime of crime and intermittent incarceration. In poor communities, both the victim and the perpetrator are trapped in the mire of despair. Similarly, the elimination of low-income housing, underemployment and unemployment, sharply curtailed and disappearing benefit programs, and unplanned and unprovided for deinstitutionalization have all conspired to create homelessness and an unconscionably large number of adults and children deprived of the basic human need for shelter.

The life event of being born black in the United States creates a trajectory with profound impact on education, employment, housing, health, and family life. For example, African Americans suffer higher death rates from most major causes. They receive less and poorer health care and die six to seven years earlier than do whites (Kilborn 1998). For another example, over the last several decades major changes have taken place in the composition of African American families. In the 1950s, 78 percent of black families were composed of couples. However, in 1991 only 48 percent were composed of couples. During the same period, white family composition experienced only a minor decline, from 88 percent to 83 percent (U.S. Bureau of the Census 1993).

When people find themselves in distressing life circumstances and dealing with stressful or traumatic life events, some become helpless, hopeless victims. They live on the margin struggling for day-to-day survival. Others somehow miraculously and astonishingly manage deeply adverse situations as survivors not as victims. Various theories attempt to explain what differentiates a victim from a survivor. Unfortunately, most of our theories have focused on the deficits and negative aspects of individual and family life. Since many of our theoretical approaches are based on people who do not rebound well from life's miseries, we know much less about those who do and how they do it. Rutter (1971) eloquently captures this pattern:

> There is a most regrettable tendency to focus gloomily on the ills of mankind and on all that can and does go wrong. It is quite exceptional for anyone to study the development of those important individuals who overcome adversity, who survive stress and rise above disadvantage. (7)

By developing knowledge about the positive as well as the negative poles of people's lives, social workers are more likely to formulate balanced assessments and responsive interventions. For example, children dealing with parental alcoholism or divorce must find ways to disengage and to develop psychological distance from daily conflicts and hassles. Adaptive distancing requires the ability to disengage internally while pursuing and sustaining external connections (Berlin and Davis 1989).

Many theoretical explanations pathologize the African American family. By evaluating and judging from the outside, however, we miss the resourceful survival adaptations, such as that: "They 1. may be comprised of several households, 2. have a multiple parenting and inter familial consensual adoptions; 3. are child-centered; 4. have a close network of relationships between families not necessarily related by blood; and 5. have flexible and interchangeable role definitions and performance" (Fine and Schwebel 1991:34). These features provide the kinds of conditions that nurture the development of "protective" factors that also promote resilience. That many poor families of color survive extreme poverty, racism, and oppression is a tribute to their resilience in overcoming overwhelming odds.

While various theories attempt to explain what differentiates a victim from a survivor, no single theory is apparently capable of providing a comprehensive explanation. We do know, however, that people's social functioning and adaptations reflect the interplay and degree of congruence and compatibility between body, mind, and environment. Sometimes people's exchanges with their environments are mutually fulfilling. The congruence and compatibility between people and their environments provide the context for realization of potential. Other times, these exchanges can lead to isolation and alienation. A poor fit limits realization of potential. How people perceive their constitutional and environmental resources and limitations, their personal attributions and social constructions, also have a profound impact. Thus, two people with similar constitutional and environmental attributes may perceive subjectively their personal and environmental resources quite differently and consequently function at differing levels. And, finally, there is the simple element of chance—good fortune and misfortune. Although our efforts to be scientific may cause us to shy away from the idea of chance, it may well enhance our understanding and feeling for the human experience.

DEMOGRAPHIC PATTERNS

Each contributing author in this text presents available demographic data about the particular life condition, circumstance, or event. *Webster's* dictionary defines *vulnerability* as "capable of being wounded; open to attack or damage." Research into physical and emotional "wounding" consistently identifies two associated risk factors for physical and emotional deterioration: *prolonged stress* and *cumulative stress.* And among many factors, chronic poverty is the major force responsible for both prolonged and cumulative stress.

In 1996, 36.5 million people lived in poverty (income less than $15,569 for a family of four). Moreover, 14.4 million people met the definition of being very poor (income of $7,500 or less for a family of four). While older adults (65 and over) represent 12 percent of the population, they comprise only 9 percent of the poor. In contrast, children under 18 represent approximately one-fourth of the population, but they comprise an astonishing 40 percent of the poor. Younger children (under age 6) are particularly vulnerable to poverty, representing 22.7 percent of the nation's poor (Lamison-White 1996). Poverty creates chronic disadvantages and problems for children. Poor children are more likely to have difficulties in school as well as attend inferior schools, more likely to become teen parents, and more likely as adults to earn less and to be unemployed more than advantaged children.

A strong correlation between poverty and family structure is evident. Namely, children living in one-parent families are more likely to be poor than those living in two-parent families. Over the last three decades we have witnessed a dramatic change in family structure and living arrangements. Between 1970 and 1996, the number of divorced persons has grown from 4.3 million to 18.3 million (more than quadrupled). During the same period of time, the number of never-married adults dramatically grew from 21.4 million to 44.9 million (more than doubled). Women living alone doubled from 7.3 million to 14.6 million, while the number of men tripled from 3.5 million to 10.3 million (U.S. Bureau of the Census 1996). The 1997 Census reported that since 1980, the number of single mothers has increased by more than 50 percent, from 6.2 million to 9.9 million (U.S. Bureau of the Census 1997).

In 1996, 28 percent of children under 18 years of age lived with one parent as compared with only 12 percent in 1970. Similarly, in 1996, 68 percent of children lived with two parents as compared with 85 percent in 1970. One quarter (24 percent) of children lived only with their mothers and 4 percent only with their fathers and 4 percent with neither (Federal Interagency Forum on Child and Family Statistics 1997:10).

Of the children under age 6 living in a single-parent female family, 58.8 percent were poor compared with only 11.5 percent of these children living in married-couple families. In 1995, the median income of married-couple households is triple that of female households and more than double of male households (Lamison-White 1996). Table 1.1 presents the actual median family income among families with children under age 18 by family type (Federal Interagency Forum on Child and Family Statistics 1997:67). The dramatic increase in single-parent, female households forebodes a worsening economic trend for our nation's children.

Black children have a significantly lesser chance of being raised in a two-parent household than do white children. In 1996, only 33 percent of black children lived with two parents as compared with 75 percent of white children. As table 1.2 indicates, more than half of black children under 18 are being raised by a single mother (Federal Interagency Forum on Child and Family Statistics 1997:64). Only 13 percent of black children in married-couple families lived in poverty as compared with 62 percent of black children living in female household families. (A similar pattern is evident with Hispanic families—28 percent compared with 66 percent [U.S. Bureau

TABLE 1.1 Median Family Income Among Families with Children Under Age 18, by Family Type, Selected Years 1979–95 (in 1995 dollars)*

Family Type	1979	1985	1991	1993	1995
Married couple	$46,579	$45,818	$47,571	$48,038	$49,969
Female household	16,881	14,271	14,560	14,209	16,235
Male household	—	—	27,046	23,570	26,990

*Table adapted and presented in summary form.

TABLE 1.2 Family Structure: Living Arrangements of Children Under Age 18, by Race and Hispanic Origin, Selected Years 1970–96*

Family Type	1970	1980	1990	1992	1994	1996
Two parents						
White	90	83	79	77	76	75
Black	58	42	38	36	33	33
Hispanic	78	75	67	65	63	62
Mother only						
White	8	14	16	18	18	18
Black	30	44	51	54	52	53
Hispanic	—	20	27	28	28	29

*Table adapted and presented in summary form. Persons of Hispanic origin may be of any race. Each race category includes Hispanics of that race.

of the Census 1996:14].) Thus, based on their structural position in the U.S. economy, single mothers and their children are at risk of prolonged and cumulative stress.

The 1998 U.S. Census Bureau reported that Hispanic persons of any race comprised 11.1 percent of the total population of 268.8 million (U.S. Bureau of the Census 1998; see table 1.3). While comprising only 11.1 of the country's population, Hispanic persons of any race comprise 24 percent of the nation's poor. In 1995, the median household income of Hispanic residents fell 5.1 percent while it rose for all other ethnic and racial groups. Goldberg (1997) noted, "For the first time, the poverty rate among Hispanic residents of the U.S. has surpassed that of blacks" (A1). Thirty percent of all Hispanic residents live in poverty—almost three times the percentage of non-Hispanic whites in poverty.

Language and schooling appear to account for the growing ethnic and racial disparity. For example, in 1994, 12.7 percent of white persons and 15.5 percent of black persons did not complete high school as compared with 34.7 percent of Hispanic persons (Goldberg 1997). By 1996 and over the last quarter century, approximately one-third of Hispanic persons ages 16 to 24 years lacked a high school degree and were not enrolled in school, with 50 percent having completed less than a tenth-grade education (The National Center for Education Statistics 1996). Moreover, Hispanic persons are the fastest-growing ethnic group in the United States. As shown in table 1.4, by the year 2050, the Hispanic population is expected to increase to 23 percent of the total projected population of 391 million (Ozawa 1997). These data suggest that in the decades to come the Hispanic population will account for an increasing proportion of poor in this country because they are insufficiently prepared to compete in a highly technical society.

TABLE 1.3 Resident 1997 Population of the United States: Estimates by Race and Hispanic Origin (Numbers in thousands)

Race	Population	Percentage
White, not Hispanic	194,926	72.5
Black, not Hispanic	32,466	12.1
Hispanic, any race	29,802	11.1
Asian/Pacific Islander	9,584	3.6
American Indian, Eskimo and Aleut, not Hispanic	1,986	0.7

TABLE 1.4 Comparison of Percentage of United States Resident Population in 1995 and Projected Population in 2050 by Race and Hispanic Origin

Race	1995	2050
White, not Hispanic	72.5	53
Black, not Hispanic	12.1	13
Hispanic, any race	11.1	23
Asian/Pacific Islander	3.6	10
American Indian, Eskimo and Aleut, not Hispanic	0.7	1

SOCIETAL CONTEXT

After a discussion of the definitions and demographics of the distressing life condition, circumstance, or event, the authors examine how social structures and institutions cushion, aggregate, or "cause" the problems in question. When social structures and institutions provide essential resources and supports, they are critical buffers, helping people cope with life transitions, environments, and interpersonal stressors (Germain and Gitterman 1996). By providing emotional, instrumental, informational, and appraisal supports, society structures influence the worldviews and self-concepts of people and fortify them against physiological, psychological, and social harm (Gottlieb 1988a, 1988b). In contrast, when these resources and supports are unavailable, or insufficient, people are apt to feel helpless and lack self-confidence and skill in interpersonal and environmental coping.

Economy. In the United States, the rich continue to become richer; the poor become poorer. In essence, the gap between the poor and the wealthy, the unskilled and the skilled is widening.[1] For example, Bill Gates has greater wealth than half of the people in the United States put together. Larder (1998) reported, "Since the 1970's, virtually all our income gains have gone to the highest-earning 20 percent of our households, producing inequality greater than at any time since the 1930's, and greater than in any of the world's other rich nations" (C1).

Broad changes in the economy have further victimized the poor. The demand for low-skilled workers has significantly declined. Over the last two decades blue-collar and lower-income workers wages have eroded. Gradually and consistently many manufacturing plants have closed, resulting in significant job losses (Danziger 1997). The loss of blue-collar and lower-income jobs has created severe economic hardships. At the same time, service industries have grown rapidly and created millions of new jobs, requiring new and advanced technical skills not possessed by many in the manufacturing industry.

Not only have these workers lost jobs, but their real wages have also declined. Among males between the ages of 25 and 44, only those who completed more than a college degree, a very small percentage, had a higher inflation-adjusted earnings in 1993 than in 1973 (Danziger 1997). The enormity of the decline in blue-collar and lower-income wages is captured by Passell (1998):

> The median wage of those with only a high school diploma fell by 6 percent, adjusted for inflation from 1980 to 1996, while earnings of college graduates rose by 12 percent. . . . In 1982, people in the top one-tenth of the work force made $24.80 an hour, 3.95 times the $6.28 an hour for workers in the bottom one-tenth. By 1996 the wage gap widened with then high-end workers averaging $25.74 an hour, or 4.72 times the $5.46 an hour of those at the bottom. (1)

Blue-collar and lower-income workers are less marketable and have difficulty competing in an information and technologically driven economy.

Not only have blue-collar and lower-income workers lost jobs and had their real wages decline, they also have suffered from significant discrepancies in job benefits and quality of work life. The comparative decline in their job benefits swells the discrepancy between high- and low-wage earners. For example, the entire compensation package in 1982 of workers earning in the top 10 percent ($35.16 a hour) was 4.56 times higher than that of workers in the bottom 10 percent ($7.72 an hour). By 1996, the disparity grew even wider with highly paid workers gaining $1.73 an hour and low-end workers losing 93 cents an hour and the ratio increasing to 5.43 to 1. Passell (1998) provides two additional examples:

> More than 80 percent of workers received paid holidays and vacations in 1996, but less than 10 percent of those in the bottom tenth received paid leave of any kind. Similarly, about 70 percent of workers have pension plans, while less than 10 percent of those in the bottom can count on any employer-financed retirement benefits. Access to health insurance follows a similar pattern. (28)

Clearly, those on the bottom of the economic ladder are competing for a decreasing pool of nontechnical jobs, at lower wages, with greater discrepancies in job benefits and quality of work life.

The transformation in the U.S. economy has not affected all groups equally. A large and growing number of young black males are hopelessly locked into a life of unemployment. The dramatic economic changes intensified by our country's long history of racism and discrimination have left the black family extremely vulnerable. Already in the 1960s, the national rate for unemployed black men between the ages of 18 to 24 was five times as high as that of white males of the same age (Clark 1965:34). Whereas the previously slave-exploited agricultural economy required relatively unskilled labor, our increasingly automated and service economy requires skilled labor. Therefore, the economy now has little need for the unskilled black male. Wilhelm and Powell (1964) suggest that our economy no longer needs the black male:

> He is not so much unwanted as unnecessary; not so much abused as ignored. The dominant whites no longer need to exploit him. If he disappears tomorrow he would hardly be missed. As automation proceeds it is easier and easier to disregard him . . . thus, he moves to the automated urbanity of "no-bidiness." (4)

Lack of employment opportunities institutionalizes poverty and its varied consequences.

The environment of poor people is particularly harsh. Because of their economic position, they are unable to command needed goods and services. Good education, preventive health care, jobs, housing, safe communities, neighborhood amenities, and geographic and social mobility are unavailable or extremely limited for the poor. They are not able to compete for societal resources and their leverage on social institutions is extremely limited. A devastating cycle of physical, psychological, and social consequences follow. And with the government reducing its role in providing a safety net, the plight of poor, particularly poor children, can only worsen.

Legislation. In 1996, President Clinton signed into law the welfare "reform" act—the Personal Responsibility and Work Opportunity Reconciliation Act (PRWORA). This federal law imposed work requirements and a sixty-month lifetime time limit, promising to "end welfare as we know it." The new law's manifest purpose was to end public assistance recipients' dependence on the government and create economic independence and self-reliance by limiting benefits to a maximum of five years and by providing job training and employment opportunities.[2] Some believe that the new legislation's latent and real purpose is to punish poor women for having children "they shouldn't have had"—through stigma, economic deprivation, work requirements, and lack of provision of child care.

The campaign to gain the public's approval and to pressure the president to sign PRWORA into law conveniently ignored the fact that in 1995 approximately two-thirds of the recipients receiving Aid to Families with Dependent Children were children and only one-third were adults (U.S. House of Representatives 1996). With the projected changes in public assistance, according to the Urban Institute, 3,500,000 children will be dropped from the rolls in 2001. By 2005, 4,896,000 children will be cut off. The new law will cause 2.6 million persons to fall below the poverty line. Those currently in poverty will be pushed further below the poverty line.

The legislation does not differentiate between short-term and long-term public assistance recipients. Yet, as an Urban Institute report indicates, they differ in important ways:

> Long-term recipients displayed more depressive symptoms, had less of a sense of personal control over their lives, and had fewer social supports than short-term recipients. Long-term recipients also provided their children with less cognitive stimulation and emotional support than did short-term recipients, and the children themselves scored lower on measures of receptive vocabulary and social maturity. Children from families who are more likely to reach the time limits thus appear to be at higher risk already. (Zaslow et al. 1998:5–6)

The question becomes, which families are more likely to be long-term recipients and, therefore, reach time limits without a viable alternative? Apparently, a surprise to many legislators (but not to most social workers) is the fact that black and Hispanic mothers and their children are at much greater risk than white mothers of reaching the time limits. While the number of people receiving public assistance has dramatically declined, white recipients are finding employment and leaving the welfare system at a disproportionately faster rate than black and Hispanic recipients.

Until recently, the majority of public assistance recipients had been white. Currently, black and Hispanic recipients outnumber whites by about a 2 to 1 ratio. In New York City, for example, white recipients have declined at almost twice the rate of black recipients and almost eight times the rate of Hispanic recipients. Specifically, 57 percent of the white population on welfare have left since 1995 as compared with 30 percent of the black population and only 7 percent of the Hispanic population. Currently, New York City's recipients are 59 percent Hispanic, 33 percent black, and 5 percent white (DeParle 1998).

Multiple forces seem to account for this striking development. Black and Hispanic recipients have less formal education than their white counterparts. Among white recipients, only 33 percent did not have a high school degree compared with 40 percent of the black and 64 percent of the Hispanic recipients (DeParle 1998). In a survey of a sample of New York City public assistance mothers conducted by New York State Social Services, the researchers found that as many as 80 percent of the

Hispanic women were not born in the United States, with 30 percent lacking a ninth-grade education compared with only 9 percent of non-Hispanic women (Swarns 1998). Hispanic persons' lag in education and language skills reflects a partial explanation for their difficulties in entering the world of work. When they attempt to improve language skills, they often have difficulty finding resources. For example, in New York City in 1998, "the city turned away hundreds of Spanish-speaking welfare mothers from English classes because they had more students than seats. Hundreds more were denied access to resume writing courses and vocational training—services available to English speaking mothers" (Swarns 1998:A1, B8).

Family Factors. Another factor in Hispanics and blacks being more likely than whites to reach welfare time limits without viable alternatives is the association between poverty and single-mother families. Minority women are less likely to marry. About 31 percent of white female welfare recipients had never been married as compared with 40 percent of Hispanic women and 61 percent of black women (DeParle 1998). As previously discussed, children living in married-couple families live in greater financial security than those living in single-parent households. A related factor is that minority women have larger families (20 percent of white recipients have more than two children as compared with 38 percent for black and Hispanic families), creating additional associated financial burdens.

Finding suitable child care is a problem for most families and significantly more so for larger single-parent poor minority families. Poor children are less likely to enter kindergarten with prior early childhood program experience than children living in families above the poverty line. In 1996, 41 percent of children whose family income was below the poverty line were enrolled in an early childhood program as compared with 58 percent of children living in families whose income is above the poverty line. Hispanic children were the least likely (37 percent) to attend an early childhood program compared with 63 percent of black children and 54 percent of white children (Federal Interagency Forum on Child and Family Statistics 1997:45). For Hispanic mothers, the cultural expectation is that the woman's primary role is to stay home and raise her children. Day care centers are often deeply distrusted. In the New York State survey, 75 percent of Hispanic mothers feared that their children would be mistreated in day care compared with 45 percent of non-Hispanic mothers (Swarns 1998).

Also contributing to the disproportionate number of minority families nearing their time limits is the fact that they are more likely than white families to live in inner-city, high-crime, and job-scarce communities. While 71 percent of black families and 63 percent of Hispanic families receiving public assistance lived in large urban inner cities, only 31 percent of white welfare families did so. As DeParle (1998) poignantly states, "Race is intertwined with place" (A12). Race is also intertwined with job discrimination.

VULNERABILITIES AND RISK FACTORS

Anthony (1987) analogizes vulnerability and risk to three dolls made of glass, plastic and steel. Each doll is exposed to a common risk, the blow of a hammer. The glass doll completely shatters, the plastic doll carries a permanent dent, and the steel doll gives out a fine metallic sound. If the environment buffers the hammer's blow by "interposing some type of 'umbrella' between the external attack and the recipient," the outcome for the three dolls will be different (Anthony 1987:10). Each contributor identifies the major vulnerabilities and risk factors for people finding themselves with the life's condition, circumstance, and event presented in this book.

As stated earlier, chronic poverty is the major force responsible for both prolonged and cumulative stress; consequently, it is the most potent risk indicator for many of the distressing life circumstances and events. Poor people are simply most likely to become unhealthy, single parents, homeless, crime victims, abused and violated, imprisoned, pregnant in adolescence, jobless, etc. And among the poor, people of color are at highest risk. Two examples follow.

Health and Poverty. Generally, people who live in societies with large income and wealth disparities are less healthy than those who live in societies characterized by a small disparity in income and wealth. In a society like the United States where differences in income and wealth are extremely large, "your chances of escaping chronic illness and reaching a ripe old age are significantly worse than if you live in place where differences are not as large (Sweden, for example)" (Larder 1998). The association between family income and health is clearly evident in the health of the country's children.

Family income directly affects the health of children. The higher the family's income, the higher the percentage of children in very good or excellent health. Eighty-eight percent of the children of families with annual incomes of $35,000 or more were in very good or excellent health as compared with 63 percent of children in families with annual incomes under $10,000 (Federal Interagency Forum on Child and Family Statistics 1997:22). A significant factor accounting for this disparity is that poorer children simply receive poorer medical care. A significant number of poor children are not covered by health insurance. In 1996, as many as 10.6 million children were without health insurance (Weinberg 1997). Most of these children live 200 percent below the poverty line. Without health insurance, poor children receive less preventive as well as restorative medical care. For example, uninsured children have been found to receive medical care half as often for acute earaches, infections, and asthma compared with children with private and public insurance. They are also less likely to receive hospital services, routine checkups, to be fully immunized, and to receive dental care than insured children (U.S. Department of Health and Human Services 1997).

Health and Race/Ethnicity. White persons are expected to live an average of seven more years than black persons (Anderson, Kochanek, and Murphy 1998). The differentials in white and black mortality rates begin at the outset of life and persist throughout the life span. In 1995, the black infant mortality rate was 14.9 percent compared with 6.3 percent for white infants. Black infants die at almost a two and a half times higher rate than white infants (Federal Interagency Forum on Child and Family Statistics 1997:24). In 1994, there were 36.5 deaths per 100,000 of white children ages 1 to 4 years as compared with 77.2 deaths per 100,000 black children of the same age (more than twice as many) (28). Among children 5 to 14 years of age, there were 20.3

deaths per 100,000 white children as compared with 34.8 deaths per 100,000 black children (29). As table 1.5 shows, the Asian and Pacific Islander mortality rate is the lowest for all age children (78).

Black adults also suffer higher death rates than whites from most major health-related causes. And the gap between black persons and white persons continues to widen in the incidence of asthma, diabetes, several forms of cancer, and major infectious diseases. For example, for every 100,000 live births in 1995, the white maternal mortality rate was 7.1 as compared with a rate of 22.1 for black mothers. For another example, since the 1980s, diabetes cases have risen 33 percent among black persons, three times the increase among whites. In relation to tuberculosis, in 1995 for every 100,000 people, 8.7 white persons contacted the disease as compared with 23.9 black persons. The pattern for heart disease (whites 108 and blacks 147 per 100,000) and stroke (whites 26.7 and blacks 45 per 100,000) is also consistent (Kilborn 1998).

For the first time since the 1930s, there has been a decline in cancer rates as well as deaths from cancer. From 1990 to 1995 the actual rates of cancer rates dropped for both races, although black persons continued to have a higher proportion of deaths from all forms of cancer (130 whites and 172 blacks for every 100,000 people). The drop in cancer rates has affected every group in the United States except black men. They have the highest rates of cancer, primarily because of a significant rise in new cases of prostate cancer. Lung, prostate, breast, and colon cancers, the four most common types of cancer, account for approximately 54 percent of all newly diagnosed cancers. And for each, except breast cancer, black persons had the highest rate. Although the rate of breast cancer is higher for white persons than black persons, black women were much more likely to die from breast cancer. Late medical detection and poor quality medical attention accounts for these differential rates of cancer and deaths (Stolberg 1998a).

The U.S. Department of Health and Human Services (1997) reported that the cumulative number of reported AIDS cases was 612,078. As table 1.6 indicates, the number of black persons reported with AIDS was somewhat less than white persons.

TABLE 1.5 Child Mortality Rates by Age, Race, and Hispanic Origin, Selected Years 1980–94 (Deaths per 100,000 Resident Population)*

Age	1980	1985	1991	1993	1994
1–4					
White	57.9	46.6	41.7	38.4	36.5
Black	97.6	80.7	79.7	79.1	77.2
Hispanic	—	48.2	47.0	42.0	39.1
Asian**	43.2	40.1	30.4	30.5	25.3
5–14					
White	29.1	24.9	22.0	21.4	20.3
Black	39.0	35.5	34.2	35.1	34.8
Hispanic	—	19.6	21.5	22.6	20.1
Asian**	22.5	20.8	15.1	17.1	16.2

*Persons of Hispanic origin may be of any race. Each race category includes Hispanics of that race.
**and Pacific Islander

TABLE 1.6 United States AIDS Cases by Race or Ethnicity

Race or Ethnicity	No. of AIDS Cases
White, not Hispanic	279,072
Black, not Hispanic	216,980
Hispanic	109,252
Other	6,774

However, the similarity in the number of reported AIDS cases among white and black persons is astonishing when one considers that black people comprise only 13 percent of the total U.S. population.

Moreover, while comprising only 13 percent of the population in the United States, black persons account for 57 percent of all new HIV infections. For black adolescents and young adults (ages 13–24), the estimate is even higher, 63 percent. For black adults (ages 25–44) AIDS has become the leading cause of death. The AIDS epidemic is ravaging black families and neighborhoods and "many worry that AIDS will become marginalized, just another inner-city problem, like crime or drugs or graffiti" (Stolberg 1998b:A1).

Race and ethnicity are associated with different sources of risk for HIV/AIDS. For example, of the reported male adolescent/adult AIDS cases, 76 percent of the non-Hispanic white males and 76 percent of Asian/Pacific males contacted the HIV virus and AIDS from sex with other men as compared with only 38 percent among non-Hispanic black males and 44 percent Hispanic males. In contrast, the exchange of needles accounted for only 9 percent and 5 percent of HIV/AIDS cases among non-Hispanic white and Asian males, respectively, as compared with 36 percent among non-Hispanic black men and 37 percent among Hispanic men. For white, black, and Hispanic women, the demographics for sharing needles are very similar: 43 percent of non-Hispanic whites, 46 percent for non-Hispanic blacks, and 43 percent for Hispanics. However, drug use accounts for only 17 percent of cases of AIDS for Asian/Pacific Islander women, the majority of whom contact AIDS from heterosexual contact (46 percent). Asian/Pacific Islander women also have by far the highest rate (18 percent) of blood transfusions responsible for AIDS (as compared with 8 percent for non-Hispanic whites, 2 percent non-Hispanic blacks, and 3 percent Hispanics). Obviously, the various subpopulations are vulnerable to different risk behaviors (U.S. Department of Health and Human Services 1997).

The total number of reported AIDS-related deaths was 379,258; the ratio of blacks and Latinos to whites was about 3 to 1. And of the children with AIDS, 90 percent are black and Latino. In 1996, the cumulative HIV births were 60 percent black, 32 percent Latino, and 6 percent white infants (U.S. Department of Health and Human Services 1997). These children's mothers carry a double burden. They are blamed for becoming infected and, then, for infecting their children. They are judged and stigmatized.

Community Violence and Poverty. Poverty breeds violence. Neighborhoods that have a large number of reported child abuse cases tend to be very poor, with poor housing and a low level of neighborhood interaction. Child abuse has been associated with lower socioeconomic status, unemployment, lack of education, childbearing at an early age, alcohol and drug abuse, and spousal violence (Hampton and Newberger 1985; Olsen and Holmes 1986). Poverty is also the most powerful correlate to wife battering.

Violence is endemic and epidemic in our society. The country's poor youth are the primary victims of violent crimes. According to a study by Ringel (1997), youth between the ages of 12 and 19 had the highest rates of violent crime victimization. This age group was twice as likely as those ages 25 to 34, three times as likely as those ages 35 to 49, and twenty times as likely as those age 65 or older to experience violent crimes. Youth in households with annual incomes of less than $7,500 were much more vulnerable to violent crimes than youth in higher-income households. Per thousand, 65.3 persons age 12 or older in the poorest households were victims of crimes of violence as compared with 30.5 persons in households with annual incomes of more than $75,000 (Ringel 1997:4).

Although the murder rate has been continually declining for several years, the murder rate is much higher in the United States in comparison to other industrial democratic societies. In 1996, for every 100,000 people living in the United States, 7.4 persons were murdered. Finland had the next highest rate, but it was only 3.2 per 100,000 people (France's rate was 1.1, Japan's 0.6, and Britain's 0.5). While the mass media and public perception frequently equate violence with minorities living in the urban inner cities of the Northeast, actually, the high American murder rate is primarily a Southern murder rate. The South has almost double the murder rate of the Northeast. This regional difference has been traced back to the nineteenth century. For example, from 1880 to 1886, the murder rate in South Carolina (then a primarily agricultural state) was four times higher than that of Massachusetts (then the most urban, industrial state). In 1996, the murder rate in South Carolina was 9 per 100,000 people as compared with 2.6 per 100,000 people in Massachusetts. Currently, "the former slave holding states of the old Confederacy all rank in the top 20 states for murder, led by Louisiana with a rate of 17.5 murders per 100,000 people in 1996" (Butterfield 1998a:1).

The American tradition of violence has its roots in the Southern code of honor. It evolved from a rich and proud culture that prospered in the antebellum rural South. Southern upper-class gentlemen were compelled to defend their personal and familial honor, risking injury and life itself for the sake of reputation and manliness. Gradually, the African American slave society adapted the Southern code of honor. Since African American slaves and their descendants could not trust or turn to the law and its white institutions, disputes were personally and often physically settled. This traditional code of honor has been transformed into modern inner-city street culture: "Don't step on my reputation. My name is all I got, so I got to keep it." As guns and semiautomatics have become available to younger and more neglected and desperate children, "the rituals of insult and vengeance" represent a lethal anachronism (Butterfield 1996). And true to the Southern tradition of defending honor and proving manliness, most murders are not committed in pursuit of a crime, but rather as an outcome of personal differences such as lovers' quarrels or bar or neighborhood brawls (Butterfield 1998a).

The cumulative impact of the exposure to violence is devastating. Exposure to violence has been "associated with feelings of depression and anxiety, higher levels of antisocial and aggressive activities, lower school attainment, and increasing risk taking" (Marans, Berkman, and Cohen 1996:106). An increasing number of inner-city children, for example, suffer from low self-esteem and a posttraumatic stress syndrome similar to that seen in the Vietnam veterans (Lee 1989). These children have been exposed to violent attacks on and murders of their parents, friends, relatives, and neighbors. They are further traumatized by domestic violence and child abuse. These experiences have long-lasting physical, psychological, and social effects.

Community Violence and Race/Ethnicity. Blacks are more likely than whites to be victims of violent crimes. For example, blacks are nearly twice as likely as whites to be victims of aggravated assault (Ringel 1997:4). Black youth are the most vulnerable to violent death. In 1994, among 15- to 19-year-olds, the total death rate for white males of this age group was approximately 109 deaths per 100,000 resident population; for black males, there were 234 deaths per 100,000 resident population. Of the 234 black male deaths per 100,000 resident population, 150 were from firearms as compared with only 25 from motor vehicles. In contrast, white adolescents suffered deaths more from motor vehicles than from firearms. Moreover, among black adolescents, death by firearms increased threefold between 1985 and 1991 (Federal Interagency Forum on Child and Family Statistics 1997:79: see table 1.7).

RESILIENCIES AND PROTECTIVE FACTORS

Yet, in spite of various vulnerabilities and risk factors, a surprisingly large number of people mature into normal, happy adults. Why do some people collapse under certain life conditions and circumstances while others remain relatively unscathed? What accounts for the remarkable individual variations in people's responses to adversity and trauma? How do people adapt, cope, and meet the challenges of physical and mental impairments, severe losses, chronic discrimination, and oppression? Why do some people thrive and not simply survive in the face of life's inhumanities and tragedies?

What accounts for their resilience? *Webster's* defines *resilience* as "the tendency to rebound or recoil, to return to prior state, to spring back." Protective factors are

TABLE 1.7 Mortality Rates Among 15- to 19-Year-Old Males, by Gender, Race,* Cause of Death, Selected Years 1980–94 (Deaths per 100,000 Resident Population, Ages 15–19)

Cause of Death	1980	1985	1991	1993	1994
All causes					
White	143.5	112.1	113.6	108.8	109.6
Black	134.5	125.3	232.6	234.3	234.3
Motor vehicle					
White	68.1	50.3	44.4	41.4	41.5
Black	24.3	21.9	29.7	26.8	29.0
Firearms					
White	21.0	18.4	29.5	29.1	30.0
Black	46.7	46.5	142.7	154.8	152.7

*Persons of Hispanic origin may be of any race. Each race category includes Hispanics of that race.

biological, psychological, and/or environmental processes that contribute to preventing a stressor, or that lessen its impact or ameliorate it more quickly. The process of "rebounding" and "returning to prior state" does not suggest that one is incapable of being wounded or injured. Rather, in the face of adversity a person can bend, lose some of his or her power and capability, yet recover and return to prior level of adaptation.

Although, as mentioned earlier, most investigations to date have focused on the negative rather than the positive aspects of people's responses to life's miseries, some research into children living in highly stressed, trauma-inducing environments has helped to inform us about the protective factors that children use to negotiate high-risk situations. The protective factors are related to the following: temperament, family patterns, external supports, and environmental resources (Basic Behavioral Task Force 1996):

1. *Temperament.* Temperament includes such factors as: (a) activity level; (b) coping skills; (c) self-esteem; and (d) attributions.
   a. activity level—children with easy temperaments are less likely than those with difficult ones to be scapegoated by parents and others. In comparison, unfriendly and overactive children often encounter much greater rejection, anger, and abuse.
   b. coping skills—some children's ability to physically remove or emotionally distance themselves reduces their exposure to family discord.
   c. self-esteem—children's concepts and feelings about themselves and their social environments play an important role in their ability to deal with life's challenges. Self-esteem is not set in early or even late childhood. How we feel about ourselves develops throughout life and is modified by life experiences. Moreover, self-esteem is a dynamic, complex concept as "individuals have not one but several views of themselves encompassing many domains of life, such as scholastic ability, physical appearance and romantic appeal, job competence, and adequacy as provider" (Basic Behavioral Task Force 1996:26). Two types of experiences seem to be primarily related to feelings of self-worth. First, positive intimate relationships, even in adult life, do much to bolster people's feelings of self-worth. Second, successful task accomplishment (e.g., academic, sports, music, employment) also strongly affects feelings of self-worth.
   d. attributions—children's attribution of responsibility for exposure to trauma-inducing environments also plays an important role. Generally, a self-condemning attribution style has a strong negative impact. For example, in a study of the relationship between the ways adult women survivors of sexual abuse attributed responsibility and the number of symptoms they exhibited found that those who blamed themselves had more symptoms than those who did not; those who blamed fate or bad luck had more symptoms than those who did not blame fate or bad luck; those who blamed both themselves and fate or bad luck had more symptoms than those who did not; and those who blamed the perpetrator had fewer symptoms than those who did not (Feinauer and Stuart 1996).

People's subjective realities, i.e., their perceptions of their inner and external resources, their attributions, and social constructions, are essential to professional understanding. Two people with similar personal and environmental resources may perceive their resources quite differently and consequently function at very different levels.

2. *Family Patterns.* In family illness studies, one good parent-child relationship served as a protective factor in cushioning dysfunctional family processes as well as in increasing the child's self-esteem. The relationship also reduced psychiatric risk. The presence of a caring adult such as a grandparent led to similar outcomes (Basic Behavioral Task Force 1996).

3. *External Support.* External support from a neighbor, parents of peers, teacher, clergy, or social worker is also a significant cushioning and protective factor. The importance of social support has been widely documented. Supportive social networks are important sources of positive self-concept and also help shape one's worldview (Miller and Turnbull 1986). Buffering or cushioning an individual in harm's way is achieved through the provision of four types of support (Auslander and Levin 1987): instrumental (goods or services); emotional (nurturance, empathy, encouragement); informational (advice, feedback); and appraisal, (information relevant to self-evaluation). These supports provide essential ingredients for effective protection and coping, including a sense of physical and emotional well-being, personal identity, and the sustainment of life itself (Heller, Swindel, and Dusenbury 1986; Thoits 1986). Simply believing that networks are available for support results in people being less anxious and more confident in dealing with new stressors (Gottlieb 1988a, 1988b).

4. *Environmental Resources.* Finally, the broader environment and the opportunity structure create the conditions for all other factors. As discussed previously, when social structures and institutions act as buffers, they enhance people's abilities to cope with life's transitions and stressors; when environmental resources are unavailable, or insufficient, people are more apt to feel hopeless and are less able to cope.

Many vulnerability or protective processes often concern *key turning points* in people's lives rather than long-standing attributes. The direction of a trajectory for the future is often determined by what happens at a critical point. The decision to remain in school, for example, represents a critical turning point, often leading to more positive trajectories than dropping out of school. In contrast, the birth of an unwanted child to a well-functioning teenager, who is then rejected by family, creates a negative trajectory (Rutter 1987).

Planning in making choices looms as a critical factor in turning-point decisions. Exercising foresight and taking active steps to cope with environmental challenges are critical factors. In a follow-up study of girls reared in institutional care, Rutter (1987) found that the extent to which they did not marry for a negative reason, such as to escape from an intolerable situation or because of unwanted pregnancy, and exercised planning in their choice of a partner, they were less likely to marry a man who was a criminal or had a mental disorder. The importance of planning as a protective factor also emerges in areas of school and work (Rutter 1987).

And then there is always the simple element of chance or God's will: good fortune and misfortune. Although our efforts to be scientific may cause us to shy away from the idea of chance or spiritual beliefs, they may well enhance our understanding of and feeling for the human experience. For example, survivors of the Holocaust know that they survived because they happened to be at the right place, at the right time. For another example, people involved with AA commit and align themselves with a spiritual force larger than themselves.

Two additional factors to planning in making choices and chance or God's will are worth noting. One factor is humor. Laughter is essential to life. Laughter "deflects, unmasks, and frees us from unreal, pretentious, and imprisoning beliefs or perceptions" (Siporin 1984:460). To be able to laugh in the face of adversity and suffering releases tension, provides hope, and takes sadness and "makes it sing." Eli Wiesel poignantly noted (as quoted in Baures 1994):

> The truth comes into this world with two faces. One is sad with suffering, and the other laughs; but it is the same face, laughing or weeping. When people are already in despair, maybe the laughing face is better for them; and when they feel too good and are sure of being safe, maybe the weeping face is better for them to see. (31)

And finally, through the processes of *helping and giving to others,* people help and heal themselves. Frankl (1963), a survivor of the Holocaust, eloquently describes that one finds meaning in life—finds meaning in suffering—not through the pursuit of self-gratification, but primarily through the processes of helping and giving to others. Essentially, when people lend their strength to others, they strengthen themselves.

PROGRAMS AND SOCIAL WORK CONTRIBUTIONS

Each contributor examines programs and social work contributions in dealing with the population's life stressors. Managed care has had a profound impact on almost all social work programs. Managed care's main objective is cost containment by either placing limits on patient services (e.g., number of days in the hospital, visits to general practitioner and specialists, total dollar expenditures per year and per lifetime) and/ or increasing copayments and deductibles. Managed care's dual emphases on minimizing costs and maximizing profit impose corporate values and ideology on health and social welfare agencies. These values and ideology differ radically from social welfare's commitment to human rights and the provision of safety nets and buffers to our capitalist system (Schamess 1998:24).

In health care, for example, social work departments are being decentralized and social work practitioners integrated into service teams. Consequently, social work directors and supervisors are yielding some of their administrative responsibilities and searching for ways to survive. The diminished administrative structure limits staff opportunities for promotion and leaves them isolated and vulnerable in ongoing turf battles with nurses. Furthermore, staff isolation and vulnerability inhibits their ability to advocate for quality patient care.

Managed care's dual emphases have a particularly deleterious affect on poor people. Medicaid consumers are being rapidly enrolled by managed care organizations. However, these organizations' primary experiences are with providing services to employed populations with low health risk. They have little experience with such needed services as outreach or case management. Consequently, Medicaid patients "may encounter difficulties obtaining the full range of health and related social services" (Perloff 1998:68).

Since each author examines the specific programs, services, and modalities and, where relevant, the impact of managed care, the discussion is limited to selected ideas about primary prevention programs. What do we do with our knowledge about populations vulnerable and resilient to various pernicious life conditions, circumstances, and events? Funding sources have placed an increasing emphasis on the public health concept of primary prevention, the primary objective of which is to anticipate and forestall some undesirable event or condition that might otherwise occur and spread (Gitterman 1988).[3] Primary prevention has two distinct strategies: (1) *specific protection*, an explicit intervention for disease prevention in which a population at risk is identified and something is done with the population to strengthen its resistance and resilience; and (2) *health promotion,* an intervention for improving the quality of life and raising the general health/mental health level of a population. Social workers also have inherited from their past a third prevention strategy, *environmental change*, i.e., doing something about the social conditions that play host to and foster the problems. In times like the present, this tradition, if not ignored, is certainly neglected. Funding and consequently professional interests are both primarily engaged in the "specific protection" aspect of prevention.

This direction can be a problem. By emphasizing specific protection, our efforts may be promising much more than they can deliver. Childhood poverty, for example, is deeply embedded in our social structure. The decline in actual earnings, decrease in public entitlements, and increase in single parenting and numerous social problems all conspire to enlarge the dimensions of childhood poverty. These children's problems are becoming more desperate, intractable, and dangerous. In this context, the premise of specific protection prevention, i.e., intervening before a problem has "struck," must be reexamined. If we identify poverty and racism as the major problems, prevention of social ills becomes elusive, if not illusionary.

Intimate partner and child abuse prevention programs, for another example, are being implemented within the context of a violent society. Our society promotes and tolerates violence and few prevention programs deal with the cultural propensity toward violence. Programs that teach selected adolescents to avoid pregnancy by saying "no" or advise parents who may potentially abuse their child to manage their angry feelings, however useful and pertinent, cannot deal with the multidimensional pathways to social problems. In fact, most new immigrant groups have shown high rates of "social pathology," but as they achieved economic security, the social pathology rates declined. These social pathologies are analogous to a high fever: in such an analogy, specific protection interventions may momentarily reduce the fever, as, for example, an aspirin does, but they disguise the problem. Social pathologies are outcomes of complex ecological chains that include attributes of the individual's genetic, biopsychosocial makeup; the structures of the family, social networks, community, school, workplace, religious organizations, and health system; recreational resources; general culture and subculture; social class; and the overall polity.

Another problem with specific protection strategies is the difficulty in identifying subpopulations at risk. Certain life problems, for example, have been associated with pathogenic family processes. The problem is what to do about these findings. A boy observing his father batter his mother does not, of course, inevitably become a wife batterer himself. Based on his experiences, he may become determined and successful at not battering his wife. Similarly, a boy growing up in a nonbattering family may, owing to unemployment or addictions, become a batterer. What do we do about aggregate data: do we attribute to the individual the characteristics of the group, thus stigmatizing and defining them to be "at risk"?

To draw a parallel, a colleague was asked to study alcohol abuse in a police department. He found that Irish policemen were particularly at risk of alcoholism. It is obvious from a logical (if not political) point of view that action, if any, can only be taken in relation to health promotion for the total police population. When we identify a subpopulation at "risk" as candidates for specific protection interventions, rather than using a universal health promotion approach, we are in danger of adding to the burdens of that population. Moreover, by seeking and accepting restrictively defined prevention funding, we are in effect promising to reduce or eliminate problems such as child abuse, drug addiction, and teenage pregnancy. And when these modestly funded specific protection programs are unable to mitigate what are probably the consequences of structurally ingrained poverty, we diminish our professional credibility.

The second strategy, "health promotion," is a viable alternative. It attempts to improve the quality of life and foster optimal health in the total population. It focuses on "wellness" and maintaining health rather than treating "sickness" and restoring health. Services based on a developmental approach scheme emphasize access to health education, recreation, and socialization activities, and cultural programs. In effect, the health promotion approach offers multiple pathways to well-being. Examples include genetic counseling, marital counseling, pregnancy planning, pre- and postnatal care, obstetrical care, well baby clinics, preschool programs and enrichment programs, and parental involvement in school programs and sex education. These programs attempt to engage social competence, cognitive and emotional coping, and achievement. Maximizing early positive experiences and minimizing negative experiences are more likely to have long-lasting effects. Thus, in social planning for universal services, programs need to be designed to strengthen major social institutions: the family, the school, the world of work, and the community. When these institutions are strengthened, general health is promoted.

Our programs also ought to reflect more involvement with the third strategy, "environmental change." We need to revitalize the community organization tradition in our practice. Community organization is essential for instrumental accomplishments (e.g., voter registration) as well as for the experience of challenging imbalance in power relations (Mondros and Wilson 1994). Participation and action can absorb hopelessness, despair, and apathy. Experiencing and developing the belief that one can take initiative to achieve some control of one's environment is a powerful strategy for promoting physical and mental health.

ASSESSMENT AND INTERVENTIONS

Most social workers provide direct services to individuals, families, and groups. We attempt to help clients adapt and cope with the tasks and struggles in day-to-day living. In their transactions with their environments, disturbances and disruptions often occur. People experience stress when they perceive an imbalance between external demands placed on them and their self-defined capability to meet the demands through the use of their own internal and environmental resources. These transactional disturbances create life stressors in three interrelated areas: life transitions and traumatic events, environmental pressures, and dysfunctional interpersonal processes.

Life Transitions and Traumatic Events. Whether a person has to adapt to depression or schizophrenia or diabetes, to homelessness or foster care status, transitions in life impose new demands and require new responses and are, therefore, often deeply distressing. All such transitions require some changes, some flexibility, and some creativity in dealing with the environment, processing information and problem solving, and relating to others. Gradual life changes usually provide the opportunity for planning and preparation, and consequently the attendant stress is more manageable than when the change is sudden and unexpected. For some clients, change represents major threats to environmental survival and to self-image. For others, change represents an opportunity for environmental enhancement and self-preservation. But for most people, all change has its difficulties. The immediacy and enormity of a traumatic life event creates a personal crisis. Traumatic life events—such as the death of a child, the violence of rape, the diagnosis of AIDS, the birth of a genetically defective child, or the aftermath of a natural disaster—represent losses of the severest kind. Such events are experienced as disastrous and overwhelming and therefore tend to immobilize us. The state of crisis is time limited in nature, during which ordinary adaptive patterns are not adequate, so that novel solutions or coping skills are required. We cannot long remain in the state of extreme discomfort implied by crises. The painful anxiety and/or grief elicits protective measures sooner or later.

Environmental Pressures. While social and physical environments can support or obstruct the tasks of daily living, the environment itself is a source of severe stress. A society riven with prejudice against people of color, women, homosexuals, and old people provides unequal opportunities for its citizens. Many clients are dealt a "stacked deck." If they are impaired physically, cognitively, and emotionally, this "deal" can be insurmountable. Organizations (schools, hospitals, etc.) established to provide essential services may in fact block access and impose harsh and restrictive policies and procedures. Social networks, i.e., relatives, friends, workmates, and neighbors, may be scarce and unavailable, so that clients are, in effect, socially isolated. Physical and spatial arrangements, e.g., density, crowding, safety, and privacy, may be unsuitable and generate a great deal of distress.

Dysfunctional Interpersonal Processes. In dealing with life transitions or unresponsive environments, families and groups may experience intensified stress because of problematic interpersonal relationship and communication patterns. Inconsistent mutual expectations, exploitative relationships, and blocks in communication are examples of problems in interpersonal communication to individual members and to the family or the group itself. Similar problems may also emerge between workers and their clients. Workers may add to the client's burden by defining his or her behavior as resistant or unmotivated rather than as a transactional difficulty between them (Gitterman 1983, 1989; Gitterman and Schaeffer 1972).

Helping people with their life stressors provides the social worker with a clear and distinctive professional function: to improve the transactions between people and their environments and to facilitate a better match (i.e., a better level of fit) between their needs and environmental resources.[4] The professional function is represented in figure 1.1.

Assessment. How people experience their daily life stressors and how effectively they manage the associated life tasks will largely depend on the perceived level of fit between their personal and environmental resources. Workers begin by assessing the client's appraisal of his or her life stressors, i.e., the meaning the client attributes to the situation. For example, a mother becomes depressed when she learns that her adolescent daughter is pregnant. The mother interprets her daughter's pregnancy as a reflection of her failure in raising her daughter. For the social worker to be helpful, the cognitive meaning of the pregnancy must be understood. The mother's appraisal of the event results in a judgment that the issue is a stressor rather than an irrelevant or a benign event (Lazarus 1980; Lazurus and Folkman 1984). The mother's continued appraisal will determine whether the stressor represents a harm or loss, or a threat of harm or loss, or a challenge.

Distinguishing between harm/loss and threat is a matter of time perspective. *Harm/loss* refers to current damage and suffering, such as losses of all kinds, while *threat* refers to an anticipated future loss or harm, such as the announced changes in public assistance or an unwanted retirement. In such instances, efforts to cope are directed to overcoming, reducing, or tolerating the stressor. In the case of threat, efforts to cope are directed to maintaining the current state of affairs, preventing the anticipated harm/loss, or easing its effects. Individuals may oscillate between harm and threat as they appraise the harm already suffered and the threat(s) that may lie ahead, as in the birth of a child with a serious, nontreatable genetic disorder. An appraisal of a stressor is accompanied by a sense of being in jeopardy, with the aroused feelings

FIGURE 1.1 Professional Function and Life Stressors

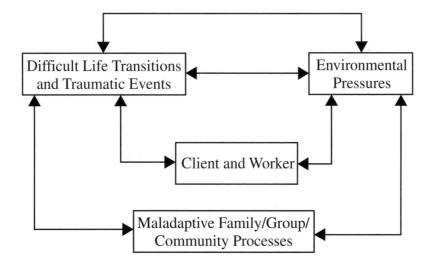

often interfering with problem solving. This process affects self-esteem, a sense of competence, relatedness, and self-direction.

After assessing clients' primary appraisals of their situations, the worker has to assess the accuracy of their perceptions and thinking. Under intense stress people may err in their evaluation of personal and environmental resources. For example, a substance-abusing client may believe that his or her peer network is a major resource in dealing with life issues when in fact it fuels his or her dysfunctional patterns. Clients may overestimate their resources for dealing with life stressors and thereby fail to cope successfully, or underestimate their resources and believe that the situation is hopeless. In assessment (as well as in intervention), client(s) and social worker need to determine whether appraisals of stressor and resources are accurate and, if they are not, work on developing greater accuracy.

The worker also assesses how the client has coped with the life situation. Coping measures include emotional, cognitive, and behavioral actions to change aspects of the stressful life situation such as oneself, the environment, exchanges between them, or all three. Coping is a process through time; stressors may be of short duration, as in job loss followed soon by another job, or they may be of long duration, as when mourning, raising an autistic child, or living as a solo mother in poverty. An ecological concept, coping expresses a particular person(s)-environment relationship, since both personal and environmental resources are required (Germain and Gitterman 1996).

In assessing personal coping resources, the worker evaluates the client's motivation; problem-solving and relationship skills; outlook on life; self-confidence; ability to search for and use information from the environment; capacity to restrain rash or impulsive decisions and actions, and to regulate negative emotions aroused by the stressor; and an ability to seek environmental resources and to use them effectively. Wheaton (1983) suggests that flexibility is also a personal coping resource. Personal resources such as optimism (Lazarus and Folkman 1984) and self-attention (Suls and Fletcher 1985) are also important.

In assessing environmental resources, the worker evaluates the availability and responsiveness of the client's formal service networks such as public and private agencies and institutions of many kinds. Potential resources also include the client's informal networks of relatives, friends, neighbors, workmates, coreligionists, and so on, who may or may not provide emotional support, material resources, information, feedback, and advice. Just the perception of the availability of informal networks can make it easier to cope with a life stressor (Wethington and Kessler 1986). Since some formal and informal support systems may be unresponsive, even hostile and destructive, and act as significant stressors rather than buffers, their responsiveness must be evaluated by client and social worker, just as personal resources are evaluated. The worker also assesses relevant dimensions of the client's physical environment such as provisions for safety, privacy, crowding, accessibility of space, and so on.

Professional judgments about the meanings clients attribute to the identified life stressors, the accuracy of their perceptions, and the level of fit between personal and environmental resources must be based on reasoned inferences and reasonable premises. To achieve such judgments, workers must have *salient data*. All inferences have to be based on and supported by data. Without data, the social worker is unable to determine an appropriate purpose and focus of help. Sources of data include: the client's verbal accounts; the worker's observations of nonverbal communication; verbal and nonverbal presentations by others (obtained only with the client's informed consent); and written reports (obtained only with client's permission, except for the agency's own earlier records). Mutually agreed upon definitions of the most pressing life stressors and agreed upon goals and methods of working on them determine the direction and the content of the data to be sought.

Workers can readily become overwhelmed by a mass of data and, therefore, need to be able to organize the data as they are being collected. The *life stressor formulation* provides a useful schema for partializing and grouping data about clients' problems. Besides providing a useful schema for problem identification, the life stressor formulation also serves as an assessment framework throughout the helping process. To illustrate: A worker is trying to help an adolescent mother mourning her decision to surrender her infant for purposes of adoption. In the fifth session, she agitatedly complains about her loneliness and isolation. The worker asks herself, is she (the adolescent), at this particular moment, requesting help for further exploration of her grief, i.e., life transition; asking for help with her feelings of isolation from her teenage friends and family and in becoming reconnected to these natural support systems; possibly requesting help in constructing new environmental support systems; or, finally, complaining obliquely about the worker's inattentiveness and, therefore, subtly pressing for attention to their own interpersonal transactions? Organizing the data by life stressor themes helps the worker select, as their work moves along, the more appropriate intervention than otherwise. A system for organizing data is apt to lend focus and direction to clinical interventions.

To develop *reasoned inferences,* the collected and classified data have to be analyzed and synthesized. Workers have to develop inferences based on the following: (1) identification and definition of the clients' life stressors; (2) the meanings these stressors have for the clients; (3) clients' strengths and limitations to deal with and work on their life stressors; (4) social and physical environments' supports and obstacles in maintaining and resolving the clients' stressors; and (5) the level of fit between the clients' (individual, family or group) and the environments' resources and deficits (Germain and Gitterman 1996). Developing inferred propositions requires two disciplined forms of reasoning—inductive and deductive. *Inductive reasoning* is the intellectual process of moving from the data to the generalizations. As professionals, we have to conscientiously distinguish data from inferences and be ever tentative about the validity of our generalizations. *Deductive reasoning* is the intellectual process of applying the generalizations, i.e., practice knowledge and research findings, to the specific case situation. Disciplined use of informing knowledge is an important aid to determining practice focus and direction. As professionals, we have to be careful that our needs for certainty, constancy, and stability do not compromise our curiosity and ability to individualize clients.

Through disciplined forms of reasoning as well as spontaneous intuition, workers assess the level of fit between the client and the environment and their respective demands, resources, and limitations. When an imbalance exists between a perceived demand and a perceived capability to meet the demand through the use of available internal and external resources, people experience stress. How much stress a frail elderly person will experience upon discharge from a hospital, after surviving a stroke and being confined to a wheelchair, will depend on the person's degree of physiological impairment and damage, amount of physical strength and resiliency, and inner resources (i.e., motivation, outlook on life, coping skills, meaning of illness, etc.). Also extremely important are the family and extended network caregivers, and their ability and willingness to provide emotional and instrumental supports. Moreover, access to such resources as medical staff, homemaker, nursing, physical rehabilitation, speech therapy, financial entitlements, medical insurance, and financial status and ability to purchase services will have a significant impact on the final prognosis. Finally, the flexibility of the physical environment, e.g., building entrance door and corridors, furniture, etc., also will affect recovery. Figure 1.2 shows the combined impact of a client's internal resources and limitations and environmental resources and limitations. Although the figure may be a bit too pat and an oversimplified view of reality, it does offer a representation of the fit between person and environmental resources.

In situations of low inner and low environmental resources (A), the client is at most serious risk. The poor person:environment fit suggests potential deterioration and disintegration. These situations require immediate attention and priority and an active and directive worker with sufficient time to become a critical resource for possibly an extended period. Situations of high inner and environmental resources (D) suggest a good person:environment fit and an optimistic prognosis. In these situations, the worker's activities may be limited to uncomplicated referrals, suggestions, and support. In situations of low inner resources and high environmental resources (B) and high inner and low environmental resources (C), less definitive statements can be made. When inner resources are low, the worker usually is required to be active, lending technical problem-solving competence and energy. Finding and connecting the client to available network and community resources to compensate for biopsychosocial deficits are essential professional activities. When environmental resources are low, the worker usually assists the client in asserting his or her needs, seeking alternative resources, or constructing new ones.

Figure 1.2 provides a diagrammatic overview of the fit between client and environmental resources and deficits and general guidelines for different practice directions. To be useful, an assessment needs to be more refined than an overview. One can never, however, collect all of the available data and can never have all of the available knowledge. All professionals must act in the context of varying degrees of ambiguity. Every worker faces an array of cues, messages, and themes, which are at times perplexing and at other times overwhelming. At every and any moment, the

FIGURE 1.2 Person:Environment Fit*

		ENVIRONMENTAL RESOURCES	
		Low	High
PERSONAL RESOURCES	Low	− − A	− + B
	High	+ − C	+ + D

*Low indicates limited resources; high, significant resources.

worker has to decide which of these to respond to and which to table or defer. There is little time to think and strategize about the "correct" intervention. Yet, within the context of uncertainty, the worker must act with a certain degree of sureness. What is being suggested here is a way to think about clients and their situations, a way to organize and analyze data and a way to systematize practice.

Interventions. All people have strengths and resilience, although for some, their strengths and resiliencies have been dampened by life circumstances. Social workers therefore must identify, mobilize, and build on people's inner and external strengths. While internal limitations and external obstacles must be noted, change occurs through the encouragement of people's positive assets. When social workers are pre-occupied with vulnerability, psychopathology, and diagnostic labels, individuals and collectivities are perceived as merely broken objects to be "fixed" (i.e., treated) by powerful experts. This practice form obscures clients' and practitioners' humanness. Too often social work education and socialization to the professional stiffens and formalizes social workers' practice. Students learn to be threatened by ambiguity rather than challenged by it. Students are taught to search for prescriptions, to become cautious and avoid taking risks. And through these and other processes, students are taught to distance and detach themselves from their clients. Wanting to confront and heal from life's troubles and pains, clients too often come into contact with professionals who themselves are hiding and avoiding.

Jourard (1971) insightfully analogizes human communication to a poker game. Players do not disclose their hands. Like in a poker game, we wear masks or poker faces and hide our inner feelings and thoughts. Professionals with poker faces and masks inhibit rather than facilitate the healing of their clients. The splitting of our personal and professional selves encourages the other person also to hide within a stereotypical role, e.g., patient or student. An artificial and false communication takes place in which neither party says what he or she really feels or means. The client-worker roles must be carried out in a mutual, reciprocal, and respectful manner and shift from those of subordinate recipient and superordinate expert to those encouraging collaboration (Germain and Gitterman 1996). By reducing social distance and power differences, the worker helps to encourage clients' competencies and strengths. When, and only when, social workers deal with the existing power differentials in their relationships with clients can these relationships empower clients rather than reinforce and fuel continued powerlessness (Cohen 1998; Gitterman 1983, 1989).

Professional interventions are directed to person(s), environments (physical and/ or social), and their exchanges in order to reduce or eliminate the life stressors. Supporting and strengthening people's adaptive capacities and problem-solving abilities to deal with life stressors requires the creative use of various professional methods and associated skills. For example, *enabling* is used to mobilize or strengthen clients' motivation to deal with difficult life stressors and the associated stress they arouse. The enabling method also helps clients to manage their negative feelings and stress that otherwise could lower self-esteem and interfere with effective coping. Enabling skills include: identifying strengths; conveying hope; offering realistic reassurance; and legitimizing and universalizing thoughts, reactions, and feelings. These skills help clients to mobilize and sustain their motivation and personal strengths. For another example, exploring and clarifying provides focus and direction to the work. The social worker draws on skills such as partializing concerns, reaching for underlying meaning, clarifying ambivalence, identifying discrepant messages, offering interpretations, providing feedback, and inviting self-reflection. Exploring and clarifying skills provide structure, direction, and depth to the work.

Guiding is used to help clients learn the steps in the problem-solving aspects of coping. Many client populations described in the book often lack the requisite skills to engage and solve their life stressors and cope with the associated stress. Some clients simply lack basic information or are handicapped by misinformation. Others may have difficulty because they are unaware of unproductive, possibly self-destructive patterns of behavior. They remain mired in helplessness. Still others may have difficulty because they cannot partialize alternatives and take action. They are too overwhelmed by their oppressive situations to accomplish daily tasks. These clients do have inherent and potential life skills to cope with their problems and associated stresses; rather, they are immobilized by a particular life event (e.g., death of a child, institutionalization of a parent) and unable to use coping strategies to manage this particular life change. In these situations, the social worker guides the problem-solving aspects of coping, selecting from a repertoire of educational interventions to influence and encourage coping strategies and skills.

Successful coping calls for an ability to: (1) identify and evaluate life stresses, (2) deal with attendant emotions, and (3) delineate and choose among alternative responses in problem resolution (Lazurus and Laumier 1978). Social workers have the potential to become critical teachers of coping skills. For example, guiding a parent to prepare a child for a hospital admission may serve as a protective factor, while the lack of preparation may serve as a risk factor. The guiding method is particularly appropriate for helping clients to cope with stressful life conditions and circumstances. For this reason, the guiding method and associated skills will be discussed more fully.

To help clients improve coping skills, social workers must attend to the different ways in which people process and learn information. Some learn primarily by doing; others learn primarily by summarizing, visualizing, and organizing perceptions into patterns and images. Still others learn primarily by abstracting and conceptualizing (Bruner 1966). Effective use of the guidance method depends on providing opportunities for activity and doing; visual means, modeling, and role play; and discussion and exchange of ideas. Guiding skills include the following: providing needed information regarding the stressor and coping tasks, clarifying misinformation, offering advice, providing feedback, specifying action tasks, and preparing and planning for task completion.

In helping a client to prepare for major surgery, for example, the social worker explores the client's beliefs and perceptions about the procedure and corrects mistaken understanding, provides relevant information about the overall features of the impending surgery, restructures some of the unhelpful thought processes, and focuses on more effective management of feelings. The worker might also role-play how to ask the surgeon relevant questions and how to listen for responses. If the client is too passive in the role play, the worker might consider teaching assertiveness skills. An assertive behavior sequence calls for four steps that can help the client complain effectively and feel more empowered and less helpless: (1) describe behavior, (2) express associated feeling, (3) request specified change, and (4) identify positive consequence (Lange and Jakobowski 1976).

Based on the discussion and role play, the worker might decide to offer specific advice to encourage the client to try a new behavior (e.g., "If you feel the nurse is too rough with you, tell him firmly that he is hurting you and that he should immediately let go of your arm"). Advice also can be offered to discourage a client's self-defeating behavior (e.g., "If you continue to pull out your IV, the nurses will have to bind your arms"). Depending on the severity of the problem and the client's level of functioning, the worker determines how direct the advice should be. This can range from "suggesting" to "urging" to "warning" to "insisting." The more directive advice is usually most helpful to anxious and impaired clients. In offering advice, the worker has to be familiar with the client and the situation, being careful not to impose his or her own values and coping style. The advice has to be responsive to what a client is actually requesting, rather than reflect a worker's own need to demonstrate helpfulness.

At times, the worker might offer an "informed" interpretation. In offering an interpretation, the worker shares meanings and inferences she or he attributes to the client's feelings, behaviors, and situations. By patterning available data, the social worker provides a potentially new frame of reference for a client to consider, e.g., "I sense a lot of your concern about your surgery, about the risks, recovery period, etc., is being expressed in disappointment and annoyance with your family. This is understandable." Timing is essential to how interpretations are received. To venture an interpretation, the worker has to have sufficient data and sense the client's trust. Premature insights distance clients from workers. The worker's interpretation may be incorrect, but, even if correct, the client may not be ready to integrate it. It has been suggested that an interpretation should not be made unless it is virtually irrefutable.

People are usually unaware of how they are perceived by others—their strengths and their limitations. By sharing one's own reactions to a client, the worker provides invaluable feedback, rarely available from friends and family. When it is offered out of an objective caring and concern rather than frustration and anger, it is more likely to be received and believed. A worker can decide to share a feeling at a particular moment—e.g., "Right now, I am feeling overwhelmed. When I try to say something, you cut me off. I feel you are running right by me, pushing me away." The worker uses his or her reactions to examine the client's experiences and transactional patterns. To be most helpful, the worker's reaction is presented in concrete, behavioral terms and expressed calmly and empathically.

Directive interventions should be followed by inviting clients' reactions (e.g., "What's your reaction to what I have suggested?"). At times, a client will respond directly whether the advice or interpretation is helpful or unhelpful. Other times, the response will be more indirect, e.g., "I guess you're right" or "Yes, but. . . ." The worker invites hesitation, lack of clarity, and negative reactions. Even if the advice or interpretation is perceived as unhelpful, the client's feedback stimulates further work. Without client feedback, the worker may sound "smart" or, in fact, be insightful, but the work may not be deepened.

ILLUSTRATION AND DISCUSSION

Each contributor follows the "assessment and interventions" section with a specific presentation of practice (individual, family, group, community, organization, program development) to illustrate and typify the stressors and situations confronted by the client population. Contributors were asked to explore the practice issues related to social class, ethnicity and race, gender, sexual orientation, religious affiliation, and developmental phase. The focus of the illustration is on the worker's professional behaviors and skills, i.e., what the worker actually does to help. Contributors were invited to pay special attention to this section and to try to capture the art and science of social work helping. This section was emphasized because of a conviction about the primacy of professional skills and competence.

As our profession has been pushed into a preoccupation with accountability, one of the consequences has been a preoccupation with practice outcomes, and a tendency to evaluate professional competence and skills primarily on the basis of outcomes specified in advance or beforehand. The client's progress or lack of progress is attributed to the worker's skills or lack of skills. This is absurd, if not dangerous, because it leads logically to working only with motivated clients and clients without serious environmental problems. Moreover, evaluating professional competence solely on the basis of outcomes also ignores and negates the reality of what happens in the helping process, i.e., a worker trying to be helpful, and a client deciding whether and how to use help from this particular person at this particular time.[5]

The worker's behaviors may be skillful and the client may not progress (or possibly even regress); the worker's behaviors may be unskillful and the client may progress. We can properly hold professionals accountable for professional skills and informed use of relevant knowledge. It has been said that clients benefit because, in spite of, and without our help. Lawyers who lose their cases may be justly praised for their fine work in a lost cause, and doctors often do well but still their patients sometimes die. In all cases, the question or issue is whether they did well or did the right thing in the circumstances and considering the state of the art and available options. And, similarly in social work, the behavior of helping has to be evaluated in its own terms and distinguished from the behavior of using help.

How can the general public and specific client populations have confidence in a profession that is unclear and uncertain about its methodology (Ellis 1984)? How will professional social workers be able to demonstrate their competence without committing educational and professional careers to the acquisition of established and newly emerging skills? As professionals, we are and become what we do! Being competent is our most reliable means to survival. Although society does not fully appreciate what our profession does and what social workers accomplish day in and day out, this book tries to capture and convey our profession's vision and our practitioners professional competence, spirit, and, in many situations, heroism.

CONCLUSION

This introductory chapter attempts to introduce the reader to the content of this book. In Part I, "Life Conditions," each contributor deals with issues related to etiology. A complex ecological chain emerges linking genetic, family, and environmental forces. Alcoholism, chronic heart disease, diabetes, learning disability, manic depression, developmental disability, and schizophrenia all appear to have in common genetic predispositions. Inherited levels of cholesterol, other blood fats, and structural defects, for example, set the conditions for heart disease. A family tradition of cooking in fats and grease increases the risk. Living in a society in which fast-food chains with high-fat hamburgers and potatoes fried in lard are desired staples, smoking by youth is pervasive, ice cream is a favorite dessert—all conspire to act on the genetically vulnerable individual. A similar chain exists for many of the life conditions described in this book: i.e., a genetic predisposition; a society and culture that either provide insufficient supports and environmental controls or encourage unhealthy behaviors; and dysfunctional family and individual behaviors. For the problematic life condition to develop, all the factors in the ecological chain are usually present in some degree. However, extreme family and environmental factors such as excessive family and work stress can also precipitate serious difficulty even though there is little constitutional basis for it.

Poverty has a pervasive impact on most distressing life circumstances and undesired events. Poor children, for example, learn early in life that they have limited control over their lives, that things happen and are done to them. Poor children are at greater risk than others of suffering various acute illnesses and specific health problems. At every age, poor children are at a relatively higher risk of death. They are more likely to be exposed to violence, malnutrition, poor education, family disruption, and institutionalization or incarceration of parents; in turn, they are more likely to respond with antisocial behavior, addiction, and depression (Nettles and Pleck 1994). Public health child development researchers using statistical models have catalogued a score of risk factors: poverty; overcrowding; neighborhood and school violence; and parental absence, unemployment, or instability. The higher the score of risk factors, "the more astronomically the odds rise" of the child ending up delinquent, addicted, or chronically mentally ill (Butler 1997:24).

Drugs and drug subcultures, for another example, ravage economically disadvantaged communities and their schools. As poor inner-city communities become poorer and as people become more alienated, escape into alcohol and drugs becomes a seductive option. People addicted to drugs relate primarily to drugs and drug-seeking behavior. The Office of National Drug Control Policy (1998) estimated that 35 percent of people 12 years of age and older have used an illegal drug in their lifetime (90 percent used either marijuana or hashish, 30 percent tried cocaine). Chronic drug users (fifty-one or more days) are estimated at 3.6 million for cocaine and 810,000 for heroin. Chronic users not only cause significant injury to themselves, but they also "maintain the illegal drug market, commit a great deal of crime, and contribute to the spread of hepatitis and tuberculosis as well as HIV/AIDS and other sexually-transmitted diseases" (7).

While crime appears to be steadily declining, arrests for drug-law violations are climbing. More than 1.5 million people were arrested for drug-law violations in 1996. Many crimes are committed out of the need to obtain money to purchase drugs and/or under the actual influence of drugs. Drug trafficking and violence go together as "more than 60 percent of adult male arrests tested positive for drugs in twenty out of twenty-three cities in 1996. In Chicago, 84 percent of males arrested for assault tested positive." Nearly three-quarters of the growth in the federal prison population between 1985 and 1995 was accounted for by the increase in drug offenders (Office of National Drug Control Policy 1998:17).[6]

In virtually every chapter, the author(s) poignantly describe the all-encompassing consequences of poverty. When there is prejudice and discrimination, when family and social network ties are weak, and when individuals have the added burdens of physical, intellectual, or emotional impairments, the impact of poverty is particularly devastating. Poor people with AIDS, homeless people, unemployed black adolescents, isolated elderly—all are at severe risk of not being able to survive in the environment. Yet some remain relatively unscathed by traumatic experiences such extreme poverty, racism, homophobia, family violence, sexual and other forms of abuse, or loss of a loved one. They do not become bitter or jaded. They somehow forge ahead when life seems unbearable—when hope and trust have been taken from them.

Social workers struggle to help people in greatest need and highest risk. Many do so with great personal commitment and zeal, and professional creativity and competence. These social workers struggle daily to provide relevant services with extremely limited resources. They refuse to abandon social agencies; they refuse to desert these most vulnerable populations and instead they continue to develop programs, provide individualized services, and offer hope. This book is a tribute to these professionals, and we hope it does them justice.

Notes

1. Martin Luther King once made the mordant observation that our society has socialism for the rich and rugged individualism for the poor.
2. PRWORA requires involvement in some work-related activities as defined by each state within twenty-four months of receiving assistance.
3. Discussion is based on author's prior publication.
4. In mediating the exchanges between people and their environments, social workers daily encounter unresponsive environments. Thus, an additional professional function is to influence social and physical environmental forces to be responsive to people's needs.
5. The author wishes to acknowledge the contribution of William Schwartz to his ideas about the nature of professionals skills.
6. Substance abuse also has a profound impact on mental illness, increasing the rates of violence by up to five times. Moreover, the violence is most often directed at family members (Butterfield 1998b).

References

Abuelo, D. N. 1983. "Genetic Disorders." In J. L. Matson and J. A. Mulick, eds., *Handbook of Mental Retardation*, pp. 105–26. New York: Plenum Press.

Anderson, R., K. Kochanek, and S. Murphy. 1998. "Report of Final Mortality Statistics, 1995." *Monthly Vital Statistics Report* 45, no. 11 (Supplement 2). http://search.cdc.gov (August 1998).

Andrulonis, P., C. Glueck, C. Stroebel, N. Vogel, A. Shapiro, and D. Aldridge. 1981. "Organic Brain Dysfunction and the Borderline Syndrome." *Psychiatric Clinics of North America* 4(1):47–66.

Anthony, J. E. 1987. "Risk, Vulnerability, and Resilience: An Overview." In E. J. Anthony and B. Cohler, eds., *The Invulnerable Child*, pp. 3–48. New York: Guilford Press.

Auslander, G. and H. Levin. 1987. "The Parameters of Network Intervention: A Social Work Application." *Social Service Review* 61(June):305–18.

Basic Behavioral Task Force of the National Advisory Mental Health Council. 1996. "Basic Behavioral Science Research for Mental Health: Vulnerability and Resilience." *American Psychologist* 51(1):22–28.

Baures, M. 1994. *Undaunted Spirits: Portraits of Recovery from Trauma*. Philadelphia: Charles Press.

Berlin, R. and R. Davis. 1989. "Children from Alcoholic Families: Vulnerability and Resilience." In T. Dugan and R. Coles, eds., *The Child in Our Times: Studies in the Development of Resiliency,* pp. 81–105. New York: Brunner/Mazel.

Blum, K. and H. Topel. 1986. "Opiod Peptides and Alcoholism: Genetic Deficiencies and Chemical Management." *Functional Neurology* 1:71–83.

Bruner, J. 1966. *Toward a Theory of Instruction.* Cambridge: Harvard University Press.

Butler, K. 1997. "The Anatomy of Resilience." *The Family Therapy Networker* 21(2): 22–31.

Butterfield, F. 1996. *All God's Children: The Bosket Family and the American Tradition of Violence.* New York: Avon Books.

——. 1998a. "Southern Curse: Why America's Murder Rate Is So High." *New York Times,* July 26, Section 4, pp. 1, 16.

——. 1998b. "Studies of Mental Illness Show Links to Violence." *New York Times,* May 15, p. A14.

Clark, K. 1965. *Dark Ghetto.* New York: Harper & Row.

Cloninger, R. 1983. "Genetic and Environmental Factors in the Development of Alcoholism." *Journal of Psychiatric Treatment and Evaluation* 5:487–96.

——. 1987. "Neurogenetic Adaptive Mechanisms in Alcoholism." *Science* 236:410–16.

Cloninger, R., M. Bohman, and S. Sigvardsson. 1981. "Inheritance of Alcohol Abuse." *Archives of General Psychiatry* 38:861–68.

Cloninger, R., S. Sigvardsson, and M. Bohman. 1988. "Childhood Personality Predicts Alcohol Abuse in Young Adults." *Alcoholism: Clinical and Experimental Research* 5: 494–505.

Cohen, M. 1998. "Perceptions of Power in Client/Worker Relationships." *Families in Society* (July–August):433–42.

Danziger, S. 1997. "America Unequal: The Economy, The Labor Market and Family Incomes." Special Plenary, Council on Social Work Education Annual Program Meeting, Friday, March 7.

DeParle, J. 1998. "Shrinking Welfare Rolls Leave Record High Share of Minorities." *New York Times,* July 27, pp. A1, A12.

Dickerson, M. U. 1981. *Social Work Practice with the Mentally Retarded.* New York: Free Press.

Dohrenwend, B. S. and B. P. Dohrenwend, eds. 1981. *Stressful Life Events.* New York: Prodist.

Ellis, A. 1984. "Must Most Psychotherapists Remain as Incomplete as They Are Now?" In J. Hariman, ed., *Does Psychotherapy Really Help People?,* pp. 24–36. Springfield, Ill.: Charles C Thomas.

Federal Interagency Forum on Child and Family Statistics. 1997. "America's Children: Key National Indicators of Well-Being." Washington, D.C. http://www.fedstats.gov/index 20.html (1 October 1998).

Feinauer, L. and D. Stuart. 1996. "Blame and Resilience in Women Sexually Abused as Children." *American Journal of Family Therapy* 24(1):31–40.

Feldman, R., A. Stiffman, and K. Jung. 1987. *Children at Risk.* New Brunswick, N.J.: Rutgers University Press.

Fine M. and A. Schwebel. 1991. "Resilience in Black Children from Single-Parent Families." In W. Rhodes and W. Brown, eds., *Why Some Children Succeed Despite the Odds,* pp. 23–40. New York: Praeger.

Foch, T. and G. McClearn. 1980. "Genetics, Body Weight, and Obesity." In A. Strunkard, ed., *Obesity,* pp. 48–71. Philadelphia: W. B. Saunders.

Frankl, V. 1963. *Man's Search for Meaning: An Introduction to Logotherapy.* Boston: Beacon Press.

Gelles R. J. and M. A. Straus. 1988. *Intimate Violence: The Definitive Study of the Causes and Consequences of Abuse in the American Family.* New York: Simon & Schuster.

Germain, C. B. and A. Gitterman. 1996. *The Life Model of Social Work Practice: Advances in Knowledge and Practice.* New York: Columbia University Press.

Gershon, E. 1983. "The Genetics of Affective Disorders." In L. Grinspoon, ed., *Psychiatry Update: The American Psychiatric Association Annual Review,* vol. 2, part 5, p. 4–34. Washington, D.C.: American Psychiatric Press.

Gitterman, A. 1983. "Uses of Resistance: A Transactional View." *Social Work* 26(March/April):127–31.

———. 1988. "Social Work Looks Forward." In Gerald St. Denis, ed., *Implementing A Forward Plan: A Public Health Social Work Challenge (Proceedings),* pp. 3–14. Pittsburgh: University of Pittsburgh Graduate School of Public Health.

———. 1989. "Testing Professional Authority and Boundaries." *Social Casework* 70(March): 165–71.

Gitterman, A. and A. Schaeffer. 1972. "The White Professional and the Black Client." *Social Casework* 53(Spring):280–91.

Goldberg, C. 1997. "Hispanic Households Struggle Amid Broad Decline in Income." *New York Times,* January, pp. A1, A16.

Goodwin, D., F. Schulsinger, L. Hermansen, S. Guzi, and G. Winokur. 1973. "Alcohol Problems in Adoptees Raised Apart from Alcoholic Biological Parents." *Archives of General Psychiatry* 38:238–43.

Gottlieb, B. 1988a. "Marshalling Social Supports: The State of the Art in Research and Practice." In B. Gottlieb, ed., *Marshalling Social Support: Formats, Processes, and Effects,* pp. 11–51. Newbury Park, Calif.: Sage.

———, ed. 1988b. *Marshalling Social Support: Formats, Processes and Effects.* Newbury Park, Calif.: Sage.

Hampton, R. and E. Newberger. 1985. "Child Abuse Incidence and Reporting by Hospitals: Significance of Severity, Class and Race." *American Journal of Public Health* 75:56–60.

Heller, K., R. Swindel, and L. Dusenbury. 1986. "Component Social Support Processes: Comments and Integration." *Journal of Consulting and Clinical Psychology* 54(4): 466–70.

Hollingshead, A. and F. Redlich. 1958. *Social Class and Mental Illness.* New York: John Wiley.

Jourard, S. 1971. *Of the Transparent Self.* New York: Van Nostrand Reinhold.

Kety, S. 1988. "Schizophrenic Illnesses in the Families of Schizophrenic Adoptees: Findings from the Danish National Sample." *Schizophrenia Bulletin* 14:217–22.

Kilborn, P. T. 1998. "Black Americans Trailing Whites in Health, Studies Say." *New York Times,* January 26, p. A16.

Lamison-White, L. 1996. "Poverty in the United States: 1996." U.S. Bureau of the Census, Current Population Reports, Series P60–198. Washington, D.C.: U.S. Government Printing Office. http://www.census.gov/pub/prod/3/97pubs/p60–198.pdf (August 1998).

Lange, A. and P. Jakobowski. 1976. *Responsible Assertive Behavior.* Champaign, Ill.: Research Press.

Larder, J. 1998. "Deadly Disparities: American's Widening Gap in Incomes May Be Narrowing Our Lifespans." *The Washington Post,* August 16, p. C1.

Lazarus, R. 1980. "The Stress and Coping Paradigm." In L. Bond and J. Rosen, eds., *Competence and Coping During Adulthood,* pp. 28–74. Hanover, N.H.: University Press of New England.

Lazurus, R. and S. Folkman. 1984. *Stress, Appraisal and Coping.* New York: Springer.

Lazarus, R. and B. Laumier. 1978. "Stress-Related Transactions Between Person and Environment." In L. Pervin and M. Lewis, eds., *Perspectives in International Psychology.* New York: Plenum Press.

Lee, F. 1989. "Doctors See Gap in Blacks' Health Having a Link to Low Self-Esteem." *New York Times,* July 17, p. A11.

Marans, S., M. Berkman, and D. Cohen. 1996. "Child Development and Adaptation to Catastrophic Circumstances." In R. Apfel and B. Simon, eds., *Minefields in Their Hearts: The Mental Health of Children in War and Communal Violence,* pp. 104–27. New Haven: Yale University Press.

Mendlewicz, J. and J. Rainer. 1977. "Adoption Study Supporting Genetic Transmission in Manic-Depressive Illness." *Nature* 268:327.

Miller, D. and W. Turnbull. 1986. "Expectancies and Interpersonal Processes." *Annual Review of Psychology* 37:233–56.

Mondros, J. and S. Wilson. 1994. *Organizing for Power and Empowerment.* New York: Columbia University Press.

The National Center for Education Statistics. 1996. "Dropout Rates in the United States, 1996: Event, Status, and Cohort Dropout Rates." http://nces.ed.gov/pubs98/dropout/98250–05.html (August 1998).

Nettles, S. M. and J. Pleck. 1994. "Risk, Resilience, and Development: The Multiple Ecologies of Black Adolescents in the United States." In R. Haggerty, L. Sherrod, N. Garmezy, and M. Rutter, eds., *Stress, Risk, and Resilience in Children and Adolescents,* pp. 145–81. New York: Cambridge University Press.

Office of National Drug Control Policy. 1998. *The National Drug Control Strategy, 1998: A Ten Year Plan.* Washington, D.C.: Executive Office.

Olsen, L. and W. Holmes. 1986. "Youth at Risk: Adolescents and Maltreatment." *Children and Youth Services Review* 8:13–35.

Ozawa, M. N. 1997. "Demographic Changes and Their Implications." Special Plenary, Council on Social Work Education Annual Program Meeting, Friday, March 7.

Passell, P. 1998. "Benefits Dwindle Along with Wages for the Unskilled." *New York Times,* June 14, pp. 1, 28.

Perloff, J. 1998. "Medicaid Managed Care and Urban Poor People: Implications for Social Work." In G. Schamess and A. Lightburn, eds., *Humane Managed Care?,* pp. 65–74. Washington, D.C.: National Association of Social Workers Press.

Rauch, J. 1988. "Social Work and the Genetic Revolution: Genetic Services." *Social Work* 33:389–97.

Ringel, C. 1997, November. "Criminal Victimization 1996: Changes 1995–96 with Trends 1993–1996." U.S. Department of Justice, Bureau of Justice Statistics, National Crime Victimization Survey, NCJ-165812. http://www.ojp.usdoj.gov:80bjs/pub/pdf/cv96.pdf (December 1998).

Rutter, M. 1971. "Parent-Child Separation: Psychological Effects on the Children." *Journal of Child Psychology and Psychiatry* 12:233–60.

———. 1987. "Psychosocial Resilience and Protective Mechanisms. *American Journal of Orthopsychiatry* 57:316–31.

Schamess, G. 1998. "Corporate Values and Managed Mental Health Care." In G. Schamess and A. Lightburn, eds., *Humane Managed Care?,* pp. 23–35.Washington, D.C.: National Association of Social Workers Press.

Schmeck, H. M., Jr. 1987a. "Genetic Abnormality Seen as Link with Alzheimer's." *New York Times,* March 13, p. A14.

———. 1987b. "Young Science of Cancer Genes Begins to Yield Practical Application." *New York Times,* October 6, pp. C1, C4.

———. 1987c. "Scientist Link an Activated Gene to Lung Cancer." *New York Times,* October 8, p. A28.

Siporin, M. 1984. "Have You Heard the One About Social Work Humor?" *Social Casework* 65(8):459–64.

Stolberg, S. 1998a. "New Cancer Cases Decreasing in U.S. as Deaths Do, Too." *New York Times,* March 14, pp. A1, A14.

———. 1998b. "Eyes Shut, Black America Is Being Ravaged by AIDS." *New York Times,* June 29, pp. A1, A12.

Suls, J. and B. Fletcher. 1985. "Self-Attention, Life Stress and Illness: A Prospective Study." *Psychosomatic Medicine* 47:469–81.

Swarns, R. 1998. "Hispanic Mothers Lagging as Others Leave Welfare." *New York Times*, September 15, pp. A1, B8.

Thoits, V. 1986. "Social Support as Coping Assistance." *Journal of Consulting and Clinical Psychology* 54(4):416–23.

U.S. Bureau of the Census. 1993, March. "Black Americans: A Profile." U.S. Department of Commerce Economics and Statistics Administration. http://www.census.gov/apsk/www/statbrief/sb93_2.pdf (August 1998).

———. 1996, March. "Marital Status and Living Arrangements." U.S. Department of Commerce Economics and Statistics Administration. Series P20–496. http://www.cenus.gov/population/www.socdemo/ms-la.html (August 1998).

———. 1997. "Press-Release." U.S. Department of Commerce Economics and Statistics Administration. http://www. census.gov/Press-Release/cb97–162.html.

———. 1998, August. "Resident Population of the United States: Estimates, by Sex, Race, and Hispanic Origin, with Median Age." http://www.cenus.gov/population/www. socdemo/ms-la.html (6 February 1998).

U.S. Department of Health and Human Services. 1997. "HIV AIDS Surveillance Report." Public Health Service, Centers for Disease Control and Prevention, National Center for HIV, SDT and TB Prevention. (Midyear Edition, Vol. 9, No. 1). http://www.cdc.gov/nchstp/hiv_aids/stats/hasrlink.htm (September 1998).

U.S. House of Representatives, Committee on Ways and Means. 1996. *Green Book.* Washington, D.C.: U.S. Government Printing Office.

Wallace, J. 1989. "Biopsychosocial Model of Alcoholism." *Social Casework* 70(June): 325–32.

Weinberg, D. 1997. U.S. Housing and Household Economic Statistics Division U.S. Census Bureau. "Press Briefing on 1996 Income, Poverty, and Health Insurance Estimates" (September 29). http://www.census.gov (August 1998).

Wender, P., S. Kety, D. Rosenthal, F. Schulsinger, J. Ortman, and I. Lunde. 1986. "Psychiatric Disorders in the Biological and Adoptive Families of Adopted Individuals with Affective Disorders." *Archives of General Psychiatry* 43:923–29.

Wethington, E. and R. Kessler. 1986. "Perceived Support, Received Support and Adjustment to Stressful Life Events." *Journal of Health and Social Behavior* 27(1):78–89.

Wheaton, B. 1983. "Stress, Personal Coping Resources, and Psychiatric Symptoms: An Investigation of Interactive Models." *Journal of Health and Social Behavior* 24(3): 208–29.

Wilhelm, S. and E. Powell. 1964. "Who Needs the Negro?" *Trans-Action* 1(September/October):3–6.

Zaslow, M., K. Tout, C. Botsko, and K. Moore. 1998. *Welfare Reform and Children: Potential Implications.* New York: The Urban Institute, Number A-23 in Series.

Zhukov, U., A. Varkof, and Y. Burov. 1987. "Effect of Destruction of the Brain Serotoninergic System on Alcohol Intake by Rats at Early Stages of Experimental Alcoholism." *Biogenic Amines* 4(3):201–4.

Part I

LIFE CONDITIONS

2

Acquired Immune Deficiency Syndrome (AIDS)

George S. Getzel
Stephen W. Willroth

Acquired immune deficiency syndrome (AIDS) has been with us for nearly twenty years, after being first recognized by the federal Centers for Disease Control and later labeled as the greatest public health threat in the United States. In the last two decades we have undergone a period of profound adjustment to the hard reality of AIDS.

The early response to the pandemic was too often the abject neglect and abuse of the historic casualties—gay men, intravenous drug users, men and women of color, and recipients of blood products. Extremist solutions of tattooing buttocks, calls for quarantine, unauthorized disclosures of medical information, and coerced human immunodeficiency virus (HIV) testing were debated by both experts and ideological opportunists. Charlantism and premature announcements of AIDS cures had devastating effects on desperately ill people and their families. People with AIDS (PWAs) faced egregious conduct from health and social service providers, and PWAs' basic human rights were routinely breached. Poor treatment included the callous discussion of an HIV or AIDS diagnosis and breaches of confidentiality even when guaranteed by law (Altman 1986; Cahill 1984; Kramer 1989; Shilts 1987).

Nearly two decades later, the course of the pandemic has assumed a too ready familiarity that is incurring yet more apathy toward the plight of PWAs and their families (Mann et al. 1989; Nichols 1987; Sontag 1988). Health care and social service providers, in some cases, have grown overly euphoric about breakthroughs that have increased the longevity and quality of life of many PWAs, at least for an uncertain period of time. For the public, it may appear as if AIDS is no longer a threat to them or others. Although we do not have the level of fear, hostility, and indifference that was characteristic of the responses by many health and social service providers in the early 1980s (Caputo 1985; Greenly 1986; Leukefeld and Fimbres 1987; Lopez and Getzel 1984), the issues currently arising present just as profound challenges for service development and effective interventive strategies as in the beginning of the pandemic.

An urgent requirement remains for professionals to keep up-to-date on the changing biopsychosocial consequences associated with HIV/AIDS, diverse populations infected and affected, the nature of the disease sequelae, and treatment options, access, and compliance. HIV prevention remains a serious issue for health and social service providers now as in the past. Rates of HIV transmission have leveled off in some population cohorts, while growing precipitously in others: This has added to the complexity of service strategies.

DEFINING AND EXPLAINING AIDS

Since much of systems thinking, such as the concept of homeostasis, as well as ecological concepts, originates from biology (Buckley 1967; Cannon 1939), a biopsychosocial system framework is particularly applicable to the variables associated with AIDS in social work practice.

René Dubos (1959) wrote that modern persons tend to deny their organismic nature and their place in biological evolution, largely because of the widespread elimination of many life-threatening infectious diseases that, in past centuries, killed infants, children, and large portions of the populations of towns and cities. Clean water systems separated from sewage outlets, fresh food, housing regulations, and mass inoculation for childhood diseases are largely responsible for human longevity and the revolution in life expectations. A likely early death has been superseded by concerns about chronic disease in old age in modern industrial and postindustrial societies.

The emergence of AIDS has made us aware that human beings are indeed organisms of exquisite complexity who are subject to parasitic and symbiotic relations with microorganisms from within and without (Bateson and Goldsby 1988). Microorganisms can disable, disfigure, and kill a larger organism when their numbers reach a sufficient level, if they are not stopped by the organism's resistance to their increase.

In the highly sophisticated and technologically advanced countries, human beings can falsely believe that they are beyond the grasp of a variety of microorganisms, such as tubercle bacilli and streptococci, as well as a multiplicity of viruses capable of bringing on life-threatening diseases and horrific symptoms. The biological reality, however disconcerting it may be, is that the tissues of the human organism are awash with a variety of bacteria, protozoa, invertebrates, and viruses that are contained because of the multilevel defenses of the immune system.

Unless the balance of microorganisms radically shifts in the host, it is perfectly possible for an individual to live his or her life oblivious of their existence. Biologists are beginning to explore the possible benefits of microorganisms, as well as their harm when resistance to them falters. An investigation of public health measures through the centuries points to social activities such as sanitation and changed behaviors such as hand washing by doctors and midwives that have altered the environments of people and the balance of life-threatening microorganisms (Dubos 1965).

Pestilences like war have caused great social changes, not only by dramatically decreasing population size, but also by challenging cultural expectations (Risse 1988; Rosenberg 1989; Sontag 1988). Camus (1952) noted that plagues and war surprise us because each assumes a size exceeding expectations and forces us to confront mass deaths, which are met with initial denial and slowness to react.

The Life Model developed by Germain and Gitterman (1996) uses an ecological system perspective that can be applied to the complexities of AIDS as a biological entity interacting with different psychological, social, and cultural dimensions. AIDS touches and influences the whole fabric of society and its cultural assumptions. Clearly, AIDS points to the Darwinian struggle for survival as human beings begin to engage in a life-and-death struggle to fit into a natural world that is also inhabited by the virus associated with AIDS. Human beings' failure on the biological, psychological, social, and cultural levels to understand and to adapt to their new place in the natural world is a matter of individual and collective life and death.

Bateson and Goldsby (1988) noted that HIV has created a new niche for itself in the natural world, supported not only by the individual human organism but also by the behavior that transmits HIV to other human organisms. Thus, the extent to which the individual human organism has favorable internal and external environments determines the individual's health and life chances, and specifically whether he or she will become infected with HIV and go on to develop AIDS. While epidemics start by growing exponentially, changes in the infected organism or in the organism's environment slow down the rate of infection. AIDS reveals how vulnerable human beings are in their biological relations with microorganisms, and for that matter with their fellow human organisms in maintaining bodily integrity and well-being.

AIDS is a worldwide natural event. Modern transportation links populations all over the world, and in time, material, ideas, and microorganisms are diffused throughout different nations and cultures with significant, and sometimes catastrophic, consequences. The resources needed to maintain the health of men, women, and children may not be available, and individuals, families, and whole communities may break down under the crisis of the worldwide AIDS pandemic.

The AIDS pandemic taxes the available resources and may call for a redistribution of material resources and expertise in the interest of the whole of the human community—to halt the spread of disease and to care for those infected and affected. AIDS also points out that the human species is highly interdependent: they inhabit a finite planet and must discover ways to ensure their mutual security and well-being.

Social work practice with PWAs demands a constant review of the emerging knowledge about the nature of the disease, its treatment, and the social and cultural impact on persons infected and ill, as well as on all those who interact with them over time. Medical discoveries related to HIV will have far-reaching effects on medical treatments, strongly affecting the longevity and quality of life, not to mention the hopes and expectations, of persons with life-threatening conditions. The ever-changing character of the AIDS epidemic requires constant updating of knowledge and systematic reflection on the interaction of biological, psychological, social, economic, political, and cultural factors. The biopsychosocial systems framework that has evolved in social work practice in health care is a useful heuristic for handling the complexity of the data emerging on AIDS and HIV infection; conversely, this tragic epidemic may be an example par excellence of the usefulness of this framework.

DEMOGRAPHIC PATTERNS

With each year, the basic understanding of the magnitude and the international scope of the HIV/AIDS pandemic grows. There are an estimated 30 million cumulative HIV cases worldwide. Two major strains of retrovirus, HIV I and HIV II have been located throughout the inhabited world. Sub-Saharan Africa, with 19 million cumulative cases of HIV infection, has the highest concentration of any global geographic area, followed by more than 6.9 million in South East Asia, 1.5 million in Latin America, 1.2 million in North America, 838,000 in Europe, and 503,000 in the Caribbean. By January 1996, the estimated cumulative number of AIDS cases worldwide was estimated at 10,375,000 with more than 9.2 million persons, or 89 percent, dead from AIDS complications (Mann and Tarantola 1996).

In the United States the estimates range between 650,000 and 900,000 HIV-infected persons (*JAMA* 1996). According to the Centers for Disease Control, from 1981 to the end of 1997, there were more than 641,000 cumulative cases (CDC 1997). Of the cumulative diagnosed cases, 49 percent have been identified as homosexual and bisexual males; 26 percent as intravenous drug users (IVDUs); 6 percent as both male homosexuals or bisexuals and IVDUs; 9 percent as adults who were infected through heterosexual contact; and the remaining 10 percent as persons who received infected blood or blood products or as infants infected before or during birth. Of the total cumulative cases of AIDS, approximately 15 percent have been women, of whom 44 percent had histories as IVDUs, 39 percent were infected through heterosexual contact, and the remaining 17 percent were infected through blood, blood products, or undetermined sources. Children under the age of 13 made up a little more than 1 percent of the cumulative cases of AIDS, 91 percent having been infected before or during birth and the remaining 9 percent having been infected through blood, blood products, or undetermined sources. Of the total cumulative cases of women with AIDS at the end of 1997, more than 76 percent were black and Hispanic, and over 80 percent of all the children were black and Hispanic, from inner-city areas where the sources of infection were IVDUs. Whole families have become sick and died in poor neighborhoods throughout the United States.

Of the more than 641,000 cumulatively diagnosed AIDS cases at the end of 1997, more than 60 percent of the persons diagnosed with AIDS were dead by end of December 1997. From the period between January 1981 and June 1997, the rate of newly diagnosed AIDS cases has declined significantly since 1992, and the mortality rate of PWAs has dropped dramatically since 1995. The decline in mortality is associated with the availability of more effective drug treatments (combination antiretroviral therapies including protease inhibitors). Perinatally acquired AIDS shows a marked decline, principally reflecting successful strategies to promote prenatal HIV testing and drugs administered during pregnancy diagnosis (CDC 1997).

SOCIETAL CONTEXT

AIDS evokes powerful psychosocial responses in persons at the point of diagnosis (and often earlier), and in all those intimates and service providers with whom they interact. Such responses reflect current and changing societal values and assume greater magnitude as more individuals, families, and communities have direct experiences with PWAs.

The meaning of AIDS on a societal and cultural level is constantly delineated and reinterpreted in the mass media, particularly as the number of persons who become ill and die grows larger. The economic costs of providing expensive, if not scarce, health and social services at the state and local levels of government to PWAs are gaining more attention as a political concern. Those who do not have AIDS and who perceive themselves as being in no danger of becoming HIV-infected may challenge the use of resources for PWAs because of their high economic and social costs. In short, compassionate concern may decrease because of self-interest and a protectionist outlook in the general population.

Powerlessness and stigma are inextricable aspects of AIDS on a societal level. Ironically, because of their prior stigmatized and isolated condition, gay and bisexual men as well as intravenous drug users and their sexual partners and newborns have had the heaviest concentrations of HIV infection.

The societal prejudice against homosexual persons now has a powerful biological analogue in the form of AIDS, which reinforces the existing enmity toward them and severely limits their civil rights and opportunities to live full and productive lives. The homophobia experienced by gay people is frequently internalized, adding to the pain that vulnerable persons feel, even before they develop HIV-related symptoms or a formal AIDS diagnosis.

The largest proportion of intravenous drug users are the inner-city poor, black, and Hispanic adults whose health, security, and life chances are greatly diminished even before they are HIV-infected. Poor-quality medical services, lack of access to care, and community distrust and suspicion effectively may deprive inner-city people of required preventive, acute, and long-term health care. Prejudice toward addicts on the part of providers and the public is accompanied by racial, ethnic, and class hostilities.

An abiding and very serious question asked by inner-city community leaders and concerned advocates for AIDS services is whether inner-city populations are being written off as expendable because they cannot be served easily and because they come with so many enmeshed problems, such as homelessness and poverty. Most HIV-infected women are from poor, inner-city, minority backgrounds, and they frequently have infected infants and children. The directing of resources of all kinds to this population, as to gay and bisexual men, was initially indifferent and typically slow in response.

On a societal level, AIDS challenged the historically new concept of what constitutes a fair share of life by devastating young adults with an exotic array of chronic, life-threatening diseases and with early deaths. AIDS links a death-dealing disease to sexual activities, with far-reaching effects on sexual attitudes and behavior. Sexual freedom and expression are now fraught with danger, microscopic mysteries, and mortality.

VULNERABILITIES AND RISK FACTORS

The epidemiological evidence gives overwhelming support to the proposition that AIDS cannot be transmitted through casual contact, such as touching, kissing, and using the same toilet; it can be transmitted only through the exchange of blood, semen, vaginal fluid, and mother's milk. Studies of persons sharing the same households indicate that transmission occurs only between those individuals engaged in sexual activities and IV drug use and to infants born of infected mothers (Friedland 1989).

Social workers dealing with AIDS should have a rudimentary understanding of the biology of HIV infection and be able to translate it clearly to clients to assist them in AIDS prevention activities and interpreting AIDS-related symptoms and infections. Social workers are increasingly called on to speak to a wide range of individuals and groups about AIDS and the transmission of HIV. Therefore, all AIDS education for social workers begins with an understanding of HIV biology and goes on to considerations of the person, dyadic relations, the family, the community, and the larger social systems. In simple, unadorned language with apt analogies designed for specific audiences, social workers must discuss the nature of HIV transmission and prevention. Social workers should be prepared to react to simple ignorance as well as to highly intellectualized arguments that reveal a person's denial of the actual modes of AIDS transmission and the real threats to their lives.

AIDS, an underlying disease of the immune system, must be understood as a metadisease process, a generator of otherwise rare opportunistic infections such as Pneumocystis carinii pneumonia (PCP), cytomegaloviral infections, toxoplasmosis, and rare cancers such as Kaposi's sarcoma and non-Hodgkin's lymphomas. According to a 1992 revision of the case definition, an AIDS definition also includes adult and children with less than a 200 CD T-lymphocyte count, cervical cancer, recurrent bacterial pneumonia, and pulmonary tuberculosis.

AIDS is a disease associated with the imminent or actual catastrophic collapse of bodily immunity and with the presence of HIV infection. As mentioned, HIV is transmitted only through the intimate exchange of bodily fluids, specifically semen, vaginal fluid, blood, and mother's milk. The activities identified with a high risk of the transmission of HIV are anal, oral, and vaginal sex; the use of infected blood or blood products; the sharing of infected drug paraphernalia; and breast feeding. HIV is also transmitted from mother to fetus in the uterus or during birth (Gallo and Montagnier 1989; Heyward and Curran 1989; Mass 1987).

Not all persons who have contact with HIV become infected, nor do all persons infected develop HIV symptoms (such as night sweats, swollen glands, weight loss, and rashes) or full-blown AIDS with the appearance of an opportunistic infection or through blood test finding. Because of the dangers of spreading infection to others and exacerbating existing infections, it is vital for all persons with or without current HIV infection to be aware of the modes of transmission; to practice safer sex through the use of rubber latex condoms during anal, oral, and vaginal sex; and to avoid the sharing of intravenous drug paraphernalia.

In the course of their direct practice with individuals, families, and groups, social workers have frequent opportunities to assist clients to examine the activities that place them at risk of infection. Social workers must develop comfort in discussing sexual practices and drug use, so that they can help clients make behavioral changes to avoid infection. Neither the induction of fear nor calls for abstinence are sufficient to encourage new, lifesaving behaviors. Social workers have created exciting approaches to teaching safer sex behaviors by positive techniques such as eroticizing the use of condoms with both gay and nongay men and women (Getzel and Mahony 1988; Shernoff 1988).

Scientific knowledge about HIV and the cellular processes of infection has grown dramatically in the 1990s as research proceeds in the United States and throughout the world. Because of its specific attraction to T4 helper lymphocytes (blood cells), HIV infects them, replicates, and thus overwhelms the individual's overall immune capacity. The growth of opportunistic infections and cancers may proceed rapidly or over a long period of time. There is strong evidence that HIV has a long latency period before replicating. Scientists are investigating the conditions or cofactors associated with the development of specific symptoms and opportunistic infections related to the flaring up of HIV infection.

HIV infection can be readily detected by the use of antibody tests and emerging new test strategies. These tests have been useful in the mass screening of blood in hospitals and blood banks. The use of antibody testing for individuals presents serious practical, clinical, and ethical questions. The tests check for the presence of HIV antibodies, which the body produces six weeks to three months or longer after infection has occurred. There is clearly a possibility of a false-negative test finding; it is therefore recommended that persons abstain from high-risk activities and be tested again within six months (Fineberg 1988; Nichols 1987; Redfield and Burke 1989; Walters 1988).

The test is a diagnostic tool, and negative test findings are not a signal that a person is immune from infection. There is a strong danger of magical thinking that turns the test into a stimulus for unsafe activities. Consequently, there is a profound need for pretest counseling about what the test is and is not, as well as for an exploration of the meaning of both a negative and a positive test finding. Skilled posttest counseling by a social worker or other qualified health professional is vital to reinforce safer sex guidelines and to handle the often strong emotional responses of those hearing about a positive test finding. A person with a positive test finding may become depressed or even suicidal. Other reactions may be a fear of informing intimates and rage at those who are perceived as the source of the infection.

In certain jurisdictions, important practical and ethical issues arise about the counselor's legal requirement to report positive test findings to government officials, to the tested person's intimates, and to other agencies (Bayer 1989; Dickens 1988). The client should know the reporting requirements in advance. Anonymous testing sites, where available, provide the opportunity to assist in teaching AIDS prevention activities and helping the client get the necessary health care. To the extent possible, test findings should be kept confidential. Some states protect test findings legally, a most difficult task in many health care agencies. The revealing of a positive test finding or an AIDS diagnosis may cause the loss of a job and benefits, breaches of civil liberties, and incidents of violence.

Medical treatment for persons with HIV infection and AIDS has changed radically since the beginning of the epidemic in 1981. Changes in the treatment of HIV infection and opportunistic diseases are occurring rapidly because of the introduction of new treatment procedures and drugs. Such developments have significantly affected the quality of life of people with HIV and AIDS. Multiple drug therapies have radically changed the clinical condition of many who have been symptomatic and facing foreshortened lives. Some longer-term survivors assumed from the premature death of their friends and family members from HIV-related conditions that they only had months or at best a few years to live. Consequently, they left jobs and were forced to use most of their financial resources. A so-called Lazarus effect has been noted among this population who have felt they have come back from the dead. It is not unusual for these survivors to have seemingly paradoxical reactions of depression, agitation, and disorientation to unexpected quality of life enhancement and increased longevity. A major emphasis of social workers in recent years has been to help those who have benefited significantly from "state-of-the-art" treatments to accept that they have a future and begin to plan for reentry into the hurly-burly of work, contact with family and friends, and reintegration into community activities.

Social workers and other professionals committed to working with PWAs also have been disoriented by these medical breakthroughs that eliminate quick death from opportunistic infection shortly after an AIDS diagnosis. HIV-related illnesses and disabilities have shifted from an overwhelming chronic syndrome with successively worsening acute life-threatening episodes to a chronic condition with indeterminate symptom display characterized by less frequent acute life-threatening episodes. Important advances also have been made in the treatment of opportunistic infections and cancers historically associated with an AIDS diagnosis. Medical treatments tend to be administered more often by health professionals in the client's home than in acute care hospitals. Social workers in health care must now work with the family as a whole in adjusting to intrusion of medical treatment in the home that may involve their participation in supporting medical treatment.

Not all persons have benefited from these revolutionary medical advances; some have initially rallied only to become acutely ill again, while others have not benefited at all. A profound sense of personal failure may be felt by such patients and those frustrated health care professionals caring for them.

RESILIENCIES AND PROTECTIVE FACTORS

While HIV/AIDS opens people to biopsychosocial vulnerabilities from forces from within and without, core resiliency and reserves of strength of people affected by HIV/AIDS represent a stunning resource for the practitioner. The early indigenous PWA movement demanded that researchers and clinicians not use terms such as *sufferer, afflicted,* and *patient,* connotive of an inherent moral weakness of the person. PWAs were also to be represented at all public forums, educational presentations, and panels and boards reviewing AIDS service projects. The dignity and humanity of PWAs were recognized as crucial to expanding human rights and enhancing public understanding (Kramer 1989; Shilts 1987). AIDS service organizations such as GMHC and the San Francisco AIDS Foundation developed legal and public policy arms to support PWAs and their families in challenging violations of their civil rights at the workplace and in public accommodation. Thus, built into the social construction of an individual's career as a PWA was the expectation or at least the possibility of standing resolutely against prejudices and other forms of societal violence. In short, participants in the AIDS movement endeavored to disabuse themselves and the public of the image of the PWA as a pitiable victim with a tainted moral status. With the support of organizations and community-based self-defense structures, the strengths and resiliency of PWAs had a sociopolitical context for recognition and support. PWAs and their loved ones saw the practical virtues of challenging threats from enemies of their interests. From a position of self-defense and identity politics, the PWA came to represent someone who not only needed assistance from time to time but also had contributions to make toward the well-being of the rest of the population who were in denial of their vulnerability to HIV infection and AIDS pandemic. Interestingly, many PWAs assumed roles as expert HIV educators and AIDS service providers after their diagnosis.

The AIDS movement provided important semantic distinctions and behavioral stances that contributed to the possibility of a wholesome identity arising out of an AIDS diagnosis or later an HIV-positive test finding. For example, a self-help organization of HIV-positive men and women in New York City was named "Body-Positive."

Paradoxically, AIDS and HIV for many affected people became an affirmative, transformative experience. Upon discovering that they are infected with HIV or have an AIDS diagnosis, some people make fundamental changes in their lives, such as the recovery from substance abuse and the assumption of a more healthful diet or lifestyle. They may even see HIV/AIDS as a gift or an opening to spiritual regeneration. In support groups and in other contexts, PWAs typically demonstrate coping styles or survival strategies that prove very useful in more effectively managing the shifting states of vulnerability associated with the biopsychosocial twists and turns of symptoms and illness.

The dangerous stances for people affected by HIV/AIDS are related to two extremes: either becoming morbidly preoccupied with HIV/AIDS or assuming an outlook of total denial of HIV/AIDS that includes continuation of poor health habits and unsafe sex. However, there are alternative strategies that have survival benefits that are continuous with social types familiar to us all from life and literature: for example, "The Hero" who valiantly fights the foe, AIDS, and although he or she may be vanquished in the end, lives bravely in others' memories. In addition to a *heroic* survival strategy, a PWA may use *beneficence,* or helping others, as a positive mode of coping while being helped him- or herself. Other PWAs become *instrumental-rational* by reading medical journals or seeking out experts in devising self-care approaches for themselves and others. For others, the use of *artistic-spiritual* expression may be their mode of transcending or understanding the boundary and the existential problems associated with illness, death, and meaning.

These survival strategies represent socially validated constructions that are personally driven efforts to avoid the extremes of morbidity and blanket denial of life-threatening conditions. Social workers should be respectful of these survival strategies as wholly human efforts to deal with existential concerns. As human actions, they reflect social connection with others, a historical period and intentionality (to move beyond the here-and-now to images of a future). These are the mechanisms to resiliency that represent strengths existing alongside vulnerabilities.

Strengths can only exist in a context of support and recognition that is imparted significantly in social workers' attitudes and actions toward people with HIV/AIDS. Despite social workers' myopic preoccupation with *disease* and *dysfunction,* the essential truth is that we work with people through their evident strengths or those reserves of strength that are hidden for the moment. Just as PWAs use maladaptive stances and positive survival strategies, social workers benefit from honest appraisals of their own stances to HIV/AIDS that support or deter PWAs' healthful efforts. For example, some social workers have been shocked and confused by PWAs who were literally dying of complications of AIDS, now having remarkable recoveries because of revolutionary new medicines. We are reaching a period when learning to live with AIDS is far more prevalent than learning to die from its complications.

PROGRAMS AND SOCIAL WORK CONTRIBUTIONS

The nearly twenty years of activities by social workers with and in behalf of PWAs have been characterized by *heroic humanitarianism* in meeting the acute, crisis-related problem of persons infected or affected by HIV (Lopez and Getzel 1987; Palacios-Jimenez and Shernoff 1986; Ryan 1987; Sonsel, Paradise, and Stroup 1988). The humanitarian strategy created an array of AIDS-specific programs either de novo in the case of voluntary community-based AIDS organizations, or through political agitation for special entitlement for PWAs—income maintenance programs, housing, mental health care, drug reimbursement, and AIDS-designated medical units and long-term facilities. In addition, some governmental units have provided PWAs with varying degree of legal protections and assistance.

Heroic humanitarianism has created an appreciable, but often shoddy, service network for PWAs. For example, in New York City it is not unusual for formerly impoverished, homeless PWAs to say, "After I got AIDS, they treated me like a human being."

This form of *exceptionalism* in behalf of PWAs, while life enhancing in many instances, creates resentment among other needy people with non-AIDS-related conditions that are no less life threatening and serious. Of particular concern now that medical breakthroughs are improving the health of many PWAs is that these critical survival benefits will be removed.

Since the early 1980s many social work programmatic efforts have been undertaken in response to the AIDS epidemic in the United States. Social workers have participated in the development of *community-based programs* for PWAs and their loved ones under gay auspices, first in the establishment of the Gay Men's Health Crisis in New York City in 1982 (Lopez and Getzel 1984), followed by the Los Angeles AIDS Project and the Shanti Project in San Francisco. These innovative programs operate through the large-scale use of nonprofessionals and professionals as volunteers providing an array of personal services to help PWAs and their loved ones to handle the multiple crises often associated with diagnosis and the subsequent biopsychosocial crises precipitated by illness, hospitalizations, financial difficulties, legal and employment problems, familial conflicts, and entitlement concerns. Hundreds of community-based programs for PWAs initially started by the gay and lesbian community now serve thousands of gay and nongay persons throughout North America and parts of Europe.

Social workers and other professionals have been particularly influential in the development of and leadership in volunteer *crisis intervention teams,* whose members are available to provide emotional support and advocacy activities to PWAs and their loved ones at critical periods of stress in the psychosocial sequence of the disease (Lopez and Getzel 1987).

Volunteer crisis workers undergo careful recruitment and require ongoing supervision and training. Another widespread innovative program uses volunteers as "buddies" who do light household chores for disabled PWAs as well as provide social contact to break down social isolation.

Community-based programs offer *support groups* for PWAs, which are generally run by social workers and other professional volunteers. Membership in these groups may be open-ended and as needed, or closed-ended and long term (Gambe and Getzel 1989). Support groups for family members and care partners are also quite common. Innovative couples' groups for both gay and nongay couples are sometimes used, as well as groups that focus on bereavement adjustment, which are generally time limited.

Educational or more *didactic-oriented group programs* are increasingly used to teach safer sex by cognitive-behavioral techniques. Support groups for persons who are HIV-positive, but who are otherwise asymptomatic, that focus on more healthful living and on social support are becoming more widespread as testing for the virus is related to experimental treatments to ward off HIV symptoms and an AIDS diagnosis. Social workers and other health care professionals may conduct such groups in community health programs or at HIV testing sites. The special problems of women who are HIV-infected, of children who have siblings with AIDS, and of survivors of multiple losses due to AIDS may be addressed through special focus groups that universalize their difficult situations with peer support.

Family counseling with persons from a variety of backgrounds, conducted by social workers, has proved promising (Walker 1987). Increasingly, social workers in private practice and agency work are seeing the direct and indirect influence of AIDS and HIV infection in their caseloads. For example, agencies serving the visually disabled are being asked to work with PWAs blinded by different opportunistic infections and cancers. Long-term-care facilities and home care programs are being pressed into service for multiply disabled PWAs, including individuals with AIDS dementia. Hospice programs tailored to the particular needs of PWAs are beginning to be established.

A primary setting for social work intervention remains the *acute care hospital* during the health crises of PWAs. Whether dispersed or in a designated area, PWAs and their families require focused crisis intervention and even short-term groups.

Increasingly, *case management work* by social workers is an area of importance because of the growth of outpatient care provision. Sensitive work with PWAs is necessary as they become more disabled and disoriented. Homelessness and poverty among inner-city hospital AIDS patients require intensive case management and the elimination of routine bureaucratic red tape. Social workers frequently become strong advocates for entitlements and prompt responses from large public agencies, especially when their clients are in crisis and are under the stresses of life-threatening conditions. A high degree of interprofessional cooperation is not unusual in hospital programs designed for AIDS patients.

Support networks of social workers have also developed in different parts of the country to allow exchanges of information as well as to provide professional recognition and emotional support. Social workers also have given expert testimony to local, state. and federal panels on AIDS and HIV infection.

The advent of so-called welfare reform, privatization, and managed care further highlight societal failures to effectively deal with a grave public health emergency. Placing money and cost containment before the needs of people has serious consequences for PWAs. The absence of a national health care program in the United States places all citizens at risk during pandemic and other health care emergencies, because there is no comprehensive system for the dissemination of public health education.

Scientists also lack accurate baseline epidemiological data on all Americans so that the progression of the pandemic can be adequately monitored.

Citizens may be wary of how for-profit insurance companies and other corporate entities will use sensitive medical information to deny them services or infringe on their privacy. The social work profession through its national association and other organizations have continued to respond slowly to the pandemic. Conflicts of interest also exist when professionals collude with managed care and insurance programs for short-run financial rewards. The federal government continues to resist funding needle exchange programs that effectively reduce HIV infection among users of intravenous drugs.

Despite these considerable limitations, there is need to generate programs that address the niche requirement of women, adolescents, older people, AIDS orphans, long-term survivors, prisoners, immigrants, the newly infected, and the cumulatively traumatized through serial bereavement. Social workers clearly have and can continue to assume leadership in these areas of emerging need.

ASSESSMENT AND INTERVENTIONS

Social work practice with PWAs must be particularly sensitive to the diversity of the people infected and affected in each case. Individuals, families, communities, and regions reflect different patterns and variations that significantly influence diagnoses, assessments, and interventions. The following case illustrations point to the complexity of understanding needed to work with persons with AIDS and HIV infection.

Peter is currently hospitalized in a room filled with cards and flowers. This is his third hospitalization in four months. He is a white 34-year-old gay man and the first college-educated member of his working-class suburban family. Peter has known that he is HIV-positive for ten years. Four years ago, his T cell count dropped below 200, and the volume of HIV infection grew in his body. Peter was among the first patients to take combination antiviral drugs. The drugs reduced viral activity and his blood work improved as did his sense of well-being. Recently, viral activity has increased because of his diminished response to combination drug treatment. He has been hospitalized three times in the last two months for hepatitis and bacterial pneumonia. Peter has lost 30 pounds. His friends and his former lover have been available to help him in the hospital and at home. He has grown depressed and agitated and has told his sister that they should plan his suicide.

Martha is a Hispanic female, aged 40, and is a recovering narcotic addict with a history of drug abuse from the age of 14 to 35. She had one child when she was 20 years old; at 6 months of age, the child was removed from her by the department of child welfare. After her second child was shot to death in a gunfight, Martha joined Narcotics Anonymous and has been drug-free for five years. She joined an AIDS support group shortly after being diagnosed six months ago. Martha, a leader in the group, says the group helps.

Warren is a white 35-year-old bisexual man who is married and has no children. His wife does not know about his AIDS diagnosis; he is frightened that she is HIV-infected.

Warren has been able to continue working but spends all his available time reading medical journals; he tells his social worker at the clinic that he will "beat" AIDS. Warren has been asymptomatic since discovering Kaposi's sarcoma lesions on his chest a year and a half ago.

Jane is a 25-year-old middle-class woman who was exposed to HIV through a six-month relationship with a man with a prison record who did tell her he had AIDS. She was diagnosed as HIV-positive after losing a great deal of weight and having recurring fevers. Her current boyfriend, Roberto, accepted the news of Jane's HIV diagnosis and he subsequently tested HIV-negative. A month later, he proposed marriage. They have expressed interest in adopting a child in a year or two.

Allan is a 16-year-old hemophiliac who became HIV-positive from infected blood products used for their clotting substance. Allan's older brother, also a hemophiliac, died several years ago from AIDS. Allan is currently unaware that his father, a hemophiliac, is HIV-positive, while his mother is not. Recently, his parents have been fighting and have discussed a trial separation.

Each person with HIV infection has a unique history, specific life experiences, social supports, and other resources. In considering how to serve this population, social workers should pay particular attention to the following assessment criteria and intervention foci. Christ, Weiner, and Moynihan (1986) indicated that at diagnosis, an individual generally goes through profound and far-reaching emotional responses to the *psychosocial* consequences of the illness. In turn, all persons intimately related to the diagnosed person may experience similar strong emotional reactions. The social worker must understand the intensity of the coping efforts that underlie the strong and sometimes confusing reactions of individuals and their families.

Psychosocial issues are expressed at the dyadic relational level between a PWA and providers of health and human service and within the family system. A person with symptoms associated with HIV or an AIDS diagnosis goes through strong responses during his or her periods of illness. Anxiety about being diagnosed may precede the development of any symptom of an opportunistic infection. Persistent respiratory infections, skin rashes, and transitory fever may occasion sleeplessness, psychosomatic symptoms, and obsessive thinking.

Panicky reactions build if a person develops night sweats, swollen glands, weight loss, and other HIV-related symptoms before the presence of an AIDS diagnosis. Paradoxically, once the PWA develops an opportunistic infection and finally receives a formal AIDS diagnosis, he or she may be emotionally relieved for a time. A PWA often feels, "At least I can now stop worrying that I'm going to get AIDS."

Pre- or postdiagnosis preoccupation with becoming ill results in social isolation. Affected individuals may see themselves as possessed by the disease—controlled at every turn by thoughts about illness—and subtly and not so subtly reminded by others that they have a potentially progressive fatal condition. Therefore, PWAs often see themselves as toxic, stigmatized outcasts worthy of others' rejections.

Susan Sontag wrote, "Any illness that is treated as a mystery and acutely enough to be feared will be felt to be morally, if not literally contagious" (1977:5–6). The association of AIDS with homosexuality and substance abuse has contributed to the public's fears and the legitimation of prejudice and aversion. Unfortunately, many

PWAs also assume these powerful negative images of themselves, which are too frequently reinforced by the actual withdrawal of kin, friends, and others who become fearful of becoming ill or tainted by their contact with AIDS.

Family members' and friends' vulnerabilities are heightened if they share PWAs' lifestyles, age, interests, and personal habits. Aversive and rejecting behaviors by providers of health and human service are particularly potent in feeding depression, diminishing self-esteem, and engendering rage in already stressed and burdened PWAs.

Mounting social isolation contributes to PWAs' feeling withdrawn, depressed, emotionally worthless, physically fatigued, and sexually void. PWAs may experience shame at being exposed as gay or as drug users or as sexually linked with these populations. Tragically, some PWAs may associate AIDS with a personal attribute and not with past activities. Defensively, these PWAs may bargain to go straight or to swear off the use of drugs, if they might be cured. This kind of magical thinking and self-condemnation becomes a dead-end approach by PWAs to overcome the crises of diagnosis, illness, and disabilities.

Social workers must carefully assess the positive coping elements in PWAs' emotional expression during crisis periods. During crises, PWAs' characteristic methods of coping with feeling states and problem solving falter. An emotional roller-coaster ride of anger, guilt, rage, sadness, and fear represents PWAs' early efforts to cope with each bit of medical information, new symptoms, and functional losses.

Social workers are most helpful when they assist PWAs to understand their reactions at a specific time. For example, sadness and depression reflect, in part, authentic grieving over actual bodily and functional losses. As PWAs are able to give themselves time and space to grieve, they can approach other aspects of personal mortality. The prospect of dying from AIDS often opens up memories of the deaths of family members and friends. PWAs may feel guilty about the burdens that they believe their illness is placing on loved ones for their care. Consequently, PWAs may be reticent to ask for help from others. PWAs' anger and rage are reflections of the injustices of falling ill and being rejected by others. Anger can be positive, if it can be channeled into being more assertive with physicians and other providers of health and social services.

Becoming a thoughtful and responsive consumer of help results from social workers' legitimating PWAs' sometimes diffuse anger and sense of impotence when approaching the staffs of hospitals and social agencies. Far too often, PWAs feel powerless as they face making new and greater demands for care. If PWAs can gain a sense of control over their care, they are apt to experience enhanced responses and practical assistance from the medical establishment, social agencies, employers, and others.

Finally, in the face of ultimate questions of life and death, PWAs show remarkable capacities for hope. Even though PWAs occasionally intimate as well as actually speak about suicide, expressions of hope are ubiquitous. In many situations, denial of being ill or of having a foreshortened existence is a necessary and useful coping strategy. Hope is supported when PWAs live as fully as they can. Just as PWAs should be allowed to deny aspects of their illness, they should be free to express concerns about dying and death, which often come up in the discussion of wills, funeral arrangements, and living wills that control quality of life while dying.

Social workers and other professionals serving people with HIV infection and

AIDS—and, for that matter, responding to a variety of other problems and conditions—should draw a broad operational definition of family, so that it includes all relatives, life companions, and friends who demonstrate a long-term commitment to caring for the person in need.

Social workers should identify a PWA's functional family as the network that provides some measure of emotional support, guidance, material resources, and help with practical, everyday routines and chores. Members of the family network play an important role in determining how PWAs receive needed health care, social services, legal assistance, and other services, particularly during crisis periods and at points of incapacitation. The family network undergoes changing patterns of closeness and social support to a PWA as he or she experiences the crises associated with HIV and AIDS. A PWA may be overwhelmed at the prospect of revealing a diagnosis to unsuspecting relatives for fear of emotional rejection and abandonment. The pressure on the PWA is heightened if family members also will discover the "secret" of homosexuality or drug use. While such fears cannot be dismissed, it is also not uncommon for relatives and friends to move closer after such revelations, paradoxically surprising the wary PWA.

The decision to inform a family of an AIDS or HIV-positive diagnosis must always be the PWA's; the social worker can be the most helpful in assisting the PWA to find the appropriate time and way to share the diagnosis with particular family members and friends. Family dynamics as well as cultural and ethnic styles may be factors in how and with whom information is first shared. Clearly, there are political consequences in and outside the family network when an AIDS diagnosis is revealed.

Very often, the social worker's balanced, nonjudgmental, and accepting attitude toward a PWA, during good times and bad, serves as an antidote to recurrent feelings of isolation, diminished self-esteem, and suspicion. One of the most powerful and effective tools for helping a PWA to break down isolation and to regain a sense of normality and trust is the PWA support group, which universalizes experiences and provides true understanding and a safe environment (Child and Getzel 1989; Gambe and Getzel 1989; Getzel and Mahony 1989).

AIDS may prompt family members to try to resolve long-standing concerns related to sexuality, drug use, and other significant historical issues in the kinship network. A PWA and a family member may share guilt and recriminations, holding themselves or others responsible for the irreversible tragedies each perceives. Gay couples may experience a breakdown in their relationship and in their capacity for trust and intimacy. Family members may be ashamed to share their feelings with friends who are perceived as too judgmental about the subject of AIDS.

Fear of HIV contagion is especially upsetting to members of the family network who fear casual contact or who are justifiably concerned about sexual, intravenous needle, or fetal transmission. Therefore, in the course of their work with family members, social workers must assess the risks of transmission and the wisdom of HIV antibody testing in the immediate and long-term interests of the members of the kinship network. Social workers have an important role in the direct teaching of families about AIDS transmission and prevention and about safer sex practices.

If spouses and life companions of PWAs are HIV-positive or believe themselves to be infected, they may fear developing symptoms or opportunistic infections. Powerful feelings of anxiety, helplessness, and even anger toward PWAs may make it difficult for spouses and life companions to acknowledge self-concerns, especially if they are providing significant caregiving. They may have recurrent fatalistic fantasies and fears of becoming ill alongside the PWA. Even if a spouse or life companion is HIV-negative, he or she may experience survivor's guilt and feelings of personal unworthiness. If a child is infected, the emotional burdens for the mother and others in the family are catastrophic.

Social workers should be aware of the ethical questions entailed in sharing information about HIV infection and AIDS. Legal requirements for reporting test results to a person's sexual partners exist in certain jurisdictions, as well as rules for strict confidentiality about sharing test findings and diagnoses.

Families of intravenous drug users may have several members who are infected and ill at different times or all at once; over time, the family network may collapse functionally and physically from within. Such families require humane and continuous survival services and ongoing grief and bereavement counseling. Child welfare services become very important (Anderson 1986). Before care can be provided and formal diagnoses made, poverty, racism, and cultural barriers must be overcome by community-based service providers and inner-city hospitals' staff who often discover HIV-infected men, women, and children who have long been ill and are severely debilitated. Intravenous drug users' survival strategies frequently entail subterfuge, criminality, and suspicion, which continue in their relationships with AIDS service providers, who in turn become antagonistic adversaries. Relapse prevention strategies have assumed central importance in the psychosocial treatment of HIV-positive addicts.

The burdens of family caregivers deepen with successive health crises. PWAs' concerns about becoming increasingly dependent on others may be expressed in strong emotional reactions to family members. Stresses from the indignities of illness and from historic conflicts within the family network are bound to overwhelm even the most even-tempered PWAs from time to time. Support groups for family caregivers provide valuable opportunities to discuss practical concerns and emotional issues with others who are having similar experiences.

When conflicts erupt in the family network, social workers should assume a mediating function. The well-being of the PWAs must always be of paramount concern. When PWAs face life-threatening health crises, family members may wish to discuss such contingencies as living wills, powers of attorney, funeral arrangements, and estate planning. If these arrangements are made carefully in advance, they help families avoid excessive conflict during periods of stress. Discussion of these practical concerns of living and dying allows anticipatory grief expressions and some partial acceptance of the prospective losses.

Many persons now appear to be living longer with AIDS. An immediate death from opportunistic infections may be less likely because of more sophisticated medical treatments and the effectiveness of antiviral medications. As PWAs live longer with AIDS, they make plans against a backdrop of incertitude. Life cycle events like baptisms, weddings, bar mitzvahs, and holiday rituals assume greater importance because they break down social isolation and allow opportunities to participate in activities that represent continuity and contribution to others. PWAs often desire ways to identify their legacies to loved ones as they review the meaning of their lives during or after life-threatening episodes.

Family members and PWAs exhibit considerable variation in their capacity to discuss illness directly, regardless of how ominous circumstances become. Caregivers may need help to accept respite from the increasing anxiety and pressures that occur during the course of the disease. Often, a PWA is relieved of guilt if the burdens of caregiving are lightened for a primary-caregiving family member. Family members continue to struggle with AIDS after PWAs die. The need for remembrance, validation, and continued expressions of grief is natural and predictable. Loved ones may benefit from bereavement groups geared to the special needs of "survivors" of AIDS. There are no simple formulas for adjusting to the loss of so many people cut off in the prime of their lives by devastating illnesses. Family members who care for PWAs may find volunteer work in AIDS service organization a meaningful way to memorialize relatives and friends, and to participate anew in life's sorrows and joys.

ILLUSTRATION AND DISCUSSION

It is in the specific case that the human face of AIDS is revealed. Understanding human responses to AIDS is important, not only in indicating how the mechanics of diagnosis and intervention may be accomplished, but also in sensitizing clinicians to the pathos of PWAs, who often must face, in addition to the indignities of disease, societal stigma and isolation. In preparation for AIDS work, practitioners may benefit from an examination of the emerging literature of firsthand encounters with AIDS (Dreuilhe 1988; Monette 1988; Peabody 1986; Whitmore 1988) or accounts by practitioners (Greenly 1986; Snow 1987).

The following case description focuses on Marcos Vega, a 24-year-old Latino man who sought out help from a community-based AIDS clinic after finding out Anita, his 20-year-old wife, was HIV-positive after a routine prenatal examination revealed abnormal blood findings. Marcos was 21 years old when he met Anita, who was completing her senior year in high school. Marcos had a history of substance abuse since the age of 13, culminating with heroin addiction.

Marcos did not know his father, who left the family when Marcos was 4 years old; he persistently dreamed of uniting with his father, but feared that he might have died. His mother had tried repeatedly to get Marcos into rehab and felt increasingly helpless in her ability to take care of him. After his mother's death, Marcos was tossed from one family member to another. After multiple rejections, he began receiving welfare benefits and continued to fail in all drug programs he was required to attend. The road to sobriety was long with many arrests, homelessness, loneliness, depression, and suicidal gestures.

Persuaded by a friend of his mother, Marcos began to attend Narcotics Anonymous (NA) regularly; he felt strong for the first time in his life. His confidence grew with each month of sustained sobriety. Marcos was well liked by others in "the rooms" of NA. He soon met Anita after being introduced by a friend from NA. They both remember it as love at first sight. Despite her father's reasonable concerns about Marcos's ability to earn a living and take care of his beloved oldest daughter, they were married. Anita success-fully completed high school and continued to work at a local grocery, con-tributing money to her family as well as pooling income with Marcos who worked as a peer educator in his drug treatment program. Marcos was widely seen by his peers as a role model of successful recovery accomplished by hard work. The Vegas both felt that they were working together to make their dreams happen. A few months into their marriage, Anita was pregnant. Al-though surprised, they felt confident that all would be fine. Unfortunately, even with all of this determination, the Vegas were going to face even more daunting challenges arising from HIV and AIDS.

Anita's first prenatal visit showed an abnormal count for white blood cells, the cells that help fight off infection. The Vegas were referred to a hospital social worker who, after a brief interview, noted factors in their history placing them at high risk for HIV infection. The worker told the Vegas that given Marcos's historic drug use, she strongly recommended that they each be tested for HIV. Anita looked confused and asked if anything bad could happen to their baby. The social worker noted if Anita were HIV-negative, the baby could not be HIV-positive. If she were HIV-positive, there were drugs that help the fetus avoid infection. Anita looked confused and disoriented.

Phase 1. In the first phase with a family affected by HIV, social workers engage and assess the condition of the persons at risk of an HIV/AIDS diag-nosis. The beginning phase of intervention also is characterized by approach-avoidance responses prompted by the at-risk person's unconscious sense of dependency and the loss of control that is associated with simply reaching for help. HIV/AIDS itself is emblematic of uncertainty and the prospect of the loss of bodily control. Therefore, the social worker working with people affected by HIV/AIDS must strive to give them a sense of control by allowing them to define their needs at their own pace and in their own terms. The interventive approach is, therefore, nonconfrontational and typically permits a PWA to ritually tell and retell his or her survival story beginning with diagnosis and attendant concerns. The social worker points out commonal-ties of the experience and acknowledges explicit and implicit painful affects, including shame, guilt, loneliness, rage and sadness.

Marcos grew extremely agitated, blaming himself for never having a complete blood workup. Avoiding his wife's eyes, he told the social worker that he was confident that there was absolutely no risk to the baby. As if he were pleading his case to the social worker, he reiterated that the only pos-sible route of infection was his multiple sexual partners from the period he was out in the streets and using. Marcos only remembers using drugs intra-venously one time with a buddy of his from high school, all the other times he did his usual snorting. Marcos felt assured that this was the first time for his friend. Marcos hadn't seen this friend in at least seven years, no one had.

After a long painful interview with their social worker, the Vegas decided to be tested for the HIV. In Anita's words, "not for themselves but for the baby."

Anita and Marcos met with their doctor and the social worker when they discovered they both tested HIV-positive. They were shocked and never had an idea of the possibility.

The next few weeks were filled with heartache and pain. In silence and secrecy, both Anita and Marcos found their attention primarily focused on the pregnancy and HIV. Anita tearfully told the worker that she had no one to talk to about her concerns. Marcos spent a great deal of time working and going to NA meetings. Anita was particularly fearful of her father's reaction and thought that it would hurt him too much. Marcos kept it quiet among his friends, only telling his Narcotic Anonymous sponsor, afraid of former addicts' reactions.

The Vegas each privately told the social worker that they were concerned about the well-being of the other and did not know where to turn. The social worker asked them how helpful it would be if they came together for a few sessions to speak about the pregnancy as a couple. During a single session they began ask each other out loud: Would we soon get ill and die? Do we need to be taking medications? What about our unborn child? The Vegas realized that they had each other for support, but they also needed other forms of help. The social worker suggested that they make active use of counseling with her and join relevant support groups that the agency offered.

Phase 2. Assisting and supporting persons with HIV/AIDS, the social worker continues to identify and to explore complex psychosocial problems with clients. The social worker must avoid the temptation to preempt self-determination out of anxiety arising from perceptions that the persons with HIV/AIDS are automatically weak and vulnerable. The worker identifies the strengths and resiliency present by their characteristic survival strategies.

Anita said to the social worker that she was afraid to be in an HIV support group. She was also concerned about her father finding out that she was HIV-positive. Anita was feeling like she was in the eye of a hurricane with everything imaginable turning in every direction around her, "Everything was a blur." Anita decided she would see the social worker weekly and when any crisis occurred. She noted that she could no longer keep herself bottled up inside.

The first in a series of crises occurred when Anita was four months pregnant. The Vegas met with a physician and a social worker, specialists in HIV treatment. This made it possible for the Vegas to get an updated physical with blood results and give a pyschosocial history that would hopefully assist them in receiving state-of-the-art treatment and much needed assistance with illness and complex treatment protocols.

Anita was told that in addition to having the HIV antibodies, she had been exposed to hepatitis; with these both, the risk of liver failure was highly possible. This stress on her body could impact the welfare of her unborn child as well. Her CD4 count, also referred to as the T cell count (number of white blood cells), was beginning to decline, probably due to, among other things, the high stress level in her life. When she was diagnosed, Anita's count was around 400, but since then consistent drops had occurred. Medications were immediately started, antiretroviral combination therapy for Anita. Her doctor told her of the importance of starting them now and how the treatment might allow the child not to contract the HIV virus.

Phase 3. A person affected by HIV/AIDS often receives quick relief by hearing similar situations and responses from peers in a support group led by a social worker. Although many group members may be locked into their own emotional world, a support group offers nonthreatening acceptance from peers and a recognition of shared experiences. They can also discuss the quality of life issues for themselves and loved ones.

Marcos's health was more robust than his wife's constantly weakening condition. His CD4 count remained at a stable 700. Although he had also signs of exposure to hepatitis A, likely arising from sharing intravenous drugs, his liver seemed to be holding up fine. Marcos and his doctor made the decision not to start medications at this time.

Marcos grew increasingly more taciturn and depressed in his contacts with the social worker who was concerned that Marcos was at a higher risk of relapse into addiction with the many stresses now evident in his life. In their interviews, the worker frequently checked in on Marcos's use of an already strong peer support system. Despite his acute depressive episodes, Marcos went to several NA meetings weekly, and several supportive friends in recovery cared about his welfare. Keeping this level of connection with the meetings and speaking daily with his NA sponsor were strongly reinforced by the social worker. Marcos also started attending a support group for newly diagnosed people who also used the same HIV/AIDS clinic. Accustomed to being in groups, Marcos shared a flood of concerns about Anita's diminishing health and whether the baby would be healthy. Marcos was gently confronted by two male members that he seemed to speak more about his wife than himself. Marcos seemed not to hear their comments.

Phase 4. It is not unusual for a person affected by HIV/AIDS to challenge the authenticity of the helping relationship and the meaning of HIV/AIDS for him- or herself. This is yet another step in the client's efforts to maintain autonomy in the face of uncontrollable bodily changes. Unexpressed rage at family members, friends, and others with better life prospects (including the social worker) may be expressed metaphorically or in strong emotional responses. People affected by HIV/AIDS are quick to pick up cues of the social worker's and others' survival guilt, death fears, and sadness.

Marcos's attendance at the support group became erratic; on two recent occasions, he called the worker to say that "something came up at work," but he surely would be there next week. When the worker told the group about Marcos's messages, members made no audible comments. The worker called Marcos before the next group session about the time and place of the meeting. Marcos told the worker not to worry, that he would attend. He came to the session as agreed and was unusually silent. Other groups members acted as if he were not present.

During a lull in the group discussion, Marcos announced, with muted affect, that he would be leaving the group. Marcos told the group that he really needed to maintain his sobriety and coming to the group interfered with a more important NA meeting. The group members grew restive and seemed unable to express their obvious shock and anger. The social worker noted that Marcos might also be angry at her for calling him to come to today's group meeting. Marcos vigorously denied he was angry at the worker or the group. The social worker stated that it was always a group member's right to leave a group, but that in this case, she felt that Marcos was flying away from the group and, perhaps, not examining some of his HIV-related concerns. A few group members wished him well, while two members said they regretted Marcos's decision to leave so quickly.

The following week, Marcos returned and told the group that he would stay. He expressed growing anxiety about Anita's health and whether the baby would survive to term. The group members commiserated with him and noted how upsetting these new developments were for him and for them. One member asked him if he ever thought that he might become sick and be unable to care for his family. Marcos sadly acknowledged he worries about that each night before he goes to sleep and looks at Anita . . .

Phase 5. The social worker supports persons affected in the family system by recognizing the possibility of foreshortened lives and yet living fully in the present. With the succession of symptoms, affected people begin to acknowledge directly the cumulative declines in functioning due to the disease process. Intimations of death are expressed metaphorically or as a contingency to be planned for and thus controlled. Events in the past assume saliency as future planning is fraught with uncertainties. A social worker should assist affected individuals and members of the family system to recognize the actual functional consequences of HIV/AIDS without encouraging either a morbid preoccupation with or a denial of the implications of specific health concerns.

Of critical significance is the social worker's powerful emotional identification with a declining PWA, which may propel the social worker to assume either premature fatalistic or magical solutions to the more tragic elements of the disease process. Through an ongoing life-review process, a PWA and others seek modes of mastery through active use of the past to make sense of the present and an uncertain future. Relationships with family members and longtime friends are examined in light of the realities of shifting life chances.

Anita presented many pyschosocial issues; she was falling into a deep depression, which was distracting herself from following proper care associated with her drug intake. Now six months pregnant, she felt alone. Marcos could not give her the attention that she felt she needed. Anita continued to keep her HIV status from everyone, but her father grew increasingly concerned and suspicious; he could sense that something was wrong. Anita denied any problems, "I have been working too hard, that's all, Father."

During an interview, Anita insisted that a support group could not help her, but she would attend if Marcos insisted. Two weeks later, Anita expressed her questions and concerns in the women's AIDS support group. A major topic in the group was the consequences of telling family and friends about their diagnosis. Some of the group members used the group as a source of guidance and support to inform their parents and friends. Anita felt group pressure to do the same. Anita wanted the support of her family but wondered if was possible. She told group members how upset she was when her father kept the mortal illness of her mother a secret until a few weeks before her death. Weeping, she said that she could not have carried out her household responsibilities caring for her siblings if she knew her mother was dying. The worker told Anita and the group that she felt some of the weight of Anita's continuing grief over the death of her mother. Anita nodded yes. The group began discussing how Anita might tell her father about being HIV-positive.

At the next session, Anita told the group that she was going to talk to her father, but something inside stopped her. Later, unexpectedly, after asking her about a recent visit to the doctor, Anita's father was dissatisfied with her response and felt she was holding something back. Anita told the group she was no longer able to hold it in. Her father asked once again and she told him the whole story. Anita began crying in the group. Marisol and Linda reached forward and held Anita's hands. Anita said sometimes you need a good cry, but expressed concern to the group about how her father would accept Marcos after the baby was born.

Phase 6. The social worker monitors and supports people affected by HIV/AIDS during episodic crises. As PWAs grow more seriously ill, they naturally become more dependent on others for care and emotional validation. The social worker assists affected people to become more observant of their changing health status, and to acknowledge the need to accept help from others. Anita's health was rapidly deteriorating. Now, seven months into her pregnancy, she was complaining that she did not have much energy in the morning and did not feel like going into work some days. When support group members suggested the possibility of her staying home, Anita's bristled, saying that it was impossible because they needed money.

Even though she now had the strong support from her father and other family members, Anita started distancing herself from Marcos and her family. She said that Marcos was too worried about her and he had plenty to do just to remain sober.

At one point in the group, the discussion turned quickly to the virtues of stopping work and going on disability benefits. Anita was concerned with falling into greater depression and isolation, if she stopped working. Going to so many medical appointments and managing her medications has become a second career. She said she envied the two members who decided to stop work and accept disability insurance.

After the eighth month of pregnancy, Anita was becoming weaker with each passing day. She also noticed a persistent cough and was fearful of it moving into her chest. Her next doctor's appointment confirmed her exposure to tuberculosis and the need to stay isolated in the hospital for its initial treatment. Visitors were required to wear a mask when in the room with Anita.

While in the hospital, Marcos and Anita spent hours talking about their hopes and dreams. Anita told the social worker she dreamt that the baby would live and she would die. Marcos discussed his fear about Anita "making it" and the chance of her missing most if not all of the child's life. The worker said even though it was difficult to discuss, his concern about planning for the child was important to him and Anita.

Phase 7. As a person with HIV/AIDS grows more seriously ill, the worker supports efforts made toward greater intimacy and more active grief work. As a person with HIV/AIDS experiences a more precipitous decline, especially in mental status and mobility, more sustainable discussion starts among the ill person and loved ones.

As her medical condition worsened, Anita became depressed, speaking only to Marcos and refusing to see the social worker. Marcos told the social worker that he asked a doctor if Anita and the baby would survive. The doctor indicated that the fetus seemed to be healthy, even though Anita was weaker. The birth would be very stressful, but hopefully she would make it. Marcos later told his support group members and sponsor that he was frightened to ask the doctor, but he felt he had to make plans for the baby even if Anita could not.

Later, Marcos and the social worker talked about a plan to speak to Anita's father about her oldest sister helping Marcos care for the baby after its birth. He said it would be hard speaking to his father-in-law, but they both shared a love for Anita and her baby. Later, Marcos spoke during a group session, to the applause of other members, about his successful conversation with his Anita's father.

Phase 8. The social worker assumes a more direct role in caring for and advocating in behalf of persons affected by HIV/AIDS. An ill PWA may not be able to discuss concerns. Caregivers become vital for their assistance at obvious points of intervention. The social worker supports and advocates for appropriate and dignified care during the often upsetting last days of life.

Anita gave birth to a baby boy. She seem to be flushed with energy after the birth, returning home a week later. Unfortunately, her health declined rapidly and she was hospitalized for bacterial pneumonia. Anita survived the respiratory distress, but she was unable to eat and required tube feeding. Marcos slept evenings and weekends in her hospital room or outside in the hall. The social worker convinced him to go home on several occasions. The social worker encouraged Marcos to follow his routine of NA attendance and going to his support group. The group assisted him in a decision to follow Anita's advance directives to withdraw all extraordinary means to keep her alive, if there were no hope of recovery. Her wish was to have maximum pain relief.

Anita's weight dropped to 60 pounds and she was transferred to a subacute facility for PWAs where she died three weeks later. Marcos continued attending the support group and had periodic contacts with the social worker prompted by bouts of grief and anxiety about how he could care for his son who turned out to be HIV-negative. He started to speak about making arrangements for the child's care if Marcos became sick or died.

CONCLUSION

It is not hyperbole to say that the measure of our society and the profession of social work will be made in how we respond to the AIDS pandemic in this country and throughout the world. Every aspect of our knowledge and our values will be challenged by the multilevel complexity of the efforts at prevention, treatment, and social reconstruction called for by the HIV infection and AIDS. Camus (1948) concluded in *The Plague* that in times of pestilence, there will hopefully be more to admire in humankind than to despise. In social solidarity, social workers, with other professionals and an educated citizenry, can and must act humanely and intelligently in the days and years ahead, as together we face the complexity and challenges of the pandemic.

References

Altman, Dennis. 1986. *AIDS in the Mind of America.* New York: Anchor Book Press.

Anderson, Gary B. 1986. *Children and AIDS: The Challenge for Children Welfare.* Washington, D.C.: Child Welfare League of America.

Bateson, Mary Catherine and Richard Goldsby. 1988. *Thinking AIDS: The Social Response to the Biological Threat.* Reading, Mass.: Addison-Wesley.

Bayer, Ronald. 1989. *Private Act, Social Consequences: AIDS and the Politics of Public Health.* New York: Free Press.

Buckley, Walter. 1967. *Sociology of Modern Systems Theory.* Englewood Cliffs, N.J.: Prentice-Hall.

Cahill, Kevin M. 1984. "Preface: The Evolution of an Epidemic." In Kevin M. Cahill, ed., *The AIDS Epidemic,* pp. 2–6. New York: St. Martin's Press.

Camus, Albert. 1948. *The Plague.* New York: Knopf.

Cannon, Walter B. 1939. *The Wisdom of the Body.* New York: Norton.

Caputo, Larry. 1985. "Dual Diagnosis: AIDS and Addiction." *Social Work* 30:62–73.

CDC (Centers for Disease Control). 1997, January. *HIV/AIDS Surveillance Report.* Atlanta, Ga.: Author.

Child, Rachel and George S. Getzel. 1989. "Group Work with Inner City People with AIDS." *Social Work with Groups* 12(4):65–80.

Christ, Grace, Lori Weiner, and Rosemary Moynihan. 1986. "Psychosocial Issues in AIDS." *Psychiatric Annals* 16:173–79.

Dickens, Bernard M. 1988. "Legal Rights and Duties in the AIDS Epidemic." *Science* 239:580–86.

Dreuilhe, Emmanuel. 1988. *Mortal Embrace.* New York: Hill & Wang.

Dubos, Rene. 1959. *Mirage of Health: Utopias, Progress and Biological Change.* New York: Harper & Row.

——. 1965. *Man Adapting.* New Haven, Conn.: Yale University Press.

Fineberg, Harvey V. 1988. "Education to Prevent AIDS: Prospects and Obstacles." *Science* 239:592–96.

Friedland, Gerald H. 1989. "Clinical Care in the AIDS Epidemic." *Daedalus* 118:59–83.

Gallo, Robert C. and Luc Montagnier. 1989. "The AIDS Epidemic." In William Heyward and James W. Curran, eds., *The Science of AIDS: Readings from Scientific American,* pp. 1–12. New York: W. H. Freeman.

Gambe, Richard and George S. Getzel. 1989. "Group Work with Gay Men with AIDS." *Social Casework* 70:172–79.

Germaine, Carel B. and Alex Gitterman. 1996. *The Life Model of Social Work Practice.* New York: Columbia University Press.

Getzel, George S. and Kevin Mahony. 1988. "Education for Life During the AIDS Pandemic." *Social Casework* 69:393–96.

——. 1989. " Facing Human Finitude: Group Work People with AIDS." *Social Work with Groups* 2:95–107.

Greenly, Mike. 1986. *Chronicle.* New York: Irvington.

Heyward, William and James W. Curran. 1989. *The Science of AIDS: Readings from the Scientific American.* New York: W. H. Freeman.

JAMA (Journal of the American Medical Association). 1996. 276:126–31.

Kramer, Larry. 1989. *Reports from the Holocaust: The Making of an AIDS Activist.* New York: St. Martin's Press.

Leukefeld, Carl G. and Manuel Fimbres. 1987. *Responding to AIDS.* Washington, D.C.: National Association of Social Workers.

Lopez, Diego J. and George S. Getzel. 1984. "Helping Gay Patients in Crisis." *Social Casework* 65:387–94.

———. 1987. "Strategies for Volunteers Caring for Persons with AIDS." *Social Casework* 68:47–53.

Mann, Jonathan M., James Chinn, Peter Pilot, and Thomas Quinn. 1989. "The International Epidemiology of AIDS." In William Heyward and James W. Curran, eds., *The Science of AIDS: Readings from the Scientific American,* pp. 51–61. New York: W. H. Freeman.

Mann, Jonathan M. and D. J. M. Tarantola. 1996. *AIDS in the World II: Global Dimensions, Social Roots and Response.* New York: Oxford University Press.

Mass, Lawrence. 1987 *Medical Facts About AIDS.* New York: Gay Men's Health Crisis.

Monette, Paul. 1988. *Borrowed Time: An AIDS Memoir.* San Diego: Harcourt Brace Jovanovich.

Nichols, Eve K. 1987. *Mobilizing Against AIDS: The Unfinished Story of a Virus.* Cambridge: Harvard University Press.

Palacios-Jimenez, Luis and Michael Shernoff. 1986. *Eroticizing Safer Sex.* New York: Gay Men's Health Crisis.

Peabody, Barbara. 1986. *The Screaming Room: A Mother's Journal of Her Son's Struggle with AIDS.* San Francisco: Old Oak Press.

Redfield, Robert R. and Donald S. Burke. 1989. "HIV Infection: Clinical Picture." In William Heyward and James W. Curran, eds., *The Science of AIDS: Readings from the Scientific American,* pp. 63–73. New York: W. H. Freeman.

Risse, Guenter B. 1988. "Epidemics and History: Ecological Perspectives and Social Responses." In Elizabeth Fee and Daniel M. Fox, eds., *AIDS: The Burdens of History,* pp. 33–66. Berkeley: University of California Press.

Rosenberg, Charles E. 1989. "What Is an Epidemic? AIDS in Historical Perspective." *Daedalus* 118:1–17.

Ryan, Caitlin C. 1987. "Statement of Challenge." In Carl G. Leukefeld and Manuel Fimbres, eds., *Responding to AIDS,* pp.1–6. Washington, D.C.: National Association of Social Workers Press.

Shernoff, Michael. 1988. "Integrating Safer-Sex Counseling Into Social Work Practice." *Social Casework* 69:334–39.

Shilts, Randy. 1987. *And the Band Played On: Politics, People and the AIDS Epidemic.* New York: St. Martin's Press.

Snow, John. 1987. *Mortal Fear: Meditations on Death and AIDS.* Cambridge, Mass.: Cowley.

Sonsel, George E., Frank Paradise, and Stephen Stroup. 1988. "Case-Management Practice in an AIDS Service Organization." *Social Casework* 69:388–92.

Sontag, Susan. 1977. *Illness as Metaphor.* New York: Random House.

———. 1988. *AIDS and Its Metaphors.* New York: Farrar, Straus & Giroux.

Walker, Gillian. 1987. "AIDS and Family Therapy, Part II." *Family Therapy Today* 2:1–6.

Walters, LeRoy. 1988. "Ethical Issues in the Prevention and Treatment of HIV Infection and AIDS." *Science* 239:597–603.

Whitmore, George. 1988. *Someone Was Here.* New York: New American Library.

3

Alcoholism and Other Drug Addictions

Meredith Hanson

These are difficult times for alcohol- and other drug-involved individuals, as well as for social workers who are committed to helping them. Despite recent declines in drug use (Substance Abuse and Mental Health Services Administration [SAMHSA] 1997), persons who suffer from addictive disorders continue to outnumber those experiencing most other types of major mental disorder in the United States. Two recent epidemiological surveys reported that from 16 percent to over 25 percent of the U.S. adult population has met the *Diagnostic and Statistical Manual of Mental Disorders (DSM)* diagnostic criteria for a substance use disorder at some time in their lives; over 10 percent qualify for a current diagnosis of substance abuse or dependence (Kessler et al. 1994; Robins and Regier 1991). Since 1990 drug-related visits to hospital emergency rooms, especially those linked with heroin and cocaine use, have increased noticeably (National Institute on Drug Abuse [NIDA] 1998b). The annual economic costs of alcohol and other drug abuse exceed $245 billion in such areas as lost earnings, decreased job productivity, higher health care and treatment costs, and crime and social welfare expenditures (NIDA 1998a).

The social costs are even higher. Neighborhoods have been devastated by drug use (Currie 1993). The prison system is populated with large numbers of persons who have been convicted of drug-related crimes and who have untreated addictions themselves (Institute of Medicine 1990b). Children whose parents abuse drugs or alcohol are nearly three times more likely to be abused and over four times more likely to be neglected than children whose parents are not alcohol- or drug-involved (Reid, Macchetto, and Foster 1999).

Clearly, alcoholism and other drug addiction continue to be among the most serious health and social problems faced in modern society. Virtually everyone seeking professional assistance has experienced—directly or indirectly—the effects of substance abuse. Yet, despite this reality, disability, financial, and other governmental benefits for persons with alcohol and other drug disorders have been restricted or eliminated (Gresenz, Watkins, and Podus 1998). Benefits continue to be cut even though there is little research showing how substance abuse affects clients' use of benefits or their experiences on welfare (Schmidt, Weisner, and Wiley 1998). Access to treatment is limited, despite growing evidence of effectiveness (SAMHSA 1998; Swarns 1998); and expenditures for law enforcement and drug interdiction programs continue to outstrip moneys spent on drug treatment, even though studies consistently report that expenditures on treatment are more cost-effective than law enforcement expenditures (Rydell and Everingham 1994).

Social workers in all fields of practice must be prepared to work with alcohol- and drug-involved individuals. Five percent of the social work workforce specializes in addictions services (Gibelman and Schervish 1995). Most alcohol- and other drug-involved persons do not find their way to addictions treatment agencies, however (Hasin and Grant 1995). Instead, they appear in mental health facilities where it is estimated that 30 percent of adults who have had a mental disorder also have had an alcohol or drug problem or both, and over 70 percent of the institutionalized adults have had both substance use and mental disorders (Regier et al. 1990). They enter work-based assistance programs, which had their origins as occupational alcoholism programs (Hanson 1993). They seek treatment via general hospitals and primary care clinics, where between 10 percent and 40 percent of some hospitals' admissions are linked to alcohol abuse (Rose, Zweben, and Stoffel 1999). They show up in children and family services agencies (Besharov 1994). They collide with the criminal justice system. Their difficulties become apparent when they grow older and seek assistance for age-related complications (Gurnack 1997).

Some experts predict that due to cost-containment efforts like managed care, "[addictions] treatment services will increasingly be delivered at the general health and social service level, with the specialized addiction treatment system focusing on cases that do not respond to less intensive efforts" (Sobell and Sobell 1995:1151). Thus, it becomes even more urgent that all social workers acquire the basic knowledge and skills needed to assist alcohol- and other drug-involved clients and their significant others.

As they struggle with the challenges posed by practice with persons who are affected by addictions, social workers will discover few clear definitions or explanations for addictive behavior or its treatment. Over the years, the characteristics of drug abusers have changed. In addition, definitions, explanations, and treatments of choice have evolved. This chapter reviews some of these changes and suggests practice approaches that have shown evidence of effectiveness and are congruent with social work's purpose and value base.

DEFINING AND EXPLAINING ALCOHOLISM AND OTHER DRUG ADDICTIONS

Defining addiction and addictive behavior has always been problematic. Although disease-based definitions tend to predominate among professionals, multiple and competing definitions of alcoholism and other drug addictions exist, and no single definition is universally accepted. Over the years, definitions of addictions have varied greatly from formulations based on the presence or absence of physiological disease to views relying more on the moral, legal, social, and/or psychological characteristics of drug users and their social contexts (Babor 1990; Berridge 1990).

How a condition is defined determines in large part where assistance is focused and how services are delivered (Germain and Gitterman 1996). To be useful, the definition a social worker constructs to characterize addictive behavior must draw attention to its core features, suggest why it exists and how it develops, and thereby indicate intervention options. Most descriptive definitions of addictive behavior draw attention to abnormal patterns of consumption (e.g., excessive consumption, ritualized and stereotyped use patterns), the functional consequences of drug use (e.g., marital and family difficulties), symptoms associated with substance use (e.g., increased tolerance, withdrawal symptoms, and drug-related health problems), the meaning and salience of addictive behavior for the user (e.g., drug use replaces other activities in an individual's life; drugs are used to cope with life stressors), the social context of drug use (e.g., addiction becomes a lifestyle and habit that becomes a primary way that individuals identify themselves), and the persistence of the behavior (e.g., development of the problem and its continuation despite efforts to eliminate it) (American Psychiatric Association 1994; Edwards, Marshall, and Cook 1997).

Addictive behavior can be thought of as patterns of alcohol or other drug use intended to alter one's physical, psychological, or social functioning, which are associated with harm to the user or others. Addiction is both a psychological obsession and a physical compulsion (Reinarman et al. 1997). Many addicted persons are aware of their "need" (desire, craving) to use drugs, but they continue to use drugs despite the presence of adverse consequences. Persons who are caught up in addictive cycles often cannot predict reliably and consistently how much of a substance they will consume or when they will stop. More severe forms of addictive behavior are characterized by increased tolerance, withdrawal symptoms, and faster reinstatement of the addictive patterns if consumption resumes following a period of abstinence (American Psychiatric Association 1994; Edwards et al. 1997).

Persons are tolerant to a drug if the usual quantity of a substance has a diminished effect or if they need markedly increased amounts to achieve intoxication or another desired effect. Withdrawal symptoms vary by drug use. In general, withdrawal is induced when drug use is stopped after a prolonged period of regular and heavy use. The presence of withdrawal symptoms suggests that an individual is dependent on a particular drug. If people who are dependent on a drug relapse after abstinence, the full blown dependence syndrome can reemerge rapidly, depending on the severity of the original dependence. For example, Edwards and his colleagues (1997) suggest that a severe alcohol dependence syndrome "which had taken years to develop can be fully reinstated within perhaps 72 hours of drinking" (40).

Definitions of addictive behavior and associated explanatory frameworks are socially constructed products of the larger societal context in which addiction exists. In many respects, they are metaphors—images that shape reality for both drug users and society. For example, defining addictive behavior in moral terms places it in the legal arena. Addicts become people who are at best "weak willed" and at worst "criminal." They are stigmatized as persons who must be controlled and from whom society must be protected.

Historically, most addiction control efforts have been morally based. In colonial times heavy drinking was the norm, and alcohol misuse was considered a matter of personal choice (Levine 1978). Alcohol was the "good creature of God"; the drunkard was "from the Devil" (Lender and Martin 1987). Efforts to control excessive drinking were confined primarily to criminal sanctions, including corporal punishment, incarceration, and public censure.

When other drug addiction became a serious concern in the latter part of the nineteenth century, it, too, was defined legally and morally. Images of crazed, out-of-control dope fiends emerged. Opium smoking was linked with racial stereotypes (Kandall 1998), and it was considered a "willful indulgence" (Morgan 1981). Like alcohol-control efforts, the primary attempts to control other drug use were legal in nature. With the passage of laws like the Harrison Act of 1914 drug use became effectively illegal (Brecher 1986; Gray 1998; Musto 1999), the drug user became a social outcast, and society was "protected" from a potent danger.

Some evidence indicates that a major consequence of moral-legal approaches to addictions was a change in the characteristics of the addict population (Jonnes 1995). For example, during the nineteenth century "the typical opiate addict was a middle-aged white woman in the middle of the upper class" (Courtwright 1982:1). In the early twentieth century, when opium was still legal and opium-based medicines could be purchased over the counter, "the typical American addict was [still] a middle-aged southern white woman strung out on laudanum (an opium-alcohol mix)" (Gray 1998:43). When drug use became illegal, drug use patterns changed. Currently, the typical opiate addict is more likely to be a male member of a deviant subculture and a person who is alienated from many aspects of conventional society. In short, a consequence of moral-legal definitions may be the emergence of a social group that is less accessible for assistance.

Although addictive behavior is still considered a moral matter by many persons, the most commonly accepted explanatory definitions appearing in the professional literature assert that addictions are diseases, symptoms of underlying unconscious processes, learned behaviors, or reflections of social dysfunction.

Disease models suggest that addictions are "rooted" in dispositional or constitutional differences that distinguish addicts from others (Miller and Hester 1995; Miller and Kurtz 1994). That is, addictions are "brain-related" medical disorders (National Consensus Development Panel 1998), which are probably caused by some combination of preexisting physiological vulnerability, heritable genetic traits, and biological changes resulting from drug use (Cloninger 1987; Dole and Nyswanger 1967; Jellinek 1960). Core premises of most disease models of addiction are as follows: Addiction is a primary condition in its own right that is not symptomatic of some other disease. It is progressive and irreversible. Substance abusers are "qualitatively different" from nonsubstance abusers and probably are predisposed to developing the disease (Kissin 1983).

The defining feature of the disease is said to be "loss of control" or impaired control over drug use (Jellinek 1952). Loss of control means that addicts can not predict reliably when they will stop their drug use once an episode starts, nor can they consistently control the amount they will consume during an episode. The inability to control drug use is not due to weak willpower or psychological inadequacies. Rather, it results from physiological characteristics that cause addicts to react differently than nonaddicts to both drug ingestion and drug withdrawal. Once an addiction has been established, according to disease theorists, addicts cannot resume drug use without reinstating the addiction. The essence of addiction becomes the physiologically determined uncontrollable, continued use of drugs, including alcohol, despite the presence of adverse consequences.

Although disease conceptualizations of addiction appeared in the eighteenth and nineteenth centuries (Levinstein 1878; Rush 1791; Trotter 1804), the "modern" disease designation, especially as it applies to alcoholism, was developed after the repeal of Prohibition, in part, to depoliticize alcohol consumption and alcohol abuse (Gusfield 1996; White 1998). Currently, support for the disease aspects of addiction can be found in research on the genetics of alcoholism, the results of twin studies, and findings on the impact of drug abuse on the brain's neurotransmitters (Begleiter and Kissin 1995; Goldman and Bergen 1998; Julien 1998).

Intervention approaches evolving from disease models of addictions assert that addicts must establish lifelong abstinence from all drugs in order to remain free from the effects of addictions. Without abstinence, addictions will progress and addicts' conditions will deteriorate. Intervention strategies, therefore, are designed to identify addicts early; educate them about the adverse consequences of addictions; break down psychological defenses, like denial, that interfere with recovery; and support efforts at maintaining abstinence, possibly through referral to twelve-step, self-help groups like Alcoholics Anonymous and Narcotics Anonymous. In some cases, pharmacotherapy (e.g., methadone maintenance; naltrexone treatment) is provided to counteract the effects of a drug of abuse (Agency for Health Care Policy and Research 1999).

Symptom models of addictions draw on a range of psychoanalytic theories, including drive theory, ego psychology, object-relations theory, and self-psychology (Yalisove 1997). Early psychoanalytic explanations of addictions evolved from drive theory and viewed addictive behavior as a regressive attempt to fulfill libidinous wishes, while minimizing stress associated with unconscious conflict (Wurmser 1978). Freud (1897/1985) described masturbation as the "primary addiction" from which other addictions emerged. Substance abuse was a "compromise solution" that enabled an addict to satisfy primitive oral-dependency needs while maintaining a facade of adult autonomy (McCord and McCord 1960), and it was a maladaptive defense mechanism aimed at resolving neurotic conflict (Fenichel 1945).

More recent psychoanalytic formulations have placed greater emphasis on impaired ego functions (e.g., poor impulse control, poor judgment), self-destructive behavior associated with a damaged sense of self and difficulty regulating self-esteem, and distorted object relations (Yalisove 1997). Chein and colleagues (1964) argued that adolescent drug use was an attempt to cope with overwhelming feelings of anxiety in anticipation of adult roles in the absence of adequate models. Khantzian (1985; Murphy and Khantzian 1995) suggested that vulnerabilities, including deficits in ego capacities, object relations, and sense of self, made it difficult for addicts to soothe themselves, care for themselves, and manage affect. Drug use is hypothesized to represent an attempt by addicts to eliminate pain associated with psychic impairment and to achieve adaptive functioning through "self-medication."

Viewing addictive behavior as a symptom or a manifestation of an addict's defective personality structure leads to helping strategies that are initially ego-supportive and ultimately personality modifying (once clients establish extended periods of abstinence). It is thought that an exclusive focus on drug use without attention to the underlying dynamics that contribute to it will produce therapeutic failure. Early in the helping process social workers must focus on impaired self-care and provide the support necessary for clients to cease drug use. As the helping process evolves, through an empathic, clarifying, interpretive process social workers promote emotional growth and more adaptive functioning by helping clients develop insight into the conflicts they are experiencing and the negative impact that drug use has on their lives.

A basic premise of **learning and conditioning models** of addiction is that addictive behavior is learned and maintained by some combination of antecedent, mediating, and consequent factors. Classical conditioning theory emphasizes the role of antecedent stimuli and automatic (reflexive) reactions in shaping addictive behavior. Research building on classical theory has demonstrated how antecedent environmental cues can trigger withdrawal symptoms without the drug of abuse being present and can condition drug tolerance among users (Childress et al. 1993; Ehrman et al. 1992). Instrumental (operant) conditioning theory draws attention to consequent environmental contingencies that reinforce addictive behavior and enable it to continue or increase.

During the latter half of the twentieth century more complex models of learning were developed (Miller and Hester 1995). Social learning models draw attention to the social foundations of addiction, particularly the role of modeling by peers that help individuals learn vicariously and develop beliefs and attitudes, which mediate their responses to environmental cues to use drugs (Bandura 1986). Cognitive models underscore the role of covert processes (cognitions, beliefs, expectancies) in addictive patterns (Beck et al. 1993). Cognitive behavioral paradigms draw attention to high-risk situations in which addictive behaviors are likely to occur and to the adaptive benefits of drug use for the user (Marlatt and Gordon 1985).

Central to all of these models is the idea that addictive behavior is learned in the same way other behaviors are learned. To understand why a person uses drugs, one must discover the antecedent stimuli that elicit addictive behavior, the social models that facilitate vicarious learning, the cognitive factors that mediate perception and response, and the consequent effects that maintain the behavior. Intervention strategies that evolve from these models focus on the drug user's behavior and contingencies that maintain it. Examples of interventions that are designed to disrupt addictive patterns and to develop alternative behaviors include aversive conditioning, contingency contracting, cognitive restructuring, community reinforcement to alter environmental contingencies, behavioral rehearsal, and skills training.

Theorists who explain addictive behavior as a function of **social arrangements** draw attention to societal and cultural factors that differentially affect availability and access to drugs, as well as produce stress, alienation, and despair that may place certain subgroups of society at greater risk for drug use (Currie 1993). Some theorists draw attention to subcultural support for deviant and alternative lifestyles like drug use (Bourgois 1995). Others argue that addictions are associated with a social disengagement from conventional values and norms (Lukoff 1980; Minnis 1988). Still others declare that alcohol and other drug use may be legitimized by social and cultural arrangements that influence individuals' behavioral patterns (MacAndrew and Edgerton 1969). Common to each of the models is the belief that sociocultural factors may be the most critical forces explaining societal and subgroup levels of consumption and subsequent addiction-related problems.

Interventions based on social models take several forms. Some aim at restricting availability and access to drugs through strategies like taxation and age limits for legal consumption. Others try to eliminate the social conditions that create stresses that lead to drug use. Another group of interventions attempts to improve drug users' access to conventional society and the legitimate opportunity structure (Currie 1993). Examples of assistance strategies that are consistent with social models include vocational training and job development programs, therapeutic communities that remove drug users from pro-use drug cultures and place them in antidrug environments, and workplace prevention programs that address organizational patterns that normalize drug use on the job.

Spiritual models of addiction can trace their origins to Alcoholics Anonymous and some of its predecessors. Although AA endorses no official view of addiction, its program of recovery has a fundamentally spiritual quality (Miller 1998; Miller and Kurtz 1994). As a "disease of the spirit," addiction is characterized by a loss of meaning, purpose, and connectedness in one's life (McCrady and Delaney 1995). Substance abusers are thought to be caught up in narcissistic, grandiose patterns in which little in their world makes sense except the quest for intoxication. For recovery to occur, substance abusers must "hit bottom" and experience an "ego deflation" (Tiebout 1957). They must "surrender" and "accept" that they are powerless over the addiction. Through this acceptance, they give up a battle for control, turn their lives over to a higher power, reconnect with others, and acquire a sense of serenity through which they can live their lives without mood-altering substances.

Programs of spiritual recovery are illustrated most clearly in the "steps" of twelve-step self-help groups. Recovery begins with "defeat" and the realization that one is "not God" and has limitations (Kurtz 1979/1991; Tiebout 1957). This realization marks the beginning of a shift from self-centeredness to self-acceptance. Assistance implications that derive from this model include encouraging clients to participate in self-help groups and examine their own sense of hopelessness. Acceptance, optimism, and self-renewal are encouraged further through tactics that promote increased self-awareness, nonjudgmental reflection, and tolerance for the actions of oneself and others (Marlatt 1994; Miller 1998; Nowinski 1999).

In summary, the preceding definitions and conceptual models are representative of the many existing addiction theories. Each contributes to the understanding of addictive behavior. Disease definitions call attention to critical biological features of addictions, including impaired control over drug use, and they legitimize addictions treatment. Psychological approaches highlight intrapsychic, learning, and characterological aspects of addictions. Social explanations reveal environmental and interpersonal factors. Spiritual models underscore the despair and loss of meaning that may accompany addiction. All the theories err, however, to the extent that they oversimplify the addiction process and underemphasize its multifaceted nature. Each definition is a necessary but insufficient view of reality (Golucke, Landeen, and Meadows 1983). If they are used in isolation from one another, they are likely to result in poor communication across disciplines, incomplete assessments of addiction problems, and ineffective assistance strategies.

Taken together, the definitions illustrate that alcoholism and other drug addictions are biopsychosocial phenomena (Kissin and Hanson 1982). As the addiction process unfolds, factors from multiple domains—the psychological, the physiological, the sociocultural, the spiritual—interact sequentially and simultaneously to influence not only the emergence of addictions but also their maintenance and interruption. To understand and to assist alcohol- and drug-involved clients, social workers must be sensitive to each of these factors and how they interrelate.

DEMOGRAPHIC PATTERNS

Addictive behavior occurs in all cultural/ethnic groups, all age groups, both genders, and all socioeconomic strata. General population surveys suggest that, for most people, drug and alcohol use begins during adolescence, peaks during young adulthood, and then gradually tapers off thereafter (e.g., Johnson et al. 1998). Use of legal drugs (e.g., cigarettes and alcohol) tends to occur before use of illegal substances (e.g., heroin, cocaine, and marijuana). While most users of illegal drugs begin their addictive careers by using legal drugs and "gateway" drugs (e.g., marijuana), most users of legal and "gateway" drugs do not progress to more serious drug involvement. Further, most casual and experimental users of any drug do not develop destructive and addictive patterns of use.

The 1996 National Household Survey of Drug Abuse (SAMHSA 1997) reported that 13 million Americans aged 12 years and older were current (past month) users of illicit drugs, down from a peak level of 25 million in 1979. More than 100 million persons were current users of alcohol, with about 11 million people being classified as current heavy drinkers. The rate of current use of illicit drugs by youths aged 12 to 17 was estimated to be at 9 percent. About 1.9 million youths aged 12 to 20 were thought to be current heavy drinkers.

These overall trends mask some interesting patterns. Within an overall pattern of stability and decreased use, especially in the past few years, one sees patterns of increase in some areas. For example, numerous reports indicate that there has been a rise in heroin use in recent years, which is attributed to the emergence of a new cohort of young users who snort, sniff, or smoke heroin (Epstein and Gfroerer 1997). Other reports indicate that an overall leveling of drug use by youths may be counterbalanced by increased consumption among young adults and the aging of the drug-using population (the proportion of drug users aged 35 years and older has increased from 10 percent in 1979 to 28 percent in 1996 as the baby boom generation has grown older; SAMHSA 1997).

Studies of alcohol consumption reveal that, while two-thirds of the adult population are current drinkers, half of all alcohol consumed is drunk by 10 percent of the drinkers (Malin et al. 1982). Heavy drinking and drinking problems are most common among young men, with women and older adults being more likely to abstain from alcohol. Although women experience fewer drinking-related problems and dependence symptoms, they tend to experience more adverse consequences associated with drinking than do heavy-drinking men (Straussner and Zelvin 1997).

Whites tend to drink more and have higher rates of heavy drinking than do Latinos and African Americans (SAMHSA 1997). Latinos have higher rates of heavy drinking than do African Americans. Native American men aged 25 to 44 years drink more than members of other ethnic groups. Native Americans suffer from some of the highest rates of drinking-related accidents, cirrhosis, fetal alcohol syndrome, and suicide (Tang and Bigby 1996). Asian Americans have some of the lowest rates of alcohol use. Americans of Japanese, Korean, and Filipino heritage drink more than persons from China. As Asian immigrants become more acculturated to the United States, their drinking patterns become more like those of other Americans (Westermeyer 1992).

Use patterns for illegal drugs tend to parallel the use patterns for alcohol. However, due to the fact that drugs like marijuana, heroin, and cocaine are illegal, higher proportions of users tend to develop drug-related difficulties. Of the major illegal drugs of abuse, marijuana is used by the largest numbers of people, with over 30 percent of the population reporting some lifetime use. Cocaine use reached its peak with about 5.8 million current users with the introduction of crack cocaine in the mid-1980s. Currently, it is estimated that cocaine (including crack cocaine) is used by 1.74 million people. Heroin is used by up to 500,000 persons (Office of National Drug Control Policy 1996; SAMHSA 1997). Different studies, however, have reached estimates of from 50,000 to more than one million chronic opiate users (Dozier and Johnson 1998).

In all ethnic/cultural groups young men tend to be at greatest risk for illegal drug use. Women users, however, seem to experience proportionately more adverse consequences associated with use (Straussner and Zelvin 1997). Regardless of gender and age, African Americans self-report lower rates of use for most illegal drugs. African Americans tend to persist with cocaine use for longer periods of time, however, and lifetime prevalence for crack cocaine is twice as high as comparable rates for whites. When analyses are controlled for neighborhood of residence, however, racial/ethnic differences in use tend to disappear (Chilcoat and Johanson 1998).

SOCIETAL CONTEXT

The United States has been described as a "drug-saturated society" (Akers 1985). The types of drugs available are innumerable. Most drug use, however, consists of the acceptable use of legal substances. The chief contribution of the societal context to drug use and abuse may be that it facilitates exposure to favorable attitudes, opportunities, and pressures to use drugs. The societal context and setting in which alcohol and other drug use occurs gives it meaning not only for users (or abusers) but also to social control agents. The sociocultural context is the most powerful factor influencing not only whether people use drugs, but also the drugs they choose.

Research with Vietnam veterans who used heroin in Vietnam revealed that "rather than equalizing the drug experience of men from different social and behavioral backgrounds, easy access [to drugs] seemed to increase their pre-existing differences" (Robins 1978:195). In other words, a facilitating context exaggerated, rather than reduced, preexisting tendencies to use drugs. Other research suggests that for individuals to use or abuse drugs in the absence of a favorable context, they must experience greater personal psychopathology (Kaufman 1974).

Drug use is a learned behavior. Regardless of an individual's predisposing vulnerability toward addictive behavior, to become a drug user, one must learn to use the drugs, recognize drug effects, attribute them to the drugs, and define the effects as positive (e.g., Akers 1985; Becker 1953). For the most part, this learning occurs in a social situation in which people learn drug-related norms and observe drug use by significant others. Like other social behaviors, learning to use drugs is the result of continuous, reciprocal interaction among people and a facilitating environment.

Cultural approval and social structure increase the accessibility of specific drugs; cultural ritual and social structure regulate their use (e.g., MacAndrew and Edgerton 1969). Favorable attitudes toward drugs like alcohol can emerge in children by the age of 6 (Jahoda and Cramond 1972). Such attitudes can interact with parental and peer norms and behaviors to influence adolescents' definitions of alcohol use and the probability that they will become heavy drinkers (Zucker 1979).

In a study of drug and alcohol use among three thousand adolescents in grades seven through twelve, social learning factors, such as *differential association*—differential exposure to drug using peers and adults and to favorable drug use norms, *definitions*—definitions favorable to drug use, *differential reinforcement*—variations in rewards and punishments for use, and *imitation*—differential exposure to admired models who used drugs, were correlated highly with the use and abuse of alcohol and marijuana (Akers et al. 1979). Variations in the same factors were related to both the continuation of drug use and its cessation (Lanza-Kaduce et al. 1984).

Most cultural and societal values are communicated to individuals through their interactions with meaningful persons, like parents and peers. The relative influence of parents and peers on drug use varies as adolescents grow older. One study suggested that peer models become more important relative to adult models as teenagers mature (Huba and Bentler 1980). Another report revealed that, while parental influences remained stable through high school, peer influence increased (Margulies, Kessler, and Kandel 1977). A third study reported that the drinking of young adolescents was affected directly by parental norms, while that of middle adolescents was a response to peer pressures. By late adolescence, parental and peer norms were equally influential (Biddle, Bank, and Marlin 1980).

These studies and others (e.g., Jessor and Jessor 1977) clearly demonstrate that drug use is learned in a favorable social context, with friends, parents, and other role models influencing an individual's decision to use drugs. Social factors interact with personal and demographic attributes to affect the onset of drug use. They continue to interact reciprocally to influence its continuance and cessation.

Despite the fact that all drug use and abuse is learned in social contexts and extends to all social strata, problems associated with use and risks for becoming addicted are not equally distributed among all social groups. Drug abuse seems to pose a greater threat to persons from society's more disadvantaged and vulnerable social groups (Cahalan 1982; Chilcoat and Johanson 1998). To understand why this is so, one must examine the functions of drug use and how they interact with the societal context. Among the reasons people use drugs are to gain peer acceptance (e.g., Akers 1985), cope with stress (e.g., Schinke et al. 1988), and escape overpowering threats and pressures (Cahalan 1970). Individual motivations to use drugs emerge in societal contexts that not only provide access to drugs and definitions favorable to drug use, but also present people with a range of environmental demands with which they must cope.

Adaptive functioning is a transactional process in which people respond to environmental demands that are mediated by social and personal resources. It is well documented that a supportive social environment is associated positively with healthier adaptive functioning (e.g., Cohen and Syme 1985). Persons from the most disadvantaged social groups are likely to experience environmental demands that are greater than, or equal to, the demands experienced by other people. However, they often lack "social margin," the relationships and resources needed to survive (Segal, Baumohl, and Johnson 1977). In settings with stressful demands, ready access to drugs, and favorable definitions for drug use, drug use and abuse become viable options for many individuals. Faced with diminished access to legitimate opportunities, persons at high risk for drug use (i.e., those with favorable attitudes and other liabilities) are more likely to use/abuse drugs. As use continues, they can become enmeshed in cultures of drug use in which drugs are a source of "status, identity, and challenge" (Currie 1993:59), and they are apt to become more alienated from conventional sources of support (Bourgois 1995).

VULNERABILITIES AND RISK FACTORS

Until the 1940s most drug problems were localized in specific geographic areas, each of which experienced difficulties with particular substances (Arif and Westermeyer 1988). For example, heroin abuse tended to be a major problem in parts of Asia and North America, while cocaine posed more serious difficulties in Latin American and South American countries. Further, in most cases affluent social groups were the first to encounter drug problems. However, as mass culture "homogenized" the world and as technological and communication advances made it smaller, differences in drug abuse patterns changed to the point where many drug problems are world wide now. Factors that are associated with increased risk for drug use in modern society include biological vulnerabilities, family characteristics, psychological characteristics, age, gender, and community characteristics (Norman 1997; Pagliaro and Pagliaro 1996).

Biological Factors. Most researchers agree that there seem to be genetically transmitted biological vulnerabilities for drug abuse, especially alcohol dependence (Begleiter and Kissin 1995). However, the mechanisms that are operating seem to lead to a variety of problem behavioral patterns of which drug abuse is just one (e.g., Goldman 1998). Some researchers suggest that men who have low sensitivity to alcohol (i.e., they must drink more to feel its effects) are at greater risk to become dependent on alcohol (Schuckit 1998). Others counter that greater reactivity to alcohol is associated with increased risk for dependence (Sher 1991). What seems clear is that alcohol and other drug addictions are biological conditions, and heritable traits contribute to the emergence of the conditions for many persons. The precise mechanisms of action remain unclear (Chilcoat and Johanson 1998). Given the weight of the evidence, it is safe to conclude that persons born in families with histories of alcoholism or drug addiction are at increased risk to develop addictive behavioral patterns and other life problems. Thus, high indexes of suspicion should be maintained when clients present with this history. Equally important to remember is that despite increased risk, most children of substance abusers do not develop addictive behaviors and most substance abusers do not have substance-abusing parents.

Individual Factors. Among the personal factors that are associated with increased risk for addiction are low self-esteem, low self-confidence, greater rebelliousness, behavioral undercontrol (e.g., impulsivity), and mental disorders (e.g., Chilcoat and Johanson 1998; Goldman 1998; Schinke, Botvin, and Orlandi 1991). In general, individuals alienated from conventional norms and institutions (e.g., schools), lacking respect for authority, and overly reliant on peer pressure are more apt to use drugs. Their drug use patterns seem to be part of a more generalized problem behavior syndrome in which drug-using individuals are likely to engage in other "antisocial" behaviors, many of which precede the onset of drug use (Jessor and Jessor 1977).

Surveys of drug use and abuse patterns have revealed consistently that addictive behavior is associated with age. For all drugs, young adults have the greatest rates of usage and the most problems related to use (Kandel 1978). A national survey of drinking practices among men found that the youngest respondents (those aged 21–24) not only drank at greater rates, they experienced the highest rates of alcohol-related problems, including loss of control, interpersonal conflicts, legal problems, and financial difficulties (Cahalan and Room 1974). Analyses of alcohol use patterns among women (Herd 1988), surveys of use and abuse patterns for specific illicit drugs such as cocaine (Chilcoat and Johanson 1998), and reviews of general American drug use patterns (Schuster 1987) have reached similar results. In one report it was concluded that the period of greatest risk for initiating illicit drug use ends by the mid-20s. Persons who start drug use at a later age not only experience less drug involvement but also are more likely to cease drug use (Kandel 1978).

Other individual characteristics are less strongly associated with drug use and abuse. Men are more likely than women to drink and use illicit drugs (SAMHSA 1997). Women are more likely to abuse prescription drugs (Gomberg 1986). In the youngest age groups, however, gender differences are less marked, and, as women gain sexual, social, and economic equality, their addictive patterns are becoming more visible and gender differences are declining (e.g., Kaestner et al. 1986).

Social Factors. Economic and social deprivation are major environmental risk factors for drug abuse (Hawkins et al. 1992; Turner 1997). Research has revealed that when other factors are controlled, persons who reside in impoverished communities are at greater risk to use drugs (Chilcoat and Johanson 1998). Risk for use increases greatly when those neighborhoods are disorganized and residents feel little attachment to the community (Hawkins et al. 1992). Favorable familial attitudes toward drug use and poor family management practices have been associated with greater risk for adolescent drug use, regardless of the presence of drug problems in the family (Hawkins et al. 1992). Communities in which social institutions are poorly developed and school systems are less effective (e.g., high dropout rates) have also been linked with addictive behaviors. Surprisingly, the presence of drug dealers, except as they reflect broader community problems, does not factor much into drug use initiation (Cohen et al. 1996). Friends, peers, and family members are much more powerful influences on drug use initiation than are drug dealers with whom users have no other interaction.

RESILIENCIES AND PROTECTIVE FACTORS

Protective factors and resilience can be categorized into biological, individual, family, and social domains.

Biological Factors. The alcohol-flush reaction exhibited by many Japanese, Korean, and Chinese individuals is a genetic factor that may protect some persons from developing serious alcohol problems (Crabb et al. 1995). Due to physiological discomfort like dizziness, nausea, and facial swelling, persons who experience flushing may be less likely to consume sufficient quantities of alcohol to produce problems. Two other characteristics that seem genetically based and associated with resilience are an easygoing temperament and intelligence (Norman 1997). Both traits are socially desirable. Thus, it is likely that easygoing and intelligent persons receive more positive feedback from others and experience less stress that may lead to drug abuse.

Individual Factors. Among the most powerful individual factors associated with resilient outcomes is perceived self-efficacy, the perception that one can have an effect on one's environment (Norman 1997). A wide range of research reveals that adolescents and adults who have greater confidence in their ability to refuse pressures to use drugs and cope in stressful situations are less apt to become addicted. In addition, persons who possess a wider range of social and general coping skills are more likely to establish and maintain abstinence if they ever initiate addictive behavioral patterns (Marlatt and Gordon 1985). A sense of purpose and meaning in one's life also seems to protect some persons from drug abuse (Norman 1997).

Family Factors. Positive family bonding and interpersonal support protects many persons from addictive behaviors (Turner 1997). In addition, family stability is a powerful prognostic variable associated with successful outcomes in addictions treatment (Smyth 1998). Children whose parents demonstrate high levels of monitoring and control (e.g., by restricting access to drug-using peers) are less likely to associate with drug-using peers and are less apt to experiment with drugs (Chilcoat and Johanson 1998). Strong family relationships and the presence of adults who model non-drug-use behavior seem to mediate stress and reduce the risk that adolescents will initiate drug use (Rhodes and Jason 1988).

Social Factors. Communities that have available resources, like recreational centers, strong churches, and parent-school involvement, seem able to protect children from alcohol and other drug abuse (Hawkins et al. 1992; Rhodes and Jason 1988). Other environmental factors that seem to reduce the risk of drug use include high response costs (i.e., drugs are less available) and the availability of alternative reinforcers (Chilcoat and Johanson 1998). In settings where social interaction patterns support linkages with conventional cultural institutions and social models for responsible consumption exist, overall rates of problem drug use decline (e.g., Vaillant 1995).

PROGRAMS AND SOCIAL WORK CONTRIBUTIONS

The Institute of Medicine (1990a) suggests that about 13 million Americans aged 12 years and older need treatment for alcohol use disorders; another 5.5 million persons need treatment for other drug use disorders. The treatment they receive is organized into a diversified—at times uncoordinated—service delivery system. Alcoholics Anonymous (AA) and other twelve-step self-help groups like Narcotics Anonymous (NA), while not part of the formal service delivery system, have reached the largest number of persons. Twelve-step and non-twelve-step self-help groups like Rational Recovery (RR) and Women for Sobriety (WFS) are fellowships that provide unconditional support and acceptance, while promoting structured programs of recovery for alcohol- and drug-involved individuals (McCrady and Delaney 1995). Consequently, they are integral adjuncts to most professional treatment systems. Several hybrids of twelve-step groups have formed to meet the needs of children, other family members, and associates of drug abusers (e.g., Al Anon, Nar Anon, Adult Children of Alcoholics groups).

Although self-help groups have been around for decades (e.g., AA was formed in the 1930s), little empirical research exists that demonstrates their effectiveness as "stand-alone" programs (Kurtz 1997; McCrady and Miller 1993). Studies in which AA is an adjunct to formal treatment, however, reveal that AA attendance is often associated with some improvement in treatment outcome (Emrick et al. 1993; Ouimette, Moos, and Finney 1998).

Like any other assistance option, self-help groups are not useful for all clients. Some research, for example, suggests that AA affiliates are more likely than nonaffiliates to have experienced loss of control and anxiety about their drinking. They also tend to have more severe drinking histories and social networks that are more supportive of drinking (Emrick et al. 1993; Longabaugh et al. 1998). However, because of the potential benefit clients can receive from self-help groups, they should be encouraged to "sample" group meetings. Preparatory assistance, like familiarizing clients with group traditions and processes and teaching them communication skills, can increase the likelihood that they will affiliate and profit from involvement with self-help groups (Anderson and Gilbert 1989). If, after attending several meetings, clients find that they are not helpful, continued participation should not be mandated.

Professional service delivery systems occupy two broad categories of settings: *specialized addictions treatment facilities* and *nonspecialized agencies*. Agency setting and mandate establish the parameters for social work assistance. Thus, the functions of social workers employed in *nonspecialized settings* may differ greatly from the responsibilities of social workers in specialized addiction agencies.

As observed earlier, most alcohol- and drug-involved persons encounter social workers in nonspecialized settings, like primary care clinics, mental health agencies, employee assistance programs, and school-based health clinics. The major professional tasks vis-à-vis addictions in these settings usually involve early identification, information, and referral. Since social workers in these settings are in position to identify addiction-related problems early—sometimes before clients are aware they exist—they must be adept at screening for the existence of alcohol and drug problems (possibly by using standardized screening questionnaires; Smyth 1998), performing "triage" to ascertain clients' needs and locate available resources, and linking clients with the proper levels of care (Pattison 1982). In addition, social workers in nonspecialized settings should be prepared to help clients reintegrate with natural support groups as they recover from addictive lifestyles.

The specialized addictions treatment system includes several levels of care, including prevention and education programs, detoxification services, early intervention and outpatient clinics, day programs and partial hospitalization centers, residential and in-patient rehabilitation services, including therapeutic communities (TCs), and dual diagnosis programs for persons with coexisting substance use and mental disorders. Social workers in these settings occupy positions ranging from case managers and clinicians, who deliver and coordinate care, to advanced generalist practitioners and administrators, who supervise staff, evaluate program effectiveness, design and develop new programs, and manage daily program operations.

Increasingly, decisions about the type of treatment clients receive are informed by "best-practice" guidelines, which are based on evidence derived from empirical research on the clinical utility, efficacy, and effectiveness of different treatment approaches (Goldman 1998; Schilling and El-Bassel 1998). The selection of the level of care a client needs often is guided by "placement criteria" developed by expert task forces composed of addictions treatment specialists and researchers. Typical of the placement criteria used by many facilities are those of the American Society of Addiction Medicine (ASAM). When making placement decisions and developing treatment plans, ASAM suggests that professionals should assess the following: acute intoxication and withdrawal potential, biomedical condition, emotional and behavioral status, relapse/continued use probability, client preference (motivation and acceptance/resistance potential), and environmental supports and resources (ASAM 1996).

Education and prevention programs are supported more in theory than in practice (Schinke and Cole 1998). Although policymakers and practitioners recognize the need for preventive services, adequate resources and legislation often are missing, and few practitioners are involved in their delivery. Educational and preventive initiatives include policy-level responses, like alcohol taxes and raising the minimum legal drinking age, and community/educational interventions (Alcohol Alert 1996). Some responses, like drug-free workplace initiatives and public service campaigns warning about drinking and driving, are aimed at the general public. Others are targeted at high-risk groups like pregnant women or teenagers who are experimenting with drugs. Among the most effective education and prevention programs are those aimed at adolescents. Group-based approaches exploit the natural peer group of the classroom and community to alter norms and reinforce the prevention message (Schinke and Cole 1998). Culturally competent approaches that target life skills and social influence models have been particularly successful (Daugherty and Leukefeld 1998; Hawkins et al. 1992; Schinke et al. 1989). In general, these approaches achieve their effects by providing information through peer models and helping clients develop both "drug-specific" problem-solving skills (e.g., drug refusal skills) and general social skills that enhance feelings of competence and self-esteem.

Detoxification services are designed "to eliminate a substance from someone who is psychoactively dependent on it by gradually tapering off of that substance, or a cross-tolerant substance [e.g., methadone for heroin dependence; benzodiazepines for alcohol dependence], so as to alleviate significant subjective discomfort, minimize observable or measurable withdrawal signs, or prevent health risks that might occur if the substance were discontinued abruptly" (Alling 1992:402). Depending on the severity of a client's dependence and the availability of social resources, detoxification may or may not be medically supervised. It can occur in inpatient or outpatient settings. Because detoxification services are rarely sufficient to help clients develop long-term abstinence, social workers employed in drug detoxification units usually provide substance abuse education to raise awareness about the risks of continued drug use, motivational enhancement therapy to encourage clients to continue in post-detoxification treatment, and discharge planning to facilitate contact with self-help groups and other aftercare services.

Outpatient and early intervention are most appropriate where minimal risk of withdrawal exists, clients are able to establish and maintain abstinence, and a supportive recovery environment is available (ASAM 1996). Some outpatient clinics provide drug-free treatment. Others offer drug substitution chemotherapy like methadone maintenance and methadone-to-abstinence treatment for opiate addiction or narcotic antagonist treatment like naltrexone therapy for opiate addiction or alcohol dependence. A primary value of outpatient assistance is that clients are able to face addictive behavioral patterns in the social contexts in which they arose. With the rise of managed care and other cost-containment efforts, outpatient stays have been curtailed greatly in recent years. Thus, it has become imperative for social workers and other professionals, like addictions counselors, nurses, physicians, and psychologists, to provide brief, time-limited interventions and to involve clients quickly in self-help groups whenever feasible.

When clients lack the social supports that will facilitate abstinence but are not debilitated enough to require inpatient or residential care, they may be involved in *partial hospitalization* or *day programs*. Generally, these programs are group and milieu oriented and provide from nine hours to more than twenty hours of structured programming per week (ASAM 1996). They expose clients to information about alcohol and other drugs, offer alternative social supports that will reinforce drug-free lifestyles, and teach new coping skills to handle pressures that lead to alcohol and drug abuse.

Residential/inpatient services and therapeutic communities (TCs) are designed to serve clients who need safe and stable living environments in order to develop recovery skills (ASAM 1996). Generally, inpatient rehabilitation services last from three to four weeks. TCs provide social therapy that can extend much longer. Although intervention strategies and techniques vary across settings, the goals of this level of care include rehabilitating and resocializing clients by fostering mutual aid and peer support. Therapeutic communities, which were pioneered by Maxwell Jones in England at the end of World War II (DeLeon 1999) and adapted for drug addicts by Charles Dederich in the late 1950s (Yablonsky 1965), try to accomplish these goals by isolating clients from pro-drug-use external environments and creating highly structured treatment systems in which they can undergo "identity transformations" from drug abusers to drug-free persons. This transformation is facilitated through encounter groups and other methods that create new family dynamics and peer relationships in which resocialization can take place (Yablonsky 1989). Social workers in these settings work in partnership with counselors who are recovering alcoholics or drug addicts to promote a recovery-oriented mutual aid system. They help prepare clients to return to their natural environments by helping them to anticipate threats to sobriety and locate resources that will support drug-free lifestyles (Hanson 1997).

In recent years services for special populations like persons with *dual diagnoses* (coexisting substance use and mental disorders) have been developed. These services arose out of the realization that significant numbers of persons with serious mental illnesses also experienced addictive disorders, but they did not respond well to mainstream addictions treatment. In general, there are three primary strategies for assisting individuals with dual diagnoses: sequential treatment, when first one condition is treated then the second condition is addressed; parallel treatment, in which treatment of both conditions occurs simultaneously in two or more settings; and integrated treatment, in which both conditions are addressed in the same treatment program

(Minkoff and Drake 1991). Most professionals agree that, where possible, integrated treatment combined with case management services produces the best therapeutic outcomes—at least for clients with severe and persistent mental disorders (Drake et al. 1996; Smyth 1998). Services themselves should be delivered in a supportive milieu in which substance abuse problems are addressed in the context of clients' overall psychosocial functioning (Hanson, Kramer, and Gross 1990).

ASSESSMENT AND INTERVENTIONS

Research and clinical experience confirm that potential clients seek, or are referred for, addictions services with varying motivational levels that are highly susceptible to professional influence (Miller and Rollnick 1991; Prochaska, DiClemente, and Norcross 1992). Thus, a first clinical task is to assess and enhance potential clients' motivational readiness to engage in the helping process by eliciting from them their interests, doubts, and concerns about treatment; their views on alcohol and drug use; their definitions of the "problem"; and any hopes or expectations they have for assistance. By encouraging potential clients to tell their own stories, social workers develop an appreciation for their perspectives. Once social workers grasp these views, they can attempt to establish common grounds that link potential clients' concerns with agency mandate and function. When this occurs, and there is agreement, potential clients become actual clients, and the helping process can proceed (Germain and Gitterman 1996).

Many individuals entering addictions treatment are "coerced" into care, and they would not be seeking assistance if it were not for outside pressure (Barber 1995). It is helpful to think of these individuals as "visitors" rather than "customers" who are ready to use the services that are offered. According to Berg (1995), visitors are persons who define their "real problem" as having to come to treatment when their true concerns lie elsewhere. Thus, they may appear unmotivated or resistant. When faced with this dilemma, social workers should respect and affirm the person's position and not aggressively challenge it. By using client-centered interview tactics like open-ended questions, reflection, and summarization, social workers can help visitors identify, explore, and understand their ambivalence, and they can help them weigh the risks and benefits of accepting assistance and considering change (Miller and Rollnick 1991). An empathic, "not knowing" style in which social workers deliberately try *not* to impose their own views on potential clients helps individuals feel understood and creates a context in which they are more apt to accept assistance. By clarifying expectations and negotiating goals, social workers can identify concerns that are meaningful to clients. By coupling these concerns with the persons' alcohol and drug use, they provide a credible basis for engaging potential clients into treatment that addresses addictive patterns.

Assessment. To assist clients and plan intervention strategies with them social workers must understand the severity and nature of a client's addiction and how addictive behaviors "fit" within the person's life context. Generally, assessment occurs at two basic levels. Screening and diagnostic strategies attempt to determine the presence and severity of an alcohol or drug problem. More comprehensive, ecologically grounded assessment strategies attempt to clarify how particular clients' alcohol- and drug-related difficulties are manifested in their lives. An ecological assessment tries to uncover the adaptive and maladaptive aspects of drug use. It attempts to determine how drug use may increase stress and discomfort for clients and others, how addictive behavior may ease stress, and how it may be a normal "way of life" for clients and their associates (Vaillant 1992).

Screening and assessment information is obtained through a variety of methods including open-ended interviews, structured clinical interviews (e.g., the Addiction Severity Index, McLellan et al. 1992; the Structured Clinical Interview for the DSM IV, First et al. 1996), client self-report instruments (i.e., screening questionnaires like the Michigan Alcoholism Screening Test, Selzer 1971, and the Alcohol Dependence Scale, Skinner and Horn 1984), and computer-assisted procedures. The CAGE questionnaire is an extremely simple screening tool that is used widely in nonspecialized addiction settings like primary care clinics (Mayfield, McLeod, and Hall 1974). Although the CAGE questionnaire was developed for alcohol use, it has been adapted for other drug use. To administer the CAGE, a social worker asks a client four questions that can be answered yes or no: Have you ever thought you should **C**ut down on your drinking? Have you felt **A**nnoyed when people criticize your drinking? Have you ever felt bad or **G**uilty about your drinking? Have you ever had a drink first thing in the morning to steady your nerves or to get over a hangover (**E**ye-opener)? Two or more yes answers are indicative of a drinking problem and should be followed up with further assessment.

A comprehensive ecological assessment of addictive behavior should occur as part of a broader examination of clients and their impinging environments. It must identify and explore the types of life tasks and demands clients face, the developmental level of clients and their communities, and the personal and environmental resources that affect adaptation and motivation (Germain and Gitterman 1996). Among the drug-specific domains that should be examined are the following: (1) the client's general drug use patterns, including type of substances used, quantity and frequency of use, method of ingestion (e.g., snorting, smoking, orally, injection), and contexts of use (e.g., where, with whom); (2) precipitants (antecedents) of use; (3) consequences of use (e.g., behavioral or mood changes, withdrawal symptoms, drug-related medical complications, social and interpersonal consequences, increased tolerance); (4) history of use, including patterns of increase and decrease and length of involvement with drugs; (5) prior efforts to stop use; (6) environmental, personal, and sociocultural factors that will support or block recovery; and (7) any other problems in living the client faces (Smyth 1998).

Since addictive behavior tends to occur in some situations and not in others, it is critical to assess closely the characteristics of the situations in which clients are at high risk to use drugs, as well as the characteristics of those situations that seem to protect them from drug use (Annis and Davis 1988; Meyers and Smith 1995). One study found, for example, that over two-thirds of all alcoholic relapses occurred in three types of situations: those evoking *negative emotional states,* like anger, anxiety, and depression; those involving *interpersonal conflict;* and situations containing *social pressures* to drink. Heroin relapse followed the same pattern. However, while alcoholic relapses were associated most strongly with negative emotional states, social pressures were the strongest determinants of heroin relapses (Cummings, Gordon, and Marlatt 1980). These findings have been replicated in other studies that found that younger drinkers relapsed in a wider range of situations and that men were more likely than women to drink in response to social pressures (Annis and Davis 1988).

Central to an analysis of high-risk drug use situations, as well as those situations in which they are less apt to use drugs, is an assessment of clients' *perceived self-efficacy,* their expectations about their capacity to cope effectively with situational demands and tasks (Bandura 1997; Marlatt and Gordon 1985). Research has demonstrated that drug use/abuse involves a process in which people with differing vulnerabilities for drug abuse enter high-risk drug use situations (sometimes unintentionally) and encounter pressures to use drugs. If they perceive that they can cope with the pressures without using drugs, the likelihood that they will resist drug use is increased. If, however, they perceive that they are unable to cope with the situational demands without using drugs, the probability that they will use and abuse drugs is increased (Marlatt and Gordon 1985).

As assessment data is gathered, social workers must organize it so that it leads logically to assistance options. They must formulate a data-based description that tells them *who the client is.* They should develop inferences that help explain *why the client is using drugs.* They must form *intervention hypotheses* that link description and explanation and suggest how to aid the client.

Interventions. As assessment information is gathered and clients accept an offer of help, social workers must align themselves with real possibilities for change within individuals and their environmental contexts (Vaillant 1995). According to Edwards and his colleagues (1997), the "basic work" of treatment builds on an understanding of a client's natural capacity for recovery, as well as potential dimensions of recovery. Practitioners' efforts consist largely of helping clients develop the personal and environmental resources and supports that will allow them to overcome addictive patterns and move along "natural" recovery pathways.

A wide range of assistance strategies are employed to help alcohol- and drug-involved persons. Core interventions include group counseling, individual therapy, family therapy, chemotherapy (e.g., methadone maintenance, disulfiram treatment), and referral to self-help groups. These interventions may be utilized (or initiated) in all service settings. Other services—detoxification, vocational and educational assistance, referral for financial aid and other benefits, medical and psychiatric care—are supplementary and may be merged to form separate systems of care (e.g., a community reinforcement approach to assistance, Budney and Higgins 1998; Meyers and Smith 1995). Supplemental services usually are not needed by all clients.

Core interventions are designed to address the central addictions-related difficulties most alcohol- and drug-involved clients face. They are aimed at helping persons establish abstinence, alter addictive lifestyles, develop more effective coping skills, and establish social support networks that will reinforce abstinent behavior. The sequence and timing of assistance efforts are determined by an assessment of clients' needs, as well as their willingness to accept the assistance offered. The "natural sequence" of intervention in order of urgency usually involves: detoxifying the client; meeting emergent social, medical, and emotional needs; providing core interventions aimed at the addictive lifestyles and behavioral patterns; and delivering additional services (e.g., vocational rehabilitation) that will strengthen a client's general adaptive capacity.

To increase the likelihood that a particular intervention package will be successful, it should have some empirical evidence for effectiveness. Controlled experimental studies and "real-world" applications of efficacious interventions have helped to dispel the "myths" that little helps substance abusers and that they are more resistant than other persons to assistance (Institute of Medicine 1997; Miller et al. 1995; O'Brien and McLellan 1996; Project MATCH Research Group 1997; Schilling and El-Bassel 1998; Smyth 1998). Clearly, not all interventions used in the addictions field are effective, and some approaches seem more appropriate for some clients than others. Effective alternatives exist, however, and social workers, who are guided by "informed" (Miller and Hester 1995), "technical" (Lazarus 1997) eclecticism, will be able to select "best-practice" options with their clients.

No single intervention approach has been shown to be consistently superior to all others in its effectiveness. For example, group therapy is considered by many to be the treatment of choice for alcohol- and drug-involved persons. However, while group approaches that promote problem solving and the acquisition of coping skills have been shown to be successful, little research documenting that group methods are comparatively more effective than other intervention methods exists (Miller et al. 1995; Smyth 1998). Intervention alternatives that are well supported by treatment outcome research include: brief interventions, motivational interviewing, decision-making approaches, social skills training, contingency contracting, community reinforcement, client-centered strategies, relapse prevention, cognitive therapy, family interventions with nonaddicted spouses, behavioral marital and family therapy, and chemotherapy like naltrexone treatment and methadone maintenance (Miller et al. 1995; Schilling and El-Bassel 1998; Smyth 1998). Addictive behaviors often can be addressed best through a combination of behavioral, social, and pharmacological interventions (Stocker 1998). Social workers wishing to improve their abilities to be responsive to their clients should consider integrating these strategies into their practice so that they have "menus" of options from which they and their clients can select.

Work with clients should be guided by several practice principles (e.g., Edwards et al. 1997): (1) Continuity of purpose should be maintained. Initial goal selection and contract should establish focus and maintain a demand for work. (2) A flexible, collaborative stance should encourage active client involvement. (3) An ecological perspective that enables clients and social workers to see the larger context in which addictive patterns exist should be maintained. (4) Whenever possible, the perspectives of family and social network members should be incorporated into the helping process (Szapocznik et al. 1989). The empirical literature links beneficial therapeutic outcomes to the involvement of social network members, when clients are invested in the relationships and the networks are supportive of abstinence (Longabaugh et al. 1995). The roles network members play should be determined by their interests and capacities, as well as the wishes of the addictive clients (Zweben 1991). (5) A balanced focus should be maintained between addictive behavior and other life problems. (6) Clients and workers should engage in continuous monitoring of the pacing, intensity, and outcomes of helping encounters. (7) Client strengths and the advantages of drug-free living should be highlighted to give meaning to the therapeutic work.

ILLUSTRATION AND DISCUSSION

The following case example illustrates the process of differential assessment, contracting, and intervention with a drug-involved client. The case illustration is not a "recipe" for social work practice. Instead, it highlights useful practice concepts.

Jerry (aged 23) and Ann Smith (aged 24) are a married Irish American couple who were referred for assistance by children's protective services (CPS) after their 2-year-old daughter was removed from their home and placed in Ann's mother's custody when allegations of neglect were filed. According to the referral materials, Jerry, who worked as a school custodian, has a history of alcohol and crack cocaine use. School authorities noticed that he was intoxicated on the job on more than one occasion. After continued efforts to help him stop using drugs through the school's employee assistance program failed, the case was referred to CPS, which determined that Jerry's actions placed his daughter at risk. Although Ann admitted to no addictive behavior herself, she acknowledged that Jerry often became loud and belligerent when he smoked crack. Since she refused to ask him to leave the home, officials removed their daughter. CPS informed the couple that they would be reevaluated and their daughter would be returned to them if Jerry entered substance abuse treatment, he established complete abstinence from crack and alcohol, and the couple entered marital counseling that addressed anger management and conflict resolution.

On their first visit, Jerry announced, "This is all a big waste of time, and we really don't need to be here. I haven't had a beer or smoked any crack in over two weeks, and I don't intend to start now. My wife and I are in marriage counseling and that is going fine." Ann volunteered, "We just want to do what it takes to get our daughter back."

The social worker assessed quickly that the couple—especially Jerry—was reluctant to engage in treatment, so he assumed they were "visitors" who were investigating the treatment program, rather than "customers" who were ready to make use of the services (Berg 1995). He thanked them for coming to the center. He commented that he had reviewed the materials CPS had sent over, and he asked them to share with him their impressions of the situation. Jerry did all of the talking and Ann sat quietly. He externalized the difficulties and minimized any drug use problem. When asked directly if he thought he had difficulties with drugs, Jerry replied, "No." Jerry's remarks indicated that he was in the "precontemplation" stage of change with respect to the addictive behavior (i.e., he did not attribute his difficulties to drug use, despite evidence to the contrary, Prochaska et al. 1992). The social worker suspected Ann might view the situation differently. However, given the history of marital conflict, he chose not to put her in a position of disputing her husband's statements.

The social worker decided that to engage the couple in the helping process, he had to discuss with them the mandated requirements of service and attempt to negotiate goals (Berg 1995; Germain and Gitterman 1996). He told them that he understood that CPS required Jerry to be sober *and* in addictions treatment, and that these conditions seemed nonnegotiable from CPS's perspective. He added, "Given that we have to be here, I'm wondering what could happen that might make this whole experience worthwhile." Both Ann and Jerry replied, "Getting our daughter back." The social worker acknowledged the goal and then asked Ann and Jerry what steps they thought needed to be taken to attain it. They replied that they did not know, to which the social worker responded, "What about what you are doing now? You've taken important steps already. Jerry is drug-free and you are here. I know that must be difficult, but it shows me how committed you are to making this work." Ann and Jerry nodded in agreement.

The social worker sensed that an initial rapport was being established, so he asked if it would make sense for them to explore ways to make their initial success last. They agreed, so he asked Jerry if he would mind telling him a little about his drug use—when it started, what he likes about it, and any concerns he has about it. He asked Ann to be a "witness" to the process and offer feedback at times to clarify the information (Zweben 1991). He thought that this tactic would keep her involved with less potential for stress.

Through the use of client-centered interviewing skills (reflection, open-ended questions, summarization), the social worker learned that Jerry was raised in a "family of alcoholics" (father, uncles, and paternal grandfather had drinking problems). He had no role model for moderate drinking. "When my family drank, they drank to feel it." Jerry remembered tasting beer at an early age. "It was around 5. I remember I liked it. It made me feel like my dad." He became intoxicated the first time he drank with friends at the age of 13. He started smoking crack with high school classmates when he was 15. He reported "no problems" associated with drug use until he was caught drinking on the job several months ago. He minimized the arguments he and Ann had when he was high.

In response to the social worker's question, Ann agreed that Jerry's history seemed accurate with two exceptions: Jerry began to drink in the mornings to calm his nerves long before he appeared intoxicated on the job, and the arguments were very upsetting to her and to their daughter, who would sometimes cry and ask them to stop fighting. Jerry seemed genuinely surprised by Ann's comments, and said, "Yes. You're right, I forgot about Calleigh (their daughter). . . . And, I guess, I was tying it on in the mornings, sometimes."

This was Jerry's first treatment for addictive behavior. A "review of systems" uncovered the following additional information: He had no physical problems. He exhibited no symptoms of major mental disorder. He tended to handle problems rigidly and reactively, responding "that's the way I've always done things." He spent leisure time watching sports on television and playing softball in a work league. Ann and Jerry went to the movies about once a month. They had few mutual friends.

A situational assessment of his addictive behavior revealed that during the past year Jerry was most likely to drink heavily and smoke crack after social events with his friends. This usually led to arguments with Ann, which precipitated more drug use. Times when he would not drink or smoke crack were generally preceded by "conscious decisions" on his part not to use. According to Jerry, "Crack and alcohol cost money. I can't go broke. Besides, sometimes, I'm not in the mood to have an argument when I get home."

Preparatory to developing an intervention plan with the couple, the social worker provided personalized feedback (Miller and Rollnick 1991). He presented the results of the situational assessments and he summarized that Jerry, by his own report, consumed much more alcohol and drugs than other people did. He observed also that given his family history he was at risk for developing more serious problems if use continued. He balanced the feedback on risks by pointing out that the couple had strengths—they were staying together and committed to resolving their difficulties and regaining custody of their daughter, Jerry still had his job, and he was able to exert control over drug use when he "put his mind to it." He concluded by saying, "Your goals are clear and there are some specific things we can do to help you. If you maintain sobriety and strengthen your ability to handle conflict without drinking or smoking crack, I will report this to CPS so that steps can be taken to regain custody of Calleigh."

Jerry commented, "Well, I just have to get my act together. As you said, when I put my mind to it, I can stay out of trouble." The social worker sided with him and suggested that they could develop a plan that would strengthen Jerry's strategies. He pointed out that some situations were more difficult than others for Jerry to handle, and that he could develop skills for coping with them and avoiding relapse. Jerry agreed to "give it a try." The social worker asked Jerry and Ann what role they wanted her to play in the addictions treatment, and they both replied that she should be "supportive" but not get too involved to avoid conflicts. Picking up on their concerns, the social worker suggested that Ann could become more involved when they addressed marital conflict. Ann and Jerry agreed.

The following objectives were established with the couple: (1) Jerry would increase his awareness of drug use cues and he would identify correctly situations in which he was at risk to use. (2) He would chart situations in which he felt tempted to use drugs and those in which he felt no temptation, keeping track of his thoughts, feelings, and actions. (3) Jerry would develop skills for handling interpersonal encounters—first general social encounters, then temptations to use drugs, finally interpersonal conflict. (4) When Jerry improved his sense of mastery and competence in other social situations, Ann and he would practice applying conflict management strategies to the marital interactions.

To attain these objectives Jerry contracted with the social worker to participate in weekly individual sessions. Ann and Jerry contracted to follow up the individual sessions with couples counseling. In addition, Jerry agreed to attend group counseling, and Ann agreed to participate in a group for wives of drug-involved men. Jerry also agreed to "sample" at least six AA meetings in the community and decide whether or not he thought they could be of assistance to him. Since CPS wanted a progress report in six months, a six-month time frame was established for the contract.

The group Jerry attended stressed problem-solving and coping skills development. Its purpose was to encourage members to complete "functional analyses" of situations in which they were at risk for using drugs and to practice alternate ways of handling those situations. Techniques included role plays, modeling, coaching, positive feedback, support, and practicing new skills in "real life" (Carroll 1998). Jerry found himself "at a loss for words" in most social encounters. So, in early group meetings he learned how to relax himself and prepare himself for the encounters. He also observed other members model social encounters without using drugs. Then, he rehearsed the situations himself. For example, he practiced making "small talk" about sports and "refusing" requests to drink. Group members gave him positive feedback and encouragement, and his confidence (perceived self-efficacy) in social situations improved.

In couples counseling Jerry applied the coping skills he learned in group to his interactions with Ann. For her part, Ann learned how to assert herself and focus on her own needs. By disengaging somewhat from Jerry's drug use behavior she was able to communicate to him not only that she did not want to be controlled by his addiction, but also that she was confident that he could come to grips with destructive addictive patterns.

Ann and Jerry continued treatment for one year. After six months of continued abstinence and steady progress, a favorable report from the social worker paved the way for Calleigh's return home. When the situation remained stable for one year, treatment ended. A two-year follow-up revealed that Jerry remained drug-free and occasionally attended AA. Ann attended a community support group for spouses of drug-involved people. The couple retained custody of their daughter.

This practice illustration highlights some important features of social work practice with alcohol- and drug-involved people. Clinical assessments and interventions were individualized to meet the clients' life circumstances. Assistance built on strengths, de-emphasized the "addict" label (stigma), and linked the offer of help to concerns as they were experienced by the clients. Once differential, situational assessments were completed, a treatment contract that established a stepwise hierarchy of assistance was negotiated. The intervention plan focused on developing both general coping skills (e.g., interpersonal skills; conflict resolution skills) and drug-specific coping skills (e.g., drug refusal skills). For recovery to progress, both categories of skills had to develop, since the general coping skills provided the context in which drug-specific skills could emerge. Finally, as Jerry improved his sense of self-efficacy and competence, environmental interventions were effected. Alternative support networks (e.g., AA) were explored and existing supports (e.g., his relationship with Ann) were strengthened.

A multidimensional intervention strategy that included the clients' total life health helped them to develop the skills needed to meet situational demands and create social networks that would be more supportive of their efforts at adaptive functioning. Consequently, two years after formal services ended the couple's progress continued, and they were coping successfully with life demands.

CONCLUSION

This chapter has offered an introduction to social work practice with persons affected by alcoholism and other drug addictions. Addictive behavior is a biopsychosocial life condition that is influenced by multiple factors affecting all areas of functioning. To understand addictive behavior and to help people who encounter drug-related difficulties, social workers must adopt a dual person:environment focus. Addictive behavior must not be isolated from other domains of functioning and it must be understood as one attempt persons make to remain adaptive in stressful life circumstances.

By adopting an ecological perspective toward addictive behavior, social workers will begin to (1) understand clients, their strengths, and their problems in their own terms; (2) accurately assess the nature and severity of their needs and resources; and (3) develop meaningful assistance strategies that help clients and others alter addictive lifestyles and develop supports for sobriety.

Addictions are major life difficulties that affect persons from all social groups. Their detrimental impact on people and society is immense. Clients who utilize the services of any social work setting may be affected by the consequences of addictive behavior. Therefore, social workers must become sensitive to a population at risk, continuously develop their knowledge base, and intervene at the personal and environmental levels to help individuals become empowered and create communities that support adaptive, drug-free functioning.

References

Agency for Health Care Policy and Research. 1999. "Pharmacotherapy for Alcohol Dependence. Summary, Evidence Report/Technology Assessment: Number 3." http://www.ahcpr.gov/clinic/alcosumm.htm (January 1999).

Akers, Ronald L. 1985. *Deviant Behavior: A Social Learning Approach,* 3d ed. Belmont, Calif.: Wadsworth.

Akers, Ronald L., Marvin Krohn, Lonn Lanza-Kaduce, and Marcia Radosevich. 1979. "Social Learning and Deviant Behavior: A Specific Test of a General Theory." *American Sociological Review* 44(August):636–55.

Alcohol Alert. 1996. *Preventing Alcohol Abuse and Related Problems.* PH370. No. 34. Rockville, Md.: National Institute on Alcohol Abuse and Alcoholism.

Alling, Frederic A. 1992. "Detoxification and Treatment of Acute Sequelae." In Joyce H. Lowinson, Pedro Ruiz, Robert B. Millman, and John G. Langrod, eds., *Substance Abuse: A Comprehensive Textbook,* 2d ed., pp. 402–15. Baltimore: Williams & Wilkins.

American Psychiatric Association. 1994. *Diagnostic and Statistical Manual of Mental Disorders (DSM-IV),* 4th ed. Washington, D.C.: Author.

American Society of Addiction Medicine (ASAM). 1996. *Patient Placement Criteria for the Treatment of Substance-Related Disorders,* 2d ed. Chevy Chase, Md.: Author.

Anderson, Jack G. and Francis S. Gilbert. 1989. "Communications Skills Training with Alcoholics for Improving the Performance of Two of the Alcoholics Anonymous Recovery Steps." *Journal of Studies on Alcohol* 50:361–67.

Annis, Helen M. and Christine S. Davis. 1988. "Assessment of Expectancies." In Dennis M. Donovan and G. Alan Marlatt, eds., *Assessment of Addictive Behaviors,* pp. 84–111. New York: Guilford.

Arif, Awni and Joseph Westermeyer, eds. 1988. *Manual of Drug and Alcohol Abuse.* New York: Plenum.

Babor, Thomas F. 1990. "Social, Scientific, and Medical Issues in the Definition of Alcohol and Drug Dependence." In Griffith Edwards and Malcolm Lader, eds., *The Nature of Drug Dependence,* pp. 19–40. New York: Oxford University Press.

Bandura, Albert. 1986. *Social Foundations of Thought and Action: A Social Cognitive Theory.* Englewood Cliffs, N.J.: Prentice-Hall.

———. 1997. *Self-Efficacy: The Exercise of Control.* New York: W. H. Freeman.

Barber, James G. 1995. "Working with Resistant Drug Abusers." *Social Work* 40:17–23.

Beck, Aaron T., F. D. Wright, C. F. Newman, and B. S. Liese. 1993. *Cognitive Therapy of Substance Abuse.* New York: Guilford.

Becker, Howard S. 1953. "Becoming a Marihuana User." *American Journal of Sociology* 59:235–42.

Begleiter, Henri and Benjamin Kissin, eds. 1995. *The Genetics of Alcoholism.* New York: Oxford University Press.

Berg, Insoo Kim. 1995. "Solution-Focused Brief Therapy with Substance Abusers." In Arnold Washton, ed., *Psychotherapy and Substance Abuse: A Practitioner's Handbook,* pp. 223–42. New York: Guilford.

Berridge, Virginia. 1990. "Dependence: Historical Concepts and Constructs." In Griffith Edwards and Malcolm Lader, eds., *The Nature of Drug Dependence,* pp. 1–16. New York: Oxford University Press.

Besharov, Douglas J., ed. 1994. *When Drug Addicts Have Children.* Washington, D.C.: Child Welfare League of America.

Biddle, Bruce J., Barbara J. Bank, and Marjorie M. Marlin. 1980. "Social Determinants of Adolescent Drinking." *Journal of Studies on Alcohol* 41(3):215–41.

Bourgois, Philippe. 1995. *In Search of Respect: Selling Crack in El Barrio.* New York: Cambridge University Press.

Brecher, Edward M. 1986. "Drug Laws and Drug Law Enforcement: A Review and Evaluation Based on 111 Years of Experience." *Drugs and Society* 1(1):1–27.

Budney, Alan J., and Stephen T. Higgins. 1998. *A Community Reinforcement Plus Vouchers Approach: Treating Cocaine Addiction.* Therapy Manuals for Drug Addiction, Manual 2. Rockville, Md.: National Institute on Drug Abuse.

Cahalan, Don. 1970. *Problem Drinkers: A National Survey.* San Francisco: Jossey-Bass.

———. 1982."Epidemiology: Alcohol Use in American Society." In Edith Lisansky Gomberg, Helene Raskin White, and John A. Carpenter, eds., *Alcohol, Science and Society Revisited,* pp. 96–118. Ann Arbor: University of Michigan Press.

Cahalan, Don and Robin Room. 1974. *Problem Drinking Among American Men.* New Brunswick, N.J.: Rutgers Center of Alcohol Studies.

Carroll, Kathleen M. 1998. *A Cognitive-Behavioral Approach: Treating Cocaine Addiction.* Therapy Manuals for Drug Addiction, Manual 1. Rockville, Md.: National Institute on Drug Abuse.

Chein, Isidar, D. L. Gerard, R. S. Lee, and E. Rosenfield. 1964. *The Road to H.* New York: Basic Books.

Chilcoat, Howard D. and Chris-Ellyn Johanson. 1998. "Vulnerability to Cocaine Abuse." In Stephen T. Higgins and Jonathan L. Katz, eds., *Cocaine Abuse: Behavior, Pharmacology, and Clinical Applications,* pp. 313–41. San Diego: Academic Press.

Childress, Anna Rose, Anita V. Hole, Ronald N. Ehrman, Steven J. Robbins, A. Thomas McLellan, and Charles P. O'Brien. 1993. "Cue Reactivity and Cue Reactivity Interventions in Drug Dependence." In L. S. Onken, J. D. Blaine, and J. J. Boren, eds., *Behavioral Treatments for Drug Abuse and Dependence.* NIDA Research Monograph 137, pp. 73–95. Rockville, Md.: National Institute on Drug Abuse.

Cloninger, C. Robert. 1987. "Neurogenetic Adaptive Mechanisms in Alcoholism." *Science* 236(April 24):410–16.

Cohen, G., N. Fleming, K. Glatter, D. Haghigi, J. Halberstadt, K. McHugh, and A. Wolf. 1996. "Epidemiology of Substance Use." In Lawrence Friedman, Nicholas F. Fleming, David H. Roberts, and Steven F. Hyman, eds., *Source Book of Substance Abuse and Addiction,* pp. 17–40. Baltimore: Williams & Wilkins.

Cohen, Sheldon and S. Leonard Syme, eds. 1985. *Social Support and Health.* New York: Academic Press.

Courtwright, David T. 1982. *Dark Paradise: Opium Addiction in America Before 1940.* Cambridge, Mass.: Harvard University Press.

Crabb, David W., Howard J. Edenberg, Holly R. Thomasson, and Ting-Kai Li. 1995. "Genetic Factors That Reduce Risk for Developing Alcoholism in Animals and Humans." In Henri Begleiter and Benjamin Kissin, eds., *The Genetics of Alcoholism,* pp. 202–20. New York: Oxford University Press.

Cummings, Claudette, Judith R. Gordon, and G. Alan Marlatt. 1980. "Relapse: Prevention and Prediction." In William R. Miller, ed., *The Addictive Behaviors: Treatment of Alcoholism, Drug Abuse, and Obesity,* pp. 291–321. New York: Pergamon.

Currie, Elliott. 1993. *Reckoning: Drugs, the Cities, and the American Future.* New York: Hill & Wang.

Daugherty, Raymond P. and Carl Leukefeld. 1998. *Reducing the Risks for Substance Abuse: A Lifespan Approach.* New York: Plenum.

DeLeon, George. 1999. "The Therapeutic Community Treatment Model." In Barbara S. McCrady and Elizabeth E. Epstein, eds., *Addictions: A Comprehensive Guidebook,* pp. 306–27. New York: Oxford University Press.

Dole, Vincent P. and Marie Nyswanger. 1967. "Heroin Addiction—A Metabolic Disease." *Archives of Internal Medicine* 120:19–24.

Dozier, Cheryl and J. Aaron Johnson. 1998. "Opiate Abuse." In Bruce A. Thyer and John S. Wodarski, eds., *Handbook of Empirical Social Work Practice,* vol. 1, pp. 223–42. New York: Wiley.

Drake, Robert E., K. T. Mueser, R. E. Clark, and M. A. Wallach. 1996. "The Course, Treatment, and Outcome of Substance Disorder in Persons with Severe Mental Illness." *American Journal of Orthopsychiatry* 66(1):42–51.

Edwards, Griffith, E. Jane Marshall, and Christopher C. H. Cook. 1997. *The Treatment of Drinking Problems,* 3d ed. New York: Cambridge University Press.

Ehrman, Ronald, Joseph Ternes, Charles P. O'Brien, and A. Thomas McLellan. 1992. "Conditioned Tolerance in Human Opiate Addicts." *Psychopharmacology* 108(1/2):218–24.

Emrick, Chad D., J. Scott Tonigan, Henry Montgomery, and Laura Little. 1993. "Alcoholics Anonymous: What Is Currently Known?" In Barbara S. McCrady and William R. Miller, eds., *Research on Alcoholics Anonymous,* pp. 41–76. New Brunswick, N.J.: Rutgers Center of Alcohol Studies.

Epstein, Joan F. and Joseph C. Gfroerer. 1997. *Heroin Abuse in the United States.* OAS Working Paper. Rockville, Md.: Substance Abuse and Mental Health Services Administration, Office of Applied Studies.

Fenichel, Otto. 1945. *The Psychoanalytic Theory of Neurosis.* New York: Norton.

First, Michael B., Robert L. Spitzer, Miriam Gibbon, and Janet B. W. Williams. 1996. *Structural Clinical Interview for DSM-IV Axis I Disorders—Patient Edition (SCID-I/P),* version 2.0. New York: Biometrics Research Department.

Freud, Sigmund. 1897/1985. *The Complete Letters of Sigmund Freud to Wilhelm Fliess.* Jeffrey M. Masson, trans. and ed. Cambridge, Mass.: Harvard University Press.

Germain, Carel B. and Alex Gitterman. 1996. *The Life Model of Social Work Practice,* 2d ed. New York: Columbia University Press.

Gibelman, M. and P. Schervish. 1995. "Practice Areas and Settings of Social Workers in Mental Health." *Psychiatric Services* 46:12–37.

Goldman, David and Andrew Bergen. 1998. "Commentary: General and Specific Inheritance of Substance Abuse and Alcoholism." *Archives of General Psychiatry* 55(11): 964–65.

Goldman, Mark S. 1998. "Alcohol Abuse and Dependence: The Process of Empirical Validation." In Keith S. Dobson and Kenneth D. Craig, eds., *Empirically Supported Therapies: Best Practices in Professional Psychology,* pp. 237–58. Thousand Oaks, Calif.: Sage.

Golucke, Ulrich, Robert Landeen, and Dennis Meadows. 1983. "A Comprehensive Theory of the Pathogenesis of Alcoholism." In Benjamin Kissin and Henri Begleiter, eds., *The Biology of Alcoholism. Volume 6. The Pathogenesis of Alcoholism: Psychosocial Factors,* pp. 605–75. New York: Plenum.

Gomberg, Edith S. Lisansky. 1986. "Women: Alcohol and Other Drugs." *Drugs and Society* 1(1):75–109.

Gray, Mike. 1998. *Drug Crazy: How We Got into this Mess and How We Can Get Out.* New York: Random House.

Gresenz, Carole Roan, Katherine Watkins, and Deborah Podus. 1998. "Supplemental Security Income (SSI), Disability Insurance (DI), and Substance Abusers." *Community Mental Health Journal* 34(4):337–50.

Gurnack, Anne E., ed. 1997. *Older Adults' Misuse of Alcohol, Medicines, and Other Drugs: Research and Practice Issues.* New York: Singer.

Gusfield, Joseph R. 1996. *Contested Meanings: The Construction of Alcohol Problems.* Madison: University of Wisconsin Press.

Hanson, Meredith. 1993. "Serving the Substance Abuser in the Workplace." In Paul A. Kurzman and Sheila H. Akabas, eds., *Work and Well-Being: The Occupational Social Work Advantage,* pp. 218–38. Washington, D.C.: National Association of Social Workers Press.

———. 1997. "The Transition Group: Linking Clients with Alcohol Problems to Outpatient Care." In L. Donald McVinney, ed., *Chemical Dependency Treatment: Innovative Group Approaches,* pp. 21–35. New York: Haworth.

Hanson, Meredith, Thomas H. Kramer, and William Gross. 1990. "Outpatient Treatment of Adults with Co-Existing Substance Use and Mental Disorders." *Journal of Substance Abuse Treatment* 7:109–16.

Hasin, Deborah S. and Bridget F. Grant. 1995. "AA and Other Helpseeking for Alcohol Problems: Former Drinkers in the U.S. General Population." *Journal of Substance Abuse* 7:281–92.

Hawkins, J. David, Richard F. Catalano, Jr., and Associates. 1992. *Communities That Care: Action for Drug Abuse Prevention.* San Francisco: Jossey-Bass.

Herd, Denise. 1988. "Drinking by Black and White Women: Results from a National Survey." *Social Problems* 35(5):493–505.

Huba, G. J. and P. M. Bentler. 1980. "The Role of Peer and Adult Models for Drug Taking at Different Stages in Adolescence." *Journal of Youth and Adolescence* 9(5):449–65.

Institute of Medicine. 1990a. *Broadening the Base of Treatment for Alcohol Problems.* Washington, D.C.: National Academy Press.

———. 1990b. *Treating Drug Problems,* Vol. 1. Washington, D.C.: National Academy Press.

———. 1997. *Dispelling the Myths About Addiction: Strategies to Increase Understanding and Strengthen Research.* Washington, D.C.: National Academy Press.

Jahoda, Gustav and Joyce Cramond. 1972. *Children and Alcohol.* London: Her Majesty's Stationery Office.

Jellinek, Elvin M. 1952. "Phases of Alcohol Addiction." *Quarterly Journal of Studies on Alcohol* 13(4):673–84.

———. 1960. *The Disease Concept of Alcoholism.* New Haven, Conn.: College and University Press.

Jessor, Richard and Shirley L. Jessor. 1977. *Problem Behavior and Psychosocial Development: A Longitudinal Study of Youth.* New York: Academic Press.

Johnson, Fred W., Paul J. Gruenewald, Andrew J. Treno, and Gail Armstrong. 1998. "Drinking Over the Life Course within Gender and Ethnic Groups: A Hyperparametric Analysis." *Journal of Studies on Alcohol* 59:568–80.

Jonnes, Jill. 1995. "The Rise of the Modern Addict." *American Journal of Public Health* 85(8):1157–62.

Julien, Robert M. 1998. *A Primer of Drug Action,* 8th ed. New York: Freeman.

Kaestner, Elisabeth, Blanche Frank, Rozanne Marel, and James Schmeidler. 1986. "Substance Use Among Females in New York State: Catching Up with the Males." *Advances in Alcohol and Substance Abuse* 5(3):29–49.

Kandall, Stephen R. 1998. "Women and Addiction in the United States—1850 to 1920." In Cora Lee Wetherington and Adele B. Roman, eds., *Drug Addiction Research and the Health of Women,* pp. 33–52. Rockville, Md.: National Institute on Drug Abuse.

Kandel, Denise B. 1978. "Convergences in Prospective Longitudinal Surveys of Drug Use in Normal Populations." In Denise B. Kandel, ed., *Longitudinal Research on Drug Use,* pp. 3–38. New York: Halsted.

Kaufman, Edward. 1974. "The Psychodynamics of Opiate Dependence: A New Look." *American Journal of Drug and Alcohol Dependence* 1(3):349–70.

Kessler, Ronald C., K. A. McGonagle, S. Zhao, C. B. Nelson, M. Hughes, S. Eshleman, H-U Wittchen, and K. S. Kerdler. 1994. "Lifetime and 12-Month Prevalence of DSM-III-R Psychiatric Disorders in the United States." *Archives of General Psychiatry* 51(1):8–19.

Khantzian, Edward J. 1985. "The Self-Medication Hypothesis of Addictive Disorders: Focus on Heroin and Cocaine Dependence." *American Journal of Psychiatry* 142(11):1259–64.

Kissin, Benjamin. 1983. "The Disease Concept of Alcoholism." In Reginald G. Smart, Frederick B. Glaser, Yedy Israel, Harold Kalant, Robert Popham and Wolfgang Schmidt, eds., *Research Advances in Alcohol and Drug Abuse Problems,* vol. 7, pp. 93–126. New York: Plenum.

Kissin, Benjamin and Meredith Hanson. 1982. "The Bio-Psycho-Social Perspective in Alcoholism." In Joel Solomon, ed., *Alcoholism and Clinical Psychiatry,* pp. 1–19. New York: Plenum.

Kurtz, Ernest. 1979/1991. *Not God: A History of Alcoholics Anonymous.* Center City, Minn.: Hazelden.

Kurtz, Linda Farris. 1997. *Self-Help and Other Support Groups.* Thousand Oaks, Calif.: Sage.

Lanza-Kaduce, Lonn, Ronald L. Akers, Marvin D. Krohn and Marcia Radosevich. 1984. "Cessation of Alcohol and Drug Use Among Adolescents: A Social Learning Model." *Deviant Behavior* 5:79–96.

Lazarus, Arnold A. 1997. *Brief But Comprehensive Psychotherapy: The Multimodal Way.* New York: Singer.

Lender, Mark E. and James K. Martin. 1987. *Drinking in America: A History,* rev. and expanded ed. New York: Free Press.

Levine, Harry Gene. 1978. "The Discovery of Addiction: Changing Conceptions of Habitual Drunkenness in America." *Journal of Studies on Alcohol* 39(1):143–74.

Levinstein, Edward. 1878. *Morbid Craving for Morphia.* London: Smith & Elder.

Longabaugh, Richard, M. Beattie, P. Wirtz, N. Noel, and R. Stout. 1995. "Matching Treatment Focus to Patient Social Investment and Support: 18-Month Follow-Up Results." *Journal of Consulting and Clinical Psychology* 63:296–307.

Longabaugh, Richard, Philip Wirtz, Allen Zweben, and Robert Stout. 1998. "Network Support for Drinking, Alcoholics Anonymous, and Long-Term Matching Effects." *Addiction* 93(9):1313–33.

Lukoff, Irving F. 1980. "Toward a Sociology of Drug Use." In Dan J. Lettieri, Mollie Sayers, and Helen W. Pearson, eds., *Theories of Drug Abuse: Selected Contemporary Perspectives.* Research Monograph 30, pp. 201–11. Rockville, Md.: National Institute on Drug Abuse.

MacAndrew, Charles and Robert D. Edgerton. 1969. *Drunken Comportment.* Chicago: Aldine.

Malin, H. J., J. Coakley, C. Kaelber, N. Munch, and W. Holland. 1982. "An Epidemiologic Perspective on Alcohol Use and Abuse in the United States." In National Institute on Alcohol Abuse and Alcoholism, *Alcohol Consumption and Related Problems,* pp. 99–153. Rockville, Md.: National Institute on Alcohol Abuse and Alcoholism.

Margulies, Rebecca Z., Ronald C. Kessler, and Denise B. Kandel. 1977. "A Longitudinal Study of Onset of Drinking Among High School Students." *Journal of Studies on Alcohol* 38(5):897–912.

Marlatt, G. Alan. 1994. "Addiction, Mindfulness, and Acceptance." In Steven C. Hayes, Neil S. Jacobson, Victoria M. Follette, and Michael J. Dougher, eds., *Acceptance and Change: Content and Context in Psychotherapy,* pp. 175–97. Reno, Nev.: Context Press.

Marlatt, G. Alan and Judith R. Gordon, eds. 1985. *Relapse Prevention.* New York: Guilford.

Mayfield, Demmie G., Gail McLeod, and Patricia Hall. 1974. "The CAGE Questionnaire: Validation of a New Alcoholism Screening Instrument." *American Journal of Psychiatry* 131(10):1121–23.

McCord, William and Joan McCord. 1960. *The Origins of Alcoholism.* Stanford, Calif.: University of Stanford Press.

McCrady, Barbara S. and Sadi Irvine Delaney. 1995. "Self-Help Groups." In Reid K. Hester and William R. Miller, eds., *Handbook of Alcoholism Treatment Approaches: Effective Alternatives,* pp. 160–75. Boston: Allyn & Bacon.

McCrady, Barbara S. and William R. Miller, eds. 1993. *Research on Alcoholics Anonymous: Opportunities and Alternatives.* New Brunswick, N.J.: Rutgers Center of Alcohol Studies.

McLellan, A. T., H. Kushner, D. Metzger, R. Peters, I. Smith, G. Grissom, H. Pettinati, and M. Argeriou. 1992. "The Fifth Edition of the Addiction Severity Index: Historical Critique and Normative Data." *Journal of Substance Abuse Treatment* 9:199–213.

Meyers, Robert J. and J. Ellen Smith. 1995. *Clinical Guide to Alcohol Treatment: The Community Reinforcement Approach.* New York: Guilford.

Miller, William R. 1998. "Researching the Spiritual Dimension of Alcohol and Other Drug Problems." *Addiction* 93(7):979–90.

Miller, William R., Janice M. Brown, Tracy L. Simpson, Nancy S. Handmaker, Thomas H. Bien, Lorenzo F. Luckie, Henry A. Montgomery, Reid K. Hester, and J. Scott Tonigan. 1995. "What Works? A Methodological Analysis of the Alcohol Treatment Outcome Literature." In Reid K. Hester and William R. Miller, eds., *Handbook of Alcoholism Treatment Approaches: Effective Alternatives,* 2d ed., pp. 12–44. Boston: Allyn & Bacon.

Miller, William R. and Reid K. Hester. 1995. "Treatment for Alcohol Problems: Toward an Informed Eclecticism." In Reid K. Hester and William R. Miller, eds., *Handbook of Alcoholism Treatment Approaches: Effective Alternatives,* 2d ed., pp. 1–11. Boston: Allyn & Bacon.

Miller, William R. and Ernest Kurtz. 1994. "Models of Alcoholism Used in Treatment: Contrasting A.A. and Other Perspectives with Which It Is Often Confused." *Journal of Studies on Alcohol* 55:159–66.

Miller, William R. and Stephen Rollnick. 1991. *Motivational Interviewing.* New York: Guilford.

Minkoff, Kenneth and Robert E. Drake, eds. 1991. *Dual Diagnosis of Major Mental Illness and Substance Disorder.* New Directions for Mental Health Services No. 50. San Francisco: Jossey-Bass.

Minnis, John R. 1988. "Toward an Understanding of Alcohol Abuse Among the Elderly: A Sociological Perspective." *Journal of Alcohol and Drug Education* 33(3):32–40.

Morgan, H. Wayne. 1981. *Drugs in America: A Social History, 1800–1980.* Syracuse: Syracuse University Press.

Murphy, Susan Lyden and Edward J. Khantzian. 1995. "Addiction as a 'Self-Medication' Disorder: Application of Ego Psychology to the Treatment of Substance Abuse." In Arnold M. Washton, ed., *Psychotherapy and Substance Abuse,* pp. 161–75. New York: Guilford.

Musto, David F. 1999. *The American Disease: Origins of Narcotic Control,* 3d ed. New Haven: Yale University Press.

National Consensus Development Panel on Effective Treatment of Opiate Addiction. 1998. *Journal of the American Medical Association* 280:1936–43.

National Institute on Drug Abuse (NIDA). 1998a. "NIDAInfofax: Costs to Society (038)." http://165.12.78.61/Infofax/costs.html (April 1998).

———. 1998b. "NIDAInfofax: Hospital Visits and Deaths (040)." http://165.112.78.61/Infofax/hospital.html (April 1998).

Norman, Elaine. 1997. "New Directions: Looking at Psychological Dimensions in Resiliency Enhancement." In Elaine Norman, ed., *Drug-Free Youth,* pp. 73–93. New York: Garland.

Nowinski, Joseph K. 1999. *Family Recovery and Substance Abuse: A Twelve-Step Guide for Treatment.* Thousand Oaks, Calif.: Sage.

O'Brien, Charles P. and A. Thomas McLellan. 1996. "Myths About the Treatment of Addiction." *The Lancet* 347(January 27):237–40.

Office of National Drug Control Policy. 1996. *The National Drug Control Strategy: 1996.* Washington, D.C.: Executive Office of the President of the United States, The White House.

Ouimette, Paige Crosby, Rudolf H. Moos, and John W. Finney. 1998. "Influence of Outpatient Treatment and 12-Step Group Involvement on One-Year Substance Abuse Treatment Outcomes." *Journal of Studies on Alcohol* 59:513–22.

Pagliaro, Ann Marie and Louis A. Pagliaro. 1996. *Substance Use Among Children and Adolescents.* New York: Wiley.

Pattison, E. Mansell. 1982. "Decision Strategies in the Path of Alcoholism Treatment." In William M. Hay and Peter E. Nathan, eds., *Clinical Case Studies in the Behavioral Treatment of Alcoholism,* pp. 251–74. New York: Plenum.

Prochaska, James O., Carlo C. DiClemente, and John C. Norcross. 1992. "In Search of How People Change: Applications to Addictive Behavior." *American Psychologist* 47(9):1102–14.

Project MATCH Research Group. 1997. "Matching Alcoholism Treatment to Client Heterogeneity: Project MATCH Posttreatment Drinking Outcomes." *Journal of Studies on Alcohol* 58(1):7–29.

Regier, Darrel A., M. E. Farmer, D. S. Rae, B. Z. Locke, S. J. Keith, L. L. Judd, and F. K. Goodwin. 1990. "Co-Morbidity of Mental Disorders with Alcohol and Other Drug Abuse: Results from the Epidemiological Catchment Area (ECA) Study." *Journal of the American Medical Association* 264:2511–18.

Reid, Jeanne, Peggy Macchetto, and Susan Foster. 1999. *No Safe Haven: Children of Substance-Abusing Parents.* New York: National Center on Addiction and Substance Abuse at Columbia University.

Reinarman, Craig, Dan Waldorf, Sheila B. Murphy, and Harry G. Levine. 1997. "The Contingent Call of the Pipe: Bingeing and Addiction Among Heavy Cocaine Smokers." In Craig Reinarman and Harry G. Levine, eds., *Crack in America: Demon Drugs and Social Justice,* pp. 77–97. Berkeley: University of California Press.

Rhodes, Jean E. and Leonard A. Jason. 1988. *Preventing Substance Abuse among Children and Adolescents.* New York: Pergamon.

Robins, Lee N. 1978. "The Interaction of Setting and Predisposition in Explaining Novel Behavior: Drug Initiations Before, In, and After Vietnam." In Denise B. Kandel, ed., *Longitudinal Research on Drug Use,* pp. 179–96. New York: Halsted.

Robins, Lee N. and Darrel A. Regier. 1991. *Psychiatric Disorders in America: The Epidemiological Catchment Area Study.* New York: Free Press.

Rose, Susan. J., Allen Zweben, and Virginia Stoffel. 1999. "Interfaces Between Substance Abuse Treatment and Other Health and Social Systems." In Barbara S. McCrady and Elizabeth E. Epstein, eds., *Addictions: A Comprehensive Guidebook,* pp. 421–36. New York: Oxford University Press.

Rush, Benjamin. 1791. *An Enquiry into the Effects of Spiritous Liquors Upon the Human Body and Their Influences on the Happiness of Society.* Philadelphia: Edinburgh.

Rydell, C. Peter and Susan S. Everingham. 1994. *Controlling Cocaine: Supply versus Demand Programs.* Santa Monica, Calif.: RAND Corporation, Drug Policy Research Center.

Schilling, Robert F. and Nabila El-Bassel. 1998. "Substance Abuse Interventions." In Janet B. W. Williams and Kathleen Ell, eds., *Advances in Mental Health Research: Implications for Practice,* pp. 437–81. Washington, D.C.: National Association of Social Workers Press.

Schinke, Steven P., Gilbert J. Botvin, and Mario A. Orlandi. 1991. *Substance Abuse in Children and Adolescents: Evaluation and Intervention.* Newbury Park, Calif.: Sage.

Schinke, Steven P. and Kristin C. Cole. 1998. "Prevention." In Janet B. W. Williams and Kathleen Ell, eds., *Advances in Mental Health Research: Implications for Practice,* pp. 359–73. Washington, D.C.: National Association of Social Workers Press.

Schinke, Steven P., Michael S. Moncher, Gary W. Holden, Gilbert J. Botvin, and Mario A. Orlandi. 1989. "American Indian Youth and Substance Abuse: Tobacco Use Problems, Risk Factors, and Preventive Interventions." *Health Education Research* 4:137–44.

Schinke, Steven P., Michael S. Moncher, Josie Pallega, Luis H. Zayas, and Robert F. Schilling. 1988. "Hispanic Youth, Substance Abuse, and Stress: Implications for Prevention Research." *International Journal of the Addictions* 23:809–26.

Schmidt, Laura A., Constance Weisner, and James Wiley. 1998. "Substance Abuse and the Course of Welfare Dependency." *American Journal of Public Health* 88(11):1616–22.

Schuckit, Marc A. 1998. "Biological, Psychological, and Environmental Predictors of the Alcoholism Risk: A Longitudinal Study." *Journal of Studies on Alcohol* 59:485–94.

Schuster, Charles R. 1987. "The United States 'Drug Abuse Scene': An Overview." *Clinical Chemistry* 33(11B):7B–12B.

Segal, Steven P., Jim Baumohl, and Elsie Johnson. 1977. "Falling Through the Cracks: Mental Disorder and Social Margin in a Young Vagrant Population." *Social Problems* 24(February):387–400.

Selzer, M. L. 1971. "The Michigan Alcoholism Screening Test: The Quest for a New Diagnostic Instrument." *American Journal of Psychiatry* 127(12):1653–58.

Sher, Kenneth J. 1991. *Children of Alcoholics: A Critical Appraisal of Theory and Research.* Chicago: University of Chicago Press.

Skinner, Harvey A. and John L. Horn. 1984. *Alcohol Dependence Scale (ADS): User's Guide.* Toronto: Addiction Research Foundation.

Smyth, Nancy J. 1998. "Substance Abuse." In John S. Wodarski and Bruce A. Thyer, eds., *Handbook of Empirical Social Work Practice, Volume 2: Social Problems and Practice Issues,* pp. 123–53. New York: Wiley.

Sobell, Mark B. and Linda C. Sobell. 1995. "Editorial: Controlled Drinking After 25 Years; How Important Was the Great Debate?" *Addiction* 90:1149–53.

Stocker, Steven. 1998. "Drug Addiction Treatment Conference Emphasizes Combining Therapies." *NIDA Notes* 13(3):1–3.

Straussner, Shulamith L. A. and Elizabeth Zelvin, eds. 1997. *Gender and Addictions.* Northvale, N.J.: Aronson.

Substance Abuse and Mental Health Services Administration (SAMHSA). 1997. *National Household Survey on Drug Abuse: Main Findings.* Rockville, Md.: Substance Abuse and Mental Health Services Administration, Office of Applied Studies.

———. 1998. *Services Research Outcome Study.* Rockville, Md.: Substance Abuse and Mental Health Services Administration, Office of Applied Studies.

Swarns, Rachel L. 1998. "Mayor Wants to Abolish Use of Methadone." *New York Times,* July 21, pp. B1, B5.

Szapocznik, Jose, William M. Kurtines, and Contributors. 1989. *Breakthroughs in Family Therapy with Drug-Abusing and Problem Youth.* New York: Springer.

Tang, Wilson and JudyAnn Bigby. 1996. "Cultural Perspectives on Substance Abuse." In Lawrence Friedman, Nicholas F. Fleming, David H. Roberts, and Steven F. Hyman, eds., *Source Book of Substance Abuse and Addiction,* pp. 41–56. Baltimore: Williams & Wilkins.

Tiebout, Harry. 1957. "The Ego Factor in Surrendering to Alcoholism." *Quarterly Journal of Studies on Alcohol* 15:610–21.

Trotter, Thomas. 1804. *An Essay, Medical, Philosophical and Chemical, On Drunkenness.* London: Longman.

Turner, Sandra. 1997. "Building on Strengths: Risks and Resiliency in the Family, School, and Community." In Elaine Norman, ed., *Drug-Free Youth*, pp. 95–112. New York: Garland.

Vaillant, George E. 1992. "Is There a Natural History of Addiction?" In Charles P. O'Brien and Jerome H. Jaffe, eds., *Addictive States*, pp. 41–57. New York: Raven Press.

——. 1995. *The Natural History of Alcoholism, Revisited.* Cambridge: Harvard University Press.

Westermeyer, Joseph. 1992. "Cultural Perspectives: Native Americans, Asians, and New Immigrants." In Joyce H. Lowinson, Pedro Ruiz, Robert B. Millman, and John G. Langrod, eds., *Substance Abuse: A Comprehensive Textbook*, 2d ed. pp. 890–96. Baltimore: Williams & Wilkins.

White, William L. 1998. *Slaying the Dragon: The History of Addiction Treatment and Recovery in America.* Bloomington, Ill.: Chestnut Health Systems.

Wurmser, Leon. 1978. *The Hidden Dimension: Psychodynamics in Compulsive Drug Use.* New York: Jason Aronson.

Yablonsky, Lewis. 1965. *Synanon: The Tunnel Back.* Baltimore: Penguin.

——. 1989. *The Therapeutic Community.* New York: Gardner Press.

Yalisove, Daniel L., ed. 1997. *Essential Papers on Addiction.* New York: New York University Press.

Zucker, Robert A. 1979. "Developmental Aspects of Drinking Through Young Adult Years." In Howard T. Blane and Morris E. Chafetz, eds., *Youth, Alcohol, and Social Policy*, pp. 91–146. New York: Plenum.

Zweben, Allen. 1991. "Motivational Counseling with Alcoholic Couples." In William R. Miller and Stephen Rollnick, *Motivational Interviewing*, pp. 225–35. New York: Guilford.

4

Borderline Personality

Nina Rovinelli Heller
Harriette C. Johnson

People who meet criteria for borderline personality disorder (BPD) present for services in almost every type of social work practice setting. Typical presenting problems are suicide attempts and gesture, family violence, substance abuse, eating disorders, reckless spending, and other problems with self-control. Social workers act therapeutically with persons with BPD not only when they are designated "therapist" but also in the roles of case manager or advocate (Goldstein 1983; Heller and Northcut 1996; Johnson 1988, 1991).

Clients with BPD are widely recognized as being difficult and frustrating to work with because of characteristics such as intense hostile-dependent feelings toward the practitioner, overidealization of the social worker alternating with rageful disappointment, suicidal or otherwise violent behaviors, impulsivity and recklessness, and the tendency to terminate treatment abruptly and prematurely when painful issues arise (Kaplan and Sadock 1998; Stone 1994). Although there are multiple theoretical perspectives regarding etiology and treatment strategies, the descriptions of problematic behaviors, course of illness, and treatment difficulties are highly consistent.

DEFINING AND EXPLAINING BORDERLINE PERSONALITY

The *Diagnostic and Statistical Manual of Mental Disorders,* fourth edition (*DSM-IV*) criteria are used throughout the United States. The International Statistical Classification of Diseases and Related Health Problems (ICD-10) is used worldwide, with increasing use in the United States. By the year 2000, *DSM-IV* codes must be identical with ICD-10 (Kaplan and Sadock 1998). Many insurers now require use of this system. However, nearly all research on BPD relies on the *DSM-IV* rather than the ICD. Moderate support for validity of *DSM-IV* criteria was found in an evaluation of content validity related to three domains: affective instability, impulsivity, and interpersonal and identity instability (Blais, Hilsenroth, and Castlebury 1997). Some writers advocate broader inclusion for people in this diagnostic category (Kernberg 1984), a dimensional rather than a categorical approach to diagnosis (Stone 1994; Tuinier and Verhoeven 1995), or regrouping the nine *DSM-IV* criteria into a different set of characteristics (Linehan 1993). A dimensional approach identifies all characteristics of an individual's profile, emphasizing specific symptoms or characteristics such as self-mutilation and dissociation, rather than including or excluding people from a diagnosis based on a list of criteria.

Some scholars emphasize certain criteria over others. For example, Cowdry (1997), using research diagnostic criteria, requires the presence of self-injurious behavior for an individual to qualify for the diagnosis, whereas *DSM-IV* requires at least five of nine characteristics that may or may not include self-injurious behavior.

Linehan (1993) sees psychic dysregulation as the core disorder. She has rearranged *DSM-IV* criteria into five rather than nine characteristics: (1) emotional dysregulation (emotional responses that are highly reactive to stimuli), including episodes of depression, anxiety, irritability, and anger; (2) interpersonal dysregulation, characterized by fear of abandonment and chaotic, intense, difficult relationships; (3) behavioral dysregulation (extreme problematic impulsivity seen in self-mutilation, suicidal attempts or gestures, substance abuse, indiscriminate sex, binge eating, reckless driving, and profligate spending); (4) cognitive dysregulation (brief nonpsychotic depersonalization, delusion, or dissociation); and (5) dysregulation of the self (feelings of emptiness and problems with self-identity).

Other salient characteristics are intolerance of aloneness (Gunderson 1996), low levels of emotional awareness, inability to coordinate positive and negative feelings, poor accuracy in recognizing facial expressions of emotion, and intense responses to negative emotions (Levine, Marziali, and Hood 1997).

Almost all observers, no matter what their preferred ideologies, agree that *highly variable mood* (extreme fluctuations in emotion) and *impulsive behavior* (e.g., overdoses, self-injury, other violent acts, and outbursts of rage) are two features that characterize most people with BPD and distinguish them from other, often overlapping, *DSM-IV* personality disorders (Cowdry 1997). There is agreement that the self-destructive behaviors often engaged in by people with BPD, such as cutting or burning themselves or attempting suicide, are very effective in alleviating psychic pain, especially anxiety and anger (Linehan 1993). These behaviors also are effective at regulating the environment (e.g., by getting others to admit the person with BPD to a hospital or otherwise to express concern and caring).

Because their pain is extreme, people with BPD may engage repeatedly in self-destructive behavior as they learn that it reduces pain. How this mechanism works is not yet known, but various theories have been proposed to explain it. Studies comparing persons with BPD who experience pain during self-injury with those who do not suggest that analgesia (not feeling physical pain) is related to neurosensory and attitudinal/psychological abnormalities, to cognitive impairment in the ability to distinguish pain, and/or to dissociative mechanisms (Kemperman, Russ, and Shearin 1997; Russ et al. 1996).

While descriptions of borderline symptomatology are similar, theories of etiology and recommendations for treatment have varied widely. The early literature strongly

favored intrapsychic and object-relations explanations, along with individually oriented analytic interventions (Frosch 1960; Kernberg 1967, 1984; Knight 1953; Kohut
1978; Mahler 1971; Masterson and Rinsley 1975; Stern 1938). While some earlier
investigators (Andrulonis et al. 1981; Hartocollis 1968; Murray 1979) noted possible
neurobiological involvement in the development of BPD, the bulk of the clinical literature continued to focus on psychodynamic explanations. More recently, evolving
knowledge regarding neurobiological factors has become incorporated into theory
development, treatment protocols and research agendas. Feminist critiques have
emerged primarily from trauma theory (Herman 1992; Landecker 1992) and reflect an
appreciation of sociocultural and gender-related influences in the development of
BPD.

Symptoms of BPD border on several Axis I disorders and also *overlap with several
Axis II personality disorders* (Cowdry 1997). Axis I disorders commonly co-occur with
BPD or are mistaken for it. These include major depressive disorder (MDD) (Alneas
and Torgerson 1997), the spectrum of bipolar disorders (Akiskal 1996), substance use
disorders (Grilo et al. 1997; Morgenstern et al. 1997; Senol, Dereboy, and Yuksel 1997),
dissociative identity disorders (Atlas and Wolfson 1996; Sar, Yargic, and Tutkun
1996), and eating disorders (Davis, Claridge, and Cerullo 1997; Grilo, Levy, et al. 1996;
Sansone, Sansone, and Wiederman 1997; Verkes et al. 1996).

Affective Disorders. Unstable mood is one of the defining characteristics of BPD.
Extensive research supports overlap between BPD and mood disorders. Depression
is a major component of many borderline states. A strong positive family history of
serious affective disorder has been found among persons meeting criteria for BPD.
Many have symptoms characteristic of bipolar, cyclothymic, and unipolar affective
disorders. Significant improvement on antidepressant medication has been reported
for clients whose BPD includes prominent affective components (Kaplan and Sadock
1998). Phobic-anxious people who meet BPD criteria also respond to antidepressants
(Klein 1977). In Turkey, 45 patients diagnosed with BPD were followed for two to
four years after discharge. Prevalence of affective disorder was 76.6 percent, with
substance use disorders the second most common Axis I diagnosis among persons
with BPD (Senol et al. 1997).

Ultrarapid-cycling forms of bipolar disorder, where morose, labile moods with
irritable, mixed features constitute the patients' habitual self, are often mistaken for
BPD (Akiskal 1996). De La Fuente and Mendlewicz (1996) found no evidence of an
endocrine biological link between BPD and MDD, suggesting that the depressive
symptoms in some patients with BPD may have different biological substrates from
those found in patients with MDD.

Substance Use Disorders. Substance abuse commonly co-occurs with BPD. For example, high prevalence of BPD was found in a multisite sample of 366 substance
abusers in treatment, with BPD and ASPD linked to more severe symptomatology of
alcoholism (Morgenstern et al. 1997).

Dissociative Disorders. Recent studies highlight overlaps between dissociative phenomena and BPD (Atlas and Wolfson 1996; Kemperman et al. 1997; Paris and Zweig-
Frank 1997; Russ et al. 1996). Dissociation is increasingly being recognized as a

characteristic of persons with BPD, and conversely, among people meeting criteria for dissociative identity disorder (DID), borderline characteristics are very common. In a cross-national study, Sar et al. (1996) found that among 35 patients diagnosed with DID, an average of 3.8 criteria for BPD were reported, only slightly fewer than the five required to meet DSM criteria for BPD. Another study of 26 adolescents with BPD showed both significant depression and dissociation, suggesting the importance of evaluating instability of mood as well as weak continuity in self-expression when identifying and treating BPD (Atlas and Wolfson 1996). Cowdry (1997) has noted the similarity of dissociative states to complex partial seizures.

Eating Disorders. Persons with eating disorders serious enough to warrant hospitalization often also meet criteria for BPD. Using blood platelet measures of serotonin (5-HT) and monoamine oxidase activity to assess monoamine functions, Verkes et al. (1996) found that bulimia could be subdivided into two groups, those with comorbid BPD, who resembled recurrent suicide attempters with BPD in levels of anger, impulsivity, and biochemical characteristics, and those without BPD.

The overlap of BPD with other Axis II personality disorders is widely acknowledged. In fact, Kernberg's *borderline personality organization* (different from *DSM-IV* BPD criteria) is a large umbrella that comprises all major forms of character pathology and appears to encompass DSM categories of borderline, histrionic, narcissistic, and antisocial personality disorders (American Psychiatric Association 1994; Kernberg 1984). The wide net cast by Kernberg yields a very high prevalence rate of between 15 and 30 percent of the population (Gunderson 1984). To identify overlaps between BPD and other personality disorders, readers can consult tables of diagnostic criteria in the *DSM-IV* (American Psychiatric Association 1994).

Neurologic Dysfunction. Various investigators have found evidence of neurologic dysfunction in persons meeting criteria for BPD, especially those for whom impulsivity is a salient characteristic (Biederman, Newcorn, and Sprich 1991; Drake, Pakalnis, and Phillips 1992; Stein et al. 1993; van Reekum 1993). It is important to distinguish the term "neurologic" from "neurobiological." All psychic phenomena have neurobiological underpinnings, whereas the term neurologic designates specific subtypes of neurobiological dysfunctions that are diagnosed and treated by the subspecialty of neurology rather than psychiatry. These distinctions are becoming increasingly fuzzy as knowledge about the neurobiology of psychiatric disorders advances, but they are rooted in medical tradition.

In a study of 91 hospitalized borderline patients, 38 percent ($n = 35$) had underlying neurologic dysfunction (Andrulonis et al. 1981), including ADHD (attention-deficit hyperactivity disorder, then called minimal brain dysfunction) or learning disability (27 percent, $n = 25$), and brain trauma, epilepsy, or a history of encephalitis (11 percent, $n = 10$). Differences by gender were highly significant, with 53 percent ($n = 17$) of males positive for a history of minimal brain dysfunction or learning disability compared with only 14 percent ($n = 8$) of females. Females more frequently bordered on major affective disorder.

Residual characteristics of ADHD are also typical of adults with BPD. ADHD often continues into adulthood and may underlie such characteristics as impulsivity, irritability, poor frustration tolerance, aggressive outbursts, temper tantrums, readiness to anger, drug and alcohol abuse, distractibility, mood swings, diminished responsiveness to rewarding events, antisocial behavior, and loneliness. There are as yet no large-scale studies indicating prevalence of overlap between ADHD and BPD.

The revolution in knowledge about biological bases of psychopathology made possible by the development of scanning and other technologies has contributed to knowledge about borderline phenomena. De La Fuente et al. (1997) used positron emission tomography (PET scan) to identify characteristics of the physiology (function or process) taking place in borderline states. They found a relative hypometabolism (low level of glucose consumption) in the premotor and frontal cortices, the anterior cingulate cortex, and thalamic, caudate, and lenticular nuclei, indicating significant cerebral metabolic disturbances in BPD. Recent studies have tested relationships between BPD and hormonal responses (Steinberg et al. 1997); BPD, subthreshold depression, and sleep disorders (Akiskal et al. 1997); association between platelet monoamine oxidase activity and stable personality traits such as impulsiveness, monotony avoidance, and aggressiveness (Stalenheim, von Knorring, and Oreland 1997); and a possible neural basis for the phenomenon of splitting so often observed in persons with BPD (Muller 1992).

Higher levels of platelet serotonin in persons with BPD predict recurrent suicide attempts within a year of follow-up, suggesting an association between suicidality and central serotonergic dysfunction (Verkes et al. 1997). Platelet 5-HT was higher in patients with BPD than in normal female controls and was positively correlated with experiencing anger.

The current understanding of the biological substrates thought to be present in BPD has been reviewed by Figueroa and Silk (1997). In persons with BPD, the type and breadth of the individual's hyperreactivity to the environment, which often manifests itself in hypersensitivity in interpersonal situations, is probably mediated through noradrenergic mechanisms. Impulsivity, a major constitutional predisposition to BPD, is mediated through serotonergic mechanisms. The combination of these two mechanisms may lead to a clinical picture, often seen in BPD, where impulsivity and self-destructive behavior are employed to deal with the stress and dysphoria of being hypersensitive to interpersonal and other environmental stimuli.

DEMOGRAPHIC PATTERNS

There are no precise data on prevalence of BPD, but it is thought to be present in about 1 to 2 percent of the population. First-degree relatives of persons with BPD have a higher prevalence than average of major depression and substance use disorders (Kaplan and Sadock 1998). In contrast with other personality and psychiatric disorders, persons meeting DSM criteria for BPD were found in a meta-analysis ($N = 783$) to have significantly higher educational achievement and younger age (Taub 1996). Persons with BPD constitute 10 to 25 percent of all inpatient psychiatric admissions and represent the most common inpatient personality disorder diagnosis (Springer and Silk 1996). Differences by race or ethnicity have not been demonstrated, although most recent studies have been based on small samples of subsets or persons meeting criteria for BPD (Else et al. 1993; Grilo et al. 1997; Snyder et al. 1985). Alarcon, Foulks, and Vakkur (1998) suggest that cultural differences and expectations in the expression of affect and certain behaviors may be implicated in any prevalence differences among ethnic and racial groups.

SOCIETAL CONTEXT

BPD is estimated to be twice as frequent in females as in males (Kaplan and Sadock 1998). Cowdry (1997) questions these differences in prevalence by gender, postulating that males with BPD often are in jail and remain undiagnosed, so that the 2:1 ratio overstates prevalence in females as compared with males. Grilo, Becker, et al. (1996) found that among 138 consecutively admitted adolescents, females were significantly more likely to meet criteria for BPD, whereas narcissistic personality disorder was diagnosed only in males. Paris (1997a, 1997b) postulates that a common base of impulsivity in antisocial personality disorder (ASPD) and BPD is expressed behaviorally in different ways due to shaping by gender.

Kaplan and Sadock (1998) note that *DSM-IV* defines personality disorders, generally, as including "enduring subjective experiences and behavior that deviate from cultural standards" (775). If this is so, an increased understanding of the culture from which one "deviates" becomes critical to both assessment and intervention. Paris (1991) hypothesizes that significant and rapid changes in cultural roles are implicated in the development of borderline traits in persons with insufficient adaptive skills. Likewise, the stresses associated with immigration have been implicated in the development of symptoms such as identity disturbance, emptiness, and abandonment, which are part of the BPD clinical picture (Laxenaire, Ganne-Devonec, and Streiff 1982). This suggested connection between cultural role changes and vulnerability to developing BPD might offer one explanation for the higher incidence of BPD in women.

While persons meeting diagnostic criteria for BPD tend to be relatively young, there is little clear research regarding personality disorders in older adults. Tyrer and Seivewright (1988) report that persons with personality diagnoses such as borderline, antisocial, and histrionic, who are characterized in part by strong affective symptoms, improve with age. They attribute this to decreases in impulsivity and activity levels. Sadavoy and Fogel (1992) suggest that persons with BPD may show a shift in symptoms as they age, with somatization and depression replacing the more impulse-ridden earlier symptoms. Murray (1988) reports that older adults who no longer meet formal criteria for a personality disorder may exhibit related traits when confronted with certain life stresses. Given that the mental health issues of the older adult have been generally overlooked both in the clinical and research realms, further investigation is warranted, particularly regarding the complex relationships between BPD and stressful life events.

At the other end of the spectrum is the adolescent. While practitioners have historically been reluctant to diagnose personality disorders in persons under 18, *DSM-IV* defines personality disorders as having an onset in adolescence or early adulthood. In a longitudinal study, Thomsen (1990) reported that children hospitalized with a diagnosis of conduct disorder between the ages of 10 and 15 had a higher rate of adult admission for treatment for personality disorder and substance abuse. Literature of the 1970s and early 1980s included many case reports of "borderline" children. However, these appeared to be more descriptive than diagnostic. Lofgren et al. (1991) reported in a prospective study: "The borderline child diagnosis remains a misnomer. Instead, this diagnostic category appears to represent an antecedent condition for the development of an array of personality disorders in adulthood" (1545). If this is so, early identification and intervention with this group of children is important.

Long-term prognosis appears to be good for the majority of persons diagnosed with BPD. Four long-term studies following persons with BPD for fifteen years showed remarkable concordance of findings (McGlashan 1986; Paris 1993; Stone 1987). BPD is a chronic disorder into middle age, by which time the majority of persons formerly diagnosed with BPD no longer meet criteria. In all four studies, mean Global Assessment Scale scores were in the normal range (mid-60s), and most former patients were working and had a social life. It is unclear whether treatment contributes significantly to outcome or whether the natural course of improvement would occur in any case. To the extent that treatment during crisis periods can deter suicide, however, it would be essential to buy time by "holding" BPD sufferers until the risk of suicide has passed.

However, about 10 percent of persons with BPD have committed suicide by the fifteenth year of posttreatment follow-up (Paris 1993). Findings are inconsistent with respect to predictors of suicide and other poor outcomes.

VULNERABILITIES AND RISK FACTORS

As is the case with most psychiatric conditions, both the anecdotal and empirical literature on BPD has been biased toward the examination of risk factors rather than factors associated with resiliency. Factors promoting resiliency in persons with BPD have typically been inferred rather than directly investigated. The preponderance of evidence now supports the view that the borderline personality represents a common or similar picture that is the outcome of a heterogeneous developmental course. Almost all observers agree that interacting biological and environmental risk factors play a role in the development of BPD. In general, the components appear to be **biological** vulnerability (predisposition for affective instability, impulsivity, or other borderline characteristic) interacting with a childhood history of abuse, lack of validation, or other unidentified environmental inputs (Cowdry 1997; Linehan 1993).

The role of **childhood trauma** as a risk factor for BPD is related to sensitivity to environmental stimuli and is proposed to be acting through noradrenergic mechanisms in the development over time of BPD in individuals with a history of childhood trauma. In multiple regressions of potential predictor variables for the borderline diagnosis, *interpersonal sensitivity* was the only significant predictor of the borderline diagnosis (Figueroa et al. 1997). The investigators postulate that at least in some cases, interpersonal sensitivity may be the constitutional/environmental substrate with which traumatic experiences interact to lead to BPD. That is, interpersonal sensitivity makes such individuals especially vulnerable to trauma. Reviewing empirical evidence, Zanarini and Frankenburg (1997) conclude that BPD is an outcome arrived at by interactions between a vulnerable (hyperbolic) temperament, a traumatic childhood, and/or a triggering event or series of events. In any particular situation, any one of these three categories may contribute most strongly

Neurobiological responses to stress were reviewed by Henry (1997). Delayed responses to severe psychological trauma (posttraumatic stress disorder, or PTSD)

present a paradoxical mix of symptoms: continuing elevation in catecholamine response mediating anger and fear, together often with normal levels of hypothalamic-pituitary-adrenal (HPA) axis activity. Reexperiencing the trauma and the arousal may be associated with dysfunction of the locus coeruleus, amygdala, and hippocampal systems. In addition, dissociation of the connections between the right and left hemispheres appears to be responsible for alexithymia (lack of awareness of one's emotions or moods) and failure of the cortisol response that so often follow severe psychological trauma. In this condition, it appears that the right hemisphere no longer fully contributes to integrated cerebral function. Children with damage to the right hemisphere lose critical social skills. Adults lose a sense of relatedness and familiarity. Henry postulates that these losses of social sensibilities may account for the lack of empathy and difficulties with bonding found in antisocial personality disorder (ASPD) as well as BPD.

Paris (1997a) critically reviews beliefs pertaining to the relationship between traumatic events in childhood and personality disorders in adulthood. He notes that attributing adult psychopathology primarily to environmental factors is problematic because personality traits are heritable, children are resilient to the long-term effects of trauma, all studies of trauma in personality disordered persons suffer from retrospective designs, and only a minority of patients with severe personality disorders report severe childhood trauma.

According to Paris, the effects of trauma in the personality disorders can therefore be better understood in the context of gene-environment interactions. Interaction is key because many biologically vulnerable persons do not develop BPD, and many persons with histories of childhood trauma or loss do not develop BPD. In cases of biological vulnerability, it should be theoretically possible to prevent later onset of BPD by recognizing vulnerabilities early and by supporting parents and educating them about these children's special, idiosyncratic needs. These vulnerable children require parenting efforts *different from* and/or *greater than* ordinary parenting behaviors successful with children lacking these vulnerabilities. At present, however, few if any preventive assessments or interventive programs are in place.

Linehan (1993) views etiology as the interaction of biological factors (due possibly to genetic factors, intrauterine events, or trauma at an early age, especially head trauma) and environmental factors characterized as "invalidating." Invalidating environments communicate to persons who later develop BPD that their responses to life situations are invalid, inappropriate, or incorrect. In such environments, all problems are viewed as motivational in origin—if only you were to try harder, the problem would be solved. Typically such environments fail to recognize or take seriously the person's (biologically based) emotional vulnerability and overly sensitive responses, seen in children who may be inhibited, irritable, or cry a great deal in infancy, children known as "difficult."

For many decades, **parents** of persons with BPD were assumed by professionals to have caused their children's disorders. In an early review, Gunderson and Englund (1981) found little evidence to support the literature's messages about parental culpability and suggested that the tendency of the persons with BPD and their therapists to see mothers as "bad" may be a function of the splitting mechanisms used so frequently by persons with BPD. They might, in fact, be projecting nonexistent negative behaviors or affects onto their mothers in the process of reconstructing their pasts.

Palombo (1983) observed that persons with BPD experience the world as hostile and chaotic and believe their caretakers have failed to provide a benign environment:

> Regardless of whether or not the parents did fail, [they] were in all likelihood helpless to provide such an environment for the child . . . the benign, responsive, caring parents may in that sense be utter failures from the perspective of the child because his needs were not adequately attended to. Conversely, neglectful parents raising a competent, well-endowed child might be experienced as loving and responsible. . . .
>
> [The person with BPD] could, and often does, pin the blame for his suffering on those around him. From his perspective, they are the causes of it. Since [the parents] are perceived as powerful and mighty, they cannot be absolved of the blame for permitting his suffering to occur. Myths are then created about the terrible things that parents did to the child, even though in reality the parents may have struggled mightily to provide for the child. (335–36)

In their study, Gunderson and Englund (1981) had expected to find empirical support for the beliefs prevailing in the late 1970s that family psychopathology for persons with BPD was characterized by overinvolved, separation-resistant, dependency-generating mothers. Instead, they found that parental underinvolvement was much more common. Neglectful parenting was also implicated in a recent study (Zanarini et al. 1997). In comparison with people with other personality disorders, three family environmental factors were significant predictors of a borderline diagnosis: sexual abuse by a male noncaretaker, emotional denial by a male caretaker, and inconsistent treatment by a female caretaker. The results suggested that sexual abuse was neither a necessary nor a sufficient condition for the development of BPD and that other childhood experiences, particularly neglect by caretakers of both genders, represent significant risk factors. Since the majority of children who experience any of these risk factors do not develop BPD, however, other variables clearly had to be present as well to account for the later development of BPD.

Gunderson, Berkowitz, and Ruiz-Sancho (1997) caution against one-sided assessment of BPD:

> Much of the preceding literature about the families of borderline patients derived solely from reports provided by the borderline patients and rarely included the families' perspectives. When you consider that borderline patients are by nature often devaluative and that they often find on entering treatment that devaluing past caretakers—past treaters as well as families— is a way to ignite the ambitions and enthusiasm of the new candidates for becoming their caretakers, it is disturbing in retrospect that we have not been more suspicious about their accounts of their families. (451)

Recently, Gunderson himself offered a mea culpa with respect to parents of people with BPD, as had another psychiatrist fifteen years earlier with respect to schizophrenia (Gunderson et al. 1997; Terkelsen 1983). "I was a contributor to the literature that led to the unfair vilification of the families and the largely unfortunate efforts at either excluding or inappropriately involving them in treatment. So it is with embarrassment that I now find myself presenting a treatment [psychoeducation] that begins with the expectation that the families of borderline individuals are important allies of the treaters" (Gunderson et al. 1997:451).

RESILIENCIES AND PROTECTIVE FACTORS

Factors promoting resilience in persons with BPD have typically been inferred rather than directly investigated. The reconsideration of existing and emerging data regarding those factors that do and do *not* promote risk for the development of BPD can be useful in the development of both clinical and research questions about resiliency factors. Masten (1994) refers to resilience as "a pattern over time, characterized by good eventual adaptation despite developmental risk, acute stressors or chronic adversities" (5). We would extend the definition of developmental risk to explicitly include biological vulnerability. Further clinical and empirical investigation regarding factors that promote resiliency in persons at risk for developing and/or sustaining BPD might focus on the following questions: Given the prevalence of BPD diagnosis in women with sexual abuse histories (Herman 1992; Landecker 1992), why do some women with similar abuse histories not develop BPD? Persons with BPD frequently experience interpersonal chaos, impulsivity, and intense affect, characteristics that presumably impair "good parenting." What impact does this parenting have on children, and are there differences among siblings? Given the presumed biological/genetic and environmental vulnerability of these offspring, are they at risk for developing BPD? If so, what are the protective factors for children of parents with BPD? What impact does early diagnosis (e.g., before age 15) have on the course of the illness? How do the social supports and treatment histories of the 10 percent of persons with BPD who commit suicide differ from those who do not? What impact does family involvement in psychoeducational efforts within the first year of diagnosis of BPD in a family member have on the course of the illness as measured by numbers of hospitalizations, parasuicidal gestures, and so on? What is the relationship between ongoing, satisfying employment and the course of the illness? What distinguishes those older adults previously diagnosed with BPD who continue to exhibit borderline traits from those who do not? How does the course of illness differ in persons who are in a long-term committed relationship and those who are not? Are persons from cultures that condone or expect high levels of affect at less risk for developing BPD, given the cultural concordance of certain related "symptoms"? Do cultures with a low rate of cultural and gender-role change have lower prevalence rates for BPD?

While these questions are critical to the formation of research questions and the promotion of further theoretical understanding of the BPD condition, our most immediate concern is within the practice realm. The identification of client strengths in the face of the disruptive symptoms of BPD is no easy task. Typically, social workers see BPD clients at their most vulnerable, often when in crisis. The impulsive behaviors and negative affect that are often present in the BPD client at these times often obscures their considerable strengths. These clients are often described, pejoratively, as "manipulative," "needy," and "crisis-ridden." The clinician must see beyond and around these terms as they perhaps better describe the interpersonal realm of the client with BPD, of which the clinician becomes a part. The clinician who is able to explore with the client the multiple function of certain behaviors will at once join with the client respectfully, inviting him or her to the task of self-reflection, and ultimately to the possibility of identifying and utilizing more adaptive responses to overwhelming affects and cognitions. In turn, this allows both the worker and the client to identify and capitalize on the client's considerable strengths.

A good and common example of both reframing and reaching for the underlying complexities and functions of difficult behaviors is self-mutilation. Self-mutilation, a form of parasuicidal behavior is not uncommon in people with BPD. It is intentional self-harm through cutting areas of one's body with the intent to hurt oneself. Family members and treatment providers often interpret this behavior as "attention-seeking" and "manipulative." Clients have different perspectives. Heller (1990), in interviews with 30 hospitalized BPD clients with self-mutilating behavior, found that these women cut themselves for a variety of reasons. Some reported a "wish to hurt myself," to "make the outside match the inside." Some further explained that they'd prefer "the physical pain to the emotional pain," or that "when I see the blood, I know I'm real." These explanations suggest the clients' attempts to "solve a problem," for example, overwhelming affect, dissociation, or trauma. Granted, the solutions are only stopgap (clients often report an immediate but short-lived release of tension), but they do demonstrate an effort to resolve an intolerable feeling state.

Paradoxically, the shifting affective and cognitive states of the BPD client may allow them, with professional help, the ability to entertain divergent perspectives about their situation. Ultimately this may be useful to them in terms of considering alternative behaviors. The person with BPD is unlikely to be an isolate; while their interpersonal relationships are often chaotic, they are typically object-seeking and crave connections with others. This in itself bodes well for the establishment of a therapeutic relationship. Although it is not reported in the literature, many clinicians observe that people with BPD often possess fine senses of humor and the ability to be self-reflective. These too are strengths with which the social worker must be able to identify and join. Finally, the typical client with BPD experiences significant psychic and social distress, and many of the behaviors that are seen by others as objectionable represent both typical and idiosyncratic means of coping and adaptation. Once the clinician can utilize this lens, that behavior is less likely to be alienating, and more available for joint exploration, modification, and change.

PROGRAMS AND SOCIAL WORK CONTRIBUTIONS

Social workers practice in virtually every setting in which clients with BPD are treated, including inpatient and outpatient mental health centers, day treatment, partial hospitalization programs, and Assertive Community Outreach programs. Social workers in host settings such as medical hospitals, correctional settings, and schools are in a unique position to bring their expertise to direct work with clients and also with organizations who may not be well equipped to handle the particular challenges that clients with borderline symptoms present. We function in multiple roles in these settings, including social work therapist, case manager, family consultant, patient and family advocates, and social and political advocates. Social workers have made particular contributions to the literature in the areas of psychosocial assessment, diagnosis, and treatment (Goldstein 1990; Heller and Northcut 1996; Johnson 1988, 1991; Marziali and Munroe-Blum 1995). Because of social workers' biopsychosocial orientation, we are particularly well poised and trained to extend our understanding of the effects of social conditions and cultural and gender variables on the etiology, course, and treatment of BPD. Persons with BPD require knowledgeable and flexible practitioners who are equally competent as psychotherapists, as advocates, and as educators, all roles familiar to the social worker.

ASSESSMENT AND INTERVENTIONS

Biospsychosocial assessment that focuses on each of those three areas, the biological, the psychological, and the social, and on their complex interactions, is critical in work with persons with BPD, given the etiological and protective factors possible in each sphere. Social work assessment should always be considered an ongoing process, particularly when working with a person with BPD who typically experiences very wide shifts in affective, behavioral, cognitive, and social functioning. A client with BPD typically presents for treatment when in a crisis state, which may not accurately reflect either her/his optimum level, or range of functioning. Reliance solely on the client's report may be problematic, because of either incomplete or distorted recollections by a client who may be flooded by affect, impulsivity, or interpersonal chaos. In this instance, information from collateral sources, with the client's permission, may be invaluable.

Many clients, particularly older ones with histories of multiple crises and hospitalizations, may not have active family involvement. Assessment of the larger social support network may yield information about the presence of a supportive and involved friend, employer, or neighbor who may be an important resource to the client and her/his treatment. With these clients the worker must make an assessment regarding the present or future inclusion of estranged family members. Comprehensive assessment, preferably interdisciplinary, combined with the use of treatment effectiveness data, is a critical factor in determining both choices of interventions and appropriate treatment settings.

By the beginning of the 1990s only a very limited number of studies of treatment effectiveness had been completed. At that time, interventive options for persons with BPD were limited primarily to inpatient and outpatient psychotherapy (psychodynamic, some early use of cognitive-behavioral strategies), inpatient group therapy, family therapy for members of the person's family, and medication (McGlashan 1986; Stone 1987). Although psychoeducation and cognitive-behavioral interventions were already widely used for persons with schizophrenia and their families, these approaches were just being introduced for BPD (Linehan et al. 1989; Schulz et al. 1988).

Since that time our repertoire of interventions has expanded. Emphasis is shifting from insight-oriented reflective therapies to skills training targeted on the most common difficulties of persons with BPD, such as intense anger, self-destructive acts, excessive drug use, binge eating and purging, or reckless spending (Springer and Silk 1996). Treatment components (inpatient or outpatient) may involve some combination of individual and group psychoeducation, behavioral strategies and skills training (such as anger management, relapse prevention, social skills training), medication, peer support groups, family psychoeducation and support, cognitive therapy, individual psychodynamic counseling, environmental changes, and advocacy. In light of the chronicity of BPD, Paris (1997a, 1997b) advocates a wide range of treatment options in a model emphasizing continuous availability and intermittent active intervention.

Advances in neurobiology have amplified and deepened our understanding of major psychiatric disorders, including BPD. Axis I disorders such as major depression and ADHD, now known to be biologically based brain disorders, often co-occur with BPD and are targeted for treatment (Cowdry 1997). In addition, specific problem behaviors of persons with BPD arising from mood or impulse control dysfunctions are targets of treatment. Concurrently, psychoeducation and cognitive-behavioral approaches have emerged as first-line interventions (Gunderson et al. 1997; Linehan 1993). Insight-oriented psychodynamic psychotherapy appears to have been effective for a subgroup of persons with BPD who are generally likable by others, motivated, psychologically minded, free of overwhelming impulsivity and substance craving, and without a history of "grotesquely destructive" early environments (Stone 1987).

However, impulsivity and/or cravings are among the defining characteristics of BPD, and where present usually appear to require more structured, behaviorally oriented interventions to help persons with BPD control self-destructive or addictive-like impulses that threaten their ability to maintain jobs or intimate relationships. Some persons with BPD may benefit from combining these different approaches (Heller and Northcut 1996; Patrick 1993). As yet there are no empirical studies that could measure relative contributions to outcomes of behavioral versus insight-oriented strategies.

Psychoeducation for persons with BPD and family members is increasingly emphasized as it has become widely recognized that information is empowering (Gunderson et al. 1997). The question "Why am I this way?" or "Why is my family member this way?" is a salient preoccupation even if not articulated. Palombo (1983) referred to the person with BPD's "maddening sense of inadequacy at coping with an imperfectly understood environment" (31). The clinician can help the client understand his or her environment (internal as well as external) by giving information about the role of biological factors in the person's borderline illness and about the ways in which the environment may interact with the client's biological vulnerability to cause symptoms and suffering. For example, when the person with BPD has a history of ADHD, head injury, or other neurological dysfunction, it is helpful to say "You know, your ADHD (head injury, epilepsy) seems to have the effect of making you fly off the handle easily" ("get distracted," "say things you're sorry for," "look for excitement all the time"). When there is a tendency to major affective disorder, the worker can point out that the client seems to have a constitutional proclivity for depression or mania that interacts with stressful life events. It is often useful to suggest reading that can help clients understand their own vulnerabilities and explain treatment options, including medication. Psychoeducation usually includes specific information about the disorder itself; benefits and risks of medication, side effects, and signs that the medication requires adjustment (larger or smaller doses or a different medication); alternative treatment options; and information about financial assistance, health benefits, community resources, employment assistance, support groups, and respite care.

Dialectical behavior therapy (DBT), now the leading cognitive-behavioral strategy in the treatment of BPD, has shown promise in reducing self-destructive behaviors in people with BPD, reducing hospital admissions, and improving social adjustment (Linehan et al. 1991). Linehan notes that standard cognitive-behavior therapy, like psychodynamic therapy, has a change orientation. It strives to change behavior through learning and experience. Where these therapies fail, according to Linehan, is the lack of acceptance of clients as they are, a posture that would reinforce clients' own ability to accept themselves. DBT begins with a posture of total acceptance (called "radical acceptance") borrowed from Eastern religions such as Zen. The term "dialectical" refers to the treatment's philosophical frame, the resolution of polarity and tension between opposites. Clients must accept themselves as they are and at the same time try to change. That is, the treatment is geared toward a balance involving supportive acceptance combined with change strategies. The treatment is behavioral because it focuses on skills training, collaborative problem solving, contingency clarification and management, and the observable present (Linehan 1993). It is directive and intervention-oriented.

Treatment includes weekly individual visits with a therapist and weekly group sessions. The treatment is manualized to follow several phases. In the pretreatment phase (sometimes called the "contracting phase" in other treatments), the therapist focuses on suicidal or other self-harming behaviors. Will the client agree to stop doing these things? Before other issues can be addressed, the client must be willing to agree to stop hurting or threatening to hurt herself or himself. Treatment requires collaborative agreement. The worker/therapist emphasizes that there are only two options, to accept one's condition and stay miserable, or to try to change it.

The worker engages with the client in active problem solving, responds with warmth and flexibility, and *validates the patient's emotional and cognitive responses.* For example, the worker recognizes that the client's coping behaviors (such as cutting, burning, or attempting suicide) have been very effective or functional for that person by supplying predictable relief from pain. Treatment focuses on figuring out ways to avoid or escape from pain other than hurting oneself.

The social worker frequently expresses sympathy for the client's intense pain and sense of desperation, creating a validating environment while conveying a matter-of-fact attitude about current and previous self-destructive behaviors (Linehan 1993). The worker reframes suicidal and other dysfunctional behaviors as part of the client's learned problem-solving repertoire and tries to focus the counseling process on active problem solving. In individual and group sessions, workers teach emotional regulation, interpersonal effectiveness, distress tolerance, and self-management skills. They openly reinforce desired behaviors to promote progress by maintaining contingencies that shape adaptive behaviors and extinguish self-destructive behaviors. They set clear limits to their availability for help. The treatment process emphasizes building and maintaining a positive, interpersonal, collaborative relationship in which the social worker's roles are teacher, consultant, and cheerleader.

Because of continual crises, following a behavioral treatment plan within the context of individual treatment may be difficult, especially if this plan involves teaching skills that are not obviously related to the current crisis and that do not promise immediate relief. Therefore, behaviorally oriented workers have developed psychoeducational group treatment modules to teach specific behavioral, cognitive, and emotional skills (Linehan 1993).

Overall, there are few methodologically sound studies of effectiveness of **group therapy** for persons with BPD, with one notable exception: Linehan's outpatient dialectical behavior therapy groups that are part of an overall multimodal treatment package (Linehan et al. 1991). Empirical findings with respect to psychodynamically oriented group therapy for persons with personality disorders have been discouraging (Springer and Silk 1996). Some researchers even noted deterioration among patients receiving psychoanalytic group therapy (Beutler et al. 1984). However, inpatients with BPD themselves have sometimes evaluated group therapies as the most effective treatment received (Hafner and Holme 1996; Leszcz, Yalom, and Norden 1986).

There has been a long-standing debate on the respective merits of **interpretive, insight-oriented individual counseling** versus a supportive, structured "holding" environment (Waldinger 1987). Kernberg (1984) viewed the origin of borderline pathology in malformed psychic structures, whereas Kohut (1978) viewed it as a deficit in the ability to hold or soothe oneself, arising from early developmental failure. According to the deficit view, the worker must be a "holding self-object" (Kohut 1978), that is, perform the holding and soothing functions that persons with BPD cannot perform for themselves (Waldinger 1987). Advocates of the holding environment believe that healing occurs not through interpretation, but by being a stable, consistent, caring, nonpunitive person who survives the client's rage and destructive impulses and continues to serve this holding function (Waldinger 1987:270). According to this view, experiential factors are more important than the content of interpretations. Buie and Adler (1982) advocated implementing the holding function by such supports as hospitalization when needed, extra appointments, phone calls between sessions, provision of vacation addresses, and even postcards sent to the client while on vacation.

In line with current thinking emphasizing the long-term and chronic nature of BPD, Links (1993) advocates the application of the **psychiatric rehabilitation** model used for persons with schizophrenia to provide a validating environment, the opportunity to enhance skills, and a mechanism to accept input from families. Specific skills are taught, such as learning to accurately label one's own emotions, general problem-solving skills, and skills to enhance self-esteem and deal with anger, as in Linehan's DBT. Often the person's lack of skills is situationally specific, so the training must be done in relation to a setting in which the deficits lead to dysfunction. Practitioners develop environments and mental health services that validate the person's experience. For example, families can be helped to create more validating environments through psychoeducation about the characteristics of the disorder and the idiosyncratic needs of the person with BPD. Hospitalization in acute psychiatric settings is viewed as not very desirable as it may be too emotionally stimulating. Other settings, such as a community agency or a work environment, must be found that mesh with the patient's characteristics and can create a sense of validation.

A current unanswered question is whether **residential and therapeutic communities** (TCs) are still justifiable for BPD given the success of Linehan's outpatient approach (Hafner and Holme 1996). The effectiveness of therapeutic programs for BPD appears to be strongly related to program structures that can meet the idiosyncratic needs of persons with BPD (Miller 1995). What are these structures, and can they be used as effectively in outpatient settings as in residential programs? At this time, the jury is still out on these questions.

Miller (1995) describes four characteristics of successful programming in a day setting for persons with BPD: affect facilitation, holding without overcontaining, ensuring client safety, and providing focused time-limited treatment (three weeks in Miller's program). The first three of these characteristics also typify some TCs specializing in longer-term treatment of persons with BPD (Hafner and Holme 1996; Schimmel 1997).

Yet the high rate of suicide in people with BPD living in the community continues (Antikainen et al. 1995; Paris 1993). Can client safety be ensured in outpatient programs? Those who argue that hospitals take away responsibility for individual self-care in persons with BPD, by removing "sharps" and other implements of suicide, emphasize the need for service providers to take a strong position that they cannot save clients from themselves; only the individuals can ensure their own safety (Linehan 1993; Miller 1995).

The emergence of **psychoeducation and family support groups** as the interventions of choice in work with families of persons with BPD is relatively recent (Gunderson et al. 1997; Johnson 1991). Recent research on BPD suggests that average or "good enough" mothering may be insufficient to protect a child with neurobiological vulnerabilities from developing borderline characteristics, and, conversely, resilient children at high risk due to traumatic environments may grow into well-functioning successful adults. A borderline outcome may be the cumulative result of interactive biological vulnerabilities and life stresses, with or without parental inadequacies. The blame/shame stigma now beginning to dissipate for other major psychiatric disorders such as schizophrenia and bipolar disorder has been slower to diminish in BPD, in our view, because persons with BPD seldom have signs of psychosis and in addition frequently exhibit irritating or upsetting behaviors. In the absence of evidence to the contrary, such as the widely publicized PET scans shown on all the major networks at the time of the assassination of two security guards at the Capitol, parents are often *assumed* to be at fault when their children grow up with problematic characteristics. Parents of persons with BPD themselves need to be educated that BPD is a neurobiological disorder, not retribution for toxic parenting; they need the support of others in similar situations to break down their sense of stigma, self-blame, and hopelessness; and they need training in ways to cope with behaviors typical of BPD. As Gunderson has pointed out (see earlier), they should be viewed as collaborators in the treatment process, not objects of therapy.

Medication may target coexisting Axis I disorders and/or specific symptoms characteristic of people with BPD (Cowdry 1997; Hirschfeld 1997). *Major depression* in people with BPD may be helped with selective serotonin reuptake inhibitors (SSRIs), usually the first-choice antidepressants, newer antidepressants such as venlaxafine (Effexor), or the older monamine oxidase inhibitors (MAOIs) or tricyclic antidepressants. These agents are also helpful in relieving dysphoria when not all criteria for MDD are met.

Residual adult ADHD in persons with BPD is often responsive to stimulant medications, notably methylphenidate (Ritalin), dextroamphetamine (Dexedrine), or pemoline (Cylert). Some symptoms of ADHD—impulsivity, aggressive outbursts, temper tantrums, distractibility, and emotional overreactivity—often can be controlled with stimulant medication such as methylphenidate (Ritalin) in adults whose borderline characteristics arise from ADHD (Cowdry 1997; Spencer et al. 1996). Wender, Reimherr, and Wood (1981) found that 60 percent of adults with ADHD responded to methylphenidate with a reduction in impulsivity and hot-temperedness and an increase in concentration, calmness, and energy. Stimulant medication has an alerting effect that may help the individual organize multiple incoming internal and external stimuli that he or she has experienced as chaotic, thus reducing anxiety, increasing confidence, and giving the individual a sense of mastery.

Some persons have ultrarapid-cycling forms of *Bipolar I,* in which morose, labile moods alternate with irritable, mixed (manic and depressive) moods, but are often mistaken for BPD. Such patients with bipolar characteristics may need mood-regulating medications, such as lithium and anticonvulsants carbamazepine and valproate, which can benefit lifelong temperamental dysregulation combined with depressive episodes (Akiskal 1996).

In *eating disorders,* several neurotransmitters and neuromodulators (brain chemicals that modify neurotransmission without meeting all the criteria to be neurotransmitters) are involved in regulation of eating behavior in animals and have been implicated in symptoms such as depression and anxiety in humans with eating disorders (Mauri et al. 1996). Antidepressants have been effective in reducing frequency of binge eating, purging, and depressive symptoms in persons with bulimia, even in cases of chronic persistent bulimia in patients who had repeatedly failed courses of alternative therapies, and even in persons with bulimia who do not display concomitant depression (Mauri et al. 1996). Medication for anorexia nervosa has been less successful and few controlled studies have been published (Mauri et al. 1996). Central serotonergic receptor-blocking compounds such as cyproheptadine can cause marked increase in appetite and body weight. Zinc supplementation or cisapride may be helpful in combination with other approaches in anorexia nervosa. Naltrexone, an opiate antagonist sometimes used to treat opiate or alcohol addiction, is also being tried.

Mood stabilizers, venlaxafine (Effexor), MAOIs, and stimulants such as Ritalin have all been found helpful in reducing *impulsivity* and *aggression* (Cowdry 1997; Hirschfeld 1997).

The antidepressants as a group, including the SSRIs, MAOIs, tricyclics, and newer antidepressants like venlaxafine, alleviate depressive symptoms even when criteria for major depression are not met. *Anxiety* is sometimes targeted with anxiolytic (anxiety-reducing) drugs, notably the benzodiazepenes such as alprazolam (Xanax). Results are mixed, with some studies reporting negative effects of anxiolytics (i.e., increased impulsivity and dyscontrol), others reporting helpfulness (Antikainen et al. 1995; Hirschfeld 1997).

Self-injurious behavior (SIB) has been reduced with risperidone (an antipsychotic that blocks certain dopamine as well as serotonin receptors) and naltrexone (an opiate antagonist used to treat addiction to alcohol and opiates) in persons with BPD (Khouzam and Donnelly 1997; Roth, Ostroff, and Hoffman 1996).

Repetitive SIB such as wrist-slashing is a dangerous and often treatment-refractory feature of many borderline personality disorders. Khouzam and Donnelly (1997) induced remission of self-mutilation in a patient with BPD using risperidone (Risperdol). Szigethy and Schulz (1997) also found risperidone effective in comorbid BPD and dysthymia. Self-injurious behaviors ceased entirely in six of seven patients receiving naltrexone whose SIBs were accompanied by analgesia (feeling no physical pain) and dysphoria reduction (acts of self-injury temporarily relieve painful feelings of sadness and emptiness) (Roth et al. 1996). Two of the patients who discontinued naltrexone briefly experienced rapid resumption of SIB, which ceased once again after naltrexone therapy was resumed.

Dissociative states in persons with BPD suggest underlying neurobiological events, such as complex partial seizures, that may call for treatment with anticonvulsants (Cowdry 1997). Schizotypal characteristics are usually transient and intermittent when they occur in patients with BPD. These clients may improve with low-dose neuroleptic medication (Schulz et al. 1988).

Cowdry (1997:9) has noted that psychotropic medications in treatment of persons with BPD occasionally result in marked improvement, but more often serve to *modulate affect* enough to make daily experiences somewhat less disruptive and to make psychotherapy more productive. In most cases, medication is only one weapon in an arsenal of individual and group interventions to help persons with BPD develop coping skills. For all persons with BPD, creative combinations of the approaches reviewed in the preceding should be individually tailored to the needs of persons with BPD and their families.

ILLUSTRATION AND DISCUSSION

The following vignettes illustrate various elements of assessment, evaluation, and practice skills in two different settings with both a fairly high-functioning and a more low-functioning chronic client with BPD.

Sandy is a 25-year-old single white woman who presents at a community mental health center walk-in clinic with the complaint that "I wish I were dead. Everybody would be better off." She reports a recent breakup with a boyfriend and states that "I am nothing without him." She reveals that in the forty-eight-hour period prior to her appointment, she cut her wrist (superficially) with "a bracelet he gave me." After doing that she left him a "terrible, furious" message on his answering machine and "he didn't even call me back." She then describes a downward spiral in which she went to bed, missed work, and refused to answer the phone, reasoning that "if he called me back I didn't want to give him the satisfaction of answering." During the interview she was alternately weepy, defiant, eager for help, and fearful that "everything is going bad again." Preoccupied with her current distress, she had little patience for questions about her past history, treatment, and so on. When the worker asked her whether she'd "ever felt just this way before," Sandy was able to recount several prior episodes in which she'd also felt alternately angry, bereft, and self-destructive in the wake of the loss or perceived loss of a relationship. When asked how she'd manage to "get through" these prior episodes, Sandy noted that she'd typically "cut myself, settle down, maybe go to a clinic, numb out and go on till the next time." She noted, however, that these episodes were occurring more frequently and more intensely and were interfering with her work. She had recently been placed on probation at her job as a secretary in a law firm because "I keep bringing my personal life to work."

Initial tasks for the social worker included the assessment for suicidality, identification, and mobilization of natural support networks, and clarification of the client's willingness to be involved in treatment. While the worker initially had difficulty eliciting relevant prior history, once she acknowledged and inquired about the client's affective state and its resonance with Sandy's history, the client was able to be quite forthcoming with information and also responsive to the worker. Further data were then gathered, including treatment history and medication history. Sandy revealed that as an adolescent she had had problems with alcohol and occasional cocaine use, but that she had not used substances for three years. She gave indications of the possibility of disordered eating but refused to discuss that further. She did note a history of sexual abuse by a neighbor, continually from ages 9 to 14. She states that "that has nothing to do with my problems, so don't even talk about it." She describes an alternately close and estranged relationship with her mother and no contact with her father who had left the family when she was age 9.

After determining that the client was not actively suicidal and was willing to contract for safety, the worker presented some preliminary treatment options. Appealing to the client's own sense "that things are getting out of control," the worker encouraged Sandy to return to the clinic for a more comprehensive assessment later in the week. Sandy agreed, providing that she would meet with the same worker. Client strengths included her admitted wish "to be close to people," her cessation of substance use, her above average intelligence, her previous good work performance, her network of women friends, and the availability of her mother to provide both emotional and financial supports. Pending the outcome of further evaluation, including differential diagnosis, the client might continue with some combination of individual, psychoeducation, and DBT, family/social support, and medication therapies.

The worker's skills of engagement were critical to the beginning work with this client. This, combined with her knowledge of psychopathology, the differences between suicidal and parasuicidal thoughts and actions, and the literature regarding treatment interventions for clients with BPD, allowed her to complete the comprehensive evaluation and access appropriate resources for the client. This worker, on the basis of this and similar cases, was also able to advocate for a revised agency policy that allowed the crisis worker to continue with the three-session evaluation with BPD clients, rather than referring them on to yet another worker. She also initiated a very simple evaluation procedure, which, after six months, revealed that clients with BPD who were screened in the crisis service and allowed to continue the evaluation with the same worker were more likely to continue with the treatment recommendations than those who were not.

Dora is a 34-year-old white woman hospitalized on the acute unit of a general hospital following her disclosure in her partial hospitalization program (PHP) that she was "going to kill myself this time." Dora is well known to the hospital staff and is assigned to a second-year social work graduate student, Rob.

Prior to meeting with Dora for the initial social work assessment, Rob reviewed her voluminous chart. When he knocked and entered her room, he was surprised to see her huddled in the corner of her bed, clutching a teddy bear. Although she'd been admitted only hours earlier, she had decorated her room with many pictures and mementos. Rob introduced himself and explained his role on the unit. Dora took notice and sat up, and quite coherently explained her current situation with great detail, noting that she was "surprised I can tell you this much . . . usually it takes me a long time to feel close to someone." While Rob felt flattered by her immediate connection to him, he found himself a bit uneasy, remembering the warnings he'd received from other staff about "the chronic complainer."

Rob met with Dora twice more before the first treatment planning meeting. Each time she said that in all the times she'd been in the hospital no one had understood her like he does. When he met with the treatment team and reported this, one staff member became quite angry, saying that "Rob, you've been taken in by her." Confused, Rob brought the situation to his supervisor, who talked with him about the phenomena of both psychological and interpersonal splitting, common in clients with BPD and on their treatment teams. She suggested readings for him and also encouraged him to talk with the program staff at the PHP regarding current treatment issues and their expectations for this hospitalization.

Rob subsequently learned that Dora had a history of idealizing new staff members and devaluing others and that this typically had resulted in conflict among team members and the obscuring of the real treatment issues. Rob was better prepared then, when at his next meeting with Dora, she refused to talk with him once he denied her the day pass she'd requested. He noted to his supervisor that "it was as if she'd entirely forgotten that three days earlier she had been acutely suicidal, or that she thought I was the 'best social worker' she'd ever had."

Rob then worked closely with the treatment team, Dora, and the PHP program to facilitate her gradual transition back to the PHP. He and Dora were able to do a review of their work together and she jokingly noted in their last session that "maybe it is possible to like *and* not like somebody!"

This was an important learning case for Rob. He learned a great deal about the complexity of the BPD diagnosis, the countertransference responses among treatment team members, and the importance of understanding the interpersonal styles of the client with BPD. He also was able to appreciate Dora's humor and to reflect it back to her in ways that she could hear. Through his work with the PHP he better understood the importance of continuity of care and of short-term hospitalization for the stabilization of the client with BPD.

Both cases reflect the need for knowledge about BPD, well-honed practice skills, and the use of colleagues and various levels of programs for the client with BPD.

CONCLUSION

How does this new expanded knowledge fit with our roles as case managers, therapists, family consultants, patient and family advocates, and social and political activists? Contemporary approaches to work with persons with BPD and their families, considered earlier, all fall within the purview of social work practice. Even with respect to psychotropic medication, social workers perform all critical functions except for writing prescriptions, doing medical evaluations, and interpreting laboratory results.

Prior to intervening, we must familiarize ourselves with current research-based knowledge about characteristics and etiologies of BPD, what interventions are effective for what types of BPD clients, and under what conditions. Research published during the past few years has given us tools for understanding and treating BPD in ways that were beyond our capability in the past. Without valid *knowledge* about the diverse forms and different underlying characteristics of BPD, and without *training in specific skills* targeted on troublesome or dangerous characteristics of the disorder, there is no reason to expect that our treatments will be effective.

We should not be discouraged by the fact that we do not know for sure whether our treatments account for the positive outcomes, years later, of many clients who in their teens and twenties have been ill with BPD for periods of years. We do know that a significant number of persons with BPD (perhaps 10 percent) commit suicide outside the hospital, so clearly efforts to prevent suicide are critical. Research suggests that if we can prevent suicide in the crisis phases of the disorder, individuals have a good chance at a satisfying life later. The process is usually very slow and gradual, however. We should have reasonable expectations that the illness will be chronic for an extended time and that relapses are to be expected. Meanwhile, until the risk of suicide is diminished, intensive therapeutic efforts must be put forth. At the same time, social workers can remind themselves and their clients with BPD that tools of self-destruction are always available in the community, that we cannot save them, and that ultimately only they can choose to stay safe.

The natural course of BPD of gradual diminution in symptoms over a period of years underscores the need for ongoing structure and monitoring the community and for short-term protected environments (hospitals or some other kind of safe haven) where clients can stay until the immediate threat of suicide has passed. Expansion of such services, rather than the contraction of services now happening under the aegis of managed care, must be vigorously advocated by social workers in the political sphere as well as on an individual basis. At the time of writing, the American public has begun to voice frustration and anger about the impact of current cost-cutting measures throughout managed care–dominated health care systems. Some social workers are taking an active role in this effort, but we need to do much more.

Skills necessary to work with persons with BPD and their families are teachable and learnable. However, it appears that training of these skills is not available in some social work programs, requiring workers to get it elsewhere. In our view, generic social work skills simply are not adequate to address the specific challenges of work related to this painful and often dangerous condition. Given the prevalence of this life condition across social work settings, social work educators should think of ways to bring these therapeutic skills training modules directly into graduate and undergraduate curricula.

The specific skills that workers may need include the following. (1) Social workers must know how to provide psychoeducation for persons with BPD and their families in group and individual venues, conveying up-to-date information about characteristics and etiology of the disorder, helping clients explore the meaning of this information for their own lives, giving information about treatment options and community resources, and explaining potential benefits and risks associated with these.

(2) Workers must know how to create a validating environment, so as to help the person with BPD accept him- or herself while at the same time working actively to change. (3) Workers must know how to clearly specify and enforce the conditions under which client and practitioner will work together, especially the boundaries of treatment. (4) Workers must learn cognitive-behavioral skills for teaching impulse control, anger management, relapse prevention, and self-soothing, which can be conveyed well in groups as well as individual sessions. (5) With respect to medication, practitioners must access up-to-date information so they can share this information with clients and their families, and so together with clients and family members they can effectively monitor the client's response to a medication and report to the prescribing physician when necessary. Workers do not need to memorize drug information, as it changes continually, but they should become adept at doing computer searches on Medline to obtain state-of-the-art information about drug effectiveness and side effects. Because these searches can be done on the Internet with only a minimal expenditure of time, "keeping up" with current knowledge is infinitely easier than it was only a few years ago. The easiest method is to get online access to Medline at home. Otherwise, Internet access to Medline can be obtained in libraries. Finally, (6) skills in advocacy and political action are required for social workers to join with other activist groups fighting to make services available to thousands of service consumers and their families *when they need them.*

At the time of this writing, the gap between these goals for service delivery and reality is great. All of the preceding should be available to persons with BPD on an as-needed basis, not only for crisis management but also to provide the continuity of a relationship with a consistent, caring person who can weather the client's outbursts of hostility, self-destructive threats and acts, and who can convey hope that a happier future is possible.

References

Akiskal, H. S. 1996. "The Prevalent Clinical Spectrum of Bipolar Disorders: Beyond *DSM-IV." Journal of Clinical Psychopharmacology* 16, no. 2 (Supplement 1):4S–14S.

Akiskal, H. S., L. L. Judd, J. C. Gillin, and H. Lemmi. 1997. "Subthreshold Depressions: Clinical and Polysomnographic Validation of Dysthymic, Residual, and Masked Forms." *Journal of Affective Disorders* 45(1–2):53–63.

Alarcon, R., E. F. Foulks, and M. P. Vakkur. 1998. *Personality Disorders and Culture: Clinical and Conceptual Interactions.* New York: John Wiley.

Alneas, R. and S. Torgerson. 1997. "Personality and Personality Disorders Predict Development and Relapses of Major Depression." *Acta Psychiatrica Scandinavica* 95(4): 336–42.

American Psychiatric Association. 1994. *Diagnostic and Statistical Manual of Mental Disorders (DSM-IV),* 4th ed. Washington, D.C.: Author.

Andrulonis, P. A., B. C. Glueck, C. F. Stroebel, N. G. Vogel, A. L. Shapiro, and D. M. Aldridge. 1981. "Organic Brain Dysfunction and the Borderline Syndrome." *Psychiatric Clinics of North America* 4(1):47–66.

Antikainen, R., J. Hintikka, J. Lehtonen, H. Koponen, and A. Arstila. 1995. "A Prospective Three-Year Follow-up Study of Borderline Personality Disorder Inpatients." *Acta Psychiatrica Scandinavica* 92:327–35.

Atlas, J. A. and M. A. Wolfson. 1996. "Depression and Dissociation As Features of Borderline Personality Disorder in Hospitalized Adolescents." *Psychological Report* 78(2): 624–26.

Beutler, L. E., M. Frank, S. C. Schierer, S. Calvert, and J. Gaines. 1984. "Comparative Effects of Group Psychotherapies in Short-Term Inpatient Setting: An Experience with Deterioration Effects." *Psychiatry* 46:66–77.

Biederman, J., J. Newcorn, and S. Sprich. 1991. "Comorbidity of Attention Deficit Hyperactivity Disorder with Conduct, Depressive, Anxiety, and Other Disorders." *American Journal of Psychiatry* 148(5):564–77.

Blais, M. A., M. J. Hilsenroth, and F. D. Castlebury. 1997. "Content Validity of the *DSM-IV* Borderline and Narcissistic Personality Disorder Criteria Sets." *Comprehensive Psychiatry* 38(1):31–37.

Buie, D. and G. Adler. 1982. "The Definitive Treatment of the Borderline Patient." *International Journal of Psychoanalysis and Psychotherapy* 9:51–87.

Cowdry, R. 1997. "Borderline Personality Disorder." *NAMI Advocate* (January/February):8–9.

Davis, C., G. Claridge, and D. Cerullo. 1997. "Personality Factors and Weight Preoccupation: A Continuum Approach to the Association Between Eating Disorders and Personality Disorders." *Journal of Psychiatric Research* 31(4):467–80.

De La Fuente, J. M., S. Goldman, E. Stanus, C. Vizuete, I. Morlan, J. Bobes, and J. Mendlewicz. 1997. "Brain Glucose Metabolism in Borderline Personality Disorder." *Journal of Psychiatric Research* 31(5):531–41.

De La Fuente, J. M. and J. Mendlewicz. 1996. "TRH Stimulation and Dexamethasone Suppression in Borderline Personality Disorder." *Biological Psychiatry* 40(5):412–18.

Drake, M. E., Jr., A. Pakalnis, and B. B. Phillips. 1992. "Neuropsychological and Psychiatric Correlates of Intractable Pseudoseizures." *Seizure* 1(1):11–13.

Else, L. T., S. A. Wonderlich, W. W. Beatty, D. W. Christie, and R. D. Staton. 1993. "Personality Characteristics of Men Who Physically Abuse Women." *Hospital and Community Psychiatry* 44(1):54–58.

Figueroa, E. F. and K. R. Silk. 1997. "Biological Implications of Childhood Sexual Abuse in Borderline Personality Disorder." *Journal of Personality Disorders* 11(1):71–92.

Figueroa, E. F., K. R. Silk, A. Huth, and N. E. Lohr. 1997. "History of Childhood Sexual Abuse and General Psychopathology." *Comprehensive Psychiatry* 38(1):23–30.

Frosch, J. 1960. "Psychotic Character." *Journal of the American Psychoanalytic Association* 8:544–55.

Goldstein, E. G. 1983. "Clinical and Ecological Approaches to the Borderline Client." *Social Casework* 64(6):353–62.

Goldstein, E. G. 1990. *Borderline Disorders: Clinical Model and Technique.* New York: Guilford.

Grilo, C. M., D. F. Becker, D. C. Fehon, W. S. Edell, and T. H. McGlashan. 1996. "Gender Differences in Personality Disorders in Psychiatrically Hospitalized Adolescents." *American Journal of Psychiatry* 153(8):1089–91.

Grilo, C. M., K. N. Levy, D. F. Becker, W. S. Edell, and T. H. McGlashan. 1996. "Cormorbidity of DSM-III-R and Axis I and II Disorders Among Female Inpatients with Eating Disorders." *Psychiatric Services* 47(4):426–29.

Grilo, C. M., M. L. Walker, D. F. Becker, W. S. Edell, and T. H. McGlashan. 1997. "Personality Disorders in Adolescents with Major Depression, Substance Use Disorders, and Coexisting Major Depression and Substance Use Disorders." *Journal of Consulting and Clinical Psychology* 65(2):328–32.

Gunderson, J. G. 1984. *Borderline Personality Disorder.* Washington, D.C.: American Psychiatric Press.

——. 1996. "The Borderline Patient's Intolerance of Aloneness: Insecure Attachments and Therapist Availability." *American Journal of Psychiatry* 153(6):752–58.

Gunderson, J. G., C. Berkowitz, and A. Ruiz-Sancho. 1997. "Families of Borderline Patients: A Psychoeducational Approach." *Bulletin of the Menninger Clinic* 61(4):446–57.

Gunderson, J. G. and D. W. Englund. 1981. "Characterizing the Families of Borderlines." *Psychiatric Clinics of North America* 4(1):159–68.

Hafner, R. J. and G. Holme. 1996. "The Influence of a Therapeutic Community on Psychiatric Disorders." *Journal of Clinical Psychology* 52(4):461–68.

Hartocollis, P. 1968. "The Syndrome of Minimal Brain Dysfunction in Young Adult Patients." *Bulletin of the Menninger Clinic* 32:102–14.

Heller, N. R. 1990. *Object Relations and Symptom Choice in Bulemics and Self-Mutilations.* Unpublished doctoral dissertation. Smith College, Northampton, MA.

Heller, N. R. and T. B. Northcut. 1996. "Utilizing Cognitive-Behavioral Techniques in Psychodynamic Practice with Clients Diagnosed As Borderline." *Clinical Social Work Journal* 24(2):203–15.

Henry, J. P. 1997. "Psychological and Physiological Responses to Stress: The Right Hemisphere and the Hypothalamo-Pituitary-Adrenal Axis, An Inquiry into Problems of Human Bonding." *Acta Physiologica Scandinavica* Suppl 640:10–25.

Herman, J. 1992. *Trauma and Recovery.* New York: Basic Books.

Hirschfeld, R. M. 1997. "Pharmacotherapy of Borderline Personality Disorder." *Journal of Clinical Psychiatry* 58(Supplement 14):48–53.

Johnson, H. C. 1988. "Where Is the Border? Issues in the Diagnosis and Treatment of the Borderline." *Clinical Social Work Journal* 16(3):243–60.

——. 1991. "Borderline Clients: Practice Implications of Recent Research." *Social Work* 36(2):166–73.

Kaplan, H. I. and B. J. Sadock. 1998. *Synopsis of Psychiatry,* 8th ed. Baltimore: Williams & Wilkins.

Kemperman, I., M. J. Russ, and E. Shearin. 1997 . "Self-Injurious Behavior and Mood Regulation in Borderline Patients." *Journal of Personality Disorders* 11(2):146–57.

Kernberg, O. 1967. "Borderline Personality Organization." *Journal of the American Psychoanalytic Association* 15:641–85.

——. 1984. *Severe Personality Disorders.* New Haven: Yale University Press.

Khouzam, H. R. and N. J. Donnelly. 1997. "Remission of Self-Mutilation in a Patient with Borderline Personality During Risperidone Therapy." *Journal of Nervous and Mental Diseases* 185(5):348–49.

Klein, D. F. 1977. "Psychopharmacological Treatment and Delineation of Borderline Disorders." In P. Hartocollis, ed. *Borderline Personality Disorders,* pp. 365–83. New York: International Universities Press.

Knight, R. 1953. Borderline states. *Bulletin of the Menninger Clinic* 17:1–12.

Kohut, H. 1978. *The Search for the Self,* Vols. I and II. New York: International Universities Press.

Landecker, H. 1992. "The Role of Childhood Sexual Trauma in the Etiology of Borderline Personality Disorder: Considerations for Diagnosis and Treatment." *Psychotherapy* 29:234–42.

Laxenaire, M., M. O. Ganne-Devonec, and O. Streiff. 1982. "Identity Problems Among Migrant Children." *Annales Medico-Psychologiques* 140:602–5.

Leszcz, M., I. D. Yalom, and M. Norden. 1986. "The Value of Inpatient Group Psychotherapy: Patients' Perceptions. *International Group Psychotherapy* 85:411–33.

Levine, D., E. Marziali, and J. Hood. 1997. "Emotion Processing in Borderline Personality Disorders." *Journal of Nervous and Mental Diseases* 185(4):240–46.

Linehan, M. M. 1993. *Cognitive-Behavioral Treatment of Borderline Personality Disorder.* New York: Guilford.

Linehan, M. M., H. E. Armstrong, A. Suarez, and D. Allmon. 1989. *Comprehensive Behavioral Treatments for Suicidal Behaviors and Borderline Personality Disorder.* Washington, D.C.: Association for the Advancement of Behavior Therapy.

Linehan, M. M., H. E. Armstrong, A. Suarez, D. Allmon, and H. Heard. 1991. "Cognitive-Behavioral Treatment of Chronically Parasuicidal Borderline Patients." *Archives of General Psychiatry* 48:1060–64.

Links, P. S. 1993. "Psychiatric Rehabilitation Model for Borderline Personality Disorder." *Canadian Journal of Psychiatry* 38 (February Supplement 1):S35–S38.

Lofgren, D. P., J. Bemporad, J. King, K. Lindem, and G. O'Driscoll. 1991. "A Prospective Follow-Up of So-Called Borderline Children." *American Journal of Psychiatry* 148: 1541–47.

Mahler, M. 1971. "A Study of the Separation-Individuation Process and Its Possible Application to Borderline Phenomena in the Analytic Situation." *Psychoanalytic Study of the Child* 26:403–24.

Marziali, E. and H. Munroe-Blum. 1995. "An Interpersonal Approach to Group Psychotherapy with Borderline Personality Disorder." *Journal of Personality Disorders* 9(3):179–89.

Masten, A. 1994. "Resilience in Individual Development: Successful Adaptation Despite Risk and Adversity." In M. Wang and E. Gordon, eds., *Educational Resilience in Inner-City America: Challenges and Prospects,* pp. 3–25. Hillsdale, N.J.: Erlbaum.

Masterson, J. and D. Rinsley. 1975. "The Borderline Syndrome: The Role of the Mother in the Genesis and Psychic Structure of the Borderline Personality." *International Journal of Psychoanalysis* 56:163–67.

Mauri, M. C., R. Rudelli, E. Somaschini, L. Roncoroni, R. Papa, M. Mantero, M. Longhini, and G. Penati. 1996. "Neurobiological and Psychopharmacological Basis in the Therapy of Bulimia and Anorexia." *Progress in Neuropsychopharmacology and Biological Psychiatry* 20(2):207–40.

McGlashan, T. H. 1986. "The Chestnut Lodge Follow-Up Study: III. Long-Term Outcome of Borderline Personalities. *Archives of General Psychiatry* 43:20–30.

Miller, B. C. 1995. "Characteristics of Effective Day Treatment Programming for Persons with Borderline Personality Disorder." *Psychiatric Services* 46(6):605–8.

Morgenstern, J., J. Langenbucher, E. Labouvie, and K. J. Miller. 1997. "The Comorbidity of Alcoholism and Personality Disorders in a Clinical Population: Prevalence Rates and Relation to Alcohol Typology Variables." *Journal of Abnormal Psychology* 106(1): 74–84.

Muller, R. J. 1992. "Is There a Neural Basis for Borderline Splitting?" *Comprehensive Psychiatry* 33(2):92–104.

Murray, G. B. 1988. "Personality Disorders in the Elderly." *Clinical Perspectives on Aging* 8:3–15.

Murray, M. 1979. "Minimal Brain Dysfunction and Borderline Personality Adjustment." *American Journal of Psychotherapy* 33:391–403.

Palombo, J. 1983. "Borderline Conditions: A Perspective from Self-Psychology." *Clinical Social Work Journal* 11(4):323–38.

Paris, J. 1991. "Personality Disorders, Parasuicide and Culture." *Transcultural Psychiatric Research Review* 28:25–39.

Paris, J. 1993. "The Treatment of Borderline Personality Disorder in Light of the Research on Its Long Term Outcomes." *Canadian Journal of Psychiatry* 38 (February Supplement 1):S28–S34.

——. 1997a. "Childhood Trauma As an Etiological Factor in the Personality Disorders." *Journal of Personality Disorders* 11(1):34–49.

——. 1997b. "Antisocial and Borderline Personality Disorders: Two Separate Diagnoses or Two Aspects of the Same Psychopathology?" *Comprehensive Psychiatry* 38(4):237–42.

Paris, J. and H. Zweig-Frank. 1997. "Dissociation in Patients with Borderline Personality Disorder." *American Journal of Psychiatry* 154(1):137–38.

Patrick, J. 1993. "The Integration of Self-Psychological and Cognitive-Behavioural Models in the Treatment of Borderline Personality Disorder." *Canadian Journal of Psychiatry* 38 (February Supplement 1):S39–S43.

Roth, A. S., R. B. Ostroff, and R. E. Hoffman. 1996. "Naltrexone As a Treatment for Repetitive Self-Injurious Behaviour: An Open-Label Trial." *Journal of Clinical Psychiatry* 57(6):233–37.

Russ, M. J., W. C. Clark, L. W. Cross, I. Kemperman, T. Kakuma, and K. Harrison. 1996. "Pain and Self-Injury in Borderline Patients: Sensory Decision Theory, Coping Strategies, and Locus of Control." *Psychiatry Research* 63(1):57–65.

Sadavoy, J., and B. Fogel. 1992. "Personality Disorders in Old Age." In J. E. Birren, R. B. Sloane, G. D. Cohen, N. R. Hooyman, B. D. Lebowitz, M. Wykle, and D. E. Deutchman, eds., *Handbook of Mental Health in Aging,* pp. 433–63. New York: Academic Press.

Sansone, R. A., L. A. Sansone, and M. W. Wiederman. 1997. "The Comorbidity, Relationship and Treatment Implications of Borderline Personality and Obesity." *Psychosomatic Research* 43(5):541–43.

Sar, V., L. I. Yargic, and H. Tutkun. 1996. "Structured Interview Data on 35 Cases of Dissociative Identity Disorder in Turkey." *American Journal of Psychiatry* 153(10): 1329–33.

Schimmel, P. 1997. "Swimming Against the Tide? A Review of the Therapeutic Community." *Australia and New Zealand Journal of Psychiatry* 31(1):120–27.

Schulz, S. C., J. Cornelius, P. M. Schulz, and P. H. Soloff. 1988. "The Amphetamine Challenge Test in Patients with Borderline Disorder." *American Journal of Psychiatry* 145(7):809–14.

Senol, S., C. Dereboy, and N. Yuksel. 1997. "Borderline Disorder in Turkey: A 2- to 4-year Follow-Up." *Social Psychiatry and Psychiatric Epidemiology* 32(2):109–12.

Snyder, S., W. A. Goodpaster, M. W. Pitts, Jr., A. D. Pokorny, and Q. L. Gustin. 1985. "Demography of Psychiatric Patients with Borderline Personality Traits." *Psychopathology* 18(1):38–49.

Spencer, T., J. Biederman, T. Wilens, M. Harding, D. O'Donnell, and S. Griffin. 1996. "Pharmacotherapy of Attention-Deficit Hyperactivity Disorder Across the Life Cycle." *Journal of the American Academy of Child and Adolescent Psychiatry* 35(4):409–32.

Springer, T. and K. R. Silk. 1996. "A Review of Inpatient Group Therapy for Borderline Personality Disorder." *Harvard Review of Psychiatry* 3(5):268–78.

Stalenheim, E. G., L. von Knorring, and L. Oreland. 1997. "Platelet Monoamine Oxidase Activity As a Biological Marker in a Swedish Forensic Psychiatric Population." *Psychiatry Research* 69(2–3):79–87.

Stein, D. J., E. Hollander, L. Cohen, M. Frenkel, J. B. Saoud, C. DeCaria, B. Aronowitz, A. Levin, M. R. Liebowitz, and L. Cohen. 1993. "Neuropsychiatric Impairment in Impulsive Personality Disorders." *Psychiatry Research* 48(3):257–66.

Steinberg, B. J., R. Trestman, V. Mitropoulou, M. Serby, J. Silverman, E. Coccaro, S. Weston, M. de Vegvar, and L. J. Siever. 1997. "Depressive Response to Physostigmine Challenge in Borderline Personality Disorder Patients." *Neuropsychopharmacology* 17(4):264–73.

Stern, A. 1938. "Psychoanalytic Investigation of and Therapy in the Borderline Group of Neuroses." *Psychoanalytic Quarterly* 7:467–89.

Stone, M. H. 1987. "Psychotherapy of Borderline Patients in Light of Long-Term Follow-Up." *Bulletin of the Menninger Clinic* 51(3):231–47.

——. 1994. "Characterologic Subtypes of the Borderline Personality." *Psychiatric Clinics of North America* 17(4):773–84.

Szigethy, E. M. and S. C. Schulz. 1997. "Risperidone in Comorbid Borderline Personality Disorder and Dysthymia." *Journal of Clinical Psychopharmacology* 17(4):326–27.

Taub, J. M. 1996. "Sociodemography of Borderline Personality Disorder (PD): A Comparison with Axis II PDs and Psychiatric Symptom Disorders Convergent Validation." *International Journal of Neuroscience* 88(1–2):27–52.

Terkelsen, K. 1983. "Schizophrenia and the Family: II. Adverse Effects of Family Therapy." *Family Process* 22:191–200.

Thomsen, P. H. 1990. "The Prognosis in Early Adulthood of Childhood Psychiatric Patients: A Case Register Study in Denmark." *Acta Psychiatrica Scandinavia* 81:89–93.

Tuinier, S. and W. M. Verhoeven. 1995. "Dimensional Classification and Behavioral Pharmacology of Personality Disorders: A Review and Hypothesis." *European Neuropsychopharmacology* 5(2):135–46.

Tyrer, P. and H. Seivewright. 1988. "Studies of Outcome." In P. Tyrer, ed., *Personality Disorders: Diagnosis, Management and Course,* pp.119–36. London: Wright.

van Reekum, R. 1993. "Acquired and Developmental Brain Dysfunction in Borderline Personality Disorder." *Canadian Journal of Psychiatry* 38(Supplement 1):S4–S10.

Verkes, R. J., D. Fekkes, A. H. Zwinderman, M. W. Hengeveld, R. C. Van der Mast, J. P. Tuyl, A. J. Kerkhof, and G. M. Van Kempen. 1997. "Platelet Serotonin and [3H] Paroxetine Binding Correlate with Recurrence of Suicidal Behavior." *Psychopharmacology Bulletin* 132(1):89–94.

Verkes, R. J., H. Pijl, A. E. Meinders, and G. M. Van Kempen. 1996. "Borderline Personality, Impulsiveness, and Platelet Monoamine Measures in Bulimia Nervosa and Recurrent Suicidal Behavior." *Biological Psychiatry* 40(3):173–80.

Waldinger, R. 1987. "Intensive Psychodynamic Therapy with Borderline Clients: An Overview." *American Journal of Psychiatry* 144(3):267–74.

Wender, P. H., F. W. Reimherr, and D. R. Wood. 1981. "Attention Deficit Disorder ("Minimal Brain Dysfunction") in Adults: A Replication Study of Diagnosis and Drug Treatment." *Archives of General Psychiatry* 38(4):449–56.

Zanarini, M. C. and F. R. Frankenburg. 1997. "Pathways to the Development of Borderline Personality Disorder." *Journal of Personality Disorders* 11(1):93–104.

Zanarini, M. C., A. A. Williams, R. E. Lewis, R. B. Reich, S. C. Vera, M. F. Marino, A. Levin, L. Yong, and F. R. Frankenburg. 1997. "Reported Pathological Childhood Experiences Associated with the Development of Borderline Personality Disorder." *American Journal of Psychiatry* 154(8):1101–6.

5

Chronic Physical Illness and Disability

Grace H. Christ
Mary Sormanti
Richard B. Francoeur

Social work with individuals coping with chronic illness and disabilities is characterized by wide variation and diversity at both individual and systems levels. Assessment and intervention problems are challenging, and social and institutional contexts are only slowly developing more relevant service systems. Indeed, the problems are so varied that skilled social workers quickly learn the value in using a structured problem-specific assessment and case formulation process and a broad range of intervention approaches and techniques to provide comprehensive, effective care. Even so, the experience of persons with chronic illness and disability includes a number of profoundly important similarities as they negotiate and adapt to their physical differences and capacities in our society.

Across formal and alternative systems of health care, changes in the perception and understanding of individuals affected by these experiences have altered the way chronic illness is treated by professionals in our society and the way patients experience and think about their condition. Gradually society is modifying some of its own rigid attitudes and perspectives on illness and disability, including the ways we attribute value to these common life experiences and confer visibility and place for them in our communities. These changes have included:

1. a greater focus on individuals' strengths and capacities as well as vulnerabilities and limitations;
2. a greater acceptance of patients' rights and abilities to advocate for themselves within our profession-based medical care system; and
3. a recognition that effective care plans must be patient/family focused.

The emergence of numerous disease-specific advocacy groups has provided an additional means of expressing patients' views, potentially influencing policy decision making. These self-help groups also have provided important networks of support for affected individuals and have become a powerful sustaining force for individuals with a broad range of illnesses.

These changes in perspective also have resulted in increasing affirmation of social work practice values, knowledge, and skills. Expertise in developing interventions that improve quality of life for the patients and families coping with chronic illness and disability is growing. However, such improvement may still be thwarted and should not be taken for granted given that important advances in services for chronic illness have been slow to develop and can be undermined by cost reductions in health care due to economic downturns.

DEFINING AND EXPLAINING CHRONIC
PHYSICAL ILLNESS AND DISABILITY

At the beginning of this century, Americans frequently died at a young age from infectious and parasitic diseases due to the limits of medical and public health knowledge. As sanitation, nutrition, and living conditions improved and medical technology advanced, deaths from infectious diseases declined steadily, and children and young adults survived longer. The increased longevity of both men and women and the greater vulnerability of older individuals to chronic illness strongly suggest that the number of people affected with these conditions will be steadily increasing. Today, more than 45 percent of Americans (about 100 million people) suffer from chronic conditions, such as diabetes, bronchitis, or arthritis. The cost of treating these conditions is estimated to be $659 billion per year (Hoffman and Rice 1996). Furthermore, these costs have steadily increased, now representing nearly 70 percent of national expenditures on personal health care.

Chronic illness is distinguished from acute illness by at least three different dimensions: illness duration, interference with ordinary functioning, and impact on quality of life (Sidell 1997). The National Center for Health Statistics considers an illness chronic if its duration exceeds three months (Lapham 1986; Pollin 1994). A chronic illness is considered to interfere with a person's ordinary physical, psychological, or social functioning and to affect the quality of life of the individual and his or her family by interfering with normal activities and routines (Dimond 1984; Miller 1983).

An illness that becomes chronic may occur gradually or suddenly and without warning, leaving residual psychological and physical disabilities after treatment that interfere with an established identity or self-concept, developmental phase, and lifestyle. The age of the individual when such an illness or disability occurs is one of the variables that shape the individual's response and the range of psychosocial problems that the patient and family confront. Others include marital status, preillness fitness, ethnicity, and education. Chronic illnesses and disabilities vary with regard to the degree of threat they pose to an individual's life. They may be fatal, potentially life-shortening, or of no consequence to one's life span. For example, diseases such as arthritis have no impact on life expectancy while illnesses such as diabetes may shorten it. Finally, chronic illnesses may be unchanging, but they may also be progressive (Rolland 1994; Sidell 1997).

Although disabilities can occur as a consequence of a chronic illness, they may also develop as a consequence of an accident or be present at birth due to a prenatal or birth injury or to a genetic disorder. A somewhat different social and psychological impact is associated with each of these conditions. A genetic etiology is more likely to be identified as an issue for disabilities that occur at birth. This biological reality creates multiple medical crises at the beginning of a child's life, often causing parents to struggle with questions of blame and responsibility. Such conditions require that individuals interact with the health care system throughout their lives around the continuous challenge of optimizing functioning at each developmental phase and with each change in treatment or condition. Disabilities from accidents occur suddenly and also confront patients and families with questions of blame and responsibility, depending upon the particular circumstances of the accident, and the preceding and subsequent events (Hockenberry 1995). They can occur at any point in the life cycle. Finally, due to a sudden occurrence, accidents may evoke a traumatic stress response in affected individuals that can impede their psychological adjustment to their disabilities. Like disabilities from birth and chronic illness, disabilities due to accidents have become more prevalent in our society as medical advances have included treatments that prolong life in situations that previously led to certain and often rapid death.

Jane was 20 years of age when she was in a motorcycle accident with her 21-year-old fiancé. They had been riding with a group when a car tried to taunt them by swerving toward their bike. Her fiancé lost control of his bike and ran into a tree. He died immediately and Jane's leg was so damaged it eventually required amputation. One year later she was seen by a social worker during her rehabilitation of the amputation. She was demonstrating signs of complicated grief and traumatic stress: continuing to live in her fiancé's room, refusing to let anyone remove his possessions from the room, delaying rehabilitation of her severed limb, and developing increasing fears and phobias. With the social worker she began to confront her anger toward her fiancé for losing control of the bike and causing her amputation, an emotion that seemed unacceptable to her since she had survived and he had not. Expressing and working through these feelings empowered her to become active in making more realistic plans for her life, including moving out of her fiancé's room.

The **severity** of the burden of a chronic illness varies considerably. For example, the most common chronic condition in the United States is sinusitis, considered a mild chronic illness (Kerson 1985). While not usually devastating in terms of overall health, it is considered to be a chronic illness. At the opposite end of the spectrum are the five most disabling chronic conditions: mental retardation, respiratory cancers, multiple sclerosis, blindness (both eyes), and paralysis of extremities (Collins 1993). The most prevalent chronic diseases with severe impact include arthritis, cancer, dementia, diabetes, epilepsy, heart disease, respiratory illness, stroke, substance abuse, and AIDS (Kerson 1985). Hobbs, Perrin, and Ireys (1985) argued that a chronic illness could be considered "severe" when it resulted in serious physical difficulties, major financial burdens, serious emotional or psychological problems for the affected individual or major disruptions in family life.

Chronic illnesses are not viewed as curable. Rather, they are often progressive. The emphasis of treatment is on effective management of the symptoms or residuals of disease (Kinzel 1993). Many conditions once considered severely disabling are now responsive to treatment, permitting the possibility of reducing disability and improving quality of life for many individuals who previously would be faced with more severe disability. Such "salvage" procedures include knee replacement surgeries for the effects of arthritis or bone cancers, cardiac surgeries, and cataract operations. These procedures may be costly, however, and they pose risks as well as likely benefits.

The increase in prevalence of chronic illness, the broad impact of associated disabilities, and the cost of care has encouraged a shift away from an almost exclusive focus on the biological nature of health problems to an emphasis on broader concerns about quality of life. This focus has increased the importance of the social worker's expertise in problem-solving approaches in enhancing quality of life and in developing interventions within the persons total ecological system as well as providing assistance at the level of the individual. Despite what today would be considered an insensitive label, these broader dimensions are nonetheless reflected in the definition of *handicapped individual* found in the Rehabilitation Act of 1973, PL 93–112, as amended by PL 95–602, Section 7:

1. Any person whose physical or mental impairment substantially limits one or more of the person's major life activities;
2. Has a record of such impairment; or
3. Is regarded as having such an impairment.

The Rehabilitation Act affirms that handicaps are sequelae of chronic illnesses and disabilities and emphasizes the contribution of societal perceptions to producing handicaps. Today, advocates are increasing public awareness about the unintentional yet stigmatizing effects of terms and labels such as "handicaps" and are replacing them with terms such as "differently abled."

A thorough examination of the problems that arise in chronic illness calls for knowledge of at least three critical areas (Dimond 1984):

1. the physiological and medical treatment aspects
2. the sociological definitions and responses to the illness on the part of family, friends, and co-workers, health care workers, and society in general
3. the context of the individual's particular response to his or her own condition, often shaped by age, gender, and cultural expectations, as well as by the degree of impairment and/or visibility of the impairment.

These three areas tend to interact with each other, and the social work challenge is to enhance a positive, mutually reinforcing interaction rather than a more limiting or even destructive one. Frequently social work interventions focus on conflicts, misunderstandings, or on the dis-synchrony between the goals, values, perspectives and preoccupations of individuals or groups in each of these areas (Christ 1982).

The knowledge base for understanding chronic illness reflects an ecosystems perspective of social work practice (Germain and Gitterman 1996; Meyer 1976, 1983) that considers the individual and family in transaction with their immediate and larger society. For the practitioner, this also means recognition that persons coping with chronic illness or disability are likely to experience greater personal difficulty and to feel less hope about the future to the extent that disabled persons and their families share society's discriminatory views of handicapped persons. Similarly, professionals who grew up exposed to those same societal prejudices may categorize clients and develop treatment strategies based on unexamined assumptions about the limitations imposed by specific physical problems. For the affected individual, the maintenance of self-esteem and a realistic sense of personal control are critical areas of focus for social work intervention. However, as will be elaborated in the following, interventions that improve the individual's self-esteem and sense of personal control may conflict with the values and goals of the family, the health care team, and the larger society.

The primary focus in this chapter is on chronic illnesses that occur throughout the life cycle. They will be compared with disabilities present from birth and with accidents. Cancer is used as an illustration of a highly prevalent illness in our society. Cancer was once considered a terminal condition that with medical advances has developed into a chronic disease with residual disabilities caused by either the illness or treatments. Cancer is prototypic of modern chronic illnesses, affecting individuals throughout the life cycle, but increasing in prevalence as individuals age. In fact, cancer comprises many diseases that require a full range of treatments, including chemotherapy, surgery, and radiation as well as organ transplants and immunotherapies. While often curable, cancer is also life-threatening, and the possibility of relapse or recurrence remains (DeVita, Hellman, and Rosenberg 1993).

DEMOGRAPHIC PATTERNS

Although estimates of the incidence of chronic illnesses and disabilities (their frequency) and their prevalence (the number of those affected by the disorders at a given time) vary with the definitions used for illness and disability, the relative contribution of severe and chronic illnesses to mortality and morbidity has increased over the last several decades (Fox 1986; Hobbs et al. 1985; Hoffman and Rice 1996; Manton, Patrick, and Johnson 1987).

The prevention of many infectious childhood diseases and improved technology for the care of newborns and young infants has allowed survival in the face of even serious health problems and disabling conditions. Many chronically ill children, who previously would have died much earlier from their illnesses, now survive into adulthood. One in four children younger than 18 years of age have a chronic illness. Hobbs et al. (1985) estimated that perhaps 1 percent of those problems in children are so severe that the health care system is unlikely to serve them more than moderately well. Definitions of severe chronic illness that were used by this study include severe burdens on physical, monetary, psychological, and family functioning.

A growing number of individuals report activity limitations due to chronic conditions. Between 1987 and 1993 there was an increase of (1) over 20 percent in the number of Americans identified as having a chronic condition that limited their activity, and (2) at least 33 percent in those identified as being unable to carry on their major activity because of a chronic condition (Collins 1993). Even those who are not disabled by their chronic condition live with the threat of recurrent exacerbations, higher health care costs, days lost from work, and the risk of long-term limitations and disabilities.

Individuals with chronic conditions are at greater risk for being underinsured (Hoffman and Rice 1996). This means that they are more likely to incur high out-of-pocket costs for medical services relative to their family income. They are also less likely to be insured by managed care plans that cover more services and preventive care, thus increasing their likelihood of incurring high out-of-pocket expenses.

For those individuals who are poor, lack education, and are from racial minority groups, the risks of chronic illness and disability are even higher. Inadequate or lack of prenatal care increases the risk of mortality or later difficulties for a baby, yet prenatal care is least likely to be obtained by poor women who are unmarried, especially if they are young, not well educated, live in rural areas, or are Hispanic (Black and Weiss 1991; Brown 1988). Poor children are likely to have more illnesses and more severe illness than their nonpoor counterparts (Starfield 1982).

SOCIAL CONTEXT

The dominant culture in American society continues to place a high value on those who go through a crisis such as illness unscathed, are able to bounce back, and then continue life without missing a beat, at least in any visible or observable way (Siegel and Christ 1990). Also valued are those who die with dignity. But that is not the experience of most individuals with a chronic, often deteriorating, illness. While life has been prolonged, ongoing disabilities, the threat of future exacerbations, and the reality of continuing physical losses challenge these individuals to maintain relationships and a meaningful quality of life under conditions of uncertainty and threat. These illnesses constitute transformative experiences in individuals' lives that alter much of the way they view themselves and the world. There are few social role models in the dominant culture for living with the day-to-day rigors of managing a chronic deteriorating illness with dignity and meaning.

Societal attitudes often shape the kinds of services provided to, or withheld from, individuals affected by illness and disability. For example, with medical advances, increasing numbers of cancer patients were cured. However, the intensive treatments sometimes led to disabling physical and psychological conditions. These conditions could occur months, even years after cancer treatment and patients found it difficult to obtain medical care for these late effects. Having cured a difficult disease, physicians wondered what more the patient could expect of them. The patient's perspective was quite different. Knowing they had a longer survival time, they were more concerned about physical problems caused by the treatments that impeded their quality of life. They wanted the loss of body parts, vision and hearing problems, and cardiac conditions to be rehabilitated. They wanted symptoms such as depression, anxiety, loss of energy, and other psychological symptoms to be treated. As the number of survivors increased, they were able to effectively advocate as a group of patients with knowledgeable professionals for attention to the residual psychosocial as well as physical effects from their disease and treatment (Christ 1987).

Society's values also shape the solutions provided for quality-of-life problems. For example, society values maximum independence for individuals with disabilities and often proposes to foster this with technological assists. However, the patient may prefer a home health aid who provides socialization rather than technological assistance that enhances independence but requires isolation. Quality of life implies an individually defined situation, and a broad range of options need to be available in order to accommodate the many different individual values and choices.

13-year-old Lee was diagnosed with osteosarcoma, a cancer of the bone in his leg.

The surgeons removed the tumor and were able to replace his knee with a metal internal prosthesis rather than amputate the leg, which was the usual treatment for this disease in past years. However, because the doctors had to remove a great deal of muscle due to the placement of the tumor, the resulting limb was fragile, and Lee's ability to walk even a moderate distance and to engage in sports of any kind was severely limited. In addition, he had several infections secondary to the surgery that required weeks in the hospital each year. Lee was very depressed about the interruption in his athletic activities not only because he enjoyed sports, but because this was a major source of social contact for him. He saw individuals with amputated limbs running marathons and skiing and he longed to be with them. He struggled with feelings of depression and hopelessness. When he was 16 years of age Lee pleaded with his father to let him have the limb amputated so that he could increase mobility. He had decided mobility was more important than the external appearance of a normal limb so compromised in its functioning. Society may think that maintaining body integrity is the most important value in selecting a treatment once survival is assured, but Lee had concluded that for him giving up the limb would have a more positive impact on his quality of life. The amputation would also permit him to be less vulnerable to infections, which required long hospital stays and treatment with antibiotics. However, his father refused to give permission since he viewed amputation as a failure, his own as well as his son's. Lee continued to discuss the situation with his surgeon and when he was 18, old enough to sign an independent consent form, the surgeon agreed to perform the amputation. Lee was immensely relieved by his improved ambulation and his ability to participate in the many athletic activities available to amputees today. His mood and self-esteem also improved markedly. Unfortunately his father maintained a bitter and resentful attitude toward his son for this decision.

Programs of comprehensive medical and social support services are needed to treat chronic illnesses as well as disabilities of all kinds (Berkman 1996; Dhooper 1997; Keigher 1997). However, despite the prevalence of chronic conditions, the health care system has found it difficult to shift from its earlier focus on the treatment of infectious diseases and acute illnesses to the provision of treatment and care systems that can more adequately address these longer-term health problems. The pressures of containing AIDS highlighted the deficiencies in current services for the chronically ill (Fox 1986). Treatment and rehabilitation programs that are community based rather than institution based are integral to making services accessible over a longer period of time. Interventions that enhance communication between multiple specialists enable the sharing of treatment information and expertise essential to effective treatment and continuity in care.

Chronic illness management also requires patients to be knowledgeable about their own conditions, and to be active participants in their own care. Informal caregivers need to be knowledgeable as well since they can help to reduce costs. Therefore, services generally encompass education for both patient and caregivers. Informal caregiving responsibilities traditionally assumed by families are becoming less feasible due to increasing numbers of scattered families, divorce, single-parent families, childless couples, as well as families with both spouses working in order to survive (State Health Coordinating Council 1992). Without access to informal caregiving, patients face higher out-of-pocket costs and are at greater risk for inpatient hospitalization and institutionalization (Vandermeer 1993). Supportive services aimed at assisting patients and families in advocating for themselves in a sometimes unknowing and/or reluctant community are integral to effective care. However, services often have a patchwork quality and the need to redress such gaps continues to be reflected in a variety of legislative initiatives and funding sources to address the needs (Hobbs et al. 1985).

Early legislative attention to children's needs came in Title V of the Social Security Act of 1935. This Act provided assistance to children through Crippled Children's Services programs in the states and territories and through other categorical programs such as those for hemophilia and pediatric pulmonary conditions. The 1970s saw the passage of the Developmentally Disabled Assistance and Bill of Rights Act of 1975 (PL 94–142), which provides assistance to children with a wide range of chronic conditions, and the Education for All Handicapped Children's Act of 1975, which provides federal subsidies to improve educational opportunities. An increased recognition of the importance of early intervention resulted in the more recent passage of PL 99–457, which supports educational services for children with special needs starting at birth. In addition, funds are available to some health-impaired children through Medicaid and the Supplemental Security Income (SSI) Program, both under the Social Security Act.

Of particular significance to adults with disabilities was the passage of Section 504 of the 1973 Rehabilitation Act, which bars employment discrimination on the basis of disability in federally funded programs. The 1974 amendments to that act also developed a comprehensive definition of disability (cited earlier) that considers the handicapping potential of society's stigmatizing views of certain disabilities.

The major cash transfer programs for disabled adults are Social Security Disability Insurance (DI) and Supplemental Security Income (SSI). Disability insurance helps those who have been workers with Social Security coverage and entitles the recipient to Medicare coverage after two years on DI. Supplemental Security Income focuses on low-income children and adults with either no work experience or too little work experience to be eligible for DI and provides medical coverage under Medicaid (Mudrick 1988).

Programs that replace wages when a worker becomes disabled or that provide income for those not in the labor force form a patchwork of supports, none of which base eligibility solely on the nature and the severity of physical disability (Mudrick 1988). Instead, eligibility rests on such non-illness-related criteria as required periods of work covered by Social Security, veteran's status, or poverty. Under these programs, disabled women in particular are less likely to achieve eligibility because household work does not qualify as gainful employment and women's more frequent patterns of part-time participation in the labor force often disqualify them from Social Security coverage (Mudrick 1988). These programs have eligibility requirements and complicated applications that can limit access to necessary financial help.

A committed gay caregiver living with his unemployed partner with AIDS-related cancer felt resentful because his partner's moderate work history qualifies him for only a minimal level of Social Security DI, which he must receive for twenty-nine months before qualifying for Medicare Part A hospitalization coverage (Kerson 1985; Montoya 1993). Ironically, the work history of the partner with AIDS-related cancer exceeded the low work history threshold to qualify for SSI and immediate Medicaid coverage. Furthermore, both programs require that various financial documents be obtained, organized, and submitted in support of the applications, which may take several months to process. Fewer disabled adults receive benefits under Aid for Families with Dependent Children (AFDC, for low-income families in which there is a disabled parent), veterans' pensions, and worker's compensation (for workers injured on the job).

The preceding review of legislation and funding confirms the gains that have been made on behalf of children and adults with serious health impairments. However, significant barriers in health care, education, employment, and income support continue to impede their attempts to participate in our society to the full extent of their abilities. Services available vary tremendously from one disease to another. For example, the presence of an interested specialist or a particular comprehensive clinic can mean a dramatically higher level of services for one disorder than for another in the same locale. The gaps in the continuity of services are often reflected in a lack of communication and coordination of services among providers for effective care of these complex diseases.

Although educational opportunities for some children with chronic illnesses and disabilities were expanded with the passage of the special education initiatives of the 1970s already described, many chronically ill children are not easily or appropriately served by special education programs. Since special education itself is often stigmatizing, many parents and children resist this designation. Additions or modifications to health services in the regular school setting transform regular education programs to be appropriate for many health-impaired children. However the decline in the numbers of school health nurses and related services represents a barrier to mainstream education for many children with chronic health conditions (Hobbs et al. 1985).

The importance of home care and other community resources for the chronically ill is reflected in the fact that a full 95 percent of home care expenditures are used for care for the chronically ill. The lack of home care services available in the community or reimbursed by health care plans represents another barrier to services for the chronically ill.

For the disabled adult attempting to participate in the labor force, antidiscrimination laws have provided leverage for combating the more obvious and extreme prejudicial barriers. More difficult to counter are strains from inadequate special education programs, architectural and transportation barriers, job structures that allow few opportunities for part-time or flexible work hours, or salary and benefits that are inadequate to cover such extra expenses as home attendants, prosthetic devices, or specialized transportation assistance. For example, most insurance does not cover the costs of prostheses for amputated limbs. These expenses can be prohibitively costly for children who require new prostheses with body growth. Each artificial limb may cost between $15,000 and $20,000. Poor-quality or inadequately fitting prostheses result in dramatic reductions in mobility, socialization, and other quality-of-life domains.

Many insurance and managed care companies seek to avoid paying benefits to individuals who have conditions that are likely to incur high medical costs. This is particularly limiting for individuals who have a condition such as cancer or cardiovascular illnesses. They often find themselves "locked in" to work for large companies who will provide more generous group benefits or to work in particular localities.

This often results in little opportunity for job advancement. For example, health insurance for a child with a chronic illness is often critical for the child and the families' economic survival. These benefits may determine the wage earner's employment opportunities. In addition, in an economic downturn, the individual with high medical expenses or physical limitations is at greater risk for job loss, adding to the already considerable uncertainties and stresses these individuals confront. A patient with advanced cancer may strive to work as long as possible to prolong his or her eligibility for COBRA health insurance. Patients may be preoccupied by the fear that their health insurance might be canceled during the terminal stage of an illness when family financial stresses are expected to be most severe (Brown and Tai-Seale 1992).

Programs for AIDS patients were viewed as highly successful not only for providing integrated systems of care for chronically ill patients, but also for advocating for patients in ways that influence the actual medical treatments recommended to patients as well as the direction of medical research. Other illness groups became more assertive as a consequence of observing the helpfulness and effectiveness of AIDS programs. For example, breast cancer organizations joined together to advocate not only for more medical research, but also for financing of behavioral research to address quality-of-life and survivor issues. Patients pushed for early release of promising new treatments and insurance coverage of preventive interventions as well as information about nutrition, exercise, cosmetic enhancements, and the development of networks of social and emotional support.

VULNERABILITIES AND RISK FACTORS

Both adults and children with chronic illnesses and disabilities are at greater risk of experiencing a broad range of psychological and social problems than individuals who do not have these conditions. Although most research on the psychosocial consequences of chronic illness has occurred within particular disease categories, some consensus has emerged about client's vulnerabilities and special needs across diseases for both children and adults. Social workers must be aware of characteristics of clients that make them more vulnerable so that they can fully appreciate the quantity as well as quality of stress the individual is experiencing and structure their interventions to mitigate the impact of vulnerabilities. Identified vulnerabilities and risk factors include (1) demographic factors, (2) illness and treatment experiences, (3) psychological symptoms, (4) personal coping style, (5) social support networks, (6) illness appraisals and attributions, and (7) concurrent stresses.

Managing a chronic illness can be a costly process; therefore, individuals who have fewer resources have greater problems with out-of-pocket costs, expensive procedures and equipment, and obtaining necessary personal assistance to meet a range of adaptive challenges. Individuals from **poorer areas** are more vulnerable to chronic illness and disability and are more severely disabled by their illnesses. Racial differentials in health status are also evident in comparisons of the percentage of persons with limitations in activity due to chronic conditions: **blacks** outnumber whites by a ratio of 4 to 1 among those 45 to 64 years of age (Trevino and Moss 1984). Among children, this vulnerability may include the child's inability to access adequate support from the school and community to help them deal with the limitations they confront.

Individuals with **less education** may have more difficulty negotiating with health professionals and managing the complex demands of current treatments. The capacity of individuals and families to take an active role in their own care is becoming increasingly important as patients are given more responsibility for decision making in the emerging health care system.

The role of gender in facilitating adaptation to chronic illness varies by type of illness, but **women** are better able to adapt to some illnesses than their male counterparts (Siegel and Christ 1990). Finally, **age** is an important demographic factor. Each stage in development brings its own particular adaptational challenges. For example, younger individuals have been found more vulnerable to emotional distress when confronting chronic illness. Disease is less expected and a great interference with normative life tasks of the young adult. Older individuals are more vulnerable to difficulties managing physical realities and resolving practical problems in functioning. They may have more experience in managing illness and stress but are more vulnerable to other concurrent illness and limitations in their physical capacities.

Specific aspects of the **illness and treatment experience** can create vulnerabilities. The greater the functional limitations imposed by illness and disability, the greater the degree to which the individual must confront the struggle of dependence versus independence. The greater the uncertainty of the outcome of the illness, the more psychological distress the patient experiences (Lapham 1986; Rolland 1994; Sidell 1997). Clients who have neurological or sensory impairments from their illness or treatment experience greater difficulty as their coping capacities may be reduced. Some illnesses require intense and life-threatening treatments such as organ transplantation. Each phase or stage of an illness brings its own challenges to the client and some clients have more difficulty with the demands of a particular stage of illness. For example, leaving the many resources and personnel of the acute care hospital can be difficult for individuals who live in an inner-city environment that has few community resources to assist them.

Adults with chronic illness are at greater risk for experiencing depression, and some illnesses, most notably AIDS, have higher rates of suicide (Mancoske et al. 1995). And while there is great variability in children's response to chronic illness, they are about twice as likely to develop some form of psychiatric disturbance relative to their healthy peers (Kliewer 1997; Stein, Westbrook, and Silver 1998). Individuals with chronic illnesses may be at risk for psychiatric disturbances, and individuals with mental illnesses are also more likely to have chronic physical conditions. Clearly the individual's mental illness is an added vulnerability and risk factor for compromised adaptation to physical illness.

Individuals who do not use active coping strategies, who feel less optimistic about their adaptation, who have low self-esteem, and who do not perceive themselves as able to master the demands of their illness are more likely to experience depression and other indicators of compromised adaptation (Nezu et al. 1994, 1999).

The importance of social support, that is, help from family, friends, and community, in facilitating adaptation to chronic illness is identified by many studies (Bloom 1982; Ell et al. 1989; Kriegsman, Penninx, and van Eyk 1995). The patient's perception of good social support appears to protect chronically ill individuals from severe depressive symptoms. However, the particular aspects of that support that are needed for a given illness may vary—for example, emotional support seems more helpful for individuals confronting a life-threatening illness, whereas instrumental or practical support is required by individuals who are functionally disabled (Penninx et al. 1998). For children, the family environment is the more critical support network. More family conflict and less cohesion in family functioning creates a greater risk for compromised adaptation to chronic illness (Kliewer 1997). School and community support systems that do not make adequate accommodations for the child with a chronic illness or disability to succeed as he or she matures also increase the ill child's vulnerability to adaptive failure. Social isolation has been identified as a consequence of the vulnerabilities of some children with chronic illness.

13-year-old Susan was from a small rural community. Neither her parents nor her older siblings had completed high school, and she was the youngest in the family. Prior to her development of osteosarcoma she had been achieving high grades in school, was an ice skating champion, and had been chosen as a class officer. After her successful knee replacement and chemotherapy, she became fearful of returning to school. Her parents were unaware of the problems of her giving in to this fear and they permitted her to remain at home. The school system had no home tutoring program. As time went on she fell further behind in her work, became isolated from friends as she watched television all day, and when evaluated at age 17 years, had never returned to school. At that time she had decided to get married and just obtained a job at a local supermarket. Her surgery was successful, her disease cured, but her disability was profound.

Some studies suggest that the professional relationship to the chronically ill client influences their ability to adapt to rigorous and long-term treatment protocols. The relationship of professionals to the chronically ill client can extend over many years. In a study of children with diabetes, mothers who reported greater perceptions of racism and family stress were significantly less satisfied with their children's medical care than those from less stressful environments (Auslander et al. 1997). These mothers who perceived racism also had more difficulty adhering to the required treatment protocol. This finding emphasizes the importance of the families' relationship with professional staff in facilitating treatment effectiveness.

Increasingly, studies have focused on how individuals' **way of thinking** about their illness affects how they feel about it and how well they adapt to it. Their level of optimism that treatments will be effective, their belief in their ability to master the many physical and psychological challenges of the illness, and their ability to maintain self-esteem while transforming identity in ways that integrate the realities of the physical illness do seem to influence their ability to adapt. Ongoing negative thoughts about the self and the illness have been found to be correlated with continuing depressed mood (Schiaffino and Revenson 1995). Pollin (1994) identified eight fears that she believed individuals with chronic illness confront: (1) loss of control, (2) loss of self-image, (3) loss of dependency, (4) stigma, (5) abandonment, (6) expression of anger, (7) isolation, and (8) death. She proposed a brief treatment to help individuals cope with these specific fears.

Finally, individuals who struggle with many other stresses in their lives as well as the chronic illness, face additional adaptive challenges. Some families experience a "pileup" of stressors (McCubbin and Patterson 1987; McCubbin et al. 1998) often secondary to or exacerbated by the chronic illness condition. Others have concurrent stresses unrelated to the patient's illness (Nezu et al. 1999; Northouse 1995). These might include other illnesses or deaths in the family, severe financial problems, or other major losses. These additional stresses can make it more difficult for individuals to adapt to the psychological and practical demands of the illness.

RESILIENCIES AND PROTECTIVE FACTORS

Identifying vulnerabilities and risk factors for individuals with chronic illness and disabilities has been accompanied more recently by a search for characteristics associated with individuals who adapt well to their illness. Becoming more active in identifying strengths, factors that seem to protect individuals from adverse consequences of the stresses of illness, and characteristics of resilience in adapting to chronic illness has increased significantly over the past decade. This has led to a focus on "coping resources" and other factors that are associated with better adaptive outcomes. This is critical in order to be able to develop interventions that aim at ways to increase resilience and strengths, as well as to mitigate the impact of vulnerabilities.

Research has shown that those who cope well with stress, whether it be a serious illness, job loss, or a natural disaster, are those who don't deny the adversity or tragedy of the situation, but who are also able to see it as a **challenge**, to make positive changes in their life and their relationships, and who can derive some positive meaning out of the situation. This is an empowering process that provides the individual with the critical tools of sense of mastery and self-efficacy, and improved self-esteem. Facilitating this process is an important role for social work. Resilience and protective factors are the converse of vulnerabilities and risk factors. Adults who adapt well to chronic illness use active coping strategies such as engaging in a partnership and dialogue with professionals about their condition. They tend to have more economic and educational resources. They work actively to identify specific problems caused by each stage in the illness process, and they focus on resolution of associated problems. While acknowledging the losses and disappointments in their situation, they view it as a challenge, and they consider ways to develop a positive meaning of this experience, using it as a source of personal growth and learning (Nezu et al. 1994, 1999).

A perception of strong **social support** is another characteristic associated with better adaptation. Better-adapted individuals reach out for help and assistance from a broad range of individuals outside the family and have families who are highly supportive of their efforts to "keep the illness" in its place rather than permitting it to dominate their total life experiences. Their reaching out often seems a recognition of the reciprocal nature of the recovery process. They feel a sense of self-efficacy, empowerment, and less conflict with their level of dependence. They feel good about what they have accomplished and are able to identify and value their positive attributes. They recognize that life has changed. and they seek to integrate that reality into their future plans. The better-adapted individuals have large support networks that include other patients, family, and friends as well as professionals. They often seek self-help groups for information and normalization as well as emotional release.

For children, active coping strategies are also related to better adjustment outcomes. In addition, families of well-adjusted children are characterized by high levels of cohesion, flexibility, and warmth. Conflict is reduced in these families. These mothers also have lower levels of depression and other symptoms of high levels of stress (Kliewer 1997).

These characteristics of resilience and protective factors are reflected in the range of interventions that are being developed to assist patients with chronic illness and disabilities. Some of these have been formally evaluated by research; others have become integrated with the ongoing clinical care of these patients and their families.

PROGRAMS AND SOCIAL WORK CONTRIBUTIONS

Social workers provide service to individuals with chronic illness in a wider array of service sites than was true just a decade ago. While many services continue to be located in acute care facilities and rehabilitation centers, there has been an expansion of treatment, rehabilitation, and assistive programs in the community, especially in the area of home care, self-help organizations, and for children, in schools (Berkman 1996; Dhooper 1997; Egan and Kadushin 1999; Keigher 1997).

In health care settings, social workers frequently function as members of multidisciplinary teams that serve persons with chronic and disabling health problems in specialty programs devoted to similar clusters of illnesses (e.g., renal, orthopedic, or gastrointestinal clinics). The social work role can vary widely from case manager, counselor, therapist, health educator, group leader, and program developer. The social worker is typically both a resource to which families turn for guidance in their negotiations with other health professionals, for referral to community resources, and for personal support at times of medical crises or changes in the course of the illness. Unfortunately, the size of workers' assignments or caseloads can often limit the numbers of patients they are able to intervene with or the range of services that they can provide.

An increasing challenge for social workers in health settings, especially acute care facilities, is effective communication with the members of the multidisciplinary team. Social workers deal with psychosocial and quality-of-life issues, rather than the more physical/biological concerns of most other professionals. On many treatment teams the social worker may be the only mental health professional. Describing the social work role and communicating about patient's and families' psychological, social, and emotional needs are critical to the social workers' effectiveness. They are often an important linkage between the patient/family system and the medical team, interpreting their needs and wishes.

Increasingly, it is necessary for social workers to define the specific outcomes of their services, to demonstrate to corporate administrators financial as well as quality-of-life benefits. This has been a difficult area for social workers not only because of the nature of their work, but also because they are often not given the time or training to fulfill this function. Nevertheless it is now a vital component of functioning in health care settings.

Through interpersonal contact with the client, family, and staff within and outside of the agency, social workers engage in a natural process of *case management* to address the needs of the client with chronic illness across all areas of functioning and daily living within the client's physical and social environment. The multiple and interacting issues that call for case management are often subtle and intricate, demanding careful and deliberate application of critical thinking and creative problem-solving approaches to meet client goals of problem prevention, amelioration, or resolution. Although a cursory view of case management might suggest a limited and simplistic focus on the provision of concrete resources to chronically ill clients and their families, a hallmark of case management appears to be its flexibility and plasticity to assume ever-changing roles and functions across broad, multiple, and interacting domains that are important to clients, their families, interdisciplinary professional teams, and human service agencies (e.g., Vandiver and Kirk 1992). This adaptability and fluidity can result in surprisingly effective outcomes.

In addition to the more apparent function of linking clients and families to services within and across agencies, case management itself may function as a "social support" linkage that may impact the client as part of a caring, meaningful, and motivating intervention. For instance, physical and mental health needs may exacerbate each other when either remains untreated; as an example, untreated and mismanaged diabetes may mimic or worsen symptoms of chronic mental illness. In effective case management for clients with both chronic physical and mental illness, clients and their families may feel a sincere and motivating sense of caring and support when they actively witness social workers who strive to assess, initiate, monitor, and advocate for ongoing linkages to community physicians and medical services while encouraging clients to seek periodic physical examinations, attend follow-up appointments, and comply consistently with medical and psychiatric care (Davis 1996; Francoeur, Copley, and Miller 1997). Positive impacts of performing case management in the presence of clients, families, and other professionals may be subtle yet profound, especially when other case management roles and functions occur simultaneously.

However, the performance of actions and tasks by the social worker and witnessed by the client should not be overreaching, for an important case management goal should concern the effective empowerment of patients and families to advocate and solve problems associated with their chronic illness situation whenever they can and to resist overdependence on the social worker, other professionals , and agencies. One of these case management concerns is strengthening the social competencies of chronically ill clients and their families through training and referrals that foster self-help and through guidance to improve social skills. This function of case management is based on the concept of self-efficacy from social learning theory (Liberman 1988; Roberts-DeGennaro 1987; Vandiver and Kirk 1992), which poses that behavior results from continuous interactions among cognitive, behavioral, and environmental factors (Bandura 1986). The role of the social worker is to intervene in ways that build the capacities of clients and their families to engage in purposeful actions and tasks that prevent, ameliorate, or resolve problems. Such interventions not only focus on improving the actual capacities of clients and families but also seek to enhance their *beliefs* that they are capable of engaging in particular actions and tasks that are likely to result in desired outcomes.

These interventions may take various forms. Through the process of direct performance, social workers may engage with clients and families to jointly work on and achieve a task, such as arranging for home health assistance. Through the process of vicarious coping, social workers may engage with clients and families to plan and role-play various ways of dealing with stressful situations, such as writing down important medical questions and learning ways of feeling less intimidated when speaking to physicians. Through the process of social persuasion, social workers provide corrective feedback, verbal persuasion, coaching, and encouragement, such as encouraging socially withdrawn clients to take the initiative to set up transportation for medical appointments. Through the process of self-monitoring, social workers may train clients and families to monitor baseline levels of key perceptions, emotions, or behaviors, followed by monitoring of changes during and after intervention(s), through the use of logs, diaries, and various types of measures (e.g., direct observations, self-anchored scales, rapid assessment instruments and longer standardized instruments).

Finally, it should be noted that the flexibility and plasticity of case management to assume ever-changing roles and functions across broad, multiple, and interacting domains often generates "multiplier effects" that enhance the effectiveness of actions and interventions by other professionals. Common positive outcomes with vested interests by various parties include improvements in the client's physical and mental health symptoms and quality of life that reduce the future prevalence of costly and inappropriate service needs (examples are delayed hospital admissions or repeated emergency room visits).

Rehabilitation programs also exist as part of the health sector but specialize in remediating disabilities and teaching alternative approaches to managing the tasks of daily living. Here also the social worker functions as a member of the interdisciplinary team that is at the core of rehabilitation services (Russell 1988). Treatment plans in rehabilitation extend into the community and often include the involvement of close family and friends. Social workers with their knowledge of family functioning and community resources are particularly equipped to make important contributions on rehabilitation teams (Russell 1988).

Social workers also work in the range of community programs and voluntary agencies that provide services for disabled persons. Social services that can benefit clients and families with chronic health problems include: (1) those that support and reinforce the caretaking abilities of the client or parent, e.g., family or mental health counseling, and anticipatory child guidance; (2) those that supplement care, e.g., respite care, homemakers, and transportation; and (3) those that provide substitute care, e.g., foster and adoption services, and long-term care facilities (Hobbs et al. 1985). Social workers employed in these non-illness-specific social service settings are critical providers of services for this population but are often hampered in their efforts by fragmentation of programs and limited resources.

Newer and expanded roles for social work have developed in a variety of new programs for individuals with chronic illness and disabilities. These include: (1) more sophisticated case management programs that permit the professional to follow the patient through in and outpatient services and provide monitoring of the patient's condition over a period of many years; (2) more comprehensive home care services where social workers now provide a very broad range of counseling, decision-making, educational, support, and continuity services (Egan and Kadushin 1999; Roberts et al. 1997); (3) expanded self-help programs that provide a broad range of information, support, and political advocacy; (4) support programs for caregivers whose economic value to the system has been recognized; (5) increasingly sophisticated intervention programs that use advanced technology such as telephone groups, Internet chat rooms, and distance learning (Galinsky, Schopler, and Abell 1997); and (6) the provision of enormous quantities of information on the Internet for patients, families, caregivers, and professionals. This accessibility of information for patients promises extraordinary help; however, professionals are challenged to develop ways to monitor its validity and provide correction and validation so that patients are not misled. This is most evident in the development of homeopathic medicine. Methods such as massage and acupuncture have become more widely available. These are treatments that are helpful, but were not studied or used in the past because they had little economic value (Cassileth 1999). A professionally developed and regularly updated Web site provides comprehensive descriptions of the support for many of these approaches. The challenge for social work is to maximize the opportunities this new information source offers while assuring clients about the validity of the information provided.

ASSESSMENT AND INTERVENTIONS

The complex interaction of psychosocial, medical, and ecological factors that affect the chronically ill can make it difficult to select a focus for social work intervention. How does the professional decide which problem to address at a given point in time? For example, when should interventions emphasize the client's internal feelings of discouragement and loss, practical problem solving, or expanding and empowering the support network? These are just a few of the decisions a social worker confronts with an individual coping with a chronic illness condition. Three processes are critical to effective intervention planning in chronic illness: (1) illness-related assessment, (2) case formulation, and (3) intervention implementation and evaluation. Assessment refers to information the social worker obtains about the client's experience and functioning. The case formulation is the social worker's analysis of this and all other pertinent information. This step is often the most overlooked part of the intervention process by mental health professionals. It requires critical thinking and analytic skills and may be the most important step in choosing a successful intervention. Implementation requires the integration of this information with clinically recommended approaches and interventions that have empirical support.

A structured illness specific **assessment** is critical in organizing the range of information required to understand the clients' adaptation to chronic physical conditions. This structure helps the worker to be comprehensive, consider the full range of stresses that may be affecting the individual, and include critical factors that the client may have overlooked or not viewed as influential. Chronic physical illness and disability imply complexity in illness course, in treatments, and in responses to treatments. The way these factors interact over time can be confusing to the professional who is gathering information. The structure of the assessment is intended to help reduce this confusion.

Presenting Problem or Chief Complaint. In chronic illness, clients need to be helped to articulate the nature of the problem that brings them to the worker as comprehensively as possible. Patients with a chronic illness may have many thick records from multiple sources that document the system's treatment of their condition over many years. The sheer volume of information can create a reaction in professionals that provokes or contributes to an undesired negative interaction with the client. Busy emergency rooms are well known as settings where arriving at rapid professional conclusions is routine. But emergency rooms are poorly suited for the often confusing, but potentially dangerous and frightening, symptoms of chronic illness. Clients who have been involved in battles during multiple encounters with the health care system may seem to have a chip on their shoulder as the result of a long history of difficult experiences. This anger can easily be projected onto the new professional. A careful, thoughtful and respectful effort to understand the client's presenting problem may facilitate the assessment interview and increase the accuracy of the information elicited.

Several dimensions of an illness have been found to be particularly important in analyzing individuals' illness experiences and in identifying relevant psychosocial tasks around which workers can organize their work (Christ 1991; Mailick 1979; Rolland 1994; Strauss and Glaser 1975). They include the illness trajectory, the level of impairment, the phase or stage of the illness, and the response to treatment.

Illness Trajectory. Increasingly, authors have pointed out the importance of understanding the illness "trajectory": how it is likely to change over time and the different demands it makes on affected individuals (Christ 1991; Corbin and Strauss 1988; Rolland 1994). The trajectory includes the course of the illness (medical) but also the way in which it is affected by the responses of the patient and the significant people in their social network. The trajectory includes the disease's onset (i.e., whether it is sudden or gradual); its duration and course, including whether it is progressive, relapsing, or constant; and its likely outcome (i.e., a shortened or normal life span). Figure 5.1 shows variations in the trajectory of a cancer illness that ranges from a cure for increasing numbers of patients with increased risk of recurrence, second cancer, or late effects of treatments to terminal illness and death following diagnosis for other cancers. The expected trajectory of an illness may change as has happened, for example, with HIV, the AIDS virus. With the development of a widening array of antiviral treatments, patients began to realize they would likely have a longer life span than they had previously anticipated. For AIDS patients who divested themselves of resources in anticipation of an earlier death, this change has created challenging financial problems (McReynolds 1998).

Functional and/or Visible Impairment. The type and severity of impairment caused by the disease or treatment also affects the adaptive challenge of the illness. The level of impairment has both a subjective and an objective dimension. The limitation may be experienced as severe by one individual and mild by another. In a study of adolescent seven-year survivors of bone cancer, patients who had limb surgery for removal of the bone tumor experienced, on average, less severe anxiety and depression if their surgery was less extensive and they had fewer postsurgical complications (Christ, Lane, and Marcove 1995). On the other hand, there were patients who had a very successful surgical result who continued to hide their scars from peers. They thought the doctors were unrealistic in their positive views of the results of their surgery, especially the appearance of the spared leg.

Breast cancer patients who have had surgery that restricts the range of motion in their arm are generally only affected by this in a limited way. However, Jane, a 32-year-old patient who made her living teaching golf was devastated by the implications this had for continuing her vocation.

The impact of the impairment on patients' usual functioning, their attitude toward the impairment, level of acceptance, adaptation, and future plans for alteration shape the adaptive challenge and their response.

FIGURE 5.1 Cancer: Variations of Illness Experience

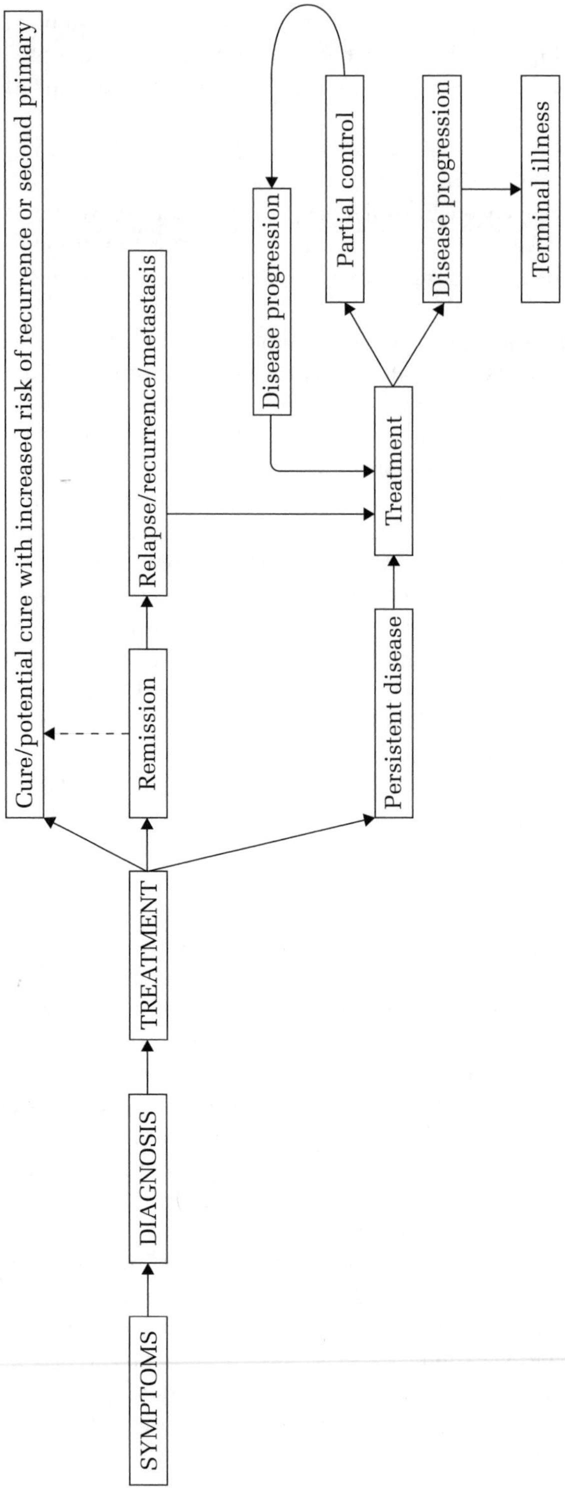

Phase/Stage of the Illness. The client's adaptive task is also shaped by the particular stage or phase of the current illness. Identification of the illness phase helps to specify the personal and professional tasks that must be addressed at these various points on the illness trajectory. While these phases vary with every illness, Rolland (1994) suggested three generic phases for all chronic illnesses. The initial crisis phase that begins before diagnosis may extend into the early period of adjustment. The second, chronic phase is the "long haul" period of the illness trajectory, whose characteristics are determined by the severity of the illness and the extent to which it is progressive, relapsing, or constant in nature. The terminal phase occurs when death looms as an inevitable event that dominates family life. Earlier, Mailick (1979) described these as the diagnostic phase, the chronic, and the ending of an episode of illness. Pollin (1994) suggests three times when individuals with a chronic illness face crucial adaptive challenges: (1) at diagnosis, (2) when the disease is exacerbated, and (3) when the disease must be managed without the constant presence of the medical team. With each particular illness, some effort to characterize typical phases and their associated psychosocial tasks helps the professional to focus quickly on critical adaptive issues (Christ 1991). The tasks associated with several phases of a cancer illness are described in tables 5.1 and 5.2 with the interventions that have been shown to be effective in helping patients meet these challenges.

At diagnosis, for example, clients are likely to be confronted with the possibility of death or permanent disability or disfigurement for the first time. Initially patients' responses may reflect shock and then denial that the illness is serious or life-threatening. They may focus on the most optimistic possibilities and have difficulty integrating the reality of negative test results. Other patients may feel they are dying immediately rather than being able to integrate the good, but not certain, possibility of newer treatments that have become effective in producing a cure or remission. The difference in the social work role during this period includes more utilization of crisis intervention techniques than when, for example, the patient is successfully completing a treatment and preparing to return to work, school, and normal family living with some new physical deficits. While the patient is in crisis at diagnosis, the social worker keeps in mind the fact that over time patients can become quite accommodated to living with a life-threatening disease. One woman who had AIDS for four years said, "I don't get upset about it. I don't think that 'I'm dying.' It's just that my life has been shortened. AIDS has taken over my body, I'm not going to let it take over my spirit as well!"

Treatment Response. The patients' responses are also shaped by the effectiveness of treatments. If their treatment response is positive and they have regained some functioning and some improvement in their quality of life, their mood and optimism may be quite high. However, if treatments have failed and the disease is progressing, patients may become discouraged, depressed, and reject or become noncompliant with additional treatment. They may search for nontraditional treatments. The patient's level of trust of the physician and other health care staff may be significantly altered by treatment failure as well. Conversely, when the patients' mood does not improve with improvement of their condition, other sources of stress need to be explored.

Past History. Often health care professionals behave as though the client's life began with the illness. There are some chronic illnesses of infancy, such as Down's

TABLE 5.1 Stage of Illness and Effective Professional Institutions

Stage of Illness	Adaptive Tasks	Social Work Role
Diagnosis	Manage acute emotional distress Confront mortality and vulnerability Move from disorientation and denial to constructive processing of medical information Make treatment decisions Cope with overwhelming emotions and initial lack of control Alter daily plans (e.g. work, school, day care) Consider disclosure of diagnosis to relevant others	Solicit illness story and health beliefs Normalize social work involvement Facilitate expression of feelings Support adaptive defenses Contain anxiety Normalize feelings, reactions, and questions Recognize developmental issues Provide information Create opportunities for patient/family control Enhance patient/family strengths Identify secretive and protective communication Address immediate practical needs Mobilize supports
Initial treatment	Understand treatment options and decide on a plan Regain emotional and interpersonal equilibrium Balance fear and hope Integrate illness experience into daily life (e.g., reorganize schedules and roles) Manage treatment requirements and routines Begin building illness-related support network Prepare for and cope with the effects of treatment including pain Strive to make illness a part of life but not the focus Grieve myriad changes resulting from illness and treatment Avoid social isolation Manage effects of illness and treatment on functioning, self-esteem, and relationships	Normalize emotional responses Provide emotional support Assist in reorganization of patient/family life through provision of resources Encourage health-promoting skills Prepare patient/family for rigors of treatment Facilitate communication with health care provider Assist with management of side effects Reinforce effective coping skills

(continued on next page)

TABLE 5.1 *(continued)*

Stage of Illness	Adaptive Tasks	Social Work Role
Continuing care	Recognize fear of less medical surveillance Confront sense of emptiness/abandonment now that crisis is over Relinquish medical care team as primary source of support Procure support from those outside medical care team Reengage with preillness activities, functions, and tasks Cope with residual physical impairments and psychological stresses Reevaluate priorities within the context of illness	Normalize fears, anxieties, and conflicting feelings Provide information about community resources Facilitate return to normative tasks and functions Encourage patient/family recognition of strengths and coping skills Facilitate grief of perceived losses Prepare patient/family for potential complications and late effects Provide structure for continued medical and social work services
Exacerbation	Integrate new medical information Evaluate treatment options and side effects Confront ambivalence about treatment Decide which course to pursue Cope with new threats to integrity and control Balance hope and fear in light of potentially poorer prognosis	Same as those during diagnosis and initial treatment
Terminal illness	Grapple with relevant existential and spiritual issues Find acceptable balance between living and letting go Relinquish self-care abilities as condition worsens Grieve for what will not be Address important unresolved issues Plan for surviving loved ones	Explore patient/family fears about the dying process Facilitate a discussion of patient/family choices for end-of-life care Propose predeath rituals to facilitate grieving Support realistic attempts at reconciliation and resolution of important issues and relationships Facilitate good-byes Assist in reallocation of roles and functions held by dying person Help patient/family to redefine hope with a focus on the present Assist patient/family with plans for practical realities (e.g., funeral)

TABLE 5.2 Empirically Supported Interventions

Behavioral Therapy
    Problem-solving therapy (Nezu et al. 1998, 1999)
    Cognitive-behavioral group therapy (van Dulmen, Fennis, and Bleijenberg 1996)
    Communication skills training (Ewart et al. 1984)
    Biofeedback (Davis 1986)
    Relaxation training (Carey and Burish 1987)
Psychoeducation
    Nursing interventions (Pless et al. 1994)
    Multifamily groups (Gonzales, Steinglass, and Reiss 1989)
Support Groups (Cella et al. 1993; Evans and Connis 1995; Kelly et al. 1993; Roberts et
    al. 1997; Spiegel et al. 1996)
Individual Psychotherapy (Forrester, Kornfeld, and Fleiss 1985; Lin, Lin, and Harris
    1982)
Family Therapy (Gustafsson, Kjellman, and Cederblad 1986)
In-Home Support (Hughes et al. 1991; Stein and Jessop 1984)
Activity Camps (Balen, Fielding, and Lewis 1998)

syndrome, or birth injuries, such as cerebral palsy, where there is no separation be-tween the **past history** and the **present illness**. Most patients have an illness-free part of their lives that antedates the onset of the illness. Dawn, described in the case il-lustration that follows, did not develop her cancer until well into or just past the growth spurt of adolescence. By then she, her parents, her teachers, and her friends had aspirations and expectations of who she was and who she might become as an adult. But it is not only what may have been lost that needs to be explored in the past history, it is also the experiences that may have strengthened or weakened the indi-vidual's adaptive resources. Previous activities, abilities, and achievements as well as vulnerabilities can be very relevant in understanding the client's responses to the illness as well as in identifying existing strengths that can be used to help them cope.

Identity Reconstitution. Reconstituting a new identity that encompasses the reality of the illness and its consequences in the patient's life is a central task for individuals living with a chronic illness (Christ 1999; Corbin and Strauss 1988).This process in-cludes grieving losses of previous abilities, relationships, and opportunities while celebrating remaining strengths and capacities, and developing new coping skills. This is an important process for patients, families, and members of their support network. They may have interacted with the patient in very different ways before the illness. The increasing access to groups of patients with similar illnesses either in person, over the telephone, or over the Internet has helped patients with the process of identity reconstitution. Finally, identity transformation is an ongoing challenge at different stages of development and with different life events.

History of Illness and Loss. Previous family illnesses or losses can also shape illness responses (e.g., level of optimism/pessimism). A patient who has known others in her life who have survived a life-threatening illness may be more likely to feel hopeful that she too will respond positively to treatment. For these reasons, previous devel-opmental, work, and medical histories are essential to a comprehensive assessment.

History of Interaction of the Ecological Systems. Especially with children, a sense of the family microsystem (Bronfenbrenner 1979; Kazak 1989) into which the patient was born, the temperament of the child (Thomas and Chess 1977), the fit with parent(s) and siblings, and the role of the child in the home/ family are some of the types of information that may be more or less important in understanding who this client is now, who she or he has been and how the chronic illness has affected her or his development. Knowledge of the individual's interaction with the school—as a site of learning to relate to adults other than the parents, and to peers other than to siblings—adds to the emerging picture. Most important for chronically ill individuals is their evolving relationship to the health care system and the available network of patients and professionals who can be an important resource for information, effective treatment, and emotional support. Conflict in those relationships or an overly passive approach to coping can signal adaptive problems.

Developmental Task Interference. A developmental perspective is very helpful in pursuing the type of information that is relevant to our understanding of a chronically ill person. At 17, Dawn, described in the following case illustration, was just discovering that she had a special appeal to young men when she was diagnosed with a bone cancer that at that time generally required an amputation. She had already discovered that she was an excellent student, was liked by teachers, and excelled in sports. She was beginning to push the edges of independence and was not yet secure about who she was with peers—boys and girls, white and black. Dawn was close to her mother, but she had only a vague understanding of her father, who spent most of his time with his work. All these streams of development were profoundly affected by the life-threatening illness and then the year of intensive treatment. Independence, rebellious or dignified, was no longer an option. One of the most difficult challenges for chronically ill individuals is the regressive pull—actually a survival reality—of needing to be much more dependent than they have ever been—for toileting, for feeding, for survival. Learning to accept help while retaining autonomy, dignity, and self-esteem is never easy.

Other Areas. Different chronic illnesses may require a greater level of concentration on specific areas, such as, for example, family history (e.g., genetic or familial illnesses such as diabetes), school history (e.g., retardation, learning disability), work history (e.g., accident, toxicity), and marital history and sexual history (e.g., HIV). The patient may also bring up very idiosyncratic factors within a given family that are integral to their management of this particular illness.

A 17-year-old cancer survivor was interviewed ten years after his diagnosis and successful treatment for bone sarcoma. He revealed that the most stressful part of his illness was his father's response of intense criticism of the patient's rehabilitation efforts. His father had had both of his legs amputated below the knee consequent to a war injury. The son's illness that included the threat of possible amputation had reawakened his father's traumatic stress responses and caused him to be quite unrealistic in his expectations of his son's performance. He seemed to be saying "At least you have one whole leg, you should be walking much better." The reality was that the knee replacement surgery for the patient had not gone well due to the size and location of the tumor and he struggled with ongoing painful complications with limited sympathy or support from his father.

Case Formulation. Clinical and supervisory experience in a cancer center, as well as teaching social work students led one of us (GHC) to elaborate a case formulation component to precede and inform treatment planning. The reason for developing this component was to encourage the worker to be very clear about the connections between assessment information and intervention decision making. The case formulation also helps the worker to organize his or her understanding in such a way that as new information becomes available, the part of the formulation altered and the way in which this in turn alters (or does not alter) the treatment approach can be clarified. The hard work this brief formulation requires is well worth the effort. At the very least, it facilitates a rational thinking process and a common source of agreement and/ or disagreement with team members or supervisor, where the disagreements and/or corrections can be based on the interpretation of the assessment data or on the specific intervention planned to deal with identified strengths or vulnerabilities. Basing an intervention on a formulation also improves the ability to develop ways of measuring the efficacy of the intervention.

There are seven headings in the formulation outline, each with one to five subheadings. The formulation outline is shown in table 5.3.

TABLE 5.3 Case Formulation Outline

A. Strengths
    1. Biological strengths
    2. Personal psychological strengths
    3. Attitudinal or attributional strengths
    4. Family strengths
    5. Sociocultural strengths
B. Vulnerabilities
    1. Biological: (neurobiological-genetic)
        a. genetic or familial vulnerability
        b. biological (general/nonspecific) vulnerability including disabilities
    2. Personal psychological vulnerability
    3. Family vulnerability
    4. Sociocultural vulnerability
C. Precipitating Event(s)
D. Diagnosis (*DSM-IV*)
E. Formulation Summary
F. Intervention Approach
    1. Central problem(s)
    2. Contract mutually agreed to between client and worker
    3. Basic approach and time frame for intervention
G. Goals and Evaluation Plan
    1. Short term
        a. address the effect of safety, salience, and cooperation of client on intervention selection
        b. address the effect of time and finances on intervention selection
        c. address the effect of individual characteristics on interventions

Strengths and Vulnerabilities. The listing of the strengths and vulnerabilities under different headings clarifies which domains might be the primary or only source of a given strength or vulnerability. It also encourages specificity: for example, a patient with a diagnosis of schizophrenia would probably have vulnerabilities in all four domains, yet separating them this way encourages the clinician to identify how each might play a different role in the client's illness and each might require a somewhat different approach.

An 11-year-old boy with a school behavior problem related to a moderately severe learning disability might have the following set of vulnerabilities and strengths: a biological familial vulnerability (both his father and older brother have or had a similar disorder), a personal psychological vulnerability (he was always a temperamentally difficult child, has a chip on his shoulder, and was considered a bully until one year ago, possibly related to his feelings of insecurity because of his chronic school failure and his father's handling of this), and a family vulnerability (his father is very punitive about his learning problem, and treats him as he was treated by his own father—with frequent threats, scolding, and occasional beatings). The strengths include biological strengths—that he is an excellent athlete and unusually well coordinated, an unusual strength in a learning disabled child—and both personal psychological and sociocultural strengths—that he quickly gave up being a bully when he transferred to the new school where he began to succeed and then excel in sports. There are no sociocultural vulnerabilities in this family. It is a middle-class family with adequate financial resources, and the school to which the boy transferred has a good attitude about youngsters with learning disabilities. The school provides good supports, counseling, and remedial help and seeks to find attributes in each child that will compensate for the low self-esteem commonly seen in children with learning disabilities.

Precipitating Event. The precipitating event is singled out in the formulation to distinguish which reactions might be related to an acute traumatic experience. For example, depression following the death of a spouse or parent could be a normal component of mourning or it could be a complicated grief response related to the nature of the death (Pynoos 1992) or to earlier life experiences (Christ 1999). Similarly, initial depression following the diagnosis of cancer and its early treatment would be an expected response, while the onset of an immobilizing suicidal depression with a family history of bipolar illness might point to the possible onset of a mental illness as well. In addition, for many multiply stressed families living in inner-city neighborhoods, the onset of a depressive symptom might be precipitated by "the last straw" stress response, being a precipitant because it is the last in a series of stressful events and conditions. Finally, it is necessary to assess the importance of the precipitating event because the individual may be unaware of its importance and therefore unable to mobilize effective coping approaches. For example, a change of a caregiver may precipitate a crisis for a chronically ill person, one that he or she finds difficult to recognize. The assessment might require a much more careful review of recent life events to place in context the importance of the precipitating event.

DSM-IV. Probably the least relevant to the formulation of chronic physical illness is the *DSM-IV* diagnosis. It helps to remember that the DSM nomenclature is atheoretical and nonetiologic and is actually geared to improve agreement about diagnoses. However, major clinical depression and anxiety are more prevalent among individuals with chronic illnesses. Indeed, major medical illness is a risk factor for suicide. Further, individuals with severe mental illnesses are more likely to have chronic physical illnesses as well. Therefore, it is an important dimension to evaluate.

Formulation Summary. Perhaps the most daunting challenge for the clinician is writing the formulation summary statement. The temptation is to write a case summary, but what is needed is a true summary of the clinician's current thinking and understanding of the case, including the role of strengths, vulnerabilities, and mediators and moderators. The summary draws on factual material provided by other professionals as well and incorporates existing literature and theoretical approaches that suggest ways in which experiences interact with the individuals in their ecological setting. In addition to clarifying the clinician's thinking about the client, the formulation provides information for others who might also have contact with the client, helping them to understand the reasoning of the clinician who wrote the summary. Especially in situations of chronic disability, the likelihood that other professionals will be involved in the care of the client is very great. The formulation summary conveys the thinking and reasoning of the previous clinician.

The **intervention planning** is listed next to underscore the importance of using the information generated in the assessment, and integrated in the case formulation, to develop a relevant intervention and evaluation plan. The intervention is also informed by practice knowledge of the adaptive tasks required by individuals and families coping with chronic illnesses and by empirical evidence of the effectiveness of a range of interventions. For example, Dawn (see the following case illustration) had already successfully negotiated the diagnosis and initial treatment stages of her illness. At the point of current social work involvement, she was considered a cancer survivor. However, she had recently experienced neurological symptoms that she feared were either long-term side effects of her cancer treatment or a recurrence of the cancer. Although tests confirmed that her cancer had not recurred, Dawn was forced to face some of the adaptive tasks associated with the exacerbation stage of an illness during the lengthy workup for her symptoms. She was coping with the emergence of new symptoms, integrating new medical information, managing threats to her newly found sense of self, and balancing hope and fear in light of the possibility of a recurrence or other condition that might result in a poorer prognosis.

The stages identified in table 5.3 were originally based on a cancer diagnosis, but they have relevance to other chronic illnesses. There is no magic in the number of stages; each illness may have more or less. The stages also may overlap in relation to the demands they make on the individual. However, they do describe the type of tasks confronting most individuals who are at a given point in their illness trajectory, and the social work role and clinically recommended interventions to help patients adapt. The table also identifies the empirically supported interventions that have shown some ability to help patients with task completion. While the interventions were generally evaluated in a research environment that cannot be fully replicated in a clinical setting, they reflect basic principles of adaptation and coping that can be integrated into a variety of intervention models. Most research interventions have focused on the period of diagnosis and treatment initiation.

ILLUSTRATION AND DISCUSSION

This case concerns Dawn, a 24-year-old African American woman who was diagnosed at age 17 with osteosarcoma, a bone cancer that affected her left femur just above the knee. Dawn was treated at a major cancer center with bone replacement surgery, essentially the substitution of metal for the affected bone, and chemotherapy. As a consequence she did not require surgery to amputate her leg thus preserving greater body integrity. This surgery has since become an option for 80 percent of patients with this diagnosis and when offered as an alternative to amputation, almost all patients elect this procedure. Dawn was eligible for this "limb salvage" procedure because of the location, size, and other characteristics of the tumor. By the time she was diagnosed, the introduction of high-dose chemotherapies had resulted in dramatically improved survival rates and osteosarcoma was considered a curable disease. Still, approximately 30 percent of adolescents diagnosed with this disease experienced recurrence and deaths. In addition the long-term effects of the surgery and chemotherapy treatments were just beginning to be clarified. At the time of the social work interview from which this history was obtained, Dawn was returning to her surgeon's office for a follow-up visit because she was pregnant. She had questions about the effect of her compromised leg on the birth process as well as questions about the possible effect of the chemotherapy she had taken on the health of her unborn child.

The social worker was asked to evaluate Dawn's adaptation to her illness. This type of assessment was a routine component of follow-up visits for patients who had been treated for cancer and were indicating significant problems around their illness adaptation. Dawn reported that in addition to her pregnancy, she had gone through a period of having neurological symptoms. These symptoms had subsequently disappeared, but she reported that tests showed there had been a brain hemorrhage of unknown etiology. Dawn was relieved when the symptoms stopped. However, her physicians worried the symptoms might also reflect psychological stress or that psychological stress had contributed to her biological condition.

Dawn was a very intelligent, articulate young woman who presented as emotionally intense but confident and in control of her situation. In spite of her compromised leg, her walk was balanced so that her limp was not immediately apparent. Such a smooth gait can only be accomplished with considerable attention to rehabilitation. However, her pressured speech, emotional intensity, and adamant optimism suggested to the interviewer that Dawn was also worried about what was happening to her body. What she presented was her concern about her pregnancy, how her compromised leg might affect her delivery, and how her leg might affect her ability to manage a small child. She was also concerned about conflict with her family over her withdrawal from law school.

Despite the fact that Dawn is considered a cancer survivor, there were really three conditions that needed to be explored with her: (1) her pregnancy, (2) her neurological symptoms, and (3) her history of cancer and her reconstructed leg.

1. Pregnancy. Dawn had been married for two years to a man her parents thought was ideal for her. He was in business and very supportive of her taking time away from her law school studies. They had not planned to have a baby at that time, but both were pleased. In fact Dawn had wondered if she would be able to conceive due to the chemotherapy treatments and she was relieved to know that she could have children. She was only worried about the delivery process, the health of the baby, and her ability to take care of her child with her fragile leg. She and her husband had adequate resources to care for the child. Dawn also was very involved with a local church that she valued highly. Her relationships with people in the church were a source of great support and encouragement. What was unclear was how much these individuals would be able to help her with her child care responsibilities.

2. Neurological Symptoms. The strokelike symptoms she had one year ago, before her pregnancy, were very frightening to Dawn and were also a source of ongoing conflict with her parents. They thought she may be malingering or using these symptoms as an excuse not to return to law school. Dawn went through many frightening tests and was relieved when the doctors said they thought they saw evidence of some bleeding into the brain that was now healing. She felt vindicated and pleased when the symptoms disappeared. During this period of heightened uncertainty and threat, Dawn had brief treatment for her anxiety and depression with a local psychiatrist who prescribed medication, which she had stopped taking when she discovered she was pregnant. She wanted to discuss this with her physician.

3. Bone Cancer. Both the neurological symptoms and her pregnancy reawakened Dawn's memories and feelings about her cancer diagnosis and treatment at the age of 17. She was an intelligent and inquisitive patient. Prior to her illness she had been studying science in high school and planning to attend medical school. She knew her treatment might have late effects. At the time of the interview, seven years after the illness, Dawn felt positively about her cancer experience. She saw herself as fortunate to be able to have had the limb salvage, to have rehabilitated so well, and to have had so much attention and support from friends and family. She was a survivor. But she was also aware that the late effects of the disease and treatment were unknown and for this reason the neurological symptoms had been especially distressing. Several of her acquaintances had had a recurrence and had died. That was the "Sword of Damocles" she knew was hanging over her (Koocher 1986). She wondered if her luck had finally run out. Because of her fear of an exacerbation of her disease, recurrence, or late effect of treatment, she said the neurological symptoms seemed even worse than the cancer experience. In addition, Dawn's family had provided much support for her during her cancer illness. She quickly returned to school after treatment and her development proceeded with little interruption. Her parents encouraged her to keep succeeding and moving ahead.

Dawn's parents had raised her father's four children before she was born. The youngest was six years older than Dawn. Dawn and her 21-year-old sister were the only children of her father and mother's marriage. Her father was a highly successful lawyer and businessman and he had high hopes that Dawn would follow in his footsteps. She was very bright, outgoing and popular with people, and an excellent student. The family had lived in the east during her grade school experience where she attended a mostly white sub-urban public school. When they moved to the west, she was for the first time attending a school that was being integrated and at the time was mostly black. She felt rejected and devalued by the students' lack of immediate acceptance even though her mother told her the students were jealous of her compe-tence. Dawn said, "In fifth grade, you don't want to hear that students are jealous of you, you just want them to like you." But gradually she became popular, was in the Honor Society, was elected to many student offices, and just before her diagnosis, was the first African American student to be elected to the homecoming court. The outpouring of concern and good wishes she received from the school, friends, and the local community was a major source of encouragement and support to her during her psychologically ar-duous cancer treatment, helping her to overcome underlying fears of her peers' rejection and devaluation.

Dawn's family had dealt with disability before her cancer; her younger sister had a fairly severe scoliosis and had to spend several years in a brace. Subsequently she had a short stature, and even after the surgeries her mal-formation was somewhat visible. Since this condition is not life-threatening and was diagnosed as a birth defect, with surgeries taking place over several years, there was much less "fanfare" than with Dawn's much more dramatic survival of cancer treatment. Her sister was jealous of Dawn's successes and the attention she received regarding her cancer, and Dawn worked hard to help her sister feel better about herself.

> She is a success story herself, but she won't see that. Her condition was so severe that they did two surgeries when she was 13 or 14 years old. When I came home from the hospital, she had her second surgery the next month. While I was having all the attention from friends and the community, she was in bed in a body cast.

These experiences strained their relationship.

The family was also strained by the demands of illness and disability in both children. However, Dawn was pleased that she had become much closer to her father during her illness. Because of his work, they had spent little time together prior to her cancer treatment. Afterward she traveled to the treatment center with him when she went for her chemotherapy. He had been able to rearrange his work to spend more time in a corporate office close to the hospital. As a consequence, she became more interested in law, and he believed she would become a success in his chosen field. But after one year in law school, Dawn realized the content of this profession was not one that interested her. She felt unhappy and confused and therefore dropped out with an agreement that she could reenter within the next couple of years. Dawn said she felt that she just needed to "sit still" for a year while she thought about herself and what she really wanted to do with her life. It was this decision that created serious conflict between Dawn and her parents.

Dawn's parents believed she was giving up after all their efforts to sup-port her. They became angry and told her how disappointed they were. They could not accept what they believed was a defeat.

I told them I was taking a "leave of absence," but they heard "quit." I have always been the one child that has gone straight through everything. I went from high school, graduated honors, went to college, graduated, and was accepted in law school with a scholarship. I married a guy my father feels he couldn't have picked better himself—he likes to take credit for finding him! So I have done everything right. And then to withdraw from law school . . . it did something to my dad. When I used to visit my father's office he would talk about me to everyone . . . I almost thought I should have a scepter and a crown on my head when I walked in. That got on my nerves, but when he stopped that, it really hurt.

Although Dawn still thought she had made the right decision, she was tremendously stressed by the conflict. Several months later she began to experience her strokelike symptoms: severe headaches and numbness. She wondered if it was related to the stress she was experiencing, but she pursued medical treatment as she believed the symptoms were too severe to be stress reactions. She also worried about the possibility of late effects of her cancer treatment or, worse yet, recurrence of her cancer. All these thoughts went through her mind during the six months of diagnostic testing. Her parents still thought she might be malingering or making an excuse to stay out of law school and the career that was their dream for her.

Once the doctors found a possible physiological basis for her symptoms, Dawn felt vindicated. Her symptoms gradually subsided, but she continued to live with the uncertainty about what had caused them. Dawn began to feel better emotionally but she continued to feel upset about her strained relationship with her parents. She finally confided in the social worker that she felt she was a failure and wondered if her parents were right. Her mother noticed that she did not complete things and that made Dawn wonder if there was something else wrong with her. She felt confused, depressed, and hopeless. Dawn was surprised that her parents were so pleased with her pregnancy; she was afraid they would see this as just another excuse to stay away from law school.

Formulation of Strengths. 1. *Biological.* Dawn was very athletic and physically active before her cancer. She responded well to the chemotherapy. The surgery was successful, and she had rehabilitated with limited residual disability given the severity of the operation. Dawn was intelligent and was reported by her parents to have an easy temperament.

2. *Psychological.* Although Dawn is depressed about her conflict with her parents, she uses her considerable intellectual skill to cope effectively. She is persistent and able to follow through on tasks and goals. She is self-reflective and reaches out for support, both professional and nonprofessional. Although Dawn's tendency to deny her vulnerability caused her stress as a cancer survivor, during the treatment and immediate posttreatment phase it helped her to survive arduous treatments while continuing to meet developmental tasks. It is only with her movement into adulthood and the challenge of establishing intimacy, and defining a stable identity and life

work, that this approach has become less adaptive. Her opposition to her parents and to her own internal compliance with their goals appears to be a strength: a reflection of the emergence of her need for greater self-definition and identity. These strengths support her ability to master the current psychological crisis she confronts.

3. *Sociocultural.* While Dawn confronts the realities of racism in society, her personal gifts and her hard work have won her admiration, affection, and esteem, not only in the African American community, but in the majority culture as well.

4. *Familial.* Dawn's family are highly educated and accomplished and have been able to acquire sufficient resources to support a large family and pay for education and the considerable medical expenses they have incurred. They are valued in their community and can obtain assistance for most problems. They care deeply for Dawn and reach out to her in spite of the current conflict in their relationship. Given their considerable experience with illness they have become quite adept in managing illness crises.

5. *Developmental.* Dawn has excelled academically, interpersonally, and socially. She has the capacity for intimate relationships. She chose a husband who not only is warmly accepted by her family but also is supportive of her needs. Her reflective capacity supports her ability to confront her current delayed identity crisis. She seems ready for and is eager to move into the developmental stage of young parent.

Formulation of Vulnerabilities. 1. *Biological/genetic.* Clearly Dawn has a life-threatening chronic illness. She survived the treatment, rehabilitated well, but confronts the uncertainty of a future recurrence and unknown effects of the aggressive treatment she endured. Dawn is currently limited in the activities she can engage in: she cannot run, ride a bike, or participate in active sports. She has a severe scar on her leg that concerns her. The rate of secondary leg problems is still unknown, but several of her acquaintances from the treatment center have had frequent rehospitalizations related to their reconstructed leg and one has had a secondary amputation. She is currently pregnant and confronts uncertain complications related to her other illnesses. She has had strokelike symptoms of unknown etiology. While osteosarcoma is not known to be a genetic disorder, there are some hypotheses that suggest this possibility. Her sister's birth defect further raises the possibility of familial vulnerability.

2. *Psychological.* Dawn has been treated with both medication and brief therapy for depression, and she currently expresses depressive symptoms such as feelings of being a failure and hopelessness. The family conflict over her withdrawal from law school was a significant stressor and the contribution of this stress reaction to her strokelike symptoms is unknown. She seems to be suffering from a delayed identity crisis that includes identity confusion and fears of independence and separation.

Dawn follows a pattern of survivors of illness who adapt by denying vulnerability, taking on increasingly demanding tasks in order to prove they are worthy to have survived, and denying the limitations imposed by their chronic illness. At times the practical demands of Dawn's illness and her family's expectations threatened to overwhelm even her considerable psychological strengths. She then experiences high levels of anxiety and depression that could threaten her health, and certainly threaten her subjective sense of well-being. Dawn's minimization of her anger in the conflict with her parents and her feelings of dependence on them, probably exaggerated by her illness, is currently contributing to her distress.

3. *Sociocultural.*   Dawn is African American and experienced feelings of rejection when she first entered a racially mixed school having attended an almost all-white elementary school. Her achievements in school were remarkable. However, they were overshadowed by her peers' jealousy and anger toward her. She feels additional pressure to achieve because of her race and fears rejection if she does not. The reality of racial discrimination in our society adds to her fears of stigma and rejection due to the combination of illness and race. It also at times creates distrust of her physicians. For example, she wonders if her first doctor made the incision on the outside of her leg rather than the inside, leaving a highly visible scar, because he had already resigned himself to doing an amputation or because he did not value her appearance needs. The reluctance of traditional health care approaches to consider late effects of cancer treatment, and the need to see illnesses as discrete events with time limits, may also have led physicians to view her neurological symptoms as psychosomatic or stress-related rather than looking for physically rooted causes. Lack of knowledge about, and denial of, the ongoing impact of illness on developmental transitions may have prevented them from exploring in greater depth her psychological adaptation to her illness. No attempt was made to uncover her family conflict or to help her resolve it.

4. *Familial-interpersonal.*   Dawn's family's resources were strained by the major illness and disability of two children. The pileup of stresses was likely considerable and may be affecting their current response to her. Her withdrawal from law school may have been a last straw to them after they had worked so hard to support their children's healthy development within the context of their illnesses and disabilities. The family conflict over Dawn's withdrawal from law school was extremely stressful to all of them. While her parents are resourceful and supportive in many ways, they are also controlling and experiencing their own difficulty with Dawn's normative need for increased independence.

5. *Developmental.*   Due to Dawn's cancer, she became reengaged with her family, especially her father, just as she was beginning to separate and feel comfortable with her independence. This increased dependence on parents at a time when greater independence is normative potentially delayed formation of an independent identity. Her neurological illness and her family conflict further compromised her confidence in her capacity to function independently.

Precipitating Event.   Dawn feared complications of her pregnancy due to her earlier cancer treatment. She experienced depression over the conflict with her family over her withdrawal from law school and together with her neurological symptoms fostered feelings of helplessness and hopelessness.

DSM-IV: Depression.

Formulation Summary.   Dawn is a 24-year-old young adult struggling with a delayed identity crisis, a common late psychological effect of the cancer illness she experienced as an adolescent. She had coped well with her cancer but decided she did not want law as a profession after a year of classes. Her parents' criticism of her withdrawal from law school exacerbated her underlying feelings of inadequacy, of being a failure and not worthy to have survived, and of depression. The subsequent development of neurological symptoms confronted her with all the emotional and practical tasks of the stage of "illness exacerbation." However, because of her family conflict she did not have the parents' support through this process, as they considered her symptoms to be psychosomatic and a further manipulation to avoid law school. Neurological symptoms also increased her fears of physical vulnerability especially in relation to her pregnancy.

Intervention Approach. Brief counseling to normalize delayed identity crisis and to reduce feelings of depression and failure by supporting Dawn's "taking time" to sort out her career direction. With her agreement, arrange a joint meeting with husband and family to educate them about this pattern of delayed identity formation, reduce conflict, and better understand their distress. Normalize feelings of apprehension about her pregnancy in the context of various chronic illnesses, increase control by providing information about her condition, assist with immediate practical needs, and expand existing support network outside of family. Locate group for survivors and/or network information or Internet chat room that will provide ongoing contact with peer survivors.

Longer-Term Goals and Evaluation Plan. Reduce anxiety and depression, normalize "survivor" experiences, reduce family conflict, expand support network to include other survivors and ongoing sources of information, increase feelings of efficacy and control. Improve communication between new network of health care providers with the health care team that treated her cancer.

Follow-Up. Three years later, Dawn had a healthy son. She and her mother had developed a new shared intimacy around the parenting of her son. Her health continued to improve and she had just completed her first year in medical school. Her father was almost reconciled to her career change and believed his new grandson would become an attorney. Her repaired leg was still holding up, but Dawn was reconciled that an amputation may be required in the future. She had occasional headaches, but none as severe as the ones she previously experienced.

CONCLUSION

Dawn's experience with life-threatening illness illustrates the continuous interaction of disease and treatment occurrences with the individual's temperament, personality, and psychological adjustment. It also highlights the fact that the individual is not an island unto herself. Her developmental progression, family relationships, and societal responses exemplify the person/ecological interaction that is so critical in the emerging individual-family adaptation to chronic illness. The social work role is to clarify these processes and to identify key barriers to effective problem solving. Optimal interventions aim to help clients, their families, and the social system find new ways to relate to each other, and to solve problems in order to improve self-esteem, affirm strengths, and promote a sense of well-being. With adequate support, clients and their families are able to grow from their experiences and may, like Dawn, develop remarkably sophisticated and strong coping capacities in the face of extraordinary disease stresses. In the context of such apparent strength, the appearance of developmental delays and transient stress reactions can be unexpected and especially when unrecognized, can lead to depression and low self-esteem. Idiosyncratic factors such as other illness in the family, or racial prejudice, may shape client's and families' responses in unanticipated ways as well. The illness of Dawn's sister and the experience of racial prejudice fueled the family's need for Dawn to quickly achieve expected professional goals. A temporary withdrawal from school and educational pursuits was feared by the family as permanent abandonment of striving. This proved not to be the case.

Social workers in all areas of work are likely to encounter individuals with chronic illnesses who are struggling to maintain an adequate quality of life with their disease. The increasing prevalence of chronic illness in our society and the complexity of associated treatments and disabilities has brought this about. Uninformed and ambivalent societal response, inadequate financial support, and a narrow focus on disease factors is only slowly giving way to a broader understanding of the importance of social, psychological, and ecological dimensions of care. Psychosocial research has identified key areas of biopsychosocial risk for poorer adaptation as well as clarified factors associated with better adaptation for a broad range of diseases. This knowledge has led to the development of a broader range of social work interventions that increase opportunities to meet patients' and their families' diverse needs. Such interventions include a widening array of options such as patient self-help and advocacy, the use of Internet technology for education and peer contact, and more sophisticated and effective case management. Still, because of the complex interaction of disease and treatment factors with developmental, psychological, social, and cultural/environmental factors that emerge episodically over long periods of time, the use of a structured assessment and problem formulation process is recommended. An accurate understanding of the specific problem and its dimensions can lead to an effective, focused intervention as occurred in the case of Dawn.

References

Auslander, W., S. Thompson, D. Dreitzer, and J. Santiago. 1997. "Mother's Satisfaction with Medical Care: Perceptions of Racism, Family Stress, and Medical Outcomes in Children with Diabetes." *Health and Social Work* 22(3):190–99.

Balen, R., D. Fielding, and I. Lewis. 1998. "An Activity Week for Children with Cancer: Who Wants to Go and Why?" *Child Care, Health and Development* 24(2):169–77.

Bandura, A. 1986. "Fearful Expectations and Avoidant Actions As Co-effects of Perceived Self-Inefficacy." *American Psychologist* 41(12):1389–91.

Berkman, B. 1996. "The Emerging Health Care World: Implications for Social Work Practice and Education." *Social Work* 41(5):541–51.

Black, R. and J. Weiss. 1991. "Chronic Physical Illness and Disability." In A. Gitterman, ed., *Handbook of Social Work Practice with Vulnerable Populations*, pp. 137–64. New York: Columbia University Press.

Bloom, J. 1982. "Social Support, Accommodation to Stress and Adjustment to Breast Cancer." *Social Science and Medicine* 16:1328–38.

Bronfenbrenner, U. 1979. *The Ecology of Human Development: Experiments by Nature and Design.* Cambridge, Mass.: Harvard University Press.

Brown, H. and M. Tai-Seale. 1992. "Vocational Rehabilitation of Cancer Patients." *Seminars in Oncology Nursing* 8(3):202–11.

Brown, S., ed. 1988. *Prenatal Care, Reaching Mothers, Reaching Infants.* Washington, D.C.: National Academy Press.

Carey, M. and R. Burish. 1987. "Providing Relaxation Training to Cancer Patients: A Comparison of Three Delivery Techniques." *Journal of Consulting and Clinical Psychology* 55(5):732–37.

Cassileth, M. 1999. *Alternative and Complementary Cancer Therapies.* New York: W. W. Norton.

Cella, D., B. Sarafin, P. Snider, S. Yellin, and P. Winicor. 1993. "Evaluation of a Community-Based Cancer Support Group." *Psycho-oncology* 2:123–32.

Christ, G. 1982. "Dis-synchrony of Coping Among Children with Cancer, Their Families, and the Treatment of Childhood Cancer." In A. Christ and K. Flomenhaft, eds., *Psychosocial Family Interventions in Chronic Pediatric Illness*, pp. 85–96. New York: Plenum.

——. 1987. "Social Consequences of the Cancer Experience." *American Journal of Pediatric Hematology/Oncology* 9:84–88.

——. 1991. "Principles of Oncology Social Work." In A. Holieb, D. Fink, and G. Murphy, eds., *American Cancer Society Textbook of Clinical Oncology*, pp. 594–605. Atlanta, Ga.: American Cancer Society.

——. 1999. *The Legacy: Children Surviving the Death of a Parent from Cancer.* New York: Oxford University Press.

Christ, G., J. Lane, and R. Marcove. 1995. "Psychosocial Adaptation of Long-Term Survivors of Bone Sarcoma." *Journal of Psychosocial Oncology* 13(4):1–22.

Collins, J. 1993. *Prevalence of Selected Chronic Conditions, U.S. 1986–1988* (Vital Health Statistics 10 (182)): National Center for Health Statistics, 87 pp. (PHS) 93-1510. PC93 16 18 18. PC A05 MF A01.

Corbin, J. and A. Strauss. 1988. *Unending Work and Care: Managing Chronic Illness at Home.* San Francisco: Jossey-Bass.

Davis, H. 1986. "Effects of Biofeedback and Cognitive Therapy on Stress in Patients with Breast Cancer." *Psychological Reports* 59:967–74.

Davis, K. 1996. "Primary Health Care and Severe Mental Illness: The Need for National and State Policy." *Health and Social Work* 21(2):83–87.

DeVita, V., S. Hellman, and S. Rosenberg, eds. 1993. *Cancer: Principles and Practice of Oncology*, 4th ed. Philadelphia: J. B. Lippincott.

Dhooper, S. 1997. *Social Work in Health Care in the 21st Century.* Thousand Oaks, Calif.: Sage.

Dimond, M. 1984. "Identifying the Needs of the Chronically Ill." In S. Milligan, ed., *Community Health Care for Chronic Physical Illness: Issues and Models*, pp. 1–14. Cleveland: Case Western Reserve University.

Egan, M. and G. Kadushin. 1999. "The Social Worker in the Emerging Field of Home Care: Professional Activities and Ethical Concerns." *Health Care and Social Work* 24(1): 44–55.

Ell, K., G. Mantell, M. Hamovitch, and R. Niskomate. 1989. "Social Support, Sense of Control and Coping Among Patients with Breast, Lung and Colo-rectal Cancer." *Journal of Psychosocial Oncology* 7(3):63–89.

Evans, R. and R. Connis. 1995. "Comparison of Brief Group Therapies for Depressed Cancer Patients Receiving Radiation Treatment." *Public Health Reports* 110(3):306–11.

Ewart, C., C. Taylor, H. Kraemer, and W. Agras. 1984. "Reducing Blood Pressure Reactivity During Interpersonal Conflict: Effect of Marital Communication Training. *Behavior Therapy* 15(5):473–84.

Forrester, B., D. Kornfeld, and D. Fleiss. 1985. "Psychotherapy During Radiotherapy: Effects on Emotional and Physical Distress." *American Journal of Psychiatry* 142:22–27.

Fox, D. 1986. "AIDS and the American Health Policy: A History and Prospects of a Crisis of Authority." *Millbank Quarterly* 64 (Supplement I):7–33.

Francoeur, R., C. Copley, and P. Miller. 1997. "The Challenge to Meet the Mental Health and Biopsychosocial Needs of the Poor: Expanded Roles for Hospital Social Workers in a Changing Healthcare Environment." *Social Work in Health Care* 26(2):1–13.

Galinsky, M., J. Schopler, and M. Abell. 1997. "Connecting Group Members Through Telephone and Computer Groups." *Health and Social Work* 22(3):181–88.

Germain, C. and A. Gitterman. 1996. *The Life Model of Social Work Practice: Advances in Theory and Practice,* 2nd ed. New York: Columbia University Press.

Gonzales, S., P. Steinglass, and D. Reiss. 1989. "Putting the Illness in Its Place: Discussion Groups for Families with Chronic Medical Illness." *Family Process* 28:69–87.

Gustafsson, P., N. Kjellman, and M. Cederblad. 1986. "Family Therapy in the Treatment of Childhood Asthma." *Journal of Psychosomatic Research* 30:369–73.

Hobbs, N., J. Perrin, and H. Ireys. 1985. *Chronically Ill Children and Their Families.* San Francisco: Jossey-Bass.

Hockenberry, J. 1995. *Moving Violations: War Zones, Wheelchairs, and Declarations of Independence.* New York: Hyperion.

Hoffman, C. and D. Rice. 1996. "Persons with Chronic Conditions: Their Prevalence and Costs." *Journal of the American Medical Association* 276(18):1473–79.

Hughes, D., M. McLeod, B. Garner, and R. Goldgloom. 1991. "Controlled Trial of a Home and Ambulatory Program for Asthmatic Children." *Pediatrics* 87(1):54–61.

Kazak, A. 1989. "Families of Chronically Ill Children: A Systems and Social-Ecological Model of Adaptation and Challenge." *Journal of Consulting and Clinical Psychology* 57(1):25–30.

Keigher, S. 1997. "What Role for Social Work in the New Health Care Practice Paradigm? National Health Line." *Health and Social Work* 22:149–56.

Kelly, J., D. Murphy, R. Bahr, S. Kalicman, B. Morgan, Y. Stevenson, J. Koab, T. Brasfield, and B. Bernstein. 1993. "Outcome of Cognitive-Behavioral and Support Group Brief Therapies for Depressed, HIV-Infected Persons." *American Journal of Psychiatry* 150:1679–82.

Kerson, T. 1985. *Understanding Chronic Illness.* New York: Free Press.

Kinzel, T. 1993. "Key Psychosocial Aspects in the Medical Management of Chronic Illness." In J. Toner, L. Tepper, and B. Greenfield, eds., *Long Term Care: Management, Scope and Practical Issues,* pp. 123–29. Philadelphia: Charles Press.

Kliewer, W. 1997. "Children's Coping with Chronic Illness." In S. Wolchik and I. Sandler, eds., *Handbook of Children's Coping: Linking Theory and Intervention,* pp. 275–300. New York: Plenum.

Koocher, G. 1986. "Psychosocial Issues During the Acute Treatment of Pediatric Cancer." *Cancer* 58:468–72.

Kriegsman, D., B. Penninx, and J. van Eyk. 1995. "A Criterion-Based Literature Survey of the Relationship Between Family Support and Incidence and Course of Chronic Illness in the Elderly." *Family Systems Medicine* 13:39–68.

Lapham, E. 1986. "Chronic Illness: Overview and Theory." In E. Lapham and K. Shevlin, eds., *The Impact of Chronic Illness on Psychosocial Stages of Human Development,* pp. 91–104. Washington, D.C.: National Center for Education in Maternal and Child Health.

Liberman, R. 1988. "Psychosocial Management for Schizophrenia: Overcoming Disability and Handicap." *The Harvard Medical School Mental Health Letter* 5(5):4–6.

Lin, M., B. Lin, and R. Harris. 1982. "Effects of Counseling for Late-Stage Cancer Patients." *Cancer* 49:1048–55.

Mailick, M. 1979. "The Impact of Severe Illness on the Individual and Family: An Overview." *Social Work in Health Care* 5(2):117–28.

Mancoske, R., C. Wadsworth, D. Dugas, and J. Hasney. 1995. "Suicide Risk Among People Living with AIDS." *Social Work* 40(6):783–87.

Manton, K., C. Patrick, and K. Johnson. 1987. "Health Differentials Between Blacks and Whites: Recent Trends in Mortality and Morbidity." *Millbank Quarterly* 65 (Supplement 1):129–99.

McCubbin, H. and J. Patterson. 1987. "Adolescent Coping Style and Measurement." *Journal of Adolescence* 10(2):163–86.

McCubbin, H., E. Thompson, A. Thompson, and G. Fromer, eds. 1998. *Stress, Coping and Health in Families: Sense of Coherence and Resilience.* Thousand Oaks, Calif.: Sage.

McReynolds, C. 1998. "Human Immunodeficiency Virus (HIV) Disease: Shifting Focus Toward the Chronic, Long-Term Illness Paradigm for Rehabilitation Practitioners." *Journal of Vocational Rehabilitation* 10:231–40.

Meyer, C. 1976. *Social Work Practice: The Changing Landscape,* 2nd ed. New York: Free Press.

——, ed. 1983. *Clinical Social Work in the Eco-Systems Perspective.* New York: Columbia University Press.

Miller, G. 1983. *Coping with Chronic Illness: Overcoming Powerlessness.* Philadelphia: F. A. Davis.

Montoya, M. 1993. "Maintaining Your Insurance." *LifeTIMES: A Wellness Service of Statlanders Pharmacy* 8(3):25.

Mudrick, N. 1988. "Disabled Women and Public Policies for Income Support." In M. Fine and A. Ash, eds., *Women with Disabilities: Essays in Psychology, Culture, and Politics,* pp. 245–68. Philadelphia: Temple University.

Nezu, A., C. Nezu, S. Friedman, S. Faddis, and P. Houts. 1994. *Helping Patients Cope: A Problem-Solving Approach.* Washington, D.C.: American Psychological Association.

——. 1998. *Helping Cancer Patients Cope: A Problem-Solving Approach.* Washington, D.C.: American Psychological Association.

Nezu, A., C. Nezu, P. Houts, S. Friedman, and S. Faddis. 1999. "Relevance of Problem-Solving Therapy to Psychosocial Oncology." *Journal of Psychosocial Oncology* 16: 5–26.

Northouse, L. 1995. "The Impact of Cancer in Women on the Family." *Cancer Practice* 3(3):134–42.

Penninx, B., T. Tilburg, J. Boeke, D. Deeg, D. Kriegsman, and J. Eijk. 1998. "Effects of Social Support and Personal Coping Resources on Depressive Symptoms: Different for Various Chronic Diseases?" *Health Psychology* 17(6):551–58.

Pless, I., N. Feeley, L. Gottlieb, K. Rowat, G. Dougherty, and B. Willard. 1994. "A Randomized Trial of a Nursing Intervention to Promote Adjustment of Children with Chronic Physical Disorders. *Pediatrics* 74:70–75.

Pollin, L. 1994. *Taking Charge: Overcoming the Challenge of Long-Term Illness.* New York: Random House.

Pynoos, R. 1992. "Grief and Trauma in Children and Adolescents." *Bereavement Care* 11: 2–10.

Roberts, C., L. Piper, R. Denny, and G. Cuddeback. 1997. "A Support Group Intervention to Facilitate Young Adults' Adjustment to Cancer." *Health and Social Work* 22(2): 133–41.

Roberts-DeGennaro, M. 1987. "Developing Case Management As a Practice Model." *Social Casework* 68(8):466–70.

Rolland, J. 1994. *Families, Illness and Disability.* New York: Basic Books.

Russell, M. 1988. "Clinical Social Work." In J. Goodgold, ed., *Rehabilitation Medicine,* pp. 942–50. St. Louis: C. V. Mosby.

Schiaffino, K. and T. Revenson. 1995. "Why Me? The Persistence of Negative Appraisals Over the Course of Illness." *Journal of Applied Social Psychology* 25(7):601–18.

Sidell, N. 1997. "Adult Adjustment to Chronic Illness: A Review of the Literature." *Health and Social Work* 22(1):5–11.

Siegel, K. and G. Christ. 1990. "Hodgkin's Disease Survivorship: Psychosocial Consequences." In M. Lacker and J. Redman, eds., *Hodgkin's Disease: The Consequences of Survival,* pp. 383–99. Philadelphia: Lea & Febiger.

Spiegel, D., G. Morrow, C. Classen, G. Riggs, P. Stott, N. Mudaliar, H. Pierce, P. Flynn, and L. Heard. 1996. "Effects of Group Therapy on Women with Primary Breast Cancer." *Breast Journal* 2:104–6.

Starfield, B. 1982. "Family Income, Ill Health, and Medical Care of U.S. Children." *Journal of Public Health Policy* 3:244–59.

State Health Coordinating Council (SHCC). 1992. *Alabama Health Plan* (Statutory Authority: 2-21-260 [4]), Code of Alabama.

Stein, R. and D. Jessop. 1984. "Does Pediatric Home Care Make a Difference for Children with Chronic Illness? Findings from the Pediatric Ambulatory Home Care Study." *Pediatrics* 73:845–53.

Stein, R., L. Westbrook, and E. Silver. 1998. "Comparison of Adjustment of School-Age Children with and without Chronic Conditions: Results from Community-Based Samples." *Journal of Developmental and Behavioral Pediatrics* 19(4):267–72.

Strauss, A. and B. Glaser. 1975. *Chronic Illness and the Quality of Life.* Saint Louis: C. V. Mosby.

Thomas, A. and S. Chess. 1977. *Temperament and Development.* New York: Brunner/Mazel.

Trevino, F. and A. Moss. 1984. "Health Indicators for Hispanic, Black, and White Americans." *Vital Health Statistics* 10(148): National Center for Health Statistics, 88 pp. (PHS) 84-1576. PB87-156976. PC A05 MF A02.

Vandermeer, J. L. 1993. "The Cost of Home-Based Care for Dependent Elders: Who Pays?" *Nursing Economics* 11(6):350–57.

Vandiver, V. and S. Kirk. 1992. "Case Management for Persons with Schizophrenia." In K. Corcoran, ed., *Structuring Change: Effective Practice for Common Client Problems,* pp. 72–94. Chicago: Lyceum Books.

van Dulmen, A., J. Fennis, and G. Bleijenberg. 1996. "Cognitive-Behavioral Group Therapy for Irritable Bowel Syndrome: Effects and Long Term Follow-Up." *Psychosomatic Medicine* 58:508–14.

6

Depression

Jay Callahan
Joanne E. Turnbull

Depression is so common in our society that it is often referred to as the "common cold" of mental illness. Depression is difficult to comprehend, assess, and treat effectively. Because it is so common in our society, social workers encounter depression in their work with clients regardless of their field of practice. Consequently, social workers have to be able to recognize and assess depression.

The impact of depression on society is enormous. At any point in time, 11 million Americans suffer from depression, and the cost in absenteeism and lowered productivity is 24 billion dollars annually. Individuals with depression are more impaired in their social functioning than those suffering from diabetes, hypertension, and arthritis. Altogether, the cost of depression to American society totals over 40 billion dollars per year (Greenberg et al. 1993).

Perhaps the most devastating consequence of depression is suicide. Depression is the single largest condition that predisposes people to suicide. Approximately 50 to 60 percent of the thirty thousand people who die from suicide in the United States annually suffered from depression (Brent et al. 1993a; Conwell et al. 1996; Shaffer et al. 1996), and about 15 percent of individuals with major depression die by suicide (Sainsbury 1986). This is a particularly important area for social workers—it is an arena in which social workers have an opportunity to make interventions with life and death consequences.

DEFINING AND EXPLAINING DEPRESSION

Depression is heterogeneous; there are several types of depression. Depression can be described as simply a mood state, often part of what people refer to as "everyday ups and downs." As such, it is simply a normal human emotion, one that everyone experiences from time to time. People frequently describe this mood state as feeling "blue," "down," "sad," "low," or "down in the dumps." However, depression can also be thought of as a cluster of symptoms, centering on sad feelings but also including a pessimistic attitude and reduced enjoyment in normally pleasurable activities. This cluster of symptoms can often be a part of a mental or emotional disorder other than depression, such as alcoholism or other substance dependence, schizophrenia, or personality disorders. Finally, in its most pure form, depression can be a mental or emotional disorder itself, and as such includes reduced ability to experience pleasure, lessened motivation and energy, and a variety of physical symptoms.

Although the popular notion of depression is limited to mood disturbance, the symptoms of depression can be grouped into four dimensions. In the cognitive dimension are memory difficulties and distorted thinking, including pervasive beliefs of futility, pessimism, hopelessness, and helplessness. In the motivation dimension are feelings of apathy, fatigue, and inactivity. In the mood or affective dimension are sad feelings, as already noted, but depressed people also frequently feel irritable, anxious, angry, and hostile and direct these feelings especially toward those close to them. In the physical (somatic) dimension are increased or decreased appetite and sleep, and psychomotor changes. These psychomotor changes include agitation and restlessness, or slowed (retarded) speech and movements. Occasionally an individual will alternate between these two states.

As described earlier, depression is also the core element of a family of mental or emotional disorders. Since it is so widely used, we will discuss the various depressive disorders using the framework of the fourth edition of American Psychiatric Association's *Diagnostic and Statistical Manual of Mental Disorders* (*DSM-IV*; American Psychiatric Association [APA] 1994). Differentiating between these disorders is relatively straightforward conceptually, although in practice some individuals' clinical pictures are confusing and unclear. The *DSM* system, as most social workers know, is a descriptive one, focusing simply on the symptoms and course of disorders, with no attempt to establish cause. Making a *DSM* diagnosis requires the social worker not only to obtain the client's "story," frequently a narrative account in chronological order, but also to assess symptoms and course over time.

Primary among the mood disorders in *DSM-IV* is **major depressive disorder** (MDD). MDD is generally thought of as the most severe depressive disorder, although it can vary from a brief (two-week) episode of fairly mild symptoms to lengthy episodes (years) with symptoms so extreme that the individual is unable to function at all. The vast majority of cases occur in episodes, although in a small minority of cases the depression becomes chronic and unremitting. About half of individuals with MDD appear to have one episode, and the other half have multiple ones (Badger and Rand 1998). The etiology of MDD is controversial, and partisans of an entirely biological or entirely psychological or entirely social causation can be found. However, the consensus of most experts is that it is biopsychosocial. That is, major depression is caused by a combination of factors, including a biological (genetic) vulnerability, constitutional temperament, early childhood experiences and family functioning, predisposing life events, traumatic stressors, presence or absence of social support, and precipitating life events. Cultural factors also play a role, although a detailed discussion of cross-cultural depression is beyond the scope of this chapter.

Major depression is common. The recent National Comorbidity Survey (NCS), a large-scale epidemiologic survey of mental disorders in the United States, found that 12.7 percent of all adult men and 21.3 percent of all adult women in the United States have or will have experienced at least one episode of major depression in their lifetime. Current rates, defined as the presence of major depression during the past thirty days, was 3.8 percent for men and 5.9 percent for women (Blazer et al. 1994). Major depression is usually precipitated by a psychosocial stressor, but some episodes begin spontaneously. Although previously thought of as a disorder of middle and old age, it has now become evident that major depression can have an onset at any age and frequently begins in adolescence or young adulthood (Sorenson, Rutter, and Aneshensel 1991).

The second disorder of depression listed in *DSM* is **dysthymic disorder** (DD). Dysthymic disorder is a milder but more chronic condition. Previously referred to as "neurotic depression," DD typically has a gradual onset, and frequently people cannot identify exactly when it started. By definition, DD lasts at least two years, and in many cases individuals state that they have been depressed "as long as I can remember." DD is less severe than major depression, and if criteria are met for both during the same period of time, MDD takes precedence. However, it is certainly possible to have both MDD and DD, in a kind of alternating fashion, and this combination is often referred to as "double depression." Double depression essentially consists of chronic mild to moderate depression over the years, with occasional more severe episodes that last a few months. DD by itself never includes psychosis.

Dysthymic disorder is less common than major depression. In the NCS, the lifetime rate for men and women ages 15 to 54 in the United States was 4.8 percent and 8 percent, respectively. The prevalence during the most recent twelve months for this population was 2.1 percent and 3 percent, respectively (Kessler, McGonagle, Zhao, et al. 1994).

A third depressive disorder is **adjustment disorder** with depressed mood. Although not technically a mood disorder, adjustment disorder is important to include, since our focus here is the range of syndromes or disorders that must be considered when a social worker encounters a client who appears to be depressed. The key concept that distinguishes an adjustment disorder is the identification of a specific psychosocial stressor that causes difficulty in coping. Along with this difficulty, clinically significant emotional or behavioral reactions begin relatively soon after the stressor occurs. "Clinically significant" means that the individual's reactions (in this case, depressive symptoms), are "in excess of what would be expected given the nature of the stressor" (APA 1994:623). For example, an individual who was demoted at work, who felt sad, and who began functioning at a lower level could be diagnosed with an adjustment disorder. An adjustment disorder is a diagnosis of last resort and can only be used when nothing else applies. An adjustment disorder can look much like a precipitated episode of major depression but is by definition milder.

Finally, it is important to differentiate **bereavement** from the various subtypes of depression. Bereavement is a normal reaction to the loss of a loved one and includes sad mood, loss of interest in normally pleasurable activities, impairment of functioning, and many of the other features of major depression. In many cases, making a diagnosis of bereavement is straightforward. In other instances, in which atypical features are present (such as a significant loss of self-esteem) or in which the death took place a year or two in the past, diagnosis is more difficult. Later in this chapter a more detailed discussion of differentiating bereavement from major depression is presented.

Mood disorders also include bipolar disorders, which are presented here briefly. Chief among these is **bipolar I disorder,** in which an individual experiences one or more episodes of mania as well as episodes of major depression. Mania can be thought of as roughly the opposite of depression: a state of heightened energy, increased self-esteem, euphoric mood, increased activity, and impulsive action with little regard for the consequences. Individuals may spend thousands of dollars, place numerous phone calls at all hours, and engage in indiscriminate sexual activity. Bipolar I disorder is much more rare than major depression, affecting only about 1.6 percent of the population on a lifetime basis (Kessler, McGonagle, Zhao, et al. 1994).

A related disorder, new to *DSM-IV*, is **bipolar II disorder**. Bipolar II disorder is similar to bipolar I, but the symptoms of the episodes are not as severe and so are termed hypomanic episodes. Many of the same symptoms are present, but to a milder degree, and functioning is not impaired. Finally, cyclothymic disorder is a rare condition consisting of numerous alternating episodes of low and high mood, none of which reach the level of major depression or mania.

Social workers must also keep in mind that depression and other mood alterations may be caused by the direct physiologic effects of medical conditions and substances. For example, several of the many medications used to treat hypertension cause depression. When the medication is discontinued, the symptoms remit. Similarly, hypothyroidism produces a syndrome that includes low mood, decreased energy, increased sleep, and many of the other symptoms of depression. Evaluation by a physician is an important aspect of all thorough assessments of mood disorders.

A word about terminology is in order. The term "clinical depression" is frequently used as a shorthand phrase, referring to major depression, bipolar depression, and/or dysthymic disorder. Clinical depression is not a technically defined term; it simply means serious enough to warrant professional help. Accordingly, social workers may encounter a variety of different definitions in practice. Similarly, "affective disorder" is an older term that is essentially synonymous with "mood disorder."

DEMOGRAPHIC PATTERNS

When general epidemiologic data such as the preceding is broken down, we find that depression affects various groups differently. In the United States, women have significantly high rates than men, and European Americans have higher rates than African Americans, and Hispanic Americans. The NCS assessed lifetime rates of major depression (and other disorders) in U.S. citizens aged 15 to 54 (Blazer et al. 1994). The rates of major depression among these groups were as follows:

	Males (%)	Females (%)	Total (%)
White	13.5	22.3	17.9
Black	7.2	15.5	11.9
Hispanic	11.7	23.9	17.7
All	12.7	21.3	17.1

One of the most frequent epidemiologic findings, both in the United States and in other countries, is the elevated frequency of depression among women as compared with men (Kessler et al. 1993; Newmann 1987; Spaner, Bland, and Newman 1994). Numerous hypotheses have been generated to explain this difference, including biology, differential exposure to stress, differential vulnerability to stress, role conflict, and role overload. Moreover, because of socialization factors, women are thought to be more willing to self-report emotional difficulties than men, and men may forget more. Men may also deny or hide their feelings not only from others but also from themselves.

Previous epidemiologic studies have found varying rates of depression among the U.S. population. The Epidemiologic Catchment Area (ECA) project (Regier et al. 1984), conducted in the early 1980s, found rates of depression that were considerably lower than in the NCS. For example, the ECA found the lifetime rate of depression among women in the United States to be about 7.2 percent (Robins et al. 1984), as opposed to the 21.3 percent found in the NCS. For men, the corresponding rates were 3 percent in the ECA (Robins et al. 1984) and 12.7 percent in the NCS. This large discrepancy between the two most sophisticated and scientifically complex epidemiologic studies ever conducted in the United States highlights the methodological difficulties in accurately measuring true rates of lifetime depression in the community (see also Bromet et al. 1986).

As noted in the preceding, NCS lifetime rates of major depression varied by race and ethnicity. African Americans had significantly lower rates than European Americans or Hispanic Americans. In the NCS, the lifetime rate of major depression among African American men was 7.2 percent, as compared with 13.5 percent for white men. Similarly, the lifetime rate among African American women was 15.5 percent, as compared with 22.3 percent for white women (Blazer et al. 1994). The rates of major depression among Hispanic Americans were similar to European American rates; rates among Hispanic men were a bit lower than European American men and Hispanic women's rates were a bit higher than European American women's rates (Blazer et al. 1994). Possible reasons for these dissimilarities will be discussed later, in the sections on risk factors and protective factors.

The rates of depression among the elderly are also somewhat unclear. Varying methods of measurement account for some of the differences. Generally, the finding of high rates of depression among the elderly is based on self-report distress scales (Husaini 1997). Studies that have used diagnostic interviews, by contrast, have found lower rates of depression among those 65 and older than among younger respondents (Newman and Bland 1998; Robins et al. 1984; Weissman and Myers 1978). Moreover, assessment of depression among the elderly is complicated by the more frequent presence of medical illnesses with symptoms that mimic or resemble that of depression, as well as medication that may cause mood changes and associated symptoms (Baker 1996).

The epidemiologic statistics reviewed here generally lump all manner of major depression together. That is, individuals with one lifetime episode, those with numerous lifetime episodes, and those with chronic depression all count the same. Similarly, mild cases of major depression, in which the individual has the fewest number of symptoms that meet the criteria (five) for the shortest length of time (two weeks), and the most severe cases, in which individuals are so seriously impaired they cannot function, or are psychotic, all count the same. But one must remember that these cases are not the same. More severe symptoms, more frequent episodes, longer chronicity, and the comorbid presence of other disorders (such as anxiety or substance dependence) clearly increase the suffering and impair the functioning of the individuals afflicted, and in treating people individually, social workers must remember the social work value of helping those most in need. In the case of depression, the most severely affected are clearly in great need.

Another important concept in understanding depression and mood disorders is comorbidity. Comorbidity is the concurrent existence of two or more mental disorders at the same time. The presence of other comorbid disorders complicates the diagnosis and treatment of depression significantly, and it is important to realize that the vast majority of individuals with major depression have other disorders as well. In the NCS, 61 percent of the respondents with major depression had some other *DSM* disorder prior to the depression. Anxiety disorders, especially generalized anxiety disorder, were the most common comorbid conditions. Posttraumatic stress disorder and substance abuse disorders were also frequent (Kessler et al. 1996). Similar high rates of comorbidity were found for dysthymic disorder in the ECA (Weissman et al. 1988). Of course, the coexistence of major depression and dysthymic disorder constitutes a special case of comorbidity—"double depression." In one study, over a third of the respondents with recurrent major depression also had dysthymic disorder (Spaner et al. 1994).

SOCIETAL CONTEXT

As is the case with many other phenomena in our society, groups that are oppressed or marginalized are at greater risk for depression than others. Although most studies suggest that racial or ethnic minority status per se does not increase one's risk for depression, several factors that are more often found in minority groups do increase the risk. Poverty or low economic level increases risk for depression (Moscicki et al. 1989; Narrow et al. 1990), as does racism (Kessler and Neighbors 1986), unemployment, and homelessness (Schwartz and Schwartz 1993).

Epidemiologic studies have provided compelling evidence that the rates of depression have been increasing with each new birth cohort, at least since World War II (Cross-National Collaborative Group 1992; Kessler, McGonagle, Zhao, et al. 1994; Lewinsohn et al. 1993). That is, individuals born during the 1950s have higher lifetime rates of major depression than those born during the 1940s. Similarly, those born in the 1960s have higher rates than those born in the 1950s, and so forth. This increase appears to be continuing through the 1990s. Better methods of identifying depression may account for some of the increase, but they do not explain it entirely. Social factors such as changes in family structure, higher divorce rates, and increased family mobility with a concomitant loss of the extended-family system may be contributing factors. These indicators often represent disrupted attachments and deficient social supports. Earlier onset may be fueled by increased social and competitive pressures, and by earlier exposure to alcohol and drugs among young people. Thus, stresses inherent in contemporary society seem to be related to depression and have turned theoretical and empirical attention to the social factors that may influence depression.

Social support may protect one against the onset of depression and may be associated with a good outcome. Alternatively, lack of social support or negative social interactions may make one vulnerable to depression. Social support can be broken down in a variety of ways. One conceptualization describes two primary types: instrumental and expressive. *Instrumental support* is practical help with the tasks of daily living. *Expressive support* is characterized by access to and use of intimate, confiding relationships. In summary, companionship, emotional support, guidance and advice, and material aid and services, as well as a sense of belonging and social role expectations, are all components of the construct of social support (Billings and Moos 1986; Coyne and Downey 1991).

However, the nature of our understanding of the relationship between social support and depression has undergone a transition in recent years. Earlier theories posited a linear cause/effect explanation, which saw depression in part as a result of lack of support. It has become clear recently that a more complex relationship, one that is reciprocal and circular in causation, is more accurate (Coyne and Downey 1991; Keitner and Miller 1990; Kendler 1997; Shrout et al. 1989; Turner, Wheaton, and Lloyd 1995). That is, lack of social support leads to vulnerability to depression, but depression also leads to a lack of social support. Disentangling the social causes of depression from the social consequences of depression is a daunting task.

Similarly, stressful life events are part of the etiology of most instances of depression. However, in life events research, it has been extremely difficult to sort out which events are independent of the behavior of the individual, as opposed to those which are possibly dependent, i.e., likely to have been caused either directly or indirectly by the individual (Brown, Bifulco, and Harris 1987; Coyne and Downey 1991; Hammen 1991). For example, the loss of a job may lead to depression, but depression may also lead to job loss.

VULNERABILITIES AND RISK FACTORS

There is ample evidence that depressive disorders are biopsychosocial in nature. That is, depression is caused by a combination of a factors, including biological (genetic) vulnerability, constitutional temperament, early childhood experiences and family functioning, predisposing life events, traumatic stressors, presence or absence of social support, and precipitating life events. Overall, the total number of risk factors, along with their nature and severity, in combination with the presence or absence of protective factors, combine to determine the probability of an episode of depression at that time. In addition, varying risk and protective factors are differentially significant for different people. Previous conceptions of categorically endogenous ("from within") or categorically reactive depression appear to simply be endpoints on a continuum of biology versus environment, with the vast majority of cases caused by some combination of both. The complexity of each of these contributors is increasingly evident. For example, different risk factors appear to be most salient for each gender, for different age groups, and for different ethnic and racial groups. In addition, previous depression is itself a risk factor for a recurrence of depression. Numerous studies have attempted to elucidate the specifics of these factors, or vulnerabilities, and are discussed in the following.

Certain demographic characteristics are risk factors for depression, such as **female gender, young age, marital status of divorced/widowed/separated/unhappily married,** and **European American ethnicity** (as opposed to African American or Hispanic American).

As noted previously, **women** have a higher risk of depression than men (Blazer et al. 1994; Newmann 1987; Spaner et al. 1994). Rates of depression are low and approximately equal for boys and girls during childhood. The increased rate among females begins with early adolescence (Angold et al. 1996; Angold and Worthman 1993; Kessler et al. 1993; Rutter 1988). The NCS found that at any given age, women had a greater risk of experiencing a first episode. After an episode took place, the risk for recurrence was identical for men and women (Kessler et al. 1993). Medical researchers have emphasized biological explanations to explain women's higher rates, such as childbirth, menopause, and hormonal factors (Blumenthal 1994; Seeman 1997). Postpartum depression and involutional melancholia (precipitated by menopause) were previously thought to be unique depressive reactions triggered by women's hormones. However, these seem to be simply major depressive episodes like any other, and that the hormonal changes are merely precipitants. Sociological theories have posited that the inherent stress in women's multiple roles are causal in women's higher rate of depression (Bromberger and Costello 1992).

Alternative explanations have included the idea that women have poorer coping abilities than men, and thus women are more vulnerable to depression. However, studies have shown that women actually experience more stress than men, particularly in that they are more emotionally involved in the lives of important people around them. It appears it is this "emotional cost of caring" that accounts for much of the difference (Kessler and McLeod 1987; Turner et al. 1995). Women in specific life circumstances are particularly vulnerable. Working-class women and women with young children in the home, no outside employment, and no intimate relationship with the opposite sex are at high risk of developing depression in the face of stressful life events (Brown and Harris 1978). In addition, certain traumatic events that are much more common in women—childhood sexual abuse, domestic violence, sexual assault—are significantly related to depression (Burnam et al. 1988; Levitan et al. 1998; Scott 1992).

Virtually all of the studies upon which these findings are based rely on respondents' answers to either interview or self-report questions. An additional factor may be that women's higher scores on depression scales partly reflect their greater willingness to admit to feelings of sadness and/or vulnerability (Newmann 1987). Furthermore, advocates of projective testing argue that the only way to accurately gauge the presence or absence of depression or other states is to include some techniques that tap unconscious mental processes. They argue that men's denial of symptoms may not be conscious avoidance so much as unconscious defense mechanisms, and thus men's apparent low level of symptoms is actually just the "illusion" of mental health (Shedler, Mayman, and Manis 1993).

Major depression was previously thought to be a disorder of middle age. However, it is increasingly clear that the **late teens** and **twenties** are the most frequent ages of onset. In one study, a full 50 percent of all cases had had their onset by age 21

(Spaner et al. 1994), and in the Los Angeles site of the ECA, over half of the cases had their onset by age 25 (Sorenson et al. 1991). In both the ECA and NCS, younger groups were at higher risk for depression (Robins et al. 1984; Blazer et al. 1994); in the ECA, the median age of onset of major depression was 24 (Christie et al. 1988). As noted earlier, despite numerous "check-list" studies that have documented high rates of distress among the elderly, research using more accurate diagnostic interviews have found lower rates of depression among those 65 and older than among younger respondents (Newman and Bland 1998; Roberts et al. 1997; Robins et al. 1984; Weissman and Myers 1978).

Marital status affects the risk for depression. Divorce, separation, and widowhood convey increased risk, and married people are at lower risk for depression (Badger and Rand 1998; Blazer et al. 1994; Weissman 1987). However, depression is highly correlated with unhappy marriages and marital distress, especially among women. In community samples, the lifetime prevalence of divorce and marital instability is higher among individuals who meet criteria for a mood disorder than for persons with other psychiatric diagnoses (Kessler et al. 1993; Turnbull et al. 1993). Divorce rates are still higher if both members of a couple are depressed, a not uncommon occurrence due to the phenomenon of "assortative mating," the tendency of depressed people to marry each other (Merikangas 1984; Merikangas, Bromet, and Spiker 1983).

As already noted, NCS lifetime rates of major depression among African Americans are significantly lower than among European Americans or Hispanic Americans. However, once again, the accuracy of these rates is controversial. The earlier ECA study found that rates of major depression among whites and blacks were not significantly different. Other studies that used rating scales of depressive symptoms (which, as noted, produce a score of overall distress, not a diagnosis of major depression) have also found similar rates for whites and blacks (Fellin 1989; Husaini 1997). Nonetheless, the NCS is usually regarded as the most methodologically sophisticated, and its findings are generally considered the most accurate. In the NCS, the lifetime rate of major depression among African American men was 7.2 percent, as compared with 13.5 percent for white men. Similarly, the lifetime rate among African American women was 15.5 percent, as compared with 22.3 percent for white women (Blazer et al. 1994).

At first glance, it seems counterintuitive that a racial and cultural minority group should have lower rates of depression than the European American majority. Certain stressful life events that are more common to African Americans, such as poverty and racial discrimination, are correlated with depression (Stevenson et al. 1997). However, these risk factors appear to be balanced by important protective factors, such as religion, intragroup social support, social participation, and cultural values of perseverance (Fellin 1989; Gary et al. 1985; Gibbs 1997).

In the NCS, the rates of major depression among Hispanic Americans were comparable to European American rates; Hispanic men's rates were a bit lower and Hispanic women's rates were a bit higher (Blazer et al. 1994). Of course, simply lumping various Hispanic groups together disguises significant ethnic differences. For example, a survey of Puerto Ricans living in New York in the early 1980s found very high rates of depression, higher than in the ECA or NCS. In this study, the lifetime rate of major depression among Puerto Rican women was 32.96 percent, and among men,

19.20 percent (Potter, Rogler, and Moscicki 1995). Risk factors for depression included low education, poor health, and disrupted marital status (divorced, widowed, separated). By contrast, a study of Mexican Americans found that 8.0 percent of males and 18.7 percent of females had high rates of depressive symptoms over the previous week. In this study, low educational achievement, low income, U.S. (as opposed to Mexican) birth, and Anglo cultural orientation were risk factors for depression. Surprisingly, in light of the acculturation finding, preferred language (Spanish vs. English) was not a risk factor (Moscicki et al. 1989).

Cuban Americans living in Dade County, Florida, were surveyed in the early 1980s. Lifetime rates of depression were found to be quite low—for males, 2.42 percent, and for females, 3.74 percent. The only risk factor that independently predicted depression was low income (Narrow et al. 1990).

For Hispanic Americans, immigration and acculturation are significant stressors. Maintenance of the culture of origin (Puerto Rico, Mexico, Cuba) or biculturalism appear to be associated with mental health; predominant acculturation into mainstream culture is a risk factor for depression (Gomez 1990; Potter, Rogler, and Moscicki 1995). As is true in the population at large, young Mexican Americans are particularly at risk (Roberts, Roberts, and Chen 1997).

Chinese Americans in Los Angeles were studied in 1993–94. The lifetime rate of major depression was 6.9 percent, much lower than the rates in the NCS for European Americans. Strikingly, the rate was virtually the same for men and women. However, when acculturation was included in the analysis, it was found that among highly acculturated individuals, women were three times more likely to have had a lifetime episode of major depression. Among low-acculturation individuals, there was no sex difference. In contrast to major depression, the rates of dysthymic disorder were roughly the same as that of European Americans. Disrupted marital status and a history of at least one traumatic stress were associated with higher rates of both major depression and dysthymic disorder (Takeuchi et al. 1998).

For the population at large, **lower socioeconomic level, lower levels of education,** and **related occupational groupings** are risk factors for depression. This vulnerability is apparently due to the increased level of stress and reduced resources, economic and otherwise, that poorer groups possess relative to other population groups (McLeod and Kessler 1990; Turner et al. 1995). In the NCS, odds ratios for the presence of current major depression were highest for the lowest income level (Blazer et al. 1994).

Biological vulnerability is a major risk factor. From a variety of research studies, it is clear that mood disorders are familial, and that there is a genetic component to the transmission of depression from one generation to another. Depression is more likely to occur among close relatives of those with the disorder than among unrelated people. Different rates of depression are observed in identical and fraternal twins; identical or monozygotic twins have higher rates of depression than fraternal or dizygotic. High rates of depression have been found among the offspring of depressed parents who have been adopted by families without a history of depression (Goldin and Gershon 1988).

A **family history of depression** is an important risk factor. In most cases, a family history contributes a combination of biological and environmental factors. A particularly elegant demonstration of this phenomena has been provided by Kendler, Neale et al. (1992), in which the authors prospectively studied 680 pairs of twins over a three-year period. One of the most powerful predictors of the onset of major depression during the study period was "genetic factors," defined as the difference between the rates of depression in monozygotic versus dizygotic twins. Other nonbiological family factors were also significant, however, such as negative "perceived parental warmth" and "childhood parental loss."

A family history of depression doubles or triples the risk of major depression (Goldin and Gershon 1988). In some studies of individuals in treatment for depression, family history has been identified as the strongest risk factor (Weissman, Kidd, and Prusoff 1982). The rate of major depression in the relatives of depressed patients, whether outpatient or hospitalized, is triple that of the general population (Weissman et al. 1982). Children of depressed parents have an increased risk of both major depression and substance abuse (Nunes et al. 1998; Weissman et al. 1987, 1997).

The specification of additional risk factors for depression is a complex task. Considerable research has been conducted on certain categories of risk factors, such as stressful life events and ongoing circumstances. On the other hand, results are often in conflict with one another, and it appears that the causal impact is bidirectional: stressful life events lead to depression, and depression leads to stressful life events (Coyne and Downey 1991; Hammen 1991; Keitner and Miller 1990; Kendler 1997; Shrout et al. 1989; Turner et al. 1995).

Predisposing (or distal) events must be differentiated from precipitating (or proximal) ones. Predisposing, or distal, events are ones that occur long in the past, often years before the onset of depression. Precipitating, or proximal, events are the "triggers" for an actual episode of depression. **Stressful events in childhood** are often considered predisposing factors for major depression during adulthood. For instance, separation from a parent during childhood or adolescence has often been found to be a predisposing factor for adult depression, but the effect is not a strong one and has not been found in all studies (Kendler, Neale et al. 1992; Paykel 1982; Roy 1987). Qualitative aspects of the loss, such as the nature of the loss (whether it was due to illness, marital separation, or death), its timing (the developmental stage when the loss occurred), the nature of the attachment, the adequacy of the care following the loss, and family stability are all critical elements that may influence the outcome (Bifulco, Brown, and Harris 1987; Breier et al. 1988; Coyne and Downey 1991; O'Connell and Mayo 1988; Rutter 1985; Tennant, Bebbington, and Hurry 1982).

The link between childhood experiences and vulnerability to adult depression is hypothesized to be a downward spiral of negative circumstances that stem from the loss and from which it is difficult to escape. For example, the loss of one's mother may be accompanied by subsequent neglect, which may impair or arrest personality development and may result in inadequate coping mechanisms and difficulty in forming close, lasting relationships. These factors, in turn, make it more difficult to adapt to losses and stresses as an adult (Coyne and Downey 1991; Ragan and McGlashan 1986; Rutter 1985).

Traumatic events are those that involve overwhelming amounts of stress and usually include an element of "death threat." Traumatic occurrences during childhood have been found to be predisposing events for the later onset of depression. Childhood sexual and/or physical abuse, perhaps the most common traumatic events of childhood, are particularly significant (Burnam et al. 1988; Duncan et al. 1996;

Levitan et al. 1998; Liem et al. 1997; Lizardi et al. 1995; Scott 1992; Valentine and Feinauer 1993). The trauma of a suicide of a family member or friend is also associated with depression (Brent et al. 1993b, 1996). Ongoing stressful circumstances can also lead to depression later, such as presence of depression or alcoholism in one or both parents (Hill and Muka 1996; Nunes et al. 1998; Reich et al. 1993; Weissman et al. 1987; Weissman et al. 1997), poor relationships with parents, including less care but more overprotection (Birmaher et al. 1996; Gotlib et al. 1988; Lizardi et al. 1995), low family support (Lewinsohn et al. 1994), and all of the possible sequelae of parental loss already outlined (Coyne and Downey 1991; Rutter 1985).

Recent negative life events are frequent precipitants, or proximate causes, of depression. A wide range of events has been identified, usually those that are perceived as losses (Coyne and Downey 1991). For example, in one study, significant associations between "fateful loss events" and depression were found in investigating the following life events: death of spouse, child, or close friend; miscarriage or stillbirth; physical attack or assault; cut in wage or salary; laid off from work; and so on (Shrout et al. 1989). These authors assert that the connections between events and depression is obscured when low-impact events are included in lists or interviews, and that the association is best highlighted "by eliminating events that would not lead to lasting behavioral changes in the lives of most normal persons who experience them" (Shrout et al. 1989:465). Examples of other important life events include health problems, teen pregnancy, family conflict during teen years (Carbonell, Reinharz, and Giaconia 1998), and corporal punishment during adolescence (Straus and Kantor 1994).

Although some reviews of the literature have found that the contribution of stressful life events to depression is relatively minor (O'Connell and Mayo 1988), most authorities see their role as more important (Coyne and Downey 1991; Kendler et al. 1995; Kessler, Abelson, and Zhao 1998; Shrout et al. 1989). Perhaps if all life events are considered together, the impact is equivocal. However, when the focus is on severe normative events, such as serious marital problems or divorce/breakup (Kendler et al. 1995) and on traumatic events (Shalev et al. 1998), the contribution to depression is more significant and convincing.

Specific life events may be particularly stressful for certain people, depending on the meaning and value they possess for those individuals. The personality characteristic of **perfectionism** may be a risk factor for depression, but only in interaction with specific stress. It appears that failures and/or difficulties in school or work are salient for people who highly value achievement (the autonomous form of depression), whereas problems with family members and/or close friends are more salient for those who highly value people and relationships (the sociotropic form of depression) (Blatt 1995; Ferguson and Rodway 1994; Hewitt and Flett 1993). For individuals who value achievement, and who have perfectionistic standards, failures perceived by others as relatively minor may assume overwhelming proportions. Perfectionism has been identified as a factor not only in depression, but in suicide as well (Blatt 1995).

For many people, but especially those who find meaning in relationships, specific interpersonal conflicts or losses, or ongoing interpersonal difficulties may precipitate depression. As noted earlier, many women in the United States have larger social networks than men and are more involved in the lives of others; when negative events happen to others, these individuals are also negatively affected (Kessler and McLeod 1987; Turner et al. 1995).

Among the elderly in particular, medical disorders and health concerns are specific risk factors for depression (Coleman et al. 1993; Husaini 1997; Roberts et al. 1997).

The impact of family interaction is an important factor. A depressed person and his or her intimate others, particularly the spouse, exerts a powerful effect in the direction of triggering and maintaining the depression. A circular process of mutual causation is postulated, in which the depressed person and family members inadvertently interact to create and maintain a stable system that resists change. Theoretically, the depressed person engages others in the intimate environment in such a way that support is lost (Coyne et al. 1987). Initial communications of hopelessness, helplessness, and irritability by the depressed person are answered with direct reassurances. The depressed person must decide whether the reassurances that he or she is worthy and acceptable are sincere or are empty responses to repeated attempts to elicit reassurances. Accelerated efforts to elicit even more positive feedback in order to answer this question have profound negative effects on interpersonal relationships (Coyne et al. 1987).

In time, depressive symptoms gain an aversive and powerful ability to arouse guilt and annoyance in others, because no amount of reassurance is ever enough. However, the depressed person's apparent dependency inhibits direct expressions of annoyance and hostility. Instead of direct expressions, manipulative attempts at non-genuine reassurance and support are made to reduce the aversive behavior of the depressed person, accompanied by simultaneous rejection and avoidance of the depressed person. As he or she becomes aware of the reactions of others, the depressed person displays more symptoms of distress, which stimulate the depressive social process further. A malignant cycle develops.

A related conception is that depressed people sometimes attempt to elicit feedback in others that serves to confirm their negative view of themselves. Although counterintuitive, research shows that people differentially prefer feedback that confirms their self-image, whatever it is, to contradictory feedback. This outcome is preferred because validation of one's perceptions of life, the world, and the self is even more important than a positive view of the self (Giesler, Josephs, and Swann 1996).

Lack of support from intimate family members, especially the spouse, and disturbed family functioning are significant contributors to recurrence of depression (Hooley 1986; Keitner and Miller 1990; Keitner et al. 1995). "Expressed emotion" (EE) is a concept that originated in the study of the families of people with schizophrenia. Studies found that schizophrenic patients relapsed sooner when they lived with families who were critical and overinvolved (labeled "expressed emotion"), as compared with patients whose families were more supportive and who assumed a moderately distant, but caring stance (Bebbington and Kuipers 1994; Jenkins and Karno 1992; Rosenfarb et al. 1995). There is no evidence that EE has any role in the etiology of the disorder, but rather it appears to be a kind of interpersonal stress that triggers relapse. Further work revealed that EE also operated in families of individuals with other disorders, such as depression (Hooley 1986; Schwartz et al. 1990). In fact, in one dramatic example of the role of family support, one researcher found that the answer to one question was the best single predictor of depressive relapse, better than any other clinical or demographic factor. That one question was, "How critical is your spouse of you?" Patients who perceived their spouses to be highly critical of them relapsed sooner than those who perceived their spouses to be less critical (Hooley and Teasdale 1989).

Another example of the crucial role spouses and family members play has been identified in an important community study carried out in London by Brown and Harris (1978). They found that housewives who had "nonconfiding" relationships with their spouses were much more likely, given certain stresses, to become depressed than others.

Another risk factor is **cognitive style**. The "learned helplessness" theory of depression posits that a perceived lack of connection between one's own efforts and outcomes in the environment results in depression. Following multiple uncontrollable events, a stable generalized belief forms that the environment is uncontrollable and independent of one's efforts. This belief inhibits active coping responses in new situations. A perception of response-reinforcement independence is acquired as the individual comes to believe that responding is ineffective (Seligman 1990). The depressed individual does not engage in actions that will challenge his or her perception of environmental control. The key rests in the tendency to interpret negative events in internal, global, stable terms. Internal attributions ("I am responsible") for events result in self-blame, while attributions to global factors ("not just in this situation, but in all situations") and attributions to stable factors ("not just this time, but every time") lead to a chronic sense of helplessness that is manifested in depression (Hamburg 1998; Lewinsohn et al. 1994; Seligman 1990). "Learned Optimism," an educational program geared to prevent depression among children and adolescents, has been developed using this perspective, in which children are taught to challenge their pessimistic thoughts (Seligman et al. 1995).

Biological factors that have nothing to do with genetic inheritance, such as stopping smoking, have been found to be precipitants for depression. Because nicotine is a mild stimulant, it is believed that one factor that leads to smoking is the use of nicotine as a form of self-treatment for depression. When the nicotine is removed, the underlying depression becomes evident (Covey, Glassman, and Stetner 1997).

In real-life practice, these various factors must be integrated. A particularly elegant study (Kendler, Kessler, Neale et al. 1992; Kendler et al. 1995) recently identified a number of etiologic factors for major depression in different domains. Researchers prospectively studied 680 pairs of twins over a three-year period, using structured interviews and a variety of other questionnaires. The role of genetic factors centered on the differences in occurrences of depression between monozygotic twins, who have identical genes, and dizygotic twins, who share some genes but only to the extent of normal siblings. Etiologic factors were hypothesized to be independent variables and intervening variables; the former were genetic factors and early family environment, and the latter were more recent events, including the occurrence of an episode of major depression in oneself and/or in one's co-twin. Nine distinct variables were found to be significant in causing a new episode of major depression during the three years of the study. These variables included childhood parental loss, low perceived parental warmth, and genetic factors. Intermediate variables that were significant were social support, neuroticism (the characteristic tendency to frequently experience negative emotions such as dysphoria, anger, etc.), and lifetime traumatic events. A recent history of major depression was also an intervening variable, and the final ones were both stressful life events and minor difficulties ("daily hassles") in the previous three months. All these variables were significantly related to the prospective prediction of an episode of major depression. This state-of-the-art study provides empirical support for the biopsychosocial model, presents a model of intermediate specificity, and rebuts any theories that attempt to reduce the phenomenon of depression to one or two etiologic factors. One major finding was that "genetic factors influence the risk of onset of major depression in part by altering the sensitivity of individuals to the depression-inducing effect of stressful life events" (Kendler et al. 1995:833).

RESILIENCIES AND PROTECTIVE FACTORS

Despite genetic vulnerabilities, early family discord, and stressful life events, some individuals do not become depressed, and, indeed, flourish. A newer line of research has attempted to identify protective factors, which are conditions and qualities that seem to shield or buffer people from the impact of adversity. "Protective factors refer to influences that modify, ameliorate, or alter a person's response to some environmental hazard that predisposes to a maladaptive outcome" (Rutter 1985:600). Individuals with sufficient protective factors to prevent depression or other psychopathology are said to be resilient (Smith and Carlson 1997).

Resilience to depression has not been studied to a great extent. To some degree, protective factors are the opposite of, and usually the absence of, risk factors. However, additional or positive factors exist in their own right. Despite the paucity of studies, certain characteristics have been identified. Three general domains of protective factors have been identified: individual factors, family factors, and external support systems (Aro 1994).

Individual factors include characteristics that are either genetically acquired or are the result of a positive family environment. A temperament that embraces equanimity, that enables an individual to "roll with the punches," appears to be protective (Beardslee 1989), as is an internal locus of control. For example, in two separate studies of adults who were sexual abuse victims as children, internal locus of control was resilience-producing, but at the same time, the abuse victims did not blame themselves for the abuse, as an internal locus of control might suggest (Liem et al. 1997; Valentine and Feinauer 1993). Higher than average intelligence appears to be a protective factor (Radke-Yarrow and Sherman 1990). A belief in one's own self-efficacy also has been found to be protective (Aro 1994; Rutter 1987; Valentine and Feinauer 1993), along with such characteristics as being flexible and adaptive (Wagnild and Young 1993), having a range of problem-solving skills, spirituality (Valentine and Feinauer 1993), and having high self-esteem (Rutter 1987; Valentine and Feinauer 1993).

However, the true meaning of self-esteem in the building of resilience is controversial. The culture at large has taken on a quest for self-esteem among youth, and schools and recreation programs have been designed to explicitly foster increased self-esteem. Some experts believe that such programs really do not build self-esteem, but rather a superficial good feeling about the self. True self-esteem, they argue, is based on succeeding at tasks, facing and overcoming challenges, and actual achievement ("task accomplishment"), as opposed to simply being told to feel good about the self (Aro 1994; Caplan 1990; Seligman et al. 1995). Self-esteem also comes about through positive interactions over time with parents, siblings, and peers, in which an individual is treated as if he or she has value (Smith and Carlson 1997).

Several researchers have developed and factor analyzed a "resilience scale," which focuses on individual variables. Two main factors emerged, which the authors labeled "personal competence" and "acceptance of self and life." The former factor included such characteristics as perseverance, determination, flexibility, and coping adaptability; the latter factor included an easygoing disposition ("I usually take things in stride"), sense of humor, and a liking oneself (Wagnild and Young 1993).

One area of resilience that has been studied extensively is that of coping. Positive or adaptive coping provides an individual with an effective or at least helpful way to address stresses and difficulties (Coyne and Downey 1991; Kessler, Price, and Wortman 1985; Rutter 1985). Coping strategies can be broadly categorized as those that directly address the problem and modify or eliminate it, those that alter the individual's perception of the meaning of the stressor, and those that keep the emotional consequences within bounds (Pearlin and Schooler 1978). A repertoire of responses is protective, and different coping mechanisms are associated with different situations and problems. For example, in "high-loss" situations, reappraisal of the problem appears to be especially protective against depression (Mattlin, Wethington, and Kessler 1990).

Family protective factors generally center around having a psychologically healthy, communicative, supportive family. For example, in one study, a "less stressful" family environment was identified as a protective factor against depression (Liem et al. 1997). Family stability itself appears to be protective (Conrad 1998). Family cohesion, good family functioning, and good communication were protective against depression in a prospective study of adolescents (Carbonell et al. 1998). In a prospective study of at-risk children, resilience in the parents and high parental aspirations for their children's education were protective (Osborn 1990).

Protective factors in the general environment consist of social support from friends and peers. In the study of resilient adolescents described in the preceding, the ability to request and use assistance from adults, and the perception of greater social support from peers, was also protective (Carbonell et al. 1998). A network of good interpersonal relationships, which provide social support, are protective (Aro 1994; Rutter 1985, 1987; Valentine and Feinauer 1993).

Additional research into resilience-producing conditions is obviously important, especially those that may be modifiable. Innovative programs and interventions that address resilience-producing factors need to be developed. This appears to be a burgeoning area of mental health research.

PROGRAMS AND SOCIAL WORK CONTRIBUTIONS

Programmatic social work responses to depression can occur at three levels: at the interpersonal level, at the organization and policy level, and through social work education. Based on theories of and research on depression, clinical programs have been developed that go beyond traditional psychotherapy. These programs tend to be readily available in clinical settings, especially those that specialize in the treatment of depression, but they also have been modified and distributed to the general public through books on self-treatment. Based on cognitive and behavioral theories, these approaches use self-control techniques, relaxation training, pleasant activities, social skills, and cognitive restructuring (Copeland 1992; Gilbert 1999; Gold 1995). Many social workers are incorporating these techniques into their clinical work with clients. Self-help groups exist both in clinical settings and in the community, and social workers can offer their skills as resource consultants.

New approaches are sensitive to the burden shouldered by families and emphasize effective coping (Jacob et al. 1987; Noh and Turner 1987). Severe depression is a mental illness with serious consequences, and when mental illness strikes a family, that family becomes intimately and indefinitely involved with the mental health system. Such families must learn to gain access to and interact effectively with the appropriate services. As such, they are viewed as equals on the treatment team and may be involved in treatment-planning decisions (Spiegel and Wissler 1987). They may even be used to train professionals in family issues related to the care of the mentally ill. In this model, social workers offer consultation as it is needed on such issues as community resources, interpersonal problems, and crisis intervention.

In hospitals, training programs and administrative changes are being implemented to increase cooperation between staff and patients' families (Bernheim and Switalski 1988). Psychoeducational groups and workshops for families maximize family strengths to enable significant others to become useful, long-term resources for their loved ones (Jacob et al. 1987). Families are taught how to recognize the early warning signs of depression so that appropriate treatment can be sought quickly in an effort to ward off serious episodes. Families can be oriented to the complex issues that surround hospitalization, and the support of others struggling with similar issues is also provided (Turnbull et al. 1993). Families are empowered through self-help groups that counteract the devastating effects of mental illness and feelings of guilt (Axelrod, Geismar, and Ross 1994). Skills-training programs for parents afford an opportunity for preventive work with offspring. For the families of those with unremitting depression, day and respite programs similar to those designed for families of the elderly are appropriate. Social workers can take a role in starting up these groups and programs where a need exists and can also serve as facilitators. They may also be advocates for these groups and may serve as resources.

On the organizational and policy level, educational programs are under way, such as National Depression Screening Day (Greenfield et al. 1997; Rapaport and Suminski 1994). Government-funded training programs and promotional materials are increasing public and professional awareness (Regier et al. 1988), and television programs are informing the public through educational programs on depression and other mental health problems. Celebrities who have experienced serious depression, such as television reporter Mike Wallace and writer William Styron, have talked publicly about their difficulties (Styron 1990). The highly publicized and unfortunate suicides of presidential aid Vincent Foster (Blatt 1995), youth leader Abbie Hoffman, and rock musician Curt Cobain (Jobes et al. 1996) have also increased public awareness of the obviously serious consequences of depression. Such interventions are critical in decreasing the stigma associated with depression and, in turn, in facilitating the search for appropriate help. Despite these constructive developments, social workers need to develop more public education programs that deal with the psychosocial aspects of these problems and to conduct workshops in their communities for the public and for professionals in other disciplines.

Grass-roots, university-based, and state-supported family support programs have emerged as important social and political movements (Weiss 1989; Zigler and Black 1989). Social workers should be actively involved in these organizations and should support other social actions that are directly or indirectly related to depression. These include feminist programs that empower women and families and lead to mastery coping, such as child care programs that enable women to work and to obtain training programs.

Social work education is becoming increasingly systematic in teaching students to recognize and assess depression. Our academic institutions need to take more responsibility for conducting research into the manifestations of depression among vulnerable subgroups of the population such as the poor and, from this research, to design effective interventions and programs.

Most people with depression do not seek help. In the ECA, only about one-third sought treatment (Regier et al. 1993). The rates may be even lower among racial and ethnic minorities. For example, one study of African Americans found that only 11 percent of those with major depression saw a psychiatrist or other mental health professional (Brown et al. 1995). A number of programs have targeted primary care physicians as recipients of education regarding depression, with the hope that their ability to identify depression will increase ("New Federal Guidelines" 1993). Social workers are in a similar position, given the wide variety of settings and populations with whom social workers interact (Levy and Land 1994). Hopefully, improved social work education will lead to better case finding and higher rates of identifying client depression in social work's various fields of practice.

ASSESSMENT AND INTERVENTIONS

The assessment of depression is straightforward in some cases, and extremely complex in others. In all cases, depression as a mental disorder is much more than simply feeling depressed. In each disorder to be described, a variety of associated symptoms are also present, and a characteristic course or trajectory over time can usually be identified. As described in the introduction to this chapter, the most widely used diagnostic framework is the *Diagnostic and Statistical Manual of Mental Disorders,* 4th edition (APA 1994). In *DSM-IV,* there are a variety of possible disorders when a client presents with a depressed mood:

1. Major Depressive Disorder
2. Dysthymic Disorder
3. Adjustment Disorder with Depressed Mood
4. Uncomplicated Bereavement
5. Depression as a part of some other clinical condition, such as substance abuse/dependence or a personality disorder.
6. Depression Due to a General Medical Condition or the Direct Effects of a Substance
7. Bipolar Disorders: Bipolar I, II, or Cyclothymic Disorder

As described earlier, the differential diagnosis of mood disorders and depression involves assessing symptoms and course, as well as understanding how the depression has affected the individual's life. Most clients who come to a social worker for help are prepared to tell their "story," a constructed narrative that describes the meaning and context of their problems. They do not usually offer specific symptoms while describing this story. Similarly, many social workers have not been trained in evaluating depression, and they may fail to inquire about specific symptoms, age of onset, course over time, and family history. Knowing which symptoms to inquire about means knowing the symptoms of each of the mood disorders in *DSM-IV,* as well as how they fit together over time.

Major Depressive Disorder. As displayed in table 6.1, major depressive disorder (MDD) is a mood disorder centering on feeling sad, blue, or down in the dumps, *or* one in which the individual has lost interest or pleasure in normally enjoyable activities, termed "anhedonia." Sometimes individuals do not state that they feel sad or depressed, but rather simply apathetic or numb. This is anhedonia. In addition to either sad mood and/or anhedonia, the individual must experience at least four other symptoms during the same two-week period (or longer), each of which are present most of the day nearly every day. These other symptoms include appetite increase or decrease, or weight increase or decrease, sleep increase or decrease, decreased energy, feelings of worthlessness, guilt, or low self-esteem, decreased ability to concentrate or make decisions, psychomotor agitation or retardation, and suicide thoughts. Although usually a moot point when a client requests help, the symptoms just listed must cause "significant distress or impairment" in functioning in one or more aspects of life.

Finally, to diagnose MDD, the social worker must determine that the mood disturbance is not caused by a medical problem or a substance. Confirming that depression is not caused by a medical problem usually involves requesting that the client obtain a medical evaluation, including routine blood work that tests thyroid function, unless the client has recently already done so. Ruling out the presence of a substance requires a careful inquiry about the client's use of alcohol, prescribed drugs, and illicit drugs. Even with assurances of confidentiality, many clients are not totally honest about their use of substances, and so this line of questioning involves paying as much attention to the process as the content. Some clients who were open and cooperative initially become defensive and resistant when questions about substances are raised, and this change may alert the social worker to the presence of a potential substance abuse problem. Virtually all drugs of abuse, including alcohol, can lead to depression, either from a pattern of excessive or prolonged use or from withdrawal effects.

As noted earlier, major depression usually occurs in episodes. The minimum duration is two weeks, but almost everyone who seeks help for depression has had a longer episode. In its most extreme form, an episode can last for years (Howland 1993). The severity of MDD can vary tremendously, from a condition that is distressing but tolerable, which in many cases the individual never identifies as depression, to a syndrome so severe that a person stays in bed virtually continuously, or attempts suicide to escape from the unbearable pain. Author William Styron's account of his own depression is an extremely articulate description (Styron 1990). Since it occurs in episodes, most individuals with major depression recognize that something abnormal is happening to them—that they are "not themselves"—although they frequently do not label it depression.

Most episodes are precipitated by a stressor of some kind, as described earlier,

TABLE 6.1 DSM-IV Major Depressive Disorder

Major Depressive Episode

A. Five (or more) of the following symptoms have been present during the same two-week period, and represent a change from previous functioning; at least one of the symptoms is either (1) depressed mood, or (2) loss of interest or pleasure.

    (1) depressed mood most of the day, nearly every day, as indicated by either subjective report (e.g., feels sad or empty) or observation made by others (e.g., appears tearful). Note: In children and adolescents, can be irritable mood.

    (2) markedly diminished interest or pleasure in all, or almost all, activities most of the day, nearly every day (as indicated by either subjective account or observation made by others)

    (3) significant weight loss when not dieting or weight gain (e.g., a change of more than 5% of body weight in a month), or decrease or increase in appetite nearly every day. Note: In children, consider failure to make expected weight gains.

    (4) insomnia or hypersomnia nearly every day

    (5) psychomotor agitation or retardation nearly every day (observable by others, not merely subjective feelings of restlessness or being slowed down)

    (6) fatigue or loss of energy nearly every day

    (7) feelings of worthlessness or excessive or inappropriate guilt (which may be delusional) nearly every day (not merely self-reproach or guilt about being sick)

    (8) diminished ability to think or concentrate, or indecisiveness, nearly every day (either by subjective account or as observed by others)

    (9) recurrent thoughts of death (not just fear of dying), recurrent suicide ideation without a specific plan, or a suicide attempt or a specific plan for committing suicide

B. The symptoms do not meet criteria for a mixed episode.

C. The symptoms cause clinically significant distress or impairment in social, occupational, or other important areas of functioning.

D. The symptoms are not due to the direct physiological effects of a substance (e.g., a drug of abuse, a medication), or a general medical condition (e.g., hypothyroidism).

E. The symptoms are not better accounted for by bereavement, i.e., after the loss of a loved one, the symptoms persist for longer than two months or are characterized by marked functional impairment, morbid preoccupation with worthlessness, suicidal ideation, psychotic symptoms, or psychomotor retardation.

Major Depressive Disorder, Single Episode

A. Presence of a major depressive episode.

B. The major depressive episode is not better accounted for by schizoaffective disorder, and is not superimposed on schizophrenia, schizophreniform disorder, delusional disorder, or psychotic disorder NOS.

C. Has never had a manic episode or unequivocal hypomanic episode. Note: This exclusion does not apply if all of the manic or hypomanic episodes are substance- or treatment-induced.

Major Depressive Disorder, Recurrent

A. Two or more major depressive episodes.

    Note: To be considered separate episodes, there must be an interval of at least two months without significant symptoms of depression.

(continued on next page)

TABLE 6.1 *(continued)*

Major Depressive Disorder, Recurrent *(continued)*

B. The major depressive episodes are not due to the direct effects of a substance (e.g., drugs of abuse, medication), or a general medical condition (e.g., hypothyroidism); are not better accounted for by schizoaffective disorder, and are not superimposed on schizophrenia, schizophreniform disorder, delusional disorder, or psychotic disorder NOS.

C. Has never had a manic episode or unequivocal hypomanic episode. Note: This exclusion does not apply if all of the manic or hypomanic episodes are substance- or treatment-induced.

but some episodes start spontaneously. With recurrent episodes, less psychosocial stress is required to trigger subsequent episodes (Post 1992). At least 50 percent of the individuals who have one episode have a second or third, and after two or three, the probability is very high that additional episodes will occur (APA 1994). Moreover, in many cases, the depression becomes "autonomous" once begun. That is, it seems to "take on a life of its own," such that if there were a specific precipitant, reversing or undoing it often does not eliminate or even reduce the severity of the depression.

One of the unique characteristics of MDD is what *DSM-IV* calls "markedly diminished interest or pleasure in all, or almost all, activities" (APA 1994:327). This phenomenon we have previously termed anhedonia, and it is a hallmark of MDD, even more than the oft-noted loss of appetite or sleep. Anhedonia is also manifested by "lack of reactivity of mood," meaning that the individual's mood state does not change in reaction to events, other people, or other stimuli. Positive occurrences do not make them feel any better, and negative ones do not make them feel worse. In the interview, the social worker may notice a client's lack of reactivity by his or her monotone voice, lack of facial expression, and particularly by the constricted range of their emotions. Social workers frequently expect that clients will temporarily feel better after discussing their depression or associated problems with an empathic and nonjudgmental listener. However, when a client has significant anhedonia with lack of mood reactivity, "venting" their feelings has no effect, and they seem just as depressed after an hour's interview as they were at the beginning. An inexperienced social worker may think he or she failed to pinpoint the central issue when the client does not exhibit a brief brightening of mood by the end of an interview, but this phenomenon frequently represents not an oversight, but an important clue to the presence of major depression.

A related phenomenon is that during an episode of depression, individuals perceive their lives, their past and future, and the world in negative and pessimistic ways (Beck 1991). One important aspect of this "cognitive distortion" is that they perceive their previous adjustment in a much more negative way than when they are not depressed. In taking a history, social workers must be aware of this distortion and not assume that the assessment the individual makes while depressed is accurate or objective (Morgado et al. 1991).

In severe cases, some individuals have psychotic symptoms. "Psychotic" means a significant loss of reality contact, and the symptoms consist of an illogical or confused form of thinking ("thought disorder"), delusions (fixed, false beliefs), and/or hallucinations (usually hearing voices). In previous years it was mistakenly thought that the presence of psychosis meant schizophrenia, but now it is clearly known that MDD (and bipolar I disorder) can include psychotic features in severe cases.

Another variation is called major depressive disorder, seasonal pattern, or simply "seasonal affective disorder" (SAD). Individuals with SAD experience depressions almost entirely during the winter months, when the amount of daily sunlight is substantially decreased. SAD may be due to excess production of the hormone melatonin in the pineal gland, which normally is suppressed by sunlight, and this excess melatonin in turn causes depression (Lam 1998). Alternatively, it may be that an abnormal shift in circadian rhythms, normally stabilized by adequate sunlight at regular intervals, is responsible (Sack et al. 1990).

When it appears that a client has a depressive disorder, it is helpful to pursue the possible presence of MDD first, as a "default option." If it is determined that the client does not have MDD, then other possible diagnoses can be considered.

Dysthymic Disorder. The second disorder to consider is dysthymic disorder (DD) (see table 6.2). DD is more chronic than MDD, but milder. It consists of a sad mood "for most of the day, more days than not" (APA 1994:349) for at least two years (or one year in children or adolescents). In addition, the individual must also have two or more symptoms from the following list: poor appetite or overeating, insomnia or hypersomnia, low energy, low self-esteem, poor concentration or difficulty making decisions, and feelings of hopelessness. During the two years or more of the disorder, there may be times when the individual feels "normal" or "not depressed," but these periods must not exceed two months at a time. If these "good times" do exceed two months, some other disorder—or no clear-cut disorder—is present. Most cases of DD begin slowly and gradually, so that the individual never really notices it at the time; only later can he or she look back and date its onset in rough fashion. Typically no specific precipitant or stressor can be identified. Most cases also go on for much longer than two years.

DD, by its chronic nature, comes to be viewed by most as simply part of their personalities, as part of themselves, not as something out of the ordinary or different from their normal selves.

Like MDD, dysthymic disorder must cause significant distress or impairment and must not be caused by a general medical problem or a substance. Psychosis is never a part of DD. Like MDD, if periods of mania have ever been present, the diagnosis of DD is ruled out, and bipolar I disorder should be considered.

A complicated association exists between DD and major depression. In cases when the dysthymic period seems to come right before or right after an episode of MDD, then MDD takes precedence. However, many people have both disorders, and this combination is termed "double depression." Double depression consists of chronic mild-to-moderate depression for years, often decades, punctuated by occasional worsenings that last several months at a time. Most people, perhaps as high as 90 percent, of individuals with DD also develop MDD (Badger and Rand 1998; Howland 1993).

Adjustment Disorder with Depressed Mood. The third depressive disorder to be considered, when both MDD and DD have been ruled out, is adjustment disorder with

TABLE 6.2 DSM-IV Dysthymic Disorder

A. Depressed mood for most of the day, for more days than not, as indicated either by subjective account or observation made by others, for at least two years. Note: In children and adolescents, mood can be irritable and duration must be at least one year.

B. Presence, while depressed, of two (or more) of the following:
  (1) poor appetite or overeating
  (2) insomnia or hypersomnia
  (3) low energy or fatigue
  (4) low self-esteem
  (5) poor concentration or difficulty making decisions
  (6) feelings of hopelessness

C. During the two-year period (one year for children and adolescents) of the disturbance, the person has never been without the symptoms in A and B for more than two months at a time.

D. No major depressive episode has been present during the first two years of the disturbance (one year for children and adolescents); i.e., the disturbance is not better accounted for by chronic major depressive disorder, or major depressive disorder in partial remission.
    Note: There may have been a previous major depressive episode provided there was a full remission (no significant signs or symptoms for two months) before development of the dysthymic disorder. In addition, after the initial two years (one year for children and adolescents) of dysthymic disorder, there may be superimposed episodes of major depressive disorder in which case both diagnoses may be given when the criteria are met for major depressive episode.

E. There has never been a manic episode, a mixed episode, or a hypomanic episode, and criteria have never been met for cyclothymic disorder.

F. Does not occur exclusively during the course of a chronic psychotic disorder, such as schizophrenia or delusional disorder.

G. Not due to the direct physiological effects of a substance (e.g., a drug of abuse, a medication), or a general medical condition (e.g., hypothyroidism)

H. The symptoms cause clinically significant distress or impairment in social, occupational, or other important areas of functioning.

---

depressed mood (AD; see table 6.3). Although technically not included in the mood disorders section of *DSM-IV,* it nonetheless must be considered when depression is the presenting problem. The concept of an adjustment disorder is that of a specific psychosocial stressor that causes difficulty in coping, responding, or adjusting to it. As such, AD almost seems to be a normal reaction to a life change. However, the criteria for AD state that the difficulty consists of clinically significant emotional or behavioral reactions that begin relatively soon after the stressor occurs. "Clinically significant" means that the individual's reactions (in this case, depressive symptoms), are "in excess of what would be expected given the nature of the stressor" (APA 1994:623). Deciding what is a "normal" response to a particular stressor is obviously a difficult judgement. In practice, though, when an individual requests help from a social worker, a clear stressor is identified, and his or her depression does not meet criteria for major depression or dysthymic disorder, an adjustment disorder is usually diagnosed. Adjustment disorder is a diagnosis of last resort and can only be used when nothing else applies. The stressor cannot be the death of an important person,

TABLE 6.3 DSM-IV Adjustment Disorder with Depressed Mood

A. The development of emotional or behavioral symptoms in response to an identifiable stressor(s) occurring within three months of the onset of the stressor(s).

B. These symptoms or behaviors are clinically significant as evidenced by either of the following:

    (1) marked distress that is in excess of what would be expected from exposure to the stressor

    (2) significant impairment in social or occupational (academic) functioning

C. The stress-related disturbance does not meet the criteria for any specific Axis I disorder and is not merely an exacerbation of a preexisting Axis I or Axis II disorder.

D. Does not represent bereavement.

E. The symptoms do not persist for more than six months after the termination of the stressor (or its consequences)

    Acute: the symptoms have persisted for more than six months

    Chronic: the symptoms have persisted for six months or longer

that is, the "adjustment" cannot be grief or bereavement, since grief is a normal response to a death.

An AD can look much like a precipitated episode of major depression but is by definition milder. In some cases, the differential diagnosis is difficult. For example, a two- or three-week depression that was precipitated by the loss of a job is major depression if four additional symptoms accompany the sad feelings, but if only three are present, the diagnosis is AD. Beyond counting symptoms, however, most experienced social workers look for some of the unique symptoms of MDD to validate its presence, such as significant anhedonia and/or lack of mood reactivity. Anhedonia is not present to any significant degree in AD or in DD.

Finally, in AD the disturbance resolves itself if the stressor is removed. Up to six months can be required for the symptoms to fade, but in an AD, removal of the stressor leads to the remission of the disorder. This is usually not true for MDD.

Grief or Bereavement. Another diagnostic possibility for the depressed individual is bereavement. In *DSM-IV,* bereavement is reserved for the death of a person, as opposed to a pet, job, hobby, or other activity, or body part, even though many of the features and dynamics of these losses are similar. Bereavement is a normal reaction to the loss of a loved one and includes sad mood, loss of interest in normally pleasurable activities, impairment of functioning, and many of the other features of major depression. *DSM-IV* offers no criteria, noting that it is a normal reaction, and that culture plays a major role in the way that grief is expressed. In many cases, making a diagnosis of bereavement is straightforward. In other instances, in which atypical features are present or in which the death took place a year or two in the past, are more difficult.

DSM-IV actually terms this phenomenon uncomplicated bereavement, which suggests the possibility of "complicated bereavement." Indeed, the literature and clinical experience suggest that there are many instances and many types of abnormal or complicated bereavement, or unresolved grief. However, *DSM* supplies no name or diagnostic criteria for such a phenomenon, although proposals have been made (Horowitz et al. 1997; Prigerson et al. 1995). *DSM* suggests that instances in which bereavement has become complicated or abnormal should simply be diagnosed according to the presenting symptoms, much like any other disorder. Most often, bereavement that has become complicated turns into MDD, DD, or substance abuse.

Differentiating MDD from bereavement can sometimes be difficult. One must keep in mind that the expression of grief is culturally specific, and that most grief reactions include many of the symptoms of MDD. However, *DSM-IV* offers some guidelines. When an apparent grief reaction includes psychomotor retardation, significant loss of self-esteem, psychotic features, anhedonia, considerable difficulty functioning for more than a few weeks, and suicidal thoughts, fantasies, or plans, the grief has probably become complicated by major depression (APA 1994).

Depression Due to a Medical Problem or a Substance. Social workers must be alert to the possibility that a depressive disorder might be caused by the direct physiological effects of a medical illness; *DSM-IV* terms this mood disorder due to a general medical condition. As noted earlier, medical evaluation by a physician is necessary to adequately address this possibility. Illnesses that may cause depression include diabetes, hypothyroidism, Cushing's disease, Addison's disease, lupus, multiple sclerosis, encephalitis, Parkinson's disease, strokes, vitamin B-12 deficiency, and many others (Gaviria and Flaherty 1993; Schwartz and Schwartz 1993).

Depression might also be due to the effects of a substance, including prescribed medication, a drug of abuse, or a toxin or poison. As noted earlier, a careful assessment of possible substance use or abuse is necessary, including inquiring about prescribed medications. Medications and drugs that may cause depression include birth control pills, reserpine, propranolol, L-dopa, corticosteroids, clonidine, the withdrawal from amphetamines and cocaine, and others (Gaviria and Flaherty 1993). In this case, the diagnosis is substance-induced mood disorder.

Depression As a Symptom. Depression is also frequently present in many other mental and emotional disorders. Social workers must be aware that a self-report of depression on the part of a client does not guarantee that the diagnosis is necessarily a mood disorder. Virtually all of the personality disorders, for example, include the mood of sadness or depression at times and are also at heightened risk for either MDD or DD. Anxiety disorders are frequently accompanied by the mood of depression, so much so that a new diagnostic proposal was included as an appendix in *DSM-IV,* mixed anxiety-depressive disorder. Psychotic disorders such as schizophrenia also cause depression, especially immediately after an individual has recovered from an episode of psychosis. Impulse control disorders, such as pathological gambling and kleptomania, are often accompanied by depression. In short, the mood of depression is ubiquitous, and social workers should not be misled by a presenting complaint of depression into assuming that that is the core problem. A thorough assessment is always needed.

Bipolar Disorders. Social workers should also consider that the depression that a client is experiencing may be one pole of a bipolar disorder, such as bipolar I or bipolar II disorder. Bipolar I disorder consists of alternating episodes of major depression (in this instance, termed bipolar depression) and mania. Mania is the opposite of depression; manic episodes tend to last for a few weeks and they are usually shorter than depressive episodes. During a manic episode an individual feels euphoric, elated, or expansive, with increased self-esteem, increased activity, talkativeness, hypersexuality, and in general a tendency to carry out impulsive actions that are poorly considered. When manic, clients spend thousands of dollars in a few weeks, and then later take years to pay off the debts and regain financial stability. Manic clients may make numerous phone calls, write novels, start businesses, and sleep little. They are grandiose, distractible, and in severe cases, psychotic. When psychotic, manic people frequently have delusions that are consistent with their elated mood. In an interview, they are often witty and clever. Manic clients are notorious for having little or no insight into the nature of their disorder, even if carefully educated about the signs and symptoms beforehand. Manic clients can also be irritable and arrogant and can become violent if others do not submit to their will. Individuals who are manic can become violent even if they would never do so under any other circumstances.

Less frequently, an individual with bipolar I disorder experiences a mixed episode, in which symptoms of mania and depression coexist. This juxtaposition seems impossible, since many of the symptoms of mania and depression are the opposite of each other. However, in practice, an individual in mixed mania has manic energy, but his or her mood is dysphoric and frequently anguished. The combination of dysphoric mood and high energy places the individual at great risk for suicide (Goldberg et al. 1998).

Bipolar II disorder is similar, except that the individual has depressive episodes alternating with hypomanic episodes. Hypomania is similar to mania, but milder, and has a lifetime prevalence of 0.6 percent (Badger and Rand 1998). Many of the same characteristics are present, but to a lesser degree, and the disorder does not interfere with functioning. An individual who is manic would be almost immediately noticeable in a social situation, whereas an individual who is hypomanic would not stand out. Indeed, in conversation, he or she would only seem like an unusually talkative person, not one who was mentally ill.

Finally, **cyclothymic disorder** is a relatively rarely diagnosed disorder that consists of numerous short periods (hours to days) of mild depression and numerous short periods of mildly hypomanic symptoms. Neither the "highs" nor the "lows" are severe enough to be diagnosed mania/hypomania or major depression. Cyclothymic disorder appears to be heterogenous, with a significant proportion of cases actually being the prodromal period prior to the onset of bipolar I or bipolar II disorders (Howland and Thase 1993).

The first step in **treatment** is obtaining a history, making a diagnosis, and formulating a treatment plan. In severe cases, it may be a difficult task to draw a history from a person whose memory is impaired and whose speech is decreased and marked by long pauses between words and sentences. Therefore, the history should be gathered not only from the client, but also from significant others who have observed the client's behavior. This expanded assessment approach provides an opportunity to develop an alliance with family members and increases the likelihood that objective, reliable data about the client's depression will be gathered.

An essential part of the evaluation of a depressed person is a suicide risk assessment. Although the details of this process are beyond the scope of this chapter, social workers must keep in mind that depression is the most frequent underlying condition in suicide. In cases of high risk, protective measures must be taken, which most often means hospitalization. In this era of managed care, the most justifiable basis for psychiatric hospitalization is high suicide risk.

An evaluation of psychosocial functioning is also important. An acute episode of depression can be conceptualized as a crisis that commands all of the individual's coping resources and leaves little energy for personal growth. As in any crisis, regression may occur during episodes of depression, and functioning typically improves after the depressive symptoms have abated. For clients who have had a long course of depressive illness marked by multiple severe episodes, it is not uncommon for the developmental tasks to be those of an earlier life stage rather than those indicated by chronological age. In this instance, the client may be fixated at the developmental stage operating when the first episode of depression occurred. Intervention planning should maximize the periods between episodes as opportunities for completing developmental tasks, advancing psychosocial functioning, and moving to a more advanced developmental stage.

The contemporary consensus of most mental health professionals, including most social workers, is that the treatment of major depression should include both **psychotherapy** and **medication**. In severe cases, in which psychotic features are present, the client is extremely suicidal, or all other treatments have failed, electroconvulsive treatment (ECT) is utilized. Although no doubt misused in the past, ECT is an effective and at times lifesaving treatment for severe depression.

The treatment of DD emphasizes psychotherapy, but medications are used at times, especially in cases whose severity approaches that of MDD. The treatment of AD is typically brief therapy and the mobilization of social support. The treatment of bereavement is a special topic with a literature of its own (e.g., Worden 1991).

Various models of psychotherapy have been used to treat depression. **Psychodynamic** conceptualizations were the earliest to provide a causal framework for depression. The role of repressed hostility is the central explanatory variable. Basically, depression is viewed as anger that is first projected onto one's parents and is later generalized to the wider interpersonal environment. In the process, the anger becomes detached from its roots in hostility, is turned inward on the self, and is experienced as a deep sense of inferiority, guilt, and dysphoria (Abraham 1911/1986; Freud 1896/1962).

Additions to the basic theory include the notion that depression is based on early childhood trauma that translates into a vulnerability to feeling helpless in the face of specific frustrations in adulthood (Bibring 1953), and the idea that adult patterns of interpersonal relationships are forged in early family life in an emotional climate that is characterized by conformity. As a result, a narrow range of relationships, characterized by dependency and sensitivity to disapproval and rejection, is developed (Cohen et al. 1954).

Other events that are thought to lead to adult depression include "early childhood experiences of being disappointed by others, from inadequate nurturing, . . . from an inability to bridge the gap between aspirations and achievements," and similar factors (Schwartz and Schwartz 1993:180).

Traditional conceptions of psychodynamic treatment were necessarily long term, involving analysis of the transference as well as extensive review of childhood events. In many ways, psychodynamic treatment for depression was no different than psychodynamic treatment of other disorders, since neurotic disorders were treated similarly. In the past twenty years or so, brief or short-term variations have also been developed, mostly of up to twenty or twenty-five sessions in duration. These short-term models usually emphasize one focal conflict to which treatment is addressed. Transference interpretation is still utilized, but only interpretations that focus on this core conflict (Book 1998; Henry et al. 1994).

There are very few empirical studies of psychodynamic treatment, for depression or any other disorder. This paucity of research is due partly to the extraordinary demands of conducting research on a long, idiosyncratic, difficult-to-operationalize undertaking. Empirical studies are somewhat easier with shorter-term models, although still complex, and thus much of the empirical work has centered on these. Overall, there is insufficient evidence to speak to the effectiveness of psychodynamic treatments for depression one way or another.

One important exception to this generalization is that of interpersonal psychotherapy (IPT). Developed by Klerman, Weissman, and colleagues twenty years ago, IPT is a short-term (approximately twelve-session) psychodynamic therapy that has been the subject of a considerable number of empirical trials. It conceptualizes depression as either being caused or sustained by problems in the interpersonal arena and offers particular strategies for four interpersonal difficulties. These four difficulties are (1) abnormal or unresolved grief, (2) role disputes, in which two people disagree about how to define their relationship, or have conflicting expectations of each other, (3) role transitions, including life cycle changes that accompany the aging process, and (4) interpersonal deficits, in which individuals suffer from too few relationships. Specific treatment manuals have been developed for IPT in general (Klerman et al. 1984) and for treatment of adolescents in particular (Mufson et al. 1993). It is the one psychodynamic therapy that has been empirically studied most often, and in general its efficacy has been validated (Elkin 1994).

The **behavioral perspective** conceptualizes depression in terms of observable behaviors that operate under the influence of antecedent events (controlling stimuli) and subsequent events (reinforcement contingencies) in the environment. Depression is viewed as a low rate of behavior and a concurrent low mood that is a function of the total amount of positive reinforcement for any available response (Ferster 1971; Lewinsohn 1986). Not only must the reinforcement be available, but the person must also respond to the reinforcement. The rate of response-contingent reinforcement available depends on three factors: (1) events that are reinforcing to the person, (2) reinforcing events that are available in the immediate environment, and (3) the ability of the person to receive the reinforcement. The events that precipitate depression affect one or more of these factors.

Cognitive theories of depression emerged from the behavioral perspective and assume that cognition determines affect; that is, affective, motivational, and behavioral deficits are secondary to negative cognitions. Beck (1967) theorized that the root of depression is a "negative cognitive triad" that consists of a gloomy view of oneself, the world, and the future. Beck also introduced the notions of negative cognitive schemata and cognitive errors. Cognitive schemata are enduring, organized negative representations of past experience that act as filters and distort incoming information from the environment. Cognitive errors include a range of illogical and erroneous conclusions about the environment, such as overgeneralizing, selective abstraction, "catastrophizing," and dichotomous thinking.

These illogical ways of thinking are elicited and examined in cognitive-behavioral therapy. The role of the therapist is not to try to persuade the client that his or her thinking patterns are erroneous, but rather in a spirit of "collaborative empiricism" to design real-world experiments to see if the patterns are accurate and valid or not. Invariably, clients discover that the global negative conclusions they have reached about themselves are inaccurate. The social worker then helps the client to design alternative self-statements that the client uses to replace his or her negative thoughts. At the same time, behavioral homework assignments are used to combat the passivity and inactivity that is frequently symptomatic of depression (Beck et al. 1979).

Beck's cognitive therapy, which has gradually transformed itself into cognitive-behavioral therapy, has been the subject of numerous empirical studies. It has generally been validated as an effective treatment for depression (Emmelkamp 1994; Hollon and Beck 1994) and also for relapse prevention (Fava et al. 1998).

In some cases, severe major depression may not respond to psychotherapy of any kind, and somatic treatments are necessary, such as antidepressant medication or electroconvulsive treatment (ECT). However, straightforward **psychoeducation** about the nature of depression, its biopsychosocial basis and what to expect during the course of an episode, is helpful and appropriate. Many social workers are unfamiliar with severe major depression and attempt psychotherapy aimed at dynamic conflicts during an episode. For clients whose depressive symptoms include severe cognitive deficits, such as memory loss and an inability to engage in abstract thinking, the experience is frustrating at best and cruel at worst. Typically, clients blame themselves for their inability to benefit from a therapeutic intervention that leaves them with an increased feeling of worthlessness and hopelessness. They may even become desperate, because they continue to feel bad despite attempts to clarify conflicts, to rectify problems in interpersonal relationships, and to formulate new goals for themselves.

Marital and family therapy is also utilized as a treatment for depression. Capitalizing on the strong interpersonal aspects of depression for many individuals, marital therapy targets conflict between spouses, expressed emotion, skill deficits such as failure to offer support, and increases in expressiveness and marital intimacy. Behavioral marital therapy (BMT) has shown some promise in this regard, as well as other modalities (Jacobson et al. 1991; Prince and Jacobson 1995).

However, it is possible for a person to be so depressed or for a partner's negative attitudes and ideas about the hopelessness of the depressed person to be so overwhelming that marital therapy is impossible. For severe major depression, when antidepressant medication is necessary, it may be wise to delay marital treatment until the symptoms are alleviated sufficiently so that the depressed person can participate actively.

Somatic treatments for depression are used for MDD and in some cases of DD. The use of antidepressant medications has greatly increased in the last decade, heralded by Prozac. Since then a number of other selective serotonergic reuptake inhibitors (SSRIs) have been introduced, including Zoloft, Luvox, Paxil, and Celexa. The SSRIs are popular because of their lower incidence of side effects and low index of toxicity, relative to the older tricyclic/heterocyclic antidepressants (Tofranil, Elavil, Sinequan, etc.). A third category, rarely used except in refractory or unusual cases, is the MAO inhibitors (Nardil, Marplan). All of the antidepressants require several weeks for their effects to take place.

In instances of SAD, bright light treatment has proved effective (Avery 1998; Lam 1998). Individuals with SAD frequently respond within a few days, but cessation of the light treatment typically brings a rapid relapse as well. The dose (brightness, duration, and distance from the light) must be titrated, and although no eye damage has ever been reported from light treatment, clients are advised to undergo a precautionary eye examination prior to beginning treatment.

For any of the mood disorders, but particularly major depression, **hospitalization** is sometimes necessary due to high suicide risk, profound functional impairment, extreme severity of symptoms, or to make a particularly complex differential diagnosis. During a hospitalization, family intervention that includes the goals of accepting and understanding the illness and the possible precipitating stressors may improve family coping with depression and may result in greater compliance with and willingness to accept professional help. Interventions can also help to form strategies to deal with stressful family interactions by interrupting negative sequences between the depressed person and the other family members. Family members also can be encouraged to avoid overinvolvement, to foster the depressed person's autonomy, and to avoid burnout (Anderson et al. 1986). Multiple family groups can decrease stigmatization and isolation and can improve communication.

It can be difficult to work with depressed clients. The social worker often feels drained after an extended interaction and may feel frustrated by the seeming lack of effort on the part of the client. The client's pessimism and hopelessness may lead the social worker to feel the same way. These feelings may be alleviated by consultation with other professionals, a mixed caseload that includes problems other than depression, and a firm sense of where one's responsibilities begin and end.

The following case illustration is used to highlight several of the important clinical issues that emerge in working with depressed clients.

ILLUSTRATION AND DISCUSSION

Catherine G. is a 33-year-old nurse who was referred three days after the birth of her daughter. She was referred for a suspected postpartum depression. The social worker immediately suspected major depressive disorder based on symptoms such as slowed movements and a flat facial expression. The interview, which was difficult to conduct because of the client's slowed speech and memory difficulties, revealed multiple psychosocial stressors, including several major life events. Catherine was married to a man who suffered from debilitating lung disease. Both Catherine and her husband worked in the field of developmental disabilities and had planned to adopt a handicapped child. These plans were interrupted by the unplanned pregnancy. Catherine's mother had died eight weeks before the baby was born. Catherine had undergone a tubal ligation immediately following the birth in accordance with her husband's wishes.

An evaluation indicated that Catherine was suffering from major depressive disorder. Her depressive symptoms responded to a course of antidepressant medication within a few weeks. She had to stop nursing her baby when she began the medication, and once the symptoms lifted, she stopped the medication to resume nursing. Unfortunately, the symptoms reemerged, and she had to stop nursing in order to begin medication again. Within four months of her mother's death, Catherine's father remarried suddenly. The social work involvement during this time consisted of evaluation, support, and education about major depressive disorder. The supportive work included the provision of hope in the face of overwhelming hopelessness, as well as continual reminders that painful symptoms such as hopelessness would remit as the depression lifted. Catherine also needed continual reminders that symptoms such as feelings of worthlessness were components of depression and not of her character.

Catherine's significant past psychosocial history included a brief hospitalization as a teenager. She remembered only feeling blamed and refusing to talk to her parents during this time. She had been raped by her gynecologist when in her early 20s but had not reported the rape. Although she had worked with a variety of mental health professionals intermittently for ten years, her problem had never been assessed as major depression, which was partly biological. The therapy had tended to focus on her passive-aggressive behavior and her hostility, and one therapist had told her she "chose to be depressed" when therapy failed to alleviate her symptoms. She worked as a filing clerk until her mid-20s, when she decided on a career in nursing and eventually obtained a graduate degree.

Catherine's family history revealed many female relatives with histories consistent with depression, as well as an overly close mother-daughter relationship. The mother seemed to have been overinvolved, yet unaware of her daughter's needs. For example, Catherine had been named after her mother's favorite doll and had been discouraged from dating or other peer activities as a teenager. The parents had an unhappy marriage and the father traveled extensively in his work. The mother had confided her long-standing marital difficulties, including her father's numerous infidelities, to her daughter.

Once the symptoms of depression were under control, Catherine asked to work with the social worker on issues related to long-term feelings of helplessness and job and marital difficulties. She expressed a desire to understand why she had become an adult who lacked confidence and fulfillment, and she wanted to put the recent events, such as the death of her mother and her depression, behind her. The working relationship lasted three years. For some periods, the work was intermittent because of financial problems. At other times, when things were going well, the work would cease and contact would be on an as-needed basis. The majority of the three years consisted of sustained work every week that intensified during episodes of severe depression.

Following the initial episode, Catherine's depressive symptoms decreased, but she continued to experience low self-confidence, little interest in sex, and lack of energy. She also had fleeting thoughts of suicide. An initial attempt at insight-oriented psychotherapy had proved minimally useful. She talked of experiencing anger interspersed with sadness and was able to describe several strengths, such as determination, insightfulness, and motivation. She was passive in response to interpretations, and while she would superficially agree when ways to improve her situation were pointed out to her, she was unable to formulate independent solutions to her problems or to grapple actively with issues.

Because of Catherine's job termination, coupled with her husband's low-paying job, the family began experiencing severe financial difficulties. They moved into a small basement apartment in a poor neighborhood, and the dampness in the apartment set off serious asthmatic problems in the baby. With many disagreements over money management and sex, the couple experienced increased emotional distance.

Things improved as some of the stresses abated. Catherine's obtaining another job relieved the financial situation somewhat. At this point, the intervention plan was modified to incorporate mutually agreed-upon cognitive strategies. Negative cognitive schemata and the use of selective abstraction were actively challenged. Catherine began to be more assertive in her marriage. At her insistence, the couple obtained credit counseling despite her husband's strong resistance. She began to explore the possibility of having her unwanted tubal ligation reversed. Her marital dissatisfaction increased, and over time, a seesaw marital pattern was revealed: When Catherine's depression lifted, her husband's chronic illness would invariably worsen. Eventually, he began to have an affair with a woman at work, which prompted Catherine's first and only suicide attempt.

Within three years, Catherine experienced two additional episodes of severe depression and was hospitalized briefly once. Each episode responded to a course of antidepressant medication, and after the second episode, she decided to continue the medication indefinitely. Eventually, she began to experience severe cardiac side effects from the medication. Numerous changes and reductions in medication ensued. Despite the serious complications, Catherine resisted stopping the medication for fear that the deep depression would return. She came to believe that the depression was entirely controlled by the antidepressant medication. The worker-client relationship ended when the social worker moved from the area. During termination, Catherine was unable to express any feelings of anger or loss, saying only that there was nothing she could do about the move.

This case clearly demonstrates the complex coexistence of major depression and dysthymic disorder. Support was critical during severe episodes of depression, to fill in deficits that were caused by the depressive symptoms and to help the client cope with the multiple uncontrollable life events that were occurring.

Support continued between episodes, and other issues were addressed. Glimmers of appropriate mastery behavior can be seen in Catherine's psychosocial history (her return to school) and in the current work (her active handling of the financial situation and her exploration of reversing the unwanted tubal ligation).

Socialization into a passive orientation to life is relevant to this case and is not uncommon in many women in our society. Inappropriate intrusiveness like that exhibited by Catherine's mother is often found in the histories of depressed women. We can surmise that the inappropriate disclosure of her father's behavior did little to foster a vision of healthy reciprocal relationships between men and women. We can also hypothesize that the developmental stage of separation and individuation that usually occurs in late adolescence was hampered by depression and hospitalization, and that the rape only reinforced Catherine's feeling of not being in control of her life. Not surprisingly, insight-oriented therapy was not the treatment of choice, as evidenced by her response to medication and cognitive strategies.

The worker-client relationship in this case reflects typical relationships between depressed clients and significant others. An alliance is easily established during the most severe episode of depression but is characterized by extreme dependence. The alliance must be renegotiated when the depression lifts, or the worker will join the larger environment by sending a message that the client perceives as saying that the client is not capable of taking control of his or her own life. An underlying current of hostility can also be read in this vignette. An inability to express feelings of anger or loss is evident in the client's attitude toward termination.

CONCLUSION

This chapter has described the theories, the social influences, and the risk and protective factors associated with depression. Assessment and intervention issues have also been described. A great deal of clinical "knowledge" about depression is based on the fallacy that it is a homogeneous phenomenon. It is not. Clear definitions of depression and a clarification of the distinguishing features of the different types of depression will enhance treatment for social workers' clients, but we need to learn more. Most information about depression has been gleaned from middle-class samples, and very little information exists about the poor. More research is needed to explore differential treatment strategies and programs for the different types of depression.

The prevalence of depression, the extensive suffering it causes, and the effective clinical interventions available stand in tragic contrast to the lack of appropriate care received by those who need it. Today, 80 to 90 percent of people with a major depressive disorder can be helped successfully, but only one person in three with depression ever seeks treatment (Regier et al. 1988).

Depression is the most treatable of any of the major psychiatric disturbances, but it goes unrecognized and untreated because it is misunderstood. Public attitudes toward depression need to be changed so that there is greater acceptance of depression as a serious health problem, rather than a moral or personality weakness. Social workers can help to alleviate or prevent problems with depression among vulnerable people by taking an active role in educating other professionals to recognize depression. The training that social workers receive in the dynamics of human behavior makes them especially suited to alert professionals in other disciplines to the need to identify and obtain treatment for depressed clients outside psychiatric settings. Social workers can also work to increase public knowledge about the symptoms of depression and the availability of effective interventions, and to develop new programs to meet the needs of the depressed.

Social workers are in a unique position to assume a critical role in ensuring that clients will be identified early and will be provided appropriate care. Social workers have the perspective, the training, and the expertise to identify the emotional distress associated with social problems, especially as it varies with the particular social problem presented, and with the characteristics of the client. With its unique person-environment perspective, social work can and should take a leading role in the identification and treatment of depression. Early recognition and proper care of depressed clients may help prevent other serious individual and social problems, including perhaps the most significant consequence of depression, suicide.

References

Abraham, K. 1911/1986. "I. Notes on Psychoanalytical Investigation and Treatment of Manic-Depressive Insanity and Allied Conditions (1911)." In J. Coyne, ed., *Essential Papers on Depression,* pp. 23–31. New York: New York University Press.

American Psychiatric Association (APA). 1994. *Diagnostic and Statistical Manual of Mental Disorders (DSM-IV),* 4th ed. Washington, D.C.: Author.

Anderson, C., S. Griffin, A. Rossi, I. Pagonis, and D. Holder. 1986. "A Comparative Study of the Impact of Education vs. Process Groups for Families of Patients with Affective Disorders." *Family Process* 25:185–205.

Angold, A., A. Erkanli, R. Loeber, and E. J. Costello. 1996. "Disappearing Depression in a Population Sample of Boys." *Journal of Emotional and Behavioral Disorders* 42:95–104.

Angold, A. and C. W. Worthman. 1993. "Puberty Onset of Gender Differences of Depression: A Developmental, Epidemiological, and Neuroendocrine Perspective." *Journal of Affective Disorders* 29:145–58.

Aro, H. 1994. "Risk and Protective Factors in Depression: A Developmental Perspective." *Acta Psychiatrica Scandinavia.* 377 (Supplement):59–64.

Avery, D. H. 1998. "A Turning Point for Seasonal Affective Disorder and Light Therapy Research?" *Archives of General Psychiatry* 55:863–64.

Axelrod, J., L. Geismar, and R. Ross. 1994. "Families of Chronically Mentally Ill Patients: Their Structure, Coping Resources, and Tolerance for Deviant Behavior." *Health and Social Work* 19:271–78.

Badger, L. W. and E. H. Rand. 1998. "Mood Disorders." In J. B. W. Williams and K. Ell, eds., *Advances in Mental Health Research: Implications for Practice,* pp. 49–117. Washington, D.C.: National Association of Social Workers Press.

Baker, F. M. 1996. "An Overview of Depression in the Elderly: A U.S. Perspective." *Journal of the National Medical Association* 88:178–84.

Beardslee, W. R. 1989. "The Role of Self-Understanding in Resilient Individuals: The Development of a Perspective." *American Journal of Orthopsychiatry* 59:266–78.

Bebbington, P. E. and L. Kuipers. 1994. "The Predictive Utility of Expressed Emotion in Schizophrenia." *Psychological Medicine* 24:707–18.

Beck, A. 1967. *Depression: Clinical, Experimental, and Theoretical Aspects.* New York: Harper & Row.

——. 1991. "Cognitive Therapy: A 30-Year Retrospective." *American Psychologist* 46: 368–75.

Beck, A. T., A. J. Rush, B. F. Shaw, and G. Emery. 1979. *Cognitive Therapy of Depression.* New York: Guilford.

Bernheim, K., and T. Switalski. 1988. "Mental Health Staff and Patients' Relatives: How They View Each Other." *Hospital and Community Psychiatry* 39:63–68.

Bibring, E. 1953. "The Mechanism of Depression." In P. Greenacre, ed., *Affective Disorders,* pp. 48–64. New York: International Universities Press.

Bifulco, A., G. W. Brown, and T. Harris. 1987. "Childhood Loss of Parent, Lack of Adequate

Parental Care, and Adult Depression: A Replication." *Journal of Affective Disorders.* 12:115–28.

Billings, A. and R. Moos. 1986. "Psychosocial Theory and Research on Depression: An Integrative Framework and Review. In J. C. Coyne, ed., *Essential Papers on Depression,* pp. 331–66. New York: New York University Press.

Birmaher, B., N. D. Ryan, D. E. Williamson, D. A. Brent, J. Kaufman, R. E. Dahl, J. Perel, and B. Nelson. 1996. "Childhood and Adolescent Depression: A Review of the Past 10 Years. Part I." *Journal of the American Academy of Child and Adolescent Psychiatry* 35:1427–39.

Blatt, S. J. 1995. "The Destructiveness of Perfectionism: Implications for the Treatment of Depression." *American Psychologist* 50:1003–20.

Blazer, D. G., R. C. Kessler, K. A. McGonagle, and M. S. Swartz. 1994. "The Prevalence and Distribution of Major Depression in a National Community Sample: The National Comorbidity Survey." *American Journal of Psychiatry* 151(7):979–86.

Blumenthal, S. J. 1994. "Women and Depression." *Journal of Women's Health* 3:467–79.

Book, H. E. 1998. *How to Practice Brief Psychodynamic Psychotherapy: The Core Conflictual Relationship Theme Method.* Washington, D.C.: American Psychological Association.

Breier, A., J. Kelsoe, P. Kirwin, S. Bellar, O. Walkowitz, and D. Pickar. 1988. "Early Parental Loss and Development of Adult Psychopathology." *Archives of General Psychiatry* 45:987–93.

Brent, D. A., G. Moritz, J. Bridge, J. Perper, and R. Canobbio. 1996. "The Impact of Adolescent Suicide on Siblings and Parents: A Longitudinal Follow-Up." *Suicide and Life-Threatening Behavior* 26:253–59.

Brent, D. A., J. A. Perper, G. Moritz, C. Allman, A. Friend, C. Roth, J. Schweers, L. Balach, and M. Baugher. 1993a. "Psychiatric Risk Factors for Adolescent Suicide: A Case-Control Study." *Journal of the American Academy of Child and Adolescent Psychiatry* 32:521–29.

Brent, D. A., J. A. Perper, G. Moritz, C. Allman, L. Liotus, J. Schweers, C. Roth, L. Balach, and R. Canobbio. 1993b. "Bereavement or Depression? The Impact of the Loss of a Friend to Suicide." *Journal of the American Academy of Child and Adolescent Psychiatry* 32:1189–97.

Bromberger, J. T. and E. J. Costello. 1992. "Epidemiology of Depression for Clinicians." *Social Work* 37(2):120–25.

Bromet, E. J., L. O. Dunn, M. M. Connell, M. A. Dew, and H. C. Schulberg. 1986. "Long-term Reliability of Diagnosing Lifetime Major Depression in a Community Sample." *Archives of General Psychiatry* 43:435–40.

Brown, D. R., F. Ahmed, L. E. Gary, and N. G. Milburn. 1995. "Major Depression in a Community Sample of African Americans." *American Journal of Psychiatry* 152:373–78.

Brown, G. W. and T. Harris. 1978. *The Social Origins of Depression.* New York: Free Press.

Brown, G., A. Bifulco, and T. Harris. 1987. "Life Events, Vulnerability, and the Onset of Depression: Some Refinements." *British Journal of Psychiatry* 150:30–42.

Burnam, M. A., J. A. Stein, J. M. Golding, J. M. Siegel, S. B. Sorenson, A. B. Forsythe, and C. A. Telles. 1988. "Sexual Assault and Mental Disorders in a Community Population." *Journal of Consulting and Clinical Psychology* 56:843–50.

Caplan, G. 1990. "Loss, Stress, and Mental Health." *Community Mental Health Journal* 26:27–48.

Carbonell, D. M., H. Z. Reinharz, and R. M. Giaconia. 1998. "Risk and Resilience in late Adolescence." *Child and Adolescent Social Work Journal* 15:251–72.

Christie, K. A., J. D. Burke, D. A. Regier, D. S. Rae, J. H. Boyd, and B. Z. Locke. 1988. "Epidemiologic Evidence of Early Onset of Mental Disorders and Higher Risk of Drug Abuse in Young Adults." *American Journal of Psychiatry* 145:971–75.

Cohen, M., G. Baker, R. Cohen, F. Fromm-Reichman, and E. Weigert. 1954. "An Intensive Study of Twelve Cases of Manic-Depressive Psychosis." *Psychiatry* 17:103–37.

Coleman, P., A. Aubin, M. Robinson, C. Ivani-Chalian, and R. Briggs. 1993. "Predictors of Depressive Symptoms and Low Self-Esteem in a Follow-Up Study of Elderly People Over 10 Years." *International Journal of Geriatric Psychiatry* 8:343–49.

Conrad, B. S. 1998. "Maternal Depressive Symptoms and Homeless Children's Mental Health: Risk and Resiliency." *Archives of Psychiatric Nursing* 12:50–58.

Conwell, Y., P. R. Duberstein, C. Cox, J. H. Herrmann, N. T. Forbes, and E. D. Caine. 1996. "Relationships of Age and Axis I Diagnoses in Victims of Completed Suicide: A Psychological Autopsy Study." *American Journal of Psychiatry* 153:1001–8.

Copeland, M. E. 1992. *The Depression Workbook: A Guide For Living with Depression and Manic Depression.* Oakland, Calif.: New Harbinger Books.

Covey, L. S., A. H. Glassman, and F. Stetner. 1997. "Major Depression Following Smoking Cessation." *American Journal of Psychiatry* 154:263–65.

Coyne, J. C. and G. Downey. 1991. "Social Factors and Psychopathology: Stress, Social Support, and Coping Processes." *Annual Review of Psychology* 42:401–25.

Coyne, J. C., R. C. Kessler, M. Tal, et al. 1987. "Living with a Depressed Person." *Journal of Consulting and Clinical Psychology* 55:347–52.

Cross-National Collaborative Group. 1992. "The Changing Rate of Major Depression: Cross-National Comparisons." *Journal of the American Medical Association* 268(21):3098–105.

Duncan, R. D., B. E. Saunders, D. G. Kilpatrick, R. F. Hanson, and H. S. Resnick. 1996. "Childhood Physical Assault as a Risk Factor for PTSD, Depression, and Substance Abuse: Findings from a National Survey." *American Journal of Orthopsychiatry* 66:437–48.

Elkin, I. 1994. "The NIMH Treatment of Depression Collaborative Research Program: Where We Began and Where We Are." In A. E. Bergin and S. L. Garfield, eds., *Handbook of Psychotherapy and Behavior Change,* 4th ed., pp. 114–39. New York: John Wiley.

Emmelkamp, P. M. G. 1994. "Behavior Therapy with Adults." In A. E. Bergin and S. L. Garfield, eds., *Handbook of Psychotherapy and Behavior Change,* 4th ed., pp. 379–427. New York: John Wiley.

Fava, G. A., C. Rafanelli, S. Grandi, R. Canestrari, and M. A. Morphy. 1998. "Six-Year Outcome for Cognitive Behavioral Treatment of Residual Symptoms in Major Depression." *Archives of General Psychiatry* 155:1443–45.

Fellin, P. 1989. "Perspectives on Depression Among Black Americans." *Health and Social Work* 14:245–52.

Ferguson, K. L. and M. R. Rodway. 1994. "Cognitive Behavioral Treatment of Perfectionism: Initial Evaluation Studies." *Research on Social Work Practice* 4:283–308.

Ferster, C. 1971. "A Functional Analysis of Depression." *American Psychologist* 10:857–70.

Freud, S. 1896/1962. "Mourning and Melancholia." Standard Edition of the Collected Works of Sigmund Freud. In J. Coyne, ed., *Essential Papers on Depression,* pp. 48–63. New York: New York University Press.

Gary, L. E., D. R. Brown, N. G. Milburn, V. G. Thomas, and D. S. Lockley. 1985. *Pathways: A Study of Black Informal Support Networks.* Washington, D.C.: Howard University Press.

Gaviria, M. and J. A. Flaherty. 1993. "Depression." In J. A. Flaherty, J. M. Davis, and P. G. Janicak, eds., *Psychiatry: Diagnosis and Therapy,* pp. 46–75. Norwalk, Conn.: Appleton & Lange.

Gibbs, J. T. 1997. "African-American Suicide: A Cultural Paradox." *Suicide and Life-Threatening Behavior* 27:68–79.

Giesler, R. B., R. A. Josephs, and W. B. Swann, Jr. 1996. "Self-Verification in Clinical Depression: The Desire for Negative Evaluation." *Journal of Abnormal Psychology* 105:358–68.

Gilbert, P. 1999. *Overcoming Depression.* New York: Oxford University Press.

Gold, M. S. 1995. *The Good News About Depression.* New York: Bantam.

Goldberg, J. F., J. L. Garno, A. C. Leon, J. H. Kocsis, and L. Portera. 1998. "Association of Recurrent Suicide Ideation with Nonremission from Acute Mixed Mania." *American Journal of Psychiatry* 155:1753–55.

Goldin, L. R. and E. S. Gershon. 1988. "The Genetic Epidemiology of Major Depressive Illness." In A. J. Francis and R. E. Hales, eds., *Review of Psychiatry,* pp. 149–68. Washington, D.C.: American Psychiatric Press.

Gomez, M. R. 1990. "Biculturalism and Subjective Mental Health Among Cuban Americans." *Social Service Review* 64:375–89.

Gotlib, I., J. Mount, N. Cordy, and V. Whiffen. 1988. "Depression and Perceptions of Early Parenting: A Longitudinal Investigation." *British Journal of Psychiatry* 152:24–27.

Greenberg, P. E., L. E. Stiglin, S. N. Finkelstein, and E. R. Berndt. 1993. "The Economic Burden of Depression." *Journal of Clinical Psychiatry* 54:405–18.

Greenfield, S. F., J. M. Reizes, K. M. Magruder, L. R. Muenz, B. Koplans, and D. G. Jacobs. 1997. "Effectiveness of Community-Based Screening for Depression." *American Journal of Psychiatry* 154:1391–97.

Hamburg, S. R. 1998. "Inherited Hypohedonia Leads to Learned Helplessness: A Conjecture Updated." *Review of General Psychology* 2:384–403.

Hammen, C. 1991. "Generation of Stress in the Course of Unipolar Depression." *Journal of Abnormal Psychology* 100:555–61.

Henry, W. P., H. H. Strupp, T. E. Schacht, and L. Gaston. 1994. "Psychodynamic Approaches." In A. E. Bergin and S. L. Garfield, eds., *Handbook of Psychotherapy and Behavior Change,* 4th ed., pp. 467–508. New York: John Wiley.

Hewitt, P. L. and G. L. Flett. 1993. "Dimensions of Perfectionism, Daily Stress, and Depression: A Test of the Specific Vulnerability Hypothesis." *Journal of Abnormal Psychology* 102:58–65.

Hill, S. Y. and D. Muka. 1996. "Childhood Psychopathology in Children from Families of Alcoholic Female Probands." *Journal of the American Academy of Child and Adolescent Psychiatry* 35:725–33.

Hollon, S. D. and A. T. Beck. 1994. "Cognitive and Cognitive-Behavioral Therapies." In A. E. Bergin and S. L. Garfield, eds., *Handbook of Psychotherapy and Behavior Change,* 4th ed., pp. 428–66. New York: John Wiley.

Hooley, J. 1986. "Expressed Emotion and Depression: Interactions Between Patients and High- Versus Low-Expressed Emotion Spouses." *Journal of Abnormal Psychology* 95:237–46.

Hooley, J. M. and J. D. Teasdale. 1989. "Predictors of Relapse in Unipolar Depressives: Expressed Emotion, Marital Distress, and Perceived Criticism." *Journal of Abnormal Psychology* 98:229–35.

Horowitz, M. J., B. Siegel, A. Holen, G. A. Bonanno, C. Milbrath, and C. H. Stinson. 1997. "Diagnostic Criteria for Complicated Grief Disorder." *American Journal of Psychiatry* 154:904–10.

Howland, R. H. 1993. "Chronic Depression." *Hospital and Community Psychiatry* 44:633–39.

Howland, R. H. and M. E. Thase. 1993. "A Comprehensive Review of Cyclothymic Disorder." *Journal of Nervous and Mental Disease* 181:485–93.

Husaini, B. A. 1997. "Predictors of Depression Among the Elderly: Racial Differences Over Time." *American Journal of Orthopsychiatry* 67(1):48–58.

Jacob, M., E. Frank, D. Kupfer, C. Cornes, and L. Carpenter. 1987. "A Psychoeducational Workshop for Depressed Patients, Family, and Friends: Description and Evaluation." *Hospital and Community Psychiatry* 38:968–72.

Jacobson, N. S., K. Dobson, A. E. Fruzzetti, K. B. Schmaling, and S. Salusky. 1991. "Marital Therapy as a Treatment for Depression." *Journal of Consulting and Clinical Psychology* 59:547–57.

Jenkins, J. H. and M. Karno. 1992. "The Meaning of Expressed Emotion: Theoretical Issues Raised by Cross-Cultural Research." *American Journal of Psychiatry* 149:9–21.

Jobes, D. A., A. L. Berman, P. W. O'Carroll, S. Eastgard, and S. Knickmeyer. 1996. "The Curt Cobain Suicide Crisis: Perspectives from Research, Public Health, and the News Media." *Suicide and Life-Threatening Behavior* 26:260–71.

Keitner, G. I. and I. W. Miller. 1990. "Family Functioning and Major Depression: An Overview." *American Journal of Psychiatry* 147:1128–37.

Keitner, G. I., C. E. Ryan, I. W. Miller, R. Kohn, D. S. Bishop, and N. B. Epstein. 1995. "Role of the Family in Recovery and Major Depression." *American Journal of Psychiatry* 152:1002–8.

Kendler, K. S. 1997. "Social Support: A Genetic-Epidemiologic Analysis." *American Journal of Psychiatry* 154:1398–1404.

Kendler, K. S., R. C. Kessler, M. C. Neale, A. C. Heath, and L. J. Eaves. 1992. "The Prediction of Major Depression in Women: Toward an Integrated Etiologic Model." *American Journal of Psychiatry* 150:1139–48.

Kendler, K. S., R. C. Kessler, E. E. Walters, C. MacLean, M. C. Neale, A. C. Heath, and L. J. Eaves. 1995. "Stressful Life Events, Genetic Liability, and Onset of an Episode of Major Depression in Women." *American Journal of Psychiatry* 152:833–42.

Kendler, K. S., M. C. Neale, R. C. Kessler, A. C. Heath, and L. J. Eaves. 1992. "A Population-Based Twin Study of Major Depression in Women: The Impact of Varying Definitions of Illness." *Archives of General Psychiatry* 49:257–66.

Kessler, R. C., J. A. Abelson, and S. Zhao. 1998. "The Epidemiology of Mental Disorders." In J. B. W. Williams and K. Ell, eds., *Advances in Mental Health Research: Implications for Practice*, pp. 3–24. Washington, D.C.: National Association of Social Workers Press.

Kessler, R. C., K. A. McGonagle, M. Swartz, D. G. Blazer, and C. B. Nelson. 1993. "Sex and Depression in the National Comorbidity Survey I: Lifetime Prevalence, Chronicity, and Recurrence." *Journal of Affective Disorders* 29:85–96.

Kessler, R. C., K. A. McGonagle, S. Zhao, C. B. Nelson, M. Hughes, S. Eshleman, H-U. Wittchen, and K. S. Kendler. 1994. "Lifetime and 12-Month Prevalence of *DSM-III-R* Psychiatric Disorders in the United States." *Archives of General Psychiatry* 51(1):8–19.

Kessler, R. C. and J. D. McLeod. 1987. "Sex Differences in Vulnerability to Undesirable Life Events." *American Sociological Review* 49:620–31.

Kessler, R. C. and H. Neighbors 1986. "A New Perspective on the Relationships among Race, Social Class, and Psychological Distress." *Journal of Health and Social Behavior* 27:107–15.

Kessler, R. C., C. B. Nelson, K. A. McGonagle, J. Liu, M. Swartz, and D. G. Blazer. 1996. "Comorbidity of DSM-III-R Major Depressive Disorder in the General Population: Results from the U.S. National Comorbidity Survey." *British Journal of Psychiatry* 168 (Supplement 30):17–30.

Kessler, R. C., R. H. Price, and C. B. Wortman. 1985. "Social Factors in Psychopathology: Stress, Social Support, and Coping Processes." *Annual Review of Psychology* 36:531–72.

Klerman, G. L., M. M. Weisman, B. J. Rounsaville, and E. S. Chevron. 1984. *Interpersonal Psychotherapy of Depression*. New York: Basic Books.

Lam, R. W., ed. 1998. *Seasonal Affective Disorder and Beyond*. Washington, D.C.: American Psychiatric Press.

Levitan, R. D., S. V. Parikh, A. D. Lesage, K. M. Hegadoren, M. Adams, S. H. Kennedy, and P. N. Goering. 1998. "Major Depression in Individuals with a History of Childhood Physical or Sexual Abuse: Relationship to Neurovegetative Features, Mania, and Gender." *American Journal of Psychiatry* 155:1746–52.

Levy, A. J. and H. Land. 1994. "School-Based Interventions with Depressed Minority Adolescents." *Child and Adolescent Social Work Journal* 11:21–35.

Lewinsohn, P. M. 1986. "A Behavioral Approach to Depression." In J. Coyne, ed., *Essential Papers on Depression*, pp. 150–80. New York: New York University Press.

Lewinsohn, P. M., R. E. Roberts, J. R. Seeley, P. Rohde, I. H. Gotlib, and H. Hops. 1994. "Adolescent Psychopathology: II. Psychosocial Risk Factors for Depression." *Journal of Abnormal Psychology* 103:302–15.

Lewinsohn, P. M., P. Rohde, J. R. Seeley, and S. A. Fischer. 1993. "Age-Cohort Changes in the Lifetime Occurrence of Depression and Other Mental Disorders." *Journal of Abnormal Psychology* 102(1):110–20.

Liem, J. H., J. B. James, J. G. O'Toole, and A. C. Boudewyn. 1997. "Assessing Resilience in Adults with Histories of Childhood Sexual Abuse." *American Journal of Orthopsychiatry* 67:594–606.

Lizardi, H., D. N. Klein, P. C. Ouimette, L. P. Riso, R. L. Anderson, and S. K. Donaldson. 1995. "Reports of the Childhood Home Environment in Early-Onset Dysthymia and Episodic Major Depression." *Journal of Abnormal Psychology* 104:132–39.

Mattlin, J. A., E. Wethington, and R. C. Kessler. 1990. "Situational Determinants of Coping and Coping Effectiveness." *Journal of Health and Social Behavior* 31:103–22.

McLeod, J. D. and R. C. Kessler. 1990. "Socioeconomic Status Differences in Vulnerability to Undesirable Life Events." *Journal of Health and Social Behavior* 31:162–72.

Merikangas, K., E. Bromet, and D. Spiker. 1983. "Assortative Mating, Social Adjustment, and Course of Illness in Primary Affective Disorder." *Archives of General Psychiatry* 40:795–800.

Merikangas, L. R. 1984. "Divorce and Assortative Mating Among Depressed Inpatients." *American Journal of Psychiatry* 141:74–76.

Morgado, A., M. Smith, Y. Lecrubier, and D. Widlocher. 1991. "Depressed Subjects Unwittingly Overreport Poor Social Adjustment Which They Reappraise When Recovered." *Journal of Nervous and Mental Disease* 179:614–19.

Moscicki, E. K., B. Z. Locke, D. S. Rae, and J. H. Boyd. 1989. "Depressive Symptoms among Mexican Americans: The Hispanic Health and Nutrition Examination Survey." *American Journal of Epidemiology* 130:348–60.

Mufson, L., D. Moreau, M. M. Weissman, and G. L. Klerman. 1993. *Interpersonal Psychotherapy for Depressed Adolescents.* New York: Guilford.

Narrow, W. E., D. S. Rae, E. K. Moscicki, B. Z. Locke, and D. A. Regier. 1990. "Depression Among Cuban Americans: The Hispanic Health and Nutrition Examination Survey." *Social Psychiatry and Psychiatric Epidemiology* 225:260–68.

"New Federal Guidelines Seek to Help Primary Care Providers Recognize and Treat Depression." 1993. *Hospital and Community Psychiatry* 44:598.

Newman, S. C. and R. C. Bland. 1998. "Incidence of Mental Disorders in Edmonton: Estimates of Rates and Methodological Issues." *Journal of Psychiatric Research* 32:273–82.

Newmann, J. P. 1987. "Gender Differences in Vulnerability to Depression." *Social Service Review* 61:447–68.

Noh, S. and R. Turner. 1987. "Living with Psychiatric Patients: Implications for the Mental Health of Family Members." *Social Science and Medicine* 25:263–71.

Nunes, E. V., M. M. Weissman, R. B. Goldstein, G. McAvay, A. M. Seracini, H. Verdeli, and P. Wickramaratne. 1998. "Psychopathology in Children of Parents with Opiate Dependence and/or Major Depression." *Journal of the American Academy of Child and Adolescent Psychiatry* 37:1142–51.

O'Connell, R. A. and J. A. Mayo. 1988. "The Role of Social Factors in Affective Disorders: A Review." *Hospital and Community Psychiatry* 39:842–51.

Osborn, A. F. 1990. "Resilient Children: A Longitudinal Study of Highly Achieving Socially Disadvantaged Children." *Early Child Development and Care* 62:23–47.

Paykel, E. 1982. "Life Events and Early Environment." In E. Paykel, ed., *Handbook of Affective Disorders,* pp. 146–61. New York: Guilford.

Pearlin, L. I. and C. Schooler. 1978. "The Structure of Coping." *Journal of Health and Social Behavior* 19:2–21.

Post, R. M. 1992. "Transduction of Psychosocial Stress into the Neurobiology of Recurrent Affective Disorder." *American Journal of Psychiatry* 149:999–1010.

Potter, L. B., L. H. Rogler, and E. K. Moscicki. 1995. "Depression Among Puerto Ricans in New York City: The Hispanic Health and Nutrition Examination Survey." *Social Psychiatry and Psychiatric Epidemiology* 30:185–93.

Prigerson, H. G., E. Frank, S. V. Kasl, C. F. Reynolds, B. Anderson, G. S. Zubenko, P. R. Houck, C. J. George, and D. J. Kupfer. 1995. "Complicated Grief and Bereavement-Related Depression as Distinct Disorders: Preliminary Empirical Validation in Elderly Bereaved Spouses." *American Journal of Psychiatry* 152:22–30.

Prince, S. E. and Jacobson, N. S. 1995. "A Review and Evaluation of Marital and Family Therapies for Affective Disorders." *Journal of Marital and Family Therapy* 21:377–401.

Radke-Yarrow, M. and T. Sherman. 1990. "Hard-Growing: Children Who Survive." In J. E. Rolf and A. S. Masten, eds., *Risk and Protective Factors in the Development of Psychopathology,* pp. 97–119. New York: Cambridge University Press.

Ragan, P. and T. McGlashan. 1986. "Childhood Parental Death and Adult Psychopathology." *American Journal of Psychiatry* 143:153–57.

Rapaport, M. H. and M. Suminski. 1994. "National Depression Screening Day: The San Diego Experience." *Hospital and Community Psychiatry* 45:1042.

Regier, D. A., J. Boyd, J. Burke, D. Roe, J. Myers, M. Kramet, L. Robins, L. George, M. Karao, and B. Locke. 1988. "One-Month Prevalence of Mental Disorders in the U.S.—Based on Five Epidemiologic Catchment Area Sites." *Archives of General Psychiatry* 45:977–86.

Regier, D. A., J. K. Myers, M. Kramer, L. N. Robins, D. G. Blazer, R. L. Hough, W. W. Eaton, and B. Z. Locke. 1984. "The NIMH Epidemiologic Catchment Area Program: Historical Context, Major Objectives, and Study Population Characteristics." *Archives of General Psychiatry* 41:934–41.

Regier, D. A., W. E. Narrow, D. S. Rae, R. W. Manderschied, B. Z. Locke, and F. K. Goodwin. 1993. "The De Facto U.S. Mental and Addictive Disorders Service System: Epidemiologic Catchment Area Prospective 1-Year Prevalence Rates of Disorders and Services." *Archives of General Psychiatry* 50:85–94.

Reich, W., F. Earls, O. Frankel, and J. J. Shayka. 1993. "Psychopathology in Children of Alcoholics." *Journal of the American Academy of Child and Adolescent Psychiatry* 32:995–1002.

Roberts, R. E., G. A. Kaplan, S. J. Shema, and W. J. Strawbridge. 1997. "Does Growing Old Increase the Risk for Depression?" *American Journal of Psychiatry* 154:1384–90.

Roberts, R. E., C. R. Roberts, and Y. R. Chen. 1997. "Ethnocultural Differences in Prevalence of Adolescent Depression." *American Journal of Community Psychology* 25:95–110.

Robins, L. N., J. E. Helzer, M. M. Weissman, H. Orvaschel, E. Gruenberg, J. D. Burke, and D. A. Regier. 1984. "Lifetime Prevalence of Specific Psychiatric Disorders in Three Sites." *Archives of General Psychiatry* 41:949–58.

Rosenfarb, I. S., M. J. Goldstein, J. Mintz, and K. H. Nuechterlein. 1995. "Expressed Emotion and Subclinical Psychopathology Observable within the Transactions between Schizophrenic Patients and their Family Members." *Journal of Abnormal Psychology* 104:259–67.

Roy, A. 1987. "Five Risk Factors for Depression." *British Journal of Psychiatry* 150:536–41.

Rutter, M. 1985. "Resilience in the Face of Adversity: Protective Factors and Resistance to Psychiatric Disorder." *British Journal of Psychiatry* 147:598–611.

——. 1987. "Psychosocial Resilience and Protective Mechanisms." *American Journal of Orthopsychiatry* 57:316–31.

——. 1988. "Epidemiological Approaches to Developmental Psychopathology." *Archives of General Psychiatry* 45:486–95.

Sack, R. L., A. J. Lewy, D. M. White, C. M. Singer, M. J. Fireman, and R. Vandiver. 1990. "Morning vs. Evening Light Treatment for Winter Depression: Evidence That the Therapeutic Effects of Light Are Mediated by Circadian Phase Shifts." *Archives of General Psychiatry* 47:343–51.

Sainsbury, P. 1986. "Depression, Suicide, and Suicide Prevention." In A. Roy, ed., *Suicide,* pp. 73–88. Baltimore: Williams & Wilkins.

Schwartz, A. and R. M. Schwartz. 1993. *Depression Theories and Treatments: Psychological, Biological, and Social Perspectives.* New York: Columbia University Press.

Schwartz, C. E., D. J. Dorer, W. R. Beardslee, P. W. Lavor, and M. B. Keller. 1990. "Maternal Expressed Emotion and Parental Affective Disorder: Risk for Childhood Depressive Disorder, Substance Abuse, or Conduct Disorder." *Journal of Psychiatric Research* 24:231–50.

Scott, K. D. 1992. "Childhood Sexual Abuse: Impact on a Community's Mental Health Status." *Child Abuse and Neglect* 16:285–95.

Seeman, M. V. 1997. "Psychopathology in Women and Men: Focus on Female Hormones." *American Journal of Psychiatry* 154:1641–47.

Seligman, M. E. P. 1990. *Learned Optimism.* New York: Pocket Books.

Seligman, M. E. P., K. Reivich, L. Jaycox, and J. Gillham. 1995. *The Optimistic Child.* Boston: Houghton Mifflin.

Shaffer, D., M. S. Gould, P. Fisher, P. Trautman, D. Moreau, M. Kleinman, and M. Flory. 1996. "Psychiatric Diagnosis in Child and Adolescent Suicide." *Archives of General Psychiatry* 53:339–48.

Shalev, A. Y., S. Freedman, T. Peri, D. Brandes, T. Sahar, S. P. Orr, and R. K. Pitman. 1998. "Prospective Study of Posttraumatic Stress Disorder and Depression Following Trauma." *American Journal of Psychiatry* 155:630–37.

Shedler, J., M. Mayman, and M. Manis. 1993. "The *Illusion* of Mental Health." *American Psychologist* 48:1117–31.

Shrout, P. E., B. G. Link, B. P. Dohrenwend, A. E. Skodol, A. Stueve, and J. Mirotznik. 1989. "Characterizing Life Events as Risk Factors for Depression: The Role of Fateful Loss Events." *Journal of Abnormal Psychology* 98:460–67.

Smith, C. and B. E. Carlson. 1997. "Stress, Coping, and Resilience in Children and Youth." *Social Service Review* 71:231–36.

Sorenson, S. B., C. M. Rutter, and C. S. Aneshensel. 1991. "Depression in the Community: An Investigation into Age of Onset." *Journal of Consulting and Clinical Psychology* 59(4):541–46.

Spaner, D., R. C. Bland, and S. C. Newman. 1994. "Major Depressive Disorder." *Acta Psychiatrica Scandinavia* (Supplement 376):7–15.

Spiegel, D. and T. Wissler. 1987. "Using Family Consultation as Psychiatric Aftercare for Schizophrenic Patients." *Hospital and Community Psychiatry* 38:1096–99.

Stevenson, H. C., J. Reed, P. Bodison, and A. Bishop. 1997. "Racism Stress Management: Racial Socialization Beliefs and the Experience of Depression and Anger in African American Youth." *Youth and Society* 29:197–222.

Straus, M. A. and G. K. Kantor. 1994. "Corporal Punishment of Adolescents by Parents: A Risk Factor in the Epidemiology of Depression, Suicide, Alcohol Abuse, Child Abuse, and Wife Beating." *Adolescence* 29:543–61.

Styron, W. 1990. *Darkness Visible: A Memoir of Madness.* New York: Random House.

Takeuchi, D. T., R. C. Chung, K. Lin, H. Shen, K. Kurasaki, C. Chun, and S. Sue. 1998. "Lifetime and Twelve-Month Prevalence Rates of Major Depressive Episodes and Dysthymia Among Chinese Americans in Los Angeles." *American Journal of Psychiatry* 155:1407–14.

Tennant, C., P. Bebbington, and J. Hurry. 1982. "Social Experiences in Childhood and Adult Psychiatric Morbidity: A Multiple Regression Analysis." *Psychological Medicine* 12:321–27.

Turnbull, J. E., M. J. Galinsky, M. E. Wilner, and D. E. Meglin. 1993. "Designing Research to Meet Service Needs: An Evaluation of Single Session Groups for Families of Psychiatric Inpatients." *Journal of Research on Social Work Practice* 4:192–208.

Turner, R. J., B. Wheaton, and D. A. Lloyd. 1995. "The Epidemiology of Social Stress." *American Sociological Review* 60:104–25.

204 I Life Conditions

Valentine, L. and L. L. Feinauer. 1993. "Resilience Factors Associated with Female Survivors of Childhood Sexual Abuse." *American Journal of Family Therapy* 21:216–24.

Wagnild, G. M. and H. M. Young. 1993. "Development and Psychometric Evaluation of the Resilience Scale." *Journal of Nursing Measurement* 1:165–78.

Weiss, H. 1989. "State Family Support and Education Programs: Lessons from the Pioneers." *American Journal of Orthopsychiatry* 59(1):32–48.

Weissman, M. M. 1987. "Advances in Psychiatric Epidemiology: Rates and Risks for Major Depression." *American Journal of Public Health* 145:445–51.

Weissman, M. M., G. D. Gammon, K. John, K. R. Merikangas, V. Warner, B. A. Prusoff, and D. Sholomskas. 1987. "Children of Depressed Parents: Increased Psychopathology and Early Onset of Major Depression." *Archives of General Psychiatry* 44:847–53.

Weissman, M. M., K. Kidd, and B. Prusoff. 1982. "Variability in Rates of Affective Disorders in Relatives of Depressed and Normal Probands." *Archives of General Psychiatry* 39:1397–1403.

Weissman, M. M., P. J. Leaf, M. L. Bruce, and L. Florio. 1988. "The Epidemiology of Dysthymia in Five Communities: Rates, Risks, Comorbidity, and Treatment." *American Journal of Psychiatry* 145:815–19.

Weissman, M. M., and J. K. Myers. 1978. "Affective Disorders in a U.S. Urban Community: The Use of Research Diagnostic Criteria in an Epidemiological Survey." *Archives of General Psychiatry* 35:1304–11.

Weissman, M. M., V. Warner, P. Wickramaratne, D. Moreau, and M. Olfson. 1997. "Offspring of Depressed Parents: 10 Years Later." *Archives of General Psychiatry* 54:932–40.

Worden, J. W. 1991. *Grief Counseling and Grief Therapy: A Handbook for the Mental Health Practitioner,* 2d ed. New York: Springer.

Zigler, E. and K. Black. 1989. "America's Family Support Movement: Strengths and Limitations." *American Journal of Orthopsychiatry* 59(1):6–19.

7 Developmental Disabilities

Claudia L. Moreno

Developmental disAbilities is an area that requires multi- and interdisciplinary involvement. Social work is an important and essential component because of the profession's practice, advocacy, programming, and social policy involvement. Further, social work contribution emphasizes the family-centered approach characterized by the provision of services within the context of the whole family. In this chapter, the *abilities* of individuals with disAbilities is emphasized; that is, the term *disAbilities* is viewed from a strengths perspective.

Developmental disAbilities are conditions and disorders that affect any areas of cognitive, physical, communication, social, emotional, and adaptive development. The federal definition of developmental disAbilities requires that an impairment must be present before the age of 22 and be severe and chronic in nature. For those under 6, the definition of disAbility encompasses limitations in the usual kind of activities in that age group, and it is also based on the receipt of services or therapy for developmental, behavioral or emotional needs (U.S. Census Bureau 1997). The definition of who is developmentally disAbled has been problematic for some groups who resist being classified as developmental disAbled because of the stigma attached to people with mental retardation (Mackelprang and Salsgiver 1996).

Developmental disAbilities can affect individuals on a temporary or lifelong basis. Individuals also move across the spectrum of disAbility or involvement in their lifetime, depending on several factors, which include the nature of the disAbility, developmental achievements, individual differences, rehabilitation services, and the environment in which they function and grow. Where individuals are in reference to the spectrum of their disAbility is an approach that social workers need to be attuned to because individuals might need different services and support across the life span that vary in need and duration. This has implications for practice, programming, advocacy, and social policy.

Developmental disAbilities affect individuals and their families in different ways, ways that depend on the nature of the disAbility, ability level, coping and stress, individual differences, culture and belief systems, society's response to a specific condition, and attitudes and value system.

DEFINING AND EXPLAINING DEVELOPMENTAL DISABILITIES

Over the last five decades individuals with developmental disAbilities and their families have been profoundly affected by social, economic, philosophical, political, and scientific changes. These changes have included scientific discoveries about drug treatment and prevention of certain conditions, medical technologies to keep at-risk children alive, deinstitutionalization of the disAbled and mentally ill, cash benefits to the disAbled and their families, physical and employment access to public places, public special education, legal protection of civil rights, and the rise of self-help movements for both the disAbled and their families.

Family caregiving is the product of social policy generated by multiple factors: clinical, fiscal, legal, and humanistic. Since ancient times families have provided care to their disAbled members. Perceptions about parental influence are related to philosophical perspectives and treatment of the time. The psychogenic theory in the early 1950s made parents responsible for the child's psychological problems and personality (DeMause 1974). This perspective was influential in portraying "mothers" as bad parents, lacking knowledge and skills and in some way responsible for their children's condition (DeMause 1974). Treatment approaches included working with parents' anxieties and frustrations and removing the child from the parent.

Over time this perspective changed, influenced by the emergence of research findings that demonstrate that developmental disAbilities, specifically those that are in the social and adaptive domain (e.g., autism, schizophrenia), are not caused by parents and have other biological and unknown causes (Rimland 1964). This approach has contributed to removing blame from parents as the cause of their children's conditions. Then in the early 1960s, parents' reaction to their child's disAbility was conceptualized from the bereavement perspectives of Kübler-Ross (1969) and Freud (1957), which suggested that parents' grief can be understood from a stage perspective, including shock, denial, guilt, shame, anxiety, hopelessness, blame, anger, fear, and acceptance.

From the 1980s, the stress and coping perspective has been influential in understanding how parents experience and cope with a disAbled child. This perspective changes the focus from considering only the caregiver's experience to considering the experiences of *all* family members (Dyson 1993). It also concentrates on parental psychological factors such as self-esteem, coping, and stress levels (including the initial crisis that parents experience when they find out that their child has a disAbility) and changes over time. Contextual aspects such as family functioning, financial burden, and the adequacy and availability of resources in the micro- and macroenvironments are considered (Pearlin et al. 1981). The ecological perspective has been helpful in understanding the broader context of the reciprocal interaction of families and children with disAbilities within a social-ecological environment (Rogers-Dulan and Blacher 1995). Gallimore et al. (1993) developed the ecocultural model by drawing from the ecological theory (Bronfenbrenner 1979) and integrating cultural aspects (the psychocultural model developed by Whiting and Whiting 1975). It considers how families adapt to tasks required by the special needs of their children's activities and development. The process of how families adapt includes ecological constraints, available resources, cultural beliefs and customs, and opportunities that are sustainable, meaningful, and congruent (Gallimore et al. 1993). This process of accommodation is extended to all family members. This ecocultural model has been embraced by the cross-cultural adaptation model that includes the ecological perspective, emphasizing the centrality of the parent's culture (belief system, religion, practices, values) in understanding how disAbility is perceived and constructed. Dilworth-Anderson and Anderson (1994) suggest that research about the effects of race on the caregiving experience needs to be informed by an understanding of the social, cultural, and psychological context in which the caregiving takes place. This perspective criticizes other models that ignore the context of culture and make generalizations based primarily on white samples.

DEMOGRAPHIC PATTERNS

The U.S. Census Bureau (1997) estimated that 1 in 5 Americans have some kind of disAbility and 1 in 10 have a severe disAbility. An estimated 4 million children and adolescents, or 6.1 percent of the U.S. population under 18 years of age, have disAbilities. Here, *disAbility* is defined broadly to include any limitation in activity due to a chronic health condition or impairment. Results for a 1994 survey indicated that 12 percent of U.S. children below 18 years of age had a chronic physical, developmental, behavioral, or emotional condition (Newacheck et al. 1998).

Lower levels of income have been associated as a stronger predictor of having a child with a disAbility. Poor families are four times more likely to have a child with a disAbility in comparison to the general population (U.S. Census Bureau 1997). Poverty has been blamed as the closest link to other social problems and conditions. Some forms of mental retardation, low birth weight, prematurity, chronic health problems and other disAbilities, and some secondary conditions have been related to low-income populations. Children in poor families present an elevated risk for disAbilities and chronic health problems. In addition, with regard to race, American Indians (27 percent) and blacks (21 percent) are more likely to have a disAbility than whites (18 percent), Hispanics (18 percent) or Asians (10 percent) (U.S. Census Bureau 1997).

SOCIETAL CONTEXT

Historically, we have neglected and rejected the notions of differences, especially when it comes to disAbility. The early conceptions of disAbility have been influenced by sociocultural and political belief systems that implied negative views of the disAbled (Mackelprang and Salsgiver 1998). Individuals with developmental disAbilities and mental retardation have been portrayed throughout history with stereotypical language, such as "evil," "deviant," "deficient," "sick" (Bryan 1996), "perpetual children," "incompetent," "biologically deficient," "deviant," "a curse or a gift from God" (Moreno 1996), and "passive and dependent" (Priestley 1998). This language also has negatively portrayed other disAbilities. Conditions such as blindness, cerebral palsy, learning disAbilities, autism, or speech problems are not necessarily accompanied by mental retardation. In addition, mental retardation and developmental disAbilities vary in severity and ability.

From the 1960s, several activist groups have demanded that people with disAbilities have access to the mainstream of society, not just in terms of social justice and equal rights, but also in terms of how they are defined as individuals. Activists reveal a macroperspective of disAbilities by enhancing awareness about how the larger society creates and perpetuates disAbilities as a result of architectural and attitudinal barriers (Mackelprang and Salsgiver 1998). Individuals with disAbilities have been pushed into rehabilitation with a "fix the individual" approach without addressing the environmental barriers that perpetuate their conditions and make them more disAbled. Upon the dawn of the twenty-first century, society has made little progress, if we consider the effort, and if activists continue to be silenced (Mackelprang and Salsgiver 1998). In addition, the voices of disAbled children have frequently been excluded. Social workers have created dependence and diminished self-advocacy, growth, and empowerment (Gilson, Bricout, and Baskind 1998).

Currently, different groups and social workers who advocate on behalf of people with disAbilities stress for alternative models and approaches. Among these approaches, the strengths and empowerment perspective provides a focus upon abilities, strengths, potentialities, and capabilities. The independent living model advocates for self-determination and social and economic justice for people with disAbilities. In addition, disAbility needs to be seen as an aspect of diversity and not as a deficiency (Mackelprang and Salsgiver 1998); individuals with any disAbility have to negotiate complex identities within a world that disAbles their own conditions (Priestley 1998). People with disAbilities have suggested that social workers need to move away from the label, listen to their specific needs, recognize the individual strengths and capabilities of individuals with disAbilities, integrate them as active participants in their own struggle, and recognize their expert advice (Gilson et al. 1998).

In working with families of children with developmental disAbilities, the new paradigm includes the family-centered approach, which stresses empowering parents rather than emphasizing solely the psychological treatment of their "emotional dysfunction." Using this approach involves shifting the focus of service and interventions to support and empower families instead of perceiving them as targets of change (Johnson et al. 1998).

VULNERABILITIES AND RISK FACTORS

The presence of a disAbility increases the likelihood of living in poverty or with lower income. According to the U.S. Census Bureau (1997), the proportion of individuals with a disAbility receiving cash assistance is 62.4 percent. Although, 77.4 percent of Americans between the ages of 22 and 64 do not receive public assistance, disAbility is relatively common among individuals who receive cash, food, or rent assistance. Low-income families have a higher incidence of children with chronic illness or a disAbility, which may be as high as 40 percent (Newacheck and McManus 1988). Poor families of children with disAbilities carry a double burden, their child's condition and financial problems (Beresford 1994). In a study conducted in California with 1,320 families, 43 percent of AFDC recipients had children with disAbilities and chronic health problems, and the severity of their children's conditions had an impact on the economic well-being of families (Meyers, Lukemeyer, and Smeeding 1998). The presence of a child with a disAbility can impose socioeconomic stress to families that includes lower income, part-time work, inability to work due to care demands of the disAbled child, and difficulties obtaining suitable employment to meet current needs (Breslau, Salkever, and Staruch 1982). Social workers must understand how financial matters affect families of children with developmental disAbilities.

In addition, lack of financial resources limits the ability of families to obtain proper care for their children, including rehabilitation services, transportation, respite care, and adequate medical services (Beresford 1994). When families are poor, high proportions of medical care are received in city hospitals and emergency rooms. Most pediatricians in the community do not see these children because they do not accept Medicaid in their private practices. When these children go to emergency rooms, their medical conditions might be more severe because of the lack of affordable medical care in the community. The financial assistance provided by governmental programs does not include out-of-pocket expenses for families such as transportation for families to schools, doctors, and therapists; modification of the living headquarters; or special equipment (not covered by Supplemental Security Income [SSI] or insurance), clothing, and food. In addition, the care of these children can impose considerable costs on families and government programs (Meyers et al. 1998). For families of undocumented children, these financial hardships are even greater. They are forced to use whatever services or equipment they can receive through charitable organizations or programs. Financial burden is also related to psychological stress and psychosocial reactions; families with lower incomes suffer from higher levels of psychological stress than families with higher incomes (Palfrey et al. 1989). They also tend to be more isolated and experience more family conflict and anxiety.

Measuring levels of stress and coping is an area that has been given much attention in working with families of developmentally disAbled children. Families of children with disAbilities are at risk for emotional and psychological difficulties (Dyson 1991, 1993). Perception of stress is complicated by differences in socioeconomic interpretation of disAbility, culture, and ethnicity (Moreno 1996), and parental educational levels. A greater perception of difficulties in accepting a child with a disAbility is reported by highly educated parents (Palfrey et al. 1989). In addition, parents are affected differently depending on the type of disAbility. In a study conducted with parents of children with Down's syndrome, with autism, and without a disAbility, parents of children with autism revealed elevated levels of stress compared with the other sets of parents (Sanders and Morgan 1997). Parents of children with disAbilities will always have to confront the fact that their child is not the one they would have. Parents begin a period of crisis when they are informed about their child's diagnosis. It is a time of painful, often overwhelming, feelings and emotional reactions such as shock, disbelief, anger, and grief (Leff-Taner and Hilburn-Walizer 1992). For social workers, this is a time to start where the client is—parents need support, guidance, and information about available resources and knowledge about their children's condition.

Grief can be present at different stages of development. In addition, parental stress varies over time, and changes in these levels will occur as children grow older. Divorce rates are higher among families of children with disAbilities (Hodapp and Krasner 1995), regardless of socioeconomic status. However, these divorce rates vary according to the type of disAbility (Sanders and Morgan 1997). DisAbilities that tend to be most stressful for the family system, such as autism and severe behavioral difficulties, are associated with higher divorce rates (Jenkins and Smith 1993).

Finally, there is a need to use sensitive language when referring to people with disAbilities and their families. Gilson and colleagues (1998) found that the language we use to talk about people with disAbilities has become more positive and affirming and is moving away from label-oriented language (e.g., autistic children) to people-first language (e.g., children with autism). Gilson et al. also criticize most research and articles about families of children with disAbilities because they do not reflect the positive aspects of raising a child with a disAbility but focus on the negative aspects, with families still portrayed as victims. Social work practice with the families of developmentally delayed children should include a strengths perspective, which is vital for accurate assessment, intervention, and development of services and programs.

RESILIENCIES AND PROTECTIVE FACTORS

Resilience in families and children with developmental disAbilities needs to be seen from a perspective of how families cope in spite of the stress, turmoil, and demands that a child with developmental disAbilities takes on parents, families, and communities. Many families thrive and become very strong and resilient. Some parents can find spiritual or religious answers to their situation, viewing it as a gift from God. Others might see the situation as a test of endurance and patience, and still others reconcile themselves by considering it a matter of luck or happening for unknown reasons.

Germenzy (1993) defines *risk factors* as the increased potential for an individual to develop emotional or behavioral disorders in comparison to the general population. Risk factors need to be contextualized to developmental disAbilities. For instance, a child with attention deficit disorder (ADD) can be at risk for developing behavioral difficulties. However, even though the presence of ADD can be a risk factor, many children do well in spite of their condition. Common risk factors for children with developmental disAbilities can be temperament, severity of the developmental delay, biological/genetic factors, and gender (Morrison and Cosden 1997). In addition, the literature associates risk factors to conditions associated with poverty (Rounds, Weil, and Bishop 1994), nutrition, and lack of resources needed for the specific condition, abuse, family disruption, and socioemotional complications. On the other hand, risk factors need to be viewed as multidimensional in terms of analyzing how disruptions in individuals, families, and communities have harmed functioning. *Resilience* has been defined as a process of bouncing back from adversity, resulting in adaptive outcomes even in the presence of challenging situations (Morrison and Cosden 1997). Resilience is also viewed as the individual strengths and capacity to recover or deal with hardship.

Many families and children with developmental disAbilities are resilient in spite of their circumstances and might be more resilient at specific stages than others. Resilience can present a challenge for social workers who might not think that a child has a good prognosis because of his or her condition. Many children develop, improve, and make dramatic changes in spite of their disAbility.

PROGRAMS AND SOCIAL WORK CONTRIBUTIONS

Social work has a long history in the delivery of direct services, advocacy, programming, and social policy for individuals with developmental disAbilities and their families. Services and entitlements for children with developmental disAbilities vary from state to state. Policies and eligibility have changed over time according to shifts in philosophies and advocacy efforts. Social workers need to be attuned to these changes in the law because they have implications for service delivery.

Over the past five decades, services and programs for individuals with disAbilities and their families have been affected by social, economic, and scientific changes. These changes have included the availability of drug treatments that have helped to alleviate conditions such as mental illness, severe conduct disorders, ADD, and other conditions. Since the deinstitutionalization of the mentally ill and the mentally retarded, the federal government and states have been forced to create programs in the community. Over the years, community services have changed and improved according to individual, community, state, and special interest groups. This process of restructuring and improving services, options, and supports has emphasized community inclusion and direct support for individuals and families (Balcazar et al. 1996). Families of children with developmental disAbilities were hardly included in the decision-making process. During the last decade, however, different interest groups have advocated for full inclusion in the decision process and the enhancement of empowerment for families. Parents need training, networking, knowledge, and leadership skills to be successful advocates.

Health Care and Insurance. In many states, every child who is born with a disAbility or a chronic condition is registered by a health professional and/or hospital. Children and families, *referred to as Case Management Units*, are followed in order to connect them with appropriate services. Many social workers are actively involved in case management and provide not only concrete services but also support and advocacy.

Some states have adopted legislation to provide cash benefits to cover the cost of uncovered medical expenses for a child with an illness, if the expenses exceed 10 percent of the family's income and are uncovered by insurance or other programs. One such fund in New Jersey, called the Catastrophic Illness in Children Relief Fund (www.state.nj.us/humanservices/article1.html), does not limit coverage to specific diseases or diagnoses, and expenses might include hospital, physician bills, medications, medical equipment, transportation for treatment, psychiatric and home health care, and specialized home and vehicle modifications.

For those families who do not qualify for Medicaid, SSI, or any other state or federal program due to their income, President Clinton signed, on August 5, 1997, the Children's Health Insurance Program (CHIP). This program provides medical coverage for those uninsured children from middle-income homes who do not have health insurance. The Department of Human Services (www.hcfa.gov/init/wh-chip7.htm) is forming task forces in many states to educate families and professionals about the potential eligibility for health insurance, because this information was not being widely disseminated.

The Social Security Act was enacted in 1935 and only until 1959 included aid to the permanently and totally disAbled, excluding children. In 1972, the SSI program was created but also excluded children. After pressure from social workers and other interest groups in 1974, Title XVI was established under SSI, and for the first time disAbled children were eligible. In 1997, the Congress revised eligibility, and some disAbilities considered "minor" were ineligible to receive SSI, which determines eligibility based on family income *and* diagnosis. Once the child reaches the age of 18, eligibility depends only on an individual's income. SSI provides cash assistance and coverage for medical and rehabilitation expenses. In 1997, welfare reform temporarily changed cash benefits such as SSI, TANF, and state-funded General Assistance programs for many immigrants (legal residents) who arrived after August 22, 1996. The changed was reconsidered after political pressure, and services were reinstated for all legal residents. However, the bad press that asserted that immigrants are a public charge, as well as the fear of interfering with naturalization services, decreased the numbers of immigrants asking for entitlements, especially for families of children with developmentally delayed children.

Some states require that Medicaid beneficiaries enroll in managed care programs. Some groups are advocating for the specific needs of children and adults with special needs to receive services according to the multiple and complex needs of their situation, such as housing, employment, and need for special equipment, that might directly affect their condition (www.families.usa.org/FCTDIS.HTM).

Education. Social workers, educators, and rehabilitation professionals have been pioneers in delivering services to children who are developmentally disAbled and their families. The Education for All Handicapped Children Act (PL-142) in 1975 gave the right to all children with special needs to receive free special education. In 1978, an educational amendment (PL 96–561) was included to allow handicapped children to be placed by local school districts into private schools.

Programs such as Early Intervention and Head Start have been significant in improving the quality of life for many children with a variety of conditions (Mahoney et al. 1998). Early interventions programs are funded by federal, state, and local funds, as well as, private organizations to provide therapies and support for children and families who have children from 0 to 3 years of age with developmental disAbilities and those who are at risk for developing a disAbility. This criterion includes gestational age, low birth weight, and presenting medical problems.

Head Start is a preschool program for low-income children and children who are identified as at risk. This program has been very successful in providing cognitive and social gains to children who otherwise might have fallen between the cracks in day care centers (Lee, Brooks-Gunn, and Schnur 1998).

Once a child with developmental disAbilities reaches the age of 3, he or she is eligible for a special preschool program as determined by the Board of Education. Children are evaluated by a multidisciplinary team of professionals who develop an individualized educational plan (IEP).

In 1990, the Americans with Disabilities Act (ADA) was signed by the federal government to protect against discrimination based on a person's disAbility. This legislation was influential in making special legislative mandates to the Individual Disabilities Education Act (IDEA) in making categories specific, identifying children with disAbilities or at risk for developmental delays, and in the development of service plans for these children (Lifter 1999). IDEA emphasizes family-centered, community-based services for children with and at risk for disAbilities as a result of conditions associated with poverty (Rounds et al. 1994). In addition, advocacy efforts have improved the education for children with developmental delays because parents and interest groups felt that just the "special needs" area was emphasized and not the academic arena. The Disabilities Education Act Amendments of 1997 significantly improved the educational opportunities for children with disAbilities.

Special education services for children with developmental delays also have shifted in approaches, from removing the child from the regular classroom for specialized education to current approaches to mainstream children. Mainstreaming emphasizes allowing special needs children to remain in regular classes with nondisAbled peers. In the past, it was very difficult to remove children with disAbilities from mainstream classes or special education classes. A recent concept that has emerged in education is inclusion. With inclusion, a child's primary placement is in the regular education class, and the child has no additional assignment to any special class. Advocates for inclusion support the provision of specialized services, not separate education.

Thus, services for children with developmental disAbilities and their families have evolved over the years and will continue to change. Social workers have an important role that consists of sharing information, providing referrals, providing specific ways parents can help their children, supportive and psychotherapeutic services, advocacy, empowerment, teaching coping skills, involving parents in the decision process, acknowledging and valuing parent's expertise about their own children and specific condition, using parents as cotherapists, keeping up-to-date with current knowledge, and informing parents of state-of-the-art services, treatment, and pertinent information (Johnson et al. 1998).

ASSESSMENT AND INTERVENTIONS

Multidimensional assessment is a process of gathering information regarding the different dimensions that are present in the micro- and macroenvironments of clients during treatment and intervention. It is used in screening, diagnosing, and determining eligibility, program planning, service delivery, and advocacy. Interventions are planned efforts to bring some form of problem solving to the personal, family, community, group, or organizational or societal level. Interventions include finding and developing different types of resources.

Families of children with developmental disAbilities have been misunderstood over time, and assessment has been influenced by pathology and maladjustment models. New models now include other aspects, such as the complexity of family functioning and ecological approaches regarding the multidimensionality of individuals. However, current models have been criticized (Masters-Glidden 1993) because of the assumptions they make, such as: (1) a family with a child with a disAbility is a family with a disAbility; (2) the child's exclusive reliance is on the mother, although generalizations are made to the entire family; (3) stress is pathological and negative in nature; and (4) researchers do not differentiate among the demands, stresses, and strains faced by families with developmentally delayed children.

In working with families of developmentally delayed children, proper assessment and intervention include looking at different dimensions of the micro- and macro-ecological systems of clients. For an accurate assessment, five dimensions of the systems need to be considered in our work with families of developmentally delayed children: family context, children characteristics, strengths, social context and supports, and cultural differences.

Family Context. Each member of a family with a child with a disAbility is different from one another. This uniqueness implies that separate and individual assessments and interventions should be conducted to identify person-specific stressors, demands, strains, adjustments, strengths, and individuals' developmental stages within the context of the family life cycle (Seltzer and Heller 1997) and availability and quality of resources.

Research has shown that mothers have higher levels of stress in parenting a child with developmental disAbilities than in parenting a child who has no disAbilities (Frey, Greenberg, and Fewell 1989). Social workers face families who are struggling financially, often as single parents, in addition to raising children with disAbilities. These families face a triple challenge: stress, depression and strains. Coping is related not only to the child's condition and demands but also to the overall family situation. The financial situation, in addition to single parenting and having a child with developmental disAbilities, can result in extra strains in the parenting role and in the way a parent feels as a person (Stokes-Gottlieb 1997).

Experiences by fathers and mothers in raising children with disAbilities tend to be different. In the past, research suggested that mothers experienced higher levels of stress than fathers (Milgram and Atzil 1988). New findings shed light on the new roles that parents are adopting in the care of their children with special needs. Fathers appear more involved in the care and rearing of the child and experience the same level of stress as mothers (Dyson 1997).

When assessing families, it is important to consider the stage and quality of relationships, marital satisfaction, and the age and developmental stage of children. For instance, some families of children with disAbilities might be experiencing difficulties with an adolescent in addition to the child with disAbilities. Families of children with disAbilities confront myriad issues like any other family. Often parents need to divide their time to meet the needs of the child with special needs and to satisfy the needs of other family members.

Of all family members, we often assume that parents of children with developmental disAbilities are the most affected. Siblings of children with disAbilities, as well as grandparents and other relatives, are also affected by having a family member with a disAbility (Atkins 1989; Bagenholm and Gillberg 1991).

Families of children with disAbilities need to balance the new demands imposed by the special care of their children. It is important to assess how family members balance the demand of children with special needs and sustain the multiple caregiving, partner, sibling, family member, and work roles.

Characteristics of Children. Developmental disAbilities do not affect parents the same way. Children who have severe cases of behavioral difficulties such as autism, severe attention-deficit hyperactivity disorder (ADHD), or severe mental retardation affect parents more than those children with milder cases (Beckman 1983). Research studies reveal that parents experience greater stress with boys and with children whose communication skills are low (Frey et al. 1989).

The child's age in the life cycle can generate more demands and greater stress for a family. For instance, some adolescents with autism experience heightened behavioral outbursts and developmental manifestations, such as sexuality (Moreno, under review), and this period can be very stressful for parents and the family in general. Younger children with severe behavioral problems in addition to limited self-help skills can transform parenting into a twenty-four-hour job. In many instances, parents need to perform all the daily activities for children such as bathing, tooth brushing, dressing, and eating. These activities demand constant energy from parents, generally mothers.

Strengths. Social workers must remove the deficit perspective and acknowledge that families of children with disAbilities have their own values, perceptions, and uniqueness (Weick et al. 1989). We need to acknowledge that families of children with developmental disAbilities are families and not disAbled families. All families go through changes, conflict, and transformation, and their experiences are not uniform (Seltzer and Heller 1997). A strengths-based perspective allows social workers to see the strengths of individual members and gain a sense of how a child with developmental disAbilities transforms a family, gives meaning, and makes parents experts and resources for other parents (Kurtz 1997). A disAbilities-strength perspective needs to incorporate the experience, values, and specific choices of families of children with disAbilities and to assist them in redefining, evaluating, and choosing their own goals and priorities. Parents need to be seen as resources, partners, and experts with regard to their own children.

On the other hand, in assessing family strengths, it is important to assess strengths in the context of personal history, current and past challenges, and the immediate social environment (McQuaide and Ehrenreich 1997). There are factors within these three dimensions that transcend individuals' situations and cannot be attributed solely to them.

Finally, services for families of developmentally delayed children should be guided based on the family's perspective and not the social worker's values. We are there to assist and not to impose. We can assist families and nurture their development in their own journey with children with specific conditions.

Social Context and Social Support. As discussed earlier in this chapter, our historical view of the disAbled has shaped policy, programs, practice, attitude, and values. The social context is a very important aspect to address within the assessment process. We used to blame parents for their children's disAbilities, and that was accepted by practitioners. Now we need to reevaluate the present social context in reference to how it influences advocacy, practice, policy development, programs, and the rights of the disAbled.

Part of the social context is the attitude and behavior of professionals toward parents. The literature discusses that parents and individuals with disAbilities are concerned about the overt behavior of professionals toward parents. Areas of concern include minimizing and devaluing parent's expertise about their children, blame attribution, explaining the scope of treatment options, teaching coping skills, sharing information, involving parents in the assessment and treatment decisions, advocacy, keeping up-to-date with latest treatments, respecting parents' beliefs in nontraditional cures, and referring parents to services beyond their expertise (Johnson et al. 1998).

Structural barriers, found within the social context, limit our practice and intervention. Managed care, for instance, has impacted on the quality and quantity of services for the disAbled. Immigration laws also restrict the care and treatment of undocumented children and their families. This area is of specific concern for social workers because we should advocate for the creation or transformation of programs, services, and laws on behalf of the disAbled and their families.

Assessing and developing interventions about the adequacy of social supports for parents of children with developmental disAbilities is one of the foundations of social work. Parents of children with developmental disAbilities experience a tremendous burden and might feel isolated, stressed, and depressed about their child's condition and the impact that it makes on the family as a whole (Seltzer and Heller 1997). The quality and the quantity of supports is an important area for social workers to assess, as the literature stresses that parents with strong social supports cope better than parents with low levels of support (Friedrich, Cohen, and Wilturner 1985; Gavidia-Payne and Stoneman 1997). Supports can be informal (natural) and formal (institutions, programs). Informal supports can be social contacts that provide assistance to families of children with disAbilities, such as family members, friends, and community and other resources available for the family. Informal supports also can consist of centers of worship, social/civic organizations, grocery stores, restaurants, beauty parlors, and support groups (Delgado 1998). Part of the social work assessment should consider the community where the family lives, because some communities have more resources than others. This area is usually neglected in assessment. Research suggests that social support might lessen the stresses and demands experienced by families of the developmentally disAbled (Weiss 1991). Formal support consists of schools, community programs, agencies, mental health centers, and hospitals. Families of children with developmental disAbilities might have frequent contact with these places in the form of rehabilitation and therapeutic services.

Cultural Differences. Families with cultural differences from the mainstream culture often cope with tensions associated with cultural differences. Parents have beliefs about their children's condition that might not match those of the larger society. Parents from different cultures have different ideas about etiology and theories of conditions; as a result, indigenous treatment techniques might be different from traditional approaches (Moreno 1996). It is important for social workers to acquire awareness of the variations between different ethnic groups with regard to child rearing, parenting, achievement, perception of disAbilities (Moreno, under review), family roles, and family styles. In addition, for proper assessment and intervention, social workers need to be aware of the values, customs, religious and folk beliefs, worldviews, boundaries, behavioral and linguistic patterns, and individual differences of their clients. Some families of children with disAbilities might seek nontraditional cures for their children's conditions. Social workers need to be sensitive to these practices and use them in positive ways instead of informing families that they are not accepted. Some innovations are occurring with nontraditional cures used in conjunction with traditional cures.

Families of children with disAbilities who have immigrated to this country present a real challenge in reference to their own journey to a new country, culture, and language. Relocation to a new environment brings the stresses that come with financial, employment, housing, and demographic changes. Immigration disrupts the family life cycle. Immigrant families of children with disAbilities need extra help not only in what matters to their children but also in learning to negotiate educational, legal, and community systems; they also must familiarize themselves with the dominant value system in the host country (Lequerica 1993). Some immigrant families leave children behind and mourn this practice. Language difficulties are common for most families who arrive in a host country. This is a real challenge for the social worker who might need to do extra work with these families.

Religion has been found to influence how parents adapt, experience, interpret, and respond to children with developmental disAbilities (Weisner, Breizer, and Stolze 1991). Many families turn to religion, faith, prayers, and celestial powers as a way of coping with their children's conditions. For social workers, assessing religious views of children with developmental disAbilities can help in developing adequate intervention and treatment plans. For instance, a mother who believes children with disAbilities are gifts from God might have different needs in the therapeutic process than a mother who thinks that children with disAbilities are a punishment from God.

ILLUSTRATION AND DISCUSSION

Working with families of children with developmental disAbilities involves a multi- or interdisciplinary approach. This means that social workers should be working along with other professionals involved in comprehensive assessment and intervention, including neurodevelopmental pediatricians, neurologists, psychologists, speech pathologists, and occupational and physical therapists. According to the presenting problem and the nature of the setting, each professional will conduct an assessment and provide recommendations for intervention; professionals also might administer tests to identify areas of need and strengths and the nature of the problem.

The case presented here happened in a center for the evaluation and treatment of developmental disAbilities. Children are referred to the center by their physicians, social workers, family members, day care centers, or friends. This is the story of Mrs. Rodriguez, who was referred by a neighbor because her 2½-year-old boy, Ramon, had some "odd behaviors," such as lack of response to people, poor eye contact, hand flapping, echolalia, aggressiveness, and being in a world of his own. The intake worker had set up an appointment with the social worker for a psychosocial evaluation. When Mrs. Rodriguez heard that the social worker was fluent in Spanish, she felt at ease and became very verbal. Speaking the same language of a client and being from the same ethnic group may facilitate rapport and the emergence of the client's story. Ramon was first seen by the social worker who, in order to have a better understanding of the case, took a history of the "problem," developmental milestones, medical events, and the family context.

Mrs. Rodriguez mentioned that she first noticed that her Ramon was "different" when he was a year old. She did not seek any help because she thought that he might be just a quiet and introverted boy. However, Ramon's behavior puzzled her because he used to play with car toys and align them with much detail. She thought that he was going to be a very well organized boy. Mrs. Rodriguez's neighbor, who has a child with speech delays, advised Mrs. Rodriguez to have the child evaluated at the same place. Ramon's developmental milestones had been achieved within normal limits except for his language and socialization skills. He currently has no language and utters a few words that he hears. Mrs. Rodriguez was not sure if Ramon's hearing was normal because he was not responsive to some noises or when spoken to. Ramon was described as a "loner" who does not play with his siblings. Rather he ignores them. He doesn't watch television and doesn't play with all kinds of toys. He screams a lot for no reason at all and hits his siblings. Mrs. Rodriguez reported that Ramon doesn't like to be touched, held, or comforted. Ramon's health has been remarkable except for a few colds and ear infections. Mrs. Rodriguez blames herself for Ramon's behavior and feels that she hasn't given enough attention to his needs. Taking a detailed history of the child's condition, developmental milestones, and behavior and the parent's response to the child's condition is essential. Mrs. Rodriguez's self-blaming is very common among parents of children with behavioral, emotional, and speech problems. Many parents feel that they are in part responsible for their child's condition.

Mrs. Rodriguez is 23 years old. She was born in Mexico, where she finished a fifth-grade education. She is currently a homemaker and married to Mr. Rodriguez, who is 44 years old. He was also born in Mexico and works as a baker in a local Spanish bakery. He earns minimum wage and works seven days a week. He also finished fifth grade and reads and writes with more difficulty than Mrs. Rodriguez. They have been married for eight years and have been in this country for six years. They crossed the border with the help of a "coyote" and lived in California for six months before moving to the East Coast. They are undocumented, but their three children were born in this country. They have a daughter, Cristina, who is 6 years old; Jose, who is 4 years old; and Ramon, who is the youngest. Cristina and Jose are in good health and have no problems. Cristina is currently attending first grade in a local public school. The family does not have health insurance. When the children are sick, Mrs. Rodriguez seeks help from women in the community who know home remedies and if it doesn't work, she takes the children to the local emergency room. For many low-income families, the emergency room is the only chance families have to see a physician, and in many circumstances the medical problems are severe. Going to healers or local botanical shops is a very common practice for many Latino low-income families. In many rural areas in Latin America the only available help is healers. Healers are cheaper, readily available, knowledgeable of the cultural practices, speak the same language, and have a level of trust and reliance for many families.

Mr. Rodriguez's brother and his brother's wife also live with the Rodriguezes. They have no children and work selling flowers. They all help with the expenses and have to send money to support Mr. Rodriguez's parents back in Mexico. The family's finances are very limited. Sending money back home is common for many recent immigrants who leave families in their countries in financial need. The adults in both families are undocumented and unable to obtain lucrative employment for this reason. In addition, their command of English is poor, and they have no other work skills. They live in fear of being deported and are very mistrustful of anyone working for the government or any public office.

In terms of social supports, the family is very religious and go to church every week. They have friends from church and seek religious and emotional support from the priest. They do not socialize outside church because of lack of time. Once in a while Mrs. Rodriguez will take her children to a local park. She mentioned that she does not like to take them all together because Ramon is a handful. He needs constant supervision when taken to public places, and she cannot manage with three kids at the same time. Mrs. Rodriguez mentioned that they do not have enough money, and the apartment is very crowded. She does not allow her children to go out because she fears the dangers of her neighborhood.

Part of the history taking involves observation of the child and mother's body language, facial expression, and dialog emergence during the interview. Mrs. Rodriguez was rather shy at the beginning, but as time went along she felt very comfortable. She did not look at the social worker eye to eye. This behavior is very common among Latinos because it can be considered disrespectful to look at someone directly in the eye. She was very affectionate with her son in spite of Ramon's inattentiveness to her. Ramon had poor eye contact. His glance was rather sporadic. He did not play with toys and was constantly grinding his teeth. He appeared "unaware" of his surroundings.

The social worker explained to the mother the procedure about the evaluations conducted at the center as well as the duties and roles of the different professionals who might evaluate her son, such as the speech and occupational therapists and neurodevelopmental pediatrician; the worker also explained other possible evaluations that might be conducted, such as psychiatric and neurological examinations. Ramon had a comprehensive evaluation by all the members of the interdisciplinary team. The main diagnosis was pervasive developmental disorder not otherwise specified (PDDNOS), commonly known as PDD, a form of childhood autism. Autism is a lifelong disorder with many levels of involvement. It varies in severity and behavioral manifestations. Autism is characterized by a sensory integration deficit: this is one reason that many children with autism do not like to be touched or held (Green 1996), which might impact negatively on parents. Many children with autism have language, cognitive, social, and behavioral difficulties. The incidence of autism has increased over the years and is more common in boys that in girls. PDD is a condition that should present before the age of 30 months, characterized by a pervasive impairment in communication, reciprocal social interaction skills, and stereotyped behavior, interests, and activities (American Psychiatric Association 1994). Ramon had many of these behaviors: poor eye contact, speech delays, echolalia, and inappropriate behaviors (hand flapping, sameness, inappropriate play activities).

Speech and occupational therapies were recommended for Ramon as well as a referral for special education and health insurance benefits. Mrs. Rodriguez also was referred to a parent's support group. Mrs. Rodriguez met with all the professionals who evaluated her child and had an opportunity to ask questions and clarify doubts she had. For many months, Mrs. Rodriguez attended individual and group sessions with the social worker. In the group, other parents shared techniques of behavior modification that work for their children, sensory integration techniques used for children with autism, and communication enhancement. During this time, the social worker and Mrs. Rodriguez focused on areas of strength and gains that Ramon had made as well as different ways of dealing with his sometimes erratic behavior. The worker also focused on Mrs. Rodriguez's parental beliefs because when the diagnosis was given, she thought that her child had a bad spirit inside and also felt that she probably did something wrong in raising her child. During the process of understanding the diagnosis, explanations are found within the cultural realm of labels (Moreno 1996). In the Hispanic culture, many odd behaviors are attributed to supernatural causes and spirit possession. These beliefs are also influenced by Catholicism. Mrs. Rodriguez felt comfortable and obligated to consult a healer in the community and to try different home remedies to cure her child. She was open with the social worker about these beliefs, and she found support to use her cultural remedies. Ramon continues with special education and intensive behavioral training with individual, occupational, and speech therapies. If Mrs. Rodriguez's beliefs had been rejected and not integrated in the therapeutic process, it is likely that she would have viewed with distrust and disbelief the approaches that were recommended. Ramon's siblings attended a siblings' support group and were very supportive of Ramon's treatment. They also tried to live as normal a life as possible and to integrate Ramon in all their activities. Mr. Rodriguez could only attended a few sessions with the social worker due to the demands of his job. However, Mrs. Rodriguez shared with him all the main issues discussed in the sessions and everything she has learned about autism.

This case illustrates the multidimensionality of clients who have children with developmental disAbilities. Developmental disAbilities vary in severity and condition. Also, many children with developmental disAbilities improve their condition. On the other hand, many conditions are lifelong and present many challenges for families. It is important to understand the conditions of clients such as immigration, culture, socioeconomic status, social support availability, religion, stress, education, and the context in which the situation occurs. It is likewise important to understand how all these elements impede, interfere, enhance, empower, and disempower people.

CONCLUSION

Early intervention, behavior modification, special education, parents' support groups, and individual and parental training are very effective in improving many conditions. Social workers play an important role in working with families of children with disAbilities. We have neglected this population for many years. We need to revisit our roots and history and serve families again at different levels: direct practice, planning and programming, community organizing, advocacy, and social policy. Children with disAbilities become adults with disAbilities; thus, our involvement is essential throughout the life span. Families are different and have different needs, which must be integrated in social work assessment, planning, and intervention. They are partners in our quest to serve individuals with disAbilities, and many times, they become experts. Let's use their expertise and join other professionals in advocating and in developing services, programs, and policies to create better living for children and adults with disAbilities. Furthermore, let's work to make others sensitive to their needs and uniqueness as individuals and families.

References

American Psychiatric Association. 1994. *Diagnostic and Statistical Manual of Mental Disorders (DSM-IV)*, 4th ed. Washington, D.C.: Author.

Atkins, S. P. 1989. "Siblings of Handicapped Children." *Child and Adolescent Social Work Journal* 6(4):271–82.

Bagenholm, A. and C. Gillberg. 1991. "Psychosocial Effects on Siblings of Children with Autism and Mental Retardation: A Population Based Study." *Journal of Mental Deficiency Research* 35(4):291–307.

Balcazar, F. E., C. B. Keys, J. F. Bertram, and T. Rizzo. 1996. "Advocate Development in the Field of Developmental Disabilities: A Data-Based Conceptual Model." *Mental Retardation* 34(6):341–51.

Beckman, P. J. 1983. "Influences of Selected Child Characteristics on Stress in Families of Handicapped Infants. *American Journal of Mental Deficiency* 88:159–66.

Beresford, B. A. 1994. "Resources and Strategies: How Parents Cope with the Care of a Disabled Child." *Journal of Child Psychology and Psychiatry* 35:171–209.

Breslau, N., D. Salkever, and K. S. Staruch. 1982. "Women's Labor Force Activity and Responsibilities for Disabled Dependents: A Study of Families with Disabled Children." *Journal of Health and Social Behavior* 23:169–83.

Bronfenbrenner, U. 1979. *The Ecology of Human Development: Experiments by Nature and Design*. Cambridge, Mass.: Harvard University Press.

Bryan, W. V. 1996. *In Search of Freedom: How People with Disabilities Have Been Disenfranchised from the Mainstream of American Society*. Springfield, Ill.: Charles C Thomas.

Delgado, M. 1998. *Social Services in Latino Communities: Research and Strategies*. New York: Haworth Press.

DeMause, L. 1974. "The Evolution of Childhood: A Symposium." *History of Childhood: The Journal of Psychohistory* 1(4):503–75.

Dilworth-Anderson, P. and N. Anderson. 1994. "Dementia Caregiving in Blacks: A Contextual Approach." In E. Light, G. Niederehe, and B. D. Lebowitz, eds., *Stress Effects on Family Caregivers of Alzheimer's Patients,* 385–409. New York: Springer.

Dyson, L. L. 1991. "Families of Young Children with Handicaps: Parental Stress and Family Functioning." *American Journal of Mental Retardation* 95(6):623–29.

———. 1993. "Response to the Presence of a Child with Disabilities: Parental Stress and Family Functioning Over Time." *American Journal of Mental Retardation* 98(2):207–18.

———. 1997. "Father and Mothers of School-Age Children with Developmental Disabilities: Parental Stress, Family Functioning, and Social Support." *American Journal of Mental Retardation* 102(3):267–79.

Freud, S. 1957. "Mourning and Melancholia (1917)." In J. Rickman and C. Brenner, eds., *A General Selection from the Works of Sigmund Freud.* Garden City, N.Y.: Doubleday Anchor Books.

Frey, K. S., M. T. Greenberg, and R. R. Fewell. 1989. "Stress and Coping Among Parents of Handicapped Children: A Multidimensional Approach." *American Journal of Mental Retardation* 94(3):240–49.

Friedrich, W. N., D. S. Cohen, and L. T. Wilturner. 1985. "Coping Resources and Parenting Mentally Retarded Children." *American Journal of Mental Deficiency* 90:130–39.

Gallimore, R., L. P. Weisner, L. Bernheimer, D. Guthrie, and K. Nihira. 1993. "Family Response to Young Children with Developmental Delays: Accommodation Activity in Ecological and Cultural Context." *American Journal of Mental Retardation* 98(2):85–206.

Gavidia-Payne, S. and Z. Stoneman. 1997. "Family Predictors of Maternal and Paternal Involvement in Programs for Young Children with Disabilities." *Child Development* 68(4):701–17.

Germanzy, N. 1993. "Children in Poverty: Resilience Despite Risk." *Psychiatry* 56 (February): 127–136.

Gilson, S. F., J. C. Bricout, and F. R. Baskind. 1998. "Listening to the Voices of Individuals with Disabilities." *Families in Society: The Journal of Contemporary Human Services* (March–April):188–96.

Green, G. 1996. "Evaluating Claims About Treatments for Autism." In C. Maurice, G. Green, and S. Luce, eds., *Behavior Interventions for Young Children with Autism: A Manual for Parents and Professionals.* Austin, Tex.: PRO-ED.

Hodapp, R. M. and D. V. Krasner. 1995. "Families of Children with Disabilities: Findings from a National Sample of Eighth-Grade Students." *Exceptionality* 5(2):71–81.

Jenkins, J. M. and M. A. Smith. 1993. "A Prospective Study of Behavioral Disturbance in Children Who Subsequently Experience Parental Divorce: A Research Note." *Journal of Divorce & Remarriage* 19(1–2):143–60.

Johnson, H. C., E. F. Renaud, D. T. Schmidt, and E. J. Stanek. 1998. "Social Workers' Views of Parents of Children with Mental and Emotional Disabilities." *Families in Society: The Journal of Contemporary Human Services* 79(2):173–87.

Kübler-Ross, E. 1969. *On Death and Dying.* New York,: Macmillan.

Kurtz, P. D. 1997. "Clients As Resources: Empowering School Social Work Practice with Students, Families, and Communities." *Social Work in Education* 19(4):211–18.

Lee, V. E., J. Brooks-Gunn, and E. Schnur. 1988. "Does Head Start Work? A 1-Year Follow-Up Comparison of Disadvantaged Children Attending Head Start, No Preschool and Other Preschool Programs." *Developmental Psychology* 24(2):210–22.

Leff-Taner, P. and E. Hilburn-Walizer. 1992. "The Uncommon Wisdom of Parents at the Moment of Diagnosis." *Family Systems Medicine* 10:147–68.

Lequerica, M. 1993. "Stress in Immigrant Families with Handicapped Children: A Child Advocacy Approach." *American Journal of Orthopsychiatry* 63(4):545–52.

Lifter, K. 1999. "Descriptions of Preschool Children with Disabilities or At-Risk for Developmental Delay: How Should a Child Be Called?" In N. E. Vazques and I. Romero, eds., *Assessing and Screening Preschoolers: Psychological and Educational Dimensions,* 2d ed., pp. 25–49. Boston: Allyn & Bacon.

Mackelprang, R. W. and R. O. Salsgiver. 1996. "People with Disabilities and Social Work: Historical and Contemporary Issues." *Social Work* 41(1):7–14.

——. 1998. *Disability: A Diversity Model Approach in Human Service Practice.* Pacific Grove, Calif.: Brooks/Cole.

Mahoney, G., G. Boyce, R. R. Fewell, D. Spiker, and C. A. Wheeden. 1998. "The Relationship of Parent-Child Interaction to the Effectiveness of Early Intervention Services for At-Risk Children with Disabilities." *Topics in Early Childhood Special Education* 18(1):5–17.

Masters-Glidden, L. 1993. "What Do We Not Know About Families With Children Who Have Developmental Disabilities: Questionnaire on Resources and Stress As a Case Study." *American Journal of Mental Retardation* 97(5):481–95.

McQuaide, S. and J. H. Ehrenreich. 1997. "Assessing Client Strengths." *Families in Society* 78(2):201–12.

Meyers, M. K., A. Lukemeyer, and T. Smeeding. 1998. "The Cost of Caring: Childhood Disability and Poor Families." *Social Service Review* 72(2):209–33.

Milgram, N. A. and M. Atzil. 1988. "Parenting Stress in Raising Autistic Children." *Journal of Autism and Developmental Disabilities* 18:415–24.

Moreno, C. L. 1996. "Understanding 'El Autismo': A Qualitative Study of the Parental Perception of Autism, A Hispanic Perspective." *Dissertation Abstracts International Section A: Humanities & Social Sciences* 56(9-A):3745.

———. (Under review). "Why Me? Parents Confronting Autism: A Hispanic Perspective."

Morrison, G. M. and M. Cosden. 1997. "Risk, Resilience, and Adjustment of Individuals with Learning Disabilities." *Learning Quarterly* 20:43–60.

Newacheck, P. and M. McManus. 1988. "Financing Health Care for Disabled Children." *Pediatrics* 81(3):385–94.

Newacheck, P., B. Strickland, J. P. Shonkoff, J. Perrin, M. McPherson, M. McManus, C. Lauver, H. Fox, and P. Arango. 1998. "An Epidemiologic Profile of Children with Special Health Care Needs." *Pediatrics* 102:117–25.

Palfrey, J. S., D. K. Walker, J. A. Butler, and J. D. Singer. 1989. "Patterns of Response in Families of Chronically Disabled Children: An Assessment in Five Metropolitan School Districts." *American Journal of Orthopsychiatry* 59(1):94–104.

Pearlin, L. I., M. Lieberman, E. Menaghan, and J. T. Mullan. 1981. "The Stress Process." *Journal of Health and Social Behavior* 22:337–56.

Priestley, M. 1998. "Childhood Disability and Disabled Childhoods: Agendas for Research." *Childhood* 5(2):207–33.

Rimland, B. 1964. *Infantile Autism.* New York: Appleton-Century-Crofts.

Rogers-Dulan, J. and J. Blacher. 1995. "African America Families, Religion, and Disability: A Conceptual Framework." *Mental Retardation* 33(4):226–38.

Rounds, K., M. Weil, and K. K. Bishop. 1994. "Practice with Culturally Diverse Families of Young Children with Disabilities." *Families in Society* 75(1):3–15.

Sanders, J. L. and S. B. Morgan. 1997. "Family Stress and Adjustment As Perceived by Parents of Children with Autism or Down Syndrome: Implications for Intervention." *Child and Family Behavior Therapy* 19(4):15–32.

Seltzer, M. M. and T. Heller. 1997. "Families and Caregiving Across the Life Course: Research Advances on the Influence of Context." *Family Relations* 46:321–23.

Stokes-Gottlieb, A. 1997. "Single Mothers of Children with Developmental Disabilities: The Impact of Multiple Roles." *Family Relations* 46:5–12.

U.S. Census Bureau. 1997. *Disability. Current Population Reports P70–33, Americans with Disabilities: 1991–92.* Washington, D.C.: U.S. Government Printing Office.

Weick, A., C. Rapp, W. P. Sullivan, and W. Kirsthardt. 1989. "A Strengths Perspective for Social Work Practice." *Social Work* 34(4):350–54.

Weisner, T. S., L. Breizer, and L. Stolze. 1991. "Religion and Families of Children with Developmental Delays." *American Journal on Mental Retardation,* 95(6):647–62.

Weiss, S. 1991. "Personality Adjustment and Social Support of Parents Who Care for Children with Pervasive Developmental Disorders." *Archives of Psychiatric Nursing* 5:25–30.

Whiting, J. and B. Whiting. 1975. *Children of Six Cultures: A Psychocultural Analysis.* Cambridge, Mass.: Harvard University Press.

8

Eating Problems

Barbara von Bulow
Susan Braiman

Eating problems such as anorexia nervosa and obesity have long been of interest to social work clinicians. More recently, with the growth in the incidence of bulimia, mental health workers have been increasingly interested in this disorder as well. An eating disorder can present as a sole problem or as one of many difficulties. These eating problems are encountered by social workers in medical settings, psychiatric clinics, community centers, and in private practice. Social workers should have a comprehensive theoretical understanding of eating disorders and be able to devise appropriate plans for helping their clients. Plans may include combinations of individual, group, and family therapy; full or partial hospitalization; and medication.

DEFINING AND EXPLAINING EATING PROBLEMS

Anorexia nervosa is a term first used in 1868 by Sir William Gull, an English physician, and refers to loss of appetite due to nervous symptoms. Gull used it to describe a "want of appetite" attributable to a "morbid mental state" (Gull 1874/1964). However, those with anorexia nervosa usually do not lose their appetite; rather, they expend enormous energy in curbing their intake of food. Anorexics are extremely thin, often to the point of emaciation, yet they do not perceive that they are underweight. The *Diagnostic and Statistical Manual of Mental Disorders,* 4th ed. (American Psychiatric Association [APA] 1994), known as *DSM-IV,* provides a common language in which mental health clinicians and researchers can communicate about psychological disorders. The diagnostic criteria for anorexia nervosa in *DSM-IV* includes body weight 15 percent below that expected, intense fear of gaining weight or becoming fat, amenorrhea, and a disturbance in the way in which one's body weight, size, or shape is experienced.

Bulimia nervosa is an eating disorder that has been increasing in incidence in recent years. The diagnosis of bulimia nervosa in *DSM-IV* includes recurrent episodes of binge eating, a feeling of lack of control over the eating behavior, an average of two binge eating episodes a week, persistent overconcern with body shape and weight, and the use of self-induced vomiting, laxatives or diuretics, strict dieting or fasting, or vigorous exercise in order to prevent weight gain.

The diagnoses of anorexia nervosa and bulimia had little in common as they were delineated in the *DSM-III* (APA 1987). However, the changes in *DSM-IV* have illuminated the common psychopathological feature in these two diagnostic categories: i.e., overconcern with shape and weight. The commonality in diagnostic criteria is underlined by the change from *bulimia* to *bulimia nervosa*.

Obesity is a medical diagnostic entity and is listed in the *ICD-9* (U.S. Department of Health and Human Services [U.S. HHS] 1980) as a subcategory under "278 Obesity and Other Hyperalimentation." *DSM-IV* does not list obesity as a psychiatric diagnosis because obese people do not have in common a characteristic cluster of psychological symptoms. In addition, many studies of psychopathology associated with obesity have not found persons who are obese to differ from those who are not obese (Halmi 1980). However, other studies have shown an increased level of depression, especially in the obese who binge, as opposed to the obese who chronically overeat slightly (Prather and Williamson 1988). Obesity is medically defined as having an excess of fat tissue and a weight of at least 20 percent over what is considered normal for age and build (Stunkard 1980). Mild obesity is defined as 5 to 39 percent over ideal weight, moderate obesity as 40 to 99 percent over ideal weight, and severe obesity as 100 percent or more over ideal weight (Austrian 1995). Obesity is further defined by appearance, circumferential measurements of the body and its parts, and skinfold tests. Approximately 12 million Americans are considered obese. The prevalence is estimated at about 35 percent of men and 40 percent of women (Hodge and Maseelall 1993).

Currently there is consideration of a new diagnostic category to be called **"binge eating disorder,"** which resembles bulimia nervosa. It is characterized by episodes of uncontrolled eating, but sufferers do not purge their bodies of excess food. They eat until they are uncomfortably full, and they have a history of weight fluctuations. People who develop bulimia and binge eating disorder typically consume huge amounts of junk food to reduce stress and anxiety (National Institute of Health [NIH] 1993). Another problematic eating pattern is "night eating syndrome," which is usually marked by anorexia in the morning, little or moderate eating in midday and evening, and compulsive consumption late at night or in the middle of the night until exhaustion or sleep.

DEMOGRAPHIC PATTERNS

Anorexia is found predominantly in girls. Stringent dieting plays a key role in triggering this disorder, which typically begins at the onset of puberty, with the aim of achieving an ideal figure. Anorexia nervosa is growing in incidence in the West (Bruch 1978). This increased incidence appears to be real, rather than apparent, and not to be related to changes in diagnostic or hospitalization practices. The incidence of bulimia nervosa has also dramatically increased in the past ten to twenty years (Garner and Garfinkel 1985). It is unclear how much of this increase is due to the revelation of a previous shameful secret, how much is due to women copying other women, and how much is due to societal and familial pressures. Although obesity does not appear to have increased in incidence recently, public censure of obesity has not lessened; indeed, there appears to be more emphasis than ever on maintaining a normal weight for health reasons.

Most epidemiological studies report that 90 to 95 percent of anorexia nervosa subjects are female, and this percentage has not changed over time: there are few documented cases of males who are truly diagnosed as having anorexia nervosa. Also, anorexia nervosa tends to occur predominantly in women from an upper socioeconomic background and to be mainly a disease of Western society. However, Garner and Garfinkel (1985) found a progressive rise in the proportion of patients from the lower social classes. Between 1970 and 1975, 70.6 percent of their patients fell into Hollingshead's Social Classes I and II, whereas between 1976 and 1981 only 52 percent of their anorexia nervosa patients were from Classes I and II. Women whose professions require that they control their weight, such as ballerinas, models, and athletes, are at higher risk of developing anorexia nervosa. Garner and colleagues (1980) found the prevalence of anorexia nervosa among professional dance students to be seven times what might be expected in young females in the general population. Anorexia nervosa is reported to be growing in incidence in Japan but is relatively rare in other non-Western societies.

Historically, anorexia nervosa usually develops during adolescence or the early 20s. Recently, there appears to be a significant increase of onset in young adulthood over the earlier age of onset (Garfinkel and Garner 1982). The actual incidence of anorexia nervosa is not clear, as one study found 1 severe case in every 100 adolescent girls (Crisp, Palmer, and Kalucy 1976) and another study reported that 10 percent of the surveyed adolescents showed some anorexic behavior (Garfinkel and Garner 1982). Although anorexia nervosa was historically almost exclusively an illness of Caucasian women, more recently there have been a few reported cases of non-Caucasian women with anorexia. Hsu (1987) reported on seven black patients (one was male), who represented 4 percent of her patient population within a forty-two-month period. Four suffered from anorexia and three from bulimia. Silber (1986) wrote about seven black and Hispanic female adolescent anorexia nervosa patients, who represented 5 percent of her patient population during a twelve-year period. Both of these studies caution that the prevailing stereotype of the victim of anorexia nervosa as a white upper-middle-class female may prevent early diagnosis in non-Caucasian clients.

Some researchers have attempted to document the incidence of bulimia nervosa and to describe the course and symptoms of this disorder (Fairburn and Cooper 1982; Halmi 1983). The incidence of bulimia has been reported to be as high as 13 percent (Halmi 1983). Bulimic women have been found to aspire to a thinner ideal body than normal controls. Also, women who are heavier than their peers tend to develop bulimia because the gap between the ideal body and the actual body is intensified by a thinner than average ideal and a heavier than average self (Johnson et al. 1982). Bulimia often begins when a woman goes on a diet. Food deprivation is followed by bingeing and subsequent purging by vomiting, laxative or diuretic abuse, excessive exercise, or starvation. Bulimics are intensely afraid of gaining weight and are acutely sensitive to small fluctuations in weight. In addition, bulimic women appear to be significantly more ashamed of their weight than other women, as bulimic women accept and internalize most deeply the societal norms of attractiveness and thinness

(Rodin, Silberstein, and Striegel-Moore 1985). Bulimia nervosa appears to be a disease that fluctuates over time, with individuals sometimes having a clinical eating disorder and at other times not meeting all the criteria necessary for a clinical diagnosis (Fairburn and Beglin 1990).

Five major studies have been done to delineate the characteristics of bulimic individuals (Fairburn and Cooper 1982, 1984; Johnson et al. 1982; Pyle, Mitchell, and Eckert 1981; Russell 1979). The results of these studies were compared by Bulow and DeChillo (1987). The average age of onset of bulimia is between 18 and 20 years, and the victims generally suffer with the illness for four or five years before seeking treatment. About half of these bulimic individuals binge daily, and more than 80 percent vomit or purge in other ways. A history of anorexia nervosa was noted for only 6 percent in the Johnson et al. study, in contrast to 57 percent in Russell's study. The majority of bulimics have an acceptable weight for their height. Menstrual irregularities (including amenorrhea) occur in one-third to three-fourths of bulimic women. Most bulimics have depressive symptomatology, and many report suicidal plans or acts. These women are also noted to have high levels of anxiety, interpersonal sensitivity, and impulsivity as measured by general personality inventories such as the Minnesota Multiphasic Personality Inventory (MMPI) or the General Health Questionnaire (GHQ) in Great Britain. The onset of bulimia appears to occur after voluntary restrictive dieting, or following a period of emotional upset (Johnson et al. 1982; Pyle et al. 1981).

Family history data are limited; however, families have been implicated in the etiology of bulimia because of the psychodynamic interactions in the family and/or a genetic loading for psychopathology. Pyle and colleagues (1981) noted that there seemed to be a high incidence of alcoholism and weight problems in the families of bulimic subjects. Half of their research participants reported alcoholism in at least one first-degree relative, and 68 percent reported obesity in one or more first-degree relative. Similarly, Fairburn and Cooper (1984) noted that 29 percent of their participants reported that a first-degree relative had received treatment from a psychiatrist, usually for a depressive disorder, and more than half the patients (59 percent) had a relative who had been advised by a doctor to lose weight. Igoin-Apfelbaum (1985) studied bulimics' family background and found a significantly higher percentage of broken homes than in the study's control population. He also found that a significant proportion of the intact families were hiding massive internal tensions.

Social environment differences have important implications for the development and maintenance of obesity. There is a marked inverse relationship between socioeconomic status and the prevalence of obesity, particularly in women; obesity in men is much less class-linked. Although obesity occurs in every social class, it is predominantly a disease of the lower classes. Stunkard (1980) surveyed midtown Manhattan and found that obesity was more prevalent among downwardly mobile people than among those who had remained in the social class of their parents. The predominance of obesity in lower-class women was 30 percent, while 16 percent of middle-class women and only 5 percent of upper-class women were obese. Religious affiliation was another social factor linked to obesity. Jews demonstrated the greatest prevalence of obesity, followed by Roman Catholics and then Protestants. The relationship between obesity and Protestant religious affiliation was that Baptists had the largest proportion of obesity, followed by Methodists, Lutherans, and Episcopalians. Ethnic factors were also demonstrated, as the percentage of obesity in first-generation Americans from Czechoslovakia, Hungary, and Italy was higher than in first-generation Americans from England or fourth-generation Americans. Black women tended to be heavier than white women at all age levels; however, when the economic levels were the same, there were no significant racial differences (Allon 1982).

SOCIETAL CONTEXT

In our stressful culture there is ample reinforcement for the development of eating disorders. Girls gain self-esteem and social acceptance for their physical appearance, whereas boys are valued for intellectual and physical prowess and success. Since the late 1960s the standard of physical beauty for women has been changing, and there has been an increasing emphasis on lean, almost boyish figures. One recent study found that when mothers are overly concerned about their daughters' weight and attractiveness, they may put them at increased risk. These girls often have fathers and brothers who are overly critical of their weight.

The desirability of thinness for women is stressed for models, dancers, long-distance runners, gymnasts, and actresses. Magazines stress diets, restaurants serve "lite" food, and as pressure mounts, self-esteem plummets.

In past eras, women were considered desirable if they were plump. Impressionist paintings glorified healthy-looking women. In some societies, where food supplies were scarce, an overweight family implied that the father was a good provider. In the Western world, there are intense and conflicting messages about weight and eating (Saunders 1985). On the one hand, we are constantly bombarded with food in television commercials and in magazine advertisements, and there are a multitude of food stores and restaurants. On the other hand, there is intense pressure to be thin exemplified by the diets in every magazine, numerous health clubs and spas, and clothes for every sport. These conflicting social pressures lead women to be enormously concerned about weight and eating behavior. A majority of women report feeling fat, although only a minority of women are actually overweight. For many women, dieting has become a way of life. A survey by Nielson found that 56 percent of female respondents between the ages of 24 and 54 were currently on a diet (Rodin et al. 1985). In addition to this enormous concern with weight and dieting, women also experience enormous shame in relation to their bodies. This shame derives from the woman's perception that her actual body does not match her internalized ideal body shape. Many females try to adhere to society's dictates of a fashionably slim body by episodes of severe dieting that lead to anorexia nervosa or to food cravings and episodic binge eating, i.e., bulimia nervosa.

Cultural and societal standards of appropriate body shape are major determinants of the perception and evaluation of one's body. A woman's ideal body image is not her individual creation but the product of a societal prescription. Beauty ideals are highly culture-bound and change with time. In America, there is a preoccupation with thinness and a negative evaluation placed on being fat. There is an inverse relationship between low body weight and high social class in Western society; the reverse is true in less developed societies. However, the longer the time immigrants have been in Western countries, the less obese they tend to be (Furnham and Alibhai 1983).

Because of the pressure in Western culture to be thin, women try to force themselves to be thin. Fallon and Rozin (1985) studied 248 male and 227 female under-graduates and found that the men were satisfied with their figures and that the women were not. Thus, one of the precipitants of the increasing incidence of anorexia nervosa and bulimia nervosa is the apparent shift in cultural preference toward thinner women (Garner et al. 1980). In an effort to document this shift, Garner and colleagues collected data from *Playboy,* the Miss America Pageant, population norms, and a number of diet articles in women's popular magazines. The results of this survey confirmed a shift toward an ideal of a thinner female figure over the twenty years from 1959 to 1979, particularly between 1969 and 1979. Furthermore, since 1970 the Miss America Pageant winners have been thinner than the average size of the other contestants, a finding that suggests that the thinnest woman is considered the most beautiful. However, spanning this same period, women's average weights actually increased. Therefore, paradoxically, as women's actual weights went up, the idealized female figure became thinner. Schwartz, Thompson, and Johnson (1982) were also interested in the interplay between sociocultural forces and eating disorders. They speculated that sociocultural pressures affect the shape of psychological symptoms. Pointing to the dramatic increase in eating disorders, the authors added sociocultural factors to the previously suggested etiological causes of eating problems, such as mother–child interaction, family system problems, and organic causes.

VULNERABILITIES AND RISK FACTORS

In addition to cultural pressure, which is a major risk factor, there are medical and psychological factors to be considered as well in the etiology of these illnesses. Eating disorders can be divided into three diagnostic categories: anorexia nervosa, bulimia nervosa, and obesity. Sometimes these diagnoses occur simultaneously in one client (e.g., an anorexia nervosa client may also purge). At other times, they follow each other (e.g., a bulimic woman may stop purging and become obese). A careful assess-ment is essential because the eating problem may be a specific illness or one symptom within a larger constellation of symptoms, or it may occur along with another illness in a single client. Depression, for example, is an illness in which an eating problem is a prominent symptom but not an exclusive one. Most individuals with severe de-pression become anorexic and lose weight; in contrast, patients with a mild to mod-erate depression often have an increased appetite, which can lead to weight gain or bulimia. However, those suffering from depression also have other symptoms, such as anhedonia, depressed mood, sleep disorder, and loss of concentration. For de-pressed clients, counseling is insufficient if it focuses only on the eating problem. In addition, an eating disorder can coexist with substance abuse. Some excessive eaters, such as obese and bulimic individuals, may also drink excessive amounts of alcohol. Increased appetite often occurs after marijuana intoxication and nicotine withdrawal. Other clients may try to curb their excessive intake of food by using cocaine, which is known to decrease appetite, and, therefore, they develop an additional problem. In these examples, counseling must be geared to both the eating problem and the sub-stance abuse.

Some family theorists believe that family dynamics account for anorexia nervosa. According to Minuchin, Rosman, and Baker's (1980) theory, families of patients with anorexia nervosa demonstrate rigidity, enmeshment, overprotectiveness, and failure to resolve conflict. Initially, Selvini-Palazzoli (1978) theorized that the seeds for anorexia nervosa lay in the mother–daughter relationship. However, over time, she shifted her focus to the whole family's interactions. Both Minuchin et al. (1980) and Selvini-Palazzoli (1978) have postulated a systems model in which certain family relationships contribute to the development of anorexia nervosa and, in turn, in which the illness maintains the family's homeostasis.

Some authors have evaluated the psychodynamics of bulimic patients' families. Strober (1981) reported that affective disorder, alcoholism, and drug abuse in the first- and second-degree relatives of 35 bulimics were all more prevalent than in the relatives of 35 anorexics or in the general population. In terms of parental personality characteristics, fathers of bulimics were more impulsive and excitable, had lower frustration tolerance, and were more dissatisfied with their familial relations. Mothers scored higher on depression, hostility, and dissatisfaction with family relationships. Ordman and Kirschenbaum (1986) compared the families of bulimics with the families of normal controls and found more conflict and less cohesion in the bulimic families. Humphrey's (1986) findings were similar to Ordman's; in addition, she found that the bulimic-anorexic families were less involved and less supportive. There are not more overweight family members in bulimics' families; however, the families of severe bulimics are highly anxious about weight and derogatory of overweight people (Wold 1985).

Eating disorders run in families, suggesting that genetic factors predispose some people to these conditions. For anorexia nervosa, there is little data about genetic factors. Mother–child concordance for anorexia nervosa is rare, although there are many reports of more than one case in a single family (Garfinkel and Garner 1982). However, anorexia in more than one female in a family may be due to environmental factors, rather than genetic factors. Regarding bulimia nervosa, the emergence of large numbers of sufferers is so recent that the incidence of bulimia in both mother and child is rare. There are no reported studies of anorexics or bulimics that indicate genetic factors, such as studies of adopted offspring or of twins reared apart. However, bulimics do tend to have a family history of psychological problems, as the incidence of affective illness and/or alcoholism in the parents of bulimics is high (Pyle et al. 1981; Fairburn and Cooper 1984). Finally, with regard to obesity, there appears to be clear evidence that genes can influence body weight and obesity; however, weight appears to be quite malleable by the environment (Foch and McClearn 1980). Twin studies have demonstrated high concordance of weights, in contrast to adoptive studies, which have shown an absence of correlations in weight between adopted children and their adoptive parents and siblings. The magnitude of the genetic contribution varies with age and sex and with the criteria used for obesity.

Bulimia nervosa and anorexia nervosa can be understood theoretically as modern-day versions of obsessive-compulsive neuroses. Social and educational factors influence the development of particular symptomatology. What is common to all anorexic and bulimic women is a constant preoccupation with food and a persistent pursuit of thinness and an ideal body size. Certain foods become forbidden and thus both strongly feared and strongly desired (Rothenberg 1986). For clients with eating disorders, the emphasis on body image and body dissatisfaction may divert attention from other stressful areas and may become a defense against dealing with other problems in life.

The dynamics of the anorexia nervosa patient can also be understood from an object-relations perspective (Selvini-Palazzoli 1978). People suffering from anorexia nervosa may view their bodies as threatening forces that must be kept in check. From this perspective, the anorexic equates her body with the incorporated object (i.e., the mother) in its negative, overwhelming aspects. The anorexic experiences her body as all powerful, indestructible, growing, and threatening. The findings of Halmi, Falk, and Schwartz (1981) also support a developmental concept of body image. Their study shows that the accuracy of self-estimation increases as adolescent girls become older. Briefly summarized, the object-relations point of view is that an unempathic, unresponsive mother results in the child's having an ego structure inadequate to the tasks of autonomy and self-regulation as well as little capacity to monitor hunger and a resulting tendency to act out conflicts over independence and self-control via the body and food intake (Bruch 1973). The process of separation-individuation is hypothesized to persist much longer in women (Beattie 1988). There is far more blurring of boundaries and identification for mothers with female children than for mothers with male children. Mothers also see their daughters as narcissistic extensions of themselves and project onto their daughters their own hopes, fears, and fantasies about femininity. At puberty, the girl's ambivalent struggle for autonomy from the mother is intense as she tries to attain psychosocial maturation. The mother, on the other hand, is often threatened by her daughter's growing sexual attractiveness and, at the same time, is heavily invested in her social success.

In discussing obesity, we must distinguish between juvenile-onset obesity and adult-onset obesity. In their work on weight reduction in obese patients, Glucksman and Hirsch (1969) found striking body image differences between severely obese persons with juvenile-onset obesity and those with adult-onset obesity. The onset of obesity during adolescence seems to be an extremely crucial factor in terms of that individual's self-concept and evaluation of body image. Obesity is an extremely visible physical deviation not unlike any other type of physical handicap. The ramifications of this handicap include teasing by peers and family and an inadequate opportunity to learn appropriate social skills. Thus, the obese youngster develops an extremely poor body image and self-concept (Leon 1982).

RESILIENCIES AND PROTECTIVE FACTORS

Eating problems are individual issues that need to be seen in a family and social context. As Shakespeare said, "Beauty is in the eye of the beholder"; therefore, how a person thinks the world and her family perceive her is vital in the establishment of self-esteem. Some obese women are quite happy and emotionally well adjusted because of feeling accepted, valued, and loved by their families. Acceptance by others can facilitate recovery from eating problems.

One of several valuable coping mechanisms for eating disordered women and their families is the use of humor. Laughter can provide an emotional catharsis, promote intimacy and humanness, and create an atmosphere of closeness (Broden 1994). Humor can break tension and ease emotional anguish. Self-reflection in an accepting, gently joking manner, can advance self-acceptance.

For some people, becoming articulate advocates for their personal issues is a means of transforming a strictly personal matter into a potentially useful "cause" that can help others. Thus, an adult with an eating disorder can start an informal group for friends, can write about the experience in fiction or nonfiction form, and can help spread information about treatment alternatives to others with similar afflictions. It may be recalled that the organization now known as MADD (Mothers Against Drunk Driving) had its origin in the personal tragedy of one family who found within themselves remarkable resilience and a coping mechanism that has helped countless others.

Protective factors also include the capacity for the development of compensatory strengths. People struggling with eating disorders often feel they have a disability; one protective factor against despair is the capacity to develop expertise, talent, and excellence in some area of strength. It is remarkable to observe how many adults with health problems and/or handicapping conditions use their strength in other areas to develop as dramatists, artists, writers, and professionals in all walks of life. If self-esteem is a function of success and pride, then patients with eating disorders should be encouraged to develop themselves in areas in which they can excel, in which they can develop new sources of self-confidence.

The more the population becomes educated about the etiology and treatment of eating problems, the less judgmental people will become. To protect a vulnerable segment of the population, social workers and other helping professionals should be vigilant in encouraging clients to take advantage of their strengths and their emotional resilience.

PROGRAMS AND SOCIAL WORK CONTRIBUTIONS

Anorexia nervosa can be a life-threatening disease, and clinicians have to know when referral to a medical doctor is essential. Even though clients with bulimia nervosa are usually within a normal weight range, this illness can also be life-threatening because of electrolyte imbalance and cardiac complications. Bulimia nervosa patients tend to be secretive about the extent of their psychopathology because of enormous shame. Therefore, referral for a medical evaluation must be very carefully handled. Obesity is also a health problem. Therefore, it is imperative that social workers be knowledgeable about intervention models for all three conditions and to be aware of the many facets of these diseases. Broad-spectrum approaches using community as well as medical resources are familiar to social work clinicians. They can provide individual family and group therapy, and they can help clients find exercise and self-help programs. It is also very important for social workers to help clients understand the health hazards implicit in these disorders and to direct them to appropriate medical facilities.

Social workers encounter eating problems in their clients in a variety of settings. Medical social workers see eating problems in both outpatient and inpatient settings because of medical difficulties caused by the bodily abuse of massive food intake and restriction. Anorexia and bulimia nervosa clients may have gastrointestinal difficulties, esophageal tears, dermatological problems, cardiac complications, etc. Obese clients run an increased risk of diabetes, hypertension, and cardiac problems. Family agencies have clients whose predominant difficulty is family interaction around a female member's food intake or lack of it. Social workers in psychiatric settings will probably be involved with both anorexia nervosa and bulimia nervosa clients. Finally, social workers in private practice may have young women in treatment who reveal their bulimic behavior only after a long period of counseling.

Many options are available to social workers who want to help clients with eating disorders. These options can be used singly or in combination after a thorough clinical assessment. In assessing an individual's eating disorder, developmental problems, psychodynamics, and environmental context, the social worker should maintain an ecological perspective. This perspective views individual psychopathology as rooted in the discrepancy between the individual's needs and the environmental resources and supports (Germain and Gitterman 1980; Goldstein 1984). Therefore, a clinician needs to assess the family and social supports of clients with eating disorders in order to determine which of the many programmatic possibilities are most suited to that client. This ecological assessment requires a nonlinear view of causality and an understanding of the meaning of the eating problems to both the client and the environment.

ASSESSMENT AND INTERVENTIONS

A comprehensive initial evaluation is essential to the appropriate counseling of clients with eating disorders. The degree of pathology in these clients is quite variable; therefore, a broad perspective is required. The evaluation process should take into account current symptomatology, including the duration and frequency of the symptoms, psychodynamics, and the degree of fit between personal and environmental resources. The client's level of object relations and degree of family pathology should be reviewed. In addition, the presence or absence of concurrent psychopathology, such as depressive symptoms or other impulse-control problems (alcohol or drugs), should be assessed. Medical evaluations are important if physical health is being jeopardized or if psychotropic medication may be indicated.

Obviously, the first consideration in the assessment of the client with anorexia nervosa is how precarious her physical condition is and whether medical intervention is necessary. The most common reason for hospitalization is weight loss. If the client is 25 percent below normal weight for her height or if weight loss is rapid (four to five pounds a week or more), hospitalization is usually indicated. Symptoms that result from weight loss include the lowering of vital signs, physical weakness, coldness, and difficulty in concentrating. The other possible indications for hospitalization include severe depression and/or strong suicidal ideation.

If the weight loss can be contained and the depressive symptomatology is not severe, outpatient counseling is indicated. Then the question becomes what form of intervention would be most helpful. Individual counseling is almost always prescribed, either solely or in conjunction with other modalities of treatment. All anorexics initially need support, realistic encouragement, and a sense that the clinician empathizes with their struggle against fat. Cognitive-behavioral techniques are often used to facilitate weight gain. An assessment of whether more dynamic counseling would be useful should be based on the client's age, capacity for insight, and psychological maturity.

As discussed earlier, it is important to evaluate not only the client, but also the family and environmental supports. Family sessions are often vitally important in altering family dynamics and facilitating change. Families of anorexics are suffering also and have a mixture of feelings, including guilt, anger, and a sense of being over-whelmed by the illness.

The assessment of the bulimic client is similar to that of the anorexic in that many factors need to be considered, including psychiatric impairment, the actual symptomatology, psychodynamics, the family, and the broader environment. Hospitalization is rarely indicated for bulimic clients unless they are severely depressed and suicidal. The other indications for inpatient care include being incapacitated by the bulimic symptoms, being addicted to other substances, or serious electrolyte imbalance.

There are major differences among bulimic clients in regard to symptomatology. The frequency of binge-purge episodes varies from many times per day to less than one time per week. Bulimics vary in how they define a binge, from consuming many thousands of calories to eating one cookie. Purging behavior also demonstrates great variability, from vomiting to laxatives or diuretic abuse to excessive exercise or a combination of these. Some women have developed major physical and dental problems, whereas others do not experience such complications. All bulimics with active symptoms should have regular medical and dental checkups to assess the development of complications. The client's degree of competence and ability to function effectively in the world fluctuate widely, as does the degree of social involvement or social isolation. Some women have been able to separate from their families, whereas others are enmeshed in pathological family systems. The psychodynamic pattern of these clients includes lack of self-esteem, distorted body image, and a paralyzing sense of ineffectiveness. Underlying conflicts over dependency-independency and passivity-assertiveness are prominent. These women often feel lonely and isolated from their peers. Bulimia is a "secret sin" and the sufferers live in terror of being exposed.

The clinician assesses all of the preceding factors to determine what modality should be recommended (individual, group, or family counseling; medication; or hospitalization) and what focus the intervention should take (cognitive, behavioral, or dynamic). For example, if a client has frequent binge-purge episodes, a combination program may be suggested, consisting of individual and group sessions and medication. Initially, cognitive-behavioral techniques could be used to get the symptoms under control, followed by dynamic interventions to uncover underlying conflicts. When clients live at home or when family enmeshment is found, family meetings are often essential.

The initial assessment of the obese client entails a consideration of whether there is concomitant psychopathology such as depression or alcohol abuse. Hospitalization is rarely indicated unless the client is markedly obese to the point of medical danger. An ecological perspective is particularly crucial for obese clients because family dynamics and social supports may have the most impact on ameliorating the obesity. Individual psychodynamic counseling seems to be quite unsuccessful in helping clients to reduce, while behavioral interventions seem to be somewhat more successful. Family sessions are often necessary for symptomatic alteration when the client is a child. Ideally, when the child is an adolescent, the family sessions are supplemented by group work because of the importance of peer support at this transitional stage. Finally, for adult obese clients, group sessions are frequently indicated, possibly to include both professionally run group sessions and self-help groups such as Weight Watchers or Overeaters Anonymous.

During midadolescence, heterosexual associations begin. However, obese girls in particular may have great difficulty in dating and developing romantic relationships; therefore, they may show an overall immaturity. Obese adolescent girls are often overly dependent on the family, have separation anxiety about leaving their mothers, and are greatly interested in sex, but only on the fantasy level. Both male and female adolescents who are obese are often the butt of comments and are often excluded from peer-group activities; thus, their social development is stunted. Some obese adolescents use their excessive weight consciously or unconsciously as a protection against sexual involvement, which they feel incapable of handling. A small percentage of obese adolescent girls go to the opposite extreme and become sexually promiscuous in their search for acceptance.

Obesity is a serious handicap in the social life of a child and even more for a teenager. Fat children often become miserable and reclusive. In obese adolescents, the preoccupation with weight and appearance may become so intense that it overshadows all other feelings and actions, as everything is experienced in terms of "weight" and "figure." Many of the personality features of obese people—their shyness and oversensitivity, their easy discouragement in the face of difficulties or when confronted with the slightest rejection, and their tendency toward depression—may be considered to be related to their constant concern with their obese appearance and the impression they make on others (Bruch 1949, 1975).

Obesity can provide a defense against dealing with the "real" problems of life (Kornhaber and Kornhaber 1975). Adults who want to lose weight must be able to reexperience all the tumultuous feelings of the adolescent period that they buried in an obese body. These adults may have a delayed a social life and professional advancement because of the vow, "First I must lose weight, then I shall . . ."

Almost all investigators have found problems in normal-weight families in which there is an obese child whom the parents have urged or demanded to lose weight. The obese child has often been ridiculed or rejected or become the scapegoat of parents and siblings. Obese children are often used as an object by one or the other parent to satisfy the parent's own needs (Wolman 1982). In addition, obese children are frequently the opposite sex of that wished for by the parent or a disappointment in some other way (Bruch 1973). This wish for an opposite-sex child can lead to the child's being confused in sexual identification. In one study, adolescents were able to move toward a more normal weight when the family did not demonstrate excessive anxiety about the overweight; in families in which there was constant preoccupation with weight, the child became increasingly overweight and psychologically less well adjusted (Daniel 1982). Disturbances in the families of obese children are frequently characterized by poor sociability among family members and much sibling fighting (Daniel 1982).

Three factors predispose an obese individual to the development of a disturbed body image: the onset of obesity before adulthood, the presence of a neurotic behavior pattern, and censure by significant family members (Stunkard and Mendelson 1967). The disturbance in relation to body image is generally not affected by weight reductions and is improved only by long-term psychotherapy. The impaired body image does not usually occur in families in which other people are large and fat, and when overweight is associated with strength and health. Therefore, a probable cause of the disturbed body image is censure or rejection by parents or significant others because of the obesity.

All of the following possibilities have been effectively used with clients with primary eating problems: individual counseling, either psychodynamic or cognitive-behavioral, group work, family therapy, medication, and hospitalization. Each treatment option is discussed next as it applies to the different disorders.

Individual counseling is the most frequently recommended treatment modality for anorexia nervosa and bulimia nervosa patients. Sometimes individual counseling is the only modality chosen; at other times, it is the major component of a plan that includes hospitalization and/or medication. The treatment approach needs to be defined: the psychoanalytic approach focuses on internal dynamics; the behavioral approach concentrates on symptoms; and a life model emphasizes interpersonal, life-transitional, and environmental task resolution. Unfortunately, despite the widespread use of individual counseling, very little research has been done to substantiate the effectiveness of the different approaches or delineate which elements of individual work are most helpful.

For anorexia nervosa clients, Bruch (1982), an analyst and a well-known authority on eating disorders, recommended an active therapy, where counseling is a "fact-finding mission" rather than a traditional interpretive analytic approach. However, some analysts still recommend intense psychoanalysis to deal with underlying conflicts regarding identity and object relations (Wilson, Hogan, and Mintz 1983). Other theorists use cognitive techniques to deal with the intellectual problems that seem to be quite common among anorexia nervosa clients, such as dichotomous thinking and overgeneralization. Behaviorists recommend behavioral techniques such as eating diaries to deal with eating pathology in terms of behavioral manifestations. Life-model-oriented social workers intervene in the dysfunctional transactions between the client and the environment.

Women with bulimia nervosa rival anorexic clients in being difficult to help. The illness is viewed by its sufferers as being a "secret sin," and merely getting the client to acknowledge the problem is an enormously difficult task. Also, bulimics frequently want "instant cures" and have unrealistic expectations about being able to stop the bingeing and purging cycle in a short time. Fairburn (1981) reported on a cognitive-behavioral approach for bulimics in which the treatment was divided into three phases and generally extended from four to six months. He emphasized increased self-control with the use of eating diaries, specific strategies for avoiding overeating, and the development of an understanding of the events that lead to a bulimic episode. In contrast to this cognitive-behavioral approach, Wilson et al. (1983) advocated a psychoanalytically oriented treatment that focuses on the underlying conflicts rather than on the overt symptoms, with an emphasis on the patient's understanding of internalized object representations and, ultimately, on an analysis of the triadic oedipal conflict. Lowenkopf (1983) used supportive psychotherapy or exploratory therapy or a combination of supportive therapy with psychotropic medication, depending on the severity of bulimic episodes.

Even though anorexia nervosa and bulimia nervosa clients are extremely difficult to help in individual counseling, perhaps the most difficult of all problem eaters are the obese. Obese people tend to be vague and nonspecific in counseling when asked about their eating habits, probably for many reasons, including shame and guilt, not thinking the quantity eaten is too much, and fearing that the food on which they are psychologically dependent will be taken away. As Bruch stated, "The basic attitude toward life of a fat person is passive and demanding and he expects to have everything done for him. His ideal of treatment is something, anything, that will melt his fat away without effort on his part" (1949:236).

Psychodynamically oriented psychotherapy with the obese focuses on obesity as a somatic manifestation of a problem in personality development. Obesity symbolizes the strength and the security that the passive-dependent obese person lacks. Anxiety is masked by chronic overeating. Focusing on these dynamic issues, however, is only moderately successful in encouraging weight reduction in the mildly obese and is not at all successful with the morbidly obese. Individual counseling of the obese that combines a respectful tolerance of initial overeating with the use of some behavioral techniques may be more successful in helping clients to lose weight gradually. In a review article on practice effectiveness, Thomlison (1984) commented that the obese appear to respond better, at least in the short run, to behavioral techniques. Weekly eating diaries, the development of a moderate diet based on the individual's needs, and counseling that facilitates an understanding of feelings may be successful over a long period of time.

Group work has increasingly been recommended as the modality of choice for eating disorders, either singly or in combination with other modalities. As in individual counseling, the approaches vary from psychoanalytically oriented to cognitive and behavioral work. From an ecological perspective, a disturbance in eating behavior may develop because of a lack of fit between an individual's ego capacity and self-identity and the expectations, stresses, and rewards of the environment. The pressure put on women by Western society to have a beautiful body is excessive and unrealistic. Therefore, acceptance by a group of peers can be enormously reassuring and ego-enhancing. In addition, practical advice is often given by other group members and the social worker about how to change eating patterns.

Anorexia nervosa clients seem to do less well in group work than do their bulimic sisters. Anorexia nervosa sufferers are often anxious and withdrawn and have extreme difficulty identifying and expressing their feelings. Although superficially socially competent, anorexics are limited in their ability to establish and maintain social relationships. Their self-esteem is quite low, and they have a limited frustration tolerance for any comment that may be experienced as even mildly critical. Anorexics often respond to the anxiety stirred up by the group with a competitive desire to be the thinnest group member and, therefore, unfortunately to lose more weight. However, in spite of all the pitfalls just listed, when the group modality is successful, it offers the anorexic meaningful social interactions and a unique experience of social acceptance. The selection of the members is crucial for a successful anorexia nervosa group; the clients must not be at a stage of extreme starvation and should have moved beyond denial to wanting help (Hall 1985).

Group work has also been successful in helping bulimic clients. Generally, these groups consist exclusively of bulimic clients rather than clients with mixed diagnoses because of the envy bulimics experience about anorexic behavior and the fear anorexics have that, like the bulimics, they will lose control of eating. Again, the particular approach varies: some groups use a short-term behavioral format; other approaches use psychodynamic understanding for long-term groups, and still others use a group format with behavioral, cognitive, and psychodynamic components (Boskind-White and White 1983; Johnson, Connors, and Stuckey 1983; Roy-Byrne, Lee-Benner, and Yager 1984; Stevens and Salisbury 1984).

Group work is perhaps the single most useful modality for helping the obese.

Most obese people do not demonstrate psychopathology beyond the single symptom of overeating; therefore, it is this symptom that needs to be addressed. In this way, obese clients are similar to alcoholics who have to stop drinking before they can deal with other possible problem areas. A group format can offer emotional support for the trials of dieting and a weekly check on progress. In addition, specific approaches, including diets that may be helpful, can be suggested.

The mutual-aid or self-help group tradition has been enormously useful for many years in addition to, or instead of, professionally run individual, family, or group sessions (Gitterman and Schulman 1994; Katz and Bender 1976). This alliance of individuals who need each other to work on a common problem can be very successful with clients who have eating disorders. Anorexics, bulimics, and obese people often respond positively to self-help programs such as Weight Watchers or Overeaters Anonymous, in addition to or instead of professionally led group sessions. Weight Watchers is an enormously successful organization that combines sound dietary recommendations with group support in an environment similar to a religious pep rally. The philosophy of Overeaters Anonymous (OA) is similar to that of Alcoholics Anonymous in that both are "twelve-step" programs with the major goal of achieving abstinence (Malenbaum et al. 1988). Abstinence in OA is defined as freedom from compulsive overeating and eating only three meals a day with no snacks. Some OA meetings are specifically focused on anorexic and bulimic women. Many obese people do not seek help through the mental health profession and go instead to Weight Watchers, OA, or Take Off Pounds Sensibly (TOPS). Stuart and Mitchell (1980) suggested that the current treatment of choice for the mildly to moderately obese is self-help groups that incorporate behavioral self-management techniques.

Family work is often recommended for clients with eating disorders, particularly if they are young and still living at home. A disturbed eating pattern is the obvious symptom of all three problems discussed: anorexia nervosa, bulimia nervosa, and obesity. However, underlying this symptom in all three conditions is a paralyzing sense of ineffectiveness, a lack of control over one's body, and an inability to discriminate hunger from other states. These deficits in autonomy and initiative have originated in the mislabeling of feelings and moods from early childhood. Family work can therefore often facilitate appropriate developmental growth so that these clients will acquire a sense of competence and autonomy.

For anorexia nervosa clients, family counseling is often not only useful, but essential. Anorexia nervosa sufferers have difficulties with independence, with not feeling in control of their bodies, and with being overprotected. These issues of separation-individuation can sometimes most effectively be dealt with by involvement of the entire family. The focus of therapy with anorexia nervosa families is to challenge the enmeshment within the family as it interferes with the developmental growth of the anorexic.

Family work is also often used with bulimia nervosa clients, especially those who are living with or near their families. Often bulimia nervosa clients (unlike many anorexics) have succeeded in separating physically from their families of origin. However, their internal life may be dominated by demands for perfection that developed because of family dynamics. Also, they are frequently overinvolved with the families of origin and have great difficulty establishing independent adult sexual relationships. Bulimic women experience performance demands by their families, are compelled to meet those demands, and, as a result, feel hugely overburdened (Jones 1985). An ecological perspective can facilitate the clinician's evaluation of how the client's family and environment have affected the client in the past and how the bulimic symptoms distort and interfere with current object relations and environmental interactions (Yudkovitz 1983). In Mintz's (1982) treatment of young women with bulimia nervosa, the primary therapy modality was individual sessions, with conjoint family sessions as needed.

Family work is discussed much less frequently as a modality of treatment for obese clients unless the client is an obese child or adolescent. Obese adolescents, according to Daniel (1982), often suffer from disruptive family relationships that delay psychosocial maturation. Family therapy can facilitate the psychological development of these adolescents. Obese children tend to lose more weight when they are accepted, not severely censured, by their families. Family therapy can promote acceptance of the child rather than harsh criticism because of the obesity.

Many *medications* have been tried with anorexia nervosa patients, including major tranquilizers, minor tranquilizers, antidepressants, lithium, anticonvulsants, insulin, and appetite stimulants. However, while some medications may prove to be helpful to some anorexics, there is no consensus in the field about the efficacy of any of these medications. There is a consensus, however, that none of these medications should be used as the sole or primary mode of treatment.

Women who have bulimia nervosa, in contrast, have been shown to be much more responsive to medications, particularly antidepressants. Bulimia may be closely related to the affective disorders, as evidenced by depressive symptomatology and a family history of affective disease. Several studies have reported significant results with different types of antidepressants. Pope and colleagues (1983) recommended tricyclic antidepressants, whereas Walsh's group (1982) demonstrated the usefulness of monoamine oxidase inhibitors (MAOIs). More recently, a new category of medications such as Prozac, Zoloft, and Paxil has been used successfully. Numerous double-blind, placebo-controlled studies have demonstrated that antidepressants help patients to reduce binge frequency; however, only a minority of patients stop bingeing completely, and there is significant relapse once the medication is stopped (Walsh and Devlin 1998). Obese clients, like anorexics, have not generally demonstrated positive response to medications.

Hospitalization should be recommended to an anorexia nervosa client only if her physical condition has become medically precarious. When hospitalization is proposed to an anorexic client, the focus should be on the symptoms of food preoccupation, irritability, and social isolation rather than on the need for weight gain. It is also important to keep an ecological perspective and to deal constructively with family and environmental supports.

Professionals disagree about the value of hospitalization for bulimic clients. Many therapists agree with Mintz (1983) that hospitalization should be reserved for patients who are in danger of dying or becoming severely medically ill, or who are suicidal or psychotic. In contrast, using the British criteria for bulimia nervosa, Russell (1979) recommended hospital admission for most patients to interrupt the vicious cycle of overeating, self-induced vomiting, other kinds of purging, and weight loss.

Hospitalization may be used as a last resort for the obese who are massively overweight, i.e., those who weigh 100 percent over normal weight. In the controlled environment of an inpatient medical unit, these obese persons do lose weight. However, follow-up studies demonstrate that most of these clients, unfortunately, regain their lost pounds over a period of months or years.

A day hospital is a variant of hospitalization which can often be useful for eating disordered patients who do not require hospitalization for suicidal behavior (Kaplan, Kerr, and Maddocks 1992). The day hospital format consists of a variety of group therapies that provide support and structure and allow critical issues to be addressed. Such intense outpatient care limits regression, promotes autonomy, and allows patients to practice eating regulation skills.

ILLUSTRATION AND DISCUSSION

As noted, many different modalities of counseling have been recommended for clients with eating problems. The clinician is left with the difficult decision of which type of intervention is best suited to the client and which intervention, if any, should be pursued for the family. For a client with an eating disorder to be treated properly, the social worker should attempt as comprehensive an initial evaluation as possible.

The following case illustrates the collaboration of two social workers in the treatment of an unhappy 14-year-old girl, referred by her mother. This case is of a mother/daughter dyad in which both are compulsive overeaters and are obese.

The mother, Mary, is a 40-year-old divorced woman, of European American heritage, who works full-time as a dentist. Her daughter, Carol, an only child, is a 14-year-old high school sophomore in a small public school.

Mary's maternal grandparents emigrated to New York as young adults and opened up a bakery shop in lower Manhattan. Mary's parents were born in New York. Her father was a dentist who died in an automobile accident when Mary was 8, leaving her widowed mother to support Mary and her younger brother. Both children stayed with their grandparents while their mother worked as a nurse. Mary loved the heavy meals served daily by her grandmother; however, her mother objected to the "unhealthy" eating habits of her parents. Mary recalls her mother and grandmother quarreling about her eating habits and her weight.

Mary's weight has vacillated since childhood. At each stage of development she was at times somewhat obese or fell into the upper end normal range. As an adult she is obese. Mary is 5 feet 5 inches tall, and her weight has remained stable for the past ten years, around 200 pounds.

Mary is the only woman in a three-person dental office; her specialty is pediatric dentistry. Her work is satisfying and reasonably lucrative; however, her specialty requires her to work nights and Saturdays because of children's school hours. Mary divorced Jack, Carol's father, when Carol was 2 because of her belated recognition that she was sexually attracted to women, not men. After a number of years alone with only casual relationships with women, she found a gay lover with whom she has been in a stable relationship for two years, although they live separately.

At the time of the initial intake Mary requested "parental guidance" in managing her relationship with Carol, a sad, lonesome, overweight girl, who weighed approximately 180 pounds on a 5-foot, 1-inch frame. Carol was allegedly a normal weight child until age 10, when she began gaining slowly by episodes of uncontrolled eating followed by normal eating and brief attempts to restrict food intake. Carol demonstrated several aspects of bulimia nervosa in her recurrent episodes of binge eating at least two times a week and her feeling of being out of control of her eating behavior. However, Carol does not purge, use laxatives or diuretics, or vigorously exercise. She is unable to strictly diet and does not fast. Her diagnosis would be in a new category called binge eating disorder. Currently this diagnosis would be in the *DSM-IV* category called "Eating Disorder, Not Otherwise Specified." Although she is obese, Mary would not be classified as having a psychiatric disorder in *DSM-IV* because her eating behavior consists of chronic overeating rather than discrete episodes of bingeing alternating with normal food intake or undereating, and she does not have a subjective sense of being out of control of her food intake.

During the past four years Mary and Carol have moved twice and Carol changed schools three times. The last school move was from an academically competitive high school to a less pressured environment. The first school change was from suburbs to city. Carol's schoolwork was no longer superlative, and her weight had become a focal issue for the family.

Both parents have been appropriately concerned about Carol and agreed that she should be medically evaluated. At 12 she was seen and followed by an endocrinologist who has medicated her with no success. After a frustrating year of treatment, the doctor recommended an alternative medication but the parents refused to allow the trial, as it was in the "fen fen" family. Instead, they then sought mental health counseling and left the endocrinologist.

Jack is a businessman who remarried and moved to a nearby city. He does not plan to have any more children and is devoted to Carol, who sees him every other weekend. He is a stable provider. He is in good health, has no eating problems, and is by all accounts supportive and affectionate toward his daughter.

The social worker met initially with Mary to gather history and understand the chief complaint. Mary described her stormy fights with Carol, largely around eating issues. Their situation was made worse by Mary's perception of Carol as a satellite of herself, as a younger version of a woman who felt helpless, out of control, unattractive. Unable to help herself, Mary could not help Carol. Mary alternated between yelling at Carol for overeating and painstakingly cooking healthy and appealing meals. At other times, Mary would be exhausted both by her long work hours and her conflicts with Carol; she then would order in unhealthy food or give Carol money for candy and other junk food. Eating was an activity they both hated and loved together, a source of strife as well as intimacy.

The initial treatment recommendation was that Mary and Carol come in together for two purposes: to observe their interaction and to devise an ongoing treatment strategy that would be realistic and effective. When the social worker evaluated Mary and Carol together, the tension in the air was palpable and they sat as far away from each other as possible. After a few sessions, it became clear that the separation-individuation process was arrested at an early level of development and that anger on Carol's part was actually a defense against intense dependency. Mary revealed that she saw Carol as a narcissistic extension of herself and that she felt as frustrated and helpless about controlling Carol's weight as she did her own. It was the social worker's clinical opinion that Carol and Mary's enmeshment was not decreasing with joint sessions, and that individual treatment supplemented by a supportive group experience might be best.

On the recommendation of the social worker, Carol agreed to consult with another therapist for her own treatment, while Mary remained with the initial therapist. Carol made her own appointment for an after-school hour, arrived promptly, and thereafter kept every appointment. Her new therapist had been given thorough background information by both the social worker and Mary. At the family's request, the girl's therapist spoke with the endocrinologist as well, who thought that other modalities might be more effective than medication at this juncture. She had given Carol "diets," to no avail.

Carol was an extraordinarily articulate, anxious, precocious girl, dressed in baggy clothing, with eyeglasses and an enormous bookbag. Her speech was pressured and in a flood of drama she described her awful fights with mother in which she threw and broke things, out of all proportion to the actual disagreement. She said she was depressed, hated herself, had no friends, was a misfit in school, and couldn't wait to move to another country all alone. She complained that people didn't trust her because she was smart, that she never got invited anywhere, felt academically pushed all the time, hated competition, had no interest in her religion, was bisexual but only a few people knew, and that she sometimes scratched and bit herself. If she could lose 5 pounds a year she would be the "happiest person on this earth." She aspired to be a professional musician (she plays the flute) and believed that she had considerable talent. For a brief period she had seen a psychiatrist and a social worker, didn't like either one of them, and had taken 40 mg of Prozac, which she hated and stopped taking.

In one session Carol gave the equivalent of many hours of information. She made little eye contact, was defiant and self-aggrandizing, and flaunted her self-loathing as if she were describing someone else. She fled from her competitive high school to a smaller place where she hoped she would "be seen as a person," and her intelligence was immediately noted in school; she was technically in tenth grade but took eleventh-grade classes, making her the youngest in her classes. The initial sessions were devoted to outlining a strategy for the future. The therapist "teamed up" with Carol to give her as much autonomy as possible in a nurturing environment where she would not be judged and where her weight was only one of many factors that defined her identity and sense of self.

It quickly emerged that Carol's obesity was one symptom within a larger constellation of issues. She was chronically depressed, anhedonic, socially isolated, highly sensitive to rejection, slept too much, was unable to "come out of the closet" with peers, and felt "doomed" by her genetic predisposition to obesity, which her mother could never conquer. This very bright teenager fully understood "what she had to do" and was sick of being nagged by every adult she knew.

In the early phase of treatment the social worker concentrated on two tasks: (1) building a comfortable camaraderie with Carol and (2) talking in depth about her dreams for the future and the many things she had done of which she could feel proud. Discussion of her weight was minimal, and emphasis was instead put on her mood disorder and the ways in which depression inhibits progress and achievement and happiness. Within a couple of months Carol was ready to accept a referral to a psychiatrist, to assess whether she might want to reconsider medication as an adjunct to her therapy. She went to see the doctor, accompanied by her father. She was diagnosed as dysthymic and given Effexor XR 75 mg daily. The social worker and psychiatrist conferred. He described her father as warm and understanding and said they had an easy and affectionate tie. He agreed that Carol was a precocious youngster, in many ways skeptical and sophisticated beyond her years and in other respects overly attached to family, socially awkward, and seriously handicapped by her obesity.

Carol remained on medication for the duration of her treatment. Approximately two months into her therapy she announced that she had joined Weight Watchers, liked the group meetings, and had lost 6 pounds. She accomplished this "on her own" and was proud to make her announcement to the therapist. She referred to how difficult it was to give up "snacking" but was matter of fact about the process, and the therapist was able to begin to use some humor and joking to relieve tension around the all important and ever dominating "obesity issue."

Thereafter Carol began concentrating on the other developmental tasks of adolescence. Her parents were supportive of all her talents and endeavors and openly enjoyed her lively intellect. Carol began volunteer community service, wrote articles, wrote songs, practiced the flute, and began to talk about college. She stopped talking about moving away. She began to explore gay and lesbian issues and to express a wish for close friendships, male and female. She constantly fought the familiar urge to become reclusive, but did not want to be part of an adolescent "therapy group."

There were many difficult phases in Carol's treatment, either directly or tangentially related to her eating disorder. Throughout her classes there were boys who teased her relentlessly and sadistically (i.e., whispering *oink oink* when she entered the room), out of teacher earshot. She was ostracized for being younger than everyone in her classes and heard peers making social plans that never included her. She was terrified to acknowledge her bisexuality, conditioned by the cruel responses to every other aspect of her that was "different."

In time she earned some respect and a few friends, for her wit, musical talent, and kind personality. Carol continued to make "private" friendships at gay and lesbian teen functions. She made plans for studying music in the summer and learned that she did not have to put her life on hold until she was no longer overweight.

Her mother remained in treatment with the social worker they had seen initially, on a less frequent basis. Although Mary made only minimal progress in losing weight, she was able to provide, on a consistent basis, a healthy diet for Carol. Perhaps even more important, Carol and Mary started to enjoy doing things together that did not involve food, such as movies and concerts, and Mary stopped trying to monitor Carol's food intake.

In therapy, Carol recognized that success in other areas might give her the self-confidence and pride she needed to take on the challenge of her obesity. It will be a long and slow process for Carol to emerge into adulthood as a happy person. She made healthy strides during treatment and went on to college, eager to pursue music, able to separate from home and feel optimistic about her future. The prognosis was good, her attitude toward the helping professions positive, and her obesity was no longer equivalent to her definition of herself. Carol's weight loss was steady but slow, but she no longer felt like a marginal person, or a "reject." She had other mechanisms than food for coping with anxiety and stress and was successfully compensating for those aspects of herself that she did not like by striving to become successful in her academic and romantic life.

Patients with an eating disorder require that the treatment interventions address aspects of life other than food. Active therapy, in which the clinician is allied with the client's strengths, can be a source of healing. Carol had a genetic problem, a divorced family, a minority sexual orientation, a precocious mind, an affective disorder, an obese mother, and years of teasing. She also had supportive parents, kind teachers, Weight Watchers, medication, and access to psychotherapy. Her problems overlapped in a tapestry that had to be seen as a whole. There is no one factor that could account either for her misery or the gradual restoration of her sense of self-worth and good health. She will probably have a lifelong struggle with food, but she knows that everyone struggles with something and that her inner resources and her family support are available to her.

CONCLUSION

Being overweight has profound psychological effects. In a study by Leon (1982) adolescent and adult patients who sought treatment for overweight were found to accept the dominant values of society, viewing obesity—and hence, their own bodies—as undesirable and, in extreme cases, as repulsive. Overweight patients such as these often feel that their bodies are grotesque and loathsome, and they exhibit low self-esteem and a negative self-concept. Obese girls have been found to display personality characteristics strikingly similar to those recognized by social anthropologists as typical of ethnic and racial minorities subjected to intense discrimination; these characteristics include passivity, obsessive concern about appearance, the expectation of rejection, and progressive withdrawal. Stunkard and Mendelson (1967) found that patients who were obese during adolescence developed an attitude toward weight that caused them to judge people in terms of adiposity; they expressed contempt for fat people and admiration for thin people. All the patients' disappointments were attributed to this handicap of obesity. The feelings of a 12-year-old child on a diet about his body image were expressed in a poem that ended, "Happy when skinny/ and sad when fat" (Collipp 1975:47).

In her studies of anorexic and obese patients, Bruch (1973) described their psychological disturbances, differentiating three areas of disordered experiences: disturbances in body image; disturbances in the perception of affective and visceral sensations, including inaccuracy in the way hunger is experienced; and an overall "sense of ineffectiveness." This sense of ineffectiveness is characterized by passivity, a sense of helplessness, difficulty in mastering bodily functions, and the conviction of being unable to change anything about one's life. These patients experience themselves as not being in control of their behavior, needs, and impulses; as not owning their own bodies; and as not having a center of gravity within themselves. Instead, they feel that they are under the influence and direction of external forces.

The importance of social work involvement with this population cannot be overestimated. Compassionate treatment can save a person's life. Social workers, combining their knowledge of clinical theory with their awareness of community resources are in a unique position to triage clients to appropriate caretakers, and to be primary care clinicians in appropriate cases.

References

Allon, N. 1982. "The Stigma of Overweight in Everyday Life." In B. Wolman, ed., *Psychological Aspects of Obesity: A Handbook*, pp. 130–74. New York: Van Nostrand Reinhold.

American Psychiatric Association (APA). 1987. *Diagnostic and Statistical Manual of Mental Disorders (DSM-III-R)*, 3d ed. Washington, D.C.: Author.

———. 1994. *Diagnostic and Statistical Manual of Mental Disorders (DSM-IV)*, 4th ed. Washington, D.C.: Author.

Austrian, S. 1995. *Mental Disorders, Medications, and Clinical Social Work.* New York: Columbia University Press.

Beattie, H. 1988. "Eating Disorders and the Mother-Daughter Relationship." *International Journal of Eating Disorders* 7:453–60.

Boskind-White, M. and W. White. 1983. *Bulimarexia.* New York, London: W. W. Norton.

Broden, S. 1994. "The Therapeutic Use of Humor in the Treatment of Eating Disorders; or, There Is Life Even After Fat Thighs." In B. Kinoy, ed., *Eating Disorders: New Directions in Treatment and Recovery*, 92–99. New York: Columbia University Press.

Bruch, H. 1949. "Psychological Aspects of Obesity." In P. Mullahy, ed., *A Study of Interpersonal Relations*, pp. 223–38. New York: Hermitage Press.

———. 1973. *Eating Disorders.* New York: Basic Books.

———. 1975. "The Importance of Overweight." In P. J. Collipp, ed., *Childhood Obesity*, pp. 75–81. Acton, Mass.: Publishing Sciences Group.

———. 1978. *The Golden Cage.* Cambridge: Harvard University Press.

———. 1981. "Developmental Considerations of Anorexia Nervosa and Obesity." *Canadian Journal of Psychiatry* 26:212–16.

———. 1982. "Anorexia Nervosa: Therapy and Theory." *American Journal of Psychiatry* 139:1531–38.

Bulow, B. and N. DeChillo. 1987. "Treatment Alternatives for Bulimia Patients." *Social Casework* 68:477–84.

Collipp, P. J. 1975. "Obesity Program in Public Schools." In P. J. Collipp, ed. *Childhood Obesity*, pp. 43–53. Acton, Mass.: Publishing Sciences Group.

Crisp, A., R. Palmer, and R. Kalucy. 1976. "How Common Is Anorexia Nervosa? A Prevalence Study." *British Journal of Psychiatry* 218:549–54.

Daniel, W. A. 1982. "Obesity in Adolescence." In B. Wolman, ed., *Psychological Aspects of Obesity*, pp. 104–17. New York: Van Nostrand Reinhold.

Fairburn, C. 1981. "A Cognitive Behavioural Approach to the Treatment of Bulimia." *Psychological Medicine* 11:707–11.

Fairburn, C. and S. Beglin. 1990. "Studies of the Epidemiology of Bulimia Nervosa." *American Journal of Psychiatry* 147:401–8.

Fairburn, C. and P. Cooper. 1982. "Self-Induced Vomiting and Bulimia Nervosa: An Undetected Problem." *British Medical Journal* 284:1153–55.

——. 1984. "The Clinical Features of Bulimia Nervosa." *British Journal of Psychiatry* 144:238–46.

Fallon, A. and P. Rozin. 1985. "Sex Differences in Perceptions of Desirable Body Shape." *Journal of Abnormal Psychology* 94:102–5.

Foch, T. and G. E. McClearn. 1980. "Genetics, Body Weight, and Obesity." In A. J. Stunkard, ed., *Obesity*, pp. 48–71. Philadelphia: W. B. Saunders.

Furnham, A. and N. Alibhai. 1983. "Cross-Cultural Differences in the Perception of Female Body Shapes." *Psychological Medicine* 13:829–37.

Garfinkel, P. E. and D. M. Garner. 1982. *Anorexia Nervosa: A Multidimensional Perspective.* New York: Brunner/Mazel.

Garner, D. M. and P. E. Garfinkel. 1985. *Handbook of Psychotherapy for Anorexia Nervosa and Bulimia.* New York: Guilford.

Garner, D., P. Garfinkel, D. Schwartz, and M. Thompson. 1980. "Cultural Expectations of Thinness in Women." *Psychological Reports* 47:483–91.

Germain, C. and A. Gitterman. 1980. *The Life Model of Social Work Practice.* New York: Columbia University Press.

Gitterman, A. and L. Shulman. 1994. *Mutual Aid Groups, Vulnerable Populations and the Life Cycle.* New York: Columbia University Press.

Glucksman, M. H. and J. Hirsch. 1969. "The Response of Obese Patients to Weight Reduction." *Psychosomatic Medicine* 31:1–7.

Goldstein, E. 1984. *Ego Psychology and Social Work Practice.* New York: Free Press.

Gull, W. W. 1874/1964. "Anorexia Nervosa." Transaction of the Clinical Society of London 7:22–28. Reprinted in R. M. Kaufman, and M. Heiman, eds., *Evolution of Psychosomatic Concepts. Anorexia Nervosa: A Paradigm.* New York: International Universities Press.

Hall, A. 1985. "Group Therapy for Anorexia Nervosa." In D. M. Garner and P. E. Garfinkel, eds., *Handbook of Psychotherapy for Anorexia Nervosa and Bulimia,* pp. 213–39. New York: Guilford.

Halmi, K. 1980. "Psychiatric Diagnosis of Morbidly Obese Gastric Bypass Patients." *American Journal of Psychiatry* 137:470–72.

——. 1983. "The State of Research in Anorexia Nervosa and Bulimia." *Psychiatric Development* 3:247–62.

Halmi, K., J. Falk, and E. Schwartz. 1981. "Binge-Eating and Vomiting: A Survey of a College Population." *Psychological Medicine* 11:697–706.

Hodge, J. R. and E. A. Maseelall. 1993. "The Presentation of Obesity." In A. J. Giannini and A. E. Slaby, eds., *The Eating Disorders,* pp. 29–43. New York: Springer-Verlag.

Hsu, L. 1987. "Are the Eating Disorders Becoming More Common in Blacks?" *International Journal of Eating Disorders* 6:113–24.

Humphrey, L. 1986. "Family Relations in Bulimic-Anorexic and Nondistressed Families." *International Journal of Eating Disorders* 5:223–32.

Igoin-Apfelbaum, L. 1985. "Characteristics of Family Background in Bulimia." *Psychotherapy and Psychosomatics* 43:161–67.

Johnson, C., M. Connors, and M. Stuckey. 1983. "Short Term Group Treatment of Bulimia." *International Journal of Eating Disorders* 2:199–208.

Johnson, C., M. Stuckey, L. Lewis, and D. Schwartz. 1982. "Bulimia: A Descriptive Survey of 316 Cases." *International Journal of Eating Disorders* 2:3–16.

Jones, D. 1985. "Bulimia: A False Self Identity." *Clinical Social Work Journal* 13:305–16.

Kaplan, A., A. Kerr, and S. E. Maddocks. 1992. "Day Hospital Group Treatment." In H. Harper-Giuffre and K. R. MacKenzie, eds., *Group Psychotherapy for Eating Disorders,* pp. 161–79. Washington, D.C.: American Psychiatric Press.

Katz, A. and E. Bender. 1976. *The Strength in Us.* New York: New Viewpoints.

Kornhaber, A. and E. Kornhaber. 1975. "Obesity in Adolescents: Contributing Psychopathological Features and their Treatment." In P. J. Collipp, ed., *Childhood Obesity,* pp. 109–15. Acton, Mass.: Publishing Sciences Group.

Leon, G. 1982. "Personality and Behavior Correlates of Obesity." In B. Wolman, ed., *Psychological Aspects of Obesity,* pp. 15–29. New York: Van Nostrand Reinhold.

Lowenkopf, E. 1983. "Bulimia: Concept and Therapy." *Comprehensive Psychiatry* 24: 546–54.

Malenbaum, R., D. Herzog, S. Eistenthal, and G. Wysbak. 1988. "Overeaters Anonymous: Impact on Bulimia." *International Journal of Eating Disorders* 7:139–43.

Mintz, I. 1983. "An Analytic Approach to Hospital and Nursing Care." In C. P. Wilson, C. C. Hogan, and I. L. Mintz, eds., *Fear of Being Fat,* pp. 315–24. New York: Jason Aronson.

Mintz, N. 1982. "Bulimia: A New Perspective." *Clinical Social Work Journal* 10:289–302.

Minuchin, S., B. Rosman, and L. Baker. 1980. *Psychosomatic Families: Anorexia Nervosa in Context.* Cambridge: Harvard University Press.

National Institutes of Health (NIH). 1993. "Eating Disorders." Publication No. 94–3477.

Ordman, A. and D. Kirschenbaum. 1986. "Bulimia: Assessment of Eating, Psychological Adjustment, and Familial Characteristics." *International Journal of Eating Disorders* 5:865–78.

Pope, H., J. Hudson, J. Jones, and D. Yurgelun-Todd. 1983. "Bulimia Treated with Imipramine: A Placebo-Controlled Double-Blind Study." *American Journal of Psychiatry* 140:554–58.

Prather, R. and D. Williamson. 1988. "Psychopathology Associated with Bulimia, Binge Eating, and Obesity." *International Journal of Eating Disorders* 7:177–84.

Pyle, R., J. Mitchell, and E. Eckert. 1981. "Bulimia: A Report of 34 Cases." *Journal of Clinical Psychiatry* 42:60–64.

Rodin, J., L. R. Silberstein, and R. H. Striegel-Moore. 1985. "Women and Weight: A Normative Discontent." In T. Sonderegger, ed., *Psychology and Gender. Nebraska Symposium on Motivation, 1984,* pp. 267–307. Lincoln: University of Nebraska Press.

Rothenberg, A. 1986. "Eating Disorder as Modern Obsessive-Compulsive Syndrome." *Psychiatry* 49:45–53.

Roy-Byrne, P., K. Lee-Benner, and J. Yager. 1984. "Group Therapy for Bulimia." *International Journal of Eating Disorders* 3:97–116.

Russell, G. 1979. "Bulimia Nervosa: An Ominous Variant of Anorexia Nervosa." *Psychological Medicine* 9:429–48.

Saunders, R. 1985. "Bulimia: An Expanded Definition." *Social Casework: The Journal of Contemporary Social Work* 66:603–10.

Schwartz, D., M. Thompson, and C. Johnson. 1982. "Anorexia Nervosa and Bulimia: The Socio-Cultural Context." *International Journal of Eating Disorders* 1:20–36.

Selvini-Palazzoli, M. 1978. *Self-Starvation.* New York: Jason Aronson.

Silber, T. 1986. "Anorexia Nervosa in Blacks and Hispanics." *International Journal of Eating Disorders* 5:121–28.

Stevens, E. and J. Salisbury. 1984. "Group Therapy for Bulimic Adults." *American Journal of Orthopsychiatry* 54:156–61.

Strober, M. 1981. "The Relationship of Personality Characteristics to Body Image Disturbances in Juvenile Anorexia Nervosa: A Multivariate Analysis." *Psychosomatic Medicine* 43:323–30.

Stuart, R. B. and C. Mitchell. 1980. "Self-Help Groups in the Control of Body Weight." In A. Stunkard, ed., *Obesity,* pp. 345–54. Philadelphia: W. B. Saunders.

Stunkard, A. J. 1980. *Obesity.* Philadelphia: W. B. Saunders.

Stunkard, A. and M. Mendelson. 1967. "Obesity and the Body Image, 1: Characteristics of Disturbances in the Body Image of Some Obese Persons." *American Journal of Psychiatry* 123:1296–1300.

Thomlison, R. 1984. "Something Works: Evidence from Practice Effectiveness Studies." *Social Work* 29:51–56.

U.S. HHS (U.S. Department of Health and Human Services). 1980. *International Classification of Diseases (ICD-9),* 9th revision. Washington, D.C.: U.S. Government Printing Office.

Walsh, B. T. and M. J. Devlin. 1998. "Eating Disorders: Progress and Problems. *Science* 280 (May 29):1387–90.

Walsh, B., J. Steward, L. Wright, W. Harrison, S. Roose, and A. Glassman. 1982. "Treatment of Bulimia with Monoamine-Oxidase Inhibitors." *American Journal of Psychiatry* 139:1629–30.

Wilson, C. P., C. C. Hogan and I. L. Mintz. 1983. *Fear of Being Fat.* New York: Jason Aronson.

Wold, P. 1985. "Family Attitudes Toward Weight in Bulimia and in Affective Disorder—A Pilot Study." *The Psychiatric Journal of the University of Ottawa* 10:162–64.

Wolman, B. 1982. *Psychological Aspects of Obesity: A Handbook.* New York: Van Nostrand Reinhold.

Yudkovitz, E. 1983. "Bulimia: Growing Awareness of an Eating Disorder." *Social Work* 28:472–78.

9

Learning Disabilities

Naomi Pines Gitterman

When we refer to someone as learning disabled, what do we mean? Many people would answer that the term *learning disabilities* refers to children with some specific cognitive deficits. This is what much of the public believes about people with learning disabilities. This is also what some in our profession currently believe. Yet such perceptions are dated and too narrow. Work on the subject during the past few decades has generated a wealth of new information, documented by research that has led to a significantly expanded perspective and to changing interpretations of the term learning disabilities.

A review of the literature suggests that social work has left much of the understanding of the learning disabled and interventions to assist this population to our colleagues in such allied professions as education, psychology, and the health field. Yet we need to pay attention! The prevalence of learning disabilities among all ages is wide and represents possibly the most common disorder of children seen in mental health settings (Gross and Wilson 1974; Silver 1987; Small 1982). These clients are referred to social agencies or are seeking help with a wide range of behavioral problems affecting their social interactions and their ability to effectively carry out certain, expected developmental tasks. We need to understand the possible etiologies of their problems if we are to effectively develop strategies to address their needs.

DEFINING AND EXPLAINING LEARNING DISABILITIES

It was not until the 1960s that the concept of *learning disabilities*, a term originated by an educator, Samuel Kirk, became known to professionals and the general public (Kirk 1962). During this same period, Clements (1966) introduced into the psychiatric literature a syndrome he called *minimal brain dysfunction,* and these two terms were used interchangeably. Johnson and Myklebust broadened this definition to refer to children "as having a psychoneurological learning disability, meaning that behavior has been disturbed as a result of a dysfunction of the brain and that the problem is one of altered processes, not of a generalized incapacity to learn" (1964:8). To understand the development of these concepts, one needs to trace two sometimes parallel and interrelated areas of study: *how people learn and what determines behavior.* In accepting the meaning and implication of these terminologies, people began to reexamine some of their earlier beliefs.

Our thinking about childhood development in the first half of this century was dominated by the introduction of psychoanalytic thought. Clinicians viewed problems in children as originating in the experiences or unresolved conflicts of early childhood, and parents, especially the mother, were viewed as critical influences (Gross and Wilson 1974). For example, difficulties in learning, as well as behavioral problems, were widely thought to be the result of some underlying emotional problem (Johnson 1999).

The professional literature prior to the 1960s was replete with descriptions of learning and behavioral problems of children that did not fit into existing classifications and were not responsive to the usual interventions based on such classifications (Ochroch 1981). In the 1930s and 1940s, a few pioneers were exploring other avenues of explanation and began to produce research and new hypotheses based on clinical observations of patients with neurological disorders. Increasingly, evidence was provided about the relationship between brain processes and various cognitive or behavioral disorders. In 1937, Samuel Orton, a neuropathologist, became interested in the relationship between cerebral dominance and language disabilities and developed a theory about how differences in specific aspects of brain functioning affected a child's capacity to read. Several years later, Kurt Goldstein's (1942) research revealed that people with brain injuries exhibited certain disordered behaviors, such as distractibility, which persisted even after healing.

Strauss and Lehtinen's classic work, *Psychopathology and Education of the Brain-Injured Child* (1947), marked the beginning of learning disabilities as a field of study (Lerner 1971). In their work, Strauss and Lehtinen carried out close observations of children with similar patterns of behavior, who had been categorized with such diagnoses as mentally retarded or emotionally disturbed. They theorized that these behavior and learning problems were the result of brain injury and were not emotionally based or caused by psychogenic factors. Their definition of the brain-injured child included the following:

> The brain injured child is the child who before, during, or after birth has received an injury to or suffered an infection to the brain. As a result of such organic impairment, defects of the neuromotor system may be present or absent; however, such a child may show disturbances in perception, thinking and emotional behavior, either separately or in combination. (Strauss and Lehtinen 1947:4)

Similarities in certain behavior manifestations between children with brain damage and a large group of children with problems of behavior and learning led to the concept of *minimal brain dysfunction.* This latter group did not give evidence of "hard" neurological impairments, such as motor weakness, but rather of "soft" signs, such as clumsiness. Compelling evidence for the existence of minimal brain dysfunction can be shown by the similarity between children with these symptoms and those with organic brain disorders, and in the response of this population to medication (Gross and Wilson 1974).

There have been changes in the nomenclature, and more important, in the definitions and working hypotheses in the field of learning disabilities since the advent of Strauss and Lehtinen's book. During this process, social workers have had to incorporate new knowledge, question old beliefs, and look at the effects of new educational, physiological, and therapeutic interventions on identified populations.

Certainly, the discovery of psychotropic medications in the 1950s, and their impact on mental illness, led to a resurgence of interest in the brain and its effect on behavior. Internal processes or the external environment could no longer be seen as the sole factor in the etiology of behavior. This discovery played a major role in dispelling long-held myths. Social workers now realized that behavioral symptoms can be, at least in great part, organically based.

Perhaps the first, and among the best-known, examples was the discovery that autism is a behavioral disorder based on some dysfunction in the brain, and not the result of a psychological disturbance (Gross and Wilson 1974; Johnson 1999). Similarly, over the years, the symptom of hyperkinesis/hyperactivity has been demonstrated to be neurobiologically based (Gross and Wilson 1974; Shin 1998).

In the 1960s, Thomas, Chess, and Birch (1963, 1968) introduced the concept that temperament was an inborn trait. In their pioneer research, they showed how a child's temperament affected family relationships. Their findings were very influential in demonstrating the reciprocity between nature and nurture. Additional findings about the impact of inborn traits, referred to as temperament, on human development were subsequently identified by Thomas and Chess (1977) and Kagan (1984).

In the 1980s a whole new body of research was developed through long-term studies of twins and adopted children that validate that the core or determinants of many behaviors and personality traits are genetically determined. These include social potency, e.g., shyness and extroversion; stress reactions, e.g., vulnerability; and aggression and control (Franklin 1989; Goleman 1986; Pines 1982). Our common understanding that physical attributes and intellectual potential are affected by heredity was enlarged to include many personality characteristics.

Now our understanding of learning has been expanded and refined to reflect that all areas of learning development and dysfunction are affected by complicated, yet subtle, brain processes. Findings demonstrate the impact of genetics and brain function on a great range of behaviors, formerly considered to be solely based on psychological, cultural, or environmental influences. Such understandings have a profound impact on how we define the disorders and syndromes of learning and behavior, and the options for intervening effectively.

The definitions of learning disabilities have been affected over the years by newly emerging information and by differences of professional orientation and opinion. Following Kirk's original definition of the term learning disabilities, the National Advisory Committee on Handicapped Children formulated the following definition in 1967:

Children with special learning disabilities exhibit a disorder in one or more of the basic psychological processes involved in understanding or using spoken or written languages. These may be manifested in disorders of listening, thinking, talking, reading, writing, spelling, or arithmetic. . . . They do not include learning problems which are due primarily to visual, hearing, or motor handicaps, to mental retardation, emotional disturbance, or to environmental disadvantage. (Lerner 1971:4)

This definition was widely quoted and became the basis for landmark legislation that resulted in the establishment of educational programs for handicapped children and the training of professionals in this arena of service, called PL 94–142. This law provided a systematic methodology for the identification, assessment, and education of children with handicaps and was followed in later years by important amendments. The significance of this legislation has been considerable. Yet the definition quickly created certain theoretical and service delivery problems. The National Joint Committee on Learning Disabilities (NJCLD; 1987) was joined by others in its position that the federal definition did not convey the heterogeneity of learning disorders, it incorrectly limited the application of the definition to children, and it did not clearly state the etiology of learning disabilities, but rather made a listing of terms.

The vast changes in this field can be seen if one compares the proposed federal definition for the term learning disabilities. It refers to: "a heterogeneous group of disorders, presumed to be due to central nervous system dysfunction and manifested by significant difficulties in the acquisition and use of listening, speaking, reading, or mathematical abilities, or of social skills" (Interagency Committee on Learning Disabilities [ICLD] 1987). This definition is particularly significant because it acknowledges that many individuals classified as learning disabled have significant difficulties in establishing and maintaining satisfying peer and adult relationships (Gershon and Elliot 1989).

The cause of learning disabilities is not known. There are various hypotheses about its origin, including the probability that in any one person there may well be multiple origins. What we can also surmise is that the cause in one person will probably differ from the cause in another, which may explain why this syndrome has many variations (Shin 1998; Silver 1979; Small 1982).

Beginning with the assumption that understanding the etiology of a problem will assist in the selection of appropriate interventions, the practitioner may need to establish the probability of a specific etiology or to rule out, at least, those that are unlikely. More than forty different causative factors of learning disabilities have been reported in the literature of the last three decades. The following paragraphs include the major etiologies.

At some time, a learning disabled person may have experienced some *brain damage.* Such injuries may have occurred during gestation, the period of prenatal development, the birth process, or the early years of life. Such injuries may have been caused by disease, by exposure to lead or other toxic substances, by trauma, or by ingestion of drugs or medication by the mother, or by anesthesia. Depending on the location, extent of damage, and time period in the life cycle, an individual may suffer severe damage or a minimal form of subtle brain dysfunction.

Maturational lag, which is defined as some delay in the development of the central nervous system, is another possible cause (Silver 1979). Another common expla- nation relates to some *biochemical or physiological dysfunction*. This hypothesis sug- gests there may be some deficiency or altered homeostasis in metabolic functioning of the body. For instance, some allergic conditions are associated with specific be- havioral manifestations. An example of this problem can be found in Feingold's (1974) work in which an *allergic reaction* to food additives can result in specific learning or behavioral problems.

As already indicated, *genetic transmission* is commonly identified as a probable etiology, although in some families with such histories, it is not a determinant. Genetic factors may be important predictors for people with certain types of learning prob- lems. Twin and foster child rearing studies further support a genetic etiology. In as many as 40 percent of learning disabled children, family histories of learning dis- abilities were discerned (Silver 1987). Reports also show that children of low birth weight are at risk for learning problems as are those with seizure disorders (ICLD 1987).

Another factor that compounds developmental outcomes has to do with prema- ture birth, which has been associated with various developmental or behavioral prob- lems, including learning disabilities (Morrison and Cosden 1997). There is a school of thought that certain *dysfunctions of the eye*, especially in its ability to effectively gather visual information, can lead to dyslexia and are correctable by special eye exercises (Friedman 1981; Small 1982). Other examples of possible causes include, *low birth weight, environmental pollutants, radiation exposure of the mother or child, cortical dysfunction*, etc.

The clinical picture of the person with learning disabilities is not homogeneous. Though each person's functioning reflects a different combination of characteristics, they all fall into the same, broad unitary syndrome. *Learning disabilities can affect cognitive, social, emotional, and physical development and functioning.* Some gen- eral characteristics commonly include: an uneven growth pattern, which results in areas of maturational lag; average or above average intelligence; and discrepancies between achievement and potential. This syndrome can affect a person's capacity to meet academic and life tasks.

DEMOGRAPHIC PATTERNS

It is complicated to determine the number of persons affected by learning disabilities from the demographic data used to describe such persons. Prevalence varies, in great part, by the definition used. Criteria for inclusionary and exclusionary measures have changed over the years and differ further depending on the perspective or source used. School-based reports are most easily obtainable, yet these exclude youngsters who are learning disabled but whose major deficits may not be in the academic sphere, and, of course, these reports exclude adults. The U.S. Department of Education re- ported in 1987 that almost 5 percent of all school-aged children received special education services. Other studies reflected higher findings among youth, ranging from 10 to 15 percent (ICLD 1987; Silver 1987). The National Institutes of Health reports that 15 percent of the total population has some type of learning disability ("Facts about Learning Disabilities" 1999). Prevalence was slightly higher among *socioeco- nomically disadvantaged* populations, and at least twice as common in *males than in females* (ICLD 1987). In 1992, males with specific learning disabilities represented 7 percent of public school enrollment, while females with this disability accounted for only 3 percent ("Education of Students with Disabilities" 1999). The population of people diagnosed with a learning disability has grown markedly, about threefold, between 1976 and 1993 (Roush 1995). Studies to date are not adequate, largely because of the problems in achieving a consensus about definition, which are further influenced by political factors such as when funds are sought to address the needs of this population (Kavale and Foreness 1998).

SOCIETAL CONTEXT

The advent of federal legislation for people with handicaps, and in particular the learning disabled, was associated with two major phenomena. In the 1960s, America learned about equal rights for minorities, and legislation for racial and ethnic minorities paved the way to consideration of the needs of other minority groups. But for people with learning disabilities to be perceived as a group with special needs, they had to be so identified. As already indicated, the labeling of this population and the growing understanding of the ways in which people with learning disabilities were disadvantaged, especially in the educational system, enabled legislators and professionals to articulate the special needs of this population. Lobbying efforts seemed especially effective, because children from middle-class families composed a sizable portion of this group. Their parents were effective in initiating efforts for legal recognition and resources.

Two profoundly important pieces of federal legislation have supported the rights and need for services for the learning disabled. In 1973, Congress passed Section 504 of the Rehabilitation Act, prohibiting discrimination on the basis of physical or mental handicap in any federally assisted program or activity. Its intent was to effect fundamental changes in the attitudes of institutions and individuals toward handicapped persons. People with a diagnosis of specific learning disabilities fell into the federal definition, if their impairment(s) were severe enough to limit one or more major life functions. This legislation provided assurances that no handicapped child would be excluded from a public education because of a disability, that these children would be educated with nonhandicapped students to the extent possible, and that their parents or guardians could object to evaluation or placement decisions. In addition to supporting the rights of children in the educational system, it also mandated that postsecondary institutions could not discriminate against its applicants or students because of a handicap. The law further stipulated that employers could not refuse to hire or promote solely because of a worker's disability and that health and welfare services must provide equal access to services to persons with disabilities (U.S. Department of Health, Education and Welfare 1978).

Then, in November of 1975, Congress adopted PL 94–142, the Education for All Handicapped Children Act, and it became effective in October 1977. The spirit of this law was to assure handicapped children a free and appropriate education, and it set forth procedures to ensure that all parts of the law were implemented. The legislation introduced important concepts, including a mandate that children be educated in the least restrictive environment; that they be provided with individual educational plans (IEPs); that decisions on evaluation and placement be made by a committee composed of representative educators, professionals from related disciplines, and parents; and that due process provisions allow parents to challenge the school system's decisions or inaction (Smith 1980). Subsequent amendments, namely the Education of Handicapped Act of 1986, extended services to handicapped infants and preschool children (National Center for Clinical Infants Program [NCCIP] 1989). The Individuals with Disabilities Act (IDEA) of 1990, reauthorized the federal law (PL 94–142) passed in 1975. The Americans with Disabilities Act (ADA) of 1990 is a civil rights law protecting people with disabilities from discrimination in such areas as employment and public accommodations.

The opportunities generated by these acts are extraordinary, but the funds to support such options are often extremely high for local and state governments to support. The federal government's good intentions far exceeded its fiscal generosity. For example, one finds local communities, large cities, and small villages torn between serving the needs of its children, some of whom are severely handicapped by physical disabilities, by retardation, by autism, etc., and at the same time, trying to keep local taxes from spiraling further. Taxpayers' pleas compete with the pleas of desperate parents. Committees on Special Education are mandated to make sound educational decisions in behalf of children, yet anyone observing such a group in action will become aware that fiscal concerns loom large in the background. Similarly, many communities cannot keep pace with the growing needs of its handicapped population.

Other issues were raised about the mandate of this legislation. The notion of the *least restrictive environment* implied that moving toward mainstreaming was the preferred option, especially for children with learning disabilities. Clearly, the requirement enabled many formerly forgotten or "hidden" children to return to neighborhood schools to learn and socialize with peers; yet for others, it was not the panacea. Assigned to regular classes meant that many would not have the opportunity for more individually designed learning and were singled out by classmates as being "stupid." Others could not keep up socially, lacking the skills or self-confidence (Diamond 1979; Johnson 1981; Thomas et al. 1968). Placing children in regular classes with resource room supports or in self-contained, special education classrooms is only a beginning. Again, unprepared or overburdened staff, with limited resources, have not been able to carry out the goals set for each child.

Special education is a contentious issue in many state governments. Some experts contend that children have been diagnosed as learning disabled when their teachers wanted to rid themselves of disruptive students. In New York State, the special education program was criticized for placing a disproportionate number of black and Latino students into separate classrooms (Hernandez 1999).

Persons with learning disabilities often have an invisible handicap. Their problems are less blatantly observable than those of a person with mental retardation or pervasive developmental disabilities. The very definition that a learning disabled person must have average or above-average intelligence may further camouflage specific limitations. It is not difficult in our society to find those who feel that learning problems are precipitated by unmotivated or lazy students or serve as a symptom of some psychological "block." They are unsympathetic to people identified as learning disabled, feeling if only they tried harder, or were not obtaining secondary gain, they could overcome whatever cognitive or behavioral problem they possess. The situation is even more difficult for adults with learning disabilities, because learning disabilities were originally deemed to be a problem for children that they would eventually outgrow. The research amply demonstrates that the characteristics of learning disabled youngsters persist into adulthood and that learning disabilities often exist, some in changing form, throughout the life span (Adelman and Taylor 1986; Buchanan and Wolf 1986; Lyon 1996). Legislation and accompanying funding have largely been geared toward youth. While some laws provide for vocational education for adults with learning disabilities, their other needs, such as for support in independent living and training, receive less attention. Finally, professional training and funding reflect society's primary concern with academic and employment issues. Society does not seem to understand the primacy of the area of social needs of the learning disabled and the ways in which such deficits have an impact on total life functioning. This lack of understanding takes its toll on all levels, from the kind of expectations we have for the learning disabled to the kinds of services and resources we make available to them.

VULNERABILITIES AND RISK FACTORS

Having a learning disability "is, in itself a risk factor; however, there are wide variations in the emotional and social adaptation of individuals with learning disabilities" (Morrison and Cosden 1997:45). Risk factors, may be internal, namely a function of neurologically based features that influence behavior, or risk factors may be external, influenced by peer, family, or societal values, expectations and interactions (Spekman, Herman, and Vogel 1993).

Studies have revealed different outcomes regarding the relationship between individuals with learning disabilities and emotional problems, specifically depression and anxiety. Some studies report that individuals with learning disabilities score higher compared with their counterparts without disabilities, whereas other studies report less than half of persons with learning disabilities present clinical symptoms. The greater risk is associated for those with a lack of social relationships or with poor social relationships (Morrison and Cosden 1997).

The incidence of learning disabilities in *delinquent populations* is considerably higher than in the general population. Estimates of prevalence range from 26 percent to 73 percent (Larson 1988). According to a study by the Learning Disability/Juvenile Delinquency Project at Fordham University, individuals with learning disabilities are 22 percent more likely to be adjudicated delinquent than those without such disabilities (Moynihan 1987). Several hypotheses attempt to explain the link between learning disabilities and delinquency, such as vulnerability to peer group pressure and school failure (Berman 1974). Current investigators postulate that ineffective problem-solving skills increase the risk for delinquency in learning disabled youth (Larson 1988). Certainly, people with problems of impulsivity who lack social judgment skills would have an increased propensity for engaging in antisocial behaviors (Waldie and Spreen 1993).

Students with learning disabilities are more likely to become *school dropouts,* and those who do drop out of school or whose academic achievements are low are at greater risk vocationally and socially (Morrison and Cosden 1997). School and employment policies or practices that are not responsive to the needs of this population contribute to feelings of failure, alienation, and disengagement. Academic and social problems persist into adulthood. One of the common characteristics of adults with learning disabilities is a prolonged dependence on families, which emerges from difficulties in finding employment, in developing independent living skills, and in maintaining social relationships (Spekman, Goldberg, and Herman 1992). Denial of this disability further affects the individual's capacity to cope, and adults who are in denial are less likely to develop strategies for vocational or academic success.

Karacostos and Fisher (1993) found that higher proportions of adolescents with learning disabilities than those without learning disabilities were classified as *chemically dependent,* although there is limited research pertaining to rates of substance abuse prevalence in this population. Factors that may put adolescents at higher risk for substance abuse are behavioral problems, peer rejection, and school failure experiences. The Office of the Inspector General (1992) reported that learning disabilities and substance abuse are the most common impediments to the employment of clients on public assistance.

Having a family member with learning disabilities often places greater stress on families. Some of these families report greater chaos, disorganization, or conflict (Morrison and Cosden 1997). Parents experience high levels of anxiety when they have a child with special needs, especially when there are limited family or community resources. Moreover, family responses to the member with learning disabilities, such as unrealistic expectations, lack of acceptance, impatience, etc., increase risk factors.

Disorders of *learning and attention* commonly co-occur. A high proportion of individuals with learning disabilities have problems with attention, especially hyperactivity. It has been estimated that 30 to 50 percent of children who have been diagnosed with learning disabilities meet criteria for attention-deficit/hyperactivity disorder (Fletcher and Shaywitz 1996). The features of this disorder, such as impulsivity and hyperactivity, are additive risks that place a person with learning disabilities in greater jeopardy.

RESILIENCIES AND PROTECTIVE FACTORS

A significant proportion of people with learning disabilities have positive outcomes in various areas of functioning and experience overall life satisfaction. Protective factors may come from the individual's other level of skills or talents, his or her temperament, or in the responsiveness of the environment to the individual.

Resilience may be viewed as protective factors that act on risk conditions to reduce the impact of the risk factors (Morrison and Cosden 1997). Factors contributing to resilience may lie in the individual or in the environment and are often created by the interaction between the two. Certain *personal characteristics,* such as strong verbal skills, athletic ability, and the completion of different milestones in education, serve as protective factors and are often predictors of positive adult outcomes. Major protective factors for depression and anxiety are self-esteem and self-awareness, which contribute to a sense of well-being and competence.

Gerber and Reiff (1991) cite the importance of self-understanding in enabling people with learning disabilities to make appropriate accommodations and to utilize compensatory mechanisms. Self-understanding also generates self-confidence, the ability to strategize in stressful situations, and the capacity to take action that helps people feel in control.

"Reframing" is a strategy used by successful adults with learning disabilities. It refers to "reinterpreting the learning disability in a more positive or productive manner," which includes recognizing the disability, accepting it, understanding its meaning and implications, and taking action appropriate to that situation (Gerber, Ginsberg, and Reiff 1992:481).

Another protective factor is the family's ability to handle stress along with the availability of *external resources.* Additional supports for resiliency are related to the degree to which a family accepts and develops realistic expectations for the member with learning disabilities and has the knowledge and flexibility to address their needs.

Schools and the workplace that make accommodations, provide supportive environments, and develop arenas for the learning and application of skills are critical protective factors that lead individuals with learning disabilities to make successful adaptations. The capacity to ensure responsive social environments for learning disabled people with behavioral or social problems is far more complicated and elusive.

PROGRAMS AND SOCIAL WORK CONTRIBUTIONS

Social workers have not been in the forefront in identifying or addressing the needs of this population. Over the past four decades, educators have played a prominent role in advocating for and developing services to meet academic needs. Public schools offer an array of options for children with learning disabilities, though there is a significant gap between actual need and available services. Private schools have also been established, which broaden options for parents with economic means to make their own choices for their children and for overburdened school districts to provide support to children referred to private resources. Libraries for teachers abound with literature on theories and specialized techniques for teaching these youngsters. Educators are even in the vanguard of the learning disability movement in now devising and offering social skills training programs.

Psychiatrists and neurologists have carried out extensive and important research in this field, as well as offering both assessment and intervention services, including medication. The community has often turned to psychologists to administer testing to children and adults, to make learning and psychological assessments and to determine the nature and extent of learning and behavioral deficits and strengths. Both psychiatrists and psychologists have been major providers of therapeutic services and also work alongside other disciplines, such as speech therapists, in serving this population's needs.

Social workers in child guidance clinics, mental health and family agencies, and school systems are receiving sizable numbers of referrals and working with people of all ages who have learning disabilities. Similarly, child welfare and criminal justice settings serve youth or adults who struggle with many problems including learning disabilities. Clients with this diagnosis come to social agencies primarily because their social, behavioral problems have led to difficulty in some aspect of their life functioning. Parents may also seek help with a range of reactions to their learning disabled child, for assistance in acting in their child's behalf, or for help in dealing with child development or management issues. In these agencies and community institutions, social workers are offering multimethod interventions ranging from evaluation to consultation to counseling to advocacy.

In response to clients' needs and requests, various other programs are available.

Beyond academic programs, there are special camps or recreational and social programs for learning disabled youth and young adults. Such settings feature structured programs in which youth with learning disabilities who have social or motoric deficits may function with needed supports and in less competitive environments conducive to growth. Parents of learning disabled children may wish to join educationally oriented or mutual aid groups to enhance their understanding of their child's difficulties, to obtain new child rearing skills, or to gain the support of others in similar situations (Gitterman 1979). Many parents or learning disabled adults have also made active use of information and referral centers.

Middle-class parents have been effective in spearheading movements for their children. They have joined together in local and national associations to lobby for legislation, funds, and services. They are active presenters at professional conferences and join boards and school committees to enlighten the community and to advocate for resources. In lower socioeconomic communities, progress is slower, probably because parents besieged with so many life problems generally have not mobilized themselves in such organized efforts. Yet the numbers of learning disabled are great and their needs are naggingly persistent. There are never enough services, and as professionals, we are still somewhat neophytes in fully developing our technology for helping the learning disabled.

ASSESSMENT AND INTERVENTIONS

To obtain a total and accurate picture, carrying out an assessment of a person with learning disabilities often involves contributions from other disciplines, including neurologists, psychiatrists, speech and occupational therapists, psychologists, and remedial specialists. Each discipline, if relevant, will administer its own set of tests to illuminate areas of strength and the nature of the problem. A social worker can make an overall assessment, which, among other things, usually includes history taking. One important aspect involves documentation of exactly how the person's functioning deviates from what is normally expected, with emphasis on information about language, motor, cognitive, and social development, including delays in reaching developmental milestones, and inconsistencies in performance (Collard 1981). Questions to determine possible etiologies would include exploration into such areas as genetic factors, nutritional and allergy problems, mixed dominance, and prenatal, birth, and medical history.

Evaluations would include interviewing the person, family, and significant collateral contacts, such as a teacher or recreation counselor. Observations may be carried out in the office, home, and/or school. It would be particularly important to see the person in his or her social environment and to understand and assess the impact of the supports or stress factors, chaos or structure, cultural norms, performance expectations, and degree of acceptance or rejection in the environment on the person's functioning. If the client is a child or adolescent, it is also important for the social worker to understand the meaning of the disability for the parent and siblings, the family environment, pressures, and resources. In making an assessment, a professional needs to inquire into the following areas of functioning where evidence of deficits or delays may exist.

An early sign of learning disabilities may emerge in the area of *language devel-*

opment. A disorder exists when there is a qualitative difference in some aspect of language behaviors from expected normal development, based on a child's chronological age. Language disorders encompass many different kinds of disruptions in the content, form, and use of language (Bloom and Lahey 1978). Sometimes children do not express themselves well conceptually because they may lack the verbal acuity or because they think in more concrete terms. Children also may not express themselves well grammatically and cannot, for example, produce full sentences or utilize the correct parts of speech. Sometimes a child will speak in an immature manner.

Thus, a frequent signal of learning disabilities is a delay in language development, e.g., children who begin to speak at the age of 3 years or later. Children may also experience difficulty in articulation and do not produce sounds correctly. This can be the result of a motoric problem in which the mouth, tongue, and lips do not function well together in producing certain sounds. Language provides a person with a means to communicate and to socially interact with others, so that significant deficiencies can have a impact on a child's social development. If the disorder is readily apparent, it can also be a form of acute, public embarrassment.

Problems in *motor coordination* may be another early sign in the learning disability syndrome. While some learning disabled children have histories of reaching early milestones in motor development and possess strong athletic skills, many more have histories of awkwardness or clumsiness. Children may have difficulties with gross motor coordination, such as running or hopping; with small motor dexterity, such as cutting with scissors, tying shoelaces, or with handwriting; or in both areas. Others have problems with balance. All these deviations usually show up as "soft" neurological signs, rather than as "hard" classical neurological symptoms (Wender 1971).

Visual perception plays an important part in learning. Problems in visual perception may take one or more of the following forms. Some people have difficulty with spatial relations, which refers to how objects are viewed together in space and of how one organizes oneself in space. For example, a person might have trouble reading or doing arithmetic because of how they view letters or numbers and their relationship to space, or they might have difficulty discriminating left from right, or they might feel disoriented or dizzy when placed in a more open environment (Lerner 1971; Silver 1979). People may have difficulty with depth perception, in which distance is misjudged, so that a person may miss a step in climbing stairs, or bump into things or fall down while trying to sit. Visual discrimination problems often occur when people reverse letters (e.g., *d* and *b*) or words (e.g., *saw* and *was*) or see symbols in reverse, as in mirror reading. They may copy incorrectly, become confused with visual directions, or experience visual motor problems, as in trying to track and catch a ball. Visual perception problems often lead to difficulties in reading, due, in this situation, to some limitation in the ability to decode correctly.

Some people's problems occur more in the area of *auditory perception*. There is no problem with hearing acuity, but people may have difficulty distinguishing subtle differences in sound, in distinguishing significant sounds to pay attention to, or in integrating different phonic sounds. Other possible difficulties occur when a person experiences auditory lag, so they cannot process quickly what they hear and the speaker must speak more slowly; or a person might have trouble with auditory sequencing, i.e., not being able to remember the order of things given in oral directions.

A particularly serious dysfunction occurs when a person has a *memory disability,* i.e., problems with either integrating, storing, or retrieving information from memory. The two primary forms of memory are short-term and long-term, and the problems may occur in visual or auditory sphere. Short-term memory refers to information that needs to be retained for a short time while a person is using it. In long-term memory, knowledge is retained and is available for retrieval when required. For instance, a person may look up and remember a number long enough to dial it on the telephone; this only requires short-term memory. When a person learns that telephone number and can retrieve it at will many hours or days later, then it has become a part of long-term memory. With constant repetition a person usually learns to store things in long-term memory. When this process fails, learning is seriously affected and impaired.

A pervasive problem that many people with learning disabilities experience is one of *disorganization,* which takes many forms and affects many areas of daily functioning and learning. People are bombarded constantly with all kinds of sensory stimuli coming from the environment. The learning disabled are often overwhelmed by the stimuli. They cannot easily process, integrate, and act on the stimuli appropriately or effectively.

Two major areas of *behavioral characteristics* coexist with learning disabilities or are viewed as part of the learning disability syndrome: (1) *problems in attention,* and (2) *social immaturity or problems in social competence.* The *Diagnostic and Statistical Manual of Mental Disorders,* 4th edition (*DSM-IV*; American Psychiatric Association [APA] 1994) classifies the first group as attention-deficit/hyperactivity disorder (AD/HD). *Hyperactivity* is physiologically based rather than anxiety based, meaning that evidence of hyperactivity can be traced to early childhood. Frequently, though not always, children with this disorder were very active since birth, frequently in motion, often colicky, and not always easy to cuddle. Their movements can be described as jittery, their cries as piercing, and their meals as fraught with difficulty (Kavanagh and Truss 1988). Such children leave their parents exhausted, with the house looking very much like a combat zone. Hyperactive people are described as "always on the go" as "if driven by a motor" (Kavanagh and Truss 1988), have difficulty sitting still, fidget excessively, and run around or climb on things excessively. Some children are more appropriately classified as *distractible,* meaning that some external stimuli are affecting their behavior and they are distracted from attending to the task at hand. To differentiate between these two sets of behavior, hyperactive persons act as if they are driven internally into motion, whereas distractible persons are excessively disturbed, for example, by the noise of a pencil dropping in the rear of the room while a teacher is speaking in the front. A much less observed symptom that people with learning disabilities sometimes have is the reverse problem, known as *hypoactivity,* where there is a lethargic appearance.

Other people have what is described as *problems with inattention,* for they lack the capacity for sustained attention or have a short attention span. They do not seem to always listen or to finish what they start. Sometimes they are described as daydreaming. Problems with impulsivity, or what is sometimes called *poor impulse control,* is a common manifestation in many people with learning disabilities (Ruffner 1994; Wender 1971). Evidence of such behaviors is seen in a person's tendency to act before thinking, to experience difficulty in delaying gratification, and generally to have a low frustration tolerance. Such people will become quickly upset when things or other people fail to react as anticipated or hoped. Impulsive people also may experience problems in disorganization or in staying with one activity for a period of time. Impulsivity often results in unplanned or socially inappropriate responses.

Children with problems in attention, especially hyperactivity, experience difficulty during infancy and in preschool years, but it is during the advent of the school years that the problems are markedly apparent. Virtually every aspect of the child's environment is affected: school, peers, and home (Kavanagh and Truss 1988). AD/HD is considerably more common in boys. It was initially thought that problems in inattention greatly subside in the early years of adolescence with the change in hormones. However, studies reflect some dissipation of gross motor symptoms but a persistence into adulthood of many of the other attentional problems (Fletcher and Shaywitz 1996; Kavanagh and Truss 1988).

For many years, the definition of *learning disability* did not include the identification of social behaviors or social adjustment. Yet, throughout this period, studies increasingly demonstrated the evidence of various patterns of *social immaturity* endemic to the learning disabled syndrome. Studies further reveal that people with learning disabilities are often poorly accepted or rejected and exhibit significant social skill deficits (Gresham and Elliott 1989). Therefore, social skill deficits can be viewed as a primary learning disability (Gresham et al. 1997; Jackson, Enright, and Murdock 1987; Kavanagh and Truss 1988; Kronick 1978, 1981; Lerner 1996; Ritter 1989). In terms of total life functioning, social ineptitude tends to be far more disabling than most cognitive deficits (Kronick 1978).

Previously, some characterized the problems observed as secondary problems resulting from children's difficulties and frustration in coping with cognitive and other previously identified deficits. Yet the proposed federal definition, coupled with extensive research, suggests that, indeed, social skill problems are an integral part of the learning disability syndrome and are the result of some physiological determinant or delay. This finding fits in with what we are now learning about the effect of genetics and brain function on many behaviors.

Characteristically, socially immature people exhibit difficulty in some of the following areas. They may lack acuity in social perception and tend to misread or ignore the cues of others. They may have problems in exercising social judgments, namely, in how they choose to handle social situations, so that behavior often appears immature or inappropriate. Such lack of sophistication also results in difficulties in social problem solving. Many experience problems in social interactions, especially with peers on age-appropriate levels. Their desire to make friends is clearly apparent, but their social behaviors are often awkward, lacking in social competence and appropriateness. The picture looks different at different age levels, but almost always it is not what would be expected at a specific age. For instance, in young children, there may be extroversion: excessive hugging and kissing; inviting friends too quickly, such as asking a stranger on the street to visit their home; or joining into games without considering possible rejection and the impact on others. They may blurt out what they think without the expected social prohibitions (e.g., "you look fat" or "your house is messy"). Children with such problems may have inappropriate expectations of others so that the judgments they make may be met with annoyance. For example, if an 8-year-old learning disabled boy is playing with a 3-year-old girl and she takes his ball away, the boy acts as if the 3-year-old were his peer, grabs the ball back, and does not take into account the age difference.

As children grow older, they will learn and integrate various age-appropriate interactions; however, these are offset by frequent lapses into less age-appropriate behaviors. Initiating and sustaining friendships and making mature social judgments will still prove to be a problem. By adolescence, the peer group takes on greater importance, but learning disabled children are often excluded by peers because they lack peer-valued attributes (Kronick 1981). Thus, the gap for social opportunities for learning and interaction is widened. The behaviors of learning disabled adolescents, and adults as well, is varied and colored by the accumulation of other life experiences. Yet one can factor out certain traits that seem to be characteristic of the learning disabled person. For example, they may miss the point of what is being said, they may overreact, or they may make inappropriate remarks, actions, or poorly timed responses. They may need to be in control, which grows out of their need to organize other people and situations from their own sense of internal disorganization. They may sometimes, incorrectly, project blame. Yet they can be simultaneously and acutely aware of the messages of others toward them, but have difficulty knowing how to effectively respond. They may seem stubborn, or they may need time alone to pull themselves together and to withdraw from bombarding and overwhelming stimuli. For some, poor judgment may result in antisocial acts (Smith 1980). The form these behavioral symptoms take is varied, but the common denominator is usually eagerness for interaction, coupled with qualities of social ineptness.

Three other behavioral traits may be seen in many people with learning disabilities. The first is what is called *emotional lability,* meaning strong vulnerability. Excessively labile people may be hurt out of proportion to what one might anticipate and then react with a corresponding degree of pain. It may be as simple as how one responds to a belonging being broken or misplaced, or to losing in a game or to teasing. The second is *perseveration,* meaning a person seems to "get stuck." The learning disabled do not easily pull themselves out of a situation to look at options, or they create a mental set, a script of expectations that may not come to fruition. One common and sad example is the child who gets into a physical fight and cannot stop. Finally, there is the problem of *slower adaptive mechanisms,* meaning that people cannot deal with unexpected changes easily and need more time to integrate changes that are nonroutine or unexpected. A change may be small (e.g., a new textbook); it may be an unanticipated visitor, a trip to a new place, or almost any change in known ritual, plan, structure, or interaction.

It is not uncommon for the learning disabled to experience *secondary emotional problems* that grow out of many years of experiencing frustration and failure and to which they react in many ways. They may develop such symptoms as withdrawal or hypochondria, or they may resort to clowning to divert attention from their problems. In one form or another, most struggle with a poor sense of self-esteem (Silver 1979).

Still, people with learning disabilities bring to their lives some very special qualities. They may display a hearty enthusiasm, spontaneity, or adventurousness (Smith 1980). Particularly impressive is the courage, resilience, and persistence they may ultimately apply, over and over again, to facing difficult life tasks. One is often captivated by the uniqueness of their personalities and their ability to draw on their resources.

In working with this population, recommended interventions are dictated by the implications of an assessment for learning disabilities. For some children, where difficulties are predominantly cognitive, academic remediation will undoubtedly be very important. Specific suggestions should be made, including the kind of individual or class structure needed and the specific remediation techniques suggested to help a person to learn required skills or to find appropriate compensatory measures. Such options abound; the following is a simple example. A child with problems in handwriting may learn to write more effectively if he can learn to draw in sand or fingerpaint, may copy over dots more readily than trying to copy from a picture, or may need wide lines rather than open space as a guide.

Speech therapists have been effective in helping children with a range of language problems, and early intervention, especially, reaps important success. In the field of medicine, the use of medication has had a profound impact in alleviating such symptoms as hyperactivity. Although the use of medication, especially on children, has been controversial, medication that has been carefully monitored to reduce possible side effects has achieved significant results (Gross and Wilson 1974). Research findings indicate that 60 to 90 percent of hyperactive children can focus their attention better and can reframe from physically and mentally responding to diversions when taking stimulant mediations (Smith 1986). Hence, there is a decrease in motor activity and an increase in attention span (Silver 1979). These medications do not affect specific learning deficits but modify the child's activity level, so that the child becomes more available to learning. Wender (1971) argued that substituting psychotherapy for medication could be viewed as malpractice, a harmful withholding of needed treatment from a child. He suggested that psychological help is popular, but as pragmatists, the question is not what is popular, but what works.

Social workers may assume various roles in working with learning disabled clients and their families. They may serve as coordinators, helping the client or family to locate appropriate resources for evaluation and future planning and to think through decisions and needed actions. Social workers often function in the role of consultants, providing information and suggestions, usually to parents, about learning disabilities and ways in which they can understand and be helpful to their child. Clients with learning disabilities and their families are often referred to or seek help from social workers for counseling, because of some interpersonal, developmental, and/or environmental problems. Finally, social workers serve as advocates or mediators and help to empower clients to act in their own behalf or in support of a family member.

Having a learning disability often means experiencing some difficulties throughout the life span. Therefore, help may be obtained to cope with tasks at different points in the life cycle, during crises as well as for longer periods of time. If one traces the path a learning disabled person takes, it is not uncommon to see him or her moving in and out of different kinds of helping relationships.

The first encounter is usually when problems are initially identified. Parents often become aware during the infant, toddler, or certainly the latency years that their child's development is different from that of the child's peers. By the time the parents seek help, they already suspect that something is wrong. They may even imagine that the problem is worse than it is (Faerstein 1986). On another level, parents go through different stages as they assimilate their observations and try to cope with emerging anxieties. Parents may begin by denying the problem, trying to minimize what they observe or are told. This stage may be followed by anger, as parents ask "why me?" These emotions are coupled with feelings of helplessness or frustration. If this anger is directed inward, they become depressed, and for some there is attendant guilt. They worry about something they may have inadvertently done that created the problem. If the anger is directed outward, the parents may begin to blame others, including their child. Parents then move into a time of grieving, as they slowly give up their hopes and dreams for a certain "kind of child." During this period, they are especially vulnerable to panaceas. From this point, they gradually begin to move toward greater acceptance, and in many cases, they begin to take needed actions (Silver 1979).

Unlike parental grieving at the birth of a child with a visible handicap, such as a physical deformity, the process of mourning for a child with a marginal and less observable handicap is prolonged (Killner and Crane 1979). The parents' reactions are staggered and not clear-cut, as they may move from panic to anger to grief, in any given situation or period of time. How parents react has implications for professional intervention.

The period of denial has many ramifications. For many parents, denial may serve an important function, as they need time to prepare to accept the painful reality and its implications. Therefore, professionals who provide evaluative interpretations may need to give parents several weeks to assimilate what they have heard before they meet with them again to plan. Still, during the time of denial, a child is often left vulnerable. The child knows something is wrong, that she or he is different, but feels "if my parents can't accept me for who I am, how will others. I must hide my problems."

Parents need guidance and support through the lengthy grieving process as well as in separating when they are irrationally angry from when their rightful expectations are not being met by other professionals. How often one hears of the frustrations of perceptive parents who have brought their concerns about their child to a pediatrician, only to be told they are being impatient and overanxious. Parents need to be relieved of their guilt. Raising a learning disabled child will have an effect on the family. Parents need to know they did not cause the problem, for if they feel so, they will then feel they can "cure" the problem. Social workers can be most helpful when they recognize the legitimate pain that raising a child with problems may cause, as well as the sadness parents must experience as their child struggles to cope.

Raising a child who has special problems means parents often need assistance in specifying expectations and learning effective techniques for helping their child gain mastery in their environment. For example, parents need to learn how to break down everyday tasks for a child who is less adept and easily overwhelmed. Learning how to put on a pullover sweater can be demonstrated to a child step by step, as can learning to brush one's teeth, or learning how to order and buy an item in a store. For those who cannot master certain tasks, alternatives need to be considered. Zippers and buckles are more easily handled than buttons and laces. Youth who adapt to new or unanticipated situations more slowly need anticipatory guidance and more time. A child who is going on a class trip needs help in thinking about what to expect and how to handle any problems, for instance, what to do if she or he gets lost. Parents tend to end up in power struggles when children insist unrealistically that an event will happen a certain way. Rather than argue, parents are more effective when they say, "That's what you wish, but that is not what may happen."

People with problems in social competence need parental assistance at many levels. They lack natural ease in relationships, and efforts at engaging and sustaining contacts can be awkward and therefore labored. When children are young, parents can take the initiative in structuring social opportunities for their child. They can play a more active role in helping their child to connect appropriately and to engage in successful play. As their child grows older, role modeling, direct advice, and active problem solving help people learn needed social skills. Since people with learning disabilities are often taken advantage of or rejected, without provocation, they need help in dealing with peer reaction. Efforts to strengthen social skills take on special relevance in view of a recent study showing that learning disabled youth have demonstrated their capability of improving social-perceptual skills, so that by late adolescence they are closing the maturational gap (Jackson et al. 1987).

Children with problems in attention may need medication. In addition, providing structured and predictable environments, setting clear boundaries, and minimizing distractions will lend important sources of support to these children. Parents need to learn how to effectively handle disciplinary issues and to evade futile power struggles and attacks on their child (Johnson 1989). For example, impulsivity in children can best be addressed by helping them develop awareness and then creating an extra moment between impulse and action, which provides youngsters with time to stop and think so they can alter their response.

Adolescents with learning disabilities do not achieve autonomy at the same rate as their peers, and therefore have a prolonged and wider dependence on adults (Margalit and Shulman 1986). They also are more vulnerable to stress and experience greater anxiety as they confront difficult tasks. The dilemma for parents and educators is to find the appropriate balance between providing needed help and offering increasing supports toward achieving independence.

People with learning disabilities face certain common tasks with which they often need help. It is the social worker who can, and indeed should, address these needs with them. By the time children develop a sense of awareness about themselves in relation to peers or siblings, they may well realize that in certain subtle ways they are different from others. It may be apparent in the difficulties they experience in mastering academic expectations (e.g., reading); in the way they behave (e.g., hyperactivity); or in the way they are perceived socially by their peers or family (e.g., ignored). The child begins to worry and thinks, "Why me? What's wrong anyway? What can be done? Will I fail? Why don't I have friends?" Those are the kinds of questions a professional or parent needs to help children with, clarifying that what they are having trouble with (e.g., sitting still or writing poorly) is not their fault and helping them specify strengths and weaknesses, and to avert gross negative generalizations (e.g., "I am dumb"). Learning disabled youth are often teased by their peers, and they need specific ideas on how to respond. For example, people make fun of them because they may attend a different school or class, or they may taunt them because they perform poorly in athletics. Expecting a youngster to ignore these comments is not realistic; rather, they need to learn to respond with straightforward answers, such as, "I know I am not good at sports."

The therapeutic context for work with people with learning disabilities should have both structure and predictability. They need a sense of organization; for some, open-ended sessions will evoke greater anxiety and loss of control. It is often necessary to depart from traditional psychotherapeutic strictures, for with the learning disabled, the worker takes on a more active role. This population responds best to a strong, positive working alliance, one in which the worker moves patiently and very supportively with the client while interceding to develop receptivity in the environment.

By adolescence, problems may intensify and family, teachers, and peers may be less patient. Adolescents may be angry about the demands made on them that they cannot meet. Those who lack social or communication skills feel deepened inadequacy and loneliness because they are not part of the teenage group. Adolescents who have poor impulse control and lack social judgment may be exploited by peers and become easy targets for involvement in antisocial acts. Parents and other adults have become worn out, are less tolerant, and express such feelings as, "It's time to shape up already. . . . Aren't you ever going to grow up?" Thus, the cycle of conflict already present in this phase of life may greatly intensify.

Adults with learning disabilities have been a less visible and identified population. As noted earlier, it was originally assumed that people outgrew these problems by the time they reached adulthood. We now know that this outcome is not necessarily valid. We see adults discovering, for the first time, that they are learning disabled. We also see learning disabled adults struggling in the job market, being discriminated against because of their handicaps or losing employment because they do not adapt well to more sophisticated workplace demands (Brown 1979).

People with learning disabilities are born into a wide range of families, some functioning more or less effectively than others. Having a learning disability cannot be attributed to a problem within the family, but rather families may need help in coping with their reactions to existing difficulties and stress. A social worker may need to reinforce and support a family's efforts to improve behavioral management, to enhance avenues of communication, to help define realistic expectations of each other, and to tolerate periods of ambiguity and frustration in the context of long-term progress (Zeigler and Holden 1988). Marital stress may be precipitated by the birth of a learning disabled child (Featherstone 1980). Parents may find themselves not able to draw strength from their relationship; rather, they may be divided by their own fears, their anger, their disappointments, and their impotence. Differences in decision making while raising a disabled child may similarly result in additional marital discord. Last, families carry extra emotional and physical burdens in living with a learning disabled member and will need assistance in locating and using resources for support within the community.

It is often helpful to focus on and offer service to the siblings of learning disabled children and to understand their reactions. Some siblings experience guilt because they function more effectively than their learning disabled sibling, especially if the sibling without the disability is younger. More frequently, however, brothers or sisters experience acute embarrassment in having to explain to their own peers their sibling's differences in behavior or achievement. They may bear the brunt of teasing. Some siblings long for a "real" brother or sister with whom they could share more, one who would more closely reflect their own feelings and experiences. Finally, siblings resent what they may experience as a double standard in their families when there are two levels of expectations, one for the learning disabled child and another for the sibling (Kronick 1973). These siblings will need help in sorting through their own reactions, opening up communication within the family, and, finally, developing strategies to deal with their peers' reactions.

A person's disability touches every family member. As a problem throughout the life cycle, we are only beginning to learn about how emerging issues will affect family members as the learning disabled person carries out his or her respective roles as child, spouse, and then, perhaps, parent.

ILLUSTRATION AND DISCUSSION

The kinds of problems for which the learning disabled and their families seek help from social workers may occur at various points in their lifetime. The tasks that they face, often coupled with and unresponsive environment, may produce situations that warrant crisis intervention, short-term consultation, or longer-term counseling. The following case was selected because it provides the opportunity to learn about a child with learning disabilities and her parents who obtained needed services intermittently over the period of a decade and a half.

This is a story of Cindy (now age 16), her brothers Barry and David (ages 21 and 23), and her parents, Edward and Lucy Stone. This is a middle-class, Unitarian family who live in southern Connecticut. Mr. Stone is a journalist and a devoted and caring father. Ms. Stone is an early childhood educator, who works part-time, and is deeply invested in the well-being of her children. Their sons are both bright, competent, and highly engaging young men who have fared very well in both their academic and social lives.

Ms. Stone's first two pregnancies were normal. She was 35 years old and pregnant with Cindy when she developed a serious respiratory infection for which she took antibiotic drugs. She remained healthy for the remainder of her pregnancy, and Cindy was born, at full term, by forceps delivery. Cindy appeared to be a healthy, quiet, content infant whose sole problem, at that time, was some colic she experienced for several months after the introduction of whole milk into her diet. Ms. Stone became concerned about Cindy's physical development when Cindy reached 9 months and still had difficulty sitting without support. Ms. Stone's worries remained dormant until she began to realize that Cindy continued to reach other physical developmental milestones at a slower pace than most of her peers. Ms. Stone's efforts to bring her questions to the pediatrician were met by reassuring statements that "some children develop more slowly than others, but Cindy would soon catch up."

Ms. Stone tried to engage her husband in listening to and acknowledging her fears that Cindy was not developing normally, but he offered reasons for any differences and cited areas in which she performed at the norm. Feeling alone in her growing anxiety, even panicked by the gloomy picture she fantasized and foresaw for her child, Ms. Stone became depressed. She was obsessed with thoughts about Cindy, impatient with the ambiguity of not knowing what was wrong, and distraught with her own impotence. She went to a local mental health clinic for help. The social worker played an instrumental role in alleviating the symptoms of depression but was not able, understandably, to offer Ms. Stone the assurances she repeatedly sought that her child would eventually achieve the capacity for normal functioning. The social worker offered to meet with Mr. and Ms. Stone jointly. She gently helped Mr. Stone to hear his wife's concerns and to move past his own denial.

Cindy began to walk at about 18 months and Mr. and Ms. Stone went through a period of relief and renewed hope. However, after several months, it became apparent that Cindy's receptive speech was limited, and she understood less than children her age who were already speaking words, if not sentences. Although a seemingly self-contented child, Cindy often played in an isolated fashion away from her peers. Family and friends began to notice and comment on Cindy's lack of ability to speak. Again Mr. and Ms. Stone became alarmed and concerned and contacted a pediatric neurologist for an evaluation. The physician pointed out uneven areas of development, ruled out retardation or autism, hypothesized what was then called "minimal brain dysfunction" and recommended speech therapy to address Cindy's delayed language development.

Cindy attended a local speech therapy clinic and made rapid strides in gaining language. Some difficulties in articulation persisted because of problems in the proper placement of her tongue in mouth coordination.

Cindy entered nursery school at the age of 4, and delays in certain areas of emotional and social development became readily apparent. The noise level and active environment of preschoolers were overwhelming to Cindy, who sometimes sought refuge by herself or under a blanket. Other times, she tried to engage with her classmates, but her judgments on how to enter play and her ongoing social interaction skills were inept. She was easily upset with changes in routines and her excessive vulnerability led to outbursts of crying, if someone, for example, sat in her chair by mistake.

During this time, her parents sought professional guidance in order to understand Cindy's behavior, to learn needed new parenting skills, and to make future educational plans. For many months, they met monthly with the social worker and provided her with examples of Cindy's behavior. She helped create a framework for understanding Cindy and frequently pointed to areas of strength and effective efforts Cindy was making to cope with a sometimes overwhelming or rejecting environment. Through these interventions, the social worker helped to alleviate some parental anxiety, offered new perspectives on Cindy's functioning and progress, and helped the Stones to learn to influence Cindy's school experience. One poignant example occurred when Ms. Stone described a recent meeting with the nursery school teacher. This teacher was critical of Cindy, saying she had entered the room of an adjoining class to play and that many of the children began to yell and ridicule Cindy. The envisaged pain of this scene caused Ms. Stone to suddenly dissolve in tears. The social worker softly asked Ms. Stone, "What did you say when the teacher told you this story?" Ms. Stone replied, "I said nothing. I felt she was telling me how my daughter misbehaved." The social worker commented, "But this was a 4-year-old not acting in malice. You should have said to the teacher 'and what did you do'?" This important lesson that parents don't have to accept someone else's definition of a problem, and that parents have the right to expect that their child be appropriately represented and protected, became a model that the Stones used over and over again in their negotiations with the programs in which Cindy was enrolled.

Cindy entered kindergarten in a small school when she was almost 6, so she could have an extra year of developmental time. Although she lacked competence in both social interaction and motor agility (especially graphomotor skills), her cognitive abilities were within the norm, and she was even precocious in reading. This was surprising because an aunt and cousin had histories of dyslexia. Cindy's behavior was seen as immature, rather than deviant, and she was not well organized. Still, Cindy was an appealing youngster, had a quick sense of humor, and related well to adults. Her perceptiveness coupled with her unusual resilience and persistence served as important strengths in facing daily problems. Throughout her latency age years, she progressed in most areas, especially in speech and academic work. Her continuing difficulty in social functioning remained a source of frustration to her and of concern and sadness to her family.

As Cindy entered adolescence, she appeared dissatisfied, if not somewhat depressed, by the disparity between her aspirations and what she could actually expect for herself. Her parents tried to locate a counseling group for learning disabled children, where she might obtain professional help in acquiring skills and feedback in this social context, but they were not successful. So they returned to a social worker to seek additional help for themselves and now also for Cindy. Mr. and Ms. Stone moved to a deeper level in sharing their worries, especially whether Cindy could move toward greater independence in functioning. They also were helped to reflect on how their frustrations were inadvertently being communicated to Cindy, and how they might try to respond positively to her new efforts to communicate and interact.

Cindy was immediately receptive to the social worker's active, interested style and the kind of support, patience, and acceptance she experienced in their work together. Cindy has been meeting weekly with the social worker for the past two years. They have explored many themes, including Cindy's feelings of being different, and her search for who she was, as she straddled two worlds, one of normally developing children and the other of the learning disabled. By the age of 14, Cindy developed some secondary problems attendant to her differences in development. Primary among them was her lack of self-esteem, which increasingly affected her expectations for herself and her communications with others. It became so marked that she sometimes walked with her head down to avert any possible peer rejection. Nevertheless, Cindy made slow, but consistently positive strides. The use of a dual educational and therapeutic focus on coping skills as she faced interactional tasks in her family, school, and social arena gave her new confidence and mastery. She also gained self-awareness, so she could "catch herself" when acting in dysfunctional ways, such as "I guess I am nervous about getting a new coat, because I am so used to the old one." She can better anticipate problems and plan accordingly, e.g., finding ways to organize her school assignments. She also learned to move from initial rigidity to greater flexibility in handling everyday situations. Finally, Cindy has been helped to handle the multiple demands of high school. At this time, Cindy was able to taper off contacts with the social worker and assume some greater responsibility for autonomous functioning and to advocate for her own needs. It is anticipated that Cindy may need to return for help when she prepares to move toward her college entrance year.

CONCLUSION

Several salient issues emerge. The first is that the learning disability syndrome is extremely common. This term serves as an umbrella category covering certain dysfunctions in cognitive, language, physical, and/or behavioral functioning. Initially, this syndrome was seen as affecting only children, but it is now a documented problem that persists, sometimes in changing form, into adolescence and adulthood. In this relatively young, and still growing field, there is ambiguity and lack of agreement about the definition and etiology of learning disabilities. Recent research attests to the effectiveness of a range of new interventive techniques and particularly highlights the usefulness of medication, counseling, psychoeducational techniques, and environmental supports. Certainly early identification, assessment, planning, and intervention have reaped important gains in ameliorating the effects of this dysfunction and its attendant secondary problems.

The challenge for social workers lies ahead. We have inadvertently played a major role in working with people with learning disabilities, because this population abounds in our social agencies and institutions. Yet we have not been in the forefront of service but have sometimes relied on old and improper diagnostic categories and models of psychotherapeutic interventions that have not been necessarily helpful. In other instances, we have focused on addressing the secondary rather than the primary problem.

Our expertise in work with individuals, families, and groups and in helping clients with their problems in the context of their environments certainly bodes well for the responsibility of our assuming increasing leadership in services to the learning disabled. Within our own range of social work settings, we have the unique opportunity to reach out, to innovate a practice technology, and, in collaboration with other disciplines, to offer much needed help to this population. We also need to join with other professionals in developing programs, influencing legislators, and educating the public about what life is like and how to support people with learning disabilities in our society.

References

Adelman, Howard and Linda Taylor. 1986. "Moving the Field Ahead: New Paths, New Paradigms." *Journal of Learning Disabilities* 19(12):602–7.

American Psychiatric Association (APA). 1994. *Diagnostic and Statistical Manual of Mental Disorders (DSM-IV)*, 4th ed. Washington, D.C.: Author.

Berman, Allen. 1974. "Delinquents Are Disabled." In Betty Lou Kratoville, ed., *Youth in Trouble*, pp. 86–96. San Rafael, Calif.: Academy Therapy Publications.

Bloom, Lois and Margaret Lahey. 1978. *Language Development and Language Disorders*. New York: John Wiley.

Brown, Dale. 1979. "Learning Disabled Adults Face the World of Work." *Learning Disability: Not Just a Problem Children Outgrow.* President's Committee on Employment of the Handicapped. Washington, D.C.: U.S. Government Printing Office.

Buchanan, Mary and Joan S. Wolf. 1986. "A Comprehensive Study of Learning Disabled Adults." *Journal of Learning Disabilities* 19(1):34–38.

Clements, Sam. 1966. *Minimal Brain Dysfunction in Children.* National Institute of Neurological Diseases and Blindness Monograph No. 3. Washington, D.C.: Department of Health, Education, and Welfare.

Collard, Jean. 1981. "The MBD Child: The Art of Definitive History Taking for Diagnostic Clarification." In Ruth Ochroch, ed., *The Diagnosis and Treatment of Minimal Brain Dysfunction,* pp. 46–62. New York: Human Services Press.

Diamond, Barbara. 1979. "Myths of Mainstreaming." *Journal of Learning Disabilities* 12(4): 246–50.

"Education of Students with Disabilities." (1999, March 8). *The Condition of Education.* http://nces.ed.gov/pubs/ce/c9746a01.html.

"Facts about Learning Disabilities." (1999, March 9). *Tell Me the Facts about LD.* http://www.ldonline.org/ccldinfo/1.html.

Faerstein, Leslie Morrison. 1986. "Coping and Defense Mechanisms of Mothers of Learning Disabled Children." *Journal of Learning Disabilities* 19(1):8–11.

Featherstone, Helen. 1980. *A Difference in the Family.* New York: Basic Books.

Feingold, Ben. 1974. *Why Your Child Is Hyperactive.* New York: Random House.

Fletcher, Jack M. and Bennett A. Shaywitz. 1996. "Attention-Deficit/Hyperactivity Disorder." In Shirley C. Cramer and William Ellis, eds., *Learning Disabilities, Lifelong Issues,* pp. 265–76. Baltimore, Md.: Paul H. Brookes.

Franklin, Deborah. 1989. "What a Child Is Given." *New York Times Magazine,* September 3, pp. 36–41, 49.

Friedman, Harold N. 1981. "The Rationale for Optometric Intervention in Learning Disabilities." In Ruth Ochroch, ed., *The Diagnosis and Treatment of Minimal Brain Dysfunction,* pp. 160–64. New York: Human Services Press.

Gerber, Paul J., Rick Ginsberg, and Henry B. Reiff. 1992. "Identifying Alterable Patterns in Employment Success for Highly Successful Adults with Learning Disabilities." *Journal of Learning Disabilities* 25(8):475–87.

Gerber, Paul J. and Henry B. Reiff. 1991. *Speaking for Themselves: Ethnographic Interviews with Adults with Learning Disabilities.* Ann Arbor, Mich.: University of Michigan Press.

Gershon, Frank M. and Stephen N. Elliot. 1989. "Social Skills Deficits as a Primary Learning Disability." *Journal of Learning Disabilities* 22(2):120–124.

Gitterman, Naomi Pines. 1979. "Group Services for Learning Disabled Children and Their Parents." *Social Casework* 60(4):217–26.

Goldstein, Kurt. 1942. *After Effects of Brain Injuries in War.* New York: Grune & Stratton.

Goleman, Daniel. 1986. "Major Personality Study Finds That Traits Are Mostly Inherited." *New York Times,* December 2, p. C1.

Gresham, Frank M. and Stephen N. Elliott. 1989. "Social Skills Deficits as a Primary Learning Disability." *Journal of Learning Disabilities* 22(2):120–24.

Gresham, Frank M., Donald L. Macmillan, Diane L. Ferguson, and Philip M. Ferguson. 1997. "Social Competence and Affective Characteristics of Students with Mild Disabilities." *Review of Educational Research* 67(4):377–415.

Gross, Mortimer D. and William C. Wilson. 1974. *Minimal Brain Dysfunction.* New York: Brunner/Mazel.

Hernandez, Raymond. 1999. "Under U.S. Threat, Albany Seeks to Overhaul Special Education." *New York Times,* June 12, p. B1.

Interagency Committee on Learning Disabilities (ICLD). 1987. *Learning Disabilities: A Report to the U.S. Congress.* Washington, D.C.: U.S. Department of Health and Human Services.

Jackson, Sara C., Robert D. Enright, and Jane Y. Murdock. 1987. "Social Perception Problems in Learning Disabled Youth: Developmental Lag Versus Perceptual Deficit." *Journal of Learning Disabilities* 20(6):361–64.

Johnson, Doris J. and Helmer R. Myklebust. 1964. *Learning Disabilities: Educational Principles and Practices.* New York: Grune & Stratton.

Johnson, Harriette C. 1989. "Behavior Disorders." In Francis Turner, ed., *Child Psychopathology,* pp. 73–139. New York: Free Press.

——. 1999. *Psyche, Synapse, and Substance.* Greenfield, Mass.: Deerfield Valley Publishing.

Johnson, Sharon. 1981. "Dissent on Mainstreaming." Spring Survey on Education. *New York Times,* April 26, p. 16.

Kagan, Jerome. 1984. *The Nature of the Child.* New York: Basic Books.

Karacostos, Dametra D. and Gary L. Fisher. 1993. "Chemical Dependency in Students with Learning Disabilities." *Journal of Learning Disabilities* 26(7):491–95.

Kavale, Kenneth A. and Steven R. Foreness. 1998. "The Politics of Learning Disabilities." *Learning Disability Quarterly* 21(4):245–73.

Kavanagh, James F. and Tom J. Truss, Jr. 1988. *Learning Disabilities: Proceedings of the National Conference.* Parkton, Md.: York Press.

Killner, Selma K. and Rochelle Crane. 1979. "A Parental Dilemma: The Child with a Marginal Handicap." *Social Casework* 60(1):30–35.

Kirk, Samuel. 1962. *Educating Exceptional Children.* Boston: Houghton Mifflin.

Kronick, Doreen. 1973. *A Word or Two About Learning Disabilities.* San Rafael, Calif.: Academic Therapy Publications.

——. 1978. "An Examination of Psychosocial Aspects of Learning Disabled Adolescents." *Learning Disability Quarterly* 1(4):86–92.

——. 1981. *Social Development of Learning Disabled Persons.* San Francisco: Jossey-Bass.

Larson, Katherine A. 1988. "A Research Review and Alternative Hypothesis Explaining the Link Between Learning Disability and Delinquency." *Journal of Learning Disabilities* 21(6):357–63, 369.

Lerner, Janet W. 1971. *Children with Learning Disabilities.* Boston: Houghton Mifflin.

——. 1996. *Learning Disabled,* 7th ed. New York: Houghton Mifflin.

Lyon, G. Reid. 1996. "The State of Research." In Shirley C. Cramer and William Ellis, eds., *Learning Disabilities, Lifelong Issues,* pp. 3–61. Baltimore, Md.: Paul H. Brookes Publishing.

Margalit, Malka and Shmuel Shulman. 1986. "Autonomy Perceptions and Anxiety Expressions of Learning Disabled Adolescents." *Journal of Learning Disabilities* 19(5):291–93.

Morrison, Gale M. and Merith A. Cosden. 1997. "Risk, Resilience, and Adjustment of Individuals with Learning Disabilities." *Learning Disability Quarterly* 20(1):43–60.

Moynihan, Daniel P. 1987. "Statements on Introduced Bills and Joint Resolutions." *Congressional Record.* June 4.

National Center for Clinical Infants Programs (NCCIP). 1989. *The Intent and Spirit of P.L. 99–457.* Washington, D.C.: U.S. Government Printing Office.

National Joint Committee on Learning Disabilities (NJCLD). 1987. "Learning Disabilities: Issues on Definition." *Journal of Learning Disabilities* 20(2):107–8.

Ochroch, Ruth, ed. 1981. *The Diagnosis and Treatment of Minimal Brain Dysfunction.* New York: Human Services Press.

Office of the Inspector General. 1992. *Report on Functional Impairments of AFDC Clients.* Washington, D.C.: U.S. Government Printing Office.

Orton, Samuel T. 1937. *Reading, Writing and Speech Problems in Children.* New York: Norton.

Pines, Maya. 1982. "Behavior and Heredity: Links for Specific Traits Are Growing Stronger." *New York Times,* June 29, p. C1.

Ritter, David R. 1989. "Social Competency and Problem Behavior of Adolescent Girls with Learning Disabilities." *Journal of Learning Disabilities* 27(7):460–64.

Roush, Wade. 1995. "Arguing Over Why Johnny Can't Read." *Science* 267(5206):1896–98.
Ruffner, Frederick G. 1994. "Attention Deficit/Hyperactivity Disorder." National Information Center for Children and Youth with Disabilities, Briefing Paper. In Linda Shin, ed., *Learning Disabilities Sourcebook,* 315–341. Health Reference Series. Detroit, Mich.: Omnigraphics Inc.
Shin, Linda, ed. 1998. *Learning Disabilities Sourcebook.* Health Reference Series. Detroit, Mich.: Omnigraphics Inc.
Silver, Larry B. 1979. "The Minimal Brain Dysfunction Syndrome." In Joseph Noshpitz, ed., *The Basic Handbook of Child Psychiatry,* 416–439. New York: Basic Books.
——. 1987. "The 'Magic Cure': A Review of the Current Controversial Approaches for Treating Learning Disabilities." *Journal of Learning Disabilities* 20(8):498–504.
Small, Leonard. 1982. *The Minimal Brain Dysfunctions.* New York: Free Press.
Smith, Corinne Roth. 1986. "The Future of the LD Field: Intervention Approaches." *Journal of Learning Disabilities* 19(8):461–68.
Smith, Sally L. 1980. *No Easy Answers: The Learning Disabled Child.* New York: Bantam Books.
Spekman, Nancy J., Roberta J. Goldberg, and Kenneth L. Herman. 1992. "Learning Disabled Children Grow Up: A Search for Factors Related to Success in the Young Adult Years." *Learning Disabilities, Research and Practice* 7(3):161–70.
Spekman, Nancy J., Kenneth L. Herman, and Susan Vogel. 1993. "Risk and Resilience in Individuals with Learning Disabilities: A Challenge to the Field." *Learning Disabilities, Research and Practice* 8(1):59–65.
Strauss, Alfred and Laura E. Lehtinen. 1947. *Psychopathology and Education of the Brain Injured Child.* New York: Grune & Stratton.
Thomas, Alexander and Stella Chess. 1977. *Temperament and Development.* New York: Brunner/Mazel.
Thomas, Alexander, Stella Chess, and Herbert Birch. 1963. *Behavioral Individuality in Early Childhood.* New York: New York University Press.
——. 1968. *Temperament and Behavior Disorders in Children.* New York: New York University Press.
U.S. Department of Health, Education and Welfare. 1978. *Section 504 of the Rehabilitation Act of 1973. Handicapped Persons: Rights Under Federal Law.* Washington, D.C.: U.S. Government Printing Office.
Waldie, Karen and Otfried Spreen. 1993. "The Relationship between Learning Disabilities and Persisting Delinquency." *Journal of Learning Disabilities* 26(6):417–23.
Wender, Paul H. 1971. *Minimal Brain Dysfunction in Children.* New York: Wiley-Interscience.
Zeigler, Robert and Lynn Holden. 1988. "Family Therapy for Learning Disabled and Attention-deficit Disordered Children." *American Journal of Orthopsychiatry* 58(2): 196–210.

10

Schizophrenia

Ellen Lukens

Schizophrenia is a disease of the brain that affects approximately 1 percent of the population worldwide, regardless of race or gender. A combination of symptoms alters a person's sense of reality and changes the ability to attend to normal life functions, such as work, school, and relationships. At its worst schizophrenia can impair an individual's ability to take care of and monitor the simplest of the activities of daily living. A chronic and multifaceted illness, it affects every aspect of an individual's life, distorting a person's sense of self and altering how he or she experiences the environment. Those affected describe a sense of loss of self, disorientation, and emptiness. As a person suffering from active psychosis reported after a session with his psychiatrist, "He wants to know what's going on inside my head, and *I don't know.*"

According to the standard set by the American Psychiatric Association in the *Diagnostic and Statistical Manual of Mental Disorders,* 4th edition (*DSM-IV*), schizophrenia is typically recognized and diagnosed by a common set of symptoms, usually referred to as the *positive* and *negative* symptoms. The positive or psychotic symptoms include hallucinations, delusions, bizarre behavior, disorganized speech, and disorganized or withdrawn behavior. The negative symptoms, which are sometimes referred to as residual or deficit symptoms, include affective flattening, alogia, or loss of volition. These symptoms are accompanied by a significant disturbance in functioning, particularly as regards work, interpersonal relations, or self-care. In situations where one set of symptoms predominates, individuals may be categorized and treated based on diagnostic subtypes such as paranoid or disorganized schizophrenia (American Psychiatric Association [APA] 1994).

In spite of this grim description, some important developments have occurred over the last several decades that provide increased opportunity and hope for persons with the illness. These include the availability of new psychotropic medications, strengths-based psychosocial interventions with an emphasis on education and rehabilitation, and an increasingly visible and active family and consumer advocacy movement.

DEFINING AND EXPLAINING SCHIZOPHRENIA

Descriptions of schizophrenia as one form of severe mental illness have been clearly documented since the turn of the century, although emphasis on particular diagnostic characteristics has varied over time. The seminal work of Emil Kraepelin and Eugen Bleuler, written at the end of the nineteenth and the beginning of the twentieth century, characterized the illness in terms of what are now referred to as the negative symptoms. Kraepelin described uniformity in the course of illness and age of onset among those diagnosed with schizophrenia and coined the term *dementia praecox* to describe what he considered a group of illnesses with related outcome. Characterizing the illness in terms of both loss of function and mental integrity, accompanied by progressive deterioration, he viewed the negative symptoms, particularly loss of will and abnormalities in attention and interest, memory and affect, as central to the illness (Kraepelin 1919/1971).

Bleuler, as an early proponent of a disease construct for schizophrenia, explained the illness in terms of presenting symptoms, vulnerability, and variability of performance, rather than focusing on course. He described a cognitive disorder, characterized by *fundamental* and *accessory* symptoms and expressed through disturbance in experience and behavior. His fundamental symptoms included abnormalities in affect, attention, and volition, as well as sense of identity or ego function; accessory symptoms included delusions, hallucinations, now considered the positive symptoms, and associated loss of orientation, memory, and attention (Bleuler 1911/1950). This emphasis on loss of functioning remained central to the understanding of schizophrenia until Kurt Schneider's work appeared in the 1950s.

Schneider concurred with Bleuler's perception that presenting symptoms were more critical to understanding the illness than was course of illness, but he veered away from underlying vulnerabilities and supports. Rather he focused on what he termed the first-rank symptoms, including delusions, hallucinations, bizarre behavior, and thought disorder (Schneider 1959/1980). Following Schneider's work, and until the publication of the *DSM-IV* in 1994 in which the negative symptoms again were included as primary symptoms of the illness, schizophrenia has been diagnosed according to the positive symptoms (APA 1994). The renewed attention to the negative symptoms has encouraged mental health professionals to look beyond distortions in thinking and belief systems and to attend to the impact of the illness on experience and functioning.

To some extent the changing diagnostic picture for schizophrenia has mirrored changes in policies, attitudes, and explanations regarding mental illness per se over the last several centuries. In the United States, changes in policy occurred as the society became increasingly industrialized and urbanized. During the eighteenth and nineteenth centuries, mental disorders were associated with indigence, immorality and poor habits. Responsibility for caring for persons with mental illness was generally assigned to the family or local community, and *lunacy* or *insanity* was considered a social and economic problem rather than a medical problem. Backup care was typically the local jail or almshouse. During the late 1700s, some medical hospitals began to admit people who were considered insane, and in 1770 the first mental hospital opened in Virginia (Fellin 1996; Grob 1994).

At the end of the eighteenth century, various reform movements in Europe influenced a slowly growing interest in the United States toward more proactive care, with cure as the hoped for outcome. In France, Phillipe Pinel developed a moral treatment approach that involved psychologically oriented care in an asylum, and in England, William Tuke established the York Retreat to help the person with illness develop mechanisms for self-control. In the United States, the work of social reformer Dorothea Dix during the 1830s and 1840s led to the development of more than thirty mental hospitals, built predominantly to serve the particular needs of those designated as mentally ill and impoverished (Fellin 1996; Grob 1994). Her efforts coincided with the increasing number of cities in the United States where informal systems of care for indigent persons were less readily available than in small communities (Starr 1982).

Over the next century some additional five thousand institutions were built. Until the end of the nineteenth century, these hospitals typically served people with more acute cases of mental illness; individuals would typically return to the community after relatively short-term hospitalizations of less than a year (Grob 1994). But as it became clear that many people did not recover, policies changed and gradually the mental hospitals became long-term care facilities where individuals with persistent illness resided for most of their adult lives. This approach to care continued through the end of World War II.

With the discovery of the first psychotropic or antipsychotic medications such as thorazine, and with increasing scrutiny of the mental hospitals among social reformers, the push toward discharge to the community became a reality, beginning in the 1950s. With the advent of the Community Mental Health Act of 1963, thousands of individuals were discharged or *deinstitutionalized* to community mental health systems on the assumption that more effective care could be provided outside a hospital setting. But the newly developed community programs were not fully equipped or prepared to handle the challenges involved in managing an illness as unpredictable and misunderstood as schizophrenia. The clients had spent a significant number of their adult years in closed environments, and because their medication needed careful monitoring both for effectiveness and to monitor untoward side effects, they could not fully manage and fend for themselves (Fellin 1996). Not surprisingly, families stepped in to fill the gaps. But they were also unprepared for this responsibility. This was not helped by the distant and uncommunicative attitudes toward families regarding any kind of illness that was so characteristic of medical professionals of the time (Starr 1982). As a consequence, the families had limited access to support services or information to alleviate burden of care. The stigma attached to mental illness, and the widely held belief that families contributed to schizophrenia, only served to promote isolation and compound the level of responsibility (Lefley 1996).

Attempts to explain schizophrenia changed over the course of the twentieth century, as did attitudes toward care and treatment. Early theoreticians and clinical researchers, following the work of Bleuler and Kraepelin and influenced by psychoanalytic theory and by their own case studies, argued that schizophrenia was caused by impaired family dynamics, particularly between mother and child (Kasinin, Knight, and Sage 1934; Levy 1931). Hence the term *schizophrenogenic mother* appeared in the literature, a phrase that served to stigmatize the family and that affected the way the illness was evaluated, managed, and treated for many years (Fromm-Reichman 1948).

The family therapy movement, which began to emerge in the 1950s, grew out of this frame of reference as well. Early family therapists such as Gregory Bateson and Theodore Lidz initially focused their interventions on the families of persons with schizophrenia, building on their observations of conflicted parental relationships and impaired communication among family members (Bateson et al. 1956; Lidz et al. 1957).

After the move toward deinstitutionalization, this fascination with the role of the family in schizophrenia reemerged in the research literature. During the 1950s, a group of researchers and clinicians in Britain, led by sociologist George Brown and psychiatrist Michael Rutter, noticed that people with schizophrenia who resided with family returned more quickly to the hospital after an acute episode than those who lived in the community. Hence they devised a series of studies to examine family dynamics among this group, based on lengthy semistructured interviews conducted in the family home (Brown and Rutter 1966; Rutter and Brown 1966). Originally the construct, which came to be known as *expressed emotion,* measured a series of attitudes and behaviors reflecting the two-directional relationship between parents and their adult child with schizophrenia. But as the variable has been typically applied in later research studies, it is single and dichotomized, measured as either *high* or *low,* and applied solely to the primary caretakers, usually the parents. Those families or family members rated as high in expressed emotion have been considered particularly critical and/or overinvolved (i.e., overly intrusive or protective) toward the person with illness.

Findings from these studies and subsequent replications in different settings and cultures reinforced the idea that when parents showed high expressed emotion, the person with illness was likely to relapse more rapidly and to require hospitalization (Kuipers and Bebbington 1988). This also contributed to the perception that somehow the family was responsible for the illness; hence, families categorized in this fashion were targeted as a means of improving the outcomes for the person with illness. The results of these intervention studies were varied and impact appeared to be time-limited, but they received much attention among the professional mental health community (Bebbington and Kuipers 1994; Goldstein et al. 1978; Leff et al. 1982). Not surprisingly they irked family members and their advocates, who observed that it was too easy to confuse impact on *course* of illness with *cause* of illness, that expressed emotion as a construct was not fully understandable or operationalized, and that the impact of low expressed emotion was generally overlooked. Rather, they argued that expressed emotion might even help families cope with a medical and psychiatric culture that tended to be withholding of both care and information (Hatfield 1987; Terkelson 1983).

These debates contributed to ongoing tensions between families and professionals, particularly since the Western model of blaming the family is an insidious one. But as research during the last several decades of the twentieth century contributed overwhelming evidence that schizophrenia is a brain disease affected by environmental stressors, the emphasis on expressed emotion as a focal target variable has receded. Recent work on the psychosocial aspects of the illness have focused on a more broad-based assessment of all members of the family, examining factors ranging from resiliency and coping, social supports, and quality of life to family burden, experiences of mourning and loss, and the impact on well siblings (Marsh et al. 1996; McCubbin and McCubbin 1988; Struening et al. 1995). More current work on expressed emotion has examined the construct in the context of broadly defined environmental variables including reciprocal or interactive responses between family member and client, social control, and availability of external supports and resources (Greenberg, Greenley, and Benedict 1994; Greenley 1986). Most recently professionals and families have made increasing effort to work together to understand and address these environmental stressors, although there is still much work to be done in this arena (Dixon and Lehman 1995). Examples of programs that are strengths based and collaborative are described later in this chapter.

DEMOGRAPHIC PATTERNS

Schizophrenia is associated with great individual, social, and financial cost. Although there is variation in prevalence across cultures with a reported range of .2 to 2 percent, the estimated lifetime prevalence rate worldwide is about 1 percent (APA 1994). Reported prevalence for men and women is approximately equal, although there are some discrepancies based on whether samples are community or hospital based.

The etiology of schizophrenia is not fully understood. There is strong evidence that it is a biological disease, which can be triggered by environmental stressors, and that it has a genetic component. A person with an identical twin with schizophrenia has twenty-five to forty-five times more chance of developing schizophrenia than the average person. But this also means that genetics alone does not explain the illness (Reiss, Plomin, and Heterington 1991).

Schizophrenia usually manifests itself in early adulthood, with a median age of onset in the early or midtwenties for men and late twenties for women (APA 1994). The initial presentation of the illness is variable; in some individuals it is abrupt, in other cases gradual. Often there is some sort of problematic or prodromal presentation of behavior that appears prior to help seeking, but this may be elusive and difficult to characterize. The course of illness is highly variable, which complicates diagnosis, assessment, and treatment. In reported studies of course of illness over time, it is estimated that about one-third of those who are originally diagnosed recover and return to baseline functioning, one-third suffer mild to moderate impairment in life functioning, and one-third have relatively poor outcome characterized by significant impairment in functioning (McGlashan 1988; Möller and von Zerssen 1995). Those who are most in need of mental health services are those who are most severely impaired, but the course of illness is not predictable. As such the illness is disruptive to the life cycle of both the client and the family.

Schizophrenia appears in all cultures. However, the manifest content of the distorted belief systems associated with the illness may be influenced by particular mores in a given culture. For example, in non-Western cultures, beliefs associated with particular religious values might be truly reflective of mental illness, or they might fall within the normal belief system for that society. This means that the illness must be understood in relation to the culture in which it appears. Certain behaviors or beliefs considered unusual, strange, or psychotic in one culture might be normal or acceptable in another and must be carefully assessed in making cross-cultural diagnoses. Language barriers between clinician and client may further confound such diagnoses.

The prevalence of schizophrenia is approximately the same across class and ethnicity, although there are certain differences and interactions that are important to consider if we are to fully understand the disease. Poverty is associated with mental disorders of all kinds, but it is difficult to sort out what aspects, if any, are specific to schizophrenia (Lefley 1996; Regier et al. 1990). Within the United States, African Americans and Native Americans are more likely to be hospitalized for schizophrenia than either Mexican Americans or Asian Americans (Manderscheid and Sonnenscheid 1992). But once hospitalized, those of white, Hispanic, and Asian descent tend to remain in hospital for longer periods of time (Manderscheid and Barrett 1987). Findings are complicated by research that suggests that individuals with less education are two to three times more likely to be hospitalized for schizophrenia than those with more education (Aro et al. 1995). Research also indicates that individuals in ethnic minority groups, who tend to have lower socioeconomic status, are less likely to use formal mental health services, relying instead on informal supports within the community such as family, friends, religious leaders, or spiritual healers. Given the potential for interaction among data and the relatively limited research in this area, it is difficult to fully explain such phenomenon. Individual clients may be more ill by the time they are in formal contact with the mental health system, thus requiring more intensive treatment. An alternative explanation might be that they are more poorly treated by the formal system because of their background; thus, they receive less adequate care and are more freely diagnosed with severe mental illness (Neighbors et al. 1992).

The illness is also associated with other factors, which make it particularly frightening to those individuals or families who must confront it. Among people with schizophrenia, approximately 10 to 15 percent actually commit suicide and approximately 20 to 40 percent attempt suicide at some point in their lives. Of those who complete suicide, about 60 percent have already made a previous attempt (Harkavey-Friedman and Nelson 1997).

People with schizophrenia are also at higher risk for drug and alcohol abuse than those in the general population. An estimated 45 to 50 percent have at least some history of substance use disorder (Drake et al. 1993; Regier et al. 1990).

Most persons with schizophrenia do not enter long-term relationships or partnerships, and only about 10 percent are able to maintain employment in competitive jobs (Anthony, Cohen, and Farkas 1990; Bond 1992). Because schizophrenia usually strikes just as a person would normally assume normal adult responsibility by seeking education and/or employment, or partnership and possibly family, he or she becomes dependent on the mental health and social service systems, and when available, the family of origin. This creates a disruption in the normal life cycle for both client and family and inevitably compounds the levels of burden and stress that contribute to the illness.

SOCIETAL CONTEXT

Schizophrenia has a profound effect on daily life. Because it attacks the brain, the very essence of who the person is, constant vigilance is necessary to help the person keep on track and avoid the demoralization and stigma attached to revolving door hospitalizations or inadequate or stultifying community care. Increasing evidence suggests that early intervention helps to assuage some of the chronicity of the illness as well. Through early identification of symptoms and the use of carefully regulated medication, the course of schizophrenia can be genuinely improved (Dequardo 1998; McGlashan 1986). Such an approach is quite easy to fathom in thinking about how to help people mange medical illnesses that do not include a psychiatric component. But the presence of psychiatric symptoms adds an immeasurable level of complexity to the presenting picture. The manifestation of these symptoms may collide with the sensibilities and understanding of the client's support system, which only serves to increase isolation, alienation, and attached stigma on the part of all involved and which quickly interferes with the monitoring needed to keep the person on track (Brewin et al. 1991).

Such monitoring requires that social workers and other mental health professionals attend to the cycles of vulnerability that the client incurs. The most significant psychosocial needs include areas that disenfranchised persons so often require help with and that are made even more complicated by this particular illness. These include housing, financial support, and structured activity if work is unrealistic or unavailable, psychiatric monitoring and medication, medical support, crisis intervention and hospitalization when necessary, and rehabilitation and support in the workplace if work is a viable possibility. If the symptoms include apathy or lack of motivation, or inability to make and maintain relationships, the challenges involved become even more complex.

The state of vulnerability that underlies a brain disease is worsened by the fact that the person does not always seem normal in behavior, speech, or appearance. Any presentation of self that differs from the norm lends itself to *labeling,* a construct that usually refers to negative beliefs or attitudes at the societal or community level that contribute to stereotyping, prejudice, ostracism, and tarnished identity. If used appropriately, as in a careful diagnosis and assessment, labeling can facilitate treatment and understanding. But if used inappropriately, it can also affect outcome negatively through associated stigma (Link, Mirotznik, and Cullen 1991; Rosenfield 1997). As a most basic example, it would seem relatively simple to describe a client with schizophrenia as someone who *suffers from an illness,* or *who has an illness,* as opposed to the typically used *schizophrenic,* a term implying that the person is solely defined by the illness itself. By assiduously avoiding such labeling and associated stigma it becomes easier to identify other areas in which the person may be functioning adequately or even well, and to help the person and those who comprise the available support system capitalize on these strengths.

Educating professionals, families, and the general public to differentiate between person and illness is not an easy task, particularly given that the illness affects both internal perception and external presentation. The task is complicated by the fact that each of these groups has very different investments in the illness and very different perspectives on how they, either individually or collectively, will be affected. Addressing labeling and stigma across system levels may serve to sensitize the general public to the illness and increase their willingness to support needed interventions, programs, and policies, both within their own communities and at a state and national level. But for the person with illness, their family members, and even professionals, the stakes are significantly higher. These individuals are constantly confronted by the illness and must address and cope with associated stigma in trying to maintain daily equilibrium and navigate the complex medical, social services, and psychiatric systems that sustain them.

VULNERABILITIES AND RISK FACTORS

Stress serves as a major risk and complicating factor for any illness, regardless of presenting symptoms (Elliott and Einsdorfer 1982; Hatfield and Lefley 1987; Nicholson and Neufeld 1992). For an illness as complex as schizophrenia, the impact of environmental stress is particularly important to consider. The Stress-Diathesis Model (or Vulnerability Stress Model) places schizophrenia in the context of both biological and environmental (psychosocial) risk factors (Zubin and Spring 1977; Zubin, Steinhauer, and Condray 1992). The model suggests an interactive or reciprocal association among stressors (which might include genetic predisposition to illness as well as environmental factors), symptom formation, protective factors, and outcome. Cumulative (or proliferating) stress may create additional burden through the buildup of stressful situations over periods of time (Pearlin, Aneshensel, and Leblanc 1997; Struening et al. 1995). Lack of support or stimulation may also serve as a source of stress, particularly given that individuals with schizophrenia can become withdrawn and isolated (Cassel 1976; Heinrichs and Carpenter 1983). At the other extreme, change and transition can be as stressful; there is strong evidence to suggest that structure and routine can help to ground and focus persons who suffer from mental disorders (Penn et al. 1997; Scheflen 1981).

External variables serve as risk factors as well, particularly availability of resources across system levels, including society, community, and family. In their work on the fundamental causes of illness, Link and Phelan (1995) consider the potential for differential impact of *proximal* and *distal* causes of illness. The distal (external) risk factors include socioeconomic status and access to resources such as power, money, knowledge, and prestige. For someone with schizophrenia, the very nature of the illness interferes with the ability to attain or maintain such access. This is magnified by the lingering Western model of assigning responsibility for control over one's life and/or illness to the individual or family by focusing on the proximal (immediate) factors associated with illness. The authors argue for a shift in assigning locus of responsibility such that both distal and proximal factors are weighed in assessing the stress associated with disease, evaluating the need for services, and developing and implementing appropriate programs and policies. Assessing risk factors across system levels is central to the social work perspective and serves to refocus attention on the role of protective factors and resiliency in promoting positive outcome.

RESILIENCIES AND PROTECTIVE FACTORS

Resiliency refers to the internal strengths that a person is able to draw on under duress and stress; protective factors represent those resources that facilitate such resiliency and promote self-determination. For someone suffering from schizophrenia, the ability to recognize and use personal strengths is easily impaired by the illness. Therefore, it becomes imperative that those surrounding the person help to identify and capitalize on these internal strengths and reinforce external supports. These include social and professional supports, the availability of continuity of care and concrete resources (including medication), and education.

Social supports and networks refer to the nature and extent of social relationships available to an individual. Social supports describe the content and process of relationships, how and to what extent other people are available to provide emotional and concrete sustenance to the individual on an ongoing basis (Breier and Strauss 1984). Social networks are more clearly operationalized in terms of existence, structure, and density (or interrelatedness) among people (Mueller 1980). Given an illness such as schizophrenia, which is frequently characterized by withdrawal and isolation, and in which interpersonal relationships are impaired, the availability of regular and ongoing support is essential to tracking and monitoring the illness. Family members can fulfill this function, as can other laypersons within the community such as friends, clergy, family, or other consumers. But for this illness even the most vigilant and caring members of a social support system may not be enough to carry a person through the changes in functioning that characterize schizophrenia, especially since the person with illness is not always aware of these changes. As a client observed sadly, "Because I don't live with people or with my family, it is difficult to recognize what I do. One way or another I wind up in the hospital whether I recognize the warning signs or not."

Availability of professional resources serves to extend the system of care so as to provide a broader support system for the person with illness. In their work on the range and defining characteristics of case management services for persons with schizophrenia, Pescosolido, Wright, and Sullivan (1995) refer to such extended or community support as a system in which professionals and laypeople, including family and involved others, work together with the individual with illness. Through such coordination, stress levels and changing needs can be monitored, both in terms of attention to symptom exacerbation at one extreme and increased challenge at the other to avoid stagnation and boredom.

Knowing when to intervene to achieve such a balance is not easy, given what can be a profound disturbance in the client's ability to merely carry on from day to day. A coordinated and sensitive effort is required on the part of professionals, family, or other community members with attention to timing and planning. Several major hurdles must be overcome in achieving such comprehensive care. Professional services must be available and accessible (Stein, Diamond, and Farton 1990). The client and those surrounding the client must be willing and able to seek care. Services must be maintained. Clients and families must be informed as to the value of using and complying with medication regimens in the treatment of schizophrenia. But they also must be informed that medication alone is not adequate treatment. The antipsychotic medicines are critical in reducing relapse, but up to 50 percent of those who are fully compliant still relapse within a year's time (Liberman 1994).

Because schizophrenia is such a complex and variable illness, there is no way to adequately predict individual outcome once the disease is present. As an adult sibling of a person with schizophrenia observed, "the personality customizes the disease." Given this, individual protective factors are still important to review and consider, particularly in the context of preliminary planning for the individual and in developing models for global treatment and rehabilitation.

Several factors are associated with better outcome over time. These include good adjustment prior to the onset of illness, particularly in the areas of school and peer relationships, more education, and an extended family *without* a history of schizophrenia. Individuals with a tendency to have more affective (i.e., depressive) symptoms than psychotic symptoms also tend to function better over the long term (McGlashan 1986; Swanson et al. 1998). Recent work in Australia suggests that although women generally have a more benign course of illness than men, those women with an early onset may have a worse course of illness overall (Gureje and Bamidele 1998).

Given such a range of findings, one of the most critical components in providing comprehensive care and promoting resilience is education across system levels. With the many changes that have occurred in understanding and defining schizophrenia, social workers and other mental health professionals must stay abreast of important developments in the field, ranging from evolving theories regarding course and prognosis and new medications, to psychosocial interventions, models, and resources that are available both nationally and locally. By so doing they can translate and share this knowledge in such a manner that the client and members of his or her family or support system can understand and use the information, both to advocate for and improve care. Maintaining open and mutually respectful lines of communication with both individual and family clients also allows the social worker to learn from and assimilate information based on the everyday experiences of those faced with the ongoing illness. Such collaboration between social worker and client enhances the potential for extending and reinforcing both the formal (professional) and informal (family and community) systems of care that are so important for enhanced resiliency and well-being (Borkman 1976; Pescosolido et al. 1995). It also helps to dispel any residual tendency to blame the family for this particular life condition.

There are several means for promoting education of clients and families. Encouraging involvement in the family and consumer organizations is one important approach. The family advocacy groups, particularly the National Alliance for the Mentally Ill (NAMI), have become increasingly sophisticated in synthesizing such knowledge for their members and teaching their members how to advocate (Sommer 1990). Their work has become an extremely rich resource for family members and professionals alike and has significantly increased national awareness and attention to the cause of severe mental illness (Lefley 1996). The advocacy groups organized by the consumers themselves also have provided valuable venues for individuals to work together, battle stigma, raise self-esteem, and create opportunities for themselves through advocacy, client-run businesses, and other important services (Deegan 1992).

Finally it is important for professionals to develop new programs and interventions that are strengths based and promote education, resiliency, and improved quality of life. Several of these are described in the following section.

PROGRAMS AND SOCIAL WORK CONTRIBUTIONS

As we have seen, perspectives on schizophrenia have changed dramatically over the course of the century. Much of the day-to-day care and monitoring of those with schizophrenia has been the responsibility of social workers, and social workers have been directly involved in or responsible for the development of many innovative programs and interventions in the community. Four of the more successful and carefully documented of these are described here. The first three are comprehensive programs and include the Assertive Community Treatment Program (Stein and Test 1980; Test and Stein 1980), the Family Psychoeducation in Schizophrenia Project (McFarlane et al. 1993, 1995), and Personal Therapy (Hogarty et al. 1995, 1997a, 1997b). Both the Assertive Community Treatment Program (ACT) and Personal Therapy (PT) are oriented toward the individual, while the Family Psychoeducation in Schizophrenia Project (FPSP) is designed to offer psychoeducational interventions to the entire family. The fourth intervention, entitled Social Skills Training (SST), is less comprehensive in nature but is highly effective when combined with rehabilitation or community day treatment programs (Bellack et al. 1990). Because of their strengths-based approach and positive outcomes, these models have been described and promoted through a recent national study conducted by the Schizophrenia Patient Outcome Research Team (PORT), in an effort to describe and effectively disseminate research models in service settings (Lehman et al. 1998). Each of these models was designed to facilitate the functioning of the person with schizophrenia in a community setting and to address the need for enhanced quality of life. The programs differ in terms of the approach that they provide for the person with illness. But they all address the complexity of the illness in a fashion that recognizes strengths and facilitates rehabilitation, growth, and the realization of potential.

Assertive Community Treatment. The Assertive Community Treatment Program (ACT) was first developed in Wisconsin by Leonard Stein and Mary Ann Test in the early 1970s in collaboration with a team of mental health professionals that included psychiatrists, psychologists, social workers, nurses, and occupational and recreational therapists. In their ongoing work these clinician researchers noted that their clients would reenter the hospital soon after discharge, and this pattern would repeat itself in revolving door fashion, with little apparent change in functioning or quality of life, despite the outreach of those who worked with them. Realizing over time that they had severely underestimated the extent and kind of help their clients needed to even begin to function adequately on their own, they began to reassess and reorganize their approach to working with clients in the community. Coining the phrase *training in community living,* they organized core services (termed *continuous treatment teams*) that would serve as primary providers and brokers of care, providing continuity of care and professional caregiving across functional areas and time. These multidisciplinary teams were on twenty-four-hour call seven days a week, with each participant receiving individualized treatment on a daily basis if needed. This treatment included distribution and monitoring of medication, crisis availability and interventions, arrangement of hospitalization if needed, and the development of long-term one-on-one relationship between team member and client. The approach facilitated optimally supportive environments, including assistance with meeting basic needs such as housing, and support in learning how to manage one's life on a daily basis, including work, social relations, and child care.

Since the early 1970s the ACT models have been meticulously studied and replicated in many settings, both in this country and abroad, and have been a highly effective means of helping individuals to live successfully in the community. Repeated assessments of the ACT programs have showed reduced symptomatology and relapse, increased community tenure, enhanced satisfaction with life, a decrease in subjective distress, and improved overall functioning, particularly in the areas of employment, social relationships, and the daily activities of living that constantly challenge those with illness, such as personal hygiene, shopping, travel, or money management (Lehman et al. 1998; Test 1998). In addition to being promoted through the recommendations of the PORT study, ACT has also been embraced and promoted by the National Alliance for the Mentally Ill as a model community treatment program (Noble et al. 1998).

Family Psychoeducation in Schizophrenia Project. The Family Psychoeducation in Schizophrenia Project (FPSP) compared two long-term models of psychoeducation for individuals suffering from schizophrenia and their families, with psychoeducation referring to a combined educational and treatment approach. The work was conducted by William McFarlane along with a team of clinicians and researchers during the late 1980s (McFarlane et al. 1993, 1995).

The first model consisted of a series of multiple-family group meetings in which six families and persons with illness met with two mental health professionals, usually social workers, for one and one-half hours on a biweekly schedule. The second model followed the identical psychoeducational format, but the structure was that of traditional single-family therapy, with one family, including the client, meeting with one mental health professional, again on a biweekly schedule. Families were randomly assigned to one of the two treatments at the point that the subject was admitted to the hospital for an acute episode of schizophrenia. Care continued throughout the hospitalization and for the two years following discharge to the community. As with the ACT model, clinicians were on call seven days a week, twenty-four hours per day.

The research was conducted in six public hospitals across the state of New York, including three hospitals in New York City and three in suburban or rural areas, and included 176 families. The goals for the treatment were to educate, support, and empower the families through the formation of a collaborative relationship with the clinicians. Effective dissemination of the model required that clinicians educate the administrators as well as families as to the principles and goals of the project (McFarlane et al. 1993).

There were two primary hypotheses for this intervention. The first was that the clients in the psychoeducational multiple family groups would fare better over the long term as regards relapse of symptoms. This was based on the assumption that the multiple-family group format would positively influence outcome for the person with illness by allowing persons with shared problems to work and learn together to address and defuse ongoing problems and challenges, and through the natural enhancement of social networks through group membership. The second hypothesis was that regardless of treatment, the clients would require less hospitalization during the two-year intervention than they had in the two years prior to entering the FPSP.

The two treatments were very specific and parallel. The stages of treatment included joining between clinician and family, and between clinician and client, a day-long psychoeducational workshop, and ongoing treatment. The joining phase, which involved one therapist working alone with each family, and separately with each client, for a period of several weeks to form a therapeutic alliance, regardless of treatment modality, served as the foundation for the intervention. During these sessions the clinicians worked to assess the family resources and strengths and to establish the foundation for a collaborative and empathic relationship that would be fostered through the ongoing work. The psychoeducational workshop involved a daylong training session in which facts and information regarding schizophrenia were presented and discussed with a group of families (for multiple-family group participants) or with individual families (for those in single-family treatment). Topics covered included diagnosis, epidemiology, medication, and crisis intervention. In addition, families were provided with specific guidelines geared toward lowering stress in the home environment. The recovery process from an acute episode was described as necessarily slow and individualized, with careful attention to readiness and timing in terms of stages of rehabilitation. This approach helped families to understand the complexity of the recovery process.

After the workshop, the ongoing treatment began. Each session included a brief period of socialization to allow group leaders to model the idea of focusing on topics other than those related to illness. An open discussion followed where each family was encouraged to identify and address problems and issues that had developed since the last group meeting. The focal part of each session centered on the use of carefully delineated techniques designed to teach families how to identify, partialize, and solve problems, and were drawn from the work of Anderson and Falloon (Anderson, Hogarty, and Reiss 1986; Falloon, Boyd, and McGill 1984). Emphasis was placed on working with families to integrate and use the knowledge they had gained through the psychoeducational workshops.

Those with illness were encouraged to join the group as they seemed ready. As the client became more healthy, he or she was also provided with information regarding various aspects of illness. The treatment itself was staged, on the assumption that individuals need time to recover after an acute episode of illness. The emphasis during the first year is on relapse prevention and during the second year on rehabilitation and transitions to work. At the end of the formal intervention, families in the multiple-family groups were encouraged to continue meeting without the professionals as a means of maintaining the support and advocacy network.

The findings from this work are important to review. The first hypothesis was supported in that among those who participated in the multiple-family groups, there was a trend in favor of fewer relapses among client participants over the two-year treatment. Sixteen percent relapsed among those persons with illness in the multiple-family groups as opposed to 27 percent in single-family treatment. Those persons who were more severely ill at discharge from hospital and who participated in the multiple-family group experienced significantly fewer relapses than did those who participated in the single-family treatment. Among this subsample, 13 percent relapsed who participated in the multiple-family groups, while 33 percent relapsed who received the single-family intervention.

The second hypothesis was also supported. Regardless of treatment there were no differences between number of hospitalizations when the individuals were compared to themselves during the two years prior to entering the project and during the first eighteen months in treatment. However, when hospitalization rates during the last six months of treatment were compared to rates during the two years prior to treatment, the differences were statistically significant, suggesting that time in treatment had a positive impact on this aspect of outcome (McFarlane et al. 1995).

These intensive family interventions need to be replicated and participants need to be followed over time to determine the long-term impact of such psychoeducational intervention on both families and clients. In future studies, the impact on outcome measures other than relapse, particularly vocational and social functioning, and quality of life also need to be carefully assessed (Strauss and Carpenter 1974). But the results are important and promising for *both* treatment interventions, given that relapse rates in schizophrenia for those treated with the typical regimen of drug therapy can run as high as 30 to 50 percent over a one-year period and 65 to 75 percent over a three- to five-year period (Anthony et al. 1990).

Personal Therapy. Although an estimated 50 to 75 percent of persons who suffer from schizophrenia reside with their families, a significant number have little or no contact with family members (Kuipers and Bebbington 1988). Hence, models that focus on the individual client are essential for providing comprehensive care. Personal Therapy (PT), developed over the last fifteen years by Hogarty and his colleagues (1995, 1997a, 1997b), is a carefully described and tested model of individual intervention for schizophrenia.

On the assumption that the functional manifestation of schizophrenia is impaired basic and social cognition, the model is based on practice principles specific to the illness, staged interventions, and response to the poorly regulated affect (i.e., losing control, inability to regulate mood), which is so characteristic of schizophrenia. As such "PT became an exercise in managing personal vulnerability through a process of guided recovery" (Hogarty et al. 1995:383). The idea was to increase the client's ability to recognize the stages and processes of recovery, and to develop and internalize coping strategies necessary to manage external stress through increased awareness and development of coping styles and adaptive strategies. As with the psychoeducational family therapy approaches as defined by Anderson and McFarlane, joining between clinician and client, gradual reentry and graduated assumption of responsibility, and reintegration served as the building blocks (Anderson et al. 1986; McFarlane et al. 1995). These approaches were combined with traditional behavioral techniques (including modeling, rehearsal, practice, feedback, and homework). The three-stage treatment is strengths based and individualized; participants must attain clearly stated objectives regarding personal functioning before moving to the next stage in the process.

The effectiveness of the model was assessed among persons discharged from the hospital after an acute episode of schizophrenia. Of this group, some lived with family; others lived alone or with nonrelatives. Those who lived with family were assigned to PT alone, PT in conjunction with family therapy, family therapy alone, or supportive therapy alone. Those who resided away from family received either PT or supportive therapy.

Findings were noteworthy because the impact on relapse per se and on other forms of adjustment was different depending on residence. Those who lived with family and received PT were less likely to relapse with either psychotic or affective symptoms than those who received either family or supportive therapy, both over the three-year treatment, and particularly during the first year. However, those who lived alone and received PT showed significantly higher levels of psychotic relapse than those in supportive therapy (Hogarty et al. 1997a). For those with family, PT contributed to higher overall functioning than did any of the other interventions. For those without families, PT led to significantly improved work performance and nonfamilial relationships when compared with supportive therapy. In both trials PT led to improved social adjustment in the second and third years of treatment, whereas the supportive therapy, regardless of family status, improved after twelve months and then leveled out (Hogarty et al. 1997b).

The findings regarding relapse outcome suggested that the treatment was enhanced when family was involved. Their presence seemed to serve a protective function; their informal care and support appeared to enhance stability (Hogarty et al. 1995). As with the FPSP, this work needs to be extended and replicated, and participants need to be followed over time. But the findings support the efficacy of a clearly defined model that is fine-tuned for the individual, and where presence of family serves as a stabilizing force. As with the findings from the FPSP, they speak to the importance of family as a powerful resource for treatment and help to effectively counter historical tendencies to pathologize and negate family influences.

Social Skills Training. As we have seen, the deficits associated with schizophrenia interfere with the person's ability to form and keep relationships, to carry out normal social roles (such as worker or partner), and to satisfactorily monitor daily needs (APA 1994; Bellack et al. 1990). In some cases, the individual never fully developed these skills; in others, the skills diminished in conjunction with the illness. Regardless of how the deficits evolved, the impact is such that the person is further handicapped by the inability to utilize social skills in a manner that is appropriate to a given situation, reinforcing the person's presentation as odd or *other than normal.* This easily contributes to demoralization, stigmatization, and isolation, which may contribute to relapse and interfere with rehabilitation and entry or reentry into the workplace. Social skills training is a behavioral model that focuses on those areas of behavior that are sanctioned within the society and that allow individuals to interact and function in a manner considered socially acceptable.

The basic assumptions of the social skills model are (1) that such skills are based on a set of component responses including expressive behaviors, perception of relevant cues, and interactive behaviors; (2) that the skills are learnable; (3) that dysfunction occurs when a person does not have a skill, uses a skill at an inappropriate point in time, or acts inappropriately; and (4) that such deficits can be decreased through training. Psychotic symptoms, motivation, affective symptoms, environmental factors, and neurobiological deficits such as impaired memory, negative symptoms, or the side effects of medication affect level of social functioning (Bellack et al. 1990; Mueser et al. 1990).

The techniques of skills training are drawn from social learning theory (Bandura 1969) and include modeling and role play, verbal reinforcement and feedback, shaping, overlearning by repeating the skill until it becomes automatic, and generalization or transfer of skill from one situation to another through practice and homework. Training in problem solving, communication skills, and conflict resolution is central to the approach. The training can be conducted in one-on-one situations, in groups, or with families or couples (Bellack et al. 1990). It follows a carefully laid out series of steps that are carefully documented for the purposes of replication and dissemination.

In this section several important community-based interventions have been described, including Assertive Community Treatment, Psychoeducational Multiple Family Groups, Personal Therapy, and Social Skills Training. All of these programs are backed by both professionals and family advocates (Lehman et al. 1998). Many other outstanding programs exist, including the intensive case management programs (Solomon 1998), and such supported employment programs as Venture House in Chicago and Fountain House in New York City (Test 1998). Other programs have been developed by families and consumers for themselves. Examples include a nine-month curriculum plan devised by NAMI for educating its family members (Burland 1992), and various businesses run by consumers alone or in collaboration with social workers or other mental health professionals (Deegan 1992). What has become increasingly clear is that for these programs to be widely replicated and disseminated at a programmatic level, they must be carefully evaluated and well described in the literature in a manner that makes them available and accessible to other professionals as potential resources for their clients. For these programs to work for the individual client, they must incorporate sound assessment and clearly defined treatment principles, which allow room for individual differences, strengths, resources, and needs, and which build on a strong alliance between professional and client.

ASSESSMENT AND INTERVENTIONS

To build such an alliance, assessment, both initial and ongoing, is essential. The collaboration of a number of key players is required, most particularly the person with the illness, the health and mental health professional(s) closely linked with his or her care, and when available, key family members or other members of the person's support network. As such, the assessment becomes a central part of ongoing care and intervention.

Schizophrenia is an illness that is episodic in nature, and knowledge of how those episodes play out for any one individual is critical if the person is to function adequately in the community. If the person and his or her caregivers are able to identify and monitor early warning signs of decompensation, significant progress can be made toward keeping the illness in check through both medical and environmental intervention (McGlashan and Johannessen 1996; Mueser et al. 1992).

Diagnosis represents a more static construct than does assessment. As already noted, it may serve to label and stigmatize, and to limit possibilities and minimize strengths. But for a disease as complex and misunderstood as schizophrenia, diagnosis is an important part of what should be an ongoing assessment. Given that medication is usually required for the treatment of the most disturbing and overt psychotic symptoms, and because knowledge of the mix of symptoms for any given individual is essential for monitoring progress, a physician, most often a psychiatrist, is necessarily involved in this process.

To date, schizophrenia is not an illness that can be diagnosed by laboratory test; rather, it is always diagnosed through clinical dialogue and observation and collaborative information. This means there is always room for diagnostic error. Moreover, formal diagnosis is related to symptoms per se and overlooks the critical environmental factors that are essential to the complex process of assessment. As such diagnosis is only a first step toward understanding the full circumstances of the illness.

As previously reviewed, several critical factors tend to interfere with this process of intervention and monitoring that follow and contribute to full assessment. The most obvious is lack of external supports and resources. Others include internal processes, the cognitive deficits and associated denial of illness or lack of insight that is frequently characteristic of schizophrenia (Amador et al. 1991; Amador and David 1998; Silverstein 1997). In his work on neuropsychological deficits, Silverstein (1997) discusses how the illness hinders a person's ability to use the internal and external cues that typically regulate behavior. The normal individual is able to utilize cues (e.g., time, place or setting, tone of voice, facial expression) to appraise situations, recall past responses, adapt these to the current situations, and act appropriately. But for someone with schizophrenia this skill is impaired such that it interferes with awareness (or even existence) of goals, intention, or even the intention of others (Frith 1992). Not surprisingly, such impairment can also impede awareness of illness, which complicates the client's ability to allow others to identify and work with his or her symptoms (Amador et al. 1991; Amador and David 1998).

The role that environmental stress plays in the course of schizophrenia also immeasurably complicates the process of effective intervention. Approaching the illness from the perspective of the stress-vulnerability theory posited by Zubin and others (Heinrichs and Carpenter 1983; Zubin and Spring 1977; Zubin et al. 1992), ordinary stress can be experienced as extraordinary by the person with schizophrenia. For example, such simple factors as the stimulation of background noise, or the lack of stimulation of unstructured time, can exacerbate existing symptoms and serve to distract and disorient the person and interfere with the ability to focus on daily tasks (Anderson et al. 1986; McFarlane et al. 1995).

These stressors are further complicated by the fact that the psychotropic (or neuroleptic) medications have side effects that mimic or exacerbate other symptoms or that interfere with functioning in and of themselves. Sorting out and distinguishing among these requires careful monitoring, again with the cooperation of the person with illness (Carpenter, Heinrichs, and Alphs 1985).

So social workers and other mental health professionals are faced with the ongoing challenge of trying to assist and work with people who because of impaired insight may be denying the existence of any need for such assistance, even in the face of multiple stressors. This clearly raises ethical concerns as well, particularly around issues of self-determination.

Timing is also critical given an illness that is cyclical in nature, where symptoms appear and recede. Therefore, maintaining engagement and developing shared goals between clinician and client becomes a primary and ongoing challenge for effective intervention and for maximizing potential for growth.

In recent years new medications have served to more effectively control symptoms and to increase levels of functioning for persons with schizophrenia. Sometimes this is associated with improved cognitive functioning and increased insight. But the improved insight can have unexpected drawbacks as well (Duckworth et al. 1997). Recognizing and admitting the profound impact of schizophrenia on the self may contribute to depression, suicidal behavior, fear, mourning, and a sense of loss of "what might have been." Paradoxically, the disappearance of familiar symptoms may also be experienced as a kind of loss. These reactions may range from mild to extremely debilitating and must be carefully assessed in helping the individual effectively cope with and reach some level of acceptance of the illness, while adjusting to a new level of functioning (Duckworth et al. 1997).

A critical part of both the assessment and intervention process is identifying, evaluating, and drawing on the person's social network and supports. In this illness more than in many others, the client needs other people (whether family or others) who serve as checkpoints for those times when the person's symptoms interfere with the ability to monitor changes in functioning or behavior for him- or herself. As with any situation with impaired self-awareness, external feedback and support are critical in enabling the person to remain on track and to forestall decompensation (Pescosolido et al. 1995). When family members are available, their level of social support must be assessed. In recent research reported by Solomon and Draine (1995), availability of social support was the strongest explanatory factor regarding adaptive coping (i.e., self-efficacy and sense of mastery) among family members.

Availability of other resources must be carefully considered as well. These include any benefits to which the person is entitled, such as Social Security Income (SSI), Social Security Disability Income (SSDI), Medicaid, Medicare, access to housing, and information as to how to use those benefits. If the person wishes to work, this must also be evaluated, and the proper supports must be in place to ensure access to employment, and then adequate functioning on the job. Again the new medications have provided hope and opportunity for people with schizophrenia. But work settings bring their own set of environmental challenges and stresses, and another arena for the individual to cope with and manage. As clients become more ready to work in competitive situations, increased attention must be paid to supports in the workplace (Bond 1992; Lehman et al. 1998).

ILLUSTRATION AND DISCUSSION

Bill T., a 36-year-old single unemployed white male, was admitted voluntarily to a local state hospital for an acute episode of schizophrenia. Presenting symptoms included active suicidal ideation, bouts of rage toward his parents and younger sister, increasing disorientation, inability to sleep, and refusal to take his medication. Bill had a fifteen-year history of chronic psychosis, characterized by prominent negative symptoms. He had attended community day treatment programs sporadically during this time, where he had been well liked. The social workers there described a quiet well-mannered man who went out of his way for other clients, particularly those who appeared most ill. Prior to developing schizophrenia Bill had completed two years of study in a local community college where he had studied horticulture and environmental science. Since that time he had been unable to work, finding the demands of a regular nine to five schedule to be stressful and overwhelming. Until the week prior to his admission, much of his free time had been spent hanging out at a local diner where he seemed to be well liked by the owner and regular patrons. He spent his time playing checkers and reading local newspapers, or just smoking. Sometimes he helped out by running errands for the owner. At the time of admission he was residing at home with his parents and 17-year-old sister.

Within the first week after admission some of the presenting symptoms had calmed down and Bill no longer felt suicidal. At this point Bill was approached by Mr. Seth, a hospital social worker, who described the psychoeducational multiple-family group model of treatment that was used on this particular inpatient unit and that continued upon discharge from hospital. Although initially skeptical of being involved in any program that included his parents, and particularly his sister, Bill was willing to meet with Mr. Seth for at least one or two individual "joining" meetings so that he could better understand the nature of the psychoeducational program.

During these initial sessions, Bill expressed anger, at his family for "getting me into this mess," at Mr. Seth for being like all other social workers, "you know, someone who says he'll help but doesn't really help at all and then kind of disappears." Mr. Seth expressed empathy, listening to Bill's experience of family and mental health professionals. But he also focused on describing the premise of the psychoeducational approaches, in which family, individual with illness, and professional collaborate to assess needs, identify goals, and problem solve, and learn from each other. He explained that the model was set up to include continuity and teamwork, such that the coleaders of the multiple-family group would work with Bill and his family over a two-year period to help Bill stay out of the hospital and cope with some of the problems that had led to hospitalization. He informed Bill that as one of the group coleaders he would work consistently with Bill and his family and had no plans to disappear. He emphasized the fact that the group leaders would be on call twenty-four hours per day. He also described the multiple-family group process, explaining that family members other than Bill's would be present, and that other individuals from the inpatient unit would be participating in the group as well, that sometimes as many as eighteen or twenty people might be in attendance in one group. He noted that the group would be ongoing so that Bill and his family could continue to attend for two years after he left the hospital. Mr. Seth said that such a plan might help Bill stay out of the hospital in the long term. Bill remained skeptical but agreed to let Mr. Seth approach his parents and to at least attend the group on a "trial" basis.

During the family joining sessions, the T's also expressed anger at the system, feeling like they had been ignored, dismissed, or misinformed by the majority of mental health professionals they had dealt with since Bill had first become ill many years before. Mr. Seth was able to calm them down by sharing a bit about his life, his work, and how he had become involved with people with mental illness. When they realized that he seemed genuinely interested in their story, they were able to talk about the stress the family had endured regarding Bill's illness, the withdrawal of Bill's siblings, their own feelings of inadequacy, and fear regarding the future. They began to talk sadly about their experience of "losing" the Bill they had known as a child and young adolescent, a person who had been "full of life, and always kept us laughing." When Mr. Seth asked the family whether they had ever attended a local meeting of NAMI, the T's noted that they had heard about the organization but hadn't really looked into it, fearing that it wasn't for them.

During the last joining session, Melissa, the 17-year-old daughter who resided at home, reluctantly participated. Mr. Seth made a point of talking directly to her about her experience with Bill, and the amount of attention her parents had had to direct toward Bill throughout her childhood and adolescence. Mr. and Mrs. T. seemed pensive and sad during this part of the meeting.

After the conclusion of the family joining sessions, the T's seemed ready and willing to attend the psychoeducational workshop along with the other five families who would participate in the multiple-family group. Following the FPSP model as defined by McFarlane and his colleagues (1993, 1995), the workshop was designed to include an overview of critical information regarding the illness of schizophrenia, presented in a manner that the families could understand and manage. Mr. Seth and his coleader, Ms. Ross, along with one of the attending psychiatrists on the inpatient unit, conducted the workshop. It was designed for the families only; the model is such that the information would be presented to the persons with illness at a later point in the process. Mr. and Mrs. T. were in attendance, as was Melissa.

During the workshop the T's were relatively quiet, seemingly a bit overwhelmed by the whole experience. But they were quite attentive and showed their engagement by asking a lot of questions, particularly about the diagnosis, medications, and some of the history and epidemiology of the illness. During the socialization period with professionals and staff, Mrs. T. became quite engaged in talking with another mother. Although Melissa was the youngest person present, and the only sibling, she seemed to be able to hold her own. At one point she entered a discussion with Ms. Ross, the cotherapist, and another parent, about how frustrating and enraging and lonely it was to cope with this illness day in and day out.

Over the course of the next two years the T's were active and regular participants in the multiple-family group. Melissa attended on an irregular basis, and Bill attended most of the time, stating that sometimes he just needed to take a break. During the first three or four sessions, much of the emphasis was on encouraging coleaders, families, and clients to get to know one another; each participant had the opportunity to talk about him- or herself and about aspects of their lives unrelated to schizophrenia. This period of socialization was considered critical in terms of group formation and promoting a relaxed and accepting atmosphere so participants could work and talk together.

Early on in the process, the T's started talking about how worried they became when Bill stopped taking his medication, knowing that it was only a matter of time until his symptoms worsened and he would need hospitalization. They also talked about more minor stresses; for example, the times when Bill would stay up all night and suddenly start playing his music so loudly that the other family members were startled awake. They acknowledged that these stresses initially seemed minor but that they had had a cumulative and exhausting effect over time. Bill talked about how angry he felt when the family tried to set limits on his behavior, and how alienated and lonely he often felt because "nobody ever listens to me; they just see my illness."

Over time the group members learned problem-solving techniques to address these concerns. The families presented problem situations on a ro-tating schedule, with one family actively working each week with the sup-port of the entire group. Initially the families resisted the process somewhat, finding it frustrating and slow. Bill and the client members also resisted the problem-solving aspect of the work at first, again feeling as though they were being singled out and labeled as the "problem." But as everybody began to see small changes, and as the stress levels at home began to abate, the families became increasingly engaged and involved. In the process the group meet-ings became more relaxed, and the level of humor and interaction among participants increased dramatically. People began to work together to de-velop creative ways of solving problems and monitoring solutions, such that the solutions would be workable outside the group. This took time, with some trial and error built in, and it took some time for the trust level among group members to build. But slowly, with much input and modeling from the group leaders, people opened up to each other. There were many ex-amples of *cross-parenting,* where one parent could say something to a client from another family that he or she could hear in a way that would not have worked if the speaker had been his or her parent. In other cases of *cross-family communication,* one client would educate the families as to what it was like to experience delusions or hallucinations in an ongoing fashion, or give feedback to another client in a manner that could only be heard and accepted from a peer. In one powerful exchange, Bill started talking to Susan S., another client, about how important it was "not to mess with your med-ication." After he said this, he suddenly stopped, hesitated, and then laughed ironically. "I guess that means I should take the stuff too." Everybody laughed and clapped good-naturedly. As the group continued, a sense of pride and hope among group members was engendered that had been lacking initially.

All the participants were encouraged to maintain contact with each other outside the sessions as a means of decreasing isolation and increasing sup-ports. In one moving sequence of events, the T's were able to successfully calm down Tricia, a client member of the group, by telephone, when she was particularly upset and angry about something that had happened in her vol-unteer job. Both Tricia and her parents felt extremely supported by this exchange.

The group leaders encouraged the families to join NAMI, and the T's in particular were able to overcome their hesitance and began attending support group meetings. Mr. and Mrs. T became very involved in the organization, and during the second year of their participation in the group, they attended both a state and national conference.

The group continued to work together for two years as per the program design. During the first year, the T. family experienced some low points. Bill was hospitalized briefly, and for about six weeks he refused to attend the group altogether. But during the second year his compliance with treatment substantially improved, and he seemed to regain some pleasure in his life. He planted a small garden at home during the second summer, which he reported on with some enthusiasm during the group meetings. He still felt unable to work in a competitive situation but was able to involve himself semiregularly in a volunteer program at the local day treatment program working with the animal rescue squad. His sister Melissa left home for college where she was doing well academically and felt socially accepted.

The preceding case study exemplifies the potential for growth and enhanced stability that can occur within a well-structured and planned psychoeducational multiple-family group following the FPSP model (McFarlane et al. 1995). Bill and his family entered the process hesitantly, with trepidation about the process and anger about past involvement with mental health professionals. Through the initial joining process, the therapist, Mr. Seth, was able to form an initial therapeutic alliance with each member of the family individually, including Bill and Melissa. During this stage he worked to partner himself with the family members as a means of helping them feel validated, accepted, and central to the treatment process. This served to engage and calm the family, so they could focus on the challenges involved in the psychoeducational process.

The case also provides examples of some of the difficulties involved in this work, particularly in the earlier stages. Families usually respond positively to the psychoeducational workshop; this is an opportunity for them to begin to understand and absorb some of the complexities and mysteries of the illness. But the information can be overwhelming as well, which is why the work done in the early stages of the two-year process may seem slow and plodding, with periods of both success and setback. This may be initially frustrating to family, client, and professional alike, but as all begin to understand that measured recovery and careful monitoring are critical to positive outcome and resiliency, group members begin to calm down and the process becomes more effective.

Because schizophrenia is such a complex and often unpredictable illness, knowing how to work with the symptoms may require creative approaches that are not obvious to families who are immersed in the situation (McFarlane and Lukens 1994). As the group becomes more coherent over time, participants, including clients, can work with the coleaders to help members of other families step back and address the problems encountered in living with the illness in a thoughtful and planned manner that diminishes stress and enriches quality of life. At its best, this work fosters a true partnership between family members and professionals in which all participants serves as educators, students, facilitators, consultants, and advocates. This is enhanced by the expanded social support system that defines the multiple-family group. In this setting both professional and practical knowledge can be exchanged, and group members have the opportunity to witness and validate each other's experiences.

CONCLUSION

In conclusion, it is important to consider what directions we as social workers might take to improve the quality of life of those with schizophrenia. As we have seen, schizophrenia can be profoundly debilitating, and intervention is clearly complicated by the fact that the client may be unaware of or unwilling to admit the presence of illness. Because of the complexity of presentation, and because someone with this illness is sensitive to even subtle changes and stressors in the environment, helping the client and significant others to monitor these changes is key to successful intervention. Particular attention must be paid to those points of transition that are particularly stressful, from hospital to home or community residence, from home to community residence or apartment, or from day treatment program to competitive employment. In each of these vulnerable situations, a lack of continuity or coordinated care may create setbacks *or* points of crisis for the client. But such situations also provide opportunities for both short- and long-term planning, which helps to generate perspective and hope. As exemplified by the previously described models (ACT, PT, FPSP, SST) and the case study, such attention requires a collaborative and ongoing effort among the professional and lay community, including the person with illness and family and friends. If the person is working or trying to work, this community may be extended to include supervisors and colleagues as well.

New medications have provided hope and opportunity for persons with the schizophrenia, in that some of the more disturbing and overt symptoms can be more adequately controlled. This may help the person to look more normal, to feel more normal, or both. But for even the most healthy person, moving to a new stage of functioning is a transition that usually requires adjustment. So whether a person with schizophrenia is helped by new medicines or not, the need for ongoing support remains critical on several fronts. In addition to well-described and evaluated community programs, these include attention to housing, rehabilitation, work, and quality of life.

Housing is a most fundamental need. Although a significant number of adults with schizophrenia reside with their families, many others have little or no access to family supports. Among the homeless population in the United States, it is estimated that approximately 10 percent have schizophrenia (Brekke and Slade 1998). For those who do reside with relatives, alternative living situations might more adequately serve their needs and the needs of their families. Matching individuals with appropriate housing, in a setting where needed supports are in place, provides an ongoing challenge, particularly given limited availability and funding support.

Because of the nature of the illness, only a limited number of people with schizophrenia have been able to function adequately in the workplace. Others function in large sheltered workshops or in vocational training programs where they are responsible for relatively unskilled or semiskilled tasks. However, as medications and other interventions become increasingly sophisticated and effective, people with schizophrenia will be more emotionally available to meet the demands required to maintain regular employment. The structure and potentially rewarding nature of the work environment may also serve to focus and ground the individual if appropriate supports are available. This demands that social workers and other mental health professionals working with this group of clients become well versed in the policies and services related to the rights of persons with disabilities in the workplace (Kurzman and Akabas 1993).

Access to housing, benefits, and employment contribute to quality of life, which can be elusive for those with schizophrenia. As the case study suggests, working with the client to build on strengths and maximize opportunities while weathering the episodic nature of schizophrenia is central to the social work mandate. This challenge demands professional involvement across system levels not only to provide day-to-day care and strategies for maximizing individual potential but also to develop and disseminate new programs and influence policies to address the changing needs of clients with this complex mental illness.

References

Amador, X. F. and A. S. David. 1998. *Insight and Psychosis.* New York: Oxford University Press.

Amador, X. F., D. H. Strauss, S. A. Yale, and J. M. Gorman. 1991. "Awareness of Illness in Schizophrenia." *Schizophrenia Bulletin* 17:113–32.

Anderson, C., G. Hogarty, and D. Reiss. 1986. *Schizophrenia and the Family.* New York: Guilford Press.

Anthony, W., M. Cohen, and M. Farkas. 1990. *Psychiatric Rehabilitation.* Boston: Center for Psychiatric Rehabilitation.

American Psychiatric Association (APA). 1994. *Diagnostic and Statistical Manual of Mental Disorders (DSM-IV),* 4th ed. Washington, D.C.: Author.

Aro, S., H. Aro, M. Salino, and I. Keskimaki. 1995. "Educational Level and Hospital Use in Mental Disorders: A Population Based Study." *Acta Psychiatrica Scandinavica* 91:305–12.

Bandura, A. 1969. *Principles of Behavior Modification.* New York: Holt, Rinehart & Winston.

Bateson, G., D. Jackson, J. Haley., and J. Weakland. 1956. "Towards a Theory of Schizophrenia." *Behavioral Science* 1:251–64.

Bebbington, P. and L. Kuipers. 1994. "The Predictive Utility of Expressed Emotion in Schizophrenia: An Aggregate Analysis." *Psychological Medicine* 24:707–18.

Bellack, A. S., R. L. Morrison, J. T. Wixted, and K. T. Mueser. 1990. "An Analysis of Social Competence in Schizophrenia." *British Journal of Psychiatry* 156:809–18.

Bleuler, E. 1911/1950. *Dementia Praecox or the Group of Schizophrenias.* Translated by J. Zinken. New York: International University Press.

Bond, G. R. 1992. "Vocational Rehabilitation." In R. P. Liberman, ed., *Handbook of Psychiatric Rehabilitation,* pp. 244–75. New York: Macmillan.

Borkman, T. 1976. "Experiential Knowledge: A New Concept for the Analysis of Self-help Groups." *Social Service Review* 50:445–56.

Breier, A. and J. Strauss. 1984. "The Role of Social Relationships in the Recovery from Psychotic Disorders." *American Journal of Psychiatry* 141(8):949–55.

Brekke, J. and E. S. Slade. 1998. "Schizophrenia." In J. B. W. Williams and K. Ell, ed., *Advances in Mental Health Research: Implications for Practice,* pp. 157–81. Washington, D.C.: National Association of Social Workers Press.

Brewin, C. R., B. MacCarthy, R. Duda, and C. E. Vaughn. 1991. "Attribution and Expressed Emotion in the Relatives of Patients with Schizophrenia." *Journal of Abnormal Psychology* 100:546–55.

Brown, G. W. and M. Rutter. 1966. "The Measurement of Family Activities and Relationships." *Human Relations* 19:241–63.

Burland, J. 1992. *The Journey of Hope Family Education Course.* Baton Rouge, La.: Alliance for the Mentally Ill.

Carpenter, W., D. Heinrichs, and L. Alphs. 1985. "Treatment of Negative Symptoms." *Schizophrenia Bulletin* 11:440–51.

Cassel, J. 1976. "The Contribution of the Social Environment to Host Resistance." *American Journal of Epidemiology* 104:107–23.

Deegan, P. E. 1992. "The Independent Living Movement and People with Psychiatric Disabilities: Taking Back Control Over Our Own Lives." *Psychosocial Rehabilitation Journal* 15(3):3–19.

Dequardo, J. R. 1998. "Pharmacologic Treatment of First-Episode Schizophrenia: Early Intervention Is Key to Outcome." *Journal of Clinical Psychiatry* 59 (Supplement 19): 9–17.

Dixon, L. B. and A. F. Lehman. 1995. "Family Interventions for Schizophrenia." *Schizophrenia Bulletin* 21(4):631–43.

Drake, R. E., S. J. Bartels, G. B. Teague, D. L. Noordsy, and R. E. Clarke. 1993. "Treatments of Substance Abuse in Severely Mentally Ill Patients." *Journal of Nervous and Mental Disease* 181:606–11.

Duckworth, K., V. Nair, J. K. Patel, and S. M. Goldfinger. 1997. "Lost Time, Found Hope and Sorrow: The Search for Self, Connection and Purpose During 'Awakenings' on the New Antipsychotics." *Harvard Review of Psychiatry* 5(4):227–33.

Elliott, G. R. and C. Einsdorfer. 1982. *Stress and Human Health: Analysis and Implications of Research.* New York: Springer.

Falloon, I., J. Boyd, and C. McGill. 1984. *Family Care of Schizophrenia.* New York: Guilford.

Fellin, P. 1996. *Mental Health and Mental Illness: Policies, Programs, and Services.* Itasca, Ill.: F. E. Peacock.

Frith, C. D. 1992. *The Cognitive Neuropsychology of Schizophrenia.* Hove: Erlbaum.

Fromm-Reichmann, F. 1948. "Notes on the Development of Treatment of Schizophrenics by Psychoanalytic Psychotherapy." *Psychiatry* 2:263–73.

Goldstein, M., E. Rodnick, J. Evans, P. May, and M. Steinberg. 1978. "Drug and Family Therapy in the Aftercare Treatment of Acute Schizophrenia." *Archives of General Psychiatry* 35:1169–77.

Greenberg, J. S., J. R. Greenley, and P. Benedict. 1994. "Contributions of Persons with Serious Mental Illness to their Families." *Hospital and Community Psychiatry* 45:475–80.

Greenley, J. 1986. "Social Control and Expressed Emotion." *Journal of Nervous and Mental Disorders* 174(1):24–30.

Grob, G. N. 1994. *The Mad Among Us: A History of the Care of America's Mentally Ill.* New York: Free Press.

Gureje, O. and R. W. Bamidele. 1998. "Gender and Schizophrenia: Association of Age at Onset with Antecedent, Clinical, and Outcome Features." *Australia and New Zealand Journal of Psychiatry* 32(3):415–23.

Harkavey-Friedman, J. M. and E. A. Nelson. 1997. "Assessment & Intervention for the Suicidal Patient with Schizophrenia." *Psychiatric Quarterly* 68(4):361–75.

Hatfield, A. 1987. "Taking Issue: The Expressed Emotion Theory: Why Families Object." *Hospital and Community Psychiatry* 38(4):341.

Hatfield, A. B. and H. P. Lefley. 1987. *Families of the Mentally Ill: Coping and Adaptations.* New York: Guilford.

Heinrichs, D. and W. Carpenter. 1983. "The Coordination of Family Therapy with Other Treatment Modalities." In W. R. McFarlane, ed., *Family Therapy in Schizophrenia,* pp. 267–88. New York: Guilford Press.

Hogarty, G. E., S. J. Kornblith, D. Greenwald, A. L. DiBarry, S. Cooley, S. Flesher, D. Reiss, M. Carter, and R. Ulrich. 1995. "Personal Therapy: A Disorder-Relevant Psychotherapy for Schizophrenia." *Schizophrenia Bulletin* 21(3):379–93.

Hogarty, G. E., S. J. Kornblith, D. Greenwald, A. L. DiBarry, S. Cooley, R. F. Ilrich, M. Carter, and S. Flesher. 1997a. "Three-Year Trials of Personal Therapy among Schizophrenic Patients Living with or Independent of Family, I: Description of Study and Effects on Relapse Rates." *American Journal of Psychiatry* 154(11):1504–13.

Hogarty, G. E., D. Greenwald, R. F. Ulrich, S. J. Kornblith, A. L. DiBarry, S. Cooley, M. Carter, and S. Flesher. 1997b. "Three-Year Trials of Personal Therapy among Schizophrenic Patients Living with or Independent of Family, II: Effects on Adjustment of Patients." *American Journal of Psychiatry* 154(11):1514–24.

Kasinin, J., E. Knight, and P. Sage. 1934. "The Parent-Child Relationship in Schizophrenia." *Journal of Nervous and Mental Disorders* 79:249–63.

Kraepelin, E. 1919/1971. *Dementia Praecox and Paraphenia.* Translated by R. Barclay and G. Robertson. New York: Robert E. Krieger.

Kuipers, L. and P. Bebbington. 1988. "Expressed Emotion Research in Schizophrenia." *Psychological Medicine* 18:893–909.

Kurzman, P. A. and S. H. Akabas, eds. 1993. *Work and Well-Being: The Occupational Social Work Advantage.* Washington, D.C.: National Association of Social Workers Press.

Leff, J., L. Kuipers, R. Berkowitz, R. Eberlein-Vries, and D. Sturgeon. 1982. "A Controlled Trial of Social Intervention in the Families of Schizophrenic Patients." *British Journal of Psychiatry* 141:121–34.

Lefley, H. P. 1996. *Family Caregiving in Mental Illness.* Thousand Oaks, Calif.: Sage Publications.

Lehman, A. F., D. M. Steinwachs, and Coinvestigators, PORT Project. 1998. "Translating Research into Practice: The Schizophrenia Patient Outcomes Research Team (PORT) Treatment Recommendations." *Schizophrenia Bulletin* 24(1):1–10.

Levy, D. M. 1931. Maternal Overprotection and Rejection. *Archives of Neurology and Psychiatry* 25:886–89.

Liberman, R. P. 1994. "Psychosocial Treatments for Schizophrenia." *Psychiatry* 57:104–14.

Lidz, T., A. R. Cornelison, S. Fleck, and D. Terry. 1957. "The Intrafamilial Environment of the Schizophrenic Patient. II. Marital Schism and Marital Skew." *American Journal of Psychiatry* 114:241–48.

Link, B. G., J. Mirotznik, and F. T. Cullen. 1991. "The Effectiveness of Stigma Coping Orientations: Can Negative Consequences of Mental Illness Labeling be Avoided?" *Journal of Health and Social Behavior* 32:302–20.

Link, B. and J. Phelan. 1995. "Social Conditions as Fundamental Causes of Disease." *Journal of Health and Social Behavior* 36(Supplement):80–94.

Manderscheid, R. W. and S. A. Barrett, eds. 1987. *Mental Health, United States, 1987.* (DHHS Publication No. ADM 87–1518). Washington, D.C.: U.S. Government Printing Office.

Manderscheid, R. W. and M. A. Sonnenscheid, eds. 1992. *Mental Health, United States, 1992.* (DHHS Publication No. SMA 92–1942). Washington, DC: U.S. Government Printing Office.

Marsh, D. T., H. P. Lefley, D. Evans-Rhodes, V. I. Ansell, B. M. Doerzbacher, LaBarbera, and J. E. Paluzzi. 1996. "The Family Experience of Mental Illness: Evidence for Resilience." *Psychiatric Rehabilitation Journal* 20(2):3–12.

McCubbin, H. I. and M. A. McCubbin. 1988. "Typologies of Resilient Families: Emerging Roles of Social Class and Ethnicity." *Family Relations* 37:247–54.

McFarlane, W. R., E. Dunne, E. Lukens, M. Newmark, J. McLaughlin-Toran, S. Deakins, and B. Horen. 1993. "From Research to Clinical Practice: Dissemination of New York State's Family Psychoeducation Project." *Hospital and Community Psychiatry* 44(3): 265–70.

McFarlane, W. R. and E. P. Lukens. 1994. "Systems Theory Revisited: Research on Family Expressed Emotion and Communication Deviance." In H. P. Lefley and M. Wasow, eds., *Helping Families Cope with Mental Illness,* pp. 79–104. Chur, Switzerland: Harwood Academic Publishers.

McFarlane, W., E. Lukens, B. Link, R. Dushay, S. Deakins, M. Newmark, E. Dunne, B. Horen, and J. Toran. 1995. "Multiple Family Groups and Psychoeducation in the Treatment of Schizophrenia." *Archives of General Psychiatry* 52:679–87.

McGlashan, T. H. 1986. "The Prediction of Outcome in Chronic Schizophrenia." *Archives of General Psychiatry* 43:167–76.

———. 1988. "A Selective Review of Recent North American Long Term Follow-Up Studies of Schizophrenia." *Schizophrenia Bulletin* 14:515–42.

McGlashan, T. H. and J. O. Johannessen. 1996. "Early Detection and Intervention with Schizophrenia: Rationale." *Schizophrenia Bulletin* 22:201–22.

Möller, H. J. and D. von Zerssen. 1995. "Course and Outcome of Schizophrenia." In S. R. Hirsch and D. R. Weinberger, eds., *Schizophrenia,* pp. 106–27. Oxford, England: Blackwell Science.

Mueller, D. P. 1980. "Social Networks: A Promising Direction for Research on the Relationship of the Social Environment to Psychiatric Disorder." *American Journal of Psychiatry* 14:147–61.

Mueser, K. T., A. Bellack, R. Morrsion, and J. Wixted. 1990. "Social Competence in Schizophrenia: Premorbid Adjustment, Social Skill and Domains of Functioning." *Journal of Psychiatric Research* 24(1):51–63.

Mueser, K. T., A. S. Bellack, J. H. Wade, S. L. Sayers, and C. K. Resenthal. 1992. "An Assessment of the Educational Needs of Chronic Psychiatric Patients and Their Relatives." *British Journal of Psychiatry* 160:674–80.

Neighbors, H., W. R. Bashshur, R. Price, S. Selig, A. Donabedian, and G. Shannon. 1992. "Ethnic Minority Mental Health Service Delivery: A Review of the Literature." *Research in Community and Mental Health* 7(1).

Nicholson, I. and R. Neufeld. 1992. "A Dynamic Vulnerability Perspective on Stress and Schizophrenia." *American Journal of Orthopsychiatry* 62:117–30.

Noble, J. H., R. S. Honberg, L. L. Hall, and L. M. Flynn. 1998. "A Legacy of Failure." http://www.nami.org.

Pearlin, L. I., C. S. Aneshensel, and A. J. Leblanc. 1997. "The Forms and Mechanisms of Stress Proliferation: The Case of AIDS Caregivers." *Journal of Health and Social Behavior* 38:223–36.

Penn, D. L., W. Spaulding, D. Reed, M. Sullivan, K. T. Mueser, and D. A. Hope. 1997. "Cognition and Social Functioning in Schizophrenia." *Psychiatry* 60:281–91.

Pescosolido, B., E. Wright, and W. Sullivan. 1995. "Communities of Care: A Theoretical Perspective on Case Management Models in Mental Health." *Advances in Medical Sociology* 6:37–79.

Regier, D. A., M. E. Farmer, D. S. Rae, B. Z. Locke, S. J. Keith, L. L. Judd, and F. K. Goodwin. 1990. "Comorbidity of Mental Disorders with Alcohol and Other Drug Abuse: Results from the Epidemiologic Catchment Area (ECA) Study." *Journal of the American Medical Association* 264:2511–18.

Reiss, D., R. Plomin, and E. M. Heterington. 1991. "Genetics and Psychiatry: An Un-Heralded Window on the Environment." *American Journal of Psychiatry* 148:283–91.

Rosenfield, S. 1997. "Labeling Mental Illness: The Effects of Received Services and Perceived Stigma on Life Satisfaction." *American Sociological Review* 62:660–72.

Rutter, M. and G. Brown. 1966. "The Reliability and Validity of Measures of Family Life and Relationships in Families Containing a Schizophrenic Patient." *Social Psychiatry* 1(1):38–53.

Scheflen, A. 1981. *Levels of Schizophrenia.* New York: Brunner/Mazel.

Schneider, K. 1959/1980. *Clinical Psychopathology.* Translated by M.W. Hamilton and E. W. Anderson. New York: Grune & Stratton.

Silverstein, S. M. 1997. "Information Processing, Social Cognition, and Psychiatric Rehabilitation in Schizophrenia." *Psychiatry* 60:327–40.

Solomon, P. 1998. "The Conceptual and Empirical Base of Case Management for Adults with Severe Mental Illness." In J. B. W. Williams and K. Ell, eds., *Advances in Mental Health Research: Implications for Practice,* pp. 482–98. Washington, D.C.: National Association of Social Workers Press.

Solomon, P. and J. Draine. 1995. "Subjective Burden among Family Members of Mentally Ill Adults: Relation to Stress, Coping, and Adaptation." *American Journal of Orthopsychiatry* 65(3):419–27.

Sommer, R. 1990. "Family Advocacy and the Mental Health System: The Recent Rise of the Alliance for the Mentally Ill." *Psychiatry Quarterly* 61(3):205–21.

Starr, P. 1982. *The Social Transformation of American Medicine.* New York: Basic Books.

Stein, L. I., R. J. Diamond, and R. M. Farton. 1990. "A Systems Approach to the Care of Persons with Schizophrenia." In M. I. Herz, S. J. Keith, and J. P. Docherty, eds., *Handbook of Schizophrenia.* Vol. 4, *Psychosocial Treatment of Schizophrenia,* pp. 213–46. Amsterdam: Elsevier.

Stein, L. and M. A. Test. 1980. "Alternatives to Mental Health Hospital Treatment I.: Conceptual Model, Treatment Program, and Clinical Evaluation." *Archives of General Psychiatry* 37:392–97.

Strauss, J. S. and W. T. Carpenter. 1974. "The Prediction of Outcome in Schizophrenia." *Archives of General Psychiatry* 31:37–42.

Struening, E. L., A. Stueve, P. Vine, D. E. Kreisman, B. G. Link, and D. B. Herman. 1995. "Factors Associated with Grief and Depressive Symptoms in Caregivers of People with Serious Mental Illness." *Research in Community Mental Health* 8:91–94.

Swanson, C. L., R. C. Gur, W. Bilker, R. G. Petty, and R. E. Gur. 1998. "Premorbid Educational Attainment in Schizophrenia: Association with Symptoms, Functioning, and Neurobehavioral Measures." *Biological Psychiatry* 44(8):739–47.

Terkelson, K. 1983. "Schizophrenia and the Family: II. Adverse Effects of Family Therapy." *Family Process* 22:191–200.

Test, M. A. 1998. "Community-Based Treatment Models for Adults with Severe and Persistent Mental Illness." In J. B. W. Williams and K. Ell, eds., *Advances in Mental Health Research: Implications for Practice,* pp. 420–36.Washington, D.C.: National Association of Social Workers Press.

Test, M. A. and L. Stein. 1980. "Alternatives to Mental Hospital Treatment III: Social Cost." *Archives of General Psychiatry* 37:409–12.

Zubin, J. and B. Spring. 1977. "Vulnerability: A New View of Schizophrenia." *Journal of Abnormal Psychology* 86:103–26.

Zubin, J., S. R. Steinhauer, and R. Condray. 1992. "Vulnerability to Relapse in Schizophrenia." *British Journal of Psychiatry* 161(Supplement 18):13–18.

Part II

Life Circumstances and Events

11

Adolescent Pregnancy

Bruce Armstrong

Even though the U.S. teen pregnancy rate is lower now than during the "baby boom," public focus on the costs and consequences of adolescent sexual behavior has intensified over the past four decades. American teenagers still have higher pregnancy, birth, abortion, and sexually transmitted disease (STD) rates than teens in other industrialized countries. Each year, nearly one million American teenagers become pregnant (nearly 85 percent unintentionally), more than half a million bear children, and three million acquire an STD.

Dramatic transformations in family and labor market structures over the past forty years have left young Americans increasingly vulnerable to the adverse health, social, and economic consequences of early, unintended pregnancy. Over 75 percent of teens who gave birth in 1996 were unmarried, compared with only 16 percent in 1960. More than ever before, adolescents need to obtain a high school, or higher, diploma and to develop interpersonal and critical thinking skills in order to secure and maintain employment in today's high-tech, service-oriented job market. The devastating effects of sexually transmitted (and often asymptomatic) bacterial infections like chlamydia, and incurable viral infections like human immunodeficiency virus (HIV) and human papillomavirus (HPV) leave sexually active teens with little room for error during the increasingly wide interval between when they typically experience puberty, when they first have intercourse, and when they marry.

The personal and public costs and consequences of early pregnancy and childbearing have been abundantly documented (e.g., Maynard 1996). Teen parents, for example, leave school earlier and have lower lifetime earnings than peers who delay having children. Children of teen parents are more likely to experience health, social, educational, and behavioral problems than the children of older mothers. The billions of public tax dollars expended for health, educational, child and foster care, and other social services for adolescent parents and their children, as well as the loss in national productivity resulting from adolescent childbearing, while impossible to precisely calculate, are staggering. The private events of pregnancy and parenting during adolescence have been transformed into public issues, and they pose perplexing policy and service delivery dilemmas for social work, other service professions, and virtually all of American society.

DEFINING AND EXPLAINING ADOLESCENT PREGNANCY

While pregnancy itself is not a "problem," and most adolescent parents competently care for and love their children, a consensus has emerged among policymakers, service providers, and the public over the past forty years that *adolescent* pregnancy is a "problem," and that it is important to prevent teenage childbearing. Little consensus exists, however, about what the exact nature of the "problem" is, how to prevent it, or how to address it once it occurs.

Adolescence and parenthood are both major life events. Even when the adolescent passage is on course and parenthood is desired, adapting to both roles generates stress. When the demands of parenting occur simultaneously with adolescence, there is great potential for a "lack of fit" between a young person's capacity to assume a parental role and the social environment's ability and/or willingness to provide the resources they need.

For some, adolescent pregnancy is a moral issue: sexual intercourse before marriage is now and always has been unacceptable. Those who believe that consensual sexual activity during adolescence is appropriate behavior remain concerned when precautions are not taken to avoid pregnancy and STDs. Still others lament the excessive costs incurred by taxpayers who subsidize the health and social services young parents and their children need. Regardless of one's moral, political, or economic position, the concern of virtually all rises exponentially when sexual activity, pregnancy, or childbearing occur among young teens.

There are many reasons why adolescent pregnancy rates are higher in the United States than in other developed countries, why teens embark on the challenging career of parenting, and why many experience difficulties raising their children. Some explanations of adolescents' risk-taking behaviors reflect a perception of teenagers as being too impulsive to avoid "accidental" pregnancies. Such attitudes are observed when clinic staff complain that teens can find time to have sex, but not to keep clinic appointments.

A more benevolent understanding recognizes that while physical maturation occurs early and rapidly, the emotional and cognitive changes of adolescence ("adolescence" in fact means "to come to maturity") happen over time and usually involves trial and error. During adolescence, cognitive skills that facilitate contraceptive behaviors may not be fully developed, increasing susceptibility to unintended pregnancy. Unprotected intercourse may be a manifestation of adolescents' "personal fable"; i.e., their sense of being invulnerable to consequences experienced by others (Elkind 1978). Awareness of normal developmental tasks diminishes the tendency to criticize youth for not thinking ahead and may suggest instead a need for school "life skills training" interventions or greater access to contraceptives.

How a problem is "defined" ultimately influences how it is addressed (Germain and Gitterman 1996), and few issues better demonstrate this connection than the public policy response to adolescent pregnancy contained in recent welfare reform legislation. Childbearing by unmarried teens was a central issue throughout the debate leading up to the *Personal Responsibility and Work Opportunity Reconciliation Act*

(PL 104–193) of 1996, and many of the new law's provisions already affect how health and social services are provided to adolescents.

It is ironic that the debate leading up to PL 104–193, which essentially overhauled the Aid to Families with Dependent Children (AFDC) "welfare" program established by the Social Security Act of 1934, occurred during a period when teen pregnancy and birthrates were decreasing. Although these declines were encouraging, Congress and the public were increasingly disturbed by the fact that over 75 percent of teen births were to unmarried teens (in 1996), compared with only 16 percent in 1960 (Wertheimer and Moore 1998). Since teen parents rarely married, virtually all were eligible for AFDC cash benefits, which automatically qualified them for Medicaid and food stamps. Congress came to believe that overly generous AFDC entitlements provided incentives for low-income teens to have children in order to establish their own households. Unwed teen childbearing thus came to be understood as both a *cause* of escalating welfare costs, and a *consequence* of a system that encouraged dependency (Wertheimer and Moore 1998).

Several provisions of the Temporary Assistance for Needy Families (TANF) block grant that replaces AFDC are thus targeted at discouraging teenage childbearing by limiting access to cash assistance and social services. Whereas AFDC obligated states to match federal funding for low-income families, TANF does not give families (including those headed by teenagers) any guarantee of financial assistance. TANF grants states a fixed amount of funding and expects each to design and implement programs according to guidelines that essentially restrict assistance to minor teen parents. For example, states have the option of requiring individuals to file separate applications for Medicaid, food stamps, and TANF. Delinking cash assistance from medical insurance has already created confusing logistical and procedural barriers for eligible families, including those headed by teenagers.

Other provisions designed to discourage unmarried teen childbearing include: providing $50 million in funding for abstinence-only programs, school attendance and adult-supervised residency requirements for minor parents, and a five-year time limit on the use of federal TANF dollars to support cash aid (states can elect to provide additional assistance). No TANF funding is designated for family planning (although states can elect to use a portion of their block grant for such services), and no additional funding is guaranteed to support child care so teens can participate in mandated educational or training activities. Moreover, Medicaid can be terminated if a minor parent who is head of household refuses to work, even though states are not permitted to rescind benefits to nonparenting minors on this basis.

One of the most significant shifts in public policy inherent in the new welfare legislation is the termination of most of the federal government's monitoring and regulatory oversight of programs that help families. Under TANF, states are free to design their own programs, set program goals, and establish eligibility guidelines. States' responses to unanswered policy and programmatic questions such as the following will have a significant impact on what and how services are provided to adolescents, adolescent parents, and their children:

▪ **Adult-supervised residency requirements:** TANF mandates that adolescent mothers who are minors live in adult-supervised settings in order to receive benefits (exceptions include teens who have a history of or are at risk for abuse). States will need to strengthen linkages between local welfare and child protection agencies and establish assessment procedures to ensure that living arrangements are appropriate. Coresidence with maternal grandmothers, for example, is usually perceived as a protective factor for teen mothers and their children. Recent studies, however, suggest that older teens may provide more effective parenting when they live apart from their mothers while continuing to receive their emotional support and help with child care (East and Felice 1996). States may also need to expand group homes for teen mothers when their parental home is unsafe, despite the high short-term costs of such residences.

■ **Abstinence education:** TANF allocates $50 million each year for five years to fund programs that exclusively promote abstinence, but it targets no funding for family planning services. Each state is free to determine who these programs will target, even though research suggests that encouraging abstinence is only effective with younger teens who are not yet sexually experienced. States will need to monitor these programs carefully, since abstinence-only programs have not demonstrated consistent or significant effects delaying the onset of intercourse (Kirby 1997).

There is considerable evidence, on the other hand, that easy access to contraceptive services encourages sexually active adolescents to use birth control and that every dollar spent on contraceptive services for teens saves taxpayers an estimated $3 that would have been spent on pregnancy-related and newborn medical care (Alan Guttmacher Institute 1998a). Congress' choice not to mandate any TANF funding for family planning appears to ignore the reality of most teenagers' lives.

■ **Teen parent school requirement:** TANF mandates that teen mothers participate in educational activities. With little federal direction or oversight, each state is expected to design its own programs that help young mothers finish schooling and/ or vocational training and move on as quickly as possible from welfare to work. How "participation" is defined and how linkages between welfare and educational agencies can be improved to monitor and assist parenting teens, however, are not clarified under current TANF guidelines. Moreover, the questions of how to provide support services tailored to the educational needs of teen parents when alternative programs are not available and how to provide infant care so teen mothers can satisfy eligibility requirements are largely left unanswered.

Many researchers believe that the disincentives to out-of-wedlock births contained in welfare reform legislation are misguided and reflect a profound misunderstanding of adolescent sexual and childbearing behaviors. The belief that teenagers "plan" to get pregnant to obtain welfare ignores the fact that teen pregnancy and birthrates have been declining since 1991, while contraceptive use has been improving (Abma et al. 1997). A study by Adams and Williams (1990) found that while three-quarters of unmarried teen mothers began receiving AFDC within five years of the birth of their first child, several years often elapsed between giving birth and receiving cash benefits. Most young women apparently were not assuming that pregnancy automatically qualified them for welfare; efforts to restrict eligibility would therefore be unlikely to change their sexual and reproductive behaviors.

The vast majority of pregnancies to teens (85 percent) and adults (over 50 percent) are **unintended** (Alan Guttmacher Institute 1994). Moreover, while three-quarters of births to teens do indeed occur outside of marriage, nonmarital pregnancy and birthrates for women of *all* ages increased during the past few decades. Teens now account for only one-third of nonmarital births (Foster and Hoffman 1996) and make up a smaller proportion of births to unmarried women in 1996 than in 1970.

Sexual and reproductive behaviors do not occur in a vacuum. Young people are aware of the societal trend separating sex from marriage. Advertising, soaps, prime-time network and cable TV, movies, and videos contain pervasive messages that glamorize sexual activity while rarely mentioning contraception. Marriage occurs three to four years later, and unmarried couples are more likely to cohabitate than in the past (and with far less stigma) (U.S. Bureau of Census 1991). Four out of ten 14-year-old females live with single parents who have never married, are separated, or divorced (Alan Guttmacher Institute 1994), and two-thirds of formerly married women and men aged 20 to 44 are sexually active (Billy et al. 1993). Adolescent children of single parents who know their parents are sexually active outside of marriage are not likely to view nonmarital intercourse and childbearing as problematic (Trent and South 1992).

Premarital intercourse is the norm in virtually all modern industrialized societies, and more than 80 percent of young Americans are sexually experienced before they turn 20 (Alan Guttmacher Institute 1994). Many argue, therefore, that contraceptives should be made accessible by expanding family planning clinics and school condom distribution programs, while also implementing programs that help teens withstand pressure from peers and media to have sex. A competing view contends that sexuality education and contraceptive services send conflicting messages that confuse adolescents, reduce sexual inhibitions, and encourage sexual activity. This view appears to underlie TANF-funded abstinence interventions that prohibit providing information about contraception but encourage informing teens that contraceptives do not provide 100 percent protection against pregnancy or STDs.

Criticism that simultaneously promoting contraception *and* encouraging teens who are not sexually experienced to remain abstinent is confusing to adolescents appears to be unfounded. Evidence indicates that young people are capable of reducing sexual activity *and* increasing contraceptive use (Kirby et al. 1994), and that the best outcomes are achieved when health education occurs prior to the onset of sexual activity and when information about abstinence, contraception, and STD prevention is provided (Grunseit and Kippax 1993).

Research increasingly suggests that reproductive behaviors and outcomes are best understood in broader social contexts that consider the impact of poverty, educational and employment opportunities, neighborhood quality, and other environmental factors that impact on adolescents' perceptions of life opportunities (Dryfoos 1990). Common underlying risk factors such as school failure, involvement in "problem" behaviors, lack of familial support and attachment, and poverty are known to be associated with unintended pregnancy (Moore et al. 1995). Manlove (1998) found that a strong attachment to school was a protective factor associated with avoiding school-age pregnancy, suggesting the programs designed to keep girls attending school may reduce the incidence of teen pregnancies.

This broader understanding of adolescent pregnancy suggests that policy and programmatic responses need to address underlying risk and protective factors, rather than focusing exclusively on sexual behaviors. According to this perspective, interpersonal skills and accessible contraceptive services help adolescents avoid risky sexual behaviors but are not sufficient to enable them to sustain motivation to avoid pregnancy. Preventive interventions need to go beyond increasing knowledge, skills, and resources to promote the healthy development of young people; bolster protective factors of individuals, families, and groups; and reduce risk factors in adolescents' schools, communities, and social environments.

Comprehensive services need to be crafted, coordinated, and sustained particularly in communities characterized by poorly functioning and inadequately funded schools, where few adults demonstrate the link between successful schooling and satisfying employment. Investing in employment training that enables disadvantaged, minority males to secure decent jobs and be able to financially support their family, for example, may be the most effective way of addressing the multiple problems of female-headed low-income households. Redesigning schools so that learning activities connect education with the world of work may be the best way to boost adolescents' beliefs in a successful future and thus increase motivation to avoid pregnancy. Expanding GED programs, child care, and other supportive services may enable welfare agencies to connect teen parents to suitable school placements so they can satisfy TANF eligibility requirements. While such efforts to address the underlying predictors of early parenthood can be costly and time-consuming, in the long run they may prove to be the most effective way of preventing the interconnected problems of teen pregnancy, school failure, and other problem behaviors.

DEMOGRAPHIC PATTERNS

Adolescents, defined as youth 10 to 19 years old, comprised nearly one-fifth of the world's population, and numbered just over one billion, in 1995—913 million in developing countries and 160 million in developed countries (Alan Guttmacher Institute 1997). There are more than 38 million youth aged 10 to 19 in the United States (U.S. Bureau of Census 1998). Nearly 40 percent of these youth (two-thirds of black and Hispanic youth) live in poor or low-income families. The number of girls aged 15 to 19 is expected to increase by more than 2 million between 1995 and 2010 (U.S. Department of Health and Human Services 1995), increasing the population at risk for pregnancy.

Several new sources of data about adolescent sexual behavior, contraceptive use, and childbearing have become available in recent years. The National Survey of Family Growth (NSFG) and the National Survey of Adolescent Males (NSAM) provide the most recent data on trends in adolescent sexual behavior, contraceptive use, and childbearing. Both data sets provide comparable information from 1988 and 1995 (Abma et al. 1997; Sonenstein et al. 1998). The Youth Risk Behavior Surveillance System (YRBSS), a national survey conducted by the Centers for Disease Control and Prevention monitors health risk behaviors among male and female high school students (Kann et al. 1998), and the National Longitudinal Study on Adolescent Health provides additional information about teenagers' health behaviors as well as the social contexts that influence those behaviors (Resnick et al. 1997).

Sexual Activity. Being sexually experienced by age 19 is the norm among adolescents of all racial and ethnic groups and across all income levels. More than half of women now are sexually experienced before 18, compared with just over a quarter of women under 18 in the mid-1950s (Alan Guttmacher Institute 1994; Kann et al. 1998). While the proportion of sexually active teenagers increased and the age of first intercourse declined during the early 1980s, the proportion of 15- to 19-year-old females who were sexually experienced decreased from 53 percent to 50 percent between 1988 and 1995, reversing a twenty-year upward trend in the rate of teen sexual activity. Recent data from the 1997 YRBSS corroborates findings of the 1995 and 1988 NSFG: the proportion of female high school students who reported having had sexual intercourse decreased by 11 percent between 1991 and 1997 (Kann et al. 1998). Despite these declines, nearly three-quarters of 19-year-old females are sexually experienced (Moore, Driscoll, and Lindberg 1998).

At age 19, 85 percent of males have had intercourse (Sonenstein et al. 1997). Rates of male sexual activity also have decreased in recent years. While the proportion of never-married sexually experienced 15- to 19-year-old males rose slightly between 1979 and 1988, it declined from 60 percent in 1988 to 55 percent in 1995 (Sonenstein et al. 1998). Data from the 1997 YRBSS showed a similar trend: 57 percent of male high school students were sexually experienced in 1991 compared with 49 percent in 1997 (Kann et al. 1998). This decrease is attributable almost exclusively to white males: rates of sexual activity among black and Hispanic males were essentially unchanged between 1988 and 1995, while the proportion of white adolescent males who had had sex declined from 57 percent in 1988 to 50 percent in 1995 (Sonenstein et al. 1998).

The proportions of female and male teenagers who have had sexual intercourse varies by race and ethnicity (Moore et al. 1998). Among 19-year-olds, almost 90 percent of black females are sexually experienced, compared with 75 percent of non-Hispanic whites and Hispanics. Black teenage males begin having sexual intercourse earlier than whites or Hispanics: 60 percent of 15-year-old black males have had intercourse compared with 35 percent of Hispanic and 18 percent of whites. Racial and ethnic variations level off through the teen years so that among 19-year-olds, 94 percent of blacks, 87 percent of Hispanics, and 83 percent of white males have had sex (Moore et al. 1998).

Adolescent sexual activity is episodic. More than a quarter (28 percent) of sexually experienced respondents in the 1997 YRBSS were abstinent during the three months preceding the survey (Kann et al. 1998). NSAM data confirms that the majority of young men are not "sexual adventurers": while males report more sexual partners at every age than females, 52 percent of sexually experienced young men have intercourse fewer than ten times in a year, and over 50 percent have only one partner (Sonenstein et al. 1997).

Contraception and Condoms. Most teenagers use contraception the first time they have intercourse. Adolescents use birth control as effectively as unmarried young adults and have unintended pregnancy rates that are lower than unmarried women in their early 20s (Alan Guttmacher Institute 1994). Trend data from the 1995 NSFG and NSAM show that contraceptive use among sexually active adolescent females and males increased over the past two decades (Abma et al. 1997; Sonenstein et al. 1998): 77 percent of teenage females whose sexual debut occurred between 1990 and 1995 reported using contraception at *first* intercourse compared with 71 percent who became sexually active between 1988 and 1990, and 53 percent who first had sex between 1980 and 1982. In 1995, 84 percent of unmarried teenage females who had sex in the past three months used some form of contraception at *last* intercourse.

Contraceptive use at first intercourse was highest among white female adolescents and lowest among Hispanics. In 1995, 83 percent of white females aged 15 to 19 used contraception at first intercourse compared with 72 percent of black and 52 percent of Hispanic adolescent females. Sexually active Hispanic female adolescents also reported the lowest rate of contraceptive use at *last* intercourse (74 percent), compared with 86 percent of black and 85 percent of white adolescent females (Abma et al. 1997; Donavan 1998).

Much of the increase in contraceptive use among teenagers over the past two decades is attributable to a dramatic rise in condom use, probably due to greater awareness of the health threat posed by HIV and other STDs. The proportion of adolescent female contraceptive users relying on condoms increased slightly between 1988 and 1995 from 33 percent to 37 percent (Donavan 1998); 78 percent of teen females aged 15 to 19 used some form of contraception at first voluntary intercourse. Most females who used a method during first intercourse relied on condoms (66 percent) (Moore et al. 1998). In 1995, 90 percent of never married, sexually experienced 15- to 19-year-old males used a condom at least once during the past year (Sonenstein et al. 1997). Sixty-seven percent used a condom at last intercourse (74 percent of black, 67 percent of white, and 58 percent of Hispanics), up from 57 percent in 1988 (Sonenstein et al. 1998).

While condom use has increased, the proportion of teen women who use the pill, withdrawal, and other barrier methods has declined. Overall, the method most commonly used by teenagers is still oral contraceptive pills (44 percent in 1995, down from 64 percent in 1982), followed by the condom (38 percent in 1995, up from 21 percent in 1982), the injectable Depo-Provera (10 percent), withdrawal (4 percent), and the implant Norplant (3 percent) (Kaiser Family Foundation, Alan Guttmacher Institute, and National Press Foundation 1998).

Although consistency of condom use has improved among sexually active males in recent years (45 percent reported using condoms at every act of intercourse in 1995, compared with 33 percent in 1988), there is still great cause for concern. Many males and their sexual partners continue to be at risk for transmission of STDs (including HIV) since almost half do not use condoms at each act of intercourse, and almost 10 percent never use them. Sexually active Hispanic males and their sexual partners are at particularly high risk: fewer than one-third used a condom consistently, compared with almost half of non-Hispanic black and white male adolescents (Sonenstein et al. 1998). While contraceptive use among females increases with age, the risk of STDs remains high since condom use declines as men get older and increasingly rely on their partners' use of hormonal contraceptives. Since females have a 40 percent chance of being infected with chlamydia as a result of even one act of unprotected intercourse with an infected partner, there is little room for error.

Pregnancy and Birthrates. Adolescent pregnancy and birthrates have declined in recent years, reflecting teens' decreasing rates of sexual activity and increasing rates of contraceptive use. Still, the United States has the highest pregnancy and birthrates of any industrialized country—nearly twice as high as Great Britain, four times that of Sweden, and fifteen times greater than Japan (United Nations 1991). While some argue that the ethnic diversity of the United States is responsible for these dramatic variations, the birthrate of white adolescents alone surpasses the birthrates of other industrialized nations.

Pregnancy rates, which include births, abortions, and miscarriages, declined among females aged 15 to 19 in the 1990s after increasing 7 percent between 1985 and 1990, and peaking at 117 pregnancies per 1,000 females in 1990. The pregnancy rate for 15- to 19-year-olds declined 17 percent between 1990 and 1996, and stood at 97 pregnancies per 1,000 in 1996, the country's lowest rate since 1975 (Alan Guttmacher Institute 1999). Among sexually experienced males 15–19, 14 percent have made a partner pregnant (Sonenstein et al. 1997).

The teenage birth rate also declined between 1991 and 1996, from 62 to 55 births per 1,000 females aged 15 to 19 (Donavan 1998; Moore et al. 1998), reflecting an overall 11 percent reduction in the national birthrate between 1990 and 1995 (Ventura et al. 1997). Birthrates among 18- to 19-year-olds (87 per 1,000) were double those of 15- to 17-year-olds (34 per 1,000) (Wertheimer and Moore 1998). Declines in teen birthrates occurred in all fifty states and among all racial and ethnic categories. As a result, the overall number of births to teens declined between 1991 and 1996, from 519,600 annually to 494,300 (Donavan 1998). The rate of second births for teens decreased dramatically (21 percent) between 1991 and 1996 (National Center for Health Statistics 1998).

Half of teenage pregnancies end in a live birth, one-third in abortion, and the remainder in miscarriage. Adoption is rare. Since fewer teenagers are becoming pregnant and fewer pregnant teens are choosing to have an abortion, abortion rates among 15- to 19-year-old females decreased 29 percent between 1985 and 1994 (Kaiser Family Foundation et al. 1998). Adolescents account for 22 percent of all abortions performed each year (Henshaw and Frost 1996).

There are significant racial and ethnic differences in teen pregnancy and birthrates. While half of pregnant teens aged 15 to 19 are white, white teenagers are less likely to give birth at any age than are blacks and Hispanics (Ventura et al. 1997). Birthrates of 15- to 19-year-old females in all racial and ethnic categories declined between 1991 and 1996; however, the largest reduction (21 percent) occurred among black teenagers. There were 92 births per 1,000 black teens aged 15 to 19 in 1996, compared with 48 per 1,000 among white teens and 102 births among Hispanic teens. Among Hispanic groups, rates were highest for Mexican American and Puerto Rican adolescents (National Center for Health Statistics 1997).

Substantial variation in the incidence of teenage childbearing is also observed across states and regions of the country. While birthrates declined in all fifty states between 1990 and 1996, they ranged from as low as 29 births per 1,000 females aged 15 to 19 in New Hampshire to 86 births per 1,000 in Mississippi. Birthrates in the Sunbelt states are typically twice as high as those in the upper New England states (Wertheimer and Moore 1998). Striking differences in pregnancy and birthrates have important implications, because many provisions of the 1996 welfare legislation are targeted at reducing teen pregnancy but allow states a great deal of autonomy in crafting welfare and educational programs for sexually active and parenting teenagers.

SOCIETAL CONTEXT

The adolescent passage from childhood to adulthood is no longer viewed as a life stage in which turmoil is unavoidable (Offer 1987). It is, however, a transitional period filled with risks and opportunities, and the demands of raising a child significantly compounds those challenges. Like any developmental stage, adolescence is "stressful." Teens need to adapt to profound and rapid physical, emotional, cognitive, social, and behavioral changes.

Mastery of stage-appropriate tasks occurs in social contexts. Families and friends, neighborhoods and schools, local employment opportunities, health and social services, physical environments, the media, public policies, and structural forces (e.g., shifts in the labor market) all potentially function as protective factors that promote competency and residency, or as risk factors that hinder development and increase the likelihood that adverse consequences will be experienced.

American adolescents are bombarded every day with sexual messages from advertising, television, music videos, films, and other media. Network and cable TV, for example, can enhance adolescents' reproductive health by providing realistic information that enables them to make informed decisions. Unfortunately, programs are more likely to glamorize and accentuate the benefits of sexual behavior while making scant reference to contraception or the risks of unprotected sexual activity: primetime TV shows contain an average of twenty-eight references to sexual behavior each hour compared with one reference to contraception, abortion, or STDs (Alan Guttmacher Institute 1994).

The interval between when adolescents are biologically capable of getting or making someone pregnant and when they get married has doubled over the past century, significantly extending the period during which sexual "risk" behaviors and adverse consequences can occur. In 1890, seven years separated when a girl had her first menstrual period and when she got married. In 1988, median ages of menarche, first intercourse, and marriage were 12.5, 17, and 24 years of age; median ages for male spermarche, first intercourse, and marriage were about 14, 17, and 27 (Alan Guttmacher Institute 1994).

Whereas puberty and sexual intercourse occur at younger ages than in the past, many transitional markers of adulthood now are delayed well into the 20s. Establishing economic and emotional independence by moving from school to full-time employment has been pushed back considerably. Over half of 20- to 24-year-olds continue to live with their parents (U.S. Bureau of Census 1998). Ten percent of American youth were disconnected (i.e., out of school, not working, not in the military, and not married) for at least one year between the ages of 16 and 23 (Brown 1996). Manufacturing jobs that once provided low-skilled workers with decent wages, benefits, and a sense of purpose have vanished from inner cities and relocated to regions with lower overhead and plentiful sources of inexpensive labor (Wilson 1996); far more than a high school diploma or GED is required for employment in today's service-oriented job market.

The impact of social and physical environments is underscored by wide discrepancies in teen pregnancy rates among the fifty states: while New Hampshire and other New England states have achieved rates as low as those of other industrialized countries, Mississippi and other southern states have rates that are three times as high (National Campaign to Prevent Teen Pregnancy 1997). Several factors account for these differences, including discrepancies in adolescents' access to health and social services in different regions of the country.

Variations in state funding for family planning and abortion services result in uneven access to reproductive health services. Nearly every state uses federal funds for family planning services for teens, but overall funding for pregnancy prevention interventions varies from zero to $78 per female aged 15 to 19 (Wertheimer and Moore 1998). All the states use federal and state Medicaid monies to pay for prenatal and childbirth services, but most allow state Medicaid monies to be used only for termination of pregnancies that result from rape or incest, or when termination is medically necessary to save the mother's life. Currently, only sixteen states use state Medicaid funds to pay for medically necessary abortions for poor women (including poor teenagers) (Alan Guttmacher Institute 1998b). While other factors explain why nearly three-quarters of accidental pregnancies to teens from affluent families are resolved by abortion compared with less than half of accidental pregnancies to poor teens, restrictions on public financing of abortion clearly play a major role.

Other adolescent health-related public policies also provide support and generate stress. With the exception of abortion, the trend in recent decades has been toward allowing teenagers to make many of their own reproductive health decisions. Opinion polls indicate that there is support for making condoms available in public schools, but only 418 high schools elected to do so during the 1997–98 academic year (Dodd 1998). School-based clinics increased from 327 to almost 1,000 between 1991 and 1996, but local policies prohibit three-quarters of clinics from dispensing contraception. Accessing care at school clinics in rural areas is particularly problematic: less than half treat STDs (compared with 68 percent in urban areas), and less than one-third offer HIV testing (compared with almost half of urban clinics) (Fothergill 1998).

Family planning and community health clinics provide adolescents with ready access to contraception since they often have convenient hours, cost less than private physicians, and do not require parental consent. Funding for the federal Title X family planning program, however, decreased over 70 percent (adjusting for inflation) between the early 1980s and 1990s (Daley and Gold 1993), resulting in fewer clinic hours and higher fees. Cutbacks also limit the ability of family planning programs to invest in initiatives that increase male involvement, since programs typically respond by limiting support for male services (Brindis et al. 1998).

Despite evidence that comprehensive sexuality education programs help adolescents delay intercourse and increase use of contraception, no federal policy mandates sexuality or HIV education. Only twenty-three states and the District of Columbia *require* that schools provide sexuality education, and only thirty-seven states and the District of Columbia *require* STD or HIV/AIDS education. The federal government also refrains from dictating the content of programs, allowing states to determine standards and curricula. Of the twenty-six states that require abstinence education, only fourteen mandate that information about contraception, pregnancy, and STDs be provided, and five states restrict discussion of abortion (Siecus Fact Sheets 1998).

Service providers and parents are environmental resources that can help teens adapt to the challenges of adolescence and parenting or contribute to maladaptive outcomes. Unfortunately, one-third of 15-year-old females say their parents have not talked to them about how pregnancy occurs, and half say their parents have not discussed birth control or STDs (Alan Guttmacher Institute 1994). Less than half of teen males receive information about contraception from parents (Sonenstein et al. 1997). Most teens are sexually experienced before turning 20, but health providers rarely discuss reproductive health issues with them. Adolescent males report that doctors and nurses are their least frequent source of contraceptive information (Sonenstein et al. 1997).

VULNERABILITIES AND RISK FACTORS

Several publications have summarized the antecedents of adolescent pregnancy in recent years (Kirby 1997; Moore et al. 1995). A number of interrelated characteristics of adolescents, their peer groups, families, and communities have been found to be associated with sexual and contraceptive behaviors. Knowledge of these character-istics enhances social work interventions with youth and guides efforts targeted at modifying environments that increase the risk of pregnancy and parenting problems.

Individual Characteristics. Adolescents at highest risk of becoming pregnant are likely to be living in poverty, doing poorly in school, involved in other problem be-haviors, and to have low expectations for their future. Girls who have low grades, a history of grade retention, and low expectations for continuing schooling are more likely to have sex at an early age (Santelli and Beilensen 1992) and to become teen parents than higher-achieving peers (Maynard 1995). White and Hispanic girls who leave school before graduating are more likely to become pregnant than girls who stay in school (Manlove 1998). Boys who are two or more years behind in school are more likely to be sexually active than those who are in a grade that is appropriate for their age (Moore et al. 1998; Sonenstein et al. 1997).

Adolescents involved in smoking and other "problem" behaviors (Robinson et al. 1998) are more likely to be sexually active. Young men who use illegal drugs and who have been arrested or been in jail are more likely to be sexually active than those who don't use drugs and who haven't been involved in the juvenile justice system (Sonenstein et al. 1997). Girls who have been pregnant are at higher risk for pregnancy than girls who have never been pregnant (Resnick et al. 1997).

Age is strongly associated with contraceptive use: the younger girls are when they begin having intercourse, the less likely they are to use contraception (Alan Guttmacher Institute 1994). While developmental issues such as a false sense of in-vulnerability (Elkind 1978) and difficulty planning ahead (Kirby 1997; Zabin 1994) contribute to the difficulties adolescents have using contraception, almost four in ten of the girls who have their first sexual intercourse at age 14 or younger say that sex was unwanted (Moore et al. 1998). Being coerced into having intercourse obviously makes it impossible for a young woman to insist that protection be used. Among males, condom use declines with age as they develop longer relationships and in-creasingly rely on female hormonal methods of contraception (Sonenstein et al. 1998). While these methods provide protection against pregnancy, STD risk remains high, since adolescent males are more likely than females to have multiple partners (Kann et al. 1998). Young men who believe condoms reduce pleasure and are inconvenient use them less (Sonenstein et al. 1997).

Other factors associated with early onset of sexual activity are early puberty; believing that one's life span will be short (Resnick et al. 1997); having favorable attitudes toward premarital sex, pregnancy, and childbearing; and believing that friends are sexually active (Robinson et al. 1998). Teens who have multiple partners, negative attitudes toward contraception, and low confidence (self-efficacy) in their ability to use contraception are more likely to engage in risky sexual behaviors (Kirby 1997).

There are significant racial and ethnic variations in adolescents' sexual and contraceptive behaviors. Black males and females have intercourse earlier than whites or Hispanics and thus experience longer periods of exposure to the risks of pregnancy and STDs. Although female Hispanic adolescents have lower rates of early sexual experiences, they are less likely to use contraception than their black or white peers (Alan Guttmacher Institute 1994). Hispanic adolescent males are less likely to use condoms than black and white males (Sonenstein et al. 1998).

Studies have documented a high incidence of sexual abuse among pregnant teens and teen mothers (Boyer and Fine 1992). Stock et al. (1997), for example, found a strong association between sexual abuse and teen pregnancy; they suggested that sexually abused girls are more likely to have intercourse with multiple partners before age 15 and are less likely to use contraception. Teenagers with a dual-risk background of sexual abuse and history of parental alcohol abuse report higher levels of risky sexual behaviors than teenagers with only one risk factor (Chandy, Blum, and Resnick 1996).

Family Characteristics. Adolescents who live in poor and low-income families with parents who have low levels of education are more likely to be sexually active, less likely to use contraception, and more likely to experience pregnancy and childbearing than their more affluent peers (National Center for Children in Poverty 1996). Daughters of mothers who gave birth to their first child before age 20 are more likely to become mothers as teenagers than daughters of women who were not teen mothers (Moore et al. 1998). Having an older sister who gave birth as an adolescent is associated with early initiation of sexual activity. Adolescents who don't feel supported by their parents are more likely to give birth as a teenager (Jaccard, Dittus, and Gordon 1996).

More than 80 percent of adolescents who give birth are from poor or near-poor families (U.S. Department of Health and Human Services 1995); as family income rises the proportion of adolescents who become teen mothers decreases. While some poor youth may be less motivated to avoid pregnancy than affluent peers because they view their future less hopefully, policies such as prohibiting Medicaid reimbursement for abortion explains much of the discrepancy in birthrates among SES groups.

Community Characteristics. Adolescents at highest risk for early, unintended pregnancy are more likely to live in communities with high rates of poverty, high residential turnover, low levels of parental education, high rates of divorce and single parenthood, high rates of nonmarital births, high unemployment, and poor labor force opportunities (Kirby 1997; Moore et al. 1995; Wilson 1996). Youth in poor neighborhoods have less proof of the link between educational success and good jobs. They see fewer working families, have limited exposure to neighbors owning or employed in local businesses, and have weaker connections to entry-level jobs. When adults do work, it is often in low-wage jobs that do little to inspire enthusiasm.

Since support for schools is closely tied to tax revenues generated in local communities, schools in poor areas are often overcrowded, in poor physical condition, and lack safe and constructive after-school activities. Funding for extracurricular athletics have been seriously reduced in many urban school districts over the past twenty-five years, limiting teens' opportunities to celebrate their competency and become attached to school through nonacademic activities. Few after-school programs meet the criteria suggested by Kerewsky and Lefstein (1982): diverse activities, time for reflection, meaningful participation, and positive interactions with adults and peers. When programs exist, participation may be discouraged by parents who fear their children being out alone in unsafe neighborhoods.

Young parents need an array of health, educational, and social services to effectively cope with the challenge of caring for children. Critically needed services, however, are often unavailable to teens who need them most. Affordable infant and child care enables young parents to participate in mandated school and employment training activities, yet the United States is one of few industrialized nations without a coherent child care policy. As discussed earlier, new TANF provisions fail to provide sufficient funding for child care that enable young mothers to participate in educational and training activities required by recent welfare legislation.

Adolescents suffer greatly from unprotected sexual activity. They are at risk of STDs, parenthood, and premature birth.

STDS. Sexually active teens are at higher risk for STDs than other age groups because they are less likely to be married than adults (and therefore more likely to have multiple sexual partners), because of the high prevalence of STDs among teens (Institute of Medicine 1996), and because condom use is sporadic. Each year three million teens acquire an STD; one in three sexually active people have had an STD by the time they are 24 (Alexander et al. 1998).

Teenage girls are very vulnerable to cervical infections such as gonorrhea and chlamydia since these STDs easily infect the immature cervix (Donavan 1993). While gonorrhea rates have fallen in the population as a whole, rates remain disproportionately high among teens and minorities (Alexander et al. 1998; Kaiser Family Foundation et al. 1998). Teenage females have the highest rate of gonorrhea, while the rate for teen males is exceeded only by 20–24 year olds (Office of National AIDS Policy 1996). In some studies, 30 to 40 percent of sexually active teenage women (Institute of Medicine 1996) and 10 percent of sexually active teenage males (Schacter 1989) were infected with chlamydia. Since bacterial infections like chlamydia frequently do not produce symptoms, adolescents are likely to delay seeking health care, leaving them at risk for complications such as pelvic inflammatory disease, infertility, and tubal pregnancy.

Incurable viral STDs also pose serious threats to adolescent health. Two-thirds of female undergraduates at a major East Coast university tested over a three year period were infected with HPV, strains of which are linked with cervical cancer (Kaiser Family Foundation et al. 1997). By the end of 1997, almost three thousand teenagers were known to have AIDS (Kaiser Family Foundation et al. 1998). While the number of AIDS cases among teens is small, adolescents account for half of the forty thousand people diagnosed each year with HIV.

Adolescent Parenthood. While many of the consequences of adolescent childbearing are associated with the educational and economic disadvantages young women experience before pregnancy, having a baby as a teenager compounds these difficulties considerably. Compared with women who delay childbearing, adolescent parents and their children are at greater risk for adverse educational and economic consequences including: less educational attainment, higher rates of single parenthood, larger families, and greater reliance on public assistance (Maynard 1996). Teenage mothers are more likely to experience violence during and after their pregnancy than older women (Gessner and Perham-Hester 1998). The 175,000 mothers who are 17 or younger and their children are at particularly high risk.

Becoming a parent during adolescence makes it less likely that mothers will complete high school and attend college: three out of ten adolescent mothers attain their high school diploma by age 30, compared with three-quarters of women who delay having children until after 20 (Maynard 1996). While the discrepancy in school achievement between adolescent and older mothers is reduced by teen mothers' higher rates of completing GEDs, the earnings gap between the two groups remains significant. Low educational levels coupled with limited work experience and child care demands contribute to adolescent parents' high levels of unemployment. As the qualifications for employment in today's service economy rise, teen mothers without a high school diploma are at a disadvantage and are often limited to low-skill, low-paying jobs.

Climbing out of poverty is challenging for young mothers since they tend to have more children than women who delay childbearing. Twenty-five percent of teen mothers have a second child within twenty-four months of their first birth, and the rate is even higher for the youngest teen mothers. Under AFDC, women who became mothers as teenagers were more likely to be relying on public assistance in their 30s than women who delayed childbearing even until their early 20s (Alan Guttmacher Institute 1994).

Children of Teen Parents. The younger a pregnant teen is, the less likely she is to receive prenatal care during the critical first trimester of pregnancy. Because of inadequate prenatal care, the children of teen mothers are more likely to be born prematurely and low birth weight (Wolfe and Perozek 1997), increasing the likelihood that they will experience respiratory infections and other chronic health problems, as well as dyslexia, hyperactivity, and other disabling conditions (Maynard 1996).

Because teen mothers themselves are still developing, they are often unable to provide the kind of environment that is optimal for an infant's development. Their children live in less supportive home environments (Moore, Morrison, and Green 1997) and are more likely to experience abuse and neglect (George and Lee 1997) than children of older mothers (Moore et al. 1995). Measured against national norms, homes headed by adolescent mothers are in worse physical condition and have fewer educational resources such as toys, books, and educational games (Maynard 1996). Children of adolescent mothers score lower on achievement tests (Moore et al. 1995), and their cognitive and developmental delays contribute to academic and behavioral difficulties that get worse over time (Alan Guttmacher Institute 1994).

Compared with children from two-parent households, the children of single adolescent parents are more likely to drop out of school, repeat a grade, have a lower grade point average, and have poorer school attendance (McLanahan 1994). As adults, they are less likely to be working than their peers whose mothers delayed having children until their early 20s (Haveman, Wolfe, and Peterson 1997). Later in life, their sons are 13 percent more likely to experience incarceration, and their daughters 22 percent more likely to themselves become teen mothers (Maynard 1996).

RESILIENCIES AND PROTECTIVE FACTORS

Just as individual and environmental factors increase adolescents' risk of pregnancy and the likelihood of experiencing problems raising children, several factors protect them from involvement in risky behaviors and increase the resiliency of those who are parents.

Individual Characteristics. Positive school experiences and feeling connected to school are among the most frequently cited protective factors that reduce adolescents' risk of pregnancy and contribute to positive educational, social, health, and economic outcomes for adolescents who are parents. Studies throughout the world have demonstrated that schooling is strongly associated with young women's motivation and ability to delay childbearing. Only 19 percent of Colombian teenagers with seven or more years of education had a child by age 20, compared with half of young girls with less than seven years of education (Alan Guttmacher Institute 1997). Feeling emotionally connected to school (e.g., feeling close to classmates and teachers) is associated with teens' decisions to delay sexual activity (Resnick et al. 1997), and academic success and high expectations for postsecondary education are associated with a reduced risk of pregnancy (Manlove 1998). Girls who stay in school and continue living with parents after giving birth have lower rates of subsequent births (Manlove 1998).

Having religious and moral beliefs that premarital sex is immoral (Moore et al. 1998) and clear intentions to avoid pregnancy and STDs (Moore et al. 1998; Resnick et al. 1997) are strong protective factors that motivate young girls to abstain from sex. Positive attitudes toward condoms and contraception, and a history of effective contraceptive use at first and most recent intercourse, also reduce an adolescent's susceptibility to early pregnancy (Resnick et al. 1997). Having friends who use condoms and feeling confident in one's ability to insist that a partner use condoms are associated with condom use.

Family Characteristics. Adolescent females raised from birth by both parents have lower probabilities of being sexually active at any age and are less likely to give birth in their teens than girls from other family situations (Moore et al. 1998). Having strong emotional attachments to parents (Blum and Rinehart 1997; Resnick et al. 1997) and receiving family encouragement and supervision (Danziger 1995) help teens delay sexual activity. Clear parental messages discouraging early dating (Santelli and Beilensen 1992) and early sexual activity (Resnick et al. 1997) appear to protect adolescents from early sexual activity and pregnancy. When dating does occur, structured and consistent rules reduce the likelihood of risky sexual behaviors, especially when limit setting occurs in the context of an affectionate parent-child relationship (Santelli and Beilensen 1992). Parental involvement in adolescents' schoolwork also is associated with a reduced risk of pregnancy (Manlove 1998).

Community Characteristics. Neighborhoods, communities, states, and regions of the country vary in the extent to which they help promote the reproductive health of adolescents. Attending a school with a high daily attendance rate, for example, is negatively associated with early sexual activity and pregnancy (Resnick et al. 1997). Seventeen percent of seventh and eighth graders report having had sexual intercourse (Resnick et al. 1997) and as discussed earlier, many of these youth have sex against their wishes. While having accessible reproductive health services, including provision of early education on how to avoid unwanted sexual advances, enables adolescents to protect themselves from the adverse consequences of unprotected intercourse, only nineteen states have an official policy requiring or encouraging pregnancy prevention programs in public schools. Two-thirds of states offer family planning services to teens statewide, but only three offer contraceptive clinics in schools (Wertheimer and Moore 1998).

Accessible prenatal and other health services, as well as social and educational services matched to the needs of pregnant and parenting adolescents, increase their resiliency and capacity to adapt to the stress of raising children. Affordable child care and support and guidance from grandparents and their children's fathers also help buffer parenting adolescent parents and their children from negative outcomes.

PROGRAMS AND SOCIAL WORK CONTRIBUTIONS

Pregnancy Prevention. Schools, churches, government, and community-based organizations have developed numerous programs to prevent unintended teenage pregnancy and to improve outcomes for young parents and their children. While there is almost unanimous agreement that preventing teenage pregnancy is a desirable goal, formative and outcome evaluations have not kept pace with these interventions. As a result, there is little consensus on what to do on an individual, community, or national level.

A summary of approaches to reduce teen pregnancy by Kirby (1997) classifies interventions according to five categories: curriculum-based programs, contraceptive access programs, programs for parents and families, multicomponent programs, and youth development programs.

Several **educational/training programs** have been implemented in schools and community-based organizations to modify adolescents' sexual behaviors and prevent unintended pregnancy (Barth 1992; Howard and McCabe 1990). While the components, intensity, target populations, and evaluation rigor vary among programs, most emphasize abstinence or delaying sexual activity, interpersonal skills training (particularly resistance and negotiation skills), and sexuality and contraceptive education. Some programs focus on STD/HIV prevention, while others increase access to contraception.

Analysis of the impact of sexuality and STD/HIV preventive educational programs has demonstrated that when interventions are well designed, they can be successful in helping teens delay intercourse (especially if younger teens are targeted), reduce the frequency of intercourse and number of sexual partners, increase contraceptive and condom use, and even reduce pregnancy (especially when teens are helped to access contraception) (Frost and Forrest 1995). The "Reducing the Risk" curriculum (Barth 1992), for example, successfully reduced the likelihood students would initiate intercourse, increased contraceptive use among sexually active youth, and increased parent-child communication about sexuality. Theory-based, well-implemented educational interventions combined with contraceptive access does not hasten the onset of intercourse or increase the frequency of sexual activity (Kirby 1997).

As discussed earlier, "abstinence-only" programs that focus on delaying sexual intercourse until marriage have received considerable attention (and funding) in recent years. These programs provide moral support and teach interpersonal skills to help young teens resist peer and media pressure, but they do not discuss contraception. A review of several published studies of abstinence-only programs failed to identify any that consistently and significantly delayed the onset of intercourse (Kirby 1997).

According to Kirby (1997), the following are characteristics shared by programs that have demonstrated positive changes in adolescent reproductive behavior:

∎ a focus on reducing specific sexual behaviors (e.g., refusing to be pressured into having sex) that lead to pregnancy or infection
∎ behavioral goals, teaching methods, and materials that are developmentally and culturally appropriate, and that are matched to the level of sexual experience of participants
∎ theoretical grounding in models of behavior change (e.g., social learning theories, social influence theories)
∎ interventions that are of sufficient duration to have an impact, and that include follow-up
∎ provision of accurate information about methods of avoiding unprotected intercourse
∎ experiential, interactive teaching methods to help participants personalize information
∎ activities that address social pressures to have sex
∎ opportunities to practice communication, negotiation, and refusal skills (e.g., role playing)
∎ selection and sufficient training for teachers and peers who believe in the program

Family planning and school-based clinics, and condom availability programs in schools, have demonstrated that it is possible to **reduce sexual risk taking** and **increase contraceptive use** by sexually active teens (Kirby 1997).

Family planning clinics provide contraception and reproductive health services including individual and group education and counseling to help adolescents learn about and use contraception. Publicly funded family planning clinics are an important source of contraceptive services for teenagers. Three in ten individuals using publicly funded family planning clinics are younger than 20 (Alan Guttmacher Institute 1998a).

In some family planning clinics, social workers provide case management services and counseling to teens who are in crisis (e.g., deciding how to resolve an unplanned pregnancy) or who are facing serious psychosocial problems (e.g., domestic violence). Social workers supervise public health, medical, and social work students and adult volunteers who design and implement psychoeducational waiting room groups, and directly provide short-term group work services for high-risk adolescents with a history of pregnancy and sexual abuse.

School-based clinics numbered almost 1,000 in 1996 (Fothergill 1998). These clinics reduce barriers to health services and increase adolescents' access to affordable medical, mental health, health education, and social services. As discussed earlier, however, obstacles still impede students from obtaining reproductive health services at these sites. Three-quarters of school-based clinics serving adolescents are prohibited by school policies from dispensing contraception.

Realizing that sexual activity is prevalent among junior high school students (Resnick et al. 1997) and that 20 percent of first pregnancies to adolescents occur within one month of initiating sexual intercourse (Hatcher et al. 1994), junior high school–based clinics in an underserved urban community implemented an intensive risk-identification and case management intervention to help teens access contraception (Tiezzi et al. 1997). Under the supervision of social workers, graduate students conducted confidential schoolwide risk factor screening surveys to identify students who were sexually active and those who had characteristics associated with sexual activity. Students identified through the survey were assessed by clinic social workers, and those at risk for pregnancy were invited to participate in yearlong groups at the school. Students received ongoing individual counseling and case management services throughout junior high school and the first year of high school. Special arrangements were made to link at-risk youth at the nearby family planning clinic and when necessary, school clinic staff met students there to help them register. As a result of these activities, pregnancy rates in program schools decreased by 34 percent.

Condom availability programs in schools make condoms accessible through specially trained counselors and teachers, vending machines, and other distribution channels. Despite opinion polls indicating overwhelming public support for these programs and research showing that distribution programs increase sexually active students' condom use without encouraging sexual activity (Guttmacher et al. 1997; Schuster et al. 1998), only 418 high schools in the United States elected to initiate such programs during the 1997–98 academic year (Dodd 1998).

Several types of **parent-child programs** have been implemented to increase communication about sexual topics, including programs for parents only, programs that bring parents and children together, and sexuality education classes that assign homework assignments requiring students to communicate with parents at home about sexuality issues. Evaluations of these programs consistently show that parent-child communication and levels of comfort around sexuality increase over the short term but dissipate over time, and that such programs do not increase adolescents' use of contraceptives (Kirby 1997).

Multicomponent programs encompass a wide array of community and media activities. One program that resulted in decreased pregnancy rates among 14- to 17-year-old participants in a rural community included sexuality education training of teachers, community leaders, and peers; implementation of sex education in all grades; health education counseling; condom distribution and family planning referrals by the school nursing staff; and community-wide broadcasting of pregnancy prevention messages by media, churches, and community groups (Koo et al. 1994). Pregnancy rates rose after parts of the program ended (i.e., links to contraceptive services were severed; key teachers left the school system), underscoring the importance of continuous programming and follow-up to help at-risk youth avoid risky, unprotected sexual behaviors.

Youth development programs build on a growing body of evidence that improving young women's educational, employment, and life options reduces pregnancy and birthrates. These programs typically do not focus directly on sexuality issues but seek to increase motivation to avoid pregnancy by building "life skills" and increasing teens' awareness of life options. Connecting youth with adult mentors and involving them in community service projects are common elements of such programs.

Youth development programs frequently link substance abuse, delinquency, pregnancy, and dropout prevention efforts on the premise that these "problem behaviors" share a common etiology. Problem behaviors such as early sexual activity and substance use are viewed as serving important functions such as satisfying human needs for group belonging and a sense of competence. These programs are typically comprehensive, targeted at young adolescents, and sustained over a prolonged period of time, in contrast to brief categorical programs that begin only after problems are well entrenched.

One extensively evaluated program that reduced pregnancy rates included weekly classroom discussions of values, decision-making and communication skills, human growth and development, interpersonal relationships, as well as volunteer community service (Allen et al. 1997). Hypothesized explanations for the program's success were that students had opportunities to develop close personal relationships with adult staff, had fewer opportunities to be involved in problem behaviors because of involvement in prosocial program activities, and developed a sense of purpose and a more hopeful view of future options because of their gratifying volunteer experiences.

Adolescent mothers, especially those who come from poor and low-income families, are more likely than mothers who delay childbearing to need assistance from their families and publicly funded programs. Even prior to the provisions set forth in TANF and throughout the new welfare reform legislation, almost three-quarters of teen parents under 18 were living with one or both of their parents (Alan Guttmacher Institute 1994).

For a variety of reasons (e.g., safety concerns, staff shortages), few programs use *home visitation* to young parents' homes to engage them in services. Recognizing that many teen parents are isolated or overwhelmed by the demands of child rearing, however, social workers in some family agencies use home visits as a primary service modality. Through aggressive and continuous outreach, parents are helped to access services, negotiate complex bureaucracies, and experience less social isolation. Home visits by nurses during pregnancy and the first two years of life have resulted in improved birth weights and reduced rates of child abuse and neglect among the children of adolescent parents (Olds et al. 1986), and lower rates of second pregnancies (Olds et al. 1997).

Pregnant and parenting teens have numerous psychosocial needs and experience a wide range of problems that require them to interact with a service delivery system that is often fragmented and confusing. *Case management programs* provide intensive, long-term, personalized support across a range of areas affecting adolescent parents and their children (Carlson, Abagnale, and Flatow 1993; Fischer 1997). Such support has been found to improve birth outcomes and child health (Smith et al. 1990). This approach requires highly trained staff different from that of welfare eligibility workers and can be expensive since caseloads need to be relatively small (forty cases or less) in order to be effective. Case managers need to be flexible and capable of locating and developing cooperative relationships with a variety of services.

As compared with a problem-centered, fragmented approach in which an agency or worker addresses only specific problems it is prepared to handle itself, case management is designed to address the many needs of adolescent parents who require services from more than one source. Core functions of case managers include assessment of parents' needs, developing individual service plans, coordinating referrals, counseling and crisis intervention, brokering and advocating for parents as they contact other service agencies, outreach to families and partners, arranging transportation, and monitoring and revising service plans as needed. In addition, case managers identify gaps in existing services, especially where client demands exceed existing services' capacity to respond.

Several teen parent programs designed to improve the economic outcomes and overall well-being of young mothers and their children have employed a comprehensive and intensive set of integrated services, including case management, and have resulted in some positive effects on adult outcomes of low-income participants who began the program as teenagers (Granger and Cytron 1998). In some cases, monthly earnings and completion of GED programs increased, and reliance on welfare decreased among participants who completed programs. While participants had higher employment rates, they also had higher job turnover than women in comparison groups. The mixed results of these interventions underscored several areas where services needed to be improved, including providing more consistent follow-up, improving family planning services, providing more continuous child care, and increasing attention to mental health needs.

Group living arrangements provide support to pregnant and parenting adolescents who lack sufficient adult and peer support, and a secure residence for youth whose parental homes are unsafe. Social workers in residential programs for young parents and their children arrange for comprehensive and coordinated services that match the multiple and shifting needs of these clients. In transitional shelters, workers help parents obtain scarce permanent housing by assisting in housing searches and coaching mothers how to interview for publicly funded apartments. Through individual and group interventions, mothers receive emotional support as well as training in parenting and independent living skills. Workers arrange for assessment and placement in educational or vocational programs and facilitate referrals to medical, day care, and recreational services. Aftercare case management is provided to ease transitions to more permanent settings.

Adolescent parents are also served in a variety of *community-based agencies.* Comprehensive parenting programs provide on-site child care while young mothers and fathers receive instruction leading to their GEDs. Young parents participate in individual counseling as well as group activities that bolster their home management skills and enable them to prepare for and obtain scarce resources. Helping mothers anticipate bureaucratic barriers and confusions stemming from recent welfare reforms that delink TANF, Medicaid, and food stamp applications increases the likelihood that services will be obtained.

In addition to learning parenting skills such as how to soothe an upset child, young parents are helped to work through unresolved issues emanating from past frustrations with their own childhood experiences. When parents are unable to attend classroom and group activities because of other more pressing needs, workers adapt by advocating for them at court hearings, or brokering for them at housing and employment interviews. Home and office visits may be alternated as the teen parent grows to trust the worker. Respite care is provided through a developmental playroom so that young mothers can use other agency services and have time for themselves. Recreational outings and activity groups (e.g., sewing classes) cultivate skills while enhancing social contact with peers. Parenting groups bolster parents' capacity to respond to their children. In addition to encouraging mutual aid, workers negotiate conflicts, as when peers challenge a mother to weigh the costs of staying in a relationship with an abusive boyfriend.

ASSESSMENT AND INTERVENTIONS

Social workers assess where a poor fit exists between what adolescents need to avoid pregnancy or to raise their children, and how environments respond to those needs. Assessments include an evaluation of protective factors that buffer adolescents from risk, as well as factors that contribute to their susceptibility to early pregnancy and problems raising children. Thorough and accurate assessments increase the likelihood that interventions will be appropriately targeted at bolstering individuals' adaptive capacities, modifying environments, or both.

Reproductive and parenting behaviors result from interactions between people and their social environments. Sexual behaviors take place in the "life space," i.e., an open system with interrelated parts that include adolescents, their families and friendship networks, service agencies, neighborhoods, and other social and physical environments. Unprotected intercourse, for example, can result from an imbalance between teenagers' basic need for accurate information, adaptive capacities such as communication or help-seeking skills, and the qualities of their real or imagined environments (e.g., availability of family planning clinics, estimations of friends' sexual activity).

Assessment entails gathering and making sense of such factors as (1) the adolescent's perception of the "problem" (e.g., whether the pregnancy was planned or not), (2) the adolescent's capacity to satisfy needs and solve problems (e.g., parenting skills), and (3) the adequacy of environmental resources (e.g., nature of the teen mother's relationship with her own mother). Connections between the system's components are also assessed (e.g., whether mother and father are willing to be resources for each other).

In addition to age, SES, and family intactness and functioning, other important considerations in assessing the risk for unplanned pregnancy are the adolescent's (1) knowledge of reproductive facts, (2) capacity to plan and communicate, (3) educational functioning and aspirations, (4) beliefs and attitudes, as well as perceptions of peer, family, and community norms about sexual and reproductive behaviors, (5) patterns of sexual activity, (6) involvement in other problem behaviors, and (7) relationships with sexual partners. The availability of health education and contraceptive, educational, and social services and supports also needs to be considered.

To make informed decisions about their reproductive health, adolescents need accurate information, as well as cognitive and interpersonal skills. Youth may be motivated to avoid pregnancy, but still take risks because of inaccurate information or because of difficulties planning ahead (e.g., "She was a virgin so I thought I didn't need a condom"; "Sex just happened"). Adolescents who are failing in school and who have low educational aspirations are at high risk for unplanned pregnancy. When conception occurs, early parenthood may be perceived as having few "costs" since positive future life options are vague or appear unattainable.

Believing that "everyone has sex but me" can be a discomforting thought for young people during a developmental stage when peer group acceptance is critical. Ambivalence about having sex, on the other hand, may contribute to delays seeking contraception (e.g., "I don't need the pill because I'm not *that* kind of person"). Young men may hesitate to discuss condoms because they think their partner will be insulted ("Don't you trust me?"). Family, peer group, and community norms and expectations in turn influence personal beliefs. Early childbearing may be reinforced by cultural expectations that a woman's place is in the home raising children, not pursuing higher education.

Substance abuse, school truancy, fighting, reckless driving, and other problem behaviors are signals that an adolescent may be involved in risky sexual behaviors. Patterns of sexual activity and the nature of relationships with sexual partners also affect reproductive decision making. For example, since adolescents' sexual activity is sporadic, planning and using contraception can be difficult. Adolescents in long-term, committed relationships may not use condoms because they trust each other, disregarding the fact that HPV and other viral infections from former relationships can be transmitted. Large age discrepancies between younger adolescents and older males are of particular concern and need to be addressed directly but without alienating and losing contact with the adolescent female.

Especially during times of scarce resources, it is easy for mismatches to occur when teens seek help from formal agencies. Free or low-cost family planning services may not be available. Clinics may not have evening or weekend hours. Uninviting attitudes of overwhelmed receptionists may discourage youth from returning for follow-up visits. Young people may view hospital- or school-based clinics as places where people with emotional problems or STDs go. Difficulties following through on referrals may arise from adolescents' perceptions and fears that parents will be informed of their sexual activity.

The availability and adequacy of family support such as help with child care need to be determined since such assistance helps buffer many of the stresses of parenthood. Family involvement can also generate stress, however, as when grandparents function as "gatekeepers" between a young couple. Paternal grandparents may blame their son's partner for interfering with his future career. Maternal grandparents may reprimand a young father for his inability to fulfill the role of "breadwinner." Even when the teen parent lives at home, tension can arise from overcrowding or a grandmother's difficulty resolving her disappointment with her child. Partner involvement can also alleviate or exacerbate the stress of parenting. A young father's "in-kind" baby-sitting contributions temporarily give a young mother respite from the demands of parenting. On the other hand, mothers who had been making great strides toward establishing independent living may withdraw from programs and become less responsive to their child because of contact with less stable partners.

Assessment may determine that helping interventions be targeted not directly at the adolescent, but at service providers and organizational policies and procedures. Difficulties experienced by young mothers at maternity residences may be intensified due to the unrealistic expectations of caretakers who act out their resentment at being excluded from agency decision making. Social work interventions might target agency practices and arrange for child care staff to be included in case conferences. Sex education programs may not be adopted in a school or school district because of concern about parents' reactions. Meeting with principals and attending parent and school board meetings to inform influential decision makers about research that demonstrates how well-implemented programs reduce sexual risk behaviors without increasing sexual activity may assuage concerns.

Numerous "teachable moments" are lost because of health and social service providers' failure to routinely ask adolescents about their sexual activity. As discussed earlier, adolescent males report that doctors and nurses are their least likely sources of contraceptive information. Only 15 percent of females said they discussed STDs with their medical provider at their first routine visit (Kaiser Family Foundation et al. 1998). A study of rural junior high school students showed that while only 11 percent had sexual intercourse, over 30 percent were involved in heavy petting. Even a well-intentioned provider's question, "Did you ever have sex?," might elicit a "no" response and fail to address the risky sexual situations in which adolescents are engaged. Social workers can make a significant contribution to improving the quality of adolescent health care by conducting in-service training for medical and nursing staff so that they feel more comfortable and competent taking thorough sexual histories during routine office or clinic visits.

Adolescents' capacity to obtain needed resources can also be bolstered if workers prepare them for encounters with agency staff and make themselves available to encourage teens to persist when difficulties are encountered. Providing pregnant teenagers with anticipatory guidance regarding the two-step process now required for TANF and Medicaid applications, helping them assertively ask for application forms, guiding them as they assemble necessary documentation, and role-playing intake interviews empowers them to secure important services.

Since all parts of an open system are related, change in one area brings change elsewhere. Linking a grandmother to a support group can reduce her isolation, diffuse some of the friction that arises over child-rearing practices, and free up more of her energies to help her parenting daughter or son. Helping a young father maintain contact with his partner and child even if they are not cohabiting can have positive effects for all involved. Advocating with school personnel for an expeditious transfer to a smaller alternative high school or a more flexible GED program may be a critical first step toward preventing a young mother from becoming demoralized, leaving school, and experiencing the negative consequences such a choice brings.

Worker roles and helping responses need to be flexible and multifaceted. A school social worker may conduct life space interviewing in the gym and hallways to improve outreach to at risk students. By venturing out of the clinic, the worker may reach more clients, make quicker assessments, and promptly discuss ways to reduce risks. Because the needs of adolescents are numerous, interventions need to employ a variety of helpers. To reduce the perception that a family planning clinic was far away, a school social worker had students make a narrated videotape of the walk from school to clinic and used it in classroom presentations. Older sisters can be encouraged to accompany younger pregnant siblings to prenatal appointments. Fathers at a young parents program can do phone outreach to their peers whose attendance is decreasing.

ILLUSTRATION AND DISCUSSION

Social workers play important roles in family planning and parenting service programs. The following practice illustration describes interventions implemented by two social workers at a community-based, hospital-affiliated family planning program in a low-income urban community. Programmatic examples and case vignettes are drawn from the workers' efforts to engage adolescent and young adult males in family planning and parenting services, an area of service delivery that is beginning to receive long-overdue national and international attention.

Family planning and parenting services for men have lagged far behind those directed at women, and the few programs that have been implemented have been difficult to sustain. Over the past decade however, there has been a growing recognition in both national and international circles that male involvement in reproductive health services can contribute to improved health, social, and economic outcomes for young men, as well as their partners and children. Research with men that can inform practice, however, is limited. Fortunately, the workers' kept themselves informed about the results of national surveys (e.g., the National Survey of Adolescent Males), maintained connections with local, regional, and national task forces and consortia that addressed men's reproductive health issues, as well as reviewed publications of model male involvement prevention and parenting programs published in recent years (Levine and Pitt 1995; Sonenstein et al. 1997).

Problem Identification. The workers were aware of research documenting the important role men played in couples' reproductive decision making and health outcomes (e.g., Drenan 1998) and were concerned over program data indicating a high incidence of repeat pregnancies and recurring STDs among female patients at their clinic. They began exploring the possibility that increasing male involvement might be an important intermediate objective to reducing adverse reproductive health outcomes among female clinic patients. They wondered why young men were so underserved at their clinic (only 2 percent of documented clinic visits were by males), despite their observations of significant numbers of men sitting with their partners in the clinic waiting room and lingering in front of the clinic building.

The workers obtained approval from clinic administration to respond to a request-for-proposals (RFP) announcement from their state health agency and were successful in securing a small grant to study males' perceived barriers to involvement in family planning, parenting, and reproductive health services. Through focus groups and in-depth qualitative interviews of adolescent and adult community residents, they learned that young men viewed the clinic as an "unfriendly" place that was "for women only," and that they were embarrassed to access its services. Coaches, teachers, and youth leaders also informed the workers that few services existed for young men to obtain physical exams needed for participation in sports, work, and school, and adolescent focus group participants suggested that emotionally "safe" entry points such as a sports medicine clinic would be needed to "hook" sexually active young men and fathers to reproductive health and parenting services.

Building on this information and the credibility earned by such intimate knowledge of the gap between community needs and resources, the workers collaborated with program administrators to obtain sufficient public and private grant funding to open a clinic session "for men only" and to "outpost" the workers to the women's family planning clinics as well as carefully selected school-based clinics and community-based organizations.

Asset Mapping. The social workers created an "ecomap" diagramming the formal and informal places men gathered (e.g., playgrounds, schools, after-school programs, social clubs) and collected information from the local community board, local school district, churches, youth associations, and informal community leaders to identify the health, recreational, employment, educational, and legal resources available to young men. The workers were particularly interested in identifying high-quality employment and alternative educational programs since adult and adolescent "key informants" indicated that many of the neighborhood's young men were "disconnected" from school and work.

Building on the clinic's close ties to nearby schools of public health and social work, graduate students were recruited to help the clinic build its knowledge of community resources. Workers organized students' explorations of TANF centers; employment and GED programs; public health STD, working paper, chest, and sports physical clinics; anonymous HIV test sites; dental clinics; and programs for young parents and incorporated findings in the clinic's referral manual. For example, a student visited local welfare offices ("job centers") to gather detailed information about application procedures for TANF, Child Health Plus, and Medicaid. The student described the facilities, created maps to show clients how to reach the centers, described the ambiance of the settings, and outlined application procedures. The student identified direct and indirect procedural barriers to accessing services, such as agency workers' failure to inform TANF and Medicaid applicants of the federal food stamp program. The student alerted staff that the centers seemed to discourage applicants by turning away those who failed to arrive early in the morning. Clinic workers utilized the students' findings to provide clinic patients with anticipatory guidance prior to their visiting the public welfare offices to begin their applications.

Outreach/Casefinding. The social workers identified and engaged sexually active young men and young fathers through a variety of methods including visits to the venues where men congregated (e.g., social clubs) as well as through "gatekeepers" such as their female sexual partners, family planning and other service staff, and peer leaders.

For example, the workers knew that men were reluctant to enter the clinic building, preferring rather to wait outside smoking cigarettes and conversing with other men, so they periodically visited those *life spaces:*

The worker noticed Mark leaning against the building smoking a cigarette, approached him and introduced himself, and engaged him in casual conversation. He learned that Mark, 22, was waiting for his 26-year-old girlfriend to learn the results of a pregnancy test. He said he had accompanied her to the clinic because "I'm part of this" and intended to support her decision to terminate the pregnancy if the test was positive. Mark said he was already the father of a 4-year-old girl by another woman. He provided some financial support, visited her periodically, and occasionally took her for day trips. He was keenly aware that he was in no position to have a second child. Mark acknowledged that he had only completed eighth grade, that he had difficulty reading, and had been unable to find work because of his limited skills and history of incarceration for drug dealing.

When the worker asked why Mark wasn't inside the clinic he responded ". . . it's a man thing . . . it's all women in there . . . it's not that I'm nervous; I just don't feel like I belong." He noticed that all the pictures on the walls were famous women, and that the HIV education film depicted a man verbally abusing his partner.

Mark said that he had not had a physical exam in several years. He had been treated for gonorrhea while he was in jail, knew that infections could be asymptomatic, but only used condoms sporadically. He had never been taught how to examine his own testicles. Mark said he often "worried" about his health but was "afraid to come to a place like this" for an examination. The worker informed Mark that the men's clinic's medical and social services were free or low-fee and specifically tailored to address the health and psychosocial needs of men and assured him that he would assist him in the registration process. By the end of the conversation, Mark agreed to come see the worker at the clinic the following week.

Mark's hesitation to enter the clinic is typical of many young men, but the worker's genuine, nonjudgmental, and proactive interest in his concerns empowered him to take a first step accessing the services he knew he needed. While Mark's use of contraceptives was sporadic, he demonstrated "responsibility" through his supportive presence at his girlfriend's pregnancy evaluation exam. The worker selectively attended to Mark's strengths, including even his small financial contributions and participation in his daughter's child care and emotional development. Through this brief exchange, the worker and Mark collaboratively identified several areas for work including: reconnecting him to education and employment and taking better care of his physical health. Mark's observations about the clinic's "unfriendly" ambiance spoke volumes and prompted the worker to propose small changes to clinic administrative staff (e.g., purchasing and hanging up pictures of accomplished African-American and Hispanic men; selecting a less provocative HIV health education film).

Female patients at the family planning clinic were key gatekeepers targeted by the social workers. The workers trained family planning nurse practitioners and reception staff to open up discussions with female patients about their male partners so that they would refer men to the clinic. Reception staff, for example, were trained to mention the men's clinic when they made telephone appointments for young women; nurses and nurse's aids were trained to offer condoms to young men returning to have their PPD tuberculin skin tests read.

Public health students designed and implemented waiting-room group education activities in the family planning clinic waiting room with the goal of increasing referrals of male partners to the men's clinic. The students first conducted focus groups to learn females' suggestions and concerns regarding male involvement, and they ultimately developed brief groups with the following foci:

▮ teaching women about testicular cancer to capitalize on their positive feelings for their partners and to suggest a "safe" way to open up conversation about men's health services,

▮ informing women about the asymptomatic STDs like chlamydia and the need for men and women to have periodic screening,

▮ brainstorming and role playing ways to initiate conversations with male partners about family planning, and

▮ providing mutual support for women publicly deciding to refer and make appointments for their partners, and arranging specific appointment dates. Public health students guaranteed that they would also be at the men's session and would expedite registration into the clinic.

Peer leaders at the local high school served as gatekeepers for sexually active and parenting adolescents at their school. A worker was outposted to the high school to lead bimonthly groups with the school's youth leadership group. The worker conducted "life skills training" including role-playing interpersonal communication skills. In return, students and their faculty liaison provided sustained broadcasting of clinic services through a variety of distribution channels within the school. Students organized and implemented classroom activities about HIV, maintained a bulletin board for announcements and information about reproductive health and parenting issues, and distributed clinic brochures in school offices, the cafeteria, at sporting events, and other venues. Youth leaders were given clinic T-shirts and key chains, and movie tickets, as a reward for their participation in outreach activities.

Young fathers often functioned as gatekeepers for the mothers of their children, informing them of services and supporting them and their children in ways that extended beyond providing financial support:

Carlos, 19, initially came to the clinic for treatment of a chlamydial infection. He was referred to the social worker by a medical student counselor who thought he was depressed. The worker helped Carlos acknowledge that he was "down" and felt stressed because his girlfriend was pregnant. He felt badly that he had to go back to Puerto Rico because his mother was ill, and was unable to commit to any further contact with the worker.

Several months later, Carlos reappeared to inform the worker that he had received a bill requesting payment for lab tests performed at his last clinic visit. The worker reassured him that this was an error and that he would resolve the issue with clinic administrators; he then proceeded to ask Carlos about his mother, the pregnancy, and his depression. Carlos was clearly pleased that the worker remembered him and reported that his mother was better, that he felt less stressed, and that his girlfriend had given birth to a baby boy. Carlos said that he had been present at the birth and had established paternity. The worker attended to his successes and praised him for acknowledging paternity. The worker asked how he could be of further assistance and learned of several areas where Carlos wanted help.

Carlos and his partner had resumed sexual relations but were not using contraception. Carlos admitted that he hated to use condoms and said that his 18-year-old partner couldn't use any birth control because "they make her sick." She was interested in the IUD but felt sure that no medical provider would give her one because of her age. The worker informed the couple that he and the family planning nurses would help them think through their options and provide some method, since neither Carlos or his partner wanted another child.

Carlos indicated that his partner and child were living with her mother and that they were not currently receiving TANF or Medicaid. Carlos said he felt too proud to let his child go on "welfare" and described a confusing, frustrating, and frightening visit to a "job center" shortly after the child's birth. The worker empathized with Carlos's desire to provide for his child "like a real man" but suggested that together they work to secure any benefits to which he, his partner, and child were entitled. The worker capitalized on Carlos's obvious love for his infant son to help him stay engaged in the TANF and Medicaid application processes. He also informed Carlos of the nearby Department of Labor employment office that was setting up a special program for young fathers who needed GED and employment skills training and arranged to meet him there for his application interview with that agency's social worker. The worker sustained contact with Carlos via telephone and letters (e.g., periodically sending him information on normal child development) to ensure that his partner's family planning appointments were kept, and his own health care, educational, and employment needs were addressed.

Provider Training. Health care providers, especially primary care physicians (e.g., family practice, pediatrics, and internal medicine) and nurses, and social service staff need to be more proactive in discussing sexual issues with male and female patients. Recent data from the NSAM and other studies suggest that numerous "teachable moments" are missed when adolescents have contact with health and social service providers.

To contribute to medical education at their affiliated medical school (thus building the clinic's reputation at the medical center), and at the same time to augment the health education and medical staff available to examine young men, the social workers recruited physicians from the hospital's pediatric and family practice residency programs, as well as undergraduate medical students looking to acquire their first glimpses of clinical practice. Resident physicians increased the numbers of providers (and thus the number of young men able to receive physical examinations) at each clinic session at no cost to the program and tightened linkages between the men's clinic and the pediatric and family practice ambulatory clinics at the hospital. In turn, physicians satisfied their adolescent medicine residency requirements.

The social workers trained volunteer first-year medical students to take comprehensive psychosocial assessments and sexual histories, to identify psychosocial needs (e.g., unemployment, depression, relationship problems), and to make referrals for social work services. The workers trained students to use the "BIHEADS" mnemonic (Cohall and Mayer-Cohall 1995) to help them comprehensively assess risk and protective factors in young men's lives:

BI body image

H   home environment, relationships with parents; general health

E   educational progress, performance, and aspirations; school environment

A   use of time, hobbies, peer networks

D   drug, alcohol, and cigarette use; depression; diet

S   sexual history, including sexual behavior, contraceptive use, pregnancy, parenting, abortion, STDs, HIV risk assessment, and relationships; sleeping patterns; history of suicidal ideation or behaviors

The counseling approach focused on identifying strengths as central to the helping process (e.g., "tell me your strongest subject at school"), rather than focusing only on deficits, dysfunctions, failures, and problems. Medical students sought to empower patients by bolstering their sense of competence so that they become "partners" with clinic staff in bringing about changes in their lives, including increasing their use of condoms, increasing their support of partners' use of contraception and, if they were a father, increasing their level of involvement with their child.

Social workers developed a training module to ensure that the health education and counseling provided by residents and medical students fit the clinic's empowerment philosophy of providing care. Students were taught to build relationships with patients by "selectively attending" to their accomplishments and health-promoting behaviors (e.g., saying to a young man who recently began using condoms after years of taking risks, "It's great that you've figured out how to make this change in your behavior; how did you manage to do that?"). In asking about school, students were trained to reword questions to empower young men (e.g., asking out-of-school youth "How did you decide to leave school before graduating?," not "Why did you 'drop out'?").

Outposting Staff. To reduce barriers between existing services, conserve institutional resources, and avoid duplication of services, collaborative arrangements were established between the clinic and selected community-based social services that served men. The workers took extra steps to establish linkages with a community employment agency that had direct ties to the Department of Labor and its computerized network of jobs and job training services. Workers from the clinic and the agency visited each other several times to establish trust and to carve out how each could help the other. The clinic workers learned that the agency needed space to conduct groups with young fathers and health services so men could complete physical exams required by employers. The agency in turn realized that young patients at the clinic (including young fathers) needed its high-tech employment services. Institutional arrangements were established to colocate staff in each agency. A "Memorandum of Understanding" (MOU) formalized linkages between the two programs. Several appointment slots were reserved at the clinic for men from the agency, and these youth were given priority status upon arrival. Similar arrangements were made for men's clinic patients at the employment agency.

Clinic social workers were periodically outposted to the employment agency and other sites. In addition to working directly with young men, workers provided in-service training to help providers at these sites expand their role and improve their comfort and skill levels for assessing and referring young men at risk for reproductive health problems. In turn, employment agency social workers were periodically outstationed to the men's clinic to broadcast their services and provide informational sessions on how to search for employment and how to apply for tuition assistance for school and vocational training. Discussions were videotaped and shown during subsequent clinic sessions when employment agency staff were unable to attend. Realizing the common concern each agency had for working with fathers, workers from both groups colead parenting education/father's groups in the clinic's attractive and spacious group room.

Case Management. Realizing that young men, especially young fathers, have multiple problems and needs and often require services from several unconnected resources, clinic social workers provided time-limited, strategic case management to high-risk young men and young fathers to promote service coordination and strengthen linkages among agencies and workers. Case management services included assessing client needs, collaboratively developing individual service plans, coordinating referrals, advocating with service providers when needed, engaging family members and female partners, monitoring delivery of services, and providing ongoing and crisis intervention counseling as needed. Workers also identified resource gaps (e.g., inadequate and developmentally inappropriate GED programs) and institutional barriers to obtaining existing services (e.g., "job centers'" failures to inform individuals of their right to apply for food stamps independent of eligibility for other programs) and intervened on a larger systemic level (e.g., blending clinic and agency missions by collaboratively seeking new sources of funding; reporting unauthorized eligibility procedures at local "job centers" to state-level social service authorities).

Group Work. Young fathers were recruited to participate in parenting workshops designed to promote positive parenting practices, foster healthy father-child relationships, and reduce the stresses associated with parenthood. A graduate public health student conducted a "needs assessment" of fathers attending the clinic to determine their social, financial, emotional, legal, and health needs; to learn of barriers to obtaining assistance they had experienced in the past; and to inquire about ways to help fathers achieve their desired relationships with their children.

Identified barriers included: lack of adequate time with their children due to geographic barriers and job requirements, relationship difficulties with their child's mother, trouble reconnecting to school and finding adequate employment, and inadequate information about parenting that undermined their confidence disciplining and educating their children. Requested services included information on developmental stages, discipline practices, education, and relationships; help finding jobs; and information about legal issues related to children. Fathers suggested that small groups be held in the early evening and on Saturday mornings, that bilingual brochures on child development be made available in clinic waiting rooms, that videotapes on child development and parenting be shown while men waited for medical exams, and that social workers be accessible by phone to answer specific questions related to parenting practices and their own psychosocial and interpersonal needs. Building on this information and the collaboration with the nearby employment agency, a monthly father's group was established at the clinic and coled by workers from both agencies. The clinic social worker continued to collect names of prospective group members at each clinic session and called fathers the day before each session took place. A monthly fathers' newsletter listing employment opportunities, tips on parenting, and brief health facts (e.g., how to lower cholesterol; how to reduce stress) was created and a computerized distribution list kept updated by public health students.

Social workers also supervised public health students who designed and conducted *waiting room groups* to (1) create a friendlier clinical ambiance while patients waited for physical exams, health education, and social work counseling, (2) provide basic education about STDs, condoms, male and female anatomy, the male reproductive health exam, and female methods of contraception, (3) practice condom use and partner communication skills, and (4) elicit, challenge, and reinforce behavioral, normative, and self-efficacy beliefs related to male reproductive health behaviors such as communicating with partners about contraception. Students let research and behavioral theory inform practice. From the NSAM, for example, they learned that diminished sexual pleasure and inconvenience interfered with males using condoms. Research and "practice wisdom" indicated that men were concerned that using a condom insulted women ("you think I have an infection?"), and that condom use declined with age as men increasingly relied on female methods of contraception. Behavior theory further suggested that skills and the intention to perform specific behaviors, as well as ready access to resources (e.g., clinics) influenced whether health behaviors occurred. Intentions were in turn influenced by (1) perceptions that the benefits of the behavior outweighed costs, (2) social norms and networks that supported the behavior (e.g., "most of my friends use condoms"), and (3) self-efficacy beliefs, i.e., that one could competently perform the behavior ("I am confident in my ability to use condoms or talk to my partner"). Students developed a slide show and discussion guide to ensure that salient beliefs were examined, and designed brief role plays to engage men in practicing condom use and partner communication skills, exploring their sexual behaviors and examining their beliefs (challenging, e.g., the belief that "women are insulted if you take out a condom").

CONCLUSION

The majority of sexually active adolescents successfully avoid pregnancy, and most young parents competently and lovingly care for their children. The serious adverse consequences of early, unintended parenthood experienced by many American teenagers, however, should cause public concern and demand creative and sustained responses by the social work profession. Far too many teens find their youth curtailed, their adulthood rushed, and their life options limited by too early pregnancy. Early parenthood brings the "psychosocial moratorium" of adolescence—i.e., that period of commitment-free time "granted to somebody who is not ready to meet an obligation" (Erikson 1968)—to an abrupt halt. Prematurely assuming the exhausting responsibilities of raising a child too often curtails educational pursuits and the development of basic skills. Lacking "employability" skills and adequate social supports, young parents are at a disadvantage when competing with their better prepared peers and often suffer serious long-term economic hardships. As a result, the stage is set for an intergenerational cycle of economic dependency, unfulfilled dreams, and underachievement.

While teen pregnancy is not a "new" problem, it should evoke an increased sense of urgency as the twenty-first century begins. There are more adolescents in the world than ever before, and the next generation will be even larger (Bos et al. 1994). Just as there is no one "cause" of unintended pregnancy, there is no one simple solution. Multiple strategies need to be crafted so that teens obtain accurate information about sexuality, develop the cognitive and interpersonal capacities that facilitate safe sexual behaviors, and have access to health and parenting support services. Adolescents also need opportunities to acquire basic skills that open up possibilities for adequately paying employment. Above all, they need to cultivate a reason for delaying parenthood built on a hopeful sense that future options are available and within their reach. Given the high personal and public costs involved, it is imperative that social workers continue to contribute to both the prevention of unintended pregnancy and the promotion of competent child rearing by adolescent parents.

References

Abma, J., A. Chandra, W. Mosher, L. Person, and L. Piccinino. 1997. "Fertility, Family Planning, and Women's Health: New Data from the 1995 National Survey of Family Growth." *Vital Health Statistics.* Hyattsville, Md.: National Center for Health Statistics, U.S. Department of Health and Human Services, PHS 97-1995.

Adams, G. and R. C. Williams. 1990. *Sources of Support for Adolescent Mothers.* Washington, D.C.: Congressional Budget Office.

Alan Guttmacher Institute. 1994. *Sex and America's Teenagers.* New York: Author.

———. 1995. *Hopes and Realities: Closing the Gap Between Women's Aspirations and Their Reproductive Experiences.* New York: Author.

———. 1997. "Issues in Brief: Risks and Realities of Early Childbearing Worldwide." http://www.agi-usa.org/pubs/ib10.html (February 1997).

———. 1998a. "Facts in Brief." New York and Washington, D.C.: Alan Guttmacher Institute (January).

———. 1998b. "Facts in Brief." New York and Washington, D.C.: Alan Guttmacher Institute (February).

———. 1999. "Facts in Brief." New York and Washington, D.C.: Alan Guttmacher Institute (September).

Alexander, L. L., J. R. Cates, N. Herndon, and J. M. Ratcliffe. 1998. "Sexually Transmitted

Diseases in America: How Many Cases and at What Cost?" Research Triangle Park, N.C.: American Social Health Association.

Allen, J. P., S. Philliber, S. Herrling, and G. P. Kuperminc. 1997. "Preventing Teen Pregnancy and Academic Failure: Experimental Evaluation of a Developmentally Based Approach." *Child Development* 64:729–42.

Barth, R. P. 1992. "Enhancing Social and Cognitive Skills." In B. C. Miller et al., eds., *Preventing Adolescent Pregnancy*, pp. 53–82. Newbury Park, Calif.: Sage.

Billy, J. O. G., K. Tanfer, W. R. Grady, and D. H. Klepinger. 1993. "The Sexual Behavior of Men in the United States." *Family Planning Perspectives* 25:52–60.

Blum, R. W. and Rinehart, P. M. 1997. *Reducing the Risk: Connection That Makes a Difference in the Lives of Youth*. Minneapolis, Minn.: University of Minnesota, Division of General Pediatrics and Adolescents.

Bos, E., M. T. Vu, E. Massiah, and R. A. Bulatao. 1994. *World Population Projections 1994–95 Edition: Estimates and Projections with Related Demographic Statistics*. Baltimore: Johns Hopkins University Press.

Boyer, D. and D. Fine. 1992. "Sexual Abuse as a Factor in Adolescent Pregnancy and Child Maltreatment." *Family Planning Perspectives* 24:4–11.

Brindis, C., J. Boggess, F. Katsuranis, M. Mantell, V. McCarter, and A. Wolfe. 1998. "A Profile of the Adolescent Male Family Planning Patient." *Family Planning Perspectives* 30(2):63–66, 88.

Brown, B. V. 1996. "Who Are America's Disconnected Youth?: Final Report." Washington, D.C.: Child Trends, Inc. Paper presented for the American Enterprise Institute.

Carlson, B. E., C. Abagnale, and E. Flatow. 1993. "Services for At-Risk, Pregnant, and Parenting Teenagers: A Consortium Approach." *Families in Society: The Journal of Contemporary Human Services* 74(6):375–80.

Chandy, J. M., R. W. Blum, and M. D. Resnick. 1996. "History of Sexual Abuse and Parental Alcohol Misuse: Risk, Outcomes and Protective Factors in Adolescents." *Child and Adolescent Social Work Journal* 13(5):411–32.

Cohall, A. T. and R. Mayer-Cohall. 1995. "Screening for Psychosocial Health Problems." *Contemporary Adolescent Gynecology* (Winter):11–14.

Daley, D. and R. B. Gold. 1993. "Public Funding for Contraceptive, Sterilization, and Abortion Services, Fiscal Year 1992." *Family Planning Perspectives* 25:244–51.

Danziger, S. K. 1995. "Family Life and Teenage Pregnancy in the Inner-City: Experiences of African-American Youth." *Children and Youth Services Review* 17(1–2):183–202.

Dodd, K. J. 1998. "School Condom Availability: The Facts." Washington, D.C.: Advocates for Youth.

Donavan, P. 1993. *Testing Positive: Sexually Transmitted Disease and the Public Health Response*. New York: Alan Guttmacher Institute.

——. 1998. "Falling Teen Pregnancy, Birthrates: What's Behind the Decline?" *The Guttmacher Report* 1(5):6–9.

Drenan, M. 1998. "Reproductive Health: New Perspectives on Men's Participation." *Population Reports*, Series J, Number 46, Baltimore, Md.: Johns Hopkins University School of Public Health, Population Information Program.

Dryfoos, J. G. 1990. *Adolescents at Risk: Prevalence and Prevention*. New York: Oxford University Press.

East, P. L. and M. E. Felice. 1996. *Adolescent Pregnancy and Parenting: Findings from a Racially Diverse Sample*. Mahwah, N.J.: Erlbaum.

Elkind, D. 1978. "Understanding the Young Adolescent." *Adolescence* 13(49):127–34.

Erikson, Erik H. 1968. *Identity, Youth, and Crisis*. New York: W. W. Norton.

Fischer, R. L. 1997. "Evaluating the Delivery of a Teen Pregnancy and Parenting Program Across Two Settings." *Research on Social Work Practice* 7(3):350–69.

Foster, E. M. and S. D. Hoffman. 1996. "Nonmarital Trends in the 1980s: Assessing the Importance of Women 25 and Over." *Family Planning Perspectives* 28:117–19.

Fothergill, K. 1998. "School-Based Health Centers Hindered in Offering Reproductive Health Care to Students." *Transitions.* 10(1):1–3.

Frost, J. J. and J. D. Forrest. 1995. "Understanding the Impact of Effective Teenage Pregnancy Prevention Programs." *Family Planning Perspectives* 27:188–95.

George, R. M. and B. J. Lee. 1997. "Abuse and Neglect of Children." In R. A. Maynard, ed., *Kids Having Kids: Economic Costs and Social Consequences of Teen Pregnancy,* pp. 205–30. Washington, D.C.: Urban Institute Press.

Germain, Carel B. and Alex Gitterman. 1996. *The Life Model of Social Work Practice: Advances in Theory and Practice,* 2d ed. New York: Columbia University Press.

Gessner, B. D. and K. A. Perham-Hester. 1998. "Experience of Violence among Teenage Mothers in Alaska." *Journal of Adolescent Health* 22(5):383–88.

Granger R. C. and R. Cytron. 1998. "Teenage Parent Programs: A Synthesis of the Long-Term Effects of the New Chance Demonstration, Ohio's Learning, Earning, and Parenting (LEAP) Program, and the Teenage Parent Demonstration (TPD)." New York: Manpower Demonstration Research Corporation.

Grunseit, A. and S. Kippax. 1993. "Effects of Sex Education on Young People's Sexual Behavior." Geneva: World Health Organization.

Guttmacher, S., L. Lieberman, D. Ward, N. Freudenberg, A. Radosh, and D. DesJarlais. 1997. "Condom Availability in New York City Public High Schools: Relationships to Condom Use and Sexual Behavior." *American Journal of Public Health* 87:1427–33.

Hatcher, R. A., F. Stewart, J. Trussell, D. Kowal, P. Guest, K. Stewart, and W. Cates. 1994. *Contraceptive Technology,* 16th rev. ed. New York: Irvington Publishers.

Haveman, R. H., B. Wolfe, and E. Peterson. 1997. "Children of Early Childbearers as Young Adults." In R. A. Maynard, ed., *Kids Having Kids: Economic Costs and Social Consequences of Teen Pregnancy,* pp. 257–84. Washington, D.C.: Urban Institute Press.

Henshaw, S. K. and K. Frost. 1996. "Abortion Patients in 1994–5: Characteristics and Contraceptive Use." *Family Planning Perspectives* 28:140–47,158.

Howard, M. and J. B. McCabe. 1990. "Helping Teenagers Postpone Sexual Involvement." *Family Planning Perspectives* 22:21–26.

The Institute of Medicine. 1996. *The Hidden Epidemic: Confronting Sexually Transmitted Diseases.* Washington, D.C.: The Institute of Medicine, National Academy Press.

Jacccard, J., P. J. Dittus, and V. V. Gordon. 1996. "Maternal Correlates of Adolescent Sexual and Contraceptive Behavior." *Family Planning Perspectives* 28(4):159–65, 185.

Kaiser Family Foundation/Glamour. 1997. *National Survey—Talking About STD with Health Professionals: Women's Experiences.* Menlo Park, Calif.: Kaiser Family Foundation.

Kaiser Family Foundation, Alan Guttmacher Institute, and the National Press Foundation. 1998. "Teen Sex, Contraception, and Pregnancy." *Emerging Issues in Reproductive Health: A Briefing Series for Journalists.* Menlo Park, Calif.: Kaiser Family Foundation.

Kann, L., S. A. Kinchen, B. I. Williams, J. G. Ross, R. Lowry, C. V. Hill, J. A. Grunbaum, P. S. Blumson, J. L. Collins, and L. J. Kolbe. 1998. "Youth Risk Behavior Surveillance—United States, 1997." *Journal of School Health* 68(9):355–65.

Kerewsky, W. and L. Lefstein. 1982. "Young Adolescents and Their Communities: A Shared Responsibility." In L. Lefstein, W. Kerewsky, E. Medrich, and C. Frank, eds., *3:00 to 6:00 P.M.: Young Adolescents at Home and in the Community,* pp. 5–22. Carrboro: University of North Carolina Press.

Kirby, Douglas. 1997. *No Easy Answers: Research Findings on Programs to Reduce Teen Pregnancy.* Washington, D.C.: National Campaign to Prevent Teen Pregnancy.

Kirby, D., L. Short, J. Collins, D. Rugg, L. Kolbe, M. Howard, B. Miller, F. Sonenstein, and L. Zabin. 1994. "School-Based Programs to Reduce Sexual Risk Behaviors: A Review of Effectiveness." *Public Health Reports* 109:339–60.

Koo, H. P., G. H. Dunteman, C. George, Y. Green, and M. Vincent. 1994. "Reducing Adolescent Pregnancy Through a School- and Community-based Intervention: Denmark, S.C. Revisited." *Family Planning Perspectives* 26(5):206–11, 217.

Levine, J. A. and E. W. Pitt. 1995. *New Expectations: Community Strategies for Responsible Fatherhood.* New York: Families and Work Institute.

Manlove, J. 1998. "The Influence of High School Dropout and School Discouragement on the Risk of School-Age Pregnancy." *Journal of Research on Adolescence* 8(2):187–220.

Maynard, R. 1995. "Teenage Childbearing and Welfare Reform: Lessons from a Decade of Demonstration and Evaluation Research." *Children and Youth Services Review* 17:309–332.

Maynard, R. A. 1996. *Kids Having Kids: A Robin Hood Foundation Special Report on the Costs of Adolescent Childbearing.* New York: Robin Hood Foundation.

McLanahan, C. S. 1994. "The Consequences of Single Motherhood." *The American Prospect* 18:48–58.

Moore K. A., A. K. Driscoll, and L. D. Lindberg. 1998. *A Statistical Portrait of Adolescent Sex, Contraception, and Childbearing.* Washington, D.C.: National Campaign to Prevent Teen Pregnancy.

Moore, K. A., D. R. Morrison, and A. D. Green. 1997. "Effects on the Children Born to Adolescent Mothers." In R. A. Maynard, ed., *Kids Having Kids: Economic Costs and Social Consequences of Teen Pregnancy,* pp. 145–80. Washington D.C.: Urban Institute Press.

Moore, K. A., B. W. Sugland, C. Blumenthal, D. Glei, and N. Snyder. 1995. *Adolescent Pregnancy Prevention Programs: Interventions and Evaluations.* Washington, D.C.: Child Trends.

National Campaign to Prevent Teen Pregnancy. 1997. *Whatever Happened to Childhood?: The Problem of Teen Pregnancy in the U.S.* Washington, D.C.: Author.

National Center for Children in Poverty. 1996. *One in Four: America's Youngest Poor.* New York: Author.

National Center for Health Statistics. 1997. *Teenage Birth in the United States: National and State Trends, 1990–1996.* Hyattsville, Md.: National Center for Health Statistics, U.S. Department of Health and Human Services.

———. 1998. *Declines in Teenage Birth Rates: National and State Patterns, 1991–1997.* Hyattsville, Md.: National Center for Health Statistics, U.S. Department of Health and Human Services.

Offer, D. 1987. "The Mystery of Adolescence." *Adolescent Psychiatry* 14:7–27.

Office of National AIDS Policy. 1996. *Youth and HIV/AIDS: An American Agenda.* Washington, D.C.: Author.

Olds, D., J. Eckenrode, C. Henderson, Jr., H. Kitzman, J. Powers, R. Cole, K. Sidora, P. Morris, L. M. Pettitt, and D. Luckey. 1997. "Long-Term Effects of Home Visitation on Maternal Life Course and Child Abuse and Neglect: A Fifteen Year Follow-up of a Randomized Trial." *Journal of the American Medical Association* 278:637–43.

Olds, D. L., C. R. Henderson, R. Chamberlin, and R. Tatelbaum. 1986. "Preventing Child Abuse and Neglect: A Randomized Trial of Nurse Home Visitation." *Pediatrics* 78:56–78.

Resnick, M. D., P. S. Bearman, R. W. Blum, K. E. Bauman, K. M. Harris, J. Jones, J. Tabor, T. Beuhring, R. E. Sieving, M. Shew, M. Ireland, L. H. Bearinger, and J. R. Udry. 1997. "Protecting Adolescents from Harm: Findings from the National Longitudinal Study on Adolescent Health." *Journal of the American Medical Association* 278(10):823–32.

Robinson, K. L., J. H. Price, C. L. Thompson, and H. D. Schmalzried. 1998. "Rural Junior High School Students' Risk Factors for and Perceptions of Teen Pregnancy." *Journal of School Health* 68(8):334–38.

Santelli, J. S. and P. Beilenson. 1992. "Risk Factors for Adolescent Sexual Behaviors, Fertility, and STDs." *Journal of School Health* 62:271–79.

Schacter, J. 1989. "Why We Need a Program for the Control of Chlamydia Trachomatous." *New England Journal of Medicine* 320:802–4

Schuster, M. J., R. M. Bell, S. H. Berry, and D. E. Kanouse. 1998. "Impact of a High School

Condom Availability Program on Sexual Attitudes and Behaviors." *Family Planning Perspectives* 30(March/April):67–72.

Siecus Fact Sheets. 1998. "Sexuality Education in the Schools: Issues and Answers." http://www.siecus.org/pubs/fact/fact0007.html.

Smith, I., M. Weil, B. Ferleger, W. Russell, C. Jo, and A. Kwinn. 1990. "California's Adolescent Family Life Program: Evaluating the Impact of Case Management Services for Pregnancy and Parenting Adolescents." Final Report. Los Angeles: University of Southern California Press.

Sonenstein, F. L., L. Ku, L. D. Lindberg, C. F. Turner, and J. H. Pleck. 1998. "Changes in Sexual Behavior and Condom Use Among Teenaged Males: 1988 to 1995." *American Journal of Public Health* 88(6):956–59.

Sonenstein, F. L., K. Stewart, L. D. Lindberg, M. Pernas, and S. Williams. 1997. *Involving Males in Preventing Teen Pregnancy: A Guide for Program Planners.* Washington, D.C.: The Urban Institute.

Stock, J. L., M. A. Bell, D. K. Boyer, and F. A. Connell. 1997. "Adolescent Pregnancy and Sexual Risk-Taking Among Sexually Abused Girls." *Family Planning Perspectives* 29(5):200–203, 227.

Tiezzi, L., J. Lipshutz, N. Wrobleski, R. D. Vaughan, and J. F. McCarthy. 1997. "Pregnancy Prevention among Urban Adolescents Younger Than 15: Results of the 'In Your Face' Program." *Family Planning Perspectives* 29:173–76, 197.

Trent, K. and S. J. South. 1992. "Sociodemographic Status, Parental Background, Childhood Family Structure, and Attitudes toward Family Formation." *Journal of Marriage and the Family* 54:427–39.

United Nations. 1991. *Demographic Yearbook.* New York: Author.

U.S. Bureau of Census. 1991. "Marital Status and Living Arrangements, 1990." *Current Population Reports.* Series P-20, Number 450, Table A, p. 1. Washington, D.C.: U.S. Government Printing Office.

———. 1998. *Statistical Abstract of the United States: 1998.* Washington, D.C.: U.S. Government Printing Office.

U.S. Department of Health and Human Services. 1995. *Report to Congress on Out-of-Wedlock Childbearing.* Hyattsville, Md.: Author.

Ventura, S. J., J. A. Martin, S. C. Curtin, and T. J. Mathews. 1997. "Report of Final Natality Statistics, 1995." *Monthly Vital Statistics Report* 45, no. 11(Supplement 2):1–22.

Wertheimer, R. and K. Moore. 1998. "Childbearing by Teens: Links to Welfare Reform." *New Federalism: Issues and Options for States.* Washington, D.C.: The Urban Institute. Series A, Number A-24.

Wilson, W. J. 1996. *When Work Disappears: The World of the New Urban Poor.* New York: Knopf.

Wolfe, B. and M. Perozek. 1997. "Teen Children's Health and Health Care Use." In R. A. Maynard, ed., *Kids Having Kids: Economic Costs and Social Consequences of Teen Pregnancy,* pp. 181–203. Washington, D.C.: Urban Institute Press.

Zabin, L. S. 1994. "Addressing Adolescent Sexual Behavior and Childbearing: Self-esteem or Social Change?" *Women's Health Issues* 4:93–97.

12

Adult Corrections

C. Aaron McNeece
Albert R. Roberts

In his famous work *On the Genealogy of Morals,* Nietzsche (1887/1989) wrote: "It is nowadays impossible to say definitely the precise reason for punishment" (8). More than a hundred years later, we are no more certain about the reasons society chooses to punish certain individuals. Originally a ritual for the redemption of sin through punishment, the rhetoric of imprisonment often takes on a decidedly theological cast (Sullivan 1990). As an integral part of the American criminal justice system, the prison provides a socially acceptable way to rationalize revenge through retribution.

Liberal ideologies about imprisonment and corrections, more likely to be espoused by social workers, assume that most of the defects of human behavior have their origins in the social environment and that the key to changing offenders lies in learning how to manipulate either these environments or their psychological consequences (Shover and Einstadter 1988). Social workers and other liberals assume that incarceration should provide treatment to rehabilitate, reeducate, and reintegrate offenders into the community. Social workers have been active with other liberals in the correctional reform movement (Cullen and Gilbert 1982) as a reaction to the conservative ideologies and punitive strategies popular in the 1970s.

Conservatives are more likely to believe that the primary cause of crime is inadequate control over a fundamentally flawed human nature (Currie 1985). They support the principle of retribution or just deserts, not necessarily as vengeance, but because it serves utilitarian purposes as well. Prisons and correctional systems are not only proper, but necessary, because they reinforce the social order. Reduced criminal behavior is an expected outcome of punishment, because punishing offenders for their misdeeds should reduce both the probability of their repeating the act (specific deterrence) and the likelihood of others committing criminal acts (general deterrence).

The incapacitation function of incarceration reflects an especially pessimistic view of human nature: Offenders probably cannot be rehabilitated, but they cannot commit other crimes against people outside the prison as long as they are incarcerated (Von Hirsch 1976).

Radical ideologies about imprisonment and corrections have never been very popular, and they seem to be losing whatever attraction they once may have held for social workers. They are based on the view that the nature and rate of crime in America are inevitable results of the structure and dynamics of the capitalist economic system (Gibbons 1979). According to Rusche and Kirchheimer (1939), the threat of incarceration was an effective capitalist device for controlling the labor supply. Radicals do not pursue the naive belief that crime can be eradicated, but they do argue that changes in the political economy could substantially affect the types and rates of crime.

DEFINING AND EXPLAINING ADULT CORRECTIONS

Throughout civilized history the usual punishments for transgressions of moral codes and threats to the social order were death, slavery, maiming, or the payment of fines. Beginning with the Enlightenment, however, the philosophy of utilitarianism dominated penal reform into the twentieth century. One of the most influential Enlightenment writers on penal reform, Cesare Beccaria (1819/1963) argued for a hierarchy of penalties, decreeing that punishment should be prescribed according to the gravity of the offense. Crime would be deterred more by the certainty of punishment than by its severity. Later reformers such as John Howard (1726–1790), the driving force behind American penology, translated this theory into specific penal reforms beginning in the late eighteenth century. John Howard also had initiated lay visiting in England's jails and prisons.

Immanuel Kant articulated an opposing philosophy, deontology, in his work *The Metaphysics of Morals* (1796/1991). The penal law was to be a categorical imperative rather than a tool for the purpose of securing some extrinsic good such as the deterrence of crime. Punishment was imposed because an individual had committed an offense (Heath 1963). Today penology has once more shifted from utilitarianism to retribution, based on the neo-Kantian principle of "just deserts."

Opening in 1773, a former military prison used by General George Washington, an old converted copper mine near Simsbury, Connecticut, was the first American prison. A few years later the Quakers created the Philadelphia Society for Alleviating the Miseries of the Public Prisons, with the goal of replacing physical torture and the death penalty with imprisonment in solitary confinement. The "penitentiary movement" began with the Walnut Street Jail in 1790, and the organization was renamed the Pennsylvania Prison Society in 1887 (Sullivan, 1990).

The John Howard Society, a voluntary advocacy and prisoners' rights organization, was established in England in 1866 and in Massachusetts in 1889. The Correctional Association of New York was formed in 1844, and the Prisoners' Aid Association of Maryland was created in 1869 (Fox 1983).

Ironically, some writers date the beginning of professional social work to 1893, the year that settlement house workers lobbied to be placed on the program of the National Conference of Charities and Correction (Fox 1983). From the beginning, social work and corrections differed sharply on certain principles. Corrections had long been a part of philanthropy and preprofessional social work, but as social work became recognized as a profession, the field of corrections came to be viewed as separate and distinct. This was partly the result of the social work emphasis on self-determination. Corrections, by its nature, is coercive and difficult to reconcile with the principle of self-determination (Fox 1983). The social worker who accepted employment in an authoritarian setting with nonvoluntary, unmotivated clients was often considered to be in violation of professional values (Treger 1983).

Somewhat later the paths of the two professions crossed again, with correctional rehabilitation in the 1950s drawing from the concept of therapeutic treatment, either psychotherapy or some form of group treatment. However, political and social events made rehabilitation in a prison setting seem impossible by the end of the 1960s (Sullivan 1990). About the same time, prison activism and violence was seen on an unprecedented scale at Soledad, California, and Attica, New York, and finally culminated in the slaughter of thirty-three inmates in Santa Fe, New Mexico, in 1980. Since those turbulent years American prisons have experienced overcrowding, violence, inmate abuse, and recidivism. Few resources have been directed at improving inmate treatment or living conditions.

Coupled with a serious questioning of the effectiveness of rehabilitation in the 1970s and the disappearance of indeterminate sentencing and parole in the 1980s, fewer social workers considered careers in the correctional system (DiNitto and McNeece 1997). As a result, employment in the field of corrections has become increasingly less attractive to professionally trained social workers. By 1991 only 1.2 percent of the membership of the National Association of Social Workers identified "corrections" as their primary field of practice (Gibelman and Schervish 1993).

For puposes of clarity, the following definitions are offered of salient terms:

> *Imprisonment* is often used interchangeably with confinement or incarceration. Its goal is to punish, deter, and incapacitate the *offender.* However, incarceration may take place in a prison, jail, boot camp, or other type of secure facility, while imprisonment occurs only in prison. For years the United States has had the highest rate of imprisonment in the Western world, and the third highest rate in the known world—after Russia and South Africa (McNeece 1995).
>
> *Community corrections* is the use of a variety of court-ordered programmatic sanctions permitting convicted offenders to remain in the community under supervision as an alternative to prison.
>
> *Probation* is the most common type of community corrections. It is a sentence of imprisonment that is suspended, usually allowing the offender to remain in the community under supervision.
>
> *Intermediate sanctions,* sometimes called *alternative sanctions,* are used as alternatives from everything from fines to imprisonment. They include split sentencing, shock probation and parole, home confinement and monitoring, shock incarceration, and community service.
>
> *Split sentence* is a sentence requiring the offender to serve a period of confinement, followed by a period of probation.
>
> *Shock probation* is the practice of sentencing offenders to prison, then allow-

ing them to apply for probationary release after a relatively short period of incarceration. It is sometimes known as *shock parole*.

Parole is similar to probation, except that instead of being an *alternative* to incarceration, it is a *conditional release* from incarceration.

Offender is a person who has been arrested and convicted for one or more misdemeanor or felony violations of the criminal code. Defining a person as an offender has several consequences. It attaches stigma as well as legal consequences to that person. The stigma of being an offender may make it difficult to obtain services, education, or employment. Greater stigma is attached to being a felony offender than to being a misdemeanor offender, and to being imprisoned or incarcerated than to being on probation or under community supervision. In some states certain classes of offenders (usually felons) may be barred from employment as child care workers, teachers, social workers, attorneys, and so forth.

In fourteen states felony offenders lose their voting rights for life, and forty-six states place some restrictions on their voting rights, resulting in the permanent disenfranchisement of a disproportionate number of minority citizens, since offenders are more often African American or Hispanic (NRA 1998). Greater stigma is attached to female than male offenders, and women may experience a real risk of losing custody of their children or having parental rights terminated because of a criminal offense (McNeece 1995).

Being an offender can work either for or against a person when it comes to the receipt of services. Some private agencies may decline to serve anyone who has been convicted of a felony offense. However, the federal Byrne program generally requires that a client be involved in the criminal justice system in order to be eligible for services.

DEMOGRAPHIC PATTERNS

Prisoners. The total number of prisoners under the jurisdiction of state or federal adult correctional authorities was 1,244,554 at the end of 1997, an increase of 5.2 percent over 1996 (Bureau of Justice Statistics [BJS] 1997). Jail inmates totaled 567,079 persons. Thirty-six states, as well as the federal system, were operating at more than 100 percent of capacity. Fourteen states were operating at more than 140 percent of capacity. Drug offenders were the largest source of growth among female inmates, while violent offenders account for the largest source of growth among males. The average annual growth rate in the prison population since 1990 has been 7.0 percent. Relative to the number of U.S. residents, the rate of incarceration in prisons in the United States in 1997 was 445 sentenced inmates per 100,000 inmates, up from 292 in 1990. The rate of imprisonment varied from 112 per 100,000 in North Dakota to 717 in Texas (U.S. Department of Justice 1997a).

Since 1992 there have been more African American than white inmates in the nation's prisons. Hispanic inmates (who are counted as either African American or white in the BJS statistics) numbered 200,400 at the end of 1996, the latest year for which that data are available. Just over a third (34.5 percent) of the inmate population were between the ages of 20 and 29, and slightly more (36.7 percent) were between 30 and 39 years. Only 3.3 percent were 55 years or older (BJS 1997).

If the recent incarceration rates remain unchanged, about 5.1 percent of all Americans will serve time in prison during their lifetime. The lifetime chances of a person in the United States going to prison are as follows:

❚ 9 percent for men, 1.1 percent for women
❚ 16.2 percent for African Americans, 9.4 percent for Hispanics, and 2.5 percent for whites

In 1996, 7 percent of all African American males in their twenties and thirties were in prison (U.S. Department of Justice 1998a).

Among state prisons, about one-third of inmates describe themselves as daily drinkers, and half of them had been in some type of alcohol treatment program prior to incarceration (U.S. Department of Justice 1998b). Although recent comparable data for prison inmates are not available, almost two-thirds of jail inmates in 1996 reported being "regular users" of illicit drugs (U.S. Department of Justice 1998c).

One final statistic regarding prisoners: about 2.3 percent of all state and federal prison inmates tested positive for HIV. The actual incidence of HIV/AIDS is probably much higher than this, since only about 60 percent of the nation's inmates have ever been tested. The rate of HIV-positive inmates varies from 0.0 percent in Vermont to 13.9 percent in New York. Florida and New York together account for about half of the nation's HIV-positive inmates (U.S. Department of Justice 1997b).

Probationers and Parolees. The great majority of adult offenders are given a sentence to be served within the community, usually probation. About 3.8 million adults are currently on either probation or parole. Parolees number 690,159 (BJS 1996). At the end of 1996, state and local probation agencies served about 3 million adult U.S. residents. Probationers accounted for 58 percent of all adults under correctional supervision, including those in jail, prison, or on parole. Fifty-eight percent of all probationers had been convicted of a felony; 39 percent of a misdemeanor, and 3 percent for other infractions (BJS 1997).

The most common violent offense for probationers in 1995 was assault (9.2 percent), followed by sexual assault (3.6 percent), and robbery (1.9 percent). Larceny/theft (9.9 percent) was the most common property offense, followed by fraud (7.2 percent) and burglary (5.8 percent). Drug possession (9.8 percent) and drug trafficking (9.7 percent) accounted for a large proportion of probationers' offenses, while the largest single offense for probationers (16.7 percent) was driving while intoxicated (BJS 1997).

Four out of five probationers are men, both for misdemeanor and felony probation. A disproportionate number of probationers are minorities, with 27.9 percent African American and 11.3 percent Hispanic. Probationers are somewhat better educated than prisoners, with more than half (58 percent) having a high school diploma, and 17.7 percent having some college or more (BJS 1997).

Men were almost twice as likely as women to be on probation for a violent offense but were about as likely as women to have been sentenced for a drug offense. African Americans were nearly twice as likely to be under probation supervision for a drug offense, compared with whites. Among older probationers (45 years and older), driving while intoxicated accounted for 27.7 percent of all offenses (BJS 1997).

The number of parolees has been in decline since the mid-1970s, when the federal and state governments began adopting mandatory or determinate sentencing policies, in which the offender serves a sentence of a specific length, with time off only for "good behavior." In 1995, Maine had only 40 parolees under supervision, having eliminated parole in 1976. Texas had the greatest number, with 108,563 (BJS 1996). The only parolees that many states are supervising are those released on parole before determinate sentencing was adopted.

SOCIETAL CONTEXT

Prison provides social supports and, at the same time, creates a great deal of stress for inmates. As noted by Sykes (1958), the prison's control of inmates is not based on an ideal type of power or authority relationship in which a group of individuals is recognized as possessing a right to issue commands and formulate regulations (guards, custodians) to another group of individuals who feel compelled to obey through a sense of duty or internalized morality (prisoners):

> Like a province which has been conquered by force of arms, the community of prisoners has come to accept the validity of the regime constructed by their rulers but the subjugation is not complete. . . . The recognition of the legitimacy of society's surrogates and their body of rules is not accompanied by an internalized obligation to obey, and the prisoner thus accepts the fact of his captivity at one level and rejects it at another. (42)

The rulers are far outnumbered by the ruled in our prisons, and symbiotic relationships develop between the two groups in which control of the inmates (and thus, the prison) is delegated to the inmates themselves. Members of the self-appointed inmate elite develop their own rules and norms for regulating some of the most important aspects of prison life (Schrag 1961). Irwin (1970) dismisses earlier descriptions of prison-adaptive modes as being too simplistic. Early studies mentioned two basic modes: (1) an individual style, withdrawal and/or isolation; and (2) a collective style, participation in a convict social system.

Irwin's typology is based first on a division between those inmates who "identify with and therefore adapt to a broader world than the prison, and those who orient themselves primarily to the prison world" (1970:67). He further divides inmates into those who wish to maintain their life patterns and their identities, and those who desire to make significant changes in life patterns and identities and view their imprisonment as a chance to do this.

The mode of adaptation for those who tend to make a world out of prison is called "jailing." To "jail" is to cut one's self off from the outside world and attempt to construct a new life within prison. Such inmates are more likely to seek positions of power or influence within the prison, seeking job assignments that will give them access to information, influence, or material goods (food, cigarettes, etc.). Those who want to keep their commitment to the outside life while viewing prison as a temporary suspension of that life, but not making any significant changes in their life patterns, adapt by "doing time." One "does time" by maximizing his or her comfort and/or luxuries in prison, minimizing discomfort and conflict, and getting out as soon as possible. Inmates who are "doing time" form friendships with small groups of other convicts, find activities to occupy their time, and try to avoid trouble. Those who try to effect changes in their life patterns and identities and look forward to their future life on the outside adapt by "gleaning" or self-improvement. Gleaners shy away from former friends or other convicts who are not also gleaners.

Prison gangs can also provide social support for inmates, especially African American or Hispanic inmates. At the same time, however, the competition and conflict between gangs may also serve as a source of considerable stress. Hispanics may be pressured into joining the Mexican Mafia, La Nuestra Familia, and the Border Brothers, among others; while African American inmates have options such as the Crips, the Bloods, and the 415s (Hunt et al. 1993). There is no doubt that these gangs provide a great deal of social support for individual gang members. However, because the support is not necessarily a positive influence in inmates' lives, and because of the violence associated with prison gangs, they would seem to serve more as sources of stress than social support.

Both **probation** and **parolee** work involves four functions: (1) presentence investigations, (2) intake procedures, (3) needs assessment and diagnosis, and (4) supervision of clients (Schmalleger 1997). In performing these functions, two conflicting images of the officer's role coexist. The *social work* model stresses a supportive and service-providing role and views the probationers and parolees as "clients." Officers are "caregivers" who assess the needs of their clients and connect them with job training/placement, medical care, family therapy, mental health/drug counseling, housing, education, and a range of other services. The *correctional* model views the offenders as "wards," and the officers' major responsibilities are to control them and to protect the community through close supervision.

Thus, probation or parole could be a source of support for the offender through the provision of badly needed services. On the other hand, some offenders may find probation or parole a very stressful experience, meeting conditions requiring them to avoid contact with previous associates, abstain from drinking, supply urine samples on demand, and submit to warrantless searches. Failure to comply can result in being sent to prison. Probation/parole revocation hearings are *administrative* hearings, without the normal due process guarantees of criminal trials (*Morrissey v. Brewer* [1972]; *Minnesota v. Murphy* [1984]).

VULNERABILITIES AND RISK FACTORS

Even to the casual observer, it is obvious that our prisons contain a disproportionate number of individuals with significant mental health problems, substance abuse problems, and other problems that are directly related to their ethnicity, race, or lack of adequate income. Approximately one million individuals with mental disorders and/ or substance abuse disorders are currently incarcerated in correctional institutions (Pepper and Massaro 1992). An estimated 3 to 11 percent of correctional populations are characterized by concurrent *Diagnostic and Statistical Manual of Mental Disorders (DSM)* Axis I mental and substance disorders (Peters and Hills 1993). Cote and Hodgins (1990) found that among a randomly selected group of Canadian prisoners, approximately 26 percent of alcohol and drug abusers had a lifetime history of major depression, bipolar disorder, or atypical bipolar disorder, and 9 percent had a history of schizophrenic disorders. Careful diagnostic assessment of prison inmates arraigned in a metropolitan jail revealed that 44 percent of jail inmates have a lifetime prevalence of substance abuse disorders and either antisocial personality disorder or depression (Abram 1990). Researchers in the Epidemiologic Catchment Area (ECA) study found that in prisons mental disorders co-occurred with addictive disorders in 90 percent of cases (Regier et al. 1990). As the number of persons convicted of drug offenses continues to rise, the number of persons in the correctional system who have a dual diagnosis of drug abuse and mental health problems will continue to grow as well.

Race is, by itself, a significant risk factor for imprisonment. Legislatures frequently impose tougher sentences for crimes committed by racial minority members (such as the possession of "crack" cocaine, as compared with the possession of an equal amount of cocaine hydrochloride) (Kleck 1981). Although the exact impact of race is variable from state to state, there is no doubt that African Americans and Hispanics, especially males, are at a far greater risk of going to prison than nonminorities (BJS 1997).

Young male inmates, especially those who are new arrivals, are especially vulnerable to homosexual assault and other types of victimization in prison. One study in New York found a victimization rate of 28 percent (Toch 1977). This is probably a substantial underestimate of the real rate of violence against inmates, since many of the respondents were undoubtedly reluctant to talk about their victimization experiences out of fear for their safety.

Incarcerated persons are at higher risk for suicide, more so in jails than in prisons, and the risk is highest in the first seventy-two hours of incarceration (Ivanoff, Blythe, and Tripodi 1994). Substantial reductions in the suicide rate have resulted where screening instruments to assess the risk of suicide have been implemented (Cox and Morchauser 1993).

Retrospective studies have found it almost impossible to delineate risk factors that would equally describe all adult offenders. The best way to determine underlying risk factors is to examine offenders' biological and genetic factors, preexisting personality types and character disorders, learning disabilities, lack of social skills, and dearth of academic and vocational skills. Since the majority of adult offenders have undetected learning disabilities, few marketable vocational skills, and academic deficits, many have repeatedly failed at school, work, and family life, as well as crime.

From the 1930s through the 1980s the prevailing view among prominent criminologists and correctional administrators was to study and apply particular theoretical frameworks on the etiology of crime and delinquency that had been developed by the criminologists William Healy, Cesare Lombroso, Edwin H. Sutherland and Donald Cressey, Walter C. Reckless, Don Gibbons, and Karl Menninger.

The **positive school,** founded by Lombroso, did the pioneering scientific work examining biological and physiological explanations of crime causation. Lombroso and his followers believed that hereditary factors, body chemistry, and physical characteristics determined whether an individual would become a criminal or not (Lombroso-Ferrero 1972). In the 1950s and 1960s, several researchers proposed a link between violent crime and sex chromosomes. Several male prisoners were found to have an extra Y chromosome, and this led some prominent criminologists and anthropologists of that era, including Walter C. Reckless, Ashley Montagu, and George Vold, to postulate that the additional Y chromosome was a causative factor in their criminality.

Psychological and psychoanalytic approaches held that certain individuals became criminals based on their subconscious motivation, childhood experiences, developmental conflicts, and behavioral conditioning. Some of the most prominent psychologists who espoused this approach were Karl Menninger, William Healey, and David Abrahamsen (Gibbons 1968; Menninger 1968).

Ecological and sociological approaches held that groups of individuals became criminals because of the criminal influences and community ties in their neighborhood and physical environment. In the 1920s, prominent sociologists at the University of Chicago (Clifford Shaw, Henry McKay, Ernest Burgess, and Robert Park) conducted a number of studies to verify their ecological theory. Their theory of concentric zones states that living in specific sections of the city of Chicago rather than in others was more conducive to involvement in crime. Professors Edwin H. Sutherland and later Donald Cressey and Ronald Akers were prominently known for *differential association theory,* which states that criminal behavior is learned in association with others who frequently violate the law, based on the frequency, duration, and nature of the interactions with criminal associates. Differential association theory was used to explain the development of violent gangs and delinquent subcultures.

The most overlooked underlying causes of habitual delinquency and adult criminality are undiagnosed and unrecognized **learning disabilities**. It is well known that a history of conduct problems, school failure, and truancy can lead to dropping out of school as well as juvenile delinquency. In the vast majority of cases, the underlying reason for school failure is a learning disability and the lack of early intervention and treatment plans (Roberts 1973; Roberts and Waters 1998). A disproportionate number of minorities have received a dismal education in poorly run ghetto schools and are incarcerated in our state prisons.

Several noteworthy studies have documented a strong connection between delinquency and various learning difficulties, such as attentional problems, information-processing deficits, ADHD, criticism and rejection by teachers, language deficits, failing grades, deficient moral reasoning skills, aggressive acts, fighting with peers, lack of social problem-solving skills, suspensions and expulsions, and low self-esteem (Brier 1989, 1994; Hinshaw 1992; Moffitt 1990; Sikorski 1991).

The two basic theories utilized to account for the linkage between learning disabilities and delinquency are *the school failure rationale* and the *susceptibility theory* (Waldie and Spreen 1993:417). The school failure rationale postulates that a sequence exists that begins with poor academic performance contributing significantly first to a negative self-image and then to delinquent behavior. The probability of delinquency is enhanced by two important factors, association with peers who are school dropouts and the desire for success in some endeavor (e.g., dealing drugs or stealing cars).

The susceptibility theory suggests that children with learning disabilities have traits that make them more vulnerable to cues and opportunities for delinquent behavior than individuals without learning disabilities. Among the traits specified are lack of impulse control, inability to predict the consequences of one's actions, irritability, persuasibility, and the tendency toward "acting out" behavior. Research indicates that youth with learning disabilities are less self-satisfied, less flexible, and lower in both social skills and sociability. Boys with learning disabilities have been shown to be more aggressive and hyperactive than similar boys without learning disabilities (Roberts and Waters 1998). Waldie and Spreen (1993) reported that the major finding in a longitudinal study of sixty-five participants (forty-seven males and eighteen females) with learning disabilities was that two factors (lack of impulse control and poor judgment) distinguished those youth with persisting records of delinquency and those who did not engage in repeated criminal activity. The researchers also pointed out that school failure and susceptibility are not mutually exclusive theories.

With respect to the self-esteem issue, there is often a dichotomous distribution for youth with histories of criminal behavior and school failure. While some report feelings of low self-esteem, others have irrationally high opinions of their worth and invulnerability.

RESILIENCIES AND PROTECTIVE FACTORS

One's ability to avert a crisis when confronted with extremely stressful life events is referred to by a number of terms such as resilience, psychological hardiness, learned optimism, and/or a strengths perspective. Individuals who are able to muster positive coping mechanisms are viewed as having high self-esteem, social supports, problem-solving skills, self-advocacy skills, positive coping skills, and team-building skills. Many of today's adult offenders are lacking in resilience and protective factors. However, they can be strengthened with a new belief system such as the importance of spirituality and religion, or academic education.

Dr. John Irwin spent several years as a young adult in California's State Prison at Folsom for armed robbery. While in prison during the late 1950s, Dr. Irwin discovered the inner power of religion as well as education. He obtained a high school equivalency diploma and two years of college credit while in prison. After release, he completed his undergraduate degree, master's degree, and Ph.D. in sociology and criminology. After approximately thirty years as a criminology professor at San Francisco State University in California, Dr. Irwin retired. At the American Correctional Association annual conference in Pittsburgh in the early 1970s, Dr. Irwin, who was then a consultant to the OEO Newgate Resource Center that had expanded prison college and study release programs to five different states, told conference attendees that the most important component for an inmate in a prison college program is giving him the opportunity for earning rewards, such as a Certificate of Appreciation or a small amount of money for winning an essay contest. We agree with the philosophy that success builds success, and interim rewards are important, particularly to adult felons who have experienced a life of failure.

In developing a theory of corrections, Schrag (1961) suggested that there are four major role configurations among inmates: prosocial, antisocial, pseudosocial, and asocial. Although the prosocial inmates are most frequently convicted of violent offenses, their offenses are situational, and they are not career criminals. While incarcerated they maintain strong ties with family, friends, and business associates, and they are generally sympathetic toward and cooperative with prison officials. They appear to have greater problem-solving skills than other inmates, to have greater understanding of legitimate role requirements, and generally to apply legitimate norms in making decisions. These are the most resilient inmates, and the most likely to benefit from treatment and rehabilitative efforts while in prison.

Antisocial inmates are more likely to come from underprivileged urban areas, have other family members who are criminals, and continue their close association with other criminals while in prison. They consistently employ deviant or illegitimate norms as standards of reference. Pseudosocial inmates are frequently middle class and are involved primarily in subtle, sophisticated, profit-motivated crime such as embezzlement or fraud. While incarcerated they are capable of shifting their normative perspectives according to the availability of instrumental awards. They also display a chameleonic skill in shifting allegiances between staff and other inmates, according to the exigencies of the situation. Asocial inmates are characterized by severe behavior disorders and commit a variety of crimes against persons and property, using bizarre methods without clear motives or reason. They frequently have been reared in institutions or foster care, and their social skills and abilities are greatly retarded. In prison they are the "troublemakers" more often involved in riots, escape plots, and assaults on staff and other inmates. They are detached from normal social conventions and moral commitments (Schrag 1961).

Saleebey (1997) eloquently stated: "There is a growing body of inquiry and practice that makes it clear that the rule, not the exception, in human affairs is that people do rebound from serious trouble, that individuals and communities do surmount and overcome serious and troubling adversity. . . . Every individual, group, family, and community has strengths" (9). There are no panaceas or quick fixes to the major problems in the criminal justice system, the nation's ghetto schools, and dysfunctional families. However, there are model offender treatment programs, good schools with caring teachers, and forensic social workers willing to advocate for inmates' basic rights to an education in a supportive (rather than rejecting and hostile) learning environment. Juvenile and adult offenders should be educated and given the full range of academic and vocational skills for a world of opportunity.

During the past decade, we have learned a great deal about the behavior of youth at risk, particularly that *no* human being can thrive by neglecting his or her physical, psychological, and social needs. If a youthful offender is to become a healthy, self-protective, and productive law-abiding citizen, then society must provide a nurturing environment. We strongly recommend the planning and development of early intervention programs, comprehensive education programs, and juvenile offender treatment programs if the goal is to break the cycle of juvenile and adult career criminals (Roberts 1998; Roberts and Waters 1998).

Penology in the 1990s is synonymous with punishment and incarceration of the offender. Generally speaking, this approach of building more and more maximum security prisons and sentencing offenders for longer periods of time goes completely against a strengths perspective. The punitive approach is a direct outgrowth of the fears among legislators and citizens that convicted felons will never change; that is, that they lack individual resilience, informal support networks, prosocial knowledge and skills, and socially acceptable goals. Therefore, no program or treatment model will ever rehabilitate them.

In sharp contrast, we firmly believe that many of the nonviolent offenders do possess personal attributes and capacities that can be strengthened in an effort to transform them into law-abiding citizens. First and foremost, there needs to be awareness on the part of correctional administrators, judges, and legislators that the punishment mind-set and its concomitants of pessimism, discouragement, and brutality only serve to reinforce the negative spiral.

We firmly believe that it is important to build on the potential strengths and capabilities and goal attainment skills of offenders. One example is giving an offender with academic and vocational skills deficits the opportunity to succeed. Correctional education programs need to be redeveloped to include an individualized assessment to uncover learning disabilities that may have interfered with the offender's ability to learn in school. Next, the adult learner needs an individualized educational plan including one-on-one tutoring. The correctional teacher needs to make a determination of which school subjects the offender had positive experiences with in childhood and allow the inmate the opportunity to succeed with short, attainable educational goals. After a few months of success in attaining short-term goals, it is important to set realistic longer-term goals for attaining a high school diploma or GED as well as an apprenticeship certificate in a marketable vocational trade. When inmates are given positive alternatives and program options, some will rise to the occasion.

PROGRAMS AND SOCIAL WORK CONTRIBUTIONS

Social work practice in criminal justice originated in the late nineteenth century. Mangrum (1976) describes "coercive" casework as the use of restraining and constraining legal authority in the process of helping offenders function in their social environments without resorting to illegal or antisocial behavior.

Professional social workers are dedicated to maximizing the dignity and worth of individuals, to fostering maximum self-determination on the part of clients, to advocating on behalf of clients, and to promoting equity and social justice (Johnson 1990). Most correctional systems or penal institutions do not subscribe to such lofty goals. This social work role in the correctional system has been called an "uneasy partnership" by some (Handler 1975), while others feel that "correctional social work" as a term might be an oxymoron.

Many social workers are concerned about the coercive nature of correctional work and see their role in social control activities as contradictory to their helping role. DiNitto and McNeece (1990) see many of these activities as "not conducive to social work practice." The two major ethical dilemmas for social workers employed in a prison setting are related to client self-determination and confidentiality.

Lister (1987) has outlined a model of direct practice social work, which may be grouped into system development, system maintenance, system linkage, and direct client intervention. While this conceptualization focuses on direct practice roles, some mezzo and macro roles such as planner, policy developer, researcher, administrator, consultant, team manager, and advocate are also described. Direct client intervention with involuntary clients may not differ in many respects from the traditional counseling of voluntary clients. However, social work's emphasis on self-determination will clearly be limited when working with offenders. For example, there is greater emphasis on surveillance and enforcement of rules and regulations, and more use of chemical testing for drug use. The prison social worker is legally bound to inform prison authorities about illicit drug use.

On the other hand, involuntary clients exist in many social work fields where neither client self-determination nor confidentiality is absolute (Johnson 1990). Child protective service workers, state hospital personnel, and social workers counseling spouse abusers must wrestle with this philosophical dilemma each day.

The great majority of the **jail and prison programs** surveyed by Wellisch, Anglin, and Prendergast (1993) claimed to offer services such as case management, relapse prevention, HIV/AIDS education, counseling, and twelve-step meetings. Many of these services were purchased from private providers, rather than provided through prison staff. In these arrangements, social workers employed by the private agency may also be expected to adhere to the same expectations regarding client surveillance and relaxations of rules of confidentiality.

Drug Abuse/Mental Health Services. While ongoing drug education programs for drug-abusing criminal offenders are clearly indicated, not all drug-involved offenders require treatment intervention. Indeed, diagnosis of drug addiction or dependency represents one of the more complex obstacles to achieving a better understanding of how best to design and target treatment resources for offenders.

By the mid- to late 1960s there was a growing realization in the criminal justice system that the prosecution and incarceration of drug-dependent offenders did little to deter future drug abuse or other antisocial behaviors. Indeed, research suggested that the labeling of drug abusers as felons and ex-convicts often had the unintended consequence of creating career criminals (Inciardi and McBride 1991:10). The federal Comprehensive Drug Abuse Prevention and Control Act of 1970 stimulated this growing recognition by sanctioning the diversion of some drug-involved offenders from the criminal justice system into the drug abuse treatment system. Similar legislation at the state level soon followed, with the primary focus on the diversion of nonviolent first offenders. It was also during the mid- to late 1960s that the still fledgling Community Mental Health system began to improve offender access to publicly supported substance abuse treatment programs.

Today, the drug-dependent offender typically accesses treatment in one of three ways. He or she can (1) avoid the sanctions of the criminal justice system by voluntarily seeking treatment for an addiction before the use of illicit drugs results in an arrest, (2) avoid criminal sanctions by voluntarily accepting treatment in lieu of prosecution following an arrest, or (3) voluntarily or involuntarily enter treatment as part of a criminal justice sanction following an adjudication of guilt.

Categorizing and describing the various approaches to substance abuse treatment for offenders is complicated by the lack of standardization in terminology, as well as a considerable amount of overlap among the various treatment interventions. Peters and Hills (1993) suggests a useful taxonomy that divides common treatment approaches into four basic categories: (1) chemical dependency/self-help approaches, (2) pharmacological approaches, (3) psychoeducational approaches, and (4) therapeutic communities.

Family Programs. Some prisons have family-oriented programs and activities that help prisoners and their families maintain and strengthen family relationships and address problems and needs precipitated or exacerbated by having a family member under correctional supervision. They include programs that take place in prison as well as community-based programs that provide services for prisoners' families during prisoners' incarceration and for prisoners and their families following release from prison. With the exception of prison visits, which have been permitted since the early 1900s, family-oriented programs are a rather new development in U.S. corrections. Although the idea that inmates need to maintain constructive relationships with persons outside the prison is stated as a formal corrections principle as far back as 1953 (Hopper 1994), most programs have emerged since the 1980s. Contemporary programs view families not only in terms of outside contacts for prisoners but also as persons who may be in need of assistance themselves.

Though programs vary considerably from one place to another, there are discernible features that permit a description of program types. The more common family programs found in prisons are visiting arrangements and activities, parenting programs, and support groups (Hairston 1997).

Starting in the 1960s a new correctional philosophy emerged, known among penologists as *reintegration*. This approach was based on the belief that the offender needed to be eased back into the **community.** Transitional programs were developed for offenders who were within thirty to ninety days of release, to bridge the artificial institutional environment with the realities of living in the community again. In the early 1960s, federal and state prison systems developed prerelease programs and guidance centers to help offenders to readjust to family, job, and community life upon release. Prison inmates needed to learn new skills and knowledge, a process termed *resocialization*. As part of the prerelease process, the offenders attended lectures on how to get a job (including role-playing of employment interviews), money management and budgeting, motor vehicle regulations, marriage and family relations, getting along with others, and community and social responsibility (Roberts 1973).

At the same time that prerelease guidance centers and halfway houses were developed, work-release and study-release programs were expanding. In a work-release program, the institution bus transports a group of offenders from the correctional facility to the nearest city early in the morning where they work all day, and the bus returns to pick them up in the evening (Roberts 1973).

Halfway houses are houses in the community where five to as many as fifty offenders live for six to twelve months following their stay in prison and before they are paroled. Generally, the offenders are given two to three weeks to find a job in the community. Halfway houses are operated by well-known organizations such as the Salvation Army, Volunteers of America, John Howard Societies, and State Correctional Associations (Fox 1974).

Probation Services. Despite limited resources, probation and parole systems in the United States increasingly encounter difficult offenders with multiple problems, including polydrug abuse, alcoholism, semiliteracy, learning disabilities, a lack of vocational skills, erratic work history, a lack of social skills, mental disabilities, and/or mental retardation. There is wide variation in the ways in which probation departments are administered, but many of them are understaffed and woefully underfunded. Although community corrections handles approximately three-fourths of offenders, their budget is usually less than 10 percent of the local and state allocations for corrections (Petersilia 1995). According Dr. Joan Petersilia, one of the leading experts in the field of probation and parole systems:

> Unfortunately, the public does not really understand the multi-faceted nature of probation and parole, nor their importance to justice system decision-making and public safety. . . . Its services are humanitarian to offenders, an important humane point of contact for crime victims, and a vital means of

public protection. Moreover, when properly funded, community-based corrections provides one of the best means for delivering effective offender rehabilitation programs, particularly substance abuse treatment. (1998:565)

In 1970 the *Manual of Correctional Standards of the American Correctional Association* recommended that all probation supervisors have M.S.W. degrees. Graduate social work education is the best preparation for effectively filling the multiple roles of probation officers: advocate, broker of services, caseworker, case manager, and so on. In general, probation officers are expected to prepare presentence reports for judges, regularly interview and supervise probationers, refer probationers to appropriate community resources (including alcohol or drug treatment, when needed), and monitor restitution orders. Presentence reports are comprehensive reports that involve a criminal history, personal and family data, an evaluative summary, and sentencing recommendations on the probationer. In addition, the presentence investigation report includes a description of the impact of the offense on identifiable victims or the community. Usually, the probation officer interviews the offender's current or former employers, close relatives, and neighbors—anyone who has knowledge of the offender's activities in the community.

Probation supervision entails assisting the offender to comply with the conditions set forth in the probation regulations. There are two types of probation conditions: standard conditions and special or discretionary conditions. Examples of standard conditions (which are applicable for all probationers in a jurisdiction) are: They must maintain regular employment and provide support to their dependents; they cannot leave the jurisdiction without permission; they cannot change their job or residence without permission; and they cannot have contact with known felons. Examples of special conditions (which are applied to offenders who have special needs) are: They are required to make restitution payments; they are required to complete a certain amount of community service; and they are required to attend alcohol or substance abuse treatment programs and comply with urinalysis testing.

The monumental reports of President Johnson's Commission on Law Enforcement and Administration of Justice made sweeping recommendations in order to optimize the availability of probation and parole services, resources, and supervision. The overall report, entitled *The Challenge of Crime in a Free Society,* made many far-reaching recommendations regarding the American probation and parole system, the most significant of which were as follows: All jurisdictions should examine their need for probation and parole offices on the basis of an average ratio of thirty-five offenders per officer, and make an immediate start toward recruiting additional officers on the basis of that examination (President's Commission on Law Enforcement and Administration of Justice 1967:167).

Although the Commission set a standard for an average caseload, it noted that it is also necessary to recognize the importance of specialized caseloads for the differential treatment of certain categories of offenders, such as first-time offenders and sex offenders. Included in these reports was the recommendation that probation officers who were assigned specialized caseloads should have graduate-level training in social work or the social sciences.

These recommendations were put into practice during the latter part of the 1960s and the 1970s. However, in the 1980s, under the Reagan administration, there were substantial funding cutbacks, and probation caseloads once again escalated. As the 1990s were drawing to a close, typical probation caseloads had once again climbed to from one hundred to three hundred clients in cities through the country. For example, there is wide variation among the twenty-one county probation departments in the state of New Jersey, ranging from a caseload of fifty to three hundred depending on the county. Many probation officers may not see the probationer for as long as six or eight months, and then only because the probationer has been rearrested. In many cities, probation officers no longer serve as traditional caseworkers or brokers of services, but instead are so overburdened with cases that they are able to respond only in emergency situations or to make court appearances to present the judge with a presentence report. It has been reported that some Los Angeles probation officers have a caseload that is close to one thousand. There are some exceptions to this bleak picture, most notably in Maricopa County, Arizona, where all cases are computerized and probation officers are generally assigned to small (approximately twenty-five to thirty-five) specialty caseloads (e.g., domestic violence offenders, sex offenders, etc.; Scott 1994).

In the early 1980s and continuing into the 1990s, *intensive supervision* in probation was expanded for adult offenders due to the following reasons:

▎ There is a need for accountability and careful controlling of probationers and parolees.
▎ Many incarcerated offenders can be safely placed in community settings.
▎ It is more humane (and also less costly) to place offenders under community supervision rather than incarcerating them.

Intensive probation supervision was primarily used with adult offenders. In general, the number of contacts between the probation officer and the probationer ranged from twice a month to three or four contacts per week. Many of these offenders had substance abuse problems. To participate in this probation alternative, the offenders were required to attend an accredited school or approved vocational training program, or to be gainfully employed and/or participate in drug treatment, community service, or restitution. Those offenders with drug problems were required to submit to unannounced visits by their probation officer, including urinalysis testing to detect whether they were using drugs. Because of the emphasis on supervision and surveillance, electronic monitoring was considered especially beneficial in a number of these programs.

Several research studies have indicated that intensive supervision does significantly reduce recidivism when the programs emphasize high-quality treatment, as distinct from programs that have an emphasis on control and surveillance (Petersilia and Turner 1990). Several studies have confirmed that intensive supervised probation is the most cost-effective and promising tool for treating drug-abusing offenders (Tonry 1998).

Intermediate Sanctions. *Home confinement and electronic monitoring* as conditions of probation have become more widespread in recent years. The stated purpose is to monitor the offender in the community—usually for 60 to 120 days—through the use of electronic monitoring devices that are tamper-proof and are usually attached to the offender's wrist or ankle. These devices are usually utilized for individuals convicted of property offenses, drug offenses, or major traffic offenses such as driving while intoxicated (Walker 1994).

In recent years, *restitution* has become an important condition of probation. It provides a much more humane and less severe sanction than incarceration while teaching the offenders to take responsibility for their unlawful actions. There are two primary forms of restitution—*monetary* and *community service:*

1. Monetary restitution mandates the offender to repay the victim(s) whatever financial losses the victims have suffered.
2. Community service restitution mandates the offender to do good deeds for the community by performing volunteer work at public parks, nursing homes, painting public buildings, removing graffiti, etc.

Split sentencing is in use in many jurisdictions, in which a judge imposes a combination of a brief period of imprisonment and probation. The offender is typically ordered to serve the confinement period in a local jail, rather than a prison. Ninety days in jail followed by two years of probation is a common split sentence.

Shock probation is similar to split sentencing. One difference is that shock probation clients must *apply* for probationary release from confinement. Another is that the release often comes as a surprise to the client, who believes that he or she must serve a relatively long period of confinement. The theory is that the offender who learns of a sudden and unexpected reprieve may forswear future criminal activity.

Shock incarceration is designed primarily for young, first-time offenders and generally utilizes a military-style "boot camp" prison setting that provides a highly regimented program involving strict discipline, physical training, and hard labor. They last three to six months, and offenders who complete the program are generally placed under community supervision. Shock incarceration programs have been especially popular because they are perceived as being "tough on criminals." Research on boot camps reveals, however, that their effect on recidivism is negligible (Schmalleger 1997).

ASSESSMENT AND INTERVENTIONS

The primary focus in correctional systems is on managing large numbers of individuals whose behavior has been deemed by society to be unacceptable (McNeece 1995). Therefore, correctional institutions and agencies place their emphasis on assessment techniques that rely largely on behavior profiles that are more helpful in organizational planning and institutional management than in designing appropriate treatment plans for clients (Ivanoff et al. 1994). For example, correctional programs place much stock in the client's criminal history, even though official criminal records may be quite misleading. Official offense records ("rap sheet," "yellow sheet," etc.) typically contain information on the *official* reason for conviction, thus ignoring the facts that (a) police exercise enormous discretion in deciding how to charge an offender, and (b) the conviction is generally the result of a plea bargain, in which the initial charges against the offender are reduced to a lesser charge in exchange for a guilty plea.

Prisons keep explicit behavioral reports on each inmate, which are used in making decisions about practically every aspect of the inmate's life while incarcerated, including which treatment, if any, he or she is in need of or eligible for. Most often those reports are used to *disqualify* an inmate for programs. For example, certain treatment programs automatically disqualify inmates who have a history of either preincarceration or postincarceration violence against persons.

Ivanoff et al. (1994) remind us that information on *competency* in a client's case records must be put into the proper context. Competency is a legal, not a clinical concept, and the term refers to the client's state of mind at the time of the trial or other legal hearings, not at the time of the alleged crime, nor at any time subsequent to conviction or incarceration (Stone 1988). Interpretation or application of the term in the manner it is normally used by social workers, psychologists, and other human services professionals could result in further injustice to the client.

There is a tendency in some settings, including correctional programs, to label as *antisocial* any individual who has been convicted of a felony or even a serious misdemeanor offense, or those inmates in a prison setting who have a history of "incident" reports. In some cases, the terms *sociopathic* or *psychopathic* might be attached to such an individual. There does not appear to be a common definition or understanding of these terms as applied to offenders' behavioral deficits and/or excesses that is useful in guiding either research or clinical practice (Sutker, Bugg, and West 1993). Therefore, the practitioner would be well advised to be very careful in using such terms, employing behavior and symptom checklists specifically designed to assess psychopathy and antisocial personality. For male offenders there is the Psychopathy Checklist-Revised (PCL-R), consisting of twenty items from both case record and interviews (Hare 1991). It is used extensively in the criminal justice system because of its ability to make predictions of recidivism, parole violation, violence, and treatment outcome. Other common instruments for mental health screening and assessment include:

- Beck Depression Inventory (BDI)
- Brief Symptom Inventory (BSI)
- General Behavior Inventory (GBI)
- Hamilton Depression Scale (HAM-D)
- Symptom Checklist 90—Revised (SCL-90-R)

Substance abuse screening and assessment instruments include:

- Alcohol Dependence Scale (ADS)
- Addiction Severity Index (ASI)
- Alcohol Use Disorders Identification Test (AUDIT)
- CAGE
- Drug Abuse Screening Test (DAST-20)
- Michigan Alcoholism Screening Test (MAST)
- Substance Abuse Subtle Inventory (SASSI-2)
- Simple Screening Inventory (SSI)
- TCU Drug Dependence Screen (DDS)

During the past two decades, probation risk assessments and model classification systems have become standardized in correctional agencies throughout the United States. Assessment and classification of the offender help determine the level of necessary supervision, the dangers and risks of recidivism, and the treatment needs of the offender.

The primary purpose of probation risk assessments is to reduce—by means of computerized risk assessment instruments and prediction scales—the risk of probationers reoffending. Thus, a major issue within criminal justice decision making is the use of statistical risk prediction to differentiate low-risk from high-risk offenders. Most large probation departments have traditionally utilized a four-level risk classification model for probationers. The four variables used in determining risk of revocation by the New York City Department of Probation consist of the following variables:

▌ Reported drug abuse at the time of the violation
▌ Recent incarcerations
▌ Selected conviction offense
▌ Age at first arrest (Jones 1996:39)

The National Institute of Corrections (NIC) model classification system includes components that have been well researched and used in a number of probation jurisdictions. The NIC classification system is useful in guiding probation officer decision making on how best to provide probation supervision and concrete services to probationers. This assessment system includes:

▌ Number of address changes in the last twelve months
▌ Percentage of time employed in the last twelve months
▌ Age of first conviction
▌ Number of prior probation/parole revocations
▌ Number of prior periods of probation/parole supervisión
▌ Number of prior felony convictions
▌ Alcohol usage problems
▌ Other drug usage problems
▌ Convictions of juvenile adjudications
▌ Attitude and motivation to change

This classification model helps probation officers anticipate the risks and behavior problems of the client.

Assessment in parole is very different from probation, and there are two major models. In the first, statutory decrees simply produce *mandatory parole,* providing time off for "good behavior" or other special circumstances. The other model is termed *discretionary parole,* and a parole board grants parole based on the board's judgments and assessments (Schmalleger 1997). Board members almost always consider the inmate's behavior while incarcerated; they often use reports of psychological tests. However, the board's decision may sometimes rely more on factors such as opposition from the victim's family, prosecutors, judges, and law enforcement personnel. In other words, parole assessments tend to be somewhat more politicized than probation assessments.

ILLUSTRATION AND DISCUSSION

Henry B. is a Caucasian male in his mid-30s. His parents divorced when he was 3 years old, and both his first and second stepfathers abused him physically and emotionally. He did poorly in school, and at one point he was identified as "mildly retarded." He had his first encounter with the police when he was 10 years old, after committing an act of vandalism in his school. For the next seven years he was in and out of both juvenile institutions and foster care. At that point he was sentenced as an adult to probation for a drug offense. Probation supervision consisted mostly of calling his probation officer once a week to give him a status report. On one occasion the probation officer did drop by his place of employment to make sure that Henry B. was there. A year later he was arrested for stealing a car, his probation was revoked, and he pled guilty to the new charge, sending him to one of the state's prisons for two years.

In his first prison experience, Henry B. spent most of his time either working in one of the prison farms, sleeping, or just spending time in his cell. The prison had one psychologist (a person with an M.A. degree, qualified to do psychological testing, but not therapy), but Henry B. never saw him. There was no social worker. He was sexually assaulted by other inmates twice during this stay in prison. Released on parole, Henry B. worked for a short period of time doing "day labor" in construction, but an economic recession in his community soon put him and most other construction workers out of a job. Henry B. began dealing drugs on a small scale, as well as "kiting" checks. His parole officer did require him to drop off a weekly urine sample, and after the third "dirty" urine his parole was revoked. He was also rearrested on a forgery charge, pled guilty, and sentenced to prison again. By this time he had also developed an alcohol abuse problem, and there was little help in prison, since the state's corrections system had moved farther away from the rehabilitative model to one of control and punishment. Parole also had been abolished in his state, and he received a "determinate" sentence of five years (subject to a reduction only by earning "good time").

This time Henry B. was sent to a prison that had a strong system of inmate gangs. He was recruited into the only white gang, the Aryan Brothers. He had again been sexually assaulted, and the gang promised him protection from any such future assaults. In fact, gang members severely beat the inmate who had assaulted Henry B. A few educational programs were offered in his unit by the local community college, but gang norms mitigated against enrolling in those classes, since the majority of students were African American and Hispanic. Henry B. again spent most of his time working first in the prison laundry, then later as a clerk in one of the prison staff's office. He attended a few AA meetings the first few months he was there, but it was mostly just to get out of his cell for a few hours.

Upon release, Henry B. had no parole officer supervising him (since parole had been abolished in his state). He found a job busing tables at a local restaurant but lost it after one of the waitresses accused him of stealing her tips. A few weeks later he got into a fight in a bar while intoxicated, and he unintentionally killed one of the other participants. This time he entered a plea of "not guilty," was assigned a public defender (who he saw once for approximately forty-five minutes before his trial), was convicted of the charges, and was sentenced to ten years in the state's maximum security prison.

By this time the pendulum had swung back in the other direction. Henry B. spent the first few days of this sentence undergoing a battery of psychological tests. He was diagnosed as having a learning disability, but not as mentally retarded. He also was diagnosed as a "Bipolar-II," and as having an alcohol dependence problem. He was seen by a psychiatrist who prescribed medication, and by the prison psychologist (with a doctorate in counseling psychology) who saw him once a week and referred him to AA meetings. He also joined a group of other inmates with alcohol problems who met with the psychologist once a week for group therapy.

Henry B. enrolled in a carpentry program conducted in the prison by the local vocational-technical college and was assigned to a work detail making repairs on prison buildings. A few months after completing the carpentry training program, he was put in charge of his work group.

Two years before his release, Henry B. became eligible for a newly implemented treatment program for dually diagnosed inmates (with both substance abuse and Axis I mental health disorders). He was transferred to a different unit and, after more psychological testing, he became a part of the therapeutic community of inmate-clients. His typical day consisted of about four hours a day on a work detail, and another four hours of therapy. The therapy was conducted mostly in a group setting (by a person with an M.A. in counseling). He did see a psychiatrist once a week during the first phase of the program, but this was later reduced to once per month.

He successfully completed the first two phases of the program, and he is expected to "graduate" and be released back into the community in another four to six months. At that point he will be referred to the state's Department of Social Services for aftercare. Henry B. has never seen a social worker during his time in prison, nor during his time on parole or probation supervision. The only social workers in the adult corrections system in his state are in administrative or planning positions.

CONCLUSION

Concerns about working with involuntary clients and conflicts between client self-determination and the prison's need for control and security have overshadowed needs for the social work profession to be engaged in the debate about criminal justice policies, programs, and services. This situation exists despite the profession's commitment to advocate for the poor and the oppressed. Justice system clients and their families are among the most oppressed, economically disadvantaged, and vulnerable populations. While we build more prisons to house a population that is increasingly poor and nonwhite, the social work profession has remained remarkably silent in advocating alternatives to incarceration, and relatively few social workers view employment in the justice system as an acceptable career choice.

Altogether social workers in policy, planning, and administrative positions have not had a significant impact on the design or implementation of services in the corrections field (Chandler and Kassebaum 1997). Social workers need to become more active in examining the effects of the laws and policies that determine the sentences, living conditions, and services available to inmates. When the Delegate Assembly of the National Association of Social Workers convened in Washington in August 1999, it adopted a policy statement on Correctional Social Work that acknowledged the qualifications of social workers to provide services in this field and contains the following principles:

▮ Advocacy for incarcerated clients, especially those of color
▮ The provision of appropriate treatment
▮ Equitable treatment of all individuals in prisons and jails
▮ Access to health care, medications, treatment, and support
▮ Specialized social work training in corrections
▮ Participation of the profession in national policy debates on corrections
▮ Engagement of social works in research on correctional issues and policies
▮ Humane treatment of correctional clients
▮ The provision of prevention services
▮ Funding for community-based options[1]

The policy statement included a call for the development of practice standards in correctional social work. The absence of such standards is somewhat of an embarrassment, since we have been involved in correctional social work since the early days of the profession, and we still have no practice standards. As Grodd and Simon (1991) said in the first edition of this book, "In relation to the broad arena of criminal justice, social workers have much to do as change agents, advocates, and program developers" (673). We appear to have made little improvement in the last decade.

Notes
1. Policy statement approved by the NASW Delegate Assembly, August 1999.

References
Abram, K. 1990. "The Problem of Co-occurring Disorders Among Jail Detainees." *Law and Human Behavior* 14(4):333–45.

Beccaria, C. 1819/1963. *On Crimes and Punishments.* Trans. Henry Paolucci. New York: Bobbs-Merrill.

Brier, N. 1989. "The Relationship Between Learning Disability and Delinquency: A Review and Reappraisal." *Journal of Learning Disabilities* 22(9):546–52.

———. 1994. "Targeted Treatment for Adjudicated Youth with Learning Disabilities: Effects on Recidivism." *Journal of Learning Disabilities* 27(4):215–22.

Bureau of Justice Statistics (BJS). 1996. Probation and Parole Population Reaches Almost 3.8 Million. Washington, D.C.: U.S. Department of Justice, Bureau of Justice Statistics Press Release, June 30, 1996.

———. 1997, December. *Characteristics of Adults on Probation, 1995.* Washington, D.C.: U.S. Department of Justice. NCJ-164267.

Chandler, S. and G. Kassebaum. 1997. "Meeting the Needs of Female Offenders." In C. McNeece and A. Roberts, eds., *Policy and Practice in the Justice System,* pp. 159–80. Chicago: Nelson-Hall.

Cote, G. and S. Hodgins. 1990. "Co-occurring Mental Disorders Among Criminal Offenders." *Bulletin of the American Academy of Psychiatry and Law* 18(3):271–81.

Cox, J. F. and P. Morchauser. 1993. "Community Forensic Initiatives in New York State." *Innovations in Research in Clinical Service, Community Support, and Rehabilitation* 2:29–38.

Cullen, F. and K. Gilbert. 1982. *Reaffirming Rehabilitation.* Cincinnati: Anderson.

Currie, E. 1985. *Confronting Crime.* New York: Pantheon Books.

DiNitto, D. and C. A. McNeece. 1990. *Social work: Issues and Opportunities in a Challenging Profession.* Englewood Cliffs, N.J.: Prentice-Hall.

———. 1997. *Social Work: Issues and Opportunities in a Challenging Profession.* Needham Heights, Mass.: Allyn and Bacon.

Fox, V. 1974. "The Future of Correctional Treatment." In A. R. Roberts, ed., *Correctional Treatment of the Offender,* pp. 311–26. Springfield, Ill.: Charles C Thomas.

———. 1983. "Foreword." In A. R. Roberts, ed., *Social Work in Juvenile and Criminal Justice Settings,* pp. ix–xxvii. Springfield, Ill.: Charles C Thomas.

Gibbons, D. C. 1968. *Society, Crime, and Criminal Careers.* Englewood Cliffs, N.J.: Prentice-Hall.

———. 1979. *The Criminological Enterprise.* Englewood Cliffs, NJ: Prentice-Hall.

Gibelman, M. and P. Schervish. 1993. *Who Are We: The Social Work Labor Force As Reflected in the NASW Membership.* Washington, D.C.: National Association of Social Workers Press.

Grodd, B. and B. Simon. 1991. "Imprisonment." In A. Gitterman, ed., *Handbook of Social Work Practice with Vulnerable Populations,* pp. 647–76. New York: Columbia University Press.

Hairston, C. F. 1997. "Family Programs in State Prisons." In C. McNeece and A. Roberts, eds., *Policy and Practice in the Justice System,* pp. 143–57. Chicago: Nelson-Hall.

Handler, E. 1975. "Social Work and Corrections: Comments on an Uneasy Partnership." *Criminology* 13:240–54.

Hare, R. D. 1991. *The Hare Psychopathy Checklist-Revised.* Toronto: Multi-Health Systems.

Heath, J. 1963. *Eighteenth Century Penal Theory.* London: Oxford University Press.

Hinshaw, S. P. 1992. "Academic Underachievement, Attention Deficits, and Aggression: Comorbidity and Implications for Intervention." *Journal of Consulting and Clinical Psychology* 60(6):893–903.

Hopper, C. B. 1994, March. "The Status of Prison Visitation." Paper presented at the annual meeting of the Academy of Criminal Justice Sciences, Chicago, Illinois.

Hunt, G., S. Riegel, T. Morales, and D. Waldorf. 1993. "Prison Gangs and the Case of the 'Pepsi Generation.'" *Social Problems* 40:398–409.

Inciardi, J. and D. McBride. 1991. *Treatment Alternatives to Street Crime (TASC): History, Experiences, and Issues.* Rockville, Md.: National Institute on Drug Abuse.

Irwin, J. 1970. *The Felon.* Englewood Cliffs, N.J.: Prentice-Hall.

Ivanoff, A., B. Blythe, and T. Tripodi. 1994. *Involuntary Clients in Social Work Practice.* New York: Aldine De Gruyter.

Johnson, H. W. 1990. *The Social Services: An Introduction.* Itasca, Ill.: F. E. Peacock.

Jones, P. R. 1996. "Risk Prediction in Criminal Justice." In A. Harland, ed., *Choosing Correctional Options That Work,* pp. 33–68. Thousand Oaks, Calif.: Sage.

Kant, I. 1796/1991. *The Metaphysics of Morals.* New York: Cambridge University Press.

Kleck, G. 1981. "Racial Discrimination in Criminal Sentencing: A Critical Evaluation of the Evidence with Additional Evidence on the Death Penalty." *American Sociological Review* 49:783–805.

Lister, L. 1987. "Contemporary Direct Practice Roles." *Social Work* 32(5):384–91.

Lombroso-Ferrero, G. 1972. *Criminal Man According to the Classification of Cesare Lombroso.* Montclair, N.J.: Patterson Smith.

Mangrum, C. J. 1976. *The Professional Practitioner in Probation.* Springfield, Ill.: Charles C. Thomas.

McNeece, C. A. 1995. "Adult Corrections." In *Encyclopedia of Social Work,* 19th ed. Washington, D.C.: National Association of Social Workers Press.

Menninger, K. 1968. *The Crime of Punishment.* New York: Viking Press.

Minnesota v. Murphy, U.S. 104, S.Ct. 1136, 1143 (1984).

Moffitt, T. E. 1990. "Juvenile Delinquency and Attention Deficit Disorder: Boys' Developmental Trajectories from Age 3 to Age 15. *Child Development* 61:893–910.

Morrissey v. Brewer, 408 U.S. 471 (1972).

National Rifle Association. 1998. The Felon Voting Bloc. *NRA Crimestrike's Crimewatch Weekly* 4(44):783–805.

Nietzsche, F. W. 1887/1989. *The Genealogy of Morals.* Trans. W. Kaufman and R. J. Hollingdale. New York: Vintage Books.

Pepper, B. and J. Massaro. 1992. "Trans-institutionalization: Substance Abuse and Mental Illness in the Criminal Justice System." *TIE Lines* 9(2):1–4.

Peters, R. and H. Hills. 1993. "Inmates with Co-occurring Substance Abuse and Mental Health Disorders." In H. Steadmand and J. Cocozza, eds., *Providing Services for Offenders with Mental Illness and Related Disorders in Prisons,* pp. 159–212. Washington, D.C.: The National Coalition for the Mentally Ill in the Criminal Justice System.

Petersilia, J. 1995. "A Crime Control Rationale for Reinvesting in Community Corrections." *The Prison Journal* 75:479–96.

———. 1998. "Probation and Parole." In M. Tonry, ed., *The Handbook of Crime and Punishment,* pp. 563–88. New York, Oxford University Press.

Petersilia, J. and S. Turner. 1990. "Conditions That Permit Intensive Supervision Programs to Survive." *Crime and Delinquency* 36:126–45.

President's Commission on Law Enforcement and Administration of Justice. 1967. *The Challenge of Crime in a Free Society.* Washington, D.C.: U.S. Government Printing Office.

Regier, D., M. Farmer, D. Rae, B. Locke, S. Keith, L. Judd, and F. Goodwin. 1990. "Comorbidity of Mental Disorders with Alcohol and Other Drug Abuse: Results from the Epidemiologic Catchment Area Study." *Journal of the American Medical Association* 264(19):2511–18.

Roberts, A. R., ed. 1973. *Readings in Prison Education.* Springfield, Ill.: Charles C Thomas.

———. 1998. "An Introduction and Overview of Juvenile Justice." In A. R. Roberts, ed., *Juvenile Justice: Policies, Programs and Services,* pp. 3–20. Chicago, Ill.: Nelson-Hall.

Roberts, A. R. and J. A. Waters. 1998. "The Coming Storm: Juvenile Violence and Justice System Responses." In A. R. Roberts, ed., *Juvenile Justice: Policies, Programs and Services,* pp. 54–56. Chicago, Ill.: Nelson-Hall.

Rusche, G. and O. Kirchheimer. 1939. *Punishment and Social Structure.* New York: Columbia University Press.

Saleebey, D., ed. 1997. *The Strengths Perspective in Social Work Practice.* New York: Longman.

Schmalleger, F. 1997. *Criminal Justice Today,* 4th ed. Englewood Cliffs, N.J.: Prentice-Hall.

Schrag, C. 1961. "Foundations for a Theory of Corrections." In D. Cressey, ed., *The Prison: Studies in Institutional Organization and Change,* pp. 309–57. New York: Holt, Rinehart & Winston.

Scott, L. K. 1994. "Sex Offenders." In A. R. Roberts, ed., *Critical Issues in Crime and Justice,* pp. 51–76. Thousand Oaks, Calif.: Sage.

Shover, N. and W. Einstadter. 1988. *Analyzing American Corrections.* Belmont, Calif.: Wadsworth.

Sikorski, J. B. 1991. "Learning Disorders and the Juvenile Justice System." *Psychiatric Annals* 21(12):742–47.

Stone, E. M. 1988. *American Psychiatric Glossary.* Washington, D.C.: American Psychiatric Press.

Sullivan, L. 1990. *The Prison Reform Movement: Forlorn Hope.* Boston: Twayne.

Sutker, P. B., F. Bugg, and J. A. West. 1993. "Antisocial Personality Disorder." In P. B. Sutker and H. E. Adams, eds., *Handbook of Psychopathology,* pp. 337–69. New York: Plenum.

Sykes, G. 1958. *The Society of Captives.* Princeton, N.J.: Princeton University Press.

Toch, H. 1977. *Living in Prison.* New York: Free Press.

Tonry, M. 1998. "Intermediate Sanctions." In M. Tonry, ed., *The Handbook of Crime and Punishment,* pp. 683–711. New York: Oxford University Press.

Treger, H. 1983. "Social Work in the Justice System: An Overview." In A. R. Roberts, ed., *Social Work in Juvenile and Criminal Justice Settings*, pp. 7–17. Springfield, Ill: Charles C Thomas.

U.S. Department of Justice, Office of Justice Programs, Bureau of Justice Statistics. 1997a. *Prisoners in 1997.* (BJS Publication No. 170014). Washington, D.C.: U.S. Government Printing Office.

———. 1997b. *HIV in Prisons and Jails, 1995* (NCJ Publication No. 164260). Washington, D.C.: U.S. Government Printing Office.

———. 1998a. *Bureau of Justice Statistics Fiscal Year 1998: At a Glance* (NCJ Publication No. 169285). Rockville, Md.: Author.

———. 1998b. *An Analysis of National Data on the Prevalence of Alcohol Involvement in Crime* (NCJ Publication No. 168632). Washington, D.C.: U.S. Government Printing Office.

———. 1998c. *Profile of Jail Inmates 1996* (NCJ Publication No. 164620). Washington, D.C.: U.S. Government Printing Office.

Von Hirsch, A. 1976. *Doing Justice.* New York: Hill & Wang.

Waldie, K., and O. Spreen. 1993. "The Relationship Between Learning Disabilities and Persisting Delinquency." *Journal of Learning Disabilities* 26(6):417–23.

Walker, S. 1994. *Sense and Nonsense about Crime and Drugs: A Policy Guide,* 3d ed. Belmont, Calif.: Wadsworth.

Wellisch, J., M. J. Anglin, and M. Prendergast. 1993. "Treatment Strategies for Drug Abusing Women Offenders." In J. Inciardi, ed., *Drug Treatment and Criminal Justice,* pp. 5–29. Newbury Park, Calif.: Sage.

13

Child Abuse and Neglect

Lynn Videka-Sherman
Michael Mancini

A society's investment in its future can be measured by its investment in its children. Despite the rhetoric concerning the centrality of children to families in the United States, the past thirty years have revealed a growing problem of abuse and neglect of children in the United States. Since Charles Kempe's pioneering work identifying the "battered child syndrome" Americans have witnessed an explosion of knowledge about the causes and consequences of child abuse and neglect (Kempe et al. 1962). Unfortunately, the rates of documented harm or danger to children as a result of abuse or neglect has dramatically increased during the same time frame. Although child abuse and neglect can occur within any socioeconomic stratum, its incidence is concentrated in sectors of our society that contain families with multiple social, economic, and personal resource disadvantages.

If there is a core setting for the practice of social work, it is in child welfare and child protective settings, the human service agencies that serve abused and neglected children. Social work is a central profession in the identification, assessment, prevention, treatment, and rehabilitation of abused and neglected children and their families.

DEFINING AND EXPLAINING CHILD ABUSE

Child maltreatment is defined by a heterogeneous grouping of types of inadequate care or protection that results in actual or potential harm to the child, and it encompasses acts of commission and omission. Although most state laws are modeled after federal legislation (PL 93–247, Child Abuse Prevention and Treatment Act), states' definitions of child maltreatment vary. In addition to laws pertaining to the definition of child abuse and neglect, states legislate family laws that specify the conditions under which state agencies and courts can intervene in family life to protect children. States also legislate criminal statutes that concern acts of violence, whether familial or extrafamilial.

Most definitions of child maltreatment encompass three components: (1) the occurrence of at least one identifiable instance of adult behavior (or behavior omission) toward a child under 18 years of age; (2) physical or psychological harm or endangerment to the child that is a result of the behavior in question; and (3) a clear causal link between the adult behavior in question and the harm resulting to the child (Faller and Russo 1981; Stein 1998).

Child maltreatment is typically further classified into six forms: physical or emotional abuse; physical, emotional or educational neglect; and sexual abuse. For the purpose of defining child abuse and neglect for this chapter, the 1996 National Incidence Study of Child Maltreatment definitions are used (U.S. Department of Health and Human Sevices [U.S. DHHS] 1998b). *Physical abuse* entails an act of commission that results in harm to the child, including physical assault resulting in injuries such as burns, bruises, fractures, contusions, lacerations, or other injuries. *Emotional abuse* results from verbal assault or chronic scapegoating of a child by an adult. Verbal assaults include conveying to a child that he or she is no good, worthless, evil, or hated. Emotional abuse also includes confinement, threats, and withholding life necessities such as sleep or food.

Sexual abuse is a specific form of physical abuse. In this form of abuse, injury to the child results from sexual contact by a caretaking person. Sexual contact includes intercourse, touching, and fondling. Other acts that use children as sexual objects, such as child pornography and subjecting children to view sexual acts performed by adults, are also defined as abusive.

Physical child neglect results from a parental act of omission; the parent fails to provide for the child's basic needs, resulting in the child's susceptibility to or experience of harm or injury. The most common type of child neglect is inadequate supervision, that is, leaving the child unattended or unsupervised. Other forms of physical neglect include failure to thrive (growth failure due to inadequate nurturance); failing to provide basic physical needs such as food, clothing, shelter, or health care; abandonment; and expulsion of the child from the home. *Educational neglect* includes failing to enroll the child in school, permitting chronic truancy, or not attending to the special educational needs of the child. *Emotional neglect* includes inadequate nurturance or affection, chronic violence in the household, and permitting alcohol or substance use by a child.

There are numerous difficulties in defining child abuse and neglect. As mentioned, each state has a different legal definition of what constitutes abuse and neglect. To complicate matters further, comorbidity rates are high for different forms of child maltreatment. For example, in 1996, 25 percent of all reports of child maltreatment were for both child abuse and neglect.

Without a universal definition of child abuse and neglect, different groups, agencies, and professionals use **different definitions** for different purposes and goals (Hutchison 1990). There is no agreed upon taxonomy of maltreatment types; the preceding taxonomy used is a broadly but not universally accepted list. Many researchers and child advocates believe that the prevailing definitions of child abuse and neglect are too restrictive and lead to an undercount of victimized children (Chalk and King

1998; Stein 1998). Several writers have expressed concern about the ambiguity and amount of interpretation that is required to identify behaviors as abusive or neglectful according to statutory requirements (Atteberry-Bennett 1987; Burns and Lake 1983; Melton and Davidson 1987). Christopherson (1983) outlines five criteria that professionals use in interpreting legal definitions of child maltreatment: statutory definitions, professional expertise (gained through education and experience), clients' subjective reports, social norms, and no criteria at all.

Various definitions of child abuse and neglect have different foci. For example, most state laws focus define child abuse and neglect as having two requirements— parental behavior (an act of omission or commission) *and* a harmful result to the child. No states outlaw physical punishment of children; none dictate basic requirements for adequate parenting. Our societal emphasis on family privacy results in a "hands-off" policy with respect to standards for adequate parenting and an absence of programs that promote adequate parenting. A parental act is not deemed deviant until it crosses the threshold of harm to the child, a threshold that is vague and subject to interpretation. One study found that personal experience as a parent and history of child abuse and neglect affected professionals' definition of child maltreatment very little. The same study found that if a professional had previously encountered a case of child maltreatment he or she was less likely to classify ambiguous acts of omission or commission to a child as abusive or neglectful (Portwood 1998).

Almost no legal definitions include societal factors that lead to the occurrence of abuse, such as poverty. What are the effects of poverty and what are the differential effects of child neglect? This distinction is very difficult to draw. Furthermore, the distinctions between different forms of child and abuse are vague. Dubowitz et al. (1993) discussed the typical definition of child neglect as focusing on the parent's acts of omission that have harmed or have the potential to harm the child. This definition does not take into account chronicity or severity of the behavior. Other important factors are also omitted from the definition, including the age of the child and many other aspects of the behavior such as the point at which lack of supervision can be defined as neglect, the circumstances under which the parent is culpable for an unintentional injury of the child, how many times a behavior occurs or does not occur, and the duration of the behavior. In defining child neglect, the reporter or investigator of the behavior is faced with many discriminations to make. Is the parent neglectful if he or she leaves a child at home alone when the parent works because they cannot afford day care? Does it make a difference if the child is 6 or 8 years old? Is missing a dose of an antibiotic negligent? Is not noting an ear infection evidence of medical neglect? Is a stressed and overtired parent who is asleep when his or her child has an accident neglectful? What about the parent who spends money on a drug habit instead of food for the child? How many times must such behavior occur to be considered neglectful? How severe must it be? And for how long must it last before we define these acts as neglectful? These examples illustrate some of the complexity in defining child neglect.

Gough (1996) suggests that there has been a historical broadening of the definition of abuse and neglect, which is largely responsible for the dramatic increases that have been found in reporting over the past twenty-five years. Kempe et al.'s (1962) pioneering work first defined physically abused babies. Now most states and most professionals include in their definitions of child maltreatment the multiple types of abuse and neglect outlined at the beginning of this section. There has also been a broadening of views of persons responsible for abuse and neglect, from a sole focus on families to a broader view of nonfamilial caregivers (baby-sitters, day care centers, other family members, friends) and societal institutions including schools and child welfare institutions. Recent years have witnessed an increased emphasis on the deleterious psychological and developmental effects of child maltreatment. There has been a growing concern for children not to have certain experiences, such as sexual contact between adults or minors, whether or not there is evidence of harm to the child. Finally, the start and endpoints of childhood have been broadened. Witness the definition of maternal ingestion of alcohol or drugs prenatally as an indicator of child maltreatment. A 17-year-old is still considered a protected minor with respect to sexual activity; a generation ago the 17-year-old would have been thought an adult.

Hutchison (1990) raised several issues with respect to the definitions of child abuse and neglect. She noted that child maltreatment has been defined as a basis to create social policies and social programs, as a set of legal statutes designed to protect children from harm and to punish inadequate parents, as a necessary requirement for research, and for case management and treatment purposes including differential diagnosis of the child's and family's needs.

We have adapted Hutchison's (1990) typology to define three distinct theoretical orientations toward the definition of child abuse and neglect. The *medical approach* focuses on physical findings and consequences of child abuse and neglect. This perspective was influential in identifying such syndromes as the "battered child syndrome" and "failure to thrive," and in aiding passage of the original 1974 Child Abuse Prevention and Treatment Act. Many statutory definitions of child maltreatment are still based on the medical approach to defining maltreatment.

The *sociological approach* defines child maltreatment through social constructs, cultural mores, and social conditions and stressors. Societal conditions and predilections are seen as creating environments that lead to child maltreatment. This point of view was dominant in the 1970s.

The *ecological approach* (Belsky 1993) ascended in the 1980s. Using a social systems approach, the ecological definition of child maltreatment sought to incorporate societal, neighborhood, parental, and child factors that lead to the occurrence of abuse or neglect. While the ecological approach is still dominant in current thinking about child maltreatment, the emphasis has shifted toward integrating a developmental perspective on childhood and on the transactions that transpire in the parent-child relationship. This approach orients the definitions of child maltreatment to disruptions in normal development of the child and to the family processes that are the immediate precursors and correlates of child maltreatment.

Belsky (1993) has advocated moving to an *evolutionary perspective* in viewing child maltreatment as a product of the struggle for survival within a family embedded in a society with limited social and personal resources. This approach has yet to gain widespread acceptance.

Perhaps the most deleterious **effect** of the ambiguity in defining child abuse and neglect is that it goes **unreported**. Even among professionals who are mandated reporters, only a minority of suspected cases of child abuse or neglect are reported to child protection services (CPS) agencies. Recent incidence studies suggest that the majority of child maltreatment cases are never identified to authorities (U.S. DHHS

1998a, 1998b) and, thus, that millions of children go unprotected and untreated in their abuse experiences.

The flip side of vague definitions is the huge numbers of **unsubstantiated** reports of child maltreatment to CPS agencies. An unsubstantiated report is one that has been formally made, investigated, and found not to constitute abuse or neglect according to the statutes of that state. Besharov (1990) reported that while only 4 to 10 percent of unsubstantiated reports are made as knowingly false reports, a full *60 to 65 percent* of all reports made to the CPS agency are ultimately unsubstantiated. He stated, "Many unfounded reports involve situations in which the person reporting, in a well-intentioned effort to protect a child, overreacts to a vague and often misleading possibility that the child may be maltreated" (37). These unsubstantiated reports are likely to reflect a confusion that has it roots in the ambiguity in definitions of child neglect and abuse.

In an earlier article Besharov (1981) identified three negative effects of the definitional ambiguities in child abuse and neglect that still pertain today. First, with vague and unequivalent definitions, there are **comparability** problems. Vague definitions make it impossible to maintain a research or a national standard in terms of protecting children from abuse and neglect. When viewed with this critical lens, it would be impossible to truly compare incidence data from one jurisdiction to another when definitions vary considerably. Second, since there is **no consistency** in what is defined as child abuse and neglect, it is difficult to reliably ascertain that a child was indeed harmed or about to be harmed in many cases of maltreatment. Finally, the lack of taxonomies of etiology or of effects makes it difficult to **describe** the full, interactional, ecological phenomenon of child maltreatment.

In some ways, the definitional wars concerning child abuse and neglect reflect our society's conflicts. These include the tension between the rights of the child and the rights of parents, the search for a simple definition and explanation of child maltreatment, and the search for simple solutions to preventing maltreatment. Even with existing, limited definitions, we are identifying abuse and neglect after harm has occurred to the child. Perhaps the most pressing definitional need is to identify specific risk or early signs for child maltreatment and to provide supports to those families so they can avoid the cycle of abuse and neglect. These supports are discussed later in the assessment and intervention section. Such definitions, however, would further increase the tension between parental rights and protection of the child.

DEMOGRAPHIC PATTERNS

The National Center on Child Abuse and Neglect (NCCAN) is mandated to conduct studies of child maltreatment incidence. Two sets of studies have been funded by this agency. The first is part of a collaborative effort begun in 1988 between NCCAN and the states to collect and analyze annual child abuse and neglect data from CPS agencies in all fifty states, the District of Columbia, the territories, and the armed forces (U.S. DHHS, 1988). This study uses the Children's Bureau's and the states' jointly sponsored National Child Abuse and Neglect Data System (NCANDS) and focuses exclusively on formal reports made to CPS agencies. The latest report of 1996 data was published in 1998.

The second major study is the National Incidence Study (NIS), also conducted by NCCAN. The third National Incidence Study (NIS-3), congressionally mandated under PL 100–294, was conducted in 1993 and published in 1998 (U.S. DHHS 1998a). This study compares the data from the following two previous incidence studies: the NIS-1, conducted in 1979 and 1980 and published in 1981; and the NIS-2, conducted in 1986 and 1987 and published in 1988. The NIS-3 is more comprehensive than the first two NIS studies and the NCANDS study because it includes unreported child maltreatment known to community agencies such as police, the court, health and social services agencies, day care centers, and schools as well as maltreatment that is reported to state CPS agencies.

The NIS-3 study uses two standards for defining abuse and neglect. The *harm standard* is conservative and requires that "an act or omission results in demonstrable harm in order to be classified as abuse or neglect" (U.S. DHHS 1998a:6). To provide a comprehensive count of the true incidence of child maltreatment as defined in the Child Abuse and Prevention Act (PL 93–247), the NIS-3 added an *endangerment standard* for child abuse and neglect. The endangerment standard includes all cases falling under the harm standard and also includes cases of children not yet harmed, but considered to be endangered by a CPS investigation (U.S. DHHS 1998a). As a result, a larger incidence of cases is identified. The data presented in this section are excerpted from these three studies. All data on incidence are limited because of sampling biases (Widom 1989).

Reports of child abuse and neglect have been steadily rising since 1974, the date of NIS-1 (U.S. DHHS 1981). In 1974, 669,000 CPS reports were made. In 1984, 1,727,000 reports were made, a 258 percent increase in eight years (American Humane Association 1986). By 1996, 2,000,000 reports were made, a 15 percent increase since 1984, and 44 children per 1,000 were found to be abused or neglected (U.S. DHHS 1998a).

In 1993, 2,815,600 children were considered endangered by abusive or neglectful behavior on the part of one or more caretakers, a 67 percent increase from the NIS-2 (U.S. DHHS 1998a). Most experts believe that heightened public awareness of child abuse and neglect accounts for much of the increase.

The NCANDS study found that 52 percent of reported cases were made for physical neglect (deprivation of necessities), and 24 percent were for physical abuse. Sexual abuse accounted for 12 percent of reported cases. Emotional maltreatment accounted for 6 percent of reported cases (U.S. DHHS 1998b). Using the harm standard, the NIS-3 found increases in physical abuse (42 percent), sexual abuse (83 percent), physical neglect (102 percent), and emotional neglect (333 percent) compared with NIS-2 data collected eight years earlier (U.S. DHHS 1998a). According to the NIS-3 study, there were 1,077 fatalities due to maltreatment in 1994 (a fatality rate of 1.9 children per 100,000). Of the fatalities, 76 percent were children under 4 years of age.

Of all CPS reports, 52 percent were made by professionals; 27 percent were made by friends, neighbors, relatives, victims, or perpetrators themselves. Twenty percent of reports were made anonymously. About 50 percent of reports made were substantiated by a CPS investigation. Two-thirds of the substantiated reports were made by professionals (U.S. DHHS 1998a).

Characteristics of families reported to CPS agencies in 1996 were analyzed by NCCAN (U.S. DHHS 1998b). Of the reported perpetrators, 77 percent were parents, 11 percent were other relatives, and 90 percent were the primary caretaker of the child. Incidence rates are 44 per 1,000 overall. They are higher for younger children, with the rate of 67 per 1,000 for infants (under 1 year old), 58 per 1,000 for 1-year-olds, and increasing each year for children each year older, peaking for 6-year-olds, at 68 per 1,000. After 6 years of age, the rates drop each year correspondingly for each year to 18 years of age.

The NIS-3 found, using the harm standard, that 72 percent of physically abused children were abused by their biological parents, and 91 percent of neglected children were neglected by their biological parents. Eighty-one percent of emotionally abused children were abused by a biological parent. But nearly half of sexually abused children were abused by someone other than a parent or parent substitute.

The NIS-3 also found that 65 percent of perpetrators of child maltreatment were female. Of biological parent perpetrators, mothers were implicated 75 percent of the time and fathers 46 percent of the time. Of the total, 21 percent were maltreated by both parents, accounting for the total being over 100 percent.

Women are overrepresented in these numbers due to the rates at which they are single parents, enhanced by the high rates of poverty for single-parent mothers. Single mothers and their rates of poverty also explain the fact that 87 percent of neglected children were found to be neglected by their female caretakers. The NIS-3 reported that, using the harm standard, children living in single-parent homes were 77 percent more likely to be victims of physical abuse and 87 percent more likely to be victims of physical neglect than children in two-parent families. The NIS-3 also reports that children living in households with incomes of less than $15,000 were at greater risk for all types of maltreatment (U.S. DHHS 1998a). Sixty-seven percent of perpetrators of physically abused children are males, and 89 percent of sexually abused children were abused by males.

More than half of indicated CPS cases were found to be cases of physical neglect; 24 percent were victims of physical abuse, and 12 percent were sexually abused. Three percent of cases were indicated for medical neglect, and emotional maltreatment accounted for 6 percent of victims (U.S. DHHS 1998b).

African American and Native American children were disproportionately reported as victims of maltreatment in the NCANDS study (U.S. DHHS, 1998b). The incidence of maltreatment is slightly greater for girls (52 percent of indicated cases) than boys (48 percent). The racial composition of reported families is 53 percent white, 27 percent black, 11 percent Hispanic, and 3 percent other. But the NIS-2 and NIS-3 found no statistical relationship between the incidence of maltreatment and the child's race or ethnicity. This crucial discrepancy can be explained by the different methodologies used by the two studies and by the probable differential response of the service system to different racial groups. The NCANDS study is based solely on CPS reports, whereas the NIS-3 is based on all known (reported and unreported) cases of child maltreatment. Eighty-one percent of the reported perpetrators were under 40 years old; 39 percent were between 30 and 39 years old.

SOCIETAL CONTEXT

The correlates and effects of community on child abuse and neglect is reaching major attention among researchers today. Coulton et al. (1995) showed that high neighborhood poverty rates, evidence of social disorganization, and alienation (fewer interactions among residents of a neighborhood) were positively related to rates of child abuse and neglect. It is interesting to note that the national incidence studies do not yet identify neighborhood correlates. Nor are most intervention programs (discussed later) targeted to neighborhoods. The systematic tracking and the intervention technology used to combat child abuse and neglect have not yet incorporated this newly discovered knowledge about the role of communities and neighborhoods. The orientation toward the causes of child maltreatment still rests on the parent as the controlling agent.

Lack of social support also has been shown to lead to child maltreatment. Wahler and Hann (1984) identified "the insular mother" as one who has few social ties, due in part to her communication patterns and lack of relationship-building skills. Other studies have found that social support and employment (indicating social integration as well as income generation) are inversely related to child maltreatment. It is clear that these social psychological factors, which indicate the interaction patterns of the family with societal resources, are important predictors of child maltreatment occurrence.

The incidence studies cited in the preceding and other studies (Dubowitz et al. 1993; Zuravin 1989) indicate that the most vulnerable children and families experience multiple disadvantages and hardships in their lives, including poverty, larger family size, and teenage parenting.

Research has clearly pointed to societal as well as individual factors in the etiology of child abuse and neglect. What is less clear are the mechanisms by which these factors predispose families toward abuse and neglect. We have yet to systematically incorporate this orientation into data system tracking and intervention technology.

VULNERABILITIES AND RISK FACTORS

In discussing risk factors for child abuse and neglect, the epidemiology of child maltreatment, the ecological framework will be used. This model is derived from Bronfenbrenner's (1979) pioneering work on the ecological context of child development. It posits multiple paths of bidirectional causation that eventually can lead to child abuse or neglect. Early research on risk for child maltreatment focused on the demographic variables previously described. With the advent of the ecological model, the stage was set for knowledge development regarding multidetermined vulnerabilities and risk factors that interact to produce conditions under which child maltreatment occurs. Under the ecological model, risk factors can be grouped under the interacting systems of parental, child, social psychological factors (how the family system interacts with the community), and community and cultural factors. For purposes of discussion, the perpetrator of the child maltreatment will be presumed to be the parent. Figure 13.1 shows the dynamic interaction of the ecological system that produces child abuse and neglect.

Figure 13.1 suggests that child maltreatment is a product of certain types of parent-child interaction and that abuse and neglect does not exist independently from certain styles of parent-child interaction within the family microsystem. The focus on the parent-child interaction has become one of the most promising areas of child abuse research.

FIGURE 13.1 Ecological Model of Risk and Protective Factors in Child Maltreatment

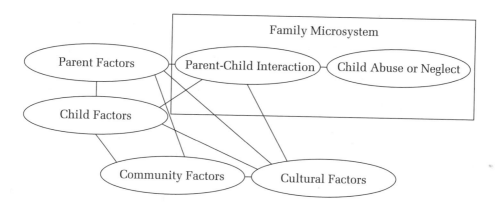

Parent-child interaction is influenced (and in turn influences) several other systems. These risk factors predispose the parent and child to interact in certain ways. Note that the direction of causation between parent-child interaction and the parent and child systems is bidirectional. The parent and the child each bring individual risk and protective factors to the family interaction. But the reciprocal causation paths also suggest that the family interaction patterns influence the parent and child subsystems. Child factors can moderate the relationship between parental style and parent-child interaction and child abuse and neglect. Community factors affect both parent and child subsystems by hosting dangers or resources within environments in which the parent and child live. Cultural factors influence the community, parent and child beliefs, and the parent-child interactions through established mores and behavioral expectations.

Parental Risk Factors. Parental factors that serve to increase risk for abuse or neglect of a child include several trait or communication-style features of the parent. Several studies have suggested that there is a causal link between *victimization as a child* and perpetrating abuse or neglect with one's own children (Conger, Burgess, and Barrett 1979; Kempe et al. 1962; Spinetta and Rigler 1972; Steele and Pollack 1968; Widom 1989). Although the majority of these studies share serious methodological flaws such as relying on retrospective (and thus possibly distorted) reports; inadequate, biased samples; or invalid and unreliable measures of childhood victimization, the few prospective well-designed studies such as Widom's (1989) show the same pattern that approximately one-third of children who were victimized as children go on to maltreat their own children.

Explanations of how childhood experience, including victimization, influences adult behavior patterns are made by both psychodynamic and social learning theorists. Learning theorists posit that through selective reinforcement and modeling, relationship and caregiving behaviors and communication styles are learned through experience. Psychodynamic theorists posit that early interactions with the parent influence the child's development, capacity for developing relationships with others, and the parent's own ego capacity and strengths. Although the mechanisms used to explain the translation of experience into behaviors vary, the end result is the same from either theoretical perspective— one's experiences as a child, especially those experiences with primary caregivers, influence one's own behavior, expectations, and caregiving patterns as an adult.

While simple unicausal models of maltreating parent psychological profiles have been rejected, many studies have found necessary, but not necessarily sufficient, risk factors for child maltreatment within the parent. *Substance abuse* is a major risk factor for child maltreatment (Young, Gardner, and Dennis 1998). *Anger management and emotion control problems* predispose a parent to abusive acts. Predisposition to *anxiety, depression,* and *hostility* increase the risk that the parent will maltreat their child. Parental anxiety, depression and hostility have been shown to be associated with more aggression, less empathy, less emotional regulation and less emotional responsiveness in parent-child interactions (Burgess and Conger 1978; Green 1976; Spinetta and Rigler 1972).

Depression and *apathy toward life* have been found to be distinguishing characteristics of neglectful mothers (Polansky et al. 1981). Neglectful parents do not know how to play and to stimulate their children. Indeed, Burgess and Conger (1978) found that neglectful families have fewer *family interactions* and more negative interactions than abusive families and both had less positive, more negative, and fewer overall interactions than nonmaltreating families. Patterson and his colleagues (1982) also show that *aggressive, antisocial behavior* on the part of the parent is associated with child maltreatment. This parental behavior, in turn, influences the child to be aggressive and antisocial, demonstrating the reciprocal nature of aversive parent-child interaction. Patterson has labeled this interactional learning process as "coercion training." The *need for control* and *pessimism regarding social relationships* as a possible source of satisfaction is another risk factor for parental maltreatment. *Lack of experience in caring for children* and *lack of knowledge of child development* can also contribute as risk factors for child maltreatment (Blumberg 1974; Steele and Pollack 1968; Whiting and Whiting 1975).

Child Risk Factors. *Prematurity* and *low birth weight* have been shown to increase the risk that a child will be maltreated (Elmer and Gregg 1967; Hunter et al. 1978; O'Connor et al. 1980). *Lack of social responsiveness* may be the mechanism by which risk for maltreatment is increased for low-birth-weight infants (Brown and Bakeman 1977; Egeland and Brunnquell 1979). A child's *attractiveness* may be an influence in child maltreatment (Dion 1974; Frodi and Lamb 1980). There may be many other child characteristics that elicit neglectful or abusive responses from parents. Most of these are likely to be mediated through interaction with the parent's own predisposition and style. Examples of other child characteristics that put the child at risk include *temperament,* the match between parent and child temperament, and *child passivity,* which could be a risk factor for neglect. There is no evidence that these relationships are either direct or unicausal. The role of the child's risk factors in the occurrence of child maltreatment is likely to be moderated and shaped (increased or decreased) through interaction with the parent's own style and attributes.

The Family System: Parent-Child Interaction. As suggested in the sections of parent and child risk factors, current thinking about child abuse and neglect focuses on parent-child interaction as the medium or process by which conditions conducive to child abuse or neglect are created and where basic aversive and harmful behavior and interaction patterns are laid. Parent-child interaction patterns of neglectful families include less *parental responsiveness* to the children, less overall *family interaction,* and less prosocial interaction than nonneglectful families (Burgess and Conger 1978). Abusive family interaction patterns include fewer *supportive interactions,* less positive *emotional interchange,* less emotional responsiveness from parent to child, more *parental controlling behavior,* more *interfering behavior,* and more *hostile behavior,* when compared with nonabusive families (Burgess and Conger 1978; Parke and Collmer 1975). These researchers have also shown how antisocial and aggressive behavior is created in the child as a response to the behaviors just listed. Maltreating parents interact less with their children, are negative in their interactions, and use physical punishments and power-asserting techniques more often in attempting to control the child's behavior. These in turn lead to the use of physical punishment to change the child, increased irritability, and, upon occasion, unintended aggression that may be defined as child abuse.

Other family indicators are also risk factors for child maltreatment. There is a high correlation of *marital problems* in abuse and neglect (Gil 1970; Hunter et al. 1978). Marital stress may increase risk for child maltreatment by decreasing the spousal support available to the maltreating parent, by increasing the level of tension and aversive interaction within the family unit, or through inducing depression or other mental illness sequelae, reducing the reserves of parents to cope with the challenges of parenting. Other family characteristics that are risk factors for child maltreatment include *poverty, large family size, early childbearing,* and *lack of labor force participation* (Zuravin 1988). Family system factors may interact with parent's early experiences to further increase risk to the child.

Community Risk Factors. Coulton et al. (1995) identified several neighborhood characteristics associated with child maltreatment. They found that *social disorganization, poverty, lack of coherence* and lack of *social connectedness* characterized neighborhoods with high rates of child maltreatment as compared with neighborhoods with lower rates. Zuravin (1989) found that the amount of vacant *housing, transience,* and a high ratio of single-family homes are associated with higher rates of child maltreatment.

Social psychological factors, or the interaction between individuals and their communities, also have been found to show risk factors for child maltreatment. Maltreating parents have been shown to have smaller, less available *social networks* (Zuravin 1989). Maltreating mothers have also been shown to use social resources less and to attend *church* less. These parents tend not to discuss problems; they do not give or get help from neighbors.

Cultural Risk Factors. In many ways our society condones violence through mass media depiction and through popular art, music, and performing arts. The vast majority of Americans use physical punishment with their children and believe that it is acceptable to do so (Straus and Gelles 1990). Slavery is part of our cultural legacy, as is tolerance of violence in families (Belsky 1993; Besharov 1990). Cultural differences in what is defined as abusive or neglectful are rarely studied in the literature. We may think of the cultural context in which we live as providing the environmental context for our values, role expectations, and behaviors.

RESILIENCIES AND PROTECTIVE FACTORS

There are resilience or protective factors for each of the domains listed in figure 13.1. Because only 30 percent of parents who were abused or neglected go on to maltreat their children, we can conclude that most abused and neglected individuals possess substantial resiliency as they grow up. Particular *cognitive mechanisms* to process one's childhood experiences can make the difference in how one behaves as a parent. Belsky (1993) and Egeland, Stroufe, and Erickson (1983) found that if one was victimized as a child, remembering the parent as rejecting *and forming a coherent account of one's own abuse and neglect* as a child can serve to protect the parent from repeating the maltreatment to his or her own child. This often takes the presence of a *therapist* or *other extremely supportive person* in the parent's life. Personal resources such as *attractiveness, social skills,* other successes or *talents, intelligence,* the presence of a *supportive partner,* and the *ability to regulate emotional experiences* are protective resilience factors for parents.

For the child, many of the same protective factors play a role in decreasing the risk for being abused. The presence of a *therapist* or *other extremely supportive person* in the child's life can reduce the likelihood that the child will be maltreated and increase the likelihood that if the child is maltreated, it will be detected. Personal resources such as *attractiveness, social skills,* other successes or *talents, intelligence,* and the *ability to regulate emotional experiences* are resilience factors for children and adolescents (Moran and Eckenrode 1992; Smith and Carlson 1997). Dorothy Allison's novel *Bastard Out of Carolina* is an excellent character study of a resilient child who is abused.

Community protective resilience factors include the presence of social support from *neighbors* as well as from *social services agencies,* including high quality *foster care,* and *community centers* and organizations. *Emergency nurseries* help parents avert child maltreatment crises, particularly leaving the child unsupervised or losing control with the child during a stressful period. *Social support* in the form of someone with whom to share the parenting role is indispensable. Communities strong in neighbor and social support structures will deter the likelihood that a stressed family will cross the line toward child maltreatment. It is interesting to note that community protective factors have received little attention in empirical studies. This may be because the attention to community-level factors has been a recent rediscovery in the epidemiological study of child maltreatment.

Cultural factors that protect against risk for child maltreatment include culturally sanctioned *experiences in caring for children* and in *preparing for the parenthood role.* Culturally sanctioned supports such as strong *religious communities, neighborliness,* and *valuing children* are other cultural factors that can reduce the likelihood that child maltreatment will occur. Similar to community factors, cultural resilience factors have received little attention in empirical research.

PROGRAMS AND SOCIAL WORK CONTRIBUTIONS

With its historical roots in ecological thinking about human problems, social work is a central profession in the fight against child maltreatment. With new thinking about how to apply preventive approaches to all phases of work with child maltreatment, we can organize intervention approaches to the needs of families and children at particular points in the child maltreatment cycle. Social work's "strengths" orientation (Saleeby 1991) is another asset in working with maltreating families. With a strengths orientation, social workers are in a position to identify and build on resiliency and protective factors against child maltreatment and its sequelae. It is important to note that while social work is a central profession in the treatment and care for maltreating families, interventions are increasingly relying on multidisciplinary approaches and on interventions that use paraprofessionals as key treatment providers; thus, social workers must have the ability to work in, and to coordinate, an interdisciplinary context.

Gordon (1988) introduced a model of prevention that has been adopted at the National Institutes of Health (National Advisory Mental Health Council Workgroup on Mental Disorders Prevention Research 1998). Adapted to child maltreatment, this model includes the following levels of prevention: *Universal prevention* for child maltreatment targets the general public that has *not* been identified on the basis of risk factors; *selective prevention* targets families whose risk is known to be higher than average for child abuse and neglect; *indicated prevention* targets families with early signs of child maltreatment or deleterious parenting behaviors; and *relapse and comorbidity prevention* targets families who have known histories of child maltreatment. The goals of relapse and comorbidity prevention are to rehabilitate the parent and to reduce long-term harm or comorbidity of mental illness, physical disorders, or behavioral problems in the children. Social interventions for child maltreatment can be conceptualized in these four categories, which are used as a heuristic tool rather than as a strict typology. They are best viewed as a continuum rather than a strict typology because levels of need and levels of prevention flow into one another rather than manifest themselves as discrete categories. There are no clear dividing points between risk for abuse and early abusive patterns, or between early neglect and entrenched neglectful interaction patterns.

Universal Prevention. Many parent and family educational services provided by social workers in health care, schools, and in family and community agencies constitute universal prevention, particularly if the services are wellness oriented and not restricted to a known risk group. Much of social work practice in maternal and child health care constitutes universal prevention of child maltreatment. Public education campaigns like those that air on public service television announcements are universal prevention programs. Unfortunately, these are seldom evaluated for their effectiveness. Universal policies such as the Family Leave Act have universal child maltreatment prevention aspects to them. While many social workers intuitively "know" that such family support programs reduce child maltreatment, there is little empirical evidence to support this assertion.

One of the few examples of universal prevention programs is a school-based child sex abuse prevention program. Such programs are now incorporated in the curricula of many school districts, although the empirical findings on these programs' effectiveness is mixed. In a meta-analysis of the effectiveness of sex abuse prevention programs, Rispens, Aleman, and Goudena (1997) found that the sixteen programs reviewed were successful in teaching children sex abuse concepts and self-protection skills, especially if the program included both components. There was reasonable retention of concepts learned, particularly when there was program repetition, boosters, in subsequent years. Programs were typically not examined for effects in reducing the incidence of sexual abuse.

Life cycle family support programs are another approach to universal support of parents and prevention of child maltreatment (Price et al. 1989; Weiss 1989; Zigler and Black 1989). Family support programs are available through community centers, health care centers, and other nonstigmatizing settings. They provide direct social, educational, and recreational services to families (Weissbourd and Kagan 1989:21) and reduce the risk for child maltreatment by providing parents with educational opportunities, social support, and support for the parenting role throughout the life cycle. Families who otherwise may be isolated or "insular" can use these programs to connect to other people, both professionals and peers, and to connect to needed services.

Selective Prevention. Most child maltreatment prevention programs are selective; that is, they target at-risk children and families for services. Interest in selective prevention has grown as we have learned more about the long-term negative effects of child maltreatment. The success of early intervention programs such as Head Start (Berrueta-Clement et al. 1984) and delinquency prevention (Hawkins and Catalano 1992) have also bolstered interest in selective prevention of child maltreatment.

Most selective prevention programs are aimed at relieving family stresses, both interpersonal and environmental, and providing social support. They typically deliver prevention services to the mother. The focus on mothers over fathers is largely a reflection of societal views of which parent is responsible for the care of children. A state-of-the-art review conducted by a panel of the National Research Council's Institute of Medicine (Chalk and King 1998:95–110) identified several selective prevention approaches. In their classification they include community-based social support programs; individual support programs, including Home Visiting Programs which have grown substantially in the past ten years; parent education and support groups; and social skills training. Some programs have had notable successes, but overall outcome findings are mixed (The Future of Children 1999; Howing et al. 1989; Videka-Sherman 1989).

Home visiting is one of the most popular child maltreatment prevention approaches. More than 550,000 children are enrolled in home visiting programs. The David and Lucile Packard Foundation's Future of Children Series (1999) conducted a review of the six current major home visiting approaches. The six models evaluated include Hawaii's Healthy Start Program (HSP). Originally developed in Hawaii, the program involves home-based parent support and education. A two year follow-up study resulted in better pediatric health care, improved parenting efficiency, decreased parenting stress, greater use of nonviolent child-rearing practices, and less violence in the home. No differences in child development were found when the intervention and control groups were compared (Duggan et al. 1999).

The Healthy Families America (HFA) program, which is being implemented in thirty-five sites nationwide, is a derivative of the Hawaii Healthy Start program. In the HFA program, peer home visitors provide links to concrete and social support for at-risk, young, poor mothers and their children. The intervention typically begins prenatally. Although home visits are conducted by paraprofessionals, social workers are often supervisors and program managers. HFA has been shown to improve parent-child interaction and to have modest effects on health care use, the prevention of child maltreatment, and improved outcomes for the mother. No significant improvements have been shown in child development or maternal social support. There has been considerable attrition and variation in outcomes across sites. These findings suggest that it is important to study more complex interactions between client-program match and program implementation.

The home visiting program with the best empirical outcomes base is David Olds's Nurse Home Visitation Program (NHVP), which identifies high-risk mothers prenatally and provides home-based services to mothers from pregnancy through the baby's second birthday. The intervention includes weekly home visits that are designed to provide health teaching concerning pregnancy, labor, delivery, and infant development and care. Nurses help mothers find concrete resources such as health care, legal assistance, and education for herself. Nurses also help mothers build social supports, including ties with their own family and the father of the baby, and provide a supportive ally (the nurse) in women's early experiences as mothers. In an article reviewing the twenty-year research findings on the model, Olds et al. (1999) describe the results of their original Elmira, New York, study and a replication study made in Memphis, Tennessee. The program produced the following positive results with the neediest families: childhood injury and ingestion rates were decreased; mothers deferred subsequent pregnancies and entered the workforce; long-term rates of abuse and neglect were reduced; and fewer rapid, successive pregnancies occurred. By age 15 the offspring of the visited mothers had fewer arrests and convictions, smoked and drank less, and had fewer sexual partners. No program effects were found on birth outcomes or children's short-term development. The program produced substantially lower results when replicated in Tennessee. Olds et al. (1999) conclude that the use of professional nurses rather than lay home visitors is the key to the program's success.

Other home visiting programs, including the Parents as Teachers Program (Wagner and Clayton 1999), the Home Instruction Program for Preschool Youngsters (HIPPY; Baker, Pietrowski, and Brooks-Gunn 1999), and the Comprehensive Child Development Program (St. Pierre and Layzer 1999), show smaller or no effects on maternal or child outcomes.

Sherman, Sanders, and Trinh (1998) developed a specialized peer visitation program for crack-addicted mothers, in which recovering crack-addicted women served as peer mentors to pregnant addicted women. Acupuncture treatment was available for the crack addiction while the peer mentors provided social support, access to necessary goods and services, and parenting preparation services. Mothers who participated in the program had fewer positive toxicology results, had fewer low-birth-weight babies, and scored lower on the Child Abuse Potential Inventory's Rigidity Scale (Milner 1986).

Certain key features distinguish successful from unsuccessful selective child maltreatment prevention programs. Successful programs provide services early in the family life cycle. Prenatal programs appear especially promising in their potential to deter child maltreatment among families at risk. Stigma is minimized when the program is implemented through health care or community centers. Effective programs involve parents and children in interaction rather than providing services to the parent alone. Most programs include a parent education component; both child development and the parenting role are covered topics. Play and positive interaction are emphasized.

There are shortcomings in these programs and the research that describes their outcomes. With the exception of Olds's NHVP study (Olds et al. 1999), most programs follow up families for two years or less. Longer-term follow-ups are needed to demonstrate program effects throughout childhood and adolescence. Some selective prevention approaches have been shown to be effective in highly controlled laboratory-like conditions with homogeneous samples that do not typically represent the typical service groups in the community. However, implementation of the same programs with community-based, heterogeneous samples show fewer and smaller effects. This performance difference is likely a result of more conscientious program implementation and the use of selected rather than representative samples. These factors should be studied so that clinicians will have the best information possible available to them.

In conclusion, selected prevention programs appear promising, but long-term outcome information is needed. Finkelhor, Hotaling, and Yllo (1988) suggested such funding as a future priority for research funding. Since many families served in selective prevention programs have limited economic, educational, and social resources, they may need episodes of support throughout the life cycle.

Indicated Prevention. Intervention during the early phase of child maltreatment, before behavior patterns are established, is the hallmark of indicated prevention. Family preservation programs such as Home Builders (Happala, Kinney, and McDade 1988) provide intensive services, which can include round-the-clock service availability, funds for emergency housing and other needs, and visits offering social support as well as immediate responsiveness to whatever needs parents have. The goals of family preservation services has been to keep the family together. The research evaluation indices show mixed outcome findings (The Future of Children 1999; Schuerman, Rzepnicki, and Littell 1995).

Out-of-home placements may be used to protect the child and to provide a period of separation to work on family and child risk vectors for child maltreatment. Widom's (1992) research on long-term sequelae of child maltreatment shows that good-quality foster care can prevent negative long-term sequelae of child abuse or neglect.

Skills-based educational and training approaches that target parent-child interactions and are delivered in an ecological context are the core components of successful indicated prevention for child abuse and neglect (Chalk and King 1998; Howing et al. 1989; Kelly 1983; Videka-Sherman 1989). Skills-based programs most often include the following components:

▮ Teaching parents to notice and reward positive child behaviors.
▮ Teaching parents alternatives to the use of verbal or physical punishment. Alternatives include withdrawing attention for the misbehavior, giving positive directives on what the child should do, and using time-out for misbehavior.

▌ Social skills or communications training.
▌ Life skills training including work readiness and problem-solving skills.
▌ Stress management and relaxation training.
▌ Concrete supports such as child care, transportation, and assistance with housing and legal needs.

Successful programs include in-session practice and homework between sessions. Practice by the family is essential for generalization and regular use of the new skills. A tripartite approach is effective in indicated prevention with maltreating families: Interventions should enhance parenting skills, bolster parents' coping skills, and provide assistance with economic and other tangible needs.

Relapse and Comorbidity Prevention. Programs targeted to this level of prevention aim to end abusive or neglectful interaction patterns that have become entrenched in the family's behavior patterns. They also aim to prevent or reverse negative long-term sequelae associated with child maltreatment. Relapse and comorbidity prevention programs may be delivered to parents and families at any point of the family life cycle. Children who are abused and neglected may receive this level of preventive service during childhood or during adulthood. Intervention may be delivered in families or individually.

Howing et al. (1989), in a review of empirically based evidence on effective interventions for child maltreatment, identified specific effective intervention approaches for each type of child maltreatment. Table 13.1 summarizes their recommendations for specific intervention focuses for specific forms of child maltreatment. Empirically based intervention is best developed for abusive families. There are fewer studies specific to the needs and outcomes of intervention for neglectful and sexually abusive families.

When we think of prevention of comorbidity and relapse, it is important to focus on the necessary intensity of intervention methods. Reversing child neglect takes steady and repeated diligence in working with neglectful parents to enhance their

TABLE 13.1 Recommended Intervention Focus for Specific Forms of Maltreatment

Type of Maltreatment	Intervention Approach
Abuse	Skills-based training programs
	Programs using ecological etiology models
	Focus on parent-child interactions
	Focus on increasing parent flexibility
	Group approaches
Neglect	Supportive services
	Focus on enhancing parental responsiveness
	Focus on increasing attachment
	Focus on increasing family cohesion
	Family therapy
	Home visiting programs
Sexual Abuse	Family interventions
	Victim protection approach

Summarized from Howing et al. (1989)

attachment capacity toward their children and to create positive interaction patterns that parents have likely not experienced in their own upbringing. Longitudinal studies have increasingly pointed to the protective role that supportive, therapeutic relationships can have for mothers and for children alike (Cicchetti 1989; Egeland et al. 1983). This can take the form of individual psychotherapy, a key supportive relationship such as spouse or member or friend for the mother, and a teacher, caregiver, or adult mentor for the child. The key is that the relationship be positive, prosocial, empathy based, and enduring. The relationship allows the parent or child to experience an empathic, prosocial relationship that supports adaptive behavior and the flowering of the individual's own skills and assets. It also allows individuals to correct the representations they have of their own experiences. It helps clients define inadequate parenting as inadequate and to distinguish between adequate parenting and abusive and neglectful parenting.

Intensity of services is also important for prevention of comorbid developmental or mental health problems for children and parents. Changing entrenched family interaction patterns is difficult, tedious work. Some successful programs have used coaching approaches, where the therapist becomes an actor in the interaction (Wolfe 1987). Others have used intensive episodic services on a crisis intervention basis (Happala, Kinney, and McDade 1988). The preference for earlier forms of prevention seems clear from an efficiency and cost-effectiveness point of view. However, no studies have systematically compared the cost-benefits of early to later intervention.

ASSESSMENT AND INTERVENTIONS

The assessment of maltreating families (or families at risk of maltreatment) should follow the ecological model outlined in figure 13.1. Although the research has not yet been this refined, the practitioner should assess risk, resilience, and protective factors within each of the model constructs in figure 13.1—parent factors, child factors, family interaction factors, community and cultural factors, and the family system. Intervention should be targeted to the risk factors and should make the greatest use possible of protective or resiliency factors in the family's life space. Assessments should also include a resource analysis for minimizing risk and bolstering the resilience and protective factors identified.

The family's point of view as well as the points of view of significant social systems supports for the family, for example, grandparents in a three-generation household, should be included in a **family-focused assessment.** Including the family's cultural and religious heritage is essential in the assessment so that the intervention can take place in a culturally relevant context for the family. Because the stress level and problems that many maltreating families experience are so pervasive and complex, a complete assessment can be daunting, adding to the family's sense of futility. Throughout the assessment process the practitioner should partialize or triage problems experienced by the family to focus on manageable goals for intervention. To build client morale for change, complex problems must be broken down into simpler components that are important for child and family well-being.

The social worker should conduct an assessment of family interaction because this construct is a critical variable in the etiology of child maltreatment and because many of the most promising interventions focus on family interaction. The best way to do this is to observe the family interacting. As suggested in the discussion about risk and protective factors, the amount of interaction, the proportion of positive to negative interactions between parent and child, the communication methods used by the parent to deal with conflict or noncompliance, and the approach the parent uses to elicit compliance from the child should be assessed. Standardized assessment tools are available to evaluate family interaction (Conger and Elder 1994). While the typical social work agency may not have the resources to conduct formal blind interaction assessments, this observation scheme can be useful as a qualitative tool to guide the social worker's clinical assessment.

Measurement tools to assess the nurturance, stimulation, and safety of the home environment are also available. These include the Home Observation for Measurement of the Environment (HOME; Caldwell and Bradley 1979) and the Environmental Hazards Scale (Lutzker 1984). Standardized assessment tools for child abuse and neglect also are available. These include the Child Abuse Potential Inventory (CAPI), a self-administered seventy-seven-item scale that has been shown to predict physical abuse, and with less accuracy, neglect (Milner 1986). Two validated scales for assessing child neglect include the Child Neglect Severity Scale (Edgington, Hall, and Rosser 1980) and the Childhood Level of Living Scale (Polansky et al. 1981). Although they cannot be used for precise identification of child abuse or neglect, they may be clinically useful because they allow the practitioners to determine the degree of maltreatment potential. If used repeatedly, they also can demonstrate progress made during intervention.

Family assessments also should include an assessment of the marital relationship, if relevant, or the parent's relationship history. This provides important information about the marriage as a source of stress or support for the parent. It also provides important information about the parent's relationship style and skills. A number of standardized assessment instruments are available for marital assessments. These include the Locke-Wallace Marital Adjustment Scale (Locke and Wallace 1959), the Dyadic Adjustment Scale (Spanier 1987), and the Index of Marital Satisfaction (Hudson 1982).

As the risk research shows, maltreating families usually experience stress in many spheres. Effective intervention should include services to met the needs of the **maltreating parent** as well as the needs of the child. Assessment of the parent's needs includes identifying sources of stress in the parent's life, which may include financial strain, unemployment, inadequate housing, substance abuse, domestic violence, the presence of children with special needs or a child with a challenging temperament, or health or emotional needs of the parent. In addition, it is important for the social worker to assess the parent's *perception* of stress as well as the presence of the stressor.

The social worker should also assess parents' coping skills and resources, such as the ability to moderate emotions and to think before acting. Other coping resources are the parent's child management and relationship skills and the ability to form nurturing attachments. These skills may be especially pertinent for abusive parents who have difficulty with anger control. Nurturing capacity has direct links to reducing risk for child neglect. Another area of coping is life management skills. These include household management, financial management, basic work role skills, grooming and self-care. A parent with substance abuse history needs treatment for the substance abuse immediately. If the family has a history of domestic violence, the adults as well as the children must have access to a safe environment.

A thorough assessment of the **child** should begin with a basic physical assessment. This includes basic observations of the child's health, grooming, and presentation. It should also include height, weight, and head circumference measurement (for infants). Growth charts that define normal growth patterns for children over childhood are available from any basic pediatric text (see, e.g., Behrman 1995). If the child is not immunized or has not received a medical examination within the time frame recommended by the American Academy of Pediatrics, an exam should be scheduled.

The social worker should also screen the child or have the child screened for cognitive and social development. A number of developmental assessment tools can be used, which include the Denver Developmental Screening Test (Frankenburg, Dodds, and Fondal 1968), the Bayley Scales of Infant Development (Bayley 1969), and the Minnesota Child Development Inventories (MCDI; Ireton and Thwing 1974).

In addition to assessing the developmental progress of the child, the school-aged child should be assessed for mental health difficulties, academic and behavioral performance at school, and the ability to make and keep friendships. The availability of standardized assessment tools such as the Achenbach Child Behavior Checklist (CBCL) can help to assess both conduct disorders (or externalizing behaviors) and internalizing disorders (such as depression) in children as young as 4 years of age (Achenbach 1991). Many maltreated children have difficulties in these spheres.

Finally, basic life skills should also be assessed for children who are preschool aged or older. These skills include dressing, toileting, and grooming themselves.

The social worker should also assess sources of **community** stress and resources for the family. The asset level and safety of the community are important contextual factors in planning to serve the child and family. The family's position in the community—how well they are known and how well they know other community members, how many friends and extended family live nearby, the nature of the family's relationship with their neighbors, and the degree of scapegoating by or isolation of the family from the community—is important information to know. It is also important for the social work practitioners to know the helping norms in the community (are neighbors expected to know and help one another?), informal helpers available to the family (extended family members, friends, neighbors), and formal help available, including recreational alternative for children and parents.

Services for child maltreatment cannot be delivered successfully unless the family's **cultural context** and the resulting risk and protective factors that this cultural heritage produces are addressed. Thus, social workers should identify the cultural reference group for the family being served. This is evident to most social workers when the family is from an ethnic or racial minority group, but it is less evident to many social workers when a white family is being served. Cultural factors include mores and beliefs about children, parent-child relationships, and the appropriate roles for extended family, friends, neighbors, and the larger society in family life. Cultural groups may also offer resources that are not immediately evident to the social worker to reduce the risk for child maltreatment. It is extremely important for the social worker to be sensitized to his or her own cultural stereotypes and to guard against such stereotypes influencing or limiting the options that the social worker sees for the family.

For example, Holton (1992) gives an excellent example of how most child abuse and neglect specialists fail to understand the effects of social structural oppression and inequalities on black families. This failure to understand the structural societal dynamics causes social workers to oversimplify the demographic findings that blacks are overrepresented in CPS reports. Without regard to social structural inequalities, racial incidence differences can be interpreted as a sign of disproportionate dysfunctionality or pathology in black families, or these differences can be misinterpreted to be influences of black culture. Culture-sensitive prevention for child maltreatment also should consider several cultural resources typical to black culture. These include the following features quoted from Holton (1992:4):

▌ The use of elders as key resources
▌ Extended family participation and influence
▌ The use of expressive (music and dance) and visual arts as vehicles for outreach and retention [and treatment]
▌ An equal emphasis on male- and female-oriented programs
▌ The incorporation of religious/spirituality via the church as a central institution for engaging community members

In a second example, consider the situation of a first-generation immigrant family from Eastern Europe who is found to have abused their child. Most Eastern European countries have no child protection laws (Videka-Sherman and Proykov 1998), and the idea of a societal representative intervening in family life for child maltreatment may be completely alien to this family. Furthermore, children are highly valued, and nurturing and protecting children are central mores to Eastern European cultures. However, in Eastern Europe, extended families who live in the same household are a typically used resource for ensuring quality care of children despite financial and other family hardships. If a family has immigrated, but without extended family, a typical resource is not present for such a family. The social worker will provide better services if these factors are known and taken into account in treatment planning.

The use of culturally similar service providers is one tool to ensure cultural sensitivity of services to prevent child maltreatment. However, this is difficult to achieve in many cases because of the underrepresentation of ethnic minorities in social work—another manifestation of some of the structural and consequent educational opportunity inequalities that exist in American society. Proponents of peer-based paraprofessional home visiting programs (Greene and Heck 1998; Sherman et al. 1998) state that cultural similarity and relevance is one of the advantages of peer-based programs. While many social workers conclude that same-culture helpers are not a necessary condition for intervention success (Proctor and Davis 1996), achieving cultural relevance is one of the challenges in delivering an intervention that is relevant and acceptable to the family's life context.

Maltreating parents, especially neglectful parents, are notoriously difficult to engage in services. To **engage** a maltreating family, the social worker must find some common ground between societal expectations for parenting behavior and the parent's own values, beliefs, cultural reference points, and resources. The social worker functions as a broker between the family and the larger society as represented by child protection services.

Setting specific and realistic goals that are priorities of the parent as well as the CPS agency enables rather than impedes the engagement process. It is important to clearly specify family and practitioner responsibilities. The more families know about the intervention process, the intervention goals, and their role in the intervention process, the more successful the intervention will be. Social workers should do all they can to demystify the intervention process. This is especially important for clients with limited verbal and other cognitive skills.

A **contract** consists of a specific statement of goals, processes, and family and social worker responsibilities in the intervention process. In a pioneering study of children in foster care, Stein, Gambrill, and Wiltse (1974) found that written contracts enhanced parents' completion of tasks necessary for the reunification of parent and child. This finding is also relevant for community-based services to abusive or neglectful families. Contracting demystifies the intervention process for social workers as well as for families. Because maltreating families typically experience a series of life crises, the contract can serve as a reference point to help the social worker and the family retain focus in their work together. Contracts also can be used in work with individuals (parents or children) in the family.

Structure and clarity of purpose are essential in working effectively with maltreating families, to avoid the frustration that can be exacerbated when social workers have allowed drift in unstructured interventions. This is disastrous in working with families for whom lack of structure is part of the problem in providing adequate parenting. While engagement may take time, there is no evidence that structure and task orientation in social work services is destructive. Furthermore, if we use the principle of informed consent, the only ethical approach to practice is to fully inform the client of the intervention components and responsibilities and to obtain their agreement and consent to participate. The mandatory nature of most child maltreatment programs does not need to deter this process. It is better to know up front if the parent is unwilling to participate in some aspect of services because then steps necessary for the benefit of the child, including removal from the home, can be taken. Structure and purpose in working with maltreating families can minimize social worker discouragement and burnout, which is a reflection of the family's own discouragement.

We know little about the necessary **duration of services** to prevent child maltreatment. Short-term programs with limited goals, such as parent-training classes, may be successful in reaching those goals, but treatment effects are likely to erode over time, particularly if social support systems are not present or not functioning in a manner that supports service goals. Nor is it clear how specific gains are related to the long-term risk for child maltreatment. Some families are referred for services or reported to CPS over and over again. Are these families failures because they need more services? Are open-ended, long-term, supportive services always necessary? These are thorny questions for which we do not have clear answers. The concept of family support programs available to families throughout the life cycle holds great appeal as a way to mount resources to respond to the ongoing stresses and dilemmas in the lives of vulnerable families.

A maltreating family's needs typically surpass the services that a single agency can provide. In addition to parent maltreatment services, substance abuse treatment or domestic violence intervention may be needed for the parent or specialized developmental or mental health services may be needed for the child. Therefore, community liaison or **case management** work is necessary to ensure coordinated services for the family. Typically, the public child welfare agency has responsibility for monitoring multiple services on behalf of the family. Social workers may provide or may supervise case coordination tasks. Coordination requires regular communication and case planning by many agencies servicing the families.

The social worker working with maltreating families must confront many **ethical issues**. In addition to being bound by the National Association of Social Workers (NASW) code of ethics and state laws and ethics codes for practicing social workers, there are special ethical challenges when working with maltreating families.

For example, one family with ten children was repeatedly referred for physical child neglect due to unsanitary conditions in the home. Chronic truancy of the school-aged children was also a problem. As a result of a CPS investigation, the family was indicated for child neglect. When the assigned social worker visited the family's home, she was taken aback by the stench and dirt, including animal excrement on the floors. Although the situation appeared to be an obvious health hazard, no family member (child or adult) was sick or had a history of illness. Several of the school-aged children were diagnosed as borderline developmentally disabled. No one in the family placed a positive value on schooling. Not a single family member defined any family interaction or lifestyle problems. Even the horrified social worker noted harmony and warmth among family members. Should the social worker attempt to modify the beliefs of the parents or school-aged children? Can this case succeed in an intervention program without this values shift? Probably not. What are the comparative harms of allowing the children to continue to grow up in an environment so deviant from American mainstream values or of removing them from their family to live in a foster home, or more likely, in a series of them?

This is an example of ethical dilemmas faced by social workers in the field of child maltreatment. Social workers are on the front line of the conflict between the mainstream American societal values and social work's commitment to individualism and self-determination. We use the concept of harm to the child as a justification for limiting the rights of the parent and family. But harm to the child, as noted in the section on definitions of child maltreatment, is a fuzzy concept. Most choices involve some benefits and some harm, and identifying the best choice is often difficult.

ILLUSTRATION AND DISCUSSION

The Bartholomews were referred for medical child neglect by the county CPS agency, when the county health department nurse called the child abuse hotline to report lack of follow-up health care for an ear infection in the 6-month-old son, Antoine. The family had been remiss in seeking health care for Antoine in several episodes of ear infections, putting him at risk for hearing damage. In addition to lack of treatment for ear infections, Antoine's parents had failed to seek regular health care for him. He had not received infant immunizations and he had been brought to the emergency room for severe, untreated middle ear infections that showed signs of being present for several weeks before the visit to the emergency room. The Bartholomews failed to give Antoine prescribed medication for the ear infections and failed to keep his follow-up medical appointments. The public health nurse made the CPS call when the Bartholomews refused to open the door when she visited their home after their last missed medical appointment. They subsequently refused to open the door for the CPS investigator until she returned to their home with a police escort.

The case was referred by CPS to a not-for-profit family service agency, serving under contract from the state department of social services. The CPS worker was not a trained social worker; she was designated as the case manager for the Bartholomew case. Her role was to coordinate the services of several agencies to which the Bartholomews were referred, including pediatric health care, early intervention for developmentally at-risk children, and counseling services to the family (the social worker's agency).

Larry and Kenisha Bartholomew were both African American, 20 years old, and mildly developmentally disabled (at the high functioning level). Neither had completed high school. Neither had held a job for more than two weeks; Kenisha has never even attempted employment. Larry had worked as a mechanic's assistant in three auto repair shops, but he lost each job for failure to show up to work. The family is supported by public assistance. Larry wants to apply for Supplemental Security Income for Disabled Individuals (SSDI).

When the social worker first attempted to contact the Bartholomews, they locked the door and drew the shades as they had for pubic health nurse and the CPS investigator. The social worker gained entry in three weeks by making regular weekly home visits, announced by letters sent four days before the visit. The family court judge made it clear to the Bartholomews that if they wanted to retain custody of Antoine, they must let the social worker and other service providers enter their home. This directive was effective, if coercive, in persuading the Bartholomews to allow the social worker to enter the home. The court order was not as effective in promoting trust on the part of the Bartholomews toward the social worker. They refused to talk to her for the first several weeks after she gained entry to their trailer.

During the first three months of the social work contact, the social worker worked carefully to gain the trust of the Bartholomews. She began each visit stating the reason for the visit, which was to ensure that the Bartholomews would do whatever was necessary for Antoine to receive good care. If Antoine received good care, he would not be removed to foster care. This cause-and-effect link motivated the Bartholomews, because they did not want to lose Antoine. Although the Bartholomews were certain that they already were providing good care for Antoine (they loved him so!), they were, although grudgingly at first, willing to do whatever was necessary to avoid the threat of Antoine's removal from the home.

After two months, Kenisha felt comfortable enough with the social worker to begin to confide in her. All that Kensiha ever wanted to be was a mother. She adored her son and was highly invested in him and in her role as a mother. To be investigated for child maltreatment was a devastating blow for her. She was extremely afraid of losing her son, yet she had no idea of why this threat had been made to her. Couldn't people tell that she loved her baby very much?

While the social worker noted Kenisha and Larry's attachment to Antoine she also noticed some serious deficits pertaining to Antoine's mental and emotional development in the home environment. Some of these stemmed from Kensiha's and Larry's lack of cognitive skills and the deprivations of their own upbringings. Kenisha grew up in foster care homes and rarely sees her biological mother whom she describes as a "junkie." Larry grew up in a the same trailer park where the couple live now. His parents are both dead; his siblings live in another city. Kenisha and Larry do not have many friends; in their own words, "We don't trust people." Larry and Kenisha are regular church attendees. Religion is very important in Kenisha's life, less so in Larry's. Larry and Kenisha denied any problems in their marriage. They also denied any substance abuse problems, although the social worker frequently noted beer on Larry's breath.

The social worker noticed that the Bartholomews kept Antoine in his own crib in a dark room with no toys nearby for long periods of time; he was always in the crib when the social worker came for visits. The Bartholomews had only two toys for Antoine; these had been given to him as baby presents from Kenisha's mother. They did not have money to purchase toys for him, and furthermore, they had never thought to do so. They did not see the need for toys or other sensory stimulation for Antoine.

The social worker was also concerned because Larry and Kenisha became highly anxious when Antoine cried. This was a relatively infrequent occurrence because Antoine was a placid baby who rarely cried. When he cried, Larry and Kenisha tried to diaper him and feed him. If that did not calm him down, they laid him in his crib and closed the door to his room so that his crying was less disturbing to them. This did not happen often, but it did happen when Antoine had ear infections.

Consistent with the preceding observations, the Bartholomews did not know much about infant or child development. They were unaware of their lack of knowledge on this subject, and they did not anticipate Antoine's blossoming development.

The social worker prioritized two goals for working with the Bartholomews. First, she wanted to ensure Antoine's well-being and optimal development by assisting Kensiha and Larry to learn about infant and toddler development and the parents' role in stimulating positive development. Specifically she wanted to bolster the Bartholomews' skills in providing a stimulating environment for Antoine and in constructive response to his crying. Second, the social worker aimed to help the Bartholomews develop better skills for interacting with the health and human services system, especially the child health care system. The social worker tried to engage the Bartholomews in goal-setting; however, they were only minimally interested. They were, however, agreeable to the goals outlined. A verbal contract was made.

The social worker referred the Bartholomews to a parent-skills group sponsored by another social worker in the agency, but Kensiha and Larry never attended the group, although they had agreed verbally to do so. When the social worker probed about barriers to group attendance, Kenisha and Larry said that they did not like to go out at night due to much crime in the neighborhood. After several attempts to get the Bartholomews to the group the social worker decided to adapt the group's content on parenting skills and child development to individual sessions between her and the Bartholomews. She instructed Kenisha and Larry about the importance of stimulation and play for a developing infant. She brought bright-colored toys to the house. Even more important, she played with Antoine and Kenisha and Larry and the toys, modeling stimulating parent-child interaction. Neither Kenisha nor Larry know how to play. They felt awkward talking to Antoine or holding up toys for him to respond to. Over a period of several months, Kenisha and Larry gained a degree of comfort in playing with and talking to Antoine. They allowed the toys to remain in his crib, and they would put toys around Antoine when they set him in the playpen. After several months, the social worker noticed that Kenisha seemed to enjoy Antoine's reactions to his toys. The Bartholomews continued to find it awkward to talk to Antoine as they were caring for him. Although they know it was good to do so, they just did not talk much, even between themselves.

To complement the parenting skills that the Bartholomews were acquiring, the county health department assigned a visiting nurse to visit the Bartholomews to provide a structured infant stimulation program for Antoine. This service also provided an opportunity to practice skills in relating to health care professionals. At first the Bartholomews refused to allow the nurse to enter their trailer. The social worker conferred with the case manager and the nurse. She gave the nurse suggestions for how to approach the Bartholomews in a nonthreatening manner. She also worked with Kenisha and Larry to explain why the nurse was visiting, to discuss the negative consequences of not allowing her in, and to give them opportunities to practice how they would respond when she came to the house. Using cognitive restructuring techniques, she coached the Bartholomews to remind themselves of how the nurse's visit would help Antoine develop in a positive way. They were to actively think about this reason before their anxiety about her visit became high. They practiced together with the social worker and eventually the Bartholomews let the nurse in, although they claimed that they still "did not like her snotty attitude."

The nurse and the social worker explained to the Bartholomews how important regular health care was for Antoine. They stood by while Kensiha called the health care center to make the 9- and 12-month well-child pediatric visit appointments for Antoine. They rehearsed pediatric visits with the Bartholomews, including how to communicate questions and concerns to the pediatric nurse practitioner (PNP). The question that was of greatest concern to Kenisha (and she *was* able to ask it at Antoine's 9-month checkup) was, "Is he developing normally?" She was delighted at the PNP's response, "He certainly is. You're doing a good job."

The social worker and the Bartholomews worked together for nine months. At this time the social worker was changing jobs, and the CPS agency and the family court decided that it was time to terminate services to the Bartholomews. Kensiha and Larry were upset about the social worker's leaving. They stated that they were afraid that the nurse would bother them again. As the termination date neared, they intermittently refused to let the infant stimulation program nurse in the trailer. On the other hand, they did take

Antoine to his well-child medical appointments independently and felt a good rapport with his PNP. Antoine was developmentally assessed and was found to be within normal limits for all indicators except language.

The Bartholomew family illustrates several points and raises questions about social work intervention with maltreating families. The case also illustrates how an indicated prevention orientation can be used with a family that is referred for early child maltreatment.

One issue illustrated by the Bartholomew case is the importance of engagement in order for services to be effective. Initially the Bartholomews distrusted all human service providers, but through careful and consistent repetition of her purpose in contacting them and through her persistent, but nonthreatening manner, the social worker was gradually able to gain Kenisha's trust. The court mandate for social work services was used as a motivation enhancer. As with many maltreating families, it is unlikely that the Bartholomews would have been engaged in services without the court mandate.

The use of contracting and a structured intervention approach was useful with this family due to their limited cognitive skills as well as their distrust of the human services. Concreteness and specificity reduced the ambiguity of the service situation for the Bartholomews, which enabled them to manage the anxiety that services and the threat of losing their son created.

Coordination of services was necessary to serve the Bartholomews effectively. In addition to referrals, recommendations for other services, and periodic communication among service providers, it was important for the professionals involved with this case to work together to enhance the family's receptivity to services. In this case the CPS worker served as the case manager, and the social worker periodically contacted her to communicate about the case.

The family needed and received information about child development and parenting skills. As Antoine moves into toddlerhood, he will voice his autonomy through normal opposition and motor activities. The Bartholomews are still at risk of becoming overwhelmed and unable to adequately socialize Antoine. Parent-skills training and child development knowledge will likely continue to be ongoing needs for the Bartholomews.

The Bartholomews' social isolation intensifies their risk for future child maltreatment. Although they made progress in relating to the health care professionals and to their son, they continued to be isolated from friends, family, and neighbors. Should the social worker have more explicitly used the church as a resource for this family?

The Bartholomews' supportive marital relationship is an asset that can serve to enhance protective factors for the family. The intervention primarily focused on Kensiha, because of her amenability. Should the social worker have attempted to engage Larry more fully in the intervention? Should the possibility of his substance abuse have been more fully assessed and referred for possible treatment? Was the family's social and cultural context taken into account sufficiently? If not what should the social worker have done differently? Should Antoine be referred to an enriched nursery to reduce the risks that he will be developmentally delayed? Should the social worker have worked on employment for Larry?

CONCLUSION

Social work has always had a historical mission to provide assistance to abused and neglected children, few service populations are as central to the mission of the profession. There are also few populations that are as challenging to serve, particularly in today's ethos of short-term episodes of services.

The last twenty years have seen great strides in the knowledge of the etiology, risk factors, and protective factors for child maltreatment. It is hopeful, indeed likely, that future intervention programs for maltreating families will be refined and improved to better serve these families. Of special priority is the development of community and neighborhood-oriented programs that support some of the recent findings on the importance of community in the etiology of child maltreatment.

References

Achenbach, T. M. 1991. *Manual for the Child Behavior Checklist/4–18 and 1991 Profile.* Burlington, Vt.: University of Vermont Department of Psychiatry.

American Humane Association. 1986. *Trends in Child Abuse and Neglect: A National Perspective.* Denver, Colo.: Author.

Atteberry-Bennett, J. 1987. *Child Sexual Abuse: Definitions and Interventions of Parents and Professionals.* Unpublished Ph.D. diss., University of Virginia at Charlottesville.

Baker, A. J. L., C. S. Pietrowski, and J. Brooks-Gunn. 1999. *The Future of Children: Home Visiting: Recent Program Evaluations.* Los Angeles: The David and Lucile Packard Foundation.

Bayley, N. 1969. *The Bayley Scale of Infant Development.* Palo Alto, Calif.: Psychological Corporation.

Behrman, R. E., ed. 1995. *Textbook of Pediatrics,* 15th ed. Boston: W. B. Saunders.

Belsky, J. 1993. "The Etiology of Child Maltreatment: A Developmental-Ecological Analysis." *Psychological Bulletin* 114(3):413–34.

Berrueta-Clement, J. R., L. J. Schweinhart, W. S. Barnett, A. S. Epstein, and D. P. Weikart. 1984. *Changed Lives: The Effects of the Perry Preschool Program on Youths Through Age 19.* Monographs on the High Scope/Educational Research Foundation, No. 8. Ypsilanti, Mich.: High/Scope.

Besharov, D. J. 1981. "Toward Better Research On Child Abuse and Neglect: Making Definitional Issues An Explicit Methodological Concern." *Child Abuse and Neglect* 5:383–91.

———. 1990. "Public Agencies Must Address Both Underreporting and Overreporting." *Public Welfare* 48(2):34–40.

Blumberg, M. L. 1974. "Psychopathology of the Abusing Parent." *American Journal of Psychotherapy* 28(1):21–29.

Bronfrenbrenner, U. 1979. *The Ecology of Human Development.* Cambridge, Mass.: Harvard University Press.

Brown, J. U. and R. Bakeman. 1977. "Behavioral Dialogues Between Mothers and Infants: The Effects of Prematurity." Paper presented at meeting of American Pediatric Society and Society for Pediatric Research, San Francisco, California.

Burgess, R. and R. Conger. 1978. "Family Interactions in Abusive, Neglectful and Normal Families." *Child Development* 49:1163–73.

Burns, G. E. and D. E. Lake. 1983. "A Sociological Perspective on Implementing Child Abuse Legislation in Education." *Interchange* 14:33–49.

Caldwell, B. and R. Bradley. 1979. *Home Observation for Measurement of the Environment.* Little Rock: University of Arkansas.

Chalk, R. and P. A. King. 1998. *Violence in Families: Assessing Prevention and Treatment Programs.* Washington, D.C.: National Academy Press.

Christopherson, R. J. 1983. "Public Perception of Child Abuse and the Need for Intervention: Are Professionals Seen As Abusers?" *Child Abuse and Neglect* 7(4):435–42.

Cicchetti, D. 1989. "How Research on Child Maltreatment Has Informed the Study of Child Development: Perspectives from Developmental Psychology." In D. Cicchetti and V. Carlson, eds., *Child Maltreatment,* pp. 377–431. Cambridge, Mass.: Cambridge University Press.

Conger, R., R. Burgess, and C. Barrett. 1979. "Child Abuse Related to Life Change and Perceptions of Illness: Some Preliminary Findings." *Family Coordinator* 28:73–78.

Conger R. and G. Elder. 1994. *Manual for the Family Interaction Scales.* Ames: The University of Iowa.

Coulton, C., J. Korbin, M. Su, and J. Chow. 1995. "Community Level Factors and Child Maltreatment Rates." *Child Development* 66:1262–76.

Dion, K. K. 1974. "Children's Physical Attractiveness and Sex As Determinants of Adult Punitiveness." *Developmental Psychology* 10(5):772–78.

Dubowitz, H., M. Black, R. H. Starr, Jr., and S. Zuravin. 1993. "Conceptual Definitions of Child Neglect." *Criminal Justice and Behavior* 20(1):8–27.

Duggan, A. K., E. C. McFarlane, A. M. Windham, C. A. Rohde, D. S. Salkever, L. Fuddy, L. A. Rosenberg, S. B. Buchbinder, and C. C. Sia. 1999. *The Future of Children: Home Visiting: Recent Program Evaluations* 9(1). Los Angeles: The David and Lucile Packard Foundation.

Edgington, A., M. Hall, and R. S. Rosser. 1980. "Neglectful Families: Measurement of Treatment Outcomes." Paper presented at the Tri-Regional Workshop of Social Workers in Maternal and Child Health, Atlanta, Georgia.

Egeland, B. and D. Brunnquell. 1979. "An At-Risk Approach to the Study of Child Abuse: Some Preliminary Findings." *Journal of the American Academy of Child Psychiatry* 18:219–35.

Egeland, B., D. Stroufe, and M. Erickson. 1983. "The Developmental Consequence of Different Patterns of Maltreatment." *Child Abuse and Neglect* 7:459–69.

Elmer, E. and G. Gregg. 1967. "Developmental Characteristics of Abused Children." *Pediatrics* 40:596–602.

Faller, K. and S. Russo. 1981. "Definition and Scope of the Problem of Child Maltreatment." In K. Faller, ed., *Social Work with Abused and Neglected Children,* pp. 3–10. New York: Free Press.

Finkelhor, D., G. T. Hotaling, and K. Yllo. 1988. *Stopping Family Violence: Research Priorities for the Coming Decade.* Newbury Park, Calif.: Sage.

Frankenburg, W.K., J. B. Dodds, and A. W. Fondal. 1968. *The Denver Developmental Screening Test Manual.* San Francisco: Ladoca Publishing Foundation.

Frodi, A. M. and M. E. Lamb. 1980. "Child Abusers' Responses to Infant Smiles and Cries." *Child Development* 51:238–41.

The Future of Children. 1999. *Home Visiting: Recent Program Evaluations.* Los Angeles: The David and Lucile Packard Foundation.

Gil, D. G. 1970. *Violence Against Children: Physical Child Abuse in the United States.* Cambridge, Mass.: Harvard University Press.

Gordon, H. 1988. *A Model of Prevention for NIH.* Washington, D.C.: National Institutes of Health.

Gough, D. 1996. "Defining the Problem: Comment." *Child Abuse and Neglect* 20(11):993–1002.

Green, A. H. 1976. "A Psychodynamic Approach to the Study and Treatment of Child-Abusing Parents." *Journal of the Academy of Child Psychiatry* 22:231–37.

Greene, R. and J. Heck. 1998. *Report of the Effects of New York State's Home Visiting Program.* Albany, N.Y.: Center for Human Services Research, State University of New York at Albany.

Happala, D., J. Kinney, and K. McDade. 1988. *Referring Families to Intensive Home-Based Family Preservation Services: A Guide Book.* Federal Way, Wash.: Behavioral Sciences Institute.

Hawkins, J. D. and R. F. Catalano, Jr. 1992. *Communities That Care.* San Francisco: Jossey-Bass.

Holton, J. 1992. "African America's Needs and Participation in Child Maltreatment Prevention Services: Toward a Community Response Toward Child Abuse and Neglect." *Urban Research Review* 14(1):1–5.

Howing, P. T., J. S. Wodarski, J. M. Gaudin, and P. D. Kurtz. 1989. "Effective Interventions to Ameliorate the Incidence of Child Maltreatment: The Empirical Base." *Social Work* 34(4):330–38.

Hudson, W. W. 1982. *The Clinical Measurement Package: A Field Manual.* Chicago: Dorsey.

Hunter, R. S., N. Kilstrom, E. N. Kraybill, and F. Loda. 1978. "Antecedents of Child Abuse and Neglect in Premature Infants: A Prospective Study in a Newborn Intensive Care Unit." *Pediatrics* 61:629–35.

Hutchison, E. 1990. "Child Maltreatment: Can It Be Defined?" *Social Service Review* 64(1):60–78.

Ireton, H. and E. Thwing. 1974. *Manual for the Minnesota Child Development Inventory.* Minneapolis: Behavioral Science Systems.

Kelly, J. A. 1983. *Treating Abusive Families: Intervention Based on Skills Training Principles.* New York: Plenum.

Kempe, C. H., F. N. Silverman, B. F. Steele, W. Droegenmueller, and H. K. Silver. 1962. "The Battered Child Syndrome." *Journal of the American Medical Association* 181: 17–24.

Locke, H. J. and K. M. Wallace. 1959. "Short Marital Adjustment and Prediction Tests: Their Reliability and Validity." *Journal of Marriage and the Family* 21:251–55.

Lutzker, J. D. 1984. "Project 12 Ways: Measuring Outcomes of a Large-in-Home Service for Treatment and Prevention of Child Abuse and Neglect." *Child Abuse and Neglect* 8(4):519–24.

Melton, G. B. and H. A. Davidson. 1987. "Child Protection and Society: When Should the State Intervene?" *American Psychologist* 42:172–75.

Milner, J. S. 1986. *The Child Abuse Potential Inventory,* 2d ed. Webster, N.C.: Psytech.

Moran, P. and J. Eckenrode. 1992. "Sequelae of Child Maltreatment in Adolescents." *Child Abuse and Neglect* 16:35–43.

National Advisory Mental Health Council Workgroup on Mental Disorders Prevention Research. 1998. *Bridging the Gap: Linking Science and Service.* Rockville, MD: National Institute of Health.

O'Connor, S., P. Vilze, K. Sharrod, H. Sandler, and W. Altmeier. 1980. "Reduced Incidence of Parenting Inadequacy Following Rooming In." *Pediatrics* 78:65–78.

Olds, D. L., C. R. Henderson, H. J. Kitzman, J. J. Eckenrode, R. E. Cole, and R. C. Tatelbaun. 1999. *The Future of Children: Home Visiting: Recent Program Evaluations.* Los Angeles: The David and Lucile Packard Foundation.

Parke, R. D. and C. W. Collmer. 1975. "Child Abuse: An Interdisciplinary Analysis." In E. M. Hetherington, ed., *Review of Child Development Research* 5:234–48. Chicago: University of Chicago Press.

Patterson, G. R., P. Chamberlain, and J. B. Reid. 1982. "A Comparative Evaluation of a Parent Training Program." *Behavior Therapy* 13(5):638–50.

Polansky, N., M. A. Chalmers, E. Buttenwieser, and D. P. Williams. 1981. *Damaged Parents.* Chicago: University of Chicago Press.

Portwood, S. G. 1998. "The Impact of Individuals' Characteristics and Experiences on Their Definitions of Child Maltreatment." *Child Abuse and Neglect* 22(5):437–52.

Price, R. H., E. L. Cowan, R. P. Lorion, and J. Ramos-Kaye. 1989. "The Search for Effective Prevention Programs: What We Have Learned Along the Way." *American Journal of Orthopsychiatry* 59(1):49–58.

Proctor, E. and L. Davis. 1996. *Race, Gender and Class: Guidelines for Practice With Individuals, Families and Groups.* Englewood Cliffs, N.J.: Prentice-Hall.

Rispens, J., A. Aleman, and P. P. Goudena. 1997. "Prevention of Child Sexual Abuse Victimization: A Meta-Analysis of School Programs." *Child Abuse and Neglect* 21(10): 975–87.

Saleeby, D. 1991. "The Strengths Perspective in Social Work Practice: Extensions and Cautions." *Social Work* 41(3):296–305.

Schuerman, J. R., T. L. Rzepnicki, and J. Littell. 1995. *Putting Families First: An Experiment in Family Preservation.* Boston, Mass.: Walter De Gruyter.

Sherman, B., L. M. Sanders, and C. Trinh. 1998. *Addiction and Pregnancy: Empowering Recovery Through Peer Counseling.* Westport, Conn.: Praeger.

Smith, C. J. and B. Carlson. 1997. "Stress, Coping, and Resilience in Children and Youth." *Social Service Review* 71(2):231–56.

Spanier, G. 1987. "Scales for Assessing the Quality of Marriage and Similar Dyads." In K. Corcoran and J. Fischer, eds., *Measures for Clinical Practice: A Source Book,* p. 424. New York: Free Press.

Spinetta, J. J. and D. Rigler. 1972. "The Child Abusing Parent: A Psychological Review." *Psychological Bulletin* 77:296–304.

St. Pierre, R. G. and J. I. Layzer. 1999. *The Future of Children: Home Visiting: Recent Program Evaluations* 9(1). Los Angeles: The David and Lucile Packard Foundation.

Steele, B. J. and C. Pollack. 1968. "A Psychiatric Study of Parents Who Abuse Infants and Small Children." In R. Helfer and C. H. Kempe, eds., *The Battered Child,* pp. 86–102. Chicago: University of Chicago Press.

Stein, T. J. 1998. *Child Welfare and the Law,* 2d ed. New York: Child Welfare League of America.

Stein, T. J., E. Gambrill, and K. Wiltse. 1974. "Foster Care: The Rise of Contracts" *Public Welfare* 55:20–25.

Straus, M. A. and R. J. Gelles. 1990. *Physical Violence in American Families: Risk Factors and Adaptation to Violence in 8,145 Families.* New Brunswick, N.J.: Transaction.

U.S. Department of Health and Human Services, Children's Bureau (U.S. DHHS). 1981. *First National Incidence Study of Child Abuse and Neglect.* Washington, D.C.: U.S. Government Printing Office.

——. 1998. *Study Findings: Study of the National Incidence and Prevalence of Child Abuse and Neglect.* Washington, D.C.: U.S. Government Printing Office.

——. 1998a. *Third National Incidence Study of Child Abuse and Neglect.* Washington, D.C.: U.S. Government Printing Office.

——. 1998b. *Child Maltreatment 1996: Reports From the States to the National Child Abuse and Neglect Data System.* Washington, D.C.: U.S. Government Printing Office.

Videka-Sherman, L. 1989. *Effective Interventions for Child Abuse and Neglect.* Final Report to the National Center on Child Abuse and Neglect. Albany, N.Y.: University of Albany Press.

Videka-Sherman, L. and T. Proykov. 1998. "The Development of Social Work in Bulgaria," Paper presented at the International Federation of Social Work Conference, Jerusalem, Israel.

Wagner, M. M. and S. L. Clayton. 1999. *The Future of Children: Home Visiting: Recent Program Evaluations.* Los Angeles: The David and Lucile Packard Foundation.

Wahler, R. G. and D. M. Hann. 1984. "The Communication Patterns of Troubled Mothers: In Search of a Keystone in the Generalization of Parenting Skills." *Education and Treatment of Children* 7:335–50.

Weiss, H. 1989. "State Family Support and Education Programs: Lessons From the Pioneers." *American Journal of Orthopsychiatry* 59(1):32–48.

Weissbourd, B. and S. Kagan. 1989. "Family Support Programs: Catalysts for Change." *American Journal of Orthopsychiatry* 59(1):20–31.

Whiting, B. B. and J. W. Whiting. 1975. *Children of Six Cultures: A Psycho-Cultural Analysis.* Cambridge, Mass.: Harvard University Press.

Widom, C. S. 1989. "Sampling Biases and Implications of Child Abuse Research." *American Journal of Orthopsychiatry* 58(2):260–70.

———. 1992. "Factors that Affect the Long-Term Sequelae of Child Maltreatment." *American Journal of Orthopsychiatry* 62(2):166–77.

Wolfe, D. 1987. *Child Abuse: Implications for Child Development and Psychopathology.* Newbury Park, Calif.: Sage.

Young, N. K., S. L. Gardner, and K. Dennis. 1998. *Responding to Alcohol and Other Drug Problems in Child Welfare.* Washington, D.C.: Child Welfare League of America Press.

Zigler, E. and K. B. Black. 1989. "America's Family Support Movement: Strengths and Limitations." *American Journal of Orthopsychiatry* 59(1):6–19.

Zuravin, S. J. 1988. "Child Maltreatment and Teenage First Births: A Relationship Mediated by Chronic Sociodemographic Stress?" *American Journal of Orthopsychiatry* 58(1):91–103.

———. 1989. "The Ecology of Child Abuse and Neglect: Review of the Literature and Presentation of Data." *Victims and Violence* 4(2):101–20.

14

Children in Foster Care

Ernst O. VanBergeijk
Brenda G. McGowan

From the earliest days of civilization, every society has had to develop some means of dealing with young children whose parents are unable or unwilling to provide adequate care. At various times in recorded history, children have been sold into slavery, donated to monasteries and convents under a process known as oblation, or left to die of exposure. Abandonment in public places was common from the days of imperial Rome until the end of the Middle Ages, when foundling hospitals were established in most European cities. Although this development marked a shift from reliance on the "kindness of strangers" to the allocation of responsibility to public institutions for the care of homeless children, the custom of abandoning children persisted. In Paris in the late eighteenth century, 20 to 30 percent of the recorded births resulted in abandonment (Boswell 1988). Thus, it is not surprising that we in the United States must still struggle with the task of finding appropriate solutions for children whose parents do not provide needed care.

Early social provisions for dependent children in this country derived from the English Poor Law tradition and relied heavily on a combination of poorhouses or orphanages for young children in urban areas and indenture or farming out for youth who could be taught a trade. Although the number of orphanages expanded rapidly in the early nineteenth century, there was no significant change in the pattern of care for young children until Charles Loring Brace established the Children's Aid Society in New York in 1853. Concerned about the need to protect poor children from the evils of urban life, Brace recruited large numbers of families in upstate New York and the Midwest and sent trainloads of homeless or destitute children to homes in these localities. This program was closely paralleled by the Children's Home Society, established by Martin Van Buren Van Arsdale in Illinois in 1883, and by the end of the century, free foster home care had become a well-established means of providing for dependent children. At the same time, many communities continued to place large numbers of children in orphanages or institutions, in part because of the concern of the Roman Catholic and Jewish leaders about protecting children's religious heritage. Although most of the large children's residential institutions have been converted in recent years to smaller facilities with more specialized functions, these two traditions of foster family care and residential group care continue today as the primary societal mechanisms for caring for dependent children.

DEFINING AND EXPLAINING CHILDREN IN FOSTER CARE

Although the rearing of children by extended family members is a time-honored tradition in the United States as in most other cultures, such kinship care was not considered part of the formal foster care systems until relatively recently. In the mid-1970s child advocates began to argue that relatives caring for children should be entitled to the same foster care benefits as nonrelatives; and in 1979, acting on a court case filed in Illinois in 1976, the U.S. Supreme Court ruled in *Miller v. Yoakim,* 440 U.S. 125 (1979) that children living in relatives' homes were entitled to the same level of foster care benefits as children living with nonrelatives. Since that time the number of children living in what is usually termed *kinship foster care,* i.e., care provided by relatives that is licensed and supported by the state, has increased exponentially. However, there are still many more children living in informal kinship arrangements in which there is no state involvement.

The term *foster care* is now commonly used to describe both family-based (relative and nonrelative) and congregate care settings, thus incorporating a wide range of substitute living arrangements for children whose parents are unable to provide adequate care temporarily or permanently. Formal foster care is distinguished from other types of temporary substitute care for children, such as informal care by relatives or friends, by the fact that it involves a change in legal custody and state sponsorship. It is distinguished from adoption by the fact that adoption involves a permanent change of legal guardianship as well as custody.

Foster care includes a wide range of placement options that are customarily distinguished as follows:

▮ *Emergency Shelter:* Group residence where children may live up to thirty days until a more permanent placement can be arranged.

▮ *Diagnostic Center:* Group residence where interdisciplinary staff conducts a full range of clinical evaluations and recommends appropriate treatment plan.

▮ *Foster Boarding Home:* Licensed private family home in which parent(s) are paid a small per diem fee to provide care for up to six children in a "normal" family environment. (An adoptive family home prior to court approval of final adoption is technically one type of foster boarding home, but it is commonly referred to as a *preadoptive home.*)

▮ *Kinship Foster Home:* Licensed private family home in which relative(s) of the child(ren) in care are paid a small per diem fee to provide care for up to six related children in a normal family environment.

▮ *Agency-Operated Boarding Home:* Neighborhood-based home that provides care for up to six children in a family-like atmosphere in which the foster parents are paid a salary and the residence is maintained by the sponsoring agency.

▌ *Group Home:* Neighborhood-based residence that provides care for six to twelve children in a group setting supervised by agency child care workers.

▌ *Group Residence:* Neighborhood-based residence that provides care for thirteen to twenty-five youngsters in a group setting that is supervised by agency child care workers and ordinarily has social work and/or other clinical staff on-site.

▌ *Child Care Institution:* Residential facility that provides care for more than twenty-five children in a setting that is separated from the community and often maintains educational, medical, recreational, and social services on-site.

▌ *Residential Treatment Center:* Residential group facility with an interdisciplinary professional staff that provides care, education, and treatment on-site for children who are emotionally disturbed or developmentally disabled.

Although foster care services developed as a solution to the needs of children who cannot remain with their own parents, the use of substitute care inevitably creates other problems. The term *foster care* itself has acquired a negative connotation for many foster children over the years because it implies a difference, and children do not like to be perceived as different. In a follow-up study of former foster children, Festinger (1983:273) reported that almost three out of five indicated there were times when they had not wanted to acknowledge that they were foster children. One of her respondents said, " 'Foster' sounds like a disease," and another commented, "You don't feel like an average kid." The discomfort that many foster children feel about their status has been compounded in recent years by changing attitudes regarding the viability of foster care as a solution for children who cannot be raised by their own parents.

As professional knowledge about the importance of the parent-child relationship and children's need for continuity and stability expanded, and as the costs of maintaining children in foster care increased, public officials, researchers, and advocates alike began to criticize child welfare agencies for their tendency to allow children to drift in foster care, moving from one placement to another with no clear plan for discharge, either to their own families or to an adoptive home. The first real challenge to foster care in this country was posed in 1959 in Maas and Engler's study of children in foster care in nine communities. Their criticisms were echoed repeatedly and reached a crescendo in the late 1970s with the issuance of a number of influential reports (see, e.g., Fanshel and Shinn 1972; Gruber 1978; Knitzer, Allen, and McGowan 1978; Persico 1979; Temporary State Commission on Child Welfare 1975; Vasaly 1976).

Foster care has since been redefined so that it is now commonly viewed, not as an open-ended option available until children reach majority, but as a temporary, planned service that should be used only when preventive services have failed and until more permanent living plans can be developed. Social work practice in foster care is now guided by the concept of *permanency planning,* which is defined as "a set of goal-directed activities designed to help children live in families that offer continuity of relationships with nurturing parents or caretakers and the opportunity to establish lifetime relationships" (Maluccio, Fein, and Olmstead 1986:5). This shift in perception of the purpose of foster care has been beneficial in forcing attention to the need for expanded services to biological parents and potential adoptive families, but it has also had the unfortunate effect of undermining the viability of long-term foster care as an appropriate option for selected youth and conveying a pejorative view of service to foster children, foster parents, and foster care workers alike.

DEMOGRAPHIC PATTERNS

National data about children in foster care are limited because the federal government has made no effort in recent years to collect systematic data on this population or even to establish standard definitions and procedures for data collection. Therefore, state statistics cannot be readily aggregated. Recent figures have supported earlier projections that the numbers of children in foster care would increase substantially. The incidence of children in foster care rose from 3.9 per 1,000 in 1962 to 6.9 per 1,000 in 1996 (House Ways and Means Committee 1998b). According to the Voluntary Cooperative Information System (VCIS), the number of children in substitute care in the United States increased 52.9 percent from fiscal year 1986 to fiscal year 1991 (Tatara 1994).[1] When the first edition of this book was published in 1991, it was estimated that the number of children and adolescents in care would reach a half million by the year 2000. The Children's Defense Fund (CDF) reported that 502,000 children were in foster care at the end of 1996. This represented a 25 percent increase from 1990 (CDF 1998). Five states, namely California, Illinois, Michigan, New York, and Texas, now account for almost half of all the children in foster care nationally (House Ways and Means Committee 1998b).With the passage of the Personal Responsibility and Work Opportunity Reconciliation Act of 1996, PL 104–193, many are concerned that the numbers of children in foster care will continue to rise well into the next century (Berrick et al. 1998).

During the late 1980s the number of kinship foster care homes increased dramatically while the number of nonrelative foster care homes decreased. In 1987 there were 147,000 nonrelative foster homes across the country. By 1990 that number plummeted to 100,000, representing a 32 percent decrease in the number of available nonrelative foster homes. However, kinship care increased from 18 percent to 31 percent of the total foster care caseload in the span of four years (1986–1990) in the twenty-five states that reported statistics to the Department of Health and Human Services (House Ways and Means Committee 1998b). Despite the increases in kinship care, the number of kinship foster care placements remains relatively unchanged among white non-Hispanics. Kinship foster care appears to be an intervention used primarily with children of color. Approximately two-thirds of the kinship caregivers are grandparents. Only half of the kinship parents are married, and 85 percent of the single kinship caregivers are female. These caregivers are less educated on average than biological parents. They are also more likely to be poor, unemployed, and receiving government assistance (House Ways and Means Committee 1998a). However, even the federal government acknowledges that the statistics on the kinship foster care population are suspect. The House Ways and Means Committee, which produces the *Green Book,* states that "little reliable national data are available" concerning kinship foster care.

Like the kinship foster care data, all the foster care data should be seen as estimates rather than an accurate representation of reality. Because of the voluntary nature of the VCIS system and the problems in implementation of the Adoption and

Foster Care Analysis and Reporting System (AFCARS) system, the numbers presented are a far cry from an actual census of children in foster care. Furthermore, the amount of time required to process the data only allows us to look at groups of children in past years rather than a contemporary snapshot of whom is currently in substitute care.[2]

About half (50.2 percent) of the children who entered care in twenty-one reporting states in fiscal year 1990 had been placed because of child abuse or neglect; 20.9 percent had entered because of a parental condition or absence; 11.3 percent had been placed because of a status offense or delinquent behavior; and 1.9 percent had entered care because of the child's disability (Tatara 1997). These findings indicate that foster care placements now occur primarily as a consequence of protective service investigation and that the vast majority of children enter care because of inadequacies in parental functioning, not because of parental death, or their own behavioral problems or developmental needs.

Data from twenty-five reporting states indicate that one-quarter of those who entered care in fiscal year 1985 were reentrants, meaning that they had been in care at least once during the previous year (Tatara 1988). Courtney (1995) cited reentry rates between 3 percent and 33 percent in his literature review of reentry studies, noting that the wide variation in reentry rates was potentially an artifact of varying definitions of reentry. Of the children Courtney studied in California, 19 percent returned to foster care within three years of being placed with their families. Festinger (1994) found 12.9 percent of her sample of New York City children returned to foster care within one year of being discharged.

Given the known trauma that repeated separations can create for children, this is a very troubling finding. No information is available about the total proportion of children who may have had placements in previous years. However, there are some preliminary data on the predictors of reentry. Shorter initial stays (i.e., less than ninety days) in foster care result in a higher probability of returning to care (Berrick et al. 1998; Courtney 1995; Festinger 1994; Wulczyn 1991). Thirty-three percent of Wulczyn's sample who were in foster care initially for less than ninety days returned to foster care. Age is another factor associated with reentry. Young adolescents who are under the age of 14 at the time they are returned to their families are more likely to reenter care than both younger children and older adolescents (Wulczyn 1991). Neither gender nor race/ethnicity of a child were found to be predictive of reentry in either Festinger's or Wulczyn's studies, both of which were based in New York State.

However, Courtney (1995) did find race to be a significant predictor of reentry in his sample of California youth. African American youth were significantly more likely to reenter foster care than any other racial group. He also found that health problems of the child contributed to reentry. Children with health problems were 1.4 times more likely to return to care. The type of placement before discharge and the sheer number of placements were also statistically significant in terms of reentry in Courtney's sample. Children who were in kinship care prior to discharge were 68.6 percent less likely to return to foster care than children who were discharged from other settings. As the number of placements prior to discharge increased, the likelihood that a child would return to foster care increased as well. Children with multiple placements were 1.1 times more likely to return to care than children who experienced stable placements. Finally, children who came from homes that were AFDC eligible were 1.6 times more likely to reenter foster care than children who were from more affluent families.

In fiscal year 1990 over two-thirds (66.6 percent) of the children who were discharged from care in thirty reporting states were reunited with parents or relatives; 7.7 percent were placed for adoption; 6.5 percent reached the age of majority or were emancipated; and 15.7 percent were discharged for other reasons, such as running away, death, incarceration, marriage, or transfer to another public agency. The percentage of children leaving foster care by being adopted has remained relatively constant at about 10 percent (Courtney 1994). In 1996 the median length of stay was 23.2 months. The degree to which the problems that necessitated placement were resolved prior to discharge is not known.

Table 14.1 presents selected demographic characteristics of children in foster care. Unfortunately, because of the lack of reliable, comprehensive national data, the figures presented in this table are derived from multiple sources, are based on different sample sizes, and refer to different reporting years. The number of reporting states, data collection year, and data source are presented next to each item. The picture that emerges from these data suggests that foster children are disproportionately adolescent and minority-group members. Although most were placed because of inadequacies in parental functioning, one out of five had a disabling condition. One-fourth of the children had three or more prior placements, and well over one-third had been in care longer than two years. These findings, together with the fact that one-fourth of those entering care had been in placement previously, raise serious questions about the amount of stability that foster care provides children.

An alarming trend in foster care centers around the racial composition of the children in care. As table 14.2 indicates, the number of African American children in care exceeds the number of white children in care. To the lay observer, the difference may not seem like an extraordinary amount, but when this information is taken in context with the fact that whites comprise 75.6 percent of the population, the disparity becomes clearer. Both Hispanic and African American children enter and stay in care at a rate that far exceeds their representation in the population. According to the American Public Welfare Association, by 1995 African American and Hispanic youth comprised more than half the children in care (House Ways and Means Committee 1998b, table 11–21).

SOCIETAL CONTEXT

Foster care is by definition a socially prescribed phenomenon and can be understood only in this context. The stresses in family functioning that bring children to the attention of child welfare authorities are a direct reflection of socioeconomic problems and racial and gender inequalities in the larger society. Moreover, the way children's needs are defined and the types of legal and service protections they are offered vary over time in accord with the prevailing norms of the communities in which they reside. Parents and children's rights are both relative concepts, as are definitions of adequate parenting. Consequently, social service agencies and courts have great latitude and are heavily influenced by structural variables in determining when and under what circumstances children should enter and leave foster care. One need only read Billingsley and Giovannoni's history (1972) of child welfare services for black

TABLE 14.1. Characteristics of Children in Foster Care

Age (N = 18)** (AFCARS DATA)* September 30, 1996

Under 1 Year	1–5 Years	6–10 Years	11–18 Years
4%	29%	27%	39%

Sex (N = 18)** (AFCARS DATA)* September 30, 1996

Male	Female
51%	49%

Race/Ethnicity of Children in Care (N = 38)** FY 1995*

White	Black	Hispanic	American Indian	Asian/Pacific Islander	Other
36.5%	45.1%	11.3%	1.6%	1.0%	2.2%

Living Arrangements (N = 18)** (AFCARS DATA)* September 30, 1996

Foster Home (Relative & Non Relative)	Group Home	Institution	Independent Living	Runaway
79%	11%	4%	1%	1%

Disabling Condition(s) (N = 18)** FY 1990*

One or More	None	Awaiting Adoption
13%	87%	72%

Total Number of Placements (N = 15)** FY 1990*

One	Two	Three–Five	Six or More
42.6%	27.5%	23.6%	6.1%

Continuous Time in Placement (N = 22)** FY 1990*

0–12 Months	1–2 Years	2–3 Years	3–5 Years	5 or more years
32.6%	23.9%	15.8%	16.9%	10.2%

Length of Stay in Months (N = 18)* (AFCARS DATA)* September 30, 1996

Median = 23.2	Mean = 34.25

Permanency Planning Objective (N = 18)** (AFCARS DATA)* September 30, 1996

Discharge to Relatives	Adoption	Independent Living	Long-Term Foster Care
60%	16%	4%	12%

*Source: House Ways and Means Committee. 1998b. *Green Book*. Washington, D.C.: U.S. Government Printing Office.

**N = Number of states reporting on each characteristic.

Percentages do not always add to 100 percent because unknowns and very small proportions have been eliminated.

children in the United States to understand the ways in which racism has shaped service provision or Gordon's study (1988) of changing responses to family violence from 1880 to 1960 to understand how the politics of family life influence problem definition.

What has not changed significantly over time is the fact that foster care is essentially a service for poor children. Although the specific reasons for children's entering substitute care, and the types of care provided, have varied throughout history, the problems necessitating placement have seldom been child-related. Instead, they have

TABLE 14.2. Race/Ethnicity of Children in Care, Fiscal Year 1995

Race/Ethnicity	Percent
African-American	45.1
White	36.5
Hispanic	11.3
Unknown	2.3
Other	2.2
American Indian/Alaskan Native	1.6
Asian/Pacific Islander	1.0

Source: American Public Welfare Association, as cited in the *Green Book* (House Ways and Means Committee 1998b).

usually reflected the inadequacies in parental functioning commonly associated with poverty. Thus, as Jenkins (1974) suggested, foster care must be understood in part as a class system that attempts to compensate for deficiencies in the social structure. Since there is little evidence that placement of children in foster care contributes to upward mobility for children or their biological parents, foster care may actually contribute to maintaining the status quo. The very availability of substitute care resources deflects attention from the structural problems such as poverty, unemployment, and homelessness that undermine parental capacity to provide adequate care.

At the same time, history suggests that society will always need some type of substitute care provision for children who cannot remain with their own parents. Although increased efforts to reduce socioeconomic deficits would undoubtedly decrease the number of children requiring foster care, structural changes alone cannot ensure equitable distribution of the emotional, cognitive, and physical resources also required for adequate parenting. Thus, some need for foster care services must be anticipated as long as the country maintains even minimal standards for child nurturance and protection. And because foster care *is* different and necessarily implies some deficit in family functioning, children in placement and their biological parents will always present special service needs.

Although social workers have traditionally assumed primary responsibility for the administration and delivery of foster care services, their practice is structured in large measure by (1) social problems in the larger society that shape the size and nature of the population entering care and (2) federal and state laws and regulations governing the conditions under which children can or must be placed in foster care and the actions taken on their behalf.

As suggested earlier, poverty and minority ethnic status have long been recognized as variables that contribute disproportionately to the risk of children entering and remaining in foster care. In an effort to examine these associations in more detail, Jenkins and Diamond (1985) conducted an analysis of samples drawn from data sets compiled for the 1980 Office of Civil Rights Children and Youth Referral Survey and the 1980 U.S. Census. Their findings confirmed the general hypothesis that foster care as an institution reflects prevailing patterns of social and economic disorganization, demonstrating significant interactions among race, percentage of children in a county living in poverty, placement rate, and length of stay in foster care. They also discovered important differences in placement patterns between large cities and other areas, suggesting that urban foster care systems may experience special problems that disadvantage all children equally.

These patterns reflect long-standing structural problems in this country that influence the delivery of foster care services. However, it is also important for social workers to recognize the ways in which recent changes in social policy shape the service needs of children entering foster care and their parents. In the 1980s, low-income families across the country suffered the consequences of the Reagan administration's mean-spirited campaign to cripple and/or dismantle many of the federal programs established to strengthen family life and enhance child development. These efforts to strip families of needed resources have been widely documented and need not be repeated here. What is important to note is that the stresses of poverty contribute to the risk of family dysfunction and child placement. In families headed by young adults today, one in three children is poor. Poverty rates increased among children in all ethnic groups during the 1980s and 1990s, and if present trends continue, all of the growth in the child population between now and the year 2000 will consist of poor children. In 1974, 14.4 percent of America's children were poor. As of 1996, 20.5 percent of our nation's children lived in poverty (U.S. Census as cited in CDF 1998). According to CDF, 40.3 percent of Hispanic children, 39.9 percent of black children and 16.3 percent of white children were poor in 1996 (CDF 1998:4). The large numbers of children in poverty occurred despite the fact that by 1996 our country was in its fifth year of economic recovery. The overall proportion of children in poverty only dropped .3 percent from 1995 to 1996. Concurrently, the "proportion of poor children living in families where an adult worked at least some of the time soared to 69 percent in 1996, up from 61 percent just three years earlier" (CDF 1998:4). Thus, it is not surprising that the number of children in foster care has again started to increase.

Three problems associated with poverty—AIDS, maternal substance abuse, and homelessness—are also placing enormous demands on child welfare agencies today, especially in urban areas, and these stresses are expected to increase. It is estimated that 80,000 to 125,000 youth are likely to be orphaned due to their mother's infection with AIDS (Michaels and Levine 1992). The overwhelming majority of the children who will lose a parent to AIDS are likely to be poor and from a community of color. Ninety percent of the children will be African American and Latino (Committee on HIV, Children and Families 1996 as cited in Taylor-Brown et al. 1998).

Many of the children of HIV-infected women are HIV-positive themselves. Eighty-five percent of the pediatric AIDS transmissions are transmitted from mother to child (Groze, Haines-Simeon, and Barth 1994). Approximately, 1,500 to 2,100 babies are born each year with HIV. Furthermore, it is estimated that 25 to 33 percent of the infants born HIV-positive will enter substitute care and that up to 60 percent of HIV-infected children will enter foster care (Hopkins 1989 as cited in Groze et al. 1994). These children have myriad medical complications and require intensive medical treatment. Consequently, these children are less likely to be adopted and more likely to remain in the foster care system. The recent increase in the foster care population is attributed in part to the influx of these special needs children (Barth 1991 as cited in Groze et al. 1994).

The exact impact of substance abuse on the child welfare system is difficult to determine. Groze et al. (1994) cited studies that estimated the number of infants born prenatally exposed to illegal drugs to be between 30,000 and 375,000 each year nationally. They contended that the best estimate is 150,000 infants each year prenatally exposed to drugs. The authors noted that only a "modest" proportion (30 to 50 percent) of drug-exposed infants are placed in foster care at birth. Yet they also cited New York State estimates that 75 percent of the children in foster care come from homes where there is substance abuse. The national estimate of 80 percent mirrors the New York numbers.

Maternal substance abuse increases the odds that a child will be born compromised by both HIV and drugs. Yet treatment for women addicted to drugs is not readily available. By providing treatment during pregnancy and by providing visiting nurse and in-home support services many infants could be raised in their own homes rather than in a foster home. Groze et al. (1994) reported that an estimated 280,000 pregnant women were in need of drug treatment and only 11 percent received it. DeBettencourt (cited in Groze et al. 1994) studied drug treatment programs in New York City; over half of those programs refused to treat pregnant women. Sixty-seven percent of those programs refused to treat pregnant women on Medicaid. The refusal rate climbed to 87 percent if the women were on Medicaid and addicted to crack or cocaine (as cited in Groze et al. 1994).

Despite a heightened awareness of the problem of homelessness during the 1980s and early 1990s we still do not know the exact nature of the homeless problem and how it affects the foster care population. According to the 1998 *Green Book* (House Ways and Means Committee 1998a, table 7–23), of the 4.8 million families receiving AFDC in 1995, less than 1 percent (.3 percent) were homeless. Yet this means that at least 14,620 low-income families were homeless, and there are likely to be many more. Among risk factors in substantiated cases of abuse and neglect, few states collect housing related data. According to the Child Welfare League of America (1998), only seven states, Hawaii, Kentucky, Nevada, New Jersey, Oregon, South Carolina, and Virginia reported "inadequate housing" as a risk factor in 1995. The percentage of substantiated cases where inadequate housing was an issue ranged from 2–23%. The average percentage of cases where inadequate housing was a factor among these seven states was only 9 percent, but the large urban areas where homelessness and inadequate housing have become such major problems are not well represented in these seven states. More research is definitely needed in the prevalence and incidence of these problems across the country.

Unlike social workers in most other settings, those working with children in foster care have explicit **legal responsibilities.** These duties are imposed as a consequence of the transfer of legal custody from a child's biological parents to the local state authority. In making decisions and taking actions on behalf of foster children, workers are acting as agents of the state. Therefore, they must observe the laws and regulations set out to ensure that the state will fulfill its obligations under the doctrine of *parens patriae,* which gives the state the ultimate responsibility for protecting the welfare of all children.

State responsibilities for children are embodied in federal and state law, administrative regulations, and court decisions. All social workers in foster care must be familiar with the core components of federal laws that set the basic framework for the current provisions of foster care services: Child Abuse Prevention and Treatment Act of 1974 (PL 93–247); Adoption Assistance and Child Welfare Act of 1989 (PL 96–272);

Personal Responsibility and Work Opportunity Reconciliation Act of 1996 (PL 104–193); and the Adoption and Safe Families Act of 1997 (HR 867).

Although protective services for children were initiated in the late nineteenth century with the establishment in a number of urban areas of Societies for the Prevention of Cruelty to Children, there were no federal laws guiding the provision of protective services until the passage of the *Child Abuse Prevention and Treatment Act of 1974*. A response to media exposés and agitation in the medical community about the newly identified "battered-child syndrome," this act established the National Center on Child Abuse and Neglect. It also provided limited funding for demonstration projects to states that comply with a series of regulations related to the establishment of statewide systems for reporting and investigating reports of suspected child abuse and neglect.

Although the title of this act implies legislative concern about prevention and treatment, the implementing regulations focus attention almost entirely on mandatory reporting and investigation. Moreover, the law fails to define precisely what is meant by *child abuse* and *neglect* or to specify the evidential standards for reporting. As a consequence, the primary effect of the law has been to enlarge the number of reports and investigations of child maltreatment, not to provide the resources or guidelines required for states to serve these cases more adequately.

Despite its limited scope and funding, this law has had a tremendous impact on the delivery of child welfare services across the country. All states have some type of mandatory reporting law that requires social workers as well as many other human service professionals to report suspected incidents of child abuse or neglect and that grants immunity from civil or criminal liability to those who make such reports. According to the American Association for Protecting Children, reports of suspected child maltreatment increased 158 percent from 1976 to 1984 (Daro 1988:13). There were approximately 2.2 million reports filed in 1986 (CDF 1989:47), and the numbers have been climbing. From 1985 to 1995 the number of children reported for suspected maltreatment increased 63 percent. Approximately 3.12 million children were reported to authorities for suspected abuse and neglect in 1995 (Courtney 1998). Thirty-six percent of these referrals were substantiated or indicated in 1995 (U.S. Department of Health and Human Services 1997), thereby necessitating continuing intervention by child protective services in the lives of 1.2 million children. The country witnessed a fourfold increase in reporting between 1976 and 1996. In 1976 the incidence of reporting was 10 children per 1,000. By 1996 the incidence increased to 47 per 1,000 (House Ways and Means Committee 1998b).

We have seen a steady decline in substantiation rates from 65 percent in 1976 to 31 percent in 1996 (House Ways and Means Committee 1998b). Although not all reports of child abuse or neglect are substantiated, enormous resources must be devoted simply to investigating these complaints. Consequently, public child welfare agencies across the country have been increasingly preoccupied with their investigatory responsibilities (Select Committee on Children, Youth and Families 1987a). Based on a study of social services at twenty-two sites, Kamerman and Kahn noted, "Child protective services today constitute the core public child and family service, the fulcrum, and sometimes, in some places, the totality of the system" (1989:10). This shift in emphasis has obvious implications for the nature of social work practice in child welfare and the quality of service provision to children in foster care.

The *Adoption Assistance and Child Welfare Act of 1980 (PL 96–272)* was en-acted after several years of congressional reform efforts aimed at addressing the well-documented problems in foster care mentioned earlier. Supported by a broad coalition of public officials, child advocates, child welfare professionals, and client organiza-tions, this act amended Title IV-B of the Social Security Law and replaced the Aid to Families with Dependent Children (AFDC) Foster Care Program with a new Title IV-E, Foster Care and Adoption Assistance Program. It adopted what Allen and Knitzer described as "a carrot-and-stick approach to redirect funds away from inap-propriate, often costly, out-of-home care and toward alternatives to placement" (1983:120). Passage of this act made prevention of placement and permanency plan-ning explicit objectives of federal child welfare policy. Moreover, by requiring states to establish standards and procedures consonant with the law in order to be eligible for federal funding, PL 96–272 ensured that these objectives would become the ex-plicit policy of the state agencies responsible for the delivery of child welfare studies.

The standards established required the states to establish case review mecha-nisms—with judicial determination of need and opportunity for parental participa-tion at specified intervals—to ensure that "reasonable efforts" are made to prevent placement, to arrange placement in the most appropriate setting, and to discharge children to permanent homes in a timely manner. Case planning must ensure that placement is arranged "in the least restrictive, most family-like setting available lo-cated in close proximity to the parents' home, consistent with the best interests and needs of the child." The law also requires that the states establish statewide infor-mation systems.

Great optimism surrounded the passage of this law, and a decline in the foster care population during the early 1980s pointed to its potential efficacy. However, numerous problems related to staff limitations and resource shortages—and perhaps even the viability of some of the assumptions underlying PL 96–272—have limited the capacity of the states to implement the intent of this legislation (Select Committee on Children, Youth and Families 1987b). Although social workers generally support the intent of this law, its implementation has created many strains for practitioners. One difficulty is that the increased demands for monitoring and accountability have resulted in an enormous expansion in reporting requirements. Many of the procedural protections designed to safeguard the interests of children and parents have been utilized in a *pro forma* way that increases workers' paperwork but does little to en-hance the quality of the services they deliver. A second, related problem derives from the need for multiple administrative and court reviews of the status of children in care. These reviews inevitably press toward standardization of decision making, thereby decreasing workers' sense of professional autonomy and their capacity to develop carefully individualized intervention plans. Finally, in a system in which success is measured in part by reduction of foster care, not by reduction of the familial and social problems leading to placement, social workers are now confronted at times by situations in which they are ordered to implement discharge or adoption plans that they do not think are in the best interests of their clients.

In response to increasing rates of child abuse and neglect and increasing numbers of children in foster care in the late 1980s and early 1990s, the states began to argue that additional federal funding was required to help them implement federal man-dates regarding improving services for families and children at risk and to reduce foster care costs. Therefore, as part of the Omnibus Budget Reconciliation Act of 1993, Congress created the *Family Preservation and Support Services Program* that authorized $930 million in federal funds to states over five years for family preservation and support services. Family preservation services are targeted to families in crisis whose children are likely to be placed in foster care without the immediate provision of services. Family support services are community-based services designed to promote the well-being of families and children and to prevent the types of cases that could lead to child and/or foster placement. The early reports on this program suggested that the vast majority of states were using these funds to initiate and expand different types of family preservation and support services and to track the results. Two large federal evaluation studies were initiated to provide assessment of program impact across states, but the results from these studies are not available yet (U.S. General Accounting Office 1997).

The social Darwinist sentiments of the 1980s culminated in the passage of the *Personal Responsibility and Work Opportunity Reconciliation Act of 1996, PL 104–193.* Although passed under President Clinton, the act, more commonly referred to as the "Welfare Reform" Act, continued the Reagan/Bush era's mission of dismantling federal programs designed to strengthen families and promote child development. It ended federal entitlements by eliminating Aid to Families with Dependent Children (AFDC). In its place Congress created Temporary Assistance to Needy Families (TANF), which not only replaced AFDC but also Emergency Assistance, and the Job Opportunities and Basic Skills (JOBS) training program. The TANF monies are distributed to the states in the form of block grants. This single payment to the states is capped at an estimated $16.4 billion from 1996 through 2003 (Courtney 1998).

Aside from capping the amount of federal funds the federal government will provide the states in their efforts to relieve poverty and promote work and eliminating individual entitlement to assistance, the Welfare Reform Act of 1996 places a number of severe restrictions on the new forms of assistance. The law imposes a five-year lifetime limit on the receipt of cash assistance. Legal immigrants who have not yet achieved citizenship are denied cash assistance and food stamp benefits as well as Title XX Social Services, child care, most Supplemental Security Income (SSI) benefits, and Medicaid (with the exception of emergency services). Persons convicted of a drug felony after the passage of this law are barred for life from receiving either cash assistance or food stamps. Unmarried minor parents are required to live with a parent, legal guardian, or in an adult supervised setting and participate in educational and training programs in order to be eligible for TANF and the other forms of assistance. Finally, the TANF Law restricts the definition of disability under Supplemental Security Income (SSI). Many children with emotional and behavioral problems are being eliminated from the rolls. The estimated number of children who will be excluded from SSI benefits by the year 2002 is about 315,000 (Super, Parrott, Steinmetz, and Mann 1996 as cited in Courtney 1998). A related sequel of this provision is that an estimated 20,000 to 45,000 of these children will also lose their Medicaid benefits (Kamerman and Kahn 1997).

The projected impact of this legislation is potentially profound. Already 14.5 million children live in poverty in the United States (CDF 1998). This translates into more than one out of every five children in this country living in poverty and one out of three children spending at least part of their childhood living below the poverty line (CDF 1998; National Center for Children in Poverty 1996). Another way to conceptualize the depth of childhood poverty is that 21 percent of our nation's children are poor. This number is almost double the adult poverty rate of 11 percent (CDF 1998). Our current treatment of children ranks us eighteenth among industrialized nations in terms of the gap in wealth between rich and poor children. As a result of the Personal Responsibility and Work Opportunity Reconciliation Act of 1996, the Congressional Budget Office estimates that between 2.5 and 3.5 million children could be affected by the five-year time limit once the law has been fully implemented (Courtney 1997, 1998). The estimates are conservative in that they consider only the number of children who will be affected by the fact that their parents are unable to meet the work requirements of the law, may be convicted of drug related felonies, are legal immigrants, or no longer meet the eligibility requirements of SSI. At best, an additional 1.1 million children could fall into poverty (The Urban Institute 1996 as cited in Courtney 1998).

If these projections are accurate, then the foster care system will undoubtedly feel the effects. Poverty is the single strongest correlate of child neglect and abuse. From the Third National Incidence Study (NIS-3) we learned that children from families whose annual income was below $15,000 were twenty-two times more likely to experience some form of maltreatment than children whose families' annual income was over $30,000. Furthermore, they were fifty-six times more likely to suffer from educational neglect (Sedlak and Broadhurst 1996a, 1996b). The children from the families who will be impacted by changes in the federal welfare law are at much greater risk of maltreatment and abandonment due to the financial hardships their families will face. They will come to the attention of public institutions such as schools and hospitals and subsequently be reported to child protective services. Ten percent of the cases that are reported to child protective services where there is a finding of abuse or neglect are likely to result in some sort of foster care placement (Waldfogel 1998). Moreover, an unknown number of foster care parents (relative and nonrelative) who are receiving TANF benefits will be affected by the five-year time limit on the receipt of cash assistance and may be forced to secure full-time employment outside the home. If so, there could be a drastic reduction in the number of foster homes available for children in need of care.

Although there is substantial research indicating that long-term foster care may not have as negative effects on children as premature efforts to return children home or disrupted adoptions (see discussion later), in 1997 Congress approved a bill designed to promote child safety and permanency, the *Adoption and Safe Families Act of 1997 (PL 105–89)*. Reflecting some of the same political sentiments as those that led to passage of the Welfare Reform Act as well as increased concern about the rise in child maltreatment and the length of time children were remaining in foster care, this act makes the safety of children a clear priority in all child welfare decision making. The law reaffirms the concept of permanency planning established under the Adoption Assistance and Child Welfare Act of 1980 and specifies again the importance of making "reasonable efforts" to preserve and unify biological family units. However, it also defines circumstances under which states are not obliged to make reasonable efforts to maintain children with or return them to their biological parents because of an assumed threat to their safety, e.g., cases in which a child has been subject to abandonment, torture, chronic abuse, or sexual abuse; cases in which a parent has committed murder or voluntary manslaughter; and cases in which parental rights to a sibling have been terminated.

Moreover, this law expedites consideration of termination of parental rights by requiring states to file a termination of parental rights petition for any child in foster care for fifteen of the preceding twenty-two months. The only exceptions are situations in which the child is in the care of a relative, or the agency documents a compelling reason why such termination would not be in the child's best interests, or the state has not provided the services deemed necessary to permit safe family reunification.

In an effort to facilitate more timely decision making and to promote earlier adoption of children who cannot return home safely, this law mandates a "permanency hearing" by an administrative body appointed or approved by the court no later than twelve months after a child enters foster care and every twelve months thereafter until the child is discharged from care. It also requires caseworkers to engage in what is called "concurrent planning," meaning that they should provide immediate family reunification services while also making plans for termination of parental rights and adoption in case the family reunification efforts are not successful. In addition, this law provides bonuses for states that increase adoptions of children waiting in foster care. It is too early to determine precisely how this law will influence the child welfare system. What is clear, however, is that the law is directed toward promoting safety and permanency for children, not family reunification. Therefore, biological parents who have problems that cannot be resolved within fifteen months or less will be at risk of losing their parental rights. And children who are not adopted may become "legal orphans" who have no legal parent.

VULNERABILITIES AND RISK FACTORS

All children in foster care, almost by definition, are children at risk. They generally come from low-income families with a high incidence of socioeconomic, physical, and emotional problems. They have frequently been exposed to repeated physical and sexual abuse and/or neglect. And many display serious developmental delays and behavioral problems. Compounding these disadvantages is the fact that these children have all been exposed to the trauma of at least one separation from a parent or parent figure and frequently more. Consequently, they often live in a state of limbo, uncertain about who is going to be caring for them or where they will live in the future.

In view of these enormous stresses, it is not surprising that former foster children tend to be overrepresented among runaways, prisoners, welfare recipients, and other "problem" groups. What is more remarkable is that repeated research has demonstrated that most current and former foster children function quite adequately, especially if they are compared with others from similarly troubled backgrounds. (For reviews of relevant research, see, e.g., Fanshel and Shinn 1978; Festinger 1983; Kadushin and Martin 1988; Maluccio and Fein 1985.)

However, most of the research on the impact of foster care was conducted on children who were in placement prior to passage of PL 96–272. As a consequence of the subsequent emphasis on permanency planning, child welfare agencies in recent years have made a strong effort to reunite children with their biological parents or place them in adoptive families as quickly as possible rather than allowing them to grow up in foster care. This trend poses some difficult questions about the comparative impact of these alternative placement outcomes. Several studies on this topic have concluded that family reunification is not necessarily a permanent plan. Recidivism or replacement in foster care has increased with more effort to achieve early discharge (Rzepnicki 1987) and now occurs in approximately one-quarter to one-third of all cases (Seltzer and Bloksberg 1987:67). Moreover, a review of recent research on placement outcomes suggests that although family reunification may be most desirable from a value perspective, it is the option least likely to protect children from abuse and to promote developmental well-being (Barth and Berry 1987:82). These findings point clearly to the fact that former foster children who are reunited with their biological families continue to be very much at risk and in need of ongoing services.

Although adoption tends to be a much more stable plan for children who have been in foster care (Seltzer and Bloksberg 1987), in a large sample study in California, Barth (1988a) found a disruption rate of 10 percent in adoptions of children over the age of 3. As might be expected, the likelihood of disruption was higher if the children were older, had a previous adoptive placement, had a number of problems, or were adopted by someone other than their foster parents. These findings again suggest that the risks for children in foster care do not end with implementation of a permanency plan and that follow-up services are needed, especially for those most likely to reenter foster care.

Unfortunately, because of the historic tendency to treat foster children as a unitary population, relatively little is known about the risks of various subgroups in care. All foster children are at somewhat higher risk of suffering abuse and/or neglect from their caretakers than are other children (Mushlin 1988). But the risk that they face more frequently is that of poor school performance. This educational deficit has been documented consistently in almost every study of the well-being of current and former foster children. Comparing a national random study of children in foster care to the national population in 1977, Gershenson and Kresh (1986:6) found that only 59 percent of children in foster care were at the modal age for their grade, compared with 80 percent of the general child population and 69 percent of those receiving child welfare services in their own homes.

A risk that has troubled child welfare experts for many years but is much harder to document relates to foster children's self-image and their capacity to handle the trauma of separation and to form other meaningful attachments. The first study of this topic (Weinstein 1960) concluded that foster children's understanding of their placement situation was a significant predictor of well-being. More recent studies have highlighted the importance of enabling children who grow up in foster care to retain contact with their foster and birth parents (Barth 1988b). Unfortunately, there is much that the profession still does not understand about psychological development and how this may be affected by foster placement. As Fanshel and Shinn concluded, despite their finding that children who remain in care do not fare badly compared with those who are reunited with their families, "we are not sure that our procedures have captured the potential feeling of pain and impaired self-image that can be created by impermanent status in foster care" (1978:479).

The findings from a longitudinal study of children in long-term foster care in a large, voluntary agency provide some basis for beginning to identify subgroups that may be at particular risk. The authors (Fanshel, Finch, and Grundy 1989) found that the more volatility children entering care in this agency had experienced in their prior living arrangements (number of placements, number of foster parents, and number of returns to birth parents), the more hostile and oppositional they were at intake. Moreover, the degree of children's hostility at entry was the best predictor of their adjustment in care, and this, in turn, was the best predictor of their condition at discharge and subsequent adult adjustment. Few of children's other experiences prior to placement added any explanatory power. This finding raises a serious question about the current practice of searching endlessly for a permanency plan for children who are unlikely to be returned home or placed for adoption successfully and suggests instead that efforts should be directed toward stabilizing such children in long-term foster care. It also highlights the potential importance of early clinical intervention designed to reduce the anger and oppositional behavior of children who are hostile at intake.

RESILIENCIES AND PROTECTIVE FACTORS

As indicated earlier, repeated research has indicated that the vast majority of children in foster care do well and adjust well in later life, especially in comparison to other children from troubled family backgrounds. The only common exceptions are that many foster children tend to have lower academic performance and more difficulty forming permanent, intimate relationships than might be expected (see, e.g., Fanshel and Shinn 1978; Festinger 1983; Kadushin and Martin 1988). However, no research has examined the predictors of resilience in foster children, and we are just beginning to get meaningful data on the predictors of childhood resilience in general.

What is known is that the key individual protective factors for children are easy temperament, competency in normative roles, a sense of self-efficacy, intelligence, good social skills, and self-esteem. The most important environmental protective factors for children are the presence of a caring, supportive adult; a positive relationship with at least one parent; opportunities for educational achievement; and the availability of strong supports in the school and neighborhood (Kirby and Fraser 1997: 24–27).

Thomlison (1997) has analyzed the protective factors for children exposed to maltreatment. Since so many children in foster care have been exposed to maltreatment, it can be assumed that these protective factors also contribute to the resiliency of children in foster care. Age is an important protective factor because the more developmentally competent children are, the more likely they will cope positively with stressors such as maltreatment or foster care placement. Other significant protective factors include a strong sense of attachment to a caring adult; the presence of siblings to whom a child is bonded; the availability of supportive family, friends, teachers, and/or neighbors; the presence of a positive adult role model in a child's life and the amount of time spent with that person; and the well-being of the community in which the child resides (Thomlison 1997:56–59).

A foster care agency can do little to ensure the presence of protective factors such as age or early parental attachment. However, social workers can try to promote the placement of children in foster care settings that facilitate the maintenance of ties with siblings, other relatives, friends, and neighbors; offer positive role models to children in care; and provide strong informal and formal community supports. Carefully designed foster placements can clearly contribute to the resiliency of children in care.

PROGRAMS AND SOCIAL WORK CONTRIBUTIONS

Foster care services are provided by both public and private child care agencies. Although any licensed agency can provide foster care for a child whose parents sign a voluntary placement agreement, court approval of the placement plan is required to secure public subsidy for the costs of placement. The local public department of social services or its equivalent is ordinarily responsible for determining whether involuntary placement is required and for securing the necessary court order. The public department may provide care directly through a foster home or group residence administered under its auspices, or it may contract for the provision of care with a licensed private agency. Since the vast majority of foster placements are ordered on an involuntary basis, it can be assumed that most placements are now arranged through a public agency. Moreover, all publicly financed foster placements are now subject to periodic administrative and court reviews. This recent shift in the legal framework has had a significant impact on the way foster care programs are organized.

Traditionally, the only service provided by many child welfare agencies was foster care. Starting in the 1920s, increasing numbers of these agencies began to offer adoption services, primarily for healthy white infants. Adoption services were expanded in the late 1960s as agencies began to seek adoptive homes for children formerly defined as "hard to place," i.e., older children, minority children, and those with physical handicaps or developmental disabilities. It was not until the 1970s that many child welfare agencies began to offer in-home services to families in which children were at risk of placement as well as to those whose children were in care.

PL 96–272 mandates that foster care today be viewed as part of a continuum of services to families in which parents need help to fulfill their basic role responsibilities. This service continuum includes supportive, supplementary, and substitute care services. Supportive services, often referred to as *preventive* or *home-based services,* are designed to strengthen parent and child functioning. They include various types of individual, family, and group counseling and education as well as a range of community advocacy efforts and concrete services.

Supplementary services are distinguished from supportive services by the fact that they are designed to fulfill at least part of parents' normal role responsibilities. Instead of aiming solely to strengthen the family, these services actually take some role in the family system (Kadushin and Martin 1988:143). The primary supplementary services are child care (full day and after-school programs) and homemaker–home help aides.

Substitute care services, which include both foster care and adoption, are designed to ensure that all parental responsibilities will be fulfilled in a setting apart from that of the birth parent(s). They include the wide range of placement options described earlier.

Although a full continuum of services is required to fulfill the mandates of PL 96–272 and to ensure that an appropriate package of services will be offered to each child and family at risk, such a continuum is easier to conceptualize than to implement. Because of the vagaries of historical tradition and current funding patterns, few social agencies provide the required range of services. Instead, most administer one or a few specialized service programs. As a consequence families often must seek services from several agencies simultaneously and experience multiple changes of worker and agency as their service needs change over time. In this context, it becomes increasingly difficult for foster care workers to provide the services required to effect family reunification in a timely manner, and parents tend to become increasingly distanced from their children in placement.

An innovative program designed to address these problems was initiated by the Center for Family Life in Sunset Park in New York City. Located in a low-income, multiethnic community of about ninety thousand, the Center was originally established as a preventive service program designed to sustain children in their own homes. Open to all families with children under 19 who reside in the community, it offers a wide range of services, including individual, family, and group counseling; a number of activity groups for parents and children; an advocacy clinic; an emergency food program; a foster grandparent program; a summer day camp; after-school child care at two local elementary schools; a teen evening center; an infant-toddler stimulation program; a mother–young child activity group; an employment program for adults; and educational forums for parents.

Concerned about the difficulties the staff experienced in trying to work with other agencies to arrange appropriate, accessible foster placements for children who could not be maintained in their own homes, the Center administrators decided to open a pilot neighborhood-based foster home program for children in the community. Called a *core-satellite model,* this program recruits foster homes in the neighborhood to serve children from the community who are in need of placement. The foster homes are conceptualized as satellites of the Center, and all of its services are available to the foster children and their biological and foster parents. Frequent visiting is encouraged so that birth parents can fulfill as many of their traditional parental responsibilities as possible. For example, a mother might be encouraged to walk her child to school or to attend a parent-toddler play group with her child. Following reunification, the families can continue as clients of the Center's family service program. The same social worker is responsible for arranging the placement and providing ongoing services to the foster and biological families during the placement and, if appropriate, after discharge.

The program was envisioned as offering several key advantages over the traditional pattern for foster care placements: (1) by placing children in close geographic proximity to their homes, frequent visiting can be encouraged, thus reducing the trauma of separation; (2) if large sibling groups cannot be placed together, they can at least be placed within easy walking distance of each other so that sibling ties are not disrupted; (3) children who are separated from their parents do not have to separate from their neighbors, friends, school, and other supportive aspects of their home environment; (4) the foster care worker can move quickly to initiate the full range of supportive and remedial services required to ensure that families will be reunited; (5) the model is economical because it utilizes resources already available in the community and saves the time often spent in travel; (6) the potential for matching foster parents and biological parents along racial, ethnic, social class, and other lines is enhanced when they are members of the same community; (7) work with community institutions during the placement period (e.g., schools, health facilities, and day care) paves the way for better relationships with these institutions after discharge; and (8) there can be a natural transition from substitute to home care when parents are encouraged to assume increasing responsibility for their children in care, and continuity of service relationships is ensured during the critical early discharge period by linking the foster care and community-based service programs ("Shaping Foster Care as a Community Service" 1989:3–4).

This is a small program that served a total of 142 children from 1988 to 1998. Because of the intensity of the services offered and the complex, multiple demands it places on workers, it requires experienced, skilled professional staff and a low worker-client family ratio. However, the early results seem very promising, as will be illustrated in the case example presented later. Of the 142 served in this program to date, 122 have been discharged, 104 to their parents and 18 to adoption. The recidivism rate has also been very low. Only three children had to reenter foster care a second time before they were finally discharged to their parents. Two additional children had to be placed in group home facilities after they were discharged to their families.

What may be most important is that this project demonstrates the feasibility of linking foster care and community-based services to promote a form of shared parenting (Gabinet 1983). This is quite different from the traditional foster care program, which removes children from their natural community, discourages informal contact between biological and foster parents, and carefully separates substitute care from the in-home services that could facilitate and sustain early discharge. Representatives from many different states have sought information from the Center in recent years because they hoped to replicate this program in their own communities. New York City also is now in the process of implementing a general decentralization of child welfare services, including the introduction of more neighborhood-based foster family homes. However, these replication efforts are likely to succeed only if they are implemented in the context of family-centered child welfare services staffed by highly skilled social workers and the local community is committed to taking responsibility for all of its children and families.

Unfortunately, although there are many positive service developments such as this in the foster care arena, a number of ill-informed politicians and journalists such as Heather McDonald (1999) started a drive in 1999 to return to antiquated solutions to the problem of children in need of alternative care. Frustrated by the many deficiencies in the foster care system, the alleged "immoral" behavior of some biological parents who are unmarried or substance abusers, and the unnecessary costs of foster care, they called for the re-creation of orphanages. These proposals reflect ignorance of the fact that the notion of the orphanage as the ideal place to raise children who cannot be cared for by their own parents was abandoned nearly a hundred years ago. Since the first White House Conference on Children in 1909, public officials, child advocates, and child welfare experts have all recognized that the best place to raise children is in their own homes or in a family-like setting.

Not only did the preceding campaign reveal ignorance of the historical reasons for the demise of orphanages, but it also demonstrated a lack of knowledge regarding the costs of institutional group care. A family-like foster care setting is not only in the best interests of a child socially and emotionally, but it is also more economically responsible. Courtney (1998) estimated that in 1993 the median foster home maintenance payment was over $100 per month more than ". . . the median monthly AFDC payment for one child ($212)." Yet, he added, "costs of care for children living in group homes and residential treatment centers, rather than foster family homes, averaged about $3,000 per month" (Courtney 1998:93). The argument that we should resurrect the orphanage as a panacea to the problems of the foster care system is neither fiscally nor developmentally sound.

ASSESSMENT AND INTERVENTIONS

Children in foster care are not a homogeneous group, nor are the reasons for their placement or their experiences in care necessarily similar. Yet in recent years, in response to increased judicial and administrative oversight, there have been increased efforts to standardize risk assessment and interventive planning for children entering foster care. This trend violates one of the core principles of social work practice, which is the need to individualize client service needs, and it denies children the right to be known and cared for as unique individuals with different potentials, interests, and worries. At the same time, some common issues and themes must be addressed to ensure that all children in foster care will receive equitable and appropriate treatment. Therefore, this section identifies the core questions that should be examined in assessing the differential needs of children entering foster care and the principles that should guide ongoing practice with this population. These themes can be understood most easily if they are considered in relation to the major phases in the placement process.

A primary objective of child welfare services is to sustain children in their own homes and strengthen family functioning. Both by law and by professional mandate, social workers are expected to provide in-home services to families in which children are at risk of placement *prior* to considering foster care as a service option. The decision to place a child prior to provision of the services that might alleviate the need for foster care can be justified only if there is evidence that a child has been harmed or is at imminent risk of such harm (Stein and Rzepnicki 1983:273).

In assessing the service needs of families in which children are at risk, the social worker should evaluate parental capacity:

To provide a physical environment that protects the child's safety and health.

To meet the child's instrumental needs for food, shelter, adequate sleeping arrangements, clothing and other essentials of life.

To meet the child's emotional needs to be valued and to feel a sense of security and belonging.

To set appropriate limits for the child and teach the values required to support moral development.

To negotiate effectively with neighbors, friends, and community organizations to ensure that the child will have access to needed environmental supports.

The social worker will also want to identify the personal and environmental stresses that may inhibit parental capacity to fulfill one or more of their normal role expectations and the resources that may be available to support enhanced parental functioning. Finally, depending on the age and developmental level of the child, the worker must assess the degree to which some problem behavior or condition in the child is undermining parental capacity to function adequately, and what resources are required to alleviate this problem (Janchill 1981:37).

In addition to evaluating the risk of imminent harm to a child, Janchill (1983:340–41) suggested three critical questions that must be assessed before deciding whether foster placement is needed: (1) Is there sufficient parental desire to maintain the child at home? (2) If the child is old enough to express a preference, is the child willing to stay at home and try to work out areas of difficulty? (3) Are the resources required to sustain the child in the family available in the community? If the answer to any of these questions is negative, the worker may have to consider foster placement.

Once it has been decided that placement is essential, the worker must address three tasks. First, the worker must select an appropriate placement site. As discussed earlier, federal law now requires that placement be arranged in the most family-like setting available in close geographic proximity to the biological parents that is consonant with the needs of the child. This means that foster families are normally considered the placement of choice, and group residences are selected only if the child cannot tolerate the intimacy of family life, requires specialized treatment that cannot be provided in a family home, or cannot be controlled in a community setting. If the child must be referred for group care, the worker should still attempt to locate a setting that is as close to the child's home as possible and that is no more restrictive or isolated from the community than necessary.

Other variables that should be considered in selecting a placement include: (1) the availability of suitable relatives who might be willing and financially able to provide kinship foster care; (2) the desirability of placing sibling groups in the same setting or in as close geographic proximity as possible; (3) the anticipated length and stability of the placement; (4) the importance of matching the foster family as closely as possible with the child's own family in relation to language, race and ethnicity, religion, and other factors that influence a child's sense of identity; and (5) the degree to which the child's biological parents are likely to interact positively with the foster parents or the child care staff.

A second task that the worker should address early in the life of a case, and prior to placement if possible, is development of a comprehensive service plan. This plan should specify the anticipated duration of the placement, the changes that must occur before the child can return home (in specific, behavioral terms), the actions that will be taken by each of the involved parties (parents, child, agency worker, and foster parents), the role of other community agencies, tentative visiting arrangements, and a schedule for periodic assessment of progress (Blumenthal 1983). If the plan is developed in collaboration with the biological parent(s), as is desirable, it can be used as a basis for an ongoing clinical contract. In many situations, such a plan must now also be approved by the court ordering continued placement.

A third critical, early task for the worker is to provide supportive counseling and education and to facilitate ongoing contact in order to decrease the trauma and pain associated with separation. Even when the parent-child relationship is very conflicted or there has been serious abuse, parents and children tend to experience a terrible sense of loss after placement. Children often feel sad, abandoned, angry, and/or guilty and may act out these feelings in dysfunctional ways in the new foster home. Similarly, parents are likely to feel sad, guilty, fearful, and/or angry. Therefore, it is important that the worker view foster placement as a hazardous event that may precipitate a crisis response in the biological parent(s) and/or the child and plan accordingly. Drawing on the principles of crisis intervention theory, the worker can help both parents and children (if age-appropriate) to gain cognitive mastery of the situation by involving them actively in planning the placement, providing anticipatory guidance and rehearsal, and sharing as much information and decision-making responsibility as possible. A preplacement visit to the foster care setting can be helpful, as can the development of a written service plan that is distributed to all participants. One of the objectives throughout the planning process should be to give the participants a realistic sense of control and as much knowledge as possible about what is happening, why, and what can be anticipated in the future.

Once children enter placement, the worker should make continued efforts to diminish feelings of loss and separation by helping them understand what is happening and facilitating ongoing contact between the birth parents and the children. It is essential that children experience a sense of continuity in their lives. Frequent parental visiting not only helps to diminish fears of abandonment but is a strong predictor of early discharge (Fanshel and Shinn 1978). When contact is limited, parents begin to experience a sense of filial deprivation, and their attachment to their children gradually diminishes (Jenkins and Norman 1972).

Parental visits to the foster home and/or group residence also can be used by the worker as a means of assessing the parent-child bond, monitoring parents' behavior, and teaching improved parenting skills. If biological and foster parents are helped to develop collaborative relationships, they can see themselves as working together to care for the child and can begin to share some parenting responsibilities, as is common with extended-family members. For example, a birth mother can be encouraged to feed and dress her infant in the foster home or to attend tutoring sessions with an older child or to accompany the child and the foster mother to a medical appointment. What is important is that the worker attempt to diminish the hostility and resentment that biological and foster parents often feel toward each other and to enable them to find ways to share their investment in the child's well-being. Even the most inadequate and abusive parents usually feel an attachment to their children that can be harnessed to work in the child's interests. Conversely, if the birth parents consistently refuse the invitation to remain involved in their child's life, the worker obtains valuable information about the feasibility of planning to reunite the family and data that can be used in court if termination of parental rights becomes necessary.

Although the worker's primary responsibility is to the child in foster care, it is important that the worker adopt a family-centered approach to practice. Repeated experience has demonstrated the futility of earlier efforts to "rescue" children from pathological family situations. Family ties are very powerful, and whether children live with their parents or not, they must deal with the fantasy and the reality of their family of origin.

Despite evidence that children who remain in long-term foster care or move into adoptive families may do as well as or better than some children who are reunited with their biological families, there is a strong social consensus in this country, now embodied in law, that children should grow up with their "natural" families whenever possible. Therefore, workers must view the biological family as the unit of attention and do everything possible to support that family system and enable the parent(s) and child(ren) to make the changes required to ensure that the family will be reunited. Thus, service plans for children in foster care may include parent education, individual and family treatment, remediation for children's developmental difficulties, vocational or educational counseling, coordination and advocacy with a range of community agencies, and/or efforts to strengthen the family's natural support network.

When foster care workers practice from a family-centered, ecosystems perspective, the therapeutic tasks they carry out may be very similar to those performed by workers providing services to at-risk families in their own homes. However, there are three important distinctions. One is the need discussed earlier to work specifically on issues related to separation. A second important difference is that foster care workers, by definition, must function as part of a service team, and they often carry lead responsibility for orchestrating the activities of various team members. No matter whether a foster child is placed in a kinship home, a nonrelative foster home or a group residence, his or her well-being will be heavily influenced by the quality of care provided. Moreover, the attitudes and behavior of the foster parents or the child staff toward the birth parents can do much to enhance or undercut their willingness to participate in the service plan. Therefore, the social worker must actively monitor what is happening in the placement and work in a collegial manner with the foster parents and/or child care workers to enhance their transactions with the child and the biological parents. The worker's actual interventions in this context might include educating the child care staff about why a particular child is acting upset or defiant, arranging respite care or finding some special equipment for a foster parent, or mediating a conflict between the foster and birth mothers about appropriate discipline or visiting hours.

In addition to working with child care personnel, the foster care worker must consult with agency attorneys and testify at frequent court hearings. To work effectively with the courts, workers have to learn how to obtain the type of evidence that will be admitted in court, to document their own and clients' activities precisely, and to present their observations and recommendations persuasively. They must also learn to function comfortably in what can be an adversarial context and to answer questions that may be posed by the foster child's attorney or lay advocates in a factual, nondefensive manner. Rather than feeling like a pawn of the court, the competent worker will try to use court processes to enforce the service plan of greatest benefit to the child and the family.

The third and perhaps most critical difference between practice with or on behalf of children in the community and those in foster care is that in addition to serving the therapeutic and socialization functions frequently performed by community-based workers, the foster care worker must assume major case management and life-planning responsibilities. He or she must decide when and under what circumstances family reunification may be feasible and, if not, whether adoption may be a suitable alternative. Although final decision-making responsibility rests with the court, judges often rely heavily on the social worker's recommendation. It is clearly much more stressful for the practitioner to be forced to take a position about what should happen to a child's life than it is for a worker to leave these decisions with the parents, emphasizing the importance of self-determination. Moreover, because of the awesome responsibilities that foster care workers assume, they are at much greater risk than social workers in other fields of practice of being held liable for a faulty decision or for failure to take an action that (only in retrospect) was essential to protect the life of a child or to preserve family unity.

Despite these pressures, the foster care worker must at some point decide whether it is realistic to continue to plan toward the child's eventual discharge to his or her own home or whether some alternative goal must be established. Although this decision should be made as quickly as possible, it must be made, except under extraordinary circumstances, prior to the mandated permanency hearing scheduled within twelve months of placement and every twelve months thereafter. Alternative planning options include placement with an extended-family member, adoption, legal guardianship, or long-term foster care, usually considered in that order. If efforts to move toward family reunification seem blocked, the worker must address two questions: (1) Should parental rights be terminated? and (2) What would be the best legal status and living arrangement for this child or this sibling group?

Unless the parent(s) is willing to sign a voluntary surrender of parental rights, termination requires court action. However, the worker must decide whether to file a petition to terminate parental rights. If the parent has essentially abandoned the child, failing to visit and to make plans for discharge, this can be a relatively clear-cut recommendation. And such action is now required by law if a child has been in foster care for fifteen of the preceding twenty-two months. A practice dilemma arises even earlier when the parent continues to insist that he or she wants to resume care of the child but visits very sporadically and makes little effort to address the problems that necessitated placement or to develop realistic discharge plans. At that point, the worker, in consultation with the agency attorney and other involved agency staff and administration, must determine whether the parent's overt behavior gives sufficient evidence of his or her inability to fulfill normal parental role expectations. Maintenance of a specific service contract and carefully documented records of the parent's behavior can become invaluable at this time because they provide the evidence required for the agency and the court to make an informed and equitable decision.

The other issue that must be considered if a child cannot return home is what would be the best alternative. This decision will be influenced by the child's age and degree of attachment to the biological parents, the willingness of foster parents to consider adoption, the availability of extended-family members to care for the child, the child's readiness to form a meaningful attachment to other parental figures, the availability of potential adoptive parents, and, if the child is old enough, his or her own preferences.

There are no clear-cut criteria for making such a judgment and few hard data are available on which to base a prediction about the alternative likely to be most successful. What is known is that the older the child, the less likely he or she is to form a meaningful attachment to a new family, and that the child's adjustment to foster care is a good predictor of later adaptation. Also, there is now relatively strong evidence that children who grow up in stable long-term foster homes do relatively well, as do children who are adopted. In addition, it seems clear that children can do as well in an "open" adoption, in which they retain some relationship with their birth parents, as they can in a long-term foster home setting, in which they maintain some links to their own parents. These latter findings are quite freeing for foster care workers because they suggest that there is no single "best" option for children in placement.

The planning process requires real individualization of the child's developmental needs, family history, and circumstances.

No matter what the permanency goal, it must be emphasized that no service plan is necessarily permanent. Children are often returned to care after being discharged to the home, adoptions are sometimes disrupted, and "long-term" foster care can be terminated. Therefore, it is essential that ongoing services be offered to the foster child and his or her "permanent" family—no matter whether this is the biological family, the extended family, the foster family, or the adoptive family—until it is certain that the child can grow up in this home with some degree of stability. Children need to know that there is at least one person committed to meeting their basic developmental needs until they are ready to live independently.

One final note: This chapter emphasizes what is unique about the placement process, but children enter foster care because they themselves or their parents have one or more psychosocial problems that prevent them from living at home. For example, in recent years child welfare agencies have observed increasing numbers of severely disturbed and violent adolescents entering care as well as a dramatic rise in the numbers of infants of drug-addicted mothers, multiply handicapped children, and children from homeless families referred for placement. Therefore, to be effective in providing foster care services, social workers must have the clinical knowledge required for practice with clients demonstrating the wide range of problems that may precipitate placement as well as the specific skills required to help children and parents deal successfully with the foster care experience.

ILLUSTRATION AND DISCUSSION

Marcia Walters, a supervisor at the city child protective service agency, telephoned the neighborhood family service center described earlier to request a foster care placement for Cindy Davis, the 2-year-old interracial daughter of Susan Bissell, a 26-year-old single white woman of German background. Ms. Bissell had been in a relationship with Cindy's father for the past six years. Gabriel Davis is a 36-year-old black man who was reputed to have both a drinking problem and a history of beating Ms. Bissell while intoxicated. Cindy was being referred for foster care because she was ready to be discharged from the hospital following a two-and-a-half-week admission for treatment of an epidural hematoma. Because the protective service investigation had strongly implicated Ms. Bissell and Mr. Davis in Cindy's injury, their other daughter, Lisa, age 4, had been removed abruptly from Ms. Bissell the preceding week while she and her daughter were walking down the street together. (Ms. Bissell later said that her visual image of the removal was one of Lisa screaming for her as she was ushered into the protective service worker's car.)

Upon referring Cindy for foster care, Ms. Walters was surprised to hear that the Center would not accept Cindy for placement unless Lisa was allowed to be moved to the same foster home with Cindy. However, Ms. Walters said that she recognized the logic in this, and she agreed to retrieve Lisa from the other agency so that she could be placed with Cindy.

At this point, the social worker at the center, Claire Shelton, began to address the tasks of preplacement assessment and planning. It was obvious to Ms. Shelton that this was a very high-risk family situation involving probable spouse and child abuse as well as alcoholism of at least one parent. Lisa had already been further traumatized by an abrupt separation from her remaining family, and Cindy was in a compromised, highly vulnerable medical state from which there could be lasting neurological effects. Ms. Walters had mentioned that both children were enrolled in a therapeutic nursery program about forty-five minutes out of the neighborhood, a program that was familiar to Ms. Shelton. Ms. Shelton called the program and reached the children's social worker, Suzanne Daly. Ms. Daly verified that the situation was extremely high risk and that, while the children were "adorable, they were both severely language-delayed and accident-prone." Ms. Daly described the children's mother as an emotionally constricted woman who had difficulty expressing any affection or positive feeling to the girls. She also said that the girls had no behavior problems and suggested that they be placed with someone who was affectionate and nurturing rather than distant and discipline-oriented.

On the basis of this information, Ms. Shelton decided to place Lisa and Cindy in the home of Yolanda Nieves, a 36-year-old Puerto Rican single mother of four children ranging in age from 20 years to 3 months. Ms. Shelton knew Ms. Nieves well because she had completed the home study on this family herself. She was concerned about the lack of ethnic match but decided that the foster mother's capacity to meet the children's immediate emotional and developmental needs was more important, especially since she hoped this would be a brief placement. Ms. Nieves was chosen because she was highly motivated to be a good foster parent, and she had special experience in raising her 9-year-old son, Robert, who is developmentally delayed and neurologically impaired. Also, she is a highly tolerant, accepting, flexible woman who disciplined her own children adequately but was not prone to rigid limit setting.

Ms. Nieves agreed to accept the children and to meet with Ms. Shelton immediately. The foster mother began to inspect her home for possible hazards to Lisa and Cindy, who were scheduled to arrive shortly. Once the children's immediate safety was ensured, Ms. Shelton was able to focus her attention upon Susan Bissell, the girls' mother. She telephoned her to introduce herself, to explain that her children would be living in the neighborhood, and to offer a visit with the children. Ms. Bissell accepted a visit for the following day and agreed to meet with Ms. Shelton prior to the visit.

This first meeting and visit were of crucial importance in creating the right atmosphere for the ongoing work in the case. Ms. Bissell was encouraged to view Ms. Shelton and Yolanda Nieves as her potential allies, and Ms. Shelton was able to begin her assessment of Ms. Bissell's relationship with her children and their respective treatment needs.

During the initial encounter between Ms. Shelton and Ms. Bissell, Ms. Bissell presented as a profoundly angry, defensive woman who was nevertheless devoted to her children and concerned for their safety. Ms. Bissell seemed relieved by the worker's comment that her anger and upset were normal and could be expected of any mother in her situation who cared about her children. Ms. Bissell quickly volunteered that she had not caused Cindy's hematoma and postulated that it could have been caused either by Cindy's excessive head banging, which was improbable, or else by a compilation of numerous head injuries that Cindy has sustained while in attendance at the therapeutic nursery program. This seemed more probable to the worker. Despite the fact that Ms. Bissell is an attractive, intelligent woman, Ms. Shelton sensed a pervasive, almost palpable sense of low self-esteem and feelings of worthlessness in her.

Immediately after the interview, Ms. Bissell had her first visit with Lisa and Cindy. Both girls appeared to be glad to see Ms. Bissell and ran to her eagerly when they entered the room. Lisa quickly settled in Ms. Bissell's lap and began talking to her, while Cindy scurried around the room looking for toys.

Initially, Ms. Bissell was reluctant to talk to the foster mother, but Ms. Shelton was able to facilitate an exchange of information between Ms. Bissell and Ms. Nieves about the children's basic eating and sleeping habits. This allowed them to converse in a factual, nonthreatening manner and set the tone for the cooperative relationship that would begin to develop between them and that would eventually contribute to the early discharge of the children.

Following the first interview and visit, Susan Bissell began to meet twice weekly with Ms. Shelton. Although she remained constricted and mistrustful, she was able to explore her lack of trust and the extreme anxiety and depression she was feeling about the children's placement. Gradually, as Ms. Bissell demonstrated her ability to keep frequent appointments and to use them as outlets to modify her hostility and mistrust, Ms. Shelton became convinced that if the necessary supportive services were put in place, Ms. Bissell might be able to utilize them to the extent that Lisa and Cindy could be returned home to her.

Another factor that contributed to the assessment that an early discharge might be feasible was the fact that both Lisa and Cindy continued to experience numerous head and bodily injuries while in the therapeutic nursery, despite the fact that there were no injuries in the foster home. This lent credence to Ms. Bissell's suggestion that Cindy's hematoma may have been caused by the injuries she sustained in the nursery program. For this reason, Ms. Shelton decided to remove the girls from the nursery and enroll them in programs in the local community. This would enable Ms. Shelton to monitor them more closely and would allow Ms. Bissell to become more involved in their education than she had been in the past. Ms. Shelton also thought that giving Ms. Bissell increased responsibilities for her children's needs while they were in care would provide a good indicator of how committed she would be to continuing remediation for Lisa and Cindy's language and developmental delays after their discharge home.

Ms. Bissell agreed to move Lisa to a neighborhood Head Start program and concurrently to enroll herself and Cindy in the center's parent-infant-toddler program. The Head Start program would provide Lisa with five-day-a-week, three-hour-a-day education and socialization, while the parent-infant-toddler program would offer both Ms. Bissell and Cindy a two-day-a-week, two-hour-a-day group experience. In this program, the parents met together for a counseling group in one room while the children had a play-stimulation group in an adjacent room.

During a joint meeting with Ms. Nieves and Ms. Bissell, it was agreed that Ms. Bissell would pick up Lisa and Cindy from the foster home in the morning, drop off Lisa at Head Start, and then continue with Cindy to the parent-infant-toddler group. Ms. Shelton clarified with both Ms. Bissell and the protective service supervisor that these responsibilities were being given to Ms. Bissell both to assess her level of responsibility to her children and to allow her to share more in the tasks of parenting with Ms. Nieves.

The intervention proved effective. Not only did Ms. Bissell succeed in keeping all of her individual and group counseling appointments and in transporting her children to their respective programs, she succeeded in convincing the children's father to accept Ms. Shelton's invitation to come in for an individual meeting. Mr. Davis eventually attended four individual counseling sessions, which were scheduled around the erratic demands of his job as a security guard. Although Mr. Davis denied being an alcoholic or ever hitting his children and minimized his physical assaults on Ms. Bissell, he was surprisingly willing to offer a detailed history of the emotional and physical abuse and neglect he had experienced as a child. In addition, although he also denied drinking currently, he gave a similarly detailed history of numerous episodes of binge drinking throughout his teen and adult years, which usually ended in blackouts and physical illness. About four weeks into the placement, as he began individual sessions, Mr. Davis began going with Ms. Bissell to visit the children. They were obviously glad to see him and physically affectionate with him.

By the inclusion of Mr. Davis as well as Ms. Bissell in the service plan, Ms. Shelton was able to gain a richer picture of the emotional deprivation and physical neglect and abuse in both of their backgrounds that had predisposed Ms. Bissell to the harsh treatment of her children and Mr. Davis to self-destructive behavior and violent behavior toward his family.

The foster mother, Yolanda Nieves, played a subtle but important role in ensuring a positive outcome of the placement. Ms. Nieves's accepting, nonjudgmental attitude toward Ms. Bissell and her calm, nonreactive demeanor, even when Ms. Bissell was explosively angry, served both to model more appropriate behavior and to reduce Ms. Bissell's mistrust in Ms. Nieves. Eventually, Ms. Nieves allowed Ms. Bissell to visit Lisa and Cindy in her home, which further alleviated Ms. Bissell's mistrust of the foster care system. The experience of visiting in the foster home gave the client an additional impetus to explore the dynamics of developing trust in others, a task that was a precursor to her ability to work through the feelings of deprivation and abandonment that had plagued her throughout her life.

When Ms. Bissell and Mr. Davis went to their second court hearing almost two and a half months after the children had been placed, Ms. Shelton sent a letter to the judge saying that although some risk to the children would remain because of Ms. Bissell's history of physically punishing the children and Mr. Davis's difficulties with alcoholism and spouse abuse, she recommended that the children be returned home provided that the parents would agree to continue all counseling and educational services currently in place. In addition, Ms. Shelton suggested that Mr. Davis enroll in an alcoholism treatment program. The judge agreed with Ms. Shelton's recommendations but carried them one step further, ordering Mr. Davis either to receive alcoholism treatment services or else to move out of the home if his children were to return. Mr. Davis adamantly refused alcoholism treatment and angrily agreed to move out in order for Lisa and Cindy to be returned home to Ms. Bissell. Mr. Davis moved out of the home the next morning, and Lisa and Cindy returned home that afternoon.

It should be noted that Ms. Shelton did not agree with the judge's decision to order Mr. Davis out of the home because she believed that in the course of individual counseling, the issue of Mr. Davis' drinking problem would eventually become so overt that he would be forced to seek help. In addition, because the judge merely stated that Mr. Davis could not live with Ms. Bissell and his daughters and did not restrict his contact with them in any other way, the judge did not remove the threat of physical harm to the children and only disrupted the family's living arrangement against their will. Following Lisa and Cindy's return home, Mr. Davis attended two additional counseling sessions, during which he expressed tremendous anger at being court-ordered out of his home. He then dropped out of counseling entirely. About five months later, he began an alcoholic binge that resulted in the loss of his job and his housing, which reduced him to living on a street close to Ms. Bissell's apartment. Significantly, Ms. Bissell continued to remind Mr. Davis of the services available to him at the center.

Ms. Bissell and Lisa and Cindy continued to receive all the clinical and educational services initiated during the children's stay in foster care, and Ms. Shelton remained the family's social worker. Individual counseling sessions with Ms. Bissell continued to focus on her need to explore the origins of her anger in a childhood that had been devoid of nurturance and to trace the ways in which that anger surfaced in her interactions with Lisa and Cindy and perpetuated itself in the physical and emotional abuse of her own children. Although the mystery of what had caused Cindy's epidural hematoma was never solved and the physical risks to her and Lisa were probably higher than they would have been if the children had remained in foster care, Ms. Bissell worked to replace physical punishments with behavioral consequences and to call either Ms. Shelton or other members of the parent-infant-toddler group if she felt herself losing control.

As Lisa and Cindy continued to attend Head Start and the parent-toddler program, respectively, they both made rapid gains in language development and socialization skills, to the extent that Lisa was attending a regular public kindergarten in the fall. Perhaps even more important is that during family sessions, Ms. Bissell was able to be more openly affectionate toward her children and more tolerant of their age-appropriate, rambunctious play. On-going work was planned to enable Ms. Bissell and Lisa and Cindy to improve their relationship and also to help Ms. Bissell to complete her enrollment in a community college where she planned to begin studies in zoology and to enroll Lisa and Cindy in the after-school and day care services available in the community. Ms. Bissell hoped eventually to obtain her bachelor's degree and to find a full-time job so that she would no longer need public assistance.

Ms. Shelton continued to be troubled about her inability to reengage the children's father after he had been court-ordered out of the home, and she remained available to work with him if he should reach the point where he was ready to address his drinking problem. What is most important, however, from the perspective of child and family functioning is that Ms. Bissell was able to separate sufficiently from Mr. Davis to set appropriate limits on his behavior, and that she began to build an independent life for herself and her children.

This case clearly illustrates the important work that can be accomplished by a skilled practitioner in a foster program designed to enhance parental capacities, normalize children's living arrangements, and sustain family life. If the social worker had not known that she could continue to monitor and support Ms. Bissell's parental functioning after the children were returned home, she might have been much more reluctant to effect an early discharge. And had Ms. Shelton not been able to form an early alliance with Ms. Bissell, to make a thoughtful assessment of her strengths and service needs, and to enable her to share parenting responsibilities with the foster mother, the case outcome would probably have been quite different. Unfortunately, the case also illustrates the ways in which court action may define and limit the practice objectives that can be achieved once children enter the foster care system.

CONCLUSION

Foster care as it is known today originated as a social invention of the mid–nineteenth century designed to ensure the well-being of children whose parents were unwilling or unable to provide adequate care. The early child welfare agencies established to deliver foster care services were important practice sites for the emerging profession of social work. Yet little over a hundred years later, long-term foster care has been redefined as a social problem, and federal legislation now mandates the provision of services designed to prevent and/or limit foster care placement.

This societal reassessment of the value of foster care, together with the admin-istrative and court review processes developed to monitor and regulate its use, have created new decision-making dilemmas and stresses for the many social workers who continue to work in this field of practice. But these changes have not eliminated the challenge and satisfaction inherent in providing effective services to children in foster care and their families. In fact, as the case illustration demonstrates, the need for professional leadership and creativity in child welfare practice may be greater now than ever before. Although children in foster care constitute a relatively small client population, they are one of the most vulnerable and disadvantaged groups in the country today. As such, they deserve attention from some of social work's most talented practitioners.

Notes

This chapter is based in part on data collected for a study by the Foundation for Child Development and another by the Annie E. Casey Foundation. The authors also want to express their appreciation to Sister Mary Paul Janchill of the Center for Family Life in Sunset Park, New York. She is responsible for conceptualizing and developing the core-satellite foster care program described as well as many other important innovations in child welfare practice. We also wish to acknowledge Emily Stutz for preparation of the case illustration.

1. This figure includes children in sixteen states who have returned home but are still receiving postplacement services and excludes children in preadoptive homes in ten states. Correcting these figures to ensure comparability of data across states, the VCIS estimated an adjusted total in care at the end of the fiscal year of 265,000.

2. In preparing the update of this chapter, the challenges of determining the scope of the foster care system and its inherent problems became glaringly evident. Until 1995 the Voluntary Cooperative Information System (VCIS) collected data from the states and the U.S. territories concerning children in foster care. As the name implies, the system was only a voluntary effort. In fiscal year 1990 only forty-one states and Puerto Rico reported data to the system. The American Public Welfare Association, which conducts the survey, had to employ statistical projection techniques to account for the missing data. The voluntary nature of the reporting system makes obtaining an accurate estimate of the number of children in foster care impossible. The best possible projection available is that approximately 502,000 children were in care at the end of 1996.

   Despite the availability of data, the time in which the information is processed is slow. At the time of this writing the VCIS data for fiscal year 1995 were still not released. The four-year lag prohibits policymakers and child advocates from addressing concerns in a timely manner. Current crises are not identified and consequently rectified without a long delay. Four years in the life of a child is an eternity. Funding needs to be allocated to help with the data management and analysis so that potential problems may be identified in a timely manner.

   In a response to the concern that the provision of data was only done on a voluntary basis, the federal government enacted legislation in 1986, creating the Adoption and Foster Care Analysis and Reporting System (AFCARS). The AFCARS system replaces VCIS. The federal legislation that created the AFCARS system also mandates that each and every state participate in data collection. States that are out of compliance with the legislation were supposed to be levied fines beginning in 1997. Now states are required to submit two reports each year to the Department of Health and Human Services (HHS). These reports are submitted every six months to HHS. However, the data collection system provides no unique identifiers to each of the cases submitted by the states. In other words, the system is unable to determine how many of the children in each six-month period were previously counted as an admission. Redundancy in the counts is unavoidable. The six-month reporting period is not an intuitive unit of analysis that most consumers of this information will be able to use. Without the ability to use unique identifiers to weed out redundant cases, child advocates are unable to put the data in a usable form to distribute to the public. Most people are accustomed to seeing data in either fiscal or calendar year formats. Making comparisons between years and six-month periods is problematic. Trends will be missed, especially the reentry rates. We know from research that children who are returned to the home of their biological parents too soon are at a greater risk for re-admission to foster care. Typically, these children who reenter are returned to the home after being in care less than six months. Will this oversight create a statistical blind spot? How will the federal government be able to address these types of issues without accurate, usable data? With the current encryption technology that is available, the use of unique identifiers is possible and will still safeguard the identity of the children who are the subject of these reports.

The Department of Health and Human Services published two sets of rules in an attempt to enact PL 103–66 and its provisions for AFCARS. These sets of rules outlined the notion of "comprehensive" child welfare data collection systems. To receive federal matching funds, states must develop State Automated Child Welfare Information Systems (SACWIS) of which AFCARS is a component. The SACWIS must include not only foster care and child welfare data but also adoption assistance, family preservation and support services, and independent living data. As of July 1997, thirty-eight states were implementing SACWIS. Nine states were in the planning phase. Twelve states were only partially operational. The implementation of the system has been slow and contributes to the inaccurate picture of the scope of the number of children in foster care. All we can say with certainty is that the problem is large and does not appear to be declining.

References

Allen, Mary Lee and Jane Knitzer. 1983. "Child Welfare: Examining the Policy Framework." In Brenda G. McGowan and William Meezan, eds., *Child Welfare: Current Dilemmas, Future Directions,* pp. 93–141. Itasca, Ill.: F. E. Peacock.

Barth, Richard. 1988a. "Disruption in Older Child Adoptions." *Public Welfare* 46(Winter):23–29.

Barth, Richard P. 1988b. *On Their Own: The Experiences of Youth After Foster Care.* Berkeley: Family Welfare Research Group, School of Social Welfare, University of California at Berkeley.

Barth, Richard P. and Marianne Berry. 1987. "Outcomes of Child Welfare Services Under Permanency Planning." *Social Service Review* 61(March):71–90.

Berrick, Jill, Barbara Needell, Richard P. Barth, and Melissa Jonson-Reid. 1998. *The Tender Years: Toward Developmentally Sensitive Child Welfare Services for Very Young Children.* New York: Oxford University Press.

Billingsley, Andrew and Jeanne M. Giovannoni. 1972. *Children of the Storm: Black Children and American Child Welfare.* New York: Harcourt Brace Jovanovich.

Blumenthal, Karen. 1983. "Making Foster Care Responsive." In Brenda G. McGowan and William Meezan, eds., *Child Welfare: Current Dilemmas, Future Directions,* pp. 295–342. Itasca, Ill.: Peacock.

Boswell, John. 1988. *The Kindness of Strangers.* New York: Pantheon.

Child Welfare League of America. 1998. *Child Abuse and Neglect: A Look at the States— The 1998 Stat Book.* Washington, D.C.: Author.

Children's Defense Fund (CDF). 1989. *A Vision for America's Future.* Washington, D.C.: Author.

———. 1998. *The State of America's Children Year Book.* Washington, D.C.: Author.

Courtney, Mark E. 1994. "Reentry to Foster Care of Children Returned to Their Families." *Social Service Review* 68 (March):81–108.

———. 1995. "Factors Associated with the Reunification of Foster Children with Their Families." *Social Service Review* 69 (June):226–41.

———. 1997. "Welfare Reform and Child Welfare Services." In Sheila B. Kamerman and Alfred J. Kahn, eds., *Report V: Child Welfare in the Context of Welfare "Reform."* New York: Cross-National Studies Research Program. Columbia University School of Social Work.

———. 1998. "The Costs of Child Protection in the Context of Welfare Reform." *The Future of Children. Protecting Children from Abuse and Neglect* 8, no. 1(Spring):88–103.

Daro, Deborah. 1988. *Confronting Child Abuse.* New York: Free Press.

Fanshel, David, Stephen J. Finch, and John F. Grundy. 1989. "Foster Children in Life Course Perspective: The Casey Family Program Experience." *Child Welfare* 63(September/October):467–78.

Fanshel, David and Eugene Shinn. 1972. *Dollars and Sense in Foster Care.* New York: Child Welfare League of America.

——. 1978. *Children in Foster Care: A Longitudinal Investigation.* New York: Columbia University Press.

Festinger, Trudy. 1983. *No One Ever Asked Us: A Postscript to Foster Care.* New York: Columbia University Press.

——. 1994. *Returning to Care: Discharge and Re-entry into Foster Care.* Washington, D.C.: Child Welfare League of America.

Gabinet, Laille. 1983. "Shared Parenting: A New Paradigm for the Treatment of Child Abuse." *Child Abuse and Neglect* 7:403–11.

Gershenson, Charles P. and Esther Kresh. 1986. "School Enrollment Status of Children Receiving Child Welfare Services at Home or in Foster Care." *Child Welfare Research Notes* no. 15 (September).

Gordon, Linda. 1988. *Heroes of Their Own Lives: The Politics and History of Family Violence.* New York: Penguin.

Groze, Victor, Mark Haines-Simeon, and Richard P. Barth. 1994. "Barriers in Permanency Planning for Medically Fragile Children: Drug Affected Children and HIV Infected Children." *Child and Adolescent Social Work Journal* 11(1):63–85.

Gruber, Alan. 1978. *Children in Foster Care: Destitute, Neglected, Betrayed.* New York: Human Sciences Press.

House Ways and Means Committee. 1998a. *The 1998 Green Book: Section 7 Aid to Families with Dependent Children and Temporary Assistance to Needy Families (Title IV-A).* Washington, D.C.: U.S. Government Printing Office. http://frwebgate.access.gpo.gov/cgi-bin/useftp.cgi?IPaddress = 162.140.64.88&filename = wm007_07.105&directory = /disk2/wais/data/105_green_book (19 April 1999).

——. 1998b. *The 1998 Green Book: Section 11 Child Protection, Foster Care and Adoption Assistance.* Washington, D.C.: U.S. Government Printing Office. http://frwebgate.access.gpo.gov/cgi-bin/useftp.cgi?IPaddress = 162.140.64.88&filename = wm007_11.105&directory = /disk2/wais/data/105_green_book (19 April 1999).

Janchill, Sister Mary Paul. 1981. *Guidelines to Decision-Making in Child Welfare.* New York: Human Services Workshops.

——. 1983. "Services for Special Populations of Children." In Brenda G. McGowan and William Meezan, eds., *Child Welfare: Current Dilemmas, Future Directions,* pp. 345–75. Itasca, Ill.: Peacock.

Jenkins, Shirley. 1974. "Child Welfare as a Class System." In Alvin Schorr, ed., *Children and Decent People,* pp. 3–24. New York: Basic Books.

Jenkins, Shirley and Beverly Diamond. 1985. "Ethnicity and Foster Care: Census Data as Predictors of Placement Variables." *American Journal of Orthopsychiatry* 55(April):267–76.

Jenkins, Shirley and Elaine Norman. 1972. *Filial Deprivation and Foster Care.* New York: Columbia University Press.

Kadushin, Alfred and Judith A. Martin. 1988. *Child Welfare Services,* 4th ed. New York: Macmillan.

Kamerman, Sheila B. and Alfred J. Kahn. 1989. *Social Services for Children, Youth and Families in the U.S.* Greenwich, Conn.: Annie E. Casey Foundation.

Kamerman, Sheila B. and Alfred J. Kahn, eds. 1997. Child *Health, Medicaid, and Welfare "Reform".* New York: Cross National Studies, Columbia University School of Social Work.

Kirby, L. D. and Mark W. Fraser. 1997. "Risk and Resiliency in Childhood." In Mark W. Fraser, ed., *Risk and Resiliency in Childhood: An Ecological Perspective,* pp. 10–33. Washington, D.C.: National Association of Social Workers Press.

Knitzer, Jane, Marylee Allen, and Brenda McGowan. 1978. *Children Without Homes.* Washington, D.C.: Children's Defense Fund.

Maas, Henry and Richard Engler. 1959. *Children in Need of Parents.* New York: Columbia University Press.

Maluccio, Anthony N. and Edith Fein. 1985. "Growing Up in Foster Care." *Children and Youth Services Review* 7:123–34.

Maluccio, Anthony N., Edith Fein, and Kathleen A. Olmstead. 1986. *Permanency Planning for Children: Concepts and Methods.* New York: Tavistock.

McDonald, Heather. 1999. "Foster Care's Underworld." *City Journal* 9, no. 2(Winter): 42–53.

Michaels, David and Carol Levine. 1992. "Estimates of the Number of Motherless Children Orphaned by Aids in the United States." *Journal of the American Medical Association* 268(24):3456–61.

Mushlin, Michael B. 1988. "Unsafe Havens: The Case for Constitutional Protection of Foster Children from Abuse and Neglect." *Harvard Civil Rights-Civil Liberties Law Review* 23(Winter):199–280.

National Center for Children in Poverty. 1996. "One in Four: America's Youngest Poor." *Child Poverty News & Issues* 6, no. 2 (Winter). http://cpmcnet.columbia.edu/dept/nccp/news/newi0009.html (20 September 1998).

Persico, Joseph. 1979. *Who Knows? Who Cares? Forgotten Children in Foster Care.* New York: National Commission on Children in Need of Parents.

Rzepnicki, Tina L. 1987. "Recidivism of Foster Children Returned to Their Own Homes: A Review and New Directions for Research." *Social Service Review* 61(March):56–69.

Sedlak, Andrea J. and Diane D. Broadhurst. 1996a. *The Third National Incidence Study of Child Abuse and Neglect, final report.* Washington, D.C.: U.S. Department of Health and Human Services.

——. 1996b. *The Third National Incidence Study of Child Abuse and Neglect, executive summary.* Washington, D.C.: U.S. Department of Health and Human Services.

Select Committee on Children, Youth and Families. 1987a. *Child Abuse and Neglect in America: The Problem and the Response.* Hearing before the Select Committee on Children, Youth and Families, U.S. House of Representatives, 100th Cong., 1st sess., 3 March.

——. 1987b. *Continuing Crisis in Foster Care: Issues and Problems.* Hearing before the Select Committee on Children, Youth and Families, U.S. House of Representatives, 100th Cong., 1st sess., 22 April.

Seltzer, Marsha Mailick and Leonard M. Bloksberg. 1987. "Permanency Planning and Its Effects on Foster Children: A Review of the Literature." *Social Work* 32(January/February):65–68.

"Shaping Foster Care as a Community Service: Early Findings." 1989. Brooklyn, N.Y.: Center for Family Life.

Stein, Theodore J. and Tina L. Rzepnicki. 1983. "Decision-Making in Child Welfare." In Brenda C. McGowan and William Meezan, eds., *Child Welfare: Current Dilemmas, Future Directions,* pp. 259–92. Itasca, Ill.: Peacock.

Tatara, Toshio. 1988. *Characteristics of Children in Substitute and Adoptive Care: A Statistical Summary of the VCIS National Child Welfare Data Base (July).* Washington, D.C.: American Public Welfare Association.

——. 1994. "The Recent Rise in the U.S. Child Substitute Care Population: An Analysis of National Child Substitute Care Flow Data." In Richard Barth, Jill Duerr Berrick and Neil Gilbert, eds. *Child Welfare Research Review ,*Vol. 1, pp. 126–45. New York: Columbia University Press.

——. 1997. *U.S. Child Substitute Care Flow Data and the Real Ethnicity of Children in Care for Fiscal Year 1995 Along with Recent Trends in the U.S. Child Substitute Care Populations.* Washington, D.C.: American Public Welfare Association.

Taylor-Brown, Susan, Judith Ann Teeter, Evelyn Blackburn, Linda Oinen, and Lennard Wedderburn. 1998. "Parental Loss Due to HIV: Caring for Children as a Community Issue—The Rochester, New York Experience." *Child Welfare* 77(2):137–59.

Temporary State Commission on Child Welfare. 1975. *The Children and the State: A Time for a Chance.* Albany, N.Y.: Author.

Thomlison, Barbara. 1997. "Risk and Protective Factors in Child Maltreatment." In Mark W. Fraser, ed., *Risk and Resiliency in Childhood: An Ecological Perspective,* pp. 50–72. Washington, D.C.: National Association of Social Workers Press.

U.S. Department of Health and Human Services, National Center on Child Abuse and Neglect. 1997. *Child Maltreatment 1995: Reports from the States to the National Child Abuse and Neglect Data System.* Washington, D.C.: U.S. Government Printing Office.

U.S. General Accounting Office. 1997. *Fostercare: State Efforts to Improve the Permanency Planning Process Show Some Promise.* GA01 HEHS 97-73. Washington, D.C.: Author.

Vasaly, Shirley. 1976. *Foster Care in Five States.* Washington, D.C.: U.S. Department of Health, Education and Welfare.

Waldfogel, Jane. 1998. "Rethinking the Paradigm for Child Protection." *The Future of Children: Protecting Children From Abuse and Neglect* 8(1):104–19.

Weinstein, David. 1960. *The Self-Image of the Foster Child.* New York: Russell Sage Foundation.

Wulczyn, Fred. 1991. "Caseload Dynamic and Foster Care Reentry." *Social Service Review* 65 (March):135–56.

15

Crime Victims and Victim Services

Albert R. Roberts
Jacqueline Corcoran

The victims' movement has grown remarkably during the past three decades. In the mid-1970s victim rights advocates and victim service and victim/witness assistance programs were rarely available in cities and counties throughout the United States. As of 1999 there were more than nine thousand victim service and witness assistance programs, battered women's shelters, rape crisis programs, and support groups for survivors of violent crimes nationwide. The proliferation of programs is a direct result of the 1984 Federal Victims of Crime Act (VOCA) funding, the 1994 Federal Violence Against Women Act, state and county general revenue grants during the 1980s and 1990s, and earmarking a percentage of state penalty assessments and/or fines levied on criminal offenders (Roberts 1990, 1995). The U.S. Congress has appropriated more than $2 billion for programs and services to assist victims of violent crime (Brownell and Congress 1998; Roberts 1990, 1996).

There has been a growing awareness among social work administrators, legislators, and prosecutors alike of the alarming prevalence of violent crimes and the rights of crime victims. Each year, millions of crime victims are physically, emotionally, and/or financially damaged by perpetrators of violent crime. In the aftermath of a violent crime, victims often have to cope with physical pain, psychological trauma, financial loss, and court proceedings that all too frequently seem impersonal and confusing. Many victims and witnesses have their first contact with the criminal justice system as a result of being victimized. This first meeting can be frightening and confusing. During the past fifteen years, a growing number of counties and cities have developed victim service and witness assistance programs, victim compensation programs, and specialized domestic violence programs to reduce the impact that violent crime has upon the lives of victims and witnesses. Whether people are victimized in a small town with a population of approximately 3,500 such as Black River Falls,

Wisconsin, or in major metropolitan areas such as Atlanta, New York City, or San Francisco, services from a victim assistance program are now available to crime victims (Roberts 1995).

Society must have estimates of the costs of victimization as measured by loss of life, physical injuries, economic losses, and mental health costs. By having estimates of the amount of past economic losses (e.g., unrecovered stolen property, lower productivity and work absenteeism, medical expenses, and mental health costs) policymakers and administrators are in a better position to develop critically needed victim/witness assistance, family violence intervention, and victim compensation programs. Recent estimates place the cost of victimization from criminal activity at a total of $625 billion annually.

> Tangible economic losses—$105 billion
> Intangible psychological/mental health costs—$450 billion
> Tangible criminal justice costs—$70 billion

> Tangible losses consist of direct losses from victimization such as the following:

> The cost of medical and mental health services
> Victim assistance and concrete services
> Loss of productivity in terms of wages and salary; days lost from school and/
> or work, etc.

DEFINING AND EXPLAINING CRIME VICTIMS AND VICTIM SERVICES

Crime victim: An innocent person who experiences loss or damage to their personal property and/or physical injury, psychological trauma or acute anxiety as a direct result of a criminal act.

Protective factors: In the aftermath of a criminal victimization, the psychosocial factors that help buffer the negative impact of victimization. These factors include coping strategies, high self-esteem, and informational and social support.

Revictimization rates: Refers to the data indicating that a large number of crime victims have been victimized more than once.

Victims of Crime Act (VOCA) of 1984: This was the first significant federal legislation with a major funding appropriation that has resulted in the development and expansion of several thousand victim/witness, victim compensation, sexual assault, and domestic violence programs.

Victim blaming: Refers to the insensitive statements made by some criminal justice employees (i.e., police and court staff) indicating that crime victims' actions had contributed to their own victim-related trauma and resulting mental health problems.

Victim service programs (also known as crisis intervention and recovery services for crime victims): Typically, these programs provide prompt intervention and a full range of essential services to crime victims such as: crisis stabilization at the crime scene; emergency financial assistance and food vouchers; transportation to the hospital or court; transportation to the local battered women's shelter; repairing or replacing broken locks or windows; and referral to social service agencies.

Victim/witness assistance programs: These programs are affiliated with prosecutors' offices and provide the following services: witness notification and case monitoring; transportation services and court escort; victim advocates during pretrial hearings and the actual trial; and child care for children of witnesses while they are in court.

DEMOGRAPHIC PATTERNS

Since 1973 the U.S. Justice Department has published an annual report (the National Crime Victimization Survey [NCVS]) documenting the number of victimizations in the categories of rape, robbery, assault, theft, household burglary, and motor vehicle theft to U.S. residents age 12 or older as reported by households that have been victimized. The NCVS also measures victimization rates—the frequency of crime among subgroups of the population. Subgroups classify victims by gender, race, national location, ethnicity, age, marital status, education, and household income. These rates are computed by dividing the number of victimizations occurring in a specific population by the total number of persons in that population (Dobrin et al. 1996).

In sharp contrast to public opinion and the repeated statements of some politicians, the NCVS as well as the Federal Bureau of Investigation's (FBI) Uniform Crime Reports (UCR) have documented that crime rates *overall* have remained stable or declined since the early 1980s. However, some groups—such as adolescents and African Americans—have had an increase in violent crime victimizations (Zawitz et al. 1993).

The largest declines were in property-related crimes. However, violent crimes also have dropped, particularly since 1995 (Rand, Lynch, and Cantor 1997). The most unexpected trend, reported by both the UCR and the NCVS has been the gradual decline in violent crime, starting between 1993 and 1994. Between 1993 and 1994 the UCR reported a decline in all violent crime, with an 8 percent decline in homicides. In addition, according to the NCVS data for 1995, a hefty drop in violent crime was reported. This two-year sharp decline becomes obvious when comparing the 1993 and 1995 statistics; specifically a 27.3 percent decline in aggravated assaults, a 30.4 percent decrease in rapes, and a 13.1 percent decline in robberies (Rand et al. 1997).

The NCVS reported that an estimated 2.9 million serious nonfatal violent victimizations occurred in 1990. Nonfatal violent crimes include rapes, robberies, and violent assaults. Internationally, this rate ranked among the world's highest levels. According to the Bureau of Justice Statistics, the decline in the total violent crime rate from 1994 to 1995 was "the largest single-year decrease ever measured." The total rate of violent crime from 1973 to 1990 has decreased 9.2 percent. Yet analyzing the year-to-year trends from 1973 to 1990 shows no real pattern, but rather some declines, steady increases, and stable rates in total violent crime for each year for the mid-1970s through the 1980s. As mentioned, the first sharp year-to-year reduction in crime actually occurred between 1994 and 1995 (U.S. Department of Justice, NCVS 1997).

While it is natural to see declines in crime rates between two consecutive years as a positive sign, the long-term trends in violent crime victimization tell the true picture in terms of demographic shift and crime factor impact. Percentages and rates can increase and decrease slightly from year to year based on infinite combinations among various factors (e.g., national economic situation, unemployment rates, region of the country, age, and gender) and mean very little in overall crime reduction as a societal pattern.

The NCVS results also have supported the finding that criminal victimization rates do not occur at the same rate across subgroups of the population. For instance, the statistics show that violent victimization rates for murder involve ethnic minority males in urban areas to a greater extent than white males. In 1994, black males had a 42 out of 1,000 likelihood of being victims of violent crime. Comparatively, the least likely members of society to be murdered during the same year were white females—with the risk being 3 per 1,000 (Bureau of Justice Statistics 1997).

Race. Black murder victimization rates have exceeded those of whites throughout this century, and black murder rates are higher than white murder rates for all age groups. Victimization rates for individuals age 12 and older follow a similar pattern when identifying race and family income as affiliated factors. For example, for all victimizations in 1992, whites experienced a rate of 63.5 per 1,000 for families with incomes less than $7,500 while the rate for blacks in the same socioeconomic bracket was 70.2 per 1,000 (Dobrin et al. 1996).

However, while the rate for blacks is significantly higher, blacks only make up 11 percent of the population compared with whites, who account for almost 70 percent of the population. Rates of victimization steadily decrease for whites and blacks as annual family income increases to $50,000 or more (National Institute of Justice 1994).

From 1994 to 1995 there was a 12.8 percent reduction in the overall violent crime rate for whites. Blacks saw a noticeable decrease of 24 percent in aggravated assault rates, with some evidence of downward trends in overall personal and violent crime rates, and in rape/sexual assault (U.S. Department of Justice, NCVS 1997; Dobrin et al. 1996).

Age. The 1994–1995 declines in victimization among the elderly were not as significant as those experienced by intermediate age groups. No notable declines occurred in the age 50 or older range (except for personal theft) while all intermediate age groups showed remarkable declines in the overall violent crime rate. While teenagers and young adults are more likely than older adults to be murdered, three-fourths of all murder victims are age 24 or older when killed.

Those children at greatest risk for any victimization, according to 1992 statistics, are children whose household income is less than $20,000, black children, and children in large cities (Dobrin et al. 1996; U.S. Department of Justice, NCVS 1997). In 1992, adolescents age 16 to 19 had the highest risk of being victims of robbery, with a rate of 15.4 per 1,000 children. This rate steadily decreased throughout the lifetime of individuals to the low end rate of 1.5 per 1,000 individuals at age 65 and older. Victims of aggravated assault were also most strongly represented in the 16–19 age category at a rate of 26.3 cases per 1,000 children (Bureau of Justice Statistics 1993). Aggravated assaults showed a significant decline (30.6 percent) among 12- to 15-year-olds in 1994–1995.

Elderly members of society are also a vulnerable victimization subgroup. For individuals over age 65, those at greatest risk of violent victimization from 1987 to 1990, were males, blacks, divorced or separated individuals, and persons residing in the city (Dobrin et al. 1996). Victimization has been shown to be linked to age and health. The 75-and-older age group is the fastest-growing segment of the U.S. population. As Roberts (1990) notes, "It has been predicted that with the rapidly increasing numbers of frail elderly people in our society, the incidence of elder abuse and neglect will also rapidly increase" (81). The type of abuse inflicted most frequently on elders is neglect, followed by physical abuse.

Gender. Overall violent crime rates declined from 1994 to 1995 for both men (10.7 percent decline) and women (14.4 percent decline). Women have approximately one-third the risk of men of being murdered, but women are four times as likely as men to be killed by a spouse or intimate partner. The rates of nonfatal victimization among women were highest for blacks (58.5 per 1,000 females), females ages 12 to 15 (102.3 per 1,000), and for divorced/separated women (86.2 per 1,000) (Rand et al. 1997; U.S. Department of Justice, NCVS 1997).

SOCIETAL CONTEXT

For decades the courts ignored the interests of victims and witnesses. Millions of dollars were spent in the 1950s and 1960s on rehabilitation programs aimed at changing convicted felons into law-abiding citizens. Millions of dollars were also spent by the courts on processing and protecting the best interest of defendants. In sharp contrast to the offender, crime victims had to wait in the halls of dreary courtrooms while the defendant sometimes threatened or intimidated them. Separate waiting rooms for witnesses and/or their children were practically nonexistent until the mid-1980s (Roberts 1990). Services were rarely provided to assist the victim and the family members, who were often shattered by the traumatic experience (McDonald 1976).

By the mid-1970s when the first victim/witness assistance and rape crisis demonstration projects were initiated, the pendulum began to shift toward providing woefully needed services for vulnerable crime victims (Roberts 1992). The changed focus corresponded to how the crime victim was treated throughout the criminal justice system, from the first contact with a police officer or detective to the testimony in court. Historically, many crime victims had been victimized twice: first during the actual crime and then, again, when insensitive and unresponsive police and prosecutors ignored their calls or requests for assistance, and/or subjected them to harsh, repeated and victim blaming questions (McDonald 1976).

During the fourteen-year period from 1984 through 1998, responsive federal, state, and county agencies have allocated over $2 billion throughout the nation to aid crime victims. A large portion of these funds came from fines and penalty assessments on convicted offenders. County probation departments provided increased sources of funds through monetary restitution and penalty assessments.

Although the crime rate has steadily declined each year from 1994 through 1997, public opinion surveys reveal that the public remains fearful of crime. Most people form their actual beliefs about crime from violence on television, the news media, and what politicians say in their speeches. Most people have no idea about their actual risk of becoming a crime victim. The two groups of people—women and the elderly—who have the lowest statistical likelihood of being victimized often are the most fearful.

VULNERABILITIES AND RISK FACTORS

Some beginning work on crime victimization has established certain vulnerabilities that might make recovery from the victimization experience more difficult. In this discussion, "risk" is defined in relation to readjustment after a crime has already occurred rather than the risk of crime occurring in the first place, as a focus on crime prevention is outside the scope of this essay.

Different types of crime are described under the rubric of crime victimization. According to a review by Denkers and Winkel (1998), a disproportionate amount of studies focus on sexual assault (38 percent). The remaining studies they reviewed were focused on victims of violence (10 percent), property crimes (12 percent), both violent and property crimes (8 percent), unspecified crimes (24 percent), and samples involving the general population (8 percent). It would be expected that victims of different crimes may have their own unique reactions. Indeed, one of the risk factors for crime victims' adaptation involves types of crime. Within certain crime types, aspects of the crime have also been associated with particular problems. The literature on sexual assault has further identified age of the victim as playing a role in adaptation. A final risk factor found in the crime victim research involves previous life distress with poor adjustment prior to the crime contributing to many of the symptoms victims may experience. Each of these risk factors is explored more completely in the following sections.

Studies have compared different **types of crime** and particular aspects of crimes (severity of assaults, identity of the perpetrator, threat of life). In a study by Wirtz and Harrell (1987), crimes were categorized as physical assault (rape, domestic assault, and nondomestic assault) or nonassaultive (robbery and burglary). While physical assault victims clearly showed greater psychological distress than the nonassault victims at both one month and six months postcrime, the pattern of scores were similar. These findings indicate that the effects of crimes may follow a certain profile, although lesser in degree for nonassaultive compared with assaultive crimes.

One limitation of this study was the lack of a comparison group. Indeed, only a minority of studies (20 percent) conducted in the last ten years have included a comparison sample of nonvictims (Denkers and Winkel 1998). The problem is that without a control group of nonvictims, distress and symptoms might be attributed to crime victimization when such problems may also be present in the general population.

Denkers and Winkel (1998) compared several crime-type samples and a matched sample of nonvictims (300 victims, 290 nonvictims) in a nationwide prospective study of the Dutch population. The reactions of victims were measured prior to the crime and within two weeks, one month, and two months after the crime. Results demonstrated that overall, victims of crime reported lower levels of well-being, and, to a lesser extent, higher levels of fear. In addition, this study also supported that victims of violent crime appear to experience more affective distress and feelings of vulnerability than those who have suffered property crimes. Victims of property crimes recovered within one month to their precrime level of affective functioning, whereas victims of violent crime did not do so until about another month later.

Other studies have examined subcategories within the category of violent crimes and report that rape victims may suffer more ill effects from their victimization (Denkers and Winkel 1998). However, one study suggested that both physical and sexual assaults, whether they were perpetrated by a woman's husband or a stranger, were equally distressing (Riggs, Kilpatrick, and Resnick 1992). Although it had been, on average, about thirteen years since the victimization, elevated levels of symptoms were found in a number of problem areas for four groups of women when compared with a group of nonvictims. The authors concluded that not only may a physical assault be as traumatizing as a sexual assault, but also that abuse by a husband may be no less distressing than an attack by a stranger. It was also recognized, however, that women who had been assaulted by husbands may have experienced a series of incidents as compared with the onetime attacks by strangers who were studied. The effects of recurring attacks, whether sexual or physical, may be associated with greater trauma.

Another study focused on the effects of particular aspects of sexual assault (Wyatt, Nutgrass, and Newcomb 1990). Wyatt et al. (1990) found that both short- and long-term negative effects of abuse were predicted from greater severity of abuse and more rapes per incident. Other than aspects of sexual assault, one study compared bank employees in the Netherlands who had experienced robberies and those who had not (Kamphuis and Emmelkamp 1998). Perceived life threat was associated with a higher negative impact of the event and with problematic psychological functioning.

In the sexual assault literature specifically, some aspects of the victim have also been a focus of study. **Age of victim** has emerged as a risk factor with older victims, defined in Wyatt et al. (1990) as ages 27 to 36, experiencing a more difficult adjustment. Cohen and Roth (1987) described younger victims of sexual assault as experiencing high and intense levels of symptoms that subsided in a relatively brief time period, whereas older victims did not experience their symptoms as intensely but they suffered more long-term negative effects. Further, Wyatt et al. (1990) found that older victims tended to have more self-blaming attributions for their assaults, which, in turn, led to more problems with adjustment in the areas of sexuality and relationships. Finally, older victims were less likely to make adaptive lifestyle changes after the victimization.

Evidence is accumulating that the reactions victims may suffer after a crime may have much to do with their **previctimization** levels of functioning. When controlling for distress prior to the crime event in a statewide, prospective study, Norris and Kaniasty (1994) indicated that the contribution victimization made to problematic functioning in a number of domains, such as fear of crime, anxiety, phobic anxiety, depression, somatization, hostility, and avoidance behavior, either diminished considerably or disappeared entirely at three months. These results indicate that while victims may suffer distress after a crime incident, they may also have experienced problematic functioning before the crime took place.

Further support for this phenomenon has been found in other studies. In the Dutch study, when life satisfaction and assumptions about the benevolence of the world were controlled, differences between victims and nonvictims faded (Denkers and Winkel 1998). Out of ten outcome measures, only problems with affect and increased vulnerability were significant after controlling for premeasurement functioning.

Another study conducted in the Netherlands also reported that the higher the number of items on a nonstandardized life events scale, the greater the negative impact of the event and the more problematic the psychological adjustment for bank robbery victims (Kamphuis and Emmelkamp 1998). To explain these findings, Winkel, Denkers, and Vrij (1994) suggest that distress and symptoms in a victim might be related to a series of stressful negative life events, which may result in a tendency to associate victimization with the self. Self-blame, in turn, may interfere with adjustment after a crime.

RESILIENCIES AND PROTECTIVE FACTORS

In addition to certain risks for the recovery of crime victims, protective factors also have been found to mediate the stress of victimization. These protective factors include cognitive coping resources, self-esteem, and social support.

Much of the literature in this area focuses on the cognitive resources people utilize to cope with unexpected, stressful life events (Folkman and Lazarus 1985; Lazarus and Folkman 1984). Coping has been defined by as "cognitive and behavioral efforts to master, reduce, or tolerate the internal and/or external demands that are created by the stressful transaction" (Folkman 1984:843). These demands include perceptions of potential loss and/or harm at which time the individual evaluates choices for coping. Folkman (1984) classified coping strategies into two main types: problem-focused and emotion-focused. *Problem-focused strategies* focus on the use of problem solving and action plans, whereas *emotion-focused strategies* involve the control of negative or distressing emotions.

Studies unrelated to crime victimization have examined emotion-focused versus problem-focused coping strategies with mixed results. Some of the research supports the use of problem-focused coping over emotion-focused coping (Aldwin and Revenson 1987; Vitaliano et al. 1985, 1987; Wells, Hobfall, and Lavin 1997), whereas other research indicates the use of both problem- and emotion-focused strategies (Folkman and Lazarus 1985, 1988; Folkman et al. 1986).

Only a couple of studies have looked at problem-focused and emotion-focused strategies with crime victims. In one study, coping strategies of sixty-seven rape victims who were seen at an emergency room were assessed (Frazier and Burnett 1994). Higher adjustment problems were associated with "staying home" and "withdrawing"; lower problems were related to "keeping busy," "thinking positively," and "suppressing negative thoughts." While the authors concluded that emotion-focused and approach-focused coping strategies were more helpful, the items listed as most associated with lower symptom levels seem to have avoidant aspects, "keeping busy" and "suppressing negative thoughts," particularly. Avoidant coping has sometimes been referred to as emotion-focused coping in the literature (Herman-Stahl, Stemmler, and Peterson 1995); however, avoidant implies that attention is drawn away from the problem. Emotion-focused coping may sometimes involve a distancing strategy, such as "withdrawal" or "denial," yet also includes strategies, such as "finding a sense of meaning" or "looking on the bright side of things," which focus attention on the stress. Suls and Fletcher's (1985) meta-analysis of fourteen studies classified coping strategies as either attention (focusing efforts on the stress or reactions to it) or avoidant (focusing efforts away from the stress or reactions to it). They concluded that, in general, there is little advantage of using one class of coping strategy over the other. However, additional analyses suggested that while avoidant strategies may lead to better initial outcomes of reducing pain, stress, and anxiety, attention was associated with better long-term outcomes of reducing stress. Similarly, for the victims of bank robberies, the authors determined from a factor analysis of coping items that a "depressive-avoidant" coping style was associated with both a greater negative impact and more psychological distress.

The only other study on crime to look at coping strategies involved a special police response to burglary victims in the Netherlands (Winkel and Vrij 1993). The program involved an immediate response (within one-half hour) of the burglary call by two trained officers. One officer attended to the criminal aspects of the case and the other talked with the victim, completing a detailed report and giving crime prevention information.

When compared with victims who received the usual police procedure for burglary crimes, the victims in the special program engaged in significantly more problem-focused coping in terms of willingness to perform prevention measures. They also increased in their use of emotion-focused coping, and their perceptions of the police were enhanced. However, it was not always clear how the measures used in the study reflected the constructs of "emotion-focused" and "problem-focused" coping. Further, it was not assessed whether positive changes translated into improved adjustment for victims.

As well as type of coping strategies employed, a theoretical and empirical focus in the crime literature involves the extent to which internal attributions (events are perceived under individual control) or external attributions (events are perceived as governed by forces outside the individual) contribute to adjustment. Winkel et al. (1994) contrast two different models in this area: the Janoff-Bulman (1979, 1992) model and the Abramson/Seligman model (Abramson, Metalsky, and Alloy 1989; Abramson, Seligman, and Teasdale 1978).

In the Janoff-Bulman model, internal attributions are assumed to contribute to better coping in that they enhance a victim's sense of control in terms of reducing fear of revictimization and increasing the use of prevention measures so crime will not occur again (Frieze and Bookwala 1996; Winkel et al. 1994). Janoff-Bulman (1979) further distinguished between two different types of internal attributions: characterological and behavioral. Characterological attributions center around enduring qualities of the individual's character, whereas behavioral attributions involve aspects of the individual's behavior that can be changed to affect outcomes.

In contrast to Janoff-Bulman, the Abramson/Seligman model presumes that external attributions for stressful events have a buffering effect on self-esteem. This effect then contributes to better adjustment.

To test these alternative models, Winkel et al. (1994) looked at external and internal (characterological and self-blame) attributions in a Dutch sample of burglary victims. Worse outcomes, in terms of perceptions of victimization risk and fear of crime, were associated with external attributions, while behavioral attributions had the most positive outcomes in these two areas. The effect of character attributions on outcome showed an improvement over the use of external attributions but did not show as beneficial outcomes as behavioral attributions. Although the authors claim their findings indicate support for the Janoff-Bulman model, their results have to be interpreted with caution given that a nonstandardized list of five items was used to measure attributions. It could also be that behavioral attributions might have optimal effects with certain types of crimes, namely those that are less severe. However, studies of sexual assault victims have not found behavioral attributions particularly helpful for victim adjustment (Abbey 1987; Frazier 1990; Meyer and Taylor 1986). Indeed, both behavioral and characterological attributions were related to increased depression in one study (Frazier 1990).

Another study examined some of the factors associated with self-blame with a community sample of sexual assault victims in the Los Angeles area (Wyatt et al. 1990). Age of the victim (older age) and greater severity of the assault (e.g., multiple assaults and physical force) predicted a greater likelihood of the use of internal attributions and self-blame. In turn, internal attributions and self-blame were associated with both deleterious short- and long-term effects.

While empirical support for Janoff-Bulman's model has not been found, neither has evidence accumulated for the Abramson/Seligman model. In the crime literature, only one recent study was located in which Meyer and Taylor (1986) found no relationship between external attribution and adjustment. Further, a review of the research unrelated to crime victimization on the association between external attribution and adaptation indicated that of twenty-seven studies, in none were external attributions related to more successful coping (Tennen and Affleck 1990). Indeed, the reviewed research associated external attributions with less successful coping. In sum, it appears that more work needs to uncover the connections between appraisals, attributions, and coping mechanisms as neither model seems to consistently explain victim adjustment.

Self-esteem has been identified as another protective factor for crime victims in both U.S. and Dutch samples. When victims of violent crime in a southern U.S. state were followed prospectively, high self-esteem was found to protect against both depression and anxiety (Kaniasty and Norris 1992). Similarly, in a Dutch study of bank robbery victims, high self-esteem helped predict improved psychological functioning.

A further protective factor identified in the literature has been **social support**, which can be distinguished by both formal and informal support. Given that crime impacts many aspects of the individual, different kinds of social support may have to be available. Kaniasty and Norris (1992) evaluated the effects of both perceived and received support, and, within each of these types, different kinds of support, on a representative state sample of 690 respondents. In terms of perceived support, appraisal support (consisting of emotional and informational support) had a positive effect on well-being no matter the crime and had a protective influence against anxiety and fear of crime. Tangible support, the availability of material assistance, produced positive effects by protecting victims of violent crime from anxiety and by buffering victims of both nonviolent and violent crime against depression.

Informational support (guidance or advice) and tangible support (material aid) had a protective influence with victims of violence on fear of crime. However, the receipt of emotional support was not associated with victim well-being for either violent or non-violent crime. Despite the benefits offered by received support, this study suggests that the effects of perceived social support extend more broadly in terms of impacting both victims of violent and non-violent crime and in the enhancement of psychological health (Kaniasty and Norris 1992).

In another part of the study reported by Kaniasty and Norris (1992), Johnson (1997) looked at the frequency and use of formal services, broadly categorized as legal (services offered by prosecutor's offices, legal aid, and private lawyers) and health-related services (medical, clergy, and mental health). First, only a small proportion of the total number of victims ($N = 327$) used either legal services (20 percent) or mental health services (between 11 and 12 percent). Most of those who used such services found them helpful: helpfulness of legal services was found for 60 to 66 percent of individuals, depending on the time of data collection; an even greater majority (between 80 and 92 percent) found mental health services helpful.

Perhaps more important, the study also addressed whether perceived helpfulness of services translated into actual recovery for victims. In the short term (up to six months after the crime), victims availing themselves of legal or health services actually had more adjustment problems than victims who were not involved with such services. Although it could be that those victims who are suffering greater distress are more likely to seek out services, the author also controlled for predistress variables and suggested that formal services were not beneficial in the short term.

At six to twelve months, victims who had received legal services were adjusting better than victims who had not used the legal system, particularly when these services were rated as at least somewhat helpful. However, the use of health services was associated with more problematic psychological functioning at the six- to twelve-month period. Health services were only helpful in reducing psychological distress if services were delivered both shortly after the crime and over time (six to twelve months later). In considering these results, it must be recognized that health services included mental health, medical, and religious services; therefore, it is impossible to tease out the effects of only mental health services.

In looking specifically at rape victims, Wyatt et al. (1990) also categorized police services and those offered in emergency rooms and counseling centers as "involvement of authorities," and such involvement was predictive of increased negative short- and long-term effects. In interpreting these results, the authors state that data collection occurred between 1980 and 1983 and on average, the most recent sexual assault incident had been five years previous. Therefore, it is hoped that the more current services offered by police and other authorities would have greater sensitivity to the needs of sexual assault victims and would be perceived more positively.

Protective factors for readjustment after crime victimization have included both individual (coping strategies and self-esteem) and environmental (social support) factors, although it is recognized that these factors may interact in a systemic nature. For example, one's self-esteem may be bolstered by the perception that one has a supportive network (Kaniasty and Norris 1992). Coping strategies may include seeking social support and having such a network available (Smith and Carlsen 1997).

Further research on factors that buffer the negative effects of victimization is required. The interplay between type of crime, coping strategies, locus of control, and attributions of the crime, and both short- and long-term adjustment needs to be better understood so that victim recovery can be bolstered. One way to approach this study would be to follow the process of recovery over time for victims, as reactions following victimization tend to subside within three to nine months (Denkers and Winkel 1998). Further, comparisons between victims who have high versus those who have low symptom levels can be investigated for an understanding of the various factors that might bolster the recovery process (Koss and Burkhart 1989).

PROGRAMS AND SOCIAL WORK CONTRIBUTIONS

Three different types of programs have been developed to assist crime victims in the aftermath of being victimized. The first type is known as prosecutor-based victim/ witness assistance programs. The coordinators of these types of court-based programs usually have an M.S.W. or a master's degree in counseling. The second type of program is commonly referred to as a victim service program and is usually under the auspices of a not-for-profit social service agency. Many of the coordinator/directors of these types of programs have an M.S.W. degree and learned about the program firsthand during their graduate school field placement. The third type of program is a crisis intervention unit or service. The coordinator is usually a social worker, psychologist, or counselor. These types of programs are generally located within a hospital, mental health center, or police department.

Prosecutor-based victim/witness assistance programs are usually located either within the local county prosecutor's suite of offices, the county court house, or across the street from the court building. These programs are designed to encourage witness cooperation in the filing of criminal charges as well as testifying in court. The program coordinator reports directly to the county prosecutor, the chief counsel to the prosecutor, or a deputy prosecutor responsible for all sex crimes (e.g., sexual assault and domestic violence cases). The primary responsibility of the victim advocates/counselors is the provision of services to witnesses, particularly witnesses to violent crimes where a person has been charged with one or more criminal offenses. Victim/witness advocates are also responsible for accompanying the witness to the prefiling hearing, preliminary hearing, deposition hearing, and/or the trial to ensure that each witness is treated fairly and compassionately by the attorneys, court clerk, and the magistrate. In addition, it is important for the coordinator or victim advocates to accompany the victim/witness to all official appointments related to the filing and processing of the criminal court cases. For example, if the victim has been sexually assaulted, the victim advocate will either accompany or meet the victim at the hospital or medical facility to make sure that the victim's rights are protected.

Victims and witness also are provided with transportation and a court escort when their appearance is required. Transportation assistance can be in the form of reimbursement to victims for travel expenses they incurred or by staff transporting victims and witnesses themselves.

According to a national organizational survey of *prosecutor-based victim/witness assistance programs* by Roberts (1990), slightly under one-third of these programs reported having some form of child care for the children of victims and witnesses while the parents testified in court. Providing responsible and structured child care for a parent while he or she is testifying in court can provide an important service. Unfortunately, most criminal justice agencies are very different from social work agencies in that they do not usually realize that victims and witnesses' children are affected by their parents' emotional reactions, losses, physical injuries, and disruptions due to being a victim of a crime. Victim/witness assistance programs should be concerned with the special needs of children not only because many parent witnesses will *not* be able to testify if they cannot find child care during a traumatizing court ordeal, but because it is the humane thing to do. An added benefit is that some children may have witnessed the crime and noticed additional identifying characteristics of the perpetrator (Roberts 1995).

The overriding objective of prosecutor-based victim/witness assistance programs and units is to assist witnesses in overcoming the anxiety and trauma associated with testifying in court, while encouraging witness cooperation in the prosecution of criminal cases. The primary objectives of these programs are as follows:

1. Providing victims and witnesses with the message that their cooperation is essential to crime control efforts and successful criminal prosecution.
2. Informing victims and witnesses of their rights to receive dignified and compassionate treatment by criminal justice authorities.
3. Providing information to witnesses on the court process, the scheduling of the case, the trial, and the disposition.
4. Providing orientation to court and tips on how best to accurately recall the crime scene and testify (Roberts 1990).

Victim service or crisis intervention programs for crime victims are not as common as prosecutor-based victim/witness assistance programs. This type of program is usually lodged in a police department, sheriff's office, hospital, probation department, or not-for-profit social service agency. Typically, these programs attempt to intervene within the first twenty-four hours after the victimization. They provide a comprehensive range of essential services for crime victims including responding to the crime scene; crisis counseling; help in completing victim compensation applications; emergency financial assistance and food vouchers to local supermarkets; transportation to court, the local battered women's shelter, the hospital, or the victim assistance program office; repairing or replacing broken locks and windows; assistance in replacing lost documents (e.g. birth certificates, marriage licenses, wills); and referrals to the prosecutor's domestic violence and sexual assault intake unit as well as community mental health centers and social service agencies for extended counseling and short-term treatment (Roberts 1990, 1997).

ASSESSMENT AND INTERVENTIONS

Assessment, which involves an understanding of the impact of the particular crime on the victim and knowledge of the risk and protective factors involved, can be conducted through a clinical interview and the use of standardized measurement instruments. The following self-report instruments can assist in assessment of the risk and protective factors that have been identified in the literature as related to crime victimization:

The Impact of Event Scale: The Impact of Event Scale (Horowitz, Wilner, and Alvarez 1979) is a fifteen-item, self-report instrument that measures how much distress is associated with a specific life event. There are two subscales, intrusion and avoidance, which reflect dimensions of posttraumatic stress disorder.

Brief Symptom Inventory: The Brief Symptom Inventory (BSI; Derogatis 1993) is a briefer (fifty-four-item versions) of the ninety-item Symptom Checklist 90-Revised (Derogatis 1977). The BSI assesses the following symptom dimensions: (1) somatization; (2) obsessive-compulsiveness; (3) interpersonal sensitivity; (4) depression; (5) anxiety; (6) hostility;

(7) phobic anxiety; (8) paranoid ideation; and (9) psychoticism. There are also three global indices of functioning: (1) the Global Severity Index; (2) the Positive Symptom Total; and (3) the Positive Symptom Distress Index.

Rosenberg Self-Esteem Scale: The Rosenberg Self-Esteem Scale (Rosenberg 1965) is a ten-item measure assessing self-esteem.

Social Support Behaviors Scale: The Social Support Behaviors Scale (Vaux 1988; Vaux, Riedel, and Stewart 1987) is a forty-five-item, Likert-type, self-report inventory designed to assess the following five different types of supportive behavior from both friends and family: emotional, socializing, practical, financial, and advice/guidance.

Ways of Coping Questionnaire: The Ways of Coping Questionnaire (Folkman and Lazarus 1988) is a sixty-six-item, self-report instrument designed to assess the cognitive and behavioral strategies that individuals use to cope with the demands of a stressful encounter. The following subscales are provided: (1) confrontive coping; (2) distancing; (3) self-controlling; (4) seeking social support; (5) accepting responsibility; (6) escape-avoidance; (7) planful problem solving; and (8) positive reappraisal.

The next section presents a case illustration to demonstrate how knowledge of these risk and protective factors may guide intervention in cases of crime victimization.

ILLUSTRATION AND DISCUSSION

Annette Miller, a white female in her early 30s, recently experienced a robbery during the night shift at her job as a convenience store clerk. Annette could only describe her assailant as a middle-aged white man as his face was concealed by a stocking cap. He had pulled a gun out of his jacket pocket, held it to her head, and said he'd kill her if she didn't immediately hand over the money in her register. She reported that he became even more agitated when a car pulled up in the parking lot, and she thought he'd panic and kill her. As it was, he grabbed the money from her and fled without being caught.

Annette has worked at convenience stores for the last three years. She usually worked the night shift since she had found this the best arrangement as a single parent raising three school-age children. This work had allowed her to be available to her children not only in the morning when she got off work but also in the afternoons when they came home from school and into the evening. An older neighbor would then come over when Annette was to leave for work, and she would spend the night to watch over the children. Annette said this worked well since the neighbor would not charge much and Annette couldn't have afforded the cost of regular child care if she worked during the day. She said she did not have family to help her as they lived out of state.

Annette said although this has been an ideal arrangement, now she blamed herself for working the night shift. "Everyone knows that's when the robberies happen. And I already had one happen to me. You'd think I'd learn." She said she had been through another robbery before, approximately eighteen months ago, but that had not impacted her as much. She described that the previous incident had involved a teenager, who was obviously nervous himself. Although he had held a gun to her and tried to conceal himself from the store video equipment by pulling his sweatshirt hood around his face, she could at least see his face, and this made it less scary to her. He was also immediately apprehended, and the case against him was strong.

However, this time the police had no suspects so she knew her assailant was still out there somewhere. Every time a middle-aged white man walked in the door, she would begin to panic to the point of having to leave work. She was having a difficult time sleeping at night. She also kept replaying the incident in her mind, and she worried about how she would support her three children if she didn't work on a regular basis.

Regarding previous life stress, Annette had experienced a divorce nine months ago from her youngest child's (age 7) father who left her for another woman. Her ex-husband was not following through with child support payments. To explain all these events, Annette says, "There must be something wrong with me for all these things to keep happening."

Annette was referred to the police victim assistance program after talking to the robbery investigator. She had become tearful and upset, realizing that nothing more was to be done on the case since there were no suspects, and the investigator told her that maybe she could benefit from talking to someone.

The assessment procedure in this case consists of a clinical interview and completion of standardized measures. A number of risk factors are indicated for Annette. First, the robbery involved a gun and threats were made on her life, so this represents a more severe type of crime. In addition, she had actually feared for her life, and life threat has been associated with increased distress for robbery victims (Kamphuis and Emmelkamp 1998).

Further, Annette's precrime functioning was less than optimal due to her financial problems, the stress of single parenting, a divorce in the last year, and another robbery eighteen months ago. Annette has suffered from an accumulation of prior negative life events, which contributed to her present level of high distress.

Neither does Annette seem to have many protective factors to buffer against the effects of victimization. The Ways of Coping Questionnaire indicates that her coping style is one of "accepting responsibility." She also makes statements such as "Everyone knows the night shift is when the robberies happen. You'd think I'd learn" and "There must be something wrong with me for all these things to keep happening," indicating that Annette seems to be making internal attributions for the occurrence of the robbery event.

Annette also scored low on the Rosenberg Self-Esteem Scale. Although it is difficult to know if the current low level is reflective of her precrime functioning, or whether the robbery experience has eroded her self-esteem (or possibly both), Annette's low self-esteem fails to provide a buffering effect against the depression and the anxiety she now experiences, as indicated by the Brief Symptom Inventory.

Another possible protective factor, social support, is low in Annette's case. She had moved to this state for her ex-husband's job, and she has no family in the area. She further says that she is so busy working and taking care of her children that she doesn't have time for socializing. She says she doesn't associate with her neighbors because they don't work and are always "partying," and she doesn't want that kind of influence on her children.

In terms of formal support, the fact that a suspect has not been apprehended and that legal involvement will now end might contribute to Annette's distress. The literature indicates that only when victim involvement with the legal system persists over time (six to twelve months) and is found to be helpful does there seem to be a positive effect on victims (Johnson 1997). The hypothesis is that when legal justice is served, the victim's vulnerability vis-à-vis the assailant is redressed.

In all likelihood it will probably be necessary for Annette's contact with the helping system to extend over time (at least six to twelve months) since immediate and continuing help has been associated with a reduction in psychological symptoms (Johnson 1997). Like many victims, Annette has experienced many life events that have depreciated her sense of well-being (Denkers and Winkel 1998). Therefore, crisis intervention efforts that concentrate only on bringing a victim's functioning to predistress levels may not be adequate (Roberts and Burman 1998). Efforts instead should focus on establishing more problem-focused coping strategies. For instance, cognitive-behavioral techniques can redress the faulty attributions and beliefs in regard to Annette's self-blame and can help Annette build her self-esteem and manage her anxiety. Annette can also be trained on problem-solving skills so that she can identify her options in terms of employment and child care arrangements (Roberts and Burman 1998).

Helping efforts should also focus on assisting Annette in building her supportive network. Examples of such a supportive network may include a single-parenting support group or a more informal circle of other parents in similar life circumstances who can assist Annette with child care responsibilities and emotional support. The important facet of a supportive network, whether informal or formal (the victim advocate), is that it should not be limited to the provision of only emotional support (Kaniasty and Norris 1992). Rather, the research suggests that more concrete and instrumental assistance (e.g., emergency financial assistance, child care, job training) may be more beneficial for victim recovery (Kaniasty and Norris 1992; Roberts 1990).

A further intervention strategy with Annette might be to identify more individualized protective factors that she has employed for coping. One method by which her unique strengths and resources can be assessed is through a solution-focused approach (e.g., de Shazer 1988, 1994). A solution-focused approach to crisis intervention with crime victims has been discussed in the literature (Greene and Lee 1996). The focus is on times when the victim demonstrates successful coping. The resources that are used are elicited, reinforced, and amplified so that the client can employ these strategies to resolve current difficulties. For example, Annette is raising three children as a single parent. What are the strengths she uses to be able to do this? How is she able to negotiate her work schedule, child care arrangements, and balance the needs of her children? How was she able to cope with her husband leaving her and the previous robbery she experienced? These strengths and capacities Annette has employed in the past can be accessed and developed to help her cope with more immediate challenges.

Social work practice methods are uniquely appropriate for work with crime victims because the major focus is on the interaction between victims and the criminal justice system and between other service delivery systems, i.e., health, and mental health. The intervention services performed by victim advocates reflect the characteristics of generalist social work practice. Social work is concerned with the interactions between people and their social environment that affect the ability of people to accomplish their life tasks, alleviate distress, improve social functioning, and realize their values.

CONCLUSION

In some communities, victim services and witness assistance programs have expanded to meet the special needs of child, adult, and elderly crime victims and their families. In the United States, services include crisis intervention, support groups, emergency food vouchers and financial aid, services for battered women, lock repair and replacement, child care for witnesses' children while they testify in court, victim advocacy in the courtroom, home visits, short-term therapy, relocation assistance to transitional housing, and intervention with witnesses' employers. At the same time, a number of cities and towns do not have a fully staffed and comprehensive victim assistance program (Roberts 1990, 1997).

The future looks promising. However, a major stumbling block to creating comprehensive twenty-four-hour victim assistance programs is the shortage of forensic social workers willing to work at night or on weekends when most violent victimizations take place.

References

Abbey, A. 1987. "Perceptions of Personal Availability versus Responsibility: How Do They Differ?" *Basic and Applied Social Psychology* 8:3–19.

Abramson, L.Y., G. I. Metalsky, and L. B. Alloy. 1989. "Hopelessness Depression: A Theory-Based Subtype of Depression." *Psychological Review* 96:358–72.

Abramson, L.Y., M. E. Seligman, and J. D. Teasdale. 1978. "Learned Helplessness in Humans: Critique and Reformulation." *Journal of Abnormal Psychology* 87:49–74.

Aldwin, C. M. and T. A. Revenson. 1987. "Does Coping Help? A Reexamination of the Relation Between Coping and Mental Health." *Journal of Personality and Social Psychology* 53:337–48.

Brownell, P. and E. P. Congress. 1998. "Application of the Culturagram to Empower Culturally and Ethnically Diverse Battered Women." In A. R. Roberts, ed., *Battered Women and Their Families: Intervention Strategies and Treatment Programs,* 2d ed., pp. 395, 401. New York: Springer.

Bureau of Justice Statistics. 1993. *Sourcebook of Criminal Justice Statistics 1992.* Washington, D.C.: U.S. Department of Justice, U.S. Government Printing Office.

——. 1997. *Sourcebook of Criminal Justice Statistics 1996.* Washington, D.C.: U.S. Department of Justice, Project grant given to the Hindelang Criminal Justice Research Center, State University of New York at Albany.

Cohen, L. J. and S. Roth. 1987. "The Psychological Aftermath of Rape: Long-term Effects and Individual Differences in Recovery." *Journal of Social and Clinical Psychology* 5: 525–34.

Denkers, A. and F. Winkel. 1998. "Crime Victims' Well Being and Fear in a Prospective and Longitudinal Study." *International Review of Victimology* 5:141–62.

Derogatis, L. R. 1977. *Brief Symptom SCL 90 Check List.* Baltimore: Johns Hopkins University Press.

——. 1993. *Brief Symptom Inventory: Administration, Scoring and Procedures Manual.* Minneapolis, Minn.: National Computer Systems.

de Shazer, S. 1988. *Clues: Investigating Solutions in Brief Therapy.* New York: Norton.

——. 1994. *Words Were Originally Magic.* New York: Norton.

Dobrin, A., B. Wiersema, C. Loftin, and D. McDowall. 1996. *Statistical Handbook on Violence in America.* Phoenix, Ariz.: Oryx Press.

Folkman, S. 1984. "Personal Control, and Stress and Coping Processes: A Theoretical Analysis." *Journal of Personality and Social Psychology* 46:839–52.

Folkman, S. and R. S. Lazarus. 1985. "If It Changes It Must Be a Process: Study of Emotion and Coping During Three Stages of College Examination." *Journal of Personality and Social Psychology* 48:150–70.

——. 1988. *Ways of Coping Questionnaire Permissions Set: Manual, Test Booklet, Scoring Key.* Redwood City, Calif.: Mind Garden.

Folkman, S., R. S. Lazarus, R. J. Gruen, and A. DeLongis. 1986. "Appraisal, Coping, Health Status, and Psychological Symptoms." *Journal of Personality and Social Psychology* 50:571–79.

Frazier, P. A. 1990. "Victim Attributions and Post-Rape Trauma." *Journal of Personality and Social Psychology* 59:298–304.

Frazier, P. A. and J. W. Burnett. 1994. "Immediate Coping Strategies Among Rape Victims." *Journal of Counseling and Development* 72:633–39.

Frieze, I. and J. Bookwala. 1996. "Coping with Unusual Stressors: Criminal Victimization." In M. Zeidner, N. Endler, S. Norman, et al., eds., *Handbook of Coping: Theory, Research, and Applications,* pp. 303–21. New York: John Wiley.

Greene, G. J. and M. Lee. 1996. "Client Strengths and Crisis Intervention: A Solution-Focused Approach." *Crisis Intervention and Time-Limited Treatment* 3(1):43–63.

Herman-Stahl, M. A., M. Stemmler, and A. C. Peterson. 1995. "Approach and Avoidant Coping: Implications for Adolescent Mental Health." *Journal of Youth and Adolescence* 24:649–65.

Horowitz, M. J., N. Wilner, and W. Alvarez. 1979. "Impact of Event Scale: A Measure of Subjective Stress." *Psychosomatic Medicine* 41:207–18.

Janoff-Bulman, R. 1979. "Characterological versus Behavioral Self-Blame: Inquiries into Depression and Rape." *Journal of Personality and Social Psychology* 37:1798–1809.

——. 1992. *Shattered Assumptions.* New York: Free Press.

Johnson, K. 1997. Professional help and crime victims. *Social Service Review, 71:* 89–109.

Kamphius, J. and P. Emmelkamp. 1998. "Crime Related Trauma: Psychological Distress in Victims of Bank Robbery." *Journal of Anxiety Disorders* 12:199–208.

Kaniasty, K. and F. Norris. 1992. "Social Support and Victims of Crime: Matching Event, Support, and Outcome." *American Journal of Community Psychology* 20:211–41.

Koss, M. and B. Burkhart. 1989. "A Conceptual Analysis of Rape Victimization." *Psychology of Women Quarterly* 13:27–40.

Lazarus, R. S. and S. Folkman. 1984. *Stress, Appraisal, and Coping.* New York: Springer.

McDonald, W. F., ed. 1976. *Criminal Justice and the Victim.* Beverly Hills, Calif.: Sage.

Meyer, C. and S. Taylor. 1986. "Adjustment to Rape." *Journal of Social and Personality Psychology* 50:1226–34.

National Institute of Justice, Office of Justice Programs. 1994. "Research in Brief." Washington, D.C.: U.S. Government Printing Office.

Norris, F. H. and K. Kaniasty. 1994. "Psychological Distress Following Criminal Victimization in the General Population: Cross-sectional, Longitudinal, and Prospective Analyses." *Journal of Consulting and Clinical Psychology* 62:111–23

Rand, M. R., J. P. Lynch, and D. Cantor. 1997, April. "Criminal Victimization, 1973–95." *Bureau of Justice Statistics, National Crime Victimization Survey.* Washington, D.C.: U.S. Department of Justice.

Riggs, D., D. Kilpatrick, and H. Resnick. 1992. "Long-Term Psychological Distress Associated with Marital Rape and Aggravated Assault: A Comparison to Other Crime Victims." *Journal of Family Violence* 7:283–96.

Roberts, A. R. 1990. *Helping Crime Victims: Research, Policy and Practice.* Thousand Oaks, Calif.: Sage.

——. 1992. "Victim/Witness Programs: Questions and Answers." *FBI Law Enforcement Bulletin* 61(12):12–16.

——. 1995. "Victim Services and Victim/Witness Assistance Programs." In R. L. Edwards and J. Hopps, eds., *Encyclopedia of Social Work,* pp. 2440–44. Washington, D.C.: National Association of Social Workers Press.

——. 1996. "Myths and Realities Regarding Battered Women." In A. R. Roberts, ed., *Helping Battered Women: New Perspectives and Remedies,* pp. 1–13. New York: Oxford University Press.

——. 1997. "The Role of the Social Worker in Victim/Witness Assistance Programs." In A. R. Roberts, ed., *Social Work in Juvenile and Criminal Justice Settings,* pp. 150–59. Springfield, Ill.: Charles C Thomas.

Roberts, A. R. and S. Burman. 1998. "Crisis Intervention and Cognitive Problem-Solving Therapy with Battered Women: A National Survey and Practice Model." In A. R. Roberts, ed., *Battered Women and Their Families,* pp. 3–28. New York: Springer.

Rosenberg, M. 1965. *Society and the Adolescent Self-Image.* Princeton, N.J.: Princeton University Press.

Smith, C. and B. Carlson. 1997. "Stress, Coping and Resilience in Children and Youth." *Social Service Review* 71:231–56.

Suls, J. and B. Fletcher. 1985. "The Relative Efficacy of Avoidant and Nonavoidant Coping Strategies: A Meta-analysis." *Health Psychology* 4:249–88.

Tennen, H. and G. Affleck. 1990. "Blaming Others for Threatening Events." *Psychological Bulletin* 108:209–32.

U.S. Department of Justice, National Crime Victimization Survey, Office of Justice Programs. 1997. *Changes in Criminal Victimization, 1994–95.* Washington, D.C.: U.S. Government Printing Office.

Vaux, A. 1988. *Social Support: Theory, Research, and Intervention.* New York: Praeger.

Vaux, A., S. Riedel, and D. Stewart. 1987. "Modes of Social Support: The Social Support Behaviors (SS-B) Scale." *American Journal of Community Psychology* 15:209–37.

Vitaliano, P. P., W. Katon, J. Russo, R. D. Maiuro, K. Anderson, and M. Jones. 1987. "Coping As an Index of Illness Behavior in Panic Disorder." *Journal of Nervous and Mental Disease* 175:78–84.

Vitaliano, P. P., J. Russo, J. E. Carr, R. D. Maiuro, and J. Beckker. 1985. "The Ways of Coping Checklist: Revision and Psychometric Properties." *Multivariate Behavioral Research* 20:3–26.

Wells, J. D., S. E. Hobfoll, and J. Lavin. 1997. "Resource Loss, Resource Gain, and Communal Coping During Pregnancy Among Women with Multiple Roles." *Psychology of Women Quarterly* 21:645–62.

Winkel, F. and A. Vrij. 1993. "Facilitating Problem and Emotion-Focused Coping in Victims of Burglary: Evaluating a Police Crisis Intervention Program." *Journal of Community Psychology* 21:97–111.

Winkel, F., A. Denkers, and A. Vrij. 1994. "The Effects of Attributions on Crime Victims' Psychological Readjustment." *Genetic, Social and General Psychology Monographs* 120:145–69.

Wirtz, P. W. and A. V. Harrell. 1987. "Assaultive versus Non-assaultive Victimization." *Journal of Interpersonal Violence* 2:264–77.

Wyatt, G. E., C. M. Nutgrass, and M. Newcomb. 1990. "Internal and External Mediators of Women's Rape Experiences." *Psychology of Women Quarterly* 14:153–76.

Zawitz, M. W. et al. 1993. *Highlights from 20 years of Surveying Crime Victims: The National Crime Victimization Survey, 1973–92*. Washington, D.C.: Bureau of Justice Statistics, U.S. Department of Justice.

16

Death of a Child

Barbara Oberhofer Dane

In the United States, clinicians, social workers, and other professionals have noted our society's view toward death as typically one of denial; that is, we have tried not to think about it. People would "pass away" without little notice after a grave illness. However, the battle against HIV infection and AIDS has altered this denial, drawing death to the front-page headlines. The role of social work is vital in assisting bereaved families to cope with the death of a loved one. Because of the profession's holistic perspective and scope of responsibility, social workers are in a unique position to understand the dynamics involved in working with bereaved families.

Death radically alters our relationships with others. And the death of a child constitutes one of the most painful experiences individuals may undergo in their lifetime; when a child dies, grief can be devastating. The death of a child strikes at the parent's core, and bereavement can appear more complicated, intense, and long lasting (Rando 1986). The aspects of the relationship between parent and child that defined its intimacy and uniqueness are those that intensify bereavement. Although there has been a social phenomenon of denying the importance of parental loss of a child at both ends of the age span, in most instances, the age of the deceased child is irrelevant. The issues of parental bereavement pertain equally to the parent who has sustained a perinatal loss and the parent whose adult child has died. Death out of turn, such as the sudden or accidental death of a child by suicide, miscarriage, earthquake, or car accidents, is initially incomprehensible and takes a longer time to assimilate given the implicit expectation that the parent will die before the child.

After the death of a child, as with the death of any other family member, the family system must reorganize itself. This occurs especially after the death of a child where there are surviving siblings and/or children born subsequent to the death of that child. It is imperative to ensure that role reorganization, role reassignments, and identity ascriptions are appropriate. Many deleterious situations and much pathology have been reported in the thanatological literature attesting to the negative consequences when this fails to occur (Rando 1988).

The process of grieving requires that the family both traditional and nontraditional acknowledge that loss is final and death irreversible. Denial of this reality, although common at various stages of the dying process and even afterward, may impede a family's recovery from loss. The family's shared acknowledgment of death is reflected in their communicating about the subject in clear terms. Language can be a powerful psychological tool. Families that avoid use of direct terminology may be sending signals that they have not fully integrated the reality of their loss. It also is important that the *entire* family share in the acknowledgment of the death. Most often, it is in families where children are deemed incapable of understanding loss that the largest incidence of difficulty in adjustment is found (Rosen 1986).

This chapter focuses specifically on families who experience the unnatural death of a child. The family often comprises other relatives and close friends, who are frequently overlooked as mourners. Death of a child always extracts more severe forms of bereavement. Helping families beyond their grief, which is the reaction to loss seen in acute mourning, and assisting them in adapting to it and accommodating to its changes are significant social work tasks. This process can go on forever, as the bereaved family learns to go on healthily and adaptively in the new life without forgetting the memories of their deceased child.

DEFINING AND EXPLAINING THE DEATH OF A CHILD

Mourning occurs on a smaller and more personal scale for most of us in private life. Our recognition of and response to death reflect the attitudes and customs of society. Thus, although the core experience of grief is much the same throughout the world, expressions of mourning may be specific to a particular culture. People in one culture may conclude that people elsewhere do not feel deeply when they are bereaved, when the fact is that the others simply express their grief differently. The American approach to dying, death, and the dead depersonalizes and isolates these phenomena from everyday life, and there has been a tendency to maintain death in a tundra of silence (Becker 1973; Gorer 1965).

As we enter the next millennium, some thanatologists have argued that the idea of death denial in American society is overstated. Death now is neither denied nor hidden from everyday life. Cemeteries are open to the public and can easily be seen from roadways. Many individuals avidly read the daily obituaries, and sympathy cards are publicly displayed and sold in all greeting card stores. In addition, a surge of interest in death and dying has emerged during the last generation. Numerous films have been produced, books published, and countless professional meetings have been organized around the themes of death and dying. Thanatology, the study of death and dying, has become institutionalized on college campuses. Many people in America today are familiar with the phrase "death with dignity," a concept that has become the rallying call of professional thanatology activity in the past two decades. The growth of the American hospice is indicative of the growing public awareness of the death-with-dignity movement (Moeller 1996). Kellehear and Moeller (1984) argued that death is not denied as much as is "organized" and managed within a technological system by the profession of medicine. The social status of dying persons is diminished.

For most of the past century, one theoretical paradigm dominated the thinking of service providers, researchers, and educators—Sigmund Freud's (1957) grief work theory. Like a great many other people, following the mass death and bereavement of World War I, Freud had difficulty coming to terms with the fact that nations priding themselves on their highly cultivated civilization could behave so brutally toward each other. The survivors had to come to terms with their individual grief but also with a sense of loss that pervaded all of society. Freud's original theory emphasized the intrapsychic response to loss, that is, how we attempt to deal with the thoughts and feelings inside us.

Interest in attachment behavior and bonding owes much to the investigations of Bowlby (1962, 1969, 1973, 1980), who provided a broad framework for understanding both attachment and loss. Bowlby made a strong connection between the biological need for survival and the phenomena of grief and mourning.

Parkes's (1987–88) contributions have focused directly on the interpersonal dimensions of bereavement, grief, and mourning. He has conducted some of the most important studies of the *psychosocial transitions* involved in coping with the loss of a loved person. Some examples of the questions that Parkes has been trying to answer are: How do people attempt to get on with their lives after bereavement? Under what conditions does grief work fail, leaving the survivor in a state of prolonged social and personal dysfunction? From his many observations Parkes has identified three basic components of grief work:

▮ *Preoccupation with thoughts of the deceased person.* This represents a continuing search process (reminding us of the attachment-seeking signals and behaviors described by Bowlby in many species).

▮ *Repeatedly going over the loss experience in one's mind.* This is a painful process in which the survivor seems to be testing out the reality of the loss (did this terrible thing really happen?).

▮ *Attempts to explain the loss.* It is somewhat easier to accept the reality of a death and get on with one's own life if the loss somehow makes sense, had a reason behind it. During this part of the grief work process the survivor is asking self and others, "Why, why, *why?*"

In an article that will probably spark controversy for some years to come, Stroebe has recently challenged the grief work theory: "Not only is there very little scientific evidence on the grief work hypothesis, but studies that bear on the issue yield contradictory results" (1992–93:23). In other words, clinicians, researchers, and educators (as well as the media) may have prematurely accepted the grief work theory without adequate examination. Relatively few studies have addressed themselves to direct evaluation of the grief work theory, and fewer were designed in a way that a clear evaluation could be made. "Taken as a whole, the empirical evidence . . . does not back the strong claims made by theorists and clinicians in favor of the grief-work hypothesis. There are insufficient studies; there are methodological shortcomings; and there are inconsistent findings. Overall . . . the grief-work hypothesis has neither been confirmed or disconfirmed empirically" (Stroebe 1992–93:27).

Many would agree that losing a child to death is one of the most painful of all human experiences. *Beyond Endurance When a Child Dies* is the title Knapp (1986) selected for his book on death of children. Peppers and Knapp (1980) introduced the term *shadow grief,* in which a child's death seems to follow a family like a shadow, after observing the reactions of mothers whose baby had died before or soon after birth. Many of the mothers were still feeling the anguish years after the death. Knapp (1986) found the same phenomenon among parents whose older child had died. The mothers were no longer completely dominated by grief, but the shadow had a way of making itself known as they moved through life.

McClowry et al. (1987) interviewed forty-nine families in which children had died of cancer seven to nine years previously. They described three patterns of grieving that the families used: first, attempting to "get over it" by accepting the death as fate or God's will; second, attempting to "fill the emptiness" by keeping busy and adopting new goals; and third, "keeping the connection" by integrating the pain and loss into their lives. In most cases, the parents expressed pain and loss even after seven to nine years, and instead of "letting go" of the dead child, the families described the continuing presence of an "empty space" in their families. McClowry et al. (1987) found considerable differences in assessment of the parents' own difficulties in coping with death. Although the sample size was too small to draw any firm conclusions, it is fair to say that the death of a child at home may reduce bereavement, that is, the grieving period, and the complexities attendant to such a loss. It seems the process of "getting over it" is quicker, or that "filling the emptiness" or "keeping the connection" was already under way at the time of death. It is not clear, however, why the few parents who indicated major difficulty in dealing with grief were parents of children who died in a hospital, since death in hospitals is still within our cultural norm. Although an inquiry would be worthwhile, there are scant comparison figures for families whose child died from accidents or other diseases.

Fish (1986) did a study of differences in grief intensity between grieving parents. The study involved seventy-seven women and thirty-five men who had been bereaved from one month to sixteen years. Fish argued that, unlike a "wound," which heals in time, the grieving process for parents is more like a "dismemberment," requiring adaptation to a loss that does not end. Klass and Marwit (1988–89) described this "metaphor of amputation" as the sense that a piece of the self has been cut out, that it is exaggerated in parental grief, and that this sense of amputation does not diminish with time. Grief tends to persist for years and may even intensify with the passage of time (Rando 1985). The effect can be devastating on the parents' health and marriage. A number of studies have documented the high distress of bereaved parents on such indicators as depression, anxiety, somatic symptoms, self-esteem, and sense of control in life. The marital relationship is particularly vulnerable after a child dies, with risk of further deterioration of marital satisfaction over time (Videka–Sherman 1982). Divorce rates for bereaved parents have been reported as high as 80 percent (Bluebond-Langner 1988; Schiff 1977). However, divorce after the death of a child is not inevitable, as will be discussed later in the resilience section.

Klass offers useful insights into the effect of a child's death on the parents' worldview:

> In the face of the overwhelming reality that their child had died, the bereaved parent must either reaffirm or modify their basic understanding about them-

selves and about the justice and orderliness of their world. Worldviews are experiential in the sense that individuals use them to orient themselves. They are the map of both visible and invisible reality. (1987:14)

Questions about the parents' core assumptions regarding the nature and purpose of life emerge when a child dies. The loss and sorrow that follows the death of the child may be intensified, then, by a crisis of belief or faith. The parents may feel that there is very little they can count on and that the world no longer makes sense. There is now some evidence to suggest that preserving an emotional connection with the deceased child helps to prevent the destruction of the parents' worldview. Klass (1987) acknowledges that parents continue to experience the "inner representation" of the dead child for many years (perhaps throughout their lives). He defines inner representations "as characterizations or thematic memories of the deceased, and the emotional states connected with these characterizations and memories." Parents can interact with their inner representations of the child through

- *memory*—bringing the child to mind often,
- a *sense of presence*—the feeling that the child is still there with them in some way,
- *hallucinations*—the experience of seeing or hearing the child, and/or
- *incorporation* of the characteristics or virtues of the child into their own personalities, such as rescuing lost animals as the child had often done

The sorrow and sense of loss are still there, but the feeling that something of the child still lives with or within parents may reduce doubts about their worldviews.

Klass (1987) further observed:

1. These symbolic interactions with the deceased are not signs of pathology; for example, it is not "crazy" to sense the child's presence or even to catch fleeting glimpses of the child. These experiences often accompany normal grief. (There are limits, of course; a person who becomes absorbed in fantasies of the deceased and cannot attend to the realities and obligations of daily life is in need of help.)

2. The positive value of continuing the relationship with the dead child seems to contradict grief work expectations. As mentioned, grief work theory has recently been called into doubt as a complete explanation of how we should recover from loss. It may be years before enough research has been conducted for an adequate evaluation of the grief work model. In the meantime, it may be wise to refrain from either pressuring bereaved parents to detach themselves from their memories or insisting that they incessantly recall the child to mind. It seems clear enough that the inner representation of the dead child can have an important role in recovery from grief, but individual differences should be respected.

Relatively little attention has been paid to the grief experienced when a grandchild dies. Parents and grandparents experience many of the same feelings of loss. Grandparents are also likely to experience vicarious grief for the parents (Kastenbaum 1993) as well as their own direct grief over the death of the child. It is even more unexpected for a grandparent to outlive a grandchild. Just as in the case of the parents, such an unexpected and "untimely" death can generate a worldview crisis. Ponzetti's (1992) research also supports the view that the grandparents seemed to be affected most in their role as parents; that is, grandparents grieved for the loss suffered by their child even more than they grieved for the death of the grandchild.

These findings provide several suggestions for service providers who work with the families of children who die. Clinicians should be knowledgeable about the behaviors that most frequently occur in bereaved children and their families. Generally, they need to know that behavior problems of an internalizing or withdrawing nature tend to increase, and social competencies may decrease after the death of a sibling. In particular, professionals can observe that children become sad, withdrawn, and lonely and that their performance in school may diminish. Their interests in other social activities may also wane and continue for long periods of time.

Professionals can educate parents about the behaviors they may expect to see in their grieving children. Further, they can advise parents to be alert to continuing patterns of sorrow and withdrawal in their children, as indications that the sibling needs additional support in coping with the death. Children who shared a close relationship with their sibling may be in need of greater support. At additional risk are children who already have a diminished self-concept, or whose families are not cohesive. Some children may be at risk of persistent sorrow, withdrawal. and depression (Knapp 1986).

Professionals also can be mindful that many siblings, in retrospect, perceive their experience in a positive light. Therefore, professionals must not make the morbid mistake of thinking that a sibling's death bodes *only* negative consequences for the surviving children. It is helpful, however, to overcome the previous assumption that a sibling's death has *no* effect on the surviving children.

DEMOGRAPHIC PATTERNS

Children do die. According to the 1995 final mortality statistics from the Centers for Disease Control and Prevention (1997), a record 2,312,132 deaths were registered in the United States, 33,138 more than the previous high of 2,278,994 deaths recorded in 1994. Age-specific death rates decreased substantially for those over 5 years of age. For those aged 1–4 years, the decrease was primarily due to decreases in mortality due to accidents.

Leading causes of death differed by age. Overall, accidents were the leading cause of death for age groups 1–4, 5–15, and 15–24. Homicide and HIV infection consistently ranked higher for the Hispanic population than for the non-Hispanic white population for all age groups. For the age group 5–14, suicide ranked as the fifth leading cause of death. Homicide and certain conditions originating in the perinatal period were among the leading causes of death for the black population.

Age-adjusted death rates did not change significantly for either black or white females. Age-adjusted death rates decreased almost every year between 1980 and 1995 for white males and females. Between 1994 and 1995, death rates for both sexes combined declined for these age groups: under 1 year (6.2 percent decline) and 1–4 years (a 5.4 percent decline). Mortality in these age groups has continued to decline steadily since the 1950s. In 1995 the average expectation of life at birth was 75.8 years, an increase of 0.1 years compared with life expectancy in 1994, and matches the high of 75.8 years recorded in 1992.

In 1995 a total of 29,583 infant deaths were reported, 6.7 percent fewer infant deaths than the 1994 total of 31,710. The infant mortality rate of 7.6 infant deaths per 1,000 live births is the lowest rate ever recorded for the United States and represents a 5 percent decline.

Historically, the gap between black and white infant mortality narrowed somewhat from 1.93 in 1960 to 1.77 in 1971. Since 1971, however, the black-white ratio has been increasing steadily (13 black to 14 white). In 1995 the infant mortality rate for black infants (15.1) was 2.4 times the rate for white infants (6.3), the same ratio as in the two previous years.

Between 1994 and 1995, the infant mortality rate decreased for three leading causes of infant death: sudden infant death syndrome (SIDS; 15.4 percent), accidents and adverse effects (10.2 percent), and disorders relating to short gestation and unspecified low birth weight (6.2 percent). Congenital anomalies was the leading cause of death for white infants, followed by SIDS, disorders relating to short gestation and unspecified low birth weight, and respiratory distress syndrome. Combined, these four causes accounted for 52.6 percent of white infant deaths. In contrast, for black infants the leading cause of death was low birth weight, followed by congenital anomalies, SIDS, and respiratory distress syndrome. These four causes accounted for 50.4 percent of all black infant deaths.

Although the difference between black and white infant mortality rates varied by cause, the risk was higher for black than for white infants for all the leading causes. The infant mortality rate for Hispanic infants under 1 year of age was 6.1 per 1,000 live births in an area comprised of forty-nine states and the District of Columbia. This rate was slightly lower than the rate for non-Hispanic white infants.

SOCIETAL CONTEXT

In many ways, the identity of a human being is formed and maintained by relationships with others. Thus, in a very important sociological sense, the death of a significant other not only means the loss of that person, but also may very well mean that an important part of personal identity is threatened. Grief, then, has to do with the emotional reaction that is elicited by the death of a significant other and its corresponding meanings for the identity and social roles of the survivors.

It has been argued that everyone does not necessarily fear death. A person who has been suffering from a serious and debilitating illness for a long time may see death as a relief from suffering. Likewise, families who have witnessed the pain and suffering of a child for an extended period of time may see death as a relief for themselves and the child. Studies have also shown that people may not fear death as much as they fear being dependent on others as they become sicker and more disabled (Bowlby 1980).

Traditional patterns of European and American death encompassed an expansive definition and application of bereavement. Death during these traditional periods was a public affair and involved not just the immediate family but the broader social community as well. Many primitive cultures today also utilize an extended application of bereavement. Some of the small American towns today, where there is a sense of stability, ethnic attachment, and extended family arrangements, also have an expansive application of bereavement. As society has modernized, and as the broad base of social community has been reduced to personal intimacy and friendship networks, a limited application of bereavement and mourning has evolved (Momeyer 1988). Mourning is the behavioral expression of the emotional anguish of grief, which is culturally prescribed. Wearing black clothes, crying at funerals, or taking tranquilizers are some examples of mourning behaviors.

Mourning clearly has strong social significance, as particular cultures have specific behavioral requirements, including duration and intensity, in the aftermath of the death of a loved one. Mourning is directly related to grief in that it is the physical-behavioral expression of the feeling of sorrow and suffering. Yet mourning expressions may not always reflect inner feelings. Zborowski (1969) has discussed how various cultures express pain and suffering differently and with varying intensity. Raphael (1983) described how some European cultures, like the Italians, are very expressive and emotional in their portrayal of grief, while the Anglo-Saxon culture is more stoic and behaviorally restrictive. Italians or Greeks obviously do not love their families more or suffer greater grief than people of the WASP culture; rather, emotional expressions of grief are simply expected.

The era of traditional death was supportive of extended grief reactions and of elaborate mourning customs. These included the wearing of mourning clothes and jewelry; significant modification of personal behaviors and lifestyles during mourning; construction of ornate tombs, mausoleums, and gravestones; and an enthusiastic recognition of death, including the ubiquitous representation of death and grief in writing, painting, and sculpture (Dracopoulou and Doxiades 1988).

The special nature of religious activity, as opposed to everyday behavior, is that it takes place in a context relative to things that are sacred. Durkheim (1951), in his study of religion, describes many of the beliefs and practices of primitive religions, but more important to his analysis are the ways in which the rituals related to religious belief are socially useful. An important function of rituals (such as bereavement and mourning rituals) is that they reaffirm the legitimacy of the broader social order. Rituals, by definition, are connected to the past and have become more individualized.

Some observers have noted that contemporary American funerals are not very sad occasions. It has also been argued that the funeral has become an empty, shallow, and increasingly worthless ritual. And it is this superficiality of the funeral, especially of the viewing activities, that has been heavily criticized for creating an image that avoids the reality of death. This controversy was stimulated by the recent death of Princess Diana. Mitford (1963, 1998) further points out that the activities of the embalmer-funeral director are often geared toward generating an illusion of life. As Irion (1990–91) indicates, the artifacts are marketed in a way that gives credence to the idea of the continued physical existence of the deceased. For example, the idea of the deceased comfortably at rest in the casket—luxuriously lined with fine fabric and appointed with a soft, opulent innerspring mattress—is a consoling one. The sense that the loved one is protected from the ravages of weather by means of a vault is also comforting. Both of these images are used as ordinary selling points in the funeral industry and may serve to convey an illusion or fuel a fantasy that physical life continues in and beyond the grave. The creation of a comforting memory image establishes a view of death that spares the living from having to confront the harsh and macabre realities for physical decomposition. While the critics of the funeral may be correct in noting that an aura of unreality surrounds modern practices (Mitford 1998), it is also useful to note that this process may be helpful in coping with the emotional impact of the death of a loved one (Jourard 1971). The importance of the funeral is also emphasized in the overall program of therapeutic support. First, parents are often advised to encourage the attendance of siblings. Second, the therapeutic thanatology literature defines the funeral as a memorable and therapeutically useful tool for grieving parents. Some authors suggest that active participation of the parents in the preparation of the child's body for the funeral viewing, i.e., washing the body, dressing the child, combing his or her hair, etc. is therapeutic (Doka 1989).

As the process of preparing a body for viewing and burial has become specialized and technically intricate, the funeral director has assumed a more dominant role in the American funeral. Some funeral directors place financial consideration above the needs of the survivors. At the same time, others are helpful during the death crisis and provide a source for knowledge and expertise in assisting the survivors.

The survivor must deal with many practical demands. If the deceased is a family member, the sheer physical and social demands of religious and cultural rituals—like family gatherings, such as sitting *shiva* or participating in a wake—help one to cope with the loss. Within contemporary American society, much of this support system has been modified or eroded by change. As a result, acute grief is becoming more complex and its resolution more difficult.

VULNERABILITIES AND RISK FACTORS

Parental bereavement does not originate at the moment of death. Throughout the period of caring for a seriously ill, dying child, parents not only live with the constant threat of death but also experience major and traumatic disruptions in their lives. Cook and Dworkin (1992), in their study of the practical, emotional, and social consequences of caring for a fatally ill child, have identified eighteen psychosocial problems that parents may encounter during the course of their child's illness. Many of these difficulties can parallel the time of mourning and add to a parent's vulnerability: (1) making child care arrangements for the ill child, (2) arranging child care for other children, (3, 4) encountering disciplinary difficulties with the ill child and siblings, (5) experiencing feelings of helplessness, (6) feeling a loss of confidence in parenting abilities, (7) confronting financial difficulties, (8) experiencing a sense of being avoided by other people, (9) feeling the need to reassure and comfort others, (10) suffering marital strains, (11) feeling excluded from participation in the ill child's life, (12) suffering the loss of religious faith, (13) experiencing the need to protect one's spouse from distressing feelings and upsetting events, (14) feeling that one's family unit is being torn apart, (15) feeling that one's spouse may be excessively preoccupied with the ill child, (16) fearing the inability to cope with the actual death of a child, (17) having to handle the inability of other family members to accept the child's illness situation, and (18) seeing the withdrawal of one's spouse from the family unit. The chronicity and ambiguity of serious childhood illness create an atmosphere of living in a framework of anticipatory death of the child.

Mothers and fathers define the experience of anticipatory bereavement in different ways. Their responses may also apply to the postbereavement period. According to Cook (1983), mothers identify the need to protect others from upsetting and distressing information as a prominent concern. They also perceive marital difficulties as being a major factor affecting the course of caring for a dying child. Mothers feel resentment from their husbands over the extent to which they themselves are involved with the dying child. In addition, they express concern over sexual problems and the sense of isolation precipitated by the social and emotional withdrawal of their husbands. Mothers believe that existing instabilities in their marriages are heightened by the bereavement experience, which often causes problems of drug usage, alcohol intake, and extramarital affairs. Mothers also feel the tremendous burden of keeping up the siblings' morale after the death. Finally, mothers believe that the experience of anticipatory bereavement and death places an overwhelming emotional strain on their lives.

Fathers, on the other hand, feel that a dominant problem stems from the emergence of dual responsibilities; namely, the need to juggle and adjust their work schedules to accommodate increased family obligations. Fathers stated that they felt excluded from family interactions, as many of the day-to-day decisions about the care of the dying child were made without their participation. In a related sense, fathers also expressed concern about what they perceived as the overinvolvement of their wives with the dying child. And last, fathers expressed a longing to be able to spend more time with their wives and ill children (Cook, 1983).

Cook also noted that the responses of mothers and fathers in postdeath bereavement are similar in some ways and different in others. For example, both mothers and fathers feel an overwhelming and intense sense of loss. Both experience sadness during significant days and holidays. Additionally—and this perhaps is the greatest similarity—both mothers and fathers have great difficulty in seeing other healthy children, especially during the first year after their child's death. However, fathers describe their sense of loss as a "void," as the feeling that there is "something missing." They also feel a loss of direction in the family and the subsequent need to "regroup," to "reorganize." On the other hand, mothers, define their sense of loss less in terms of family impact and more in an intimate and personal way. While both parents experience an intense and overwhelming impairment, the death of a child disrupts the father's external world, whereas, for the mother, the death of a child is often experienced as an obliteration of self and of personal identity.

Crucial differences in postdeath bereavement are clearly related to the traditional gender expectations of men and women. Fathers, in connection with their largely instrumental worldview and the norm of American male inexpressiveness, emphasize their feeling of responsibility for managing the grief of the family unit. Many fathers shoulder the emotional burden of grief in a solitary and private way. Mothers may suffer from repeated visualizations of the deceased child, see painful reminders of the child around the house, and experience emptiness related to the child's absence from their daily routine. The more personal dimensions of the mother's grief—her deep loneliness and feeling of personal diminishment—make her grief typically more profound and difficult to handle. Mothers also are more likely to express feelings of distance from their husbands and are less likely than fathers to be satisfied with the support they receive from their spouses. Fathers, on the other hand, are less likely to be distressed by an absence of support, real or imagined, as they typically cope with the emotional burdens of grief in a self-contained, private sphere (Mulhern, Laurer, and Hoffman 1983).

Mirroring gender prescriptions of the society at large, bereaved mothers are therefore more likely to express their feelings and needs than are fathers. In this way, not only are the parents using different coping strategies, but their differing reactions create distinct psychosocial patterns of need that make it difficult for them to find comfort in each other. In the absence of guiding norms for bereavement and in the cultural framework of isolated grieving, men and women understandably rely on gender prescriptions that have influenced them all of their lives to provide some sense of stability and familiarity to the turbulence generated by the death of a child (Spinetta, Rigler, and Karon 1981).

A major shortcoming in the contemporary literature on parental bereavement is that studies typically involve parents living in the traditional nuclear family. A somewhat outdated framework is thus shaping the state of research on parental bereavement. Obviously, many parents live and grieve within the traditional nuclear family, but to focus exclusive attention on the problem of bereavement from this perspective is to ignore an entire spectrum of other modern lifestyles and living arrangements. In addition to traditional and modified nuclear families, contemporary families are organized around dual-career couples; cohabitation; gay and lesbian families; single-parent families through widowhood, separation, and divorce; and reconstituted families, with one or both of the spouses or partners bringing children from former marriages to the relationship (Herz-Brown 1988).

There is an institutionalized expectation in American society that parents should begin to mourn the death of their child through a funeral. Although there is limited research to support the view that the funeral is therapeutically helpful, participation does seem to provide a base of stability in a situation plagued by uncertainty and anxiety from the moment of initial diagnosis through the bereavement period. It is also important to note that other systems of support, such as assistance of friends, support of a caring physician, or involvement in a counseling program, are helpful.

Death of a child is certainly a disruptive event in a family's life (Holmes and Rahe 1967). The primary goal is helping the family to achieve an open system. For this state of openness to exist, two essential ingredients are necessary: (a) family members must feel the freedom to express themselves without fear of censure or disenfranchisement; and (b) the system must allow family members to leave and return freely, both physically and metaphorically. The family as a whole needs to create an atmosphere that allows all family members, including children, to heal the wounds of grief (Rosen 1986, 1990; Martinson 1991).

RESILIENCIES AND PROTECTIVE FACTORS

In our society, children are not supposed to die. When a child dies, parents face the disruption of personal, marital, and family patterns and live in the midst of multiple profound changes. Part of this whirlwind of change entails the creation of a new role. The process of grieving requires that the family as a whole acknowledge that loss is final and death irreversible. Although common at various stages of the dying process and even afterward, denial of this reality may impede a family's recovery from the child's death.

What clinicians attend to is that the distress continues long beyond the acute phase and that the lives of the grieving family members may be altered in many ways. When the emotional response to a loss remains a dominant aspect of a person's life over a long period of time, it is sometimes referred to as *chronic grief*. This is a useful descriptive term because it differentiates between the intense immediate response (*acute grief*) and responses that sometimes can persist through an extended period of time. Sometimes the term *chronic* means that a condition is unalterable and permanent. It might then seem that a family suffering prolonged grief after the death of a child is destined to remain in this painful state forever. This is not necessarily true. Chronic grief can be relieved, and the survivors can once again find meaning and pleasure in life, although they never forget their loss and are never quite the same.

Parents whose child has died often feel that their own lives changed at that moment. They may not want to relinquish their grief. The pain is part of the memory—and the memory is precious. Few people would choose to experience the intense anguish of acute grief. But the twinge of sorrow and the sharp but passing pain of memory may be something the family needs to keep their lives whole (Knapp 1986).

The parent-child relationship is by definition the closest and most intense that life can generate, not only physically but psychologically and socially as well. In this situation, the other—that is, the child—"has sprung from" the mourner. Therefore, the child is "part of, and the same as" the parent. Such a different relationship mandates a different disengagement after a death, since what the parents have lost is also very much a part of them; it is often extremely difficult for parents to disengage. Each child has a particular accumulation of meanings to the parent (McGoldrick and Gerson 1985).

Another factor contributing to the unique trauma of parental loss of a child comes from the normal process of parents incorporating a number of roles into their parental identity. Parents are accustomed to being self-sufficient and in control of what happens to and with the child. They can "fix" what happens to the child, be it soothing feelings of rejection from a peer or repairing a broken toy. Parents are protectors, providers, problem solvers, and advisers (Knapp 1986). All these roles combine to define parents' sense of self, role, and identity.

Finally, parents are exposed to the most inappropriate and unrealistic set of social expectations that exist. Parents are expected to be superhuman and to be all loving, all good, all concerned, totally selfless, and solely motivated by the child and his or her welfare. These expectations leave no room for normal human ambivalence or healthy assertiveness. Unfortunately, these expectations are not only socially assigned by culture and society; they are internalized by the parents as well.

This is one of the primary reasons why bereaved parents tend to have the greatest guilt feelings of all mourners, and why they feel such failures in their parental roles. Because of the death, parents are robbed of the ability to carry out the functional role of parent. This causes an oppressive sense of failure, the loss of power and ability, a deep sense of violation, a monumental decrease in self-esteem, and an overwhelmingly confused identity. In turn, these assaults lead to additional secondary losses, which derive from the diminished sense of self and include disillusionment, emptiness, and insecurity. Ultimately, these culminate in the necessity for a profound identity shift, in which the old identity must be mourned and relinquished, along with former beliefs and assumptions about the self and the person's capabilities as a parent, and a new identity must be formed to reflect the reality of the death and its specific effects on the parent.

"Death ends a life, but it does not end a relationship," says Anderson (1968:5), in his powerful drama *I Never Sang for My Father*. Significant relationships resound across generations, enriching the family and adding to the complexity of its communal psyche. For these relationships to have meaning and for the family to be a resource needed for healing, it is imperative that the system be as open as possible, particularly in terms of allowing children the latitude necessary for grieving.

Although the notion that mourning takes about a full year has become a generally accepted maxim in the field (Glick, Weiss, and Parkes 1974; Parkes and Weiss 1983), many a clinical error has been made in treating families who present with grief-related symptoms more than a year after a death. Families may be in need of individual or family psychotherapy or other interventions, and it is vital that a careful assessment of family function be made. The four seasons—or holidays, birthdays, and other events—are difficult times and challenge the healing process. By the first anniversary of the death, the family reshaping internal relationships and reorganizing itself may be prepared to consider a new life without the physical presence of the deceased child. However, in many families at least one family member will offer evidence that suggests to the observer that the family is not prepared for the next steps in its life. Frequently, that one family member is the deceased child's sibling (Martinson 1991).

After the death, it is reasonable to expect that families will experience some breakdown in the system that will likely result in a period of "anarchy," which may not be entirely destructive. What the breakdown can create is an opportunity to abandon old patterns and to adopt a new, more functional structure.

Almost all studies have found excessive mortality rates for bereaved persons (Stroebe and Stroebe 1983). This pattern holds true for Europe and Japan as well as North America. At this point adequate data do not seem to be available to determine differential mortality in less-developed countries. The fact that bereaved people have had excessive mortality throughout the twentieth century is a further indication of the substantial reality behind these statistics. The overall picture, however, is more positive than it has usually been assumed. Many parents have proven themselves quite resilient when tested by loss.

Notwithstanding the stresses and burdens the loss of a child can place on even the healthiest and strongest marriage, it is absolutely untrue that the death of a child inevitably leads to divorce. Some studies have estimated that the divorce rate can be as high as 75 to 90 percent. This is an unsupported, although prevalent, myth! Certainly, parents do suffer significant distress after the death of a child, but many marriages remain intact or even improve. Recent evidence suggests that when there is a divorce after a child's death, it often stems from the reordered priorities and newly recognized strength of one of the bereaved parents who decides that he or she no longer wants or has to stay in an unsatisfactory marriage tolerated before the child's death (Klass 1986–87). Far too many parents have been traumatized by incorrect data on divorce based on inappropriate conclusions from poorly designed studies. They need to be informed that marriages can and do survive. In fact, some marriages actually become healthier as partners determine that they will make some good come out of the tragedy, for example, reordered priorities, deeper family commitments, and greater personal growth.

With so many intensely mourning individuals all living together in the same space, it is amazing that the roof doesn't blow off with the volatility of the acute emotion being experienced. Related to this is the dilemma of trying to modify and balance the particular idiosyncratic needs of one member versus another in the family.

It can become quite a thorny issue when what one needs to minimize the pain or assist in the mourning is diametrically opposed to what another requires. For example, one parent needs to display the photographs of the deceased child while another needs to put them out of sight. Such discrepancies are bound to occur in the mourning process. In practical day-to-day existence, finding a compromise to meet family members' needs is a challenging task.

Sometimes a family's move toward reorganization can also be maladaptive, particularly when it involves the premature adoption of a replacement for the deceased. Because families naturally adapt toward stability rather than toward change, this action is an attempt to restore equilibrium. The replacement can be a new person invited to join the family system, such as a boyfriend or girlfriend, in-law, or new spouse. It can also be manifested in a physical move, the selling of a house, job relocation, or divorce.

One potent method for helping a family to heal emotionally is fostering in them a sense of empathy, which is best accomplished by open and honest sharing. Helping the family achieve a broader perspective on the importance of multigenerational loss helps the development of this empathy. When, for example, a parent is able to share personal experiences of loss with their surviving child/children, openly expressing the pain of that loss, the child is given an accessible model for experiencing his/her own grief and confusion. In working with families where a death has occurred, encouraging the adults to talk about themselves is a most effective method for providing a coping model for the surviving children. This kind of dialogue fosters the shared acknowledgment of the harsh reality of death as well as a sense of hope for personal survival (Videka-Sherman 1982).

PROGRAMS AND SOCIAL WORK CONTRIBUTIONS

Families do not necessarily need counseling or psychotherapy when death enters their lives. Sometimes the needed strength can be drawn from friendship, a familiar environment, and their own religious and spiritual beliefs, values, and coping resources. Financial security and competent nursing and medical care are also likely to help a child and their family through the dying process and death. Before considering counseling or therapy, it is helpful to assess the entire family situation. Perhaps what a father needs is a more effective pain management regime; for the mother an opportunity to spend some time with a sibling she has not seen for years. Therapy is worth considering to provide a safe place to express one's feelings, worries, and concerns and to find emotional comfort and peace of mind.

An important goal of the clinician is to enable parents to focus on their inner strengths. A sense of helplessness can reduce the parent's ability to cope with the death. The clinician can help to restore self-confidence, reduce guilt, and create a renewed sense of being a valuable and lovable person. The success of a healing-oriented approach depends on the family's personality.

Grief is both destiny and possibility for all who care. Inherent in the sadness of loss is the potential for emotional gain and a renewed contract with life. As Thomas Mann has so eloquently stated, "To meet adverse conditions gracefully is more than simply endurance; it is an act of aggression, a positive triumph" (Stern 1985). As an act of aggression, grief links itself to the larger picture of survival.

Bereaved families may find great solace in the rituals associated with their faith, especially those used at times of death. At a time in our society when many of our traditions regarding mourning have disappeared, religious institutions can provide some structure through ritual. Religions having congregational worship can provide a source of ongoing community support after the death of a child. Religious clergy can offer spiritual assistance to families in times of grief.

Boyd-Franklin (1989) has emphasized that therapists, when assessing strengths and coping skills of black families, must be sensitive to the central role that religion and spirituality play in their lives: "Training in the mental health fields largely ignores the role of spirituality and religious beliefs in the development of the psyche and in its impact on family life. In the treatment of black families, this oversight is a serious one" (78). Kalish and Reynolds (1976) found that black families were almost twice as likely as other ethnic groups to identify religion as the main influence on their attitudes toward death. They will often frame their loss in the context of religion ("God gives you no more than you can carry," "The Lord will hear my prayers and heal me"). Unless the clinician respects these beliefs, clients are likely to feel alienated. For many, the church functions essentially as a type of extended family, and the minister is often contacted in times of emotional distress. Boyd-Franklin (1989) recommends that therapists working with black families use ministers as a resource.

Although spiritual and religious beliefs are usually a comfort in times of grief, this is not always the case. After a death, some people stop going to a church, mosque, or synagogue, stating that their religion no longer provides satisfactory answers about life and death. If the deceased was a "good person," doing all the things the devotee is supposed to do, then it's hard to understand the cause of a painful or sudden death (Kushner 1981).

A means of overcoming the parents' sense of isolation is provided by bereavement self-help groups. Such groups have become established in response to the overwhelming sense of isolation and individualism that characterize the drift of our times. In an age of alienation, the self-help group fosters healing by building a community of people who help themselves by helping others (Klass 1984–85).

One such organization, Compassionate Friends, is a nationally organized self-help group. In his study of the dynamics of the Compassionate Friends organization as a vehicle for healing parental grief, Dennis Klass has (1984–85) identified three distinct phases of parental involvement: the decision to attend, the process of affiliation, and the transition to helping others.

Initial attendance is sparked by a variety of personal and social factors. The venues through which parents become connected to the self-help organization are varied and often haphazard. They may be referred by a wide range of sources, such as friends, clergy, and health care professionals. Often, contact with self-help groups takes place in conjunction with bereavement counseling or psychotherapy. Sometimes, after a period of aimless floundering, grieving parents themselves reach out and initiate contact with the group. At other times, parents become reluctantly involved in order to please someone else. In any event, feelings of estrangement and isolation commonly motivate attendance. Parents who make the decision to participate in Compassionate Friends often feel separated from other sources of support and comfort, such as family and friends. In the face of loneliness and in the absence of social support, the idea of participating in a voluntary planned bereavement group can motivate the grieving parent.

Regardless of how or why they become involved, many parents begin their participation with a sense of timidity and uncertainty. While some parents do feel that attending will be helpful, they are often unsure of precisely what to hope for. Others are simply confused about why they are there and ambivalent about the value of belonging to the group.

The process of becoming actively involved in the group, of making it part of oneself, and of making oneself a part of it has been termed "affiliation." The first part of the process involves "catharsis." This occurs when the bereaved parent takes emotional energy (sense of grief, pain, or loss) and begins to share it with the group. By telling stories and showing pictures of the deceased child, the bereaved parents initiate a strong and special emotional interconnection and bonding. Sharing emotional energy with the group not only provides emotional release but also builds collective unity and support. Thus, during a time of grief and mourning in the parents' life, a collective vibrancy and energy begins to emerge. Klass (1987) relates:

> The sense of unity with those whose lives have been shattered, the sense of hope at seeing that others have made it, the sense of finding an appropriate object on which to attach the energy formerly given to the child, the sense of family in a supportive community, and the special relationship with someone very much like the self but further along are all part of the cathartic dimension. (13)

The second part of the affiliation process is called the "experiential dimension." Whereas catharsis means the sharing of emotions, the experiential dimension involves the sharing of experiences and information, as individuals reveal their own strategies for survival and coping; newcomers are presented with a wide array of situations and alternatives. Thus, involvement in Compassionate Friends does not entail adhering to fixed guiding norms to facilitate grief work. Rather, it provides an awareness of some possible options and encourages individualized responses appropriate to each parent's personal needs and circumstances.

The final phase of the self-help process is termed "transitions": the movement from being helped to helping others. It entails a forward motion toward the investing and reinvesting of the energies of the self in relationships with others and involves a reaching out to others, specifically the newly bereaved, to provide support and help in the immediate aftermath of their postdeath trauma. It is important to recognize that this transition does not diminish the therapeutic value of the group for the helper. Indeed, not only does the helping role give the parents an opportunity to continue a symbolically meaningfully relationship with their dead child, it enables them to continue to participate in the cathectic and experiential aspects of the group process.

ASSESSMENT AND INTERVENTIONS

Initial bereavement is a time of contradictions, numbness, disbelief, and preoccupation. It is a time of feeling separate and unconnected. In Picasso's (1903) painting *The Tragedy*, displayed in the National Gallery of Art, Chapter Dole Collection, in Washington, D.C., one can see and feel the family's withdrawal from the outside world. The figures use their own bodies as consolation. In their agony, each person is alone. The toneless mood and monochromatic coloring of the painting, all in blues, could be viewed in light of the death of a child and sibling.

Let us assume that missing from this family grouping is the dead child. Bluebond-Langner's work (1988) shows that the well siblings of a dead child live in houses of chronic sorrow. Whether the sorrow is spoken of or not, the sibling sees the tears, hears the hushed conversations, and experiences the physical and emotional unavailability of the parents. In the painting, the boy's hand tentatively reaches out to his father's thigh. What is the meaning of this gesture? Is the child to be the consoler? Caretaker to the parent? Is he about to tug at his father's clothing for the attention and support he needs? Is the child a personification of what Goffman (1963) calls "non-persons," who are there but not there. In this scenario, though absent from it, one might conclude that the deceased child is the subject of the painting.

Taking liberties with the arts, thus engaging them in dialogue, can be enlightening. Remove the mother from the picture and we are confronted with the impossibility of one parent assuming the other's role. As a matter of fact, it is doubtful that the remaining parent can fulfill his own parental role at this time. Being father must conflict with being husband: a bereaved man needs to grieve for his wife. We become acutely aware of a new terror for a bereft child: the loss of one parent, and the symbolic or temporary loss or unavailability of the other makes the actual loss of the lone surviving parent a threatening reality.

The painting underscores Rando's (1988) point that parents need to mourn their separate relationships with the child. We can appreciate the conflicting demands both to let go of the parent role (in the case of the child who died) and, at the same time, to continue to be parent to the remaining sibling. Furthermore, parents are losing not only their child, and their roles in terms of family, they are losing their planned-for future: their hopes, dreams, expectations, fantasies, wishes. Martinson (1991) has us consider how families respond to the empty space left behind by the death of a child. Literally remove the youngster from this group of three and continue to speculate. What would we assess? How would we intervene?

Effective intervention requires that social workers acknowledge and incorporate the client's belief system into their interventions. In all cultures, the meaning of loss is interpreted within a broader scheme of beliefs and attitudes, often referred to as a "worldview," which encompasses basic beliefs regarding illness, death, and healing (Lewis 1985).

The overall goal of an assessment is to answer the following questions: Who is this person (personality and coping style)? What were the circumstances of the loss? and What type of intervention is needed to facilitate the grief process? To accomplish this, the social worker must gather information on two levels. These can be described as content and process. The first level of information gathering is direct and concrete; the second is subtler, employing primarily nonverbal information. Factual information includes the context of grieving, coping styles, physical condition, support system, spirituality and religion, and cultural influences. The second level of assessment includes information learned through the process of interaction with the client and attention to nonverbal client behaviors. (Cook and Dworkin 1992; Raphael and Nunn 1988; Walsh and McGoldrick 1991).

When the process of mourning and moving on becomes blocked, several processes may occur: time stops, relationships rigidify, and the family closes itself off, and feelings are blocked by various forms of denial (Cook and Oltjenbruns 1982;

Hogancamp and Figley 1983). These patterns must be assessed as part of any clinical evaluation.

1. Time stops. When families cannot mourn, they become locked in time—either in dreams of the past, in the emotions of the present, or in dread of the future. They may become so concerned about potential future losses that they are unable to engage in the relationships they do have, fearing that to love again will mean further loss. Others focus exclusively on their dreams of the future, trying to fill in the gap left by the loss with new relationships formed in fantasy and to escape from the pain. Usually those who cut short their mourning by rushing toward other relationships find that, when the dreams give way to the realities of the new relationship, their pain comes back to haunt them. Problems that families have in other developmental transitions, such as marriage, the transition to parenthood, or launching their children, often reflect this stoppage of time.

2. Relationships rigidify, and sometimes the family closes down entirely, with an inability to attach to anyone. If survivors draw in other family members to replace the dead, their relationships may appear stable though rigid. This may work until the replacement person expresses any individuality, which makes apparent that he or she is not the dead person. This may then trigger a delayed reaction, even long after the original loss experience.

When families are unable to accept a death, they tend to develop fixed ways of relating to handle their fears of further loss. Another indication of denial is a family's unwillingness to make any changes following the death. They may make the dead person's room into a memorial.

3. The family uses denial or escape into frenetic activity, drugs, alcohol, fantasy, or myth. The myths, secrets, and expectations that develop around a critical loss may be incorporated into the rules of the family and be passed down from parents to children. Some families stop all mention of the deceased, as if they could thus banish all the pain. It is as if they attempt to blot the person out of existence.

Many of the patterns we routinely observe in families—drivenness about one's activities, affairs, continuous unresolved conflict, alienation, isolation and fear of outsiders, frequent divorce, depression, workaholism, escaping into TV sports or soap operas—may reflect the inability to deal with loss, which has finally become the inability to connect with anyone else out of fear of further loss.

Myth-making to avoid the realities of a loss entails delusional responses that bind family members to one another in pathological ways and, at the same time, create great psychological rifts among them, since these responses relate only to the delusion, not to the real person. Such myths naturally affect children who become replacements for family members who have died, even though they may be totally unaware of the connection. People develop serious emotional problems when they have been raised as stand-ins for the unburied ghosts of the past. To become free to be themselves, they must discover the mystery behind their identity and find a way of "exorcising" the ghost or dybbuk (Paul 1976; Paul and Grosser 1965; Paul and Paul 1989).

Walsh and McGoldrick (1991) state that the primary goal of therapeutic intervention around death is to empower and strengthen families to mourn their losses. This involves:

1. Shared acknowledgment of the reality of the death. To normalize the loss and diminish any sense of mystification, family members are encouraged to learn about the death and face their own and each other's reactions to it. If facts about the death have not been admitted, a therapist can facilitate their learning the facts and accepting the realities.

2. Shared experience of the loss and putting it in context. This usually involves funeral rituals and other experiences through which families can share the emotional legacy of the loss—mourning, anger, pain, regret, lost dreams, guilt, sadness, and missing the dead person. A part of this sharing is joint storytelling about the life and death of the dead person. Such sharing helps families integrate the loss experience into their lives by promoting their sense of familial, cultural, and human continuity and connectedness and empowering them to regain a sense of themselves as moving in time from the past, through the present, and into the future. To develop a sense of control, mastery, and the ability to survive in the face of loss, family members, especially men, may need encouragement to open up relationships with the living and learn more about their family overall—its history, its culture, and the perspectives and stories of different family members.

Sharing memories and stories of the dead can help family members develop more benign, less traumatic perspectives on the role of loss in their lives. Such sharing helps them tolerate their own and each other's differing emotional reactions to the loss, patterns of mourning, and pathways for moving on. It seems important for families to be free to remember as well as to let go of memories. Clarifying and elaborating family stories and narratives about their history are ways to promote this resolution. One of the most difficult aspects of denied or unresolved mourning is that it leaves families with no narratives with which to make sense of their experience. If events cannot be mentioned or if the family "party line" cannot be expanded upon, it is almost impossible for family members to make sense out of their history altogether and gives the next generation no models or guidelines for integrating later losses. Therapy can aid families to create narratives that facilitate and enhance their integration of loss (Laird 1989).

3. Reorganizing the family system. Where the system has been unable to complete the adaptive tasks of reorganizing without the dead person, therapy can help families accomplish this complex and often painful task. This may entail a shift in caretaking roles or organizational and leadership functions, a reorientation of the social network, a shift in family focus when a child dies.

4. Reinvestment in other relationships and life pursuits. Death can be an important spur to life. Families can be strengthened by the shared experience of loss to focus more clearly on what they want to do in life and on how they want to relate to others. The experience of death can release creative energies, and therapists should foster this development. Clinicians can help family members to redefine their commitments and life priorities and redirect their relationships and activities toward the dying.

Creating appropriate rituals for the expression of grief and referring parents to the nearest chapter of a self-help group of bereaved parents or a professionally led mutual aid group can be helpful. Through mutual sharing, support, modeling, and learning that they are not "going crazy," the mutual aid group process is particularly helpful for bereaved parents who lack emotional and social support for the expression and resolution of grief.

Social workers helping bereaved families must be aware of the factors that make family bereavement unique. Without an understanding of these special dynamics, the clinician will often misapply techniques, sustain inappropriate counseling expectations, or possibly miss valuable opportunities for intervention leading to the successful resolution of grief. The work of grieving entails mourning not only the person who has died but the hopes, wishes, dreams, fantasies, unfulfilled expectations, feelings, and needs one has for and with that person.

Social workers who view adjustment to sorrow as a time-bound process will view clients who experience repeated sorrow as dysfunctional. On the other hand, those who view chronic sorrow as a natural reaction to an ongoing tragic experience will offer a continuum of appropriate support services (Rosenblatt 1983).

ILLUSTRATION AND DISCUSSION

Few experts would discount the importance of the family as a vital healing resource. The family is the central stage on which the drama of our psychic life begins and is ultimately shaped and nurtured. The centrality of the family is so powerful that it accompanies us throughout all of our lives. In working with families in the aftermath of a child's death, the treatment process can be normalized to grief and mourning.

In the following example, a mother called and requested help for her 13-year-old son after the death of his sister from cancer. I conveyed that in this situation, i.e., death in the family, it would be helpful if all family members could come for the session.

Theresa and Paul Jenko, 42 and 45 years old, were married for seventeen years. They had a difficult time conceiving a child and felt God blessed them when Paul Jr., now 13 years old, was born followed by a daughter, Kathleen, aged 11 when she died. The family lived with Theresa's mom after Paul was born. It was about one year after the maternal grandfather died and the rambling house in Long Island seemed tailored to fit everyone's needs. It was commutable for Mr. Jenko and the school district was noted for its excellent standards of student achievements.

I met with the family a week after the telephone contact and after a few preliminaries, Mrs. Jenko began to tell me through sobs about Kathleen's illness and sudden death. Kathleen was born with a heart defect and had surgery several weeks after her birth. She recovered rapidly and seemed to live a normal life. There were, however, doctor visits to maintain and monitor Kathleen's condition. Mrs. Jenko felt it stabilized about 4 years of age, and she returned to work knowing her mother was accepting of being with the children for a few hours a day before she would come home from work. Kathleen's condition suddenly became acute about eight months ago when she would complain of difficulty breathing and tightness in her chest. After multiple visits to specialists, the family went to Maryland to a specialty children's hospital that treated this type of illness. "The rhythm of our lives seemed to dramatically change," said Mr. Jenko. "We have been in a fog ever since. We can't believe Kathleen is dead."

"Why God visited this suffering on us we cannot understand. I asked and prayed that God will take me," said Mrs. Jenko, "and he took our Kathy."

Paul Jr. sat silently in the chair between his parents. He played with his hat and did not make any eye contact. I invited him into the discussion and wondered how he was feeling. He described his sister as his pal and remembered two early memories of them fishing and swimming in the Long Island Sound. He expressed his guilt about being smarter than his sister and receiving the annual merit award last year when his sister was sick. He noted his parents were also busy with Kathy and only his grandma attended the awards celebration.

During the first session all members made some contributions and spoke only to the worker. No interaction took place among them. Each family member cried, but Paul Jr. wept inconsolably after he spoke and throughout the remainder of the session. The family agreed to at least twelve sessions since Mr. Jenko's insurance would reimburse them for brief treatment.

During the initial phase of work, it emerged that Mr. Jenko drank heavily and had been in recovery since Paul Jr.'s birth. Paul Jr. was shocked, and Mrs. Jenko worried that if Mr. Jenko felt overwhelmed with sadness and despair, he might begin drinking again. He acknowledged his concern and stated he would return to weekly AA meetings. Mrs. Jenko's mother requested she attend the family meetings because she too was affected by Kathleen's death.

Grandma came for the next eleven sessions and helped the family return to weekly Mass attendance to alleviate some of their spiritual pain. Although the family had gone through the traditional waking of the body, funeral mass, and burial rites, they were having a difficult time visiting the grave and making the necessary arrangements for a headstone. The worker was supportive, and in future sessions, they formulated a ritual that was "their own" and not bound by traditions of culture or religious beliefs.

Present and future work focused on attending to Mr. Jenko's reaction to the death of his daughter. He described a pattern of withdrawal, sadness, and low energy. He had previously been a man with a great zest for life, who had participated in the community both with his children at soccer and pizza parties and in a number of church societies. At present, it sounded as if his life was on hold. He said that his future was shattered and that his dreams and expectations could never be fulfilled. The social worker asked how Mrs. Jenko was reacting to the death of her daughter. It appeared that some of her former coping had emerged, such as hoping for another child. One difference was her flight into activity in relation to her past withdrawal. The couple began to see how their relationship was mirrored in their son.

Both parents reported after a number of family sessions that they had thought a great deal about what the worker had said about keeping their lives on hold and also feeling the support of normalizing this feeling. They recognized that they were stuck and felt they would like to begin to live again, recognizing they had another child who needed nurturing, support, and their emotional and physical availability. At the family's request, the eighth through the tenth sessions included the paternal grandparents, since they too were mourning the death of their granddaughter. In the eleventh session Mrs. Jenko conveyed how the extended family visited the cemetery and placed flowers on the grave. They sobbed and consoled each other. She felt Kathleen's presence at that moment. At the last extended-family session, Paul Jr. was able to express his anger at his parents for giving so much attention to Kathy. He also showed his displeasure at his grandparents for not being available and helpful to him during Kathy's hospitalization.

Counseling with the Jenkos lasted about six months. I always saw them together as a family. My primary goal was to encourage all four members to see themselves as a family that needed to heal their wounds and work through their enormous pain of loss and isolation and some of the behavioral difficulties that Paul Jr. was experiencing.

Working with children after a sibling's death is a complex and delicate task. Siblings protect and help to care for one another. For example, Paul Jr. came to Kathleen's defense on the playground, and often against Grandma, in the form of sibling alliance. Relatively little has been written about the impact of a child's death on siblings (Rosen 1990).

The initial phase of the Jenkos' counseling focused on each family member's reaction to the death and the impact other loss was having on the family system. Earlier losses, hopes, and expectations were articulated, and the significance of these losses emerged but was not necessarily resolved. Patterns of coping and adapting to life losses became conscious, and numerous examples were used and related to present coping. During the middle phase, some acceptance of the loss began to emerge. Inclusion of extended-family members in treatment and the discussion of the family's pet were used as part of a life review and a thrust toward the future. A ritual designed by the family acted as a form of empowerment and helped them in their grief work.

The final counseling phase, although very painful, suggested the beginning of healing. Paul Jr. was able to express his anger at the family and gained permission to externalize his feelings to reduce the future pain he would experience. The family decided to stop weekly counseling for a time but to return on a monthly basis.

Herz-Brown (1988) suggested several important interventions for families dealing with death. First, open, direct, clear, and factual language should be used, and euphemistic and technical language should be avoided. Second, the worker should combat the family's tendency to avoid issues related to the death by establishing an open relationship in the family. The death has to be discussed within the family. Third, the worker should remain calm. Families often seek help when their stress or tension level is high and they have been unable to reduce it. While the worker may experience strong emotions, if her or his interventions are determined by emotional reactivity, it can increase rather than decrease the stress level in the family. Fourth, the worker should encourage the family to mourn the death in ways consistent with their personal and religious customs, rituals, styles, and beliefs.

Successful intervention following the death of a child requires a combination of well-developed family assessments and counseling skills, a knowledge of issues related to death and dying, and the capacity to cope personally with the powerful emotions associated with the loss. Often, it is necessary for the worker to maintain a balance between having the family revisit the past to express unresolved feelings of grief and encouraging them to face the future so that family life can continue to develop.

As part of life, human beings have always struggled with the knowledge of personal death and coping with the death of a loved one. The overriding issue that faces us in all our determination to cope with loss and to help others cope with the loss is the place accorded to death in our lives today. Mourning is not only normal, but also essential.

CONCLUSION

One of the hardest things for all of us to accept may be the death of a child. As in most cases of grief, support from those who have suffered a similar trauma can help to reduce the feeling of being alone and misunderstood. Both family and group therapy can often be helpful after a child's death (Figley 1978). The tendency of some families to distance themselves from painful emotions that are part of the death is contrary to what is actually needed. The social worker must accept the task of challenging the client to approach his or her feelings even though expressing them may be an intense and, at times, an overwhelming experience.

The families of clients—both nuclear and nontraditional—can have a potent effect on the dynamics and outcomes of interventions. Clinicians of all orientations will want to acknowledge the importance of the family's culture and ethnicity, which can provide valuable assistance during treatment. Use of a supportive family network can help clients tolerate emotional discomfort and minimize negative outcomes of a loss.

The existence of support systems and the ability of the bereaved to use them will greatly influence the grief process. Grieving is, to a significant degree, a lonely experience, but healing comes, in part, through reconnecting with the world. One way to reconnect is by sharing one's experience and receiving the acceptance and care of others. Limited social support during bereavement has been shown to be associated with high distress and poor outcomes as measured by physical and mental health.

Spiritual and religious beliefs can be of great comfort to the person who is grieving. "Spiritual" means the way one makes sense of life and death; "religion" can be the structure in which the bereaved may exercise his or her sense of this meaning. Exploring this realm helps the therapist understand how the client operates in the world, including the value system that he or she uses.

Increasingly, school systems are providing therapeutic services for students. Since groups are a very efficient way to address personal concerns that are affecting school learning and behavior, the recent trend has been toward the use of issue-specific groups within the schools—for bereaved children, for children of divorce, for adolescents with chronic illness. Many schools have well-trained social workers to respond when a large number of students in one locality experience loss (e.g., a tornado striking a small town and resulting in fatalities, a rash of adolescent suicides occurring in a community, children witnessing a murder on the playground).

Working as a social worker in the area of grief and loss requires an awareness of yourself and your own issues. Who you are as a person affects the way you interact with clients and how you conduct therapy. With issues related to death, the worker client dynamics are even more complex than with other types of therapy. Issues surrounding grief and loss are highly emotional, touching our deepest fears as human beings. As a social worker in this field, you will come face-to-face with your own mortality and your own fears of dying and death of loved ones. If you are not in touch with your own issues in this area, your work with clients can be seriously compromised. An awareness of your own vulnerabilities can have a positive effect on your empathic attunement to clients and their grief.

References

Anderson, R. E. 1968. "Where's Dad? Paternal Deprivation and Delinquency." *Archives of General Psychiatry* 18:4–19.

Becker, E. 1973. *The Denial of Death.* New York: Free Press.

Bluebond-Langner, M. 1988. "Words of Dying Children and Their Well Siblings." *Death Studies* 13:1–16.

Bowen, M. 1976. "Family Reaction to Death." In P. J. Guerin, ed., *Family Therapy: Theory and Practice,* pp. 335–348. New York: Gardner.

Bowlby, J. 1962. "Processing of Mourning." *International Journal of Psychoanalysis* 42:317–40.

——. 1969. *Attachment and Loss.* New York: Basic Books.

——. 1973. *Separation.* New York: Basic Books.

——. 1980. *Loss: Sadness and Separation.* New York: Basic Books.

Boyd-Franklin, N. 1989. *Black Families in Therapy: A Multisystems Approach.* New York: Guilford Press.

Centers for Disease Control and Prevention. 1997. *Monthly Vital Statistics Report* 45(11):5.

Cook, A. and D. Dworkin. 1992. *Helping the Bereaved: Therapeutic Interventions for Children, Adolescents, and Adults.* New York: Basic Books.

Cook, A. S. and K. A. Oltjenbruns. 1982. "A Cognitive Developmental Approach to Death Education for Adolescents." *Family Perspective* 16:9–14.

Cook, J. 1983. "A Death in the Family: Parental Bereavement in the First Year." *Suicide and Life Threatening Behavior* 13:42–61.

Doka, K. J. 1989. *Disenfranchised Grief: Recognizing Hidden Sorrow.* Lexington, Mass.: Lexington Books.

Dracopoulou, S. and S. Doxiades. 1988. "Greece, Lament for the Dead, Denial for the Dying." *The Hastings Center Report* 18, no. 4(Supplement):15–16.

Durkheim, E. 1951. *Suicide: A Study in Sociology.* New York: Free Press.

Figley, C. R. 1978. "Psychosocial Adjustment Among Vietnamese Veterans: An Overview of the Research." In C. R. Figley, ed., *Stress Disorders Among Vietnamese Veterans: Theory, Research, and Treatment,* pp. 57–70. New York: Brunner/Mazel.

Fish, W. 1986. "Differences of Grief Intensity in Bereaved Parents." In Therese Rando, ed., *Parental Loss of a Child,* pp. 415–28. Champaign, Ill.: Research Press.

Freud, S. 1957. "Mourning and Melancholia." In J. Strachey, ed., *The Standard Edition of the Complete Psychological Works of Sigmund Freud,* pp. 243–58. London: Hogarth Press.

Glick, I. O., R. Weiss, and C. M. Parkes. 1974. *The First Year of Bereavement.* New York: John Wiley.

Goffman, E. 1963. *Stigma: Notes on the Management of Spoiled Identity.* Englewood Cliffs, N.J.: Prentice Hall.

Gorer, G. 1965. *Death, Grief and Mourning.* New York: Doubleday.

Herz-Brown, F. 1988. "The Impact of Death and Serious Illness on the Family Life Cycle."

In B. Carter and M. McGoldrick, eds., *The Changing Family Life Cycle: A Framework for Family Therapy*, pp. 457–82. Boston, Mass.: Allyn & Bacon.

Hogancamp, V. and C. Figley. 1983. "War: Bringing the Battle Home." In C. Figley and H. McCubbin, eds., *Stress and the Family: Coping with Catastrophe,* pp. 2, 148–65. New York: Brunner/Mazel.

Holmes, T. H. and R. H. Rahe. 1967. "The Social Work Rating Scale." *Journal of Psychosomatic Research* 11:213–18.

Irion, P. E. 1990–91. "Changing Patterns of Ritual Response to Death." *Omega, Journal of Death and Dying* 22:159–72.

Jourard, S. M. 1971. *Disclosing Man to Himself.* Princeton, N.J.: Van Nostrand Reinhold.

Kalish, R. A. and D. K. Reynolds. 1976. *Death and Ethnicity: A Psychocultural Study.* Los Angeles: University of Southern California Press.

Kastenbaum, R. 1993. "Reconstructing Death in Postmodern Society." *Omega, Journal of Death and Dying* 27:75–89.

Kellehear, A. and D. W. Moeller. 1984. "Are We a Death Defying Society?" *A Sociological Review. Social Science & Medicine* 18(9):714.

Klass, D. (1984–85). "Bereaved Parents and the Compassionate Friends." *Omega, Journal of Death and Dying* 15:353–73.

———. 1986–87. "Marriage and Divorce Among Bereaved Parents in a Self-Help Group." *Omega, Journal of Death and Dying* 17(3):237–49.

———. 1987. "John Bowlby's Model of Grief and the Problem of Identification." *Omega, Journal of Death and Dying* 18(1):13–32.

Klass, D. and S. Marwit. 1988–89. "Toward a Model of Parental Grief." *Omega, Journal of Death and Dying* 19(1):31–50.

Knapp, R. 1986. *Beyond Endurance When a Child Dies.* New York: Shocken.

Kushner, H. 1981. *When Bad Things Happen to Good People.* New York: Avon Books.

Laird, J. 1989. "Women and Stories: Restoring Women's Self-Constructions." In M. McGoldrick, C. M. Anderson, and F. Walsh, eds., *Women in Families,* pp. 427–50. New York: Norton.

Lewis, R. 1985. "Cultural Perspective on Treatment Modalities with Native Americans." In M. Bloom, ed., *Life-Span Development: Bases for Preventive and Interventive Helping,* pp. 458–64. New York: Macmillan.

Martinson, I. M. 1991. "Grief Is an Individual Journey: Follow-up of Families Postdeath of a Child with Cancer." In D. Papodatou and C. Papodatou, eds., *Children and Death,* pp. 255–65. New York: Hemisphere.

McClowry, S., E. B. Davies, K. A. May, E. J. Kulenkamp, and I. M. Martinson. 1987. "The Empty Space Phenomenon: The Process of Grief in the Bereaved Family." *Death Studies* 11:361–74.

McGoldrick, M. and R. Gerson. 1985. *Genograms in Family Assessment.* New York: W. W. Norton.

Mitford, J. 1963. *The American Way of Death.* New York: Simon & Schuster.

———. 1998. *The American Way of Death Revisited.* New York: Alfred A. Knopf.

Moeller, D. W. 1996. *Confronting Death-Values, Institutions and Human Mortality.* New York: Oxford University Press.

Momeyer, R. W. 1988. *Confronting Death.* Bloomington: Indiana University Press.

Mulhern, R., M. Laurer, and R. Hoffman. 1983. "Death of a Child at Home or in the Hospital: Subsequent Psychological Adjustment of the Family." *Pediatrics* 71:743–47.

Parkes, C. M. 1987–88. "Research: Bereavement." *Omega, Journal of Death and Dying* 18(4):365–77.

Parkes, C. M. and R. S. Weiss. 1983. *Recovery from Bereavement.* New York: Basic Books.

Paul, N. 1976. "Cross-Confrontation." In P. J. Guerin, ed., *Family Therapy,* pp. 329–45. New York: Gordnost.

Paul, N. and G. Grosser. 1965. "Operational Mourning and Its Role in Conjoint Family

Therapy." *Community Mental Health Journal* 1:339–45.

Paul, N. and B. B. Paul. 1989. *A Marital Puzzle.* Boston: Allyn & Bacon.

Peppers, L. G. and R. J. Knapp. 1980. *Motherhood and Mourning.* New York: Praeger.

Picasso, P. 1903. *Tragedy.* Washington D.C.: National Gallery of Art, Chapter Dole Collection.

Ponzetti, J. 1992. "Bereaved Families: A Comparison of Parents' and Grandparents' Reactions to the Death of a Child." *Omega, Journal of Death and Dying* 25:63–71.

Rando, T. 1985. "Bereaved Parents: Particular Difficulties, Unique Factors, and Treatment Issues." *Social Work* 3(1):19–23.

——, ed. 1986. *Parental Loss of a Child.* Champaign, Ill.: Research Press.

——. 1988. *Grieving: How to Go on Living When Someone You Love Dies.* Lexington, Mass.: Lexington Books.

——. 1996. "Parental Adjustment to the Loss of a Child." In C. Corr and D. Corr, eds., *Handbook of Childhood Death and Bereavement,* chap. 20. New York: Springer.

Raphael, B. 1983. *The Anatomy of Bereavement.* New York: Basic Books.

Raphael, B. and K. Nunn. 1988. "Counseling the Bereaved." *Journal of Social Issues* 44(3):191–206.

Rosen, E. 1986. *Unspoken Grief: Coping with Childhood Sibling Loss.* Lexington, Mass.: Lexington Books.

——. 1990. *Families Facing Death.* Lexington, Mass.: Lexington Press.

Rosenblatt, P. C. 1983. *Bitter, Bitter Tears: Nineteenth-Century Diarists and Twentieth-Century Grief Theories.* Minneapolis: University of Minnesota Press.

Schiff, H. S. 1977. *The Bereaved Parent.* New York: Penguin Books.

Spinetta, J., D. Rigler, and M. Karon. 1981. "Anxiety in the Dying Child." *Pediatrics* 56(6):1034–37.

Stern, E. M. 1985. *Psychotherapy and the Grieving Patient.* New York: Haworth Press.

Stroebe, M. (1992–93). "Coping with Bereavement: A Review of the Grief Work Hypothesis." *Omega, Journal of Death and Dying* 26:19–42.

Stroebe, M. S. and W. Stroebe. 1983. "Who Suffers More? Sex Differences in Health Risks of the Widowed." *Psychological Bulletin* 93:279–301.

Videka-Sherman, L. 1982. "Coping with the Death of a Child: A Study over Time." *American Journal of Orthopsychiatry* 52:688–98.

Walsh, F. and M. McGoldrick. 1991. *Living Beyond Loss. Death in the Family.* New York: W. W. Norton.

Zborowski, M. 1969. *People in Pain.* San Francisco: Jossey-Bass.

17

Death of a Parent

Nancy Boyd Webb

The Book of Ecclesiastes proclaims that "to everything there is a season . . . a time to be born, and a time to die" (Eccl. 3:1). However, family members may not experience the death of a parent with this attitude of quiet acceptance, but instead complain that the death occurred "too soon" (out of season). Admittedly, a death of a person in young adulthood or midlife *is* untimely, and the death of a parent is always difficult.

Because of the implicit role of parents as nurturers and caretakers, their loss stirs up distressing feelings of anxiety based on the ongoing attachment relationship and the dependency needs of the survivors, regardless of their age. Different issues emerge, however, when a 4-year-old child, a 40-year-old married parent, or a 65year-old retired grandparent loses a parent through death. Personal vulnerabilities and challenges related to the impact of the death depend on many factors, in addition to age. The unique circumstances of each case require that we take both a wide and a narrow view of each situation in order to assess whether help is needed, and if so, what kind.

This article presents a life cycle perspective on parental bereavement, applying an understanding of developmental and family systems theory to the situation of parental loss. The emphasis is on the death of a parent in *childhood,* but the impact on the entire family and their responses are also considered, and some comparisons are made to the experience of parental death among older individuals.

DEFINING AND EXPLAINING THE DEATH OF A PARENT

A parent's death has an impact, not only on the family, but also on the wider community, including service providers. For example, the death of a 45-year-old mother from ovarian cancer will be treated differently from that of a 45-year-old father who was shot while dealing drugs. The children in each case suffer the loss of a parent, but the shameful circumstances of the father's death create complicated emotions that inevitably make the grief process more difficult for his family. In addition, services to each family will differ because of the unique circumstances of each death, one of which may involve law enforcement investigation.

Other factors about the death of a parent that impact on the family and wider community relate to whether the death was anticipated (as with terminal illnesses) or sudden and/or accidental, sometimes raising concerns about whether it might have been prevented. For example, when a mother diagnosed with metastasized uterine cancer has hospice services in the home, the children, relatives, and friends gradually come to realize that the woman is getting weaker, and that she requires increasingly more pain medication. Even young children may begin to wonder if their mother will *ever* get better. Relatives may struggle with the issue of adequate pain medication and sometimes with the dying person's requests for assisted suicide. These matters reach far beyond the family and are currently being discussed by medical ethicists, religious, and legal scholars. They ultimately have great political, religious, and community impact.

When a parent of a child or adolescent dies, a primary question for the surviving family and the community always is, "Who will take care of this dependent youth?" The parent's previous role as a caretaker now has to be assumed by others. This can be quite complicated in many small ways that make life difficult and stressful for the child and for the survivors. For example, when a mother dies, and the father must leave for work by 6:30 a.m. and the child's school bus does not come until 7:30, who will take care of the child during this one-hour period five days a week? Similarly, who will be responsible for the child after school until the father returns from work, sometimes as late as 7 p.m.? Although many day care programs typically provide for very early drop-off, and some even serve breakfast, few public schools provide this option for school-age children whose single parents (whether widowed or not) have to struggle to arrange before- and after-school child care. Arrangements for the child's care during school vacation periods and holidays when the parent has to work also highlight the failure of community services to deal adequately with significant numbers of children in one-parent families. Sometimes family members and friends of the deceased parent can provide assistance, but where these options are not available, the community should provide alternative resources.

DEMOGRAPHIC PATTERNS

About 5 percent of children lose a parent to death before they reach the age of 18 (Wessel 1983:125). This means that teachers and schools must be prepared to face the certainty that some of their pupils will become bereaved during the course of the school year. Schools must help teachers face this inevitable occurrence by offering training and guidelines to help them respond appropriately when a child's parent dies.

The U.S. Census Bureau statistics provide information about the comparative rates of male/female deaths of blacks and whites. The projection for 1996 (U.S. Census 1998) was a death rate of 9.2 for white males, 9.0 for white females, 9.4 for black males, and 7.5 for black females per 1,000. This resonates with prevalent knowledge that males die at a higher rate than females. The higher rate of death for black males is possibly due to environmental risk factors, such as homicides. I was not able to obtain statistics about *parental deaths,* since the Census Bureau collates data by age, geography, race, and cause of death, but *not* with reference to the family status of the deceased.

SOCIETAL CONTEXT

The responses of members of an individual's surrounding environment can either help or hinder his or her mourning process. When the manner of death cannot be discussed openly as in a suicide, some homicides, and in AIDS-related deaths, the individual and family must cope with the strain of secrecy at the very time that their feelings of grief are surging within them. By contrast, when a parent dies a heroic death such as in fighting a house fire (see the case of the Turner family presented later), the outpouring of support from the community can be tremendously validating and comforting to the survivors. Of course, the pain of the loss of one's parent is just as vivid whether he or she dies in a drug-related murder or as a hero in battle. However, the drastically different response of the surrounding community in each case will have a very significant effect in the family members' ability to express their grief openly, receive support, and come to some form of eventual acceptance of the death.

Different religious practices also influence the mourning process. The Jewish religion, for example, prefers immediate burial, without viewing of the body, in contrast to the Catholic practice of a wake of several days, with the casket open, followed by a funeral. The process of remembering and honoring the person who died is accomplished in Jewish families through sitting *shiva,* a mourning ritual of several days following the burial, which can be considered analogous to the Catholic wake.

However, the participation of children in rituals of this sort often is abbreviated because of children's inability to tolerate long periods of sadness and of talking associated with the reminiscing process. Counselors must help families understand that children's short sadness span is no reflection of their lack of respect or love for the dead person.

Unfortunately, many people in the United States are uncomfortable discussing death, and others believe that it is inappropriate to expose young children to this distressing topic. This **death taboo** means that many bereaved children are ignored or avoided. There is a distinct role for social work professionals in addressing the needs of a vulnerable population (children) who do not have the knowledge, the words, or the political clout to speak for themselves. A range of bereavement services, staffed by trained personnel, should be available to children and families.

A similar insensitivity and inability to deal with the impact of a parent's death can occur with reference to the elderly. Kastenbaum (1998) describes standing beside a 74-year-old man, "with tears running down his cheeks because his 97-year-old father was dead." Kastenbaum comments:

> An outsider might rush to the conclusion that the death of a very old parent should not mean so much to a child also advanced in years. Consider, however, how long this relationship had to develop and flourish and what a blow it now was for this man to go on without the father he had known for three-

quarters of a century. *Parent-child bonds may continue strongly for many decades* (emphasis added). (333)

When children, of any age, cannot grieve the death of a parent with the understanding and support of their kinship and social network, they are at risk of unresolved mourning. There is a clear need for educational and professional intervention to meet their needs.

VULNERABILITES AND RISK FACTORS

The loss of a parent to death signals a major life transition that usually includes a harshly felt confrontation with the fragility of life and the fear of additional future losses. The reasoning of both child and adult concludes that if the all-powerful parent cannot vanquish the unseen ghost of death, then *everyone* now must be vulnerable! Children do not have a mature understanding about death until about the age of 9 (Nagy 1948). They often become clingy after the death of a parent, seeming to fear that the surviving parent will now also disappear. Middle-age adults who experience the death of a parent also may feel profound anxiety, to which some respond with heightened worries about their own mortality. They sometimes express their anxiety through preoccupation about bodily aches and pains (somatization) or with "acting-out" behaviors devoted to frantic pleasure-seeking (live in the moment). The underlying meaning of the death of a parent, whether at age 4 or 44, is that one's life has been drastically affected. Self-protective functions in the form of defenses should be understood in the context of the stress of a *major* life transition.

Most studies of parental bereavement have focused on the death of the *father.* Consistent differences have been found, as reported by Kastenbaum (1998), between children whose father died and children who have both parents alive. Children whose **father died** "tend to exhibit the following characteristics: [They]

I Are more submissive, dependent, and introverted
I Show a higher frequency of maladjustment and emotional disturbance, including suicidality
I Show a higher frequency of delinquent and criminal behavior
I Perform less adequately in school and on tests of cognitive functioning

[In summary] parental bereavement must be regarded as a *potential problem* in many areas of a child's life." (291–92, emphasis mine)

We must not be deterministic, however, since many children who lose their parents in childhood grow into achieving and well-adjusted adults. Whereas the death of a parent in the life of a child does seem to create a risk, *many other factors,* as will be discussed in the following, can intervene to help and support the child with his/her ongoing growth and development.

In several previous publications I have presented an assessment tool (*The Tripartite Assessment*) to help conceptualize the impact of the multiple interacting factors associated with a particular crisis or death experience (Webb 1991, 1993, 1996). This conceptualization (see figure 17.1) was originally developed for application to children in crisis and bereavement, but it can also inform our understanding of the experience of bereaved adults. The three groups of interacting factors in the Tripartite Assessment include:

▌ Factors related to *the individual*
▌ Factors related to the *crisis/bereavement situation*
▌ Factors related to *the support system*

In examining these diverse factors, some constitute risk factors, while others contrib-ute to the individual's resiliency. For example, in situations involving the death of a parent, *individual factors* such as the person's or the family's past history of death and loss may seriously complicate the grieving process. In other cases, *the nature of the death* itself may have repercussions that impact on the responses of the individual and family. This would be true, for example, following a suicidal death or in a situation of violent or traumatic death. Regardless of the specific factors related to either the individual or to the death itself, *the support* from the extended family, friends, and community serves as a balancing/protective influence that can ease the pain of

FIGURE 17.1. The Tripartite Assessment of the Bereaved Child

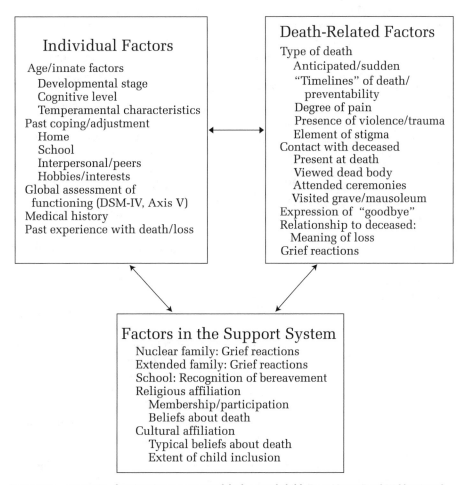

Interactive components of a tripartite assessment of the bereaved child: From Nancy Boyd Webb's *Social Work Practice With Children*, pg. 254. Copyright 1996 by The Guilford Press. Reprinted with permission.

bereavement and therefore contribute to an individual's resiliency following a death. When this support is absent, the risk factors may prevail.

As indicated in figure 17.1, **individual factors** in parental bereavement include:

▌ The individual's age/developmental/cognitive/temperamental factors
▌ Past coping/adjustment (prior to the death)
▌ Global assessment of functioning (*DSM-IV,* Axis V)
▌ Medical history
▌ Past experience with death/loss

The relative importance of these factors will vary in different cases, but the nature of the attachment relationship between the child and the deceased is especially important, as are developmental considerations that influence the child's ability to comprehend the reality of death.

The **attachment bond** between the child and parent serves as "the secure base" from which the toddler gradually reaches out to explore the world (Ainsworth and Wittig 1969). In a review of the attachment literature (see, e.g., Ainsworth 1979; Ainsworth and Bell 1971; Mahler, Pine, and Bergman 1975; Sroufe 1979a, 1979b; Sroufe and Waters 1977), Remkus summarizes that "a secure attachment bond . . . is the basis for subsequent development. . . . It is through this relationship that the infant learns about trust, love, and social interactions" (1991:144). Because the young child invests almost all of his feelings in his parents (in comparison with adults who distribute their love among several meaningful relationships), the impact of a parent's death in childhood is all the more devastating. "Only in childhood can death deprive an individual of so much opportunity to love and be loved and face him with such a difficult task of adaptation" (Masur 1991:164, referring to Furman 1974).

Most children do not know the "facts of death"—namely, that it is inevitable, personal, irreversible, and universal—until they are 9 or 10 years of age, unless they have had experiences with deaths of animals or family members (Wass and Stillion 1988). Their understanding progresses gradually from an egocentric and immature view to a more mature conceptual understanding. Thus, the preschool child whose parent dies may believe that his own "bad" behavior *caused* the death, or that the dead person can "wake up" if he screams loud enough (Saravay 1991). Preschoolers also do not comprehend the loss of bodily sensations or functions that occurs in death (Fox 1985). As children grow, their understanding improves, so that by age 9 or 10 they understand that death is final and that it will happen to everybody "sometime." They also can comprehend the difference between the body and the soul, as taught by many religions (Webb 1993).

Studies of children's responses to the death of a parent (Silverman, Nickman, and Worden 1992) have found that children maintain their attachments to their deceased parents through their memories, and that this process continues over the years, "serving an important function in terms of the child's and, later, the adult's development" (Webb 1993:10).

Important differences exist between the manner in which children and adults **express their grief.** They include (Webb 1993:14) the following:

▌ Children's immature cognitive development interferes with their understanding about the irreversibility, universality, and inevitability of death.

- Children have a limited capacity to tolerate the emotional pain of grieving (they have a "short sadness span"; Wolfenstein 1966).
- Children have limited ability to verbalize their feelings.
- Children are sensitive about "being different" from their peers (having a deceased parent makes them feel different and embarrassed).

In contrast to these distinctions between the grief process of children and adults, certain reactions to the death of a loved one occur regardless of age. These include responses of denial, anger, guilt, sadness, and longing. Miller (1995) states that "for children, as well as adults, bereavement is a cognitive and emotional process that weaves the experience of the death, the meaning of the loss, and a changing relationship with the deceased into the fabric of their lives over time" (100).

RESILIENCIES AND PROTECTIVE FACTORS

The importance of protective factors to balance risk factors is demonstrated in the *case of Sabrina,* a 7-year-old child whose mother died of cancer following several months of steady decline (Webb 1996). The child's reactions had to be evaluated in the context of the responses of her father and the extended family. The fact that Sabrina's half-brother had died of a drug overdose one year prior to her mother's death certainly was a complicating factor and an added risk in this child's bereavement experience. However, these two tragic deaths occurred in the life of a child who had previously been doing well socially and academically. In addition, the paternal grandparents were able and willing to help with Sabrina's care before and after school. Furthermore, a child and family therapist coordinated effectively with the school social worker to alert the school about Sabrina's situation. Sabrina was a very resilient child. Even the dual losses of her half-brother and her mother did not seriously interfere with her ongoing development. The fact that her paternal grandparents lived close by, as did many aunts, uncles, and cousins kept this child from feeling isolated and abandoned. The extended family system served as essential "protectors" for a child whose adjustment might otherwise have been seriously compromised.

In a different example, the *case of Mario, age 13, and Maria, age 10* (Webb 1996), the *absence* of any family supports put the children at great risk. These children were half-siblings who were orphaned by their mother's death of probable AIDS, which resulted in their subsequent placement in foster care. Although they attended their mother's funeral, they were moved out of state shortly thereafter, and then later abandoned by their former baby-sitter who changed her mind about caring for them. The lack of family support, added to other unfortunate life circumstances, put these children at great risk.

As indicated in figure 17.1, death-related factors in parental bereavement include:

- The type of death
- Contact with the deceased
- Expression of "good-bye"
- Relationship to the deceased
- Grief reactions

As previously discussed, the responses of children and other family members will vary considerably depending on the circumstances of the death. The extent to which the child was given the opportunity for closure provided by contact with the deceased and/or through attendance at a funeral or memorial service must be determined.

The issue of a "stigmatized death," such as that from AIDS, constitutes a risk factor that seriously complicates the mourning process for survivors. Public disapproval of the illness prevents open acknowledgment of the manner of death, leading family members to feel shame and isolation. Doka (1989) refers to this type of bereavement as "disenfranchised grief" (as if they are not entitled to mourn).

In Maria's case, the girl did not seem able to recognize the cause of her mother's death and referred to it as a "heart attack." This may, in fact, have been what she was told at age 5. However, now at age 10, Maria knew that she herself was infected with HIV, and she had been given literature explaining the different means of transmission of the illness. Maria had not asked how *she* contracted the illness and, apparently, could not cope with the impact of acknowledging her mother's probable role in transmitting HIV to her. It is possible that her denial defended her from feelings of anger toward her mother that would have been inevitable had she identified her mother as the source of her own illness. This protective defense (denial), may have been appropriate at a younger age, but it will no longer help Maria when she enters adolescence and/or when she becomes sexually active. She will probably need counseling at a future time when she recognizes and has to deal with her feelings about her mother and her illness.

As indicated in figure 17.1, support system–related factors in parental bereavement include:

I Grief reactions of nuclear family
I Grief reactions of extended family
I School's recognition of bereavement
I Religious affiliation (level of participation and beliefs about death)
I Cultural affiliation (extent of child inclusion)

As already discussed under Societal Context, different cultures, religions, and individual families respond differently to death, and hold varying beliefs about expected mourning practices. For children, the most important factor is the extent to which they are included in the family's mourning observances, and the extent to which the family and community allow children to mourn at their own pace. In summary, protective factors that seem to counteract and reduce the risk factors include the concern and love from the extended family, and the religious and secular (school) community.

PROGRAMS AND SOCIAL WORK CONTRIBUTIONS

The social work profession has played a pivotal role in establishing and staffing bereavement programs to assist bereaved individuals following the death of a parent. The range of these programs includes hospital-based individual, family, and group counseling; home and agency-based hospice programs to assist family members of terminally ill patients; and time-limited mental health agency (Ormond and Charbonneau 1995) and school-based grief support programs to help children who have lost a parent to death (Tait and Depta 1993). Because death often occurs in hospital settings, medical social workers have a central role either in providing such services or in referring families to community-based programs, suitable for their specific needs. For example, the American Cancer Society has a wide range of groups for patients and relatives affected by cancers of a specific type. Many of these groups are coled by a social worker and a nurse.

The hospice movement, in which many social workers offer services, has grown from a single program in the United States in 1973 to more than two thousand programs at the end of the century (Kastenbaum 1998). It now has a variety of services specially targeted to family members. A growing number of services and programs that have been developed especially for children utilize art, storytelling, and play. This is due to the growing awareness in the professional community about effective interventions with bereaved children.

Bereavement Groups. Because children dislike being considered "different" from others, bereavement groups should be considered the treatment of choice for bereaved children. These groups, frequently led by social workers, may be school- or community-based. They offer the peer support that the bereaved child so greatly craves, since the group helps him/her realize that *other children* have also lost a parent to death.

Bereavement groups typically are time-limited (eight to ten weeks) with a planned agenda that utilizes various activities such as drawing, writing, and group exercises to assist the children express their feelings about death. Casey-Tait and Depta (1993) describe the process of one such eight-session group consisting of ten children, ages 7 to 11, each of whom had experienced the death of a parent, stepparent, grandparent, or other family members. There were two coleaders, which the authors recommend in order to make it possible for one leader to attend to individuals who may become upset during the group sessions, while the other leader can continue with the group process. The groups give the child the opportunity to ask questions, either verbally or anonymously through use of a question box. They serve an important role in combating the isolation of bereaved children. In an earlier publication (Webb 1993) I pointed out that bereavement groups are *not appropriate* for traumatically bereaved children or for children bereaved by suicide. The special needs of these individuals can be more appropriately met initially in one-to-one therapy.

Other School and Community-Based Programs. In their effort to respond appropriately to situations involving student suicides or traumatic deaths, many schools and colleges have created crisis teams consisting of counseling, social work, administrative, and guidance staff who have received training about how to respond following these events. Friends of the deceased are often targeted to receive special outreach, because clinical research documents the special vulnerabilities of peers whose immaturity and lack of ability to express their grief may lead them to imitate the self-destructive behavior in what have been called "copycat suicides."

Most school-based crisis teams assign special guidance counselors and/or social workers to help students who may need to discuss their complicated reactions following traumatic deaths, such as shootings, car accidents, and suicides. Elsewhere (Webb 1986) I have discussed guidelines for schools to help with prevention of suicides and to deal with reactions of faculty and students following such a death. Many schools now have trained crisis teams prepared to deal with the emergency of traumatic deaths. However, it seems ironic to me that most schools do not have similar staff training programs and response protocols for the far more *common* type of bereavement, that of the death of a parent.

Many resources about death are available in the form of storybooks for young children, information and support books for teenagers, and textbooks and curriculum guides for teachers (Cassini and Rogers 1996; O'Toole 1998; Stevenson 1996). The availability of these resources, however, does not mean that they are being used. Because of the discomfort of many adults in discussing the topic of death, classroom teachers may shy away from it. This is analogous to the discomfort of schools and communities in dealing with issues related to sex education.

Teachers need help and guidance about how to help students following a death, and it is preferable that they receive some in-service training *prior to the need to implement this.* The following discussion describes a community-based program focused on helping schools prepare to respond to deaths and other losses by offering in-service programs on these topics to teachers.

The Westchester (NY) Task Force on Children and Loss. I am a member of a community-based task force dedicated to helping schools and community agencies deal with death and loss situations of various kinds. Composed of school guidance counselors, social workers, funeral directors, mental health practitioners and college-level faculty who volunteer their services, the mission of the task force is to offer educational and supportive services about death and loss to schools upon request. The program has been in existence for about six years, and although it is offered at no charge, it is underutilized. We have sponsored several conferences, open to both professionals and the public, but they have been poorly attended.

The most successful component of the task force has been a six-session staff in-service training seminar on a variety of topics related to loss. The two-and-one-half-hour program occurs once a week, after school. School staff (teachers, guidance counselors, administrators) who sign up in advance, receive in-service credit for attendance. Topics included in the six-session training seminar include the following:

- Children's understanding of death
- Talking to children and parents about death
- Children and funerals: understanding and participation
- Suicide bereavement
- Hospice and its role in helping children and families
- Children's reaction to divorce and talking about loss to groups of children

The anonymous evaluations at the end of the program have been unanimously favorable. However, these programs (available twice a year), have been subscribed to by only a fraction of the schools we would like to reach. The death taboo may play some role, and although we deliberately chose to use the word *loss* rather than *death* in the task force title, administrators may prefer to avoid confronting staff with issues that appear to have negative overtones. We continue to offer our services and hope to make incremental steps that will have some modest impact over time.

ASSESSMENT AND INTERVENTIONS

Use of the Tripartite Assessment, as already described, can greatly assist the practitioner in evaluating the impact of a parent's death on an *individual.* However, when a parent dies, the impact of the death reverberates across the entire nuclear and extended family and a family systems perspective gives the practitioner a broader view of the repercussions of the death.

The family's responses usually reflect both personal, familial, and religious/cultural expectations and values. According to Walsh and McGoldrick (1991) "death poses shared adaptational challenges, requiring both immediate and long-term family reorganization and changes in a family's definitions of its identity and purpose" (7). Apart from the major task of grieving the loss of a pivotal person when a parent dies, accommodations must be made within the family to carry out the specific duties and role functions of the deceased person. For example, in the Turner family case to be discussed more fully later, after the death of a fireman while fighting a house fire, his widow and four children needed to find someone to complete the painting of their home, which the father had been working on at the time of his death. Similarly, after a mother's death, the family must identify and make plans about how to complete the many tasks the mother routinely performed in the course of her average day and week.

Walsh and McGoldrick (1991) refer to the following two major adaptational tasks for family members following a death: (1) acknowledging the reality of the death and sharing the experience of loss, and (2) reorganizing the family system and reinvesting in other relationships and life pursuits (8–11). A new equilibrium must occur within the family. This process of shared grief and planning for the future usually results in increased solidarity in the family (Goldberg 1973). The social work practitioner working with a family following the death of a parent must pay attention both to the family as a whole (how it is functioning and how it is carrying out its adaptational tasks) and also to the reactions of individual family members.

Because the mourning process occurs over time, different helping approaches may be appropriate at different stages of bereavement. Baker, Sedney, and Gross (1992) refer to the grief process as a series of psychological tasks that must be accomplished in stages. In the *early phase,* the individual must "gain an understanding of what has happened, while employing self-protective mechanisms to guard against the full emotional impact of the loss. *Middle phase tasks* include accepting and reworking the loss and bearing the intense psychological pain involved. *Late tasks* include the . . . resumption of developmental progress on age-appropriate developmental issues" (105). It is imperative that the counselor identify the family's and the individual's stage of bereavement in order to plan help that will be most appropriate and acceptable at a particular time.

Depending on the specifics of each case, the social worker may offer help through **family** therapy, **group** therapy, **individual** therapy, or a **combination** of different approaches. Certain methods may be more acceptable to different individuals at different stages of their bereavement process. It is important to move at the clients' pace and to be respectful of their wishes. Although children usually do not have the autonomy or sufficient awareness to participate fully in selecting a treatment method that appeals to them, we must try whenever possible to include children in treatment decisions since this will enhance their subsequent motivation to participate. The child, obviously, had no control over the death, but many children can voice their preference about whether to see a counselor by themselves, with their family, or in a group with other bereaved children if the choice is presented to them. For example, in the case of Sabrina mentioned earlier, Sabrina declined my suggestion that she attend a weekend "summer bereavement camp," which would have necessitated her being away from her father for two nights. At the time, her mother had been dead for approximately seven months, and I had been seeing her with her father in bimonthly counseling sessions. I thought that she might be ready to deal with her grief issues in the company of other bereaved children. However, as an only child (now that her brother had also died) Sabrina was not comfortable with the prospect of being separated from her one surviving parent even for a weekend. I respected the child's wishes and continued to see Sabrina with her father in joint sessions, helping each of them express their anxieties about safety and separation issues.

In contrast, a 12-year-old girl in the fireman's family (see later case illustration) did not want to commit to either family or individual therapy after one family session four months following her father's sudden death. However, this girl did agree to attend a school-based bereavement group, and, according to her mother, she benefited greatly from the experience. Her three younger siblings participated regularly and enthusiastically in one-to-one individual play therapy over a period of five months following the death. The widowed mother attended a bereavement group during this period. In summary, choices about different treatment options should be offered in the spirit of respecting the clients' preferences.

Family Counseling/Therapy. Whenever possible, it is important to see the family together for at least one session, following the death of a parent. This is to acknowledge that they have all experienced the same loss and also to point out that different people in the family will respond differently to this loss. The social work counselor models a tolerance for differences, which can be particularly important for the children, who may feel guilty because they still want to go out and play and have fun with their friends, while their surviving parent may be sitting sadly in the house.

During the family session it is also helpful for the worker to indicate that most people's feelings change over time, and that their preference for counseling at one point may change later. The worker also should state that sometimes it will be helpful to see different family members alone or together in sibling groups. A model of flexibility respects everybody's changing needs.

It is almost always valuable to see the surviving parent alone to offer him/her support and guidance in reorganizing the family tasks and to review with the parent some typical reactions of children after the death of a parent. It is helpful to have some written educational materials to give to the parent, since if she or he is actively grieving, it is unrealistic to focus primarily on the children and to present psycho-educational information orally. In situations when the worker considers that the parent is depressed and not functioning well, this session alone with the parent can be used beneficially to help the parent grieve, to make a referral when appropriate, and to also locate helping persons within the family network to provide assistance to the children and to the parent on a temporary basis. It is important that the parent not begin to use one of the children as a confidante in place of the bereaved spouse. This can be openly discussed with the parent at the same time the worker normalizes the parent's need for an *adult* friend and source of support.

Referral to a bereavement group is also helpful for the surviving parent. In my own experience, I have found that many parents are reluctant to attend such groups soon after the death. They seem to fear being overwhelmed by the feelings of other bereaved spouses at a time when they feel that they cannot cope with their own grief. Matters of timing and personal readiness to accept a referral cannot be predicted with certainty. A group experience is very valuable for either adults or children, but only when the bereaved individual is ready. Sometimes it is helpful to suggest that the person try the group once or twice, rather than automatically rule it out.

Individual Therapy/Counseling. "Some of the distinct advantages of individual therapy over group or family therapy are that it permits maximum attention to the particular needs of the child, and allows the therapist to move at the child's pace in a careful in-depth exploration of the child's underlying feelings about the death" (Webb 1993:51). Individual counseling is *always* recommended in situations of traumatic bereavement or following a suicidal death. This is because the individual (child or adult) must deal with their frightening ideas/images about the gruesome nature of the death before they can engage in the normal mourning process. Mourning, by definition, requires remembering the person who died. When the death has been traumatic, very frightening elements become superimposed upon these memories and interfere with peaceful and healing recollections. Counseling the traumatically bereaved is a stressful process for both the individual and for the social work counselor/therapist. Before undertaking this anxiety-producing work, the worker should have received specialized training in counseling traumatized individuals.

ILLUSTRATION AND DISCUSSION

The Turner Family		
Betty (mother)	Age 34	Part-time cashier
Greg (father)	Age 35	Policeman and volunteer fireman; killed in house fire
Mary	Age 12	Seventh grade
Greg, Jr.	Age 9	Fourth grade
Brian	Age 6	First grade
Lisa	Age 4	Nursery school

Three months following Greg's death, the policeman/MSW social worker who was on the "crisis debriefing team" who visited the family immediately after the death suggested to Betty that it would be a good idea for her to consult a play therapist for the children because of the traumatic nature of their father's death. The policeman/social worker telephoned me to provide information and to alert me to expect a call from Betty. When no call came after ten days, I telephoned the referral source and he said that he would call Betty again. About three weeks after the initial referral I received the telephone call from Mrs. Turner. She agreed to bring all the children for a family session. I mentioned that following this initial meeting I would like to see each family member, including her, individually. I said that depending on my assessment of their individual needs, we would agree on a plan of how to proceed. Mrs. Turner mentioned that her husband's and Mary's birthdays were coming up soon, and she thought that this was going to be "hard" on all of them. The birthdays also coincided with an upcoming ceremony planned by the fire department and the town to name a street after her husband. I indicated my understanding of the combined honor and stress of this event and mentioned my wish to do whatever I could to help her get through this difficult period.

First Family Session. This consisted of an opportunity for me to meet all the family, to acknowledge the terrible loss they had each experienced, and to explain some of the ways I might be helpful to them. I described my role as someone who "helps children and families with their troubles and worries, and that sometimes we talk and sometimes we play" (Webb 1996:68). I suggested that we begin by everyone making a drawing of a happy memory of their family. The boys each drew a picture of an outing in the park, the mother helped Lisa draw a snowman, and Mary drew some flowers. The purpose of this warm-up exercise was to help the children begin to feel comfortable with me. I also used the drawings to refer to their father, asking his whereabouts in the scene each drew. I had suggested that Mrs. Turner bring some pictures of her husband with her to this session, and she shared them at this time, pointing out the individual children with their father when they were much younger. I was impressed by Mrs. Turner's ability to focus on her children when I knew that she had suffered a great loss herself.

The pictures also showed some older family members and other relatives. I learned that Mrs. Turner's parents had both died during the past year, as had her mother-in-law. I said with great feeling, "This family has lost a lot of important people in a very short time!" Mary said that she believed in reincarnation, and that she thought that life continues in other forms. She elaborated that several of her aunts had had babies this year, and she thinks that her grandparents' spirits will be felt in these new lives. I said that I was very impressed by her spiritual beliefs. Addressing the younger members of the family, particularly, I mentioned that no matter what happens after death, we still miss the person and wish he was still with us. There was some discussion among the boys about who would own their father's fire helmet and jacket.

Lisa was getting quite squirmy, and I suggested that we all play a board game called, "The Goodbye Game." This is a therapeutic game that incorporates the stages of grief (denial, anger, bargaining, acceptance) by permitting the players to respond to questions (printed on different-colored cards) about death when they land on corresponding color sections of the board. Because Lisa couldn't read (and it turned out that Brian couldn't either), Mary read their cards for them. One of Greg's questions was, "Draw a picture of death." He drew a picture of a narrow casket with a thin figure in it. As Greg drew, Brian asked if he could draw also, and, of course, I agreed. Brian drew a burning house. When we were looking at the drawings, I commented that they were both probably thinking about their father. I noticed that Mary's eyes filled with tears several times while playing the game.

At the end of the session I set up appointments to see Mrs. Turner and each child separately. I said that I knew it was hard to think and talk about someone you loved who had died, but that I thought it would be helpful to them. I also mentioned again that we could play as well as talk.

Comment. This family was fairly easy to engage, despite the mother's initial delay in acting on the referral. The challenge here was the wide age range of the children, between 4 and 12 years. Because of this I knew that there was a vast difference in Lisa's and Mary's understanding of death. I realized that in a family session such as this, it is difficult to meet the individual needs of different family members. Nonetheless, the family session served the purpose of engagement and beginning the therapeutic relationship with each individual. I knew that in future sessions with the individual children I would use play therapy techniques with the two younger children, mostly talk with Mary, and combine talking and playing with Greg.

Individual Session with Mrs. Turner. I used this meeting to go over many of the points mentioned earlier in this article with regard to helping the spouse of someone who died. I made a referral to a bereavement group for Mrs. Turner, and she said she didn't feel ready yet but that she might want to go "later." We also discussed the status of each child individually. Mrs. Turner stated that Mary told her after the family session that she didn't want to come back for individual sessions. The mother felt that Mary was "doing very well," and that she didn't really need help, in contrast to the other children. She was concerned about Greg, who had started to be aggressive with other children in school; also, his school work was deteriorating. Brian had always been disorganized, according to Mrs. Turner, and she felt that now he was "in a daze." Lisa simply did not comprehend what had happened, according to Mrs. Turner. She would say, "My Daddy died in a house fire," but then hearing someone enter the house the very next moment, she would say, "That's Daddy!"

I reviewed some of children's expectable responses to a parent's death, and helped Mrs. Turner understand that many of their reactions were normative. At the same time, I asked for permission to contact the boys' schools and to confer with the school social worker about their academic and behavioral status. Mrs. Turner was glad to have me do this and she signed the necessary release forms.

Summary of Sessions with Children. As planned, I saw each child individually for several play therapy sessions. Greg was able to admit that he was losing his temper "a lot lately." We spoke together about how much stress he was under because of his father's death, and I referred to the fact that many people, adults and kids, feel angry when someone they love dies suddenly. He made a picture of a volcano, at my suggestion, and we talked about when feelings are held in they can "explode like a volcano." I also gave him clay to mold and twist as we talked about what it's like now that his father isn't home, and he reminisced about some of the things he used to enjoy doing with his dad.

Within three weeks I noticed a visible relaxation of Greg's tension. His mother said that there had been no more negative reports from school, and the school social worker reported that he was spending time with Greg every week talking about their shared interest in basketball.

Brian's reactions and behavior in therapy were quite different. He typically brought an assortment of toys with him from home and dumped them in the middle of the office floor, creating a very chaotic scene. He would use my firemen dolls, trucks, and the whole array of police and medical dolls in my collection, together with an assortment of family dolls of all sizes, ethnicities, and ages. Brian re-created on my playroom floor the chaos he was feeling internally. I understood the symbolic meaning of his play and verbalized to him that "everything seemed all mixed up and confused." His play came to no resolution or conclusion, and he would not permit me to "play out" any rescue efforts. About three months after I began seeing him, and on the last day before I was to go away on an extended leave, he played out a house fire, the deaths of many people, and the inability of the hospital to save the people. This was a very sad scene, and I verbalized the feelings of sadness and helplessness for Brian. He permitted me to cover up the "dead bodies" (with Kleenex), and he joined me in doing this. After a quiet, but intense interval I said something about missing those people very much, and trying to remember how much they loved us. This very active child became quite focused and serious during this play, which I believe had deep meaning to him.

When I first began seeing Brian I was concerned about his poor speech and encouraged his mother to request an evaluation at school. In the midst of the period of therapy, she reported to me that the school was arranging special help for him. I felt quite certain that these difficulties were independent of his father's death. But it also seemed likely that his problems with speech and learning were increased by the death.

Lisa also had a speech impairment, but it was not serious, considering her young age. However, because I had some difficulty understanding her, I subsequently suggested that her mother have her evaluated. In the play sessions with me Lisa turned all the adults in the dollhouse family into females, even those who were clearly male. When I asked her to tell me who was in the family, she did not name a father. I asked her "What happened to the Daddy?" and she responded, "We can't find him." This response is understandable in view of Lisa's young age. On the one hand she has heard people say that her father is dead, but she doesn't understand that death is irreversible. That is why she can switch from saying that her father died in a house fire to announcing his arrival at the front door. My response (and one I later suggested that mother repeat to Lisa) was that "maybe the Daddy is dead, and when people are dead, we don't see them anymore and they don't come back." It was not necessary to continue play therapy sessions with Lisa, because I believed that her mother would respond patiently and appropriately to the child whenever necessary.

This case illustrates some important factors that must be considered when a parent dies. First, children will comprehend and interpret the death according to their ability, based on their age and developmental level. Second, the anxiety and stress associated with a death will magnify preexisting conditions, or lead to acting out behaviors that require a therapeutic response that recognizes the underlying meaning of the behavior. Third, the ability of the surviving parent to focus on the children's needs and to maintain structure and routine in the home will influence the children's adjustment. Fourth, a parent's ability to interact appropriately with the children depends strongly on the support the parent receives from the extended family, friends, and the community. In this case, there was a large extended family who rallied around and offered help. In addition, the community and the father's work associates also provided ongoing support. Finally, this family appeared to have been functioning well prior to the crisis of the death. They were already resilient, and although the sudden death certainly was a drastic loss, the extensive support they received contributed to their ongoing growth and development.

CONCLUSION

Death is a part of life, and parents cannot guarantee their ongoing survival throughout the life span of their children. Social workers, therefore, must be prepared to provide services to families following parental death and to assist schools and community agencies with the creation and provision of programs for bereavement counseling. Depending on the nature of the death and the age of the surviving relatives, services may be offered through hospice programs, schools, mental health clinics, religious organizations, and funeral homes, or by private practitioners. Regardless of the locale of the services, the bereavement counselor should make an assessment of the individuals, taking into account the various components of potential risk and resilience factors, as enumerated in the Tripartite Assessment. Special attention should be given to the age and level of cognitive understanding of the survivors, as well as to the nature of the death and the quality of existing support. The outcome of this assessment will point to the type of intervention that is appropriate.

A variety of treatment options should be considered, depending on the circumstances of each case. Among these are bereavement support groups, individual and family therapy, or a combination of various treatments. The social work value of client self-determination argues for participation of the client in the choice of the particular treatment modality.

Whereas a death is the end of a life, it must not result in despair and depression for the families of the survivors. Social work can lend a vital service by setting up appropriate programs, referring bereaved clients to them, and providing bereavement counseling on an age-appropriate level.

References

Ainsworth, Mary. 1979. "Infant-mother Attachment." *American Psychologist* 34:932–37.

Ainsworth, Mary and Sylvia Bell. 1971. "Attachment, Exploration, and Separation: Illustrated by the Behavior of One-Year-Olds in a Strange Situation." In S. Chess and A. Thomas, eds., *Annual Progress in Child Psychiatry and Child Development,* pp. 41–60. New York: Brunner/Mazel.

Ainsworth, Mary and Barbara A. Wittig. 1969. "Attachment and Exploratory Behaviors of One-Year-Olds in a Strange Situation." In B. M Foss, ed., *Determinants of Infant Behavior,* pp.111–36. London: Methuen.

Baker, John E., Mary Ann Sedney, and Esther Gross. 1992. "Psychological Tasks for Bereaved Children." *American Journal of Orthopsychiatry* 62(12):105–16.

Casey-Tait, Donna and Jo Lynn Depta. 1993. "Play Therapy for Bereaved Children." In N.B. Webb, ed., *Helping Bereaved Children. A Casebook for Practitioners,* pp. 169–185. New York: Guilford Press.

Cassini, Kathleen K. and Jacqueline L. Rogers. 1996. *Death and the Classroom. A Teachers Guide to Assist Grieving Students,* rev. ed. Toledo, Ohio: Griefworks.

Doka, Kenneth J., ed. 1989. *Disenfranchised Grief. Recognizing Hidden Sorrow.* New York: Free Press.

Fox, Sandra Sutherland. 1985. *Good Grief. Helping Groups of Children When a Friend Dies.* Boston: New England Association for the Education of Young Children.

Furman, Erna. 1974. *A Child's Parent Dies.* New Haven: Yale University Press.

Goldberg, Stanley. 1973. "Family Tasks and Reactions in the Crisis of Death." *Social Casework* 54(7):398–405.

Kastenbaum, Robert J. 1998. *Death, Society, and Human Experience,* 6th ed. Boston: Allyn & Bacon.

Mahler, Margaret, Fred Pine, and Anni Bergman. 1975. *The Psychological Birth of the Human Infant: Symbiosis and Individuation.* New York: Basic Books.

Masur, Corinne. 1991. "The Crisis of Early Maternal Loss. Unresolved Grief of 6-year-old Chris in Foster Care." In N. B. Webb, ed., *Play Therapy with Children in Crisis. A Casebook for Practitioners,* pp. 164–76. New York: Guilford Press.

Miller, Mary Anderson. 1995. "Re-grief as Narrative: The Impact of Parental Death on Child and Adolescent Development." In D. W. Adams and E. J. Deveau, eds., *Beyond the Innocence of Childhood: Helping Children and Adolescents Cope with Death and Bereavement,* Vol. 3, pp. 99–115. Amityville, N.Y.: Baywood.

Nagy, Maria. 1948. "The Child's Theories Concerning Death." *Journal of Genetic Psychology* 73:3–27.

Ormond, Eileen and Heather Charbonneau. 1995. "Grief Responses and Group Treatment Interventions for Five- to Eight-Year-Old Children." In D. W. Adams and E. J. Deveau, eds., *Beyond the Innocence of Childhood: Helping Children and Adolescents Cope with Death and Bereavement,* Vol. 3, pp.181–202. Amityville, N.Y.: Baywood.

O'Toole, Donna R. 1998. *Growing Through Grief. A K–12 Curriculum to Help Young People Through All Kinds of Loss,* rev. ed. Burnsville, N.C.: Compassion Books.

Remkus, Joyce. 1991. "Repeated Foster Placements and Attachment Failure." In N. B. Webb, ed., *Play Therapy with Children in Crisis: A Casebook for Practitioners,* pp. 143–63. New York: Guilford Press.

Saravay, Barbara. 1991. "Short-Term Play Therapy with Two Preschool Brothers Following Sudden Paternal Death." In N. B. Webb, ed., *Play Therapy with Children in Crisis. A Casebook for Practitioners,* pp. 177–201. New York: Guilford Press.

Silverman, Phyllis R., Steve Nickman, and J. William Worden. 1992. "Detachment Revisited: The Child's Reconstruction of a Dead Parent." *American Journal of Orthopsychiatry* 62(4):494–503.

Sroufe, Alan L. 1979a. "The Coherence of Individual Development. Early Care, Attachment, and Subsequent Developmental Issues." *American Psychologist* 34:834–41.

——. 1979b. "Socioeconomic Development." In J. D. Osofsky, ed., *Handbook of Infant Development,* pp. 462–516. New York: John Wiley.

Sroufe, Alan L. and Everett Waters. 1977. "Attachment as an Organizing Construct." *Child Development* 48:1184–99.

Stevenson, Robert G. 1996. *Teaching Students About Death. A Comprehensive Resource for Educators and Parents.* Boston, Mass.: Charles Press.

Tait, Donna Casey and Jo-Lynn Depta. 1993. "Play Therapy Group for Bereaved Children." In N. B. Webb, ed., *Helping Bereaved Children. A Casebook for Practitioners,* pp.169–85. New York: Guilford Press.

U.S. Census Bureau. 1998. *Statistical Abstracts of the United States.* Washington, D.C.: Government Printing Office.

Walsh, Froma and Monica McGoldrick, eds. 1991. *Living Beyond Loss. Death in the Family.* New York: W. W. Norton.

Wass, Hannelore and Judith Stillion. 1988. "Dying in the Lives of Children." In H. Wass,

F. Berardo, and R. Neimeyer, eds., *Dying: Facing the Facts,* pp. 201–28. Washington, D.C.: Hemisphere.

Webb, Nancy Boyd. 1986. "Before and After Suicide. A Preventive Outreach Program for Colleges." *Suicide and Life-Threatening Behavior* 16(4):469–80.

———. 1991. *Play Therapy with Children in Crisis. A Casebook for Practitioners.* New York: Guilford Press.

———. 1993. *Helping Bereaved Children. A Casebook for Practitioners.* New York: Guilford Press.

———. 1996. *Social Work Practice with Children.* New York: Guilford Press.

Wessel, Morris A. 1983. "Children, When Parents Die." In J. E. Showalter, P. R. Patterson, M. Tallmer, A. H. Kutscher, S. V. Gallo, and D. Peretz, eds. *The Child and Death,* pp. 125–33. New York: Columbia University Press.

Wolfenstein, Martha. 1966. "How Is Mourning Possible?" *Psychoanalytic Study of the Child* 21:93–126.

18

Divorce

Ellen B. Bogolub

▌ "I know leaving Tom was the right thing, but now he's really mad, and he's got that violent temper. I'm afraid he's going to come after the kids and me."

▌ "I'm 60 years old and spent the best years of my life as a full-time homemaker. I never thought my husband would dump me. Now he doesn't want to give me alimony. At my age, I'll never find a job. I'm all alone, and I don't want to go on."

▌ "I try to be a devoted father. When I wanted to leave work early to take my son to the doctor, my boss made it clear that the answer was no, and that I was not to raise the subject again. I'm really in a bind."

Each of these dilemmas results from divorce, which currently occurs in approximately half of U.S. marriages (Doherty, Kouneski, and Erikson 1998). Every year, numerous divorcing and divorced families are assisted by social workers in fields of practice such as family service, child welfare, school social work, and mental health. This chapter provides information and ideas for these social workers.

To help the diverse population of maritally disrupted parents and their offspring, social workers need awareness of divorce as a multifaceted process that unfolds over time, and a broad, contextual knowledge about divorce. They also need an eclectic practice orientation that includes community involvement and prevention in addition to psychosocial intervention with people who seek help. Finally, social workers need to see that while divorce is unquestionably stressful, it offers many people the opportunity to end an untenable situation and improve life quality.

DEFINING AND EXPLAINING DIVORCE

Some have defined divorce as an **individual flaw;** individuals who leave marriages are seen as devoid of "family values" and are thought not to care about their children's lives (Kurz 1995). This definition implies that people's reasons for exiting a marriage are often selfish or frivolous, and it ignores three points. First, departures from situations such as chronic spouse abuse and/or chronic child abuse promote rather than destroy family life. Second, such departures generally require tremendous effort and coping skill (Carlson 1997). Third, empirical research indicates that "parenting concerns and children's well-being are as salient to the well-being of . . . divorced mothers as they are to that of married mothers" (Demo and Acock 1996:405).

The individual flaw definition of marital dissolution is not helpful to social workers. It implies that little can be done to help divorced adults re-vision themselves or improve their child rearing, since they are morally deficient. Further, the definition's narrow individual perspective and lack of emphasis on the social environment rules out the consideration of public policy changes that would improve life for the divorced and their children.

A preferable, more widely used definition is divorce as a **many-sided process that unfolds over time** (Buchanan, Maccoby, and Dornbusch 1996; Hines 1997; Schwartz and Kaslow 1997; Whiteside 1998). In a classic and still-cited (e.g., Geasler and Blaisure 1998; Schwartz and Kaslow 1997) article, Bohannon (1970) may have been the first to draw attention to the various facets of divorce: emotional (i.e., a couple's changing relationship), legal (i.e., court proceedings and establishment of remarriageability), economic (i.e., termination of the single financial unit the couple comprised), coparental (i.e., arrangements for postdivorce care of children), community (i.e., changes in each spouse's social support network), and psychic (i.e., each spouse's efforts to attain a new autonomy). Although Bohannon's conceptualization is fairly inclusive, later authors have added other divorce dimensions for professionals to consider. For example, Schwartz and Kaslow discuss the spiritual and religious aspects of divorce.

The definition of divorce as a many-faceted process that unfolds over time has much to offer. Social workers may utilize the dimensions identified by Bohannon and others to develop assessments, interventions, policies, and programs that take into account clients' social and physical environments as well as their emotional and family lives. With its nonjudgmental orientation, and implication that divorced families are as worthy of acceptance as other families, this definition may also encourage a public view of divorced families as a respectable component of the broad range of families extant today (Acock and Demo 1994).

DEMOGRAPHIC PATTERNS

During the mid-1960s, the U.S. **divorce rate** began to increase rapidly (Arendell 1995; Simons and Associates 1996). It continued its rise during the 1970s, stabilized in the 1980s, and dropped very slightly during the 1990s (Masheter 1997; Schwartz and Kaslow 1997). This recent leveling off should not blind us to the overall trends: the U.S. divorce rate in the 1990s is much, much higher than it was several decades ago (Simons and Associates 1996); it is also the highest in the industrialized world (Carter and McGoldrick 1999). Specifically, at present, about 50 percent of first marriages end in divorce (Doherty et al. 1998), with the rate slightly higher for second marriages (Arendell 1995; McGoldrick and Carter 1999).

What accounts for this trend of widespread marital dissolution? Most divorces are initiated by women (Ahrons 1999; Amato and Rogers 1997; Carter and McGoldrick 1999), and a major reason for the high divorce rate is generally thought to be women's labor force participation (Ahrons 1999; Johnson and Wahl 1995). Paid employment lessens women's economic dependence on men and increases their ability to reject objectionable marital situations that they previously endured. Such situations include incompatibility, lack of affection, lack of communication, infidelity, spousal substance abuse, spousal unemployment, and domestic violence.

Additionally, the changing social norms of the 1960s, 1970s, and 1980s may have enabled adults to consider divorce. The "sexual revolution" permitted men and women to have intimate relationships outside of marriage more freely than previously (McLanahan and Sandefur 1994). The folk wisdom that parents should stay together because of their children was questioned (Hiedemann, Suhomlinova, and O'Rand 1998). Individual fulfillment was emphasized—or overemphasized (Lawson and Thompson 1995). And feminism, which promotes the value and social acceptability of women regardless of marital status, developed (Bogolub 1997). While these norms have undoubtedly influenced many people, other people—for example, Hispanic Americans and Asian Americans reared traditionally—may believe in traditional gender roles and lifestyles and remain unaffected by shifting norms.

Marital rupture is most common among ordinary young couples. Specifically, divorce correlates with **low socioeconomic class** (i.e., lower middle class or poor) (Ahrons 1999; Amato 1996; Amato and Rogers 1997), which can lead to economic hardship, emotional stress, and marital conflict (Amato 1996; Hatchett, Veroff, and Douvan 1995). Further, divorce correlates with **young age at marriage** (i.e., late teens or early twenties), which may indicate emotional neediness, or the desire to escape from parents (Ahrons 1999; Amato 1996; Amato and Rogers 1997; Hiedemann et al. 1998). Both of these factors can cause or increase marital instability. Perhaps because of the stresses generated by low socioeconomic class and young age, most divorces occur early in marriage, with fully half taking place within the first seven years (Bee 1994).

Although divorce is most common among young adults, it is on the rise among midlife and late-life couples with marriages of long duration. The principal factors in the increase in midlife divorce appear to be wives' employment and financial independence, while the exit of grown children from their parents' homes may be a lesser factor (Hiedemann et al. 1998). Among late-life couples, increased health and longevity make divorce increasingly possible (Hiedemann et al. 1998; Schwartz and Kaslow 1997).

There is widespread consensus that marital disruption is extremely common among **African Americans** (e.g., Lawson and Thompson 1995, 1996; Rank and Davis 1996); their divorce rate is generally estimated to be one and one-half to two and one-half times higher than that of whites (Ahrons 1999; Hatchett et al. 1995). The high divorce rate among African Americans stems from several factors. First, African American husbands often experience underemployment or unemployment, due to long-standing, pervasive labor market discrimination (Lawson and Thompson 1995). Male economic marginalization can lead to anxiety about the provider role (Hatchett et al. 1995; Lawson and Thompson 1996), financial strain, and marital conflict. Such conflict increases when African American wives find work more easily than their husbands do and assume significant economic roles in their families (Hatchett et al. 1995).

Second, the high female-to-male ratio among African Americans (Tucker and Mitchell-Kernan 1995) may destabilize marriages. Husbands may feel that they are in demand, and have alternatives to the current marriage, while wives may feel possessive and jealous; this dynamic leads easily to marital tension and separation (Lawson and Thompson 1995).

Third, compared with white couples, African American couples are more likely to see the alternatives to marriage in a positive light (Rank and Davis 1996). That is, adult peers in the African American community are increasingly likely to be unmarried (Lawson and Thompson 1995; Rank and Davis 1996), and African American men and women both tend to have abundant self-reliance, because of their history of fighting racial injustice. Taken together, these phenomena may suggest to African Americans that life without a spouse is not to be dreaded. The African American tradition of supportive extended families (Anderson 1999), which can buffer the stresses of single life, may also contribute to this perception.

In contrast to the abundant literature on divorce among African Americans, relatively little information is available about divorce in other ethnic groups. Nonetheless, some trends can be identified. Although the overall divorce rate of Hispanic Americans tends to be lower than that of non-Hispanics, the percentage of divorced individuals in some Hispanic subgroups is as high or higher than that of non-Hispanics (Longres 1995). Asian Americans are at very low risk for marital disruption, in part because of a powerful cultural value regarding the sanctity of the family (Yu 1993). Jewish divorce rates have risen along with Jewish assimilation, and now approach those of the general population (Rosen and Weltman 1996).

The lack of material about divorce among Hispanic Americans, Asian Americans, Pacific Islanders, Native Americans, and other ethnic groups is striking (Hines 1997; Schwartz and Kaslow 1997). Further scholarly work in the area divorce and ethnicity is clearly needed.

SOCIETAL CONTEXT

Inevitably, marital dissolution brings adults and children into contact with the law, frequently for the first time. On the one hand, the law is a support, in that a legal settlement can minimize misunderstanding and formally create arrangements for family life when the informal processes of the intact family are no longer available. On the other hand, specific aspects of the law create stress—sometimes severe—for adults and children. To guide their clients, and make appropriate referrals, social workers need to understand the five parameters of divorce settlements, as well as the role of the legal professional (i.e., attorney or divorce mediator).

Divorce settlements consist of five parameters: (1) child custody; (2) child visitation, (3) child support, (4) alimony, and (5) property divisions.

Child Custody. Custody refers to parental rights and responsibilities. Currently, 85 to 90 percent of children with divorced parents reside in mother-custody homes (Arendell 1995; Hines 1997). However, in the last twenty years, divorcing parents have received support from a broadened array of custody options; paternal custody and joint custody (both legal and legal/physical) are now increasingly used (Buchanan et al. 1996; Cancian and Meyer 1998; Kissman 1997; Schwartz and Kaslow, 1997; Seltzer 1998; Wilcox, Wolchik, and Braver 1998).

Most custody decisions are made without parental disagreement. If parents cannot agree, and turn to the courts, they may face the stress of judicial bias. For instance, judges may impose undesired joint custody, which can incite serious interparental conflict (Arendell 1995; Buchanan et al. 1996; Kurz 1995). Judges may also arbitrarily deny custody to gay and lesbian parents (Causey and Duran-Aydintug 1997; Schwartz and Kaslow 1997), or grant it to violent fathers (Kurz 1995; Schwartz and Kaslow 1997). Thus, clients are better off if they can avoid this stress and select a custody option on their own. The decision-making process may be eased by keeping in mind that the postdivorce relationship between former spouses is far more important for children's life quality than the specific custody form (Buchanan et al. 1996; Hines 1997; Whiteside 1998).

Child Visitation. The majority of nonresidential divorced parents are fathers. Despite recent increased interest in the father's postdivorce role, the contact of nonresidential divorced fathers with offspring usually declines over time (Doherty et al. 1998). However, a formal agreement about visitation is important even if a father lacks interest in his children. Such an agreement provides support for a custodial mother, in that visitation terms serve as "insurance" against a father's unpredictable future behavior. Further, when one parent has been physically or sexually abusive, the use of court-mandated supervision during that parent's visits needs formalization. And in more benign situations, a visitation agreement may support the postdivorce family by preventing arguments or escalation of extant interparental conflict.

Child Support. In the last ten years, the federal and state laws governing child support amounts and collection procedures have tightened considerably (Kurz 1995; Meyer and Bartfield 1998) and have improved the societal support for custodial parents (usually mothers). For example, awards are now determined by state guidelines rather than the previous judicial discretion method (Kurz 1995; Schwartz and Kaslow 1997). Likewise, child support payments are now routinely removed from the paychecks of noncustodial parents (usually fathers); previously, payment delinquency was necessary for such action, and custodial parents and children had to do without income until new arrangements were made (Kurz 1995; Meyer and Bartfield 1998).

However, numerous drawbacks remain. First, child support awards for custodial parents are not automatic. An in-person application in court is necessary, and parents (usually mothers) who do not speak English or who have difficulty leaving work often do not get awards (Kurz 1995). Second, although the suggested amounts in state guidelines have risen, they still usually do not cover even half the cost of rearing the couple's children (Kurz 1995; Schwartz and Kaslow 1997). Third, in a clear double standard, custodial parents who receive public assistance (generally mothers) get only $50 per month in child support, no matter how much the noncustodial parent contributes; the rest of the contribution replenishes government revenue (Dail and Thieman 1996). In contrast, other custodial parents get the full contribution. Fourth, noncustodial parents may evade financial responsibility (e.g., solicit employers not to report income, disguise income when self-employed; Meyer and Bartfield 1998). Overall, the child support system contains many inequities that stress custodial parents (mainly mothers).

Alimony. Only about 15 percent of divorced women receive alimony, or spousal support (Fine and Fine 1994; Kurz 1995). Often, these women are middle-aged or older (Schwartz and Kaslow 1997). The current trend toward short-term, "rehabilitative" alimony is based on the erroneous notion that women, with training, can earn incomes commensurate with their husbands'. Further, like child support, alimony is not always paid in full. Overall, the financial support that alimony offers to divorced women is temporary and limited.

Property Division. Although property settlements among the wealthy garner much media attention, most divorcing couples have very little property to divide (Kurz 1995). This lack of property may be particularly characteristic of divorcing couples who see social workers, because of the professional commitment to oppressed and vulnerable populations.

When property division *is* a concern, *equitable distribution laws,* operant in most states, create the potential for battle (Schwartz and Kaslow 1997). These laws empower judges to decide on a fair distribution of assets. The prevailing trend is for judges to award approximately two-thirds of the marital property to the man, and one-third to the woman, despite the fact that the woman's household usually includes minor children. Typically, judges discount the wife's homemaking contributions to the marital household and assume that property is "really" the man's, since he held a paying job. This judicial mentality clearly creates stress for custodial mothers working to obtain a fair property distribution for themselves and their children.

Most divorces do not involve courtroom litigation over custody, visitation, child support, alimony, or property (Emery 1995). Rather, they involve out-of-court contact with attorneys or mediators, who help create divorce agreements that are then implemented by a family court judge.

With attorneys (either private or legal service), each adult has her (or his) own, and a combative or competitive mentality may operate (Emery 1995). With mediation, a couple has one mediator, who helps them discuss disputes, and, if possible, resolve them cooperatively (Emery 1995; Gentry 1997). Even though some mediators do not have advanced professional training, most are attorneys, psychologists, or social workers (Emery 1995). Mediation, which is often available for minimal or no fee through the family courts, is associated with decreased levels of postdivorce litigation and seems to be associated with increased levels of long-range compliance with the original divorce agreement. For these reasons, mediation is often desirable, but it is not a panacea. For example, if a woman has a violent or psychotic husband, and prefers (with good reason) to avoid contact with him, she needs her own attorney.

A competent attorney or mediator is clearly a source of support for a divorcing adult. On the other hand, selecting or using an attorney or a mediator can be stressful. Adults who can afford private attorneys must be careful consumers during an upsetting period when clear thought may be difficult. The many low-income adults who rely on legal services may encounter lack of privacy for consultations, delays, and overworked attorneys. Again, in such cases, self-assertion at a time of emotional drain is required. Finally, couples who choose mediators must often face confusion, due to controversy over the training and background that should be required for use of the title *mediator* (Emery 1995).

When compared with the predivorce intact family, the postdivorce **mother-custody** home almost always experiences a sharp, lasting decrease in standard of living (Ahrons 1999; Catlett and McKenry 1996; Kurz 1995; Peterson 1996; Weitzman 1996). As a result, 39 percent of mother-custody families live in poverty, and many more are near-poor (Kurz 1995). Other mother-custody homes experience the devastating transition from a predivorce upper-middle- or middle-class lifestyle to one considerably more modest (Bogolub 1995; Kurz 1995). Further, middle-aged and older divorced women whose children are grown may also face severe postdivorce financial difficulties as they begin supporting themselves, often for the first time (Arendell 1995; Schwartz and Kaslow 1997; Sweeney 1997).

Income decline for mother-custody households occurs in part simply because the same amount of money that sustained one household predivorce now sustains two. Child support and/or alimony, which may or may not be available, do not fully compensate for the male salary provided before divorce (Meyer and Bartfield 1998; Schwartz and Kaslow 1997).

Income decline also occurs because a divorced woman who attempts to earn a living faces many societally imposed obstacles. For instance, she often begins or continues work that is in a low-pay, sex-segregated field. Alternately, she may be subject to the gender-wage gap: When women work in fields that are not sex-segregated, they receive less pay than do men doing the same work (McLanahan and Sandefur 1994). Younger women, particularly those lacking supportive extended families, may not be able to locate the child care that will help them enter or reenter the labor force. Middle-aged and older women are often hampered by out-of-date or nonexistent work skills, or employers' age discrimination.

When such constraints make it impossible for a woman to support herself and any children, public assistance becomes necessary. However, the income public assistance provides is poverty level (Kurz 1995). Further, the Personal Responsibility and Work Opportunity Act of 1996 (i.e., welfare reform) mandates a five-year lifetime limit on benefits, and prohibits single parents with a child older than 5 from claiming lack of child care as a reason for not working (Dickinson 1997). Welfare reform also mandates public assistance recipients to cooperate in locating ex-husbands or suffer financial penalty; this creates an untenable situation for women fleeing domestic violence, who may endanger themselves by any direct or indirect contact with former spouses (Kurz 1995; Pirog-Good and Amerson 1997). Welfare reform appears to seriously compromise the already meager ability of public assistance to relieve divorced women's financial stress.

Two-thirds of divorced women remarry (Kurz 1995); most of these experience some improvement in their financial situation (Ganong and Coleman 1994). However, because slightly more than half of remarriages dissolve in fewer than five years (Norton and Miller, as cited in McGoldrick and Carter 1999), the bonus is frequently temporary. In addition, compared with white women, African American women are less likely to remarry (Acock and Demo 1994; Hines 1997; Kurz 1995), in part because of the high female to male ratio among African Americans (Tucker and Mitchell-Kernan 1995). Hispanic women are also less likely to remarry, in part because of Roman

Catholic views about divorce (Hines 1997). Overall, remarriage has been overemphasized as a support that can compensate for divorce-engendered poverty (Carter and McGoldrick 1999; Catlett and McKenry 1996). Rather, it is the social conditions that confront divorced women (e.g., low pay, lack of affordable child care, age discrimination, welfare reform, loopholes in child support enforcement) that must be emphasized—and remediated.

For several reasons, financial stress in **father-custody** and **joint-residential-custody** families is less. First, the parents involved tend to have relatively high incomes (Buchanan et al. 1996; Cancian and Meyer 1998). Second, in these family types, the financial commitment of the father (who generally earns more than the mother) is not limited by the amount of a child support award. Third, in father-custody homes, child care expenses are fewer, as the offspring involved tend to be older (Fox and Kelly 1995).

Still, some monetary stress does arise in father-custody and joint-residential-custody families. We have seen that in mother-custody families, monetary stress results from *both* the divorce-engendered need to distribute maternal and paternal income across two households, *and* from societally imposed obstacles to women's labor force participation. In father-custody and joint-residential-custody families, impediments to female earning are much less of a factor, due to the advantaged situation of sole-custody and joint-residential-custody fathers. However, the increased expense stemming from two postdivorce households does operate in father-custody and joint-residential-custody families. They too experience financial sacrifices and worry about money.

Although the skipped child support payments (Meyer and Bartfield 1998) and postdivorce financial gains (Peterson 1996; Weitzman 1996) of nonresidential "deadbeat dads" are well publicized, the financial stresses of father custody and joint residential custody may not be as widely known. Thus, awareness that some fathers have increased postdivorce material responsibility, and an accompanying sense of burden, prevents stereotyped thinking about divorced men, and their financial contributions to their children's lives.

We have seen that the changing **social norms** of the 1960s, 1970s, and 1980s may have enabled adults to consider divorce. On the other hand, other norms create stress for divorced adults once marital disruption has occurred.

First, consider divorced fathers. Although many of these fathers withdraw from their children's lives, emotionally as well as financially (Doherty et al. 1998), others (both residential and nonresidential) want to cooperate with their ex-wives, and to nurture and provide for their children. Yet in the United States today, a divorcing man is expected to "win a war" against his ex-wife, rather than to negotiate with her about what is best for the children (Arendell 1995; Doherty et al. 1998). He is also expected to keep his child care responsibilities out of sight at work, and to emphasize job performance exclusively. Because of such adversarial, career-oriented norms, caring men often experience isolation and role confusion as they struggle to remain cooperative, involved fathers (Arendell 1995).

Second, consider noncustodial mothers. Most frequently, a noncustodial mother lives apart from her children for good reason, because the father is better able to provide them with financial and/or emotional stability (Babcock 1997; Greif 1997b). Even though she does what is best for her children, a noncustodial mother typically suffers guilt, depression, and social stigma. Underlying the rejection by self and others are widely accepted norms that (1) all mothers should reside with their children, and (2) mothers who live apart from their offspring are incompetent and should be denigrated.

When we consider the total impact of law, social conditions, and social norms, we see that there are more sources of stress for the divorced than there are of support. Although settlements help divorcing families reorganize and attain stability, judicial bias (e.g., against gays and lesbians) and specific laws (e.g., withholding of full child support payments from families on public assistance) create problems. The many impediments to female economic parity (e.g., gender-wage gap) create a chronically shortchanged group of mother-custody homes. Finally, although some norms enable adults to leave dead-end situations, other norms create stress once divorce takes place.

VULNERABILITIES AND RISK FACTORS

For those leaving dysfunctional, unhappy, and/or violent marriages, divorce can be an emotional relief (Simons and Associates 1996), an empowering act of resistance to an oppressive situation (Catlett and McKenry 1996; Kurz 1995), or an opportunity to develop latent personal strengths (Schwartz and Kaslow 1997). In these cases, the perceived benefits of divorce may exceed its perceived stress, i.e., its perceived taxing of personal capacity (Carlson 1997; Smith and Carlson, 1997). In other cases (e.g., being left by a spouse), perceived benefits may be nonexistent, and stress is the dominant experience. In any divorce, the stressful aspects create the possibility of negative outcomes (Smith and Carlson 1997), viz., compromised health, well-being, or social performance (Voydanoff and Donnelly 1998).

For women, negative divorce outcomes include depression (Simons and Associates 1996), substance abuse (Hines 1997), and diminished parenting ability, e.g., inconsistent discipline, lax monitoring and supervision, decreased affection, and loss of zest for family activities (Bogolub 1995; Buchanan et al. 1996). For men, negative divorce outcomes include somatization (De Garmo and Kitson 1996), substance abuse (Schwartz and Kaslow 1997), and gradual disengagement from children, with regard to both visitation and financial support (Doherty et al. 1998). These gender patterns are not absolute; men may experience negative outcomes typical of women, and vice versa. For offspring, negative outcomes of parental divorce include decreased self-esteem, difficulties interacting with peers, low educational attainment (Anderson 1999; Gentry 1997), substance abuse (Hines 1997), low level of labor force participation (McLanahan and Sandefur 1994), "drifting" during young adulthood (Wallerstein and Blakeslee, 1989), and divorce (McLanahan and Sandefur 1994).

Most divorced adults and their offspring do *not* experience these negative outcomes. Rather, most divorces result in at least one capable, effective parent, who is able to raise children to competent adulthood (McLanahan and Sandefur 1994; Simons and Associates 1996). However, divorced parents and their offspring are at somewhat greater risk for these negative outcomes than are people who have not experienced their own or their parents' divorce.

Negative divorce outcomes must be distinguished from unpleasant emotions, such as anxiety, anger, guilt, and sadness. These emotions frequently occur among adults, children, and adolescents while separation is considered, and may continue for several years following divorce. Usually these emotions are transient, appropriate responses to stress and are likely to diminish after divorce, when lives have been rebuilt (Ahrons 1999; Bogolub 1995).

Risk Factors for Adults and Offspring. Among divorced adults and their offspring, negative outcomes result from risk factors on three levels: *individual, family,* and *external* (Smith and Carlson 1997). (Smith and Carlson's three-level conceptualization pertains to protective factors, but we may apply it to risk factors as well.) For both adults and offspring, *individual*-level risk factors include: predivorce history of extreme emotional sensitivity, extreme dependence, substance abuse, or mental illness (Bogolub 1995; Schwartz and Kaslow 1997). For adults, additional individual risk factors are high salience of marriage as a component of predivorce identity (De Garmo and Kitson 1996) and, among women, increased age (Schwartz and Kaslow 1997). Additionally, on an individual level, ethnic heritage may generate risk for negative divorce outcome. For example, because of traditional upbringing, some Hispanic women may be more oriented to homemaking than to economic self-sufficiency (Longres 1995); such women may experience conflict as they consider divorce-necessitated job searches.

For adults, *family*-level risk factors include: severe conflict with former spouse (e.g., violence, intimidation, heated arguments; Masheter 1997); time poverty and role overload (common among custodial parents juggling child care and employment responsibilities); and lack of social support from extended family (common among recently emigrated adults without kin nearby). For offspring, family level risk factors include: diminished parenting (Bogolub 1995; Buchanan et al. 1996), particularly in the residential parent; severe interparental conflict (e.g., repeated litigation about custody, child support, or visitation; sabotage of the other parent's visits) (Masheter 1997; Whiteside 1998); and lack of involved extended family who can compensate for parental deficits (Acock and Demo 1994; Anderson 1999).

For both divorced parents and their offspring, *external*-level risk factors typically occur in a chain or sequence (Kirby and Fraser 1997). Specifically, divorce-related downward economic mobility often leads to a residential move, which in turn can lead to substandard housing, inferior schools, and neighborhoods more dangerous than those occupied while married (McLanahan and Sandefur 1994). Dangerous neighborhoods can lead to social isolation and lack of connection to neighborhood resources, as "latchkey" children of divorced parents must frequently stay indoors after school, and both divorced adults and their offspring may be afraid to travel in high-crime areas (Hines 1997; McLanahan and Sandefur 1994).

Risk Clusters and Psychosocial Needs of Divorced Families. This identification of risk factors for negative divorce outcomes among adults and children confirms recent thinking that risk factors do not generally occur in isolation (Kirby and Fraser 1997; Smith and Carlson 1997). For example, among the risk factors identified, time poverty, role overload, living in a dangerous neighborhood, social isolation, and lack of connection to neighborhood resources tend to occur together, among families headed by low-income custodial mothers.

Identification of this risk cluster suggests attention to its cause, which appears to be the previously discussed disadvantage that besets women in the labor force.

Fundamentally, a woman who is prevented from earning a living wage is faced with a group of related risks, while a woman who can earn an adequate living is spared most of these. Thus, a significant psychosocial need of divorced families is improved economic conditions for working women. These would include closing of the gender-wage gap, more part-time and flex-time jobs, more affordable, high-quality child care, and, for women temporarily unable to sustain employment, increases in public assistance amounts and decreases in public assistance restrictions (Simons and Associates 1996).

Another psychosocial need of divorced families is improved economic conditions for all low-income adults, both female and male. Although better child support enforcement would improve life quality in mother-custody homes, so would increased ability of low-income men to provide such support voluntarily. Sometimes, their failure to pay simply indicates a lack of resources after basic needs are met (Robertson 1997). An increase in the minimum wage would be the first step in improving the situation for all employed, low-income adults (Arendell 1995).

On the other hand, not all risk clusters affecting the divorced directly reflect broad social or economic trends. For example, another risk cluster among divorced adults would be predivorce history of extreme dependence, high salience of marriage as a component of predivorce identity, and severe conflict with former spouse. In this case, remedies lie in development of individual strengths and improved relationship with the former spouse. Whether risks stem primarily from lack of economic opportunity, or from dysfunctional ways of relating, it is not divorce per se that leads to difficulty, but sequelae that can be modified.

RESILIENCIES AND PROTECTIVE FACTORS

While risk factors increase the possibility of negative divorce outcomes for adults and youth, protective factors buffer the impact of risk factors. Protective factors create the possibility of resilience, i.e., coping, and recovery from trauma (Gilgun 1996; Saleebey 1996; Smith and Carlson 1997). For example, although diminished parenting is a serious risk factor for offspring of divorced parents, other people in the family and external environment (e.g., grandparents, teachers) can moderate this effect. As a result of association with these people, parental divorce may lead youth to develop early maturity (Hines 1997) and the ability to form connections outside the family, rather than the negative divorce outcomes described earlier (e.g., low educational attainment, low level of labor force participation).

Protective Factors for Adults. *Individual*-level factors that can protect against negative divorce outcomes include self-esteem, an optimistic and independent temperament, vocational skills, and, for women, young age (Bogolub 1995). Sometimes ethnic heritage may generate helpful individual attitudes. For example, the long history of earning a living among African American women may inspire continued independence at stressful times (Hatchett et al. 1995).

Family-level protective factors include cooperation with the former spouse (Buchanan et al. 1996; Whiteside 1998) and the financial, concrete (e.g., child care), and emotional support of extended family. For younger divorced adults, such support is typically provided by parents and other relatives in the parents' generation. For middle-aged and older divorced adults, it is typically provided by grown or near-grown children. Overall, such extended family support is generally more intense among members of nonwhite ethnic groups than among white people, with residential doubling up (and the associated reduction in housing costs) a stronger possibility among nonwhite (Lee and Aytac 1998). *External*-level protective factors include employment that is financially and personally rewarding, adequate housing, adequate child care, friends, new sexual partners, and involvement in community activities perceived as rewarding.

Protective Factors for Children and Adolescents. For offspring of divorced parents, *individual*-level protective factors include self-esteem, and an optimistic or independent temperament (Hines 1997). The cognitive ability to understand parental divorce as an adult decision not caused by offspring misdeeds is also helpful, although this ability is not generally present until early adolescence (Hines 1997). Interests (e.g., sports, music) can deflect youth's emotional energy from parents' troubles to enjoyment and age-appropriate development; due to environmental deficits, low-income children may not have sufficient opportunity to develop these.

On the *family* level, the most important protective factor is a loving relationship with at least one caring, involved parent (Hines 1997; Kirby and Fraser 1997). Note that although the input from a second parent is helpful, a strong relationship with one parent is sufficient. If both parents are involved, their ability to create consistent environments across households and to refrain from disparaging each other is critical (Buchanan et al. 1996; Whiteside 1998). Siblings and extended family can also be supportive, sometimes partially compensating for parental deficit (Bogolub 1995; Hines 1997). Extended family is particularly likely to participate extensively in child rearing in black and Hispanic families (Lee and Aytac 1998).

On the *external* level, depending on the youngster's age, appropriate after-school care or activities can make a difference (Schwartz and Kaslow 1997). So can friends, friends' families, quality schools, interested teachers, and housing that is not overcrowded. In the African American community, the church has long promoted pro-social behavior for youth by providing formal programs, and informal contact with caring adults (Rivers and Scanzoni 1997; Tatum 1997). In the Hispanic community, children of divorced parents may benefit from contact with nonblood kin created through the cultural institution of *compadrazgo* (godparenting) (Longres 1995).

PROGRAMS AND SOCIAL WORK CONTRIBUTIONS

For many years, social workers in family agencies have worked to minimize risk factors and maximize protective factors among those affected by marital rupture, by providing direct service to individuals (children, adolescents, and adults), divorcing/divorced couples, and divorcing/divorced families. Intervention typically focuses on clients' life tasks (e.g., applying for child support, job hunting), emotional struggles (e.g., mourning of divorce-related losses) and postdivorce relationships (e.g., formation of coparental partnerships between former spouses) (Anderson 1999; Bogolub 1997). Intervention often involves advocacy (e.g., for clients seeking child care or public assistance), and collaboration with other professionals (e.g., teachers, lawyers) as well as client contact (Bogolub 1995; Smith and Carlson 1997).

Additionally, family agency social workers provide mutual aid groups for divorced adults, addressing topics such as custodial parenting (Strand 1995), noncustodial parenting (Babcock 1997; Greif 1997a), finances, and loneliness and the fear of risking (Shulman 1994). Mutual aid groups for children of divorced parents address topics such as mastery of loss and coping with changed family relationships (Bonkowski 1997) and are offered in both agency and school settings (Bonkowski 1997; Smith and Carlson 1997). Beyond their overt content, these adults' and children's groups reduce members' isolation. They also normalize the situation of divorced families, thus raising group members' self-esteem (Strand 1995).

In recent years, education for divorcing adults has proliferated (Geasler and Blaisure 1998; Gentry 1997; Landers 1996). As a form of family life education (FLE), divorce education conveys knowledge (e.g., postdivorce reactions typical of adults and children), skills (e.g., management of ex-spousal and parent-child conflict), and attitudes (e.g., respect for divorced families) (Riley 1995). The overall goal is to influence parent behavior and prevent lasting negative outcomes in children (Bussey 1996). Increasingly, parallel educational programs are being developed for children and adolescents, again with the goal of lessening the impact of family disruption (e.g., Davenport, Gordy, and Miranda 1993; Short 1998).

Divorce education is essentially preventive and emphasizes delivery of prescribed content (Bussey 1996). It is not a substitute for individual, family, or group intervention. While divorce education can often prevent negative outcomes in families with a midrange level of divorce-engendered conflict, it is unlikely to help high-conflict families, who need more intensive assistance (Landers 1996; Masheter 1997; Whiteside 1998).

While divorce education is carried out by members of various professions, social workers are frequently the providers (Landers 1996). Often, a prepared curriculum with specific objectives is employed (Geasler and Blaisure 1998). Divorce education programs are typically single sessions of several hours, although some are longer, and take place over several weeks (Landers 1996). Divorce education can be voluntary, court-urged, or court-mandated (Fischer 1997; Gentry 1997; Landers 1996).

Overall, we note a diverse and fairly responsive array of services for divorcing and divorced families. Nonetheless, programming for divorced families could be even more responsive. For example, busy agency-based social workers assisting custodial mothers and offspring are sometimes tempted to skip the time-consuming task of outreach to noncustodial fathers (Bogolub 1995); the initiation of agency practices crediting workers for such efforts might result in more attention to these fathers and better services to families. Likewise, with regard to divorce education, Bussey (1996) suggests that programs need better integration of content about "nondivorce" problem areas that frequently impact the lives of the divorced and their offspring (e.g., substance abuse, child maltreatment [Bussey 1996], and domestic violence [Carlson 1997; Kurz 1995]). Like all programming, programming for the divorced can benefit from ongoing revision and should be seen as evolving rather than as a finished product.

ASSESSMENT AND INTERVENTIONS

Whether working with an individual, couple, or family, the social worker conducts a family-centered, ecosystems assessment. Specifically, the worker gathers data about the divorcing/divorced spouses, offspring, maternal and paternal grandparents, other maternal and paternal extended family members, significant others, remarried family members, and the social and physical environments. Thus, consistent with the definition of divorce as multifaceted, the social worker employs a wide-angle lens that extends vertically, over two, three, or even four generations, and horizontally, across households, employment sites, schools, neighborhoods, and so forth. This enables the social worker to assess a broad range of individual, family, and external risk factors (e.g., history of extreme individual sensitivity, custodial parent's time poverty, dangerous neighborhood) and individual, family, and external protective factors (e.g., optimism; supportive grandparents; caring, competent teachers) that she or he can refer to in planning intervention. Further, use of the strengths perspective and a normative-adaptive view of divorce enable the social worker to give protective factors sufficient attention and to avoid the potential mistake of overemphasizing deficits (Gentry 1997; Saleebey 1996; Whiteside 1998).

Throughout assessment, close attention is given to adult and offspring reactions to economic decline (e.g., maternal guilt; adolescent worry, and consequent initiation of after-school employment), and to adult and offspring reactions to divorce-generated family shifts (e.g., maternal anger at a son who physically resembles a father who "just walked out," a daughter's extreme passivity during visits with her father). Such reactions may constitute, or reflect, additional risk and protective factors that warrant the social worker's attention. Further, close attention is given to ethnicity as both a risk factor (e.g., long-standing employment discrimination against African American men [Lawson and Thompson 1995]), and a protective factor (e.g., tradition of employment among African American women [Hatchett et al. 1995]).

Divorce has been defined as a *process* that unfolds over time (Carter and McGoldrick 1999; Schwartz and Kaslow 1997). In assessment, the social worker considers where in that process the clients are: contemplating divorce, living through it, or accommodating themselves to a postdivorce reality. Even though these phases of the divorce process overlap, and people vary in their experience of them, clients at each phase do tend to experience unique issues and emotions.

Before the actual departure of one spouse, key issues are intense marital conflict and contemplation of separation. For adults, ambivalence about divorce (Ahrons 1999), guilt about anticipated consequences of separation for family members (Ahrons 1999), and fear of the future (Bogolub 1995) are common. Among offspring (particularly younger offspring), ambivalence about parental separation is unlikely, except in cases of severe parental brutality. However, aversion to the idea of parental separation, and anxiety, are common (Bogolub 1995).

During the massive concrete upheaval of the actual physical separation, key issues include the departure of one parent, financial decline, residential moves, employment changes, school changes, and legal involvement (Bogolub 1995). Many authors (e.g., Buchanan et al. 1996; Carter and McGoldrick 1999; Schwartz and Kaslow 1997; Whiteside 1998) suggest that the divorce transition takes at least two years to complete. Throughout this period, among both adults and offspring, negative feelings such as loss, loneliness, anger, and disorientation may alternate with positive feelings such as relief and independence (Ahrons 1999).

Eventually, people accommodate to an altered life. As previously indicated, although adults frequently remarry, they frequently redivorce too, so remarriage should not be considered the solution to divorce-engendered difficulties (Carter and Mc-Goldrick 1999). For both adults and offspring, negative divorce-engendered feelings often fade, while positive feelings often become stronger. However, a minority of adults, mainly middle-aged and older women left by their former husbands, do remain chronically depressed postdivorce. Likewise, a minority of youngsters experiencing parental divorce arrive at adulthood burdened by chronic feelings of anger, inadequacy, or confusion about relationships (Bogolub 1995).

When assessing *mutual aid groups* and *divorce education seminars,* social workers generally cannot deliberately gather comprehensive data on each client. Rather, they integrate information offered by referral sources with information that emerges during client contact. Then they conceptualize risk and protective factors likely to be present in the unit where they intervene.

For example, to assess school-based mutual aid groups, social workers use information from teachers and guidance counselors, and what children reveal as they discuss how they cope with parental divorce. Then workers conceptualize risk factors that should be ameliorated (e.g., lethargic attitude to homework among some group members, stemming from divorce-engendered depression), and protective factors that should be maximized (e.g., warm relationships with grandparents among some group members). Likewise, in divorce education seminars for parents, social workers use information from referring judges or mental health professionals, and what seminar participants reveal as they discuss how they handle their children during divorce. In this case, because of the structured nature of divorce education, assessment of risk factors (e.g., substance abuse history among some participants) and protective factors (e.g., history of benefiting from mental health services among some participants) may not always affect seminar content. However, it can affect a social worker's presentation of content. It can also heighten the worker's comfort level with participants and promote effective postseminar referrals.

To assist people facing their own or their parents' divorce, the social worker relies on assessments incorporating ecosystems and phase-of-divorce-process conceptualizations. Such assessments facilitate interventions that (1) create, support, or enhance protective factors and (2) minimize risk factors, or decrease client exposure to them.

For example, people contemplating marital separation—particularly women locked into abusive marriages—often display protracted indecision. In these cases, the social worker is respectful and patient, which can build the client's self-esteem (Anderson 1999). The social worker may also help clients identify protective factors (e.g., parenting skills, vocational skills) that they themselves think will help them face the future (McQuaide and Ehrenreich 1997).

If marital separation will create deficits in the areas of safety, income, or housing, the social worker helps the client make plans to minimize these risks. Along these lines, social workers frequently refer clients for orders of protection, legal services, vocational training, public assistance, and shelters for domestic violence victims. When clients need these services to proceed with marital separation, and do not speak English, or are very frightened, social workers may advocate as well as refer. They may even accompany a client to an unfamiliar location, such as family court, where orders of protection are obtained (Bogolub 1995). When traditional gender roles (e.g., among Hispanic or Asian women) inhibit the proactive behavior necessary for a woman to pursue these services, the social worker helps the female client consider her conflict and resolve it for herself.

Moreover, using ecosystems thinking, the social worker may work to remediate gaps or weaknesses in the network of resources for divorcing clients. For example, work with divorcing clients may make a social worker aware of a lack of shelters for victims of domestic violence, or a lack of police or judicial responsiveness to women using orders of protection. Likewise, awareness of women's experiences with the limitations of public assistance under "welfare reform" may raise troubling questions as to whether women, including those married to violent or substance-abusing men, are becoming more reluctant to consider marital dissolution due to concerns about postdivorce income (Kurz 1995). In such cases, the social worker may want to work through organizations such as the National Association of Social Workers for the modified funding allocations, changed attitudes, and revised legislation that could increase the feasibility of exit from seriously troubled marriages.

Once physical separation occurs, much intervention focuses on relationships within the new households created by marital disruption. When working with custodial parents and their offspring, social workers communicate the view that the divorced family is not deficient or substandard. They do this, in part, by recognizing specific family strengths (Anderson 1999; Proctor, Davis, and Vosler 1995); for example, employed custodial mothers of young children often demonstrate impressive physical stamina and organizational abilities.

When a custodial parent's diminished parenting ability is a concern during the divorce transition period (Buchanan et al. 1996), the social worker strengthens that parent's family executive role (Anderson 1999). Specifically, the social worker helps a custodial parent meet challenges such as discipline, affection, appropriate demands on offspring of different ages, living on reduced income, and maintenance of contact with schools within the constraints of a time-poor life. When working with custodial fathers on parenting, the social worker may rely on cognitively based approaches, such as psychoeducation, since men may be somewhat uncomfortable with approaches emphasizing emotion (Bogolub 1995). A complementary approach to diminished parenting is to encourage youngsters' connections with supportive adults in the extended family, school, and neighborhood (Anderson 1999; Bogolub 1995).

When conflict between former spouses creates risk for both adults and children (Curtner-Smith 1995; Whiteside 1998), the social worker, insofar as possible, helps former spouses develop a business-like, cooperative relationship. She or he also helps them refrain from using offspring to express emotions such as anger or attachment. To further reduce the impact of ex-spousal conflict, youngsters are encouraged to pursue their own interests, and—if they are old enough—their growing independence from parents' difficulties.

When assisting divorced families, social workers often reach out to noninvolved noncustodial parents (overwhelmingly fathers), who may not pay child support, or visit their offspring (Anderson 1999, Bogolub 1997). The purposes are to facilitate interparental communication, and to heighten paternal involvement with offspring. However, social workers should not reach out to all noninvolved noncustodial fathers (Curtner-Smith 1995); both children and their mothers are better off without men with a history of violence or sexual abuse.

Although intervention during the divorce transition generally emphasizes problem solving and the reworking of family relationships, mourning of divorce-generated losses (e.g., loss of life shared with the absent spouse/parent, loss of social status) may also be part of the help clients need to move ahead (Anderson 1999; Bogolub

1997). Bereavement issues may be buried or readily accessible; many adults, adolescents, and children utilize professional assistance as they express, control, and ultimately let go of divorce-generated pain.

Most adults and children weather the divorce transition well; in general, the greater the time since the divorce, the less the need for professional assistance (Bogolub 1995). When assisting the minority of women who remain chronically depressed postdivorce because of loneliness and/or financial deprivation that are likely to persist, social workers use limited goals around development of social networks and employment options. They also help clients to "see the glass as half full, rather than half empty." When assisting the minority of children, adolescents, and young adults who remain "adrift" after their parents' divorces, social workers use skills normally applicable to troubled youth (e.g., help them verbalize rather than act out emotions, help them become interested in age-appropriate activities). At the same time, social workers attend to possible divorce-generated feelings of "difference," and to possible yearning for the nonresidential parent, and the now-defunct two-parent family (Bogolub 1995).

Social workers conducting mutual aid groups for divorced adults usually encounter clients divorced within the last several years. Generally, they help clients support each other, and problem-solve about matters such as child rearing (custodial and noncustodial), the former spouse (e.g., coparental relationship, lingering anger or attachment, conflict around child support payments), employment, and new relationships. Throughout, awareness of divorced adults' current real-world environment (e.g., changed child support enforcement procedures, the challenge of new sexual relationships in the age of AIDS) increases rapport with clients, and the helpfulness of intervention. When working with divorced adults, the social worker pays particular attention to gender; once group bonds are established, both men and women may learn to understand former spouses better through the group mixed-gender experience (Greif 1997a).

When leading mutual aid groups for children and adolescents whose parents have divorced, the social worker again facilitates mutual support and problem-solving. Topics that arise in such groups include: coping with multiple life changes (e.g., departure of noncustodial parent, residential move, new school), understanding divorce-engendered feelings (e.g., anger, loss, powerlessness, yearning for parental reconciliation), communicating divorce-engendered feelings to parents, obtaining support from peers, and substance abuse prevention (Bogolub 1995; Bonkowski 1997).

When working with younger children (ages 6 through 12, approximately), parent involvement (sometimes in the form of a parallel group meeting at the same time as the offspring group) is beneficial, and the issue of what is shared with parents and what remains confidential requires explicit discussion (Bonkowski 1997). Similarly, if the group is school based, the issue of what is shared with teachers and/or other professional staff, and what remains confidential, requires explicit discussion.

When leading groups for divorced parents, or their offspring, the social worker must work with social agency or school personnel as well as clients. Specifically, the social worker needs to plan groups, obtain referrals, and carry out ongoing communication with professional staff in a way that demonstrates respect for other agency or school programs (Gitterman 1994). If this work does not occur, referrals will dwindle, and eventually it will not be possible to conduct the groups.

When leading curriculum-based, short-term (frequently one meeting) divorce education seminars for adults, the social worker uses varied communication skills to deliver content in areas such as developmental needs of children, cooperative co-parenting, and books and community resources for the divorced (Geasler and Blaisure 1998). These skills include minilecture, video presentation, guided group discussion, and role play (Bussey 1996; Fischer 1997; Geasler and Blaisure 1998). When providing divorce education to children on topics such as family changes and self-esteem, the social worker uses many of the same communication skills, as well as age-appropriate activities such as drama, drawing, and creation of stories about divorce (Bonkowski 1997; Davenport et al. 1993). If an extant curriculum is used to avoid "reinventing the wheel," social workers may receive training in content and communication from the organization that created the curriculum (Geasler and Blaisure 1998).

In contrast to mutual aid groups, divorce education seminars generally require the social worker to move efficiently through prescribed content. However, traditional social work skills (e.g., creating a nonjudgmental climate, working with mandated clients, identifying mental illness in a group member, making referrals for more intensive intervention) clearly heighten the social worker's proficiency as a divorce educator.

Parallel to mutual aid groups, divorce education requires social workers to work not only with clients, but also with those who refer clients, or help them on an ongoing basis. When attempting to establish a divorce education program, a social worker might enumerate advantages to professionals such as agency executives, boards of directors, judges, lawyers, and school administrators. For example, divorce education has repeatedly been described as helpful in clients' exit reports from various programs (Bussey 1996). Further, divorce education is thought to promote prompt settlements ("Calling a Truce" 1998) and decrease litigation for divorcing couples (Fischer 1997), thus easing the burden on families, on courts, and eventually, on taxpayers.

ILLUSTRATION AND DISCUSSION

Children Cope with Divorce (CCWD) is a four-hour, one-session divorce education program for adults. It was created in 1988 by Families First, an agency in Atlanta, Georgia, after Cobb County judges decided to mandate attendance at an educational seminar for both parties in divorce cases. After success in Cobb County, Families First began offering training to professionals from other agencies interested in leading the seminar (Fischer 1997).

Currently, CCWD is presented annually to over 8 percent of U.S. divorcing adults with children under 18 (Fischer 1997). Training is offered both in Atlanta, and on-site, at local agencies ("Training Options Available" 1998). As of January 1998, more than 170 providers (e.g., social work agencies) in thirty-eight states were licensed to provide the seminar. Materials for Roller-coasters, a companion divorce education program for children, have also been developed (Weaver 1998).

A CCWD seminar is led by two master's level professionals, male and female. Topics covered are: (1) dimensions of the divorce process (emotional, coparental, legal, economic, community, and psychological), (2) how children react to divorce, (3) child adjustment and parents' role, (4) new family structures, and (5) getting help when needed. Lecture, video presentation, guided group discussion, and role play are used (Fischer 1997).

Linda A., a social worker, reported how CCWD was implemented in a county in a midwestern state in the mid-1990s. An area judge felt a court-connected educational program would benefit divorcing families. The judge and a law clerk contacted Agency B, a local family service agency that responded positively to the idea of such a program. They also contacted Families First. Then, the judge appeared before a local governing body and was successful in obtaining funds for the Families First training of Agency B staff. A major national charity that funded the agency agreed to provide additional funds once CCWD actually began. Parallel to the original Georgia situation, the divorce education program was initiated because of a recognized community need for agency services.

After receiving training, and doing outreach work to build awareness of the program, Linda and George C., another social worker, led the seminar on various occasions. Referrals came from local agencies and from judges. Generally, clients were urged to attend by judges, although they were not required to do so. Advance registration was necessary, and an attempt was made to keep the number of participants in any seminar between twelve and fifteen. A fee of $30 per attendee was charged, but a sliding scale ensured that no one was turned away because of inability to pay. As per Families First policy, each participant received a manual to take home. In part because of the local demographics, most participants were white. A broad range of income levels was represented. Former spouses were discouraged from attending the same seminar. Grandparents and stepparents were permitted to attend.

As previously noted, a social worker's ability to assess increases his or her comfort with seminar participants, and the ability to connect with them, even though the prescribed seminar curriculum remains stable. In one instance, a man arrived for a seminar drunk. Linda took him aside and told him gently but firmly that it appeared he had been drinking. She then explained he would not be able to attend today's seminar. She also told him that his interest in the seminar was important, and she hoped he would come back another time. Her assessment skill led her to accept rather than deny the alcohol abuse, so that the integrity of the day's seminar was preserved for other participants. It also led her to avoid unnecessary harshness toward the man, as she kept in mind a strength (interest in attendance), not just the inebriation. Further, employing an ecosystems perspective, she explored the possibility of obtaining a guard for CCWD meetings, in the event that future substance-abusing participants might be violent.

At other times, Linda used her assessment skills during seminar breaks. Once, she noticed women exchanging phone numbers to form a follow-up group of their own. Another time, she was approached by a female participant who told her it was wonderful to be in the group because she never knew before that there were men who communicated by talking rather than hitting. From these cases, Linda concluded that separate and apart from curriculum content, the experience of being with other people in the CCWD seminar catalyzed personal growth.

As previously noted, the social worker leading a divorce education seminar relies not just on just on curriculum delivery skills (e.g., lecture, guided discussion), but also on traditional social work intervention skills. In this regard, Linda felt that her ability to be nonjudgmental and draw people out served her well. She felt the discussions, while not excessively personal (inappropriate for an educational seminar), sometimes had particular emotional depth. In one case, she elicited a man's response to curriculum content on business-like communication between former spouses. He stated that his wife had left him, and attempting to conduct such communication was "the hardest thing I ever did." He also stated that "I had to do it for my son." Responding to the same content, a custodial father (a police officer) shared that communicating with his ex-wife was difficult because he was not "the communication type," but now he realized that this was necessary for "the kids." In each case, Linda had reached out verbally and nonverbally, without being excessively forceful. Her social work skills led to emotional disclosures that seemed to demonstrate that the seminar content was being absorbed.

Linda also felt the skill of self-awareness heightened her ability to facilitate the seminars. For instance, on those rare occasions when she found curriculum content or a participant's response to be upsetting, she relied on her coleader to take charge. Likewise, because of the intensity of discussing fundamental life changes with people one has never met before, she also relied on her coleader for "debriefing" sessions after each seminar. This allowed her to discharge potentially counterproductive emotion, and to clarify ideas for future meetings.

With its emphasis on reducing interparental conflict and preventing harm to offspring, CCWD reminds us that divorce per se is not inherently detrimental to children. That is, like all good practice with disrupted families, CCWD is built on the premise that while divorce has a destructive potential, this potential can be decreased through intervention.

Further, CCWD reminds us of the multimodal nature of social work practice. Ideally, a social worker does not view divorce education (or any form of FLE) as a discrete endeavor. Rather, she integrates divorce education with other modalities. For example, she may refer an adult client whom she sees in family sessions to CCWD, expecting that CCWD will supplement family intervention. Alternately, she may begin intervention with a client referred by a CCWD leader. In either case, even if she does not lead CCWD seminars herself, she must discuss them knowledgeably and respectfully, as part of her use of a family or individual modality.

The experience of Agency B with CCWD raises the issue of cooperation between social workers and external systems (e.g., family courts, schools). Families First, which developed the original CCWD program, and Agency B, which implemented CCWD, were approached by progressive judges. However, in other cases, social workers reach out to judges and their staffs, and make court personnel aware of extant or planned divorce education programs.

Outreach to the family court system has particular importance. Divorcing adults often have difficulty focusing on children's concerns and may not seek divorce education when they need it (Fischer 1997). Usually, the judges with whom divorcing adults have contact can mandate or urge divorce education, but they are not required to do so. Thus, social work encouragement of judicial referrals becomes critical. When encouraging judicial referrals, social workers should remind judges of their power to help, and point out that widespread mandating does not simply cause adults to attend classes, but may actually generate a positive attitude (rather than a feeling of stigma); Bussey (1996) found that when "all parents from a certain judge's court are referred, no one parent feels singled out; the mandate to attend may . . . normalize the issue" (146).

When promoting divorce education for children (e.g., Rollercoasters), social workers reach out not just to potentially referring judges, but also to potentially referring guidance counselors and school social workers, and sometimes to the principals who oversee them. When addressing educators, social workers should mention that a child preoccupied with parental divorce may have difficulty learning, and raise the option of divorce education offered in the school. Overall, we are reminded that in addition to mentioning program benefits, social workers need to individualize outreach to potential referral sources and "speak their language."

CCWD also raises the issue of research about divorce education. For example, Families First, which originated CCWD, conducted a nationwide survey of referring judges focusing on judges' opinions on CCWD effectiveness (Fischer 1997). On a local scale, Agency B, which implemented CCWD, routinely conducted exit surveys of seminar participants focusing on participants' demographics and their opinions on CCWD effectiveness. Although methodological concerns might be raised about each study (e.g., judges' or participants' reports as the sole effectiveness rating), each study found the program to be beneficial.

Research about CCWD reminds us that research on divorce education (or any form of FLE) can be used for two broad purposes. First, findings can be shared with funding sources and referral sources, to demonstrate why a program should be initiated or continued. For example, the summarized findings of Agency B exit surveys, which demonstrate a high degree of satisfaction and learning, were sent to the office of the judge who initiated CCWD programming at Agency B.

Second, research findings can be used to improve programs. For example, in his survey of judges who refer to CCWD, Fischer (1997) found several suggestions arose frequently: an advanced program for adults who have completed CCWD, a program for separating couples who have never been married, and a program for children. The development of Rollercoasters suggests that Families First may have used Fischer's findings when expanding its offerings.

In a like vein, it appears that future research could improve divorce education by increasing its attention to diversity; a perusal of current divorce education programs indicates a pervasive lack of attention to social class, ethnicity, and gays and lesbians. Many intriguing questions arise. For example, even though CCWD has been well received, might satisfaction rates increase with insertion of material on the postdivorce material situation of blue-collar and poor families? Or material on the disclosures to offspring about sexual orientation by formerly married homosexuals? In the area served by Agency B, was local demographics the only reason a very small number of African American adults attended CCWD, especially given the high divorce rate among African Americans? Would insertion of ethnic-sensitive content into CCWD increase African American attendance rates? Do judges refer African American adults to CCWD less frequently than they refer white adults? Are there any African American judges? If so, what is their referral pattern? Answers to such questions could lead to important modifications of (1) divorce education materials and (2) efforts to initiate divorce education.

CONCLUSION

Divorce is common, and likely to remain so. As a result, social work practice with divorcing and divorced families will continue to be widespread. While based on time-honored social work essentials (e.g., ecosystems assessment, intervention encompassing outreach to initially uninvolved family members), practice with disrupted families is continuously evolving. Promising current developments include divorce mediation, divorce education, and increased attention to client strengths and client diversity.

Practice with divorcing and divorced families demands that we view this population in a broad context. Both social norms (e.g., those governing acceptable male behavior toward women and children) and social policies (e.g., the restrictions of "welfare reform," which may cause some to reject consideration of exit from severely troubled marriages) must be considered. This broad perspective encourages the social and political action that augments direct practice, and improves life for divorcing and divorced families, as well as other vulnerable populations.

Acknowledgment

The author wishes to thank Marian Bussey, M.S.W., for contributing to this chapter by generously sharing information about Family Life Education (FLE) for divorced parents.

References

Acock, A. C. and D. H. Demo. 1994. *Family Diversity and Well-Being.* Thousand Oaks, Calif.: Sage.

Ahrons, C. R. 1999. "Divorce: An Unscheduled Family Transition." In B. Carter and M. McGoldrick, eds., *The Expanded Family Life Cycle,* pp. 381–98. New York: Allyn & Bacon.

Amato, P. R. 1996. "Explaining the Intergenerational Transmission of Divorce." *Journal of Marriage and the Family* 58(3):628–40.

Amato, P. R. and S. J. Rogers. 1997. "A Longitudinal Study of Marital Problems and Subsequent Divorce." *Journal of Marriage and the Family* 59(3):612–24.

Anderson, C. M. 1999. "Single-Parent Families: Strengths, Vulnerabilities, and Interventions." In B. Carter and M. McGoldrick, eds., *The Expanded Family Life Cycle,* pp. 399–416. New York: Allyn & Bacon.

Arendell, T. 1995. *Fathers and Divorce.* Thousand Oaks, Calif.: Sage.

Babcock, G. M. 1997. "Stigma, Identity Dissonance, and the Nonresidential Mother." *Journal of Divorce and Remarriage* 28(1/2):139–56.

Bee, H. 1994. *Lifespan Development.* New York: HarperCollins.

Bogolub, E. B. 1995. *Helping Families Through Divorce: An Eclectic Approach.* New York: Springer.

——. 1997. "Divorce." In R. L. Edwards, ed., *Encyclopedia of Social Work* (supplement to 19th ed.), pp. 91–101. Washington, D.C.: National Association of Social Workers Press.

Bohannon, P. 1970. "The Six Stations of Divorce." In P. Bohannon, ed., *Divorce and After,* pp. 29–55. Garden City, N.Y.: Doubleday.

Bonkowski, S. 1997. "Group Work with Children of Divorce." In G. L. Greif and P. H. Ephross, eds., *Group Work with Populations at Risk,* pp. 94–104. New York: Oxford.

Buchanan, C. M., E. E. Maccoby, and S. M. Dornbusch. 1996. *Adolescents after Divorce.* Cambridge, Mass.: Harvard University Press.

Bussey, M. 1996. "Impact of Kids First Seminar for Divorcing Parents: A Three-Year Follow-up." *Journal of Divorce and Remarriage* 26(1/2):129–49.

"Calling a Truce on Divorce Warfare." 1998. *New York Times,* December 31, p. A18.

Cancian, M. and D. R. Meyer. 1998. "Who Gets Custody?" *Demography* 35(2):147–57.

Carlson, B. 1997. "A Stress and Coping Approach to Intervention with Abused Women." *Family Relations* 46(3):291–98.

Carter, B. and M. McGoldrick. 1999. "The Divorce Cycle: A Major Variation in the American Family Life Cycle." In B. Carter and M. McGoldrick, eds., *The Expanded Family Life Cycle,* pp. 373–80. New York: Allyn & Bacon.

Catlett, B. S. and P. C. McKenry. 1996. "Implications of Feminist Scholarship for the Study of Women's Postdivorce Economic Disadvantage." *Family Relations* 45(1):91–97.

Causey, K. A. and C. Duran-Aydintug. 1997. "Tendency to Stigmatize Lesbian Mothers in Custody Cases." *Journal of Divorce and Remarriage* 28(1/2):171–82.

Curtner-Smith, M. E. 1995. "Assessing Children's Visitation Needs with Divorced Noncustodial Fathers." *Families in Society* 76(6):341–48.

Dail, P. W. and A. A. Thieman. 1996. "Improving Parental Partnerships in Low-Income Families As a Means for Increasing Noncustodial Parental Compliance with Child Support Orders: A Research Report." *Journal of Family Issues* 17(5):688–701.

Davenport, M. A., P. L. Gordy, and N. A. Miranda. 1993. *Children of Divorce.* Milwaukee: Families International.

De Garmo, D. S. and G. C. Kitson. 1996. "Identity Relevance and Disruption As Predictors of Psychological Distress for Widowed and Divorced Women." *Journal of Marriage and the Family* 58(4):983–97.

Demo, D. H. and A. C. Acock. 1996. "Singlehood, Marriage, and Remarriage: The Effects of Family Structure and Family Relationships on Mothers' Well-being." *Journal of Family Issues* 17(3):388–407.

Dickinson, N. S. 1997. "Federal social legislation from 1994 to 1997." In R. L. Edwards, ed., *Encyclopedia of Social Work* (supplement to 19th ed.), pp. 125–31. Washington, D.C.: National Association of Social Workers Press.

Doherty, W. J., E. F. Kouneski, and M. F. Erickson. 1998. "Responsible Fathering: An Overview and Conceptual Framework." *Journal of Marriage and the Family* 60(2):277–92.

Emery, R. 1995. "Divorce Mediation: Negotiating Agreements and Renegotiating Relationships." *Family Relations* 44(4):377–83.

Fine, M. A. and D. R. Fine. 1994. "An Examination and Evaluation of Recent Changes in Divorce Laws in Five Western Countries: The Critical Role of Values." *Journal of Marriage and the Family* 56(2):249–64.

Fischer, R. L. 1997. "The Impact of an Educational Seminar for Divorcing Parents: Results from a National Survey of Family Court Judges." *Journal of Divorce and Remarriage* 28(1/2):35–48.

Fox, G. L. and R. F. Kelly. 1995. "Determinants of Child Custody: Arrangements at Divorce." *Journal of Marriage and the Family* 57(3):693–708.

Ganong, L. H. and M. Coleman. 1994. *Remarried Family Relationships.* Thousand Oaks, Calif.: Sage.

Geasler, M. J. and K. R. Blaisure. 1998. "A Review of Divorce Education Program Materials." *Family Relations* 47(2):167–75.

Gentry, D. B. 1997. "Including Children in Divorce Mediation and Education: Potential Benefits and Cautions." *Families in Society* 78(3):307–15.

Gilgun, J. F. 1996. "Human Development and Adversity in Ecological Perspective, Part I: A Conceptual Framework." *Families in Society* 77(7):395–402.

Gitterman, A. 1994. "Developing a New Group Service: Strategies and Skills." In A. Gitterman and L. Shulman, eds., *Mutual Aid Groups, Vulnerable Populations, and the Life Cycle,* pp. 59–77. New York: Columbia University Press.

Greif, G. L. 1997a. "Group Work with Noncustodial Parents." In G. L. Greif and P. H. Ephross, eds., *Group Work with Populations at Risk,* pp. 84–93. New York: Oxford.

——. 1997b. "Working with Noncustodial Mothers." *Families in Society* 78(1):46–52.

Hatchett, S. J., J. Veroff, and E. Douvan. 1995. "Marital Instability Among Black and White Couples in Early Marriage." In M. B. Tucker and C. Mitchell-Kernan, eds., *The Decline in Marriage Among African Americans: Causes, Consequences, and Policy Implications,* pp. 177–218. New York: Russell Sage Foundation.

Hiedemann, B., O. Suhomlinova, and A. M. O'Rand. 1998. "Economic Independence, Economic Status, and Empty Nest in Midlife Marital Disruption." *Journal of Marriage and the Family* 60(1):219–31.

Hines, A. M. 1997. "Divorce-Related Transitions, Adolescent Development, and the Role of the Parent-Child Relationship: A Review of the Literature." *Journal of Marriage and the Family* 59(2):375–88.

Johnson, G. B. and M. Wahl. 1995. "Families: Demographic Shifts." In R. L. Edwards and J. G. Hopps, eds., *Encyclopedia of Social Work,* 19th ed., vol. 2, pp. 936–41. Washington, D.C.: National Association of Social Workers Press.

Kirby, L. D. and M. W. Fraser. 1997. "Risk and Resilience in Childhood." In M. W. Fraser, ed., *Risk and Resilience in Childhood: An Ecological Perspective,* pp. 10–33. Washington, D.C.: National Association of Social Workers Press.

Kissman, K. 1997. "Noncustodial Fatherhood: Research Trends and Issues." *Journal of Divorce and Remarriage* 28(1/2):77–88.

Kurz, D. 1995. *For Richer for Poorer: Mothers Confront Divorce.* New York: Routledge.

Landers, S. 1996, July. "Divorce 101: Parents Given a Primer." *National Association of Social Workers News,* p. 3.

Lawson, E. J. and A. Thompson. 1995. "Black Men Make Sense of Marital Distress and Divorce: An Exploratory Study." *Family Relations* 44(2):211–18.

——. 1996. "Black Men's Perceptions of Divorce-related Stressors and Strategies for Coping with Divorce." *Journal of Family Issues* 17(2):249–73.

Lee, Y. J. and I. A. Aytac. 1998. "Intergenerational Financial Support among Whites, African Americans, and Latinos." *Journal of Marriage and the Family* 60(2):426–41.

Longres, J. 1995. "Hispanics: Overview." In R. L. Edwards and J. G. Hopps, eds., *Encyclopedia of Social Work,* 19th ed., vol. 2, pp. 1214–22. Washington, D.C.: National Association of Social Workers Press.

Masheter, C. 1997. "Healthy and Unhealthy Friendship and Hostility Between Ex-spouses." *Journal of Marriage and the Family* 59(2):463–75.

McGoldrick, M. and B. Carter. 1999. "Remarried Families." In B. Carter and M. McGoldrick, eds., *The Expanded Family Life Cycle,* pp. 417–35. New York: Allyn & Bacon.

McLanahan, S. and G. Sandefur. 1994. *Growing Up with a Single Parent: What Hurts, What Helps.* Cambridge, Mass.: Harvard University Press.

McQuaide, S. and J. H. Ehrenreich. 1997. "Assessing Client Strengths." *Families in Society* 78(2):201–12.

Meyer, D. R. and J. Bartfield. 1998. "Patterns of Child Support Compliance in Wisconsin." *Journal of Marriage and the Family* 60(2):309–18.

Peterson, R. R. 1996. "A Re-evaluation of the Economic Consequences of Divorce." *American Sociological Review* 61(June):528–36.

Pirog-Good, M. A. and L. Amerson. 1997. "The Long Arm of Justice: The Potential for Seizing the Assets of Child Support Obligors." *Family Relations* 46(1):47–54.

Proctor, E. K., L. E. Davis, and N. Vosler. 1995. "Families: Direct Practice." In R. L. Edwards and J. G. Hopps, eds., *Encyclopedia of Social Work,* 19th ed., vol. 2, pp. 941–50. Washington, D.C.: National Association of Social Workers Press.

Rank, M. R. and L. E. Davis. 1996. "Perceived Happiness Outside of Marriage Among Black and White Spouses." *Family Relations* 45(4):435–41.

Riley, Donald P. 1995. "Family Life Education." In R. L. Edwards and J. G. Hopps, eds., *Encyclopedia of Social Work,* 19th ed., vol. 2, pp. 960–65. Washington, D.C.: National Association of Social Workers Press.

Rivers, R. M. and J. Scanzoni. 1997. "Social Families Among African Americans: Policy Implications for Children." In H. P. McAdoo, ed., *Black Families,* 3d ed., pp. 333–48. Thousand Oaks, Calif.: Sage.

Robertson, J. G. 1997. "Young Nonresidential Fathers Have Lower Earnings: Implications for Child Support Enforcement." *Social Work Research* 21(4):211–23.

Rosen, E. and S. Weltman. 1996. "Jewish Families: An Overview." In M. McGoldrick, J. Giordano, and J. K. Pearce, eds., *Ethnicity and Family Therapy,* pp. 611–30. New York: Guilford.

Saleebey, D. 1996. "The Strengths Perspective in Social Work Practice: Extensions and Cautions." *Social Work* 41(3):296–305.

Schwartz, L. L. and F. Kaslow. 1997. *Painful Partings: Divorce and Its Aftermath.* New York: John Wiley.

Seltzer, J. A. 1998. "Fathers by Law: Effects of Joint Legal Custody on Nonresident Fathers' Involvement with Children." *Demography* 35(2):135–46.

Short, J. L. 1998. "Evaluation of a Substance Abuse Prevention and Mental Health Promotion Program for Children of Divorce." *Journal of Divorce and Remarriage* 28(3/4):139–55.

Shulman, L. 1994. "Healing the Hurts: Single Parents." In A. Gitterman and L. Shulman, eds., *Mutual Aid Groups, Vulnerable Populations, and the Life Cycle,* pp. 349–63. New York: Columbia University Press.

Simons, R. L. and Associates. 1996. *Understanding Differences between Divorced and Intact Families.* Thousand Oaks, Calif.: Sage.

Smith, C. and B. E. Carlson. 1997. "Stress, Coping, and Resilience in Children and Youth." *Social Service Review* 71(2):231–56.

Strand, V. C. 1995. "Single Parents." In R. L. Edwards and J. G. Hopps, eds., *Encyclopedia of Social Work,* 19th ed., vol. 3, pp. 2157–64. Washington, D.C.: National Association of Social Workers Press.

Sweeney, M. 1997. "Remarriage of Women and Men After Divorce: The Role of Socioeconomic Prospects." *Journal of Family Issues* 18(5):479–502.

Tatum, B. D. 1997. "Out There Stranded? Black Families in White Communities." In H. P. McAdoo, ed., *Black Families,* 3d ed., pp. 214–33. Thousand Oaks, Calif.: Sage.

"Training Options Available As CCWD Continues Growth." 1998, Spring. *Children Cope with Divorce Newsletter,* pp. 1, 4.

Tucker, M. B. and C. Mitchell-Kernan. 1995. "African American Marital Trends in Context." In M. B. Tucker and C. Mitchell-Kernan, eds., *The Decline in Marriage Among African Americans: Causes, Consequences, and Policy Implications,* pp. 345–61. New York: Russell Sage Foundation.

Voydanoff, P. and B. W. Donnelly. 1998. "Parents' Risk and Protective Factors As Predictors of Parental Well-being and Behavior." *Journal of Marriage and the Family* 60(2):344–55.

Wallerstein, J. S. and S. Blakeslee. 1989. *Second Chances.* New York: Ticknor & Fields.

Weaver, R. M. 1998, Winter. "Message from the Executive Director of Families First." *Children Cope with Divorce Newsletter,* p. 1.

Weitzman, L. 1996. "The Economic Consequences of Divorce Are Still Unequal: Comment on Peterson." *American Sociological Review* 61(June):537–38.

Whiteside, M. F. 1998. "The Parental Alliance Following Divorce: An Overview." *Journal of Marital and Family Therapy* 24(1):3–24.

Wilcox, K. L., S. A. Wolchik, and S. L. Braver. 1998. "Predictors of Maternal Preference for Joint or Sole Legal Custody." *Family Relations* 47(1):93–101.

Yu, M. 1993. "Divorce and Culturally Different Older Women: Issues of Strategies and Interventions." *Journal of Divorce and Remarriage* 21(1/2):41–72.

19

Families in Sparsely Populated Areas

Joanne Gumpert
Joan E. Saltman

Families clustered in small towns and scattered across the countryside of rural America are frequently characterized as "The People Left Behind." Responding to a National Advisory Commission on Rural Poverty report, the Congressional Rural Caucus, in the early 1970s, focused national attention on this long neglected segment of the country (Martinez-Brawley 1981). The heightened visibility brought renewed recognition of the insufficient numbers, inferior quality, and often cultural incompatibility of social services provided in rural areas. A concomitant resurgence of interest in rural America took place within the social work profession. The Rural Social Work Caucus, formed in the early 1970s, organized more than twenty years of nationwide annual institutes focused on rural problems and practice issues, and spearheaded development of the periodical *Human Services in the Rural Environment*. This group's abiding efforts heightened the visibility of rural social problems within the professional community, initiated the development of practice models for use within this context, and generated the emergence of a literature on social work practice in the rural arena (Martinez-Brawley 1981).

Despite these concentrated efforts, the nonmetropolitan segment of the U.S. population continues to struggle with insufficient resources. Population shifts due to waves of in- and out-migration over the last thirty years, as well as more recent national and global economic changes, have added to the existing problems for many rural families. The decline in the U.S. manufacturing industry and the farm crisis of the 1980s has so affected small towns that rural people appear to be as "left behind" as they were in the 1960s (Wilkinson 1986). Myths and stereotypes of the bucolic countryside dotted with white farmhouses and red barns combined with the relative isolation and lack of visibility of rural social problems and related inability to organize on a national level continue to keep these families in the background of the nation's concerns. With limited resources, rural people continue to grapple with adaptations to rapid economic and social change in their communities while attempting to hold on to the strengths inherent of their way of life (Ginsberg 1998).

DEFINING AND EXPLAINING SPARSELY POPULATED AREAS

Although the environment in which these families live defines this population, scholars and researchers have not agreed on a single definition of rurality. The literature most frequently defines the rural context in terms of demographics, culture, and needs. Demographic definitions encompass both population size and distance from a metropolitan area (Flora et al. 1992). Federal nomenclature distinguishing between metropolitan, nonmetropolitan, and rural areas is not consistently used. The Census Bureau defines *metropolitan* as (1) core counties with one or more central cities of at least 50,000 or a total metropolitan area population of 100,000 and (2) fringe counties that are economically tied to the core counties. *Nonmetropolitan* counties are outside the boundaries of metropolitan areas and have no cities with as many as 50,000 residents. *Rural* areas are comprised of places with fewer than 2,500 residents and open territory. "Frontier" states refers to those with fewer than six persons per square mile (Bull 1998). Despite these designations by the Census Bureau, most literature uses the terms rural and nonmetropolitan interchangeably to describe any area with a population of less than 50,000 (Whitaker 1984).

Rural and urban communities are considered in relation to one another and are characterized as a continuum rather than a dichotomy (York, Denton, and Moran 1993). Generally, a population of 50,000 is consistently used in the literature for distinguishing between rural/nonmetropolitan and urban/metropolitan (Ginsberg 1998). This definition parallels Deavers's (1992) three characteristics of rurality: small-scale, low-density settlements; distances from large urban centers; and specialization of rural economies. These ecological characteristics that define rural communities can lead to differing social and cultural characteristics. Due to geographic barriers and distances and social and cultural isolation, rural populations tend to be peripheral to the larger society and are not fully integrated into centers of information, innovation, technology, and finance (Davenport and Davenport 1995).

The traditional specialization, rather than diversity, of economies in rural areas has resulted from historical competitive advantages such as ready access to natural resources, the location of large manufacturing branches or plants within a community due to inexpensive land or labor, or from the impossibility of small communities to achieve diversification of employment. Rural settings, previously characterized by traditional lifestyles symbolized by the family farm, fishing, or other land-related occupations (Whitaker 1984; York et al. 1993), are changing as the service sector becomes the largest growth area in rural economies (Davenport and Davenport 1995).

Social interaction in small communities is characterized by intimate, face-to-face relations (*gemeinshaft*) rather than formal, bureaucratic role-related social relations (*gesellshaft*) (Martinez-Brawley 1990; Flora et al. 1992). Specific cultural norms and values include positive valuing of self-reliance, local autonomy, and helping neighbors, reliance on tradition and resistance to change, respect for institutions, conservative political positions and use of informal systems to conduct the business of daily life (Buxton 1978; Davenport and Davenport 1984; Ginsberg 1976; Mermelstein and

Sundet 1995; Waltman 1986). In an empirical study of rural practitioners we found that over 80 percent of these workers encountered the rural cultural norms and values of slower pace of life, importance of informal communications, suspicion of outsiders, and suspicion of professional jargon. Over 70 percent of the respondents encountered the norms of pride in local community history, suspicion of government control, and pride in "rugged individualism" (Gumpert, Saltman, and Sauer-Jones 2000). Some might say these lists of characteristics belie the diversity among rural communities and the more rapid rates of change that have occurred over the past two decades through improved economies, influx of new populations, and technological advances (Mermelstein and Sundet 1998).

In an attempt to measure county differences in degree of rurality or isolation from the mainstream U.S. culture, Cleland (1995) developed a complex "Rurality Index." This index incorporated eleven elements identified from the literature as significant to rural counties: (1) metropolitan access via interstate highway, (2) high/low education ratio, (3) percentage employed in retail trade of all employed, (4) percentage employed in professional and related services of all employed, (5) percentage employed in public service of all employed, (6) median family income in1989, (7) persistent poverty, (8) number of local newspapers, (9) percentage of population change 1980 to 1990, (10) retirement destination, and (11) population density. The index is a step toward measuring the differences in degree of rurality and isolation among counties across the country, using criteria that reflect the shifting characteristics of rurality (Cleland 1995).

Rural practitioners constantly confront the frustration of more social problems with fewer resources than their urban counterparts (Ginsberg 1998; York et al. 1993). This reality contributes to negative perceptions of practice in small towns and problems in recruiting master's-level professionals (Sullivan, Hasler, and Otis 1993). The difficulties in recruiting professional social workers are further exacerbated by lack of recreational facilities, cultural opportunities, and stimulating social contact (Ginsberg 1993; Miller and Ray 1985; Waltman 1986; Webster and Campbell 1977). These constraining life circumstances combined with lower salaries paid by rural social service agencies have developed the general perception that practice in small communities is less than an ideal position. However, despite these limitations, we found that 90 percent of the rural practitioners in our sample enjoyed working in the rural setting. Almost two-thirds of these respondents were raised in a rural setting, although only one-third were native to the community in which they were practicing (Gumpert et al. 2000). Familiarity with rural life appears to be an important factor in professionals embracing the challenges of rural practice.

DEMOGRAPHIC PATTERNS

Life in small town America has many faces. Rural communities are diverse in relation to economic character, culture, ethnicity, distance from metropolitan center, and topography. Some are farm communities and others are not; some are old and others are newly developed. Some people living in rural communities are recent migrants from urban areas while others have lived in the same small town for generations (Coeyman 1998). Today, rural communities differ more among themselves than they do from urban areas (Flora et al. 1992).

Approximately 66 million Americans, or one-fourth of the population of the United States, live across the rural areas of this country (Riche 1996). The South, with 29.9 million people, has the largest rural population (43.6 percent), followed by the Midwest, with 17.7 million rural residents, or 26.7 percent of the rural population. Although more than three-quarters of Americans live in the country's 837 metropolitan counties, 81 percent of the nation's land is in its 2,304 nonmetropolitan counties (Edmondson 1997; Johnson and Beale 1995). About 4.8 million persons (7.25 percent) of the rural population live on farms, a percentage that has steadily declined during this century (Atkinson 1994; U.S. Bureau of the Census 1990, 1992).

Most rural families are comprised of married couples (79.2 percent) and 23 percent have children under the age of 6. Rural families average 2.1 children, with rural parents having children at a relatively young age (O'Hare 1991). Rural parents are less likely than their urban counterparts to get divorced or have a child out of wedlock, but some researchers contend the difference may be shrinking (Atkinson 1994; Lichter and Aggebeen 1992). In 1990 the earnings of rural workers, controlled for education and type of employment, were lower than earnings of urban workers. The median annual income for rural families is $27,591, with 56.8 percent of the rural women over the age of 15 in the labor force (U.S. Bureau of the Census 1992). In contrast, the median income for urban families was $37,896. The 1990 rate of rural children's poverty was 23 percent compared with the nonrural rate of 20 percent. On the whole, America's rural population has lower incomes, lower employment levels, and higher poverty levels than urban and suburban locales.

Although the predominate group is white, racial differences exist between rural areas. In 1990, 87.58 percent of all nonmetropolitan residents were white; 8.07 percent were African American; 2.19 percent were American Indian, Eskimo or Aleut; 9.43 percent were Asian or Pacific Islander; and 4.27 percent were Hispanic. The Census Bureau points out that the Hispanic category may overlap with other categories (U.S. Bureau of the Census 1990).

Since the early 1970s a new population shift within the country emerged. Reversing a trend of several decades, rural areas of the country began to grow at a more rapid rate than their urban counterparts. Families in search of a different life style began to leave the cities, moving to several nonmetropolitan areas of the country. Although this trend slowed in the late 1970s and 1980s, a nonmetropolitan renaissance appears to be continuing. Two million more Americans have been estimated to have moved from metro to nonmetro areas between 1990 and 1994, and additional evidence in the 1990s showed that rural areas have begun to experience the rapid growth they saw in the early 1970s (Baldauf 1996; O'Malley 1994).

SOCIETAL CONTEXT

Families living in rural areas profit from and pay a price for their geographic locations. Unencumbered by tall buildings, air and noise pollution, and massive crowds of people, small town and rural families have an opportunity to enjoy the beauty of the land and the wonder of nature as an integral part of their daily routine. They can experience the solace of seclusion, the sense of industry from a day's physical labor on the land and the ever-changing beauty of the countryside. The slower pace of life allows for a stronger engagement with communities, neighbors, and friends. However, the other side of this existence can be isolation, loneliness, and long travel distances over rough terrain to secure services, goods, and sometimes even human interaction, and a lifestyle that is vulnerable to the impact of severe weather conditions. Some families have known this way of life for generations and cannot conceive of wanting anything different; others describe a rural life as a constraining and unstimulating existence. And still others are leaving metropolitan areas in search of the advantages rural life can provide.

Although small town communities have moved with the entire country in the direction of urbanization, there is continued recognition that differences exist between rural and urban communities. Small community relationships are personal; a person's worth is based more on who they are rather than what they do; the culture is relatively homogenous and people have a strong attachment to each other and to the countryside. Most rural communities provide a context in which individuals are known. Individuals relate to one another through a number of overlapping roles, adhere to a unified set of norms and values, and build a sense of solidarity among community members (Flora et al. 1992). However, such a tightly structured community can make it very difficult for outsiders to move into such a system or for new ideas to be accepted (Bull 1998). In many such communities, a family must have lived within it for generations before they move to the status of old-timers rather than newcomers (Ginsberg 1993).

Impacted by national and global forces in the last two decades, many rural communities are in the midst of rapid transition. The in-migration of newcomers, often more affluent than their old-timer counterparts, has introduced different values and lifestyles. In many communities, this has led to conflict among community residents, which often is played out over such community decisions as increased school taxes, better availability of social services, and stronger environment codes. While newcomers value a fine educational system, citizens' right to quality social services, and environmental conservation, many of these changes have detrimental effects on oldtimers. Additional taxes needed to support these resources are difficult for community residents who are already selling some of the land on their homestead to make ends meet. The values underpinning these ideas are a strong intrusion into old-timers' valued sense of rugged individualism and ways of farming that have been passed on for generations.

Advances in technologies and communication systems have also brought rural residents more quickly into contact with rapidly changing ideas and lifestyles. The most recent widespread use of computers has afforded worldwide information sources to those small town residents who can afford to purchase a computer. Although these forces appear to diminish the historical isolation of rural families, not all rural residents readily embrace new urban ideas and lifestyles (Bull 1998), rather, they attempt to hold on to their traditional ways of live.

National and global economic changes have significantly affected many rural communities through boom and bust town phenomena. The decline in U.S. manufacturing as capital flows to areas of cheap labor and little regulation has robbed some small town communities of their major source for employment. Conversely, other rural communities have experienced populations explosions as people moved into towns seeking retirement communities or recreation centers (O'Malley 1994). Systemic effects related to loss of payroll taxes, property taxes, and even charitable contributions, as well as sharp increases in the demand for assistance and social services, have devastated many communities, while others have not been able to meet the increase in demands for housing, services, and the development of an infrastructure to support the expanding population (Davenport and Davenport 1998; Flora et al. 1992; Ginsberg 1998).

The farm crisis of the 1980s, symbolized by the loss of the family farm, has been connected with national and global shifts in lower agricultural prices from overproduction, reduced international demands due to world recession, plunging land values, high interest rates, high costs of farm equipment and supplies, decline in numbers of farm workers, and lack of safety net programs such as unemployment compensation for farms (Edmondson 1997). Since the early 1980s there have been more bank closings and farm foreclosures than in any time since the Great Depression, and a large number of farmers are left with dangerous debt-to-asset rations. The Office of Technology Assessment predicted that given the current trends in agricultural technology and the general economy, up to 50 percent of all family farms are in danger of becoming insolvent during the next decade (Van Hook 1990b). The impact of this change is better understood as the loss of the "farm as a way of life" not simply a "means of income."

Rural families across the country have been affected by these numerous transitions in their communities. Social problems associated with urban areas—e.g. addiction, gangs, violence, homelessness—are multiplying. Once exhibiting a traditional family structure where the husband is the breadwinner and the wife cares for the family and the home, rural family members have been forced to switch roles. As men have lost jobs in manufacturing and farming, women have had to join the workforce in service positions outside the home to keep the family financially solvent (Mermelstein and Sundet 1998). Men in small town families have had to take a second job in addition to farming to hold on to their homestead. The recent film *The Farmer's Wife* by David Sutherland aired on the Public Broadcasting System depicts the many interconnections between economic hardships and family stress in farm families: for example, the shame and reluctance to accept federal benefits, the tensions between husband and wife due to the role changes, and the decreased time for parents to spend with children. One scholar reports, "From the perspective of the inner life of youths, economic difficulties and accompanying family tensions [caused by the farm crisis] have created an intense sense of pressure as well as feelings of helplessness, loneliness, depression, and anger toward those who contributed to the economic difficulties of their families" (Van Hook 1990a).

VULNERABILITIES AND RISK FACTORS

Poverty, economic hardship, and inequality have been part of life for many residents of rural communities. In 1990, the poverty rates in nonmetropolitan areas were consistently higher than those in metropolitan areas. The results of the 1990 census identified a rural poverty rate of 16.3 percent or over 9 million poor people as compared with a metropolitan poverty rate of 12.7 percent or 24.5 million people (U.S. Bureau of the Census 1992). The total population of poor people living in rural communities is 71.3 percent white, 25 percent black, and 5.6 percent Hispanic. Of particular significance are the higher rates of poverty among persons of color who live in rural regions. The poverty rate for rural whites was 13.5 percent; for rural blacks, 40.8 percent; for rural Hispanics, 32 percent; and for rural Native Americans, at least 30 percent.

The distribution of poor rural Americans by region are the South (55.3 percent), the North Central region (25 percent), the Mountain region (8.4 percent), the Pacific region (5.3 percent), the Middle Atlantic region (4.7 percent), and New England (2.1 percent). Poor African Americans are concentrated in the South (96.8 percent). Poor rural Hispanics or Latinos are concentrated in the Southwest and on the West Coast. Poor rural Native Americans are concentrated in several areas: the Southwest, where Arizona, Colorado, New Mexico, and Utah meet; the Upper Great Plains, especially North and South Dakota; and eastern Oklahoma (Summers and Sherman 1997).

Rural poverty is related to the availability of jobs in small communities. High-paying, highly skilled jobs are frequently not found in rural areas, where schools are often of lesser quality and educational levels of residents are low. Destitution for many rural families is perpetuated since low-wage, unskilled jobs flow into these communities (Flynt 1996). Most poor rural families (64.6 percent) have at least one family member with a job; and about 25 percent have two or more members with a job. Only 17 percent of the rural poor live in female-headed families with children at home, the same proportion who live in married couple families with children at home (17.6 percent). Even if all single-parent poor rural families were lifted out of poverty, 80 percent of the rural poor would still be in poverty (Summers and Sherman 1997).

Although the metro/nonmetro poverty gap has narrowed greatly in recent years, 39 percent of rural families had near poverty incomes (under 200 percent of the poverty line in 1995), compared with 29 percent of urban families (Summers and Sherman 1997). Within the entire country, the effects on poverty on children have been especially troubling, and the effects of poverty on children in rural communities have been particularly disturbing. In 1990, the rate of rural child poverty was 23 percent compared with a nonrural rate of 20 percent (Flynt 1996). With the advent of the 1996 welfare reform measures, the welfare caseloads have dropped sharply. However, the rates of child poverty and extreme poverty in urban and rural areas have increased as welfare allotments have been lowered or abolished and potential wage earners are able to obtain only low-income employment (Flynt 1996).

Rural poverty is linked to **housing problems and homelessness** for individuals and families. Although housing costs tend to be lower in rural communities, there is no advantage to living in a rural area because incomes are also lower. In 1985, 42 percent of the rural poor spent at least half of their income on housing while 26 percent spent 70 percent or more. These figures are much higher than the Department of Housing and Urban Development standard that states affordable housing should be 30 percent of income or less (Flynt 1996).

A lack of decent affordable housing is a serious issue in rural communities. Whereas rural Americans constitute only 14 percent of the nation's households, they occupy 23 percent of the poor homeowners' households and 27 percent of poor renter units that have severe physical deficiencies (National Coalition for the Homeless [NCH] 1999). More than a half million rural homes in the United States do not have clean running water or adequate waste removal (Flynt 1996). The effect on family life for isolated families living in substandard housing often hidden away in the hollows of the mountains of Appalachia or in the fields of the South is devastating.

Poverty and homelessness are inextricably tied. In rural communities, poor people often find it difficult to pay for food, health care, and housing. Because housing absorbs a high percentage of family income, it is the first expenditure that the rural poor are forced to forgo. Research has documented there has been a dramatic rise in homelessness over the past fifteen to twenty years due to a shortage of rental housing and a simultaneous rise in poverty. Not only has the number of homeless people risen, but also the number of homeless families with children has increased dramatically over the past ten years. In rural areas white families, single mothers, and children make up the largest percentage of people who are homeless (NCH 1999).

Abused women and children in rural areas face special problems because of their distance from shelters and services and their lack of transportation. Rural women often have particular difficulty realizing that the abusive situation is not their fault. In rural communities, the norms for families often include traditional gender roles, high rates of poverty, exaggerated inequities in employment and wage structures, and limited family and public resources (Cummins, First, and Toomey 1998). Because the family has been and remains the central institution in many small communities, to publicly acknowledge that one wants to leave one's family home is often both a personal and family embarrassment. The hardest challenge for rural women who have been abused is to reach out and to ask for help. Living in a culture that values independence, self-reliance, and pride, women find it difficult to admit to a violent and abusive marital relationship. These women often feel they must have been bad wives and deserve what abuse and violence they are experiencing.

Many women who are victims of domestic violence are very isolated and may not be able to receive the services they need if, indeed, these services are available. These women may have no telephone and are not seen by relatives or friends for days unless they make a trip into town. Shelters, if available, offer short-term assistance, but eventually women need to leave the shelters or in many cases leave the community in order to be safe.

In sparsely settled areas of the rural countryside many families have problems in obtaining **health care.** A shortage of medical care providers and medical care facilities frequently exists. In 1990, half a million Americans lived in counties with no obstetrician, and more than 300,000 lived in counties that had no physician (Flynt 1996). In the same year, 18 percent of the residents of sparsely populated areas, where one in six residents lived in poverty, also lacked health insurance. Since that time more Americans have lost their health insurance benefits (Flynt 1996). For example, a 1989 survey found that 46 percent of small businesses in rural areas do not sponsor health insurance for their employees (Summers 1991).

The rate of rural hospital closings has increased, leaving these communities without the ancillary services these facilities provide. As a result, those services can only be obtained by individuals traveling long distances with little or meager transportation to larger neighboring cities. For those living in urban areas, large inner-city hospitals have provided emergency room treatment for poor people. Often these facilities are unavailable in rural communities, and those services that are available are threatened by HMOs and by changes in Medicare and Medicaid (Flynt 1996).

In general, the health of rural residents is not as good as their urban counterparts. For the years 1985 to 1987, fair or poor health was reported by 12.6 percent of nonmetropolitan residents as compared with 9.3 percent of metropolitan residents (Summers 1991). Because of fatalistic values characteristic of some rural communities, public health or preventive health care—both physical and mental—have been a low priority. Living in areas where there is a lack of medical care and difficulty with transportation in obtaining it, some families tend to rely on folk medicines and herbal methods of treating illness. In addition, poor people in these communities tend to focus on immediate concerns such as food, clothing, and immediate emergency health needs (Flynt 1996).

Many rural families send their children to **educationally deficient schools.** In rural communities the school expenditure per child is often lower than in urban areas. Taxpayers in urban school districts are more willing to tax themselves for better schools. Partly as a result of funding inequities, students in rural and small community schools tend to rank lower in educational achievement. Educational gaps also occur because adequate funding is not available for transportation, for services for children with developmental challenges, and for professional development of teachers (Flynt 1996).

Schools as well as families play an important role in teaching children values and behaviors. In many rural schools children are taught values and skills that reflect the industrial age (i.e., the traditional values of obedience, punctuality, and good organization) rather than those needed to be increasingly competitive in an increasingly technical and global society. For rural students to be educationally prepared for the information age, they must know how to gather and assimilate new information and how to solve problems creatively (Van Hook 1993).

Rural areas **lack public transportation** and have limited access to costly private transportation. Owning a car is often difficult for those who work for low wages or who are unemployed. At the same time, people need to travel long distances to obtain needed health, education, recreation, and social services. The new welfare law adds a new burden regarding transportation to those receiving public assistance. The Personal Responsibility and Work Opportunity Reconciliation Act passed in 1996 does not allow exemptions to any requirements because of lack of transportation. Thus, for those individuals where there is virtually no public transportation in a geographically isolated community and for whom public funds cannot be used to purchase a vehicle in its entirety, the new welfare reform regulations create a nightmare (American Friends Service Committee 1999).

Transportation serves as the key to the network of services that may be available in a community. A major obstacle to effective public transportation in rural areas is the high cost of providing door-to-door service and of maintaining bus routes for a few passengers over large geographic areas (Koff 1992). Even in communities where there is bus service, there is usually no service on nights or weekends.

The small scale of rural community life and inherent visibility of residents, coupled with the cultural value of rugged individualism, exacerbates the stigma attached to individuals needing to use **social services**. The informal communication system of small communities, referred to as the "gossip mill," literally provides the mechanism for "everyone knowing everyone else's business." Families who are forced to seek formal and informal services can be quickly labeled and sometimes ostracized by neighbors. The presence of a worker's car in someone's front yard, of a resident's car in front of a mental health center actually announces to most of the community that he/she is a recipient of service. Attempting to avoid this stigma can cause families to resist requesting help because of the price they would pay in terms of the social context for receiving services.

RESILIENCIES AND PROTECTIVE FACTORS

At this time of rapid transition in rural communities, families are coping with many stressors in their daily lives. Yet there exist within that same environment, resiliencies and protective factors that can balance the impact and provide support to enhance coping. *Resilience* has been defined as the "self righting tendencies of the person, the capacity to be bent and not break, and the capacity, once bent to spring back" (Goldstein 1997:30). Protective factors, influences that modify, ameliorate, or alter a person's response to some environmental hazard that predisposes to a maladaptive outcome, play a significance role in resilience. Two types of protective factors have been identified: (1) individual factors within the person and (2) support systems within the wider environment (Smith and Carlson 1997).

Inherent in the definition of rural communities is a **lifestyle** that includes a close relationship with the land, weather, and other aspects of nature. Searles (1996) suggested that relatedness with the natural world (1) ameliorates various painful and anxious feelings, (2) fosters self-realization, (3) deepens one's feeling of reality, and (4) fosters appreciation and acceptance of people. Perhaps it is the search for serenity and wonder, which comes from a closer relatedness to nature, that pulls the population continuing to spill out of metropolitan areas in search of a different way of life.

Rural communities themselves are a protective factor for the families who live within them. Rural communities meet three needs: a place to belong, an arena in which to make a difference, and a sense of security (Flora et al. 1992). The **small scale** of rural communities, consistency of community members' norms and values, and overlapping roles among the residents provide community members with a sense of belonging and support which promotes a sense of personal confidence, acceptance, and self-esteem. These traits have been identified as enhancing coping and providing protection for individuals at times of stress (Smith and Carlson 1997). Several external support systems available to families are afforded through extended family members, neighbors, friends, religious leaders, and natural helpers who are always at close proximity. Cultural norms of friendliness and neighborliness through more intimate relationships prevalent in nonmetropolitan communities support mutual exchange when residents need resources. Simultaneously, this strong identification with place and solidarity among residents, these networks of mutual support, and community norms that foster mutuality and reciprocity contribute to a competent community that can respond to need and rebound from external impacts (Cottrell 1976).

Studies have identified two specific characteristics of small communities that particularly promote resilience. Faith in a higher power or a religious philosophy of life has provided important support at times of stress (Anthony 1987, as cited in Smith and Carlson 1997; Werner and Smith 1984, as cited in Smith and Carlson 1997). While a 1985 Gallup poll reported that seven out of ten Americans are members of a church or synagogue, rural families tend to be more **religiously oriented** than other groups (Meyerstedt and Smith 1984). A study by Furman and Chandy (1998) provides further support for the role of religion and spirituality in rural culture. A representative sample of licensed social workers in North Dakota, one of the most rural states in the country, reflected that 43 percent of the respondents indicated that religion and spirituality were of importance in their clients' lives and provided a positive resource for persons in solving their problems.

Natural helpers also promote resilience and act as protective factors. Several recent studies have provided a wealth of knowledge about natural helpers as preventive mental health agents in rural communities. Patterson and Brennan (1983) distinguished a natural helper—"one to whom people turn naturally in difficult times because of his or her concern, interest, and innate understanding" (22)—from other types of informal helpers. Natural helpers also have a reputation in the community for being effective providers of help. Relationships between natural helpers and those whom they help (relatives, friends, and neighbors) are marked by equality and mutual exchange. Natural helpers appear to use three styles of helping: facilitative (expressive), doing (instrumental) or a combination of both styles (Patterson and Brennan 1983). The type of problem involved in the helping situation appears to be crucial to determining a natural helper's style and perceptions of the recipient's responsibilities in creating and solving the problem (Memmott and Brennan 1988).

Patterson, Memmott, and Germain (1993) studied patterns of natural helping in rural areas. Using a modified reputational sampling of natural helpers in the New England state of Connecticut and the midwestern state of Kansas, they identified and interviewed two hundred natural helpers about their helping experiences. Analysis of collected data yielded additional information about the natural helper's characteristics and the helping situation.

These natural helpers claimed they helped because they cared about people, because it was morally right to do so, or because they were repaying the recipient for help offered in the past. Over three-quarters of these natural helpers offered help at the time they became aware of the recipients' needs (before it was requested) and were available to help recipients twenty-four hours a day (Patterson et al. 1993).

Characteristically, helpers had known recipients for a long period of time (approximately fifteen to thirty-five years) and assisted with the following types of problems: home care needs, physical illness, transportation, death, farming needs, health needs, child care, divorce and loneliness, and other crises. The majority of the helpers used a doing (instrumental) style in helping neighbors and relatives, while the facilitative (expressive) helping styles was used two to three times more often with friends than with relatives or neighbors (Patterson et al. 1993).

The general social and physical quality of life, mutuality and reciprocity among neighbors and friends, and prevailing values that foster concern for others, as well as the related significance of religious institutions and identified roles of effective resident helpers provide resources that can be utilized throughout an individual's life course to enhance coping with the stressors of life and to foster resilience in rural families.

PROGRAMS AND SOCIAL WORK CONTRIBUTIONS

Because of the dearth of rural social services, the needs of families in rural areas are not being met sufficiently. Most social service programs have been developed to meet the more visible needs of urban populations. The replication of these programs throughout the country in order to comply with federal and state funding guidelines often makes it difficult for social service agencies to tailor service for delivery in rural communities. The majority of rural social service agencies mirror the service delivery systems of metropolitan areas but make some adaptations for a better fit with the rural environment. Many nonmetropolitan programs are community based at the same time they must serve large geographic areas. Mobile health and mental health units that move through a schedule of specific days in adjoining communities is one attempt to solve the problems inherent in catchment areas that cover hundreds of miles and clients' lack of transportation. Use of public buildings, e.g., the grange, school, church, or courthouse, to provide services lowers the visibility of clients to the rest of the community and guards against the stigma that others in the community may attach to clients. Home visits are extensively used from necessity because families cannot get to service buildings.

Public social services are often provided through health departments and public social service departments. For example, a county health department may offer the following services: psychiatric evaluations, medication monitoring, crisis intervention and hospital prescreenings, psychiatric/mental health mobile treatment, and in-home services that include parenting programs and medical services. Another important public social service in rural communities are the Medical Centers sponsored by the Department of Veterans Affairs (VA). These regional centers provide inpatient and outpatient services in general medicine, psychiatry, and surgery. In many rural communities the VA centers have a strong focus on geriatric patients. Specialized services include programs for substance abuse, posttraumatic stress disorder, contract community nursing home, community residential care, homemaker/home health aide, and contract adult day health care programs. Social workers are expected to make assessments, treatment planning, discharge planning, counseling (individual and group), community referrals, participate on a health care team, nursing home placement, and to be a case manager. They are also expected to relate to a wide variety of community agency personnel and to clients' families.

Social workers provide services through private, nonprofit settings where they are expected to carry a wide variety of roles and responsibilities. They provide social work services in family service agencies, child development centers, rape and domestic violence information centers, long-term residential centers, community councils, hospices, substance abuse programs, and schools. They may also be involved with 4-H clubs and rural extension services.

Recent innovative approaches to service delivery include social work practice by telephone and on the Internet. Telephone support groups are a new and feasible means of support service delivery in rural areas. By communicating on the telephone, participants do not have to commute long distances and they are able to maintain their anonymity (Rounds, Galinsky, and Stevens 1991). Information and referral networks are now available on the Internet to rural residents seeking information about services, agencies, and programs in rural areas (West Virginia University Center on Aging 1997). On the Internet there is a growing number of on-line support groups that provide a worldwide link for people who need information on a variety of topics and a connection to others with similar issues and concerns.

ASSESSMENT AND INTERVENTIONS

The rural practitioner must be a community-based generalist who possesses a wide array of direct and indirect practice knowledge and skills, an understanding of rural culture, and an ability to work with a variety of client systems (Buxton 1978; Gibbs, Locke, and Lohmann 1990; Ginsberg 1976, 1993, 1998; Granger 1980; Martinez-Brawley 1986, 1993, 1998; Mermelstein and Sundet 1976, 1995; Morrison 1976; Raspberry 1977; Southern Regional Educational Board 1998). Development of a generalist model of social work practice and a model of practice for rural areas occurred in tandem. The small scale of rural communities, dearth of social service agencies, and lack of professional workers in nonmetropolitan areas mandate that rural workers must be generalists who can practice with individuals, families, groups, organizations, and communities as well as have the ability to supervise, develop grant proposals, administer agencies, and deal with community representatives.

Community-based practice incorporates three basic ingredients: debureaucratization, partnership with clients, and autonomy in practice. Although a newly developed framework has been recently imported from Europe, these attributes have always described good rural social work practice. This community-relevant practice suggests that workers identify the community informal networks of help beyond family and friends and develop working partnerships with these entities as they interweave formal and informal resources through their work (Martinez-Brawley 1998).

Community assessment is baseline knowledge for the rural practitioner. Local history, cultural norms and values, relationships between and among ethnic, racial, or socioeconomic groups and community formal and informal power structures are requisite knowledge for the social worker regardless of agency function or population served. This information will help identify community resources to meet clients' needs and provide the broad understanding that shapes locality-relevant and culturally sensitive practice. Community functioning is a concern that practitioners must attend to in order to strengthen the systems in which clients live so that the community can better meet its responsibilities to its residents. Agencies must foster development and change on the community level in order for their clients' needs to be more fully met. Interventions must be focused on individual, family, or group need and simultaneously foster and enhance community functioning.

Focus on work with smaller networks and systems within rural communities that strengthen the community as a whole has been discussed. Practice with natural groups of children, adolescents, and adults in the rural environment is discussed as a preferred model of group practice because it taps preexisting relationships for focused mutual support and simultaneously strengthens existing informal networks and structures within the community (Gumpert and Saltman 1998).

More recent literature has identified collaborative roles that the professional can assume with community-based systems to simultaneously provide service and strengthen communities. A study of rural practitioners suggests the following collaborative roles for workers in relation to self-help groups: referring clients, publicizing the groups, consulting about problems, helping to develop resources, and providing training and direct leadership (Gumpert et al. 2000). Findings of a study of natural and professional helpers suggest practice connections between the two. Professionals should make referrals to natural helpers, make the formal helping system better known to natural helpers so that they can channel help seekers to appropriate formal support systems and services, and facilitate mutual support among natural helpers so that they can rely less on professionals for consultation (Memmott 1993).

This community-focused framework resonates in literature on resilience. In his discussion of community development and individual resilience, Saleebey (1997) suggests, "A community is a dynamic whole that emerges when a group of people participate in common practices, depend on one another, make decisions together, identify themselves as part of something larger than the sum of their individual relationships and commit themselves for the long term to their own, one another's and the group's well-being" (201). Growing evidence suggests that individual and familial resilience and the characteristics of the communities in which people live are inseparable. Resilience is a process and an effect of the connection between what happens within you as a person and the environment. Essentially, competent communities foster resilience in the individuals who make up that community. The root idea of community development is to identify local capacities and mobilize them, which involves connecting people with capacities to other people, associations, institutions, and economic resources.

Since the early identification of models of rural practice, a focus on community development as the province of the professional social worker has existed (Martinez-Brawley 1990). Reflecting on twenty years of identification and development of rural social work practice, Mermelstein and Sundet (1998) again sound the call, made at the first National Institute on Rural Social Work, for the practitioner as community developer. They state that in light of the rapidly changing environment of small communities, it is the unique niche of the social work profession to address the issues of community building and save the rural community.

For a rural practitioner, assessment must be done in context of the surrounding community and its many parts; intervention must utilize both formal and informal resources; strategies must be reviewed for changes on an individual, family, or group level as well as the community level; and strengthening community functioning must be an integral part of service delivery. Multiplicity of relationships between clients and practitioners, a characteristic common to rural practice (Miller 1998), may actually facilitate use of professional knowledge to further these goals. Although professional ethics (National Association of Social Workers 1996) warn against the misuse of dual or multiple relationships, rural workers usually cannot escape them. To live in the same or nearby community in which one works means overlapping roles between practitioners and clients. While this requires internal vigilance against exploiting vulnerabilities of clients through a well-developed sense of self-awareness, it also allows practitioners to use their knowledge and skills in multiple roles within the community. Although the practitioner may be engaged in a community activity as a resident, he or she can use professional knowledge of organizing to further community functioning, gain knowledge about the community that will aid assessment of clients and identify potential resources, and use relationships developed in both roles to foster trust and confidence with client systems.

ILLUSTRATION AND DISCUSSION

Northernport is a town fifty miles south of the nearest metropolitan areas in the heart of the mountains with an ever-decreasing population of twelve hundred. It has one stoplight (which is flashing most of the time). Main Street consists of one bank, one very small grocery store, a barber shop, a hardware store, the post office, and two churches—Presbyterian and Methodist. There is bus transportation three times a day and only to the one nearest metropolitan area. If someone doesn't have a car and needs to go anywhere else, it is necessary to ask a friend or family member to drive. There is a senior center building that has a family service agency, Mountain Family Services, attached to it. The senior center staff can call the county-owned taxi to take persons to the larger grocery store two miles away for a cost of 25 cents. Medical services consist of two doctors and a rural health clinic which serves the indigent and Medicaid population. The closest hospital is fifty-seven miles away.

Northernport is a town where people really might go next door to borrow a cup of sugar. It's a town where it's expected that people wave at each passing car—whether or not they know the people inside—but residents usually recognize the car before they can focus on the driver and passengers. It's a town where it is difficult to purchase a dead-bolt lock because nobody bothers to lock their doors. It's a town where word travels fast, and if people need to catch up on the hometown gossip, they either go to Happy's Barber Shop, or to the local hardware store. Happy, the barber, is also a member of the Northernport Board of Aldermen and his wife is a Sunday school teacher at the Methodist Church. Most of the town aldermen decisions are made at Happy's before the actual meeting. In the fall, there is a four-day Walnut Festival, organized by the local volunteer fire department, when the side streets are closed to traffic except for the vendors and there is music all day long. The high school band leads the parade on the first day of the festival and the school is closed on that Friday. It is said that Northernport is a town where kids count the days until they can leave, and adults count the days until they can return.

Mountain Family Services is an agency devoted to stabilizing and improving the quality of life for families. Mountain is staffed with skilled professionals who provide home-based care to families and other related services in communities throughout the state. There are nine different offices of Mountain that serve all of the counties in the state. The variety of locations is advantageous for both potential clients and the staff of Mountain. If a family member hears about the services of the agency in one part of the state, he or she can receive services in another part.

Approximately 80 percent of the cases are court referred. Other clients are self-referred who have heard about the agency from a family member or friend. Even though there are centrally located offices of Mountain, most of the social workers spend a majority of their time on the road traveling to clients' residences or community sites to provide services.

Mountain provides a complete range of services, virtually meeting every family need. These include nutrition and parenting education, as well as child and family counseling to help clients gain stability and to learn better problem-solving and communication skills. Since family preservation is a large part of Mountain's program, a client must show some ability or willingness to improve the family situation. The agency offers a toll-free twenty-four-hour emergency telephone number to ensure that the clients have access to a social worker at any time.

Each client is assigned a treatment team of workers when their case is opened. The job of the direct service team member is to provide basic living skills. The job of the team leader, a social worker with a master's degree, is to provide individual and family and group counseling. The third worker, a social worker with an undergraduate social work degree, is the case manager. These workers link the client to a continuum of services from housing to employment to financial aid for college. All of the direct service team members can provide advocacy or other support that the clients may need.

The agency has had trouble forming parent groups in the community. One reason is that most of the clients do not have adequate transportation to attend meetings. The agency social workers also offer parenting groups for teenage mothers at local high schools. At one branch there is a home for pregnant women. At this site there is a school, counseling services—including substance abuse counseling—parenting classes, and counseling for families. Pregnant women from all over the state may choose to live at the school while they are pregnant.

All of the social workers perform a variety of roles that include the direct service roles of individual and family counseling, group work services, and educator; the system linkage roles of broker and case manager; the system maintenance roles of facilitator, team member, and consultant, as well as system development roles of program developer, planner, and advocate. The role of researcher is yet to be developed (Hepworth, Rooney, and Larsen 1997).

A Day in the Life of a Rural Social Worker. Bill, the social worker, began his day by driving fifty miles to his scheduled appointment at 10 a.m. His job requires that he cover a five county catchment area. This means that he could drive 90 to 120 miles a day. In his car is a suitcase containing toys, crayons, and paper for use in play therapy with some youngsters during the day. He also carries his barn boots so that he can see the many prize animals raised by children on his caseload.

When the Bill first met Debbie, she was 29 years old, a high school graduate, and seven months pregnant. She was unmarried and living with a female friend, age 30; her boyfriend, age 32; and their five children. All eight people were living in a very small three-bedroom, run-down trailer situated in a trailer park in a hollow of the mountains. The trailer had a mud driveway and was surrounded by dogs including two tied under the trailer. The ground was littered with beer cans. When Bill walked into the trailer, Debbie was drinking. Even though she knew he was coming that day, she was irate. She clearly stated she didn't need any help and she didn't care that she might be harming the unborn baby. Since she flatly denied she needed any help, Bill was offered no alternative but to leave the trailer and to report her to child protective services (CPS).

The agency did not hear anything from Debbie for four months. Bill knew that after the baby was born, the CPS worker removed the baby from the trailer and placed the child in foster care. When Debbie called the agency for help, she very much wanted her baby back. She agreed to become involved with Mountain Family Services and Bill began weekly visits to Debbie who was still living in the trailer and still drinking. Debbie began to develop parenting skills and through cognitive restructuring-focused counseling be-gan to deal with self-esteem issues. Bill linked her to vocational counseling. She moved in with the baby's father and both she and the baby's father worked with Bill around relationship issues. She desperately wanted to stop drinking and she began to ride her bicycle five miles a day to the court-ordered AA meetings.

One year after she began her association with Bill and the Mountain Family Services, Debbie went to court and obtained physical and legal cus-tody of her child. Three years later she continues to go to AA meetings and has became a sponsor. Now she is looking for a job to help pay the bills, since due to the new welfare laws, her welfare checks are only temporary. She tries to attend classes but the bus service does not go to the adjoining town in which the community college is located. She is experiencing a great deal of stress but she feels she has learned a great deal about herself, has gained knowledge about parenting her baby, has maintained a positive relationship with the baby's father, and is optimistic about the future.

On the way to his afternoon appointment back in Northernport, Bill stopped at Al's General Store for lunch and to chat with Maggie Mullins, Al's wife. Maggie often provides transportation and child care for neighbors who need help getting to a doctor's appointment, shopping for needed items, or to the senior center for meetings. He talked with Maggie about the possibility of providing transportation for Debbie to the local junior college to begin taking an evening class on Wednesdays. Maggie said she had heard that Deb-bie was still "on the straight and narrow" and had her baby returned to her, and she would be willing to drive her to Butlerville. Maggie, herself, could stop in and see her aunt in the nursing home there while Debbie was in class.

Bill arrived at the Northernport school just in time to meet his group of sixth-grade boys as they got out of school. They usually use the blacktop area of the school to shoot baskets and "shoot the bull," and then they go for pizza. Bill then drives each boy home because they have missed the school bus and have no other way to get home. Joey, one of the boys on his caseload, was sent to the principal's office today and is afraid to go home because his folks are going to "give it to him." As they shoot baskets, the other kids and Bill talk with Joey about how else he could have handled his anger when the teacher didn't believe that he had lost his homework. This led to a long discussion of how his parents had been arguing a lot more this past week about how to deal with the upcoming mortgage payment or they would lose their farm. On the ride home, the kids helped Joey rehearse what he could say to his dad when he got home about how he would control his temper in the future.

As they drove by the Lincoln farm, John Lincoln flagged Bill down to tell him the senior citizens' center board meeting was to be held at the Moose Lodge tonight because the AA folks has already booked the Episcopal Church. Bill thanked him for telling him and said he would see him there. Around the next bend in the road, the car came to a screeching halt and everyone piled out as fast as they could. Mrs. Green's dry cows had broken through the fence and were all over the road. Bill and the kids knew that Mr.

Green was in the hospital for surgery yesterday and Mrs. Green was probably there now visiting him. The kids herded the cows back into the pasture and Bill mended the fence with the tools in his car. Then it was on to get the rest of the boys home, home for dinner himself and then to the board meeting.

Bill had been asked to sit on the board of the senior center for at least two reasons. His mother had been attending the center and getting Meals on Wheels for three years now since his father had died. The other board members felt as though he had a family attachment to the center and wanted people like that to be on the board. In addition, the other board members knew that Bill had grant writing skills, and they needed that kind of help, too.

The meeting tonight was going to be a tough one. The center wanted to apply for some federal monies available for serving lunch to senior citizens. Many of the board members had heard about the dissatisfaction with Meals on Wheels from others in the community and wanted to suggest that the center try to get this money because they could do a better job of making meals and delivering them than Meals on Wheels, which was run through the county home health program. Bill knew that it was not going to help the community to become split in this manner and wanted to convince this board to work cooperatively with Meals on Wheels to jointly apply for the funds and work together on the tasks. Everyone knew that County Home Health was short staffed and underfunded, which contributed to their problem of providing lunches. The large number of volunteers at the senior center probably could relieve some of the person power problem at County Home Health and the program would be improved. This was going to be rough riding though unless both Jim and George, the local ministers, as well as some of the town elders, would back this plan. Bill has talked with many of them at Happy's Barber Shop in preparation for this meeting. He was fairly sure that at least three of the six would speak out for the plan and one other might vote for the plan, but it was hard to know how the total vote would go. The meeting was over about 9; the board had decided to join with County Home Health only because two of the board members from that agency came to the meeting and also supported this plan. One of the clergymen Bill had spoken with had talked with them last week. Bill was tired and glad to climb into bed. He had a telephone message from Jim who ran the AA meeting asking if he could stop by tomorrow. Jim had some problems in his group that he wanted to talk with Bill. Bill thought he might be able to stop at 9 tomorrow morning after the court hearing for the Hill family to have their two daughters returned.

"A Day in the Life of a Rural Social Worker" conveys how the rural practitioner becomes part of the community fabric. His familiarity with the culture, the people, and the problems becomes an essential part of his practice. His communication with natural helpers, clients, neighbors, and friends is characterized by equal informality, although Bill is always professionally purposeful in his interactions with clients. His use of a car for travel and transporting clients is essential. Bill is valued for his professional role, knowledge, and skill, but more so because he is someone who genuinely cares about people, can be trusted, and is a person of integrity.

CONCLUSION

Rural America must adapt to a complex interconnected global world and utilize external resources in combination with internal community strengths to preserve the inherent health-sustaining qualities of small town life. Despite a century of essentially hidden and neglected social problems for which resources were underfunded, of lesser quality, and often through service models developed for urban populations, the 1990s influx of population can swing the spotlight back to this segment of the country, as occurred in the 1970s. The country's focus could be utilized to gain a variety of resources that would stabilize communities that are undergoing cultural change and economic depletion or boom. The challenge will be to maintain a way of life that is humane and encourages and fosters reciprocity among people and between the environment and the population, while adapting to change and adapting elements of change to fit the rural context.

At this time of transition, social workers can play a significant role in helping rural communities to identify and utilize their strengths and to plan and effectively implement community decisions. Social work practitioners' community-based perspective and knowledge of community development provides the broad framework needed to build and sustain effective rural communities at the same time that service is provided to individuals, families, and groups. Utilizing formal and informal community resources and fostering community-wide participation and decision making will play a significant role in this process. Organizations such as the Rural Social Work Caucus have the opportunity to organize rural communities on a regional, national, and global basis to rally for resources and to influence decisions that have significance for rural areas. As rural communities strengthen their functioning, resilience and protective factors can provide resources to sustain and promote rural families.

References

American Friends Service Committee. 1999. "A Brief Guide to Welfare Changes." Charlston, W.V.: AFSC-WV Economic Justice Project.

Atkinson, M. 1994. "Rural and Urban Families' Use of Child Care." *Family Relations* 43(1):16–23.

Baldauf, S. 1996. "More Americans Move Off the Beaten Track." *Christian Science Monitor* 88(177):1.

Bull, C. 1998. "Aging in Rural Communities." *National Forum* 78(2):38–42.

Buxton, E. B. 1978. "Delivering Social Services in Rural Areas." In L. H. Ginsberg, ed., *Social Work in Rural Communities,* pp. 29–40. New York: Council on Social Work Education.

Cleland, C. 1995. "Measuring Rurality." *Human Services in the Rural Environment* 18/19(4/1):13–18.

Coeyman, M. 1998. "Make Way for Urbanites." *Christian Science Monitor* 91(9):11.

Cottrell, L. 1976. "The Competent Community." In B. Kaplan, R. Wilson, and A. Leighton, eds., *Further Explorations in Psychiatry*. New York: Basic Books.

Cummins, L., R. First, and B. Toomey. 1998. "Comparisons of Rural and Homeless Women." *Affilia: Journal of Women and Social Work* 13(4):435–53.

Davenport, J., III and J. A. Davenport. 1984. "Theoretical Perspectives on Rural/Urban Differences." *Human Services in the Rural Environment* 9(1):4–9.

——. 1998. "Rural Community in Transition." In L. H. Ginsberg, ed., *Social Work in Rural Communities*, 3d ed., pp. 39–54. Alexandria, Va.: Council on Social Work Education.

Davenport, J. and J. Davenport, III. 1995. "Rural Social Work Overview." In R. Edwards, ed. *Encyclopedia of Social Work*, 19th ed., vol. 3, pp. 2076–85. Washington, D.C.: National Association of Social Workers Press.

Deavers, K. 1992. "What Is Rural?" *Policy Studies Journal* 20(2):183–89.

Edmondson, B. 1997. "A New Era for Rural America." *American Demographics* 17(9): 30–31.

Flora, C., J. Flora, J. Spears, and L. Swanson. 1992. *Rural Communities: Legacy and Change.* Boulder, Colo.: Westview Press.

Flynt, W. 1996. "Rural Poverty in America." *National Forum* 96(76):32–39.

Furman, L. and J. Chandy. 1998. "Religion and Spirituality: A Long Neglected Cultural Component of Social Work Practice." In L. H. Ginsberg, ed. *Social Work in Rural Communities*, 3d ed., pp. 135–48. Alexandria, Va.: Council on Social Work Education.

Gibbs, P., B. Locke, and R. Lohmann. 1990. "Paradigm for the Generalist-Advanced Generalist Continuum." *Journal of Social Work Education* 26(3):232–43.

Ginsberg, Leon. 1976. "An Overview of Social Work Education for Rural Areas." In L. H. Ginsberg, ed., *Social Work in Rural Communities: A Book of Readings*, pp. 1–14. New York: Council on Social Work Education.

——. 1993. "Introduction: An Overview of Rural Social Work." In L. H. Ginsberg, ed., *Social Work in Rural Communities*, 2d ed., pp. 2–17. New York: Council on Social Work Education.

——. 1998. "Introduction: An Overview of Rural Social Work." In L. H. Ginsberg, ed., *Social Work in Rural Communities*, 3d ed., pp. 3–22. New York: Council on Social Work Education.

Goldstein, H. 1997. "Victors or Victims?" In D. Saleebey, ed., *The Strengths Perspective in Social Work Practice.* New York: Longman Press.

Granger, B. P. 1980. "Extension as a Practice of Intervention." In J. Gumpert, ed., *Toward Clarifying the Context of Rural Practice*, pp. 16–26. Lexington, Mass.: Ginn.

Gumpert, J. and J. Saltman. 1998. "Social Group Work Practice in Rural Areas: The Practitioners Speak." *Social Work with Groups* 21(3):11–22.

Gumpert, J., J. Saltman, and D. Sauer-Jones. Forthcoming. "Toward Identifying the Unique Characteristics of Social Work Practice in Rural Areas: Voices from the Practitioners." *Journal of Baccalaureate Social Work* 6(1).

Hepworth, D., R. Rooney, and J. A. Larsen. 1997. *Direct Social Work Practice: Theory and Skills.* Pacific Grove, Calif.: Brooks/Cole.

Johnson, K. M. and C. L. Beale. 1995. "The Rural Rebound Revisited." *American Demographics* 17(7):46–52.

Koff, T. 1992. "Rural Issues." *Generations* 16(2):53–56.

Lichter, D. and F. Aggebeen. 1992. "Child Poverty and the Rural Family." *Rural Sociology* 57:151–72.

Martinez-Brawley, E. 1981. *Seven decades of Rural Social Work.* New York: Praeger.

——. 1986. "Beyond Cracker-Barrel Images." *Social Casework* 62(2):101–7.

——. 1990. *Perspectives on the Small Community.* Silver Spring, Md.: National Association of Social Workers Press.

——. 1993. "Community-Oriented Practice in Rural Social Work." In L. H. Ginsberg, ed., *Social Work in Rural Communities*, 2d ed., pp. 67–81. Alexandria, Va.: Council on Social Work Education.

——. 1998. "Community-Oriented Practice in Rural Social Work." In L. H. Ginsberg, ed., *Social Work in Rural Communities*, 3d ed., pp. 99–114. Alexandria, Va.: Council on Social Work Education.

Memmott, J. 1993. "Models of Helping and Coping: A Field Experiment with Natural and Professional Helpers." *Social Work Research and Abstracts* 29(3):19–34.

Memmott, J. and E. Brennan. 1988. "Helping Orientation and Strategies of Natural Helpers and Social Workers in Rural Settings." *Social Work Research and Abstracts* 24(2): 15–20.

Mermelstein, J. and P. Sundet. 1998. "Rural Social Work is an Anachronism: The Perspective of Twenty Years of Experience." In L. H. Ginsberg, ed., *Social Work in Rural Communities,* 3rd ed. pp. 63–82. Alexandria, VA: Council on Social Work Education.

Mermelstein, J. and P. Sundet. 1976. "Social Work Education for Rural Program Development." In L. H. Ginsberg, ed., *Social Work Practice in Rural Communities: A Book of Readings,* pp. 15–28. New York: Council on Social Work Education.

———. 1995. "Rural Social Work Is an Anachronism: The Perspective of Twenty Years of Experience and Debate." *Human Services in the Rural Environment* 18/19(4/1):5–12.

———. 1998. "Rural Social Work Is an Anachronism: The Perspective of Twenty Years of Experience." In L. H. Ginsberg, ed., *Social Work in Rural Communities,* 3d ed., pp. 63–82. Alexandria, Va.: Council on Social Work Education.

Meyerstedt, E. and R. Smith. 1984. "Religion and the Rural Population: Implications for Social Work." *Social Casework* 65:219–26.

Miller, P. 1998. "Dual Relationships and Rural Practice: A Dilemma of Ethics and Culture." In L. H. Ginsberg, ed., *Social Work in Rural Communities,* 3d ed., pp. 55–62. Alexandria, Va.: Council on Social Work Education.

Miller, R. S. and R. Ray. 1985. "The Satisfaction of Community Mental Health Professionals with Life and Work in Rural Areas." *Human Services in the Rural Environment* 10(2): 5–11.

Morrison, J. 1976. "Community Organization in Rural Areas." In L. H. Ginsberg, ed., *Social Work in Rural Communities: A Book of Readings,* pp. 57–62. New York: Council on Social Work Education.

National Association of Social Workers. 1996. *Code of Ethics.* Washington, D.C.: Author.

National Coalition for the Homeless (NCH). 1999. "Who Is Homeless." http://www2.ari.net/home/hch/who.html (2 Feb. 1999).

O'Hare, W. 1991. "Gonna Get Married: Family Formation in Rural Areas." *Population Today* 20:6–8.

O'Malley, S. 1994. "The Rural Rebound." *American Demographics* 16(5):24–30.

Patterson, S. and E. Brennan. 1983. "Matching Helping Roles with the Characteristics of Older Natural Helpers." *Journal of Gerontological Social Work* 5:55–66.

Patterson, S., J. Memmott, and C. Germain. 1993. "Patterns of Natural Helping in Rural Areas: Implications for Social Work Research. In L. H. Ginsberg, ed., *Social Work in Rural Communities,* 2d ed., pp. 22–36. New York: Council on Social Work Education.

Raspberry, B. H. 1977. "Building Rural Content into Undergraduate Curriculum." In R. K. Green and S. A. Webster, eds., *Social Work in Rural Areas: Preparation and Practice,* pp. 137–47. Knoxville, Tenn.: University of Tennessee Press.

Riche, M. 1996. "A Profile of America's Diversity—The View from the Census Bureau." In *The World Almanac Book of Facts.* 377–78. Mahwah, N.J.: World Almanac Books.

Rounds, K., M. Galinsky, and M. Stevens. 1991. "Linking People with AIDS in Rural Communities." *Social Work* 36(1):13–18.

Saleebey, D., ed. 1997. *The Strengths Perspective in Social Work,* 2d ed. New York: Longman.

Searles, J. 1996. "The Non-Human Environment." In C. Germain, C. Gitterman, and A. Gitterman, eds., 1996. *The Life Model of Social Work Practice,* 2nd ed. New York: Columbia University Press.

Smith, C. and B. Carlson. 1997. "Stress, Coping and Resilience in Children and Youth." *Social Service Review* 71(2):231–56.

Southern Regional Educational Board. 1998. "Educational Assumptions for Rural Social Work." In L. H. Ginsberg, ed., *Social Work in Rural Communities,* 3d ed., pp. 23–27. Alexandria, Va.: Council on Social Work Education.

Sullivan, W. P., M. D. Hasler, and A. G. Otis. 1993. "Rural Mental Health: Voices From the Field." *Families and Society* 74(8):493–502.

Summers, G. 1991. "Minorities in Rural Society." *Rural Sociology* 56:117–88.

Summers, G. and J. Sherman. 1997. *Who's Poor in Rural America? Working Together for a Change.* Madison, Wis.: Rural Sociological Society.

U.S. Bureau of the Census. 1990. "Residents of Farms and Rural Areas: 1989." *Current Population Reports.* Washington, D.C.: U.S. Government Printing Office, Series P 20 #457.

——. 1992. "Residents of Farms and Rural Areas: 1990." *Current Population Reports.* Washington, D.C.: U.S. Government Printing Office, Series P 20 #257.

Van Hook, M. 1990a. "Impact of Farm on Youth: School Responses." *Social Work in Education* 12(3):166–77.

——. 1990b. "Family Response to the Farm Crisis: A Study in Coping." *Social Work* 35:425–34.

——. 1993. "Educational Aspirations of Rural Youths and Community Economic Development: Implications for Social Work." *Social Work in Education* 15(4):215–25.

Waltman, G. H. 1986. "Main Street Revisited: Social Work Practice in Rural Areas." *Social Casework* 67(8):466–74.

Webster, S. A. and P. Campbell. 1977. "The 1970's and Changing Dimensions in Rural Life—Is a New Practice Model Needed?" In R. K. Green and S. A. Webster, eds., *Social Work in Rural Areas: Preparation and Practice,* pp. 75–94. Knoxville, Tenn.: University of Tennessee Press.

West Virginia University Center on Aging. 1997. "Caregiver Support Network." http://www.hsc.wvu.edu/som/ctr-on-aging/coa.htm.

Whitaker, W. H. 1984. "A Survey of Perceptions of Social Work Practice in Rural and Urban Areas." *Human Services in the Rural Environment* 9(3):12–19.

Wilkinson, K. 1986. "The Small Town Community: Its Character and Survival." Address to the Third Biannual GITAP Interdisciplinary Conference, *Down to Earth: People on the Land—Questions of Food, Work, People, and Land.* Grand Forks, North Dakota, sponsored by the Group for Interdisciplinary Theory and Praxis (GITAP), November 16–21, University of North Dakota.

York, R., R. Denton, and J. Moran. 1993. "Rural and Urban Practice: Is There a Difference?" In L. Ginsberg, ed., *Social Work in Rural Communities,* 2d ed., pp. 23–27. Alexandria, Va.: Council on Social Work Education.

20

Family Caregivers
of the Frail Elderly

Ronald W. Toseland
Gregory C. Smith
Philip McCallion

Family care to frail elders represents a normative behavior that most American families strive to fulfill. Family members provide approximately 60 percent to 80 percent of long-term care for dependent elderly members (Bengtson, Rosenthal, and Burton 1996). Factors that motivate family caregivers to both assume and endure this tremendous responsibility include (a) altruistic motives such as love, affection, empathy, and feeling close; (b) self-serving motives that range from guilt over not doing more to a sense of personal satisfaction; (c) a sense of "mattering," which refers to caregivers' beliefs that they are valued by others because of the difference they make in their lives; (d) feelings of reciprocity or wanting to return the assistance and support they received in the past from their now dependent elders; (e) the "sick role" occupied by the care recipient, which offers an exemption from their need to reciprocate the provision of support; and (f) social norms of "family solidarity" and "filial responsibility" as reflected in the commitment of individuals to their loved ones, regardless of the costs or what the loved one is able to return (Gatz, Bengtson, and Blum 1990; Pearlin et al. 1996).

Even though it is often demanding and stressful, caregiving is frequently perceived as a rewarding experience. Rewards include greater intimacy and love, finding meaning through the experience of caregiving, personal growth, improved relationships, experiencing satisfaction, and appreciation of received social support from others. It is important for social workers to realize that experiencing caregiving as rewarding has been associated with better health among caregivers and reduced perceptions of burden or stress (Kramer 1997). Thus, social workers should not simply focus on problems and stressors but also help caregivers to articulate the positive feelings and experiences that are generated by providing care to a loved one.

There is also evidence that caregiving can negatively impact the health and well-being of caregivers. Physical problems that have been reported by caregivers include exhaustion and fatigue from constant and seemingly never-ending attendance to the care recipient's needs. This situation is often exacerbated because a number of caregivers are older adults themselves, sometimes with their own health problems. Physical exhaustion and deteriorating caregiver health, in turn, often contribute to psychological problems such as depression or increased anxiety. The revival of forgotten sibling and parental conflicts, and the frustrations and misunderstandings endemic to caring for someone, frequently produce additional psychological distress. Social problems may occur because the long duration of some chronic illnesses and disabilities combined with the lack of hope for improvement, and the guilt many caregivers feel about their own negative feelings, can lead to a restriction of caregivers' contacts with friends, neighbors, and other social contacts in the community (Toseland, Smith, and McCallion 1995).

Numerous studies have documented how the stress of caregiving to frail older persons is associated with physical, psychological, social, and emotional problems among family members. Recognition of these strains has led to the development of various supportive interventions. Less studied have been the positive aspects of caregiving and the resilience of families when faced with demanding caregiving situations. This chapter describes the nature, prevalence, and impact of family caregiving; discusses the strengths and resilience present in families as they assume caregiving responsibilities; reviews the intervention programs that have been designed to support family caregivers; and presents guidelines for practice with this population.

DEFINING AND EXPLAINING CAREGIVER AND CAREGIVING

Tremendous variability occurs across the situations of different family caregivers. Caregivers differ considerably in such factors as health; marital, employment, and economic status; family constellation and dynamics; personality; coping styles; and the nature of the relationship with the care recipient. Caregiving situations also vary considerably depending on the nature, extent, and duration of the disabilities experienced by the care recipient, as well as each caregiver's unique response to the different responsibilities of an evolving caregiving situation. Recognition of this variability is essential in developing differential assessment and intervention strategies to best meet the needs of caregivers.

The kinds of help family caregivers provide varies. Family caregiving arises out of needs created by chronic and acute functional disabilities. For some chronic diseases, the needs of frail elderly family members can be episodic; for example, in the early stages of diseases such as cancer. For other situations, for example, in the immediate aftermath of experiencing a stroke, physical caregiving demands are very intensive for several weeks or months until through recovery the care recipient regains some independence. Generally, however, with chronic progressive illnesses such as Alzheimer's, the need for care increases over time. Although there may be some reduction in the physical demands of caregiving when a frail family member is hospitalized or institutionalized, the emotional demands of caregiving continue for as long as the family member lives. Thus family caregiving frequently involves a long-term, open-ended commitment that wanes and waxes with the vicissitudes of the care recipients' condition.

Caregivers are confronted with many different tasks that vary depending on the problems experienced by their frail relative. Although caregiving is not characterized by any one type of assistance, emotional support, rather than physical or financial support, is the most common and most important type of assistance provided by family caregivers. Other frequently provided types of assistance include transportation; shopping; doing household chores; coordinating assistance from social service and health care providers; routine health care such as administering and monitoring medications; personal care such as bathing, feeding, toileting, and dressing; supervision; financial management; financial assistance; and the sharing of a common household (Toseland and McCallion 1997).

The responsibility for the care of a frail elderly family member is rarely shared equally by all family members. It is primarily, but not exclusively, a female responsibility, explained partly by the greater prevalence of females among frail elders in need of assistance (Lee, Dwyer, and Coward 1993; Marks 1996). This trend has encouraged an exclusive focus on the needs of female caregivers in many studies (Kramer 1997). Social workers should, however, recognize that there are also many male caregivers for whom they may be asked to provide assistance (Harris 1998; Kaye and Applegate 1990).

A family generally has one primary caregiver. It has been suggested that the decision about who will provide care follows a "principle of substitution," with one family member providing most of the care (Shanas 1968). If a spouse is available, he or she is most likely to provide care. If not, then an adult daughter is most likely to become the primary caregiver. In the absence of an adult daughter, a son or daughter-in-law is most likely to provide care. If none of these family members are available, other relatives, neighbors, and friends are the next most likely to provide care. The identification of a primary caregiver has led many social workers and other service providers to focus attention solely on this family member. However, there is increasing evidence of the importance of the additional support provided by siblings (Connidis 1997), sons (Archer and MacLean 1993; Harris 1998), spouses of adult daughter primary caregivers (Kleban et al. 1989), adolescent grandchildren (Beach 1997), and even favorite nephews and nieces (Atchley and Miller 1986). Evidence also indicates that these other family members are affected by caregiving and influence the stress experienced by the primary caregiver (Beach 1997; Kleban et al. 1989; Toseland, Smith, and McCallion 1995).

DEMOGRAPHIC PATTERNS

The average primary caregiver to a frail older person is an adult daughter or daughter-in-law, aged 46, with a high school education or some college, who is married and has a 40 percent likelihood of also having a child under 18 in the household. Sixty-four percent of caregivers are still working, but one-third of those not currently working did work at one point during their caregiving responsibilities. The older person being cared for is most frequently a female relative, aged 75 or older, with a chronic illness or condition. Only 5 percent of caregivers report taking care of a spouse, yet 23 percent of caregivers over 65 are spouses, and spouses are more likely to be caring for individuals with major caregiving needs (National Alliance for Caregiving/American Association of Retired Persons 1997). This profile also masks some other important trends; for example, the growing role of men as primary caregivers. Marks (1996) reports that as many as one in seven of older adult men are primary family caregivers. Also, a focus on primary caregivers does not recognize the contributions of other family members to maintaining the caregiving situation. Nevertheless, the profile reflects several important demographic trends influencing traditional views of caregiving patterns in families.

An important social trend influencing social work practice with family caregiving is the increasing longevity of the elders who are care recipients (Cantor 1991). Already the number of elderly persons has almost doubled from nearly 17 million in 1960. It is projected that there will be 51.1 million elderly persons by 2020, and 66.6 million by 2040. The most rapid growth will occur among those 85 and older (Biegel and Blum 1990; Cantor 1991). It is also estimated that the number of persons aged 65 and older who are experiencing difficulty with activities of daily living will increase from 8.7 million in 1990 to 11.5 million by 2010, a 30.7 percent increase in just twenty years (Jette 1996).

As the population ages, family caregivers are being expected to care for increasingly aged family members who are likely to be in poorer health, to have more chronic disabilities, and to function less independently (Jette 1996). This trend has been greatly accelerated by changing health care policies, which have shortened hospital stays for both physical and mental health problems and have resulted in the discharge of increasingly frail older people who are in greater need of intensive home health care than ever before (Hooyman and Kiyak 1996). As care recipients become older and more disabled, so too do their family caregivers. In fact, spousal caregivers sometimes become so disabled themselves that they can no longer provide certain types of care, particularly care that requires lifting and other physical exertion. This increases the likelihood that the responsibility must be borne by younger family members. The aging of the population also means that the number of families comprising four and five generations will continue to expand. Increasingly, middle-aged relatives will become responsible either sequentially or simultaneously for the care of family members from two older generations (Cantor 1993).

Other important trends are the dramatic increase in single-parent families and lowered birthrates, which are resulting in older persons having fewer spouses and adult children available to care for them. Greater participation by women in the workforce is increasing the potential for conflict between work and caregiving responsibilities (Doty, Jackson, and Crown 1998). Increased participation in the workforce also means that adult daughters are delaying childbearing, which creates the potential for conflict between child care and elder care responsibilities. Findings already indicate that women born in the most recent cohorts are more likely to be caregivers than their predecessors and that they will experience two or more caregiving episodes in their lifetime (Jenkins 1997; Robinson, Moen, and Dempster-McClain 1995).

Social workers must recognize that these trends have increased the likelihood that adult children will assume caregiving roles. Also, traditional divisions of caregiving roles by gender are being eroded, caregiving demands are being placed on all available family members, and family caregivers are increasingly likely to be stressed by their multiple responsibilities (Kaye and Applegate 1990; Sanborn and Bould 1991; Toseland, Smith, and McCallion 1995). Rather than focusing exclusively on one individual, the primary caregiver, social workers should recognize the growing need for family-based interventions. For example, they should be sensitive to differential sharing of caregiving responsibilities among family members that can cause conflict, particularly among siblings, who may become angered by the lack of involvement of brothers or sisters in the care of a parent. Also, social workers should be prepared to respond to conflicts that arise in families when time spent on caregiving for a frail elder is seen as impeding other family activities and relationships (Smith, Smith, and Toseland 1991; Strawbridge and Wallhagan 1991; Toseland, Smith, and McCallion 1995). Attention directed to the family caregiving system is most likely to result in benefits for caregivers and care recipients.

A critical population trend is that older persons from minority groups are a rapidly growing segment of the population (Angel and Hogan 1992; Aponte and Crouch 1995). People of color constituted 20 percent of elderly in 1980, and 26 percent of elderly by 1995. They are projected to represent 33 percent of elderly by 2050 (Markides and Miranda 1997). Also, their needs for service are often greater than those of the majority. For example, on most health status indicators, black and Hispanic/Latino elderly are less healthy than white elderly (Gibson 1991; Stump et al. 1997). On other measures, black and Hispanic/Latino elderly have less formal education and lower occupational status, are overrepresented in the lower socioeconomic strata of society, and have fewer retirement resources (Nickens 1995; Shay, Miles, and Hayward 1996). Caregivers of color also have been found to have lower incomes and to be less educated and in poorer health (for a review see Pruchno, Patrick, and Burant 1997). Nevertheless, relatively little attention has been paid to minority caregivers, and their participation levels in interventions and in research studies have been low (Schulz et al. 1995; Toseland and McCallion 1997).

Some studies suggest that little is actually known about how minority caregivers respond to specific stressors, or about whether intervention programs designed to alleviate caregiving stress are effective with minority populations (Toseland and McCallion 1997). Therefore, greater attention to the needs of minority family caregivers by social work practitioners and researchers is urgently needed. Investigations of lower usage of caregiver intervention programs by members of cultural minorities have found a greater reliance on filial piety, greater availability of extended family supports, distrust of formal structures, and cultural beliefs that one should take care of "one's own" (for a review see McCallion, Janicki, and Grant-Griffin 1997). However, social workers must also recognize and respond to society's structural barriers to service use that may result in needy caregiving families of color receiving the least amount of services. These barriers include the experience of historical discrimination for all, legal status concerns for some, and alienation from services that have been developed for rather than by the families to be served (Johnson 1995; Lockery 1991). In addition, there are economic, religious, transportation, financial, and insurance barriers, and caregivers of color report not feeling welcomed by other participants, feeling like outsiders in the locations chosen for the intervention, and interventions do not meet their needs (Henderson et al. 1993; McCallion et al. 1997). Social workers can respond by developing and implementing culturally sensitive interventions, involving locally based multicultural service agencies in outreach and service delivery, and having participants of color choose the intervention leader, the location of the intervention, the timing of the sessions, and the range of issues to be addressed (Henderson et al. 1993; Henderson and Gutierrez-Mayka 1992; McCallion et al. 1997; McCallion and Grant-Griffin 2000; Toseland and Rivas 1998).

SOCIETAL CONTEXT

Social workers who are concerned about the welfare of families caring for frail elders must be knowledgeable about key policy issues affecting this population. Those policies are shaped by (1) conflicting perspectives on how best to support family caregiving, (2) a view among policymakers that government action should be a last resort, and (3) changes in health system and employer roles.

Policymakers are faced with contradictory imperatives when considering how best to **support family caregiving.** These imperatives are to (a) relieve families from their voluntary assumed burden of care or (b) provide incentives to ensure that families will fulfill caregiving responsibilities they will otherwise avoid. Pursuit of one or the other of these imperatives has led to sometimes conflicting policies designed to (1) engage families in caregiving who would not otherwise do so, (2) maximize the amount and duration of caregiving, (3) enable families to provide better care, (4) make the job of caregiving less burdensome for families, and (5) ensure that the expectation of family caregiving is appropriate and equitable (Kane and Penrod 1993; Winbush 1993). The policy "picture" is further obscured by racial, ethnic, socioeconomic, geographical, and cohort differences among caregiving families (Townsend 1993); the "families with young children" bias in family policy (Neiderhardt and Allen 1993); the differing patterns of "family" involvement in family caregiving (Kane and Penrod 1993); and the impact of other policy concerns such as family versus public responsibility, using institutional versus community supports, primacy of women's versus men's issues, and addressing equity issues among the generations (Winbush 1993).

Social workers face a major challenge to expand the definition of family and to convince policymakers to give priority to the alleviation of the burdens of family caregiving for elders. The pursuit of assistance has not been helped when the debate has been couched in terms of redistributing scarce resources from families with young children to older families. Instead, the strategy should be to focus on multigenerational concerns and to emphasize the prevalence of caregiving at all stages of the family life cycle, and the need for supports to sustain all family caregiving.

Society has responded in many ways to the changing needs of family caregivers. Overall, **governmental response** has been driven by beliefs that public supports should only occur after family resources are exhausted, or the family is not able to meet basic standards of care. In those situations, services have been focused on the care recipient elder in need, rather than the family (Moen and Forest 1995; Wilcox and O'Keefe 1991). However, to address concerns about the potential for collapse of family care, and to reduce the costs associated with the premature institutionalization of elderly persons, foreshadowed by the previously mentioned demographic trends, governmental agencies have considered a number of policy initiatives, such as the following: (1) meeting intensive-care needs by increasing the availability of formal home care programs and case management services, (2) subsidizing formal services to supplement family care, (3) providing financial relief in the form of cash payments or expanded tax allowances, (4) compensating for the opportunity cost of foregone employment, and (5) providing respite and educational and counseling programs for caregivers (Hooyman and Kiyak 1996). For example, the 1987 amendments to the Older Americans Act permit limited services for the families of frail elders, and eligibility for dependent care tax allowances has been expanded. However, the Family Caregiver Support Act introduced in 1993 and providing caregivers with an entitlement of $2,400 for supportive services for caregivers of individuals with functional disabilities was not passed by Congress. Similarly, some steps have been taken to reduce the likelihood of spousal impoverishment upon entry of one partner into a nursing home, but the financing of long-term care remains a thorny and divisive issue (Stone and Keigher 1994). There is a belief that the motivations for family caregiving are primarily emotional. Monetary incentives such as cash grants or tax allowances are perceived as unlikely to motivate families to provide home care that they would not otherwise provide, and risk encouraging families who are providing care to rely upon government rather than themselves (Gatz et al. 1990). Thus, a policy approach has emerged that tends to be crisis oriented rather than prevention or support oriented. Equally important, the absence of data demonstrating the cost effectiveness of family and caregiver support programs does not encourage consideration of a different orientation. Providing the rationale and supportive evidence for preventive and supportive policy approaches represents a major challenge for social workers (Toseland and McCallion 1997).

Several factors have come together both to maintain the lack of governmental response to the needs of family caregivers and to involve **health delivery systems and employers** in the debate. For example, fiscal concerns, particularly fears for the financial viability of both Medicare and Medicaid, have impeded efforts to have health providers expand home health care and intensive case management programs. Although evaluations of numerous home care demonstration programs have indicated that family members benefit from expanded home care coverage and that such programs effectively supplement but do not reduce informal family caregiving, long-standing evidence indicates that such programs are not cost-effective in regard to reducing health care costs for frail older persons (Kemper, Applebaum, and Harrigan 1987).

There have been calls for public policy to emphasize programs aimed at alleviating the emotional stress associated with caregiving such as support groups, counseling, and respite services (Buck et al. 1997; Jutras and Levoie 1995). This is consistent with observations that the emotional stresses of caregiving are often more difficult for caregivers to cope with than are either the physical or the financial aspects of caregiving. Indeed, a wide array of religious, civic, and governmental health, mental health, and social service agencies have begun to offer programs of respite, support, and counseling for family caregivers. However, here too the absence of cost-effectiveness data for these interventions has made it difficult to find reimbursement for caregiver support services, and there are concerns that under increasingly prevalent managed approaches to health care existing money for psychosocial and health education programs will shrink (Mizrahi 1993). A challenge facing social work researchers and practitioners is to better measure the impact of interventions on the well-being of caregivers and care recipients and to connect those outcomes to health care utilization and cost outcomes to justify support for psychosocial programs for caregiving families (Toseland and McCallion 1997).

The pervasiveness of family caregiving, combined with the high employment rate of females, has begun to stimulate a response from employers. The Family Care and Medical Assistance Act of 1993 offers job protection to workers who take short-term leaves from their jobs to care for a dependent parent or child. However, 50 percent of private firm employees do not qualify because of the size of their employer. Nevertheless, realizing that caregiving responsibilities may result in absences by key employees and can affect morale and productivity, a number of corporations now provide programs of education and support through employee assistance programs, as well as flexible benefit packages that enable employees to continue to fulfill caregiving responsibilities (Barr, Johnson, and Warshaw 1992; Helfrich and Dodson 1992). Some programs are funded directly by employers. However, many are supported through the behavioral health component of employer-provided health care plans. Similar to publicly funded programs, continued support and expansion of these programs will depend on the ability of social work researchers and practitioners to demonstrate the cost effectiveness of such programs.

Society's responses to the needs of caregivers at the health system and employer levels have been limited. They suggest that there will continue to be an expanding role for social work practitioners in advocating for, developing, and implementing caregiver support programs.

VULNERABILITIES AND RISK FACTORS

Primary caregivers to the frail elderly and their families are at risk for a variety of adverse outcomes arising from the many stresses associated with providing care to an older adult with significant cognitive and/or physical impairments. Although numerous theoretical models to predict and explain caregiving outcomes have emerged in the literature (see, for review, Raveis, Siegel, and Sudit 1990), the predominant conceptual model assumes that the onset and progression of chronic illness and physical disability is stressful for the care recipient, the primary caregiver, as well as other family members and, as such, is best studied within the framework of traditional stress and coping models (Schulz and Quittner 1998). Key outcome variables that have been studied within this framework include emotional distress, physical illness, reduced social participation, altered relationships with family members (including the elder who is being cared for), and demands on finance and worklife (Gatz et al. 1990).

Emotional Risks. Recent evidence clearly indicates that emotional health is the one aspect of primary caregivers' lives that is most affected by caring for a frail elderly family member. Some of the problems that family caregivers find most difficult to cope with emotionally include: loss of control over one's time, which may lead to anger and frustration; guilt, as though he or she is not being fair to the care receiver or other family members; loss of privacy if the elder lives with the caregiver; and consistent or periodic grieving over the care receiver's decline, which may lead to feelings of guilt and depression because that person is still alive (Bass 1990). In terms of coping behaviors, it is known that caregivers' use of fantasy, wishful thinking, passive avoidance, and self-blame or internal attribution are associated with lower well-being, burden, depression, and anxiety (Neundorfer 1991).

When compared with either population norms or control groups, primary caregivers have been found by researchers to be more depressed and anxious, express higher levels of negative affect, more likely to use psychotropic medications, and have more symptoms of overall psychological distress than the general population (see, for reviews, Neundorfer 1991; Schulz et al. 1995; Schulz and Williamson 1994). Among these adverse emotional outcomes, however, depression seems to represent the greatest risk. Clinical reports show that 50 percent of caregivers get depressed in the first year of caregiving (Butler 1992), while empirical studies have led to the belief that "a substantial number of caregivers may be experiencing depression of a severity that could warrant intervention and treatment" (Schulz et al. 1995:772).

Significant shortcomings of the research that has yielded these findings should be noted, however, before conclusions about the emotional risks to family caregivers of the frail elderly can be drawn with certainty. One problem is that those investigators who have found high levels of emotional distress often obtained their samples through support groups or local media solicitations, whereas the few researchers who studied more representative samples of family caregivers have found much lower rates of symptomatology (Schulz and Williamson 1994).

Much of the research on caregiver's emotional health may also be criticized on the grounds that it does not adequately reflect the great diversity that exists among both the personal characteristics of caregivers and the nature and severity of the disability (Schofield et al. 1997; Schulz and Quittner 1998). Because the vast majority of researchers have focused on caregivers to Alzheimer's patients, for example, very little is currently known about the emotional impact of caregiving for elders with other disorders such as stroke, heart disease, or cancer.

Another limitation of the existing research in this area involves failure to distinguish normal distress from psychiatric illness. Although episodes of grief, despair, helplessness, and hopelessness may be much more common among family caregivers, they are usually circumscribed enough to allow them to retain a problem-focused orientation in coping with the care recipient's needs (Schulz and Williamson 1994).

Physical Risks. Family caregivers to the frail elderly often report that caregiving has caused their physical health to deteriorate, expressing such changes as interrupted sleep, chronic fatigue, muscle aches, irregular eating, and lack of time to take care of themselves as common complaints. Yet when caregivers are compared to noncaregiver aged peers on objective indicators of physical health (e.g., reported illnesses, symptomatology, health care utilization, health-related behaviors, or indicators of cardiovascular functioning), the evidence that caregivers have poorer health is inconclusive (Neundorfer 1991; Schulz et al. 1995).

Several possible explanations exist regarding the lack of objective physical health changes found among family caregivers despite their subjective complaints. It may be, for example, that physical health effects are difficult to detect because they take a long time to develop and do not appear until after the caregiving role is over (Schulz et al. 1995). Another possibility is that only those individuals who are in excellent health to begin with are likely to take on the demands of being a primary caregiver (Neundorfer 1991). Studies on the effects of caregiving on physical health also have suffered from many of the same methodological limitations noted earlier for research on the emotional well-being of family caregivers (Schulz and Williamson 1994). Thus, at the present time, it seems risky to conclude that family caregivers to the frail elderly are without risk to their physical health status.

Financial and Work-Related Risks. Numerous circumstances surrounding family caregiving to the frail elderly place families at risk financially. These include added medical, therapeutic, and equipment costs that are often not covered by insurance, as well as additional expenses such as those for increased use of utilities (e.g., washer and dryer due to incontinence) or for special food or clothing (Bass 1990). Perhaps the greatest financial risk associated with caregiving, however, involves lost opportunity costs due to reduced or ended employment.

In a national survey of family caregivers, Stone, Cafferata, and Sangl (1987) found that 20 percent of employed caregivers experienced conflict. This was evidenced by the additional findings that 20 percent of these working caregivers had reduced their work hours, 29 percent rearranged their schedules, and 19 percent took time off without pay. Moreover, working caregivers who had to adjust their employment because of caregiving seemed to suffer higher levels of emotional strain from caregiving than those who did not. The demands of caregiving can also result in leaving the workforce, thus sacrificing earnings, employee benefits, retirement benefits, as well as a source of personal satisfaction (Anastas, Gibeau, and Larson 1990).

Data from a national survey of working caregivers indicate that this population also possesses high needs for assistance within the workplace (Anastas et al. 1990). Few employees reported access to such family-related benefits as day care for dependent adults or children, and only 2 percent had received relevant information from employee assistance programs. The majority of the sample, however, said that they would have liked access to such employee benefits as information and referral about elder care, the flexibility to make individual decisions about work hours, reduced work hours with access to full benefits, flexible or cafeteria benefit plans, and elder day care. Interestingly, 77 percent of these respondents said that they would be willing to share the cost of such benefits.

Social and Family Risks. Family caregiving to the frail elderly also can contribute to social and interpersonal problems. Leisure and recreational activities of primary caregivers are often restricted, and they frequently report feeling trapped, isolated, and alone in this role (Farkas 1980).

There has been increased attention by gerontologists to the fact that the risks of family caregiving extend well beyond the primary caregiver to encompass the entire family system. Tasks faced by primary caregivers that may radiate to other family members and disrupt family equilibrium include: (1) maintaining family communication and the exchange of information, (2) balancing the needs of the care recipient with the needs of other family members, (3) managing feelings toward the other family members who do not help, (4) maintaining the family as an effective decision-making group over a long period of time, and (5) designating other responsible caregivers when necessary (Couper and Sheehan 1987). (See Toseland, Smith, and McCallion 1995 for a discussion of the impact of caregiving on individual family members other than the primary caregiver.)

Families themselves typically perceive caregiving to affect overall family functioning. Strawbridge and Wallhagan (1991), for example, reported that as many as 40 percent of the caregiving families they surveyed had experienced family conflict. Strain on the entire family system may result from such issues as conflict between caregiving obligations and other family tasks, disagreements among family members about the form or amount of caregiving, readjustments in family roles, the emotional impact of caregiving on all involved family members, and feelings of family stigma (Bass 1990; Gatz et al. 1990). Families with the greatest risk for negative outcomes are those having poor communication skills, limited resources, many demands on their time and resources, suppressed or open conflicts, poor parent-child relationships, and high resistance to change (Moore 1987).

Racial/Ethnic Differences. Social workers who serve caregiving families should also recognize that the effects of caregiving may vary according to the racial or ethnic background of the family. Recent evidence, for example, suggests that African American families may be more resilient to negative psychological effects of the stress of caregiving than are white families (Connell and Gibson 1997; Haley et al. 1993). White caregivers generally report higher levels of adverse emotional responses (e.g., depression and burden), but caregiving appears to produce similar social consequences for black and white families, including restriction of social activity and increased visits and supports by family from outside the home. In contrast, Aranda and Knight (1997) concluded that Latino caregivers experience at least similar and possibly higher levels of burden and depression than Anglos.

Social workers should interpret the preceding findings cautiously, however, because comparing racial or ethnic groups is made questionable by the risk of attributing to race or ethnicity what may instead be due to socioeconomic, educational, cultural, or historical differences. In fact, when such confounding factors were taken into account, several authors concluded that racial differences in the caregiving experience were minimal (see, for review, Connell and Gibson 1997). Therefore, stereotyping families by ethnicity may lead social workers to assume a level of adjustment to caregiving and availability of extended family support that is not true for a particular caregiving family. This may result in social workers not recognizing a caregiver's need for assistance (McCallion et al. 1997). Moreover, the possibility that differences exist within and between subgroups of various racial or ethnic populations of family caregivers has been insufficiently examined to date.

RESILIENCIES AND PROTECTIVE FACTORS

Despite the many risks associated with family caregiving to the frail elderly described in the previous section, gerontologists and family scholars have recently acknowledged that caregiving is not always bad for the primary caregiver, the care recipient, or other family members (Schulz and Quittner 1998; Toseland, Smith, and McCallion 1995). It is also important for social workers to realize that even though caregiving families are confronted by a great deal of stress, they typically are not troubled families requiring psychological treatment or family therapy. Instead, caregiving is best viewed as a "normative" family stress and "to apply models from psychopathology is to ignore the essential strengths of both recipients and families" (Gatz et al. 1990:405).

The situation of providing care to a frail elderly family member is, thus, best conceptualized as a family systems problem. As such, traditional models from the stress and coping literature, which have dominated the family caregiving literature to date, appear to possess three major limitations (Gatz et al. 1990): (1) They focus rather narrowly on the concerns of the primary caregiver; (2) they make little revision for including the perspective of other family members, especially the elder; and (3) positive outcomes are rarely recognized or explored.

Positive Aspects of Family Caregiving. In light of the overriding emphasis on risk and negative outcomes within the existing family caregiving literature, it is often difficult for practitioners and researchers alike to focus on the positive aspects of family caregiving to the frail elderly (Kramer 1997). Nevertheless, numerous potential gains to primary caregivers have been identified, including a sense of competence in managing the caregiving tasks, self-respect or recognition by others for taking on care-giving duties, satisfaction that they have proved their love or returned the type of care that they received at an earlier time from the care receiver, resolution of earlier un-resolved feelings or issues, and a sense of feeling needed or useful (Bass 1990; Gatz et al. 1990; Pearlin et al. 1996). Possible gains for the entire family include feeling secure in a strong kinship system, attaining a better understanding of each other's needs, and reaching a greater tolerance for other people's problems (Bass 1990; Beach 1997).

In a recent literature review, Kramer (1997) pointed out that the strong emphasis on the negative aspects of family caregiving to the frail elderly is consistent with the tendency among social scientists to focus on general measures of psychological dys-function. Of much relevance to clinical social workers, however, she went on to assert four important reasons to study the positive aspects of family caregiving: (1) Positive outcomes are reported by many caregivers and are something they want to talk about; (2) by recognizing the ways in which individuals feel enriched by caregiving, prac-titioners may more appropriately validate feelings and experiences; (3) attending to positive outcomes is consistent with a strengths perspective that recognizes the con-tinued growth in each individual; and (4) the positive features of caregiving may be important determinants of the quality of care provided to the frail elderly.

The Family Resilience Model of Adaptation. In view of the deficiency of traditional stress and coping models to both not recognize the positive aspects of family caregiv-ing and not encompass a family systems perspective, social workers may wish to embrace the newly emerging "family resilience" perspective as a means of under-standing how families respond to the challenge of caring for the frail elderly. The concept of family resilience, which refers to those qualities that enable a family to maintain its equilibrium as it experiences crisis, involves three important character-istics that make it particularly relevant to families with care responsibilities for the frail elderly (Hawley and DeHaan 1996; McCubbin, McCubbin, and Thompson 1993): (1) Resilience is believed to surface during periods of family strain or hardship, in-cluding times of normative family stress such as providing care to sick or dependent family members; (2) resilient families are presumed to return to a level of functioning at or above their precrisis level; and (3) families are viewed in terms of wellness rather than pathology, thus focusing on the ways in which families are successful rather than on how they fail.

The family resilience perspective is especially useful in identifying why some families are shattered by crises or persistent stresses like family caregiving to the frail elderly, while others emerge strengthened and more resourceful from such events. Walsh (1996), for example, described several important attributes that characterize resilient families. For one thing, research has shown that family resilience is associ-ated with such key family processes as cohesion, flexibility, open communication, problem solving, and affirming belief systems. Another essential feature of family resilience noted by Walsh is the availability of community resources and a family's willingness to use them. The importance of community resources to families providing care to the frail elderly is discussed in a later section of this chapter.

The most crucial characteristic of resilient families, however, concerns how they make sense of a crisis or stressful situation and endow it with meaning (Hawley and DeHaan 1996; McCubbin et al. 1993; Walsh 1996). McCubbin et al. (1993), for example, referred to this as the "family schema," which encompasses the family's shared values, goals, priorities, expectations, and worldview. According to these authors, "Families who reveal their schema tend to emphasize their investment in themselves, their values and goals, their investment in the family's collective we rather than I, their sense of shared influence, trust in others, as well as their optimistic view of life situations complemented by a relativistic view of life circumstances and willingness to accept optimal rather than perfect solutions to all their demands" (156).

Although virtually none of the extant research on family caregivers to the frail elderly has drawn on the family resilience perspective (see, for exception, McCubbin et al. 1993), it is quite interesting that many variables indicative of family schema (e.g., motivations for helping, and caregiving ideology) appear to be associated with caregiver gain (see, for review, Kramer 1997). Noonan and Tennstedt (1997), for example, found that meaning in caregiving was negatively associated with depressive symptoms and positively associated with self-esteem, even after the objective stresses of caregiving were taken into account. Similarly, Farran (1997) has concluded that even the most stressful aspects of caring for dementia patients may "provide caregivers the opportunity to find provisional and ultimate meaning; that the process of finding meaning or seeing the positive is a choice that caregivers can make; that their pre-existing values provide a basis for meaning; and that caregivers have responsibility for right action and conduct" (252). An important area for future social work research and practice, therefore, is determining how and if the meanings that primary caregivers attach to caring for a frail elderly relative are derived from their underlying family schema.

In summary, the family resilience model of adaptation has several important clinical implications for social workers who serve caregiving families (Hawley and DeHaan 1996; Walsh 1996). First, whenever possible, practitioners should encourage primary caregivers and their families to discover positive meanings within the family caregiving situation. Second, clinicians should realize that resilience is best detected by observing families over time and within their unique context. Thus, not only is it crucial to identify interaction patterns that helped families exhibit resilience at points in their past, but it must also be realized that the processes needed for effective family functioning may vary depending on differing sociocultural contexts and developmental challenges. Thus, an important caveat is that what worked to weather past family crises (e.g., divorce or widowhood) may not necessarily be relevant for dealing with current stresses related to family caregiving. Finally, social workers should also recognize that successful adaptation to family caregiving requires the availability and use of both intrafamilial and environmental resources.

PROGRAMS AND SOCIAL WORK CONTRIBUTIONS

For many years, social work programs and services were focused directly on older adults. Programs and services were targeted to three subgroups: (1) helping well older adults to engage in social and recreational activities with their peers in community centers and settlement houses (Kubie and Landau 1953; Maxwell 1952; Wilson and Ryland 1949), (2) providing protective and preventive casework services to frail older adults in in-home community settings (Blenkner et al. 1974), and (3) providing remedial services to very frail older adults in nursing homes and psychiatric facilities (Linden 1953; Shore 1952; Silver 1950). When family caregivers were actively involved in the care of a frail older person, they were not ignored, but they were rarely recognized as the target of intervention. Over the years, an increasing awareness of the importance of family caregivers has led to the development of programs targeted specifically at them. The current programmatic response, therefore, consists both of programs for frail elderly persons that indirectly benefit family caregivers, and of programs specifically designed to benefit family caregivers directly.

Many different programs, sponsored by a broad mix of public, voluntary, and private social service providers and delivered by paraprofessionals or professionals, have been developed to support family caregivers. These programs can be categorized into (1) respite and medical and social day care, (2) support groups, (3) individual and family counseling, and (4) specialized educational and training.

Respite programs are designed to provide periodic relief to family caregivers. There are two broad types of respite programs: (1) temporary inpatient placement in residential facilities, nursing homes, or hospitals; and (2) in-home respite by paid homemakers or home health aides (Gallagher 1985; Gallagher, Lovett, and Zeiss 1989). Most of these programs do not provide psychotherapeutic interventions for the family member or the patient. Instead, they provide personal care for a fixed period of time, often not exceeding one or two weeks. *Medical and social day care programs* provide a more extended form of respite. Although programs vary, some adult day care programs provide personal care for frail older adults in a congregate setting for as much as eight or nine hours each weekday, thereby enabling working caregivers to continue part-time or full-time employment.

Time off from the unrelenting demands of caregiving are believed to be directly therapeutic for the caregiver, and indirectly therapeutic for the care receiver (Lawton, Brody, and Saperstein 1989). However, relatively little is actually known about the effectiveness of respite services (Flint 1995; Shantz 1995). In one study, respite services produced caregiver satisfaction and enabled care receivers to remain in the community longer, but they were ineffective in reducing caregivers' burdens or in improving the caregivers' mental health (Lawton et al. 1989). Koloski and Montgomery (1995) found that the amount of respite care used was negatively associated with nursing home placement. Yet a rigorous review of the literature by Flint (1995) concluded that there were only five high-quality studies, and these studies indicated little evidence that respite care had a significant effect on caregivers' function, psychiatric status, or physical health; or on patients' cognition, function, physical health, or rate of institutionalization. Also, there is some question about how receptive family caregivers and older adults are to using respite services (Beisecker et al. 1996; Cohen-Mansfield et al. 1994; Montgomery and Borgota 1989; Rudin 1994; Worchester and Hedrick 1997), and whether the effectiveness of respite programs is sufficient to warrant government expenditures (Callahan 1989).

Different kinds of respite programs may be used in combination for various purposes, depending on the needs manifested in a particular situation. For example, a

52-year-old single daughter who lived alone with her frail 78-year-old mother paid homemakers to care for her parent while she was at work. The caregiver felt that this arrangement helped her to maintain her ability to care for her mother while getting some relief from what she described as an "extremely close, sometimes too close, relationship with my mother." Twice a year, the daughter also arranged for inpatient respite care at a local nursing home so that she could enjoy vacations away from her job and her caregiving responsibilities.

There are also many different types of *support group programs* for family caregivers. Most mix education, discussion, and social activities in a warm, empathic atmosphere that emphasizes mutual sharing and mutual help, but some are more psychoeducationally oriented, focusing on the acquisition of specific problem-solving and coping skills (McCallion, Diehl, and Toseland 1994; McCallion and Toseland 1996; McCallion, Toseland, and Diehl 1994; Toseland and McCallion 1997). Groups may be short term or long term and may have closed or open membership policies. Support groups can prevent and alleviate stress in many ways: (1) providing caregivers with a respite from caregiving; (2) reducing isolation and loneliness; (3) encouraging the ventilation of pent-up emotions and the sharing of feelings and experiences; (4) validating, universalizing, and normalizing caregivers' experiences; (5) instilling hope and affirming the importance of the caregivers' role; (6) educating caregivers about the aging process, the effects of chronic disabilities, and community resources; (7) teaching effective problem-solving and coping strategies; and (8) helping caregivers to identify, develop, and implement effective action plans to resolve pressing problems related to caregiving (Toseland and Rossiter 1989).

The early clinical literature, which was largely based on case studies of individual groups, indicated that family caregivers found participation in support groups highly beneficial and satisfying (Toseland and Rossiter 1989). More recent studies that have utilized larger sample sizes and more rigorous research designs are somewhat more equivocal but indicate, in most cases, that groups can improve caregivers' mental and physical well-being, increase their knowledge of community resources and the size of their informal support networks, and alleviate pressing problems associated with caregiving (see, for reviews, Bourgeois, Schulz, and Burgio 1996; McCallion, Diehl, and Toseland 1994; McCallion and Toseland 1996; McCallion, Toseland, and Diehl 1994; Toseland and McCallion 1997; Toseland and Rossiter 1989).

Less information is available about *individual and family-oriented counseling programs* for caregivers, perhaps because family caregivers often seek help through the regular, scheduled counseling programs of family service and community mental health agencies, where their problems are defined not as family care per se but as marital, family, or mental health problems. Studies of individual counseling programs for caregivers have yielded promising results. For example, Gallagher and her colleagues (Gallagher and Czirr 1984; Gallagher et al. 1989) found that individual therapy reduced depression among caregivers and helped them cope with anticipatory grief over the impending loss of a frail elderly family member. Toseland and Smith (1990) found that short-term individual counseling was effective in decreasing symptoms of psychological distress and in increasing feelings of competence and well-being. Mittelman and colleagues developed an intervention program for caregivers of Alzheimer's patients that used a combination of individual, group, and family intervention strategies, which was very effective in increasing the psychosocial well-being of caregivers as well as delaying the institutionalization of care recipients (Mittelman et al. 1993, 1995, 1996).

In one of the few studies that have compared individual and group intervention modalities, it was found that individual intervention had more impact on caregivers' psychological well-being, whereas group intervention had more impact on the social support that was available to caregivers (Toseland et al. 1990). A meta-analytic study of caregiver intervention programs also found that individual intervention may be more effective than group intervention in alleviating caregiver burden and psychological distress (Knight, Lutzky, and Macofsky-Urban 1993). However, Zarit, Anthony, and Boutselis (1987) found that a program of individual and family counseling was no more effective than no treatment in reducing the burden and psychological problems associated with caregiving, and Toseland, Blanchard, and McCallion (1995) found only modest effects for a program of individual counseling for caregivers of cancer patients.

There is little doubt that caregiving is associated with increased family conflict and with heightened concerns and anxieties about neglecting other family members (see, e.g., Horowitz 1985). However, despite the extensive attention that has been given to the impact of caregiving on marital and family relationships, "very few program descriptions or evaluations are published in family or gerontological journals" (Brubaker and Roberto 1993:218). In a review article, Zarit and Teri (1991) suggested that the lack of attention to family interventions may be because of their cost and the limited availability of third-party reimbursement. Others, however, have suggested that the paucity of attention to these interventions may reflect gerontological practitioners' discomfort with family strife (Couper and Sheehan 1987) or primary caregivers' reluctance to ask other family members to become involved in family counseling because of long-standing family conflicts and fears that the care recipients' feelings will be hurt (Toseland, Smith, and McCallion 1995). Most of the reports of family counseling for caregivers are based on accumulated clinical practice experience, case examples, studies without randomized control groups, or multimodal intervention programs that included family counseling along with other types of interventions. These sources indicate that when family members are willing to participate, family therapy can be a particularly effective modality for improving communication and reducing interpersonal conflict, for developing coordinated care plans, and for resolving specific problems that arise as the caregiving situation develops and evolves over time (see, e.g., Carter and McGoldrick 1980; Ferris et al. 1987; Herr and Weakland 1979; Lowy 1985; Quayhagen and Quayhagen 1994).

Many *specialized education and training programs* have also been developed for family caregivers. Some are one-session community forums sponsored by religious, civic, and governmental agencies where service providers describe the available community programs and services, and caregivers are encouraged to ask questions and to find out how to apply for service. These programs reach out to caregivers who might not otherwise learn about the programs and services available to help them care for a frail relative. Other educational programs provide weekly or monthly seminars that focus on different topics related to caregiving. Specialized training programs also have been developed for family and professional caregivers. Toseland and colleagues (McCallion, Toseland, and Freeman 1999; Toseland and McCallion 1998), for example, have developed a program for improving communication and interaction with older adults with dementia that can be used by both family caregivers and professional caregivers. These programs are particularly exemplary because they demonstrate that a partnership can be forged between social workers and family caregivers, with social workers helping caregivers to maximize their abilities to provide high-quality care to frail older adults.

The emotional ties that family caregivers have to their frail elderly relatives means that any social service program that benefits frail older people has the potential to benefit family caregivers. In fact, some programs designed for frail older persons have been found to have at least as profound an effect on family caregivers as they have had on frail older persons (Kemper et al. 1987). Therefore, to be maximally effective when working with family caregivers, social workers should be familiar with all the community programs and services that are available for the frail elderly, not just those that are specifically focused on family caregivers.

In most localities, the county department of aging, the area agency on aging, or the local community-planning agency have an up-to-date list of all the services that are available for older persons. Because frail older persons have most of the same needs as other older people, a general list of programs and services for older persons is indispensable for effective practice. It is usually best to begin with an existing directory of community services, focusing on program descriptions, contact persons, and eligibility requirements for the kinds of programs and services that are particularly likely to be helpful to frail older persons. In some communities, resource guides may have to be updated or expanded. They should include services for older persons in the following areas: (1) financial, (2) legal, (3) housing, (4) home repair, (5) assisted living, (6) emergency response systems, (7) telephone reassurance, (8) friendly visiting, (9) congregate and in-home nutrition, (10) respite care, (11) day care, (12) home care, (13) outpatient and inpatient health care, (14) outpatient and inpatient mental health care, (15) adult home and nursing home care, (16) socialization, recreation, and education, (17) information and referral, (18) case management, (19) counseling, and (20) employment.

Social workers find that a combination of programs and services are often needed to effectively serve frail older persons and family caregivers. For example, a 52-year-old married daughter was willing and able to function as case manager for her 79-year-old father who lived by himself. After a careful assessment of the needs of the care receiver and the family member, the social worker helped them to arrange for Meals on Wheels, a part-time home health aide, and a twenty-four-hour medical emergency notification system made available by a local hospital. Also, a home energy assistance program, a reverse mortgage program, and a low-cost home repair program were all used to ensure that the elderly gentlemen would be able to remain in the home where he had lived for the past forty years.

ASSESSMENT AND INTERVENTIONS

Social work practice with family caregivers and their frail elders is similar to practice with other groups in that it is necessary to engage the client; to establish a therapeutic relationship; to assess needs; and to plan, implement, and monitor beneficial interventions (Toseland 1997). However, specific adaptations in these intervention processes are needed when working with family caregivers. Two sources are particularly useful for making these adaptations. Lazarus and Folkman's (1984) work on stress and coping provides a helpful theoretical orientation for practice with family caregivers. The life model's focus on adaptation to life transition problems such as family caregiving, its emphasis on people in the context of their social and physical environments, and its compatibility with a stress and coping theoretical orientation make it a particularly useful guide for practice with family caregivers (Germain and Gitterman 1980). Together, these two sources, as well as extensive clinical experience with family caregivers, form the basis for the adaptations for practice with family caregivers described here.

Making initial contact with caregivers can be more difficult than with some other client groups. Caregivers tend to be reluctant to ask for help. Most believe that it is their filial responsibility to provide care, and that relinquishing the responsibility would be like abandoning the person for whom they are caring. Because of their perceived self-competence, and because many have never had to ask for help before, pride may also be an obstacle. The anticipation or actual experience of resistance or refusal of "outside help" by the frail older person, as well as the bewildering complexity of the social service and health care system, can present obstacles even for highly motivated caregivers.

Some active outreach efforts, which may be needed to engage family caregivers, are feature newspaper stories; personal or telephone contact with social service, health care, and religious organizations that frequently come into contact with frail older persons; public service announcements on radio and television; appearances on local radio and television programs; and educational forums sponsored by community agencies. Special recruitment efforts may be needed for Hispanic, Afro-American, and Asian minorities, who do not respond well to these recruitment methods. Extensive personal contact with religious and civic leaders, networking with community organizations trusted in minority communities, and spending time getting to know a community and gaining the trust of its residents are more effective approaches (Damron-Rodriguez, Wallace, and Kington 1994; Gallagher-Thompson et. al. 1994; Henderson et al. 1993; McCallion, Janicki, and Grant-Griffin 1996; Toseland 1995).

In practice with family caregivers, engagement may mean reaching out beyond the family caregiver. In some situations, caregivers clearly seek help only for themselves. They want to learn to cope more effectively and do not want the care receiver, or other family members, involved. In such situations, the caregivers' wishes should be respected. But when resistance is not a problem, it can be useful to take a broader perspective. Although the perceptions of the caregiver are extremely important, a direct assessment of the care receiver, as well as one or more family meetings, can give the social worker a more complete understanding of the situation. The resulting information may also change the focus of the work. For example, instead of focusing exclusively on the caregiver, a family assessment may lead to additional service provision to the care receiver, or to other family members.

Once initial contact has been made, the worker should act as a supporter and an enabler. As a supporter, the social worker listens empathically to the caregivers' pent-up feelings and emotions. Many caregivers have not had the opportunity to express their feelings and welcome the opportunity. The worker validates and affirms the caregivers' experiences, applauding efforts by caregivers to take better care of themselves and to view their caregiving efforts more positively. An emphasis should be placed on caregivers' positive coping skills and their resilience in the face of a difficult, twenty-four-hour-a-day job. As an enabler, the social worker provides hope and encouragement, helping caregivers to mobilize their coping resources and their motivation, so that they can begin the process of working on troubling problems and concerns.

When conducting assessment and intervention planning, social workers should be aware of two important characteristics of family caregivers. First, caregivers are often reluctant to admit to difficulties, although they may be nearly overwhelmed by them. Instead of describing their emotional reactions, they tend to talk extensively about the care receiver and the circumstances surrounding the caregiving situation. They fear that their emotional reactions may be seen as complaining or uncaring. To encourage caregivers to acknowledge and accept their own thoughts, feelings, and actions in the caregiving situation, attentive, focused, and empathic listening is essential.

To familiarize the social worker with the development and evolution of the caregiving situation, it is helpful to begin assessments by taking a fairly detailed history of family relationships and interactions. Once this is completed, the worker assesses the current physical, psychological, and social functioning of the caregiver and the care receiver, as well as the environment context in which care is provided.

Because of the importance of the physical capacities and limitations of both the caregiver and the care receiver, social workers need to assess this area carefully. Any unmet health care needs should be addressed immediately. It is useful to obtain medical records and to conduct a thorough assessment of the functional status and mental health of the care receiver. For a detailed discussion of assessment techniques, see Kane (1990), Knight (1996) and Kaszniak (1996); for assessment instruments, see Kane and Kane (1981) and Kaszniak (1996).

In many health care settings, the social worker may be expected to focus on the psychological, social, and environmental needs of caregivers. Information about the course of illnesses, the effects of medications, the physical abilities of the caregiver and the care receiver, and any other health problems and needs may be provided by doctors, nurses, and physical therapists. When a team approach is used, the social worker is also often called on to coordinate input from other disciplines, developing a comprehensive helping plan based on a holistic view of the caregiver and the care receiver.

In the psychological realm, the worker assesses caregivers' emotional reactions to caregiving and their commonly used coping strategies. The worker should avoid focusing solely on deficits and maladaptive coping strategies. It is important to focus on protective as well as risk factors. Thus, workers should also assess the strengths and adaptive capacities of caregivers, and their resilience in the face of adverse situations.

Some evidence suggests that individual counseling is more effective than group counseling in helping caregivers to cope with depression, anxiety, and other commonly experienced psychiatric symptoms (Toseland et al. 1990). Individual and group defenses against the expression of painful and highly personal emotions tend to prevent their expression in caregiver support groups (Schmidt and Keyes 1985; Toseland et al. 1990; Toseland and Smith 1990). The privacy of individual counseling encourages caregivers to discuss severe difficulties in marital relationships, long-standing emotionally charged interpersonal conflicts with family members, and mental health problems that are not as likely to be shared in a support group (Smith, Tobin, and Toseland 1992; Toseland et al. 1990).

In the social realm, assessment and intervention planning should focus on the quality of the relationship between the caregiver and the care receiver, on the impact of caregiving on family life, and on the adequacy of social supports for the caregiver and the care receiver. Support groups should be considered the modality of choice when planning interventions for caregivers experiencing mild and moderate social and interpersonal problems (Toseland et al. 1990). Because they put caregivers in contact with others experiencing similar problems and concerns, support groups are particularly effective in reducing feelings of loneliness and isolation, and in increasing social support, and in helping caregivers to get feedback and suggestions about how to handle difficult interpersonal interactions (Toseland 1995; Toseland and Rivas 1998).

The social worker should also carefully appraise the caregivers' environmental problems. Features of the physical environment are particularly important. Walkers, lifts, ramps, handrails, and other special modifications to the physical environment can make providing care easier and can contribute to the physical well-being of both the caregiver and the care receiver.

It is also important to assess whether caregivers are making use of the available community-based services. Sometimes professional social workers forget how confusing the patchwork network of community services is for clients. One caregiver stated it well when she said, "I've been a high school math teacher for twenty-five years. I have a master's degree. I believe I am a fairly intelligent person. Do you know it took me nearly six months and endless phone calls to figure out how to get my mother the help she needed? Nobody seemed to know what anybody else was doing, and what's worse, a number of people gave me the wrong information. It was one of the most frustrating experiences I've ever had." Educational programs and resource guides that inform caregivers about available community services; the mutual sharing of information about community resources and services that takes place in a support group; and individual consultation, information, and referral can all be effective means of helping caregivers to make effective use of the available community services and resources. But because caregivers are often reluctant to reach out for services, social workers must follow up, making sure that caregivers receive the services they need. Also, when needed community services are unavailable, social workers should spend at least a portion of their time advocating for these services.

When intervening with family caregivers, social workers can act as *consultants, coordinators,* or *case managers.* Social workers adopt the *consultant role* in situations where the caregiver is functioning relatively well, has the necessary capacities and abilities to provide care, and desires only limited assistance. Before assuming a consultant role, social workers assess whether or not they can rely on the client to acknowledge a need and to request appropriate help. Ethical issues can arise when the worker's assessment suggests that the family caregiver needs more help than has been requested. In this situation, a general practice principle is that unless caregivers or care receivers are in jeopardy of endangering themselves or some other third party, their request for autonomy should be respected.

568 | *Life Circumstances and Events*

When assuming a consultant role, the worker recognizes and acknowledges the caregivers' competency and expertise. The worker relies heavily on the caregivers' input during assessment and intervention planning and assumes that the caregiver will take day-to-day responsibility for the implementation and monitoring of any intervention plan that is developed. Generally, an intensive period of consultation is followed by occasional contact to ensure that the caregiver will be able to implement the agreed-upon plan of action. Workers may also respond on an "as-needed basis" to specific requests for information, advice, or other help.

As a consultant, the social worker may be asked to provide guidance on how to handle a wide variety of problems and concerns. Some of the most frequent are (1) nursing-home placement; (2) adjustments in living status, such as when a frail older person moves in with the caregiver; (3) behavioral and emotional problems; (4) resistance to some aspect of care that the caregiver believes to be in the best interests of the care receiver; (5) alcoholism; and (6) help in dealing with mental or physical impairments such as those arising from Alzheimer's (Tonti and Silverstone 1985).

As *coordinators,* social workers take on greater responsibility for implementing and monitoring intervention plans. The social worker may provide needed individual, family, or group counseling services directly to the caregiver or may see to it that these services are delivered in a timely and well-planned fashion. By being an enabler, a broker, and an advocate, the worker also helps the caregiver to arrange for needed services for the care receiver.

Once services are in place, the worker maintains regular contact with the caregiver. The caregiver is encouraged to take responsibility for the day-to-day implementation of the intervention plan. The worker's role is to ensure that any ongoing difficulties in implementing the plan will be resolved in a timely fashion, and to help the caregiver with needs that arise as care continues.

The *case management role* is assumed when social workers' assessments reveal that caregivers are unable, or unwilling, to fulfill the duties and responsibilities necessary to the care of a frail older family member. As a case manager, the worker involves the caregiver and the care receiver to whatever extent is possible in the development and implementation of an intervention plan. Generally, however, the worker helps the caregiver by removing some, or all, of the responsibility for the day-to-day care of the frail relative.

As a case manager, the worker (1) completes a comprehensive assessment of the needs of the caregiver and the care receiver without relying solely on information provided by the caregiver, (2) develops a comprehensive intervention plan that considers the needs of both the caregiver and the care receiver, (3) implements the plan by providing and coordinating the provision of health care and social services to meet the needs of the caregiver and the care receiver, and (4) maintains frequent and regular contact to monitor the day-to-day implementation of the plan and to ensure that the caregiver and the care receiver will continue to receive the appropriate services (Applebaum and Austin 1990; Austin and McClelland 1996).

In actual practice, social workers may be expected to perform all three roles. A typical case mix may require social workers to serve as consultants to some caregivers, and to provide case coordination and case management services for others. Also, a social worker may be called on to perform multiple roles with the same caregiver. For example, a caregiver may need only consultation to resolve a particular concern but may need help with coordination to resolve other concerns. Also, the changing health status of the caregiver or the care receiver may necessitate a change in the social worker's role, such as moving from case coordination to case management. The choice of roles is guided by the wishes and desires of the caregiver and the care receiver, and by a careful assessment of the situation. The worker guards against the tendency to take over too much responsibility, thereby robbing the caregiver and the care receiver of their autonomy, promoting the atrophy of their existing coping skills and resources, and reducing their resiliency.

ILLUSTRATION AND DISCUSSION

Work with Mrs. Joan Dicks, age 52, the oldest of the two daughters and one son, illustrates some of the clinical social work practice processes that take place when working with family caregivers. A social worker at a family service agency, Mr. Dixon, first encountered Mrs. Dicks when she requested couple counseling, complaining primarily of marital problems that caused arguments leading to prolonged periods of silence, sleeplessness, lack of appetite, moodiness, heightened irritability, and tearfulness. During the intake interview, Mrs. Dicks also mentioned problems with her son, her sister, and her self-esteem. During the course of twelve individual and couple counseling sessions, Mr. Dixon helped Mrs. Dicks and her husband to make significant improvements in their marital relationship. Near the end of these sessions, the following interaction took place:

> *Mrs. Dicks:* Things are going really well with Ted [her husband] and me, but there's never any peace. Now I'm getting concerned about my mother and father. My dad is 77, and in the last few years, there's been a reversal in their roles. Even though my mom is five years older than my dad she has always been in better health and always took care of him. But now she has hardening of the arteries in her brain—at least, that's what her doctor says—and my dad has had to spend more and more time taking care of her. She can be really forgetful. *(Silence.)*
>
> *Mr. Dixon:* It's sad to see your parents decline, isn't it?
>
> *Mrs. Dicks:* Yeah. It's not only that. My dad has heart disease and his cardiologist just told him he's got to take it real easy. Caring for her is a big strain on him.
>
> *Mr. Dixon:* Well, I'm sorry your husband couldn't come today, but you are doing really well together. *(Mrs. Dicks nods.)* It gives us an opportunity to talk about your parents and what to do about them.

Already familiar with her psychosocial development from the previous work he had done with her and her husband, the worker encouraged Mrs.

Dicks to talk about her current relationship with her parents, and about their abilities and disabilities. Mr. Dixon learned that Mrs. Dicks's relationship with her parents was much closer than her sister's relationship, and that she, rather than her sister, was called on by her parents when they needed assistance. He also learned that she anticipated being the primary caregiver when her father could no longer take care of her mother, and that a nursing home placement was not an option she would consider.

Mr. Dixon: It sounds as if your mother's condition is worsening and you're worried because you don't know what the future will hold. You mentioned a family physician, but have you ever had your mother checked by a specialist who might be able to give you a clearer picture of what to expect in the future?

Mrs. Dicks: No, Mom is very attached to her doctor. She's been going to him since I was a little kid, at least forty years, probably longer. He's almost as old as she is!

Mr. Dixon: Well, you have to respect her wishes. It's too bad because there's a program in Troy for the assessment of individuals who have health problems—forgetfulness and confusion—like your mom's. It's staffed by an excellent geriatrician.

Mrs. Dicks: I don't think Mom or Dad would go for that, but I'll ask. I wonder if there's a place I could go to learn more about my mother's condition.

Mr. Dixon: Yes, as a matter of fact, there's an Alzheimer's disease support group that meets at St. Peter's Hospital. I think it's sponsored by the Alzheimer's Disease and Related Disorders Association, a self-help-oriented organization. Don't be put off by the name. It's really there to help anyone caring for a forgetful or confused older person; it doesn't matter whether or not your mom has Alzheimer's disease. I've heard really good things about it. I've referred a few people in the past couple of years, and they've all said how satisfied they were with the information and the support they received.

Mrs. Dicks: What do they do, and when do they meet?

Mr. Dixon: Let me look *(looking through a file box filled with cards with information about community agencies).* The president of the chapter is Mrs. Lot. You can contact her by calling 737-4445. I'll write that down for you. They have their meetings once a month in the main conference hall at St. Peter's, seven to nine in the evenings on Thursday. There's no charge. As for what they do, the format is that they have a speaker on a selected topic each month, and then there is a discussion. For example, they might invite a nurse to talk about home care techniques and resources, a so-cial worker to talk about how to cope with stress, or a legal expert to talk about guardianships, wills, and so forth. I think a friend of mine spoke on nursing-home placement a couple of months ago.

Mrs. Dicks: Sounds good. I'm free on Thursday evenings. I'll try it.

The first part of Mr. Dixon's dialogue with Mrs. Dicks illustrates that individuals may seek service for other concerns and then gradually bring up problems related to family caregiving. It also reveals that by playing a con-sultant role, the worker recognized the caregiver's competence. He did not push the notion of a medical consultation, knowing that it would meet with resistance. Instead, he followed the client's lead, referring her to a resource targeted at caregivers. In this way, the worker made use of the caregiver's active problem-solving coping skills. The transcript also illustrates the im-portant connection between professional social workers and self-help orga-nizations. The worker was not hesitant to refer the client to the self-help support group, and he gave it an enthusiastic recommendation.

After one additional session that both Mr. and Mrs. Dicks attended, Mr. Dixon and Mr. and Mrs. Dicks mutually decided to end their work together. Mr. Dixon did not see Mrs. Dicks again for almost two years; then, one day, he received a phone call from her, asking if she could see him again. When she came in, she explained that she and her husband were continuing to do much better together.

Mrs. Dicks: Things are much better between us. I'm here because of my parents.

Mr. Dixon: Your parents? Oh, yes. I recall. We talked about them briefly at the end of our sessions together, and you decided to go to the Alzheimer's support group at St. Peter's. How did that go?

Mrs. Dicks: Well—I didn't go. I was going to call, but I'm really not sure if my mother has Alzheimer's disease. I re-member you said it would be OK for me to go anyway, but I felt funny.

Had the practitioner followed up on the referral by suggesting that he and Mrs. Dicks talk about it by telephone a few weeks after their last session together, he might have prevented the failure of the referral. As the record continues, the interdependence of family members and the effects of caring for an increasingly frail older relative are revealed.

Mr. Dixon: Well, why don't you tell me about what's going on?

Mrs. Dicks: Since I saw you last, Mom has gotten worse. She is really forgetful. Sometimes, she can't remember where things are. She forgets people's names, neighbors she's known all her life. Recently, she left the stove on, and my father is afraid that she's going to burn the house down.

Mr. Dixon.	How is he doing?
Mrs. Dicks:	Well, that's just it. He's not doing well at all. His heart problems, combined with the arthritis in his hips and knees, make it difficult for him to keep up with the house, and with Mom. His cardiologist has told him he's a good candidate for bypass surgery, but Dad is avoiding that.
Mr. Dixon:	And you?
Mrs. Dicks:	I'm really worried about it. My dad can't handle the stress. My mom is a real handful. I'm over there constantly now, and I just don't know what to do. I've got a big place to care for myself—you remember my husband's job means he's out of town all the time—and my son is just returning from the army.
Mr. Dixon:	Oh yes, the one that was giving both of you all that trouble.
Mrs. Dicks:	Yeah, and I don't think the army made it any better. I think he will still be using drugs, and I just don't want him in my house under those conditions!

It was clear that Mrs. Dicks was feeling somewhat overwhelmed. Mr. Dixon and Mrs. Dicks continued to discuss the situation, and the topic of her sister and brother came up.

Mr. Dixon:	Yes, we'll have to talk about what you're going to do with him [the son], but first, should we focus on your parents? Sounds like you're really upset about them.
Mrs. Dicks:	Yes, my son won't be home from Germany for almost three months.
Mr. Dixon:	Good. Well, let's talk about what else I should know about the situation with your parents. How about your brother and sister?
Mrs. Dicks:	Jean and Bob?
Mr. Dixon:	Yup.
Mrs. Dicks:	They're concerned about it, too, but that really is a problem, too.
Mr. Dixon:	A problem, too?
Mrs. Dicks:	Well, I've always been my parents' favorite, and Jean is resentful. I can understand that. They don't treat her right. But sometimes, her reactions are out of line. She takes it out on me. And Bob just isn't around much. He says he wants to help, but he never seems to come through. He's always got an excuse. So I get stuck with all of it. Not that I mind—I want to take care of my parents—but it's hard, especially now with my mother. I was going to go to the Alzheimer's meeting as you suggested, but I couldn't find the number, and I thought I'd give you a call.

This part of the transcript illustrates some of the complexities of the situation. Mrs. Dicks was struggling not only with how best to provide care for her frail elderly parents, but also with problems regarding her sister, her son, and her own emotional response to the situation. The worker did an effective job of helping to clarify what they would work on first. He also drew the client into the work by asking her to make a decision about what they should focus on first.

Mr. Dixon:	My father is frail, so I understand some of what you're going through. It's going to require a lot of work on your part, but if you follow through, I think you will feel less stressed than you do now.
Mrs. Dicks:	I know I'm going to have to do something. Even if they [her parents] are not agreeable to it.

Mr. Dixon and Mrs. Dicks spent the remainder of the session and the next session discussing the situation in depth, exploring options and alternative plans of action. At one point, Mr. Dixon suggested a plan of action that included a home visit by another agency.

Mr. Dixon:	Since you've told me that you don't have confidence in your mom's physician, and you really need some help in figuring out how best to help her, I suggest that you call Mrs. Eaton at the Capital District Psychiatric Center, and she will do a home visit. If she feels it is warranted, she can have your mother seen by the nurse or the doctor in the outpatient geriatric unit. They will help you get an accurate diagnosis of your mom's condition and will refer you to the appropriate resources. They also have a day treatment program.
Mrs. Dicks:	Day treatment?
Mr. Dixon:	Yes, a program for older people with memory impairments. Five days a week. They serve lunch, and there's a van service to transport all those who attend. *(Pause.)* Would you like me to call Mrs. Eaton right now?
Mrs. Dicks:	Yes. Oh, on second thought, let me tell Mom and Dad first. I'll tell them tonight and call myself tomorrow. Can I have her number?
Mr. Dixon:	Sure. But do you feel comfortable with this?
Mrs. Dicks:	Well, something has to be done. I'll definitely call.
Mr. Dixon:	I've met Mrs. Eaton on several occasions. She's really a lovely person. Really warm. She has a special gift when it comes to working with older people.
Mrs. Dicks:	I sure hope Mom doesn't do anything too crazy. She can really be nasty with strangers.
Mr. Dixon:	Mrs. Eaton is used to that, but let her know anyway. OK?
Mrs. Dicks:	Yes. I definitely have to do something.
Mr. Dixon:	It's almost time for us to stop. I'm looking forward to hearing how you make out. But before we end, I want

to clarify how we will proceed. Let's let Mrs. Eaton help you with the plans for caring for your mom and dad. There are all kinds of options, like home health care and day care, and I bet she'll have some good ideas about home safety and your mom's care. I think it might be best for us to focus on how you're feeling about it all, and also about your relationship with your sister and your parents. OK?

Mrs. Dicks: That would be fine. Maybe I'll try to have my sister come in with me. Would that be OK?

Mr. Dixon: Sure.

Mrs. Dicks: See you next week, and I'll let you know what happens when I call.

Mr. Dixon and Mrs. Dicks met the following week. She informed him that she had called Mrs. Eaton, who had made an appointment to come out to see her and her parents later in the week. She also told Mr. Dixon that she had invited her sister to come to the session, but that she had refused. However, she said that her sister was interested in what she and Mr. Dixon had talked about and would like to get together with her over "a cup of coffee to discuss it." Mrs. Dicks viewed this reaction quite positively, as she had been wanting an opportunity to have a "heart-to-heart talk" with her sister.

During the remainder of this session and six subsequent sessions, Mrs. Dicks and Mr. Dixon followed the plan they had agreed upon during the prior session, focusing primarily on Mrs. Dicks's relationship with her sister and her emotional reaction to the caregiving situation. The sessions also provided an opportunity to help Mrs. Dicks with her relationship with her son and provided Mr. Dixon with an opportunity to monitor the delivery of services to Mrs. Dicks's parents. At one point, when Mrs. Dicks complained that she was not being kept informed about her mother's enrollment in the day treatment program, Mr. Dixon called Mrs. Eaton and asked her to clarify the matter with Mrs. Dicks. This telephone contact proved helpful, because Mr. Dixon and Mrs. Eaton discussed their independent assessments and intervention goals and coordinated some of their efforts. During their last weekly meeting together, the following interaction took place between Mr. Dixon and Mrs. Dicks.

Mrs. Dicks: I'm going to miss our sessions. You've really been helpful. When I opened up to my sister—I mean, when we both really talked about how we felt—it seemed we grew closer. Things are still not great between us, but they're much better. Mrs. Eaton's suggestion about asking my sister and brother to help out during specific times helped, too. My sister is happy to take care of my mother Saturday mornings, and my mother seems to be a little nicer to my sister these days. Between that and my brother's getting more involved— he comes over on Sundays now quite regularly—and

	I have more time, especially on the weekends when Ted is home, and I need it.
Mr. Dixon:	Wonderful!
Mrs. Dicks:	That program [day treatment] has been really good, too. My mom goes three times a week, and that gives Dad a real break. Also, I noticed she seems to be a little more with it. They do memory exercises and all. *(Pause.)* And I've been able to go back to that part-time bookkeeping job I had. I go two of the days my mom is at the program.
Mr. Dixon:	Good. Yes, they really have a good program. With your son coming home and the situation with your parents subject to change at any time, I think we should stay in contact, at least for the time being. How about planning to meet monthly, at least for a while, and so we can see how things continue to go?
Mr. Dicks:	That's fine. I also think I'm going to go to that support group you mentioned before. I have the number right here (pointing to her handbag).

Mr. Dixon and Mrs. Dicks continued to meet monthly for the remainder of the year, and Mrs. Dicks began to attend the Alzheimer's support group on a regular basis. Her son's return did not present the problems she had anticipated, and her relationship with her sister continued to improve. Mrs. Eaton continued to help Mrs. Dicks with the care of her mother and father. A year after their last contact, and almost four years after they had first met, Mrs. Dicks wrote Mr. Dixon a letter, explaining that her mother had died two months before of a cerebral hemorrhage, and thanking him for all his help. She also explained that Mrs. Eaton was no longer working with her but had been helpful in getting her connected to a home health agency for assistance with her father, who was becoming increasingly frail.

CONCLUSION

Family caregivers play a vital role in maintaining the physical and emotional well-being of frail elderly people. Their role will almost certainly increase in importance as the numbers of frail older persons expands rapidly in the next few decades. Social workers and other helping professionals have a crucial role to play in supporting family caregivers, but until recently, this role was largely neglected. This chapter has described the characteristics and needs of family caregivers, as well as what is known about ways to assist them. It is hoped that it will serve to stimulate additional interest in the development and implementation of public policies and intervention programs for the support of family caregivers and frail older persons.

References

Anastas, J. W., J. L. Gibeau, and P. J. Larson. 1990. "Working Families and Eldercare: A National Perspective in an Aging America." *Social Work* 35:405–11.

Angel, J. L. and D. P. Hogan. 1992. "The Demography of Minority Aging Populations." *The Journal of Family History* 17:95–114.

Aponte, J. and R. Crouch. 1995. "The Changing Ethnic Profile of the United States." In J. F. Aponte, R. W. Rivers, and J. Wohl, eds., *Psychological Interventions and Cultural Diversity,* pp. 1–18. Boston: Allyn & Bacon.

Applebaum, R. and C. Austin. 1990. *Long Term Care Case Management: Design and Evaluation.* New York: Springer.

Aranda, M. P. and B. L. Knight. 1997. "The Influence of Ethnicity and Culture on the Caregiver Stress and Coping Process: A Sociocultural Review and Analysis." *The Gerontologist* 37:342–54.

Archer, C. and M. MacLean. 1993. "Husbands and Sons As Caregivers of Chronically Ill Women." *Journal of Gerontological Social Work* 21(1/2):5–23.

Atchley, R. and S. Miller. 1986. "Older People and Their Families." In C. Eisdorfer, ed., *Annual Review of Gerontology and Geriatrics,* pp. 337–69. New York: Springer.

Austin, C. and R. McClelland. 1996. *Perspective on Case Management Practice.* Milwaukee, Wis.: Families International Inc.

Barr, J., K. Johnson, and L. Warshaw. 1992. "Supporting the Elderly: Workplace Programs for Employed Caregivers." *The Milbank Memorial Fund Quarterly* 70:509–33.

Bass, D. 1990. *Caring Families: Supports and Intervention.* Silver Spring, Md.: National Association of Social Workers Press.

Beach, D. 1997. "Family Caregiving: The Positive Impact on Adolescent Relationships." *The Gerontologist* 37:233–38.

Beisecker, A., L. Wright, S. Chrisman, and J. Ashworth. 1996. "Family Caregiver Perceptions of Benefits and Barriers to the Use of Adult Day Care for Individuals with Alzheimer's Disease." *Research-on-Aging* 18(4):430–50.

Bengtson, V., C. Rosenthal, and L. Burton. 1996. "Paradoxes of Families and Aging." In R. H. Binstock and L. K. George, eds., *Handbook of Aging and the Social Sciences,* 4th ed., pp. 254–82. New York: Academic Press.

Biegel, D. and A. Blum, eds. 1990. *Aging and Caregiving: Theory Research and Policy.* Newbury Park, Calif.: Sage.

Blenkner, M., M. Bloom, M. Nielsen, and R. Weber. 1974. *Final Report: Protective Services for Older People: Findings from the Benjamin Rose Institute Study.* Cleveland: Benjamin Rose Institute.

Bourgeois, M., R. Schulz, and L. Burgio. 1996. "Interventions for Caregivers of Patients with Alzheimer's Disease: A Review and Analysis of Content, Process, and Outcomes." *International Journal of Aging Human Behavior* 43(1):35–92.

Brubaker, T. and K. Roberto. 1993. "Family Life Education for the Later Years." *Family Relations* 42:212–21.

Buck, D., B. Gregson, C. Bamford, P. McNamee, G. Farrow, J. Bond, and K. Wright. 1997. "Psychological Distress Among Informal Supporters of Frail Older People at Home and in Institutions." *International Journal of Geriatric Psychiatry* 12:737–44.

Butler, R. 1992. "Aging and Mental Health: Prevention of Caregiver Overload, Abuse and Neglect." *Geriatrics* 47:53–58.

Callahan, J. 1989. "Play It Again Sam—There Is No Impact." *The Gerontologist* 29(1):5–6.

Cantor, M. 1991. "Family and Community: Changing Roles in an Aging Society." *The Gerontologist* 31:337–46.

——. 1993. "Families and Caregiving in an Aging Society." In L. Burton, ed., *Families and Aging,* pp. 135–44. Amityville, N.Y.: Baywood Publishing.

Carter, B. and M. McGoldrick. 1980. *The Family Cycle.* New York: Gardner.

Cohen-Mansfield, J., J. Besansky, V. Watson, and L. Bernhard. 1994. "Underutilization of Adult Day Care: An Exploratory Study." *Journal of Gerontological Social Work* 22(1/2):21–39.

Connell, C. M. and G. D. Gibson. 1997. "Racial, Ethnic, and Cultural Differences in Dementia Caregiving: Review and Analysis." *The Gerontologist* 37:355–64.

Connidis, I. 1997. "Sibling Support in Older Age." *Journals of Gerontology* 49(6):S309–S317.

Couper, D. P. and N. W. Sheehan. 1987. "Family Dynamics for Caregivers: An Educational Model." *Family Relations* 36:181–86.

Damron-Rodriguez, J., S. Wallace, and R. Kington. 1994. "Service Utilization and Minority Elderly: Appropriateness, Accessibility and Acceptability." *Gerontology and Geriatrics Education* 15(1):45–63.

Doty, P., M. Jackson, and W. Crown. 1998. "The Impact of Female Caregivers' Employment Status on Patterns of Formal and Informal Elder Care." *The Gerontologist* 38(3):331–35.

Farkas, S. 1980. "Impact of Chronic Illness on the Patient's Spouse." *Health and Social Work* 5:39–46.

Farran, C. J. 1997. "Theoretical Perspectives Concerning Positive Aspects of Caring for Elderly Persons with Dementia: Stress Adaptation and Existentialism." *The Gerontologist* 37:250–56.

Ferris, S., G. Steinberg, E. Shulman, R. Kahn, and B. Reiserg. 1987. "Institutionalization of Alzheimer's Disease Patients: Reducing Precipitating Factors Through Family Counseling." *Home Health Care Services Quarterly* 8(1):23–51.

Flint, A. 1995. "Effects of Respite Care on Patients with Dementia and their Caregivers." *International Psychogeriatrics* 7(4):505–17.

Gallagher, D. 1985. "Intervention Strategies to Assist Caregivers of Frail Elders: Current Research Status and Future Research Directions." In C. Eisdorfer, M. Lawton, and G. Maddox, eds., *Annual Review of Gerontology and Geriatrics.*, vol. 5, pp. 249–82. New York: Springer.

Gallagher, D. and R. Czirr. 1984. "Clinical Observations on the Effectiveness of Different Psychotherapeutic Approaches in the Treatment of Depressed Caregivers." Paper presented at the annual meeting of the Gerontological Society of America, San Antonio, Texas, November.

Gallagher, D., S. Lovett, and A. Zeiss. 1989. "Interventions with Caregivers of Frail Elderly Persons." In M. Ory and K. Bond, eds., *Aging and Health Care: Social Science and Policy Perspectives,* pp. 167–90. United Kingdom, London: Routledge.

Gallagher-Thompson, D., R. Moorehead, T. Polich, D. Arguello, C. Johnson, V. Rodriguez, and M. Meyer. 1994. "A Comparison of Outreach Strategies for Hispanic Caregivers of Alzheimer's Victims." *Clinical Gerontologist* 15(1):57–62.

Gatz, M., V. Bengtson, and M. Blum. 1990. "Caregiving Families." In J. E. Birren and K. W. Schaie, eds., *Handbook of the Psychology of Aging,* 3d ed., pp. 404–26. San Diego: Academic Press.

Germain, C. and A. Gitterman. 1980. *The Life Model of Social Work Practice.* New York: Columbia University Press.

Gibson, R. C. 1991. "Age-by-Race Differences in the Health and Functioning of Elderly People." *Journal of Aging and Health* 3:335–51.

Haley, W. E., C. West, V. Wadley, G. Ford, F. White, J. Barrett, L. Harrell, and D. Roth. 1993. "Psychological, Social and Health Impact of Caregiving: A Comparison of Black and White Dementia Family Caregivers and Noncaregivers." *Psychology and Aging* 10:540–52.

Harris, P. B. 1998. "Listening to Caregiving Sons: Misunderstood Realities." *The Gerontologist* 38(3):342–52.

Hawley, D. R. and L. DeHaan. 1996. "Toward a Definition of Family Resilience: Integrating Life-span and Family Perspectives." *Family Process* 35:283–98.

Helfrich, T. and J. Dodson. 1992. "Eldercare: An Issue for Corporate America." *Journal of Case Management* 1(1):26–29.

Henderson, J. and M. Gutierrez-Mayka. 1992. "Ethnocultural Themes in Caregiving to Alzheimer's Disease Patients in Hispanic Families." *Clinical Gerontologist* 11(3/4):59–74.

Henderson, J., M. Gutierrez-Mayka, J. Garcia, and S. Boyd. 1993. "A Model for Alzheimer's

Disease Support Group Development in African-American and Hispanic Populations." *The Gerontologist* 33:409–14.

Herr, J. and J. Weakland. 1979. *Counseling Elders and Their Families.* New York: Springer.

Hooyman, N. and H. Kiyak. 1996. *Social Gerontology,* 4th ed. Boston: Allyn & Bacon.

Horowitz, A. 1985. "Family Caregiving to the Frail Elderly." In C. Eisdorfer, M. P. Lawton, and G. L. Maddox, eds., *Annual Review of Gerontology and Geriatrics,* vol. 5, pp. 194–246. New York: Springer.

Jenkins, C. 1997. "Women, Work, and Caregiving: How Do These Roles Affect Women's Well-Being?" *Journal of Women and Aging* 9:27–45.

Jette, A. 1996. "Disability Trends and Transitions." In R. H. Binstock and L. K. George, eds., *Handbook of Aging and the Social Sciences,* 4th ed., pp. 94–116. New York: Academic Press.

Johnson, T. 1995. "Utilizing Culture in Work with Aging Families." In G. C. Smith, S. S. Tobin, E. A. Robertson-Tchabo, and P. W. Power, eds., *Strengthening Aging Families: Diversity in Practice and Policy,* chap., 10, pp. 175–201. Thousand Oaks, Calif.: Sage.

Jutras, S. and J. Levoie. 1995. "Living with an Impaired Elderly Person: The Informal Caregiver's Physical and Mental Health." *Journal of Aging and Health* 7(1):46–73.

Kane, R. 1990. "Assessing the Elderly Client." In A. Monk, ed., *Handbook of Gerontological Services,* 2d ed., pp. 55–89. New York: Columbia University Press.

Kane, R. and R. Kane. 1981. *Assessing the Elderly: A Practical Guide to Measurement.* New York: Lexington Books.

Kane, R. and J. Penrod. 1993. "Family Caregiving Policies: Insights from an Intensive Longitudinal Study." In S. H. Zarit, L. I. Pearlin, and K. W. Schaie, eds., *Caregiving Systems: Informal and Formal Helpers,* pp. 273–92. Hillsdale, N.J.: Lawrence Erlbaum.

Kaszniak, A. 1996. "Techniques and Instruments for Assessment of the Elderly." In S. Zarit and B. Knight, eds., *A Guide to Psychotherapy and Aging,* pp. 163–219. Washington, D.C.: American Psychological Association.

Kaye, L. and J. Applegate. 1990. "Men As Elder Caregivers: A Response to Changing Families." *American Journal of Orthopsychiatry* 60:86–95.

Kemper, P., R. Applebaum, and M. Harrigan. 1987. "Community Care Demonstrations: What Have We Learned?" *Health Care Financing Review* 8:87–100.

Kleban, M., E. Brody, C. Schoonover, and C. Hoffman. 1989. "Family Help to the Elderly: Perceptions of Sons-in-law Regarding Parent Care." *Journal of Marriage and the Family* 51:303–12.

Knight, B. 1996. *Psychotherapy with Older Adults,* 2d ed. Thousand Oaks, Calif.: Sage.

Knight, B., S. Lutzky, and F. Macofsky-Urban. 1993. "A Meta-analytic Review of Interventions for Caregiver Distress: Recommendations for Future Research." *The Gerontologist* 33:240–49.

Koloski, K. and R. Montgomery. 1995. "The Impact of Respite Use on Nursing Home Placement." *The Gerontologist* 35:67–74.

Kramer, B. 1997. "Gain in the Caregiving Experience: Where Are We? What Next? *The Gerontologist* 37(2):218–32.

Kubie, S. and G. Landau. 1953. *Group Work with the Aged.* New York: International Universities Press.

Lawton, M., E. Brody, and A. Saperstein. 1989. "A Controlled Study of Respite Service for Caregivers of Alzheimer's Patients." *The Gerontologist* 29:8–16.

Lazarus, R. and S. Folkman. 1984. *Stress, Appraisal, and Coping.* New York: Springer.

Lee, G., J. Dwyer, and R. Coward. 1993. "Gender Differences in Parent Care: Demographic Factors and Same Gender Preferences." *Journals of Gerontology: Social Sciences* 48:59–516.

Linden, M. 1953. "Group Psychotherapy with Institutionalized Senile Women: Study in Gerontologic Human Relations." *International Journal of Group Psychotherapy* 3:150–70.

Lockery, S. 1991. "Family and Social Supports: Caregiving Among Racial and Ethnic Minority Elders." *Generations* 15:58–62.

Lowy, L. 1985. *Social Work with the Aging: The Challenge and Promise of the Later Years,* 2d ed. New York: Longman.

Markides, K. and M. Miranda. 1997. "Minority Aging and Health: An Overview." In K. S. Markides and M. R. Miranda, eds. *Minorities, Aging, and Health,* pp. 1–14. Thousand Oaks, Calif.: Sage.

Marks, N. 1996. "Caregiving Across the Lifespan: National Prevalence and Predictors." *Family Relations* 45:27–35.

Maxwell, J. 1952. *Centers for Older People: A Project Report.* New York: National Council on Aging.

McCallion, P., M. Diehl, and R. Toseland. 1994. "Support Group Intervention for Family Caregivers of Alzheimer's Disease Patients." *Seminars in Speech and Language* 15(4):657–70.

McCallion, P. and L. Grant-Griffin. 2000. "Redesigning Services to Meet the Needs of Multicultural Families." In M. P. Janicki and E. Ansello, eds., *Aging and Developmental Disabilities,* pp. 381–406. Baltimore, Md.: Paul Brookes.

McCallion, P., M. Janicki, and L. Grant-Griffin. 1996. "Exploring the Impact of Culture and Acculturation on Older Families Caregiving for Persons with Developmental Disabilities." Paper presented at Conference on Research Advances in Later Life Family Caregiving of Adults with Disabilities, Chicago, Illinois, June.

———. 1997. "Exploring the Impact of Culture and Acculturation on Older Families Caregiving for Persons with Developmental Disabilities." *Family Relations* 46(4):347–58.

McCallion, P. and R. Toseland. 1996. "Supportive Group Interventions with Caregivers of Frail Older Adults." *Social Work with Groups* 18(1):11–25.

McCallion, P., R. Toseland, and M. Diehl. 1994. "Social Work Practice with Caregivers of Frail Older Adults." *Social Work Practice Research* 4(1):64–88.

McCallion, P., R. Toseland, and K. Freeman. 1999. "An Evaluation of the Family Visit Education Program." *Journal of the American Geriatrics Society* 47(2):203–14.

McCubbin, H., M. McCubbin, and A. Thompson. 1993. "Resiliency in Families: The Role of Family Schema and Appraisals in Family Adaptation to Crises." In T. H. Brubaker, ed., *Family Relations: Challenges for the Future,* pp. 153–77. Newbury Park, Calif.: Sage.

Mittelman, M., S. Ferris, E. Shulman, G. Steinberg, A. Ambinder, J. Mackell, and J. Cohen. 1995. "A Comprehensive Support Program: Effect on Depression in Spouse-Caregivers of AD Patients." *The Gerontologist* 35:792–802.

Mittelman, M., S. Ferris, E. Shulman, G. Steinberg, and B. Levin. 1996. "A Family Intervention to Delay Nursing Home Placement of Patients with Alzheimer's Disease." *Journal of the American Medical Association* 276:1725–31.

Mittelman, M., S. Ferris, G. Steinberg, E. Shulman, J. Mackell, A. Ambinder, and J. Cohen. 1993. "An Intervention That Delays Institutionalization of Alzheimer's Disease Patients: Treatment of Spouse Caregivers." *The Gerontologist* 33(6):730–40.

Mizrahi, T. 1993. "Managed Care and Managed Competition: A Primer for Social Work." *Health and Social Work* 18:86–91.

Moen, P. and K. B. Forest. 1995. "Family Policies for an Aging Society: Moving to the 21st Century." *The Gerontologist* 35(6):825–30.

Montgomery, R. and E. Borgota. 1989. "The Effects of Alternative Support Strategies on Family Caregiving." *The Gerontologist* 29(4):457–64.

Moore, S. T. 1987. "The Capacity to Care: A Family Focused Approach to Social Work Practice with the Disabled Elderly." *Journal of Gerontological Social Work* 12:79–97.

National Alliance for Caregiving and the American Association of Retired Persons. 1997. *Family Caregiving in the U.S.: Findings from a National Survey.* Final Report. Bethesda, Md.: The National Alliance for Caregiving. Washington, D.C.: The American Association of Retired Persons.

Neiderhardt, E. and J. Allen. 1993. *Family Therapy with the Elderly.* Newbury Park, Calif.: Sage.

Neundorfer, M. M. 1991. "Family Caregivers of the Frail Elderly: Impact of Caregiving on Their Health and Implications for Interventions." *Community Health* 14:48–58.

Nickens, H. 1995. "The Role of Race/Ethnicity and Social Class in Minority Health Status." *Health Services Research* 30(1):151–62.

Noonan, A. E. and S. L. Tennstedt. 1997. "Meaning in Caregiving and its Contribution to Caregiver Well-Being." *The Gerontologist* 37:785–94.

Pearlin, L., F. Aneschel, J. Mullan, and C. Whitlach. 1996. "Caregiving and Its Social Support." In R. H. Binstock and L. K. George, eds., *Handbook of Aging and the Social Sciences,* 4th ed., pp. 283–302. New York: Academic Press.

Pruchno, R., J. H. Patrick, and C. J. Burant. 1997. "African American and White Mothers of Adults with Chronic Disabilities: Caregiving Burden and Satisfaction." *Family Relations* 46(4):335–46.

Quayhagen, M. and M. Quayhagen. 1994. "Differential Effects of Family-based Strategies on Alzheimer's Disease." *The Gerontologist* 29:150–55.

Raveis, V., K. Siegel, and M. Sudit. 1990. "Psychological Impact of Caregiving on the Caregiver: A Critical Review of Research and Methodologies." In D. E. Beigel and A. Blum, eds., *Aging and Caregiving: Theory, Research and Policy,* pp. 53–75. Newbury Park, Calif.: Sage.

Robinson, J., P. Moen, and D. Dempster-McClain. 1995. "Women's Caregiving: Changing Profiles and Pathways." *Journal of Gerontology* 50B(6):S362–S473.

Rudin, D. 1994. "Caregiver Attitudes Regarding Utilization and Usefulness of Respite Services for People with Alzheimer's Disease." *Journal of Gerontological Social Work* 23(1–2):85–107.

Sanborn, B. and S. Bould. 1991. "Intergenerational Caregivers of the Oldest Old." In S. K. Pfeifer and M. B. Sussman, eds., *Families: Intergenerational and Generational Connections,* pp. 125–42. New York: Haworth.

Schmidt, G. and B. Keyes. 1985. "Group Psychotherapy with Family Caregivers of Demented Patients." *The Gerontologist* 25:347–50.

Schofield, H. L., B. Murphy, H. E. Herrman, S. Bloch, and B. Singh. 1997. "Family Caregiving: Measurement of Emotional Well Being and Various Aspects of the Caregiving Role." *Psychological Medicine* 27:647–57.

Schulz, R., A. O'Brien, J. Bookwala, and K. Fleissner. 1995. "Psychiatric and Physical Morbidity Effects of Dementia Caregiving: Prevalence, Correlates, and Causes." *The Gerontologist* 35:771–91.

Schulz, R. and A. L. Quittner. 1998. "Caregiving for Children and Adults with Chronic Conditions: Introduction to the Special Issue." *Health Psychology* 17:107–11.

Schulz, R. and G. Williamson. 1994. "Health Effects of Caregiving: Prevalence of Mental and Physical Illness in Alzheimer's Caregivers." In E. Light, G. Niederehe, and B. Lebowitz, eds., *Stress Effects on Family Caregivers of Alzheimer's Patients: Research and Interventions,* pp. 38–63. New York: Springer.

Shanas, E. 1968. *Old People in Three Industrial Societies.* New York: Atherton.

Shantz, M. 1995. "Effects of Respite Care: A Literature Review." *Perspectives* 19(4):5–11.

Shay, D. G., T. Miles, and M. Hayward. 1996. "The Health-Wealth Connection: Racial Differences." *The Gerontologist* 36(3):342–49.

Shore, H. 1952. "Group Work Development in Homes for the Aged." *Social Service Review* 26(2):181–94.

Silver, A. 1950. "Group Psychotherapy with Senile Psychiatric Patients." *Geriatrics* 5:147.

Smith, G., M. Smith, and R. Toseland. 1991. "Problems Identified by Family Caregivers in Counseling." *The Gerontologist* 31(1):770–77.

Smith, M., S. Tobin, and R. Toseland. 1992. "Therapeutic Processes in Professional and Peer Counseling of Family Caregivers of Frail Elderly. *Social Work* 37(4):345–51.

Stone, R., G. L. Cafferata, and J. Sangl. 1987. "Caregivers of the Frail Elderly: A National Profile." *Clinical Gerontologist* 1(1):87–95.

Stone, R. and S. Keigher. 1994. "Toward Equitable Universal Caregiver Policy: The Potential of Financial Supports for Family Caregivers." *Aging and Social Policy* 6:57–76.

Strawbridge, W. and M. Wallhagen. 1991. "Impact of Family Conflict on Adult Child Caregivers." *The Gerontologist* 31(6):770–77.

Stump, T., D. Clark, R. Johnson, and F. Wolinsky. 1997. "The Structure of Health Status Among Hispanic, African American, and White Older Adults." *The Journals of Gerontology* 52B(Special Issue):49–60.

Tonti, M. and B. Silverstone. 1985. "Services to Families of the Elderly." In A. Monk, ed., *Handbook of Gerontological Services,* pp. 211–39. New York: Van Nostrand.

Toseland, R. 1995. *Group Work with the Elderly and Family Caregivers.* New York: Springer.

———. 1997. "Aging: Direct Practice." In *Encyclopedia of Social Work Supplement and Online Version.* Washington, D.C.: National Association of Social Workers Press.

Toseland, R., C. Blanchard, and P. McCallion. 1995. "A Problem Solving Intervention for Caregivers of Cancer Patients." *Social Science and Medicine* 40(4):517–28.

Toseland, R. and P. McCallion. 1997. "Trends in Caregiving Intervention Research." *Social Work Research, Special Issue, Social Work Intervention Research* 21(3):154–64.

———. 1998. *Maintaining Communication with Persons with Dementia.* New York: Springer.

Toseland, R. and R. Rivas. 1998. *An Introduction to Group Work Practice,* 3d ed. Needham Heights, Mass.: Allyn & Bacon.

Toseland, R. and C. Rossiter. 1989. "Group Intervention to Support Caregivers: A Review and Analysis." *The Gerontologist* 29(4):438–48.

Toseland, R., C. Rossiter, T. Peak, and G. Smith. 1990. "The Comparative Effectiveness of Individual and Group Interventions to Support Family Caregivers." *Social Work* 35:209–19.

Toseland, R. and G. Smith. 1990. "The Effectiveness of Individual Counseling for Family Caregivers of the Elderly." *Psychology and Aging* 5:256–63.

Toseland, R., G. Smith, and P. McCallion. 1995. "Supporting the Family in Elder Care." In G. Smith, S. Tobin, E. Robertson-Tchabo, and P. Power, eds., *Strengthening Aging Families: Diversity in Practice and Policy,* pp. 3–24. Thousand Oaks, Calif.: Sage.

Townsend, A. 1993. "Methodological Issues Confronting Research and Service Use Among Caregiving Families." In S. H. Zarit, L. I. Pearlin, and K. W. Schaie, eds., *Caregiving Systems: Informal and Formal Helpers,* pp. 293–301. Hillsdale, N.J.: Lawrence Erlbaum.

Walsh, F. 1996. "The Concept of Family Resilience: Crisis and Challenge." *Family Process* 35:261–81.

Wilcox, B. and J. O'Keefe. 1991. "Families, Policy, and Family Support Policies." *Prevention in Human Services* 9:109–26.

Wilson, G. and G. Ryland. 1949. "The Friendship Club." In G. Wilson and G. Ryland, eds., *Social Group Work Practice: The Creative Use of the Social Process,* pp. 514–29. Boston: Houghton Mifflin.

Winbush, G. 1993. "Family Caregiving Programs: A Look at the Premises on Which They Are Based." In L. Burton, ed., *Families and Aging,* pp. 129–33. Amityville, N.Y.: Baywood Publishing.

Worchester, M. and S. Hedrick. 1997. "Dilemmas in Using Respite for Family Caregivers of Frail Elders." *Family and Community Health* 19(4):31–48.

Zarit, S., C. Anthony, and M. Boutselis. 1987. "Interventions with Caregivers of Dementia Patients: Comparison of Two Approaches." *Psychology and Aging* 2:225–34.

Zarit, S. and L. Teri. 1991. "Interventions and Services for Family Caregivers." In K. W. Schaie, ed., *Annual Review of Gerontology and Geriatrics,* vol. 2, pp. 241–65. New York: Springer.

21

Gay and Lesbian Persons

Carol T. Tully

The gay and lesbian population in the United States is largely an invisible one that makes itself visible in varying degrees depending on the prevailing societal climate. Because the lesbian and gay identity is not marked by identifiable physical characteristics, gay and lesbian persons can be easily overlooked as a vulnerable and yet highly resilient population group. This chapter explores the current and historic sociocultural definitions of same-sex relationships, demographic estimates about the population, and the societal context in which gay men and lesbians function. Further, the chapter analyzes vulnerabilities and risk factors associated with the population and explores the resiliency of lesbians and gay men living in a heterocentric society. Programs available to same-sex persons are described and distinctive intervention issues associated with dealing with gay men and lesbians are presented. Finally, a practice illustration is presented that delineates assessment and intervention themes, practice issues, and how social workers can play an important role when working with lesbian and gay clients.

DEFINING AND EXPLAINING GAY AND LESBIAN PERSONS IN A NONGAY WORLD

Homosexuality is a socially constructed term that has recent origins, although same-sex relationships have existed in all cultures and during all eras (Altman 1982; Bullough 1979; D'Emilio and Freedman 1988). Originally coined by a Hungarian physician named Karoly Benkert (also known as Kertbeny), the term *homosexual* was introduced in 1869. It came into more current usage toward the end of the nineteenth century when it was used by psychiatrists and medical doctors to define it as an unacceptable alternative to the more "normal" heterosexual behavior (D'Emilio and

Freedman 1988). From the early 1700s, where same-sex behavior was merely a sin for which someone could atone, to the early 1900s when homosexuality became an issue of personal identity, a significant and culturally defined view of lesbians and gay men evolved. Currently, same-sex relationships are defined in a variety of ways depending on who is constructing the definition.

Generally, there are two disparate views on homosexuality. Some individuals believe it to be an unnatural, abnormal, and pathologic variation of sexual expression; others believe it to be a natural, normal expression of sexuality along the sexual continuum (Bieber 1965; Bieber et. al 1962; Kinsey, Pomeroy, and Martin 1948; Kinsey et al. 1953; Masters and Johnson 1966, 1979; Miller 1998; Nicolosi 1991; Reisner 1998; Socarides 1978). These polarized views are found both inside and outside the gay community and are the basis of homophobia, confusion, and myth.

Historically, same-sex sexual relations have been an accepted part of life, outlawed, ignored, flaunted, ridiculed, and blasphemed (D'Emilio and Freedman 1988). Although always not as usually practiced as heterosexual behaviors, homosexual patterns have existed since antiquity. And it was not until after the acceptance of Christianity as a mainstream religious belief that same-sex sexual behaviors became a "sin" (Boswell 1980; Greenberg 1988; Mondimore 1996). The tolerance for the sin ebbed and flowed depending on the societal beliefs of the era. For example, there was an increased tolerance for same-sex relations during the mini-Renaissance of the ninth through eleventh centuries that gave way to open condemnation of it during the following two centuries. While this condemnation lasted well into the nineteenth century and reemerged during the latter part of the twentieth century, the middle of the nineteenth century and the first part of the twentieth century saw the construct of homosexuality being defined as an identity issue (Walker 1999).

Those who define homosexual behaviors as pathological believe that as a sexual behavior, it is learned and therefore, because it is a chosen activity, can be made extinct. Proponents of the illness model of same-sex sexual behavior view it as abnormal and a mental illness to be cured through programs of psychological counseling, medication, electroconvulsive (shock) therapy, conversion therapy, aversion therapy, prayer, or combinations of therapeutic approaches. Citing such religious dogma as canon law, the Bible, and historical religious proscriptions against homosexuality and relying on interpretations of Freudian theory, reparative therapists attempt to cure the homosexual of her or his homosexuality (Bieber 1965; Bieber et. al 1962; Miller 1998; Nicolosi 1991; Reisner 1998; Socarides 1978). Their success rate is unknown and usually considered extremely low, but a full-page advertisement in the July 13, 1998, issue of the *New York Times* showed a photograph of a large group of people who claimed they had been saved from their homosexuality by their faith in God. The caption under the photograph read, "We're standing for the truth that homosexuals can change" (Miller 1998).

This definition of same-sex behavior as **pathological and therefore curable** represents one end of the definitional continuum as related to homosexuality and homosexuals. It is a definition that is accepted by some gays and nongays as definitive and is used in some current social work practices. The other end of this continuum presents a definition that is contradictory to this and one that is generally held in higher esteem.

Research focusing on same-sex relationships evolved steadily during the 1900s.

Moving from an examination of the etiology of homosexuality to an exploration of similarities and differences between heterosexual and homosexual women and men and then to an examination of gay and lesbian lifestyles, current research explores lesbians and gay men as part of the fabric of society. In doing so researchers have discovered the culturally diverse, economically disparate, and multiethnic hetero-geneity of the lesbian and gay community. While early studies focused on white, well-educated, usually professional, young lesbian and gay samples, recent studies have explored a variety of issues in the gay and lesbian community, including such things as aging, racism, sexism, adoption, marriage, health, coming out, domestic partner-ships, law, ethnicity, and child care (Bailey et al. 1991; LeVay 1991, 1996). The as-sumption of the majority of researchers in the field is that a homosexual sexual iden-tity is **innate** as opposed to learned, is **natural** for some portion of the general population, can be a healthy way of life, and is an acceptable lifestyle.

To support this definition, proponents cite studies that indicate physiological differences between gay and nongay samples, data that demonstrate lesbians and gay men may be psychologically healthier than their nongay counterparts, studies that show no differences between nongay and gay samples, and studies that conclude many issues related to homosexuality are the result of homophobia created and fur-thered by the heterosexual world (Belote and Joesting 1976; Bullough and Bullough 1977, 1995; Gagnon and Simon 1973; Mallen 1983; Saghir and Robins 1969, 1973; Telljohann and Price 1993). Those who believe same-sex relations are an acceptable form of behavior also cite the Bible as a source of support by noting biblical same-sex couples such as Ruth and Naomi and David and Jonathan (Swigonski 1998). But per-haps the most powerful support comes from the American Psychiatric Association's 1972 position statement that removed homosexuality from its diagnostic manual of mental illnesses. The National Association of Social Workers (NASW) also has a po-sition statement supporting the rights of lesbians and gay men, the Council on Social Work Education mandates content related to this population be included in schools of social work (Council on Social Work Education 1994; National Association of So-cial Workers 1981), and various laws and policies protecting same-sex relationships are becoming more common (Human Rights Campaign 1998b).

While many believe homosexuality to be an acceptable lifestyle that is normal to some portion of the general population, conflicting definitions, persistent stereotypes and myths, and homophobia continue to impact the larger (heterosexual) community, service providers (often in traditional agencies), and users of services (gay men and lesbians in need of such services).

Stereotypes and **myths** continue to surround the lesbian and gay community and its inhabitants. Evolving from and perpetuating myths and stereotypes, homopho-bia—the irrational fear of homosexuals and homosexuality—continues. Some of the more popular misconceptions (and realities) about gay men and lesbians appear in figure 21.1. No doubt stemming from the persistent religious proscriptions against same-sex sexual behaviors and the sodomy laws that developed in a parallel fashion, homosexual behavior continues to be viewed as less than acceptable by many. Chil-dren are not usually taught that a lesbian or gay lifestyle is as good as a nongay one. In fact, most are instructed as to the horrors of being queer (Gay, Lesbian, and Straight Education Network 1998). Many churches preach about the sinful nature of same-sex sexual activities, and in many localities gay men or lesbians can be denied basic civil rights on the basis of their sexual orientation (National Gay and Lesbian Task Force 1998a, 1998b). Such are some of the inevitable outcomes of homophobia.

Homophobia has been defined as negative feelings about lesbians and gay men, their sexual activities, and their communities. The fear may be at the phobic level, indicating an irrational fear of homosexuality and homosexuals, and the term has been identified as a prejudice similar to anti-Semitism or racism (Herek 1991). Generally there are three identified forms of homophobia—institutional, individual, and internal. *Institutional homophobia* derives from a general societal hostility toward gay men and lesbians that is manifested in sodomy laws outlawing same-sex sexual activity, religious prohibitions against homosexual behaviors, and a general perception that lesbians and gay men are not a significant part of the population. *Individual homophobia* is demonstrated by nongays continuing attacks on lesbians and gay men that come in the form of gay jokes, verbal taunts, physical assaults, and the generalized belief that all persons are heterosexual. *Internal homophobia* is self-loathing and fear manifested in the individual gay man or lesbian who, because of institutional and individual homophobia has internalized the negative attitudes and feelings about homosexuality. Each of these forms of homophobia plays a role in the delivery of services to gay and lesbian clients.

Institutional homophobia impacts social service agencies in terms of policies and procedures that tend to perpetuate myths and stereotypes about lesbian and gay clients. For example, gay or lesbian couples are prohibited in many localities from becoming foster parents. Likewise, lesbian or gay couples with children are prohibited in many jurisdictions from jointly adopting children (McClellen 1998). Often social service agencies still define families in a heterosexual fashion (perpetuating the myth that all persons are heterosexual) and fail to develop policies that are reflective of their entire caseload. Because gay and lesbian couples are not legally allowed to marry, some services available to heterosexually married couples may not be available to lesbian or gay couples. Offices in traditional social service agencies may not be seen as "homosocial" (accepting of lesbian and gay clients) because waiting areas are devoid of gay-friendly reading materials, intake forms are heterosexually biased, and personnel perceive all clients as heterosexual. These institutional issues, while slowly changing, are also reflected in the individual homophobia of many service providers who through ignorance, insensitivity, or intent may cause gay or lesbian clients to avoid services.

Social workers have been found to be just as homophobic, if not more so, than members of the general population and other helping professionals (DeCrescenzo 1983–84; DeCrescenzo and McGill 1978; Tate 1991; Wisniewski and Toomey 1987). Those individuals who actually provide services are in a position to soften institutional homophobic policies and procedures, but they are also in a position to further institutional homophobia by displaying individual homophobia. Individual homophobia becomes operationalized through an individual's assumption that all clients are heterosexual (the heterosexual assumption), the belief that lesbian or gay clients require services because of their sexual orientation, or falling victim to believing any lesbian or gay myth or stereotype (see figure 21.1).

Finally, internal homophobia can play a significant role in the ability of a gay man or lesbian to seek services in the first place. Growing up and living in a predominantly heterosexual world where institutional and individual homophobia are

FIGURE 21.1. Myths, Stereotypes and Realities

Stereotypes and Myths

The following myths and stereotypes are commonly associated with lesbian and gay persons. They have no basis in fact, are based in institutional homophobia, and must be eliminated.

I Gay men and lesbians are not capable of maintaining long-term relationships.
I Lesbian and gay relationships are prone toward addictive behaviors.
I Children are not a part of gay or lesbian families.
I Children raised by same-sex couples become gay or lesbian.
I Lesbians and gay men are sexually promiscuous.
I Gay men and lesbians are easily identifiable by the way they look.
I Gay men prey on children for sexual gratification or molest children.
I Lesbians and gay men convert children to homosexual lifestyles.
I Sexual orientation is a lifestyle choice.
I Homosexuality is an illness.
I Reparative therapy or prayer can cure homosexuality.
I Lesbians and gay men dislike members of the opposite sex.
I Gay men and lesbians have unstable relationships with their parents.
I Lesbians and gay men are less psychologically fit than their nongay counterparts.
I Gay men and lesbians are not religious.
I All lesbians and gay men are financially well off.
I Gay men and lesbians play masculine/feminine (butch/female) roles.
I There are no lesbians or gay men who are members of ethnic minorities.
I There are no older gay men or lesbians.
I Lesbians and gay men live in only urban areas.
I Gay men and lesbians do not hold positions of authority or importance.
I Gay men and lesbians are not victims of domestic violence.
I The lesbian and gay community is made up only of bars.
I All lesbian and gay men have sexual problems related to their sexual identity.
I All gay men and lesbians come out at the same time and in the same way.

Realities

While reality is relative, the following represent what has been determined about lesbians and gay men from research data that have been collected since the early 1900s.

I Lesbians and gay men can and do maintain long-term relationships.
I While some gay men and lesbians abuse liquor or drugs, most do not.
I Children are, and always have been, part of lesbian and gay families.
I Children raised by gay or lesbian parents are no more likely to be lesbian or gay than children raised by nongay parents—in fact, children raised by gay or lesbian parents are more likely to have higher levels of tolerance for difference than children raised by nongays.
I Gay men and lesbians are no more sexually promiscuous than their nongay counterparts.

Continued on next page

FIGURE 21.1. *(continued)*

∎ It is impossible to identify a lesbian or gay person based only on physical appearance.

∎ Gay men do not prey on or molest children for sexual gratification—most pedophiles and child molesters are heterosexual men.

∎ Lesbians and gay men do not convert children to homosexual lifestyles.

∎ There is no scientifically proven determinant of sexual orientation, but most now think sexual orientation (both heterosexual and homosexual) is genetically determined and not a chosen lifestyle.

∎ While some believe homosexuality to be a mental illness, the general consensus in the psychiatric community is that homosexuality is a normative state for some portion of the population and is not to be considered pathological.

∎ While some believe homosexuality can be cured through reparative therapy or prayer, these approaches have extremely low success rates, work only marginally and for short periods with those who find their homosexual behavior grossly incompatible with their psychological well-being, and may be psychically damaging—professional organizations like NASW warn social workers to avoid such interventions.

∎ Lesbians and gay men get along well with members of the opposite sex, although there are some lesbian separatist groups who try and avoid men when possible.

∎ Relationships between gay and lesbian persons and their parents have no more conflict or instability than relationships between nongay persons and their parents; however, parents often have difficulty accepting that any of their children are gay or lesbian.

∎ Data indicate that gay men and lesbians are as mentally healthy as their nongay counterparts—in some areas gays and lesbians are psychologically better able to cope.

∎ While the traditional religious sects condemn homosexuals and homosexuality, gay men and lesbians are as religious and spiritual as others.

∎ While many gay couples have dual incomes, data show a significant number of lesbians and gays could be at or below the poverty line.

∎ While some lesbian and gay couples may play butch/femme roles, most do not.

∎ A gay and lesbian sexual orientation knows no racial, ethnic, sexual, socioeconomic, regional, religious, professional, or age boundaries—lesbians and gays are found throughout society.

∎ Although not discussed until the 1980s, gay men and lesbians can be the victims of domestic violence, spousal abuse, and hate crimes.

∎ While there are bars in the lesbian and gay community, the community also includes restaurants, spas, grocery stores, shoe shops, gift shops, beauty salons, real estate brokers, coffee shops, garden supply stores, and others.

∎ Gay men and lesbians may have problems related to their sexual orientation, but they have problems similar to their nongay counterparts, too, and social workers should not assume sexual orientation to be the primary problem.

∎ Data demonstrate that lesbians and gay men can come out at any point in their lives—from adolescence through old age.

real, the symptoms of internal homophobia can range from mild anxiety to suicide. Certainly traversing the route to become a client in what may be viewed as a traditional institution filled with prevailing stereotypes about sexual orientation and being confronted with personnel who are homophobic could have a tendency to justify internal homophobia.

DEMOGRAPHIC PATTERNS

To get a general sense of how widespread homosexuality may be, the following demographics may be interesting. As has been noted, it is not possible to identify a lesbian or gay person just by appearance. Therefore, it is easy for gays and lesbians to hide in a population and society that are primarily nongay. So although it has never been possible (and never will be possible) to identify the entire population that is lesbian or gay, that has not stopped researchers from trying to estimate what percentage of the general population of the United States fits into that population category. One of the earliest estimates came from the Kinsey data that were generated during the last part of the 1940s and early part of the 1950s (Kinsey et al. 1948; Kinsey et al. 1953). These data, collected on the sexual behaviors of both men and women, suggested that between 3 percent and 10 percent of the total population were gay or lesbian. Others who study such phenomena agree that these percentages are probably fairly accurate (National Opinion Research Center 1989–1992; Rogers 1993), but these are merely estimates.

Assuming the estimates to be somewhere around reality, and based on current census data that show approximately 260 million persons living in the country (U.S. Bureau of the Census 1992), it would mean that, in the latter part of the twentieth century, a total of between 7.8 million to 26 million persons in the United States were lesbian or gay. Using the same percentages across ethnic or racial lines, data demonstrate there could be from 1 million to 3.6 million African American gay men and lesbians, from 213,000 to 710,000 Pacific Islander or Asian lesbians and gay men, and from 6.5 million to 21.7 million Caucasian gay men and lesbians living in this country.

When examining these statistics by sex, data show that the U.S. population is comprised of 135.2 million women (52 percent) and 124.8 million men (48 percent) (U.S. Bureau of the Census 1992). Again, using the generally accepted percentages of lesbians and gay men (3–10 percent), it is possible there are from 4 million to 13.5 million lesbians and 3.7 million to 12.5 million gay men in the country. Of lesbians, 524,100 to 1.8 million may be African American, 390,000 to 1.3 million Hispanic, 111,000 to 370,000 Pacific Islanders or Asian, and 3.4 million to 11.3 million Caucasian. Of gay men, 48,800 to 1.6 million may be African American, 360,000 to 1.2 million Hispanic, 102,000 to 340,000 Pacific Islanders or Asian, and 3.1 million to 10.4 million Caucasian.

Social services, while offered to all socioeconomic groups, are traditionally used more by those with lower income levels. The census data presents a graphic picture of annual household incomes in the United States (*Annual Demographic Survey* 1997). In 1996, there were a total of 100.1 million households in the country. Of those, 18.8 million households (19 percent) had annual incomes of less than $17,500. Of those 18.8 million households, 10.9 million were classified as "nonfamily households" (households comprised of persons not related by blood or marriage). Of those in the nonfamily category with incomes at or below the poverty level, 1.9 million households were African American and 94,000 were Hispanic.

While the 1990 census did make some attempt to identify persons who were living together but were not married, no data were gathered that specifically asked about sexual orientation. It may be logical to conclude that data on lesbian and gay households were captured in the "nonfamily" category, but even doing that is risky. Having so noted, if one assumes that data on gay and lesbian households are embedded in the general census data, and that between 3 percent and 10 percent of all families in this category are lesbian or gay, then it may be that of the 100.1 million total households, between 3.3 million to 10 million households are lesbian or gay households. And, of that number, between 738,000 to 2.4 million gay or lesbian households could be living in or very close to poverty. In racial lesbian or gay households at or near poverty, 500,000 are African American, 330,000 are Hispanic, and 1.8 million are Caucasian.

Caucasians in nonfamily households are more likely to live closer to poverty than family households. For the two ethnic minorities for which data were available (African Americans and Hispanics), members of these two groups tended to live in family households as opposed to nonfamily households. However, whereas 22 percent of all Caucasian households (family and nonfamily) lived with less than $17,500 annually, 38.8 percent of African American households and 40 percent of Hispanic households did so. And while it is unknown how many of these ethnic minority households are lesbian or gay, it seems logical to deduce that if one is a gay man or lesbian of color, then it is more likely he or she will be impoverished than if he or she were Caucasian.

It seems that great numbers of gay men and lesbians may be living at or near poverty and likely recipients of social services. Such services may be related to socioeconomic status, being a member of a despised and often misunderstood disenfranchised minority group, or other factors associated with a societal context that is heterocentric.

Since gays and lesbians are generally invisible as adults, they are virtually seen as nonexistent as adolescents or aged persons. Research related to lesbian and gay youth is still in its infancy, and as recently as 1980, Woodman and Lenna warned social workers that the topic of gay and lesbian adolescents was "too sensitive" (88) for general discussion. Despite this caution the topic has been and continues to be one of interest for social workers. Again, if one assumes that 3 percent to 10 percent of the adolescent population of 27.5 million persons (U.S. Bureau of the Census 1992) is lesbian or gay, then there could be anywhere from 82,500 to 2.75 million lesbian or gay persons between the ages of 12 and 19 years old in the United States. Similarly, data related to older gay and lesbian persons has only been collected with any regularity since the late 1970s. But just as adolescent gays and lesbians exist, so, too, do older lesbians and gay men. And while in 1995 one could estimate there to be between 996,000 to 3.3 million lesbians or gay men in the overall population of 33.2 million older Americans (U.S. Bureau of the Census 1997), by 2050 with the increasing numbers of elders the total number of gay or lesbian persons in this age range could be between 2.4 million to 8 million persons.

SOCIETAL CONTEXT

To be a member of an invisible and often despised minority within a societal context that is overwhelmingly heterocentric can be a potentially stressful activity. This section explores stressors and supports found both in the larger, heterocentric society as well as in the smaller homocentric gay and lesbian community.

All lesbian and gay persons grow up and live in a society dominated by a majority whose sexual orientation is different from theirs. In doing so they are confronted with a social structure that does not support their lifestyle. In fact, each major societal institution (legal, economic, religious, educational, and familial) is corrupted by institutional homophobia at some level and therefore is a source of stress. But just as each institution is homophobic, each, too, offers varying levels of support to its gay and lesbian members.

The **legal system** is one where institutional homophobia and hence a potential for stress is readily apparent. Legal prohibitions against same-sex sexual activity trace their antecedent roots to early canon laws (Walker 1999); by 1998, laws outlawing consensual sex between same-sex persons still existed in twenty-one (42 percent) of the fifty states. Forty states (80 percent) still allow discrimination on the basis of sexual orientation and thirty-one states (62 percent) do not protect lesbians and gay men from hate crimes (National Gay and Lesbian Task Force 1998b). **Workplace discrimination** on the basis of sexual orientation is still possible, domestic partnership benefits are not the norm, same-sex marriages are not permitted in any state, one hundred antigay initiatives were passed in forty states in 1996, and in 1997 state legislatures were introducing antigay bills at the rate of two per day (National Gay and Lesbian Task Force 1998b). There are 474 active hate groups in the United States, and no state is spared from having one or more hate groups represented (Southern Poverty Law Center 1998); hate crimes against gay and lesbian persons are increasing at an alarming rate ("Hate Crime Statistics" 1996); and discharges of lesbian and gay service personnel from the military have increased 67 percent in the 1990s (National Gay and Lesbian Task Force 1998b). The legal arena is still one that must undergo significant changes in order to avoid causing stress to lesbians and gay men.

Not immune from institutional homophobia, the **economic sector** is also contaminated by a fear of gays and lesbians. Although gay men and lesbians have been making significant contributions to the economy since antiquity, many employers at the end of the 1990s still have no policies governing domestic partners, it is still legal to discriminate on the basis of sexual orientation in the workplace, institutional homophobia is not uncommon among workers, and gay men and lesbians face unnecessary hardships in the workplace. Because many gays and lesbians must be economically independent, it is important that they have some marketable skill. Lesbians and gay men can be found employed across the socioeconomic spectrum from chief executive officers of Fortune 500 companies to migrant laborers. Their contributions would, no doubt, be missed, yet many prefer secrecy and anonymity to possible job loss. For example, an employee of the Cracker Barrel Restaurant chain in Atlanta was fired on the basis of her lesbianism and an assembly-line worker in a large automobile factory was subjected to verbal taunts and threats of physical abuse because he appeared at a gay rally ("Out at Work" 1999).

While the legal and economic arenas are filled with institutional homophobia, so, too, is the **religious community.** As mentioned, the first legal proscriptions against same-sex sexual behavior evolved from early canon law, and vestiges of these remain. These proscriptions can be seen in teachings and beliefs of the conservative southern Baptists, Catholics, and in organizations like the Christian Coalition, John Birch Society, the Family Research Council, and the Ku Klux Klan. The Christian Right (called the Radical Right by some) characterizes homosexuality as a mental illness that is curable through reparative therapy and prayer. It is seen by many mainstream denominations as a lifestyle choice and therefore an optional behavior that is sinful and goes against all religious teachings. While some extreme right-wing groups call for the extermination of homosexuals (as in Nazi Germany), most profess to "love the sinner, but hate the sin." Citing biblical scripture and reparative therapists, and ignoring professional admonitions against reparative therapy (National Committee on Lesbian and Gay Issues 1992), the Christian Right has included homosexuality as an issue for attack on its agenda for the new millennium (Christian Coalition Worldwide 1998; Goodman 1998; Grigg 1994; John Birch Society 1998; Ku Klux Klan 1998; People for the American Way 1998). So with little support either from traditional religious sources or the legal or economic arenas, how do lesbians and gays fare in the educational sector?

Institutions of learning are designed to teach students about societal mores, values, and skills. In the United States it is the right of each child to receive an education. However, public elementary, middle, and senior high schools are the source of and promulgate institutional homophobia with what can be devastating effects to the lesbian and gay students in attendance (Gay, Lesbian, and Straight Education Network 1998). The thought that prepubescent adolescents are sexual or would have need of any kind of sexual information is still ignored. And by the time children enter adolescence when sexual information is a necessity, schools have limited sex education content and even less content about the realities of lesbian or gay lifestyles. Information provided about gays and lesbians is often taught by faculty uncomfortable with the subject and who are unable to provide a realistic view. Coming to grips with a sexual orientation that is deviant from the norm is difficult under the best circumstances. It can be devastating in schools where there are no built-in support networks. And support networks for adolescent and underage gays and lesbians are not easily found. If such do exist, they are closely monitored to ensure older lesbians and gays are not taking advantage of younger persons; and in some cases parental permission must be obtained before an underage teen is allowed to join such a group. School counselors may be banned from discussing sexual orientation because of existing laws, school libraries are not a source of accurate information on lesbian and gay lifestyles, and teachers are often ignorant about the topic (Child Welfare League of America 1991; Grossman 1997; Hetrick and Martin 1987; Martin and Hetrick 1988; Morrow 1993; Savin-Williams 1989a, 1989b; Telljohann and Price 1993; Uribe and Harbeck 1991). While data indicate that college-age students are becoming more tolerant of same-sex relationships, junior- and senior-high-age students are the most negative group in their hatred of same-sex relationships (Child Welfare League of America 1991).

Institutions of higher education are under no obligation to provide content related to gay men or lesbians, but the Council on Social Work Education does mandate that such content be included at both the baccalaureate and master's levels of social work education (Council on Social Work Education 1994). Even so, the inclusion of such content is spotty, and accreditation site teams routinely overlook how well content on lesbians and gay men is being provided. It seems the educational system is as guilty of institutional homophobia as the legal and religious sectors.

With little support evident in the legal, economic, religious, or educational institutions, what is offered in the family? Many gay and lesbian children are raised by *nongay parents* who have to come to grips with the reality that a son or daughter has a sexual orientation that differs from the norm. Lesbian and gay youth learn that being different is not good, and that being a homosexual is awful. Parents generally do not understand the developmental and coming-out processes. Gay and lesbian youth are at risk of familial verbal abuse, physical abuse, rejection, emotional distancing, and isolation. Coupled with the institutional homophobia encountered at school these possibilities can cause the young lesbian or gay to become depressed, quit school, run away, abuse alcohol or drugs, or commit suicide (Child Welfare League of America 1991; Grossman 1997; Telljohann and Price 1993).

The **legal system,** while still largely not supportive of legislation that protects same-sex behaviors and lesbian and gay families, is slowly becoming more accepting and supportive of same-sex issues. National statistics on hate crimes now include information on hate crimes against lesbians and gay men ("Hate Crime Statistics" 1996), the 105th Congress was one vote short of proving federal legislation that would prohibit workplace discrimination against lesbians and gays but the legislation had more cosponsors than ever (Human Rights Campaign 1998b; Stachelberg 1997), and federal legislation designed to prohibit gay or lesbian couples from adopting children failed to pass (National Gay and Lesbian Task Force 1998b). Domestic partnership ordinances were passed in several cities, numerous colleges and universities passed nondiscrimination policies that included gays and lesbians, scores of businesses expanded personnel policies to include benefits for same-sex couples, openly lesbian and gay persons ran for and were elected to public office, and more and more states deleted outdated sodomy laws. Vermont's legal system is currently examining whether or not gay or lesbian couples can legally wed and New Jersey allows both persons in gay and lesbian couples to jointly adopt children (Human Rights Campaign 1999).

In the latter part of the 1990s, gay men and lesbian women are becoming more visible and more demanding of their legal rights, and candidates no longer disregard the gay vote as not important. Members of gay and lesbian **political organizations** such as the Human Rights Campaign (HRC) and the National Gay and Lesbian Task Force (NGLTF) actively lobby federal and state legislators on issues related to gays and lesbians. Their influence is not without political clout as, in 1997 and 1998, both the president and vice-president of the United States attended functions of such political organizations (Human Rights Campaign 1998b).

The legal and political systems are far more tolerant of dealing with the gay and lesbian political agenda in the 1990s than they were in the 1950s, when the mere idea that there would ever be a political debate related to anything having to do with same-sex behaviors or relationships was thought of as preposterous. That there even is a national lesbian and gay political agenda is testimony to the reality that the legal and political systems can and do change. In relation to legal conquests made by gay men and lesbians, while not yet universal, small skirmishes are fought and won each year and do provide some amount of support and hope for lesbians and gay men who continue to struggle for basic civil rights.

The **religious community,** too, has made strides in providing support for gay and lesbian individuals, couples, and families. Created in the 1970s, the Metropolitan Community Church (MCC) was the first church created by and for the lesbian and gay community (Perry 1971). By the end of the century, MCC had congregations in every major U.S. city and a following of hundreds of thousands. And despite the antigay thrust of the Christian Right, even conservative churches like the Catholic Church have organizations designed to minister to gay and lesbian parishioners, and more and more mainstream denominations are grappling with issues related to gay men and lesbians. Increasingly, Christian and Jewish churches and synagogues are willing to perform commitment ceremonies for lesbian or gay couples, and while not legally binding, such unions are religiously sanctioned. Religious institutions also are struggling with the ordination of gay men and lesbians. In some mainstream denominations it is acceptable to ordain lesbian and gay priests or ministers, and, increasingly, gay and lesbian clergy are ministering to a variety of congregational flocks (Vaid 1995; Witt, Thomas, and Marcus 1995). In sum, religious organizations are still generally not accepting of homosexuality and gay or lesbian lifestyles, but some are making significant changes to include lesbians and gays in all facets of church life. Many gay men and lesbian women consider themselves extremely religious and it is no longer impossible for lesbians or gay men to be divorced from a religion that is accepting of their lifestyle.

Just as the legal and religious systems have made significant changes in relation to their views about lesbians and gays, the **educational system** is also slowly coming to terms with the reality of its gay and lesbian students. The Gay, Lesbian, and Straight Education Network (GLSEN), created as a public school–oriented group in 1990, participates in curriculum development for elementary and secondary level schools and works with parents, teachers, students, and concerned citizens to end homophobia in the school setting. With more than forty chapters nationwide, GLSEN creates and develops curricula for in-school programs, community organizing, and advocacy. Their primary aim is to work with and create change in the homophobic belief systems of those educational leaders and policymakers who control the public school system (Gay, Lesbian, and Straight Education Network 1998). One public school initiative undertaken by GLSEN in 1998 was to challenge federal legislation prohibiting teenage children Internet access to gay- and lesbian-oriented materials through public school access networks. GLSEN believed to deny teens access to honest, helpful materials that could bolster self-esteem and perhaps reduce suicide was immoral and potentially damaging (Einhorn 1998). Some high schools have allowed same-sex couples to attend junior or senior proms together, but this still is not customary, and one Orleans Parish, Louisiana, public school official declared there were no lesbian or gay students in the New Orleans public school system.

Postsecondary institutions tend to be more liberal in their approach to same-sex behaviors and relationships. Many universities have nondiscrimination policies that protect gay and lesbian students, campus organizations for gays and lesbians, and provide housing for same-sex couples. Sororities and fraternities for lesbians and gays have been established, and some schools have tried housing lesbian and gay students on specific floors of dormitories. In the middle 1990s, "queer studies" emerged as a legitimate topic of scholastic pursuit, and lesbian and gay faculty can now openly act as mentors for gay and lesbian students. And, like the legal and religious sectors, while not totally embracing the gay or lesbian experience, primary, secondary, and postsecondary institutions of education are beginning to grapple with issues related to their lesbian and gay students and provide curricula designed about the realities of being a gay or lesbian person. In doing so, such educational institutions are providing some supports for lesbian and gay learners.

Family systems, too, are following similar paths in relationship to lesbian and gay family members. Once considered such a stigma that the disclosure of a homosexual identity to a family member was deemed unthinkable, by the end of the twentieth century more and more gays and lesbians were sharing their sexual orientation with various family members. And although responses to this disclosure vary, more supports are now in place than ever before to help struggling family members with this information. The best-known such organization is Parents, Family, and Friends of Lesbians and Gays (PFLAG). Comprised primarily of parents of gays and lesbians and family members with gay and lesbian relatives, PFLAG is concerned with the rights of lesbian and gay children, adolescents, and young adults. One of PFLAG's initiatives, Project Open Mind (POM) is to inform the general population about the realities of lesbian and gay Americans. Begun in 1995 as a counterbalance to increasing hatred, intolerance, and attacks on the gay and lesbian community, POM seeks to provide factual information to counter myths, stereotypes, misinformation, and ignorance about the gay and lesbian lifestyle. It is a multimedia public awareness campaign centered on ending discrimination against lesbians and gays and has support in major cities such as Atlanta, Houston, Seattle, and Tulsa (Parents, Families, and Friends of Lesbians and Gays 1998). By supporting family members, PFLAG helps families provide support for their gay and lesbian children. And with chapters in every major metropolitan area, families who want to be a support system for their lesbian or gay family member can do so.

Whether or not parents and siblings of gay and lesbian family members are involved with PFLAG, families are generally not immune from the media attention currently given to gay men and lesbians. Increasingly, lesbians and gay men are being portrayed on the small and large screen as normal, psychologically healthy, attractive people struggling, like everyone else, to cope with the realities of life. Lesbian travel companies have purchased advertising time during prime time, gay couples are used in major media campaigns, those accused of hate crimes against gays are publicly condemned, and gay men and lesbians are favorably portrayed on the covers of popular press magazines. Family members have opportunities to play a supportive role for their lesbian and gay relatives, and many do. However, it is not within families of origin where gays and lesbians garner the preponderance of their support—it is within their families of choice.

Families of origin certainly can play an important supportive role to lesbians and gay men, but the families chosen by gays and lesbians to be their support network provide the most support. Because same-sex couples are banned from forming legally sanctioned family units, they create their own by forming relationships that may be short term or long term and settling into the routine of living their lives. Friendship networks provide the primary source of these familial configurations, and they can be as simple or as intricate as any traditional family structure and may or may not include members of the biological family of origin.

For example, Chris and Sally, a lesbian couple had been together for twenty-five years. Chris had no close family of origin family members, but Sally had six bothers. Three of the brothers were supportive of Chris and Sally's relationship, two were not, and one was uncertain. As a result, the three supportive siblings became part of the couple's family of choice that also included gay male, lesbian, and nongay persons as well. The two brothers who did not accept the relationship did so on the basis of their religious beliefs and were isolated from and ignored by the couple.

As an overall societal system, sources of support for lesbians and gay men are increasingly visible and acceptable. It has been postulated that eventually all sodomy laws will be done away with, that same-sex couples will be allowed to marry, that religious organizations will accept lesbians and gays as normal, that schools will teach sexuality as a continuum of various approved behaviors, and that discrimination on the basis of sexual orientation will no longer exist. Small glimmers of hope that these will occur in the next century seem to exist, time will tell whether or not such will occur. In the meantime, being gay or lesbian in a heterocentric society is cause for more stress than comfort, and the support systems need constant bolstering and attention.

VULNERABILITIES AND RISK FACTORS

Lesbian and gay persons are vulnerable and at risk in the heterocentric society primarily because of their differing sexual orientation and society's continuing efforts to disavow homosexual behavior and homosexuality; this struggle has been documented since antiquity (Boswell 1980; D'Emilio and Freedman 1988; Mondimore 1996). Although some positive steps to ensure equal rights for gay and lesbian persons are being implemented, the population is still vulnerable and at risk. Lesbians and gays are most vulnerable primarily in the larger heterocentric society where they are likely to be employed, have family, and function within societal norms. However, gay men and lesbians may also be at risk in the smaller homocentric society where they seek refuge, create families of choice, and socialize. This section explores major vulnerabilities of the population and identifies pressing psychosocial needs.

Gay and lesbian persons cannot exist totally outside the larger, heterocentric social order. This social structure is predominantly heterosexual where norms and mores mirror those of the dominant members. At best, gay men and lesbian women are seen as productive members of society; at worst they are seen as mentally ill deviants. As there is no prevailing view of lesbians and gay men, just knowing when it is acceptable to acknowledge a deviant sexual orientation or not can be a source of anxiety and risk. Generally, there are various points across a gay or lesbian life where one is more vulnerable and at risk than at other times. And while developing a lesbian or gay identity is not a linear activity, one way of highlighting these is to explore them from a life-span perspective within both the heterosexual society and the smaller gay subculture.

Youth and Adolescence. The topic of sexuality as related to preadolescent children is still one that is infrequently discussed, and the topic of lesbian or gay sexuality among young children is generally ignored. Although some gay men and lesbians acknowledge having same-sex sexual feelings during childhood (Herdt 1989; Rust 1993; Telljohann and Price 1993; Troiden 1989; Tully 1983), most authors confine themselves to discussions on adolescent sexuality. The exploration of gay or lesbian adolescent sexuality is one begun in the early 1980s and is still in its infancy. However, from the research that has been conducted, several vulnerabilities and risk factors emerge for young lesbians and gays (see figure 21.2). From the nongay society a young gay or lesbian faces possible verbal, physical, or sexual assault; sexual exploitation; or victimization simply on the basis of a differing sexual orientation. To be considered a member of an illegal minority is for many adolescents a stigma that causes victimization, scapegoating, oppression, and social isolation (Child Welfare League of America 1991; Grossman 1997; Telljohann & Price 1993).

Because of lingering fears that adult lesbians and gay men prey on adolescents for sexual gratification, or recruitment into a homosexual lifestyle (Christian Coalition Worldwide 1998), adult gays and lesbians can be reluctant to interact with underage self-identified lesbians and gays. Further, school policies related to sexual education may ban any discussion of homosexuality as an acceptable lifestyle and prohibit gay or lesbian teachers from being employed (Gay, Lesbian, and Straight Education Network 1998). With this schism between younger lesbians and gays and similarly situated adults, there is a lack of appropriate role models for gay and lesbian teens. The gay community places gay and lesbian teens at risk mostly out of ignorance and fear of becoming involved, which creates few safe havens for younger lesbians and gays.

Within the family of origin young gays and lesbians are also at risk. Parents, wanting their children to be normal, generally assume all children to be heterosexual. This is simply not realistic. When family members either discover on their own or are told of their child's not normative sexuality, reactions vary, but seldom, if ever, do parents explode with pride and joy over the news. So youthful gays and lesbians are at risk even within their own families. It is not uncommon for young gay teens to be the victim of verbal or physical abuse; it is also not uncommon for a young lesbian to be rejected and isolated in the family. Parents may emotionally distance themselves from the teenager, a family crisis may erupt where one or both parents feels guilty about the child's sexual orientation, or parents may hospitalize the adolescent for treatments and cures (Child Welfare League of America 1991; Cramer and Roach 1988; Morrow 1993; Savin-Williams 1988, 1989a, 1989b, 1996).

Adulthood. Growing up gay or lesbian has its risks, but several risk factors also are associated with being an adult lesbian or gay person (see figure 21.2). As has been said, remaining myths and stereotypes associated with homosexuality still color the way many view gay men and lesbians. These, coupled with institutional homophobia, tend to create situations in which adult gays and lesbians may be vulnerable and at risk. Such situations include legal proscriptions that make same-sex sexual behaviors illegal and employment and other discrimination based on sexual orientation. Because no universal laws exist to provide civil rights for gay men and lesbians or protect them from discrimination, lesbians and gay men are at risk for civil rights violations and discrimination in employment or housing. As a result, often gay men and lesbians simply hide their sexual orientation and pass as normal heterosexuals. However, this secretive lifestyle can create low self-esteem, depression, anxiety, guilt, isolation, or suicide (Appleby and Anastas 1998; Berger and Kelly 1995; Tully 1995).

However, being open about sexual orientation in a heterocentric society also has its risks. Hate crimes are those crimes in which the perpetrator intentionally selects a victim on the basis of the perceived or actual race, color, ethnicity, national origin, sexual orientation, gender, or disability of that victim ("Hate Crimes: A Definition" 1994). Hate crimes against lesbians and gay men are increasing (National Coalition of

Anti-Violence Programs 1998). The most recent example is that of Matthew Shepard, who was brutally beaten, tied to a Wyoming fence on a frigid night in October 1998, and left to die because he was gay (Tully, 2000). Lesbians and gays who are open about their sexual orientation risk possible murder, assault, or verbal abuse and may be the focus of jokes. Further, gay men and lesbians may lose their jobs or homes because of their sexual orientation (Human Rights Campaign 1998b).

But it is not only from within the nongay society that adult lesbians and gays may be at risk. Families of origin also can create risk for the adult lesbian woman or gay man, because of nonacceptance that can cause a lack of family support, emotional distancing or rejection, and even violence or abuse toward the lesbian or gay family member (Appleby and Anastas 1998; Tully 2000). Individual homophobia of various family members can be the source of tremendous anxiety, guilt, or depression in the lesbian or gay family member.

Just as families of origin can cause potential risks for adult gay men and lesbians so, too, can families of choice. Although it would seem that families of choice would provide support and buffer the adult lesbian or gay men from institutional and individual homophobia, these socially constructed units can cause stress and put members at risk. Commonly the areas for vulnerability and risk center on how to create, maintain, and terminate relationships; whether or not the relationships should be monogamous; and how to best deal with sexual openness and coming out. Creating and maintaining same-sex relationships in a heterocentric world is fraught with risk— should the couple live together, should the dyad be monogamous, how should financial matters be dealt with, should the couple have children, should both partners work, who should know about the nature of the relationship, should the partners obviously share a bedroom, or how long will the relationship last are questions with which each gay or lesbian couple must grapple (Mallon 1998; Shernoff 1995, 1998; Tully 1995). Because no legal bonds connect them, gay and lesbian couples also must consider issues associated with jointly owned property, shared custody of children, legal encroachments made by family of origin members, and powers of attorney. Each question and activity shared by the same-sex couple poses risk simply because it is never certain where one will encounter goodwill and acceptance or ill will and homophobia. Coming out is a continuing struggle throughout adulthood. It is often greeted with genuine acceptance; but too often, sharing one's sexual orientation puts the lesbian or gay man in a vulnerable position and at risk. And these risks are found in both the gay and nongay worlds.

Old Age. Younger gays and lesbians are at risk because of their youth, adult lesbians and gays are vulnerable simply because they are seen to lead a deviant lifestyle, and older gay men and lesbians are vulnerable and at risk because (like their adolescent counterparts) they are virtually invisible. Social work did not generally embrace the older community as an important source of potential clients until the early part of the 1970s. Since then programs in gerontology have been developed in several universities, and social workers have played an important role as one of many professions currently interested in services for older adults. Interest in gay and lesbian aging began almost a decade after social work began to deal with aging populations (Berger 1980, 1982; Kelly 1977; Tully 1983). In the almost twenty years that lesbian and gay aging has been a focus of limited study, it has been determined that, like their

FIGURE 21.2. Risk Factors Associated with Being Lesbian or Gay

I. **Risk Factors During Youth and Young Adulthood**

From the Nongay Society

- Verbal, physical, or sexual abuse
- Sexual exploitation
- Victimization
- Scapegoating
- Oppression
- Stigmatization
- Isolation

From the Family of Origin

- Family disruption or crisis
- Verbal, physical, or sexual abuse
- Rejection
- Emotional distancing
- Guilt
- Isolation

From the Gay/Lesbian Community

- Lack of appropriate role models
- Insufficient resources and services
- Racism
- Legal restraints
- Fear of interpersonal relationships between adults and adolescents
- Ignorance of adolescent issues and needs

From the Young Lesbian or Gay Person

- Coming out
- Dealing with school, families, society

II. **Risk Factors During Adulthood**

From the Nongay Society

- Legal proscriptions
- Prevailing stereotypes and myths
- Employment discrimination
- Hate crimes
- Institutional homophobia
- Inadequate support systems

From the Family of Origin

- Nonacceptance
- Lack of familial support
- Violence, physical, or sexual abuse
- Isolation, emotional distancing, or rejection
- Individual homophobia

Continued on next page

FIGURE 21.2. *(continued)*

From the Gay/Lesbian Community

- ▮ Inadequate support systems
- ▮ Racism
- ▮ Sexism

From the Family of Choice

- ▮ Creating, maintaining relationships
- ▮ Monogamy v. nonmonogamy
- ▮ Coming out
- ▮ Children, adoptions
- ▮ Sexual orientation openness
- ▮ Health
- ▮ Employment
- ▮ Finances
- ▮ Internalized homophobia

III. **Risk Factors During Old Age**

From the Nongay Community

- ▮ Prevailing myths and stereotypes about gays and lesbians aging
- ▮ Lack of adequate support systems
- ▮ Invisibility
- ▮ Institutional homophobia

From Families of Origin

- ▮ Lack of support or understanding
- ▮ Emotional distancing or rejection
- ▮ Familial confusion or crisis around coming out

From the Gay/Lesbian Community

- ▮ Prevailing myths and stereotypes
- ▮ Invisibility

From Families of Choice

- ▮ Declining health
- ▮ Death and dying
- ▮ Ensuring adequate finances
- ▮ Ensuring appropriate legal protections

nongay counterparts, older gay men and lesbians are a vulnerable and an at-risk population. Like other populations of lesbians and gays, older gay men and lesbians find themselves at risk both in the larger heterocentric society and in the smaller gay and lesbian subculture.

Society at large tends to overlook and ignore older populations generally (Hooyman and Kiyak 1999), and this is also true in the gay and lesbian community (Berger 1996; Tully 1983). Doomed to invisibility in both the nongay larger social order and in the lesbian and gay community, aging gay men and lesbians are often assumed to be nonsexual beings whose issues and familial structures are similar to other groups of older women and men. This invisibility makes older gays and lesbians vulnerable and at risk simply because their needs are neither known nor cared about. But perhaps invisibility is preferable to prevailing myths and stereotypes in both the nongay and gay/lesbian worlds about older persons generally and older lesbian and gay persons specifically.

Older gays and lesbians are frequently viewed as peculiar, ugly, unhappy, pathetic creatures who prey on young persons for sexual gratification (if they have sex at all), and who are unable to maintain long-term relationships (Berger 1980, 1982, 1996; Kehoe 1986a, 1986b, 1988; Kelly 1977; Laner 1979; MacDonald and Rich 1983; Moss 1970; Tully 1989). Although according to research these myths and stereotypes have no basis in fact, many in both the larger society and the gay and lesbian subculture continue to accept them as real. So older gays and lesbians are also at risk of being perceived in unflattering and unrealistic terms and being treated accordingly.

Families of origin and families of choice, too, can place older gay men and lesbians at risk. Because the coming-out process can occur at any point in a lifetime when an older person decides to come out, familial crises can occur. Many older lesbians and gay men have been heterosexually married, raised families, and lived conventional lives prior to acknowledging their nontraditional sexual orientation (Berger 1980, 1982, 1996; Kehoe 1986a, 1986b, 1988; Tully 1989). Coming out to themselves, their heterosexual spouse, their children, their friends, or other family members can be a crisis that may lead to lack of family support, social rejection, isolation, or emotional distancing from family members. These stressors can cause anxiety, depression, lowered self-esteem, guilt, or other psychically damaging consequences.

By the time older gays and lesbians have survived to old age, most have adapted to their sexual orientation and dealt with members of their biological families. Family members who are supportive of the gay or lesbian relative remain as a family of choice member; those who are not supportive are often ignored and not considered "family" (Tully 1983). But for those older gays and lesbians who have hidden their sexual origin from their families of origin and who face providing care to parents or siblings, there are untold risks. Can the elderly parent of a gay couple move in with the aging couple? Should an older gay man abandon his home and partner of forty years to move in with his father? What should the growing older couple do with a younger mentally ill brother? Is it acceptable to expect an aging lesbian to leave her home and job to take care of parents? These and scores of other dilemmas face aging gay men and lesbians who have living family of origin members and can cause a number of consequences. Relationship stress, depression, anxiety, and guilt can lead to more damaging behaviors such as substance abuse and withdrawal.

While families of origin can cause problems for the older gay man or lesbian, their families of choice may also. Declining health, the death and dying of a partner, ensuring adequate financial reserves, and securing adequate legal protections are all issues for older lesbians and gay men that may put them at risk. Older gays and lesbians face similar health issues as their nongay counterparts, but also face health issues related to a gay or lesbian lifestyle. Because older gays and lesbians tend to be invisible, their sexual orientation may not be taken into account in diagnostic considerations. Since many older lesbians and gays do not feel their sexual orientation has anything to do with why they seek various professional services, they may very well not disclose their sexual orientation to service providers (Berger 1996; Kehoe 1986a, 1986b, 1988; Tully 1989). When an aging gay or lesbian's partner begins to experience declining health, the services traditionally available do not usually consider sexual orientation. Such service organizations tend to overlook a partner as a source of support and information, preferring instead to call on legal relatives.

Legal protections for older gay or lesbian persons reflect the institutional homophobia of the heterocentric society. It is not uncommon for the surviving partner of a gay or lesbian couple to be the sole beneficiary of the partner's estate only to have the will legally challenged. Too often, family of origin members, children, or other legal relatives will be seen as the lawful heir. Dividing household items between an unacknowledged partner and "legal" heirs can be particularly devastating to the gay or lesbian surviving partner. Likewise, ensuring for financial security in old age can be potentially risky for the aging lesbian or gay man.

Many older gay and lesbian persons have worked throughout their lives and older couples may enjoy the benefits of a dual retirement income. But, if one partner is more financially secure than the other there are no legally binding measures that will ensure financial security for both partners. If portfolios are not jointly held, financial security between partners can become a gesture of goodwill, which may put the less financially secure partner at risk.

As described in the preceding, significant risk factors are associated with being lesbian or gay, and they are all associated simply with a sexual orientation that differs from most of the population. As a result, this population is vulnerable to a variety of unhealthy possibilities. While all gay and lesbian persons face similar heterocentric societal challenges, not all gay and lesbian persons see themselves as either vulnerable or at risk. However, data indicate that at some point in every lesbian or gay life the individual has been vulnerable and at risk due to institutionalized, individual, or internal homophobia. What follows is a summary of some of the consequences of existing in a social order that is lukewarm to hostile about the existence of lesbian women and gay men (see figure 21.3).

Adolescent gays and lesbians may suffer from increased anxiety; lowered self-esteem; poor school grades; an increased rate of school dropout; substance abuse—alcohol, drugs (illegal), sexual or physical abuse; tobacco; sexual promiscuity—both heterosexual and homosexual; higher levels of sexually transmitted diseases and HIV; social isolation or withdrawal; developmental delays; depression; suicide; acting out; running away from home; or internalized homophobia (Child Welfare League of America 1991; Hetrick and Martin 1987; Martin and Hetrick 1988; Morrow 1993). Lesbian and gay adults are not immune to similar distress and may be victims of depression; anxiety; increased abuse of drugs (both illegal and prescription), alcohol, or tobacco; lowered self-esteem; guilt; poor communication and relational skills; social isolation; sexually transmitted diseases or HIV/AIDS; domestic violence; hate crimes; social stigmatization; or employment or legal discrimination. Finally, older gay men and lesbians may be socially isolated and ignored; rendered invisible by both the gay/lesbian subculture and the larger society; depressed; stigmatized; the victims

FIGURE 21.3. Possible Consequences of Being Vulnerable and At Risk

Data indicate lesbians and gays are at risk in several ways. The following represent possible outcomes of being a lesbian woman or gay man in a traditionally heterocentric social order.

I. Gay and Lesbian Youth

- Increased anxiety
- Lowered self-esteem
- Poor school grades
- Increased rate of school dropout
- Substance abuse—alcohol, drugs (illegal), tobacco
- Sexual promiscuity—both heterosexual and homosexual
- Victim of physical or sexual abuse
- Higher levels of sexually transmitted diseases and HIV
- Social isolation or withdrawal
- Developmental delays
- Depression
- Suicide
- Acting out
- Running away from home
- Internalized homophobia

II. Lesbian and Gay Adults

- Depression
- Anxiety
- Substance abuse—alcohol, drugs (prescription and illegal), tobacco
- Lowered self-esteem, self-worth
- Poor relational skills
- Victim of domestic violence or a hate crime
- Social isolation or withdrawal
- Increased risk of HIV/AIDS
- Social stigmatization or scapegoating
- Job loss or employment discrimination
- Child custody loss
- Few legal protections
- Internalized homophobia

III. Older Gays and Lesbians

- Social isolation and loneliness
- Depression
- Stigmatization
- Elder abuse
- Substance abuse—prescription drugs, alcohol, tobacco

of financial, physical or verbal abuse; or overuse of prescription drugs, alcohol, or tobacco. In sum, surviving a lifetime as a gay man or lesbian woman in a frequently hostile social climate is filled with risks, but history corroborates the continuing existence of lesbians and gays since written records have been kept (D'Emilio and Freedman 1988), which rather dramatically demonstrates their resiliency.

RESILIENCIES AND PROTECTIVE FACTORS

Resiliency has been defined as an ability to recover quickly from misfortune or change, and the word *protective* is defined as that which is intended to afford protection (*The American Heritage Dictionary* 1985). Resiliency and protective factors, then, are seen as those things both tangible and intangible that enable gay men and lesbian women to exist and function in an often hostile environment. This section explores how gays and lesbians manage to survive in a heterocentric world. Throughout this chapter the overarching conceptual framework has centered on the person-in-environment where the environment has been defined as including legal, economic, religious, educational, and familial systems. These systems are defined by the majority heterosexual society, and yet gay men and lesbians exist and function surprisingly well within each. Using these five systems, this section explores how, because of resiliency and protective factors, lesbians and gays manage to cope, sustain relationships, create resources, and exist in the predominantly nongay world.

As stated earlier in the chapter, it may appear that **legal remedies** for lesbians and gays are not abundant. However, the law is not static but evolutionary, changing slowly as social values and mores change. The social construct of homosexuality as an identity is one of recent history (Walker 1999), as mentioned earlier, and while there is no known cause for same-sex behavior, evidence points toward a genetic rather than a learned origin (Bailey et al. 1991; LeVay 1991, 1996). Thus, if one is genetically predisposed to the condition (like being left-handed or blue-eyed), there tends to be less stigma attached to it. With less stigma comes more social tolerance and acceptance; with more acceptance of the behavior comes less discrimination and more legal protections. This seems to be what is happening with relation to gays and lesbians. National Opinion Research Center (NORC) data from 1989 to 1992 reveal more tolerance of homosexuals and homosexuality than previously noted (National Opinion Research Center 1982–1992), and laws are gradually beginning to reflect that change.

Federal legislation includes gays and lesbians in its hate crimes legislation as a protected category, federal law no longer requires members of the armed forces to disclose sexual orientation, state sodomy laws are gradually being struck down, some states allow both members of gay or lesbian couples to adopt a child, and there have been several successful state initiatives to ban discrimination on the basis of sexual orientation. Coupled with the reality that scores of localities, municipalities, universities, and corporations have passed domestic partnership laws or policies and openly gay and lesbian people run for (and are elected to) federal, state, or local office, it seems only a matter of time before lesbians and gays are given full civil and legal rights.

To ensure that attention continue to be given to the legal agenda, such lesbian and gay run organizations as the previously mentioned NGLTF and the HRC have emerged. Founded in 1973, NGLTF is a grassroots politically oriented organization designed to provide the gay, lesbian, bisexual, and transgender communities support in their quest for social justice at the local, state, and national levels (National Gay and Lesbian Task Force 1996, 1998a). The HRC, begun in 1980, has an almost identical mandate—ensuring civil rights for lesbians and gays—but seeks to create change from the top down. Based in Washington, D.C., HRC is a lobbying force whose emphasis is first at the federal level, then the state level, and finally at the local level (Human Rights Campaign 1998a). Both provide hope for lesbians and gays seeking equal protection under the law.

Gay men and lesbians earn a living within the **economic** sector. Although there are no universally legally mandated protections to ensure nondiscrimination in the workplace, the 105th Congress in 1998 grappled with the issue of whether or not sexual orientation should be a protected category. While the legislation narrowly failed to pass, it will be reintroduced and, hopefully, passed in a subsequent session. Data demonstrate that most Americans do not believe gays or lesbians should be discriminated against in the workplace. In support of that, many U.S. corporations openly encourage lesbian and gay applicants, have domestic partnership policies, and help find suitable employment for partners (Human Rights Campaign 1998b; National Gay and Lesbian Task Force 1998b). These are reflections of changes since the 1970s and are encouraging economic indicators that lesbian women and gay men will continue to find adequate employment opportunities within the nongay world.

To survive in times and places not as favorably inclined toward gays and lesbians, they have created unique survival tactics. By simply disappearing into the assumed heterosexual economic structure, many gays and lesbians work unnoticed and ignored. Becoming self-employed or being employed in fields where sexual orientation is not an issue were other ways to survive. Some lesbians chose to marry and become financially dependent on their husbands, some gay men stayed on the family farm and were seen as prospective bridegrooms. Most interesting though is the fairly recent development of a gay and lesbian subculture that includes gay-owned and -run businesses.

All major cities in the country now boast openly run lesbian- or gay-owned establishments that cater to gay and lesbian clientele. While there have, no doubt, always been such businesses, it is only since the 1980s that they have become fashionably chic enough to include a large nongay clientele as well. Mainstream magazines have covers sporting lesbian or gay couples, ad campaigns for major corporations use gay or lesbian images to sell their goods, and the lesbian and gay community seems to thrive.

The **religious community** has historically been the source of homophobia and not charitable toward gay or lesbian relationships. But, as with the legal sector, incremental changes that favor same-sex relationships exist. Support systems for lesbian and gay parishioners now exist within even the most conservative denominations. Churches and synagogues for gay and lesbian persons have existed in this country since the 1970s. One of the first, the Metropolitan Community Church, founded by Reverend Troy Perry now boasts churches in every major city in the United States and has thousands of members. But not all lesbians and gays opt to attend churches or synagogues defined by sexual orientation, and by the end of the 1990s most mainstream religious institutions have gay and lesbian members, lay leaders, or officials.

Openly gay or lesbian clergy have ministries in nongay churches, several Protestant denominations ordain lesbians and gays, and many Jewish and Protestant religious institutions perform holy unions of gay or lesbian couples (Cherry and Mitulski 1990; Porter-Chase 1987; Witt et al. 1995). More than 350 churches in the country voted to be included as "welcoming churches" for the gay and lesbian community and a created a publication called *Open Hands* to provide resources for ministries whose parishioners include lesbians and gays (Witt et al. 1995).

Perhaps because traditional religious structures have not been viewed as a source of support for gay men or lesbians, many lesbians and gay men shun religion altogether and are simply not part of any organized religion. For those with strong religious beliefs who are open about their sexual orientation but do not seem to fit into more traditional structures, churches and synagogues with almost exclusively gay and lesbian members can provide an answer. Openly gay and lesbian persons are members and leaders in many nongay mainstream denominations, and for those who prefer to keep their sexual orientation private, just as gay men and lesbians tend to disappear into the heterocentrist economic mainstream, so, too, can they disappear within the church and its community.

The elementary and secondary **school systems** are not often thought of as being an area of strong support for gay and lesbian students. And while this part of the social structure provides fewer supports than it could for its at-risk lesbian and gay students, some positive changes are starting to occur. Perhaps one of the most troubling, yet worthwhile, is the reality that lesbian and gay youth do exist and that they are at risk. By acknowledging their reality, no matter how disturbing, positive steps can be taken to decrease this population's risk factors. The GLSEN organization provides one means of ensuring this. Because gay and lesbian youth often do not want to be perceived as different from their peers, they usually cope by pretending to be nongay. Organizations such as GLSEN provide curricula to elementary and secondary schools that portray the realities of lesbian and gay youth and make the process of coming out somewhat less traumatic.

In addition to hiding, more open lesbians and gays in the elementary and secondary school systems cope by participating in activities in the gay and lesbian community or support groups designed for them. For example, the New Orleans lesbian and gay community center encourages younger lesbians and gays to participate in group activities at the center as well as providing an after-school place to meet.

More encouraging activities are occurring in the postsecondary arena. The academic pursuit of knowledge in the area now known as queer studies provides scholars with information related to and about the gay and lesbian lifestyle, communities, and history. As more and more information about this population is amassed and made common knowledge, the hope is that stereotypes and myths will be replaced with truth and that hatred and discrimination will vanish.

Gay men and lesbians manage to survive in **family settings** in a variety of ways. Coping in the family of origin may not always be easy, but every gay man and lesbian has been part of the challenge to do so. Camouflage is a useful protection in a hostile environment and one that serves gays and lesbians well. If camouflage is not possible, other coping mechanisms include distancing from the family (in teens this may mean running away), denial of sexual orientation, or honesty and attempts to work things out. But perhaps the most adaptive coping strategy used by gay men and lesbians is the creation of supportive family units. Comprised of gay or lesbian couples with other friends and family or comprised of single lesbians or gay men with identified support systems, these families of choice historically have been and continue to be the mainstay of lesbian and gay endurance. Gay and lesbian people have always existed and have always managed to find one another and to provide support for one another even in historically grim times (Appleby and Anastas 1998; Mallon 1998; Shernoff 1995, 1998; Tully 1995; Walker 1999). No legal marriage vows bind gay or lesbian couples, traditional heterocentrist society creates barriers for them, and yet in rural, urban, and suburban areas lesbians and gay men exist and even flourish.

In sum, the most protective armor worn by lesbians or gay men is their cloak of invisibility. While some may argue that to be invisible is to deny a vital part of one's identity, to not do so might be more injurious. But increasingly lesbians and gays are choosing not to remain invisible, but rather to share their sexual orientation in the workplace, at church, at school, and with family members. Sharing what has been defined as a deviant and often illegal lifestyle may carry risks, but it also carries the reward of not denying part of the self. As more role models emerge in the media (such as Ellen DeGeneres or Nathan Lane), are historically claimed (such as Edith Head or Laurence Olivier), or are found in major films (like *Philadelphia* or *High Art*) or in theatre (*M. Butterfly* or *The Children's Hour*) more gays and lesbians will find it easier to come out. And as more legal, economic, religious, educational, and familial supports emerge, lesbians and gay men will find it less necessary to camouflage themselves to part of the world. Until a more tolerant societal situation evolves, gay men and lesbians will cloak themselves in certain situations, will create opportunities to sustain themselves within the gay and lesbian community, and will continue to cope in a heterocentric world.

PROGRAMS AND SOCIAL WORK CONTRIBUTIONS

Microlevel programs are customarily defined as those social work services and interventions designed to be used with individuals, couples, groups, and families. Such interventive strategies have been part of social work since the emergence of the profession. There are still few social service agencies whose services are aimed solely at members of the lesbian and gay community, although there are social work practitioners in private practice whose clientele are primarily gay or lesbian, and within traditional social service agencies programs for gays and lesbians may exist. Generally, the lesbian woman or gay man seeking social services will be confronted with the same array of service providers as their nongay counterparts. And, also like their nongay counterparts, services provided to gay or lesbian persons may be voluntary, suggested, or mandated.

Because gay and lesbian people voluntarily may seek services for depression, anxiety, low self-esteem, relationship problems, substance abuse, health issues, sexual dysfunction, coming out, and having and raising children, social workers play roles similar to when working with nongays. Thus, it is appropriate for the social worker's roles to include those of social broker, enabler, teacher, mediator, and advocate, as each of these interventive roles has its appropriate place when working with lesbians and gays.

Although common presenting problems and interventive roles are similar for nongay and gay populations, the social worker must avoid both the "heterosexual assumption" (the assumption that all clients are heterosexual) and all forms of homophobia. Often gay men or lesbians seek social services for reasons totally unrelated to their sexual orientation, but when issues about coming out, sexual dysfunction, HIV/AIDS, or sexual identity issues are the presenting problem, social workers must know how to create a homosocial space that is safe for gay or lesbian self-disclosure. It has been demonstrated that social workers are as homophobic as the rest of the general population (DeCrescenzo 1983–84; DeCrescenzo and McGill 1978; Tate 1991; Wisniewski and Toomey 1987), and that many social service agencies still have policies that assume heterosexuality or otherwise discriminate against gays and lesbians (McClellen 1998). This is particularly acute in hospital settings and in agencies that deal with children where social work professionals must struggle against institutional homophobia.

Social work roles that have been particularly evident since the outbreak of HIV/AIDS include those individual and group services developed for persons who are HIV-positive. Since the early 1980s social workers have played a key role in providing support services, caregiving, and finally hospice services to countless numbers affected by the AIDS pandemic.

When gay men or lesbians are referred to social workers for reasons other than on a voluntary basis, the professional must be alert to both overt and covert realities. If, for example, a lesbian has been arrested for murdering her "friend" it would be helpful to know whether or not the relationship was more than platonic. Or if a "business partner" of a stroke victim shows up at the emergency room wanting to see his partner, will he be dismissed as a nonrelative and denied access to the patient?

Mezzolevel programs that revolve around community have, like microlevel interventions, been part of professional social work since its beginning. They are concerned with advocacy, mobilization, service, and organization within communities and seek to promote change at the community level (Kahn 1995). Both the larger heterocentric community and the smaller lesbian and gay communities have been described. And social work professionals provide services on behalf of gay men and lesbians within both of these communities. In the heterocentric community, social workers have participated in demonstrations for gay and lesbian civil rights, have helped create laws and policies aimed at eliminating discrimination on the basis of sexual orientation, and have worked toward erasing institutionalized homophobia. Within the gay and lesbian community social workers have created agencies dedicated to gay and lesbian youth, have mobilized gay and lesbian community members to demand appropriate funding for HIV/AIDS research and medications, have created elaborate political action committees to ensure their civil and legal rights, and have worked tirelessly to protect gay and lesbian existing freedoms.

Although the focus of social work is more on practice with individuals, couples, families, and groups, community organization has a vibrant place when working with gays and lesbians. Social work practitioners should remember that gay men and lesbians create their own communities and as such may require help in negotiating barriers constructed by the heterocentric social order. For example, when no services were available for lesbian and gay homeless youth, social workers created an agency to meet the need. In this instance, not only were the roles of advocacy, mobilization, service, and organization within the community effectively used, change at the community level occurred.

Macrolevel programs are those professional social work activities related to the social institutions with which persons must interact in the course of daily living. Working with large systems seems of interest to only a few social work practitioners, but it can be that intervention on behalf of gay men and lesbians and their communities could have the most lasting change. At the agency level, social workers working in local agency settings where homophobic policies and practices exist should work toward the institutionalization of a homosocial space that accepts diversity and avoids vestiges of institutional homophobia. Those working in state agencies should be similarly active, and those advocates and policy practitioners employed by such progay organizations as HRC or NGLTF should seek to ensure the legal and civil rights of all lesbian women and gay men. Both HRC and NGLTF have professional positions that fit well within social work's values and ethics, and both organizations have a national scope designed to conquer institutionalized homophobia (Human Rights Campaign 1998a, 1998b; National Gay and Lesbian Task Force 1998a, 1998b).

ASSESSMENT AND INTERVENTIONS

It has been noted that gay men and lesbians often seek services for similar reasons as their nongay counterparts. This section explores some of the unique issues and situations associated with being gay or lesbian that will help the social work practitioner with assessment and intervention when working with this population. The constructs of assessment and intervention seem to be two sides of the same coin, and as such both need exploration to ensure appropriate services for gay and lesbian clients. The first part of this section examines distinctive person-in-environment issues that are generally seen as being related to the gay or lesbian lifestyle, and the second part explores interventive strategies that have utility when working with clients who do not, in some ways, conform to the demands of the heterocentrist social order.

The term *assessment* can mean the process of evaluating or appraising (*The American Heritage Dictionary* 1985), or understanding and evaluating (Germain 1979; Meyer 1995). In social work, assessment is usually conceptualized as the professional process undertaken by the social worker to reach an understanding of the presenting problem, the client, and the current situation in order that appropriate interventive strategies can be developed and utilized to alleviate or solve the problem (Compton and Galaway 1994; Germain 1979; Germain and Gitterman 1996). Because the lesbian and gay population is heterogeneous, it is impossible to detail assessment strategies for every social service need of the group. Rather, this section will present what have generally been seen as unique issues facing gay men and lesbian women—invisibility and the heterosexual assumption, homophobia and its impact, and developing a sexual identity and coming out.

A key element in the assessment process is that of client and worker understanding of the current situation and the person in that unique situation. Being a lesbian or gay person is not unlike being left-handed—it is not readily apparent, may be extremely awkward at times, but is always part of the person. It may or may not be relevant to the reason a client is in need of services. For example, Cecelia, a 54-year-old lesbian who was the guardian of her 90-year-old hospitalized terminally ill mother, was referred to the hospital social worker to assess the mother's pending death and the impact it might have on Cecelia. Her sexual orientation was not germane to the immediate problem, but it would be important to know that Cecelia's partner of thirty years was the primary caretaker of Cecelia's mother and more likely to need the services. But in the case of Bob, a 27-year-old married man who had recently had his first sexual experience with a male lover and was confused about his sexual identity, knowing his sexual orientation would be important to the assessment process. The reality is that many social workers still assume their clients to be heterosexual. This denies the opportunity for honest dialogue and assessment from the beginning of the client/practitioner relationship.

To be skilled at assessing the sexual orientation of a client, social workers can make their offices and waiting rooms "homosocial." Including gay- or lesbian-oriented journals, popular newspapers, or magazines is one simple yet effective means to convey acceptance. Similarly, intake forms should be designed to include routine questions about living situations that are not biased toward a heterocentric model—rather than asking about a "spouse" or "relatives," one could ask about important people in the client's life and let the client provide the nature of the relationship. Also, social workers need to listen closely when clients are sharing their unique situations. Possible keys to sexual orientation may (but not always) include long-term relationships with members of the same sex, living with a member of the same sex, being involved in lesbian or gay organizations, or referring to a same-sex relationship with such terms as "significant other," "partner," "lover," "mate," "co-vivant," or "good friend." Clues to sexual orientation may be provided if clients are known to frequent gay or lesbian restaurants or bars, or are frequently seen involved with activities in the gay or lesbian community, or subscribe to popular gay press publications. However, extreme caution must be used when following what may be seen as stereotypic and generalities because many nongay persons also use similar terminology, frequent similar establishments, and read similar publications.

While it is acceptable to ask about sexual orientation, nongays may be put off by the suggestion that they were perceived as something else, and gays and lesbians may not be immediately forthcoming with the information. The discussion of anything sexual is still highly emotionally charged and must be handled with dignity and sensitivity. A huge hurdle is simply having the social work practitioner overcome personal fears of discussing sexual matters. Social workers must also realize that just because a person is lesbian or gay may or may not be the reason for the visit and that gay men and lesbians tend to reveal their sexual orientation (or come out to the worker) when there is some need to do so (Tully 1989).

Likewise it is acceptable to have clients inquire as to the sexual orientation of a social work professional. Although data indicate gays and lesbians do not tend to choose professionals on the basis of the professional's sexual orientation (LeBlanc and Tully 1999; Tully 1989), revealing one's sexual orientation to a client can have positive or negative effects (Anthony 1981–82; Goodman 1985; Woodman, Tully, and Barranti 1995). The prevailing professional wisdom is for the practitioner to use discretion and have some compelling reason for sharing the information. For example, Rocky, an 18-year-old gay high school student living in a rural area was involuntarily placed in therapy to cure him. His social worker, a 35-year-old successful gay man accurately assessed Rocky as suicidal and shared with him possible coping strategies. But, Juanita, a 76-year-old lesbian who had lived with her partner for forty years, was horrified when her social worker shared her personal sexual orientation and then questioned Juanita about her sexual orientation. Her reply was that sexuality was a matter of privacy and that she and Anna simply shared a one-bedroom apartment to save money.

In sum, when making initial assessments social workers must not assume that all clients are heterosexual, and they must be cautious about labeling. Creating a homosocial space that is safe for gay men and lesbians, having the ability to discuss sexual issues professionally, and being alert to the subtle nuances of the client's story are also vitally important when working with lesbians and gay men.

Invisibility would not be an issue in the gay and lesbian population were it not for homophobia. Homophobia is found in every crevice of the social structure and impacts gays, lesbians, and nongays at very basic levels. Homophobia is at the root of discrimination and hatred toward lesbian women and gay men. It is overtly recognizable in jokes about faggots and dykes, in hate crimes against gays and lesbians, in legal and religious proscriptions against lesbians and gays, in gay and adolescent suicide, and in basic beliefs about differing sexual orientations. It is covertly found in the heterosexual assumption, the acceptance of heterocentric norms and mores, the denial of job promotions, and the devaluation of the gay and lesbian lifestyle.

Certainly not every gay or lesbian person has experienced every form of homophobia, and while some may deny having ever experienced homophobia, it is virtually impossible to grow up in a nongay world and be totally immune to some facets of homophobia. Homophobia can be as overt as the killing of Matthew Shepard or as subtle as not being given a scholastic honor. It is ubiquitous, and social workers must be aware of its impact on the client, the client's unique situation, and the system. Further, social workers must be aware of the impact of homophobia on themselves. All these dynamics can play an important role in the assessment process.

That homophobia has impacted a lesbian or gay client at some point in time is a reality, but whether or not homophobia is involved in a presenting problem may not be immediately clear. In overt cases of discrimination or abuse, homophobia may be easily identified in the assessment process. However, if the homophobia is subtle, even the client may not recognize it as such and overlook it as an issue. For example, Cathy had applied for a scholarship to attend graduate school. Her grades were excellent, she thought she had the inside track on the award because her female lover had "connections," and the other finalists were outclassed by her performance and ambitions. She was not awarded the scholarship. The official reason for the rejection was that Frank was deemed a more "suitable candidate." Cathy accepted the committee's stated reason, but later heard that she was denied the scholarship because someone on the awards committee had heard a rumor that Cathy was a lesbian. Since Cathy had known all the committee members since she was a child, she could not believe they would deny her the award and decided that indeed Frank was the better candidate.

Clients may internalize homophobia and the resulting consequences of this may include low self-esteem, depression, suicidal ideation, substance abuse, isolation, self-loathing, heterophobia, or acting out. And while these symptoms are not symptomatic of lesbians and gay men exclusively, in the assessment process they must be considered as a possible consequence of homophobia. Internalized homophobia, like other issues associated with homophobia, may or may not be related to the need for interventive services. It is from the client's narrative that a discerning social work practitioner will be able to determine the extent to which homophobia relates to the situation of the client and the client's present psychosocial environment.

In addition to assessing the extent to which homophobia is related to the presenting problem of the client, social workers must also be aware of the levels of homophobia in the social service sector in which the services are offered, and the amount of homophobia in the social work practitioner. As mentioned earlier, many agency policies still reflect homophobic attitudes, and many social work practitioners still hold homophobic values, beliefs, and ideas (DeCrescenzo 1983–84; DeCrescenzo and McGill 1978; Tate 1991; Wisniewski and Toomey 1987). The assessment phase will not be successful if the lesbian or gay client is faced with a homophobic worker in an unsupportive agency, and appropriate interventive services will be aborted. For example, Jon and Theo, a gay couple, were anxious to adopt a baby through a religiously conservative agency. When the social worker, a member of the Christian Right, did the home visit, their sexual orientation was discovered; and although the couple was well suited otherwise, the adoption process was halted immediately.

In sum, homophobia is a reality in the lives of every gay man or lesbian, but the extent to which it manifests itself varies from person to person, situation to situation, and community to community. But because of its insidious nature, it may be difficult to grapple with and may not be seen as a problem for the person experiencing it. Social workers and their gay and lesbian clients must assess the extent to which homophobia plays a role and then move forward.

Invisibility and the denial of discrimination on the basis of homophobia are fairly effective coping mechanisms when confronted with life in a hostile environment and perhaps could be seen as adaptive strategies. While these two curiously lesbian and gay phenomena may tend to hide the gay man or lesbian from view, the coming-out process thrusts the fledgling lesbian or gay individual directly into overt confrontation with everything nongay.

The sexual developmental process for adolescents is seen as more or less linear where certain physiological developmental changes give way to predictable psychological responses resulting in an adult who is psychosexually intact (and heterosexual). For the gay or lesbian, the process of developing a sexual identity has been characterized as nonlinear and occurring at any chronological age. The coming-out process has been described as one of possible crisis, confusion, and disquiet (Cass 1979; Chapman and Brannock 1987; Coleman 1981–82; Morris 1997; Savin-Williams 1989a, 1996). While there are several models for coming out, they have the following things in common:

▌ The coming-out process is not linear and is not related to chronological age.
▌ It is multidimensional, including cognitive, behavioral, emotional, and sexual aspects.
▌ At some point, the individual feels different from nongays because of strong emotional attachments or sexual feelings for members of the same sex. These feelings can be ignored, repressed, questioned, denied, accepted, or acted on.
▌ Once having identified the awareness and accepted its reality, the individ-

612 ¦ *Life Circumstances and Events*

ual defines the concept of homosexuality in an attempt to make it an acceptable part of the personality. This may include identity confusion, involvement with the gay and lesbian community, alienation from the nongay community, hetero- or homosexual experimentation, ambivalence, denial, or acceptance.

▎ Having adopted a positive internalized acceptance of homosexuality, the individual tends to become more involved with the gay and lesbian community by developing intimate same-sex relationships, the internalization of a gay or lesbian identity, disclosure of this identity to others, and a psychologically healthy view of the self in spite of institutional homophobia.

Each of these need to be considered during the assessment phase, but as with other issues of lesbian and gay assessment, coming out may or may not be the primary reason for intervention. However, it has been documented that during the early phases of coming out is a time when gay men and lesbians may need intervention (Cass 1979; Child Welfare League of America 1991; McDonald 1982; Morris 1997; Savin-Williams 1989a, 1989b, 1996). It is important for the social worker to assess at what point in the coming-out process the client is in, as appropriate interventive services for a teenager confused about her or his sexual identity will vary considerably from services developed to help an aging lesbian who has a positive sexual self view but is dying.

In sum, the assessment phase is a dynamic one where gay and lesbian clients have an opportunity to engage in the social work process and to honestly evaluate whether or not sexual orientation has any relevance to the psychosocial factors precipitating the need for services. Those things that are unique to lesbians and gay men in the United States include a generalized belief that there are no gay men or lesbians or that the number of them is too small to warrant serious attention to their issues, thus making them an insignificant and invisible minority; that every lesbian and gay man in this country has, at some point in his or her lifetime, been touched at some level by homophobia, and that coming out is a lifelong continuing process of personal affirmation for gay men and lesbians. To ensure the development and implementation of appropriate interventions, each of these should play some role in the assessment phase.

The term *intervene* means to come or lie between two things so as to hinder or modify or to enter into a suit as a third party to protect an interest (*The American Heritage Dictionary* 1985). Coming from this construct, the social work concept of intervention is usually described as those professional social work activities defined by interventive roles used to achieve the goals that emerge as the result of the assessment phase (Compton and Galaway 1994). While the assessment phase is used to identify and clarify problems and possible solutions, the intervention phase is designed to develop and operationalize a feasible scheme for addressing or solving those problems. The traditional interventive social work roles of social broker, enabler, teacher, mediator, and advocate (Compton and Galaway 1994; Pinderhughes 1995) all have utility when dealing with gay men and lesbians; how each role can be applied is discussed next.

Social brokering is linking those in need with existing services that may be of benefit. Gay men and lesbians have varying knowledge of what supportive services and community linkages are available. Those new to a lesbian or gay identity may have fewer resources available simply because their knowledge is limited. Social work practitioners have an excellent opportunity to link gays and lesbians to resources only if the social worker is aware of existing possibilities. A powerful tool available to the gay and lesbian community as well as the social work professional is that of the Internet. Abundant resources related to the gay and lesbian experience are easily accessed. Popular websites include those of HRC (http://www.hrc.org), NGLTF (http://www.ngltf.org), GLSEN (http://www.glstn.org), and PFLAG (http://www.pflag.org). All provide links to other equally worthwhile sites and all provide a realistic glimpse into the gay and lesbian community.

Coupled with a working knowledge of lesbian and gay resources available in the worker's own community and an ability to link clients with the appropriate service will fulfill an important function. For example, Todd a 28-year-old sexually promiscuous gay man confides to his social worker that he has not been practicing safe sex and is fearful he may be HIV-positive. To be unable to tell him where to be tested and of available services would be untenable. Or if parents suspect one of their children to be gay or lesbian, it is helpful to use the resources of the local PFLAG group as a referral.

Another tool of intervention is the role of enabler. Enablers assist clients to discover within themselves strengths and resources to cope with and create changes necessary to accomplish the goals of the agreed to service contract. The enabler allows the client to create the needed environmental changes by supporting client activities through encouraging articulation of issues, allowing for ventilation, providing encouragement, or providing logical discussion (Compton and Galaway 1994). This role can have utility when working with members of the gay or lesbian community.

It is not uncommon for lesbians or gay men to have internalized aspects of homophobia that may lead to depression or lowered self-esteem. Coming out can lead to sexual identity confusion, and a perceived lack of generalized social support for their lifestyle can cause gays and lesbians to feel disenfranchised. However, as noted earlier, gay men and lesbians have a tremendous capacity for resiliency. This strength may be eclipsed by heterocentrism, however, and social workers may find it necessary to help gay and lesbian clients discover the power within themselves and within the gay and lesbian community. For example, the police referred Stella, a physician, to the social worker. She complained of being physically abused by her "friend." Through the assessment phase it became clear that her live-in lesbian lover had beaten Stella. While she was angry, hurt, and upset at what had happened, Stella was not certain what to do next. After assessing that Stella was not in need of medical treatment and that she had a safe place to spend the night, the social worker encouraged Stella to verbalize her feelings and ventilate. This allowed for an examination of the relationship and began to provide steps for a possible solution. With encouragement and reassurance, Stella formulated an appropriate goal and steps by which to attain that goal on her own.

A third interventive role that has profound implications for working with gay and lesbian clients is that of teacher. The teacher role is one where the social worker is in a position to provide new information needed for coping or remedying situations faced by the client. There is a vast amount of misinformation, myths, and stereotypes associated with lesbian women and gay men. Both social work practitioners and clients benefit from the role of teacher. Clients have an opportunity to teach professionals what it is really like to be a member of a frequently despised, disenfranchised minority group, and social workers have a chance to provide information to gays and lesbians related to differing ways of addressing problems. Enabling and teaching have overlapping functions. Enabling encourages clients to use existing resources, and teaching encourages the introduction of new resources designed to help clients cope with and solve problems (Compton and Galaway 1994).

Social work practitioners may look to their gay and lesbian clients for information related to the lesbian and gay experience. From information learned about the realities of a gay or lesbian lifestyle, social workers should start to see similarities between the needs of gay men and lesbians and other stigmatized groups. Although not identical, similar experiences may provide new avenues of exploration for problem solving. The teaching role then becomes a reciprocal one where both the client and the professional provide and create new ways of thinking.

For example, Juan and Chuck, a gay couple, were having severe disagreements over how open they should be because of homophobia in the workplace. They referred themselves to the local mental health center at the suggestion of a friend. The social worker, a woman who had grown up in the slums of Honduras, knew and understood about hatred, racism, and sexism, but was not as well educated about gay men. Through a series of sessions the couple learned of various coping mechanisms to deal with discrimination, and the social worker learned about homophobia and the experience of being a gay couple.

A fourth interventive role appropriate for use with lesbian or gay clients is that of mediator. Mediation is that activity designed to resolve or settle disputes between the client and systems in which they operate. A social worker who is knowledgeable about the gay and lesbian lifestyle and resources available can provide countless services on behalf of clients who because of legal or religious proscriptions may have been silenced. For example, a gay couple terminating a relationship of many years is unable to equitably divide their property. Their disputes have become so disruptive to the neighbors that a friend suggested mediation. Through a series of mediation sessions where each had an opportunity to negotiate terms, a legally binding settlement agreement was signed.

Mediation can take many forms including disputes related to terminating gay or lesbian relationships, financial issues, monogamy versus nonmonogamy concerns, sexual openness, domestic violence, property settlements, coming-out dilemmas, or parent-child arguments. Again, the caveat must be that the social worker understand the gay and lesbian condition in order to be successful at mediation.

The fifth interventive role that can be successfully used with lesbian and gay clients is that of advocate. Advocacy is the process whereby the social worker becomes the client's speaker and presents information on behalf of the client. For example, a young lesbian mother living in a conservative rural Louisiana town was engaged in a custody battle with her alcoholic ex-husband. The two children, both girls, were aged 5 and 7. Both wanted to live with their mother, but the father was unwilling to allow that because of his ex-wife's lesbianism. The mother's lawyer contacted a social worker to testify as an expert witness and advocate on behalf of the mother. Based in part on this intervention sole custody was granted to the mother. Had the social worker not had a detailed knowledge of the realities of lesbian parenting and related research associated with homosexuals and homosexuality, the chances are good that the outcome might have been different.

ILLUSTRATION AND DISCUSSION

Gay and lesbian persons are as diverse as the society in which they live. They are not identifiable by race, ethnicity, socioeconomic status, age, religion, intellectual abilities, physical capacity, or sex. Because of this diversity and because clinical issues that may require social service interventions vary, the following three case situations and discussions are presented. They include the case of Kay, an adolescent struggling with her sexual identity; Rolf, a victim of domestic violence; and Juanita, a hospice client.

Kay, a 16-year-old adolescent, was hospitalized because of a suicide attempt. She is one of four children who live with a single 40-year-old, Dana. Dana is a devout member of the Christian Coalition and has raised her children following strict biblical instructions. Kay had attended Sunday school and church-related activities three times a week since she could remember and considered herself a Christian. She also thought of herself as somewhat different from her peers at school and always had close best friends who were girls.

As Kay went through puberty and became sexually mature, her emotional feelings for her best friends deepened and she began to have same-sex sexual fantasies. Knowing this was unacceptable, she hid her feelings from her friends and herself. However, one of her best friends wrote Kay what could only be described as a love letter and Kay responded in kind. The couple became inseparable, riding to school together, attending church-related activities together, writing poetry to one another, talking on the phone daily.

Dana paid no attention to these activities until one afternoon when she discovered one of the Kay's more passionate letters that described in detail her same-sex sexual desires. This discovery caused Dana to confront her daughter, and when confronted with the evidence, Kay did not deny her feelings and said she felt relieved that her mother now knew the truth. Dana demanded that the relationship between the teenagers stop. To ensure Kay's mental health, Dana contacted her pastor, who referred Dana and Kay to a reparative therapist who could cure Kay of any homosexual tendencies she might be developing.

Kay had been in treatment with the reparative therapist for one year. In that time she had been placed on antidepression medication, had been subjected to aversion therapy, and was forbidden contact with any of her old friends. Her mother had placed her in private school and kept a close watch on her activities. Despite prayer, various group and individual therapies, and medication, Kay still found herself sexually attracted to members of her own sex. Feeling utterly worthless and alone, she overdosed on her prescription medications and her mother's sleeping pills. Her sister found her in time to save her life, and she is receiving services from the hospital social worker.

The assessment phase of intervention began when the social worker met with Kay alone. The medical records indicated the attempted suicide but little else. The name of the reparative therapist was listed as a contact. Kay presented as a scared, but intelligent young woman who said she wanted no contact with the reparative therapist. She also said she was not interested in seeing her mother at the moment because it was her mother's fault that she was in her current situation. When asked to explain this, she stopped talking. The social worker had recognized the name of the reparative therapist as one whose practice centered on sexuality and questioned Kay about her association with this person. Through probing, Kay began to share information about her deep spirituality, interest in the church, and her "best friend." She successfully managed to ignore her past relationship with the therapist. But she did weave a tale that included her mother's intense dislike of the best friend, pastoral counseling sessions designed to rid the soul of sin, and finally of reparative therapy to "fix" her and make her "normal." When asked what normal meant, she cried, "You know, not queer!" and burst into tears.

Once the sexual orientation issue was identified, Kay was able to share her year of what she described as "torture" while the therapist worked with her to cure her of her sinful ways. Although she said she had tried, she was psychologically and sexually attracted to women and because she knew she could never change, she decided that she would be better off dead and that her family would be better off in the long run not having a queer in the family. She was still uncertain about how she would relate to her mother, because she believed strongly that her mother's inability to accept her for who she really was had caused her to go through the horrors of reparative therapy and forced her to her suicide attempt.

It was important to assess what goals Kay could define in relation to her situation. She had come close to death and found life to be the better option. She wanted to work on things that would make it possible for her to feel okay about herself. First, the social worker explored the relationship between Kay and her mother further and discovered a long-term bond between them had been severed because of Kay's sexual confusion. This deeply saddened Kay and she wondered whether or not the bond could be re-created. She said she would like to work on that. The social worker was acquainted with the gay and lesbian lifestyle and community and asked Kay what she knew about them. The answer was clouded with stereotypes and myths, and they agreed to include this as a goal. A third goal revolved around Kay's deep Christian faith and its compatibility with same-sex desires. The final goal was related to Kay's continuation with reparative therapy. As her mother was responsible for the therapy, a goal to work with Dana to cease this intervention was agreed to.

These goals will require the social worker to be an enabler, a teacher, a mediator, an advocate, and a social broker. As an enabler the social worker will support Kay's strengths, desire to live, and encourage her to achieve her goals. As a teacher the social worker can teach Kay and her mother about the realities of the gay and lesbian lifestyle, and as a social broker, the social worker can link Kay with such resources as the Metropolitan Community

Church or other Christian churches that welcome lesbians and gays. As a mediator, the social worker can help resolve differences between Kay and her mother around the issue of sexual orientation, and as an advocate, the social worker can speak to Dana on behalf of Kay in relation to the cessation of reparative therapy with the knowledge that the NASW condemns such therapies.

Rolf is a 38-year-old lawyer who has lived with his partner Eric for six months. Eric is a 30-year-old member of the police force. Eric was hired as part of a diversity initiative and was recruited, in part, because he was openly gay. Rolf is terrified that his wealthy clients will discover his sexual orientation, so he hides his gay identity except on those few occasions when he and Eric participate in discrete gay gatherings. This difference in sexual openness has been the source of frustration and anger between the two, but recently the quarrels have escalated. Eric assaulted Rolf and threatened him with his semiautomatic; Rolf threw a baseball bat at Eric and threatened him with a kitchen knife. This fight was followed by the couple renewing their love for one another and promising such behavior would never reoccur. Sadly, when, Eric wanted to take Rolf to the exclusively gay Mardi Gras ball and Rolf balked at the idea, the battle began again. After the last fight, when Eric severely beat Rolf, Rolf shot Eric, using Eric's weapon. The police arrived, Eric was transported to the emergency room in critical condition and subsequently died. Rolf went to city lockup, where he was booked for first-degree murder. As part of the jail's intake process, Rolf was required to be interviewed by a social worker.

When interviewed, Rolf was almost unable to understand what had happened. He was upset, outraged at his own behavior, shocked at the death of his "friend" and "roommate," and horrified at the idea of being in jail (what would his clients think?). He was aware of his legal rights and requested ongoing social services from the social worker as long as he was in jail. The first meeting went badly. Rolf denied wrongdoing, stating it was self-defense, that he, not Eric, had been the victim, that Eric had gotten what he deserved. His hostility evident, Rolf paced and smoked during the entire session. While he said he wanted someone to talk to, Rolf was not forthcoming. The meeting ended with an agreement to meet again.

The second session was more productive as Rolf had been incarcerated for more than a week and had no prospect of being released on bail. He presented himself as poised, reserved, and introspective. He was calm and apologized for his previous temper tantrum with the social worker. When asked about the nature of his relationship with Eric, his temper flared momentarily, then he simply stated the two were friends and shared an apartment to save money. When asked about his momentary defensiveness, Rolf said that some people thought he and Eric were gay and that "really pissed him off." When asked why he had such a visceral reaction to being thought of as gay he stated that "being a faggot and a lawyer in the south are not compatible."

When asked what precipitated the shooting and caused his obvious cuts and bruises, Rolf was quiet. When asked about his general relationship with

Eric, he was quiet for a time and then related how the two had met at a seminar on linkages between the legal and police communities where they had been randomly assigned as buddies. The relationship grew from that point and the two had drinks, ate quiet dinners alone, went to the theatre, and eventually decided to move in together. They had lived in what was widely known as a "gay ghetto," although Rolf described it as a "reclaimed and developing section of the city." He made no mention of his sexual orientation.

When asked again what had caused the relationship to crumble, Rolf began to share that on occasion the two would argue over "stupid little things, like where to go to dinner." He said the frequency and the intensity of the fights increased over a four-month period. He stated he had become progressively more and more afraid of Eric and his temper, but he had failed to contact the police because Eric was on the force and "it would just look like these two queer types were having a fit." On more than one occasion Eric had battered Rolf to the point where Rolf needed medical attention.

Rolf's continuing references to "queers" and his description of his relationship with Eric provided the first clues to his actual sexual orientation. The social worker, while fairly certain that Rolf was gay, provided a safe, nonhomophobic space where Rolf could tell his own story, in his own way. But Rolf's continuing denial of his lifestyle and internal homophobia was a concern that needed attention.

At a subsequent session the worker brought in a copy of one of the local gay newspapers and laid it on the table. A large picture of Eric was the cover photo and the headline read "Gay Cop Murdered by Lover." Rolf's immediate reaction was to turn bright red and stammer something that sounded like "Oh shit." He then sat down, lighted a cigarette, and told the social worker exactly what had happened during the last fight.

His story was classical in its theme of domestic abuse and the spiral of violence. As he had noted in previous sessions, the first couple of months with Eric had been paradise, but then Eric wanted to be more out than Rolf felt he could be, which led to increasingly frequent and volatile disagreements between the two. Always initiated by Eric, the fights became so brutal that on two occasions Eric had to take Rolf to the emergency room for stitches. Both always covered up how the wounds had been inflicted and following the fights the two entered into the usual honeymoon phase common to such situations. The night of the shooting the theme of the argument had been the same, but the intensity of the fight was more vicious. Eric threatened to kill Rolf and pistol-whipped him with his service weapon. Rolf managed to wrestle the gun away from Eric and shot at him once. The bullet hit Eric in the chest. This story told, the only thing Rolf wanted was to be released from jail.

Domestic violence and abuse in the gay and lesbian community is often not acknowledged, and few resources exist to deal with this reality. For Rolf, as a male gay victim of domestic violence, no programs exist to help him. The social worker in this case was confronted with Rolf's internal homophobia and willingness to deny who he was as well as with institutional homophobia. Often hate crimes and domestic violence goes unreported to the police because of the fear that reporting it to homophobic officers may be worse than the event. Rolf's narrative unfolds over a period of time, and the social worker allows this to happen by enabling the dialogue and moving it closer and closer to the truth. Confronting Rolf with the newspaper occurred only after a relationship between the client and worker had been established, which allowed for a more honest dialogue between the two. In this case the assessment phase took several sessions and the goal established at the end was simple—to get Rolf out of jail. The goal can be realized by the social worker continuing to enable Rolf to share the truth that supports his claim of self-defense.

Juanita is an 85-year-old terminally ill hospice patient who has been living beside Rose in a double house for thirty-seven years. Privately they acknowledge their great love for one another; publicly their "forbidden love" is no one's business but their own. They have separate addresses and enter their home through separate front doors. They each have their own telephone numbers, separate bank accounts, and two cars. At first glance it would seem these two were merely good friends. But once inside the house it is obvious that the double house has been converted into a single-family dwelling.

Juanita was diagnosed with inoperable colon cancer a year ago and was placed in a hospice five months ago. It is thought she has less than a month to live. She is mentally alert and is deeply concerned over how Rose will manage after her death. She is terrified that members of her estranged family will contest the terms of her will in which she has left everything to Rose. Juanita and the hospice social worker have established an excellent relationship. The social worker had to visit Juanita in her home prior to the placement and was taken into the couple's confidence about the true nature of their relationship. The worker was asked to keep this information confidential even following Juanita's death but could share the knowledge when both were dead.

Rose visited daily and no barriers prevented her from continuing her relationship with her friend. In fact, those at the hospice, both patients and professionals, enjoyed the caring relationship evident between the two old ladies. When Juanita died, all the careful planning the two had done seemed to come unglued. A brother of Juanita's who had not been seen in decades arrived to claim the body, stating he was going to take Juanita home to rural Kentucky for burial. Juanita had stated she "would rather die than spend eternity in the ground" and wanted to be cremated. Fortunately, the couple had prepaid their cremations, and the funeral home, with the help of the social worker, intervened. Juanita was cremated, but, as feared, the family contested the will. Family members were certain they were due her share of the house and its belongings, her finances, and her personal effects.

During this time Rose was in a grief support group at the hospice and had not severed her ties with the hospice social worker. Rose sought help from the social worker. The immediate goal was simply to ensure that Juanita's original will be honored.

The most effective way to ensure that outcome is for the social worker to act as a social broker and connect Rose with a lawyer who has detailed knowledge about lesbian and gay legal affairs. But making the linkage is only one part. The social worker can also act as an enabler so that Rose is supported in her decision to pursue legal intervention and to encourage her to be honest with the lawyer.

These three cases, while not coming close to the variety of case situations social work practitioners will encounter in their work, do illustrate some of the complexities that exist when working with this population. Assessment is seen as key, but arriving at an honest and feasible assessment may be complicated by sexual identity and homophobia. Interventive roles are seen as the means by which goals are attained. These do not vary because of sexual orientation, but for effective implementation, they require significant knowledge of gays, lesbians, and their communities.

Relationships between clients and social workers need to be built on trust, mutuality, and honesty. Actions toward individuals should promote self-esteem, teach coping skills, reduce psychic discomfort, provide information, and strengthen adaptive capacities (Germain 1979). Social workers who are ignorant about gay and lesbian realities have little hope of creating this kind of dynamic interrelationship with lesbian or gay persons. Figure 21.4 presents information relative to working with gay and lesbian clients at the micro-, mezzo-, and macrolevels of social work. And while the focus of the case studies has been at the microlevel, social workers must not overlook the need for intervention at the community and organizational levels as well.

In sum, as these cases illustrate, social workers have an opportunity for creative problem-solving and interventive strategies when working with clients, communities, or organizations that are involved with gays and lesbians.

CONCLUSION

The values and ethics of professional social work are well articulated in the NASW's Code of Ethics. The Code defines six core values that are central to the profession— service, social justice, dignity and worth of the person, importance of human relationships, integrity, and competence (National Association of Social Workers 1996). Embedded in these are the central roots of the profession that historically defined social work: a belief in the inherent worth of the individual and an individual's right to self-determination (Bartlett 1970; Reynolds 1934/1982, 1935).

Pursuant to the professional value stance related to the unique nature of the individual, the Code of Ethics states that, "social workers should not practice, condone, facilitate, or collaborate with any form of discrimination on the basis of race, ethnicity, national origin, color, sex, sexual orientation, age, marital status, political belief, religion, or mental or physical disability (National Association of Social Workers 1996:4.02). This emphasis on nondiscrimination can also be seen in the following NASW policy statement related to homosexuality and written in 1977:

The National Association of Social Workers realizes that homosexuality has existed under varying circumstances throughout recorded history and in

FIGURE 21.4. Intervention with Gay Men and Lesbians: Micro-, Mezzo-, and Macro-levels

To provide effective social work services to gay men and lesbian women, the social worker must consider the following.

At the Microlevel

- Avoid the heterosexual assumption.
- Accept that sexual orientation is determined by many factors including genetics and environments.
- Understand the coming-out process and its effect on the individual and their social environments.
- Become familiar with issues related to families of origin and families of choice.
- Be aware of the heterogeneity of lesbians, gay men, and their communities.
- Understand the differences between gay men and lesbians (e.g. relationships, sexual activities, at-risk behaviors, etc.).
- Develop a willingness to talk honestly about matters of sexual activity and sexual orientation.
- Avoid gay and lesbian stereotyping.
- Be comfortable with your own sexual orientation.
- Discover the reasons individuals are seeking intervention—sexual orientation may not play a role in the presenting problem.
- Allow individuals to dialogue at their own pace and with support.
- Understand homophobia (insitutional, individual, and internal) and its impact.
- Never engage in any form of homophobia.
- Respect client confidentiality.
- Understand the ramifications of reparative therapy and spiritual interventions designed to "cure" homosexuality.
- Have a knowledge base and know how to access information and resources related to those groups that are culturally different from your own (e.g., racial and ethnic minorities, hearing impaired, blind, etc.).

At the Mezzolevel

- Be able to distinguish between the nongay and gay/lesbian communities.
- Identify formal and informal structures in the gay/lesbian community.
- Understand legal dilemmas facing lesbian and gay persons.
- Recognize institutional homophobia and oppression.
- Get to know the resources within the gay/lesbian community.
- Utilize the resources of the gay/lesbian community.
- Encourage dialogue between the gay/lesbian community and the social service sector.
- Evaluate action plans in light of resources in the gay/lesbian community.
- Support the gay/lesbian community.
- Become a resource person for the gay/lesbian community.

Continued on next page

FIGURE 21.4. *(continued)*

At the Macrolevel

▮ Understand the societal proscriptions associated with being lesbian/gay.
▮ Confront institutional homophobia.
▮ Lobby congressional appointees.
▮ Prepare lesbian/gay friendly testimony for policy hearings.
▮ Build constituency networks and coalitions that promote the lesbian/gay agenda.
▮ Learn to negotiate for an agreeable outcome.
▮ Be gracious, even in the face of homophobia and defeat.

most cultures. A substantial number of women and men in American society are identified with a lifestyle that includes homosexual behavior. Homosexuality may properly be considered a preference, orientation, or propensity for certain kinds of lifestyles. Millions of women and men whose sexual orientation includes homosexuality are subject to severe social, psychological, economic, and legal discrimination because of their sexual orientation.

NASW views discrimination and prejudice directed at any minority as inimical to the mental health not only of the affected minority, but of the society as a whole. The Association deplores and will work to combat archaic laws, discriminatory employment practices, and other forms of discrimination which serve to impose something less than equal status upon homosexually oriented members of the human family. It is the objective of the social work profession not only to bring health and welfare services closer to people, but also help alter the unequal policies and practices if health and welfare institutions.

NASW affirms the right of all persons to define and express their own sexuality. In choosing their own lifestyle, all persons are to be encouraged to develop their potential to the fullest extent possible as long as they do not infringe upon the rights of others (National Association of Social Workers 1981:1).

Because social workers have a mandate to work with vulnerable and at-risk populations, it is imperative that they work with gay men and lesbians with the knowledge necessary to be effective. Social workers have always worked with members of this minority, but without recognizing it. It is past time for this to continue.

References

Altman, D. 1982. *The Homosexualization of America.* Boston: Beacon Press.
American Heritage Dictionary. 1985. Boston: Houghton Mifflin.
Annual Demographic Survey. 1997. March supplement [On-line]. http://ferret.bls.census.gov/macro/031997/hhlnc/3–001.htm.
Anthony, B. D. 1981–82. "Lesbian Client–Lesbian Therapist: Opportunities and Challenges in Working Together." *Journal of Homosexuality* 7(2/3):45–57.

Appleby, G. A. and J. W. Anastas. 1998. *Not Just a Passing Phase: Social Work with Gay, Lesbian, and Bisexual People.* New York: Columbia University Press.

Bailey, J. M., R. C. Pillard, M. C. Neale, and Y. Agyei. 1991. "Heredity Factors Influence Sexual Orientation in Women." *Archives of General Psychiatry* 50(3):217–23.

Bartlett, H. M. 1970. *The Common Base of Social Work Practice.* Washington, D.C.: National Association of Social Workers Press.

Belote, D. and J. Joesting. 1976. "Demographic and Self-Report Characteristics of Lesbians." *Psychological Reports* 39:621–22.

Berger, R. M. 1980. "Psychological Adaptation of the Older Homosexual Male." *Journal of Homosexuality* 5(3):161–75.

——. 1982. "The Unseen Minority: Older Gays and Lesbians." *Social Work* 27(3): 236–42.

——. 1996. *Gay and Gray: The Older Homosexual Man,* 2d ed. New York: Harrington Park Press.

Berger, R. M. and J. J. Kelly. 1995. "Gay Men: Overview." In R. L. Edwards, ed., *Encyclopedia of Social Work,* 19th ed., pp. 1064–75. Washington, D.C.: National Association of Social Workers Press.

Bieber, I. 1965. "Clinical Aspects of Male Homosexuality." In J. Marmor, *Sexual Inversion: The Multiple Roots of Homosexuality,* pp. 248–67. New York: Basic Books.

Bieber, I., H. J. Dain, P. R. Dince, M. G. Drellich, H. G. Grand, R. H. Gundlach, M. W. Kremer, A. H. Rifkin, C. B. Wilbur, and T. B. Bieber. 1962. *Homosexuality: A Psychoanalytic Study.* New York: Basic Books.

Boswell, J. 1980. *Christianity, Social Tolerance, and Homosexuality: Gay People in Western Europe from the Beginning of the Christian Era to the Fourteenth Century.* Chicago: University of Chicago Press.

Bullough, V. L. 1979. *Homosexuality: A History.* New York: New American Library.

Bullough, V. L. and B. Bullough. 1977. "Lesbianism in the 1920s and 1930s: A Newfound Study." *Signs* 2(4):895–904.

——. 1995. *Sexual Attitudes: Myths & Realities.* Amherst, N.Y.: Prometheus Books.

Cass, V. 1979. "Homosexual Identity Formulation: A Theoretical Model." *Journal of Homosexuality* 4(3):219–35.

Chapman, B. E. and J. C. Brannock. 1987. "Proposed Model of Lesbian Identity Development: An Empirical Examination." *Journal of Homosexuality* 14(3/4):69–80.

Cherry, K. and J. Mitulski. 1990. "Committed Couples in the Community." *Christian Century* 107(7):218–20.

Child Welfare League of America. 1991. *Serving Gay and Lesbian Youths: The Role of Child Welfare Agencies.* Washington, D.C.: Author

Christian Coalition Worldwide. 1998. News releases [On-line]. http://www.cc.org/publications/ccnews.html.

Coleman, E. 1981–82. "Developmental Stages of the Coming Out Process." *Journal of Homosexuality* 7(2/3):31–43.

Compton, B. R. and B. Galaway. 1994. *Social Work Processes,* 5th ed. Pacific Grove, Calif.: Brooks/Cole.

Council on Social Work Education. 1994. *Handbook on Accreditation Standards and Procedures.* Alexandria, Va.: Author.

Cramer, D. and A. J. Roach. 1988. "Coming Out to Mom and Dad: A Study of Gay Males and Their Relationships with Their Parents." *Journal of Homosexuality* 15(3/4):79–91.

DeCrescenzo, T. A. 1983–84. "Homophobia: A Study of Attitudes of Mental Health Professionals Toward Homosexuality." *Journal of Social Work and Human Sexuality* 2(2/3):115–36.

DeCrescenzo, T. and C. McGill. 1978. *Homophobia: A Study of Mental Health Professionals Attitudes Toward Homosexuality.* Unpublished manuscript. Los Angeles: University of Southern California School of Social Work.

D'Emilio, J. and E. B. Freedman. 1988. *Intimate Matters: A History of Sexuality in America.* New York: Harper & Row.

Einhorn, J. 1998. "GLAAD and GLSEN Disturbed by Senate Legislation Promoting Internet Censorship" [On-line]. http://www.glstn.org/pages/sections/library/news/9807–6.article.

Gagnon, J. H. and W. Simon. 1973. *Sexual Conduct.* Chicago: Aldine.

Gay, Lesbian, and Straight Education Network. 1998. "About GLSEN" [On-line]. http://www.glstn.org/pages/sections/about.

Germain, C. B. 1979. "Introduction: Ecology and Social Work." In C. B. Germain, ed., *Social Work Practice: People and Environments,* pp. 1–22. New York: Columbia University Press.

Germain, C. B. and A. Gitterman. 1996. *The Life Model of Social Work Practice: Advances in Knowledge and Practice, 2d ed.* New York: Columbia University Press.

Goodman, B. 1985. "Out of the Therapeutic Closet." In H. Hidalgo, T. Peterson, and N. J. Woodman, eds., *Lesbian and Gay Issues: A Resource Manual for Social Workers,* pp. 140–47. Silver Spring, Md.: National Association of Social Workers Press.

Goodman, E. 1998. "Reframing Anti-gay Rhetoric." *The Times-Picayune,* July 24, p. B7.

Greenberg, D. F. 1988. *The Construction of Homosexuality.* Chicago: University of Chicago Press.

Grigg, W. N. 1994. "The Lavender Revolution: Undermining America's Traditional Values." *The New American* [On-line]. http://jbs.org/tna/1994/vol10no02.htm.

Grossman, A. H. 1997. "Growing Up with a 'Spoiled Identity': Lesbian, Gay, and Bisexual Youth At Risk." *Journal of Gay and Lesbian Social Services* 6(3):45–56.

"Hate Crime Statistics." 1996. [On-line]. http://www.civilrights.org/lcef/hcpc/stats/table1.htm.

"Hate Crimes: A Definition." 1994. [On-line]. http://www.civilrights.org/lcef/hcpc/define.html.

Herdt, G. 1989. "Introduction: Gay and Lesbian Youth, Emergent Identities, and Cultural Scenes at Home and Abroad." *Journal of Homosexuality* 17(1/2):1–42.

Herek, G. M. 1991. "Stigma, Prejudice, and Violence Against Lesbians and Gay Men." In J. C. Gonsiorek and J. D. Weinrigh, eds., *Homosexuality: Research Implications for Public Policy,* pp. 60–80. Newbury Park, Calif.: Sage.

Hetrick, E. S. and A. D. Martin. 1987. "Developmental Issues and Their Resolution for Gay and Lesbian Adolescents." *Journal of Homosexuality* 14(1/2):25–43.

Hooyman, N. and H. A. Kiyak. 1999. *Social Gerontology: A Multidisciplinary Perspective,* 4th ed. Boston: Allyn & Bacon.

Human Rights Campaign. 1998a. "HRC Mission" [On-line]. http://www.hrc.org/hrc/mission.html.

——. 1998b. "HRC News" [On-line]. http://www.hrc.org/hrc/hrcnews/index.html.

——. 1999. "HRC News" [On-line]. http://www.hrc.org/hrc/hrcnews/index.html.

John Birch Society. 1998. "Pending Legislation" [On-line]. http://www.jbs.org.

Kahn, S. 1995. "Community Organization." In R. L. Edwards, ed., *Encyclopedia of Social Work,* 19th ed., pp. 569–76. Washington, D.C.: National Association of Social Workers Press.

Kehoe, M. 1986a. "Lesbians Over 65: A Triply Invisible Minority." *Journal of Homosexuality* 12(3/4):139–52.

——. 1986b. "A Portrait of the Older Lesbian." *Journal of Homosexuality* 12(3/4): 157–61.

——. 1988. "Lesbians Over 60 Speak for Themselves." Special Issue. *Journal of Homosexuality* 16(3/4).

Kelly, J. 1977. "The Aging Male Homosexual: Myth and Reality." *The Gerontologist* 17(4):328–32.

Kinsey, A. C., W. Pomeroy, and C. Martin. 1948. *Sexual Behavior in the Human Male.* Philadelphia: W. B. Saunders.

Kinsey, A. C., W. Pomeroy, C. Martin, and P. H. Gebhard. 1953. *Sexual Behavior in the Human Female*. Philadelphia: W. B. Saunders.

Ku Klux Klan. 1998. "FAQ about the KKK" [On-line]. http://www.kkk.com/klanfaq.htm.

Laner, M. R. 1979. "Growing Older Female: Heterosexual and Homosexual." *Journal of Homosexuality* 4(3):267–75.

LeBlanc, J. and C. T. Tully. 1999. *Social Support Systems of Hearing Impaired Gays and Lesbians*. Unpublished manuscript, Tulane University at New Orleans.

LeVay, S. 1991. "A Difference in Hypothalamic Structure between Heterosexual and Homosexual Men." *Science* 253:1034–37.

——. 1996. Q*ueer Science: The Use and Abuse of Research into Homosexuality*. Cambridge, Mass.: MIT Press.

MacDonald, B. and C. Rich. 1983. *Look Me in the Eye: Old Women, Aging, and Ageism*. San Francisco: Spinsters.

Mallen, C. A. 1983. "Sex Role Stereotypes, Gender Identity, and Parental Relationships in Male Homosexuals and Heterosexuals." *Journal of Homosexuality* 9(1):55–74.

Mallon, G. P. 1998. "Knowledge for Practice with Gay and Lesbian Persons." In G. P. Mallon, ed., *Foundations of Social Work Practice with Lesbian and Gay Persons*, pp. 1–30. New York: Harrington Park Press.

Martin, A. D. and E. S. Hetrick. 1988. "The Stigmatization of the Gay and Lesbian Adolescent." *Journal of Homosexuality* 15(1/2):163–83.

Masters, W. H. and V. E. Johnson. 1966. *Human Sexual Response*. Boston: Little, Brown.

——. 1979. *Homosexuality in Perspective*. Boston: Little, Brown.

McClellen, D. 1998. "Second Parent Adoption in Lesbian Families: Legalizing the Reality of the Child." Unpublished paper presented at the annual program meeting of the Council on Social Work Education, Orlando, Florida.

McDonald, G. J. 1982. "Individual Differences in the Coming Out Process for Gay Men: Implications for Theoretical Models." *Journal of Homosexuality* 8(1):47–60.

Meyer, C. H. 1995. "Assessment." In R. L Edwards, ed., *Encyclopedia of Social Work*, 19th ed., pp. 260–70. Washington, D.C.: National Association of Social Workers Press.

Miller, M. 1998. "The Right: Going to War Over Gays." *Newsweek*, July 27, p. 27.

Mondimore, F. M. 1996. *A Natural History of Homosexuality*. Baltimore, Md.: Johns Hopkins University Press.

Morris, J. F. 1997. "Lesbian Coming Out As a Multidimensional Process." *Journal of Homosexuality* 33(2):1–22.

Morrow, D. F. 1993. "Social Work with Gay and Lesbian Adolescents." *Social Work* 38(6):655–60.

Moss, Z. 1970. "It Hurts Being Alive and Obsolete: The Aging Woman." In R. Morgan, ed., *Sisterhood Is Powerful: An Anthology of Writings from the Women's Movement*, pp. 170–75. New York: Random House.

National Association of Social Workers. 1981. *Policy Statement on Gay Men and Lesbians*. Washington, D.C.: NASW National Committee on Lesbians and Gay Issues.

——. 1996. *Code of Ethics*. Washington, D.C.: Author.

National Coalition of Anti-Violence Programs. 1998. *NCAVP Annual Report: Assaults, Injuries, and Weapons* [On-line]. http://www.avp.org/assaults.html.

National Committee on Lesbian and Gay Issues. 1992. *Position Statement Regarding "Reparative" or "Conversion" Therapies for Lesbians and Gay Men*. Washington, D.C.: National Association of Social Workers Press.

National Gay and Lesbian Task Force. 1996. *1996 Year End Report*. Washington, D.C.: Author.

——. 1998a. "Homepage" [On-line]. http://www.ngltf.org/main.html.

——. 1998b. "Press Releases" [On-line]. http://www.ngltf.org/pr.html.

National Opinion Research Center. 1989–1992. *General Social Survey*. Chicago: Author.

Nicolosi, J. 1991. *Reparative Therapy of Male Homosexuality*. Northvale, N.J.: Jason Aronson.

"Out at Work." 1999. *America Undercover Series*. Home Box Office, January 14.

Parents, Families, and Friends of Lesbians and Gays. 1998. *Project Open Mind* [On-line]. http://www.pflag.org/pom/pom2.html.

People for the American Way. 1998. "Ralph Reed v. Pat Robertson: Christian Coalition Director Calls for Civility and Tolerance While His Boss Rips Opponents and Preaches Extremism" [On-line]. http://www.theshop.net/tia-ok/2voices.htm.

Perry, T. 1971. *The Lord Is My Shepherd and He Knows I'm Gay*. West Hollywood, Calif.: Metropolitan Community Church.

Pinderhughes, E. 1995. "Direct Practice Overview." In R. L. Edwards, ed., *Encyclopedia of Social Work*, 19th ed., pp. 740–51. Washington, D.C.: National Association of Social Workers Press.

Porter-Chase, M. 1987. *Circles of Love: A Woman's Unity Ritual*. Cotati, Calif.: Samary Press.

Reisner, N. 1998. "Christians Run Ads Urging Gay People to Change Their Lives." *The Times-Picayune*, July 16, p. A19.

Reynolds, B. C. 1934/1982. *Between Client and Community: A Study in Responsibility in Social Case Work*. Silver Spring, Md.: National Association of Social Workers Press.

——. 1935. "Discussion by Bertha C. Reynolds." In Family Welfare Association of America, ed., *Diagnosis and Treatment Process in Family Social Work*, pp. 25–27. New York: Family Welfare Association of America.

Rogers, P. 1993. "How Many Gays Are There?" *Newsweek*, February 15, p. 46.

Rust, P. 1993. " 'Coming out' in the Age of Social Constructionism: Sexual Identity Formation Among Lesbian and Bisexual Women." *Gender and Society* 7(1):50–77.

Saghir, M. F. and E. Robins. 1969. "Sexual Behavior in the Female Homosexual." *Archives of General Psychiatry* 2:147–54.

——. 1973. *Male and Female Homosexuality: A Comprehensive Investigation*. Baltimore: Williams & Wilkins.

Savin-Williams, R. C. 1988. "Parental Influences on Self-Esteem of Gay and Lesbian Youth: A Reflected Appraisals Model." *Journal of Homosexuality* 17(1/2):93–109.

——. 1989a. "Coming Out to Parents and Self-Esteem Among Gay and Lesbian Youth." *Journal of Homosexuality* 18(1/2):1–35.

——. 1989b. "Gay and Lesbian Adolescents." *Marriage and Family Review* 14(3/4): 197–216.

——. 1996. "Self-Labeling and Disclosure Among Gay, Lesbian, and Bisexual Youth." In J. Laird and R. J. Green, eds., *Lesbians and Gays in Couples and Families: A Handbook for Therapists*, pp. 153–82. San Francisco: Jossey-Bass.

Shernoff, M. 1995. "Gay Men: Direct Practice." In R. L. Edwards, ed., *Encyclopedia of Social Work*, 19th ed., vol. 1, pp. 1075–85. Washington, D.C.: National Association of Social Workers Press.

——. 1998. "Individual Practice with Gay Men." In G. P. Mallon, ed., *Foundations of Social Work Practice with Lesbian and Gay Persons*, pp. 77–103. New York: Harrington Park Press.

Socarides, C. 1978. *Homosexuality*. New York: Jason Aronson.

Southern Poverty Law Center. 1998. "Active Hate Groups in the U.S. in 1997." *Intelligence Report* 89:29–33.

Stachelberg, W. 1997. "Position of Strength: ENDA Reintroduced with More Cosponsors, Momentum." *HRC Quarterly* (Summer):12.

Swigonski, M. E. 1998. "Social Work, Judeo-Christian Scripture and Lesbian/Gay/Bisexual/ Transgendered Empowerment." Paper presented at the annual program meeting of the Council on Social Work Education, Orlando, Florida.

Tate, D. D. 1991. "Homophobia Among Rural and Urban Social Work Students: A Pilot Study." *Human Services in the Rural Environment* 15(1):16–18.

Telljohann, S. K. and J. H. Price. 1993. "A Qualitative Examination of Adolescent Homosexuals' Life Experiences: Ramifications for Secondary School Personnel." *Journal of Homosexuality* 26(1):41–56.

Troiden, R. R. 1989. "The Formation of Homosexual Identities." *Journal of Homosexuality* 17(1/2):43–73.

Tully, C. T. 1983. *Social Support Systems of a Selected Sample of Older Women.* Unpublished Ph.D. diss., Virginia Commonwealth University, Richmond, Virginia.

———. 1989. "Caregiving: What Do Midlife Lesbians View As Important?" *Journal of Gay and Lesbian Psychotherapy* 1(1):87–103.

———. 1995. "Lesbians Overview." In R. L. Edwards, ed., *Encyclopedia of Social Work,* 19th ed., pp. 1591–96. Washington, D.C.: National Association of Social Workers Press.

———. 1999. *Violence Against Lesbian Women and Gay Men.* Unpublished manuscript.

———. 2000. *Empowering Gay and Lesbian Persons.* New York: Columbia University Press.

Uribe, V. and K. M. Harbeck. 1991. "Assessing the Needs of Lesbian, Gay, and Bisexual Youth: The Origins of PROJECT 10 and School Based Intervention." *Journal of Homosexuality* 22(3/4):9–28.

U.S. Bureau of the Census. 1992. *1990 Census of the Population: Vol. I Characteristics of the Population.* Washington, D.C.: U.S. Government Printing Office.

———. 1997. *Households by Type: March 1997* [On-line]. http://www.bls.census.gov/cps/pub/1997/hhldtype.htm.

Vaid, U. 1995. *Virtual Equality: The Mainstreaming of Gay and Lesbian Liberation.* New York: Anchor Books.

Walker, E. J. 1999. *Historical Views on Homosexuality.* Unpublished manuscript.

Wisniewski, J. J. and B. G. Toomey. 1987. "Are Social Workers Homophobic?" *Social Work* 32(5):454–55.

Witt, L., S. Thomas, and E. Marcus, eds. 1995. *OUT in all Directions: The Almanac of Gay and Lesbian America.* New York: Warner Books.

Woodman, N. J. and H. R. Lenna. 1980. *Counseling with Gay Men and Women: A Guide for Facilitating Positive Life-Styles.* San Francisco: Jossey-Bass.

Woodman, N. J., C. T. Tully, and C. C. Barranti. 1995. "Research in Lesbian Communities: Ethical Dilemmas." *Journal of Gay and Lesbian Social Services* 3(1):57–66.

22

Homeless People

Marcia B. Cohen

Widespread homelessness exploded on the American landscape in the late 1970s and 1980s. It was a social dislocation to an extreme that the country had not witnessed since the Great Depression. While initially choosing to deny the existence of homelessness, the press and the public eventually responded to this phenomenon with outrage and shock. Advocates and elected officials bitterly debated the extent and causes of homelessness. As the conservative eighties faded into the moderate nineties, homelessness became a fixed feature in our environment. We are still disturbed by the sight of homeless people who force us to confront the visible manifestation of poverty. But we are no longer shocked. Homelessness has become one in a long list of social problems to be researched, studied, and chronicled. As Holloway (1991) predicted, homelessness has indeed become a field of practice in social work. The emergence of the homelessness field suggests social work's continued interest in addressing problems of severe poverty. But it also reveals the extent to which homelessness has become an established social fact, a topic for professional conferences, doctoral dissertations, and research funding.

Homelessness is not a new phenomenon; it existed long before the 1980s. There is documented evidence of homelessness in this country going back to the seventeenth century when transients were "warned out" out of New England towns (Miller 1991). The "wandering poor" of the nineteenth century included single men and women, families, and unattached youths. In the late nineteenth and early twentieth centuries, homelessness became increasingly associated with industrialization and immigration (Blau 1992). Homelessness grew to unprecedented proportions during the economic upheavals of the 1930s, when millions of homeless families and "hobos" camped out and rode the rails, searching for work (Holloway 1991). Blau (1992) describes the wave of homelessness associated with mature American industrialization as beginning "with the first major upsurge of tramping in the 1870s and end(ing) 100 years later with the alcoholics of skid row" (9).

Homeless people have frequently been characterized as isolated, disaffiliated, unfit, and vulnerable (Arce et al. 1983; Bahr 1973; Blau 1992; Grigsby et al. 1990; Holloway 1991; Lipton, Sabattini, and Katz 1983). There is, however, a small body of literature that has documented the adaptive capacities and survival skills of homeless people who overcome powerful and life-threatening circumstances on a daily basis (Cohen 1994; Dordick 1997; Golden 1992; Martin 1982; Snow and Anderson 1993; Wagner 1993, 1994; Wright 1997). Homeless people are indeed vulnerable. They are vulnerable to the whims of elected officials and policymakers, the reduced accessibility of affordable housing, the vagaries of the job market, and the uncertain availability of other economic resources. Homeless people are also vulnerable to the rules and requirements of social agencies and to the social workers who serve them. But the continued survival of homeless people despite the many risks they confront speaks to their considerable resiliency.

DEFINING AND EXPLAINING HOMELESS PEOPLE

Establishing an agreed upon definition of homelessness has proven to be a challenge for governmental agencies, advocacy groups, and social scientists. During most of the 1980s, the lack of a consistent definition reflected and fed political disputes about the size of the population. The now widely accepted official governmental definition of a homeless person is "one who lacks a fixed permanent nighttime residence, or whose nighttime residence is a temporary shelter, welfare hotel, or any other public or private place not designed as sleeping accommodations for human beings" (Institute of Medicine 1988:137). This definition, while broader than its predecessors, fails to include institutionalized or incarcerated individuals who, if released, would have no place to return to. It also excludes people who have inadequate shelter or are precariously housed, many of whom have been homeless in the past and are likely to become so in the future.

Differences in political ideology and their attendant debates abound in the homeless literature. As indicated, even the size of the homeless population has been widely contested. During the early years of the Reagan administration, the very existence of widespread, involuntary homelessness was disputed by elected officials. In 1982, a homeless advocacy group in Washington, D.C., released data that suggested as many as three million people were homeless in the United States (Hombs and Snyder 1982). In response, the Department of Housing and Urban Development (HUD) released their estimate of the numbers of homeless people nationally as being between 250,000 and 350,000 (U.S. Department of Housing and Urban Development 1984).

In addition to the differing political agendas that are reflected in this tenfold disparity, significant methodological problems thwart all efforts to measure the extent of homelessness in the United States (Holloway 1991). Although fairly reliable "bed counts" generally exist for most homeless shelters, homeless people sleeping on the street, living out of cars, squatting in abandoned buildings, and doubled and tripled up with friends defy the attempts of the most persistent social scientists to count them. Homeless people are often not readily identifiable. Many are intentionally inconspicuous, "passing" as domiciled in order to survive in dangerous urban environments.

Outside of the cities, the homeless population is even less visible; hence, the extent of rural homelessness is particularly hard to gauge (Nord and Luloff 1995). The most current available estimate of the number of people homeless in the United States is more than 700,000 on any given night and up to two million during the course of one year (National Law Center on Homelessness and Poverty 1999a).

The causes of homelessness were bitterly debated during the 1980s. More recently, all but the most conservative social scientists have agreed on at least three interrelated causes: eroding work opportunities, cuts in public benefit programs, and the shortage of affordable housing (National Coalition for the Homeless 1999). Broad economic forces associated with deindustrialization have generated unemployment and underemployment for many Americans (Mishel, Bernstein, and Schmitt 1999). Severe cuts in public benefits during the 1980s and 1990s have made the circumstances of poor Americans even more precarious. During the same time period, gentrification and cuts in public housing expenditures greatly reduced the availability of low-income housing nationwide (Hopper and Hamburg 1984).

Other factors, most notably the lack of affordable health care, domestic violence, mental illness, and substance abuse, are also associated with homelessness. These factors are not considered primary causes of widespread homelessness, however, because absent unemployment, inadequate public benefits, and the lack of affordable housing, it seems unlikely that they would lead to homelessness (National Coalition for the Homeless 1999). For example, when large numbers of psychiatric patients were deinstitutionalized in the 1960s and early 1970s, widespread homelessness did not result. It was only when psychiatric disability interacted with the low-income housing shortage and sharp cuts in Supplementary Security Income (SSI) that homelessness and mental illness became associated (Blau 1992).

Although it can be important to count and demarcate homeless people, homelessness must be understood as a particular manifestation of poverty, rather than as a distinctly separate entity. Marcuse (1988) has pointed to the dangers of conceptually dividing the homeless from the larger poor population, which serves to minimize and marginalize homelessness, implying that it is unrelated to economic recession, housing shortages, racism, or domestic violence. Marcuse warns against "specialism," the tendency of social scientists to slice and dice the homeless population into a series of subcategories, with labels such as "mentally ill homeless," and "substance abusing homeless," which shifts the discourse "to ascertaining the precise characterizations of the victims rather than the causes of their victimization" (88).

Conservative scholars and public officials have been particularly quick to marginalize and stigmatize homeless people, characterizing them as disabled, substance abusing, mentally ill, incompetent, and socially deviant (Main 1986). There are clear political benefits to characterizing homelessness as reflective of individual rather than structural and societal inadequacies. This view shifts the responsibility for addressing the problem of homelessness from the government and places it squarely on the shoulders of homeless people. Proponents of this perspective recommend that public policy responses to homelessness, if they should exist at all, be in the form of "separate policies for separate sub-populations" (Main 1986:31), rather than constituting a comprehensive attack on problems of housing, unemployment, or the dearth of social services (Marcuse 1988). Indeed, some conservative scholars have been quick to blame the liberal social policies of the 1960s for the phenomenon of widespread homelessness in the 1980s (Baum and Burnes 1993).

The liberal response to homelessness has been under attack from the left as well as the right. While conservatives denounce liberal advocates and policymakers for wastefully spending public dollars on private problems, radical scholars criticize the liberal "politics of compassion," which portray homeless people as helpless, vulnerable victims (Hoch and Slayton 1989). Wagner (1993) contrasts the compassionate politics of the liberal homeless advocates with the more militant and confrontational politics of earlier social movements. He points out that, unlike the poor people's movements of earlier eras, the homeless social movement of the 1980s was led by advocates in behalf of homeless people, rather than involving the homeless themselves. The advocates were successful in the courts, winning dramatic increases in shelter beds, soup kitchens, voting rights, and eligibility for social benefits (Blau 1992). But homeless people have paid a price for the politics of compassion. While liberal advocates, social scientists, and policymakers eschewed the more conservative moralizing and victim-blaming stance of conservatives, they did so "at the cost of portraying the homeless as dependent, isolated, and different from the rest of the population" (Hoch and Slayton 1989:208). According to these authors, the politics of compassion led to a policy of "shelterization," framing homelessness as an issue of containment and treatment.

Cohen and Wagner (1992) suggest that the liberal emphasis on the pathos and pathology of the homeless has served to obscure their strengths, implying that they are lacking in political awareness or the skills to advocate on their own behalf. Liberal advocates have been accused of minimizing the historical consistency in the treatment of the poor and the radical changes necessary for eliminating poverty, in order to maximize political attention to the problem of homelessness (Wagner 1993). It has been suggested that advocates, researchers, and social service providers have some self-interest in framing the problems of homelessness in terms of pathology and disaffiliation. Professionals, however compassionate, tend to define social problems in ways that imply that only they can treat and resolve them. (Hoch and Slayton 1989; Wagner 1993). We do the homeless a disservice when we begin with the assumption that they can only be helped through the aid and guidance of professionals.

DEMOGRAPHIC PATTERNS

Although the methodological problems described in the preceding make precise statements about the demographics of homelessness difficult, some fairly consistent findings have emerged. The recent survey of the U.S. Conference of Mayors (1998) found the urban homeless population to be comprised of single men (45 percent), single women (14 percent), families with children (38 percent), and a small but growing percentage of homeless youth (3 percent), defined as individuals under the age of 18 who lack parental, foster, or institutional care. Research indicates that the proportion of homeless families is particularly high in rural areas, where families, single mothers, and youth represent the largest group of people who are homeless (Vissing 1996).

Homeless families are one of the fastest-growing segments of the homeless population. Requests for emergency family shelter increased by an average of 15 percent between 1997 and 1998 (U.S. Conference of Mayors 1998). In 88 percent of the cities surveyed, a further increase in such requests was projected for 1999. These cold statistics reflect stagnating wages, the demise of the Aid to Families with Dependent Children (AFDC) program, and an ever-shrinking supply of affordable housing units. Domestic violence also impacts on homelessness among families, single mothers, and youth. In a ten-city study of 777 homeless parents (mostly mothers), close to one-fourth had left their last residence because of domestic abuse (U.S. Conference of Mayors 1998). Lack of affordable housing and limited residential options force many women to choose between certain violence in the home and likely violence on the streets. When the number of homeless mothers are added to those of homeless single women, approximately one-fourth of adult homeless people are women (U.S. Conference of Mayors 1998). The role of **domestic violence** and sexual assault in contributing to female homelessness has been well documented (D'Ercole and Struening 1990).

Sexual and physical abuse also are factors in homelessness among youth, many of whom leave family homes and foster care settings to escape violence and/or neglect (U.S. Department of Health and Human Services 1996). Others "age out" of residential and institutional settings, often discharged without housing, income, or family support. Some youth become homeless when their families lose their homes as a result of low wages, unemployment, and/or inadequate public assistance benefits. Many subsequently become separated from their families due to shelter arrangements, segregated transitional housing programs, and child welfare policies (Shinn and Weitzman 1996).

Children under the age of 18 are thought to comprise roughly 25 percent of the homeless population (U.S. Conference of Mayors 1998). A study by the Urban Institute found 31 percent of the homeless population to be over 45 years of age (Burt 1992) and the age 60 + population has been estimated to be as high as 19 percent (Institute of Medicine 1988). The literature emphasizes the fact that the contemporary homeless population is younger than its predecessors, largely due to the increase in homeless families (Blau 1992; Holloway 1991; Hopper and Hamburg 1984; Thrasher and Mowbray 1995). A special 1930 study of denizens of New York's Bowery district found 59 percent of the population to be over 40 (Bureau of the Census, Special Census of the Bowery 1930, as cited in Blau 1992). Recent data suggest that although the proportion of elderly individuals in the homeless population has declined considerably during the past two decades, their absolute numbers have increased (Cohen 1996).

The U.S. Conference of Mayors (1998) survey indicates the following **ethnic** composition of the urban homeless population: 53 percent, African American; 35 percent, Caucasian; 12 percent, Hispanic; 4 percent, Native American; and 3 percent, Asian. The ethnic makeup of the homeless population varies considerably from one region of the country to another. In rural areas, the population is primarily white (U.S. Department of Agriculture 1996). Nationally, however, the vast overrepresentation of people of color suggested by the research is striking, although quite consistent with the familiar relationship between poverty and race in the United States.

Veterans are also overrepresented in the homeless population. Approximately 40 percent of homeless men have served in the armed forces as compared with 34 percent of the general adult male population. Women make up an estimated 1.6 percent of the homeless veteran population. Homeless veterans are more likely to be white than homeless nonveterans (Rosenheck 1996). Research studies indicate that among veterans, the group most at risk for homelessness are those who have served during the late Vietnam and post-Vietnam era. These veterans had limited exposure to combat but have been found to have increased rates of mental illness and substance abuse problems, possibly as a result of recruitment patterns (Rosenheck 1996).

The extent and implications of **mental illness and addiction disorders** within the homeless population has been the subject of considerable research and debate (Koegel 1996; Marcuse 1988; National Coalition for the Homeless 1992; Oakley and Dennis 1996; Snow et al. 1986; Wagner 1993). Recent research estimates suggest that as few as 20 percent to 25 percent of homeless people have some form of severe and persistent mental illness (Koegel 1996) while approximately 33 percent suffer from a substance abuse disorder (Blau 1992; National Coalition for the Homeless 1997a). It is important to note that these statistics represent overlapping groups; many of the same people counted as mentally ill are also included in the numbers of substance abusers. Advocacy groups have suggested that serious methodological errors and definitional problems have led to exaggerated reports of the size and composition of these groups, such as the frequently cited 65 percent figure of substance abuse in the homeless population (National Coalition for the Homeless 1997a). Political considerations also play a role. Mental illness and substance use have long been convenient scapegoats for those who do not acknowledge the economic forces reflected in widespread homelessness. In fact, the vast majority of drug addicts, alcoholics, and psychiatrically diagnosed people are not homeless (National Coalition for the Homeless 1997a). Nevertheless, in the context of poverty, cuts in disability benefits, and shortages in low-income housing, people with psychiatric difficulties and addiction disorders are at an increased risk of becoming homeless.

SOCIETAL CONTEXT

As has already been suggested, the societal context of homelessness has its roots in the conservative ideology and social policies of the 1980s. During the Reagan administration, **social benefit programs** were slashed as military spending soared. Means-tested programs were reduced by almost 17 percent from 1980 to 1984 while inflation lowered the real value of benefits by 7 percent (Hopper and Hamburg 1984). Many of these cuts came as part of the Omnibus Budget Reconciliation Act (OBRA) of 1981. Eligibility criteria for AFDC were made more restrictive and benefit amounts were reduced, making unemployed and underemployed poor women and their children particularly vulnerable to homelessness. Cuts in food stamp benefits and Medicaid intensified the plight of people who increasingly had to choose between paying the rent and paying for food and medical care.

Cutbacks in Old Age Survivors Insurance (OASI) eliminated minimum monthly social security allowances for three million sporadically employed recipients, three-quarters of whom were women (Blau 1992). Cuts in Unemployment Insurance (UI) and the freezing of the hourly minimum wage during the 1980s served to further increase the economic vulnerability of low-wage workers. The number of unemployed Americans covered by unemployment insurance benefits hit a record low of 31.5

percent in 1987. The drastic reductions in benefits for the working poor occurred in the context of deindustrialization, which was reflected in the demise of the American labor movement, the flight of manufacturing jobs, and declining wages (Blau 1992).

Cuts in Social Security Disability Insurance (SSDI) and SSI benefits swelled the ranks of the homeless population as half a million people were removed from the disability rolls. The Reagan administration projected that eliminating these recipients would yield a five-year savings of $3.45 billion. Despite official pronouncements that no one who was entitled to disability benefits would be terminated, a 1984 class action suit ruling, *The City of New York v. Heckler,* found the federal government to have acted in an arbitrary and capricious manner. The ruling led to the reinstatement of disability benefits for two thousand people, approximately half the disabled people who appealed their terminations (Blau 1992).

Policy analysts emphasize the strong causal relationship between contractions in disability benefits in the 1980s and widespread homelessness (Blau 1992; Koegel 1996). Psychiatrically disabled people were the group most frequently targeted for termination. Although recipients with psychiatric disabilities comprised only 11 percent of all recipients of federal disability benefits, they represented a full third of the those whose benefits were eliminated (Hopper and Hamburg 1984). Due to the nature of their disabilities, many of these individuals lacked the internal and external supports to fight the discontinuation of their benefits. Once removed from the rolls, many were unable to pay their rent and were quickly evicted into homelessness.

The drastic reduction in the affordable **housing stock** during the 1980s and since greatly increased vulnerability to homelessness on the part of unemployed and low-wage workers, single parents, and disabled people. Gentrification and decreased federal support for low-income housing has created a widening gap between the number of affordable housing units and the number of people needing them. Between 1973 and 1993, 2.2 million low-rent units disappeared from the housing market, either abandoned or converted into more expensive dwellings. By 1995, the number of low-income renters was 4.4 million greater than the number of low-income units, a record shortfall (Daskal 1998). The rapid decline in affordable housing began with sharp cuts in expenditures for public housing during the Reagan and Bush administrations. Federal appropriations for housing dropped from 32.1 billion in 1978 to 9.8 billion in 1988. Measured in terms of people, the number of new households provided with public housing assistance during this period fell sharply, from 316,000 to 82,000 (Blau 1992).

The societal context for the steep rise in homelessness in the 1980s was a conservative political climate characterized by victim blaming and skepticism about the appropriateness of social programs. This ideology was operationalized at the social policy level by sharp cutbacks in a wide range of social benefit programs, including public housing. The growth in the numbers of homeless people in America during this decade closely parallels these policy developments.

Although the social context of the current homeless crisis emerged in the 1980s, the 1990s bipartisan quest to "end welfare as we know it" is already taking a further toll. The Personal Responsibility Act of 1996 carries its intention in its name. It was labeled so as to evoke the American glorification of individualism and underscore the pernicious view that holds poor people, rather than society, to be responsible for their plight (Katz 1996). Under this legislation, the forty-year-old AFDC program was abolished and replaced by Temporary Assistance to Needy Families (TANF). Under TANF restrictions, states are encouraged to impose two-year maximum benefit periods and mandated to restrict lifetime benefits to no more than five years.

The effects of this policy were just beginning to be felt as the century came to a close. A strong correlation between the termination of welfare benefits under TANF guidelines and increased numbers of homeless families has already been documented in those states that were among the first to implement "welfare reform." A November 1998 study conducted by the National Coalition for the Homeless found that half of the homeless families in Atlanta had recently lost their welfare benefits. In one county in Wisconsin, homelessness increased by 50 percent for children, while rising only 1 percent for adult men, a group largely unaffected by the TANF regulations. In Los Angeles, 12 percent of homeless families surveyed were found to have become homeless as a result of TANF benefit cuts (National Coalition for the Homeless 1998). In Boston, the number of homeless families rose by 11.6 percent in 1998, according to a count conducted twenty-four days after TANF limits cut six thousand people from the welfare rolls (Boston Mayor's Office 1998). Nationally, 15 percent more homeless families requested shelter in 1998 than in the previous year. Many of the cities surveyed by the U.S. Conference of Mayors (1998) reported that welfare reform had already had a negative impact on homelessness. Predictions are that this trend will intensify as more states implement the highly restrictive TANF regulations.

VULNERABILITIES AND RISK FACTORS

Life on the streets and in the homeless shelters is highly **dangerous.** Street and shelter life is highly precarious, fraught with daily uncertainties about meeting basic survival needs. The constant threat of starvation, exposure, violence, and arrest can rob homeless people of any sense of control over their environment (Berman-Rossi and Cohen 1988). This potentially disempowering existence is usually compounded by the experience of profound loss. Along with their housing, homeless people lose possessions, neighborhood, family ties, customary roles, status, daily routine, privacy, and the ability to maintain or secure employment. Such losses can easily trigger depression, anger, and reduced self-esteem (Holloway 1991). Homeless people frequently encounter rejection from the dominant society. They are treated with fear, contempt, and indifference. At least seventy-two cities have sought to criminalize activities associated with homelessness, including panhandling and sleeping in public areas. In downtown Seattle, the police have begun vigorously enforcing laws preventing homeless people from sitting down in public areas (National Law Center on Homelessness and Poverty 1999b).

Criminalized, stigmatized, and routinely disempowered by societal attitudes and institutions, homeless people are at high risk for **emotional difficulties**. They are also at risk for **incarceration** within psychiatric facilities and the criminal justice system. These ever-present dangers can also put homeless people at risk for increased **substance use.** Lack of proper nutrition, shelter from the elements, and uninterrupted periods of sleep can lead to and exacerbate a host of **physical illnesses** (Bassuk et al. 1996). Frostbite, leg ulcers, and upper respiratory infections are often the direct result of homelessness. Chronic conditions that require regular medical attention, such as tuberculosis, hypertension, and diabetes, are extremely difficult to treat or control on the streets. AIDS and HIV are highly prevalent among homeless people. Homeless people are also at greater risk of trauma from muggings, beatings, and rape (National Coalition for the Homeless 1997b).

Homeless children are particularly vulnerable to health problems, developmental delays, anxiety, depression, behavioral problems, and lower educational achievement (Shinn and Weitzman 1996). As with homeless people of other ages, unaccompanied homeless teens have been found to suffer from severe anxiety and depression, poor health and nutrition, and low self-esteem. They face particularly severe challenges in obtaining education and supporting themselves financially (National Coalition for the Homeless 1998). With few legal sources of income available to them, homeless youth often resort to exchanging sex for food, clothing, and shelter. These young people are at very high risk for contracting AIDS, HIV, and other sexually transmitted diseases (Athey 1991; Robertson 1996).

Homeless people clearly need the stability and sense of mastery over their environments that comes with housing and a dependable source of income. Other needs include affordable health care, education, job training, and employment at livable wages. Some homeless people have special needs for low-barrier mental health services, intensive case management, transitional housing, substance abuse treatment, crisis intervention, and advocacy. The overriding need is clear, however. Homeless people will remain at risk for a variety of life-threatening conditions unless permanent housing and income supports become and remain available to them. Moreover, without affordable housing, employment, and adequate public benefits, large numbers of poor people will remain continually at risk for becoming homeless people.

RESILIENCIES AND PROTECTIVE FACTORS

Homeless people are resilient. Their lives depend on their ability to **think on their feet**, survive by sheer wit, cope, overcome substantial odds, and rebound. Their survival often hinges on the social supports that exist within the homeless community. Recent research (Dordick 1997; Snow and Anderson 1993; Toth 1993; Wagner 1993; Wright 1997) contradicts earlier characterizations of homeless people as socially isolated and lacking in competence. These newer, ethnographic accounts emphasize the **dense social networks** of street communities, the prevalence of mutual aid within the homeless culture, and the resourcefulness that life on the streets demands. The homeless population is an unusually resilient one; indeed, its continued survival depends on the ability of homeless people to master the environment in the face of enormous obstacles.

Wagner (1993) studied a community of homeless people who lived in and around Checkerboard Square, a small plaza in a New England city. His ethnographic investigation revealed the existence of elaborate social networks, complex forms of social organization, and strong social cohesion. Wagner identified a form of political resistance in the culture of this community, one in which alternatives to the family and work ethics of the dominant society had been developed. For example, many members of Wagner's community had escaped from abusive families of origin. On the street, largely cut off from those families, they replaced these ties with friends, partners, and "fictive kin," clusters of socially constructed street families. Robbed of the dignity of work due to eroding job opportunities and hostile treatment in the low-wage service sector, many of these homeless people toil long hours in income-generating activities such as day labor, panhandling, and collecting deposit bottles, as well as more illicit activities such as exchanging sex for money and selling drugs. These individuals valued the autonomy of "being their own bosses" even when the working conditions (for example, going through garbage bins in foul weather looking for food) were worse than what they may have encountered in low-paying service jobs. Snow and Anderson refer to this kind of labor as "shadow work," which they define as "compensatory non-wage labor subsistence strategies . . . (involving) . . . recognition and exploitation of whatever resources and official markets happen to be available whenever a few dollars are needed" (1993:46).

The presence of mutual aid within the street community was particularly notable in Wagner's study. Resilience took the form of people caring for each other, watching each other's back, sharing food, shelter, and other resources. These homeless people had also made some connections to the more middle-class community, through linkages with several churches and social agencies. The staff of two grass-roots, community-based, "consumer-centered" agencies had gained the trust of many homeless people in this city. A consumer-run mental health social club and a low-barrier (no eligibility requirements) homeless day shelter offered a variety of tangible resources and social services, but they were mostly seen as places to hang out, see friends, chat with staff, and be treated with respect. The homeless people in Wagner's study drew a sharp distinction between these two settings and more social control–oriented institutions, such as the welfare and mental health systems, which they worked hard to avoid.

Dordick (1997) studied four homeless communities in New York City, located in a bus terminal, a large municipal men's shelter, a small church-run shelter, and a shanty town. Like Wagner, she found strong bonds of friendship and numerous examples of mutual aid among homeless people. Material resources were shared or bartered. As one middle-aged man in the shanty town put it, "We work together and have our ups and downs. Living up on this hill, it's like a great big family" (Dordick 1997:73). Some of the women of the shanty town remarked on the safety they experienced in that community, where they could count on others to watch out for them. At the bus terminal, Dordick spent time with homeless people as they gossiped, shared meals, and even sang together.

Fifteen years prior to Dordick's research, Martin (1982) found similar relational behavior among women at the same bus terminal. Toth (1993), another investigator into homeless life in New York City, discovered hundreds of homeless communities in tunnels, deep beneath the city streets. Each community had different norms. For example, some served as crash pads for addicts, while others were designated as "dry tunnels," where taboos against substance use were strictly enforced. Most emphasized mutual aid and protection from the world above and outside.

Street people often need more than mutual aid to ensure their safety. Homeless people at the bus terminal community (Dordick 1997) were frequently harassed and sometimes brutally beaten by police. A number of these resourceful individuals negotiated "deals" with individual police officers, making themselves scarce during rush hour in exchange for protection at other times of the day. Many of the women at the bus terminal interviewed by Martin (1982) intentionally allowed their appearance to deteriorate and become malodorous to protect themselves from rape and assault.

Homeless people at municipal shelters, such as those studied by Dordick (1997), live in constant danger of violence from other homeless individuals and from shelter guards. Dordick found that shelter residents had developed distinctly separate cliques but engaged in **protective relationships** across these subgroups. The "crew," a ruling elite of approximately fifteen African American men, provided protection and assistance to other shelter residents. The crew engaged in complex trade-offs with the shelter staff, the source of much of their power. As a result of the crew's internal government, the shelter was made a safer and more predictable environment for its residents (Dordick 1997). As several murders had been committed at this shelter, at least one by a shelter guard, the importance of such protection cannot be minimized.

Dordick contrasts this overcrowded and institutional environment, with its internal cohesion and norms of reciprocity, with the private, church-run shelter. Ironically, it was in this setting, the most professionalized and physically attractive of the four that Dordick studied, that she found relatively less mutuality, cohesion, and bonding among homeless people. In this setting, identification was with the staff and their disdain for the homeless. This internalized oppression appears to have worked against the formation of a strong social network among the residents whose lives were strictly controlled by a daily regimen of rules and routine. The autonomy of the streets, the terminal, the shanty town, and even the municipal shelter had been exchanged for the physical comforts of the private shelter. Compliance with the "administered social world" (Dordick 1997:166) of shelter life, where residents were constantly scrutinized and written up in a daily "log," took the form of deferring to the authority of volunteers and staff, who wielded the constant threat of eviction. In the municipal shelter, alliance with "the crew" yielded prestige and self-respect. In the private shelter, alliance with the staff was an acknowledgment of a power structure in which homeless people were on the bottom and an acceptance of a value system characterized by what Dordick terms an "ideology of moral betterment" (162). This self-negating atmosphere kept residents dependent on staff and separate from each other, hence the relative absence of mutual aid norms. A similar dynamic was identified by Cohen (1998) in a study of homeless residents in a not-for-profit transitional residence in New England.

Like the denizens of the Wagner and Snow and Anderson's studies, most members of the communities investigated by Dordick engaged in **shadow work.** Many consciously choose this alternative rather than applying for the welfare benefits they were eligible for, because of the degradation involved in negotiating the labyrinthine welfare system. Rather, they hustled, performed casual labor, sold items found in the trash, redeemed deposit bottles, engaged in sex work, washed car windows, and/or panhandled (Dordick 1997). Although some of these activities may not conjure up images of resiliency, they provided subsistence living and were viewed by the homeless people who engaged in them as considerably more dignified than the available alternatives.

PROGRAMS AND SOCIAL WORK CONTRIBUTIONS

The first programmatic response to widespread homelessness, from both the public and private sectors, was provision of **emergency shelter** at the local level. By the late 1980s, it had become clear that widespread homelessness had outlived its designation as a temporary phenomena and that locally and privately funded shelters were insufficient to meet the needs of homeless people. The landmark McKinney Act of 1988 provided federal monies for emergency shelter, food, transitional housing, rehabilitation of low-income housing units, health care, mental health services, substance abuse services, and vocational services. The McKinney Act has been amended several times since its passage, expanding its funding in the areas of mental health, substance abuse, AIDS, disabilities, education for preschoolers, rural housing assistance, and health-oriented outreach to homeless children.

McKinney grants have been used by localities across the country to fund a host of service programs for homeless people. These have ranged from temporary housing assistance, emergency food stamps, outreach services, and day care programs for preschoolers, to intensive case management programs and supported transitional housing services for homeless mentally ill and substance-abusing people. A 1995 evaluation of the McKinney programs administered through HUD concluded that they had "assisted significant numbers of homeless persons to regain independence and permanent housing . . . at reasonable costs." Critics, however, have noted that while passage of the McKinney Act represented significant legislation, its programs have been consistently underfunded (National Coalition of the Homeless 1997c). Moreover, McKinney grants are focused on emergency measures aimed at the outward symptoms of homelessness, rather than addressing its causes, specifically through employment, public benefits, and affordable permanent housing.

McKinney funding, like state-level funding for homeless services, has targeted specific "subgroups" of the homeless population, most notably people who are mentally ill, substance abusing, or dually diagnosed with both afflictions. As Hoch and Slayton (1989) predicted, this has been advantageous for the helping professions. Thousands of jobs have been created for mental health case managers, substance abuse counselors, transitional residence staff, outreach workers, community psychiatrists, social workers, and clinical supervisors. Despite the proliferation of programs, however, homelessness has shown no sign of abating. As noted by Marcuse (1988), the careful classification of homeless subgroups and the provision of services accordingly can create an illusion that we are actually doing something about the causes of homelessness rather than just addressing the symptoms.

The ethnographic literature provides some insight into what kinds of social work programs and services homeless people find helpful. Research suggests that they are most likely to accept and benefit from services such as linkage and advocacy, which are **user friendly.** Homeless people generally avoid services settings that require compliance to rigid rules and eligibility standards, such as the mandate that service recipients be diagnosed and receive psychiatric treatment in order to receive assistance in obtaining housing and public entitlements. Settings that have been experienced as effective tend to be geared toward the provision of outreach services and tangible resources. They are community based and readily accessible to homeless people. These agencies are most often characterized by a conscious commitment to client-centered practice and a strengths-oriented focus (Cohen 1998; Saleebey 1997). Homeless people have experienced many programs as carrying with them the price of humiliation, subordination, and social control (Wagner 1993; Wright 1997).

Research indicates that homeless people are most likely to accept services that respond to **self-identified needs,** rather than needs that professionals attribute to them. In a study of five programs for homeless mentally ill people, Plapinger (1988) found the degree of agreement between client and social worker regarding service needs to have a major impact on the effectiveness of service linkage. Lack of fit between client and worker expectations, for example, accounted for 88 percent of the obstacles to engaging clients in substance abuse services. Homeless people feel stigmatized and oppressed by societal neglect and abuse. It is a mark of resilience that many are able to respond to this rejection with resistance rather than compliance. Approaches to service delivery that emphasize client strengths and promote client dignity are likely to be most effective in engaging homeless people in social work services (Cohen 1989).

Wagner (1993) suggests that housing and other service programs for homeless people be designed to build on existing social ties within street communities. He asks: "What if homeless people were offered the opportunity of collective mobility and collective resources rather than individual scrutiny, surveillance, and treatment? What if the dense social networks and cohesive subcultures that constitute the homeless community were utilized by advocates and social workers?" (180). Wagner also suggests that housing programs for the homeless be located near the geographic areas where street people congregate, so they are not forced to leave their community in order to be housed. Apartment buildings could be renovated (through government programs, using and paying for homeless people's labor) that would provide adequate space to house entire small communities. Such programs could enable homeless people to obtain much needed shelter and privacy without sacrificing social connection. Recognition of homeless people as comprising viable communities also has programmatic implications for collective work projects, collective distribution of social benefits (as was done during the early 1930s), and for community organizing strategies that promote collective empowerment (Wagner 1993).

While creative, collectively oriented approaches are very important, simple access to existing services such as health and mental health care, advocacy and case management, housing, and other entitlements continue to be sorely needed. To be effective, these resources need to be provided in or near the locus of the homeless community and reflect a recognition of homeless people's need for autonomy, respect, and control over their environment.

ASSESSMENT AND INTERVENTIONS

Assessment of homeless people, as with other service recipients, is most effective when it focuses on **strengths, resilience,** and **protective factors** (Cowger 1994; Saleebey 1997; Smith and Carlson 1997) as well as on vulnerabilities. While assessment of homeless people takes into account a complex interplay of a wide array of biological, psychological, social, cultural, and environmental factors, particular attention should be paid to the histories of homeless people, including prior successful living situations and methods used for coping and survival on the streets. An assessment process that involves the service recipient in a mutual identification of coping abilities, survival skills, and external resources can facilitate the mobilization of these strengths. Since social work with homeless people frequently focuses on assistance in securing transitional or permanent housing, it is particularly important to assess what living situations have worked best in the past, and why (Cohen 1989). Recipients' prior experiences, as well as preferences, provide useful data in shaping future housing choices, within the limits of resource scarcity.

Identification of concrete **environmental supports,** including food, shelter, organizational linkages, income supports, and other benefit programs, is important to a comprehensive assessment. Information on natural support systems and social networks is critical; these resources can often be mobilized for support and assistance in addressing unmet needs. Because street life carries considerable risk for a variety of health and mental health problems, these areas are important to evaluate. Educational and vocational assessments can also be helpful with specific subpopulations of homeless people, most obviously children and youth. In addition to assessing adaptive capacities for survival on the streets, daily living skills needed for independent domiciled living should be evaluated. These include the traditional skill areas of shopping, cooking, and budgeting (Holloway 1991) but also encompass self-advocacy and collective advocacy in relation to landlords, social service providers, and the wider social and political arena (Wagner and Cohen 1991).

Most homeless people have had negative, disempowering experiences with service providers. **Outreach** and **engagement skills** are critical to establishing helping relationships with homeless people. This process will be enhanced if the worker displays respect for client strengths and a genuine desire for mutuality in the helping relationship (Cohen 1989). Homeless people, in a study of client perceptions of their relationships with social workers, indicated a marked preference for interventions that actively included them in goal setting and decision making (Cohen 1998). A three-year study of homeless, mentally ill service recipients in Virginia identified the following social work practice principles as essential to an effective model for intervention with homeless people: client-centered practice; the identification of natural support systems and social networks; client empowerment and involvement in decision making; flexible, creative, and proactive service approaches; and the creation of new services where existing ones are insufficient (Sheridan, Gowen, and Halpin 1993). The practice model articulated by these authors seeks to mobilize client resiliency rather than emphasizing pathology, deficit, and incompetence.

Given the documented existence of relational needs and affiliative abilities among homeless people, **group work** can be a highly effective intervention strategy. The group work literature contains many examples of the use of groups with homeless people in drop-in centers, soup kitchens, single-room-occupancy hotels, shelters, and transitional residences (Berman-Rossi and Cohen 1988; Brown and Ziefert 1990; Cohen 1994; Cohen and Johnson 1997; Cohen and Mullender 1999; Glasser and Suroviak 1988; Martin and Nayowith 1988; Pollio 1994, 1995). The focus on group work is consistent with Wagner's (1993) recommendation that social work practice build on the powerful group structures in the street community. Groups have been used successfully with homeless people to foster empowerment, promote mutual aid, stimulate creativity, build skills, provide community education, increase consumer input into agency decision making, and generate social action.

The social-action-focused, self-directed group work model developed by Mullender and Ward (1991) has been particularly effective in developing collective empowerment strategies for homeless people (Cohen 1994; Cohen and Mullender 1999). Self-directed group work targets external goals that are identified by group members through a process that focuses on *what* are the major problems in their lives, *why* these exist, and *how* to tackle them. This model emphasizes six practice principles: the avoidance of labels, the rights of group members, basing intervention on a power analysis, assisting people to attain collective power through coming together in groups, opposing oppression through practice, and group workers facilitating rather than leading (Mullender and Ward 1991).

ILLUSTRATION AND DISCUSSION

The **Community Group,** a task group of homeless men and women in an urban day shelter, used a self-directed group approach. The organizational context was a private, nonprofit agency serving homeless and low-income people. The day shelter provided meals and a range of social work services to approximately fifteen clients annually, operating with a small paid staff, several social work student interns, and a cadre of volunteers.

The agency mission statement emphasized empowering homeless and hungry people and advocating for solutions to social problems associated with poverty. The day-to-day work of the agency, however, was largely geared toward meeting the immediate needs (food, clothing, shelter, income supports) of homeless people. While the staff took great pride in its client-centered approach to practice, the agency had historically offered few mechanisms through which consumers of service might participate in agency decision making. The agency board of directors, for example, had consistently voted down proposals for the inclusion of consumer representatives.

The Community Group was developed by two social workers (a board member and a staff member, respectively), using the format of a weekly community meeting. The group purpose, from its inception, was explicitly stated as increasing consumer involvement in agency decision making. The group was seen, by the workers, as a vehicle for building leadership skills among consumers that could be used to affect change within the agency and the larger community. Homeless day shelter clients welcomed the opportunity to have a voice in agency decision making and adopted this as an overriding group goal. Consistent with a self-directed group work approach (Mullender and Ward 1991), the workers helped group members to set their own direction and determine group goals and objectives.

The group was designed as open-ended and task-centered. Weekly group meetings were structured through the mechanisms of agenda, minutes, and chair. This format was suggested by the workers who initially took responsibility for chairing meetings, taking minutes, and helping the group set the following week's agenda. Gradually, consumer group members began to take over these tasks and make the group their own. As an open-ended group, the size of community meetings varied weekly with member self-selection determining group composition. Attendance ranged from three to eighteen members, with an average size of ten. Participants generally reflected the demographics of the agency client population with white homeless males between the ages of 21 and 45 predominating. During the course of eighteen months, eight individuals emerged as core group members. These core group members played significant roles in the group's leadership structure. The core group consisted of five white men, two black men, and one white woman.

Over time, the group members became more secure in their ownership of the group and increasingly comfortable with the workers' nondirective, consultative roles. Despite initial resistance from some of the staff, the group was ultimately successful in gaining a sanctioned power base within the agency. The Community Group achieved one of its original goals during its second year of existence: the creation of two consumer seats on the agency's board of directors. Community Group members had advocated long and hard for direct representation on the board and had begun attending and participating in open board meetings prior to the change in policy. They had also become increasingly active in fund-raising efforts in the agency's behalf, which brought them into contact with board members. Board members' perceptions of recipients improved as a result of increased social contact. They were finally swayed to include consumers as board members, although the number of consumer representatives was limited to two, one-tenth of the total number of board directors.

Following that victory, the group expanded its focus to broader structural concerns that went beyond the boundaries of the host agency. Group discussion and analysis included topics such as the local shortage of affordable housing, the stigmatizing and discriminating tendencies of the social service system, and the punitive nature of the city's workfare program. The group developed a strategy to tackle this latter issue but quickly discovered that the public officials who administered the system were immune to their arguments. Having already been successful in attaining a collective voice within the agency, group members did not blame themselves for their lack of success in pursuing wider goals. This would have required a far longer time frame, alliances extending well beyond the group itself, and strategies that went beyond negotiation with local public officials. Instead, the group shifted its focus to fund-raising and program planning activities in conjunction with the agency's planned purchase of a building, as the organization had outgrown the space they had rented for many years.

Consumer input into plans for the new building was accomplished through several mechanisms. Staff and consumers polled clients who did not regularly attend community meetings regarding their ideas about the new building. Staff were invited to community meetings, and consumers to staff meetings, to discuss specific programmatic issues. Consumer representatives on the board of directors participated in overseeing the purchase and design of the building. As renovations were completed and moving day drew near, the consumer group expressed a sense of ownership, not only over their group but over the agency as a whole.

The group had matured over time. These resourceful consumers, with their considerable survival skills, managed of necessity to develop a leadership structure that enabled the group to persist, despite the considerable fluctuations in group participation that were inevitable given the unpredictable and precarious nature of members' day-to-day existence. Participation levels among core group members tended to vary over time, with periods of intense involvement interrupted by personal crises, hospitalizations, demands of city workfare, and other exigencies of street life. As the group developed, a top-down indigenous leadership structure within the core group gave way to a more flexible, participatory arrangement in which different members filled a variety of group leadership and maintenance roles, encompassing both task and socioemotional functions. The scope of group activities broadened, permitting members to pursue diverse interests and meet a range of needs. Instrumental and affective foci increasingly complemented each other, propelling group development (Berman-Rossi 1993). The tasks involved in organizing a sale of artwork of homeless people had an explicitly instrumental purpose, that of raising funds for the new building. The success of the art sale led to the formation of an art group, which designed and executed a highly visible, outdoor wall mural, celebrating the building and themselves. These activities combined a task focus with community building and mutual aid.

The Community Group was designed as a social action group, drawing on the vast potential for collective mobilization that exists within the homeless community. In the process of implementing collective action and organizational change, a strong mutual aid system emerged among group members. This mutuality was actively fostered by the two group workers. The internal support mechanism established within the group enhanced members' abilities to sustain their more activist pursuits. Mutual aid functioned in the service of social change goals; in times of frustration and discouragement it was the glue that held the group together. Similarly, the group's attention to its own affective process was critical to the group's survival. For example, when Gabby, one of the group's original members announced that he would be leaving town, the group initially was devastated. Gabby was a warm and charismatic man who had played a crucial leadership role in the group. Group members, with the support of the facilitators, were able to communicate their feelings of anger and love toward Gabby, openly expressing emotions of pain and abandonment. This uncensored process helped the group members to renew their commitment to one another and to their shared goals, allowing them to move forward after Gabby's departure.

The role of the workers in this self-directed group was an active but largely nondirective one. They were facilitators, consultants, and resource people, helping the group identify and periodically reexamine its goals, encouraging the group to discover the means to achieve its ends. The workers struggled with the sometimes fine distinction between intervention and direction as they learned to highlight group process without trying to manage it. They sought to create an empowering environment in which group members could "set their own goals, and take collective action, . . . drawing out the best from group members and helping them determine where they want the group to go" (Mullender and Ward 1991:129). This was a politicized group, characterized by and proud of its collective awareness and activism.

Groups such as the Community Group have the power to transform the client role from that of passive, stigmatized, recipient of services to one of active participant in the environment. The rich potential for social cohesion and social action within communities of homeless people can be tapped, fostered, and strengthened through empowerment-oriented group work. Such groups can have an impact within immediate organizational contexts, the agency setting, and, possibly, the local political level. It will be necessary, however, to mobilize much larger collectivities, through community organizing strategies, to bring about the broader social changes desperately needed by homeless and other poor people in this society.

CONCLUSION

Social work's simultaneous focus on change at the individual, family, group, and community levels makes it an effective vehicle for addressing the immediate and long-range needs of homeless people. As has been discussed in the preceding, there continues to be a desperate need for housing resources and income supports. It is also necessary to meet the health and nutritional needs of homeless people, particularly the oldest and youngest members of this population. Mental health and substance abuse services can be extremely helpful for some homeless people, and support and advocacy services are needed by many. But social work services for homeless and other poor people will not be effective if they rest on assumptions of individual pathology and deficit.

Studies such as those conducted by Plapinger (1988), Wagner (1993), and Cohen (1998) point to the importance of a partnership role between consumers and providers of services. Homeless people, like all people, do not respond well to professionals who claim to know what is best for them, disregarding their preferences. Whether in the mental health system, the criminal justice system, or the growing homeless service system, many homeless people have had a history of pathology-oriented treatment, often from well-meaning professionals. Few service recipients experience this approach as helpful (Cohen 1998). In contrast, service provision that starts where the client is (Goldstein 1983) and actively involves homeless people in decisions about service goals and objectives has been found to be effective in meeting the immediate needs of homeless people. Increased emphasis on resiliency and empowerment-based practice in social work education and practice bodes well for the provision of services that build on the considerable strengths of homeless people and harnesses these capacities in the service of client-driven goals and service plans (Cowger 1994; Saleebey 1997; Smith and Carlson 1997).

Client-centered case management programs that improve people's access to resources on a one-by-one basis, however, can only begin to scratch the surface of what is required to tackle the problems of homelessness and poverty. Social action group work, as demonstrated in the Community Group example, represents a potentially powerful approach to helping homeless people generate collective responses to social problems. Social action groups can affect organizational change, provide community education, raise public awareness, mobilize potential allies, join with other constituencies, and bring about meaningful changes in the environment. Social workers are often well positioned to develop and promote such groups. As a profession, we have the theoretical knowledge and practice wisdom necessary to do so.

The problems of homelessness stem directly from poverty and the unequal distribution of resources in our society. More fundamental changes will be necessary to rectify these deeply embedded imbalances than can be brought about through individual and group interventions by social workers. Wagner (1993) suggests that, historically, "only indigenous social movements among groups of poor people have substantially altered the social welfare system, the national political balance of power, and government policy generally" (184). He points to the broad exclusion of poor people, as historical actors in their own right, from much of the current strategy of professional homeless advocates.

The welfare rights movement of the 1990s demonstrates the ability of homeless and other poor people to organize collectively and use social action tactics to combat poverty and homelessness (Baptist, Bricker-Jenkins, and Dillon 1999; Dujon and Withorn 1996). Social workers have at times played an important role in the welfare rights movement, but it has explicitly been a movement *of* and *by* poor people. That is, social workers have acted as resources, consultants, and participants in many movement events, but leadership has come from the ranks of the poor. This indigenous poor people's movement is exemplified by the Kensington Welfare Rights Union (KWRU), a unit of the National Welfare Rights Union. KWRU was organized in the early 1990s by a group of women on welfare. Their mission was to organize a mass movement, led by poor people, that would end poverty (Baptist et al. 1999). One of the activities of KWRU was the 1998 New Freedom Bus event, a nationwide bus tour in which more than fifty people, including poor and homeless adults, children, unemployed workers, students, social workers, and others, traveled around the country, participating in local demonstrations against the implementation of Clinton's "welfare reform." Social workers were active participants in the New Freedom Bus tour, but they did not lead it. Members of the Bertha Capen Reynolds Society, a national organization of radical social workers, were particularly involved in organizing local educational and protest events in conjunction with the bus tour. Social workers continue to be important allies in the welfare rights movement. In the words of several Freedom Bus activists:

> The emphasis on individual and collective leadership by the poor should not obscure the role of allies in the struggle. Indeed, it is central to KWRU's analysis that the mission of ending poverty is inherently, and must become explicitly, the business of the majority of Americans. Most especially, social workers have a material and moral stake in the struggle—not as "supporters," but as "partners in crime." Increasingly, social workers are asked not only to implement the programs that criminalize poverty, but themselves are victimized by layoffs, downsizing, privatization, and declassification. This is not a transient circumstance affecting ever greater numbers of individual social workers, but an inevitable consequence of current economic forces with an inexorable collective impact. Professional ideology notwithstanding, the class interests of social workers lie with the bottom fifth of the population, not with the top fifth. (Baptist et al. 1999:25)

Although the ideology and activism of KWRU and other groups in the National Welfare Rights Union is encouraging, the larger political environment continues to be very conservative. The late twentieth century was characterized by an absence of political unrest and mass pressures for economic and social change. Even the most militant poor people's organizations, such as KWRU, have been forced to fight a rearguard action, protesting against welfare cuts rather than fighting for a more equal distribution of material resources within our society.

The conditions necessary for ending poverty and homelessness in the United States seem elusive at the present time. But the needs of homeless people persist. Social work can make important contributions at the individual, group, family, community, and social policy levels—as consultants, supporters, allies, and partners—in minimizing the vulnerabilities and maximizing the resiliencies and resources of homeless people.

References

Arce, Anthony, Marilyn Tadlock, Michael J. Vergare, and Stuart Shapiro. 1983. "A Psychiatric Profile of Street People Admitted to an Emergency Shelter." *Hospital and Community Psychiatry* 34(9):812–17.

Athey, Jean. 1991. "HIV Infection and Homeless Adolescents." *Child Welfare* 70(5): 517–25.

Bahr, Howard. 1973. *Skid Row: An Introduction to Disaffiliation.* New York: Oxford University Press.

Baptist, Willie, Mary Bricker-Jenkins, and Monica Dillon. 1999. "Taking the Struggle on the Road: The New Freedom Bus—Freedom from Unemployment, Hunger, and Homelessness." *Journal of Progressive Human Services* 10(2):7–29.

Bassuk, Ellen, Linda Weinreb, John Buckner, Angela Browne, Amy Salomon, and Shari Bassuk. 1996. "The Characteristics and Needs of Sheltered Homeless and Low-Income Housed Mothers." *Journal of the American Medical Association* 276(8):640–46.

Baum, Alice and Donald Burnes. 1993. *A Nation in Denial.* Boulder: Westview Press.

Berman-Rossi, Toby. 1993. "The Tasks and Skills of the Social Worker Across Stages of Group Development." *Social Work With Groups* 16(1/2):69–81.

Berman-Rossi, Toby and Marcia B. Cohen. 1988. "Group Development and Shared Decision Making: Working with Homeless Mentally Ill Women." *Social Work With Groups* 11(4):63–78.

Blau, Joel. 1992. *The Visible Poor: Homeless in the United States.* New York: Oxford University Press.

Boston Mayor's Office. 1998. "Annual Homeless Head Count Shows Increase." http://www.ci.boston.ma.us/mayorsoffice/index.html (25 December).

Brown, Karen and Marjorie Ziefert. 1990. "A Feminist Approach to Working with Homeless Women." *Affilia: Journal of Women and Social Work* 5(1):6–20.

Burt, Martha. 1992. *Over the Edge: The Growth of Homelessness in the 1980s.* New York: Russell Sage Foundation.

Cohen, Carl. 1996. *The Aging Homeless.* New York: State University of New York Health Sciences Center.

Cohen, Marcia B. 1989. "Social Work Practice with Homeless, Mentally Ill People: Engaging the Client." *Social Work* 34(6):505–12.

——. 1994. "Who Wants to Chair the Meeting? Group Development and Leadership Patterns in a Community Action Group of Homeless People." *Social Work With Groups* 17(1/2):81–87.

——. 1998. "Perceptions of Power in Client/Worker Relationships." *Families in Society* 79(4):433–42.

Cohen, Marcia B. and Julie Johnson. 1997. "Poetry in Motion: A Self-Directed Community Group for Homeless People." In Jeanne Gill and Joan Parry, eds., *From Prevention to Wellness Through Group Work,* pp. 131–42. New York: Haworth Press.

Cohen, Marcia B. and Audrey Mullender. 1999. "The Personal in the Political: Exploring the Group Work Continuum from Individual to Social Change Goals." *Social Work With Groups* 22(1):13–31.

Cohen, Marcia B. and David Wagner. 1992. "Acting on Their Own Behalf: Affiliation and Political Mobilization Among Homeless People." *Journal of Sociology and Social Welfare* 19(4):21–40.

Cowger, Charles. 1994. "Assessing Client Strengths: Clinical Assessment for Client Empowerment." *Social Work* 39(3):262–67.

Daskal, Jennifer. 1998. *In Search of Shelter: The Growing Shortage of Affordable Rental Housing.* Washington, D.C.: Center on Budget Priorities.

D'Ercole, Anne and Elmer Struening. 1990. "Victimization among Homeless Women: Implications for Service Delivery." *Journal of Community Psychology* 18(2):141–52.

Dordick, Gwendolyn. 1997. *Something Left to Lose: Personal Relations and Survival Among New York's Homeless.* Philadelphia: Temple University Press.

Dujon, Diane and Ann Withorn. 1996. *For Crying Out Loud: Women's Poverty in the United States.* Boston: South End Press.

Glasser, Irene and Jane Suroviak. 1988. "Social Group Work in a Soup Kitchen: Mobilizing the Strengths of Guests." *Social Work With Groups* 11(4):95–109.

Golden, Stephanie. 1992. *The Woman Outside: Meaning and Myths of Homelessness.* Berkeley: University of California Press.

Goldstein, Howard. 1983. "Starting Where the Client Is." *Social Casework* 64:267–75.

Grigsby, Charles, Donald Baumann, Steven Gregorich, and Cynthia Roberts-Gray. 1990. "Disaffiliation to Reintrenchment: A Model for Understanding Homelessness." *Journal of Social Issues* 46(4):141–56.

Hoch, Charles and Richard Slayton. 1989. *New Homeless and Old.* Philadelphia: Temple University Press.

Holloway, Stephen. 1991. "Homeless People." In A. Gitterman, ed., *Handbook of Social Work Practice with Vulnerable Populations,* pp. 584–617. New York: Columbia University Press.

Hombs, Mary Ellen and Mitch Snyder. 1982. *Homelessness in America: A Forced March to Nowhere.* Washington, D.C.: Community for Creative Non-Violence.

Hopper, Kim and Jill Hamburg. 1984. *The Making of America's Homeless: From Skid Row to New Poor.* New York: Community Service Society.

Institute of Medicine. 1988. *Homelessness, Health, and Human Needs.* Washington, D.C.: National Academy Press.

Katz, Michael B. 1996. *In the Shadow of the Poorhouse: A Social History of Welfare in America.* New York: Basic Books.

Koegel, Paul. 1996. "The Causes of Homelessness." As cited in National Coalition for the Homeless Fact Sheet #1. "Why Are People Homeless?" http://www.nch.ari.net/causes (February 1999).

Lipton, Frank R., Albert Sabattini, and Steven E. Katz. 1983. "Down and Out in the City: The Homeless Mentally Ill." *Hospital and Community Psychiatry* 34(9):817–21.

Main, Thomas. 1986. "What We Know About the Homeless." *Commentary* 85(5):26–31.

Marcuse, Peter. 1988. "Neutralizing Homelessness." *The Socialist Review* 18(1):69–96.

Martin, Marsha. 1982. "Strategies of Adaptation: Coping Patterns of the Urban Transient Female." Unpublished Ph.D. diss., Columbia University School of Social Work.

Martin, Marsha A. and Susan A. Nayowith. 1988. "Creating Community: Group Work to Develop Social Support Networks with Homeless Mentally Ill." *Social Work With Groups* 11(4):79–93.

Miller, Henry. 1991. *On the Fringe: The Disposed in America.* Lexington, Mass.: Lexington Books.

Mishel, Lawrence R., Jared Bernstein, and John Schmitt. 1999. *The State of Working America: 1989–99.* Washington, D.C.: Economic Policy Institute.

Mullender, Audrey and David Ward. 1991. *Self-Directed Groupwork: Users Take Action for Empowerment.* London: Whiting & Birch.

National Coalition for the Homeless. 1992. *Addiction on the Streets: Substance Abuse and Homelessness in America.* Washington, D.C.: Author.

———. 1997a. Fact Sheet #6. "Addiction Disorders and Homelessness." http://www.nch.ari.net/addict (October).

———. 1997b. Fact Sheet #8. "Health Care and Homelessness." http://www.nch.ari.net/health (October).

———. 1997c. Fact Sheet #18. "The McKinney Act." http://www.nch.ari.net/mckinneyfacts (November).

———. 1998. Fact Sheet #11. "Homeless Youth." http://www.nch.ari.net/youth. (May).

———. 1999. Fact Sheet #1. "Why Are People Homeless?" http://www.nch.ari.net/causes (February).

National Law Center on Homelessness and Poverty. 1999a. *Out of Sight—Out of Mind? A Report on Anti-Homeless Laws, Litigation, and Alternatives in 50 United States Cities.* Washington, D.C.: Author.

———. 1999b "Causes of Homelessness in America." http://www.nlchp.org//legal.htm (January).

Nord, Mark and A. E. Luloff. 1995. "Homeless Children and Their Families in New Hampshire: A Rural Perspective." *Social Service Review* 69(3):461–78.

Oakley, Deirdre and Deborah Dennis. 1996. "Responding to the Needs of Homeless People with Alcohol, Drug, and/or Mental Disorders." As cited in National Coalition for the Homeless Fact Sheet #6. "Addiction Disorders and Homelessness." http://www.nch.ari.net/addict (October 1997).

Plapinger, Jane. 1988. *Program Service Goals: Service Needs, Service Feasibility, and Obstacles to Providing Services to the Mentally Ill Homeless.* New York: New York State Psychiatric Institute.

Pollio, David. 1994. "Wintering at The Earl: Group Structures in the Street Community." *Social Work With Groups* 17(1/2):47–70.

———. 1995. "Hoops Group: Group Work with Young 'Street' Men." *Social Work With Groups* 18(2/3):107–22.

Robertson, Marjorie. 1996. *Homeless Youth on Their Own.* Berkeley, Calif.: Alcohol Research Group.

Rosenheck, Robert. 1996. "Homeless Veterans." As cited in National Coalition for the Homeless Fact Sheet #9. "Homeless Veterans." http://www.nch.ari.net/veterans (April 1999).

Saleebey, Dennis. 1997. *The Strengths Perspective in Social Work Practice.* New York: Longman.

Sheridan, Michael, Nancy Gowen, and Susan Halpin. 1993. "Developing a Practice Model for the Homeless Mentally Ill." *Families in Society* 74(7):410–20.

Shinn, Marybeth and Beth Weitzman. 1996. "Homeless Families Are Different." As cited in National Coalition for the Homeless Fact Sheet #7. "Homeless Families with Children." http://www.nch.ari.net/family (April 1999).

Smith, Carolyn and Bonnie E. Carlson. 1997. "Stress, Coping, and Resilience in Children and Youth." *Social Service Review* 71(2):231–56.

Snow, David and Leon Anderson. 1993. *Down on Their Luck.* Berkeley: University of California Press.

Snow, David, Susan Baker, Leon Anderson, and Michael Martin. 1986. "The Myth of Pervasive Mental Illness among the Homeless." *Social Problems* 35(5):407–23.

Thrasher, Shirley P. and Carol T. Mowbray. 1995. "A Strengths Perspective: An Ethnographic Study of Homeless Women with Children." *Health and Social Work* 20(2): 93–101.

Toth, Jennifer. 1993. *The Mole People.* Chicago: Chicago Review Press.

U.S. Conference of Mayors. 1998. *A Status Report on Hunger and Homelessness in America's Cities.* Washington, D.C: Author.

U.S. Department of Agriculture, Rural Economic and Community Development. 1996. *Rural Homelessness: Focusing on the Needs of the Rural Homeless.* Washington D.C.: Author.

U.S. Department of Health and Human Services. 1996. *Report to the Congress on the Runaway and Homeless Youth Program of the Family and Youth Services Bureau for Fiscal Year 1995.* Washington, D.C.: Author.

U.S. Department of Housing and Urban Development. 1984. *Report to the Secretary on the Homeless and Emergency Housing.* Washington D.C: Author.

Vissing, Yvonne. 1996. *Out of Sight, Out of Mind, Homeless Children and Families in Small Town America.* Lexington, Ky.: University Press of Kentucky.

Wagner, David. 1993. *Checkerboard Square: Culture and Resistance in a Homeless Community.* Boulder: Westview Press.

———. 1994. "Beyond the Pathologizing of Nonwork: Alternative Activities in a Street Community." *Social Work* 39(6):718–27.

Wagner, David and Marcia B. Cohen. 1991. "The Power of the People: Homeless Protestors in the Aftermath of Social Movement Participation." *Social Problems* 38(4):601–19.

Wright, Talmadge. 1997. *Out of Place: Homeless Mobilizations, Subcities, and Contested Landscapes.* Albany: State University of New York Press.

23

Immigrants and Refugees

Diane Drachman
Angela Shen Ryan

Immigrants comprise a sizable segment of the U.S. population. They are seen in service settings, such as health and mental health organizations, schools, community agencies, and in the workplace. Although the social work literature pays considerable attention to the ethnic diversity of immigrants, there is limited discussion of their experiences of migration. These include the cumulative stresses of leaving family, friends, community, and homeland and arriving in a new country, where immigrants need to find housing, learn a new language, secure education for their children, and find employment. Discussions of the policies that affect immigrants and the services available to them are limited. Since the literature is dispersed along specific immigrant and refugee groups, uniquenesses and differences among the groups are highlighted. Thus, common phenomena associated with immigration are not synthesized. This chapter examines some of the common experiences immigrants and refugees encounter in the process of migration and adaptation to their new country. It also delineates issues that social workers need to address in order to effectively provide assistance.

DEFINING AND EXPLAINING IMMIGRANTS AND REFUGEES

To understand the experiences of immigrants and refugees and explain the phenomenon of migration, consideration of both emigration and immigration is necessary. The classical paradigm of population movements explains them by the push and pull forces of sending and receiving countries and assumes that emigration and immigration are parts of a unitary process. *Push forces* from the country of origin commonly include political upheavals, severe economic circumstances, and social problems, such as persecution or discriminatory practices against an individual or group and limited educational opportunity. *Pull forces* in the receiving country are generally economic, social, or educational as immigrants anticipate better opportunities in these areas in their new country.

Recent historical and sociological analyses have widened and modified our understanding of the influences on migration beyond the macro push-pull of the classical explanation (Morawska 1990; Tilly 1990; Yans-McLaughlin 1990). These explanations of emigration and immigration incorporate support networks, communities, and families in both sending and receiving countries and discuss their influence on decisions to migrate, the point of destination, and the degree of adaptation to the new country. They also emphasize linkages between support networks in both sending and receiving countries (Morawska 1990; Tilly 1990). For example, support networks in the old country that are connected to networks in the new country may enable recent immigrants to secure housing, employment, or other needed services.

Network structures also facilitate an understanding of a recent phenomenon in migration: transnationalism. *Transnationalism* refers to migrating populations whose networks, activities, and patterns of life encompass both home and host countries (Charles 1992; Glick-Schiller, Basch, and Blanc-Szanton 1992; Wiltshire 1992). Transnational immigrants are therefore individuals whose lives and networks cut across national boundaries and whose social fields exist in two countries.

Many recent arrivals from Mexico, Guatemala, India, Pakistan, Africa, and the Caribbean are transnational immigrants. They return often to their home country for visits, some for long periods, and many send back remittances to family members. Their contacts with families in the home country may involve them in decision making on health care or the education of children. While visiting, they may take part in political, social, or religious activities. Some return to the home country permanently. Concurrently, these immigrants are involved with their U.S. families: in the U.S. schools their children attend and in their places of employment, religious organizations, and ethnic communities in the United States.

Networks of transnational immigrants benefit individuals and families in both sending and receiving countries. For example, family members in the home country often provide care for those children who did not migrate with their parent(s). Remittances from immigrants supplement the incomes of those who remain behind, while networks in the new land commonly provide concrete help and social support for recent arrivals.

Although migration studies emphasize linkages between support networks in home and host countries, the strength of those linkages may vary. In circumstances of forced and unplanned migration, for example, linkages may be weak or nonexistent (Tilly 1990). Hmong refugees who fled Laos during the war in Southeast Asia arrived in the United States when there were no preexisting Hmong communities in this country. Consequently, the Hmong not only experienced the trauma of violence and flight, having abruptly left homeland, family, and friends, but also arrived in a country where they had no natural supports. The absence of linkages between support networks in the home and the new country can add to immigrants' stress and impede their adaptation during resettlement.

The life event of immigration to the United States is also defined by the immigration status assigned to the newcomer by the Immigration and Naturalization Service (INS). Numerous legal immigrant classifications fall within the broad categories of lawful permanent residents, people fleeing persecution, individuals with work authorization, and people allowed to enter the United States with special-purpose visas (Padilla 1997). In addition, some immigrants do not have legal authorization to either enter or remain in the country. Most important, each of the statuses carries different entitlement to services, reflecting different policies for different classes of immigrants (Drachman 1995).

The statuses of refugee, lawful permanent resident, and undocumented person are discussed in the following as they illustrate the differences in service entitlement ascribed to each and the different ideological views underlying each. The erosion of entitlement to benefits and services that derive from recent legislation is also discussed.

According to the Refugee Act of 1980, a *refugee* is a person who is outside his or her country and unable to avail him- or herself of the protection of the home country because of fear of persecution on account of race, religion, nationality, membership in a particular social group, or political opinion. Humanitarianism underlies the admission of refugees, who are generally forced to leave their home countries, often suddenly, with few or no possessions. In recognition of these circumstances, the Refugee Act of 1980 created the Refugee Resettlement Program, which provides relocation allowances, job-training services, and access to federal benefits, such as Temporary Assistance to Needy Families (TANF), Supplemental Security Income (SSI), and Medicaid (Drachman 1995; Padilla 1997). Despite a significant reduction in spending for this program (Fix and Zimmerman 1995:10), refugees remain exempt from the harsh rulings established in the 1996 Personal Responsibility and Work Opportunity Reconciliation Act, which renders other classes of immigrants either ineligible for important federal benefits or significantly curtails their access.

Beyond humanitarian considerations for refugee admissions, other interests, including foreign policy and ideological preconceptions, influence the assignment or denial of refugee status. When these forces come into play, some groups are welcomed and others barred. An examination of those accepted and rejected as refugees illustrates the controversy surrounding refugee status (Drachman 1995).

Following World War II and during the cold war, large groups of people from communist countries were admitted into the United States. The United States responded to uprisings in communist Hungary and Cuba by admitting thousands of people from these countries. Later, involvement in the Vietnam War gave the United States a special obligation to countries in Indochina, although anticommunism was also an underlying reason for the admission of refugees from Southeast Asia. In 1989, 94 percent of refugees approved for admission came from communist countries (Howe 1990). In addition, INS procedures were operationalized differently for individuals from communist countries. In accordance with the 1980 Refugee Act, all individuals seeking asylum were required to demonstrate a well-founded fear of persecution should they return to their native country. However, approval for refugee applications from Soviet Armenians who arrived in the late 1980s was "virtually automatic even though they did not claim persecution when interviewed by the I.N.S." (Taubman 1988:A1). This group was, therefore, permitted to bypass the eligibility requirement for refugee status established by law.

In sharp contrast to the humanitarian response the INS accorded people fleeing communist countries was the policy applied to Haitians of detention, deportation, and interdiction at sea. Although their oppression and persecution under the Duvalier regime were amply documented, the United States persistently defined Haitians seeking entry as "economic migrant." From 1981 to 1989, only 6 of the 21,369 Haitians interdicted at sea were permitted entry (U.S. Committee for Refugees 1989:11). Many Haitians on U.S. territory were apprehended and placed in detention centers to await a decision on deportation or entry. Stays in detention centers ranged from months to years. The INS assertion that Haitians were economic migrants rather than refugees was viewed by many as motivated by either a political interest in maintaining Haiti as an ally in its anticommunist foreign policy or by racism (DeWind 1990).

Thus, two populations who viewed themselves as refugees were differently defined in the United States. These different definitions resulted in different receptions and different access to services. Members of one group were legally admitted into the country, where they received resettlement services and the same entitlements as U.S. citizens. Members of the other group were detained, deported, or slipped into the undocumented population, with limited access to services (Drachman 1995).

A *lawful permanent resident* is granted permission to reside permanently in the United States. In response to laws designed to prevent immigrants from becoming dependent on welfare (Hutchinson 1981:390–92, 410–14, 449–50), many newcomers seeking permanent resident status are required to have sponsors. A sponsor is a person or organization that guarantees economic support for the immigrant for a set period of time.

Two laws enacted in 1996, the Personal Responsibility and Work Opportunity Reconciliation Act (the welfare law), and the Illegal Immigration Reform and Immigrant Responsibility Act (IIRIRA), enact sweeping changes that either curtailed immigrants' access to benefits and services or set up obstacles to family reunification (Newman 1997; Scaperlanda 1997; Stickney 1997). In contrast to prior law, the 1996 welfare law renders immigrants who arrived after 1996 ineligible for SSI or food stamps. They are also ineligible for federally funded means-tested benefits for five years following arrival. After that, their eligibility is based on their own income plus the income and resources of their sponsor. The eligibility requirement that regards a sponsor's income as a resource available to an immigrant is lifted once the immigrant completes ten years of work or becomes a citizen. At that time, eligibility for federal means-tested benefits is based on the same criteria for immigrants as it is for citizens. These provisions dismantle the safety net for future legal immigrants, making them ineligible for federal assistance should they become disabled, aged, and/or poor. The new law also makes immigrants ineligible for important federal benefits, shifts immigrant policy in the United States toward exclusion, even though immigrants pay taxes, may serve in the military, and contribute to their communities.

New enforcement provisions in the IIRIRA also threaten those who sponsor immigrants. These provisions empower federal or state agencies that provide means-tested benefits to sue sponsors for failure to provide the promised support and to recover monies spent on an immigrant in the event that the individual received public assistance (Stickney 1997). The immigrant may also sue the sponsor in order to enforce the affidavit of support. Therefore, the law sets the stage for family disruption. For example, some families who intend to economically assist a newly arrived member may be incapable of providing the support because of unexpected economic difficulties. Since these families will either be sued or threatened by a suit from the government, they are likely to blame the immigrant for the suit. An immigrant who is upset by the responsibility placed on him or her for the lawsuit may also use the government-supported option to sue the family.

The IIRIRA also requires the INS to provide the names of all sponsors to benefit-providing agencies, enabling these agencies to track down sponsors of immigrants who request benefits. Also new is a requirement that individuals who sponsor the immigration of a family member have an income that is at least 125 percent above the federal poverty line, a figure calculated on the number of individuals to be supported, including spouses, children, other family members, and the sponsored immigrant (Stickney 1997). Since there is evidence that many families have insufficient income to sponsor the immigration of a relative at the newly required standard (Dugger 1997; Fix and Zimmerman 1995:25; Pendleton 1997:64; Scaperlanda 1997:1589; Stickney 1997), family reunification is likely to become more difficult. Thus, spouses will remain divided, children will remain separated from parents, and siblings will continue to live apart.

In contrast to prior law, the 1996 welfare law gives states the option to determine the following for current and future legal immigrants: to bar, to limit, or to provide full access to three federal programs: TANF, Medicaid, and Title XX Social Services; to deny, limit, or provide full access to state cash assistance; and to include sponsors' incomes in determining immigrants' eligibility for state public benefit programs. The option for states to deny, to limit, or to provide immigrants with full access to the above federally funded programs implies that national benefits and services for a class of individuals will vary from state to state. Thus the right to equal protection under the law is compromised, and legal challenges are likely to follow (Fix and Zimmerman 1995:27–28; Spiro 1997).

Undocumented people are individuals who have no current authorization to be in the United States. Some enter the country illegally. Others, who enter legally under a nonimmigrant status for a period of time (e.g., tourists or students) and who remain in the United States after their visas expire also fall into this category. All undocumented people are subject to deportation.

As its title indicates, the 1996 IIRIRA targets undocumented persons. In addition to previous legislation that rendered undocumented persons ineligible for most federal benefit programs, the IIRIRA now also renders them ineligible for state or locally funded programs, unless a state should pass a law affirming their eligibility. Confidentiality regarding an undocumented person's immigration status also has eroded. Currently federal, state, and local government personnel cannot be prevented from providing information on an individual's immigration status to the INS or to any other government agency. Thus, state and locally funded organizations that desire to protect the confidentiality of an undocumented person's status can no longer do so. These regulations are likely to generate many ethical dilemmas for service personnel employed in government agencies.

The expedited removal section of IIRIRA also authorizes the immediate expulsion of persons who arrive without valid travel documents. Although this section of the law is aimed at undocumented persons (and terrorists), it has consequences for persons legitimately seeking asylum in the United States. For example, persons fleeing persecution are often unable to provide valid travel documents. They commonly have trouble telling their story in a persuasive way, either because of difficulties with spoken English or mistrust of INS officers. As a result, INS inspectors may misunderstand their circumstances and make errors in deportation decisions—errors that could result in the return of persons legitimately seeking asylum to a country that will persecute, torture, or kill them. A law primarily aimed at illegal immigration, therefore, may have deadly consequences for legitimate asylum seekers.

The undocumented population is obviously a marginalized group. Not surprisingly, a common fear of deportation leads them to avoid public institutions. Some will not report assaults to the police (Gonzalez 1989). Some refuse to report landlords for housing violations. Some keep their children out of school and health care centers (Gelfand and Bialik-Gilad 1989). Beyond their limited work opportunities, many receive wages so low that their subsistence is jeopardized. Because of their limited rights and their vulnerability to deportation, they are easily exploited by employers who offer wages below minimum standards (Drachman 1995).

The life event of immigration in the United States is therefore defined by diverse phenomena—push forces propelling people to leave their home country, pull forces of a new country, the nature and strength of the support structures in the home and receiving countries, and the policies of the receiving country that establish parameters for inclusion or exclusion in the new land.

DEMOGRAPHIC PATTERNS

The United States is in its third decade of a major wave of immigration. In 1970, 9,619,302 foreign-born individuals were living in the United States (U.S. Bureau of the Census 1970). By 1980, that number had grown to 14,079,906 (U.S. Bureau of Census 1980), and, by 1990, it had reached 19,767,036 (U.S. Bureau of the Census 1990). Thus, between 1970 and 1980 the population of newcomers increased 46 percent, and between 1980 and 1990 it grew an additional 40.4 percent.

Since 1990 the number of immigrants entering the United States is approximately **one million** persons per year (Fix and Passel 1994:22; Suro 1996:17). Most new arrivals enter legally through family or employment-sponsored immigration. A second legal immigrant population is composed of refugees and asylees whose yearly numbers range from 100,000 to 150,000 (Fix and Passel 1994:22). Although the size of the undocumented population is often exaggerated, estimates derived from comprehensive studies indicate that four million undocumented persons were living in the United States in 1994 (Passel 1995:3).

In contrast to the last immigration wave at the end of the nineteenth and the early part of the twentieth centuries, when most people came from Europe, the new immigrants are coming from Asia, Central America, Eastern Europe, Africa, North America, and the Middle East. Asian and Latino immigrants arriving after 1965, when the current wave began, account for more than 80 percent of the immigration to the United States (Ong Hing 1996:2; Passel and Edmonston 1994:32). The diverse Asian population comes from China, the Philippines, India, Pakistan, Bangladesh, Sri Lanka, Korea, Vietnam, Cambodia, Laos, and Thailand. The Latino population, which is also diverse, includes immigrants from Mexico, Guatemala, El Salvador, Nicaragua, Columbia, Ecuador, Chile, Cuba, and the Dominican Republic. Eastern Europeans, particularly persons from the republics of the former Soviet Union, account for the largest number of immigrants from Europe. Although relatively small in number, African migration to the United States is also increasing, accounting for 3 percent of the legal immigration flow (Passel and Edmonston 1994).

Over 75 percent of the foreign-born population live in six states: California, New York, Texas, Florida, New Jersey, and Illinois (Rohter 1993). However, immigrant populations have increased in other states, as well. Massachusetts now has more than 500,000 foreign-born residents, and Minnesota, North Carolina, and Georgia's immigrant populations have each passed 100,000 (Fix and Passel 1994:29). Within states, most of the increases in the Asian population are attributable to immigration. During the 1980s, Rhode Island's Asian population increased 245 percent to 18,325; Alabama's, 124 percent to 22,000; Mississippi's, 76 percent to 13,000; and Louisiana's, 73 percent to 41,000 (Butterfield 1991:A22).

The educational level of immigrants, compared with U.S.-born persons, falls at the extremes of the educational spectrum (Fix and Passel 1994:32). Immigrants are more likely than natives to have low educational attainment (less than high school education) and more likely to have advanced degrees (college or beyond). Among the factors associated with the hourglass distribution is immigration status. Many at the low end have arrived as undocumented persons. Another group at the low end arrived in the 1980s as refugees (Fix and Passel 1994). At the high end of the educational scale are legal immigrants who either exceed or fall slightly below the educational level of U.S.-born persons. Therefore, the way people arrive in the United States—as undocumented persons, refugees, or legal immigrants—appears to be associated with the extremes in the distribution.

Although the rate of poverty during the 1980–1990 decade increased both for immigrant and U.S.-born households, the increase is significantly higher for immigrant households: 42 percent, compared with 11 percent for native households (Fix and Passel 1994:37–38). A larger share of immigrant households (12.3 percent) also lives in poverty (Fix and Passel 1994). The recent arrival of immigrants within the past ten years explains, in part, the income disparity, since long-term immigrants' incomes match or exceed those of U.S.-born persons (Lee and Edmonston 1994:129). The large population of refugee and undocumented immigrants may also explain the income disparity, for these populations tend to fare less well than other immigrant groups and persons born in the United States (Fix and Passel 1994:31). Moreover, lack of proficiency in English exacts a price on one's earnings. Since language proficiency develops over time, the recency of arrival may in part account for their low incomes. Yet despite the factors that contribute to immigrant poverty, a sizable segment of the immigrant population lives at a low level of subsistence. Although their incomes tend to increase with longer residence in the United States, their poverty nonetheless renders them vulnerable.

The growth and composition of the immigrant population have implications for U.S. society in the educational, labor force, and political arenas. It is estimated that 33 to 40 percent of the nation's population growth is attributable to immigration (Suro 1991). By the year 2010, children of immigrants will account for half the growth in the school-age population (Fix and Passel 1994:43). The political constituencies of the ethnically and racially diverse immigrant populations will influence future elections and, ultimately, the policies of the nation. These data suggest that the well-being of the immigrant population is critical to the well-being of the nation.

SOCIETAL CONTEXT

The ambivalent welcome experienced by immigrants in the United States is reflected in the public debate on immigration. Underlying the debate are economic, humanitarian, racial, and ethnic issues and xenophobia. These forces are analyzed in this section as they provide a picture of the societal context for immigrants.

Economic arguments in the current debate revolve around different views: the fiscal drain on communities created by immigrants' use of public services; contributions to the economy through revenues received from immigrants; and reduced job opportunities and wage depression of U.S. workers generated by immigrant labor.

The view that immigrants are an economic burden to communities focuses on both legal immigrants and undocumented persons. Many California residents and the state's former governor hold the undocumented population in California responsible for absorbing a disproportionate share of the resources of public schools, public hospitals, and prisons—institutions that are supported primarily through the taxes of U.S.-born persons and legal immigrants. Thus, the ex-governor of California claimed that two-thirds of all infants born in Los Angeles's public hospitals were children of undocumented parents; a disproportionate share of the state's prison population was made up of undocumented individuals; the state paid $1.7 billion per year to educate students, many of whom were undocumented children; and the cost to taxpayers from 1988 to 1994 for the use of health services, prisons, and schools by undocumented persons was $10 billion (Wilson 1996).

The cost to taxpayers of services utilized by the undocumented population was the overt reason for the passage, in 1994, of California's Proposition 187, the state initiative that denied most social services—including basic health care and schooling for children—to undocumented immigrants (Ayres 1994; Rayner 1996; Suro 1996). In 1997, Proposition 187 was held to be unconstitutional.

During the 1996 presidential election, an advertisement by the Republican Party brought this issue before a national audience by asking two questions: "Do you know there are 5 million illegal immigrants in the United States?" and, "Do you know that you spend $5.5 billion a year to support them with welfare, food stamps and other services?" (Schmitt 1996). Inasmuch as undocumented persons have been ineligible for benefits from major federal welfare programs for the past seventeen years, the fiscal picture of their public service utilization is misrepresented.

In a small midwestern city, Wausau, Wisconsin, a similar view was presented regarding the increased costs to taxpayers for the use of public services by Southeast Asian refugees—a legal immigrant group (Beck 1994). The issues raised in Wausau included the overcrowding of schools due to the large Southeast Asian student population; the costs to U.S.-born residents for the construction of additional schools to accommodate the larger student population; the limited job opportunities that led to a 70 percent use of public assistance by refugees; and a rise in property taxes by over 10 percent—three times that of an adjoining community with few immigrants (Beck 1994). Based on the preceding views, a moratorium on immigration has been supported by some congressional leaders, states, groups, and individuals (Brimelow 1995; Clad 1996; Lamm and Inhoff 1985).

Countering the previous argument is evidence that immigrants contribute more to the economy than they use in services. Their contributions include the taxes paid by immigrant workers; the taxes paid and jobs created by immigrant businesses; the goods and services purchased by immigrants; and the rebuilding by immigrants of neighborhoods that were previously in disrepair (Gosh 1996; Park 1996; Fix and Passel 1996; Pear 1997; Rayner 1996; Rohter 1993). These phenomena create a ripple effect in the economy that is not always captured in the analysis of costs and benefits.

A report highlighting companies founded by Asian Pacific immigrants emphasizes the economic benefits to the community derived from their job creation and the size of their combined revenues. The report calculates that monies spent on the education for Asian Pacific immigrant children are offset years later when the children become adults and pay taxes (Ong Hing 1996). This conclusion is supported by a national study on the fiscal impact of immigration that indicates that, despite initial high costs, immigrant households produce fiscal gains once schooling is finished and working adult children begin to pay income and payroll taxes (Pear 1997; Smith and Edmonston 1997). The report also estimates that immigration adds $10 billion to the nation's annual economic output (Smith and Edmonston 1997).

Although immigration may result in a fiscal gain for the nation, questions arise regarding the distribution of the gain. Businesses profit from the lower wages of workers, and consumers from the lower prices for goods and services. However, some studies indicate that U.S.-born workers at the low end of the wage scale, where they compete for jobs with low-wage unskilled immigrants, may find both their wages and employment opportunities reduced (Altonji and Card 1991; Borjas 1996).

A significant humanitarian force embedded in immigration law is the preference given to **family reunification.** Through a hierarchical system of categories established by the Immigration and Naturalization Act Amendments of 1965, family members of immigrants are given preference for admission. The family-based preference accounts for the largest number of new arrivals (Borjas 1996:74; Fix and Passel 1994:22). (Recent rulings that require sponsors of immigrants to have incomes of 125 percent of the poverty level are likely to result in a decline in the number of families reuniting.)

Other humanitarian forces include legislation and policies supporting the admission of **refugees,** such as the Refugee Act of 1980. In addition, human rights, religious and service organizations, and community groups also advocate on behalf of immigrants. A recent example of community advocacy involves the Golden Venture, a ship from China that ran aground in New York in 1993. Since the ship's passengers were undocumented, they were placed in detention centers around the country. In a Pennsylvania detention center, community advocacy led to the following actions: local newspapers sued to open the asylum hearings to the public; volunteers held weekly vigils on behalf of the immigrants, visited the immigrants in the detention center, provided housing and employment assistance for the few that were released, and raised a sizable amount of money for their assistance (Fisher 1997).

Humanitarianism is also expressed in the popular image of the United States as a refuge for oppressed peoples from other lands. The words of Emma Lazarus welcoming the tired masses yearning to be free summarizes the historic connection between humanitarianism and immigration—a view that is embedded in the nation's self-concept.

Coexisting with humanitarianism are racist, antiethnic forces, and xenophobia. Recent widely discussed literature favoring **restrictions** on new immigration on the basis of color and ethnicity reflects these forces. Examples include the suggested return of the nation to its white origin (Brimelow 1995:264); the comparison of the INS waiting room to a New York City subway, "where you find yourself in an underworld that is not just teeming but is almost entirely colored" (Brimelow 1995:28); and the prediction that the changes in the ethnic character of the United States will result in "American patriots fighting to salvage as much as possible from the shipwreck of their great republic" (Brimelow 1995:265).

Others describe new immigrants as unassimilable because they can't leave their cultures behind. They are described as stressing group identity and separatism, as opposed to American individualism, and their difficulties with English are attributed to their "nationalistic ghettos" (Zuckerman 1996:109–11).

Xenophobia finds expression in vigilante groups patrolling airport terminals to deter undocumented persons from traveling around the country (Schmitt 1996). It is illustrated by the violence erupting at the border between the United States and Mexico (Kadetsky 1996:103). It is reflected in the Mexican government's protest against the violence perpetrated by California police against Mexican nationals, presumed to be undocumented individuals, who were beaten after a car chase. It is articulated in a statement by Mexico's long-ruling Institutional Revolutionary Party that the violence by California police illustrates "how far racist and xenophobic attitudes have reached in the U.S." (Preston 1996:A10).

Attitudes toward immigration and immigrants have had historic swings between **inclusion** and **exclusion**. Inclusion is based on a "communitarian" model that emphasizes immigrants' contributions to the nation's general welfare through their productivity and diversity (Schuck 1984). Exclusion is based on the view that community resources need to be protected, and the restrictions on immigrants' entry or, if admitted, on their entitlements are necessary to achieve community goals. The erosion of immigrants' entitlement to benefits, the family reunification regulations that discriminate against low-income families, the immediate return without judicial review of persons who arrive with improper documents, the rulings that personnel in government agencies cannot be restricted from reporting an individual's immigration status to the INS or other government agencies—all lead to the conclusion that the pendulum has swung toward exclusion.

However, support and inclusion are provided by the immigrant communities. These communities, which consist of previous arrivals and family and friends, provide concrete help and social support. The immigrant businesses in the communities provide employment for both new arrivals and previous immigrants. Their news publications, which are printed in immigrants' native languages, provide local, national, international, and home country news. Stores stocked with indigenous foods and restaurants that prepare home country meals are part of the immigrant community. Community life is enriched by immigrants' religious organizations and their political constituencies. In essence, the immigrant communities assist individuals in adapting to the United States while concurrently preserving their cultures.

VULNERABILITIES AND RISK FACTORS

The word *stress* refers to the psychosocial discomfort or distress people frequently experience in daily life, especially while adjusting to new environments. The literature on immigration suggests that the process of adaptation to the host culture can be stressful enough to threaten the psychosocial well-being of many immigrants (Hull 1979; Tran and Ferullo 1997), whether admitted to the United States for economic advancement, reunification with their families, or humanitarian reasons. Studies reveal that the newcomers' stressful life experiences seem to have contributed to their psychosocial problems. The most prevalent problems include domestic violence, alcoholism, juvenile delinquency, alienation of the elderly, marital and intergenerational conflicts, and mental disorders (Hulewat 1996; Padilla et al. 1988). A list of stressors experienced by immigrants includes the following.

The term *culture shock* was coined to characterize severe anxiety-provoking situations experienced by those who must act under unfamiliar social norms and behavior cues (Oberg 1960). It implies that the experience of a new culture is an unpleasant surprise—a shock—partly because it is unexpected and partly because it may lead to a negative evaluation of one's own culture. Researchers have seen culture shock as a normal reaction, part of the routine process of adaptation to culture stress, and the manifestation of a longing for a more predictable, stable, and comprehensible environment (Furnham and Bochner 1986). Some have also suggested that the greater the difference between the culture of origin and the host culture, the higher the rate of psychosocial dysfunction (Berry et al. 1987).

Since members of any cultural group are not all alike, the differences within a cultural group may be greater than the differences between the dominant culture and a minority culture. One major difference among members of various ethnic and cultural groups is the degree to which they have immersed themselves in the culture of the United States. *Acculturation* can be defined as a process that begins when individuals from different cultures come into continuous firsthand contact and that leads to changes in the original cultural patterns of either or both groups. The task faced by new immigrants is to adapt to the host society. Not surprisingly, the stress of adapting—i.e., acculturation—may result in anxiety, depression, psychosomatic symptoms, and identity confusion (Williams and Berry 1991). For some immigrants, cultural conflicts continue to cause inner confusion and stresses even after many years of settled lives in their new environment (Derbyshire 1969).

The processes of adaptation and acculturation involve dynamic and synergistic changes in the immigrants' intrapsychic characters, interpersonal relationships, and social roles and status. The challenges they face are enormous: They include shifting ideas and realities of space and time, roles and relationships, cultural identities, social networks, employment, and, of course, language.

Our conduct is dictated by the predictions that we make about our **physical** and **social environments**. Consider an immigrant family that leaves its village or town in an underdeveloped country one day and finds itself the next day in one of the most advanced industrial countries in the world. The members of the family are instantly plunged into an unpredictable new environment that, given their ignorance of the social structure, the norms of behavior, and the timetable of natural events (Mirdal 1984), they are unprepared to survive, let alone thrive in. Most of us deal with our environment automatically, recognizing cues and responding automatically, without daily reflection upon social expectations and regulations. Immigrants, however, cannot take this nonverbal language for granted. They need to consider each situation individually and reflect quickly on their own role in it. For immigrants whose contacts with others were once limited to their own family and extended family, to live in a new land means to reorganize, structure, and predict their lives on a daily basis. This is stressful.

Immigrants often sustain **multiple losses**. The loss of social status and social roles may create a sense of deprivation and insecurity. Among immigrants, the discrepancy between anticipated and actual social status, namely, goal-striving stress, seems to exert substantial negative effects on their mental health (Kuo 1976; Parker and Kleiner 1966). Some immigrants continue to experience lower social status throughout their lives.

Female immigrants generally suffer more dramatic changes in role status than do their male counterparts (Freidenberg, Implivale, and Skovron 1988), and role reversal is a major stress in the families of several immigrant groups (Brown 1982) in which the wife can find employment more easily than the husband. When she becomes the breadwinner while the husband stays home and does the housework, many immigrants—particularly men who come from countries where traditional families are the rule—find the reversal of roles intolerable.

Migration, however, may also result in a deterioration of women's positions for those who do not work outside the home. The roles that they have been socialized to fulfill are no longer viable in their new land. Wives and mothers who do not speak the language may be more dependent on their husbands and children, as well as either more overworked or more isolated than they were in their home country (Rhee 1996). As mothers, they are confronted with primary responsibility for their children's schooling. Yet they are unprepared to understand and cope with an institution such as the school. Thus, children and husbands, experienced in schools and in workplaces, become the interpreters of this new culture and its institutions for the homebound mothers and wives, causing further role strain.

As primary providers for the families' immediate needs, women worry a great deal about the parent-child conflict accompanying a migration experience (Rhee 1996). Extreme differences between Western, Asian, African, and Latin cultures with regard to family values, authority patterns, and degree of individualism sharpen this conflict.

The search for identity and/or the **re-creation of identity** are complicated processes for immigrants. They must reexamine and change their attitudes toward themselves, toward other ethnic groups, and toward the dominant culture—an experience stressful enough to create repeated crises of identity. Most immigrants, particularly children and adolescents, must sort out and decide which parts of their cultural heritage to retain and which aspects to modify or replace in order to function effectively in their new country (Le 1983).

Immigrants, particularly refugees, often have experienced profound loss, not just in terms of status and material goods but also in seeing their native land transformed politically and culturally. Losses also are associated with **separation** from members of their families and other social support networks. These multiple losses add up to a stressful, if not traumatic, experience.

Persons living below the **poverty** level in the United States include an inordinate number of ethnic/racial/cultural group members, many of whom are immigrants. Factors such as housing, employment, educational opportunities, and life expectancies are often associated with poverty among members of culturally diverse immigrant populations.

For those immigrants who are vulnerable to social distress because of genetic or psychological factors, the added stress of poverty can lead to symptom manifestations and mental health problems. A cursory review of the literature identifies social class and environmental risk factors as having negative effects on the immigrant's adjustment. Some studies show that the negative effect may largely derive from the congested, low-income, and depressed neighborhoods where immigrants reside (LaVietes 1979; Ponizovsky and Perl 1997). A study examining the effects of a child's immediate environment on his or her mental health (Homel and Burns 1989) concluded that children who reside in commercial and industrial areas of inner cities "stood out from all others in their feelings of loneliness, dislike of other children, feelings of rejection, worry, fear, anger, and unhappiness and dissatisfaction with their lives and with their families in particular" (152–53). Residence in inner cities exposes the immigrant to overcrowded and unsafe buildings, as well as to too-frequent environmental changes that require quick adaptation. Inner-city living may present immigrants and their children with multiple stresses that, cumulatively, may be more damaging to healthy functioning than a single acute stress would be.

Migration may not be a labor migration, but if immigrants want to survive, to attain an independent income, and to regain or achieve a desirable socioeconomic status, they have to rely on **employment**. In this country, foreign-born and native-born workers generally do not share the same economic locations or labor-market rewards (North 1974). Gender adds another dimension to the stratification of immigrants within both the workplace and the larger society. Immigrant women experience the restrictions of a sex-segregated occupational structure, in which women's jobs are characterized by lower wages, fewer opportunities for advancement, and less job security (Philzacklea 1983). Immigrant women's jobs are located disproportionately in the poorly paid labor-market sectors where they work as domestics, sewing machine operators, waitresses, and so on.

Immigrants often suffer the frustration of being unemployed and regarded as fringe wage earners. Many immigrants willingly accept menial or semiskilled jobs in order to survive. They share the problems of unskilled workers throughout this country: double workloads, repetitive and fatiguing jobs, unhealthy working conditions, an absence of benefits, and the like. Many immigrants held professional or white-collar jobs in their countries of origin. Some are able to maintain their former occupational and social status, but many cannot find similar or comparable occupations in the United States. In spite of their economic mobility, they have not resolved the problem of status inconsistency.

How generous should this country be to those who do not speak standard English? This question has been asked with increasing urgency within the dominant culture. Some writers have suggested that **language** is perceived by certain white Americans as the one mutable feature of culturally diverse groups; therefore, it is the place to take a stand and demand assimilation (Hurtado and Rodriguez 1989). To them, the ability to speak English serves as a symbolic measure of assimilation. As a corollary, many of these same Americans hold in contempt individuals whose spoken language is noticeably different from what they perceive as standard English.

Far from serving as a simple vehicle for describing an objective world, language is the key facet of a person's self-concept and active shaper of the way people think and act (Rubin 1981). Learning a new language is a gradual process, for a shift from one language to another requires a change of thought processes, cultural attitudes, and self-concepts. Immigrants to the United States often feel lost and disoriented when they cannot achieve a level of proficiency in English that makes them comfortable in their new environment. Among immigrant children, for instance, behavior directly or indirectly related to the lack of linguistic proficiency is the most frequent reason for psychiatric referral of students whose primary language is not English (Canino and Spurlock 1994). Many of the behaviors considered problematic by teachers are, in reality, characteristics of students who are in the process of second-language acquisition. Often, a child undergoing acquisition of a second language is diagnosed incorrectly as learning disabled.

Evidence has shown that much of the history of culturally diverse groups in the United States has often been unpleasant, with **racism** and **prejudice** fueling the oppression of minorities. Certainly, many immigrants have experienced racism and negative stereotyping. Not surprisingly, these have in some instance led to emotional strain and social dysfunction. The current political environment is characterized by strong anti-immigrant feelings (Keigher 1997). There is a growing concern among the indigenous population that newly arrived immigrants are taking away jobs from the native-born lowest paid workers. Huddle (1993) found that for every one hundred unskilled immigrants who were working, twenty-five or more unskilled American workers were displaced from jobs. The cost of public assistance for these 2.1 million displaced American workers was $11.9 billion. Some people feel that too many immigrants come to this country to take advantage of taxpayer-funded education, health care, and other social services without ever contributing to the systems. In fact, as mentioned earlier, the costs of immigration are justified by the revenue that immigrants help produce for U.S. employers (Fix and Passel 1994; Padilla 1997).

Many immigrants come from homogeneous nations, where they were not accustomed to racial and ethnic diversity, and are unfamiliar with the kind of racism, both overt and covert, so often experienced in this country. The existence of so many unfamiliar cultural and ethnic groups, particularly in cities, where they live in close proximity to one another, often leads to stress that is exacerbated by crisis situations, such as social violence, racial profiling, and police brutality. Obviously, these experiences and the fears they generate lead to stress.

RESILIENCIES AND PROTECTIVE FACTORS

Coping has been distinguished as a mediator of social stress (Pearlin et al. 1981). Individuals may differ in their stress-reducing coping patterns, despite having similar external and internal mediating variables. Some immigrants withdraw from stress, whereas others try to diminish it by finding creative and useful solutions. Some immigrants approach stressful situations with optimism and confidence; others look to surrogates to resolve them.

At the core of immigration lies issues of cultural identity. These usually involve unstable and stormy transactions, with multiple losses and intensive external and internal changes (Grinberg and Grinberg 1989; Lin 1986). If it is thought of as the intersection of the individual and society, then its formation involves finding a place within that larger social world. For immigrants and refugees, this means giving up some components of their previous identity and establishing a new self in a social world whose dimensions may be vague or unknown.

In the process of changing behavior, values, attitudes, and identity, immigrants face two general issues: whether to retain the cultural identity and characteristics of the country of origin and/or whether to participate in the larger society (Berry et al. 1987). Four types of acculturation have been proposed: (1) assimilation, when the original cultural identity is rejected and only participation in the larger society is accepted; (2) integration, when the original cultural identity is retained and participation in the larger society is accepted; (3) separation, when original cultural identity is maintained and participation in the larger society is rejected; and (4) marginalization, resulting from the rejection of both original cultural identity and participation in the larger society (Pawliuk et al. 1996).

Researchers investigating the process of acculturation have suggested that an integrated, or **bicultural,** style is associated with better psychological functioning in adults (Berry et al. 1987; Fabrega 1969). People who can maintain a balance between two cultures have fewer psychological disorders than the groups at the extremes—the least or the most acculturated (Ramirez 1984). Studies have shown that more acculturated individuals who have become alienated from their own ethnic support systems are more likely than less acculturated individuals to suffer psychological disorders (Graves 1967).

Immigrants have both positive and negative perceptions of the United States. Though they may see it as a land of opportunity, particularly for their children, many feel lost without a sense of community and fear losing themselves (Adams 1989). Some who feel marginalized develop strategies for personal development. Quoting Marlin (1993), Mathews (1994) wrote that immigrants tend to cope with this situation by one or more of the following strategies: (a) nostalgic re-creation of past association; (b) being critical of the new culture; (c) idealizing the home country; and (d) superficial adjustment to the new reality. Since not all members of any given cultural group are alike, the acculturation pattern or style will differ from person to person. Age, gender, and social class are among the variables to be considered in relation to vulnerability, as well as adaptive behavior, in coping with cultural conflicts.

Studies have shown that the psychological functioning of children of immigrants is related to parental adaptation to the host society. Some suggest that children of immigrant parents who adopt an integrational mode of acculturation function better than those of separated or marginal parents (Berry et al. 1987). Other researchers have noted that parental social variables, such as language ability, socioeconomic status, and social support, are correlated with the psychological functioning of their children. Not surprisingly, the better-functioning children have parents who speak the language of the host culture well, enjoy professional social status, and have supportive friends (Lipson 1992; Sluzki 1979). Conversely, difficulties have been found in children whose parents do not speak the host language well and lack the supports of social status and social networks. Children in the process of learning coping skills and seeking role models will develop similar strategies in order to survive (Pawliuk et al. 1996).

A Southeast Asian young woman wrote about her coping experience while growing up in the United States:

Starting out as a six-grader, I was placed in an unfamiliar environment without any knowledge of English. I had never believed in education before. From my personal experience over a million Cambodians were executed during the Khmer Rouge Regime, between 1975 and 1979. I had never wanted to go to school but now it was something that I had to do. So I went because I had no other choice. Everyone just had to go to school here, plus I did not know where to go or what else to do if I did not go to school. At first, I hated school because I did not understand the lessons or what the teachers were saying. I remember that I would fall asleep in class almost every day. I did not learn much in Junior High School and even in High School, because I did not really want to learn. I kept telling myself that this country is not a place for me and that some day in the near future I would be going back to Cambodia. While in school I had very few friends. I did not speak English well, plus I was shy and quiet. In my old country I had been an outgoing person and was always surrounded with many friends. Now, as a shy and quiet person, I hardly spoke to anyone. My daily routine was going to school and completing my homework. With time and effort, I managed to graduate from High School.

But when I entered College, I began to see things differently. In College, I enjoyed attending classes every day. Education gave me a clearer view in understanding what is offered in the real world. I was inspired by the professors idealism, a feeling that was shared by many students. This new ideology and philosophy allowed me to observe and to learn more about every day life. I started to ask questions when I did not understand and I made a lot of new friends.

Now I believe that I am back to my own self again. Only now I consider myself a bi-cultural, bilingual professional with a strong sense of identity.
(Refugee Women's Council, 1998)

Immigrants can show resilience, as well as vulnerability, and not all immigrants will be traumatized by their experiences. Garmezy (1983), discussing stress-resistant children, identified a triad of protective factors: (1) a positive personality disposition; (2) a supportive family; and (3) an external societal agency that functions as a supply system to reinforce a child's coping efforts.

Individual Factors. Researchers have identified various personality traits that act as internal mediators of stress. These include locus of control, self-esteem, social orientation, achievement motivation, and cognitive style (Canino and Spurlock 1994). Rutter (1987) identified four specific coping mechanisms in children that protect them against stress: (1) reduce the impact of stress; (2) avoid negative chain reactions; (3) establish self-efficacy and self-esteem; and (4) seek new opportunities. These mechanisms are also applicable to adults. Those who cope effectively are likely to come away with enhanced coping abilities; those who deal ineffectively are likely to experience poor outcomes.

One internal mediator seems to be the perception of the place of one's culture within the dominant culture. This perception often affects a person's attitude toward his or her ethnicity and the intensity of ethnic identification. Immigrants who perceive the place of their ethnic culture positively tend to preserve it in their identity, either fully or partially, whereas those who perceive it as inferior tend not to identify with it (Berger 1997).

The employment status of immigrants and refugees in the host society is probably an indicator of their integration of adjustment (Tran 1991). The 1988 national survey of current employment status of Indochinese refugees, conducted by the Office of Refugee Resettlement, found that factors influencing the refugees' employment-seeking behavior included English language proficiency, pursuit of education, family needs, and health status (U.S. Department of Health and Human Services 1989). It is safe to say that immigrants and refugees who arrive in the United States with a knowledge of English, good educational background, social skills, manageable family obligations, and good health status will achieve a higher rate of employment than those who lack these characteristics.

Other studies suggest that age, gender, number of years in this country, socioeconomic background in their original countries, and number of children are crucial for their labor-force participation in the host country (Caplan, Whitmore, and Buie 1984; Tran 1991). Other protective factors may include the individual's level of anxiety and risk taking, ways of handling loss and mourning, and the family's tolerance of differences.

Social Support. Social supports—resources made available through interrelationships with significant others—provide both emotional and tangible benefits to individuals. These include a sense of meaning, belonging, and acceptance; affection and nurturing; and information, transportation, and help with daily living (Choi 1997; Hill and Christensen 1989). Research has found that social supports directly affect immigrants' adaptation with respect to job satisfaction, depression, health outcomes, and life satisfaction (Payne and Jones 1987; Turner 1981).

The literature has indicated that social support has positive effects on individuals who are exposed to demands or are experiencing stress. Some writers have begun to focus on the relationship between life events, such as migration, and social support; they suggest that the latter buffers the former (Monroe 1983; Williams, Ware, and Donald 1981). Vulnerability to depression among members of immigrant groups has been attributed to a decreased social support. Conversely, those receiving adequate social support are less impaired when confronted with stress (Lin 1986).

Family Support. Immediate family members, as well as extended family, play key roles in many immigrant families. Clinical studies have documented the importance of family support, a widely appreciated aspect of many cultures. In general, more disturbed clinical cases tend to rely on formal institutions, while less severe cases find social support among family members. Family support moderates stress, and the mobility of family support systems is likely to act as a preventative measure, alleviating stress.

Implicit within all cultures are norms that enhance growth and development in their children and that serve as additional sources of support and strength when families are exposed to adversity. The literature indicates that resilient children come from homes in which rules are consistently enforced; a good relationship with and between the parents exists; and where an adequate identification figure is present in the household (Rutter 1987).

In immigrant families, differences in acculturation style of parents and children may create family conflict. Such conflicts may also arise when some members represent the values of the country of origin and others represent the values of the new society. A family's ability to adapt to life in the new country—such as maintaining contact with formal or informal institutions and peers without giving up ethnic identity—serves as a strong protective factor. Parents who speak the language of the host culture or who have friends in the host culture may be more likely to enroll their children in team activities and organizations, activities that will result in higher levels of social competence.

Researchers have shown that the poor utilize informal social networks to alleviate poverty (Martin and Martin 1985). Social networks, especially the extended family, may point the way to housing and jobs, incorporating several income earners, relocating work responsibility, and lowering household expenses. If it does nothing more, the presence of family and extended family members helps to reduce loneliness and stress throughout the process of resettlement (Allodi and Rojas 1983).

Community Support. Newly arrived immigrants depend on their own ethnic communities for a social support system to reduce the stress of immigration and integration. Immigrants express their culture through their own social and institutional community networks, and it is the community as a whole that integrates them with the larger society. By setting up, in the host country, social networks based on both kinship and friendship, and by establishing ethnic associations and religious institutions, immigrants are able to respond adequately to their most important sociocultural needs within a community that mediates between them and the larger society. These organizations provide a place for social relationships to develop that satisfy the immigrants' need for communication and enable them to avoid isolation (Jacob 1994).

For such networks and organizations to provide social support, the immigrant community must have within it a relatively large proportion of well-integrated and educated individuals able to serve as mediators. These men and women usually share deeply ingrained core cultural values and/or support from the host society. Immigrant groups with support and funding from federal and state governments are able to express their culture and identity through their own social networks and community organizations.

PROGRAMS AND SOCIAL WORK CONTRIBUTIONS

Voluntary agencies have taken a major role in the resettlement process of refugees in this country as well as other Western countries (Tran 1991; Wright 1981). In the beginning of the arrival of refugees from Southeast Asia, the government established several refugee camps in this country to receive, process, and resettle refugees in American communities. The second-wave refugees from Southeast Asia and refugees from Latin American countries, the Soviet Union, and other Western countries came to the United States either directly or would spend a period of time in their first asylum country. Once refugees received a visa for entry to the United States, they were assigned to one of the voluntary agencies, known as VOLAGs. The VOLAG agencies included the United States Catholic Conference, the Lutheran Immigration and Refugee Service, the International Rescue Committee, Church World Services, Hebrew Immigrant Aid Society, and others. The VOLAGs were responsible for finding sponsors for refugees who were allowed to leave camps only when sponsorship in the communities was obtained (Tran 1991).

The VOLAG agencies, which continue to provide services to refugees throughout the world, have had cooperative agreements with the Bureau of Refugees Programs of the Department of State to resettle the new refugees. When no sponsors are found by the VOLAGs, local voluntary agencies, such as the New York Association for New Americans (NYANA), directly take responsibility to settle refugees. The goal of sponsorship is to assist the refugees to become integrated in the host country and to become economically self-sufficient. These international and local agencies are responsible for initial food, shelter and clothing needs and for counseling the refugees and immigrants about health, employment, and social services.

Each state has a federally funded program for assisting newly arrived refugees and immigrants. These programs, through contracts with voluntary agencies, provide services such as English as a second language training, job development, employment placement, information and referral, interpreters, and social adjustment programs.

With the establishment of **settlement houses** in the late 1800s, educated middle-class individuals moved into poor neighborhoods to work directly with immigrants and other poor populations to bring about community and social changes (Iglehart and Becerra 1996). The settlement house workers saw a part of their goal as assisting immigrants in adapting to American life. At present, many settlement houses continue to provide immigrants with social services, educational, and vocational programs.

During the early 1900s, the mutual aid and **self-help activities** of ethnic communities began to flourish. This practice was much influenced by African Americans' belief that their survival was strongly linked to self-reliance in the face of exclusionary and separatist practices (Martin and Martin 1985). Black communities began to take on the task of addressing their own community needs. Other ethnic communities organized their own self-help programs. For example, early Chinese immigrants developed benevolent associations for their communities, and Mexican American organizations emerged to address their community needs. The goal of the early ethnic community organizations was to address problems identified by the community and provide services that were endorsed by the community. Today, ethnically run services for ethnic communities continue to grow and flourish.

As the complexion and culture of the population becomes more diverse, more attention is directed toward the need for **social service agencies** to provide culturally sensitive services. The ethnic agencies became a model for the provision of such services (Iglehart and Becerra 1996). Some of these ethnic agencies, with the help of governmental funding, became multiservice centers. These centers usually are capable of providing culturally and linguistically appropriate services to the community. In a study of three multiservice centers in Chinese American immigrant communities, Chow (1999) found that these centers, in recognizing the multiple problems immigrants can face, provide a wide array of services, making the idea of one-stop service shopping possible. Services provided by these multiservice centers often include information and referral, case management, efficacy and networking services, as well as counseling, youth, health, mental health, protective, and vocational services. Some also provide housing, employment services, and services for families and children. These agencies and those in other ethnic communities are active in developing programs for the empowerment of the communities and the new immigrants.

ASSESSMENT AND INTERVENTIONS

A stage of migration framework provides a context for understanding and helping immigrants and refugees by linking the migration experiences in the country of origin with experiences in the country of destination (Drachman and Ryan 1991). Since service personnel are not in contact with "newcomers" until they arrive in the final destination country, the framework offers a way for workers to consider the intermingling between migration experiences that occur in the original country with resettlement experiences in the United States.

The framework has generic and specific utility as it can be applied to all immigrant groups and specific groups (Drachman and Halberstadt 1992). It can also be applied to the individual immigrant as it offers a lens for assessment of the individual in the particular circumstance of migration. It is based on concepts drawn from migration studies, particularly ideas revolving around migration as occurring in stages (Cox 1985; Keller 1975; Kunz 1981). It includes a three-stage process: premigration or departure, transit or intermediate country, and resettlement. Variables of age, family composition, socioeconomic and educational level, occupation, culture, rural or urban background, belief system, and social support are assumed to influence the individual or family in each of the stages. In the following discussion of the framework, the experiences of immigrants from Korea and the Dominican Republic are presented to illustrate its ability to secure salient information for assessment of different groups. Table 23.1 illustrates the factors associated with each of the stages.

1. Premigration/Departure Stage. Social, political, economic, and educational factors surrounding the premigration and departure stage are significant. This phase may involve abrupt flight, exile, or a situation in which individuals choose to depart. Expectation for a better future, separation from family and friends, leaving a familiar environment, decisions regarding who leaves and who is left behind, experiences of persecution, violence, loss of significant others, or a long wait and living in limbo prior to departure are some of the issues individuals face in this stage. Among the issues in resettlement that emerge from this phase are concern for those left behind, depression associated with the multiple losses, incongruity between expectations and the reality of life in the new land, and survivor guilt and posttraumatic stress for persons who witnessed and/or experienced violence and the loss of others.

The desire for greater economic and social opportunities underlies the migration of many individuals and families from the Dominican Republic. **Dominican** migration usually involves the departure of an individual family member versus the total family. Therefore, children, spouses/companions, parents, and so on are left behind. For a departing mother, caretaking arrangements for a child(ren) who remains in the home country is a central issue. The strong commitment in Dominican families to assist its members as well as the Dominican family structure, which includes immediate and generations of extended family as well as nonblood kin, facilitates the departing parent's ability to secure child care. The caretaking arrangements, however, could range

TABLE 23.1. Stages of Migration Framework

Stage of Migration	Critical Variables	Factors that Influence Each Migration Stage
Pre-migration	Social, political, economic and educational factors Separation from family and friends Decisions regarding who leaves and who is left behind Long wait and living in limbo prior to departure Leaving a familiar environment Life-threatening circumstances Experiences of violence and/or persecution Loss of significant others	Age Family composition Urban/rural background
Transit/Intermediate	Perilous or safe journey of short or long duration Refugee camp or detention center stay of short or long duration Awaiting a foreign country's decision regarding final relocation Loss of significant others	Education Culture Socioeconomic background Occupation Belief system
Resettlement	Cultural issues Reception from host country Opportunity structure of host country Discrepancy between expectations and reality Degree of cumulative stress throughout migration process Different levels of acculturation among family members	Social support

Drachman and Halberstadt, 1992

from consistent and nurturing to disruptive and problematic. For example, a relative (often a grandmother) could assume caretaking responsibilities for the emigrant's child(ren). Health-related problems of the individual, however, could disrupt child care, necessitating different caretaking arrangements and creating another adjustment for the child. Thus the nature of child care at the point of parental departure and during parental absence requires consideration by service personnel in contact with Dominican families if family reunification occurs during the later stage of resettlement. Similarly, the child's age at the point of parental departure may also influence resettlement if family reunification occurs. Specifically, the experiences of a child are likely to be different if separation occurs when a child is an infant versus a child who is 10, and when reunification occurs when a child is 7 versus a child who is 14 (Drachman, Kwon-Ahn, and Paulino 1996).

Competition and limited opportunities for higher education in Korea and opportunities for higher education in the United States have been significant push and pull factors in the migration of **Koreans** (Kim 1978:188–89; Kwon-Ahn 1987:101–2). Underlying the educational force propelling the migration are Korean tradition and culture, which emphasize education as a means to success, power, and status. Korean families, therefore, place high value on university education for their children. However, competition for university admission in Korea is intense. The competition coupled with the high value placed on education have led many families to prepare their children for college when they are very young, and for parents and teachers to exert considerable pressure on children aimed at school success. The U.S. educational system, which is viewed as less intense and less difficult than the Korean educational system, is therefore appealing; and migration is viewed by parents and children as a way to overcome one of the most difficult challenges they experience in Korea (Drachman et al. 1996).

Korean migration usually involves the departure of a family unit versus an individual member. The long wait for U.S. admission often fosters a state of family confusion, uncertainty and ambivalence regarding migration as members prepare to leave but don't know when departure will occur. Although children continue in school, they begin to lose motivation and interest in maintaining their studies while mothers become increasingly anxious throughout the waiting period. Meanwhile family members hold unrealistic expectations toward their prospective lives in the United States. Children who attend school six days a week with homework as the primary weekend activity look forward to weekends in the United States free from classes and homework. Thus, they expect their U.S. school life will be easier than their Korean school life. Parents anticipate they will be able to start a small business with the money saved in Korea for the United States and eventually achieve wealth in the new land (Drachman et al. 1996).

2. Transit/Intermediate Stage. In the transit phase, experiences may range from a perilous sea journey on a fragile boat (e.g., Haitians and Cubans) to an uncomplicated arrangement for travel on a commercial flight (many Asians, Caribbean Islanders, and Europeans). The duration of the transit phase may vary from hours to years. For example, an individual might live in limbo in a refugee camp for years while awaiting a final destination (Southeast Asians). The transit phase could also involve a long stay in a detention center while awaiting the decision of a receiving country regarding entry or deportation (Haitians). On the other hand, an individual may leave the country of origin and within hours connect with family or friends in the new country (many Asians, Caribbean Islanders, and Europeans).

For Dominicans and Koreans, the experiences in the transit/intermediate phase are generally uneventful. Most families and individuals apply for a U.S. visa in their home country and wait and prepare for eventual departure. After U.S. approval for entry, they arrive directly in the United States.

3. Resettlement Stage. Common issues in resettlement include the degree of cumulative stress experienced by the family, the discrepancy between expectations and actual quality of life in the United States, the reception and the opportunity structure of the receiving country, and the extent of services available to the family. Cultural issues assume prominence and include different views between the home and "host" country on health, mental health, help-seeking behavior, education, child-rearing practices, gender role behavior, and different levels of acculturation among family members. Cultural issues also surface in the interactions between service personnel and immigrant families. Depression, suicide ideation and suicide attempts, substance and chemical abuse, parent/child conflict, and wife and child abuse are among the commonly reported problems. As men and women shift in their traditional marital roles (particularly when wives are employed and husbands are unemployed or earn less than the wives), marital conflict or dissolution surface even among cultures where divorce is rare.

Family reunification issues commonly occur during the resettlement of Dominicans. Among these are different views between parent and child regarding migration. The parent often believes the migration will provide a better life for the child. Migration for the child, however, may be accompanied by a sense of lack of choice, and feelings of rejection by the immigrant parent who initially left the child for the new country and who is now considered responsible by the child for his/her leaving "loved ones" and the familiar environment of the home country. Complexity is added when parent/child separation is of long duration and the caretaker in the home country is viewed by the child as the "real" parent (Drachman et al. 1996).

If the caretaking arrangements formed in the premigration stage and during parental absence are unsatisfactory, the child may be resentful for the initial separation from the parent, the problematic caretaking arrangements, and finally the upheaval of his/her recent migration. The parent, on the other hand, may feel guilty about the difficulties created for the child by the migration or view the child as ungrateful for the sacrifices made on the child's behalf. These issues may be expressed in family conflict such as a child's or adolescent's oppositional behavior at home and/or in school, acting out in the community, substance abuse, a parental response of increased discipline resulting in little situational change or conflict escalation and finally parental sense of loss of control over the child (Drachman et al. 1996).

A child may reunify with his/her family that has a different structure—stepfather/ mother or step- or new biological siblings. Thus the child and family members may experience each other as strangers. The "family/stranger" quality may be compounded if the step- or biological children have grown up or have acculturated to the United States, while the behavior of the reunified child is culturally different and perceived by the siblings as "strange." Moreover, the reunified child may be viewed as the intruder. In some families, these issues are expressed in scapegoating the reunified child, divided loyalties between parents regarding their children, marital conflict, and depressed or defiant behavior of the reunified child, often reflected in withdrawal or acting out in home, school, or community (Drachman et al. 1996).

Parental authority and strong discipline of children are highly valued parental responsibilities in the Dominican Republic. When Dominican children assume ways of thinking and behaving similar to their U.S. peers by asserting levels of independence deemed inappropriate by their parents, and when they question and challenge parental discipline and authority, parent/child friction often surfaces. Anger and disappointment in a child who is perceived by the parents as rebellious and defiant and for whom the parent has sacrificed are common parental reactions. Children, on the other hand, view their parents as inflexible, overly strict, and "out of step" with the "ways of Americans."

Resettlement may be experienced as inordinately stressful when several of the preceding family reunification and cultural adjustment issues are present or occur concurrently. In desperation, some parents respond by returning a child to relatives in the Dominican Republic. Thus, parent/child separation reoccurs and the child's experiences of loss, separation, and a sense of rejection multiply (Drachman et al. 1996).

Although Dominicans are Catholic, their cultural belief in spiritism is practiced throughout the migration process and during stressful periods in resettlement. Spiritism is a belief system that assumes the visible world is surrounded by an invisible world of good and evil spirits that influence life events and behavior (Delgado 1988:36). It is both a worldview and a healing tradition. As a worldview, spiritism assumes outside forces have significant control over one's life. Thus, a practice approach with a Dominican client that emphasizes control over one's destiny may be discordant with the client's worldview.

Dominicans may seek the assistance of a folk healer for help with an illness or a social, interpersonal, or mental problem as it is assumed these problems may be caused by forces in the invisible world. Service personnel, therefore, require familiarity with the cultural help-seeking behavior of Dominicans and their healing traditions.

U.S. race relations heavily influence Dominican resettlement. Dominicans whose ancestry is a blend of African, American Indian, and Spanish peoples range in color from dark, medium, or light brown to white. Although race is a factor in Dominican society, it is intertwined and confounded by social class (Charles 1992; Wiltshire 1992). Specifically, money, power, education, and social class mediate and qualify a societal preference for European physical traits over African physical traits. In contrast to the United States, race alone in the Dominican Republic does not translate into a social structure of hierarchy and exclusion. Moreover, race does not assume an important role in ascribing a subordinate position for individuals with "African features" and color (Charles 1992:107). Thus, in the Dominican Republic an individual with "African features" and color is not defined primarily by physical traits or race. The experiences of Dominicans with African features and color living in the United States, however, are different, as they tend to be viewed as black. Therefore, these individuals encounter racist experiences similar to those of African Americans (Wiltshire 1992:184). Although they migrated for a better life, they are placed in a minority status in the United States. To protect themselves from identification with a minority status and racist society, some immigrants "cocoon themselves in their national identity" (Wiltshire 1992:184).

Many Dominican families live in poverty and "doubled up" in housing with other families during resettlement. Thus, the motive for the migration—better economic opportunity—may be unrealized; and the common stresses associated with migration cited earlier add complexity to the unrealized expectations.

Dominicans maintain strong ties to family members on the island. In addition to sending remittances to families, they are active in decision making regarding their children and other family members living in the Dominican Republic. On their return visits to the island, they participate in family, community, and other institutional activities. Since they are transnational immigrants, service personnel require an understanding of their two-country social field and the linkages between social networks in both countries (Drachman et al. 1996).

The arrival of the family as a group facilitates resettlement for Koreans as the family remains as a unit and the labor of individual members assists the family economically. However, the presence of the whole family also contributes to difficulties, because all members simultaneously face adjustment in a country that is vastly different in culture and language from Korea; and each member experiences unique stress (Drachman et al. 1996).

Language presents significant barriers. Although most newly arrived children unfamiliar with the language of their new land experience discomfort, Korean children may have added difficulties due to limited opportunity for bilingual education. There are also unrealistic expectations held by school and parents that the children will easily "catch up." These issues are compounded by the Korean value for education as a means to success, which fosters parental expectations of children's high-level school performance despite language difficulties. Thus, the newly arrived child who is expected to "catch up" while receiving little language assistance and whose parents expect high-level school performance may become anxious (Drachman et al. 1996).

Language difficulties for adults (which may persist) limit opportunities to move beyond low-paying labor-intensive jobs or employment outside the ethnic community (Hurh and Kim 1984:101–7; Nah 1993). Language problems limit understanding of the U.S. system of business and its regulations, creating confusion in initiating and maintaining a business. Well-educated Koreans who have not acquired sufficient English often experience shame and guilt that results in a sense of responsibility for problems in the family's existence. Also, parents whose acquisition of English remains limited often experience a sense of inadequacy as they are unable to help children with their studies or school-related issues.

Employment issues exert a significant influence on the family. Many Koreans who start a small business a few years after their arrival work long hours on weekdays and weekends (7:00 a.m.–10:00 p.m.) with most family members working in the business (husbands, wives, older children, grandparents). The multiple roles for wives may be overwhelming as they begin work early in the morning; some return home at 4:00 p.m. to cook and care for children; return to work by 6:30 p.m.; and finally assist in closing the business at 10:00 p.m. (Yu 1982:53). Children who are expected to complete their studies and perform well in school may also work in the business. Physically and mentally exhausted at the end of the day, parents have limited energy or time to interact or confer with their children on their interests or needs; and couples who are together twenty-four hours a day tend to neglect their marital relationship (Drachman et al. 1996).

The economic needs of the family that require wives to work often create a shift in the traditional Korean family structure, which ascribes the role of husband as breadwinner and absolute authority and wife as homemaker and subordinate to the husband. Since wives contribute to the economic support of the family and as they achieve greater economic independence, some become more assertive and demand more equality in their marital relationship. Husbands, however, remain strongly attached to the patriarchal tradition. Thus, marital conflict may surface, culminating in separation or divorce for some families (Nah 1993).

Intergenerational conflicts between parents and children as well as grandparents, their adult children, and grandchildren assume prominence during resettlement. For example, conflicts between parents and children often occur when children develop ways of thinking and behaving comparable to their U.S. peers by communicating independence; expressing individual desires, choices, and thoughts; and conveying parity in their relations between generations. Parents commonly experience this "individualistic way of thinking" as a loss of the Korean heritage and tradition that values mutuality, interdependence, and filial piety—values that constitute for parents family unity and integrity. Moreover, some parents are fearful that the children's way of thinking will create selfishness and indifference to parents. Children, on the other hand, are often frustrated, angry, or contemptuous toward parents' inability or unwillingness to learn the "U.S. life style and ways of behaving," Thus, separate social worlds between parents and children emerge; and some parents who are concerned about the loss of control over their children exercise greater authority over children, which results in continued or escalated conflict (Drachman et al. 1996).

Conflicts between the aged, their adult children, and grandchildren may occur as a result of a shift in status for the aged. In Korea, older persons are revered; they are assigned high status in all social settings; and their views are important in family decisions. In the United States some experience a sense of devaluation. For example, many older persons care for grandchildren whose behavior and communication with grandparents may be experienced by the elders as disrespectful.

The vast differences in culture between Korea and the United States add complexity to resettlement. Beliefs in harmony, patience, contentment, and simplicity derived from Taoism are central to Korean culture. Through Buddhism, Koreans stress the importance of strength to overcome difficulties, endurance of pain, and calmness while facing difficult circumstances. Filial piety derived from Confucianism is expressed in families as children defer to parents who are revered. It is expressed in school as teachers are treated with great respect by students. In turn, teachers are expected to demonstrate a level of dedication to students comparable to that of parents. It is expressed in the workplace as employers are entitled to respect and love from employees while employers are responsible for the welfare of employees in important aspects of their lives—economic, psychological, physical. These beliefs foster a cultural emphasis on interdependence, interrelatedness, and high value for the collective unit such as the family, the community, and the society.

The significant cultural differences between Koreans and Americans, with the former group emphasizing the primacy of the collective and the latter emphasizing the primacy of the individual, not only influence resettlement in realms of family, work, social, and educational life but also have implications for practice. Specifically, helping approaches that are undergirded by notions of self-determination, individual choice, and control over one's life are likely to be discordant with the belief systems and social functioning of Korean clients (Ewalt and Mokuau 1995).

As illustrated in the preceding discussion the premigration experiences of Dominicans and Koreans influence the nature of their resettlement. For Dominicans, who generally leave their country as single individuals, family reunification becomes a central issue in resettlement. Since Koreans commonly depart as a family unit, all members simultaneously experience the stresses of migration. The social, economic, or educational reasons for each group's migration are different. The different belief systems and value orientations held by each group color their experiences in each phase. In resettlement, both groups experience different levels of acculturation among family members, intergenerational conflict, and discrepancy between expectations and actual quality of life in the United States and cumulative stress associated with the migration.

ILLUSTRATION AND DISCUSSION

The couple described in the following example emigrated from Russia and arrived in the United States in 1988. The case illustrates the intermingling of experiences in the different migration stages and their cumulative effect. The role age plays in the migration process, the client's vulnerability and resilience, and the supports provided by a service organization and the couple's family are also portrayed.

Anna (63) and Yacov (74) were well educated. Anna had been employed as an engineer in Russia; Yacov was a mathematician. In addition to Russian, their native language, both were fluent in German. Upon arrival, they could not speak English. Although both were Jewish, they were not religious. Resettlement and counseling services were provided by a Jewish Family Service agency. Their worker was a Russian émigré who had recently completed graduate social work training in the United States.

Many crises occurred shortly after the couple arrived. Anna, who became ill, was hospitalized and diagnosed as having heart and liver disease and gastrointestinal problems. Following hospital discharge, her psychological functioning declined. She cried often, and she couldn't sleep or eat. She stared out the window most of the day. Yacov told the worker he had never seen her behave this way. He also said she threatened to kill herself.

When questioned about a history of depression, the couple indicated there was none. Shortly thereafter, Anna was rehospitalized for depression. While in the hospital, she wouldn't talk to the psychiatrist. It was discovered later that she feigned taking the antidepressant medications prescribed by the psychiatrist because she was suspicious of them.

In the first few months Anna's moods alternated between depression and anger. The mood shifts were associated with the following issues, which were prominent in the client/worker discussions.

Anna was angry at Yacov for pressuring her to leave Russia. She had worked her adult life and was a highly respected professional in her native country. She was active in her community. Her family was together, and she had friends. Here she had no one. She couldn't work. She couldn't speak English. She believed there was no time in her life to rebuild what was lost. Her son Alexei, and granddaughter, Natasha, with whom she was close and who had lived with Anna and Yacov for years, were still living in Russia. Her son Ivan, his wife, Katya, and their two sons, who also had emigrated, were detained in Rome. No one knew if they would be allowed to come to the United States. Although Anna was concerned about them, she also blamed Katya for their problems, as Katya initiated the decision to leave.

Katya's desire to emigrate grew out of a rise in anti-Semitism. Although the Soviet government at the time supported more openness, the openness also permitted overt anti-Semitic expression. Thus, virulent attacks against Jews by grassroots organizations increased. Concerned about the future for her sons, Katya therefore wanted to leave the country. Since Yacov was close to Ivan and his grandsons, he supported their decision to emigrate. He also wanted to accompany them and pressured Anna into agreeing that they, too, should leave.

Anna discussed her disappointment in U.S. life. She criticized the U.S. hospitals and doctors. In Russia, she said one has time to recuperate in a hospital or recuperate in a dacha (country home). Doctors in Russia made housecalls. Medicines there were paid for. Their streets were clean and safe. She ruminated over the past—the losses of her parents and brother during World War II, and the years of starvation at that time.

Yacov, however, was overwhelmed by concern that Ivan and his family would not be able to come to the United States. He insisted the worker pressure the "bureaucrats" to admit them. Although the worker explained she had no power over immigration matters, Yacov persisted in his request. The worker agreed she would explore the issue. The following outlines the results of the worker's exploration and the issues discussed with Yacov regarding the detention of Ivan's family.

Yacov knew that prior to the late 1980s, few people were permitted to leave the Soviet Union. He was also aware that emigration regulations in the Soviet Union were relaxed as a result of the new policies of openness (glasnost) and restructuring (perestroika). Thus many people were permitted to emigrate and many arrived in the United States. The reasons for the detention of many, the worker explained, was due to U.S. law, which involved a per country limit for the number of persons permitted to enter the United States. Since so many émigrés from the Soviet Union arrived in the United States, the Soviet Union country quota was exhausted. Also, the United States no longer considered the émigrés as refugees because of their newly acquired freedoms in the Soviet Union. Thus, they could not enter the United States as refugees. The exhausted country quota and the denial of refugee status therefore left many individuals from the Soviet Union stranded and living in limbo in Rome.

The worker's explanation of the detention, however, was met with distrust and skepticism as Yacov said, "she sounded like a Russian bureaucrat." Since the worker was bicultural and bilingual, she sensed Yacov's response was rooted in the different views held by Russians and "Americans" on institutions and their employees. Specifically she knew it was common in Russia to view institutional personnel as "bureaucrats" who followed government rules and procedures and who ultimately blocked the requests of people. She also knew Russians commonly manipulated "bureaucrats" or persisted in their request in order to receive what was needed. Although she explained that many organizations in the United States were not government controlled, Yacov's distrust persisted as he pressured her to "pull strings" so that Ivan's family could come to the United States. Yacov's lack of information regarding Ivan's situation, which made him anxious, and his lingering skepticism of the worker's reason for the detention led the worker to pursue other avenues to help. Ultimately she found a group of émigrés in a neighboring state who were participants in a Jewish organization that was pursuing the situation of Russian detainees. The worker connected Yacov to this group. She also connected him to an émigré family in the community whose family members were also detained. The agency provided transportation for Yacov, Anna, and the other family to attend the group meetings. Yacov welcomed the connection to the group and was actively involved in it. The advocacy efforts of this group (and others) led to the eventual release of many detainees. Ivan's family was among them.

Upon arrival, the agency assisted Ivan's family in locating housing close to Anna and Yacov's apartment. Anna assumed the caretaking of her grandsons, which enabled her son and daughter-in-law to attend English language classes and pursue employment. Anna also began to learn English and her depression began to subside.

Eight months after Ivan's family arrived, Yacov experienced severe headaches, which were the precursor to a stroke. He died from the stroke two and a half years after arrival in the United States.

Anna relapsed into another depression. She accepted the worker's referral to a psychiatrist. She was able to discuss her concerns with him and took the antidepressant medications he prescribed.

Anna's grief from the loss of Yacov was intense as it was intertwined with the other recent losses. Nonetheless, she was able to regain functioning in a few months. She continued to learn English. She took care of her grandchildren, and she became active in a Russian émigré community.

Although immigrants commonly experience losses of family, friends, community, work, and natural support systems, these losses often have a different meaning for the aged. As Anna indicated, "there was no time to rebuild what was lost." Thus, the sense of time and hope to build a new and better future—a view commonly held by younger immigrants is muted for Anna as well as for other older newly arrived individuals.

Health and mental health issues affect all immigrants. Older immigrants, however, are particularly vulnerable. Anna experienced both health and mental health problems that occurred shortly after her arrival. She was hospitalized for physical ailments of heart and liver diseases and she suffered from depression. Yacov, who arrived in the United States at age 74, died of a stroke at age 76. Anna, who arrived at 63, was a widow living in a new land at 65. Thus it is reasonable to assume the interaction between the age of the couple and the losses and stresses associated with their migration placed them at further risk.

The cumulative effect of experiences in the different migration stages are apparent in the case. In the premigration phase, the couple struggled with numerous issues that revolved around the "pros and cons" of emigration. Based on a desire to be with their son's family, the couple decided to leave their country. However, in the transit phase, one family was detained in Italy and the other arrived in the United States. Thus, a desire to be with one's family led to family separation. In resettlement, the separation of the two families was a major problem.

The case also illustrates how immigrants' lives may be caught between the governments of different countries. When this occurs, it is necessary for workers to explore and understand the complex immigration issues that create clients' personal problems. The understanding leads to different types of interventions, such as helping a client obtain legal assistance or connecting a client to another system that addresses the immigration issue relevant to the client's situation. The latter was the intervention used by the worker as she connected Yacov to an organization that was advocating on behalf of Russian detainees.

Cultural issues surfaced in several areas of the work. Anna's refusal to talk to a psychiatrist during her hospitalization was in part due to her life in Russia where psychiatrists were often used as a form of social control. Also in Russia talking therapy as a helping approach was not used. These factors, combined with a United States helping approach that involved an open discussion with a psychiatrist who was a stranger, led Anna to be suspicious. Thus, she feigned taking the antidepressant medications prescribed.

Yacov's expectation of the worker's power with regard to the release of Ivan's family was culturally based. His skepticism and distrust of the worker's rationale for the Russian detainees was also culturally based. Since the worker was bicultural she was able to recognize the roots of the cultural misunderstanding and intervene in accordance with this understanding.

The mediators of stress included the couple's strengths, the support of the family, and the provision of services by the agency and the Russian émigré community. The couple's high level of education was helpful background for adjusting to the complexities of U.S. life. Anna's fluency in two languages facilitated the learning of English. The caretaking of grandchildren that Anna assumed provided her with a sense of contribution to the family and increased her social interaction. Yacov's persistence enabled him to become active in pursuing the reunification of the families and increased his social interaction as well. Needless to say, Ivan's family was a support for Anna and Yacov, and Anna and Yacov were supports for Ivan's family.

The agency acted as a buffer of stress by connecting the family to medical facilities and medical personnel, assisting in family reunification, locating housing, and providing counseling. The strong Russian émigré community where the families resettled enabled Anna to pursue her future life without Yacov.

CONCLUSION

Many immigrants in the United States have adapted well. However, the difficulties associated with the migration process have rendered others vulnerable and in need of services. The unique stresses that accompany migration, the supports that buffer the stress, and the migration framework presented in the discussion provide background knowledge to understand and assist immigrants in need. Although the background is important for serving individuals, families, and groups, social workers also need to address the recent policies that disqualify immigrants from benefits and services and curtail the number of families able to reunify. These policies are likely to limit immigrants' social and economic integration in U.S. society. Documentation of the problems for individuals and families that derive from the new policies is necessary to adequately advocate on behalf of this group. Social workers will also need to join with other groups working on behalf of immigrants to strengthen the existing humanitarian force—a force that has had an historic influence on the nation's policies toward newcomers. Since immigrants and their children will account for 27 percent of the U.S. population by 2040 (Fix and Passel 1994:40), their well-being is critical to the nation.

References

Adams, J. 1989. "A Description of Some Perceptions and Psychological Features of Jamaican Immigrants." In V. J. Clarke and E. River, eds., *Establishing New Lives. Selected Readings on Caribbean Immigrants in New York City,* pp. 11–14. New York: Caribbean Research Center, Medgar Evers College.

Allodi, F. and A. Rojas. 1983. "The Health and Adaptation of Victims of Political Violence in Latin America." In P. Pichot, P. Berver, R. Wolf, and K. Tan, eds., *Psychiatry: The State of the Art.* New York: Plenum Press.

Altonji, J. and D. Card. 1991. "The Effects of Immigration on the Labor Market of Less Skilled Natives." In J. Abowd and R. Freeman, eds., *Immigration Trade and the Labor Market,* pp. 44–67. Chicago: University of Chicago Press.

Ayres, D. 1994. "Feinstein Faults Aliens Proposal." *New York Times,* October 22, p. A1.

Beck, R. 1994. "The Ordeal of Immigration in Wausau." *Atlantic Monthly* (April):84–97.

Berger, R. 1997. "Adolescent Immigrants in Search of Identity: Clingers, Eradicators, Vacillators and Integrators." *Child and Adolescent Social Work Journal* 14:263–75.

Berry, J. W., U. Kim, T. Minde, and D. Mok. 1987. "Comparative Studies of Acculturative Stress." *International Migration Review* 21:491–512.

Borjas, G. 1996. "The New Economics of Immigration." *The Atlantic Monthly* (November):72–80.

Brimelow, P. 1995. *Alien Nation: Common Sense About America's Immigration Disaster.* New York: Random House.

Brown, G. 1982. "Issues in the Resettlement of Indochinese Refugees." *Social Casework* 62:155–59.

Butterfield, F. 1991. "Asians Spread Across a Land and Help Change It." *New York Times,* February 24, p. A22.

Canino, I. A. and J. Spurlock. 1994. *Culturally Diverse Children and Adolescents: Assessment, Diagnosis, and Treatment.* New York: Guilford Press.

Caplan, N., J. K. Whitmore, and Q. L. Buie. 1984. *Southeast Asian Refugee Self-Sufficiency Study.* Ann Arbor, Mich.: Institute for Social Research.

Charles, C. 1992. "Transnationalism in the Construct of Haitian Migrants' Racial Categories of Identity in New York City. In N. Glick-Schiller, L. Basch, and C. Blanc Szanton, eds., *Towards a Transnational Perspective on Migration: Race, Class, Ethnicity and Nationalism Reconsidered,* pp. 101–23. New York: New York Academy of Sciences.

Choi, G. 1997. "Acculturative Stress, Social Support, and Depression in Korean American Families." *Cross-Cultural Practice with Couples and Families* 2:81–97.

Chow, J. 1999. "Multiservice Centers in Chinese American Immigrant Communities: Practice Principles and Challenges." *Social Work* 44:70–81.

Clad, J. 1996. "Slowing the Wave." In R. E. Long, ed., *Immigration,* pp. 151–60. New York: H. W. Wilson.

Cox, D. 1985. "Welfare Services for Migrants: Can They Be Better Planned?" *International Migration Review* 23:73–93.

Delgado, M. 1988. "Groups in Puerto Rican Spiritism: Implications for Clinicians." In C. Jacobs and D. Bowles, eds., *Ethnicity and Race: Critical Concepts in Social Work,* pp. 24–32. Washington, D.C.: National Association of Social Workers Press.

Derbyshire, R. 1969. "Adaptation of Adolescent Mexican Americans to United States Society." In E. Brody, ed., *Behavior in New Environments.* Beverly Hills, Calif.: Sage.

DeWind, J. 1990. "Haitian Boat People in the United States: Background for Social Service Providers." In D. D. Drachman, ed., *Social Services to Refugee Populations,* pp. 7–56. Washington, D.C.: National Institute of Mental Health.

Drachman, D. 1995. "Immigration Statuses: Their Influence on Service Provision, Access and Use." *Social Work* 40(2):188–97.

Drachman, D. and A. Halberstadt. 1992. "Stage of Migration Framework As Applied to Recent Soviet Emigres." In A. S. Ryan, ed., *Social Work with Immigrants and Refugees* 63–75. New York: Haworth Press.

Drachman, D., Y. H. Kwon-Ahn, and A. Paulino. 1996. "Migration and Resettlement Experiences of Dominican and Korean Families." *Families in Society* 77(10):626–38.

Drachman, D. and A. S. Ryan. 1991. "Immigrants and Refugees." In A. Gitterman, ed., *Handbook of Social Work Practice with Vulnerable Populations,* pp. 618–46. New York: Columbia University Press.

Dugger, C. 1997. "Immigrant Study Finds Many Below Income Limit." *New York Times,* March 16, p. A17.

Ewalt, P. and N. Mokuau. 1995. "Self Determination from a Pacific Perspective." *Social Work* 40(2):168–75.

Fabrega, H. 1969. "Social Psychiatric Aspects of Acculturation and Migration: A General Statement." *Comprehensive Psychiatry* 140:1103–05.

Fisher, I. 1997. "A Town's Strange Bedfellows Unite Behind Chinese Refugees." *New York Times,* February 21, p. A1.

Fix, M. and J. Passel. 1994. *Immigration and Immigrants: Setting the Record Straight.* Washington, D.C.: The Urban Institute.

———. 1996. "Myths About Immigrants." In R. E. Long, ed., *Immigration,* pp. 161–70. New York: H. W. Wilson.

Fix, M. and W. Zimmerman. 1995. *Immigrant Families and Public Policy: A Deepening Divide.* Washington, D.C.: The Urban Institute.

Freidenberg, J., G. Implivale, and M. L. Skovron. 1988. "Migrant Careers and Well-Being of Women." *International Migration Review* 22:208–25.

Furnham, A. and S. Bochner. 1986. *Culture Shock: Psychological Reactions to Unfamiliar Environments.* New York: Methuen.

Garmezy, N. 1983. "Stressors of Childhood." In N. Garmezy and M. Rutter, eds., *Stress, Coping and Development in Children,* pp. 43–84. New York: McGraw-Hill.

Gelfand, D. and R. Bialik-Gilad. 1989. "Immigration Reform and Social Work." *Social Work* 34:23–27.

Glick-Schiller, N., L. Basch, and C. Blanc-Szanton. 1992. "Transnationalism: A New Analytic Framework for Understanding Migration." In N. Glick-Schiller, L. Basch, and C. Blanc-Szanton, eds., *Towards a Transnational Perspective on Migration: Race, Class, Ethnicity and Nationalism Reconsidered,* pp. 1–24. New York: New York Academy of Sciences.

Gonzalez, D. 1989. "Poor and Illegal Mexicans Lose Hope in New York." *New York Times,* pp. 43–84, p. B1.

Gosh, S. 1996. "Understanding Immigrant Entrepreneurs: Theoretical and Empirical Issues." In B. Ong Hing and R. Lee, eds., *Reframing the Immigration Debate,* pp. 131–54. Los Angeles: Leadership Education for Asian Pacifics and UCLA Asian American Studies.

Graves, T. 1967. "Psychological Acculturation in a Tri-Ethnic Community." *Southwestern Journal of Anthropology* 23:337–50.

Grinberg, L. and I. Grinberg. 1989. *Psychoanalytic Perspectives in Immigration and Exile.* New Haven: Yale University Press.

Hill, C. and A. Christensen. 1989. "Afflictive Need, Different Types of Social Support, and Physical Symptoms." *Journal of Applied Social Psychology* 19:1351–70.

Homel, T. H. and A. Burns. 1989. "Environmental Quality and the Well-Being of Children. *Social Indicators Research* 21:133–58.

Howe, M. 1990. "Study Asks New Safeguards for Refugees Seeking Asylum." *New York Times,* March 16, p. A11.

Huddle, D. 1993. *The Costs of Immigration.* Washington, D.C.: Carrying Capacity Network.

Hulewat, P. 1996. "Resettlement: A Cultural and Psychological Crisis." *Social Work* 41:129–35.

Hull, D. 1979. "Migration, Adaptation and Illness: A Review." *Social Science and Medicine* 3A:25–36.

Hurh, W. M. and K. C. Kim. 1984. *Korean Immigrants in America: A Structural Analysis of Ethnic Confinement and Adhesive Adaptation.* New Jersey: Fairleigh Dickinson University Press.

Hurtado, A. and K. Rodriguez. 1989. "Language As a Social Problem—The Repression of Spanish in South Texas." *Multilingual and Multicultural Development* 10:401–19.

Hutchinson, E. P. 1981. *Legislative History of American Immigration Policy 1798–1965.* Philadelphia: University of Pennsylvania Press.

Iglehart, A. P. and R. M. Becerra. 1996. "Social Work and the Ethnic Agency: A History of Neglect." *Journal of Multicultural Social Work* 4:1–20.

Jacob, A. G. 1994. "Social Integration of Salvadoran Refugees." *Social Work* 39:307–12.

Kadetsky, E. 1996. "Bashing Illegals in California." In R. E. Long, ed., *Immigration,* pp. 102–8. New York: H. W. Wilson

Keigher, S. M. 1997. "America's Most Cruel Xenophobia." *Health and Social Work* 22: 232–37.

Keller, S. 1975. *Uprooting and Social Change: The Role of Refugees in Development.* Delhi, India: Manohar Book Service.

Kim, B. C. 1978. *The Asian-Americans' Changing Patterns, Changing Needs.* Montclair, N.J.: Fairleigh Dickinson University Press.

Kunz, E. 1981. "Exile and Resettlement: Refugee Theory." *International Migration Review* 15:42–51.

Kuo, W. 1976. "Theories of Migration and Mental Health: An Empirical Testing on Chinese-Americans." *Social Science and Medicine* 10:297–306.

Kwon-Ahn, Y. H. 1987. "The Korean Protestant Church: The Role in Service Delivery for Korean Immigrants." Unpublished Ph.D. diss., Columbia University School of Social Work, New York.

Lamm, R. and G. Inhoff. 1985. *The Immigration Time Bomb: The Fragmenting of America.* New York: E. P. Dutton.

LaVietes, R. 1979. "The Puerto Rican Child." In J. D. Noshpitz, ed., *Basic Handbook of Child Psychiatry,* vol. 1, pp. 264–71. New York: Basic Books.

Le, D. D. 1983. "Mental Health and Vietnamese Children." In G. J. Powell, ed., *The Psychosocial Development of Minority Children,* pp. 373–84. New York: Brunner/Mazel.

Lee, S. and B. Edmonston. 1994. "The Socioeconomic Status and Integration of Asian Immigrants." In B. Edmonston and J. Passel, eds., *Immigration and Ethnicity,* pp. 102–33. Washington, D.C.: The Urban Institute.

Lin, K. M. 1986. "Psychopathology and Social Disruption in Refugees." In C. William and J. Westermeyer, eds., *Refugee Mental Health in Resettlement Countries,* pp. 61–73. Washington, D.C.: Hemisphere.

Lipson, J. 1992. "The Health and Adjustment of Iranian Immigrants." *Western Journal of Nursing Research* 14:10–29.

Marlin, O. 1993. "Special Issues in Psychotherapy with Immigrants from Diverse Cultures." Paper presented at Spring Workshop Series, New York University, Washington Square Series.

Martin, J. and E. Martin. 1985. *The Helping Tradition in the Black Family and Community.* Silver Spring, Md.: National Association of Social Workers Press.

Mathews, L. 1994. "Social Workers' Knowledge of Client Culture and Its Use in Mental Health Care of English-Speaking Caribbean Immigrants." Unpublished Ph.D. diss., City University of New York, New York.

Mirdal, G. 1984. "Stress and Distress in Migration: Problems and Resources of Turkish Women in Denmark." *International Migration Review* 18:984–1003.

Monroe, S. M. 1983. "Social Support and Disorder: Toward an Untangling of Cause and Effect." *American Journal of Community Psychology* 11:81–97.

Morawska, E. 1990. "The Sociology and Historiography of Immigration." In V. Yans-McLaughlin, ed., *Immigration Reconsidered: History, Sociology and Politics,* pp. 187–240. New York: Oxford University Press.

Nah, K. 1993. "Perceived Problems and Service Delivery for Korean Immigrants." *Social Work* 38(3):289–96.

Newman, G. 1997. "Admissions and Denials: A Dialogic Introduction to Immigration Law Symposium." *Connecticut Law Review* 29(4):1395–1410.

North, D. S. 1974. "Immigrants and the American Labor Market." *Manpower Research Monograph, No. 31.* Washington, D.C.: U.S. Department of Labor.

Oberg, K. 1960. "Cultural Shock: Adjustment to New Cultural Environments." *Practical Anthropology* 7:177–82.

Ong Hing, B. 1996. "Reframing the Immigration Debate: An Overview." In B. Ong Hing and R. Lee, eds., *Reframing the Immigration Debate,* pp. 1–30. Los Angeles: Leadership Education for Asian Pacifics and UCLA Asian American Studies Center.

Padilla, A., R. Cervantes, M. Maldonado, and R. Garcia. 1988. "Coping Responses to Psychosocial Stressors Among Immigrants from Mexico and Central America." *Journal of Community Psychology* 16:418–27.

Padilla, Y. 1997. "Immigrant Policy: Issues for Social Work Practice." *Social Work* 42:595–606.

Park, E. 1996. "Asian Matter: Asian American Entrepreneurs in the High Technology Industry in Silicon Valley." In B. Ong Hing and R. Lee, eds., *Reframing the Immigration Debate,* pp. 155–78. Los Angeles: Leadership Education for Asian Pacifics and UCLA Asian American Studies Center.

Parker, S. and R. Kleiner. 1966. *Mental Illness in the Urban Negro Community.* Glencoe, New York: Free Press.

Passel, J. 1995. *Illegal Immigration: How Big a Problem?* Washington, D.C.: The Urban Institute.

Passel, J. and B. Edmonston. 1994. "Ethnic Demography: U.S. Immigration and Ethnic Variations." In B. Edmonston and J. Passel, eds., *Immigration and Ethnicity,* pp. 31–54. Washington, D.C.: The Urban Institute Press.

Pawliuk, N., N. Grizenko, A. Chan-Yip, P. Gantous, J. Mathew, and D. Nguyen. 1996. "Acculturation Style and Psychological Functioning in Children of Immigrants." *American Journal of Orthopsychiatry* 66(1):111–21.

Payne, R. L. and J. G. Jones. 1987. "Measurement and Methodological Issues in Social Support." In S. V. Karl and C. L. Cooper, eds., *Stress and Health: Issues in Research Methodology,* pp. 167–205. New York: John Wiley.

Pear, R. 1997. "Academy's Report Says Immigration Benefits the U.S." *New York Times,* May 18, p. A1.

Pearlin, L., M. Lieberman, E. Monoghan, and J. Mullin. 1981. "The Stress Process." *Journal of Health and Social Behavior* 22:337–56.

Pendleton, G. 1997. "Lawful Permanent Residence and the New Grounds of Inadmissibility." In I. Gomez, R. Berkower, N. Brill, S. Ignatius, N. Kelly, M. O'Sullivan, and E.

Stickney, eds., *Understanding the New Immigration Law* (97–14.02), pp. 55–67. Boston: Massachusetts Continuing Legal Education.

Philzacklea, A. 1983. "Introduction." In A. Philzacklea, ed., *One Way Ticket: Migration and Female Labor,* pp. 1–12. London: Routledge & Kegan Paul.

Ponizovsky, A. and E. Perl. 1997. "Does Supported Housing Protect Recent Immigrants from Psychological Distress?" *International Journal of Social Psychiatry* 43:79–86.

Preston, J. 1996. "Beating Increases Tension on Immigration." *New York Times,* April 6, p. A10.

Ramirez, M. 1984. "Assessing and Understanding Biculturalism-Multiculturism in Mexican American Adults." In J. L. Martinez and R. H. Mendoza, eds., *Chicano Psychology.* San Diego: Academic Press.

Rayner, R. 1996. "What Immigration Crisis?" *The New York Times,* January 7, section 6, p. 28.

Refugee Women's Council Inc. 1998. *Newsletter,* 1(1).

Rhee, S. 1996. "Effective Social Work Practice with Korean Immigrant Families." *Journal of Multicultural Social Work* 4:49–62.

Rohter, L. 1993. "Revisiting Immigration and the Open-Door Policy." *New York Times,* September 19, p. E3.

Rubin, G. 1981. "Language Policy and the Refugees." *Journal of Refugee Resettlement* 1:59–63.

Rutter, M. 1987. "Psychosocial Resilience and Protective Mechanisms." *American Journal of Orthopsychiatry* 57:316–31.

Scaperlanda, M. 1997. "Who Is My Neighbor? An Essay on Immigrants, Welfare Reform and the Constitution." *Connecticut Law Review* 29(4):1587–1626.

Schmitt, E. 1996. "Two Senior Republican Lawmakers Buck Party Effort to Bar Education for Illegal Aliens." *New York Times,* June 22, p. A6.

Schuck, P. 1984. "The Transformation of Immigration Law." *Columbia Law Review* 84(4):1359–1411.

Sluzki, C. E. 1979. "Migration and Family Conflict." *Family Process* 18:379–90.

Smith, J. and B. Edmonston. 1997. *The New Americans: Report on the Economic, Demographic and Fiscal Effects of Immigration.* Washington, D.C.: National Academy Press.

Spiro, P. 1997. "Learning to Live with Immigration Federalism." *Connecticut Law Review* 29(4):1627–46.

Stickney, E. 1997. "The Public Charge: Ground of Inadmissibility and the Affidavit of Support." In I. D. Gomez, R. Berkower, N. Brill, S. Ignatius, N. Kelly, M. O'Sullivan, and E. Stickney, eds., *Understanding the New Immigration Law* (97–14.02), pp. 123–75. Boston: Massachusetts Continuing Legal Education.

Suro, R. 1991. "Behind the Census Numbers, Swirling Tides of Movement." *New York Times,* March 30, p. B1.

——. 1996. *Watching America's Door.* New York: Twentieth Century Fund Press.

Taubman, P. 1988. "U.S. Holding Up Visas for Soviet Emigres." *New York Times,* July 8, p. A1.

Tilly, C. 1990. "Transplanted Networks." In V. Yans-McLaughlin, ed., *Immigration Reconsidered: History, Sociology and Politics,* pp. 79–95. New York: Oxford University Press.

Tran, T. V. 1991. "Sponsorship and Employment Status Among Indochinese Refugees in the United States." *International Migration Review* 25:536–50.

Tran, T. V. and D. L. Ferullo. 1997. "Indochinese Mental Health in North America: Measures, Status, and Treatments." *Journal of Sociology and Social Welfare* 24:3–20.

Turner, R. J. 1981. "Social Support As a Contingency in Psychological Well-Being." *Journal of Health and Social Behavior* 22:357–67.

U.S. Bureau of Census. 1970. *U.S. Census of Population.* Final Report, P.C. (1)-(1). Washington, D.C.: U.S. Government Printing Office.

——. 1980. *U.S. Census of Population.* Final Report, P.C. 80(1)-(1). Washington, D.C.: U.S. Government Printing Office.

———. 1990. *U.S. Census of Population*. Final Report. Washington, D.C.: U.S. Government Printing Office.

U.S. Committee for Refugees. 1989, October 20. *Refugee Reports: Update*. Washington, D.C.: U.S. Committee for Refugees.

U.S. Department of Health and Human Services. 1989. *Report to the Congress: Refugee Resettlement Program*. Washington, D.C.: U.S. Government Printing Office.

Williams, A. W., J. E. Ware, and C. A. Donald. 1981. "A Model of Mental Health Life, Events, and Social Supports Applicable to General Populations." *Journal of Health and Social Behavior* 22:324–36.

Williams, C. L. and J. W. Berry. 1991. "Primary Prevention of Acculturation Stress Among Refugees: Application of Psychological Theory and Practice." *American Psychologist* 46:632–41.

Wilson, P. 1996. "Securing Our Nation's Borders." In R. E. Long, ed., *Immigration*, pp. 96–101. New York: H. W. Wilson.

Wiltshire, R. 1992. "Implications of Transnational Migration for Nationalism: The Caribbean Example." In N. Glick-Schiller, L. Basch and C. Blanc-Szanton, eds., *Towards a Transnational Perspective on Migration: Race, Class Ethnicity and Nationalism Reconsidered*, pp. 175–88. New York: New York Academy of Sciences.

Wright, R. C. 1981. "Voluntary Agencies and the Resettlement of Refugees." *International Migration Review* 15:157–74.

Yans-McLaughlin, V. 1990. "Introduction." In V. Yans-McLaughlin, ed., *Immigration Reconsidered: History, Sociology and Politics*, pp. 3–18. New York: Oxford University Press.

Yu, E. Y. 1982. "Koreans in America: Social and Economic Adjustments." In S. K. Byong and H. L. Sang, eds., *The Korean Immigrant in America*. Montclair, N.J.: The Association of Korean Christian Scholars in North America.

Zuckerman, M. 1996. "Beyond Proposition 187." In R. E. Long, ed., *Immigration*, pp. 109–12. New York: H. W. Wilson.

24

Intimate Partner Abuse

Bonnie E. Carlson
Deborah Choi

Although violence toward intimates has undoubtedly existed for centuries, it was not until recently that violence and abuse in the context of adult intimate relationships was considered a social problem. Since being placed on the social problem agenda in the 1970s much has been learned about the nature of violence and abuse directed toward intimates as well as associated risk factors and consequences of such abuse. Although the etiology and risk factors for domestic violence have been a concern from the beginning, discussions of intimate partner abuse have rarely included a consideration of protective factors that may buffer those at risk from becoming violent or from becoming symptomatic as a result of victimization. This is a significant oversight insofar as a more complete understanding of protective factors as well as risk factors have implications for social policy, prevention, and treatment of partner abuse. This chapter examines partner violence in intimate relationships, specifically how it is defined, its prevalence, associated and contributing factors, risk and protective factors, consequences, and services and interventions to ameliorate it.

DEFINING AND EXPLAINING INTIMATE PARTNER ABUSE

From the time that it first emerged as a social problem, defining and explaining violence against women has been surrounded by controversy. Although most commonly called domestic violence, violence toward female intimate partners has acquired a wide variety of other labels, including woman abuse, woman battering, wife battering or abuse, marital violence, and most recently intimate partner violence or abuse. Examination of these different terms reveals several sources of variation: whether it is called violence or abuse, whether it is seen exclusively as a woman's problem, and whether it affects only married or heterosexual people.

As research has emerged identifying violence and abuse in the relationships of cohabiting and dating couples as early as junior high school (Burcky, Reuterman, and Kopsky 1988), scholars have been less inclined to label violence against women as marital violence or wife abuse unless they are referring to abuse in the context of marriage. Feminists tend to believe strongly that intimate partner violence should be framed as a gender-related problem of women. Others prefer to frame it in more gender-neutral terms, noting that women not only are victims of violence and abuse but also can be its perpetrators. The argument that men can be victims and women can be perpetrators has been made perhaps most persuasively by gay men and lesbians committed to ameliorating violence and abuse in same-sex partnerships (e.g., Carlson and Maciol 1997). The term "intimate partner violence" is increasingly preferred by federal agencies addressing this problem, such as the Centers for Disease Control and Prevention. Taking into account all of these concerns, the term "intimate partner abuse" will be used here in that "violence" connotes a narrower range of behavior, i.e., physical aggression, than the term "abuse," as elaborated below. At the same time, we acknowledge that although we are using a more gender-neutral term, it is the case that women are more likely to be victims of intimate violence than men, as will be discussed.

Intimate partner abuse can be defined as a pattern of behavior involving the threat or use of physical or sexual violence or emotional or psychological abuse perpetrated by an intimate partner with the potential to cause injury, harm, or death. Physical violence consists of pushing, shoving or slapping, punching, choking, beating up, cutting someone with a knife, and other acts of physical aggression. Examples of sexual violence include forcing someone to have sex against their will or to have sex with another person while the perpetrator watched. A wide range of potential behaviors have been classified as emotional or psychological abuse, such as ridicule; threats of violence; harming someone's children, pets, or property; isolating an individual from loved ones; and so forth.

A long-standing controversy has existed between advocates for abused women and scholars and researchers regarding the nature of intimate partner abuse, resulting in two different perspectives. The **feminist perspective** sees partner violence as a problem in which men victimize women in a pattern of escalating violence and abuse that will not stop on its own, having its origins in men's need or desire to control their female partners. In contrast, the **family violence perspective** has described intimate violence as a behavior that can be initiated by either men or women, not necessarily frequent or escalating in severity, and not always motivated by the desire to control. Johnson (1995) has attempted to resolve this debate by asserting that these two different points of view are informed by two different bodies of literature and arrive at two different conclusions regarding the nature of intimate partner violence, largely because they are studying essentially different phenomena. He labels these two phenomena as patriarchal terrorism and common couple violence.

> Patriarchal terrorism, a product of patriarchal traditions of men's right to control "their" women, is a form of terroristic control of wives by their husbands that involves the systematic use of not only violence, but economic subordination, threats, isolation, and other control tactics. . . .
>
> The common couple violence that is assessed by the large-scale random

survey methodology is in fact gender balanced, and is a product of a violence-prone culture and the privatized setting of most U.S. households. The patriarchal terrorism that is tapped in research with the families encountered by public agencies is a pattern perpetrated almost exclusively by men, and is rooted deeply in the patriarchal traditions of the Western family. (Johnson 1995:284, 286)

For the most part, in this chapter we consider what Johnson calls patriarchal terrorism.

How we define and conceptualize intimate partner abuse is important because these definitions will communicate what we see as the nature of the problem, who is affected by it, and what we should do about it. To the extent that intimate partner abuse is framed as a problem of women, male victims cannot exist. Thus gay men (or heterosexual men) who are victimized by their partners are rendered invisible. Similarly, lesbians who are victims of abuse will have difficulty being heard, and lesbians who inflict violence on their partners will find it difficult to get help to stop abusive behavior if our conception of an abuser is male. Similarly, if our definition of abuse is narrow, for example, consisting only of physical aggression, we will not be alert for indications of emotional or sexual abuse in the context of an intimate relationship.

Two recent sources of data are available on physical and sexual violence in the context of adult intimate relationships. The first is the National Violence Against Women (NVAW) telephone survey conducted jointly by the National Institute of Justice and the Centers for Disease Control and Prevention. A representative national sample of eight thousand women and eight thousand men was interviewed between November 1995 and May 1996 (Tjaden and Thoennes 1998). This study found that 25 percent of women and 8 percent of men reported physical or sexual assault by an intimate partner over the course of their lifetimes; 7.7 percent of women reported rape, whereas 22 percent of women reported being physically assaulted (Tjaden and Thoennes 1998).

The National Crime Victimization Survey (NCVS) collected information on crime from U.S. residents age 12 and older (Greenfeld et al. 1998). This study found women's one-year prevalence of violent victimization by a male partner to be 8 in 1,000 during the years 1992 to 1996. During that same period the authors estimated that there were nearly one million violent victimizations of women by intimate partners each year. Like other studies, the authors concluded that women are far more likely to be victimized by a loved one or acquaintance than by a stranger (Greenfeld et al. 1998). Rape and sexual assault data from 1992–1993 from the same survey indicate that as many as a half million rapes and sexual assaults occur yearly in females over age 12, a quarter of which are committed by intimates (Bachman and Saltzman 1995).

However, the NVAW and NCVS studies found substantially lower one-year incidence rates than previous studies such as the 1985 Second National Family Violence Survey conducted by Straus, Gelles, and colleagues on a national probability sample of individuals. These researchers found that acts of physical violence such as slapping, punching, and beating up were reported by about 11 percent of women during the previous year and by about 10 percent of men (Straus and Gelles 1986). Numerous other studies of adult domestic violence have found comparable rates for men and women. Other, more recent, smaller-scale studies generally concur with these findings. Using data from couples, some researchers have concluded that both genders tend to underreport their own violence when rates reported by their partners are used for comparison. It appears that men are especially likely to underreport their own severe violence (Fagan and Browne 1994). Overall, these studies suggest that at least 1.3 million women over age 18 experience physical violence at the hands of an intimate partner (Tjaden and Thoennes 1998).

In terms of the nature of intimate violence, minor acts of violence are more prevalent than severe acts (e.g., more pushing and slapping than beating up or kicking) across most studies (Aldarondo 1996; Pan, Neidig, and O'Leary 1994). To a large extent, it appears that physical violence is accompanied or preceded by verbal aggression or psychological/emotional abuse (O'Leary, Malone, and Tyree 1994). Studies that have considered both physical and emotional abuse have found them to be highly correlated for both males and females (e.g., .63 for women and .74 for men in Magdol, Moffitt, and Silva [1999] and .55 for women and .60 for men in Capaldi and Crosby [1997]). Furthermore, partner violence has been found to be a bidirectional experience. That is, in couples where there is violence, more than likely both partners have used violence toward one another (e.g., Magdol et al. 1997). Finally, to a considerable extent, when violence occurs in an intimate relationship it tends not to be a onetime occurrence. A growing literature has examined intimate partner violence over time. For example, Aldarondo's (1996) longitudinal analysis following violent men from the 1985 National Family Violence Survey found that almost half of the men violent in one year (18 percent of the sample) were also violent for two years (8 percent), and half of those were violent for all three years.

Some have speculated that **rape** of wives by their husbands may be the most common type of sexual assault (Russell 1990). Marital rape is said to occur in approximately one-third to one-half of all violent marriages, most commonly in severely violent relationships (Campbell 1989a). Men rape their wives for a variety of reasons such as the need to assert their power and feel a sense of ownership over their wives, a sense of entitlement to sex, or due to sexual jealousy (Bergen 1998). Survivors of marital rape have been described as using a variety of strategies to manage or cope with sexual assault by their husbands. Initially, some women fail to label their experiences as rape or tell themselves that what has occurred will never happen again. As time goes on, if the rapes continue, victims develop strategies to minimize their risk of sexual assault or injury through active resistance, by giving in to avoid injury, by avoiding their husbands altogether, or by placating their husbands. Emotional survival strategies included dissociating themselves from the experience or using cognitive distortions that help them minimize the severity of the experience or focus on better times (Bergen 1998). Studies suggest that marital rape is not less harmful to women than rape by a stranger (Koss et al. 1994).

In summary, interpersonal violence in the context of intimate relationships has been defined in various ways, with the preferred current terminology being intimate partner abuse. This terminology encompasses violence against men as well as women in the context of a couple relationship, and abuse in dating and cohabiting as well as marital relationships. One-year prevalence of violence against women has varied across different studies from a low of less than 1 percent (Greenfeld et al. 1998) to more than 10 percent of adult women (Straus and Gelles 1986). Violence rates in dating and cohabiting relationships are significantly higher. Most violence consists of minor rather than serious acts of physical aggression, and intimate partner violence is often bidirectional. Emotional and sexual abuse often co-occur with physical violence in intimate relationships, with marital rape occurring most often in the context of severe physical abuse.

DEMOGRAPHIC PATTERNS

A number of demographic variations in incidence of intimate partner violence have been found. First, studies have consistently found that **low-income and poorly educated** women are more likely to experience violent victimization by an intimate partner than women from higher socioeconomic classes. For example, Greenfeld et al. (1998) report that women with incomes under $7,500 had a violence rate of 21 percent, whereas women with incomes over $75,000 had a violence rate of only 3 percent.

Research has consistently found that **younger women** are more likely to be violently victimized by an intimate partner. For example, 20 percent of 16- to 19-year-olds and 21 percent of 20- to 24-year-olds have reported nonlethal violence in contrast to 7 percent for 35- to 49-year-old women and 1 percent for 50- to 64-year-old women (Greenfeld et al. 1998).

Based on a recent review of the literature, it appears that lesbians are about as likely to be assaulted by an intimate partner as heterosexual women, although there are no methodologically sound studies of domestic violence in the lesbian community due to the difficulty of obtaining a representative sample (Carlson and Maciol 1997). There is more research on the prevalence of lesbian abuse than abuse of gay men by their partners. Depending on the definition of abuse used, and in particular whether it includes sexual and/or emotional abuse in addition to physical violence, studies have reported abuse in one-third to two-thirds of previous lesbian relationships (Lie and Gentlewarrier 1991; Lockhart et al. 1994; Renzetti 1992; Schilit et al. 1991). The growing literature on **lesbian violence** suggests that contributing factors and dynamics are also similar, although there are some unique risk factors that affect lesbians.

Research indicates that it is not only married women who are subject to victimization by their partners. Research on individuals who **cohabit** suggest that rates of physical violence are significantly higher than rates for married couples or those in dating relationships (Lane and Gwartney-Gibbs 1985; Magdol et al. 1998; Stets and Straus 1990). Furthermore, a growing body of research on violence in dating relationships has found even higher rates, with one study concluding that prevalence rates for dating violence range from 22 percent to 56 percent (Magdol et al. 1997). Women who are separated and divorced from their intimate partners also experience violence and abuse, especially divorced women who were *twenty-five times* as likely to experience violence as married women in the NCVS (Bachman and Saltzman 1995; Fagan and Browne 1994).

Substantial controversy has surrounded the issue of gender differences in rates of intimate partner violence. On the one hand are the recent government surveys, already discussed, that conclude unambiguously that **women** are far more likely than men to be violently victimized by an intimate. For example, the 1992–1993 rate of women's violent victimization by an intimate is 9.3 percent compared with a rate of 1.4 percent for men (Bachman and Saltzman 1995). Similarly, Tjaden and Thoennes (1998) report lifetime rates of physical or sexual assault by an intimate partner to be

25 percent for women compared with 8 percent for men. But other large-scale surveys such as the 1985 National Family Violence Survey reported comparable annual participation rates for men and women, 10 percent to 11 percent (Straus and Gelles 1986). In addition, a wide range of surveys of smaller, nonrepresentative samples of college and high school students report rates that are comparable for males and females (e.g., Burke, Stets, and Pirog-Good 1988). Some of these studies have concluded that women are as violent as men. However, these studies have been criticized for looking only at participation rates without taking into account frequency and severity of violence, which are often higher for males, as well as injury, which is far more likely to occur among women as a consequence of violence (Koss and Heslet 1992; Stets and Straus 1990).

Numerous studies have compared rates of intimate partner violence across **ethnic** groups, but there are no consistent conclusions regarding whether rates are higher, lower, or the same among people of color as compared with whites. For example, the recent NCVS survey found rates of nonlethal violence against white women to be somewhat lower (8.2 percent) than for African American women (11.7 percent), whereas rates for non-Hispanic women were 8.7 percent and Hispanic women 7.2 percent. Bachman and Saltzman (1995) concluded that there were no statistical differences in the 1992–1993 rates of intimate violence across ethnic/racial groups. However, other studies have found higher rates for Hispanic women. Using the 1985 NFVR, Straus and Smith (1990) reported substantially higher rates of marital violence, especially severe husband-to-wife violence in Hispanic as compared with white, non-Hispanic respondents, to some extent reflecting the younger age distribution of Hispanic Americans. Another difficulty with comparing across ethnic groups is the higher average socioeconomic status of whites compared with some nonwhite ethnic groups. This means that studies finding higher prevalence of partner violence in samples of ethnic minorities might be detecting the effects of poverty or lower educational attainment rather than ethnicity. Thus, racial and ethnic comparisons should control for such social class differences. However, aside from whether there are differences of prevalence across different ethnic groups, there may be other effects of **ethnicity** and **culture.** For example, definitions of violence or abuse may vary in different ethnic groups, risk factors may differ, the consequences of abuse may differ, and perceived options for addressing violence and abuse may differ.

SOCIETAL CONTEXT

Violence against women in the context of intimate relationships has existed for centuries. In fact, the right of married men to chastise their wives physically is said to have been granted when the Romans passed the first laws governing marriage in 753 B.C. (Dobash and Dobash 1977–78). English common law, too, on which American legal traditions are based, gave men the right to beat their wives, although this right was regulated. It has only been about 120 years since the legal prohibition against men beating their wives was established in the United States (Dobash and Dobash 1977–78). Thus, from a historical perspective, violence against women in the family has been tolerated by our legal system for centuries and had strong social support. It is against this backdrop of patriarchy that feminists first began to bring the issue of wife abuse to public attention in the 1970s. Given husbands' long-standing legal right to use violence against their wives, it is not surprising that our criminal justice system, largely administered by men, has been reluctant to end the right of men to use violence to control women and hold men accountable for their abuse. Nor is it surprising that women who have sought protection and assistance to leave abusive relationships have found it difficult to access the resources and services that would enable them to terminate such relationships. Thus women encountered at every turn a hostile environment that communicated that they should accept their plight. These contextual factors have been considered to contribute to partner abuse.

However, since the 1970s there have been extensive changes in our laws and in the criminal justice system, as well as in the social services and mental health systems designed to help ameliorate violence against women in the context of intimate relationships. For example, abusive men are more likely to be arrested than ever before, as well as convicted. Shelters are available to battered women in every state in our country, supported in most cases by the local departments of social services. Increasing numbers of health and mental health professionals are recognizing the impact of victimization on women's well-being. Although progress has been made, many issues remain to be addressed.

Societal factors have long been considered by feminists and others to be the primary explanations for intimate partner abuse. However, there is evidence that other kinds of factors can also play a contributing role or increase risk for becoming an abuser or victim. Although men as a group in our society are exposed to patriarchal values and traditional gender roles that dictate that men should be dominant and women should be passive, most men do not become physically and sexually abusive to their partners. And although studies find that abuse festers in a climate of poverty and deprivation, most poor women are not victims, nor are most of their partners abusive toward them. Researchers have found prediction of intimate partner abuse to be very complex, influenced by a multitude of factors beyond macro factors. For example, much research has shown that growing up in a violent home increases risk of becoming both abuser and victim (Magdol et al., 1999), although most who are exposed to such violence do not become abusers or victims.

VULNERABILITIES AND RISK FACTORS

A substantial literature has developed on the extent to which intimate violence creates risk and vulnerability in those who have been victimized. In general, three kinds of outcomes are of concern: homicide; injuries and other physical health sequelae; and psychological or mental health consequences or aftereffects.

Since the middle 1970s, of all female **murder victims,** about 30 percent were killed by intimates. Of the almost two thousand homicides committed by intimates in 1996, almost three-quarters of the victims were female (Greenfeld et al. 1998). National surveys have shown that female victims of homicide are substantially more likely to be killed by intimate partners such as a husband, ex-husband, or boyfriend than are male victims (Bachman and Saltzman 1995; Greenfeld et al. 1998).

Two recent national surveys, the NCVS and the NVAW, queried respondents about **violence-related injuries.** The NCVS reported that about half of all victims of violence from 1992 to 1996 said they were injured and of those, only one in five sought treatment, most often in emergency rooms (Greenfeld et al. 1998). The NVAW found that 31.5 percent of female rape victims and 39 percent of female physical assault victims were injured, only about one-third of whom received medical care. As with the NCVS, most of those who received care did so in an emergency setting (Tjaden and Thoennes 1998). The authors concluded that

> According to estimates generated by the NVAW survey, hospital emergency department personnel treated approximately 1.3 million adults for injuries related to rapes and physical assaults in the 12 months preceding the survey (128,700 female rape victims and 546,900 female physical assault victims). (10)

In addition, the Survey of Victims of Violence reported on 243,000 victims of intimate violence treated in hospital emergency departments. The most common injuries were bruises (48.6 percent) and cuts/stab wounds/internal injuries (24.1 percent) (Greenfeld et al. 1998). Thus, we can conclude that although injuries are common in the aftermath of partner abuse, most injured victims fail to receive treatment. This has contributed to the conclusion that there is a significantly higher need for medical services among abused as compared with nonabused women (Plicta 1996).

However, injuries are not the most common sequelae of intimate violence. Health sequelae of intimate partner violence have been extensively studied in recent years. The emerging consensus from this research is that abused women are very likely to experience compromised health related to their victimization. The more severe the emotional, physical, or sexual abuse, the greater the number of symptoms that are likely to be experienced (Follingstad et al. 1991), suggesting a "dose-response" effect. These findings are not surprising in light of what we know about the correlation between stress and physical health (Leserman et al. 1998). A variety of nonspecific symptoms are associated with partner abuse: poor appetite and other eating problems; dizziness; low energy, chronic fatigue and feeling weak; heart racing; headaches; difficulty sleeping; breathing problems; gastrointestinal problems (nausea, vomiting, diarrhea, constipation); back pain; muscle tension or soreness; and gynecological problems (Drossman et al. 1990; McCauley et al. 1995; Sutherland, Bybee, and Sullivan 1998). Thus, it is clear that abused women as a group tend to have poorer health than nonabused women. The implications of these abuse-related health problems are substantial for society, because abused women tend to have significantly higher health care utilization rates than nonabused women (Leserman et al. 1998).

With regard to **mental health** or psychological vulnerabilities resulting from partner abuse, a wide range of outcomes has been observed. Some women appear to function quite well despite being abused, whereas others function very poorly. A recent study of New Zealand 21-year-olds used the Diagnostic Interview Schedule to obtain psychiatric diagnoses on victims of intimate partner violence and nonvictims. Over half of victimized women met diagnostic criteria for one or more of fifteen diagnoses (six anxiety disorders, three mood disorders, two eating disorders, two substance use disorders, antisocial personality disorder and nonaffective psychosis), compared with 38.4 percent of nonvictimized women. Over one-third of the victims had a mood disorder and one-third had an anxiety disorder, significantly higher rates than nonvictimized women (Danielson et al. 1998).

In some cases victims who exhibit serious problems while being abused improve dramatically shortly after abuse ceases (Koss et al. 1994). However, in other cases women continue to exhibit mental health problems after abuse ends and require much support and professional assistance. For example, Goodman, Koss, and Russo (1993a) reported that postrape symptoms subside for most victims after about three months, but about one in four continue to experience severe symptoms long term. The most common psychological aftereffects for both rape and physical violence include shame, guilt, self-blame, and humiliation; depression and suicidal behavior; fear and anxiety; substance abuse; and in particular posttraumatic stress disorder (PTSD). In addition to the preceding, sexual assault survivors also commonly experience sexual dysfunction (Goodman et al. 1993a).

Depression is considered by some to be the most common response to battering (Campbell et al. 1997). Symptoms of depression have been reported by 38 percent (Cascardi and O'Leary 1992) to 78 percent of abused women (Follingstad et al. 1991). Depression was experienced by 41.6 percent of severely abused women in one study based on a nationally representative sample (Gelles and Straus 1988). Depressive symptoms as well as low self-esteem have been found to be significantly associated with the severity and frequency of abuse (Campbell et al. 1997; Cascardi and O'Leary 1992). Risk of suicide is elevated for women victimized by partner violence, especially African American women (Heron et al. 1997).

There is a growing consensus that PTSD may be the best diagnosis for many violence victims. Among the advantages of this diagnosis is that it conceptualizes the symptoms as a normal response to abnormal circumstances, thereby depathologizing characteristic victim response patterns (Goodman, Koss, and Russo 1993b). In addition to the intrusion and avoidance symptoms that are central to the PTSD diagnosis,

> other responses suggested as indicative of PTSD include dissociation, increased arousal, irritability, angry outbursts, hypervigilance, and sleep disturbances. Symptoms of depression and anxiety, although not included among symptom criteria for a diagnosis of PTSD, are nevertheless commonly found among trauma victims. (Goodman et al. 1993b:124)

However, there have been widely varying estimates of the extent of PTSD in samples of abused women. For example, PTSD has been found in 25 percent (Weaver et al. 1997), 33 percent (Cascardi et al. 1995), and 84 percent of physically abused women (Kemp, Rawlings, and Green 1991). Several reasons may account for these differences, including different samples (e.g., sheltered battered women versus those seeking help from counseling agencies) and different instruments used to measure PTSD. Part of the difference may also be due to differential exposure to trauma and to variations in vulnerability and coping as discussed later. It is not surprising that women who feel helpless in response to life-threatening violence would develop symptoms of PTSD such as nightmares, intrusive memories of the abuse, attempts to avoid situations that are reminiscent of the abuse, and difficulty sleeping and concentrating (Saunders 1994).

Substance abuse has also been found to be a problem in some battered women

(Gondolf 1998). For example, Plicta (1996) found that abused women were significantly more likely to have used illegal drugs in the past month (7 percent versus 1 percent of nonabused women) and in their lifetimes (40 percent versus 24 percent). In addition, abused women were significantly more likely to have received treatment for a substance abuse problem (23 percent versus 12 percent of nonabused women). Unfortunately, because most studies have cross-sectional designs they do not allow us to determine with certainty that partner abuse leads to substance abuse.

The literature on psychological aftereffects associated with abuse indicates wide variation in outcomes. One explanation for this variation pertains to the abuse itself. Victims experience differences in the types of abuse to which they are exposed (physical, emotional, and/or sexual), as well as variation in the frequency, severity, and duration of each type. It appears that there is increased risk for more adverse outcomes with exposure to more frequent, severe, and long-lasting abuse, as well as when a broader range of different types of abuse is experienced (Cascardi and O'Leary 1992; Koss et al. 1994). Abuse involving injury or life threats is likely to be more traumatic (Weaver and Clum 1996).

But variation in the extent of abuse to which one is exposed does not explain all the variation in mental health vulnerability, suggesting that there are mediating or moderating factors beyond those associated with the abuse itself that might account for the diversity of outcomes observed. Two kinds of mediating factors might help explain this variation: the presence of other risk factors as well as the presence of protective factors, discussed in the next section.

One factor associated with increased risk for poor mental health outcomes is a history of childhood sexual or physical victimization (Leserman et al. 1998; Weaver and Clum 1996). Such a history can make women more vulnerable to revictimization as an adult (Plicta 1996), as well as make it more difficult for victims to extricate themselves from abusive relationships due to abuse-related sequelae such as poor health, substance abuse, distress, and self-injurious behaviors (Weaver et al. 1997). This added risk factor is important for social workers to be aware of because substantial numbers of abused women have such histories, approximately one-third to one-half (Astin et al. 1995). Other risk factors that can exacerbate harm include existence of prior trauma (Goodman et al. 1993b), lack of social support, and presence of other stressors (Leserman et al. 1998), all common in the lives of abused women.

In summary, the vulnerabilities and risk factors resulting from intimate partner abuse are numerous. The most serious risks are homicide and suicide. A substantial subgroup of women who are victimized by intimate partners experience physical injury, some of them requiring medical care, most often received in emergency settings. Other health problems are even more common sequelae of abuse, such as gastrointestinal problems, chronic fatigue, difficulties breathing and sleeping, and other stress-related somatic complaints. As a result, abused women tend to experience poorer health than their nonabused counterparts. Mental health consequences include depression, PTSD, and substance abuse. Although some of these problems remit when abuse ceases, in other cases abuse-related problems continue long term. Substantial variability exists in abuse-related physical and mental health problems, in part related to the range of types of abuse experienced as well as their severity, frequency, and duration. But the seriousness of abuse cannot account for all the variability seen among abuse victims.

RESILIENCIES AND PROTECTIVE FACTORS

Another set of factors that may help to explain the diverse mental health outcomes in the aftermath of partner abuse are protective factors that buffer individuals from the harm normally associated with stressful or traumatic experiences. Some individuals, despite exposure to multiple risk factors, fail to succumb to the expected harmful effects; that is, they are resilient and well functioning. Many abused women, despite experiencing serious, traumatic violence and other forms of abuse, function remarkably well.

Little research exists regarding specific factors known to buffer victims from the harmful effects of intimate abuse. However, there is a growing literature on factors that buffer adults from the harmful effects of stress in general. This literature indicates that numerous factors are associated with resilience in the face of exposure to high levels of stress: social support, positive self-regard, cognitive appraisal strategies, the perception of control, maintaining a positive outlook, self-efficacy, spirituality, good health, and type of coping strategies used (Benishek and Lopez 1997; Valentine and Feinauer 1993; Wheeler and Frank 1988). Although some of these factors may be aspects of personality or temperament and thus relatively fixed, others are quite malleable and have implications for intervention.

Cognitive appraisal refers to the process by which responses to stress are mediated by our subjective perceptions of potentially challenging or traumatic events; that is, the meaning we attach to them (Lazarus 1991). People can attach quite different meanings to even overwhelmingly stressful or traumatic events such as rape or assault, of which the individuals themselves may or may not be aware. Bringing such meanings to awareness allows for the possibility of altering them. Stressors that are perceived to be outside of one's control can lead to feelings of helplessness or hopelessness, which are commonly experienced by some abuse victims (Campbell 1989b; Goodman et al. 1993b).

Social support has been extensively studied as a stress buffer and has been noted to be deficient in abused women (Mitchell and Hodson 1983). Support is thought to buffer stress in several ways, such as enhancing self-esteem, affecting perceptions of stressful events, and increasing knowledge of coping strategies. In addition, merely having a confidante available to talk to about one's problems has been shown to be beneficial (Cohen and Hoberman 1983).

As a group, abused women tend not to have a generous supply of protective factors. For example, abused women have been found to have little social support (Mitchell and Hodson 1983). They also tend to have insufficient material resources insofar as intimate partner violence is often correlated with poverty, especially for women of color (Heron et al. 1997; Sullivan et al. 1994). In addition, abused women often have physical and mental health problems resulting from the abuse, in particular depression, which can interfere with coping (Mitchell and Hodson 1983). They have little control over the abuse itself and are likely to use more emotion-focused than problem-focused coping strategies (Finn 1985), which are generally regarded as less effective in reducing stress. They have also been found to have problem-solving deficits (Arias, Lyons, and Street 1997; Benishek and Lopez 1997; Campbell 1989a). Conceptualized from a stress and coping perspective, battered women are deficient in coping resources, such things as good health, positive beliefs, problem-solving skills, social skills, material resources, and social support that can assist in mobilizing coping strategies (Heron et al. 1997; Lazarus and Folkman 1984).

Finn (1985) found that compared with people in general, his sample of help-seeking abused women used more passive coping strategies (such as trying to ignore the problem) and used fewer active, problem-solving behaviors such as reframing and seeking social support and spiritual support to cope with a variety of stressors. The higher the stress is, the more likely abused women are to use passive strategies, suggesting that overwhelming stress may interfere with effective problem solving (Finn 1985; Mitchell and Hodson 1983).

Others have suggested that the **coping strategies** used by abused women change over time as abuse escalates, particularly in regard to the attributions for why abuse occurs and what can be done about it. When violence occurs once or twice, it tends to be viewed as an aberration on the part of the abuser that will not occur again (Carlson 1997; Mills 1985). But when violence occurs repeatedly, women must manage it in some way, that is, attach some meaning to it and cope with its occurrence and aftermath. Most women work actively at denying that violence will reoccur as well as trying to prevent its reoccurrence. This may involve trying to change aspects of themselves to placate the abuser in the attempt to avoid his anger and dissatisfaction. These can be considered active coping strategies that are designed to modify the source of the stress, which they initially perceive to be themselves. During this time many women are quite active and creative in their attempts to protect themselves and their children from harm.

But because these kinds of strategies usually are not effective in stopping the abuse, women may begin to change their attributions about the source of the problem and come to see their partner as the cause of the abuse. At this point they may shift their coping and problem-solving efforts to their partner's behavior, his drinking, for example, or the way he deals with his anger. It appears that victims at these stages may not seek social support, and in fact may be attempting to hide the abuse from people they are close to, withdrawing from potentially supportive relationships. The abuser may also be trying to isolate the woman from sources of social support at this time. Most abuse victims are not seeking professional help for abuse at this time, although they may seek help for the effects of abuse, such as depression (Mitchell and Hodson 1983). At a later point in time, women may begin to accept that their abusive partners are not likely to change, despite their efforts, and may succumb to a sense of despair, using passive or avoidant coping, in a state that some have called learned helplessness (Walker 1977–78).

However, despite the lack of protective factors that have been found by researchers to buffer stress, many abused women are very active in their coping and have substantial strengths that they bring to bear upon their situations. It is important to remember that abused women are typically coping not only with the abuse itself and its effects on their own and their children's well-being, but also with many other stressors such as financial problems, their partner's extreme jealousy and possessiveness, substance abuse, and chronic conflict and tension (Finn 1985).

Through all of this, many strengths are evident in women victimized by intimate partners. Some of the characteristics of abused women that are viewed as liabilities can be reframed as strengths, such as **loyalty** to their partners, **persistent attempts to improve the relationship** based on the belief that children need a father in the home, and being **sensitive to the needs and desires** of other family members. Although all of these behaviors have been viewed as barriers to women's terminating abusive relationships, they can also be seen as indicators of their strengths. **Perseverance, humor,** and **spirituality** have also been identified as strengths (Gondolf 1998).

Despite the statistics provided earlier on the mental health sequelae of partner abuse, the majority of abused women continue to function as wives, mothers, employees, sisters, and friends. They are resilient in every sense of the word. It is important to remember that many of the samples studied in research on mental health problems were clinical samples of sheltered or help-seeking abused women who almost by definition were having difficulty coping. The majority of abused women, who experience "minor" acts of violence, do not seek help from professional providers. Although some abused women are socially isolated, others do receive social support, validation, and practical assistance from friends and family members (Davis and Srinivasan 1995; Sullivan et al. 1994). Although some may lack effective problem-solving and coping skills, others are extremely resourceful and creative about maintaining their own and their children's safety and well-being.

To some extent the needs of women victimized by partner violence will vary depending on their stage in relation to the change process (Prochaska, DiClemente, and Norcross 1992). That is, a woman who is in a violent relationship but not thinking about taking any action is likely to have different needs from a woman exiting a domestic violence shelter and contemplating a divorce. Whereas women who are in the precontemplation stage may need information about what constitutes abuse, women at the point of contemplating doing something about the abuse may need information about legal options and financial resources.

However, several critical psychosocial needs transcend the stage of readiness for change: support, validation, respect for decision making (i.e., self-determination), information about abuse, and concrete services. In addition, women in a chronically abusive relationship at any stage—even if they are no longer living with the abuser—need the protection afforded by law enforcement.

For example, three-quarters of the women in one shelter study had contacted the police in the previous six months an average of 3.43 times (Sullivan et al. 1992a). At the point of leaving the shelter, the most commonly needed resources of the women in this sample were material goods and services (84 percent), social support (79 percent), education (71 percent), financial aid (64 percent), legal help (62 percent), employment services (62 percent), transportation (58 percent), and child care (58 percent) (Sullivan et al. 1992a). Almost half the women exiting a domestic violence shelter in another study also needed housing (Sullivan 1991). Sullivan et al. (1992a:273) note that

> If a woman chose to end her relationship with her assailant, she was more likely to indicate the need to work on obtaining transportation, legal assistance, financial assistance, social support, and to further her education. Women of color were more likely than white women to mention needing health care, material goods, and resources for their children.

Research "suggests that alleviation of physical health symptoms, anxiety, and depression following cessation of abuse could be expected to be slow and gradual rather than immediate" (Sutherland et al. 1998:63). Thus, professional counseling or therapy, while not needed by all abused women, is needed by a subgroup of victims who do not improve after the violence stops, even following a supportive shelter stay. This is especially true for women with symptoms of PTSD, depression, or substance abuse.

PROGRAMS AND SOCIAL WORK CONTRIBUTIONS

Over the past three decades, awareness of domestic violence and the needs of abused women have grown dramatically in the mental health, criminal justice, health, and social service sectors. For the most part, social workers have not been in the forefront of service delivery for victims of intimate partner violence, although they have played a prominent role in delivering services to batterers, as described in the following. Programs and services for abused women, their abusive partners, and their children have also expanded.

Services for Abused Women. From the beginning, battered women's shelters, which first opened in the middle 1970s, have been in the forefront of programs designed to serve victims of intimate partner violence. Shelters have been especially important because of the role they have played in pressing for social change on behalf of victims of partner violence in addition to providing services to abused women and their children (Koss et al. 1994). By the mid-1990s, millions of dollars were being allocated to fund the more than 1,250 shelters across the country (Roberts 1998). States have played a key role in the development and support of services for victims of partner violence and are often the conduit for federally supported domestic violence services. Most shelters rely heavily on state and/or county funds for survival (Roberts 1998). A 1989 survey of statewide coalitions and state agencies dedicated to services for abused women found that the most widely available services were supportive counseling, support groups, specialized domestic violence shelters, and hotlines. The most significant deficiencies in services identified at that time were insufficient shelter services, especially for rural women, services for nonsheltered women, and lack of transitional housing (Davis, Hagen, and Early 1994; Koss et al. 1994).

Many battered women's advocates believe that many—perhaps most—abused women will eventually leave the relationship. However, most who eventually leave need and receive help to end the abusive relationship, and research documents that battered women are active in their help-seeking efforts (Sullivan et al. 1994). They receive such assistance from a combination of informal and formal sources. A qualitative study of fifty-five formerly abused women across seven cities identified two major sources of assistance: shelters and other professional help sources such as lawyers, counselors, and clergy; and informal sources, in particular parents, siblings, and friends. The kinds of assistance offered from both types of sources included validation, information about resources and alternatives, emotional support, and practical help (Davis and Srinivasan 1995; Horton and Johnson 1993). Survivors in some studies have indicated mixed feelings about the help offered by professionals and even shelters (Bowker and Maurer 1986; Davis and Srinivasan 1995). Clergy in particular were identified in one large study as more harmful than helpful (Bowker and Maurer 1986). In contrast, three studies have indicated that abused women rate agency-based services and shelters as somewhat to extremely helpful (Bowker and

Maurer 1986; Horton and Johnson 1993; McNamara et al. 1997). The women studied by Horton and Johnson (1993) rated shelters, physicians and hospitals, and professional counselors as the most helpful resources. The most helpful kinds of professionals were those who had been trained to understand the plight and constraints of victims.

Few controlled evaluations exist regarding the effectiveness of services for abused women. One exception is the advocacy intervention program of Sullivan and Campbell and their colleagues in Michigan. These researchers demonstrated the effectiveness of providing highly trained (but nonprofessional) advocates who assisted women who were leaving domestic violence shelters for ten weeks in identifying, accessing, and mobilizing needed resources (Sullivan et al. 1992b). Compared with women in the control group, women who received advocacy services were significantly more successful in obtaining resources such as material goods and services, emotional support, and education. Both groups reported lower levels of physical and psychological abuse, depression, anxiety, and emotional attachment to their assailant compared with where they were at the point of shelter entrance (Sullivan et al. 1992b). However, six months after the intervention ended, those who received advocacy services were no less likely to be abused (43 percent were still being abused across both groups) than those who did not receive advocacy. The authors concluded that "although providing advocacy services to women upon their shelter exit resulted in short-term positive results, this intervention by itself was insufficient to create long-term change in the lives of women with abusive partners" (Sullivan et al. 1994:118). These findings suggest that at least some women abused severely enough to require shelter services also need more than advocacy to extricate themselves from abusive relationships and ameliorate the effects of abuse on their mental health.

Services for Abusive Partners. Treatment of abusive partners has been controversial for a host of reasons, not the least of which is its effectiveness. Since the middle 1970s batterer intervention programs (BIPs) have proliferated, and since many states passed proarrest policies in the late 1980s, court-mandated programs have increased (Gondolf 1997). Several social workers have played a prominent role in the development of programs and policies to address the needs of abusive partners, most notably Jeffrey Edleson, Daniel Saunders, and Richard Tolman. There is a strong consensus in the field that group interventions are most effective, with variation in format, length of treatment, content of treatment (e.g., education versus therapy, cognitive behavioral versus psychodynamic), and extent to which concomitant mental health and substance abuse concerns are addressed (Gondolf 1997). Gondolf (1997) has noted that there is agreement on a "gender-based, cognitive behavioral modality: Men are confronted with the consequences of their behavior, held responsible for their abuse, have their rationalizations and excuses confronted, and are taught alternative behaviors and reactions" (85). Regarding BIP effectiveness, program evaluations indicate that fewer than half up to 80 percent or 90 percent of men who complete programs refrain from physical violence after program completion. The percentage of men who are violence-free decreases with the length of the follow-up. Cessation rates for verbal and emotional abuse are lower (Gondolf 1997).

Numerous issues exist regarding effectiveness of BIPs. For example, dropout rates tend to be very high (40 percent to 60 percent), with as few as half of those referred for treatment even showing up for the first session. Concerns also exist regarding the extent to which victims may have a false sense of safety when their abuser participates in a BIP. Few programs exist specifically for abusive men from ethnic minority groups despite the fact that "minority participants often perceive, interpret, and justify their abuse differently, and their experiences with the criminal justice system and social services in general are often different than those of other men in batterer groups" (Gondolf 1997:92). Nonetheless, there is the need for intervention programs designed to assist men in changing their abusive behaviors, and there is some evidence that programs can be successful in helping certain types of men desist from violence.

Services for Child Witnesses. A large body of literature now documents the deleterious effects on children of witnessing partner abuse between their parents (see Carlson 1996). To summarize briefly, problems linked to witnessing violence can be identified in virtually all areas of development: cognitive, behavioral, and socioemotional. Both internalizing (e.g., depression, withdrawal) and externalizing (e.g., aggression toward peers or family members, noncompliant behavior) problems have been documented. In extreme cases children can be traumatized by observing adult partner abuse, manifesting symptoms of PTSD (see Lehmann and Carlson 1998 for a discussion of the trauma perspective as applied to child witnesses to partner violence). These problem behaviors can be the result of witnessing abuse where aggression is modeled by powerful figures but may also be caused by other difficulties associated with chronic abuse, such as material deprivation, stress, observation of ongoing conflict between parents, and threats to end the relationship.

Several well-documented group intervention models have been described in the literature to address the problems of such children (e.g., Wilson et al. 1989). These groups have been offered under a variety of auspices beyond shelter settings such as social agencies that see abused women as clients. Structured group interventions last six to ten weeks, with sixty- to ninety-minute sessions involving three to six children of approximately the same age. Topics covered include what violence is, who is responsible for it, emotions, communication and problem solving, self-esteem, secrets, self-protection skills, and how to obtain social support. Because participation in such a group often reverberates throughout the family, parent involvement is strongly recommended (Peled and Edleson 1995).

Where group interventions are not available, practitioners may wish to see children who witnessed partner violence on an individual basis. Assessment should include an evaluation of the extent of violence and abuse to which children have been exposed, whether they have been physically or sexually abused or neglected themselves, their behavioral adjustment, posttraumatic symptoms, coping mechanisms, perceptions of the abuse and whether they feel responsible for it, and access to social support beyond the immediate family. Interventions should be geared to the kinds of problems the child is presenting as well as safety skills and understanding who is responsible for the abuse (Jaffe, Suderman, and Reitzel 1992).

ASSESSMENT AND INTERVENTIONS

In this section, we discuss assessment and intervention with women abused by their intimate male partners. As mentioned earlier, intimate partner abuse intervention encompasses other groups as well, in particular abusers and children exposed to violence between their parents. We have chosen to focus on female victims of male violence because they are probably the group most frequently seen by social workers. In our patriarchal society, abused women are one of the most vulnerable populations that social workers encounter. However, we believe that many of the interventions proposed in this section can be applied to other groups as well, such as abused lesbians, if sensitivity to each group's unique needs and concerns is maintained.

This section is based on a **feminist perspective** of intimate violence etiology. It is based on the belief that the violence inflicted by a man against his female partner is a problem in itself, not "just a symptom" of relationship problems or substance abuse problems of the abuser (Petretic-Jackson and Jackson 1996:189). For obvious reasons, the theoretical framework adopted will determine the direction of assessment and intervention.

We assume the context of intervention to be an outpatient mental health clinic or counseling setting such as a family service agency. There are several reasons for this assumption. First, the majority of battered women tend to encounter their first helping situation not with a specific domestic violence program, but through more generic therapeutic/counseling services. They may first seek help for their own or their children's mental health issues. Through the assessment and intervention process, either the social worker or the battered woman herself might realize that violence by the intimate partner is the problem that needs attention. Second, because many battered women seek help at mental health centers for their psychological problems resulting from the abuse (Gondolf 1998), there is a danger of pathologizing the battered woman when intimate partner violence is a social problem (Gondolf and Fisher 1988). For this reason, some of the assessment and intervention tools frequently used by domestic violence advocates should be integrated into social work practice in mental health settings (Gondolf 1998). For instance, safety planning is discussed in this section. In settings that are funded largely through third-party payments, the social worker may need to give a formal diagnosis for battered women. Thus, issues pertaining to psychiatric diagnosis also are discussed in this section.

In working with victims of partner violence, assessment and intervention often occur simultaneously. In fact, the assessment process itself may be a powerful intervention for battered women. For many of these women, it may be the first time that anyone has asked about whether they have been physically and/or emotionally abused by an intimate partner. Acknowledging that domestic violence is a serious problem and validating their experience can be a source of support for battered women. They also learn that they are not alone in the struggle and that help is available. This allows them to feel less shame, guilt, and self-blame about the abuse.

Because intervention and assessment are so frequently intertwined, they are not discussed separately. Instead, the discussion of assessment and intervention is organized topically in terms of safety planning, recognizing strengths and survivor therapy, posttraumatic stress reactions and posttraumatic therapy, alcohol and other substance abuse, and other diagnostic issues. Both assessment and intervention are discussed under each topic, reflecting the reality of social work in agency settings with battered women.

Safety Planning. The first and most important area of assessment must address the safety of the client and her children. If they are in immediate danger, establishing their safety should take precedence over other interventions. Each woman defines violence and safety differently (Hanks 1992). It is important to remember that the client is the expert regarding her own situation. Client-centered intervention is especially important for battered woman because it can impart a sense of power (Gondolf 1998).

The need for social support can first be discussed in the context of finding a safe place to stay in the event that violence appears imminent. Abused clients may not have support readily available or may not want to jeopardize the safety of supporters. In that case, the social worker needs to introduce the domestic violence shelters as a safety option. The social worker can explain the array of services that a battered women's shelter can provide. The reality of positive (safety, support, information) and negative (less privacy due to sharing space with other women and children, disruption in children's lives, needing to follow rules such as responsibilities for chores) aspects of going to a shelter should be discussed, but with strong emphasis on the importance of safety for the client and her children.

Regarding the safety plan,

> The content of the plan should be specific to the needs and situation of the individual woman. Minimally, it should include attention to a means of escape if escape is necessary, and other resources necessary to put the plan into effect. The plan may involve others, such as children trained to run to a neighbor's home during an argument or trusted friends or family members who agree to provide a place to stay in an emergency or call the police when signaled. It might entail hiding a set of car keys or cab fare in a secret place or keeping a hidden suitcase packed with necessities. If the plan includes a possible shelter stay, information necessary to be admitted to the shelter should be acquired ahead of time, such as the phone number and location, eligibility requirements, and so forth. (Carlson 1997:296)

An example of a generic safety plan can be found in *Substance Abuse Treatment and Domestic Violence* (Fazzone, Holton, and Reed 1997). Making referrals to other social service agencies to ensure that basic needs are met (food, clothing, and shelter) is another aspect of addressing the immediate crisis.

Safety planning is equally important for women who are not ready to leave, do not see the reason to leave at the present time, or have already left. Most battered women fall into these categories. Putting a safety plan into effect can serve a preventive function by helping a woman to avoid violence. By the end of the first session, it is crucial to assess all aspects of safety and to create an initial safety plan. This safety plan should be reviewed at every point of contact during the duration of the intervention. In addressing safety, it is important to respect clients' rights to self-determination (Dutton 1992). Except in cases of child abuse or threats to self or others, the social worker needs to respect the woman's decision irrespective of the worker's opinion concerning the decision.

Another area needing assessment and intervention pertains to legal issues. These include marital status, immigration status, and custody status. For an immigrant woman, finding out her residency status is important. In some cases the abusive husband might use his wife's illegal status to exert control over her. Furthermore, due to unfamiliarity with her legal rights and protective laws, she may fear deportation and feel forced to stay with her abusive husband. In this case, the worker needs to educate the woman about the provisions of the Violence Against Women Act of 1994, which allows abused women and children to petition for permanent residency without the abusive husband sponsoring them (Victims Services 1999). A plan to obtain necessary documentation of the abuse must be developed in these cases.

Recognizing Strengths and Survivor Therapy. As a result of abuse, many battered women may not be aware of their own strengths. Gondolf defines strengths as "the qualities that resist attack and defeat and maintain survival and personal growth" (Gondolf 1998:95). Some psychological symptoms of battered women may in fact be coping strategies or normal responses to abuse. Treatment based on a medical model treatment may focus exclusively on the client's deficits without identifying their strengths (Gondolf 1998). What is unique about the strengths approach is the assumption that even the most troubled victims have strengths. It is crucial for the social worker to assess strengths that abused women have developed in order to survive the trauma of battering and abuse and be willing to see psychological symptoms as attempts at coping (Dutton 1992). For instance, staying in an abusive relationship may appear to be masochistic, but it can also be seen as persistence. In conducting a strengths inventory the client is assumed to be an expert on her own strengths and must be actively involved in their identification. Only after the client has had the opportunity to share her strengths does the worker offer her perceptions of client strengths (Gondolf 1998).

One of the most important goals in survivor therapy is to empower a battered woman so that she will be able to gain control over her life, which Walker (1991, 1994) calls "reempowerment." Many battered women feel powerless to protect themselves against abuse; no matter what they do, the beatings seem to happen without any clues or warning. Learned helplessness, which can develop when women have made many unsuccessful attempts to stop the violence, is an area that also needs to be assessed (Carlson 1991). Campbell, Sullivan, and Davidson (1995) recommend that "reestablishing feelings of control should be a primary focus of therapeutic interventions" (252). Social workers can help clients understand that they can still control some aspects of their lives even though they are not able to stop the violence (Walker 1994). Providing education about the abuse and violence is also an empowering intervention (Dutton 1992).

Cognitive-behavioral techniques are useful to help women develop positive coping strategies and reduce cognitive distortions. Four steps are used in a cognitive-behavioral intervention: giving an overview and rationale for the intervention, showing the desired behavior through modeling and role play, having the client practice and rehearse new behaviors, and evaluating and making necessary modifications (Webb 1992). Some specific techniques are stress reduction, relaxation, cognitive restructuring, role playing, skills development, problem solving, and use of imagery (Carlson 1997; Dutton 1992; Webb 1992).

Posttraumatic Stress Reactions and Posttraumatic Therapy. Posttraumatic stress reaction (PTSR) is defined as, "set of conscious and unconscious behaviors and emotions associated with dealing with the memories of the stressors of the catastrophe and the period immediately afterwards" (Dutton 1992:129). It is important to create a safe environment for clients before encouraging them to remember the past or discuss continuing trauma related to violence and to avoid revictimizing clients (Dutton 1992).

The social worker needs to assess and recognize posttraumatic reactions resulting from battering and follow up with appropriate interventions. Failure to identify posttraumatic stress effects can have dire effects because there is evidence that merely providing support and focusing on problem solving without also specifically addressing the trauma is less effective in alleviating trauma symptoms (Koss et al. 1994). In using standardized testing or questionnaires (e.g., the Trauma Symptom Checklist authored by Briere and Runtz 1989), the client's PTSR might be mistaken for other psychiatric disorders such as personality disorders (Walker 1991). Educating the woman about the reasons behind her reactions is important in helping her understand how her symptoms are "normal" in the context of the "abnormal" situation of the man-made trauma. This can help her feel less fearful about her being "crazy" and allow her to have an increased sense of control over her reactions. Walker (1991) states that the primary goal of intervention for PTSR is to reempower the battered woman. Explaining to the client the course of the treatment, including possible difficulties during the process, is empowering. The client can control the pace of treatment, reducing her anxiety and also providing her with a feeling of control. The therapeutic process should consist of helping the client to gradually reexperience the trauma in a safe environment, manage stress, reduce shame and rage, facilitate expression of grief, find meaning in the victimization, and rebuild a new life (Dutton 1992; Saunders 1994).

Alcohol and Other Substance Abuse. For many battered women, substance use is a way of self-medicating (Dutton 1992). Some battered women's use of alcohol and/or other substances is due to the abuser's influence (Fazzone et al. 1997). Even for women who had a substance abuse history prior to the onset of abuse, it is important to recognize the role of substance use in "numbing the pain associated with the trauma" (Dutton 1992:91). When substance abuse is determined as a result of assessment, the worker needs to discuss the client's use of the substance in relation to the abuse and point out the importance of substance abuse treatment. For example, because most shelters have rules requiring residents to be sober during their stay, intoxication might create problems in getting admitted to a battered women's shelter or being allowed to stay once admitted. If treatment priorities of the counseling agency and the substance abuse treatment program are different (safety versus abstaining from alcohol or drugs), it will be important to work with a substance counselor who is familiar with domestic violence survivors and understands the importance of safety. Because many battered women use alcohol and other substances as a way to cope with distress and pain, it may be necessary for the client to find alternative coping strategies when trying to achieve abstinence (Fazzone et al. 1997). Safety should continue to be a focus during the substance abuse treatment. Safety-related issues, such as not involving the abusive partner in the treatment process, should be discussed with the substance abuse treatment counselor.

When abused women are using substances to self-medicate for depression, anxiety, and other emotional problems, as discussed in the following (Dutton 1992), it is important to consider a referral for medication. A thorough medical and psychiatric checkup is necessary before providing appropriate psychotropic medication. Close monitoring of the woman's use of prescribed medication is necessary to prevent possible relapse involving misuse of the medication (Fazzone et al. 1997). The social worker should function as a case manager to integrate all different treatments and services the woman is receiving.

Other Diagnostic Issues. Some battered women have psychiatric disorders that need appropriate attention, including medication, treatment, and even hospitalization. It is important for the social worker to document symptoms in the context of the violence. For example, depression is a common diagnosis with battered women (Gondolf 1998). Using a tool such as the Beck Depression Inventory (Beck et al. 1979) can be beneficial to assess and monitor depression in battered women (Petretic-Jackson and Jackson 1996). Techniques such as cognitive restructuring can be useful to help the depressed woman to change her distorted beliefs (Webb 1992). Referral to a psychiatrist might be needed to provide medication therapy. In case of suicidal ideation, lethality needs to be assessed, and hospitalization might be necessary to ensure the safety of the woman.

ILLUSTRATION AND DISCUSSION

Helen is a 35-year-old Korean American woman. She walked into an outpatient mental health clinic without an appointment to discuss her son's behavioral problems. She explained that her 5-year-old son just started kindergarten two months ago. He has been getting into fights with other children, throwing things in the classroom, and swearing at other children and his teacher. She told the social worker that his teacher recommended that she get counseling for him.

To get a better understanding of the factors that might be affecting the son's behavior and to observe interaction among family members, the worker asked Helen to bring the whole family in for the next session. With hesitation, Helen reported that her husband, who is also Korean, does not know about her seeking help and that it would be difficult to get him to come to counseling. Using the "funneling" technique (Brekke 1987), the worker was able to gather more information about family dynamics and conflict resolution and found out that Helen's husband beats her frequently.

Helen reported that she didn't realize how violent her husband was before she got married. She said she got married within two months of meeting her husband and soon after moved to the United States where her husband was living. None of her family and friends lived in the United States, and she felt very isolated. Although she had several years of work experience in Korea, she felt inadequate about working outside of home in the United States, plus her husband did not want her to have a job.

Her husband first beat her when he saw Helen with a male classmate in the front of the adult school where Helen was learning English and subsequently forbid her to attend school anymore. Her husband appeared to be very controlling, often following her even when she was just going to the market. But despite her husband's beating and jealousy, she did not want to leave him, in part because she was afraid of not getting her green card. Due to her limited English skills, not having legal status, and not having any social network in the United States, she was very dependent on her husband in all aspects of her life. Her husband's beating continued during her two pregnancies, often because she was "paying too much attention to the fetus," rather than her husband. She was also beaten by her husband for reasons such as food being too salty, dust on the TV stand, or children not being finished with their homework. Oftentimes, he beat her in front of her children.

Helen reported that she felt depressed most of the time and sometimes even thought about killing herself. She said she usually changed her mind when she thought about her children and how they needed her. She reported starting to feel nervous each day around the time her husband came home from work, because she did not know what kind of mood he would be in. She often had headaches that she had to take medications for.

Assessment and intervention themes include the need for validation and support, the family's immigrant status, safety concerns, the need for information, and mental health concerns. In the first session the worker acknowledged the seriousness of the situation, validating Helen's experience, complimenting her on the courage she showed in admitting the abuse, and noting other strengths, such as concern for her children.

The fact that Helen and her family are Korean immigrants means that the worker needed to be both sensitive to and knowledgeable about Korean culture. Lack of such awareness might mean not understanding the cultural norms against married Korean women becoming employed, especially if they are mothers, for example. Getting a divorce—bringing shame upon the family—is also not normative for Koreans. The worker also needed to become knowledgeable about immigration law and be prepared to advocate for this client with the Immigration and Naturalization Service. Recent regulations mean that Helen may be successful in seeking legal status on her own, even if she is divorced from her husband, assuming that she can document her abuse. This may mean contacting the police the next time she is beaten so there is a record of her abuse. Obtaining an order of protection (called a restraining order in some states) would be another way of documenting her husband's violent behavior.

Another theme pertains to safety. It was important for the worker to conduct a safety assessment for Helen and her children to determine if they were in immediate danger. Because Helen has mentioned thoughts of suicide, this should be addressed specifically. The worker questioned Helen in detail regarding the children's well-being to determine if they have been neglected or physically or sexually abused by either parent and the extent of their exposure to the violence between their parents. The worker also developed a safety plan with Helen regarding what she could do the next time violence occurred and informed her about the local domestic violence shelter. It would be ideal if there was a shelter with cultural sensitivity to the needs of immigrant women, although this may not be an option in many locations.

The worker also used psychoeducational interventions to assist Helen in understanding the nature and dynamics of partner violence, its effects on victims, and its effects on children who witness such abuse. The worker linked the presenting problem of Helen's son's problematic behavior at school to her knowledge of the effects of abuse on child witnesses. Oftentimes, explicit awareness that exposure to chronic conflict and abuse can be harmful to children helps to increase women's readiness to take positive steps toward ending abuse. The worker noted several strengths, including Helen's obvious concern about her children, her willingness to follow up on the school's referral for her son, and not following through on her thoughts of suicide due to her concern for her children.

The worker addressed Helen's mental health concerns by administering a depression inventory and an evaluation of possible PTSD symptoms, concluding that Helen was in the moderate range for depression but was not exhibiting many PTSD symptoms. Because of her depression score, the worker chose to use cognitive-behavioral techniques such as cognitive restructuring and reframing to address her depression and cognitive distortions, which should eventually improve her self-esteem. In addition, teaching her relaxation techniques should help Helen to control her anxiety. Other interventions included helping Helen to see that the abuse was not her fault and that she did not deserve to be treated this way. The worker was careful not to pressure Helen to leave her husband to avoid alienating her and making her reluctant to return for fear of disappointing the worker if she chose not to leave.

CONCLUSION

Intimate partner abuse is increasingly recognized as a common problem seen by social workers and other mental health professionals. The demographics of this problem indicate that it is disturbingly frequent among the clients social workers commonly see: the poor and vulnerable. Because many, perhaps most, abused women do not seek help from formal domestic violence programs, it is important for social workers employed in a wide variety of settings to be knowledgeable about partner violence— its manifestations, risk factors, dynamics, and consequences. Among helping professionals, social workers are uniquely well qualified to be of assistance to abused women because of our person-in-environment perspective and basic social work values such as self-determination and the strengths perspective that are essential to working effectively with this group.

References

Aldarondo, E. 1996. "Cessation and Persistence of Wife Assault: A Longitudinal Analysis." *American Journal of Orthopsychiatry* 66:141–51.

Arias, I., C. M. Lyons, and A. E. Street. 1997. "Individual and Marital Consequences of Victimization: Moderating Effects of Relationship Efficacy and Spouse Support." *Journal of Family Violence* 12:193–210.

Astin, M. C., S. M. Ogland-Hand, E. M. Coleman, and D. W. Foy. 1995. "Posttraumatic Stress Disorder and Childhood Abuse in Battered Women: Comparisons with Maritally Distressed Women." *Journal of Consulting and Clinical Psychology* 63:308–12.

Bachman, R. and L. E. Saltzman. 1995. *Violence Against Women: Evidence from the Re-*

designed Survey. Washington, D.C.: U.S. Department of Justice, Bureau of Justice Statistics.

Beck, A., A. Rush, B. Shaw, and G. Emery. 1979. *Cognitive Therapy of Depression.* New York: Guilford.

Benishek, L. A. and F. G. Lopez. 1997. "Critical Evaluation of Hardiness Theory: Gender Differences, Perceptions of Life Events, and Neuroticism." *Work & Stress* 11:33–45.

Bergen, R. K. 1998. "The Reality of Wife Rape: Women's Experiences of Sexual Violence in Marriage." In R. K. Bergen, ed., *Issues in Intimate Violence,* pp. 237–50. Thousand Oaks, Calif.: Sage.

Bowker, L. H. and L. Maurer. 1986. "The Effectiveness of Counseling Services Utilized by Battered Women." *Women & Therapy* 5:65–82.

Brekke, J. S. 1987. "Detecting Wife Abuse and Child Abuse in Clinical Settings." *Social Casework* 68:332–38.

Briere, J. and M. Runtz. 1989. "The Trauma Symptom Checklist (TSC-33): Early Data on a New Scale." *Journal of Interpersonal Violence* 4:151–63.

Burcky, W., N. Reuterman, and S. Kopsky. 1988. "Dating Violence Among High School Students." *The School Counselor* 35:353–58.

Burke, P. J., J. E. Stets, and M. Pirog-Good. 1988. "Gender Identity, Self-Esteem, and Physical and Sexual Abuse in Dating Relationships." *Social Psychology Quarterly* 51: 272–85.

Campbell, J. C. 1989a. "Women's Responses to Sexual Abuse Intimate Relationships." *Health Care for Women International* 10:335–46.

——. 1989b. "A Test of Two Explanatory Models of Women's Responses to Battering." *Nursing Research* 38:18–24.

Campbell, J. C., J. Kub, R. A. Belknap, and T. N. Templin. 1997. "Predictors of Depression in Battered Women." *Violence Against Women* 3:271–94.

Campbell, R., C. M. Sullivan, and W. S. Davidson. 1995. "Women Who Use Domestic Violence Shelters: Changes in Depression Over Time." *Psychology of Women Quarterly* 19:237–55.

Capaldi, D. M. and L. Crosby. 1997. "Observed and Reported Psychological and Physical Aggression in Young, At-Risk Couples." *Social Development* 6:184–206.

Carlson, B. E. 1991. "Domestic Violence." In A. Gitterman, ed., *Handbook of Social Work Practice with Vulnerable Populations,* pp. 471–502. New York: Columbia University Press.

——. 1996. "Children of Battered Women: Research, Programs and Services." In A. R. Roberts, ed., *Helping Battered Women,* pp. 172–87. New York: Oxford University Press.

——. 1997. "A Stress and Coping Approach to Intervention with Abused Women." *Family Relations* 46:291–98.

Carlson, B. E. and K. Maciol. 1997. "Domestic Violence: Gay Men and Lesbians." In R. Edwards, ed., *Encyclopedia of Social Work, Update,* 19th ed., pp. 101–11. Washington, D.C.: National Association of Social Workers Press.

Cascardi, M. and D. K. O'Leary. 1992. "Depressive Symptomotology, Self-Esteem, and Self-Blame in Battered Women." *Journal of Family Violence* 7:249–59.

Cascardi, M., D. K. O'Leary, E. E. Lawrence, and K. A. Schlee. 1995. "Characteristics of Women Physically Abused by Their Spouses Who Seek Treatment Regarding Marital Conflict." *Journal of Consulting and Clinical Psychology* 63:616–23.

Cohen, S. and J. M. Hoberman. 1983. "Positive Events and Social Supports of Life Change Stress." *Journal of Applied Social Psychology* 13:99–125.

Danielson, K. K., T. E. Moffitt, A. Caspi, and P. Silva. 1998. "Comorbidity Between Abuse of an Adult and DSM-III-R Mental Disorders: Evidence from an Epidemiological Study." *American Journal of Psychology* 155:131–33.

Davis, L. V., J. L. Hagen, and T. J. Early. 1994. "Social Services for Battered Women: Are They Adequate, Accessible, and Appropriate?" *Social Work* 39:695–704.

Davis, L. V. and M. Srinivasan. 1995. "Listening to the Voices of Battered Women: What Helps Them Escape Violence." *Affilia* 10:49–69.

Dobash, R. E. and R. P. Dobash. 1977–78. "Wives: The 'Appropriate' Victims of Marital Violence." *Victimology* 2:426–42.

Drossman, D. A., J. Leserman, G. Nachman, A. M. Li, H. Gluck, T. C. Toomey, and C. M. Mitchell. 1990. "Sexual and Physical Abuse in Women with Functional or Organic Gastrointestinal Disorders." *Annals of Internal Medicine* 113:828–33.

Dutton, M. A. 1992. *Empowering and Healing the Battered Woman.* NewYork: Springer.

Fagan, J. and A. Browne. 1994. "Violence Between Spouses and Intimates: Physical Aggression Between Women and Men in Intimate Relationships." In A. Reiss and J. Roth, eds., *Understanding and Preventing Violence,* vol. 3, *Social Influences,* pp. 115–292. Washington, D.C.: National Academy Press.

Fazzone, P. A., J. K. Holton, and B. G. Reed. 1997. *Substance Abuse Treatment and Domestic Violence.* Rockville, Md.: U.S. Department of Health and Human Services.

Finn, J. 1985. "The Stresses and Coping Behavior of Battered Women." *Social Casework* 66:341–49.

Follingstad, D. R., A. F. Brennan, E. S. Hause, D. S. Polek, and L. L. Rutledge. 1991. "Factors Moderating Physical and Psychological Symptoms of Battered Women." *Journal of Family Violence* 6:81–95.

Gelles, R. J. and M. A. Straus. 1988. *Intimate Violence.* New York: Simon & Schuster.

Gondolf, E. W. 1997. "Batterer Programs: What Do We Know and Need to Know." *Journal of Interpersonal Violence* 12:83–98.

——. 1998. *Assessing Woman Battering in Mental Health Services.* Thousand Oaks, Calif.: Sage.

Gondolf, E. W. and E. R. Fisher. 1988. *Battered Women as Survivors.* Lexington, Mass.: Lexington Books.

Goodman, L. A., M. P. Koss, and N. F. Russo. 1993a. "Violence Against Women: Physical and Mental Health Effects. Part I: Research Findings." *Applied and Preventive Psychology* 2:79–89.

——. 1993b. "Violence Against Women: Mental Health Effects. Part II. Conceptualizations of Posttraumatic Stress." *Applied and Preventive Psychology* 2:123–30.

Greenfeld, L. A., M. R. Rand, D. Craven, P. A. Klaus, C. A. Perkins, C. Ringel, G. Warchol, C. Maston, and J. F. Fox. 1998. *Violence by Intimates: Analysis of Data on Crimes by Current or Former Spouses, Boyfriends, and Girlfriends.* Washington, D.C.: U.S. Department of Justice, Bureau of Justice Statistics.

Hanks, S. E. 1992. "Translating Theory into Practice: A Conceptual Framework for Clinical Assessment, Differential Diagnosis, and Multi-modal Treatment of Maritally Violent Individuals, Couples, and Families." In E. C. Viano, ed., *Intimate Violence: Interdisciplinary Perspectives,* pp. 157–75. Washington, D.C.: Hemisphere.

Heron, R. L., D. P. Jacobs, H. B. Twomey, and N. J. Kaslow. 1997. "Culturally Competent Interventions for Abused and Suicidal African American women." *Psychotherapy* 34:410–24.

Horton, A. L. and B. L. Johnson. 1993. "Profile and Strategies of Women Who Have Ended Abuse." *Families in Society* 74:481–92.

Jaffe, P. G., M. Suderman, and D. Reitzel. 1992. "Child Witnesses of Marital Violence." In R. T. Ammerman and M. Hersen, eds., *Assessment of Family Violence: A Clinical and Legal Sourcebook,* pp. 313–31. New York: Wiley.

Johnson, M. P. 1995. "Patriarchal Terrorism and Common Couple Violence: Two Forms of Violence Against Women." *Journal of Marriage and the Family* 57:283–94.

Kemp, A., E. I. Rawlings, and B. L. Green. 1991. "Post-traumatic Stress Disorder (PTSD) in Battered Women: A Shelter Sample." *Journal of Traumatic Stress* 4:137–48.

Koss, M. P., L. A. Goodman, A. Browne, L. F. Fitzgerald, G. P. Keita, and N. F. Russo. 1994. *No Safe Haven: Male Violence Against Women at Home, Work, and in the Community.* Washington, D.C.: American Psychological Association.

Koss, M. P. and L. Heslet. 1992. "Somatic Consequences of Violence Against Women." *Archives of Family Medicine* 1:53–59.

Lane, K. E. and P. A. Gwartney-Gibbs. 1985. "Violence in the Context of Dating and Sex." *Journal of Family Issues* 6:45–59.

Lazarus, R. S. 1991. "Cognition and Motivation in Emotion." *American Psychologist* 46: 352–67.

Lazarus, R. S. and S. Folkman. 1984. *Stress, Appraisal and Coping.* New York: Springer.

Lehmann, P. and B. E. Carlson. 1998. "Crisis Intervention with Traumatized Child Witnesses in Shelters for Battered Women." In A. R. Roberts, ed., *Battered Women and Their Families: Intervention Strategies and Treatment Programs,* 2d ed., pp. 99–128. New York: Springer.

Leserman, J., Z. Li, Y. J. Hu, and D. A. Drossman. 1998. "How Multiple Types of Stressors Impact on Health." *Psychosomatic Medicine* 60:175–81.

Lie, G. Y. and S. Gentlewarrier. 1991. "Intimate Violence in Lesbian Relationships: Discussion of Survey Findings and Practice Implications." *Journal of Social Service Research* 15:41–59.

Lockhart, L. L., B. W. White, V. Causby, and A. Isaac. 1994. "Letting Out the Secret: Violence in Lesbian Relationships." *Journal of Interpersonal Violence* 9:469–92.

Magdol, L., T. E. Moffitt, A. Caspi, J. Fagan, D. L. Newman, and P. Silva. 1997. "Gender Differences in Partner Violence: Bridging the Gap Between Clinical and Epidemiological Approaches." *Journal of Consulting and Clinical Psychology* 65:68–78.

Magdol, L., T. E. Moffitt, A. Caspi, and P. A. Silva. 1998. "Hitting Without a License: Testing Explanations for Differences in Partner Abuse Between Young Adult Daters and Cohabitors." *Journal of Marriage and the Family* 60:41–55.

Magdol, L., T. E. Moffitt, and P. A. Silva. 1999. "Developmental Antecedents of Partner Abuse: A Prospective-Longitudinal Study. *Journal of Abnormal Psychology* 107: 375–89.

McCauley, J., D. E. Kern, K. Kolodner, L. Dill, A. F. Schroeder, H. K. DeChant, J. Ryden, E. B. Bass, and L. R. Derogatis. 1995. "The 'Battering Syndrome': Prevalence and Clinical Characteristics of Domestic Violence in Primary Care Internal Medicine Practices." *Annals of Internal Medicine* 123:737–46.

McNamara, J. R., M. A. Ertl, S. Marsh, and S. Walker. 1997. "Short-Term Response to Counseling and Case Management Intervention in a Domestic Violence Shelter." *Psychological Reports* 81:1243–51.

Mills, T. 1985. "The Assault on Self: Stages in Coping with Battering Husbands." *Qualitative Sociology* 8:103–23.

Mitchell, R. E. and C. A. Hodson. 1983. "Coping with Domestic Violence: Social Support and Psychological Health Among Battered Women." *American Journal of Community Psychology* 11:629–54.

O'Leary, K. D., J. Malone, and A. Tyree. 1994. "Physical Aggression in Early Marriage: Prerelationship and Relationship Effects." *Journal of Consulting and Clinical Psychology* 62:594–602.

Pan, H. S., P. H. Neidig, and D. K. O'Leary. 1994. "Predicting Mild and Severe Husband-to-Wife Physical Aggression." *Journal of Consulting and Clinical Psychology* 62: 975–81.

Peled, E. and J. L. Edleson. 1995. "Process and Outcome in Small Groups for Children of Battered Women." In E. Peled, P. Jaffe, and J. L. Edleson, eds., *Ending the Cycle of Violence: Community Responses to Children of Battered Women,* pp. 77–96. Thousand Oaks, Calif.: Sage.

Petretic-Jackson, P. A. and T. Jackson. 1996. "Mental Health Interventions with Battered Women." In A. R. Roberts, ed., *Helping Battered Women: New Perspectives and Remedies,* pp. 188–221. New York: Oxford University Press.

Plicta, S. B. 1996. "Violence and Abuse: Implications for Women's Health." In M. M. Falik and K. S. Collins, eds., *Women's Health: The Commonwealth Fund Study,* pp. 237–72. Baltimore, Md.: Johns Hopkins University Press.

Prochaska, J. O., C. C. DiClemente, and J. C. Norcross. 1992. "In Search of How People Change: Applications to Addictive Behaviors." *American Psychologist* 47:1102–13.

Renzetti, C. M. 1992. *Violent Betrayal: Partner Abuse in Lesbian Relationships.* Newbury Park, Calif.: Sage.

Roberts, A. R. 1998. "The Organizational Structure and Function of Shelters for Battered Women and Their Children: A National Survey." In A. R. Roberts, ed., *Battered Women and Their Families: Intervention Strategies and Treatment Programs,* 2d ed., pp. 58–75. New York: Springer.

Russell, D. E. H. 1990. *Rape in Marriage.* New York: Macmillan.

Saunders, D. G. 1994. "Posttraumatic Stress Symptoms Profiles of Battered Women: A Comparison of Survivors in Two Settings." *Violence & Victims* 9:31–44.

Schilit, R., G. Y. Lie, J. Bush, M. Montagne, and L. Reyes. 1991. "Intergenerational Transmission of Violence in Lesbian Relationships." *Affilia* 6:72–87.

Stets, J. E. and M. A. Straus. 1990. "The Marriage License as a Hitting License: A Comparison of Assaults in Dating, Cohabiting and Married Couples." In M. A. Straus and R. J. Gelles, eds., *Physical Violence in American Families,* pp. 227–44. New Brunswick, N.J.: Transaction.

Straus, M. A. and R. J. Gelles. 1986. "Societal Changes in Family Violence from 1975 to 1985 as Revealed by Two National Surveys." *Journal of Marriage and the Family* 48:465–79.

Straus, M. A. and C. Smith. 1990. "Family Patterns of Primary Prevention of Family Violence." In M. A. Straus and R. J. Gelles, eds., *Physical Violence in American Families: Risk Factors and Adaptations to Violence in 8,145 Families,* pp. 507–26. New Brunswick, N.J.: Transaction.

Sullivan, C. M. 1991. "The Provision of Advocacy Services to Women Leaving Abusive Partners." *Journal of Interpersonal Violence* 6:41–54.

Sullivan, C. M., J. Basta, C. Tan, and W. S. Davidson. 1992a. "After the Crisis: A Needs Assessment of Women Leaving a Domestic Violence Shelter." *Violence & Victims* 7:267–75.

Sullivan, C. M., R. Campbell, H. Angelique, K. K. Eby, and W. S. Davidson. 1994. "An Advocacy Intervention Program for Women with Abusive Partners: Six-Month Follow-Up." *American Journal of Community Psychology* 22:101–22.

Sullivan, C. M., C. Tan, J. Basta, M. Rumptz, and W. S. Davidson. 1992b. "An Advocacy Intervention Program for Women with Abusive Partners: Initial Evaluation." *American Journal of Community Psychology* 20:309–32.

Sutherland, C., D. Bybee, and C. Sullivan. 1998. "Long-Term Effects of Battering on Women's Health." *Women's Health: Research on Gender, Behavior, and Policy* 4:41–70.

Tjaden, P. and N. Thoennes. 1998. *Prevalence, Incidence, and Consequences of Violence Against Women: Findings from the National Violence Against Women Survey.* Washington, D.C.: U.S. Department of Justice, National Institute of Justice Centers for Disease Control and Prevention.

Valentine, L. and L. L. Feinauer. 1993. "Resilience Factors Associated with Female Survivors of Child Sexual Abuse." *American Journal of Family Therapy* 21:216–24.

Victims Services. 1999. *Current Issues: Immigration and Domestic Violence.* http://www.dvsheltertour.org/immigration.html

Walker, L. E. 1977–78. "Battered Women and Learned Helplessness." *Victimology* 2:525–34.

——. 1991. "Post-Traumatic Stress Disorder in Women: Diagnosis and Treatment of Battered Woman Syndrome." *Psychotherapy* 28:21–29.

——. 1994. *Abused Women and Survivor Therapy.* Washington, D.C.: American Psychological Association.

Weaver, T. L. and G. A. Clum. 1996. "Interpersonal Violence: Expanding the Search for Long-Term Sequelae within a Sample of Battered Women." *Journal of Traumatic Stress* 9:783–803.

Weaver, T. L., D. G. Kilpatrick, H. S. Resnick, C. L. Best, and B. E. Saunders. 1997. "An Examination of Physical Assault and Childhood Victimization Histories within a National Probability Sample of Women." In G. K. Kantor and J. L. Jasinski, eds., *Out of Darkness: Contemporary Perspectives on Family Violence,* pp. 35–46. Thousand Oaks, Calif.: Sage.

Webb, W. 1992. "Treatment Issues and Cognitive Behavior Techniques with Battered Women." *Journal of Family Violence* 7:205–17.

Wheeler, R. J. and M. A. Frank. 1988. "Identification of Stress Buffers." *Behavioral Medicine* 14:78–89.

Wilson, S. K., C. Cameron, P. Jaffe, and D. Wolfe. 1989. "Children Exposed to Wife Abuse: An Intervention Model." *Social Casework* 70:180–84.

25

Older Persons in Need of Long-Term Care

Toby Berman-Rossi

Writing this chapter at the turn of the twenty-first century is both an extraordinary and disturbing experience. Without question, the lives of older persons reveal significant gains and accomplishments, and this pattern is expected to continue. Overall, longevity is increasing, physical health is improving, chronic illness is declining, and for many, financial status is improving. Healthier and longer lives provide additional opportunities for the creation of life's pleasure. At the same time, a large portion of our older population, particularly women, ethnic minorities, and the oldest-old, live lives of unnecessary hardship, hardship created and secured by our capitalist economy. Without structural rearrangements and a more equitable distribution of society's economic and social resources there is little hope that such deprivation will decline.

Newer theories and burgeoning ideas provide invigorating opportunities to reexamine valued beliefs and to develop new ways of thinking about older persons and the society in which they live. Cultural, humanist, and critical gerontology bring welcome relief from the dominant medical paradigm that for so long has constructed our vision of the aging experience. An emphasis on the meaning of aging and on creating and sustaining meaning in life draw us away from our fixed view of older persons as a medical problem to be solved. Resiliency theories point to the myriad ways older persons successfully cope with a variety of stressors in their lives. The offering of alternate ways of thinking about aging creates new pathways for working with older persons in need of long-term care.

As exciting as the last decade of intellectual thought has been, there remains cause for concern. At the heart of the controversies are profound differences concerning how a responsive society should provide for older persons. Intellectual support for cuts in Medicare through our "balanced budget" process, for rationing health care for older persons, for establishing a means-test for Medicare, and for free market managed-care control of health care for older persons are but a few of the popular ideas that reflect a growing conservatism and a rising negativity toward older persons. Having recently celebrated the one hundredth birthday of the profession of social work, we recognize that our profession has a long history of standing with clients and working toward a more just society. An examination of the issues facing older persons in need of long-term care reaffirms that history and reasserts the intrinsic value of our professional function between client and community.

DEFINING AND EXPLAINING OLDER PERSONS IN NEED OF LONG-TERM CARE

The population of older persons in this chapter is often called the *frail elderly*. In the literature and in our mind's eye, *frail* conjures up a stereotypic image—an elusive, vaguely generalized image, characteristic of the concept itself. At first glance, the most striking characteristic of the term is that it derives its meaning from the union of two concepts: frail and elderly. The term *frail* is used to suggest fragility, weakness, feebleness, infirmity, decrepitness, brittleness, perishableness, things easily broken, and a quality of being easily crushed, destroyed, or wanting in power (*Funk and Wagnall's* 1968; *Longman Synonym Dictionary* 1986; Simpson and Weiner 1989; *Webster's New Dictionary of Synonyms* 1968).

Even when gerontologists define the concept operationally, the concept *frail elderly* contains a strong deficit orientation centering on incapacity, that is, what the older person is unable to do. Thus, older persons are often viewed not in their wholeness as individuals, but in their limitations and dependence on others. Consider, for example, the following definitions: "Older persons with mental, physical, and/or emotional disabilities that limit their independence and necessitate continuing assistance; persons 75 years or older" (Harris 1988:75), or "By frailty is meant reduction of physical and emotional capacities and loss of social-support systems to the extent that the elderly individual becomes unable to maintain a household or social contacts without continuing assistance from others" (Federal Council on the Aging 1978:15).

These definitions of *frail elderly* suggest an individualistic, medical orientation as well as a linearity of approach. "Personal attributes" are viewed as primary factors in the older person's situation. The environment serves principally as backdrop, rather than as principal player in the creation of the "condition." "Disabilities" become intrinsic to the individual and not a function of social creation and an inadequate person:environment fit. Thus, the individual, not the environment, becomes the target for change. The logical outcome of a deficit medical model, focused on individual pathology, is a linear orientation to causality. As we shall see later, the medicalizing of aging underlies and dominates long-term-care services. This is epitomized by the fact that the Health Care Financial Administration funds and administers most federal long-term-care programs (Kane 1987). Medicaid and Medicare are the primary sources of funding for long-term health care (Garner 1995; Meiners 1996). "Although nursing homes serve less than a fifth of the disabled elderly they dominate long-term care financing. Fully 82 percent of the total expenditures for long-term care was allocated to nursing homes in 1988. Of the total cost ($43.1 billion), nearly 47 percent was paid by the public sector, primarily through the poverty Medicaid program" (Lamphere-Thorpe and Blendon 1993:80). Such views are also consistent with a historical trend in which older persons gradually became viewed as a class—a class in need, a class embodying social problems. Eventually, older persons came to be equated with the social problems themselves (Dunkle 1984; Hazan 1998).

Characterizing older persons in terms of their limitations conflicts with our developing understanding of the ways in which a stable sense of self and a positive self-identification enable older persons, especially the very old, to age well (Bergeman and Wallace 1999; Gadow 1983; Kaufman 1986; Tobin 1988). In fact, describing oneself as aged and frail is associated with poorer mental health, a perceived loss of control of one's life, and lowered physical and psychological health (Burnette and Mui 1994; Furstenberg 1989; Neeman 1995). A sense of control in one's life directly connects to psychological well-being (Bergeman and Wallace 1999; Lieberman and Tobin 1983; Perlmutter and Eads 1998). Negative self-definitions also conflict with our growing understanding of resilience in old age and the knowledge that the capacity to maintain oneself in the face of considerable challenge is an accomplishment worthy of positive notation (Ryff et al. 1998).

Our discussion of "frail older persons" contrasts with current discussion of the needs of an entirely different population: busy business and professional persons (Bader 1999). These persons, many of whom use assistance to manage their households and personal lives, accrue status by virtue of their ability to purchase assistance. Need under these circumstances is quite acceptable. A comparison of these two groups suggests that it is neither need nor dependence that distinguishes them, but power. In this instance, power takes three forms: first, the power to define the situation in the manner most advantageous to the definer; second, the power to command the necessary resources directly or through others; and third, the power of a strong voice, strong enough to resist forces tending to destroy. In short, deficit is a matter of definition and the power of the definer to enforce that definition is required. Thus, frailty has to do with "liability to failure or destruction, . . . an incapacity for dealing with forces or powers opposed to it, or tending to destroy it . . . lack of power to resist," (*Webster's* 1968:882) rather than any physical or mental impairment unto itself. Logically then, when resources are available and coping capacities are strengthened, "frailty" declines. Under such circumstances resiliency is most likely to be evident and the power to resist is more evident.

Taken together, these attributes of the frail elderly suggest a complex interaction between older persons and their environment. Frailty is best understood by understanding the context with which the older person must contend. The strength of the "forces tending to destroy" must be included in the discussion. When these elements in the environment are responsive to long-term need, the older person's strength will be more likely to meet its environmental demands. An unresponsive or menacing environment is one in which even greater strength is required to maintain the status quo, much less improve it. In such a situation, the capacity of the older person may not be equal to the tasks at hand. In such circumstances, needs increase and greater personal resources are required to maintain one. Thus, the balance in the transactions between the older persons and their environment is reflected in the character of their life experience. The need for long-term care or what others call frailty results not from attributes of older persons alone, but from a lack of congruence between their needs and capacities and the environment's demands and resources. What is defined as belonging to the individual more accurately belongs to the relation between the individual and his or her environment. As Kane (1987) notes, institutionalization in a long-term-care facility is brought about by the interaction between social circumstances and the characteristics of the individual, not solely the individual. Medical problems and the need for services are not significant predictors of institutionalization (Sommers et al. 1988).

Being dependent on others in coping with chronic illness, chronic pain, and physical, emotional, and cognitive change, as well as economic and social losses, is at best very trying even when the relevant resources are available. Under the best of circumstances, this adaptive challenge requires and consumes extraordinary personal capacities, capacities that are inevitably more and more difficult to replenish. Under the worst of circumstances, where capacities and resources are modest and limited, extreme stress is inevitable. The societally induced diminishing of mental, physical, and social health creates the very condition that long-term care is designed to mitigate (Harel 1988). Within the general population of older persons in need of long-term care there are populations with special needs (Mellor 1996). As is true of older persons in general, this segment of the older population is also heterogeneous. It includes those older persons who have experienced significant disadvantaging economic, physical, mental, and emotional conditions and circumstances throughout their lives. These stressors and their consequences, when carried into advanced age, further stress coping capacity. For example, the coping abilities of older persons who are blind (Weber 1991), developmentally disadvantaged (O'Malley 1996; Parkinson and Howard 1996), formerly hospitalized in psychiatric facilities (Feldstein 1985), homeless (Tully and Jacobson 1994), experiencing long-term disabling physical and mental conditions (Gilson and Netting 1997; Kelly 1993), Holocaust survivors (Safford 1995), and persons living with AIDS (Crisologo, Campbell, and Forte 1996) are further taxed by the stressors of aging. Special populations also include those persons stressed by life events and life circumstances especially associated with aging, for example, illness, loss of a life partner, institutionalization, decreased income, and, increasingly, grandmothers raising grandchildren.

These older persons who are dependent on others (i.e., those designated as "frail") are the fastest-growing group in the older population (Dunkle and Norgard 1995; U.S. Bureau of the Census 1996). For them, the system has not worked nearly as well. The focus of this essay is on this poor, lower- and middle-class group of older persons who need long-term care. By long-term care we mean care in home, institutional, and noninstitutional settings. The numbers of older persons needing long-term care is expected to double between 1990 and 2030, while those needing nursing home care is expected to triple (Hooyman and Kiyak 1996). These persons do not receive an adequate share of America's bounty. For them, relief from public policy that provides insufficient income and inadequate services is difficult to achieve. A grudging societal response becomes a powerful factor influencing the quality and nature of their lives.

Though the need for long-term care defies age, sex, culture, and economic class, older women and ethnic minorities are particularly disadvantaged in coping with the challenges before them and in living the last part of their lives. A sexist, racist, classist, and homophobic society, exacerbated by ageism, imposes on the older person a daunting and powerful combination of obstacles and challenges, especially on those older persons who depend on formal and informal supports to maintain their lives either in the community or in long-term care institutions.

The need to serve this group is compelling because this population is most at risk for increased morbidity, abuse, neglect, institutionalization, and death. These vulnerable older persons, especially older women and ethnic minorities, are the specific populations to which social workers must attend. There is a pressing and clear need for leadership in social policy, in planning and the organization of services, and in direct practice with this large and growing group of vulnerable persons. While agreeing with Atchley and Lawton (1997) that gerontology has paid greater attention to the problems of aging rather than the resiliency of aging, thereby distorting our portrait of older persons, and while we certainly are obligated to present a more accurate view, nevertheless, those in need *are* the appropriate purview of the social work profession. A balance between the needs and capacities of the older person and the demands and resources of the environment is an outcome "devotedly to be wished" and striven for by social workers. Ryff et al. (1998) point out that their objective in studying resilience in adulthood and later life was to "look carefully at those who, as they age, experience notable quality of life vis-à-vis the problems that come their way" (91). Moving away from the concept of frailty and toward the concept of resilience will help us achieve this objective.

DEMOGRAPHIC PATTERNS

On the whole, the nation's older persons are overall enjoying the highest standard of living and the most satisfying lifestyle they have ever known. They are living longer, are more financially secure, better educated, more content with their lives, and more politically active than ever (U.S. Bureau of the Census 1996). Less worried about financial matters, they are more likely to look forward to retirement, and those with the best retirement incomes often elect to retire earlier. This new status makes possible the development of new interests and a return to neglected pleasures. Retirement is now presented not as an age but rather as "an expanding state of mind" (Stock 1999:1). Options for older persons have vastly increased, and the concepts of work and retirement have blurred. Many persons work longer, others work less, and still others combine work and retirement (Quadagno and Hardy 1996). While this life circumstance is true for the majority of older persons, the demographics of aging also reveal another story. The story of older persons who, for a variety of reasons, have become increasingly dependent on others for assistance in managing their lives and often for sustaining a view that it is possible to successfully cope with significant life stressors. It is this tale that falls within the purview of social work. It is this tale that demands our attention. It is these older persons whose resiliency is strained by the weight of significant personal, interpersonal, and environmental stressors in the face of insufficient protective forces.

To understand the risks and vulnerabilities of those requiring long-term care, sociodemographic, economic, health, physical, and mental health characteristics must be examined. Perhaps more than for any other age group, these elements are closely interdependent, and their combined effects constitute critical elements of the aging experience. Coping with change in these areas becomes a dominant feature of growing old in America. The awareness that aging is affected not only by what occurs to those 65 and older, but also by experiences of a lifetime, makes knowledge of the ongoing effects of sex, race, and class upon older persons central to our understanding. Sex, race, and class determine the quantity and quality of economic and service resources available to older persons and inform our understanding of which older persons are most at risk. The scarcity of essential environmental resources necessarily requires us to focus on those in greatest need.

The United States is currently experiencing a dramatic increase in the number and proportion of very old persons within the general population and within the population of older persons in general. The numbers of persons over 65, particularly those over 85, are growing more rapidly than those younger. Only 4 percent of the total population at the beginning of this century, by 2030 the percentage of those over 65 will be 22 percent (National Institute on Aging 1987; Torres-Gil and Puccinelli 1995). In 1994, those aged 65 and over constituted 12.5 percent of the total population (U.S. Bureau of the Census 1996). The projected increase of older persons between 1989 and 2050 will represent an increase from 1 percent to 5 percent of the total population (Dunkle and Norgard 1995). By 2050, those 85 and over will represent 22 percent of those 65 and over (Dunkle and Norgard 1995). Fertility rates, decreased mortality, and immigration patterns have all contributed to the growth of older persons at a rate faster than that of any other population group (Olson 1994b). Concomitantly, there has been a striking increase in those over age 75, and those above 85 have doubled each decade since 1940.

In 2000, the projected proportion of the over 85 group will be 14.1 percent (Rosenwaike and Dolinsky 1987). From 1960 to 1994 persons 85 and over increased by 274 percent (U.S. Bureau of the Census 1996). By all standards, the proportion of older persons in the general population will continue to rise dramatically, well into the twenty-first century (Easterlin 1996).

Of those older, the segment growing most rapidly is those over 75, particularly **women** and **ethnic minorities** (Dunkle and Norgard 1995). By 2050, the proportion of white, non-Hispanic older persons is expected to decrease to 67 percent, down from 87 percent in 1990 (U.S. Bureau of the Census 1996). Nationally, between 1990 and 2030 older Hispanic Americans are expected to increase by 395 percent, older African Americans by 247 percent and white, non-Hispanics by 92 percent (Dunkle and Norgard 1995). From 1990 to 2050 the black population of older persons will increase from 8 to 14 percent of the total population. Hispanic older persons will double from 1990 to 2010 and by 2050 will increase tenfold (Tauber and Allen 1993). Without question, Latinos are the fastest-growing minority group in the United States (Applewhite 1998). During the same period, "Asians, Pacific Islanders, American Indians, Eskimos and Aleuts combined would increase from less than 2 percent of the total elderly population to 7 percent from 1990 to 2050" (Tauber and Allen:17–18). Sex and minority statuses have remained critical variables in life expectancy. For white males and females born in 1990, there is an almost seven-year life expectancy advantage for women and for African Americans an eight-and-a-half-year advantage for women. While the life expectancy for African American women is greater than for white men, racial comparisons between white and African American males still favor white men by 6.6 years. White women have an advantage of 4.8 years in comparison with African American women (Gottlieb 1995). A disadvantaged status in health care, social and economic conditions, preventive and health education services, and income significantly contribute to the shortened life expectancy of minority older persons (New York State Office for the Aging 1989:25). Gender continues to be a salient dimension of the aging experience. Women continue to live longer than men and disparities between men and women increase with age. In 1989, for example, among those over 85, there were 39 men to 100 women (Dunkle and Norgard 1995). This male:female ratio indicates that the aging of women will continue to predominate in comparison to the aging of men.

The living arrangements of older persons are directly affected by life expectancy and marital and childbearing practices. Within this realm, significant differences exist between men and women (U.S. Bureau of the Census 1996). The 1996 U.S. Census report notes that 80 percent of older persons living alone were women. Though representing only 52 percent of the older population, white women represented 71 percent of those living alone. The greatest increase in those living alone was for persons 85 and over. This figure rose from 39 percent in 1980 to 48 percent in 1993. In 1993, 75 percent of older men were married and living with their partner in comparison with 41 percent of women (U.S. Bureau of the Census 1996). The percentage of women living alone increases with age. In 1993, 51 percent of women aged 75 to 84 lived alone. For the same year 57 percent of women 85 and over lived alone (U.S. Bureau of the Census 1996). The portrait of older persons living alone varies by ethnicity. African Americans, in comparison with other ethnic minorities, were more likely to be living alone. When older blacks and Hispanics live alone, they are also likely to be living in poverty (Choi 1996). African American females with 37 percent represented the ethnic group with the highest percentage of persons living alone. The U.S. Bureau of the Census (1996) reports that there was a 29 percent increase in the percentage of older persons institutionalized between 1980 and 1990 and that the majority of older persons living within nursing homes are widowed, older women, with a high percentage of inhabitants childless or never married. In 1990, 70 percent of older persons living in nursing homes were women and one-third of this female population was 85 years and older (U.S. Bureau of the Census 1996). By 2018, 13.3 million older persons are expected to be living alone, 85 percent of whom will be female (Kasper 1988). Social isolation is positively correlated with increased age, a single or widowed status, few nearby informal supports, retirement, and decreased physical capacity (Shanas et al. 1968). Social isolation can lead to serious emotional, cognitive, and social difficulties (George 1996). Mui and Burnette (1994) report that while physical health is greater for those living alone, this population reports greater loneliness, social isolation, and depression. Associated poverty and decreased social supports clearly place this population of single women living alone most at risk of increased morbidity, neglect and abuse, institutionalization, and death. The much smaller percentage of older men living alone with few social supports are also at risk. For those older persons living with families, a different set of needs is generated.

To truly understand the **economic characteristics** of older persons, the formula by which poverty is calculated must be understood. The poverty index, as developed in 1964 by the Social Security Administration, established that older healthy persons

... have lower nutritional requirements than younger people and therefore the poverty threshold is higher for persons under age 65. ... The poverty threshold in 1992 was $6,729 compared to the $7,299 used for single house-holders aged 15 to 64. For a two-person elderly household with no related children, it was $8,487 compared with $9,443 for younger households. (U.S. Bureau of the Census 1996:4–16)

This means that the poverty threshold for older individuals is only 92 percent of that for those younger than 65, and for older couples it is only 89.8 percent of the rate for those under 65 years. Rogers, Brown, and Cook (1994) found absolutely no justification for establishing this lower standard and recommended its elimination. If we took their advice, and if we recognized (as does the U.S. Bureau of the Census [1996]) that if a single poverty threshold were established for all persons, the poverty rates for older persons would increase, we would then have a more realistic portrayal of the poverty of older persons. Even using the current formula, Moon and Mulvey (1995) indicate that "[i]f poverty thresholds were increased for persons of all ages, the share of the elderly in poverty would thus rise faster than for other groups. At 150% of poverty 23.6% of the under-age-65 population would be poor, compared to 27.6% of those over 65" (18). In addition, reported poverty comparisons between older persons and children fail to acknowledge the 6 percent of older persons who are institutionalized, most of whom are poor (Schutz 1994). Thus, all poverty statistics and all economic indicators for older persons must be read with this reality in mind.

Over the last fifty years, there have been major gains in the economic status of older persons. A poverty rate for older persons of 75 percent in 1936 had been reduced to 18.6 percent by 1972 and to 12.4 percent by 1984 (U.S. Department of Health and Human Services 1985–86). The U.S. Bureau of the Census (1996) notes that the current percentage of those 65 years and older below the poverty threshold is 12.9 in comparison with 14.7 for those under 65 and 21.9 percent for those under 18 years. Such figures must be viewed with the cautions identified earlier. Social Security, the major governmental program for decreasing poverty in older persons, has a greater impact on this reduction than all other governmental benefit programs combined (Porter, Larin, and Primus 1999; Tracy and Ozawa 1995). Without social security, 47.6 percent of those 65 and older would have been poor in 1997. In a high percentage of states 75 percent of all older persons would be poor were it not for social security (Porter et al. 1999).

While the overall reduction in the poverty rate for older persons is certainly encouraging, a more detailed analysis reveals considerable cause for concern, particularly for women, ethnic minorities, and those oldest. First, older persons are poorer than are other adults. Data from the 1990 census (U.S. Bureau of the Census 1996) indicate that the percentage of older persons living below 150 percent of the poverty rate was 27.6 percent in comparison to 23.6 percent for all other adults. Second, the poverty rate increases as one ages (Porter et al. 1999). Those over 75 are significantly poorer than those 65 to 74. The poverty rate of 19.8 percent for those over 85 years is "not statistically different from that of children" (U.S. Bureau of the Census 1996:4–17). Third, poverty for females at all ages is greater than poverty for males. Women 75 years and over experience almost twice as much poverty as men that age, and 41.7 percent of women 75 years and over in comparison with 24.3

percent of same-aged men live below 150 percent of the poverty threshold. Poverty of a lifetime, minimum social security benefits as a result of a high degree of economic dependence on men, lessened employment opportunities, a widowed status, and few other sources of income lock women into economic positions they are unable to alter (Jones 1987). Gender biases in the social security system further disadvantage older women (Gottlieb 1995; Tracy and Ozawa 1995). And finally, older minority persons experience poverty at a rate disproportionate to their percentage in the total population. While 10.9 percent of older whites lived below the poverty level, that figure was 33.3 percent for blacks and 22 percent for those of Hispanic origin. Black women over 75 years had a poverty rate of 42.8 percent higher than that of all other older persons (U.S. Bureau of the Census 1996). The lower lifetime earnings of blacks and other minorities ultimately form the basis for their social security retirement income. In this regard, recent immigrants who have not amassed significant social security benefits are particularly disadvantaged (Porter et al. 1999). Poverty rates make clear that minority older persons are the poorest of all populations irrespective of age and that economic differences between majority and minority older persons continued to increase from 1970 to 1990 (Choi 1997).

Clearly, economic status controls the options available to older persons in need of long-term care and influences the degree of independence and hardship older persons have in managing their lives. An analysis of sources of income for older persons indicates that poor older persons are highly dependent on federal, state, and local programs for their minimum standard of living and have little opportunity to move beyond a poverty level through their own efforts. Social security continues to be the single most important income program for older persons, particularly minority older persons (Choi 1997). The inability to purchase services also increases the poor older person's dependence on family, public, and not-for-profit sources of support for the provision of long-term care. As deterioration in the financial status of older persons occurs, the pattern of reciprocity between them and their informal support network also declines (Stone, Cafferata, and Sangle 1987). As options for ameliorating poverty decrease with age, particularly for minority older persons, the current increase in poverty for children and families bodes poorly for decreasing poverty for older persons in the future.

While poor older persons are the most disadvantaged, lower- and middle-income persons in need of long-term care also experience disadvantaging economic conditions. The costs of long-term care that is provided by both the private and not-for-profit sectors are so prohibitive that all lower- and middle-income older persons are at risk of impoverishment (Freeman 1997). In only one year, 90 percent of those needing daily home care would be impoverished under our present system, where all are required to "spend down" to a Medicaid level. Seventy percent of those needing nursing home care would be impoverished in only thirteen weeks (Select Committee on Aging 1987). Maldonado (1987) points out that the increasing pattern of spending limited dollars on fuel, rather than food, further compromises many older persons already at risk because of their dependence on others to plan meals, shop, and cook. Hospitalization and institutionalization are too frequently an outcome (Ludman and Newman 1986). As a result, most older persons will eventually have decreased possibilities of purchasing long-term care and will become more dependent on programs for which they qualify as a result of financial eligibility. Fewer supportive and preventive programs will be used, as well, if older persons must choose between fuel and "luxuries," such as attendance at a senior service center. The growing control of long-term care facilities by the for-profit market increases the likelihood that poorer older persons will have decreased access to necessary services (Olson 1994b).

For obvious reasons, the **health and physical status** of older persons are of primary concern to them. Quality of life is intimately associated with health and physical ability (George 1996). Along with economic status, more than any other variable, poor health and disability can significantly decrease the older person's capacity for self-care and for a satisfying life. The resulting dependence on informal and formal supports brings with it psychological and social consequences. To need others for one's very survival generates profound feelings that are always present.

From the vantage point of health and physical characteristics, older persons, as a group, are highly diverse. While disease and disability increase with age, they are not necessary accompaniments of aging. Most older persons enjoy good health and have no serious physical disabilities that significantly limit their ability to live in the community (Bould, Smith, and Longino 1997; Jette 1996; U.S. Bureau of the Census 1996). Overall, chronic illness and disability have declined among older persons. Nonetheless, advanced age brings with it an increased probability of a greater number of chronic illnesses and a greater need for assistance with activities of daily living (George 1996; U.S. Bureau of the Census 1996). Chronic conditions, including arthritis, hypertension, hearing loss, heart conditions, visual and orthopedic impairments, and arteriosclerosis, rather than acute disease, tend to generate the limitations in self-care of greatest concern (Maldonado 1987; U.S. Bureau of the Census 1996). Disability associated with chronic health conditions is frequently increased for low-income persons owing to poorer housing, health care, and nutrition (Eustis, Greenberg, and Patten 1984; U.S. Bureau of the Census 1996). Therefore, not surprisingly, minority older persons and women are reported to have a higher prevalence of chronic illnesses and are reported to need greater assistance with daily activities (George 1996; U.S. Bureau of the Census 1996). Blacks 65 and over have a significantly higher rate of functional limitations (59 percent) than whites (49 percent) (U.S. Bureau of the Census 1996). Though Markedis and Black (1996) put forth that the "double-jeopardy" theory of disadvantage based on socioeconomic status applies most for the "young-old" and levels out for the oldest-old, minority older persons overall are reported to need greater assistance with daily activities (George 1996; U.S. Bureau of the Census 1996). Older persons with AIDS are a particularly vulnerable population, and from 1987 to 1992 the numbers of older persons dying from AIDS nearly doubled (U.S. Bureau of the Census 1996). As longevity for persons living with AIDS increases overall, we can expect the numbers of older persons living with AIDS to also increase. As with younger persons living with AIDS, older persons living with AIDS are a stigmatized, neglected population (Crisologo et al. 1996).

Reduced capacity for self-care becomes associated with chronic disease and is first in importance to older persons and their informal and formal caregivers. A significant decrease in the capacity for self-care in the following areas increases the need for long-term-care services: (1) *home management activities,* including preparing meals, shopping for personal items, managing money, using the telephone, doing light housework, and doing heavy housework; (2) *personal care activities,* including bathing, dressing, using the toilet, getting in and out of bed or a chair, and eating;

(3) *mobility status;* and (4) *continence status* (National Center for Health Statistics [NCHS] 1989). Consistent with data on the double jeopardy of ethnicity and income, poor minority older persons also experience more difficulty in these respects than majority older persons do (NCHS 1989). Further, chronic ailments have a demonstrable negative effect on social functioning particularly when long-term care services are insufficient. This is shown by a positive correlation between health and morale, social behavior, and leisure activity (Brody and Brody 1987). Living alone has been linked to social isolation and depression. Depression has been linked to lessened self-care and poorer health (Mui and Burnette 1994).

The distinction between personal care tasks and household management tasks is important. Evidence suggests that the likelihood of institutionalization increases in accordance with increases in the degree of personal care tasks required (Gonyea 1987). At the same time, twice as many older persons with similar health and functioning live in the community than in the institution (Olson 1994b). This observation confirms the need to understand well why some older persons remain in the community while others are institutionalized. The literature suggests that the critical variable increasing the likelihood of institutionalization is not physical need but whether family and community care supports are available and sufficient (Garner 1995). An increase in neglect and abuse associated with overburdened caregiving can also increase institutionalization (Tatara 1995).

Female sex, minority ethnicity, lower educational level, and lower socioeconomic status join increased age as significant factors negatively affecting health and physical status particularly for the young-old. Health differences between African Americans and whites remain greatest throughout the life span (Markedis and Black 1996). Additionally, social factors play a critical role in physical health and well being and "have been convincingly demonstrated to be strong predictors of health and mortality" (George 1996:248). The health effects of double jeopardy (race and ethnicity) are found most strongly for the young-old and diminish for the old-old when a "black-white crossover" occurs around 75 to 85 years and health risks for minority older persons decline (George 1996).

The medically oriented biological model of aging has increased negative stereotypes toward older persons in general and older women in particular. The reality is that most older persons do quite well in meeting the life tasks before them (Feldman and Netz 1997). Prior reports of the **mental health** of older persons distort the picture by dwelling on psychopathology and not stressing the resiliency of older persons (Bergeman and Wallace 1999; Feldman and Netz 1997; Padgett, Burns, and Grau 1998). Commonly characterized as the absence of mental illness, the concept of mental health "fails to address individuals' capacities to thrive and flourish, that is, go beyond the absence of illness, or neutrality, into the presence of wellness" (Ryff et al. 1998:69).

Without question, as a group older persons are quite resilient and there is significant "evidence that older persons manifest a lower prevalence of mental disorders compared with those under 65" (Padgett et al. 1998:393). Psychopathology is not a necessary accompaniment of aging and of all the psychiatric disorders noted in the *Diagnostic and Statistical Manual* (American Psychiatric Association 1994), only late life dementias are associated with aging. Many more disorders are associated with childhood and adolescence. Of the dementias associated with aging, the Alzheimer's type is most common (Hooyman and Kiyak 1996). Hooyman and Kiyak's review of the literature suggests that while estimates of prevalence are difficult to establish, there is some agreement that the incidence of Alzheimer's increases with age. Approximations of 5 to 15 percent for those 65 and over have been noted with the highest percentage occurring in those 85 and over. The most common mental disorders noted for older persons are depression, dementia, and paranoia, with depression the most commonly diagnosed of these three (Hooyman and Kiyak 1996). Despite its rank among these disorders, depression in not considered an expected part of the aging process (Salzman 1997).

Padgett et al. (1998) observe that although the proportion of those 65 and over needing mental health services is small, there is a high level of need not met by existing services. The level of unmet need is especially true for minority older persons (Allen 1983). The White House Conference on Aging listed mental health needs as the third highest priority for older persons (Rosen and Persky 1994). In an analysis of recent suicide data from the United States, Baker (1996) found that though older persons constituted only 13 percent of the population, they completed 39 percent of the suicides. For the 1980 to 1990 period, the U.S. National Center for Health Statistics (cited in Ivanoff and Riedel 1995) records an increase in suicide rates from 52.8 to 70.3 suicides per 100,000 for white males 85 and over. Of this group, older white males living alone have the highest suicide rate of all (Kalish 1985). Comparatively, the highest rates for white males under 65 is 27.5, for those 55 to 64. The rate for white females 85 and over is 5.4 per 100,000. This latter female rate is lower than all other age groups excepting those 5 to 24 years. While older women attempt suicide three times more often than their male counterparts, older men are three times more successful (Reker and Wong 1985).

For these older persons and those who attempt suicide but are unsuccessful, life no longer contains enough elements to justify existence. Whether one believes that suicide is generated by rational decision making or by feelings of hopelessness and helplessness fueled by depression, there is no question that overpowering life conditions, circumstances, and events provide the energy for such a decision. Loss of satisfying roles and relationships, lack of meaningful activity, conflicts around needing others and the resultant feelings of lessened self-esteem, depression, loneliness, and hopelessness may provide explanations for suicides among older persons (Reker and Wong 1985). The loss of personal resources increases the older person's sense of being at the mercy of the environment. Financial limitations, a major loss of independence, a sudden decision to give away important possessions, and a general lack of interest in the physical and social environment should be listened to carefully (Hooyman and Kiyak 1996). For older men living alone, despair prompted by insurmountable losses may be a salient explanation. Another explanation posits that a state of psychological impotence is believed to develop when psychological or social coping devices used in the past are insufficient to cope with present adaptive changes (Engel 1968). Hopelessness can induce morbidity as well as death (Lieberman and Tobin 1983). The more hopeful the individual and the greater the perceived control over a stressor (Neeman 1995), the greater is the likelihood that perceived negative events will not have aversive and harmful effects. The greater the buffering forces, the less the risk and the greater the resilience of the individual.

Hopefulness and perceived control over a stressor are especially difficult to achieve when far-reaching events occur and conditions arise over which little control can be exercised. Depression associated with the stress of loss (Rzetelny 1985), dementia, and paranoia, the three most prevalent later-life mental health conditions of concern, make hopefulness and a feeling of control difficult to sustain. Alzheimer's disease makes independent living an improbability. Decreases in attention span, learning, memory, language, judgment, and relational skills, coupled with a depressive reaction to the disease itself, can increase the risk of institutionalization.

Hope, associated with predictability and a perception of being able to master life's events, is not easily achieved at a time in the life course characterized by enormous uncertainty. While functional limitations can be measured and quantified once they occur, they often cannot be foreseen. A calm of today can unpredictably explode under the power of tomorrow's life events. A broken hip, the death of a spouse, the loss of sight, the loss of an apartment, or the closing of a neighborhood store, for example, can dramatically change the lives of older persons who had once managed quite independently. Those who felt they had escaped the experience of needing others for instrumental assistance and expressive support discover the contrary. Intellectual acknowledgment of the possibility does not prepare one for the actuality. The need for informal and formal supports can arise instantaneously, propelling the individual into previously not experienced role relationships with families, friends, neighbors, and formal service organizations. Under such circumstances mental health needs increase dramatically.

While suicide statistics are clearly more dire for males, Padgett et al. (1998) believe that ageism and sexism are factors raising the risk for women of "mental disorders and inadequate or inappropriate treatment" (391). They believe that of the population of older persons, women 75 and older have the greatest mental health needs and lowest rates of service use. Distress tends to be underreported in women, and therefore older women may experience states for which mental health services would be helpful. They also believe that because most older persons, and in particular women, are treated in the general medical sector and because most mental health concerns are largely undetected in that arena, most mental health needs go undetected and untreated. Unmet mental health needs of persons in nursing homes are much higher than those of the aged living in the community. Given that those institutionalized are primarily women, there are significant numbers of older women who could use mental health services if available, accessible, and offered. This is particularly true for those 75 and older (Padgett et al. 1998).

Though Padgett et al. (1998) discuss barriers to service utilization on the part of women, clearly, these barriers are applicable to men as well. They specify three categories of service barriers: system, cost, and ageism. System barriers include the lack of mental health services and fragmentation of existing service, low levels of reimbursement that decrease the provision and development of services, and an insufficient number of qualified service providers. Cost barriers include low reimbursement for high out-of-pocket care costs and high copayments for medication management. Mental health coverage under Medicare is limited by: a ceiling on lifetime benefits, restrictions on the numbers of days in specialty hospitals, the requirement of a 50 percent copay for mental health care, and a 20 percent copayment for management of prescription drugs. Strikingly, ". . . mental health costs comprise only 2 percent of the total Medicare budget, amounting to only $71 per annum per enrollee for all mental health and substance abuse services in 1990" (Padgett et al. 1998:408). While Medicaid does cover mental health services, the low rate of reimbursement discourages professionals from accepting clients with Medicaid insurance.

Ageism on the part of service providers includes biases toward older persons in the form of negative views of the capacities of older persons to change and use mental health services. While these conditions apply across all populations, Biegel, Farkas, and Song (1997) suggest that staff/agency and individual/family barriers represent two additional barriers with particular significance to African American and Hispanic older persons. Lack of culturally sensitive practice only serves to exacerbate individual/family hesitancy to utilize mental health services. A sense of stigma, negative prior experience, and an emphasis on self-reliance become three elements that must be transcended if engagement is to occur. Limitations of professional interest and vision, and limited services readily result from such ageist views. For all these reasons the mental health needs of older persons, especially those with limited economic means, go largely unmet.

SOCIETAL CONTEXT

An association between being over 65 and being frail is commonly assumed. In fact, this perspective is socially constructed. Sixty-five years, though still an arbitrary benchmark, should no longer bespeak the image of old age. It should no longer evoke a homogeneous picture. As Germain (1987) discusses, human development and human accomplishment increasingly defy established stage-related designations. While there remains, for some, a homogeneous portrait with frailty as its premise, for others there is a more vigorous and diversified representation. It is now commonplace to speak of the "young-old" and the "old-old" (Neugarten 1982), the "healthy-aged" and the "frail-aged" (Mayer 1983). Some suggest that an age entitlement marker of 75 be substituted as the age at which specialized services should be offered (Federal Council on the Aging 1978). The very nature and meaning of *old* have been redefined. It is generally accepted that diversity increases with age and that older persons are the most diversified segment of our population (Feldman and Netz 1997). This is not to suggest that hardship is not experienced by many with increased age, particularly those in need of long-term care. Rather, I suggest that the characterizing of an entire group in deficit terms derives from the complex interaction of social, economic, and political forces. Even gerontologists are thought to be guilty of ageism, owing to their emphasis on the problems of aging without sufficient emphasis on the myriad ways older persons cope well and live productively and meaningfully (Atchley and Lawton 1997). Diverting attention from the societal context of the aging experience perpetuates two powerful, but mistaken, beliefs: (1) older persons are responsible for their own difficulties, and (2) frailty is an inevitable outgrowth of the aging process.

No issue is more imposing on the lives of those needing long-term care than the public policy that specifies need, creates the conditions under which need comes about, and sets up the service systems to meet the very need it has helped create. As an embodiment of values and philosophy, public policy expresses a point of view about the proper role of government in the lives of its citizens, about the varied beliefs and interests of those governed, and about the powerful groups that govern and create social services. Thus, public policy is both proactive in creating the social context of older persons and reactive to the social context in which it finds itself. Holstein (1998) is poignantly eloquent in describing how public policy emerges from a socially constructed definition of need. Under such conditions, definitions of need are almost always established by those in power and rarely include the view of the recipients of such decisions.

The demographics presented earlier emerge from these "dominant power relations" and reflect an ageist society. The term *ageism* was coined by Butler (1969) to convey a prejudicial societal context that results in stereotyping and bias toward older persons. These biases have profound effects on how society behaves and are especially oppressive when internalized. Ageism is an insidious process that creeps into every aspect of private and public life. Within public life the most devastating and far-reaching effect of ageism is social policy that enacts the view that older persons constitute a class apart from the mainstream of society, where they are less worthy of social investment and less capable of acting in their own behalf. The needs of older persons, especially the vulnerable aged, are increasingly counterposed to those of other groups, particularly children, who are viewed as a "better investment" (Callahan 1987). The belief that older persons are well off and profiting at the expense of children is at the center of debates concerning how society should distribute its resources (Hewitt and Quadagno 1997). The view that health care should be rationed and the length of life should be limited is an increasingly troublesome voice (Binstock 1994; Rakowski and Post 1997; Schneewind 1994). This latter view assumes a utilitarian approach to the ethical question of the disposition of scarce resources. Services that are thought to achieve a "lesser return" for the investment are valued less highly than services thought to offer a "higher return" (Monk and Abramson 1982; Rohan et al. 1994). Negative views of the capacities of older persons support policies that diminish opportunities for the older persons to make even the most ordinary choices about their own lives. Forced retirement was a prime example of such a policy (Hooyman and Kiyak 1996). Devaluation and marginalization of older persons are exacerbated by such views, and the creation of responsive social policy is thus constrained.

When ageism is internalized by older persons, as it inevitably is, the price paid is lowered self-esteem and a self-concept that often mirrors the definitions of others. Such negative self-perceptions insult one's sense of self. When not countered by protective forces, an emotional state of helplessness and hopelessness can induce and maintain disease itself (Engel 1968; Mercer and Kane 1979). These feelings profoundly affect a person's level of assertiveness, a high level of which is believed to be necessary to survival (Berman-Rossi 1994; Tobin and Lieberman 1976). The sense of oneself as potent has direct bearing on the ability to cope successfully with life events over which older persons have diminished control as they age (Seligman and Elder 1986; Neeman 1995).

These effects of ageism are felt even more strongly by the vulnerable aged who are struggling with the impact of chronic illness, lessened physical vigor, and an uncertain future. While ageist policies and practices disadvantage all older persons, those who need a high degree of instrumental and expressive support to survive are further disadvantaged. Handicapping conditions are always most disadvantaging for those with the fewest personal and environmental resources. Risk always remains risk, but when protective processes exist, risks can be nullified or their impact lessened (Cowan, Cowan, and Schulz 1996). Those least powerful to resist are always most negatively affected by "forces tending to destroy." In these circumstances, morbidity, abuse and neglect, institutionalization, and death are more likely to increase.

One policy debate of central importance is the question of whether old age, sex, and ethnicity as such are associated with the need for long-term care, or whether such an outcome is a consequence of social, political, and economic policies. Those on either side of this policy dispute have very different recommendations to offer older persons and society. Needs versus age entitlement, as well as separatist versus integrated orientations, frame the bases for these differing recommendations.

Estes (1977), Estes, Linkins, and Binney (1995), Neugarten (1982), and Olson (1982, 1994a, 1994b) are unequivocal in advocating the view that old age itself does not create the disadvantage. They share the view that "aging and old age are directly related to the nature of the society in which they occur and, therefore, cannot be considered or analyzed in isolation from other societal forces and characteristics" (Estes et al. 1995:346). These policy theorists believe that the major problems older persons face are the ones we create for them. Lifetime disadvantages in the distribution of income, education, occupational skills, pension, and health care benefits, more than anything else, produce the nature and quality of the troubles experienced by older persons. Ageist social and economic policies, which perpetuate and institutionalize negative definitions of older persons, combine to produce the powerful dialectic with which older persons must contend. Incrementalist and individualistic public policy do little to mitigate inequities. The failure to correct past abuses limits the lives of older persons and frames the central challenge of social policy and planning for older persons (Estes, Swan, and Gerard 1982).

The distribution of income overshadows all other policy decisions in the potency of its effects on the lives of older persons. Income defines the degree of freedom available for problem solving and determines the degree to which individuals can partake of the country's growing standard of living. As income becomes restricted, and for some severely restricted with retirement, and as the poverty of a lifetime is brought to advanced age, particularly for women and ethnic minorities, the ability to command the long-term care resources necessary for a satisfying life is further diminished.

The older person's dependence on the "aging enterprise" and the dependence of the "aging enterprise" on the older person for their own existence generate a potent dialectic (Estes 1977). This dialectic structures the meeting ground and influences the terms of engagement between older persons and the aging service system. While this symbiosis should theoretically contain the elements necessary for a satisfying balance between older persons and their social institutions, social, political, and economic forces and inherent inequities in power act to distort this balance. The central effect of the creation of a separate, "nonproductive," and therefore dependent class is the devaluation of an entire segment of society. Age-segregated policies stigmatize the aged. As the needs generated for some normative aspects of aging are converted into social problems, older persons are moved further from the center of society. As we move toward structurally segregated, piecemeal policies, the aged are blamed for their needs and are viewed as a drain on society, especially by the young. Antagonistic perceptions of the aged support restrictive services. Recent discussion of the adequacy of the social security fund and rising health care costs are evident in current debates on social security (Niskanen and Moon 1997; Phillips and Ghilarducci 1997). Pitting the needs of one group against those of another, according to need entitlement proponents, becomes easier when an age entitlement orientation frames the formulation of social and economic policy. Age-based programs are also believed to increase the relative disadvantage of minority older persons. The higher mortality rates for minorities ensures that advanced age as a basis for entitlement will also ensure inequality of opportunity because the minority aged do not have an equal chance to reach advanced aged (Jacobson 1982). In addition, because the aged are a heterogeneous group, age is increasingly a poor predictor of lifestyle or need. Thus, age provides a limited basis for formulating policies and programs. Chronological markers only serve to isolate the older persons and separate their needs from those of society (Neugarten 1982).

The Federal Council on the Aging (1978) took an opposing stance in a position paper on public policy and the frail elderly. The Council was not prepared to abandon the present age-based social welfare structure and believed that, if older persons are to receive more of their fair share of scarce resources, their needs must be singled out for attention. The Council recommended continuing age as a determinant of benefits and suggested a second stratum of age entitlement upon attainment of 75 years. The belief that advanced age correlates directly with increased functional impairment prompted this group to advance 75 and over as the necessary age entitlement for increased benefits. They offered the view that the inadequacies and uneven availability of services that normatively occur within the organization of social welfare become experienced more harshly by those who, because of increasing frailty, cannot adequately negotiate the important service systems in their lives. Receiving limited services for both their normative and extraordinary needs thus further restricts the lives of these older persons. The use of an age designation, the Council argued, would more widely ensure access to vital services. Mandated additional income for the normative increase in need and ensuring a significant person to assist the older person in managing his or her life would significantly increase the service base for those in need of long-term care who do not have access to service themselves and/or who do not have a significant other who can assist with such tasks. It is the Council's belief that the separation of social services from income maintenance has been a failure for those older persons with "a weakened voice" who have difficulty negotiating their service environment.

The views of the Federal Council on the Aging are readily understandable to social workers who work daily with older persons. When needs are ignored in more broadly organized services, establishing specialized services at least ensures the delivery of services to older persons (Russell 1997). Every advantage and benefit we can secure for our clients should be secured. Nonetheless, we must understand that the private troubles of our clients reflect public issues in society and that all public issues are lived in private lives (Mills 1959; Schwartz 1969). Attending to the connection between the pain of the individual and the tribulations of the many is the pathway to relieving both.

VULNERABILITIES AND RISK FACTORS

Originating in the fields of commerce and insurance centuries ago, the concept of risk has evolved from its earliest definition concerning the categorical probability of a negative outcome occurring in a particular population (Cowan et al. 1996). This original idea shifted as researchers tried to make sense of the reality that similar outcomes did not necessarily occur even when persons were similarly situated in the same risk category. Rutter (1987) proposed that it was not the risk and vulnerability factors themselves, nor the protective factors alone, but rather the vulnerability and protective processes and mechanisms that connect risk and adverse outcome that critically influence whether risk results in negative outcomes. Risk then is what predisposes "individuals and populations (identifiably groups of people) to specific negative or undesirable outcomes" (Cowan et al. 1996:9). What is important is that a predisposing risk is not a guarantee of an adverse result. The questions to be asked are at risk for what and what links risk and outcome?

Cowan et al. (1996) offer that "[v]ulnerability increases the probability of a specific negative or undesirable outcome in the presence of a risk" (10). What is most important here is that vulnerability only has viability and potency when risk is present. Vulnerability can be located in individual persons, in the external environment, or in the relation between the two. The relevant question is always: to what risk is the vulnerability linked and what are the vulnerability processes and mechanisms that increase the probability of negative outcomes in the face of risk?

Ryff et al. (1998) add two additional concepts that are especially useful to our understanding of vulnerability and resilience in later life: cumulation of adversity and cumulation of advantage. Both concepts apply to all the domains of a person's life demonstrating the robustness of the concepts. Cumulation of adversity has two distinguishing features: (1) the notion of "pileup" of hardship, and (2) the enduring or chronic nature of problems. Cumulation of advantage speaks to the pileup of advantage, which has protective benefits and may be central to an understanding of resilience. Later life is a time when individuals bring with them a lifetime's cumulation of adversity and advantage, as well as being a period in which there is a natural accretion of life challenges.

The following presentation of the risks and vulnerabilities for older persons is organized around the material previously presented in the categories of demographics and social context.

Age. The oldest-old are at greatest risk for the following: a negative view of their capacities, living alone, increased poverty, social isolation, chronic illnesses, the fewest social supports, needing assistance with activities of daily living, decreased physical and mental capacity, loneliness, depression, late life dementia, neglect and abuse, morbidity, mortality, and institutionalization.

Sex. Males are at risk for the following: shortened longevity, acute illnesses, completing suicide (particularly white males 85 and over), and poverty (especially older minority males).

Females are at risk for living alone, fewer income sources, lifetime poverty that increases poverty with aging, widowhood, chronic illnesses, social isolation, attempting suicide, inadequate or inappropriate mental health treatment, and institutionalization.

Minority Status. Minority older persons are at risk for the following: shortened longevity; living alone (notably if an African American woman); extreme impoverishment (particularly African American and Native American women and recent immigrants); inadequate housing and environmental resources; fewer long-term care services; increased chronic illnesses; higher functional limitations; and racism in the provision, availability, and adequacy of necessary services.

Class. Poorer persons are at risk for shortened longevity, poorer health, poor nutrition, increased disability and the need for assistance with activities of daily living, chronic stress, fewer available physical and mental health services, more limited access to all services, and poorer quality of all services and benefits. Lower- and middle-class older persons are at risk for impoverishment with institutionalization. Cutting across all populations irrespective of age, class, sex, and minority status is that insufficient and inadequate social supports place *all* older persons at risk for increased morbidity, abuse and neglect, institutionalization, and death.

Occupying status in more than one of the preceding categories increases overall risk and illustrates the concept of cumulation of adversity. The greater the cumulation of disadvantage, the greater the need for protective factors and processes/mechanisms to mitigate or nullify the negative outcomes associated with risk. The more negative outcomes are decreased or eliminated, the greater is the likelihood that older persons will be able to *maintain, recover,* or *improve in mental or physical health following challenge,* thus both demonstrating and experiencing resilience.

The risks identified in the preceding are those that are primarily person based, though some system-based risks are included. The risks are all associated with being situated in a particular demographic category. The case is made, once again, that these categories of age, sex, minority status, and class become risk categories because the larger *societal context* creates them as such, and therefore the environmental context itself operates as a constellation of risk factors. In this instance, the whole of society is greater than the sum of its parts. On a societal level, ageism, sexism, classism, racism, and homophobia act to predispose older persons to negative outcomes. Public policy, which emerges from these conditions, institutionalizes disadvantages for older persons and increases their vulnerability. Public policy that generates these conditions also increases vulnerability The case has been made that personal risks and societal risks are intertwined and both must be addressed if the lives of older persons are to significantly improve. Once again, poverty and low income are the most powerful risk factors for older persons, substantially predisposing them to notable disadvantages, the effects of which are increasingly more difficult to nullify or lessen as one ages. These disadvantages remain most potent for women and ethnic minorities.

In identifying and separating risks and vulnerabilities, it is apparent that the distinction between the two is sometimes difficult to establish. In addition, that which operates as a risk in one instance (e.g., poverty) can operate as vulnerability in another instance (e.g., poverty increases the risk of poorer health outcomes). In addition, the same factor can sometimes function as a risk factor and at other times as protection from risk, for example, being a grandparent can protect against isolation and depression but can be a risk factor for health and depression for grandmothers raising grandchildren. Much more can be specified concerning the risks associated with old age, and many more levels of refinement can be established; for example, advanced Alzheimer's increases the risk of institutionalization, poverty of a lifetime increases the risk of poverty of old age, severe and persisting mental illness increases the risk of poverty, poor health increases the risk of depression, and depression increases the risk of poor health.

RESILIENCIES AND PROTECTIVE FACTORS

The demographics and societal context of aging combine to present a bleak picture for a large portion of older persons. How is it then that most older persons manage well, are able to sustain meaningful lives, and, in the main, believe that life is worth living? On the positive end of the continuum are protective factors, processes, and mechanisms and resilience.

Protective factors, processes, and mechanisms are those that serve to "decrease the probability of a negative or undesirable outcome in the presence of a risk" (Cowan et al. 1996:12). Rutter (1987) cautions that to describe a situation as high in protective mechanisms is not to describe a situation of low risk; rather, it describes the processes by which risk does not result in the probable negative outcome. Such a caveat is important because it points to the necessary separation of risk and protective factors and protective processes and mechanisms and, as such, opens up multiple routes to lessening the impact of risk, for example, reducing risk, and/or strengthening protective factors, processes, or mechanisms. A second caveat is that protective factors only exist in the face of risk. There is no function to protective factors if risk does not exist. Three categories of protective factors include: (1) sociological/social, (2) psychological, and (3) social/relational (Ryff et al. 1998). Sociological/social buffers include sociodemographic resources; psychological protections point to how individuals cope with and react to the events and challenges before them, and social/relational includes the arena of social supports.

Resilience operates as a process and represents the outcome of a process. The concept includes the notion of resources that can be called upon in periods of need and that operate to facilitate, at minimum, the return to the stability of the prestress state (Bergeman and Wallace 1999). At times, the prestress state can be surpassed, as when individuals, families, or groups achieve even more positive outcomes. In such instances, crises have been turned into opportunities for growth (Cowan et al. 1996). These gains can occur in the areas of mental and physical health (Ryff et al. 1998). Thus, how can we particularize these ideas for older persons in need of long-term care? What can counter the deleterious effects of the risks and vulnerabilities previously identified? Which protective factors, processes, and mechanisms operate differentially for older persons? On a certain level there are obvious answers to the task of defining protective factors. For example, economic resources protect against poverty, psychological well-being protects against depression, health protects against illness and depression, social supports protect against isolation and depression and thus increase physical well-being, and so on. These examples demonstrate the systemic, interacting nature of protective factors and the concept of cumulation of advantage. The greater the number of protective factors, the more likely it is that protective processes will be fortified. Income and resources dramatically increase options and freedom in life. By aiding in survival, stress is decreased and physical and psychological well-being is increased. Hobfoll and Wells (1998) also believe that more heavily resourced persons can invest more meaningfully in life. By having "reserves" one can risk and engage more. Having little prompts conservation and decreases opportunities for participation in life's pleasures and challenges.

Social supports promote resilience by linking personal resources and resources of the larger environment (Hobfoll and Wells 1998). In this sense, these supports function as "conduits" fostering connections between individuals and social systems of importance to them. A sense of group membership, whether familial or peer, is particularly sustaining. Membership in a meaningful peer group can especially buffer the pain of loss of family (Safford 1995). A sense of ongoing participation in life through reciprocal relationships, for example, volunteering, promotes a positive sense of oneself (Paulino 1998).

Self-concept also has a profound effect on how older persons cope with, and adapt to, life challenges. A strong, continuous self-concept operates as a resilience mechanism by organizing life experience and by preserving a sense of coherence over the life span (Bergeman and Wallace 1999; Staudinger et al. 1999). Moreover, a sense of coherence is based in one's sense that life is comprehensible, manageable, and meaningful (Korotkov 1998). Comprehensibility fosters resilience by increasing the older person's sense of an ordered world in which experiences can be anticipated. If events can be envisioned they can be planned for. Planning fosters mastery and decreases stress. Manageability promotes resilience by increasing the older person's view that he or she has sufficient resources to cope with life's challenges. By anticipating and thinking through how one might manage, persons feel strengthened. A sense of meaningfulness is most central to resilience and the perpetuation of a sense of self. In addition, ". . . if individuals' experiences are characterized by participatory decision making in which they are free to select their own outcomes, a strong sense of meaningfulness develops. However, when individuals have no say in any matter, they tend to see life as devoid of meaning" (Korotkov 1998:55). For older persons in need of long-term care, where so much is beyond their control, the ultimate right to participate in their own life and to express their selves is directly linked to the preservation of the self. Exercising one's voice reaffirms a strong sense of self (Meador and Blazer 1998).

The literature on resiliency in later life is just developing. Ideas concerning the preservation of a sense of self and a sense of coherence, that is, a self that finds expression with others and maintains meaning and a sense of purpose, appear particularly compelling. Adding the power of resourceful environments links older persons to their community and to the society at large. These ideas are at the heart of resilience and provide a persuasive conception of successful aging, a conception that far transcends the medicalized definition of ". . . low risk of disease and disease-related disability; high mental and physical function; and active engagement with life" (Rowe and Kahn 1998:38). Taken together, these ideas about resilience provide a direction for policy, planning, and practice.

PROGRAMS AND SOCIAL WORK CONTRIBUTIONS

Historically, some older persons, with no other recourse, turned to "strangers" when family systems failed. Designed as deterrents to poverty, almshouses (the precursor to long-term care facilities) became the choices of last resort (Holstein and Cole 1996). Others, for example, African Americans, learned early that public support was closed to them and that their survival was dependent on kith and kin and the formation of mutual-aid societies (Berman-Rossi and Miller 1994; Walker 1985; Williams 1905). This long-standing pattern of depending on one's own in the face of hostility from the external environment is part of a proud self-help tradition and bears significant benefits for older African Americans (Martin and Martin 1985; Milligan 1990). For many African Americans, the church remains an influential force in the development and sustaining of informal social supports and offers a salutary, buffering hub of social connections (Chatters and Taylor 1990; Martin and Martin 1995; Solomon 1976; Taylor and Chatters 1986). Whether by choice, or by default, other older persons in need of long-term care also cope with the challenges before them through the use of a mixture of formal and informal supports. Understanding this pattern of use and factoring out the elements that influence the utilization of each system are exceedingly challenging. The requirement to do so is especially pressing if we are to develop culturally competent and relevant long-term care services for diverse populations (Purdy and Arguello 1992; Wallace et al. 1997).

Natural helping networks are important to all older persons, especially minority older persons to whom formal social supports are less universally available (Cantor, Brennan, and Sainz 1994; Delgado 1995; Roy, Dietz, and John 1996; Tsai and Lopez 1997). Estimates are that 80 to 90 percent of care for an older person is informal and consists of family and relative-based care (Foster and Brizus 1993). Nonetheless, we must be cautious in the inferences we draw regarding patterns of use and preferences. The desire to care and the ability to care do not always coincide, particularly when the instrumental needs of older persons increase and demands on the family unit also increase (John, Roy, and Dietz 1997; Tran and Phooper 1996). In some instances, minority and majority older persons appear to receive similar amounts of informal and formal care, particularly when attributes of the caregiving situation and attributes of the older person are controlled (Tennstedt, Chang, and Delgado 1998). Ethnicity is less important than functional ability and economic resources in establishing a use pattern of informal and formal support services (Cantor et al. 1994). This is especially true in institutional placement where racism in admission practices, rather than ethnic preferences, is a greater predictor of institutionalization (Morrison 1995). A double standard for placement should not be confused with a preference for caring for minority older persons at home (Morrison 1995).

Older persons learn quickly that formal supports are biased toward institutional care and that an adequate continuum of care is not available. To whom would older persons turn, and for what, if the formal service system were accessible and their own financial and personal resources were adequate for securing, coordinating, and monitoring long-term care? What would the older person's preferred balance be between familial and organizational assistance? How do ethnicity, class, and sex influence the answers to these questions? The inadequacy of the formal service system and class inequities compromise our ability to develop "pure" answers. We do know that because health care policy favors payment for institutionalization over noninstitutional care that whites are advantaged in receipt of health care dollars. Blacks have more functional limitations than whites, use nursing homes less (by choice or default), and therefore are the recipients of fewer health care dollars (Wallace et al. 1997).

Though formal long-term-care services are commonly thought of as institutionally based, actually they are one among three categories of services provided: noninstitutional and nonhome community-based; home-based; and congregate, residential- and institutional-based. Using an "impairment continuum" Tobin and Toseland (1985) highlighted thirty-seven different types of services and showed how services typically become segregated according to professional definitions of clients' capabilities. They noted that where clients are served has more to do with a patchwork response to older persons than an overall plan about how needs can best be met. For example, there is no reason that mental health services for those with the greatest cognitive needs could not be integrated within community mental health centers, rather than segregated into medical and psychiatric day care programs (Federal Council on the Aging 1979). In contrast to an "impairment model," Hooyman (1983) developed a model around clients' problems in living and how community resources, both informal and formal, can be used to respond to these problems. For example, for persons needing assistance with personal care, she suggested a variety of formal organizations providing such assistance, the possibility of student help where such help can be secured, and home sharing involving an exchange of assistance for room and board.

While many different types of programs exist, the services and the service system itself are woefully inadequate. Ten major problems with long-term care programs are repeatedly discussed in the literature: (1) persistence of unmet needs in the population, (2) bias toward institutionalization, (3) racism and the explicit disadvantaging of minority older persons, (4) low levels of quality care, (5) geographical inequity and maldistribution of benefits, (6) excessive burdens placed on families, (7) rapidly rising public and private expenditures, (8) fragmentation among services and financing, (9) lack of case management function, and (10) barriers to use (Brody and Brody 1987; Harel, McKinney, and Williams 1990; Holstein and Cole 1996; Kane 1987; Minear and Crose 1996; Morrison 1995; Olson 1994a, 1994b; Tobin and Toseland 1985; Toseland and Smith 1991; Tran and Phooper 1996). The great physical, psychological, and emotional energy and resolve required to transcend these deterrents to service use strain already strained personal resources. The failure of our society to develop a coherent and caring long-term care policy exerts major hardship on those in need (Harrington et al. 1994). Society's failure is also reflected in the fact that the Older Americans Act does not promote the redistribution of income as one of its primary objectives (Olson 1982). The tragedy of growing old in America is deeply intertwined with our failure to adopt humane economic policies (Butler 1990).

Though all problems negatively influence the lives of vulnerable older persons, the bias toward institutional care has a direct influence on the creation of significant problems. The medicalizing of aging can be seen in the fact that as of 1993, institutional care consumed about 83 percent of Medicaid's payment for long-term care (Meiners 1996). Furthermore, estimates are that 80 percent of these facilities and 75 percent of nursing home beds are operated by profit-making enterprises (Kane 1987). Thus, enormous sums of public money, made possible through Medicare and Medicaid, are funneled directly into private hands that operate facilities according to minimum federal standards, at best. Professional social workers have virtually no contact with thousands of older persons living in for-profit nursing homes. The few monthly hours of required "social work consultation," if they are provided, offer a negligible amount to the institution and nothing directly to its inhabitants. In many instances the "social work designee" has no social work training whatsoever (Garner 1995). A social work presence is more likely to be felt in not-for-profit facilities, where concern for human need, rather than profit, is the guiding organizational principle. Paradoxically, if all facilities became not-for-profit, the social work profession would not have the personnel to staff the programs, not even at the rate of one social worker per facility. The privatization of services with limited public accountability is a major problem for older persons. It also poses a particular dilemma for social workers who are concerned about the quality of care for the aged in for-profit facilities yet may not wish to work in for-profit facilities.

The needs of the vulnerable aged do not support such a proliferation of institutional facilities, nor do they support the majority of available long-term-care funds being channeled to institutional settings. Admissions to long-term-care facilities have more to do with socially constructed definitions of need, social policy decisions, and economic incentives than with qualities intrinsic to those in need of long-term care (Knight and Loiver Walker 1985). Estimates are that for each person institutionalized, there are two to three individuals with similar problems in living within the community (Kane 1987; Olson 1994b). Many who have been institutionalized could be better served in their homes or in other less restrictive environments (Kaye 1985). In truth, there are no long-term personal conditions that necessitate caring for older persons behind large institutional walls, if formal and informal supports are sufficient. While the professional community may believe that many older persons live fuller, better-cared-for, less isolated lives in nursing homes, the choice is always the older person's to make.

Paralleling the bias toward institutional care have been simultaneous efforts to increase noninstitutionally based alternatives to care. Social workers and older persons and their families have long advocated for a better continuum of long-term-care services. The quadrupling of skilled-nursing-facility costs from 1965 to 1985 prompted policymakers to join in a search for alternatives (Brody and Brody 1987). Although some progress has been made and the development of long-term care institutions has slowed, noninstitutional, community-based long-term-care services remain woefully inadequate (Callahan 1996). The bias toward institutional care has taken its toll on the quantity and the quality of in-home and community-based care. For example, Kaye (1985), Lowy (1985), and Rathbone-McCuan and Coward (1985)—in discussions of home care, multipurpose service centers and respite, and adult day care, respectively—have amply demonstrated how these services beneficially address the needs of at-risk older persons at a lower level of cost yet receive low priority in the continuum of provided services. Nonmedical long-term-care services constitute the bulk of need for these at-risk older persons (Brody and Brody 1987). Medical prescription as the primary basis for most long-term-care services has conditioned the nature of the care provided, has limited access to services, and has made qualified social workers dependent on physicians to prescribe nonmedical care. The options remain greater for those not dependent on Medicaid, who can gain access to non-medically based programs. The emphasis on impairment and limitation, once the condition has occurred, means that the older person must fail before the service system is triggered. Supportive and preventive services, if available, are provided after the "functional impairment." The degree of freedom available to the older person, their families, and the social work profession are directly related to the funding, organization, and structure of long-term-care programs.

Social work services for older persons in need of long-term care have developed sketchily. The aging field of practice has had to contend with external public policy, a funding environment with a "Band-Aid approach" to service development (Estes and Lee 1985), and the profession's own ageism and preference for other fields of practice. The reluctance of large numbers of social workers to work with older persons is particularly sad in light of the growing numbers of older persons within society. The development of a national movement toward private, for-profit "geriatric care managers" and "fee-for-service" programs reflects the further movement of social workers away from the public and voluntary sectors and away from poor and low-income older persons.

Despite a seemingly baleful picture, some bright spots are created by those social workers who labor long and hard with, and in behalf of, the older persons in need of long-term care. These efforts take place through age-segregated programs for older persons (e.g., nursing homes, multipurpose senior settings, Meals on Wheels, and sheltered residential facilities), as well as through age-integrated programs (e.g., acute hospitals, community mental health centers, and outpatient health services). Both demonstrate the flexibility and resourcefulness of social workers as they respond to the needs of older persons. The following areas of service delivery are illustrative.

Long-Term-Care Facilities. Social work's role in not-for-profit long-term-care facili-ties predates the consciousness of need and opportunities created through Medicare's financing of nursing homes in the 1960s. This role flows out of our long-standing interest in the relationship between persons and their environment (Getzel and Mellor 1982) and directs itself toward older persons, their families and friends, the interdis-ciplinary team, and the nursing-home milieu. In this setting, social workers provide a wide range of services aimed at helping residents with their life transitional con-cerns, with the interpersonal tensions that normatively arise within a congregate set-ting, and with environmental obstacles to a more satisfying life. Life stressors can be addressed through individual, family, and group services (Brody 1974; Germain and Gitterman 1996). Group services decrease isolation, foster a sense of belonging and well-being, and mitigate feelings of loneliness and helplessness by increasing expe-riences in which control over the environment can be exercised (Berman-Rossi 1990, 1994; Kelly and Berman-Rossi, in press; Miller and Solomon 1979). Families also do well in groups, where the pain brought on by the crisis of institutionalizing a loved one can be shared with others experiencing similar feelings, and families can use each other's strengths to assist in negotiating the nursing home environment (Berman-Rossi and Gitterman 1999; Brubaker and Ward Schiefer 1987; Cox and Ephross 1989; Sol-omon 1982).

Hospitals. Though commonly not thought of as a primary service setting for older persons in need of long-term care, the acute care hospital, in actuality, is inextricably linked to the future lives of older persons. Diagnostic related group (DRG) treatment and managed-care discharge policies frame the organizational context in which social workers practice. Poised at this critical decision-making juncture, social workers pro-vide a major contribution to the lives of older persons by (1) helping patients and families cope with illness and hospitalization, (2) thinking through discharge options and arranging community supports, (3) educating the staff to the needs of older pa-tients, and (4) providing support for others who work with these "low-status" clients (Blumenfield 1982). In addition to their direct practice role, social workers sometimes assume a leadership role in assisting medical centers to expand the definition of their domain to include a preventive and community medical orientation. Such a definition allows the institution to create services lacking in the community and to assist older persons in securing services to which they are entitled (Lurie and Rich 1984). This same preventive role is actualized in hospital emergency rooms, where family members bring their relatives as a first step toward nursing home placement (Shepard, Mayer, and Ryback 1987). Because many poor and underserved older persons use emergency room services, social workers are afforded a distinctive opportunity to assess and provide for critical and ongoing needs (Barnett, Harnett, and Bond 1992). These collective efforts decrease fragmentation of services and allow the older person and the social worker a wider range of options from which to choose. Without the buffering efforts of hospital social workers, it is likely that an even greater number of older persons would fail or would require institutionalization. The services of social workers are also imperative for older persons experiencing long stays in acute care hospital as they wait for long-term-care community facilities. These patients and their families are often neglected when the need for acute medical services decreases (Sulman et al. 1996).

Rehabilitation Programs. Rehabilitation programs, whether attached to nursing homes or acute care hospitals, provide short-term rehabilitation care (Adelman et al. 1987; Seltzer and Charpentier 1982). These programs are designed to enable older persons to cope with specific medical traumas so that they have the option of returning to the community. The social worker provides service links during hospitalization and upon release and helps the older person and his or her family cope with the current medical trauma. Most important, the social worker holds, for all to see, a vision of the possibility of the older person's returning to the community.

Sheltered Residential Facilities. For example, in New York State, enriched housing is a program regulated by the State Department of Social Services, with a fee-for-service monthly charge (Baker 1985). On a small scale, it is intended to offer housing plus coordinated homemaker and housekeeper services. The social worker, who often administers the program, provides help with all problems experienced by the participants: familial and interpersonal concerns, financial matters, health worries, negotiation of the service environment, loss, and change. Group meetings for members provide a supportive medium in which members help one another with similar troubles. The strength of the program lies in the provision of a responsive physical environment, personal and household management care, and a social worker who provides an integrating force in residents' lives through the provision of all instrumental and expressive assistance.

Adult Day Care. A more recent service option, adult day care, has been developed for two purposes: to benefit older persons through an alternative to institutionalization and to control the costs of nursing-home care (Goldstein 1982; Rathbone-MaCuan and Coward 1985). Designed to serve those who wish to remain independent, adult day care tends to serve those older persons who often fall outside the "safety net" of other programs, that is, those who are isolated and do not reach out to others and those with lessened mental and physical vigor. The social work, rehabilitation, recreational, transportation, nursing, and medical services combine to provide a comprehensive program that eliminates the splintering of services found elsewhere. As the older person improves and is meaningfully engaged during the day, families often feel less need of institutionalization. Toward that end, group services provide a means for preserving human connection and increasing a sense of well-being (Kelly 1999). Such programs can be effective in supporting the independence of older persons (Sakadakis and MacLean 1993).

Home Care Services. Were it not for home care services, life in the community would not be possible for thousands of older persons who remain at home, are unable to manage on their own and without family, or whose needs for long-term care exceed the family and support system's resources. Home care services can include ". . . technology-enhanced, medically intensive services, hospice care, social support, long-term maintenance and custodial care, or periodic friendly visiting and reassurance" (Kaye 1995:1–2). As the tide of managed care has more quickly discharged patients from hospitals, skilled nursing and high technology services have been increased (Kaye and Davitt 1995). Administered by the for-profit, not-for-profit, and public sector, these services are provided through home care agencies, community agencies serving the aged, or institutions with community-based home care services. In 1994, 15,027 home care agencies were identified in the United States, with a growth rate of 15 percent to 20 percent per year. For-profit chains are rapidly increasing their holdings (Kaye 1995). In 1993 alone, $33 billion was spent on home and nonnursing home, community-based long-term care. Of this amount Medicare supplied 32 percent of the cost; Medicaid, 22 percent; and private sources, 46 percent (Rosenzweig 1995). Rosenzweig notes that a lack of uniform funding will continue to necessitate private payment and those without sufficient financial resources will continue to do without necessary services. Once again, class is a critical factor in the receipt of services. The lack of a well-integrated system for the provision of home health care services creates significant problems for providers and significant hardship for receivers of service. A medical, crisis-oriented, "cure-oriented approach" predominates in the payment and provision of services (Handy 1995). Social work's role in assisting clients with home care needs is of long standing and dates back to the 1920s (Kaye 1985). Social work's counseling role in home care services is well established and well documented (Kerson and Michelsen 1995). In executing this role, we are guided by our person-in-situation view. This vision enables us to understand the ways in which the need for home care services may be part of a total need for service. In this manner, a more holistic approach to service is developed.

If these services are not reflective of the dominant service delivery pattern for the older persons in need of long-term-care services, what enables the vulnerable aged to survive as well as they do? Extensive evidence indicates that, like persons of all ages, older persons turn first to family, friends, and neighbors and, as noted earlier, 80 to 90 percent of all home care is provided by kith and kin (Coward 1987; Foster and Brizus 1993; Hooyman and Lustbader 1986). While some are pleased with this phenomenon from a financial standpoint, and others have visions of close ties between older persons and their families, a cautionary note is in order for social workers. Social workers must take care not to overtax already burdened families (Gratton and Wilson 1988) or to neglect demands on policymakers and formal service organizations (Moody 1985). The notion that long-term care services should be organized "without eroding family care and the private purchase of help" (Kane 1987:61) is curious, as there is little to suggest that increasing formal social supports decreases family caregiving and merits suspicion. Women are expected caregivers, often taken for granted as they bear responsibility for the majority of family caregiving (Sánchez-Ayéndez 1998). They and their families deserve more responsive and more readily available home care services. Charting the proper role for the formal sector in supporting, while not abusing, efforts of informal caregivers is a major challenge for policymakers (Stone et al. 1987) and practitioners alike. Given the rapid increase in older persons this challenge takes on an imperative.

ASSESSMENT AND INTERVENTIONS

Hundreds of *instruments* have been developed for "assessing the older persons" in need of long-term-care services (Kane 1985; Kane and Kane 1981). These instruments include single-dimensional tools measuring physical, mental, and social functioning, as well as multidimensional measures inquiring into more than one performance area. Assessment of need centers on the functional limitations of the older persons and their resulting dependence. These instruments quantify attributes located within the individual and believed stable enough to measure. In the main, they represent a snapshot of the older persons—a moment frozen in time, extracted from a field of interacting forces.

It is not surprising that few of these instruments assess the environment or the congruity between client need and environmental resources. Geared toward geriatrics, and emerging from a medical model, they logically incorporate a view of aging as a medical experience. Such linear approaches use a medical model of study, diagnosis, and treatment. A strong separation between assessor and assessed is established. The "greater knowledge" (and power) of the assessor, or diagnostician, is presumed. As in the case of medicine, "fixing" the older person is at the heart of the venture.

The point of these measurement instruments is to assist service providers in deciding what type and amount of service to provide individual clients (Kane 1985). Kane believes that such tools have the potential to produce a functional computation that can serve as a reliable indicator for a service plan. Of course, how the tools are actually used in practice with older persons is the critical question for practitioners. This is where the payoff lies. Without discussion of what the practitioner does once armed with such "indicators," it is as if the measurements themselves are the ends of their own utilization. In social work, assessment and practice with older persons are better served by another tradition, a tradition in which the process of "knowing" and moving from "knowing to doing" is a complex, sometimes puzzling, often difficult, nonlinear enterprise. Knowledge does not carry its own prescriptions for action (Millikan 1959; Schwartz 1962). The properties of individuals, families, groups, and communities are not rigid and fixed but adapt and vary in interaction with the environment through a process of reciprocal adaptation (Germain and Gitterman 1996). Better suited to our work are the Interactionist Model (Schwartz 1977, 1994) and Life Model (Germain and Gitterman 1996). These models suggest that the character of an entity is created by the interaction of its parts. To understand individuals, families, groups, and communities, we must understand them in interaction with their environment.

The tie between them is symbiotic (Schwartz 1961). The older person's story is never finally written until death. Who older persons are includes who they can still become. Each instance presents life anew, affording older persons the opportunity to create their lives again and again. While certain functional measures can be achieved, the totality of an older person's life and its potentiality in a responsive environment do not hold still for easy measurement. It is this potentiality that social workers must understand as they work with older persons.

Because risk and vulnerability predispose and increase the likelihood of negative outcomes without causing them and because protective factors and processes and resilience increase the likelihood of nullifying and lessening the negative outcomes associated with risk and vulnerability, without causing them, assessment must be a dynamic and not a linear process. Only when all factors and intervening processes are considered in relation to each other, and to the client(s)' focus of concern, can we comprehend the relative influence of each. Only under these conditions will helping strategies and the helping process itself be most directly related to what is real and meaningful in clients' lives. After all, unless we understand how clients cope with and adapt to the life conditions, life events, and life circumstances of their lives, what will we have gained? These ideas are at the heart of the dynamic process of assessment by which workers and clients come to understand how these factors, processes, and mechanisms, in combination, affect and are affected by an individual, family, group, or community.

To be authentic, an accurate appraisal of older persons must include both concepts of wellness and illness, for both are true. Given the sociodemographics identified earlier, it should be obvious that if older persons are living longer and healthier, they are quite able to cope with and adapt to the changes in their personal, interpersonal, and environmental lives. The ability to cope does not mean that significant stress is not experienced; it does mean the ability to cope in the face of challenges, not in the absence of challenge. In fact, ". . . resilient individuals are those who do not simply avoid the most negative outcomes associated with risk, but demonstrate adequate or more than adequate adaptation in the face of adversity" (Cowan et al. 1996:14).

The ecological concept of *person:environment fit* is at the heart of the ideas expressed in the preceding (Germain and Gitterman 1996) and Gitterman (1996). This person:environment emphasis is particularly useful in understanding older persons and their ever-changing needs (Buffum 1987–88; Coulton 1979; French, Rodgers, and Cobb 1974; Germain 1979; Kahana 1974, 1982). Perhaps more than any other, this group is subject to experience a state of disequilibrium in which balance is thrown askew by three possible sources: the person, the environment, or the person:environment. Gitterman's (1991) distinction between life conditions, life events, and life circumstances fosters clarity in assessment. Each of these, whether a condition, event, or circumstance, can represent risk and vulnerability factors. Identifying these stressors provides a possible entry point for beginning work with clients (Gitterman 1996). The first, life conditions, includes those conditions commonly attributed to the person, for example, aphasia as a result of a stroke, a disease such as Alzheimer's, or loss of mobility because of arthritis. In these instances, individual attributes are relatively fixed and "knowable" and are viewed as independent of the external environment. The second, life events, can include events occurring to an individual, for example, a stroke, a broken hip, or loss of a spouse or partner, and can also include situations commonly defined as originating in the larger environment, for example, poverty, the loss of an apartment with gentrification, or the discontinuation of income benefits as a result of changed eligibility requirements. In these instances, environmental factors are viewed as measurable and independent of the individual. Understanding the third source of disequilibrium, life circumstances, poses the greatest challenge to the social worker. This source includes those events, situations, or circumstances where a clear separation between person and environment is difficult to establish. An example would be a decline in cognitive functioning precipitated by depression associated with social isolation and fewer orientation cues, or a weight loss instigated by ill-fitting dentures associated with poor health care benefits, or low-benefit utilization associated with cognitive and physical loss. What is distinctive about this third arena is that clients' situations and their experiences with them are not "knowable" by measuring the person and the environment separately. Rather, they can only be understood through comprehension of the reciprocal interaction between the person and the environment. The flow of energy and experience between the older person and his or her environment, actually creates the phenomenon itself. While the person, the environment, and the person-in-environment can each act as a primary trigger of a state of disequilibrium, it is the degree of congruity between the needs and capacities of the individual and the demands and resources of the environment that ultimately determines the nature of the consequences for the individual. To be of help, we must understand both the degree of congruity and the person:environment reciprocal transactions so that this understanding informs our helping strategies and professional practice. Achieving such an understanding is difficult and challenging for social workers practicing with the older persons in long-term care. Complexity is a distinguishing feature of such an effort. The effects of quickly changing physical, social, economic, psychological, cognitive, and organizational forces make achieving an assessment of any particular phenomenon, no less an entire situation imbedded in a life, difficult and subject to change. Adopting the view that assessment is an ongoing, continuous process will strengthen practice with older persons.

Assessment in work with older persons does not stand apart from practice with older persons; that is, the what of assessment and the how of practice are intimately intertwined (Schwartz 1994). From the initial moment of contact between worker and client, the helping process itself is invoked. How one begins, what one says, the skills one uses are as vital a part of beginnings with clients as they are with middles and endings. Practice with older persons begins with worker and client(s) searching for a shared definition of need. The concept of a shared definition immediately sets in place the idea that the worker-client relationship is one of a joint venture. Within this arrangement, the client becomes "coassessor" and, in whatever manner possible, director of his or her own life. Whether the "units of direction" are large or small, whether they entail where to live, what to wear, or what to eat, the older person must be placed, once again, in the director's chair. Ownership of the problem generates and releases energy for the tasks at hand. Agreement on what the problem is also provides the driving force and guiding spirit in determining what data must be collected. The fullness of older persons' lives does not permit the gathering of a lifetime of information, yet the complexity of defining problems requires a breadth of knowledge. The press of current concerns militates against a leisurely, open-ended exploration of a life. Purposefulness strengthens physical and psychological energy, particularly when that energy is limited. Finally, it is more possible to live in the here and now when the present, at least some of the time, is subject to one's own influence. Choice remains essential to maintaining or reestablishing a sense of oneself as competent (Lee 1983, 1994).

From the beginning of the working relationship, the worker fosters autonomy by providing information and helping clients arrive at their own direction, without co-ercion, even when other views are preferred by the worker (Monk and Abramson 1982). For the older person highly dependent on others, the belief that one can influ-ence one's environment encourages hope. These ideas about the relation between assessment and practice are particularly fitting for older persons in need of long-term care. Severely disenfranchised by our political, economic, and social system; severely discriminated against as a result of ageism, racism, classism, and homophobia; and coping with a wide range of disheartening life conditions and circumstances, these older persons do not enter helping relationships imbued with their own power. This is particularly true for older minority clients. Fear of domination by professional helpers is very real, rightly so (Gitterman and Schaeffer 1972; Lee 1994; Lum 1996; Pinderhughes 1989). A practice strategy that maximizes strengths, provides for choice, and encourages self-direction is the preferred strategy. This strategy applies even when the client, on the face of it, seems to have "accepted" a high degree of dependence on others. Not to encourage self-direction is to deny the older person the right and opportunity to exert influence.

The following *older person:environment fit assessment tool* is proposed to prac-titioners. It allows salient data to be organized in keeping with the concepts of balance between older persons and their environment and incorporates the distinction be-tween informal and formal social supports. It incorporates recent ideas on risk, vul-nerability, protective factors and processes, and resiliency. Such a tool can be used by workers alone, or with clients. When the guide is used with clients, clients can add their ideas about personal, interpersonal, and environmental stressors; resources; and protective processes. Most important, clients provide the clues that reveal pro-tective processes that diminish the probability of negative outcomes associated with risk. Clients are invariably strengthened when they are an integral part of a search to understand the problem at hand and the resources that may diminish its potency. It is they who can find the pathway to their own resiliency. Using these concepts is challenging, much more challenging than thinking linearly and categorically, for ex-ample, directly linking risk and outcome. But the knowledge that few risk outcomes are preordained should be encouraging to social workers. Resiliency theory's hope-fulness emerges, not from a denial of risk or vulnerability, but from a recognition that protective factors and processes can protect against risks inherent in the aging expe-rience, particularly for women and minority older persons. Something, no matter how small, can always be done to contribute to the lives of our clients. Often it is the "small things" that can yield powerful outcomes, for example, setting up a system by which medicine can be delivered.

Centered in the client's initial concerns, this tool helps the worker to generate salient background information and information on significant life conditions, life circumstances, and life events. The initial formulation of need provides the beginning impetus and direction for the assessment and for determining salience. As the problem shifts, changes, or is expanded upon, and other facets of the work become revealed, worker and client can then search for other relevant information and protective processes. Germain and Gitterman's (1996) Life Model informs the formation of this assessment tool.

1. *Definition of the problem.* What is it? When and under what circumstances did it develop? How has the client dealt with the problem? What are her or his strengths and struggles in dealing with the problem? How much stress has been generated by it? What inferences can be made about the problem and the client's way of coping with it?

2. *Client's expectations of agency and worker.* Under what circumstances did the client's need come to the attention of the agency? What is the client's degree of choice? Is the service sought, offered, or mandated? What are the client's expectations of the agency and the worker? What kinds of experiences has the client previously had with social workers or organizational helpers? What inferences can be made about the client's expectations of the agency, the worker, and the helping situation? How might past experiences with helpers influence the present?

3. *Knowledge about the client's life condition, life event, or life circumstance.* What is generally known about the condition, event, or circumstance with which the client is struggling? What are the predominant associated risks and vulnerabilities, which predispose and increase the probability of the problem's perpetuation? What are the predominant associated protective factors, forces, and mechanisms that nullify or lessen probable negative outcomes and increase resilience on the part of persons experiencing this life condition, life event, or life circumstance?

4. *Client's strengths and limitations.* What are the client's strengths and limitations in dealing with the problem (consider physical, economic, social, psychological, cognitive, religious, and class dimensions)? How able is the client to negotiate organizational systems? What inferences can be made about the client's strengths and limitations in dealing with her or his problem(s) in the past and currently?

5. *Environmental supports and obstacles.* What is the client's physical environment, including the home, neighborhood, and organizational environment? What social supports are available, including informal supports (family, extended kin, friends, neighbors, and community associations) and formal supports (health and social welfare)? What inferences can be made about the client's environmental supports and obstacles and their relevance to problem resolution or problem persistence?

6. *Degree of congruity between personal and environmental resources.* What personal and environmental risks and vulnerabilities promote perpetuation of the problem? What personal and environmental protective factors, forces, and mechanisms promote problem resolution? What inferences can be made about the degree of congruity between personal and environmental resources? What is needed to establish a better person:environment fit?

7. *Practice direction.* Based on your assessment, what additional data would be helpful? What will be your approach to the problem? What will you do to help? How will you and the client work together?

Using this tool, at least three points in time capture change and strengthen evaluation and planning. *Time 1* records the state of the older-person-environment fit, in relation to the problem, at the beginning of contact between worker and client. *Time 2* records the state of the older-person-environment fit, with planned personal and environmental changes designed to respond to the older person's unmet needs. *Time 3* records the state of the older-person-environment fit after a reasonable period of time has elapsed. The entire process would be reinitiated with a new event, condition, or circumstance. Social workers and clients are encouraged to think together about the ways in which changes in any one part of the older person's life can affect changes elsewhere.

Even when there is a high degree of congruence between older persons and their environment, an element of caution and a need for professional judgment obtain. Though positive value is commonly associated with a high degree of congruence, balance or homeostasis does not define the desirability of the state, or that all is well. Rather, it represents a statement that balance exists. The social worker must understand, and understand well, the basis of that state of congruence. For example, Kahana (1982) suggested that congruence models of person-environment interaction could be used to place older persons in particular environments. But what happens when this congruence is based on a high degree of institutional authoritarianism and a lifetime of oppression, resulting in a low desire for assertion on the part of the older person? Should the client be placed in such an environment?

Helping strategies of partnership, mutuality, and encouraging a strong voice on the client's part, coupled with an understanding of older persons in interaction with their environment, are all equally important during the ongoing phase of work. It is during this phase that the worker becomes most tempted to "do for" clients, rather than painstakingly involving clients in their own lives. While the temptation to shortcut the process is understandable, doing so can only undermine clients' growing sense of confidence in their ability to influence those around them. When they are encouraged to make their own choices and are "lent a vision" of their own possibilities, then the potential of the helping relationship is being fulfilled. In a sense, it portends clients' potential in other relationships as well.

Of course, at times social workers must assume a protective role in work with older persons: situations where older persons are unable to manage money, are unable to protect themselves against abuse and neglect, are unable to make decisions, and are without reliable personal relationships (Tatara 1995). These times require the highest level of skill, lest our protective role inadvertently violate clients' rights and weaken their voices. The decision to act paternalistically must be carefully thought through (Kelly 1994). Schwartz (1994) and Shulman's (1999) discussions of skills are helpful in highlighting how social workers strengthen clients' voices. Workers prepare to receive client communication by "tuning in" to the meaning of clients' struggles and their ambivalence about expressing strong sentiment, especially toward those on whom they are dependent. Elaborating skills help older persons tell their story, moving from the general to the specific, containing the worker's instinct to solve everything; reaching inside of silences; and asking questions to learn more. Only when the practice is specifically tailored to clients can their energy come to the fore to direct the helping relationship. Empathic skills encourage clients to attach affect to the work at hand by reaching for feelings, displaying understanding of clients' feelings, and putting clients' feelings into words. The same set of values and principles that guide our "doing with" clients should guide our "doing for." These include the principle of the least restriction, a strategy of "partnership," and honoring the client's wishes, to the extent possible without endangering their well-being. Even persons with Alzheimer's disease can communicate preferences. It is we who must learn to listen well enough to hear and respond to such communications.

Ensuring the place of all older persons in the helping process demands a great deal of the social worker. The press of myriad demands pushes us quickly on and urges us to avoid attention to detail, to process, to feeling, to the complexity of the person-in-environment, to the worker-client relationship, and to the strength of the relationship that can develop when we and older persons work closely together. However, such avoidance fosters unnecessary dependency, stifles autonomy, perpetuates the passivity associated with withdrawal and a failure to thrive, and ultimately becomes oppressive.

ILLUSTRATION AND DISCUSSION

The following practice example illustrates service to a group of older persons living within Metro Home and Hospital for Aged (MHHA), a not-for-profit, long-term-care facility that has a 140-year history of serving older persons within the institution and within their homes. As funding priorities changed, and as ideas shifted toward serving older persons in less restrictive environments, MHHA developed an even wider range of noninstitutional home-based services. A broad range of programs and services, allowing older persons and their families a range of options, is one of MHHA's distinguishing features.

The Floor Group was designed to provide an ongoing opportunity for residents who lived on the same floor of MHHA to work together on shared matters of importance concerning the broad arena of their lives as older persons and the more specific domain of their lives as older persons within an institutional setting. All personal, interpersonal, and environmental issues were deemed to be important to the members. The group was conceived as a system of mutual aid wherein the worker's attention was directed toward individual participants, toward strengthening the group as a whole, and toward developing a network of helping relationships (Schwartz 1961).

As an open-ended group that met weekly, the members, the worker, and the Floor Group as a whole would face certain challenges. These developmental challenges are normative for open-ended groups (Galinsky and Schopler 1985; Schopler and Galinsky 1984). The amount and frequency of member turnover are key elements affecting group development. Open-ended, institutionally based groups for older persons are especially challenging (Kelly and Berman-Rossi, in press). In this Floor Group a central core of four residents consistently attended. It was they who carried forth the developing culture and work of the group. As time passed they assumed greater leadership and brought new members on board.

Members who attended came from a pool of thirty-one residents living together on the same floor. Consistent with national demographics for nursing home residents, the average age of residents was 86 years and 90 percent

(n = 28) were female. Ninety percent were majority and 10 percent were minority.

The worker was a 27-year-old, white, Jewish female who was new to MHHA. At the time of this group practice example she had been at MHHA for about two months. The following practice example is fleshed out from the worker's practice log. She kept this journal so that she could study her practice with her supervisor and colleagues at MHHA. The worker writes:

The following illustration of organizational influence and change occurred within my first few months as a floor social worker at MHHA. It has remained with me since. It constituted a very powerful example of how a group service strengthens individual and collective resiliency, thereby prompting and achieving organizational change. The story begins.

Defining the Problem. As a social worker for three floors, it was natural for me to compare my floors. As I thought about the residents, I was struck by the fact that the appearance of residents on one of my floors looked significantly more unkempt than the appearance of residents on my other floors. I noticed messy hair, lipstick applied in a crooked manner, ties on crooked, and a general lack of attention to physical appearance. As a new worker I thought the differences might be associated with the fact that these residents, who were sicker, might be less inclined and less able to "fix" themselves up. When I realized that healthier residents, who used wheelchairs for transportation, also had an unkempt appearance, I felt confused and was unsure of what to do with my impressions.

Our first two floor group meetings had been spent in getting acquainted. Though group members lived together, they felt they knew little about each other personally. Not only did they need to get to know me, they needed to learn more about each other as well.

At our third group meeting eight residents were present. After greetings and the sharing of refreshments I asked group members how their week had been. Four residents spoke. The sentiment was the same: nothing special had occurred. They said life was pretty much the same; nothing changed. I said I had the sense that they felt pretty resigned in their lives at MHHA. My remarks were greeted with silence. I waited a bit and when no one responded, I said I noticed how quiet they were and wondered if they could share a little of what they were thinking. No one responded. I waited. Mrs. Bauer was the first to speak. Slowly, very slowly, she said that her life was over and little mattered to her. Needless to say, I was surprised by Mrs. Bauer's remarks. It was only our third meeting and we hardly knew each other. I had not expected such strong feelings to be expressed so early in the life of the group. I waited, to give others a chance. No one said anything. The silence was heavy again. Looking at Mrs. Bauer I said I thought she had shared some pretty strong feelings and I wondered if anyone else felt so resigned, as if their lives were over too and that little mattered to them. Hesitatingly, Mrs. Domingo said she felt the same way. Ever since her husband died and she *had* to come to MHHA, she didn't care about much. She said she used to enjoy dressing up each day, but now there was no one to appreciate how she looked. Her children were far away, and people in her family were all old, too. Mrs. Schwartz said she felt the same way. Her appearance didn't matter to anyone else and certainly didn't matter to her. Mr. Smith, who had never spoken before, said that, anyway, even the Home didn't care about them and didn't think of them as people. Hearing his words, I felt very startled and disturbed. I felt so optimistic about my work and suddenly saw myself so out of tune with the residents. I couldn't imagine that this was really how the Home felt. Mrs. Bauer said she thought they had done enough talking about depressing things and wanted to know what else *I* wanted to talk about today. I said I hoped maybe we could spend a few more minutes talking about what they had raised. Mrs. Bauer said if we did, she would leave. She didn't want a group just to talk about upsetting things that would never change. The others who had spoken shook their heads in agreement. I said I was sorry. I didn't mean to push them to talk if they didn't want to, but I hoped the group could be a place where we could discuss important things to them. Mrs. Bauer said this wasn't important. It was just how things were. She again asked what else *I* wanted to discuss with them. There was an air of expectancy. I said I thought we were just getting to know each other and I hoped we could continue that process and that we could think about what they might like to discuss in the group . . . any issues, topics, or matter of interest to them. Mrs. Bauer was called for a bath and suggested we discuss this next week. Others said they had enough as well and began to leave. I asked if they wouldn't be willing to talk for just a few more minutes since I sensed that some of them were disturbed by our discussion. They said no and left. Only Mrs. Archer, who had slept through the meeting, was left. As I left the room I saw that residents were getting ready for lunch even though lunch was an hour away. I wanted to approach group members but didn't know what to say. I left the floor feeling very badly, as if I had encouraged too much self-revelation too quickly in the life of the group. I feared that residents would not return and that they had been hurt by the experience. Having previously worked with very expressive adolescents, I was unaccustomed to such an abrupt ending to such important content.

During the ensuing week I resolved to try and get a better feel for what the residents were saying by observing life on the floor. In addition, I decided to reach out to group members who had expressed such disturbing sentiments. I came on the floor very early the following morning to better understand how residents were assisted in getting ready for breakfast. As I came on the floor I noticed Mr. Smith sitting in his wheelchair, looking straight ahead into the hall, and putting on his tie. I was struck by how he did this without ever looking in a mirror. The result was a disheveled appearance. Next I came upon Mrs. Bauer who, also sitting in her doorway, was combing her hair. As I approached her, I instinctively took a mirror out of my purse and offered it to her. She looked up and said, "I used to be able to use one of those." Naively I asked what she meant. Lifting her hands she said her arthritis was so bad she could no longer hold a mirror. I said I was sorry, I didn't realize. A nursing assistant came and wheeled Mrs. Bauer to breakfast. My confidence as the floor social worker was plummeting quickly.

It was then that I realized what should have been perfectly obvious from the start. What I had originally attributed to depression was really related to the fact that all residents could not negotiate small, handheld mirrors, and other residents who used wheelchairs could not see the mirror over the sink in the bathroom. A walk through the Home's three buildings confirmed my hunch. There were no floor-length mirrors in the hallways of two of my three floors. Residents in the two other buildings had hall mirrors, and residents in this building did not. I felt embarrassed by my psychologizing of the issue. Though the problem clearly had a depressing effect on residents, the matter before us was undoubtedly environmental in origin. A nursing assistant helped me understand that the Tower Pavilion was the oldest of the three building. When renovations were conducted on the other two buildings, hall mirrors were hung. Though I wasn't sure that residents would even want hall mirrors, I reasoned they might. There was no compelling reason to believe they would not.

Understanding the Problem. Certainly I couldn't be the only one to think that full-length mirrors were in order. I spoke with a floor head nurse and a floor nursing assistant with whom I had a good working relationship. The nursing assistant immediately agreed that residents' appearances left something to be desired. She said she had difficulty encouraging residents to take an interest in how they looked. She thought anything that helped with that would be great. In contrast, while the head nurse agreed that residents didn't always look as well groomed as they might, she feared that they would be upset with what they saw and therefore it would be better to be without mirrors. Besides, the residents weren't really pushing for this addition. Sensing a veiled criticism I said, "Are you thinking that this is really 'my thing'?" She said, "I know you mean well but you are new here and young. Maybe you don't quite understand what it is like to be old." I said perhaps she was right. I knew I had a lot of learning to do and I hoped she could help me learn. Working with older persons was new to me. As she left to care for a resident she said, "Besides, the residents had their 'time of attractiveness.' " She also said, "I'm sure you will figure this all out." I must admit to being quite surprised. It never occurred to me that a staff professional would want to "protect" older persons from dealing with the visual impact of their physical changes by denying them access to mirrors. I had no doubt that my colleague had not "caused" the problem, but rather, she had a rationale as to why it would be better not to work for change. Once again, I felt at a loss about what to do.

I thought it prudent to better understand the problem. The organization's view was as yet unknown to me. What *I* perceived as a problem had gone on for a long while. I would have to learn why. I assumed that understanding the organization's stake in the status quo would help me develop a strategy for change. I was strengthened by my belief that hallway mirrors would not be a startling addition and surely seemed to be in the residents' self-interest.

It was shortly after a team meeting that I learned what was probably the reason mirrors were not installed. The head nurse and nursing assistants were speaking about their frustration with not having bathrooms in each of the resident's rooms. They said they knew the Home was applying to conduct a major renovation of the Tower Pavilion and that the construction would probably be completed within two years. At that time many of their problems would be solved but it sure felt like a long time to wait, particularly for the residents who wouldn't live to see the day. They added that they knew the Home didn't want to make any changes now that might be undone by the new construction. I thought that adding mirrors might fall into that category. While I was tempted to comment about the mirrors, I realized that raising the issue prematurely might risk a negative response. Such a response would be harder to undo than raising the issue when the team, hopefully, felt positive.

Developing a Strategy. Determining how to proceed in the development of my strategy was not clear. Brager and Holloway (1978) recommend a "force field analysis," which, like all assessments, considers the forces for and against change. Patti (1980) supports such an analysis, stressing that the development of a strategy for change is integral to and required for organizational change. Analyzing the strengths and limitations of the organizational environment would be an integral component of this organizational assessment. As a new staff member, there were few people in the larger organization whom I knew well and with whom I had a close working relationship. I was unknown to most and my efforts alone would not bring about change. Even if they could have, I wasn't sure that my timing was correct. I reasoned I had more to lose through my "rightness" if my team did not support the change than if the problem persisted for a while longer. It was more important to move with the team in relation to residents' needs than to press for change only I valued. Importantly as well, I didn't know how the group members felt about hall mirrors. While the Home did not need the residents' permission to add mirrors, it seemed important to tap the members' thinking. Including group members in the process could only serve to strengthen residents' sense of their own potency. In addition, doing so would strengthen the group as a whole, thereby strengthening connections among members and between residents and the team. The floor community as a whole could only gain from the process.

As I thought about my working relationships in the facility, I realized that my strongest relationships were with the nursing staff on my floors, the other team members, and my social work colleagues. If there were to be any change I would need to think in terms of an alliance of interests. And certainly, the head nurse and I were not necessarily on opposite sides. The head nurse was worried that residents would be too upset—too upset for their own good. While I did not have that concern, I could appreciate that she did. Several others thought it might be better to leave well enough alone. I knew if I were to engage the nurse, I would need to find ways to align with her caring and her interest in the residents as well as attend to her fear that the residents might become too upset.

Engaging other team members seemed easier. I knew the head nurse might feel that it was easier for others to advocate for change, as they would not be the ones to soothe the hurts, should that actually occur. I thought locating each discipline's stake in the change would increase their support for the change. I knew the nursing assistants were supportive of the change.

Involvement with grooming and appearance fell directly to them. Gaining support from physical and occupational therapy seemed possible, too. I could present hair brushing as an upper body range of motion exercise, in the same way wheeling oneself to the mirror would strengthen upper extremities. The doctors certainly were interested in their patients' general well-being and knew there was an important connection between mind and body. Certainly, the psychiatrist in particular would support most things that countered alienation and depression. The recreational therapist too might be excited by either specific programs she could provide pertaining to appearance or just the additional ways in which residents might involve themselves in activities when they looked and felt better about themselves.

I defined the steps in my strategy as follows:

1. Developing consciousness about the problem among residents and floor staff.
2. Developing a base of support within the floor group and among my team members.
3. Working on the change strategy with the head nurse, determining the points of tension between us, and the specifics of what would lessen her worries and increase her support.
4. Talking with the social workers from the two other floors in the Tower Pavilion to determine their assessment of the problem, their view of the possibilities of change, and whether they would lend support to the effort toward gaining mirrors in the hallway.
5. Garnering the enthusiasm of the director of social services so that she might support the effort with administration, with whom she had a close working relationship.

Utilizing the Strategy. I began by testing out my ideas with the head nurse. Our conversation meandered toward our earlier difference, and I said I was planning to bring my observations and ideas to the floor meeting next week and wondered what she thought about that. She said she guessed that was okay. I said, "You don't sound so sure." She replied, "Well, it's just that because you think the mirrors are a good idea you might pressure the residents to think the same way and besides, the residents aren't used to being asked about what they thought about floor matters." I said I could see she really had a lot of questions about my group work on the floor. What would she think of our meeting some time so that I could tell her more about the group service and what the Social Work Department was hoping to achieve? I said I had wanted to sit down with her but had only managed a brief conversation about the group because she was so busy and I was so new. She told me not to worry. We would have a chance to talk. I said, "It just occurred to me that perhaps you might like to join me for the portion of the group when I raise the matter of residents' appearances and no hall mirrors." She laughed and said, "Believe me, I have enough to do." I persisted a bit saying, that's a real invitation. She smiled and said, no . . . it was ok, she wasn't opposed and didn't feel the need to be there. I smiled and said, "Okay, thanks. I'll let you know how it goes."

Sensing that mornings were very busy for residents, with their agreement, I changed our meeting to the afternoon. At the next floor meeting Mrs. Bauer, Mrs. Domingo, Mrs. Archer, and Mr. Smith and eight additional residents were present. After refreshments were served, Mrs. Bauer asked what I wanted to discuss with them. After reaching for their agenda and finding them fixed on my raising matters, I said that I had some observations and an idea I wanted to share with them. I said that when I came on the floor I frequently noticed residents trying to groom themselves in the morning without having any mirrors to look in. I cited several examples and then noted that Mrs. Bauer had taught me that many of them found it too difficult to use a little mirror and so they did the best they could. I said I also knew many of them could not stand long enough to use the mirror over the sink in the hall bathroom. The room was quiet. No one said anything. Mrs. Bauer, who in only five meetings was emerging as a floor leader, said, "So?" I smiled and said, "Well . . . I was wondering whether you might like to have mirrors in the hallway so that you can see yourselves when you are getting ready in the morning." Silence. I waited. More silence. I waited. Mrs. Domingo was the first to speak. She said, "A mirror is not important to me. I told you already, I don't care about that stuff . . . there's no one to dress up for anymore." Waiting 30 seconds felt like eternity. Just as I was about to speak Mrs. Carver said, with a big smile, "You could get dressed for me! We could get dressed for each other." Mrs. Carver pointed out that because they were roommates they were always helping each other. Mrs. Domingo looked at Mrs. Carver intently but said nothing. I said, "Mrs. Carver, I have the sense that you are saying that things are not the same as they used to be but life continues." She said, "Right, honey, if we have to be here and have to look at each other, why shouldn't we look as nice as we can." Slowly other members began to discuss the idea of hall mirrors. Most denied their importance for them but were willing to support the idea if others wanted them. I shared with them the support of nursing staff and my intention of speaking with other team members. I also noted that I would like to bring to them, each week, how the matter was developing. Many acknowledged that they would like to hear. Mrs. Domingo was quiet throughout the meeting. Before summarizing the consensus of group, I turned to Mrs. Domingo and said that I noticed how quiet she was. I imagine many of us are interested in what you are thinking. She was quiet and then began to cry. She said this conversation only helped her miss her husband more. Mrs. Carver took her hand and said, "I know, I miss my husband too and my daughter." Others lent support. It was a tender moment in the group. Intimacy among the members was growing. We agreed I would bring feedback on the mirrors each week, and in response to my invitation a few said maybe in the future they might want to talk about missing people. People lingered together after the meeting.

Once I felt secure with the support of my team, I began talking with the social workers on the other floors in the Tower Pavilion. I was mindful of the fact that neither of them had raised the issue for their residents, though each had been there for several years. I wasn't sure that moving beyond the bounds of my floor would be a wise thing to do. Once others became involved I would lose a measure of control. On the other hand, I knew my efforts could and should not be secret. Outreach to my co-workers was strengthened by my belief that a broader base of support might be useful, and I was self-conscious about raising an issue for change for only the residents on my floor. All residents were entitled to mirrors. Attending to one's appearance was a common human need. From a pragmatic position I assumed that administration or the director of social service would eventually ask the other social workers what they thought of the idea, and I wanted to be there first.

The social workers were enthusiastic. In the hustle and bustle of all their work, hallway mirrors felt like a low priority. They suggested that because I was new and not yet involved with all the problems they were charged to address, I still had time to devote to "extras." We agreed that I would carry the major responsibility for engaging the change and theirs would be a supportive role.

When I had spoken with enough people individually, and had a sense that most supported the change, I decided to bring the matter up in team. The head nurse seemed willing to go along since everyone else seemed to want them. I thought there was enough positive sentiment to counter any remaining negatives. The team, as a whole, seemed to enjoy the idea of working together on this project. Once raised, there was consensus that mirrors were important. Team members felt especially strongly that since there were mirrors in the newly remodeled buildings, their patients should not be discriminated against.

We problem-solved about how to proceed. We needed to know one important piece before we could move on: were there mirrors lying around or did the Home have to buy them? The head nurse was friends with the head of the Engineering Department and found out that there were no extra mirrors. New mirrors would have to be bought.

All along I had been using a parallel strategy with staff and residents. As the issues were discussed in team, they were discussed in weekly floor group meetings. These meetings were new to residents and having "an issue" provided a kind of galvanizing force. Residents were becoming connected to each other through their collective interest in getting mirrors on the floor. Even the more hesitant residents seem to be captured by the energy on the floor.

Eventually the team and residents decided to invite Administration to a team meeting and to a resident floor group meeting to discuss the problem and to present the request for mirrors in the hall. By this time, the heads of social work, nursing, physical therapy, occupational therapy, and recreational therapy all supported the change. The director of social work informally cued in the Home's administrator, so she was prepared.

As we planned, both meetings occurred in the same week for maximum effect and support to residents. The residents were eloquent in their presentation. In team, the head nurse took the lead. She began her presentation by appealing to the administrator's sense of furthering the goals of the institution and her sense of fair play as other floors had mirrors. A few days after these meetings, the other floors made the same request. Shortly after, the mirrors were purchased and installed.

There was a great deal of excitement on the floors the day the mirrors were installed. The team and residents shared a sense of pride in having been effective. Residents peeked out of their rooms as the workers hung the mirrors. When all was cleaned up there was a quiet on the unit. It was as if residents were privately deciding who would go first. Ms. James, the head nurse, was watching, too. Mrs. Bauer, who had emerged as a leader in the floor group, slowly wheeled herself to the mirror closest to the nursing station. Staff members "hung" in the background, knowing that residents should be allowed sufficient space to decide when, how, and if they approached the mirror. Mrs. Bauer finally arrived and sat in front of the mirror. She turned to staff and just looked at us without words. I quietly smiled in return. She continued to view herself, not moving at all. I had no idea of how long it had been since she had really seen herself. This was her moment. Residents and staff seemed to sense that and didn't intrude. After a few more minutes Mrs. Bauer began to sob quietly. Ms. James immediately moved toward her. I suggested she wait a moment. Mrs. Bauer and the staff were only a few feet away from each other. She began to cry a little more. Ms. James and I walked over to her. Ms. James looked at me. I put my hand on Mrs. Bauer's shoulder and smiled gently at her. She smiled and said, "It's o.k. I'm all right. It's been a while since I've taken a good hard look at myself and I suppose I wasn't prepared." Ms. James held her hand. I said it seemed that she was a little upset and I wondered what she was feeling as she looked at herself. She smiled again and said, "Well, I certainly have wrinkles, and I certainly am not a 'young chippy,' " but laughing she added, "I'm o. k. This is who I am and it is nice to know." I smiled and said, "Yes, I can imagine." I moved away a little and by this time Ms. James and Mrs. Bauer were hugging each other. Many of us had watery eyes. As I looked up I noticed that residents had quietly wheeled themselves to where we were.

Mrs. Bauer invited others to come up to the mirror. Residents and staff shared the experience. It was a moving time. The floor was never the same.

The preceding example demonstrates many themes. These themes are about the salutary value of groups, the importance of professional skill, the symbiosis between private troubles and public issues, the power of the group to strengthen individual and collective resilience, the professional's obligation for social change, and the possibility and process of social change. We see a social worker encouraging group members to engage with life, to risk the possibility of disappointment, and to risk expressing their voice after being quiet for so long. We hear a social worker fostering connections among members, asking them to taste remembered pleasures when they had friends and were part of a hub of activity. We watch a social worker encouraging caring about each other and about themselves. The social worker has developed a slow, nurturing, partnership style with the group members. She understands well that loneliness and alienation prompt caution and uncertainty. More important than the mirrors was the worker's relationship with the members and their relationships with each other. After all, they were now family and community to each other with the potential for affectional ties. Receiving the mirrors would be meaningless, if in the process the members felt violated and oppressed. While the mirrors had intrinsic value, the risk of oppressing the residents far outweighed any good that might have come from adding an environmental resource. The worker also understood the group members' underlying fear that their assertion would cause institutional retaliation. Her careful attention to the process and the pains she took to attend to the dialogues between the residents and all facets of the institution, for example, nursing staff, administration, served as a protective factor diminishing the risk. With the staff and institution, too, the worker was guided by the desire to establish a close working partnership centered on the Home's relationship with the group members. Moving too quickly and risking alienating the team and administration would ultimately be a disservice to the floor residents. Jeopardizing her position within MHHA would not have served the residents well. Here too, the residents had more to gain from enhancing the tie between them and the institution. Securing the mirrors paled in comparison with diminishing this connection. The social worker's belief in the possibility of change emerged from her belief in the symbiotic connection between the residents and the institution. She held to the idea that greater than the objective of the mirrors was strengthening the dialogue between the residents and their floor and institutional community. Her emphasis on the connection between clients and their environment reflected her definition of professional function between client and community.

CONCLUSION

The subject of this chapter has been serving older persons in need of long-term care. The demographics of aging provide a dramatic picture of the social, economic, and political context in which such older persons live. Social workers must heed this picture as they plan, organize, and deliver social services to a population made vulnerable by public policy insufficiently responsive to its needs. Of the older persons in need of long-term care, older women, particularly older minority women living alone, are especially disadvantaged by poverty. These older persons are most at risk of abuse and neglect, morbidity, institutionalization, and death. Older white men living alone are at risk for suicide. The notion that these persons are at risk because of personal attributes rather than society's failure is an example of societal ageism, in which older persons are blamed for their problems in living. Viewing the individual as independent of the environment is consistent with the medicalizing of aging. The transformation of older persons' needs into social problems pushes older persons further to the margins of society and pits their interests against the interests of others. Frailty, as in the "frail elderly," is socially defined and socially created. It comes about when we separate older persons from the environment and fail to provide the resources necessary for a satisfying life. The incongruity between older persons' needs and capacities, on one hand, and society's demands and resources, on the other, taxes diminishing and difficult-to-renew personal and environmental resources. Under such conditions, weakened voices are created. An unresponsive social context produces inadequate resources and fragmented services. It also produces isolating, age-segregated policies, the very situation long-term-care services are designed to mitigate.

The task for social workers is a difficult one. Though it is beyond our profession's capacity to bring about the redistribution of economic resources, it is not beyond our ability to advocate for responsive public policy centered on an adequate economic standard. Similarly, though it may be beyond our capacity to integrate fragmented long-term-care services, it is not unrealistic to undertake to plan integrative programs to serve the whole of our clients' lives by connecting them to services that our own agencies cannot provide. Moreover, though we cannot ensure the responsiveness of others, we can bring the plight of the most vulnerable older persons to center stage in our own work and professional activities.

Practice with the older persons in need of long-term care requires a helping strategy directed toward assisting older persons in making the strongest claim possible on society, through the strengthening of their voices. Placing older persons at the head of this effort, to whatever extent possible, maximizes their strengths. At least within our relationships, self-determination and a better balance of power should prevail. Under these conditions of partnership, the resiliency of older persons is most likely to be realized.

This helping strategy is consistent with Holstein's (1998) and Shklar's (1990) view that for meaningful justice to prevail, service providers and policymakers must move from the "demands of justice to the experience of injustice" (Holstein 1998:7). In writing about the power of truly understanding the experience of those who suffer from injustice, Holstein writes:

> Once we can imagine what it feels like to be an older woman, especially an older women of color, we can recognize why we must think about injustice. Logical criteria of fairness might tell us how we ought to structure society to achieve greater justice, but until we hear the voices of those who have been treated unjustly or know the unfairness ourselves, it is unlikely that we will be moved to act. What would it mean for aging policy if we documented the injustices that raise our ire, that anger us, that make us cry out that something is " 'wrong' "? . . . Inaction makes us complicit in the humiliation of others. The view from injustice in contrast to the view from justice forces us to attend to real practices, to real people, and to real groups; this vision is the source of social action. (7)

It is from this view of injustice that the best social work practice with older persons in need of long-term care emerges. Under these conditions the link between private troubles and public issues is palpable. Under these conditions both clients and social workers are most empowered. Under these conditions coalitions among older persons, service providers, community organizers, and policymakers can best join together on behalf of older persons in need of long-term care.

However sanguine we may feel about the overall picture, the efforts of social workers who work with the most vulnerable older persons are often brave and creative. Their unflagging spirit, energy, and skill reflect the best in the social work profession.

Note

I am appreciative of discussion with Dr. Irving Miller on the concept of frailty and its relation to the aging field of practice and for his editorial suggestions on the first edition of this essay. My ideas about the profession of social work and the function of the social worker within society have been profoundly influenced by the work of Dr. William Schwartz, to whom I shall remain ever grateful.

References

Adelman, R. D., K. Marron, L. Lebow, and R. Neufeld. 1987. "A Community-Oriented Geriatric Rehabilitation Unit in a Nursing Home." *The Gerontologist* 27(2):143–46.

Allen, J. A. 1983. "Mental Health, Service Delivery in Institutions, and the Minority Aged." In R. L. McNeely and J. L. Cohen, eds., *Aging in Minority Groups,* pp. 174–84. Beverly Hills, Calif.: Sage.

American Psychiatric Association. 1994. *Diagnostic and Statistical Manual of Mental Disorders,* 4th ed. Washington, D.C.: Author.

Applewhite, S. L. 1998. "Culturally Competent Practice with Elderly Latinos." *Journal of Gerontological Social Work* 30(1/2):1–15.

Atchley, R. and M. P. Lawton. 1997. "Is Gerontology Biased Toward a Negative View of the Aging Process and Old Age?" In A. E. Scharlach and L. W. Kaye, eds., *Controversial Issues in Aging,* pp. 185–96. Boston: Allyn & Bacon.

Bader, J. L. 1999. "Relying on the Competence of Strangers." *New York Times,* April 1, pp. B1, B11.

Baker, M. E. 1996. "Service Needs, Usage, and Delivery: A Look at the Imbalance for African American Elderly." *Journal of Poverty* 1(1):93–108.

Baker, R. 1985. "Housing for the Frail Elderly: A Model." *Journal of Gerontological Social Work* 8(3/4):257–64.

Barnett, L., P. T. Harnett, and A. F. Bond. 1992. "Patterns of Emergency Department Use of Geriatric Patients." *Journal of Gerontological Social Work* 19(1):77–98.

Bergeman, C. S. and K. A. Wallace. 1999. "Resiliency in Later Life." In T. L. Whitman, T. V. Merluzzi, and R. D. White, eds., *Life-Span Perspectives on Health and Illness,* pp. 207–25. Mahwah, N.J.: Lawrence Erlbaum.

Berman-Rossi, T. 1990. "Group Services for Older Persons." In A. Monk, ed., *Handbook of Gerontological Services,* pp. 141–67. New York: Columbia University Press.

———. 1994. "The Fight Against Hopelessness and Despair: Institutionalized Aged." In A. Gitterman and L. Shulman, eds., *Mutual Aid Groups, Vulnerable Populations, and the Life Cycle,* 2d ed., pp. 385–409. New York: Columbia University Press.

Berman-Rossi, T. and A. Gitterman. 1999. "A Group for Relatives and Friends of Institutionalized Aged." In C. LeCroy, ed., *Case Studies in Social Work Practice,* 2d ed., pp. 212–21. Homewood, Ill.: Wadsworth Press.

Berman-Rossi, T. and I. Miller. 1994. "African-Americans and the Settlements During the Late Nineteenth and Early Twentieth Centuries." *Social Work with Groups* 17(3):77–95.

Biegel, D. E., K. J. Farkas, and L. Song. 1997. "Barriers to Use of Mental Health Service by African-American and Hispanic Elderly Persons." *Journal of Gerontological Social Work* 29(1):23–44.

Binstock, R. H. 1994. "The Clinton Proposal and Old-Age Based Rationing: A Plea for Informed Public Debate." *Journal of Aging and Social Policy* 6(1/2):167–77.

Blumenfield, S. 1982. "The Hospital Center and Aging: A Challenge for the Social Worker." *Journal of Gerontological Social Work* 5(1/2):35–60.

Bould, S., M. H. Smith, and C. F. Longino. 1997. "Ability, Disability, and the Oldest Old." *Journal of Aging and Social Policy* 9(1):13–31.

Brager, G. and S. Holloway. 1978. *Changing Human Services Organizations: Politics and Practice.* New York: Free Press.

Brody, E. M. 1974. *A Social Work Guide for Long-Term Care Facilities.* Rockville, Md.: National Institute of Mental Health.

Brody, E. M. and S. J. Brody. 1987. "Aged: Services." In R. L. Edwards, ed., *Encyclopedia of Social Work,* pp. 106–26. Silver Spring, Md.: National Association of Social Workers Press.

Brubaker, E. and A. Ward Schiefer. 1987. "Groups with Families of Elderly Long-term Care Residents: Building Social Support Networks." *Journal of Gerontological Social Work* 10(1/2):167–75.

Buffum, W. E. 1987–88. "Measuring Person-Environment Fit in Nursing Home." *Journal of Social Service Research* 11(2/3):35–54.

Burnette, D. and A. C. Mui. 1994. "Determinants of Self-Reported Depressive Symptoms by Frail Elderly Persons Living Alone." *Journal of Gerontological Social Work* 22 (1–2):3–19.

Butler, R. N. 1969. "Ageism: Another Form of Bigotry." *The Gerontologist* 9(4):243-46.

———. 1990. "The Tragedy of Old Age in America." In P. R. Lee and C. L. Estes, eds., *The Nation's Health,* pp. 363–73. Boston: Jones & Bartlett.

Callahan, D. 1987. *Setting Limits.* New York: Simon & Schuster.

Callahan, J. J. 1996. "Care in the Home and Other Community Services." In R. H. Binstock, L. E. Cluff, and O. Von Mering, eds., *The Future of Long-Term Care,* pp. 169–88. Baltimore: Johns Hopkins University Press.

Cantor, M. H., M. Brennan, and A. Sainz. 1994. "The Importance of Ethnicity in the Social Support Systems of Older New Yorkers: A Longitudinal Perspective (1970 to 1990)." *Journal of Gerontological Social Work* 22(3/4):95–128.

Chatters, L. M. and R. J. Taylor. 1990. "Social Integration." In Z. Harel, E. A. McKinney, and M. Williams, eds., *Black Aged: Understanding Diversity and Service Needs,* pp. 82–99. Newbury Park, Calif.: Sage.

Choi, N. G. 1996. "Changes in the Composition of Unmarried Elderly Women's Households Between 1971 and 1991." *Journal of Gerontological Social Work* 27(1/2):113–31.

———. 1997. "Racial Differences in Retirement Income: The Role of Public and Private Income Sources." *Journal of Aging and Social Policy* 9(3):21–42.

Coulton, C. 1979. "A Study of Person-Environment Fit Among the Chronically Ill." *Social Work in Health Care* 5(1):5–17.

Cowan, P. A., C. P. Cowan, and M. S. Schulz. 1996. "Thinking about Risk and Resilience in Families." In E. M. Hetherington and E. A. Blechman, eds., *Stress, Coping and Resiliency in Children and Families,* pp. 1–38. Mahwah, N.J.: Lawrence Erlbaum.

Coward R. T. 1987. "Factors Associated with the Configuration of the Helping Networks of Noninstitutionalized Elders." *Journal of Gerontological Social Work* 10(1/2):113–32.

Cox, C. and P. H. Ephross. 1989. "Group Work with Families of Nursing Home Residents: Its Socialization and Therapeutic Functions." *Journal of Gerontological Social Work* 13(3/4):61–73.

Crisologo, S., M. H. Campbell, and J. A Forte. 1996. "Social Work, AIDS and the Elderly: Current Knowledge and Practice." *Journal of Gerontological Social Work* 26(1/2): 49–70.

Delgado, M. 1995. "Puerto Rican Elders and Natural Support Systems: Implications for Human Services." *Journal of Gerontological Social Work* 24(1/2):115–30.

Dunkle, R. E. 1984. "An Historical Perspective on Social Service Delivery to the Elderly." *Journal of Gerontological Social Work* 7(3):5–18.

Dunkle, R. E. and T. Norgard. 1995. "Aging: Overview." In R. L. Edwards, ed., *Encyclopedia of Social Work,* 19th ed., pp. 142–53. Washington, D.C.: National Association of Social Workers Press.

Easterlin, R. A. 1996. "Economic and Social Implications of Demographic Patterns." In R. H. Binstock and L. K. George, eds., *Handbook of Aging and the Social Sciences,* 4th ed., pp.73–93. New York: Academic Press.

Engel, G. L. 1968. "A Life Setting Conducive to Illness: The Giving-Up-Given-Up Complex." *Bulletin of the Menninger Clinic* 32(6):355–65.

Estes, C. L. 1977. *The Aging Experience: A Critical Examination of Social Policies and Services for the Aged.* San Francisco: Jossey-Bass.

Estes, C. L. and P. R. Lee. 1985. "Social, Political, and Economic Background of Long Term Care Policy." In C. Harrington, R. J. Newcomer, C. L. Estes, and Associates, eds., *Long Term Care of the Elderly: Public Policy Issues,* pp. 17–39. Beverly Hills, Calif.: Sage.

Estes, C. L., K. W. Linkins, and E. A. Binney. 1995. "The Political Economy of Aging." In R. H. Binstock and L. K. George, eds., *Handbook of Aging and the Social Science,* pp. 346–61. San Diego: Academic Press.

Estes, C. L., J. S. Swan, and L. E. Gerard. 1982. "Dominant and Competing Paradigms in Gerontology: Towards a Political Economy of Ageing." *Ageing and Society* 2(2):151–64.

Eustis, N. N., J. N. Greenberg, and S. K. Patten. 1984. *Long-Term Care: A Policy Perspective.* Monterey, Calif.: Brooks/Cole.

Federal Council on the Aging. 1978. *Public Policy and the Frail Elderly.* Washington, D.C.: U.S. Government Printing Office.

——. 1979. *Mental Health and the Elderly: Recommendations for Action.* Washington, D.C.: U.S. Government Printing Office.

Feldman, S. and Y. Netz. 1997. "Beyond Menopause: Vulnerability Versus Hardiness." In D. E. Steward and G. E. Robinson, eds., *A Clinician's Guide to Menopause,* pp. 203–25. Washington, D.C.: Health Press International.

Feldstein, D. 1985. "Permanent Patients: On Working with the Chronic Mentally Frail in the Community." *Journal of Gerontological Social Work* 8(3/4):121–40.

Foster, S. E. and J. A. Brizus. 1993. "Caring Too Much? American Women and the Nation's Caregiving Crisis." In J. Allen and A. Pifer, eds., *Women on the Front Lines,* pp. 47–73. Washington, D.C.: The Urban Institute.

Freeman, I. C. 1997. "Nursing Home Reform: Fait Accompli or Frontier." *Journal of Aging and Social Policy* 9(2):7–18.

French, J. R. P., W. Rodgers, and S. Cobb. 1974. "Adjustment as Person-Environment Fit." In G. C. Coelho, D. A. Hamburg, and J. E. Adams, eds., *Coping and Adaptation,* pp. 316–33. New York: Basic Books.

Funk and Wagnall's Modern Guide to Synonyms and Related Words. 1968. New York: Funk and Wagnall's.

Furstenberg, A. L. 1989. "Older People's Age Self-Concept." *Social Casework* 70(5): 268–75.

Gadow, S. 1983. "Frailty and Strength: The Dialectic in Aging." *The Gerontologist* 23(2):144–47.

Galinsky, M. and J. Schopler. 1985. "Patterns of Entry and Exit in Open-Ended Groups." *Social Work with Groups* 8(2):67–80.

Garner, J. D. 1995. "Long-Term Care." In R. L. Edwards, ed., *Encyclopedia of Social Work.* 19th ed., pp. 1625–34. Washington, D.C.: National Association of Social Workers Press.

George, L. K. 1996. "Social Factors and Illness." In R. H. Binstock and L. K. George, eds., *Handbook of Aging and the Social Sciences,* 4th ed., pp. 229–52. New York: Academic Press.

Germain, C. B. 1979. "Introduction: Ecology and Social Work." In C. B. Germain, ed., *Social Work Practice: People and Environments, An Ecological Perspective,* pp. 1–22. New York: Columbia University Press.

——. 1987. "Human Development in Contemporary Environments." *Social Service Review* 61(4):565–80.

Germain, C. B. and A. Gitterman. 1996. *The Life Model of Social Work Practice: Advances in Theory and Practice,* 2d ed. New York: Columbia University

Getzel, G. S. and M. J. Mellor. 1982. "Introduction: Overview of Gerontological Social Work in Long-Term Care." *Journal of Gerontological Social Work* 5(1/2):1–6.

Gilson, S. F. and F. E. Netting. 1997. "When People with Pre-Existing Disabilities Age in Place: Implications for Social Work Practice." *Health and Social Work* 22(4):290–98.

Gitterman, A. 1991. "Introduction: Social Work Practice with Vulnerable Populations." In A. Gitterman, ed., *Handbook of Social Work Practice with Vulnerable Populations,* pp. 1–32. New York: Columbia University Press.

——. 1996. "The Life Model Theory and Social Work Treatment" In F. J. Turner, ed., *Social Work Treatment,* pp. 389–408. New York: Free Press.

Gitterman, A. and A. Schaeffer. 1972. "The White Professional and the Black Client." *Social Casework* 53:280–91.

Goldstein, R. 1982. "Adult Day Care: Expanding Options for Service." *Journal of Gerontological Social Work* 5(1/2):157–68.

Gonyea, J. G. 1987. "The Family and Dependency: Factors Associated with Institutional Decision-Making." *Journal of Gerontological Social Work* 19(1/2):67–77.

Gottlieb, N. 1995. "Women: Overview." In R. L. Edwards, ed., *Encyclopedia of Social Work*, 19th ed., pp. 2518–28. Washington, D.C.: National Association of Social Workers Press.

Gratton, B. and V. Wilson. 1988. "Family Support Systems and the Minority Elderly: A Cautionary Analysis." *Journal of Gerontological Social Work* 13(1/2):81–93.

Handy, J. 1995. "Alternative Organizational Models in Home Care." In L. W. Kaye, ed., *New Developments in Home Care Services for the Elderly: Innovations in Policy, Program, and Practice,* pp. 49–65. New York: Haworth Press.

Harel, Z. 1988. "Coping with Extreme Stress and Ageing." *Social Casework* 69(9):575–83.

Harel, Z., E. A. McKinney, and M. Williams, eds. 1990. *Black Aged: Understanding Diversity and Service Needs.* Newbury Park, Calif.: Sage.

Harrington, C., C. Cassel, C. L. Estes, S. Woolhandler, and D. U. Himmelstein. 1994. "A National Long-term Care Program for the United States: A Caring Vision." In C. Harrington and C. L. Estes, eds. *Health Policy and Nursing,* pp. 490–507. Boston: Jones & Bartlett.

Harris, D. K. 1988. *Dictionary of Gerontology.* New York: Greenwood Press.

Hazan, H. 1998. "The Double Voice of the Third Age: Splitting the Speaking Self As an Adaptive Strategy in Later Life." In J. Lomranz, ed., *Handbook of Aging and Mental Health: An Integrative Approach,* pp. 183–96. New York: Plenum Press.

Hewitt, P. S. and J. Quadagno. 1997. "Are the Elderly Benefiting at the Expense of Young Americans?" In A. E. Scharlach and L. W. Kaye, eds., *Controversies in Aging,* pp. 69–80. Boston: Allyn & Bacon.

Hobfoll, S. E. and J. D. Wells. 1998. "Conservation of Resources, Stress, and Aging: Why Do Some Slide and Some Spring?" In J. Lomranz, ed., *Handbook of Aging and Mental Health: An Integrative Approach,* pp. 121–43. New York: Plenum Press.

Holstein, M. 1998. "Opening New Spaces: Aging and the Millennium." *Journal of Aging and Social Policy* 10(1):1–11.

Holstein, M. and T. R. Cole. 1996. "The Evolution of Long-Term Care in America." In R. H. Binstock, L. E. Cluff, and O. Von Mering, eds., *The Future of Long-Term Care,* pp. 19–47. Baltimore: Johns Hopkins University Press.

Hooyman, N. R. 1983. "Social Support Networks in Services to the Elderly." In J. K. Whittaker, J. and J. Garbarino, eds., *Social Support Networks: Helping in the Human Services,* pp. 133–64. New York: Aldine de Gruyter.

Hooyman, N. R. and H. A. Kiyak. 1996. *Social Gerontology,* 4th ed. Boston: Allyn & Bacon.

Hooyman, N. R. and W. Lustbader. 1986. *Taking Care: Supporting Older People and Their Families.* New York: Free Press.

Ivanoff, A. and M. Riedel. 1995. "Suicide." In R. L. Edwards, ed., *Encyclopedia of Social Work,* 19th ed., pp. 2358–72. Washington, D.C.: National Association of Social Workers Press.

Jacobson, S. G. 1982. "Equity in the Use of Public Benefits by Minority Elderly." In R. C. Manuel, ed., *Minority Aging: Sociological and Social Psychological Issues,* pp. 161–70. Westport, Conn.: Greenwood.

Jette, A.M. 1996. "Disability Trends and Transitions." In R. H. Binstock and L. K. George, eds., *Handbook of Aging and the Social Sciences,* 4th ed., pp. 94–116. New York: Academic Press.

John, R., L. C. Roy, and T. L. Dietz. 1997. "Setting Priorities in Aging Populations: Formal Service Use Among Mexican American Female Users." *Journal of Gerontological Social Work* 29(1):69–85.

Jones, L. E. 1987. "Women." In R. L. Edwards, ed., *Encyclopedia of Social Work,* pp. 872–81. Silver Spring, Md.: National Association of Social Workers Press.

Kahana, E. 1974. "Matching Environments to Needs of the Aged: A Conceptual Scheme." In J. F. Gubrium, ed., *Late Life: Communities and Environmental Policy,* pp. 201–14. Springfield, Ill.: Charles C Thomas.

———. 1982. "A Congruence Model of Person-Environment Interaction." In M. P. Lawton, P. G. Windley, and T. O. Byerts, eds., *Aging and the Environment: Theoretical Approaches,* pp. 97–121. New York: Springer.

Kalish, R. A. 1985. "Services for the Dying." In A. Monk, ed., *Handbook of Gerontological Services,* pp. 531–46. New York: Van Nostrand Reinhold.

Kane, R. A. 1985. "Assessing the Elderly Client." In A. Monk, ed., *Handbook of Gerontological Services,* pp. 43–69. New York: Van Nostrand Reinhold.

———. 1987. "Long-Term Care." In Ann Minahan, ed. *Encyclopedia of Social Work,* pp. 59–72. Silver Spring, Md.: National Association of Social Workers Press.

Kane, R. L. and R. A. Kane. 1981. *Assessing the Elderly.* Lexington, Mass.: Lexington Books, D.C. Heath.

Kasper, J. D. 1988. *Aging Alone: Profiles and Projections.* Baltimore, Md.: Commonwealth Fund Commission on Elderly People Living Alone.

Kaufman, S. R. 1986. *The Ageless Self.* Madison: University of Wisconsin Press.

Kaye, L. W. 1985. "Home Care." In A. Monk, ed., *Handbook of Gerontological Services,* pp. 408–32. New York: Van Nostrand Reinhold.

———. 1995. "Introduction." In L. W. Kaye, ed., *New Developments in Home Care Services for the Elderly: Innovations in Policy, Programs, and Practice,* pp. 1–6. New York: Haworth Press.

Kaye, L. W. and J. K. Davitt. 1995. "The Importation of High Technology Services into the Home." In L. W. Kaye, ed., *New Developments in Home Care Services for the Elderly: Innovations in Policy, Program, and Practice,* pp. 67–94. New York: The Haworth Press

Kelly, T. B. 1993. "Educational Needs of Older Adults with Mental Illness: A Review of the Literature." *Educational Gerontology* 19:451–64.

———. 1994. "Paternalism and the Marginally Competent: An Ethical Dilemma, No Easy Answer." *Journal of Gerontological Social Work* 23(1/2):67–84.

———. 1999. "Mutual Aid Groups with Mentally Ill Older Adults." *Social Work with Groups* 21(4):63–80.

Kelly, T. B. and T. Berman-Rossi. In press. "Advancing Stages of Group Development Theory: The Case of Older Institutionalized Persons." *Social Work with Groups* 22(3/4).

Kerson, T. S. and R. W. Michelsen. 1995. "Counseling Homebound Clients and Their Families." In L. W. Kaye, ed., *New Developments in Home Care Services for the Elderly: Innovations in Policy, Program, and Practice,* pp. 159–90. New York: Haworth Press.

Knight, B. and D. Loiver Walker. 1985. "Towards a Definition of Alternatives to Institutionalization for the Frail Elderly." *The Gerontologist* 25(4):338–63.

Korotkov, D. 1998. "The Sense of Coherence: Making Sense Out of Chaos." In P. T. Wong and P. S. Fry, eds., *The Human Quest for Meaning,* pp., 51–70. Mahwah, N.J.: Lawrence Erlbaum.

Lamphere-Thorpe, J. and R. J. Blendon. 1993. "Years Gained and Opportunities Lost: Women and Health Care in an Aging America." In J. Allen and A. Pifer, eds., *Women on the Front Lines,* pp. 75–104. Washington, D.C.: The Urban Institute.

Lee, J. A. B. 1983. "The Group: A Chance at Human Connection for the Mentally Impaired Older Person." In Shura Saul, ed., *Group Work with the Frail Elderly,* pp. 43–55. New York: Haworth Press.

———. 1994. *The Empowerment Approach to Social Work Practice.* New York: Columbia University Press.

Lieberman, M. A. and S. S. Tobin. 1983. *The Experience of Old Age: Stress, Coping and Survival.* New York: Basic Books.

Longman Synonym Dictionary. 1986. Harlow Essex, Great Britain: Robert Hartnoll, Bodmin.

Lowy, L. 1985. "Multipurpose Senior Centers." In A. Monk, ed., *Handbook of Gerontological Services,* pp. 274–301. New York: Van Nostrand Reinhold.

Ludman, E. K. and J. M. Newman. 1986. "Frail Elderly: Assessment of Nutritional Needs." *The Gerontologist* 26(2):198–202.

Lum, D. 1996. *Social Work Practice and People of Color: A Process-Stage Approach,* 3d ed. Pacific Grove, Calif.: Brooks/Cole.

Lurie, A. and J. C. Rich. 1984. "The Medical Center's Impact in the Network to Sustain the Aged in the Community." *Journal of Gerontological Social Work* 7(3):65–73.

Maldonado, D. 1987. "Aged." In R. L. Edwards, ed., *Encyclopedia of Social Work,* 18th ed., pp. 95–106. Silver Spring, Md.: National Association of Social Workers Press.

Markedis, K. S. and S. A. Black. 1996. "Race, Ethnicity, and Aging: The Impact of Ethnicity." In R. H. Binstock and L. K. George, eds., *Handbook of Aging and the Social Sciences,* 4th ed., pp. 153–70. New York: Academic Press.

Martin, E. P. and J. M. Martin. 1995. *Social Work and the Black Experience.* Washington, D.C.: National Association of Social Workers Press.

Martin, J. M. and E. P. Martin. 1985. *The Helping Tradition in the Black Family and Community.* Silver Spring, Md.: National Association of Social Workers Press.

Mayer, M. J. 1983. "Demographic Change and the Elderly Population." In S. Saul, ed., *Group Work and the Frail Elderly,* pp. 7–12. New York: Haworth Press.

Meador, K. G. and D. G. Blazer. 1998. "The Variability of Depression in Old Age: Narrative as an Integrative Construct." In J. Lomranz, ed., *Handbook of Aging and Mental Health: An Integrative Approach,* pp. 483–95. New York: Plenum Press.

Meiners, M. R. 1996. "The Financing and Organization of Long-Term Care." In R. H. Binstock, L. E. Cluff, and O. Von Mering, eds., *The Future of Long-Term Care,* pp. 191–214. Baltimore: Johns Hopkins University Press.

Mellor, J. 1996. "Special Populations Among Older Persons." In J. Mellor, ed., *Special Aging Populations and Systems Linkages,* pp. 1–10. New York: Haworth Press.

Mercer, S. O. and R. A. Kane. 1979. "Helplessness and Hopelessness Among the Institutionalized Elderly: An Experiment." *Health and Social Work* 4(1):91–116.

Miller, I. and R. Solomon. 1979. "The Development of Group Services for the Elderly." In C. B. Germain, ed., *Social Work Practice: People and Environments,* pp. 74–106. New York: Columbia University Press.

Milligan, S. E. 1990. "Understanding Diversity of the Urban Black Aged." In Z. Harel, E. A. McKinney, and M. Williams, eds., *Black Aged: Understanding Diversity and Service Needs,* pp. 114–27. Newbury Park, Calif.: Sage.

Millikan, M. 1959. "Inquiry and Policy: The Relation of Knowledge to Action." In D. Lerner, ed., *The Human Meaning of the Social Sciences,* pp. 158–80. New York: Meridian Books.

Mills, C. W. 1959. *The Sociological Imagination.* New York: Oxford University Press.

Minear, M. and R. Crose. 1996. "Identifying Barriers of Service for Low-Income Frail Elders." *Journal of Gerontological Social Work* 26(3/4):57–64.

Monk, A. and M. Abramson. 1982. "Older People." In S. A. Yaleja, ed., *Ethical Issues in Social Work,* pp. 139–55. Springfield, Ill.: Charles C Thomas.

Moody, H. R. 1985. "Book Review." *Journal of Gerontological Social Work* 9(1):1–5.

Moon, M. and J. Mulvey. 1995. *Entitlements and the Elderly.* Washington, D.C.: The Urban Institute.

Morrison, B. J. 1995. "A Research and Policy Agenda on Predictors of Institutional Placement among Minority Elderly." *Journal of Gerontological Social Work* 24(1/2):17–28.

Mui, A. and D. Burnette. 1994. "A Comparative Profile of Frail Elderly Persons Living Alone and Those Living with Others." *Journal of Gerontological Social Work* 21:5–26.

National Center for Health Statistics (NCHS). 1989. *Vital and Health Statistics: Physical Functioning of the Aged, United States, 1984.* Hyattsville, Md.: U.S. Department of Health and Human Services.

National Institute on Aging. 1987. *Established Populations for Epidemiologic Studies of the Elderly,* eds. J. Cornoni-Huntley, D. B. Breck, A.M. Qustfeld, J. D. Taylor, R. B. Wallace and M. Lafferty. Washington, D.C.: U. S. Government Printing Office.

Neeman, L. 1995. "Using the Therapeutic Relationship to Promote and Internal Locus of

Control in Elderly Mental Health Clients." *Journal of Gerontological Social Work* 23 (3/4):161–76.

Neugarten, B. L. 1982. "Older People: A Profile." In B. L. Neugarten, ed., *Age or Need? Public Policies for Older People,* pp. 33–54. Beverly Hills, Calif.: Sage.

New York State Office for the Aging. 1989. *Minority Elderly New Yorkers: The Social and Economic Status of a Rapidly Growing Population.* New York: Author.

Niskanen, W. A. and M. Moon. 1997. "Should Eligibility for Medicare be Means-Tested?" In A. E. Scharlach and L. W. Kaye eds., *Controversies in Aging,* pp.13–21. Boston: Allyn & Bacon.

Olson, L. K. 1982. *The Political Economy of Aging: The Stage, Private Power and Social Welfare.* New York: Columbia University Press.

——. 1994a. "Introduction." In L. K. Olson, ed., *The Graying of the World: Who Will Care for the Frail Elderly?,* pp. 1–23. New York: Haworth Press

——. 1994b. "Public Policy and Privatization: Long-Term Care in the United States." In L. K. Olson, ed., *The Graying of the World: Who Will Care for the Frail Elderly?,* pp. 25–58. New York: Haworth Press.

O'Malley, P. E. 1996. "Group Work with Older People who are Developmentally Disabled and Other Caregivers." *Journal of Gerontological Social Work* 25(1/2):105–19.

Padgett, D. K., B. J. Burns, and L. A. Grau. 1998. "Risk Factors and Resilience." In B. L. Levin, A. K. Blanch, and A. Jennings, eds., *Women's Mental Health Services,* pp. 390–413. Thousand Oaks, Calif.: Sage.

Parkinson, C. B. and M. Howard. 1996. "Older Persons with Mental Retardation/Developmental Disabilities." *Journal of Gerontological Social Work* 25(1/2):91–103.

Patti, R. 1980. "Organizational Resistance and Change: The View from Below." In H. Resnick and R. J. Patti, eds., *Change from Within: Humanizing Social Welfare Organizations,* pp. 114–31. Philadelphia: Temple University Press.

Paulino, A. 1998. "Dominican Immigrant Elders: Social Service Needs, Utilization Patterns and Challenges." *Journal of Gerontological Social Work* 30(1/2):61–74.

Perlmutter, L. C. and A. S. Eads. 1998. "Control: Cognitive and Motivational Implications." In J. Lomranz, ed., *Handbook of Aging and Mental Health: An Integrative Approach,* pp. 45–67. New York: Plenum Press.

Phillips, M. H. and T. Ghilarducci. 1997. "Should Social Security Benefits be Reduced for High-Income Individuals?" In A. E. Scharlach and L. W. Kaye, eds., *Controversial Issues in Aging,* pp. 1–12. Boston: Allyn & Bacon.

Pinderhughes, E. 1989. *Understanding Race, Ethnicity, and Power: The Key to Efficacy in Clinical Practice.* New York: Free Press.

Porter, K. H., K. Larin, and W. Primus. 1999. *Social Security and Poverty Among the Elderly: A National and State Perspective.* Washington, D.C.: Center on Budget and Policy Priorities.

Purdy, J. K. and D. Arguello. 1992. "Hispanic Familism in Caretaking of Older Adults: Is It Functional?" *Journal of Gerontological Social Work* 19(2):29–42.

Quadagno, J. and M. Hardy. 1996. "Work and Retirement." In R. H. Binstock and L. K. George, eds., *Handbook of Aging and the Social Sciences,* pp. 325–45. New York: Academic Press.

Rakowski, E. and S. G. Post. 1997. "Should Health Care be Rationed by Age?" In A. E. Scharlach and L. W. Kaye, eds., *Controversies in Aging,* pp. 69–80. Boston: Allyn & Bacon.

Rathbone-MaCuan, E. and R. T. Coward. 1985. "Respite and Adult Day-Care Service." In A. Monk, ed., *Handbook of Gerontological Services,* pp. 456–82. New York: Van Nostrand Reinhold.

Reker, G. T. and P. T. P. Wong. 1985. "Personal Optimism, Physical and Mental Health." In J. F. Birren and J. Livingston, eds., *Cognition, Stress, and Aging,* pp. 47–71. Englewood Cliffs, N.J.: Prentice-Hall.

Rogers, B. L., J. L. Brown, and J. Cook. 1994. "Unifying the Poverty Line: A Critique of

Maintaining Lower Poverty Standards for the Elderly." *Journal of Aging and Social Policy* 6(1/2):143–66.

Rohan, E. A., B. Berkman, S. Walker, and W. Holmes. 1994."The Geriatric Oncology Patient: Ageism in Social Work Practice." *Journal of Gerontological Social Work* 23(1/2): 201–21.

Rosen, A. L. and T. Persky. 1994. "Meeting Mental Health Needs of Older People: Policy and Practice Issues for Social Work." In C. Corley Saltz, ed., *Social Work Response to the White House Conference on Aging: From Issues to Action,* pp. 45–54. New York: Haworth Press.

Rosenwaike, L. and A. Dolinsky. 1987. "The Changing Demographic Determinants of the Growth of the Extreme Aged." *The Gerontologist* 27(3):275–80.

Rosenzweig, E. P. 1995. "Trends in Home Care Entitlements and Benefits." In L. W. Kaye, ed., *New Developments in Home Care Services for the Elderly: Innovations in Policy, Programs, and Practice,* pp. 9–29. New York: Haworth Press.

Rowe, J. W. and R. L. Kahn. 1998. *Successful Aging.* New York: Pantheon Books.

Roy, L. C., T. L. Dietz, and R. John. 1996. "Determining Patterns of Formal Service Use among Mexican American Elderly: Improving Empirical Techniques for Policy and Practice." *Journal of Gerontological Social Work* 26(3/4):65–81.

Russell, R. 1997. "The Senior Outreach Program of Park Ridge Mental Health: An Innovative Approach to Mental Health and Aging." *Journal of Gerontological Social Work* 29(1):95–104.

Rutter, M. 1987. "Psychosocial Resilience and Protective Mechanisms." *American Journal of Orthopsychiatry* 57(3):316–31.

Ryff, C. D., B. Singer, G. D. Love, and M. J. Essex. 1998. "Resilience in Adulthood and Later Life." In J. Lomranz, ed., *Handbook of Aging and Mental Health: An Integrative Approach,* pp. 69–96. New York: Plenum Press.

Rzetelny, H. 1985. "Emotional Stresses in Later Life." *Journal of Gerontological Social Work* 8(3/4):141–51.

Safford, F. 1995. "Aging Stressors for Holocaust Survivors and Their Families." *Journal of Gerontological Social Work* 24(1/2):131–53.

Sakadakis, V. and M. J. MacLean. 1993. "The Role of the Social Worker with Ethnic Elderly People in Geriatric Day Hospitals." *International Social Work* 36(1):47–59.

Salzman, C. 1997. "Depressive Disorders and Other Emotional Issues in the Elderly: Current Issues." *International Clinical Psychopharmacology* 12(Supplement 7):S37–S42.

Sánchez-Ayéndez, M. 1998. "Middle-Aged Puerto Rican Women As Primary Caregivers to the Elderly: A Qualitative Analysis of Everyday Dynamics." *Journal of Gerontological Social Work* 30(1/2):61–74.

Schneewind, E. H. 1994. "Of Ageism, Suicide, and Limiting Life." *Journal of Gerontological Social Work* 23(1/2):135–50.

Schopler, J. and M. Galinsky. 1984. "Meeting Practice Needs: Conceptualizing the Open-Ended Group." *Social Work with Group* 7(2):3–19.

Schutz, J. H. 1994. "Ask Older Women: Are the Elderly Better Off?" *Journal of Aging and Social Policy* 9(1):7–12.

Schwartz, W. 1961. "The Social Worker in the Group." In *The Social Welfare Forum, 1961 Proceedings of the National Conference on Social Welfare,* pp. 146–77. New York: Columbia University Press.

——. 1962. "Toward a Strategy of Group Work Practice." *The Social Service Review* 36(3):268–79.

——. 1969. "Private Troubles and Public Issues: One Social Work Job or Two?" In *The Social Welfare Forum,* pp. 22–43. New York: Columbia University Press.

——. 1977. "Social Group Work: The Interactionist Approach." In J. B. Turner, ed., *Encyclopedia of Social Work,* 17th ed., pp. 1328–38. Washington, D.C.: National Association of Social Workers Press.

———. 1994. "Social Work with Groups: The Search for a Method." In T. Berman-Rossi, ed., *Social Work: The Collected Writings of William Schwartz,* pp. 1–193. Itasca, Ill.: F. E. Peacock Press,.

Select Committee on Aging. 1987. *Long Term Care and Personal Impoverishment: Seven in Ten Elderly Living Alone Are At Risk.* House of Representatives, Committee Publication Number 100–631. Washington, D.C.: U.S. Government Printing Office.

Seligman, M. and G. Elder, Jr. 1986. "Learned Helplessness and Life-Span Development." In A. B. Sorensen and F. E. Weiner, eds., *Human Development and the Life Course: Multidisciplinary Perspectives,* pp. 377–428. Hillsdale, N.J.: Erlbaum.

Seltzer, G. B. and M. Charpentier. 1982. "Maximizing Independence for the Elderly: The Social Worker in the Rehabilitation Center." *Journal of Gerontological Social Work* 5(1/2):661–79.

Shanas, E., P. Townsend, D. Wedderburn, H. Friis, P. Milhos, and J. Stehouwar. 1968. *Old People in Three Industrial Societies.* New York: Atherton.

Shepard, P., J. B. Mayer, and R. Ryback. 1987. "Improving Emergency Care for the Elderly: Social Work Intervention." *Journal of Gerontological Social Work* 10(3/4):123–40.

Shklar, J. N. 1990. *The Faces of Injustice.* New Haven: Yale University Press.

Shulman, L. 1999. *The Skills of Helping Individuals, Families, Groups, and Communities.* Itasca, Ill.: Peacock.

Simpson. J. A. and E. S. C. Weiner. 1989. *The Oxford English Dictionary,* 2d ed. Oxford: Clarendon Press.

Solomon, B. B. 1976. *Black Empowerment: Social Work in Oppressed Communities.* New York: Columbia University Press.

Solomon, R. 1982. "Serving Families of the Institutionalized Aged: The Four Crises." *Journal of Gerontological Social Work* 5(1/2):83–96.

Sommers, I., D. Baskin, D. Specht, and M. Shively. 1988. "Deinstitutionalization of the Elderly Mentally Ill: Factors Affecting Discharge to Alternative Living Arrangements." *The Gerontologist* 28(5):653–58.

Staudinger, U. M., A. M. Freund, M. Linden, and I. Maas. 1999. "Self, Personality, and Life Regulation: Facets of Psychological Resilience in Old Age." In P. B. Boltes and K. U. Mayer, eds., *The Berlin Aging Study: Aging from 70 to 100,* pp. 302–28. New York: Cambridge University Press.

Stock, R. W. 1999. "Not an Age, but an Expanding State of Mind." *New York Times,* March 21, 1999, section 15, pp. 1, 15.

Stone, R., G. L. Cafferata, and J. Sangl. 1987. "Caregivers of the Frail Elderly: A National Profile." *The Gerontologist* 27(5):616–26.

Sulman, J., C. J. Rosenthal, V. W. Marshall, and J. Daciuk. 1996. "Elderly Patients in the Acute Care Hospital: Factors Associated with Long Stay and Its Impact on Patients and Families." *Journal of Gerontological Social Work* 25(3/4):33–52.

Tatara, T. 1995. "Elder Abuse." In R. Edwards, ed., *Encyclopedia of Social Work,* 19th ed., pp. 834–42. Washington, D.C.: National Association of Social Workers Press.

Tauber, C. M. and J. Allen, 1993. "Women in Our Aging Society: The Demographic Outlook." In J. Allen and A. Pifer, eds., *Women on the Front Lines,* pp. 11–45. Washington, D.C.: The Urban Institute.

Taylor, R. J. and L. M. Chatters. 1986. "Church-Based Informal Support Among Elderly Blacks." *The Gerontologist* 26(6):637–42.

Tennstedt, S. L., B. H. Chang, and M. Delgado. 1998. "Patterns of Long-Term Care: A Comparison of Puerto Rican, African-American, and Non-Latino White Elders." *Journal of Gerontological Social Work* 30(1/2):177–99.

Tobin, S. S. 1988. "Preservation of the Self in Old Age." *Social Casework* 69(9):550–55.

Tobin, S. S. and M. Lieberman. 1976. *Last Home for the Aged.* San Francisco: Jossey-Bass.

Tobin, S. S. and R. Toseland. 1985. "Models of Services for the Elderly." In A. Monk, ed., *Handbook of Gerontological Services,* pp. 549–67. New York: Van Nostrand Reinhold.

Torres-Gil, F. M. and M. A. Puccinelli. 1995. "Aging: Public Policy Issues and Trends." In R. L. Edwards, ed., *Encyclopedia of Social Work,* pp. 159–64. Washington, D.C.: National Association of Social Workers Press.

Toseland, R. W. and G. Smith. 1991. "Family Caregivers of the Frail Elderly." In A. Gitterman, ed., *Handbook of Social Work Practice with Vulnerable Populations,* pp. 549–83. New York: Columbia University Press.

Tracy, M. B. and M. N. Ozawa. 1995. "Social Security." In R. L. Edwards, ed., *Encyclopedia of Social Work,* 19th ed., pp. 2186–95. Washington, D.C.: National Association of Social Workers Press.

Tran, T. V. and S. S. Phooper. 1996. "Ethnic and Gender Differences in Perceived Needs for Social Services Among Three Elderly Hispanic Groups." *Journal of Gerontological Social Work* 25(3/4):121–47.

Tsai, D. T. and R. A. Lopez. 1997. "The Use of Social Supports by Elderly Chinese Immigrants." *Journal of Gerontological Social Work* 29(1):77–94.

Tully, C. T. and S. Jacobson. 1994. "The Homeless Elderly: America's Forgotten Population." *Journal of Gerontological Social Work* 22(3/4):61–81.

U.S. Bureau of the Census. 1996. *Current Population Reports. Special Studies, P23–190. 65+ in the United States.* Washington, D.C.: U.S. Government Printing Office.

U.S. Department of Health and Human Services. 1985–86. *Aging in America: Trends and Projections.* Washington, D.C.: U.S. Government Printing Office.

Walker, J. 1985. "The Social Welfare Policies, Strategies and Programs of Black Fraternal Organizations in the Northeast United States, 1896–1920." Unpublished Ph.D. diss., Columbia University, School of Social Work.

Wallace, S. P., L. Levy-Storms, R. M. Andersen, and R. S. Kington. 1997. "The Impact by Race of Changing Long-Term Care Policy." *Journal of Aging and Social Policy* 9(3): 1–20.

Weber, N. 1991. "Vision and Aging: Issues in Social Work Practice." *Journal of Gerontological Social Work* 17(3/4).

Webster's New Dictionary of Synonyms. 1968. Springfield, Mass.: G. and C. Merriam.

Williams, F. B. 1905. "Social Bonds in the 'Black Belt' of Chicago: Negro Organizations and the New Spirit Pervading Them." *The Survey* 25(1):40–44.

26

Single Parenthood

Aurora P. Jackson

Substantial increases in the rates of divorce and nonmarital births have led to fewer children living with two parents. Some estimate that nearly one-half of all children will live in a one-parent family before reaching age 18 (Castro and Bumpass 1989). These changes in family structure have focused attention on the role of single parenthood in the well-being of children.

DEFINING AND EXPLAINING SINGLE PARENTHOOD

My classification scheme is based on two criteria: (1) whether a child is living with two parents (either biological parents or a biological parent and a stepparent) and (2) whether a child is living with only one biological parent without a coresiding stepparent. Not all scholars classify stepfamilies as two-parent families. Indeed, some believe that the latter is a serious distortion of the families' experiences because nearly all children in stepfamilies have lived in a single-parent family at one time and often have more than two parents now (McLanahan and Sandefur 1994). Single parents may be divorced, separated, never married, or widowed.

I do not attempt to distinguish between children born outside of marriage and those born within marriage in the paragraphs that follow. This distinction has become increasingly blurred over time, as divorce and cohabitation have become more common. While single parents can be fathers or mothers, most of these families are headed by women and most nonresident fathers have little contact with their children (Crockett, Eggebeen, and Hawkins 1993). I focus primarily on mother-only families and the consequences of this arrangement for young children. The terms "single parent" and "single mother" are used interchangeably to refer to families headed by single women; the term "nonresident father" refers to absent fathers.

DEMOGRAPHIC PATTERNS

According to the Federal Interagency Forum on Child and Family Statistics (1998), only 68 percent of American children lived with two parents in 1997, down from 77 percent in 1980. White children are much more likely than black children and somewhat more likely than Hispanic children to live with two parents. Among children living with one parent, most live with a single mother (National Center for Health Statistics 1995). Such children are more likely to live in poverty than children of married parents (McLanahan 1995; Ventura et al. 1997). This is important because nearly a third of all children born in the United States today are born to unmarried parents. The proportion is even higher among poor and minority populations; 40 percent among Hispanics and 70 percent among blacks (Ventura et al. 1995).

In 1996, 10 percent of children in two-parent families were living in poverty, compared with 49 percent in female-headed families. As already indicated, this contrast by family structure is especially pronounced among certain racial and ethnic minorities. For example, 14 percent of black children in married-couple families lived in poverty, compared with 58 percent of black children in female-headed families. Twenty-nine percent of Hispanic children in married-couple families lived in poverty, compared with 67 percent in female-headed families. Moreover, black and Hispanic children are less likely than white children to have a parent working full-time all year. Also in 1996, 56 percent of blacks and 64 percent of Hispanics had a full-time full-year working parent, compared with 79 percent of whites (Federal Interagency Forum on Child and Family Statistics 1998). This is important because children living in poverty are much less likely to have a parent working full-time all year than children living at or above the poverty line.

SOCIETAL CONTEXT

Researchers have found that growing up in a single-parent family diminishes children's school achievement and family stability (McLanahan 1988). Indeed, although early studies found only limited evidence of a negative effect of living in a single-parent family on the cognitive and behavioral functioning of children (Heatherington, Camara, and Featherman 1983), recent studies provide more consistent evidence of a positive association (Crockett et al. 1993; Entwistle and Alexander 1995, 1996; Luster and McAdoo 1994; Mulkey, Crain, and Harrington 1992). Children who grow up in single-parent families show more behavior problems and score lower on measures of school-based competence and cognitive achievement.

Although single mothers are capable of raising well-adjusted children, especially if economic resources are sufficient (Hawkins and Eggebeen 1991), there are three predominant explanations of the relationship between single parenting and both behavioral and cognitive outcomes. First, families headed by single mothers possess fewer financial resources than do those with two parents. Economic hardship has been linked to material conditions (fewer books and games) and behavior (parental conflict, inconsistent and harsh parenting practices) in the home that diminish intellectual stimulation and growth (Conger et al. 1994; Duncan, Brooks-Gunn, and Klebanov 1994; McLoyd 1990). Second, some have found that single mothers, in comparison with their married counterparts, possess less human capital—especially education—and lower educational aspirations for themselves and their children (Garfinkel and McLanahan 1986; Thompson, Entwistle, and Alexander 1988; Thomson, Hanson, and McLanahan 1994). Those for whom this is so might be less able than others to provide an intellectually stimulating environment that develops the cognitive abilities of their children (Teachman et al. 1998). Third, it is probable, and some have found, that two parents—all else being equal—are better able than a single parent to schedule activities such as reading to children, regulating TV viewing, supervising homework, and monitoring activities outside the home that are related to cognitive achievement and prosocial behavior (Astone and McLanahan 1991). Indeed, a consistent theme in the literature is the extraordinary scarcity that single-parent families experience with respect to fathers' input of time and financial resources (Cooksey and Fondell 1996; King 1994; Thomson et al. 1994).

The 1996 welfare reform legislation—a main component of which is TANF (Temporary Assistance for Needy Families)—places time limits on welfare receipt and requires most recipients to enter the paid labor force. This law aims to force poor, mostly single, mothers into the labor force and fathers to assume financial responsibility for their children. In this chapter, I focus on single black mothers because they are disproportionately represented among the very poor and the welfare dependent, and their employment does not forestall poverty (Duncan 1991; Wilson 1987, 1996). As such, their children are at greatest risk for negative well-being and developmental outcomes (see, e.g., Duncan and Brooks-Gunn 1997; Huston 1991; Huston, McLoyd, and Garcia Coll 1994). Understanding the consequences of low-wage employment for these mothers and their children as well as the role of nonresident fathers in their well-being is urgent.

Indeed, the links between fathers' absence and negative child outcomes have led some to assume that involving fathers, including nonresident fathers, in their children's upbringing can moderate the likely harmful effects of single parenting (Furstenberg and Harris 1992; Hawkins and Eggebeen 1991). Although there is limited evidence to support this hypothesis (King 1994), most people believe that children would be better off if their parents lived together and their fathers were involved in their upbringing. It is probable, nevertheless, that the quality of the relationship between nonresident fathers and their children is important, not just for the children, but for the functioning of their mothers as well.

VULNERABILITIES AND RISK FACTORS

Risk factors are those characteristics or variables that increase the incidence or maintenance of a problem or condition. Risk factors, moreover, are individual predispositions that heighten vulnerability to negative outcomes; contextual properties are environmental conditions that are contributory or conducive to risk. The latter can be indirect (e.g., neighborhood poverty, high unemployment, or deficient opportunity structures) or direct (e.g., inadequate parenting). Links between different risk factors can occur, forming risk "chains" (Smokowski 1998). For example, poverty frequently coexists with parental unemployment, single-parent status, low educational attainment, and parenting stress, as well as an aggregation of other stressful events. Resilience, on the other hand, implies positive adaptation despite the presence of substantial risk.

Research into risk and resilience has become quite complex. Risk factors and protective processes are considered to interact, with manifestations on individual, familial, and societal levels. In addition, levels of risk, resilience, and protection are believed to fluctuate across developmental periods, to vary by gender, and to show variations by race or ethnicity (Cohler, Stott, and Musick 1995). Commonly employed strategies to defining risk in resilience models include life events approaches that involve a summation of the number of negative events experienced by a child, and the use of individual stressful experiences such as single parenthood. A third approach involves the simultaneous consideration of multiple familial and sociodemographic indices, such as impaired psychological functioning, low parental occupation and income, absence of a parent, and minority group membership. Empirical evidence indicates that such factors often have a synergistic effect, such that the effects of coexisting stressors far exceed the effects of any single factor considered individually (Rutter 1987; Sameroff and Seifer 1983).

In sum, the literature on single-parent families identifies a variety of risk factors that accompany this status. These include unemployment, poverty, low maternal education, low maternal psychological well-being, father absence, little social support, and—when combined with the preceding—racial or ethnic minority group status. A simple *additive* model is one in which poor children are assumed to do less well because they experience more poverty risk factors than their nonpoor counterparts (Huston 1991; Parker, Greer, and Zuckerman 1988). For example, poor children are more likely to have a mother with low educational attainment, a mother who is single, a mother with low social supports, and a mother with depression (Huston 1991; McLoyd 1990). The *cumulative* model assumes that an accumulation of risks, rather than individual risk factors, accounts for poorer developmental outcomes in some children (Sameroff and Seifer 1983; Werner and Smith 1992). The assumption here is that as risks increase, the consequences for children become more portentous. For example, since not all poor families are exposed to multiple negative events, this model attempts to explain why some children in poor families do well and, conversely, why some children in affluent families do not. The *interactive* model considers moderating mechanisms in the relationship between risk and resilience (Rutter 1987), asking, for instance, which processes or attributes are associated with enhanced resilience, for which families and children, and in what specific circumstances.

RESILIENCIES AND PROTECTIVE FACTORS

Research concerning the effects of family poverty on children's development has documented the association between economic hardship and greater parental psychological distress (Belle 1990; Conger et al. 1992; Elder 1974; McLoyd 1990; McLoyd and Wilson 1991). Psychological distress, in turn, may lead to inadequate or impaired parenting and adverse child outcomes (Conger et al. 1992; McLoyd 1990; McLoyd and Wilson 1991). For example, Conger et al. (1992) posit that objective economic circumstances (i.e., income level, unstable work or unemployment, income loss) affect parents' psychological well-being and the quality of family relations through their effect on parenting behavior. Parental depressed mood is postulated to provide a principal mechanism through which economic hardship influences parenting behavior and, thereby, child outcomes. McLoyd and her colleagues (1994; McLoyd and Wilson

1991) posit that an accumulation of risks is associated with economic hardship (e.g., female headship, low social supports, constricted choices, little sense of personal control over events). These risks may have different effects on children's development, depending on the presence of protective factors (principal among them, maternal psychological well-being, helpful social supports) that may mediate between economic hardship and child developmental consequences (see, also, Elder 1974; Garmezy and Rutter 1983; Rutter 1987).

While risk and vulnerability models assert that particular children or groups of children are at risk for decrements in well-being (Brooks-Gunn 1990; Garmezy and Rutter 1983; Werner and Smith 1992), due to environmental conditions that include parental characteristics, parental beliefs and attitudes, and parental resources, scholars of development in poor and minority populations emphasize a risk and resilience model (McLoyd 1990; Spencer 1990). Rather than regarding poor and minority children in high-risk environments as uniformly at risk for negative well-being and developmental outcomes, this model takes an individual difference approach. In so doing, it highlights the differential and interactive influences of individual, family, and environmental variables in determining which children (and their parents) are at risk for negative outcomes and the circumstances under which resilience is most likely. An important issue, for example, is how and why some individuals maintain good mental health and high self-efficacy despite facing the same hardships that bring about distress, hopelessness, and failure in others (Rutter 1987). Indeed, a question worth asking is how it is that some single, low-income, black mothers are able to access resources and social supports that they can use effectively while others are not.

Although direct tests of the latter are sparse, a few clues are available. For example, parents' personal skills have been found to be important mediating variables for parent-child interaction and parents' involvement in their children's education and development (Cleary 1988; McLoyd 1990; Parker, Greer, and Zuckerman 1988). Furthermore, studies have found that maternal depression is associated with women's perceptions of parenting as more difficult and less satisfying (Crnic and Greenberg 1987; McLoyd and Wilson 1991), and that mothers with higher levels of depression express more negative attitudes toward their children than those with lower levels (Richman, Stevenson, and Graham 1982). Others have found that maternal depression increases the risk for behavior problems in young children (Downey and Coyne 1990). However, social supports have been found to moderate depression in single and welfare-dependent mothers, to have a beneficial effect on parenting behavior, and to be associated with more positive attitudes toward children (Colletta and Lee 1983; Crnic and Greenberg 1987; Zur-Szpiro and Longfellow 1982). These studies suggest that single mothers' feelings about their social roles and their children, as well as their ability to provide developmentally appropriate learning and physical conditions and to access helpful social supports, are probable factors contributing to resiliency in poor black children of single mothers who live in high-risk environments.

Garmezy (1985) has distinguished three categories of factors that protect against stress: (1) dispositional attributes of the child, (2) family cohesion and warmth, and (3) the availability and use of external support systems by parents and children. In the context of dispositional attributes, children with adverse temperaments are more likely than are other children to be the target of parental irritability, criticism, and hostility (Rutter 1987). Protective aspects of gender also have been found, indicating that boys—in comparison to girls—are more vulnerable to out-of-home day care (Gamble and Zigler 1986), and that they react to stressful family circumstances with greater emotional and behavioral disturbances (Rutter 1987). As indicated earlier, a great deal of evidence highlights the beneficial effects of family attachments and social support. In addition, Caspi, Bolger, and Eckenrode (1987) found that chronic ecological conditions (e.g., high-risk environments defined by mothers' perceptions of the safety and adequacy of their neighborhoods' physical and social environment) potentiate the effects of daily stressful events on maternal mood, whereas social supports (the availability of family, friends, and neighbors) mitigate the enduring effects of such events on mood. Furthermore, poor and single parents, compared with their affluent counterparts, experience more chronic stresses. Because affluent parents can purchase services to reduce parental strain and make their parenting roles easier to perform, it is probable that social support is more beneficial for the poor than the nonpoor (Hashima and Amato 1994).

Guided by these notions, my recent work examines—both concurrently and over time—the interplay among work, welfare, and social supports and their associations with maternal and child outcomes in a sample of economically disadvantaged families headed by single black mothers who were current and former welfare recipients in New York City in the fall of 1995. Of particular interest is understanding the effects of low-wage employment on maternal psychological functioning and parenting behavior, examining the effects of these on child well-being and development, and gaining an understanding of the conditions under which employment is most beneficial for poor and near-poor single black mothers and their children.

The discussion that follows briefly outlines some of the findings of this research, along with early childhood programs and social work contributions.

PROGRAMS AND SOCIAL WORK CONTRIBUTIONS

Single mothers do not seek help for being single. Poverty, however, puts many at risk for a variety of problems. The social programs that arguably will have the greatest impact on low-income single parents are a direct result of the previously mentioned Personal Responsibility and Work Opportunity Reconciliation Act of 1996. Its goal and, to a lesser extent, that of previous welfare reforms is and has been to move women—most of whom are single—and children off the welfare rolls. This law has two prongs: (1) the TANF work requirements and (2) the stricter child support enforcement regulations. As indicated earlier, it aims to force mothers into the labor force and fathers to assume financial responsibility for their children. Recent research on low-wage employment by single black mothers is relevant to the TANF work requirements and provides knowledge and insights for social work service provision with single parents affected by this legislation.

As a result of the 1996 legislation, many more mothers in single-parent households are (or soon will be) **working.** What might be the effects of this change in social conditions and family circumstances? Scholars have proposed two conflicting views concerning the effects of maternal employment on children from low-income families. One is that maternal employment, poverty, and single-parent status function as cumulative burdens on families, thereby resulting in poorer developmental outcomes among low-income children of employed mothers. The other is that the financial and psychological benefits associated with maternal employment are so considerable that children whose mothers are employed demonstrate better social and academic outcomes than low-income children whose mothers are not employed (Desai, Chase-Lansdale, and Michael 1989; Vandell and Ramanan 1992). Policies mandating employment for welfare recipients with young children are based on the assumption that maternal employment has positive effects in low-income families. Although plausible, this assumption is largely untested.

Recent research (Jackson 1998, in press-a, in press-b; Jackson and Huang 1998; Jackson et al. 1998) assesses the roles of maternal psychological well-being and parenting in linking employment in the low-wage job market to developmental outcomes for young black children. It focuses on a group of single mothers who are of special interest for several reasons. First, few studies to date have focused specifically on former welfare recipients now in the job market. Second, most of the maternal employment research is focused on middle-class, married, mostly white mothers. Employment may have different consequences for single black mothers and their children than for their middle-class white counterparts, because the former are less affluent and the earnings of black mothers make up a greater proportion of total family income than those of white mothers. Single black mothers are more likely than others to experience stressful events that put them at risk for psychological distress. As indicated earlier, high levels of psychological distress may lead to inadequate or impaired parenting and adverse child outcomes. Third, because single employed mothers represent a conjunction of work and parenting in one person, the impact of work-related events on parenting and children's development may be extreme. This is important because a large number of young black children are being raised by a single mother.

Findings from this research reveal that nonemployed mothers were significantly higher in depressive symptoms and parenting stress and significantly lower in perceived self-efficacy than their employed counterparts (Jackson 1998, in press-a, in press-b; Jackson and Huang, in press; Jackson et al. 1998). In addition, this work suggests that employment seems to matter for its moderating effects on the relationship between the mothers' psychological functioning and their decisions to use harsher discipline techniques and for the mothers' need of nonresident fathers' support. Concerning the latter, infrequent contact between nonresident fathers and their children had more negative psychological effects for nonemployed mothers (Jackson, in press-b). Consistent with the findings of others—that is, that fathers' involvement with children can have beneficial effects (Baydar and Brooks-Gunn 1991; King 1994)—the latter findings were interpreted to mean that although young black children seem to benefit from the presence of nonresident fathers, being employed may be a protective factor for the mothers, particularly when social and economic support from the fathers is uncertain.

The finding that employment in the low-wage job market seems to be associated with better well-being outcomes than receipt of welfare—a not uncontroversial issue (see, e.g., Edin and Lein 1997)—prompts conjecture about the differences among single black mothers who are employed. Jackson and Huang (1998) examined the effects of such mothers' concerns about their child's well-being and development on their own psychological well-being. They found that beliefs that maternal employment can be detrimental to young children and lower pay contributed to enhanced maternal psychological distress. Also, mothers were less comfortable with their main child care arrangement when their child was a boy. Perhaps they were more concerned about their sons because boys are more aggressive than girls and, as such, more difficult for less capable child care providers to manage (see, also, Maccoby and Martin 1983). Recall also that boys are more vulnerable to negative effects of out-of-home care (Gamble and Zigler 1986). These findings suggest that wages that, respectively, allay mothers' concerns about their children's employment-related care and "make work pay" (Ellwood 1988) might improve both parental and child well-being in such families.

The response of professional social workers to the problems and predicaments of poor single parents depends on how they define the problem for work and the particular services specific agencies offer. Agencies have attempted to understand and respond to the risks associated with single parenthood; indeed, fostering access to economic and social supports that promote resiliency has been a persistent concern. However, an overabundance of acute and chronic stressors in the lives of economically deprived minority families often makes participation in agency services particularly burdensome and of low priority (Jackson and Sedehi 1998). Nevertheless, some structured programs have been developed to show parents how to provide stimulation for their children and improve parent-child interactions (Smith and Carlson 1997). Moreover, important components of early interventions like Head Start often include parental education and involvement, and social workers usually are involved in these efforts.

In recent years, there has been a growing commitment to national dissemination of **early childhood programs,** due to research findings that show lasting, positive gains in behavioral and social functioning for children in high-quality programs (Smokowski 1998). For example, an ongoing evaluation of the High/Scope Perry Preschool Program—a prevention program for 3- and 4-year-old black children (and their mothers) in which participants attended classes five times a week for seven months a year for two years—revealed that by age 19, Perry participants had higher academic achievement, better jobs, higher earnings, and less unemployment than those in a control group. These findings have been held up as exemplary within the early intervention field (Smokowski 1998). The Chicago Longitudinal Study of the Child Parent Centers (CPC), a large early intervention program for low-income children and their parents, has yielded similar results vis-à-vis how comprehensive services that include parent participation and implement child-centered approaches to social and cognitive development for children can be critical in maintaining initial intervention success over time (Smokowski 1998). However, investigations of Head Start have yielded mixed results. Some have found that cognitive and academic gains made by program participants in preschool and kindergarten often decline in the elementary school years (Zigler and Styfco 1993). Others have found that Head Start children do maintain substantive gains over children without preschool experience (Lee, Brooks-Gunn, and Schnur 1990).

In summary, early childhood programs are an example of resilience-based practice. Such programs try to offset the risks associated with childhood poverty. Social work contributions usually include interventions that enhance parent-child interaction, family support, and access to needed resources. This work fosters a more positive family environment and more family time invested in educational endeavors, protective factors that benefit children vis-à-vis subsequent social and academic experiences in school.

ASSESSMENT AND INTERVENTIONS

Practice scholars have argued that persuasion, credibility, giving, and motivation are important variables in relationship formation and favorable intervention outcomes with poor and minority populations. Beutler and Clarkin (1990) argue that persuasion is best accomplished within the context of a collaborative, caring, and respectful relationship and that such a relationship is not accidental. In their perspective, persuasion is a process that derives its power from feelings of respect, credibility, and empathy. These feelings, in turn, emanate from specific interactions that are connotative of what others call a "working alliance" (see, e.g., Ivanoff, Blythe, and Tripodi 1994). Sue and Zane (1987) discuss two key processes that bring about a working alliance: credibility and giving. In their formulation, credibility refers to the client's perception of the practitioner as an effective and trustworthy helper. Giving is the client's perception that something will be received from the encounter. The perception that a "gift" of some sort has been received from the social work encounter is related to notions of "expectancy." Gold (1990) defines expectancy as "the probability held by an individual that a particular reinforcement will occur as a function of a specific behavior on his/her part in a specific situation" (51). Expectancy is further defined as the pivotal variable that transforms a person's motivational disposition into an action tendency, such as participation in an agency's services.

In their discussion of the critical role of the practitioner's **credibility** in favorable intervention outcomes, Sue and Zane (1987) emphasize the importance of two factors: ascribed and achieved status. Ascribed status is defined as the position or role that the practitioner is assigned by others. For example, one can be perceived as credible based on his/her credentials, gender, age, or race. Achieved status, or credibility, refers more directly to the practitioner's skills. Through the social worker's conduct and demeanor, for instance, clients come to have faith, trust, confidence, or hope. In efforts to engage poor, single parents these behaviors might involve explanations of the purpose of the professional contact—and the probable outcomes of active participation in the helping process—in language that conveys an understanding of the client's situation. In short, credibility is best established in terms of three areas: (1) conceptualization of the problem for work; (2) means for problem resolution; and (3) goals (Sue and Zane 1987).

Correspondingly, Germain and Gitterman (1996) discuss the importance of understanding transactions with the environment that can create problems in living. In their formulation, such problems occur in three interrelated areas: life transitions (developmental changes, status and role changes, and crisis events), environmental pressures, and maladaptive interpersonal processes. For example, the 1996 welfare law can represent not only a life transition (e.g., changes in statuses and roles), but also an environmental pressure (e.g., few available opportunity structures in the job market; constriction of choices and little sense of personal control over events such as preferring to stay home rather than to be employed; inadequate child care resources; and few helpful social supports that make the transition to employment less stressful). In addition, maladaptive interpersonal processes can come in many shapes and sizes, including conflicts between mothers and nonresident fathers (concerning children's needs, behaviors, and their respective parenting responsibilities), high levels of maternal psychological distress (a risk factor for poor and single mothers), inordinate parenting stress (which can lead to harsh or inadequate parenting practices), and children with difficult temperament (which can lead to behavior problems, parental irritability, and harsh discipline techniques). Not mentioned in this array of life conditions, circumstances, and events are crisis situations and developmental issues that require special skills—both general (e.g., crisis intervention) and specific (depending on the particular crisis or stage of development)—which are beyond the scope of this chapter.

In sum, the earlier discussions—of risk and resilience in poor and single-parent populations and the research literature vis-à-vis these risks and the circumstances under which resilience is most likely—can inform assessment and intervention efforts with clients and prospective clients of social work agencies who are at greatest risk for problems in living and perhaps least likely to seek out professional services for several reasons. First, a profusion of acute and chronic stresses makes participation in agency-based services difficult (even onerous) and of low priority (McLoyd 1990). Second, prior experiences with various mainstream professionals and the organizations they inhabit may not have been particularly pleasant (see, e.g., Jackson and Sedehi 1998). Third, many are suspicious of the motives of social workers whose ascribed status is derived, at least in part, from a presumed connection with public assistance, child support, and child welfare agencies; ergo, with agents of social control who can—and often do—take something important away from those occupying society's least advantaged statuses and roles. Thus, practitioners must achieve credibility based on planned and disciplined behavior rooted in an understanding of how participation in agency-based services might solve some problem that is important *to the prospective client.*

Intervention plans must start with a **credible assessment.** Assessment involves gathering factual data about relevant people and situations. If the client seeks the services of a particular agency, then the social worker should begin by asking the client why she/he has come. Usually, in these circumstances, the client is more than happy to inform the worker of his/her problems in living. However, this is not how most poor and minority single parents begin their contacts with social workers. More likely than not, for these individuals and families, services either are proffered or imposed. Such clients, or prospective clients, must be actively engaged. As indicated earlier, they must be persuaded to participate in the proposed (more accurately, the prospective) intervention through highly focused explanations of the purposes of the agency encounter that do not violate their dignity.

Still and all, regardless of how the client and agency come together, facts must be assembled in an effort to understand what the problem is (i.e., problem conceptualization), what the person would like to do about it (the client's perception of what needs to be done), how the worker and client will proceed (means for problem resolution), and what the expected outcomes will be (goals). Taken together, these data constitute an assessment. Guidelines vis-à-vis a credible person:environment assessment with respect to poor and near-poor single-parent families begin with knowledge of the likely risks attending this status together with some understanding of what the research evidence shows about factors associated with resilience; that is, a research:practice nexus.

Thus, data gathering from single parents for assessment purposes should be guided by the links explicated previously. For example, being a single parent is associated with financial strain, less optimal parenting, and a considerable risk for depressive symptoms. Recall that psychological well-being is presumed to be a protective factor, as are a network of helpful social supports. Depressive symptoms, in turn, are associated with being nonemployed, having few social supports, having children with increased behavior problems, and having increased parenting stress. The quality of parenting is associated with children's development. (Recall that more money—which seems to be associated with better parenting—is associated with more stimulating toys, games, and books, and more time to use them with children.) Information regarding these links needs to be systematically explored as part of the assessment process.

Plausible and competent **interventions** are guided by the data (assessment), the clients' preferences vis-à-vis problem resolution and goals, and the worker's skill and creativity. Much is variable in the foregoing statement. However, all else being equal, issues for work with poor single mothers can include efficacious negotiation of the physical environments of high-risk neighborhoods, gaining access to resources and supports that might enhance their psychological well-being (and, thereby, their parenting adequacy), increasing their educational aspirations (and, thereby, their human capital and employability), supporting and encouraging the provision of developmentally appropriate learning and physical conditions for their children in the home, encouraging nonresident fathers to maintain contact with their children, and helping mothers to better manage their own relationships—with nonresident fathers, family members, other romantic partners, and children.

Issues relevant to the larger environment might include working with other systems on the single parent's behalf, such as the welfare agency, schools, and/or child care agencies in which children may need special services or resources, or modeling how to approach such systems for the single parent who needs it and giving appropriate feedback.

The research reviewed in this chapter suggests that young black children seem to benefit from the presence of nonresident fathers. This is important information. The research suggests also that maternal employment—even low-wage employment—may be more beneficial for single mothers and their children than welfare receipt, but that child care resources of quality are an important consideration for mothers who are unable to afford the arrangement of their choice (see, also, Jackson 1997). This too is important information. Assessments and interventions can and should be guided by such knowledge. Studies suggest, as well, that single mothers are capable of raising well-adjusted children, especially when economic resources are sufficient. Helping mothers to assemble financial packages—involving economic resources from a variety of sources, including nonresident fathers, employment, subsidized child care, public housing, food stamps, relatives—that support them is certainly a logical intervention plan. But first, factual data must be obtained from the mothers regarding financial, material, and social supports. They will need to know why this information is important. Capable social work practitioners are able to provide a rationale for their questions such that clients can easily discern the relationship of the questions to the goals of their work together and, thereby, provide meaningful answers.

Finally, the evidence shows that economic hardship is linked to negative outcomes both for single mothers and their children. Thus, job availability and an increase in the minimum wage are important policy considerations. Direct practitioners can advocate for such policies. Moreover, if employment is to replace welfare for poor single mothers and if we care about the ability of employed mothers—particularly those in low-wage jobs—to parent their young children optimally, achieving an understanding of the conditions that produce parenting problems could assist in the design of effective prevention programs. I hope this chapter is one step in that direction.

ILLUSTRATION AND DISCUSSION

Dekota Yeates is a 27-year-old single black mother of two young children, a 4-year-old son (Steven) and a 7-year-old daughter (Jordan). Ms. Yeates lives in a small apartment in Brooklyn and works in a clerical capacity for a lab in lower Manhattan. She came to the attention of our research project as one of 150 randomly selected former welfare recipients with a 3- or 4-year-old child. The sample was drawn and recruited—from a sampling frame provided by the New York City Human Resources Administration (HRA)—using a multiple-step procedure involving 150 nonemployed welfare recipients and 150 employed former welfare recipients in zip codes representing Central Harlem in Manhattan, Bedford-Stuyvesant in Brooklyn, and Jamaica in Queens, areas with substantial numbers of low-income black families (Jackson 1998; Jackson and Ivanoff 1999). This case illustrates issues of engagement, assessment, and intervention, using knowledge of risk and resilience, the research evidence vis-à-vis poor and near-poor single black mothers, and practice principles that flow from these knowledge bases.

Initial telephone contacts with Ms. Yeates were for the purpose of persuading her to become a participant in the ongoing study mentioned in previous sections; that is, by setting up an appointment to interview her in her home. Had this not been a research study, these contacts would be called outreach, inasmuch as Ms. Yeates had not *sought* participation in the study. Much like involuntary clients, she was very reluctant to agree to an interview, stating that she didn't "have time." Indeed, the first telephone contacts were very brief, because she usually was "too busy to be bothered," suggesting that we "call back some other time." Using the persistence discussed earlier, I called back several times to explain the purposes of the research and the importance of her participation. (This might easily have been a situation in which an agency worker was attempting to engage a prospective client.)

Although Ms. Yeates did eventually agree to be interviewed, she called the day before to cancel (a strength, inasmuch as many overburdened individuals who have not sought "the service" simply do not keep the appointment). In the course of *persuading* her to make and keep a second appointment (via a number of telephone calls), I learned that she might lose her apartment, because—although she had Section 8 (a rent subsidy)—her rent was being withheld until her landlord facilitated needed repairs about which they were in dispute. She indicated that negotiating with her landlord (and Section 8 representatives) concerning this matter was interfering with her job, which she did not want to lose; nor did she want to end up homeless.

Encouraging her to discuss these environmental pressures and listening empathically (without offering any solutions, prematurely) must have demonstrated some degree of credibility, because Ms. Yeates did agree to another appointment that she subsequently kept. In any event, I had certainly demonstrated persistence by not giving up—despite her angry and dismissive attitude—which she acknowledged with (parsimonious) respect.

During the face-to-face interview, it soon became apparent that Ms. Yeates was depressed, angry, and isolated. She also was overwhelmed by her desire to be a good parent to her children, whom she dearly loved, but whose needs, she felt, were beyond her current capacities. She described being distracted at work and estranged both from members of her extended family and the nonresident father of her children. She did not trust the people in her immediate neighborhood and kept her children in the apartment when she herself could not schedule outings with them. In due time, she stated: "Nobody cares what happens to me and my kids." Then, tearfully, she said that she was concerned that her patience was diminished and lately her discipline practices had been—although short of abusive—unduly harsh. Actually, the research interview is structured and there are a number of questions assessing psychological well-being and parenting behaviors, including discipline practices. Often, a well-constructed interview helps individuals to gain cognitive clarity vis-à-vis some of their experiences. When this happens, they perceive it as a direct benefit; that is, a "gift" (see, e.g., Sue and Zane 1987). Moreover, in some instances, normalization (i.e., ". . . a process by which individuals come to realize that their thoughts, feelings, or experiences are common and that many people encounter similar experiences . . ." [Sue & Zane 1987:42]) is a gift. Thus, I responded with the following: "It is no wonder you feel as you do; you're handling too many things alone. Anyone would be overwhelmed."

I suggested that she needed to be referred to an agency that might help her to get a handle on the issues she had raised. She disagreed, asking, "How can they help me?" Then, somewhat sarcastically: "They're going to give me money? a better apartment? a better job?" Thus, my plan (an "intervention") was to motivate Ms. Yeates to become a voluntary client of a social agency with a range of services, including mental health services to evaluate her depression and after-school services for her children that would ease some of her worry about them while providing stimulating activities.

Recall that credibility is best established through three activities: conceptualization of the problem for work, means for problem resolution, and goals (Sue and Zane 1987). The problem for work was motivating Ms. Yeates to accept a referral to an appropriate agency to ease her depression and to provide needed emotional and instrumental support. The means for problem resolution was cognitive; that is, appealing to her reasoning. The goals were to get her to actually go to the agency, and, ultimately, to enhance her psychological well-being. To persuade Ms. Yeates to use the referral I wanted to make, I would need to achieve credibility and she would need to become *motivated* enough to follow through (see, e.g., Gold 1990; Sue and Zane

1987). So, in response to her concerns regarding what, if anything, an agency could do for her, the following exchange occurred.

Ms. Yeates: What can a social worker in an agency do for me? They don't know me and they don't care. They'd just be doing their job. I need money and a better place to live. My kids need someone who cares about them. It'd be a waste of my time, especially since they'd just want to get into my business.

The author: Let me suggest some ways the *right* agency might help, and I promise that I'll find the right place for you. Now, in my experience, the problems you're experiencing are not good for you or your children. I'm most concerned about the depression you mention. Then, I'm concerned about your impatience lately with your children. It sounds like you're handling the housing problem very well and it sounds like you're managing to do your job (at work) so far. My experience tells me that your job is very important, inasmuch as without it you'd have less money. However, you can't keep your job while worrying about your housing problems *and* your children's well-being. Also, you don't seem to have anyone (like family or your children's father) who is helping you. I'm worried about this too, because everybody needs supportive people in their lives in times of unusual difficulty.

So, what might an agency do? Give you someone to talk to about these things, for one thing; evaluate your depression, for another. Depression can be treated. An agency might also give you some respite from your children. Wouldn't it be nice for them to be engaged in stimulating activities—that don't involve you—several days a week? Wouldn't that take some of the pressure off of you?

How about the problems you're having with your landlord and Section 8? Wouldn't it be nice to get some consultation on these issues?

Ms. Yeates: Yeah, but they [agency social workers] don't know me, so why would they care? They'd just treat me (and my kids) like everybody else . . . it's their job to be nice and to pretend they care.

The author: Yes, it is their job to be professional. It will be up to you to help them to individualize you. You can tell them about yourself. Actually, you've done some pretty impressive things. Your children are smart and well behaved; clearly, you're a good parent. You've taken on your landlord, gotten Section 8, and maintained your job. These are very difficult things to do, especially when money is tight. Why wouldn't they be impressed? I am.

Ms. Yeates: But I don't like people in my business—not even my family. It's rarely helpful and they can be awfully critical.

The author: I think you don't want *some* people in your business; but you've been quite open with me. This tells me that you're capable of making good decisions about *who* might be helpful. Let me find an agency for you—that's my job. Your job is to help the *right* people to help you. By this, I mean that you will need to help the agency to individualize you and your children.

Ms. Yeates: (Thoughtfully) I work and agencies aren't open at night and on the weekends.

The author: Some agencies do have evening and weekend hours. I know you're tired when you get off work, but what you're doing now isn't good for you or your children—as you yourself have said.

Ms. Yeates: Okay, but I'm not promising anything.

The author: I understand and will be in touch.

I did find a community-based multiservice agency. Ms. Yeates did agree to call for an appointment (inasmuch as I believe that people are more committed when they make the call, rather than having the agency call them) and was given the name of the social worker (who expected her call and would work with her). Several appointments were arranged and missed before Ms. Yeates kept one. The agency worker—with my encouragement—called Ms. Yeates after each missed appointment. (Recall that Ms. Yeates responded positively—albeit grudgingly so—to my persistence in early contacts.) Hopefully, through their work together, Ms. Yeates will be able to keep her job, keep her apartment or find a better one, get the needed after-school activities for her children, and have reduced depressive symptoms. Recall that maternal psychological well-being and helpful social supports are protective factors that may mediate between economic hardship and child developmental consequences (Garmezy and Rutter 1983; McLoyd 1990; Rutter 1987).

Not all interventions are long term. Some are brief, as was my intervention in this case. With poor and minority clients, brief therapies can work very well. Ms. Yeates did indeed become a voluntary client of an agency that will be available to her over time. Who knows, she might eventually increase her human capital by returning to school, thereby increasing her job prospects. This, in turn, might result in better housing, a better neighborhood, and better schools for her children. Based on the research evidence reviewed in this chapter, Ms. Yeates's educational aspirations as well as her relationships with extended family and her children's relations with their father are issues worthy of exploration in time. However, beginning work in this case needed to focus on the issues the client considered most pressing; namely, her depressive symptoms, the needs of her children for cognitively stimulating social activities, and her desire to maintain both her job and a safe home environment (see Germain and Gitterman 1996, for a discussion of practice decision making).

CONCLUSION

There is considerable documentation of the problems of poor single parents and their children. Most of this research focuses on differences between these families and middle-class (mostly white) families. Much less attention has been paid to individual differences among poor (mostly black) single-parent families. Examinations of within-group differences are important if we are to better understand how and why some cope well with their social roles, including employment and parenting, in high-risk environments. Indeed, there is little empirical evidence on how single parents in low-wage jobs, who often are exposed to bleak working conditions, cope with the demands of parenting. We know that poverty has ramifications for parenting, the quality of the home environment, family structure, and access to resources. We know, as well, that poverty does not invariably lead to poor outcomes for young children. Hence, it is important to understand the processes that mediate the impact of economic hardship on children in high-risk environments, too many of whom are being parented by a single black mother. Social workers are in a unique position to better understand how those who cope well in dire economic circumstances are able to do so and to help these who cope less well to gain access to the resources they need to cope more efficaciously. We also must advocate for policies, programs, and services that are responsive to the needs of society's least advantaged, too many of whom are children.

References

Astone, N. and S. McLanahan. 1991. "Family Structure, Parental Practices, and High School Completion." *American Sociological Review* 56:309–20.

Baydar, N. and J. Brooks-Gunn. 1991. "Effects of Maternal Employment and Child-Care Arrangements in Infancy on Preschoolers' Cognitive and Behavioral Outcomes: Evidence from the Children of the NLSY." *Developmental Psychology* 27:932–45.

Belle, D. 1990. "Poverty and Women's Mental Health." *American Psychologist* 45:385–87.

Beutler, L. E. and J. F. Clarkin. 1990. *Systematic Treatment Selection: Toward Targeted Therapeutic Interventions.* New York: Brunner/Mazel.

Brooks-Gunn, J. 1990. "Identifying the Vulnerable Young Child." In D. C. Rogers and E. Ginzberg, eds., *Improving the Life Chances of Children At Risk,* pp. 104–24. Boulder, Colo.: Westview Press.

Caspi, A., N. Bolger, and J. Eckenrode. 1987. "Linking Person and Context in the Daily Stress Process." *Journal of Personality and Social Psychology* 52:184–95.

Castro, T. and L. Bumpass. 1989. "Recent Trends in Marital Disruption." *Demography* 26:37–51.

Cleary, P. D. 1988. "Social Support: Conceptualization and Measurement." In H. B. Weiss and F. H. Jacobs, eds., *Evaluating Family Programs*, pp. 195–216. Hawthorne, N.Y.: Aldine de Gruyter.

Cohler, B. J., F. M. Stott, and J. S. Musick. 1995. "Adversity, Vulnerability and Resilience: Cultural and Developmental Perspectives." In D. Cicchetti and D. J. Cohen, eds., *Developmental Psychopathology,* vol. 2, *Risk, Disorder and Adaptation,* pp. 753–800. New York: Wiley.

Colletta, N. and D. Lee. 1983. "The Impact of Support for Black Adolescent Mothers." *Journal of Family Issues* 4:127–43.

Conger, R. D., K. J. Conger, G. H. Elder, Jr., F. O. Lorenz, R. L. Simons, and L. B. Whitbeck. 1992. "A Family Process Model of Economic Hardship and Adjustment of Early Adolescent Boys." *Child Development* 63:526–41.

Conger, R., X. Ge, G. Elder, F. Lorenz, and R. Simons. 1994. "Economic Stress, Coercive Family Process, and Developmental Problems of Adolescents." *Child Development* 65:541–61.

Cooksey, E. and M. Fondell. 1996. "Spending Time with His Kids: Effects of Family Structure on Fathers' and Children's Lives." *Journal of Marriage and the Family* 58:693–707.

Crnic, K. and M. Greenberg. 1987. "Maternal Stress, Social Support, and Coping: Influences on Early Mother-Child Relationship." In C. Boukydis, ed., *Research on Support for Parents and Infants in the Postnatal Period,* pp. 25–40. Norwood, N.J.: Ablex.

Crockett, L., D. Eggebeen, and A. Hawkins. 1993. "Father's Presence and Young Children's Behavioral and Cognitive Adjustment." *Journal of Family Issues* 14:355–77.

Desai, S., P. L. Chase-Lansdale, and R. T. Michael. 1989. "Mother or Market? Effects of Maternal Employment on the Intellectual Ability of Four-Year-Old Children." *Demography* 26:545–61.

Downey, G. and J. Coyne. 1990. "Children of Depressed Parents: An Integrative Review." *Psychological Bulletin* 108:50–76.

Duncan, G. J. 1991. "The Economic Environment of Children." In A. Huston, ed., *Children in Poverty: Child Development and Public Policy,* pp. 23–50. New York: Cambridge University Press.

Duncan, G. and J. Brooks-Gunn, eds. 1997. *Consequences of Growing Up Poor.* New York: Russell Sage Foundation.

Duncan, G., J. Brooks-Gunn, and P. Klebanov. 1994. "Economic Deprivation and Early Childhood Development." *Child Development* 65:296–318.

Edin, K. and L. Lein. 1997. *Making Ends Meet: How Single Mothers Survive Welfare and Low-Wage Work.* New York: Russell Sage Foundation.

Elder, G. H., Jr. 1974. *Children of the Great Depression.* Chicago: University of Chicago Press.

Ellwood, D. T. 1988. *Poor Support: Poverty in the American Family.* New York: Basic Books.

Entwistle, D. and K. Alexander. 1995. "A Parent's Economic Shadow: Family Structure versus Family Resources As Influences on Early School Achievement." *Journal of Marriage and the Family* 57:399–409.

———. 1996. "Family Type and Children's Growth in Reading and Math Over the Primary Grades." *Journal of Marriage and the Family* 58:341–55.

Federal Interagency Forum on Child and Family Statistics. 1998. *America's Children: Key National Indicators of Well-Being.* Washington, D.C.: U.S. Government Printing Office.

Furstenberg, F. F. and K. M. Harris. 1992. "The Disappearing American Father: Divorce and the Waning Significance of Biological Parenthood." In S. South and S. Tolnay, eds., *The Changing American Family: Sociological and Demographic Perspectives,* pp. 197–223. Boulder, Colo.: Westview Press.

Gamble, T. J. and E. Zigler. 1986. "Effects of Infant Day Care: Another Look at the Evidence." *American Journal of Orthopsychiatry* 56:26–42.

Garfinkel, I. and S. McLanahan. 1986. *Single Mothers and Their Children.* Washington, D.C.: Urban Institute Press.

Garmezy, N. 1985. "Stress-Resistant Children: The Search for Protective Factors." In J. E. Stevenson, ed., *Recent Research in Developmental Psychopathology,* pp. 213–33. Oxford: Pergamon Press.

Garmezy, N. and M. Rutter. 1983. *Stress, Coping, and Development in Children.* New York: McGraw-Hill.

Germain, C. B. and A. Gitterman. 1996. *The Life Model of Social Work Practice: Advances in Theory and Practice,* 2d ed. New York: Columbia University Press.

Gold, N. 1990. "Motivation: The Crucial But Unexplored Component of Social Work Practice." *Social Work* 35:49–56.

Hashima, P. Y. and P. R. Amato. 1994. "Poverty, Social Support, and Parental Behavior." *Child Development* 65:394–403.

Hawkins, A. J. and D. J. Eggebeen. 1991. "Are Fathers Fungible? Patterns of Coresident Adult Men in Maritally Disrupted Families and Young Children's Well-Being." *Journal of Marriage and the Family* 53:958–72.

Hetherington, E. M., K. Camara, and D. Featherman. 1983. "Achievement and Intellectual Functioning of Children in One-Parent Households." In J. Spence, ed., *Achievement and Achievement Motives,* pp. 205–84. San Francisco: W. H. Freeman.

Huston, A. C., ed. 1991. *Children in Poverty: Child Development and Public Policy.* New York: Cambridge University Press.

Huston, A. C., V. C. McLoyd, and C. Garcia Coll. 1994. "Children and Poverty: Issues in Contemporary Research." *Child Development* 65:275–82.

Ivanoff, A., B. J. Blythe, and T. Tripodi. 1994. *Involuntary Clients in Social Work Practice: A Research-Based Approach.* New York: Aldine de Gruyter.

Jackson, A. P. 1997. "Effects of Concerns About Child Care Among Single Employed Black Mothers." *American Journal of Community Psychology* 25:657–73.

———. 1998. "The Role of Social Support in Parenting for Low-Income, Single, Black Mothers." *Social Service Review* 72:365–78.

———. In press-a. "Maternal Self-Efficacy and Children's Influence on Stress and Parenting Among Single Black Mothers in Poverty." *Journal of Family Issues.*

———. In press-b. "The Effects of Nonresident Father-Involvement on Single Black Mothers and Their Young Children. *Social Work.*

Jackson, A. P. and C. C. Huang. 1998. "Concerns About Children's Development: Implications for Single Employed Black Mothers' Well-Being." *Social Work Research* 22:233–40.

———. In press. "Parenting Stress and Behavior Among Mothers of Preschoolers: The Mediating Role of Self-Efficacy." *Journal of Social Service Research.*

Jackson, A. P., P. Gyamfi, J. Brooks-Gunn, and M. Blake. 1998. "Employment Status, Psychological Well-Being, Social Support, and Physical Discipline Practices of Single Black Mothers." *Journal of Marriage and the Family* 60:894–902.

Jackson, A. P. and A. Ivanoff. 1999. "Reduction of Low Response Rates in Interview Surveys of Poor African-American Families." *Journal of Social Service Research* 25:41–60.

Jackson, A. P. and J. Sedehi. 1998. "Homevisiting: Teaching Direct Practice Skills Through a Research Project." *Journal of Social Work Education* 34:283–90.

King, V. 1994. "Nonresident Father Involvement and Child Well-Being." *Journal of Family Issues* 15:78–96.

Lee, V. E., J. Brooks-Gunn, and E. Schnur. 1990. "Are Head Start Effects Sustained? A Longitudinal Follow-Up Comparison of Disadvantaged Children Attending Head Start, No Preschool, and Other Preschool Programs." *Child Development* 61:495–507.

Luster, T. and H. McAdoo. 1994. "Factors Related to the Achievement and Adjustment of Young African American Children." *Child Development* 65:1080–94.

Maccoby, E. D. and J. A. Martin. 1983. "Socialization in the Context of the Family: Parent-Child Interaction." In E. M. Hetherington, ed., *Mussen Manual of Child Psychology,* vol. 4, 4th ed., pp. 1–102. New York: Wiley.

McLanahan, S. 1988. "The Consequences of Single Parenthood for Subsequent Generations." *Focus* 11:16–21.

———. 1995. "The Consequences of Nonmarital Childbearing for Women, Children, and Society." In National Center for Health Statistics, *Report to Congress on Out-of-Wedlock Childbearing.* Hyattsville, Md.: National Center for Health Statistics.

McLanahan, S. and G. Sandefur. 1994. *Growing Up with a Single Parent: What Hurts, What Helps.* Cambridge, Mass.: Harvard University Press.

McLoyd, V. C. 1990. "The Impact of Economic Hardship on Black Families and Children: Psychological Distress, Parenting, and Socioemotional Development." *Child Development* 61:311–46.

McLoyd, V. C., T. W. Jayarantne, R. Ceballo, and J. Borquez. 1994. "Unemployment and Work Interruption Among African American Single Mothers: Effects on Parenting and Adolescent Socioemotional Functioning." *Child Development* 65:562–89.

McLoyd, V. C. and L. Wilson. 1991. "The Strain of Living Poor: Parenting, Social Support, and Child Mental Health." In A. C. Huston, ed., *Children in Poverty,* pp. 105–35. New York: Cambridge University Press.

Mulkey, L., R. Crain, and A. Harrington. 1992. "One-Parent Households and Achievement: Economic and Behavioral Explanations of a Small Effect." *Sociology of Education* 65:48–65.

National Center for Health Statistics. 1995. *Report to Congress on Out-of-Wedlock Child-bearing.* Hyattsville, Md.: National Center for Health Statistics.

Parker, S., S. Greer, and B. Zuckerman. 1988. "Double Jeopardy: The Impact of Poverty on Early Child Development." *The Pediatric Clinics of North America* 35:1227–40.

Richman, N., J. Stevenson, and P. Graham. 1982. *Preschool to School: A Behavioral Study.* London: Academic Press.

Rutter, M. 1987. "Psychosocial Resilience and Protective Mechanisms." *American Journal of Orthopsychiatry* 57:316–31.

Sameroff, A. J. and R. Seifer. 1983. "Family Risk and Child Competence." *Child Development* 54:1254–68.

Smith, C. and B. E. Carlson. 1997. "Stress, Coping, and Resilience in Children and Youth." *Social Service Review* 71:231–56.

Smokowski, P. R. 1998. "Prevention and Intervention Strategies for Promoting Resilience in Disadvantaged Children." *Social Service Review* 72:337–64.

Spencer, M. B. 1990. "Development of Minority Children: An Introduction." *Child Development* 61:267–69.

Sue, S. and N. Zane. 1987. "The Role of Culture and Cultural Techniques in Psychotherapy: A Critique and Reformation." *American Psychologist* 42:37–45.

Teachman, J., R. Day, K. Paasch, K. Carver, and V. Call. 1998. "Sibling Resemblance in Behavioral and Cognitive Outcomes: The Role of Father Presence." *Journal of Marriage and the Family* 60: 835–48.

Thompson, M., D. Entwistle, and K. Alexander. 1988. "Household Composition, Parental Expectations, and School Achievement." *Social Forces* 67:424–51.

Thomson, E., T. Hanson, and S. McLanahan. 1994. "Family Structure and Child Well-Being: Economic Resources versus Parental Behaviors." *Social Forces* 73:221–42.

Vandell, D. L. and J. Ramanan. 1992. "Effects of Early and Recent Maternal Employment on Children from Low-Income Families." *Child Development* 63:938–49.

Ventura, S. J., C. A. Bachrach, L. Hill, K. Kaye, P. Holcomb, and E. Koff. 1995. *The Demography of Out-of-Wedlock Childbearing.* Report to Congress on Out-of-Wedlock Childbearing. Washington, D.C.: Department of Health and Human Services.

Ventura, S. J., J. A. Martin, S. C. Curtin, and T. J. Mathews. 1997. "Report of Final Natality Statistics, 1995." *Month Vital Statistics Report* 45, no. 11(Supplement 1). Hyattsville, Md.: National Center for Health Statistics.

Werner, E. E. and R. S. Smith. 1992. *Vulnerable But Not Invincible: A Longitudinal Study of Resilient Children and Youth.* New York: McGraw-Hill.

Wilson, W. J. 1987. *The Truly Disadvantaged: The Inner City, the Underclass, and Public Policy.* Chicago: University of Chicago Press.

———. 1996. *When Work Disappears: The World of the New Urban Poor.* New York: Knopf.

Zigler, E. and S. Styfco. 1993. *Head Start and Beyond: A National Plan for Extended Childhood Intervention.* New Haven: Yale University Press.

Zur-Szpiro, S. and C. Longfellow. 1982. "Fathers' Support to Mothers and Children." In D. Belle, ed., *Lives in Stress: Women and Depression,* pp. 145–53. Beverly Hills, Calif.: Sage.

27

Suicide and Suicidal Behavior

André Ivanoff
Prudence Fisher

Suicide is the intentional taking of one's own life. What pain is so intense, what circumstance so desperate, that it leads an individual to consider suicide? Suicide has provoked political, religious, and social debate since the time of the Greek philosophers. Understanding its cause and general prevention remain a source of study, speculation, and sleepless nights among those who make it their work and among those who live with its consequences. Few practitioners specialize in working with suicidal clients; however, many practitioners are called on to respond to a suicidal crisis in their work. The need to respond to this crisis immediately and accurately is a professional responsibility. The absence of appropriate and timely intervention may result in loss of life. Unfortunately, little training is provided within general social work curricula in the assessment and treatment of suicidal behavior. Available training is generally attended by those who work only in the highest risk settings, so that a majority of practitioners face the problem without benefit of training.

Crisis intervention theory and method provide a framework for dealing with suicidal crises (Dattilio and Freeman 1994; Roberts 1990). The ability to efficiently conduct a functional assessment, that is, an assessment focused on the actions within and the interactions between a client's individual, interpersonal, and environmental domains, is essential. Within assessment, a behavior analytic strategy provides a systematic blueprint of problem behavior. Knowledge of client strengths as well as vulnerabilities is also necessary in developing clinical management intervention strategies. Not all suicidal behavior, however, is crisis in nature. Some clients think, talk, or act in suicidal ways as an ongoing means of coping with life distress. Vulnerabilities to suicide and suicidal behavior may originate within the individual, or within interpersonal or environmental domains. The clinical manifestation of these vulnerabilities, however, directly indicates that they affect other domains as well. This dynamic perspective, incorporating biological, social, and environmental factors, has the highest potential of providing a comprehensive view of the problem and support the design of prevention and intervention strategies at the personal, program, and policy levels.

DEFINING AND EXPLAINING SUICIDE AND SUICIDAL BEHAVIOR

Suicide is a relatively rare event that is generally preceded by observable forms of nonfatal suicidal behavior. There are many more individuals who think and talk about harming themselves or wishes to be dead than there are those who actually go on to kill themselves. Attempted suicide and other nonfatal suicidal behaviors have been traditionally viewed as problems primarily because they carry with them an increased risk of suicide. More recently, however, nonfatal suicidal behaviors, including suicidal ideation and attempted suicide, have received attention as problems in their own right. This change in approach is based on evidence that suicidal behavior does not lie along a continuum from least to most serious, but that individuals who engage in different suicidal behaviors may also possess other individual differences important in assessment and intervention (Linehan 1986).

The most frequently described nonfatal suicidal behaviors include suicidal **ideation** (thinking about suicide), suicidal **verbalization** (talking about suicide), and suicide **threats** or informing others of plans or intent to engage in an act of self-harm. The term *suicide gesture* refers colloquially to an act of self-harm in which the intention to die is judged as low. The lethality, or medical seriousness, of a suicide gesture is generally, but not always, also low. Attempted suicide is regarded as a failed effort to die. Based on our inability to reliably assess the intention of these acts after the fact, the term *parasuicide* has been suggested as a replacement for all categories of self-harm. Parasuicide is a deliberate, nonfatal act of self-harm; it describes a suicide-like activity without inferring the actor's intent (Kreitman 1977). Although originally intended to describe acts where suicidal intent was presumed, parasuicide has been expanded to include any act of self-harm, and like in the literature (Hirsch, Walsh, and Draper 1982), we will use *self-harm, parasuicide,* and *attempted suicide* interchangeably.

The major obstacle to the accurate collection of suicide statistics and research findings and to the development of theory about the nature and causes of suicide is that there is no agreed-upon definition of actual suicide. Although an examination of the many classification systems of suicidal behavior underscores the complexity of defining suicide, it serves little utility in direct practice settings. In practice, there is one primary definitional questions: What is suicidal behavior?

The common *definition* of suicide is a simple one: "a human act of self-inflicted, self-intentional cessation" (Shneidman 1976:53). The focus is on the intent of the actor and on the goal of the action. If this definition is broken down further, six factors are generally involved in defining suicide: the initiation of an act that leads to the death of the initiator; the willing of an act that leads to the death of the willer; the willing of self-destruction; the loss of will; the motivation to be dead or die; and the knowledge by an actor that his or her own action is likely to produce death (Douglas 1967). These dimensions are important in determining whether a death is a suicide. Those responsible for making these determinations are concerned both with "false positives" (i.e., that which should not be classified as suicide; e.g., accidental overdoses or sexual asphyxiations ruled as suicides) and "false negatives" (i.e., a case in which evidence of suicide is concealed and the death is ruled as accidental; e.g., a single occupant motor vehicle accident). There has been much debate over the accuracy with which medical examiners and coroners assign the verdict of suicide to death—in most instances, systematic underreporting or biased reporting is suspected—and the validity of these assignments and of official mortality statistics has been the subject of numerous investigations (Gould and Shaffer, in press; Jobes, Berman, and Josselson 1987; Monk 1987; O'Carroll 1989). In the end, official mortality data appear to be a fairly valid indicator of suicide (Gould and Shaffer, in press; Monk 1987; Moscicki 1995).

Intent is an important concept in the assessment of suicide risk. Intent is how serious an individual is about ending his or her life (Beck, Schuyler, and Herman 1974). Acts judged to be of low intent are frequently labeled as "less serious" or "manipulative." However, despite our best clinical efforts, there is little evidence suggesting that distinctions among levels of intent can be accurately or reliably made. Whether an individual truly wanted to die is simply too difficult to know after the fact; this is even true in nonfatal suicidal acts, when the individual may not be able to accurately report his or her intent.

Parasuicide may be used on the part of some severely distressed individuals to escape, cope with, or solve problems rather than to cause death. The ability to differentially assess intention plays an important role in choosing appropriate interventions and management strategies. Efforts to classify nonfatal suicidal behavior have been even less successful than those concerned with suicide. There is currently no widely accepted classification system in use.

Theories of suicide extend far back into recorded history. Early philosophical explanations and debates focused on individual rights, the rights of the community or state, and the morality of taking a life or the notion of "higher right." Research into the causes of suicide is a more recent activity, formally beginning with Durkheim's *Le Suicide* in 1897. Designed to illustrate the development of the sociological method, rather than to directly study suicide, Durkheim's classification efforts resulted in three categories of suicide: (1) egoistic suicide, resulting from lack of or poor social integration into family, religious, or state communities; (2) altruistic suicide, resulting from excessive integration and identification, often identified with the "honorable" suicides of some Eastern cultures; and (3) anemic suicide, resulting from a loss of integration through trauma or catastrophe accompanied by alienation, social isolation, and loneliness (Durkheim 1897/1952).

Since Durkheim's work there have been many classification systems describing the motives and intent of suicide. Common to the definitions used in most classification systems are the dimensions noted earlier: initiation, intent or motivation, and knowledge of the desired consequence (Douglas 1967). The theories used to inform current social work practice with suicidal individuals are based on sociological, psychodynamic, biological, cognitive, and learning perspectives.

Sociological theories view suicide as a function of individual role and status within social systems; that is, suicide is an understandable behavior given a person's situation or position in society (Braucht 1979; Douglas 1967; Durkheim 1897/1952; Gibbs and Martin 1964; Henry and Short 1954; Zilboorg 1936). Originally, two characteristics of society, social regulation and social integration, were thought to determine social conditions and therefore the suicide rate. Social meaning, social restraint, norms, political knowledge, and the stability and durability of social relationships are now also regarded as important concepts and have contributed to the reformulation of these theories. Sociological theories are useful for predicting changes in suicide rates for total populations or subgroups; however, they are of limited utility for the practitioner interactionist perspective, suggesting that suicide is the result of the interaction between types of individuals and the environment, rather than the result of the individual or the environment alone (Braucht 1979).

Psychodynamic theories view suicide as largely the product of internal, often unconscious, motives. Classic analytic theory defines suicide as an unconscious hostile impulse that is turned inward toward an introjected and ambivalently viewed love object. According to this theory, if this impulse is acted out against oneself, it will not be acted out against others. Menninger (1938) described three parts of this hostility: the wish to kill, the wish to be killed, and the wish to die. As Freud's thoughts about suicide evolved, factors in addition to aggression, such as maladaptive anxiety, guilt, dependency, and rage, were also acknowledged as potentially resulting in suicide-prone coping mechanisms. Rebirth, reunion with one's mother, identification with a lost object, and revenge are also suggested as motives. Feelings of abandonment and helplessness, as well as hopelessness, are also components of the psychodynamic formulation of suicide (Furst and Ostow 1979).

Biological theories suggest that either genetic predispositions or biochemical imbalances precipitate drives toward suicide. Despite results that are not uniform, family relations appear to greatly influence the possibility of suicide. Although there is evidence of higher rates of suicide among male children of suicide victims (Stengel 1964), Wandrei (1985) found no evidence of higher rates among families of female suicides. A study of twin pairs in which one twin committed suicide did not find suicide in the other twin up to forty-nine years later (Kallman et al. 1949). In youth suicide, a familial history of suicidal behavior has often been found to be a risk factor for suicide, as is parental psychopathology (Brent et al. 1994; Gould et al. 1996). However, whether this suggests genetic vulnerability, environmental stress, modeling, or some combination of all three, is not yet determined. Therefore, despite evidence linking genetic factors to major affective and psychotic disorders, no clear relationship to suicide has been found (Motto 1986).

One of the most frequently replicated studies of biological indicators found low concentrations of a serotonin metabolite (5-HIAA) in the cerebrospinal fluid of suicide attempters and completers (Asberg, Thoren, and Traskman 1976; Greenhill et al. 1995; Mann and Stoff 1997). Serotonin regulates mood and reactivity; persons with low levels of this neurotransmitter can be more emotionally volatile and impulsive, perhaps increasing vulnerability to suicide. Based on small postmortem positron emission topography (PET) studies of suicide victims and biological challenges of suicide attempters, Arrango, Underwood, and Mann (1997) noted that the serotonin abnormality is most likely localized in the ventrolateral prefrontal cortex and brainstem, the parts of the brain that regulate behavioral inhibition. Thus, an abnormality in this area may make it hard for a person with suicidal impulses to control his or her urges. However, this evidence is of little utility because the number of participants in these studies was low, and because we do not yet have information about normative levels of 5-HIAA in nonsuicidal populations (Motto 1986; Shaffer et al. 1988). Currently, there is no biochemical indicator of suicidality useful in clinical work (Motto 1986).

Cognitive theories regard suicide and suicidal behavior as attempts to communicate or solve problems that cause intense interpersonal or environmental distress. The often-heard phrase "the cry for help" is used to convey the message contained in suicidal behavior (Farberow and Shneidman 1961). Beck (1963) posited that suicidal behavior is caused by an individual's belief that current problems are insoluble. Hopelessness is strongly associated with suicidal behavior (Beck, Resnik, and Lettieri 1974; Beck, Kovacs, and Weissman 1975a) and disordered patterns of thinking. Suicidal behavior has been conceptualized as a form of problem solving by several theorists (e.g., Applebaum 1963; Levenson and Neuringer 1971) and as an effort to get rid, of rather than cope with, problems through "manipulation" or death (Beck, Kovacs, and Weissman 1975a; Olin 1976; Stengel 1964). Others have suggested that suicide attempts may be usefully regarded in some individuals as an attempt to cope with extremely difficult life situations (Linehan 1986, 1993a; Maris et al. 1992).

Learning theories define suicidal behavior as a function of: (1) past responses in similar situations and (2) motivating, reinforcing, and environmental conditions. Suicidal behavior is acquired through social learning methods and becomes part of the individual's repertoire of coping responses if it is supported and receives positive or desirable consequences from the environment. The probability of suicidal behavior is based on expectations of the act by the individual and others, on the opportunity to engage in the act, and on the presence or absence of preventive efforts by others (Diekstra 1973).

A **psychiatric disease model** posits that suicide occurs within the context of a psychiatric disease and that an underlying condition, such as a mood disorder, substance abuse or dependence, aggressive traits, or other disorder must be present for suicide to occur. Support for this model comes from several large "psychological autopsy" studies (Brent et al. 1993; Martunnen et al. 1991; Rich, Young, and Fowler 1986; Robins et al. 1959; Shaffer et al. 1996) in which 90 percent or more of the victims were found to have suffered from a psychiatric disorder at the time of death. While the psychiatric community widely supports this model, it is of limited value for the social work practitioner. First, the data upon which it is based are drawn from victims who have died from suicide—persons who make suicide attempts, feel suicidal, or harm themselves are a different population than those who die by suicide (most will not go on to kill themselves), and this population is more likely to be seen by social workers. Second, the model, to a large extent, ignores the multiplicity of social and environmental variables that can also influence suicidal death and behavior.

Linehan (1993a) proposed a *biosocial model* of suicidal behavior, integrating elements of the preceding models. This model regards the emotional picture of the suicidal individual as one of chronic, aversive emotional dysregulation. From a biosocial perspective, suicidal behaviors are viewed as problem-solving behaviors that operate to reduce negative emotional arousal and distress directly (e.g., by ending all life, and presumable pain, via sleep or distraction from emotional stimuli) or indirectly (e.g., by eliciting help from the environment) or are inevitable outcomes of unregulated and uncontrollable negative emotions. Although suicidal behaviors are not logically in-evitable outcomes, paradigms of escape conditioning suggest the strong urges to es-cape or actual escape behaviors can be so well learned that they are automatic for some individuals when faced with uncontrollable and extreme physical or emotional pain. Suicide, of course, is the ultimate escape from problems in this life.

DEMOGRAPHIC PATTERNS

The demographic risk factors increasing the likelihood of suicide and nonfatal sui-cidal behavior are **sex, age,** and **race** or **ethnicity.** Men commit suicide at rates nearly five times higher than women. In young adults, the ratio of male suicides to females is even higher; young men are six times more likely to commit suicide than their female counterparts (National Center for Health Statistics 1998). Suicide is extremely rare before puberty—only seven children under age 10 died by suicide in 1995 (Gould and Shaffer, in press). Overall, the suicide rates for both sexes are highest among those aged 65 and older. The suicide rates are almost twice as high among whites (12.7/100,000) as among nonwhites (6.7/100,000; National Center for Health Statistics 1998). Among whites, the rates generally increase with age; males aged 80 to 84 have the highest reported rates (20.2/100,000). Among blacks and other racial minorities, however, the rates remain relatively constant in later life, peaking at 25 to 34 years (National Center for Health Statistics 1998). Among youth aged 15 to 24, suicide is third only to accidents and homicide as a cause of death (National Center for Health Statistics 1998) and accounts for about twice as many deaths as all natural causes combined (Shaffer and Craft 1999). In young white youth, it is the second leading cause of death. In contrast to patterns found in other age groups, the rate of suicide among males aged 15 to 19 has increased markedly from 1964 to 1994, with no sig-nificant change in the rate for young females. The suicide rate of 20- to 24-year-olds showed a twofold increase from 1964 to 1980, at which time they leveled off. The increase in the rate among teenagers was due to a notable increase in the suicide rate for 15- to 19-year-old African American males—the white rate remained relatively constant during that time. Several explanations are suggested to account for this in-crease in suicide by young males during these three decades, including the increased prevalence of substance abuse (Shaffer et al. 1996) and increased availability of fire-arms (Boyd and Moscicki 1986; Brent et al. 1991) for the population, as well as the increased media exposure and contagion described earlier.

The markedly higher suicide rates among elderly white men than among elderly black men have been examined from perspectives trying to explain each. Theories offer a variety of social, demographic, and individual factors as being responsible for these differences, such as the status and respect accorded to the black elderly, the earlier exit of vulnerable black men from mainstream society because of homicide or incarceration, and the higher rates of alcoholism and depression among white men.

Lower suicide rates found among Mexican Americans are hypothesized to be a function of differences from Anglo culture, including the supportive characteristics of family interaction (Hoppe and Martin 1986). Rates are not available for Hispanics as a whole since it is only since 1997 that this additional classification has been included on death certificates in all states (previously, Hispanics could be included in both white and nonwhite categories).

The suicide rates among Native Americans vary widely; they range from being similar to overall U.S. rates to being thirty times higher among some tribes (Hoppe and Martin 1986). Wallace et al. (1996) reported that the adolescent and young adult suicide rate for those residing in Indian Health Service Areas was the highest of any group in the United States (62/100,000).

Attempted suicide is not recorded in any systematic fashion in the United States. Approximately 11 percent of admissions to some inpatient psychiatric units are reported precipitated by suicide attempts (Wexler, Weissman, and Kasl 1978). Based on population statistics, this suggests a rate of 103 attempted suicides for every 100,000 people. The ratio of female to male attempters reported in the literature ranges from 1:1 to 5:1, although a ratio of 3:1 is most commonly cited. Among adolescents, the ratio of female to male is highly dependent on the sample: studies of community populations show a lower female to male ratio than those samples gathered from emergency rooms (Shaffer and Pfeffer, in review). Attempted suicide or parasuicide rates decline with age. Black women attempt suicide less than their white counterparts (Baker 1984). The higher supports available within the black community for individuals alienated from the dominant society may be responsible for some of this difference (Christian 1977; Davis 1979; Poussaint 1975). Among teenagers, African American high school students report as many suicide attempts as whites, and Hispanic adolescents have the highest suicide attempt rate (Centers for Disease Control 1998).

SOCIETAL CONTEXT

Suicide was the ninth leading cause of death in the United States in 1996, resulting in 30,903 deaths; 11.6 per 100,000 (National Center for Health Statistics 1998). The overall rates have remained relatively stable over the past one hundred years with slight fluctuations. Reported rates are highest in the western states (Nevada, 20.9/100,000; Montana, 19.8/100,000; Alaska, 19.8/100,000; New Mexico, 18.6/100,000) and lowest in the East (New York and New Jersey, 7.3/100,000; Washington, D.C., 6.4/100,000) (National Center for Health Statistics 1998).

Historically, suicide and suicidal behavior were judged primarily within religious contexts. More recently, social science and mental health research have altered social attitudes, as well as the legal and religious responses to both fatal and nonfatal suicidal behavior. As evidence mounts correlating suicidal behavior and severe intrapersonal, interpersonal, and environmental stress, social and cultural responses to the problem evolve. As we learn more about the multiple pathways to suicide, however, it becomes apparent that a permanent solution to or equation for explaining or preventing suicide is not likely to result. The social, psychological, and legal consequences of suicide are far-reaching.

Reluctance to label a death as suicide or an act of self-harm as a suicide attempt remains common. Several attitudes are responsible. The strong associations between mental illness and suicidal behavior possess negative social connotations that many victims and their families try hard to avoid. There are also still vestiges of religious sanction, long-standing beliefs that suicide is murder and a sin against God. Most churches, however, including the Catholic rites, no longer prohibit the burial of suicide victims in church cemeteries.

Beginning in the early 1960s and continuing through the early 1990s, we witnessed a threefold increase in the rates of suicide among male teenagers and young adults, which has since leveled off. During that same time, there was an increase in the attention paid to suicide among youth in the popular media. This attention took many forms, including movies, youth-oriented music, and heavy news coverage of youth suicides. Suicide is portrayed in highly romanticized fashion, with the victims often taking on folk hero status. Little or no acknowledgment is made of the individual mental health or family functioning problems that promote suicidal behavior, and the victims are presented as misunderstood but rational. Suicide is regarded as a reasonable solution to what are presented as the normal social pressures and problems of adolescence. The consequences have been twofold: (1) the widespread perception among some youth that suicide is *not* tied to severely impaired functioning or psychiatric disorder (Shaffer et al. 1987), and (2) an increase in the rates of parasuicides and calls to suicide hotlines in the days following such portrayals (Gould and Shaffer 1986). Suicide and suicidal behavior among young people have been found to increase following exposure to real or fictional accounts of suicide (Gould and Kramer 1999; Gould, Shaffer, and Kleinman 1988; Gould, Wallenstein, and Kleinman 1990; Velting and Gould 1997), with a magnitude of increase being proportional to the amount of publicity (Bollen and Phillips 1982; Phillips 1974; Wasserman 1984). This appears to be a youth, not adult, phenomenon (Kessler et al. 1989). The phenomenon of a suicide cluster, defined as three or more suicidal deaths occurring within a limited geographical area within a three-month period (M. Gould, personal communication), is thought to be related to imitation (Davidson et al. 1989); and in youth suicide, it is estimated that about 1 to 5 percent of suicidal deaths will occur as part of a suicide cluster (Gould and Kramer 1999). Efforts are now being made to reduce the positive publicity given to suicide. Of paramount importance in this effort is the message that suicidal behavior is not an effective means of solving life problems and that it is not chosen by rational and well-adjusted individuals as a way of solving problems.

VULNERABILITIES AND RISK FACTORS

A working knowledge of the risk factors associated with suicidal behavior is essential to identifying individuals at imminent and long-term risk. Risk factors are based on the characteristics of the populations in which rates of suicidal behavior are higher. They operate interactionally across the environmental, interpersonal, and individual domains. It is not at all clear how many or which risk factors place an individual at "high risk." Are more worse? Yes. Is not possessing one or even many of the characteristics a guarantee of low risk or insurance against suicidal behavior? Definitely not (Farberow and MacKinnin 1970; Lettieri 1974a, 1974b; Motto 1986).

The literature on suicide and parasuicide suggests that the *social environments* linked to suicidal behavior have four characteristics: lack of social support, high negative stress, links to others or "models" of suicidal behavior, and possible positive consequences for suicidal behavior (Linehan 1981).

Unemployed or retired status is correlated with suicide. These individuals potentially lack the support and the social integration that a work setting provides. This is true for all groups except young employed professional women; rates of suicide in this group have recently been rising. A similar finding has been found in youth suicide: difficulties in school, especially lacking an affiliation with peers (e.g., drifting), is a factor for completed suicide in adolescents (Gould et al. 1996). Many child suicides (committed by those under the age 15) happened following a period of school absence (Shaffer 1974); a similar observation was made by Teicher and Jacobs (1966) for young suicide attempters.

The lack of social support in a suicidal person's life may also be due to immigrant status (Coombs and Miller 1975) or lack of shared social characteristics with neighbors (Braucht 1979). Living alone is linked both to those who commit suicide and to suicides with a history of parasuicide (Bagley, Jacobsen, and Rehin 1976; Shneidman, Farberow, and Litman 1970; Tuckman and Youngman 1968). Women who attempt and then later commit suicide are more isolated and may also receive less helpful care from service providers (Wandrei 1985). Unfortunately, little information exists to inform our clinical speculations about the quality of the social supports available to many suicidal individuals. Some data suggest that the relatives of attempters are hostile (Rosenbaum and Richman 1970), while successful suicides may lack even a hostile support system. Numerous studies have reported high rates of psychopathology among the parents of adolescent suicide victims (e.g., Brent et al. 1988, 1994; Gould et al. 1996), which would be expected to impact on the child's familial relationships.

Although stressful life events, in and of themselves, are rarely a sufficient cause for suicidal behavior, suicidal behavior is widely regarded as a response to stressful, negative life events. Loss in general and patterns of negative life events distinguish suicide attempters and completers from other psychiatric inpatients (Birtchnell 1970; Levi et al. 1966). Suicide attempters report higher numbers of distressing, uncontrollable events than do nonsuicidal depressed individuals (Paykel 1979). Other studies have found that it is not the number or type of stressful life events involved that distinguishes suicidal individuals from others, but the perception of stressful negative events, that is, a tendency for negative events to be regarded as more stressful by suicide attempters than by others (Linehan 1988).

While most individuals with low social support and experiencing stressful life events do not go on to suicide or parasuicide, those who do may have suicidal behavior in their problem-solving response repertoires. Additionally, they may have positive expectations about the consequences of such action (Chiles et al. 1985; Kreitman, Smith, and Tan 1970; Shaffer and Gould 1987).

Following a parasuicide, major environmental changes may occur in the direction desired by the attempter (Rubenstein, Moses, and Lidz 1958). These changes increase the positive expectations about suicidal behavior and may increase the risk of future attempts and of suicide (McCutcheon 1985).

Both observation and self-report of *interpersonal interaction patterns* suggest that suicidal and parasuicidal individuals may be lacking important social skills. Suicides and parasuicides exhibit low levels of social involvement and interaction. They are also less likely to ask for support or attention. There are some data suggesting that suicidal individuals are less hostile and more passive and dependent than nonsuicidal individuals (Buglass and McCulloch 1970; Kreitman 1977).

Parasuicides are more likely to express dissatisfaction with treatment and to report discomfort around people in general (Cantor 1976). The interpersonal relationships of attempters are often characterized by high levels of conflict (Hawton and

Catalan 1987; Linehan 1986); this finding is also well substantiated by clinical observation. In conjunction with interacting environmental factors, the preceding characteristics suggest a lack of mutually satisfying relationships, which may increase emotional pain, the perception of unmitigated stress, and the sense that help is unavailable.

Individual risk factors can be divided into three areas: cognitive, affective, and behavioral. As subsets of these, we discuss previous suicidal behavior and psychiatric disorder as correlates of increased risk.

Cognitive risk factors include those of cognitive style, or the processing, organization, and use of information, and those of cognitive content, or what an individual thinks about. The cognitive style most commonly linked to suicidal behavior is one of rigidity rather than reflectiveness (Patsiokas, Clum, and Luscomb 1979), impulsivity rather than deliberation (Farberow 1970; Fox and Weissman 1975), field dependence rather than independence, and poor problem-solving ability (Levenson and Neuringer 1971; Linehan et al. 1987).

Hopelessness is generally regarded as the dominant cognitive feature of suicidal behavior (Beck 1963; Bedrosian and Beck 1979, Overholser et al. 1995). Hopelessness is more strongly associated with current suicidal intent than is depression (Beck, Kovacs, and Weissman 1974, 1975a, 1975b; Wetzel 1976). The available data make a case for the relationship between suicide and hopelessness, however, not between attempted suicide and hopelessness. Recent studies of attempted suicide have found mixed results concerning hopelessness, with higher levels of hopelessness among attempters found in some population samples (Ivanoff and Jang 1991; Paykel and Dienelt 1971; Wetzel 1976), although not among teenaged minority female suicide attempters (Rotheram-Borus and Trautman 1988).

Behavioral risk factors are somewhat narrowly defined as those activities or physical states associated with increased risk. The single strongest risk factor for future suicidal behavior is a previous suicide attempt or parasuicide. The presence of a suicide note at the time of a previous parasuicide has also been linked to subsequent suicide (Leenaars 1992). Highly disputed evidence exists linking the lethality of a prior attempt to subsequent suicide or parasuicide: some studies have found higher lethality in the prior attempts, while others have found no relationship between lethality and subsequent suicidal behavior (Linehan 1981).

Substance abuse and alcoholism are widely associated with an increased risk of suicide in both adults and adolescents. Up to 20 percent of all suicides are alcoholics (Roy and Linnoila 1986). Suicide attempters are significantly more likely to have used alcohol or drugs to alter their mood within the twenty-four hours preceding hospitalization than other psychiatric patients, even those thinking about suicide (Chiles et al. 1986). Evidence of a criminal record is also associated with increased risk among young men (Lettieri 1974a, 1974b). Recklessness and running away overnight are also associated with increased risk for completed suicide in adolescents, as is aggressivity (Shaffer et al. 1996).

The presence of physical illness, whether terminal, chronic, or acute, is also linked to suicide and parasuicide. Efforts to obtain medical help are often made by those who are suicidal; most suicides and parasuicides have seen a physician within the six months prior to their act (Linehan 1981, 1988). Numerous investigators have reported that HIV infection may increase the risk of suicide and suicidal behavior in adolescents and young adults (Cote, Biggar, and Dannenberg 1992; Kizer et al. 1988); however, these findings are not uniform (Dannenberg et al. 1996).

Mental health or psychiatric disorders, generally indicated by the presence of a psychiatric diagnosis, are also indicators of increased risk. Only a very small proportion of suicides among either adults or adolescents appear to be free of psychiatric symptoms (Shaffer et al. 1988, 1996). Among adult suicides, recurrent affective disorders (major depression and bipolar disorder) and schizophrenia are prevalent, while among repeated parasuicides, there is evidence that sociopathy is linked. About 10 to 15 percent of persons suffering from major depression and 20 to 25 percent of those with bipolar disorder will go on to kill themselves; often the mood disorder is accompanied by significant substance abuse problems (Slaby 1998). In depressed persons, suicide risk is greatest when there are neurovegetative signs (e.g., increased agitation and insomnia), suicidal ideation, substance abuse, and few social supports (Slaby 1998). For those with bipolar illness, suicide usually occurs during a depressive episode but may also occur during a mixed manic episode (Isometsa et al. 1994), although this is usually when the person is in a mixed state (Dilsaver et al. 1994). A similar proportion (10–15 percent) of persons with schizophrenia will go on to die by suicide (Slaby 1998). Young schizophrenics are at particular risk—suicide is the leading cause of death for this group (Caldwell and Gottesman 1990). Adults diagnosed as schizophrenic are particularly vulnerable, especially if hopelessness is high (Beck, Kovacs, and Weissman 1974; Wetzel 1976). Some other risk factors for schizophrenics include good premorbid functioning, short duration of illness, and an awareness of how the future will be impacted by their mental state (Clark and Fawcett 1992).

Among adolescent suicides, less schizophrenia is reported and the evidence on manic-depressive disorders is mixed; major depression is the most common diagnosis. In addition to depression, a variety of disorders labeled as psychiatric are found among teenaged suicides, including substance use disorders (particularly for boys), antisocial behavior, anxiety disorders (especially for girls), and learning disorders. Most adolescent suicide victims have more than one psychiatric diagnosis at the time of death (Shaffer and Gould 1987; Shaffer et al. 1996).

The **consequences of suicide** require discussion of the involved survivors. The experience of losing a parent, a child, a partner, or a close friend to suicide significantly marks a life. The reactions of guilt and anger, coupled with profound loss, can be extremely difficult to resolve without outside assistance. Unfortunately, the social sentiment toward suicide militates against survivors receiving adequate attention or support. Suicide remains a "shameful" death, generally regarded as best not discussed in detail. Ironically, one of the strongest needs among those attending suicide survivors' groups is to lay out, often in great detail, the immediate circumstances surrounding the suicide. Specifically, these may include finding the body, efforts to save the victim, and cleaning up any mess. Survivors not immediately present at the death may need to carefully describe the sequence of events as they understand it. Many report that they have had no opportunity to discuss these things before and experience great relief in doing so (Samaritans of the Capital District, personal communication, April 1987). Practical negative consequences may also ensue from a suicide, involving estate settlement, insurance claims, and worker compensation benefits. For a further discussion of the problems of survivors and the recommended interventions, see *Suicide and Its Aftermath* (Dunne, McIntosh, and Dunne-Maxim 1987).

Unfortunately, the circle of survivors extends far beyond the victim's immediate family and friends. Intervention with survivors may be needed in school, at work, or in religious communities. These interventions, sometimes referred to as postvention, are carried out in large and small groups, as well as in individual formats. As noted under "Societal Context," these situations must be carefully constructed with adolescents: postvention should be careful to convey the sadness associated with the loss while not romanticizing the victim or the act, and consistently maintain that suicide is not a reasonable or good solution to problems.

The social consequences of attempted suicide or parasuicide may be viewed as both positive and negative. For a desperate individual who is feeling that there is no place and no one to turn to, suicidal behavior may mobilize enough resources to find a solution to the immediate problem. From a learning perspective, this is unfortunate for the individual, because the act has been effective; that is, it was successful in bringing about change in the desired direction. Interpersonally, attempted suicide may draw family and friends closer to the victim, as evidenced by such statements as "we had no idea how bad she was feeling until this happened," or may change the behavior of an estranged partner or spouse, who returns to the relationship following the parasuicide. Repeated parasuicide tends eventually to generate hostility and push others, even in primary significant relationships, away emotionally. When important social supports intentionally make themselves unavailable, further parasuicide, often of higher lethality, may occur as a way of trying to elicit a more caring response. Systematically, nonfatal suicidal behaviors drain helping resources and place a chronic burden on the health care system, particularly on mental health and emergency services (Hawton and Catalan 1987; Kreitman 1977).

RESILIENCIES AND PROTECTIVE FACTORS

Individuals may move in and out of suicidal crises over the course of a lifetime as a result of the disruption of the balance of risk and protective factors. As we truly do not understand whether suicide is the same phenomenon in youth as it is among the elderly, we also do not understand whether suicide has different meanings and different risk factors across the life cycle. The most comprehensive summary on this topic suggests that while similar risk factors appear to operate throughout life, their proportionate weights differ. Protective factors operate similarly (Vaillant and Blumenthal 1990).

Although understanding how risk and protective factors operate across the life cycle is beyond the scope of this chapter, there is some general agreement about factors that function protectively against suicide. Youth, or younger age, is widely accepted as epidemiological "protection" with recent increases in youth suicide viewed as the result of temporal and cohort effects.

The availability of active clinical and social intervention is an important protective factor against suicide. A combination of formal and informal resources create the most stable conditions. Social work assessment and intervention frequently target barriers to intervention and support (Vaillant and Blumenthal 1990). Depression, physical illness, loss, and stressful life events, even when cumulative, rarely result in suicide when adequate social support is present. Hope is the second protective factor (Beck et al. 1985), as evidenced by the fact that hopelessness as a cognitive state identifies a high percentage of completed suicides. Unfortunately, we know little about how hope functions and why its absence seems so critical.

PROGRAMS AND SOCIAL WORK CONTRIBUTIONS

The social worker plays an important role in the interdisciplinary programmatic response to suicide and suicidal behavior. Across all types and levels of service, including crisis intervention, case management, and primary intervention, social workers may have more contact with suicidal individuals and their families than most other professionals. In communities, social workers often direct and coordinate crisis intervention services. In schools, preventive and postventive education is frequently a social work task. In health and mental health emergency settings, social workers are often the first to see suicidal individuals.

Crisis intervention or suicide prevention agencies may provide services such as telephone hotlines, walk-in counseling, and direct access to emergency medical and psychiatric services. Self-help groups dealing with surviving the loss due to suicide or coping with a suicidal loved one may also be offered through crisis intervention agencies. Most services of this types are locally run and are staffed by trained volunteers, often under the direction of a social worker. The types of specialized programs, the accessibility of the service, and the level of collaboration with other community agencies vary widely and should be known prior to client referral. Clients should also know whether crisis hotlines immediately notify police or mobile crisis units when suicide intent is expressed. For example, the Samaritans, an international organization with several branches in the eastern United States, generally do not initiate contact with medical authorities unless the caller gives permission to obtain help (Hirsch 1981).

School-based prevention programs tend to be broadly based, focusing on suicide education as the primary interventive method. The rationale behind these programs is that increased knowledge and sensitivity will help identify and get help to at-risk adolescents. While this approach may make theoretical sense, it has been criticized as ineffective and inefficient. The only systematic controlled evaluation of school-based programs found no significant increase in appropriate attitudes or accurate knowledge about suicide, particularly its correlation with mental illness (Shaffer and Gould 1987). The group at highest risk, effectively disturbed young men, has not been successfully targeted by most school-based prevention programs (Shaffer et al. 1988). By defining the population at risk as all youth in the schools, we ignore much of what has been learned over the past two decades about adolescent suicide, and we dilute prevention efforts.

Family service agencies, counseling services, mental health clinics, and even some psychiatric inpatient programs are beginning to respond more programmatically to the problems of suicide and suicidal behavior. In clinic or outpatient settings, skills training groups may be available that focus specifically on suicidal behavior (Linehan 1993a) or on depression. In inpatient hospital settings, special programs have been designed to help the individual recover most quickly and to begin more adaptive problem solving. Examples of such of these programs are available in Hawton and Catalan (1987) and in Swenson, Sanderson, and Linehan (1996).

ASSESSMENT AND INTERVENTIONS

Practitioners encounter suicidal individuals in many service settings. There are several issues worth thought before one confronts a suicidal client. Nonfatal suicidal behaviors, including parasuicide, were noted earlier as sometimes being used as single or repetitive problem-solving or coping strategies by individuals who lack adequate skills or emotion regulation mechanisms. Suicidal behavior is a response to a problem the client views as unsolvable. Accordingly, it should be regarded by the practitioner as problem-solving in nature. An often used alternative is to describe the individual as a "manipulator," someone who probably does not really want to die but uses suicidal behavior to accomplish other means. The negative connotations tied to this view evoke hostility toward suicide attempters and may compromise a practitioner's ability to provide care. Individuals who engage in parasuicide, particularly those who engage in repeated parasuicide, are likely to receive less care as well as lesser-quality care from service providers (Wandrei 1985).

The practitioner's personal philosophy is also important to consider: Under what circumstances should you prevent, and under what circumstances should you perhaps not prevent suicide? Is suicide an inalienable personal right? Those who argue so view all coercive forms of suicide prevention as maligning and disrespectful (Gomery 1997; Szasz 1986). The rational suicide movement also supports the right of individuals to choose suicide as an act of self-deliverance, most often in response to unremitting physical pain or terminal illness. Based on clinical experience, however, there is evidence that in many instances, suicidal intent may change dramatically within a few days. Providing control until the individual is able to regain self-management is regarded as humane and caring from this perspective. The authors strongly believe that outside specific hospice situations, the role of the mental health practitioner is life preserving. From a legal perspective, agencies and individual practitioners alike worry about litigation and liability if suicide occurs. As a result, many agency policies require practitioners to enact restrictive means of prevention, such as involuntary hospitalization, in all cases where the practitioner is concerned about self-harm. In circumstances where no policy exists, workers must exercise greater self-awareness, risk assessment, and decision-making skills. Useful reading on this subject is found in Comstock (1992), Ivanoff (1997), and Linehan (1993a).

Finally, the need for ongoing consultation while working with suicidal clients cannot be overstated. The degree of judgment and the number and quality of decisions made require discussion with another professional, preferably one experienced in working with suicidal clients. The immediate and ongoing assessment of risk, the review of intervention strategies, and the exploration of other available prevention resources are three functions that this consultation can serve.

Another important reason to maintain close consultation while a client is actively suicidal is to maintain self-awareness and to help deal with one's own personal responses engendered by the client's suicidal behavior. The possibility of losing a client to suicide and the consequent feelings of frustration, anger, and impotence are reasonable and normal; however, they can prevent a worker from being effective during this time. In cases of repeated parasuicide, consultation can be useful in helping maintain one's own problem-solving perspective and focus when feeling uncomfortably caught by the client's maladaptive efforts. Individual vulnerabilities such as psychiatric disorders, poor problem-solving abilities, or inadequate coping mechanisms that may increase vulnerability to suicidal behavior can be worsened by environmental stress. An ecological perspective assessing the interaction between individuals and their social and physical environments is important in acquiring an understanding of suicide risk. Although the social worker practicing outside a mental health setting may have less occasion to assess suicide risk, such knowledge remains nonetheless necessary, given the possible consequence. In addition to mental health and counseling agencies, where one might typically find suicidal individuals, social workers also deal with clients at risk in public assistance or child welfare settings, in hospitals or health clinics, and particularly in institutional settings such as nursing homes, juvenile detention centers, jails, and prisons.

When seeing a client in an agency setting who presents several risk-population characteristics, it is best to ask directly about previous suicidal behavior. As part of a general assessment interview, the question can be incorporated into discussing ways in which the client has previously tried to cope with his or her problems, a standard component in social work assessment interviews (Hepworth, Rooney, and Larsen 1997). Contrary to myth, it is not advisable to avoid discussing suicide, nor is there any evidence that simply asking an adult about suicidal ideation or behavior plants the idea, that is, "Well, no, I hadn't thought of it before, but that's not a bad idea!" In fact, clinical experience suggests that if clients are thinking about suicide, most feel relieved to be asked about it. Clients may be uncertain or fearful about the social worker's reaction to suicidal ideation and may hesitate to bring it up on their own; open talk about suicide and matter-of-fact questions can make discussion easier. A good question to begin with is "Have you ever thought about doing or done anything to hurt yourself?" The question should be asked directly, and the response should be explored immediately if it is affirmative.

Although most clients do not seek help for suicidal ideation, a client may seek help for problems of depression or hopelessness tied to a downward spiral in mood, feelings of self-worth, and success in solving or coping with life problems. Client comments that require further exploration include indirect statements of how others might be better off if the client were gone, comments such as "I can't stand it" or "I am at the end of my rope," or expressed wishes to be with dead relatives or pets. Such expressed wishes must be explored carefully in adolescents and adults for evidence of concrete thinking that may indicate a thought disorder. Direct statements of wanting to end it all," "check out," or "go to sleep and never wake up" also require immediate follow-up with a question asking directly about ideation and self-harm.

Finally, social workers may see clients referred to them for ongoing individual or family intervention following a suicide attempt. In situations where the practitioner has prior knowledge that suicidal behavior has occurred in the recent past, it is important to establish quickly whether suicidal ideation or intent remains. Whether the issue of suicide risk surfaces during the initial assessment or later, the social worker proceeds with the same follow-up questions.

There are two assessment goals in working with suicidal clients: (1) assessment of the long-term and immediate risks of suicide and suicidal behavior; and (2) construction of a chain or behavioral analysis of what led to the suicidal behavior. The behavioral analysis is one of the single most important assessment tools; it identifies the antecedents and the consequences that led to the problem as well as the vulnerabilities and strengths that may contribute to solving the problem. Table 27.1 describes the basic procedures in a chain analysis.

While high-risk characteristics provide information about the long-term risk, they do not precisely predict the likelihood of future suicide or parasuicide. Unknown are the combination and the number of risk characteristics necessary to place an individual at high risk. A number of suicide prediction scales have been developed to identify at-risk individuals. These scales alert the practitioner that a client is part of a risk population. However, individuals lacking one or many of the characteristics associated with suicide or parasuicide are not without risk, nor are they in any way immune to risk. Population risk characteristics are a useful indicator of increased risk, generally at some unspecified time in the future. They do not provide the information needed most by a practitioner about the likelihood of suicide or parasuicide in the next few days.

The assessment of suicide or parasuicide in the immediate or near future is indicated in several situations, including (1) when an individual possesses several risk-population indicators; (2) when a history of suicidal behavior becomes apparent during the course of an assessment interview; and (3) when a client communicates an intent to commit suicide, either in a crisis situation (e.g., in the middle of the night over the telephone) or during a regularly scheduled appointment.

Unfortunately, as in assessing long-term risk, no known set of factors can predict imminent risk. There are, however, direct, indirect, and situational indicators (see table 27.2). These indicators discriminate suicidal or parasuicidal individuals from those who are not and describe circumstances associated with suicide or parasuicide within the next few days. This list of empirically derived indicators was originally compiled by Linehan (1981), but it has been updated for this purpose.

In the assessment and intervention planning with a client manifesting suicidal behavior, six topical areas must be thoroughly covered by the clinician: (1) complete

TABLE 27.1. Steps in Chain Analysis

1. Describe the specific suicidal behavior or self-harm. Detail exactly what the client did, said, thought, and felt, including the intensity of the feelings.
2. Identify the specific precipitating event that began the chain. Start with environmental events; for example, "Why did the problem occur yesterday rather than the day before?"
3. Identify factors such as physical illness, poor sleeping, drug or alcohol abuse, or intense emotions that heightened the client's vulnerability to the problem at this time.
4. Describe the moment-by-moment chain of events. Examine thoughts, feelings, and actions, and determine whether there were any possible alternatives to these.
5. Identify the consequences of the problem behavior.
6. Generate alternative solutions: for example, what skills might the client have used to avoid the problem behavior as a solution?
7. Identify a prevention strategy to reduce future vulnerability to this problem chain.
8. Repair the significant consequences of the problem.

TABLE 27.2. Factors Associated with Immediate Risk of Suicide or Parasuicide

I. Direct Cues If Imminent Risk for Suicide or Parasuicide
  1. Current suicide ideation
  2. Current or recent suicidal threats
  3. Current or completed suicide planning and/or preparation
  4. Parasuicide in the last year, especially if suicide intent expressed at time
II. Indirect Cues of Imminent Risk for Suicide or Parasuicide
  5. Patient falls into suicide or parasuicide risk populations
  6. Indirect references to own death; arrangements for death
  7. Recent disruption or loss of interpersonal relationship; negative environmental changes in past month
  8. Recent medical care
  9. Current hopelessness or anger, or both; increased psychological perturbation
  10. Indifference to or dissatisfaction with therapy; elopements and early pass return by hospitalized patients
III. Cues Associated with Suicide and/or Parasuicide in the Next Several Hours
  11. Suicide note written or in progress
  12. Methods available or easily obtained
  13. Precautions against discovery or intervention; deception or concealment about timing, plans, etc.
  14. Alcohol consumption; current overuse; isolation
  15. Major depression with:
    a. Severe agitation. Psychic anxiety, panic attacks, severe obsessive ruminating/compulsive behaviors
    b. Global insomnia
    c. Severe anhedonia
    d. Diminished concentration, indecision
    e. Current episode of cycling affective disorder
  16. Isolation; first 24 hours of jail incarceration
  17. Recent media publicity about a suicide

Source: Adapted from M. M. Linehan. 1993a. *Cognitive Behavioral Treatment of Borderline Personality Disorder.* New York: Guilford Press.

description of suicidal behavior (including all ideation, planning, threats, and parasuicidal acts) and information about frequency, duration, intensity, and magnitude; (2) history of previous suicidal behavior of client and his/her family members; (3) preceding and consequent situational and behavioral events associated with suicidal behavior; (4) preceding and precipitant problems and stressors impinging on the client; (5) client's description of problem that led to suicidal behavior; and (6) a "chain" or behavioral analysis of most recent self-harm or suicidal behavior.

In conducting the behavior analysis, the following four steps, adapted for suicidal behavior from the functional analysis interview model of Pomeranz and Goldfried (1970), should be followed:

1. Individual, interpersonal, and environmental factors that increase and decrease risk. Individual characteristics, including demographic, cognitive, affective, and behavioral risk factors. Environmental and interpersonal characteristics including social support, models for suicidal behavior, and consequences of suicidal behavior.

2. Individual and environmental factors relevant to intervention. Client's personal assets, such as aptitudes; cognitive, intellectual, and emotional abilities; skills;

and cultural and religious values. Client's deficits or hindrances in the same areas. Characteristics of the environment that may help or hinder intervention.

3. Problem list with targets clearly specified. Outcome criteria and how progress will be measured.

4. Immediate steps to reduce risk of suicidal behavior. List of intervention strategies with problem targets from the preceding.

All forms of intervention are ineffective with a dead client (Mintz 1968). Crisis intervention is the social worker's frontline strategy with a client at immediate risk of suicidal behavior. The standard method of crisis intervention is described in detail elsewhere (Butcher and Maudal 1976; Roberts 1990). A summary of the recommended procedures is presented in table 27.3.

Once a worker determines that the client is at immediate risk through assessing the listed indicators, action must be taken to prevent further suicidal behavior. First, this means making certain that the client is physically safe: Does the client require hospitalization? Is there someone in the client's home environment willing and able to stay with the client until the crisis passes? Is this individual willing and able to call emergency services for assistance if the client appears unable to maintain control? A bias toward maintaining the client's sense of self-control and personal management whenever possible should be demonstrated in assessing how to best deal with a crisis.

The decision to hospitalize a client is generally made in conjunction with a physician or emergency room staff. The question to ask when considering this decision is "Can I prevent a suicide now by hospitalization?" Though there is no empirical evidence that involuntary hospitalization prevents suicides from being completed, hospitalization is a final hope for families and practitioners that there may be a way to save the patient's life. There can be several levels of involuntary care that occur

TABLE 27.3. Crisis Management Procedures

1. Offer emotional support.
2. Provide opportunity for catharsis.
3. Communicate hope and optimism.
4. Be interested and actively involved.
5. Listen selectively; sift out material useful in bringing about change; leave defenses intact.
6. Provide needed factual information.
7. Formulate the problem situation; provide statement of problem to the client.
8. Be empathetic and to the point.
9. Predict future consequences of various courses of action.
10. Give advice and offer direct suggestions.
11. Set limits; establish rules.
12. Clarify and reinforce adaptive action and problem solving.
13. Confront the client's ideas or behaviors directly.
14. Terminate a session if the client is not at the point of working on his or her problems.
15. Place concrete demands or requirements on the client before the next contact.
16. Work out explicit, time-limited contract.
17. Enlist the aid of significant others.

Source: Butcher and Maudal 1976.

before a patient is hospitalized. The patient may be persuaded to go to a practitioner by his or her family. It also happens when a patient no longer has the will to refuse the requests made by the family and practitioner to be medicated. This does not imply in any way that all parasuicides should result in hospitalization, nor does it imply that hospitalization is on par with therapy or medication. Hospitalization is the last result when the patient cannot be maintained at home or in a community. Ethically, a practitioner must take all steps, no matter how drastic, to save the life of a patient. Though most of the time outpatient programs are more desirable for patients, there are times when the strain felt by family members is so tremendous that the patient loses his or her support system. Brief hospitalization may allow patient and family to refocus if a suitable outpatient plan cannot be found (Ivanoff 1997). Some psychiatric disorders linked to increased suicide risk, such as delusional depression, schizophrenia, schizoaffective disorder, and panic disorder, are best treated in the hospital during their acute phases. In other cases, however, the negative consequences of hospitalization, including social stigma, loss of a feeling of control, and the unfavorable treatment received from hospital staff, are also considerations worth weighing. The more general question of whether hospitalization will prevent suicidal behavior from occurring in the future cannot be answered unequivocally, but hospitalization for this reason has found little positive endorsement.

The use of agreements, both verbal and written, is reported to be quite useful between suicidal individuals and practitioners. In this situation, the agreement refers only to suicidal behavior, not other agreements for service that the client makes with the worker. Prior to leaving the social worker's office, the client is asked to agree not to commit suicide and, if feeling strong urges to do so, to contact the worker or some other stipulated service provider. If the client reports not feeling able to enter into this contract with the worker, a brief voluntary hospitalization may be discussed as a self-initiated method of regaining control.

If a suicide attempt has already been made or is in progress when the social worker is notified, it may be necessary to call the police or the emergency rescue squad for immediate action. If the worker knows that local emergency services are apt to be less than immediately responsive, an involved and supportive family member or friend may be called to go to the client and stay there until help arrives.

Ideally, the best way to manage a crisis is to predict and plan for it. If a client has experienced intermittent intense suicidal ideation or has acted on this ideation in the past, it is useful to acknowledge that the ideation will probably not end immediately after the first few sessions, that it may be useful to view it as a "habit," and that the client and the worker will together develop strategies for managing it in the future. Based on the information about cognitive strengths and resources obtained in the assessment (e.g., important reasons for living, any positive hopes for the future, and acknowledgment that suicide is not an effective solution to problems), a plan for coping is kept on a "crisis card," a business card containing the phone numbers of emergency contacts on one side and a list of coping strategies to help maintain control on the other. Carried in a wallet or pocketbook at all times, the card can be used as a self-instructional device for periods when the client is afraid of losing control.

Based on cognitive-behavioral and learning theories, dialectical philosophy, and Zen, **dialectical behavior therapy** (DBT; Linehan 1993a, 1993b) is the first intervention for chronic suicidal behavior, with published empirical support based on randomized experimental design. Developed by Linehan and colleagues at the University of Washington, DBT was originally begun as a treatment for chronically suicidal women. Over time, it became clear that most of these women also met the criteria for borderline personality disorder (BPD) and the treatment evolved accordingly. Standard DBT is a one-year outpatient treatment that simultaneously combines weekly individual psychotherapy with skills-training groups that run two and a half hours per week (Linehan 1993a, 1993b). The skills training groups teach adaptive coping skills in the area of emotion regulation, distress tolerance, interpersonal effectiveness, and identity confusion and maladaptive cognition reduction; each of these skills areas addresses one of the four primary problem areas of BPD clients. The individual treatment addresses maladaptive behaviors while strengthening and generalizing skills. Corollary treatment components of DBT include telephone consultation, team supervision, and casework and therapist consultation.

DBT treatment strategies are divided into four basic sets: (a) dialectical strategies, (b) core strategies (validation and problem solving), (c) communication strategies (irreverent and reciprocal communication), and (d) case management strategies (consultation to the patient, environmental intervention, supervision, consultation with therapists). These strategies can be divided into those most related to acceptance and those most related to change (see table 27.4). The DBT practitioner must balance the use of these two types of strategies within each treatment interaction. A major objective is to help the client understand that behaviors may prove both appropriate or valid and also dysfunctional or in need of change.

Validation begins with empathy. The worker then proceeds to analyze the client's response in relationship to its context and function. The function of validation is to make the unreasonable reasonable, and to help clients learn how and when to trust themselves. Validation can also serve as acceptance to balance change and can func-

TABLE 27.4 Dialectical Behavior Therapy Treatment Strategies: Acceptance and Change

Acceptance Strategies and Procedures

1. Dialectical strategies
2. Validation strategies
3. Relationship strategies
4. Environmental intervention
5. Reciprocal communication

Change Strategies and Procedures

1. Dialectical strategies
2. Problem-solving strategies
3. Contingency management
4. Capability enhancement and skills acquisition
5. Cognitive modification
6. Exposure
7. Consultation to the client
8. Irreverent communication

tion to strengthen the clinical process and the therapeutic relationship. There are three types of validation: (a) verbal (direct communication that a statement is valid: for example, "Yes. I can see that you are really upset"), (b) functional (behavioral response that indicates the therapist accepts the client's statement as valid: for example, "Let's take a look at what's upsetting you"), and (c) cheerleading (validating client's capacity, not necessarily beliefs: for example, client says "I can't do it," and the worker replies, "I know that you think that you can't do it, but I have complete faith that you really can do it").

Based on a primary assumption that clients' lives are currently unbearable, DBT places great emphasis on change. **Problem-solving procedures,** such as skills training, contingency management, cognitive modification, and exposure, are adopted directly from the cognitive-behavioral literature. Client and worker together identify public and private problematic behaviors and the factors that are associated with the initiation and maintenance of these problem patterns. Next, the client's behavioral excesses and deficits that interfere with engaging in goal behaviors are identified, as well as what the client must learn, experience, and do to perform the goal behavior.

Suicide crisis behavior, parasuicide, self-harm, and intrusive, intense suicidal thought, images, and communications, as well as significant changes in suicidal ideation or urges to self-destruct, are always addressed in individual therapy immediately following their occurrence. Although nonsuicidal self-mutilation or other self-injurious behaviors may not seem as critical as actual suicide attempts to the therapist, they are never ignored in DBT: these behaviors are good predictors of future lethal acts and can also cause substantial harm.

A behavioral or chain analysis, outlined earlier in table 27.1, is the standard tool used to understand problematic behavior. Using information about the event, the client's emotional and cognitive responses, overt actions that precedes the client's behavior, and the consequences of the behavior for the client and the environment, a chain analysis provides a moment-to-moment description of the problem behavior. This analysis indicates one or more of four change strategies: (a) *skills training* addresses the client's inability to engage in more adaptive responses; (b) *contingency management strategies* address the reinforcement strategies that support the client's problematic behavior; (c) *cognitive modification procedures* address faulty beliefs and assumptions that interfere with the client's problem-solving capabilities; and (d) *exposure-based strategies* address anxiety, shame, or other emotional responses that interfere with the client's adaptive problem-solving attempts.

The role of the worker in the change process frequently includes three simultaneous activities. The first is to provide hope, in the absence of the client's own, that her or his problems can eventually be managed or solved. While providing hope is clearly important in the beginning phase of work, it is also common for the automatic, "What's the use? I may as well give up" thoughts to return intermittently as problem solving becomes more difficult for the client. The practitioner should not be discomfited by the notion of lending his or her own hope to the client during the slow, gradual process of rebuilding the client's hope.

Second, the worker must model adaptive problem solving for the client through the worker's own behavior. This includes securing information and referrals for concrete services, generating alternatives when needed, accurately identifying problem situation, and consistently evaluating the effectiveness of problem-solving efforts.

Finally, the worker's response to the client's efforts should be supportive and encouraging, but also collective. If a client persists in attempting to solve problems in an ineffective or maladaptive manner, change has not occurred, nor has the likelihood of future suicidal behavior decreased. Learning new ways of solving problems, however, is difficult. Each step toward adaptive problem solving should be verbally identified or even pointed out for clients, as they may not recognize the accomplishment. Warmth in responding to not-quite-right efforts, help in adjusting them, and encouragement of future efforts are frequently repeated worker tasks.

An important assumption underlying DBT is that many of the problems experienced by BPD clients are due to a combination of motivation problems and behavioral skills deficits; that is, the necessary skills to regulate painful affect were never learned. For this reason, DBT emphasizes **skills building** to facilitate behavior change and acceptance. In standard DBT, skills are taught weekly in 2.5 hour psychoeducational skills-training groups. These skills are outlined and described in detail (Linehan 1993b). The function of the skills group is to teach individuals specific behavioral patterns. The DBT group emphasizes skills-building procedures through modeling, instructions, behavioral rehearsal, feedback and coaching, and homework assignments.

Group skills training works in tandem with individual therapy Simultaneous group and individual treatment creates a dedicated time to learn much-needed skills and a separate context for coached individual application. Group skills training has several advantages over individual skills training. Group members learn from each other and can practice skills with group members engaged in the same tasks; skills practice is coached by the group leader's extra set of expert eyes, and group membership often decreases isolation and increases clients' sense of being understood.

The four DBT skills-training modules directly target the behavioral, emotional, and cognitive instability and dysregulation of BPD: mindfulness, interpersonal effectiveness, emotion regulation, and distress tolerance. In standard DBT, the first two weeks of any given module are spent on mindfulness and the remaining six weeks are spent on the particular module.

Mindfulness is a psychological and behavioral translation of the meditation skills usually taught in Eastern spiritual practices. The goal of this module is attentional control, awareness, and sense of true self. Three primary states: (a) reasonable mind (the logical, analytical, problem-solving state), (b) emotional mind (the opposite; allows creativity, passion, and drama), and (c) wise mind (the integration of both the reasonable and the emotion mind). Wise mind allows the appropriate response—one responds as needed, given the situation.

Distress tolerance focuses on the ability to accept both oneself and the current environmental situation in a nonevaluative manner. While implying acceptance of reality, it does not imply approval. Self-soothing, adaptive, activity-oriented distraction, and consideration of the pros and cons of distress tolerance are skills within the module.

Similar to standard **interpersonal problem solving** and assertion, these skills include effective strategies for asking for what one needs and saying no to requests. Effectiveness here is defined as obtaining wanted changes or objectives, maintaining the relationship, and building and maintaining self-respect.

Emotional regulation is defined as the ability to (a) increase or decrease physiological arousal associated with emotion, (b) reorient attention, (c) inhibit mood-dependent actions, (d) experience emotions without escalating or blunting, and (e) organize behavior in the service of external nonmood dependent goals. Emotion regulation begins with the identification and labeling of current emotions. This occurs through observing and describing events that prompt emotions and one's interpretations of these events and through understanding the physiological responses, emotionally expressive behaviors, and aftereffects of emotions. Reducing vulnerability to emotional reactivity is also targeted.

ILLUSTRATION AND DISCUSSION

Elizabeth, a 22-year-old white unmarried woman, had previously attempted suicide three times. She initially came to the mental health clinic on a pass from the psychiatric unit of the local hospital, where she had been hospitalized for three weeks following a highly lethal overdose that she had acknowledged as an attempt to end her life. Her discharge from the hospital had been made contingent on beginning outpatient treatment. She presented as a very bright, depressed young woman and expressed amazement and ambivalence at still being alive. She acknowledged current suicidal ideation and at first insisted it was constant. However, upon closer questioning by the practitioner it appeared the ideation was more intermittent, occurring three or four times per day, usually when she was thinking about the "fucked-up mess my life is" and "this empty feeling inside me that makes me think there's no hope."

The second of five children, Beth had grown up in an upper-middle-class two-parent family in a western state. She described her physician father as caring but critical and her mother as distant and aloof. She reported no history of mental illness or emotional disorder among her parents or siblings and noted that her siblings were "wonderful and normal."

Her first suicide attempt was at age 16, while she was living at home. Following an argument with her parents, she ingested a potpourri of pills from the family's well-stocked medicine closet, became ill, and vomited. She received no medical attention and told no one of the incident at the time. Each of her attempts had been precipitated by a two- to three-month period of slowly deepening depression and lowered daily functioning. In addition, Beth reported that she had withdrawn from her few friendships and the activities that had provided satisfaction. She had increased her use of maladaptive coping methods, including alcohol and drug abuse, and spent long periods of time in bed.

The immediate precipitants of all the attempts had been interpersonal in nature, involving conflict or perceived or real rejection by an important other. The most recent attempt had been in response to a roommate and close friend's moving out of the apartment that the two were sharing and the news one week later that the therapist she had been seeing was leaving her position. Beth described how quickly life began to look empty and how thoughts of past relationship failures and feelings of being uncared for had crowded out all motivation to "keep my life together." Beth had had few long-term relationships, jobs, or avocational pursuits. Her strengths included her intellect, her ability to break down problems in living toward solving them (when not severely depressed), and her artistic abilities, most notably painting. She had been trained in art from an early age, and spending time painting afforded her a sense of self unavailable through other activities alone or with others. Her previous psychiatric diagnoses included both major depression and borderline personality disorder. Numerous problems with the use of psychiatric diagnoses have been described elsewhere in the social work literature (Kutchins and Kirk 1986), and it was not automatically assumed that these diagnoses were accurate or useful in providing social work intervention. The criteria for a diagnosis of major depression were consistent with the pattern of behavior, affect, and cognition that Beth described during each of the periods leading up to her parasuicides. The earlier diagnosis of BPD was used as an indicator of previous practitioners' views of the severity and pervasiveness of Beth's inability to regulate her feelings when distressed and the possible forms and targets of her conflictual interpersonal style.

In assessing Beth's suicidal behavior and life situation, it became clear that her pattern of unsuccessful relationships and aborted occupational ventures had left her feeling quite hopeless about the future. While conveying strong sensitivity and empathy for how overwhelmed Beth felt, the practitioner told Beth she did not believe suicide was the best or only solution to Beth's problems. Beginning with the first contact, the practitioner let Beth know that although she understood Beth's feeling of desperation, she did not share Beth's feeling of hopelessness about her situation: she believed there were ways to work toward solving Beth's problems and to create a life worth living. The practitioner did believe that Beth's life could be improved, and she communicated this sincerely.

Initially, Beth was skeptical: "I know this is just your job! You don't really care! How could you know how to fix my life? What happens if I can't do it? What makes you think there's anything here worth saving?" The practitioner explained that she didn't know how to fix Beth's life, but that there were things they could do together to improve it. The worker frankly admitted that she didn't have the "right" answers but would help generate some alternatives during this time when Beth's capacity for solving problems was diminished by her depression and hopelessness. The practitioner went on to tell Beth that she regarded their work together as a collaborative enterprise, Beth's portion of which was, initially, to commit to trying (treatment) and to work toward her goals.

Beth was vague in describing what she wanted to change in her life. She defined her problems in global terms that contributed to feeling overwhelmed by them. With the worker's help, she was able to identify two major areas that she wanted to work on: getting along better (with and without people) and finding work she was interested in doing. These goals were further broken down, as assessment indicated Beth's previous problem patterns in these areas. A chain analysis of the events (internal and external) that led up to Beth's most recent suicide attempt was completed.

Beth was willing to agree to come to every appointment and to be honest in discussing her feelings and in discussing her work toward the two goals. Beth expressed worry about lying to the worker about doing positive things when she hadn't really done them or, worse yet, being caught having agreed to do something particularly distasteful. For this reason, the worker and Beth initially agreed to individually negotiate and contract between-session tasks.

Contracting to avoid parasuicide, however, was somewhat more difficult. As Beth pointed out, "If I really want to do it, I'll do it, right? Just because I tell you I'll call someone if I feel like I want to knock myself off doesn't mean I have to do it, does it?" The worker, wishing to maximize Beth's sense of self-control, told Beth that she was absolutely correct, that the option to parasuicide was not being taken away from her by the contract. The practitioner described the contract as serving two purposes: to remind Beth of the purpose of their work together during periods when "automatic" suicide ideation may have taken over and to assure the practitioner that Beth felt confident enough in her own control to live at home. Possible scenarios were discussed: "What happens if . . . ?" "What if I forget until it's too late and call after I've taken something?" "If I screw up will you stop seeing me?" These questions, as well as when rehospitalization might be considered, were discussed in detail. A problem-solving perspective was maintained, meaning that future suicidal behavior was regarded as an eventual probability, not to be punished (or praised via the practitioner's overattention), but to be dealt with as part of ongoing work. Beth made a verbal contract and following that, she and the practitioner made up a short written contract renewable monthly that was signed by the two of them and placed in Beth's file. Beth was also given a copy to keep.

Beth agreed to keep a weekly diary card, logging her suicidal ideation, mood, urges to hurt herself, drinking, and substance use. Over time, Beth also used a checklist to indicate which skills she practiced each day.

Each session initially began reviewing Beth's diary card and a behavioral chain analysis was completed on any suicidal behavior occurring since the last contact. Positive emphasis was placed on what skills Beth used to cope with the suicidal thoughts or urges to hurt herself. Less successful efforts at coping with suicidal thoughts were examined in view of how they could be strengthened. The log detailed her thoughts about "giving up," the situation she was in at the time, how strong the urge to "do something" (negative) was on a 1–10 scale, and how she coped with the situation. Beth managed to avoid further parasuicide, despite episodes of intense ideation that occurred almost every other day at first. By six months later these had decreased to approximately one episode a month.

Early on Beth confided that she kept a cache of psychotropic prescription drugs under her bed in case she decided she "couldn't take it any more." Sometimes Beth would get the box of pills out and take it out to the living room and play with it, counting out how many of each drug or drug combinations she would have to take to kill herself. She was highly conversant with lethal dosages of these medications. For some time after beginning work she found these thoughts comforting, a sort of "entertaining of options." She acknowledged that having the drugs represented an independence and sense of control for her. The practitioner told Beth she was uncomfortable with the risk posed by the accessibility of the drugs, although understood her feelings of lack of control and wish to attain it. Beth noted that times when she was most likely to get out the drugs were when she was depressed or when angry with the practitioner for "trying to make her live." As Beth had faithfully followed the terms of the suicidal behavior contract despite severe ideation depression during this period, the worker was not certain hospitalization was the appropriate action. Following consultation with her immediate supervisor and another senior colleague, the worker did not suggest hospitalization at this time, identifying the sense of control Beth derived from the cache of drugs as important until it could be replaced by control gained through more adaptive means. (In retrospect, suggesting hospitalization may have enabled Beth to take adaptive control sooner.) Three months later Beth came in and announced she had flushed all the pills down the toilet, having decided it was "stupid to keep these things around the house anymore." This provided the impetus to review her progress and highly praise the adaptive efforts Beth was now making to maintain her sense of control over life.

Through discussion with the worker and information, testing, and guidance from the Department of Vocational Rehabilitation, Beth went on to identify a new vocational pursuit, art restoration. While this work involved great technical knowledge and ability, the challenge for Beth was positive. A long apprenticeship followed months of study. During this time, many recurring doubts about the decision to study restoration plagued Beth, sometimes interrupting work. The focus in her work with the practitioner shifted to building a broader and more competent support system. Beth found a broader network of friends, which enabled her to manage periodic feelings of loss and rejection better. She learned to adaptively use others for "perception checks," and to buffer the stress of normal change and transition via comparing experiences. Episodes of severe depression continue, on an almost annual basis. These are not tied to suicide ideation, but regarded as "circuitry overload" and necessitate reflection, time out from everyday activities and occasional medication. Beth has learned ways to manage (or not manage, as she chooses) these episodes in such a way that the important sustaining structures of her career and friends are left intact.

CONCLUSION

Because of its person-in-situation perspective, social work is well suited to designing interventions, programs, and policies for working with the problems of suicide and nonfatal suicidal behavior. The similarities between suicidal individuals and the multiproblem clients seen in social service agencies are marked. Although there have been no studies of professionals who work specifically with suicidal clients, social work appears to hold a considerable role in service provision. Given this role, social work should also take an active role in the development of intervention methods and models. To date, social work has contributed little to the literature that can help to inform prevention or intervention. With notable exceptions, most social work literature on suicidal behavior is reactive, examining the loss of a client to suicide rather than the effectiveness of intervention programs. There is significant potential for social work to contribute to the development and testing of effective treatment models for treating suicidal behaviors.

While the development of broad-based primary prevention programs that are focused on education about suicide does not appear to hold the answer (Shaffer et al. 1988), the information available on risk factors can provide population and problem targets for designing interventions. Although suicide cannot be predicted on a case-by-case basis, the evidence cited in this essay suggests that intervention models can be developed. This task involves the systematic description, application, and evaluation of specific intervention components. This work must necessarily take place through individual practitioners reporting their intervention results to others. The dual focus on suicide and nonfatal suicidal behavior is necessary both to reduce the suffering of individuals and their families and to improve the use of costly health care resources.

Note

The authors wish to acknowledge Jennifer F. Dwork for her assistance in the preparation of this chapter.

References

Applebaum, S. 1963. "The Problem Solving Aspects of Suicide." *Journal of Projective Technique* 27(1):259–68.

Arrango, V., M. Underwood, and J. Mann. 1997. "Biological Alterations in the Brainstem of Suicides." *Psychiatric Clinics of North America* 20:581–83.

Asberg, M., P. Thoren, and L. Traskman. 1976. "Serotonin Depression: A Biochemical Subgroup Within the Affective Disorders?" *Science* 191:478–80.

Bagely, C., S. Jacobsen, and A. Rehin. 1976. "Completed Suicide: A Taxonomic Analysis of Clinical and Social Data." *Psychological Medicine* 6(3):429–38.

Baker, F. 1984. "Black Suicide Attempters in 1980: A Preventative Focus." *General Hospital Psychiatry* 6:131–37.

Beck, A. 1963. "Thinking and Depression: Idiosyncratic Content and Cognitive Distortions." *Archives of General Psychiatry* 9:324–33.

Beck, A., K. Kovacs, and A. Weissman. 1974. *The Prediction of Suicide.* Bowie, Md.: Charles Press.

———. 1975a. "Assessment of Suicide Intention: The Scale of Suicide Ideation." *Journal of Consulting and Clinical Psychology* 47(2):343–52.

———. 1975b. "Hopelessness and Suicidal Behavior: An Overview." *Journal of the American Medical Association* 234:1146–49.

Beck, A., H. Resnik, and D. Lettieri. 1974. *The Prediction of Suicide.* Bowie, Md.: Charles Press.

Beck, A., D. Schuyler, and L. Herman. 1974. "Development of Suicidal Scales." In A. Beck, H. Resnik, and D. Lettieri, eds., *The Prediction of Suicide.* Bowie, Md.: Charles Press.

Beck, A., R. Steer, M. Kovacs, and B. Garrison. 1985. "Hopelessness amd Eventual Suicide: A 10-year Prospective Study of Patients Hospitalized with Suicidal Ideation." *American Journal of Psychiatry.* 142(5):559–63.

Bedrosian, R. and A. Beck. 1979. "Cognitive Aspects of Suicidal Behavior." *Suicide and Life-Threatening Behavior* 9:87–96.

Birtchnell, J. 1970. "The Relationship Between Attempted Suicide, Depression, and Parent Death." *British Journal of Psychiatry* 116:307–13.

Bollen, K. and D. Phillips. 1982. "Imitative Suicides: A National Study of the Effect of Television News Stories." *American Sociological Review* 47:802–9.

Boyd, J. and E. Moscicki. 1986. "Firearms and Youth Suicide." *American Journal of Public Health* 76:1240–42.

Braucht, G. 1979. "Interactional Analysis of Suicidal Behavior." *Journal of Consulting and Clinical Psychology* 47(532):653–69.

Brent, D., J. Perper, C. Allman, G. Moritz, M. Wartella, and J. Selenak. 1991. "The Presence and Accessibility of Firearms in the Homes of Adolescent Suicide: A Case-Control Study." *Journal of the American Medical Association* 266:2989–95.

Brent, D., J. Perper, C. Goldstein, D. Koklo, J. Allan, C. Allman, and J. Zelenak. 1988. "Risk Factors for Adolescent Suicide: A Comparison of Adolescent Suicide Victims with Suicidal Inpatients." *Archives of General Psychiatry* 45:581–88.

Brent, D., J. Perper, G. Moritz, C. Allman, A. Friend, C. Roth, J. Schweers, L. Balach, and M. Baugher. 1993. "Psychiatric Risk Factors for Adolescent Suicide: A Case Control Study." *Journal of the American Academy of Child and Adolescent Psychiatry* 32: 521–29.

Brent, D., J. Perper, G. Moritz, L. Liotus, J. Schweers, L. Balach, and C. Roth. 1994. "Familial Risk Factor for Adolescent Suicide: A Case Control Study." *Acta Psychiatrica Scandinavica* 89:52–63.

Buglass, D. and J. McColloch. 1970. "Further Suicidal Behavior: The Development and Validation of Predictive Scales." *British Journal of Psychiatry* 116:483–91.

Butcher, J. and G. Maudal. 1976. "Crisis Intervention." In I. Weiner, ed., *Clinical Methods of Psychology*, pp. 206–10. New York: Wiley.

Caldwell, C. and I. Gottesman. 1990. "Schizophrenics Kill Themselves Too: A Review of Risk Factors for Suicide." *Schizophrenia Bulletin* 16(4):80–97.

Cantor, P. 1976. "Personality Characteristics Found Among Youthful Female Suicide Attempters." *Journal of Abnormal Psychology* 85:324–29.

Centers for Disease Control. 1998. "Attempted Suicide Among High School Students—United States, 1997." *Morbidity and Mortality Weekly Reports* 47:47–49.

Chiles, J., K. Strosahl, L. Cowden, R. Graham, and M. Linehan. 1986. "The 24 Hours Before Hospitalization: Factors Related to Suicide Attempting." *Suicide and Life-Threatening Behavior* 16(3):335–42.

Chiles, J., K. Strosahl, L. McMurtray, and M. Linehan. 1985. "Modeling Effects on Suicidal Behavior." *Journal on Nervous and Mental Diseases* 8:477–81.

Christian, E. 1977. "Black Suicide." In C. Hatton, S. Valente, and A. Bink, eds., *Suicide: Assessment and Intervention*, pp. 143–59. New York: Appleton-Century-Crofts.

Clark, D. and J. Fawcett. 1992. "Review of Empirical Risk Factors for Evaluation of the Suicidal Patient." In B. Bongar, ed., *Suicide: Guidelines for Assessment, Management, and Treatment*, pp. 16–48. Belmont, Calif.: Wadsworth.

Comstock, B. 1992. "Decision to Hospitalize and Alternatives to Hospitalization." In B. Bongar, ed., *Suicide: Guidelines for Assessment, Management, and Treatment*, pp. 204–17. Oxford: Oxford University Press.

Coombs, D. and H. Miller. 1975. "The Scandinavian Suicide Phenomenon: Fact or Artifact? Another Look." *Psychology Reports* 37:1075–78.

Cote, T. R., R. J. Biggar, and A. L. Dannenberg. 1992. "Risk of Suicide Among Persons with AIDS: A National Assessment." *Journal of American Medical Association* 268(13):1084–86.

Dannenberg, A., J. McNeil, J. Brundage, and R. Brookmeyer. 1996. "Suicide and HIV infection. Mortality follow-up of 4147 HIV-Positive Military Service Applicants." *Journal of the American Medical Association* 276(21):1743–46.

Dattilio, F. and A. Freeman. 1994. *Cognitive-Behavioral Strategies in Crisis Intervention*. New York: Guilford Press.

Davidson, L., M. Rosenberg, J. Mercy, J. Franklin, and J. Simmons. 1989. "An Epidemiologic Study of Risk Factors in Two Teenage Suicide Clusters." *Journal of the American Medical Association* 262:2687–96.

Davis, R. 1979. "Black Suicide in the Seventies: Current Trends." *Suicide and Life-Threatening Behavior* 9:131–40.

Diekstra, R. 1973. "A Social Learning Approach to the Prediction of Suicidal Behavior." Seventh annual International Congress on Suicide Prevention. Amsterdam, The Netherlands.

Dilsaver, S., Y.-W. Chen, A. Swan, A. Schoaib, and K. Krajewski. 1994. "Suicidality in Patients with Pure and Depressive Mania." *American Journal of Psychiatry* 151: 1312–15.

Douglas, J. 1967. *The Social Meanings of Suicide.* Princeton, N.J.: Princeton University Press.

Dunne, E., J. McIntosh, and K. Dunne-Maxim. 1987. *Suicide and Its Aftermath.* New York: Wiley.

Durkheim, E. 1897/1952. *Le Suicide (Suicidal).* New York: Free Press of Glencoe.

Farberow, N. 1970. "Self Destruction and Identity." *Humanitas* 6:45–68.

Farberow, N. and D. MacKinnon. 1970. "Prediction of Suicide in Neuropsychiatric Hospital Patients." In C. Neuringer, ed., *Psychological Assessment of Suicidal Risk.* Springfield, Ill.: Charles C Thomas.

Farberow, N. and E. Shneidman. 1961. *The Cry for Help.* New York: McGraw-Hill.

Fox, K. and M. Weissman. 1975. "Suicide Attempts and Drugs: Contradiction Between Method and Intent." *Social Psychiatry* 10:31–38.

Furst, S. and M. Ostow. 1979. "The Psychodynamics of Suicide." In L. Hankoff and B. Einsidler, eds., *Suicide: The Theory and Clinical Aspects,* pp. 165–78. Littleton, Mass.: PSG.

Gibbs, J. and W. Martin. 1964. *Status Integration and Suicide: A Sociological Study.* Eugene: University of Oregon Press.

Gomery, T. 1997. "Suicide Prevention Does Not Justify Placing Suicidal Clients in Care." In E. Gambrill and R. Pruger, eds., *Controversial Issues in Social Work Ethics,* pp. 68–74. New York: Wiley.

Gould, M., P. Fisher, M. Parides, M. Flory, and D. Shaffer. 1996. "Psychological Risk Factors of Child and Adolescent Suicide." *Suicide and Life-Threatening Behavior* 53:1155–62.

Gould, M. and R. Kramer. 1999. "Reporting a Suicide." Pamphlet containing guidelines for the media. New York: American Foundation for Suicide Prevention.

Gould, M. and D. Shaffer. 1986. "The Impact of Suicide in Television Movies: Evidence of Imitation." *The New England Journal of Medicine* 315:690–94.

———. In press. "The Epidemiology of Youth Completed Suicide." In R. King and A. Apter, eds., *Child and Adolescent Suicide.* Cambridge: Cambridge University Press.

Gould, M., D. Shaffer, and M. Kleinman. 1988. "The Impact of Suicide in Television Movies: Replication and Commentary." *Suicide and Life-Threatening Behavior* 18:90–99.

Gould, M., S. Wallenstein, and M. Kleinman. 1990. "Time-Space Clustering of Teenage Suicide." *American Journal of Epidemiology* 131:71–78.

Greenhill, L., B. Waslick, M. Prides, B. Fan, D. Shaffer, and J. Mann. 1995. "Biological Studies in Suicidal Adolescent Inpatients." *Scientific Proceedings from the Annual Meeting of the American Academy of Child and Adolescent Psychiatry* 11:124.

Hawton, K. and J. Catalan. 1987. *Attempted Suicide: A Practical to Its Nature and Management.* New York: Oxford University Press.

Henry, A. and J. Short. 1954. *Suicide and Homicide.* London: Free Press; Glencoe, Ill.: Collier-Macmillan.

Hepworth, P., R. Rooney, and J. Larsen. 1997. *Direct Social Work Practice Theory and Skills,* 5th ed. Chicago: Dorsey.

Hirsch, S. 1981. "A Critique of Volunteer-Staffed Suicide Prevention Centers." *Canadian Journal of Psychiatry* 26:406–10.

Hirsch, S., C. Walsh, and R. Draper. 1982. "Parasuicide: A Review of Treatment Interventions." *Journal of Affective Disorders* 4(4):299–311.

Hoppe, S. and H. Martin. 1986. "Patterns of Suicide Among Mexican Americans and Anglos." *Social Psychiatry* 21:83–88.

Isometsa, E., M. Henriksson, H. Aro, and J. Lonqnquist. 1994. "Suicide in Bipolar Disorder in Finland." *American Journal of Psychiatry* 151:1020–24.

Ivanoff, A. 1997. "Suicide Prevention Does Not Justify Placing Suicidal Clients in Care." In E. Gambrill and R. Pruger, eds., *Controversial Issues in Social Work Ethics,* pp. 64–68. New York: Wiley.

Ivanoff, A. and S. Jang. 1991. "The Role of Hopelessness and Social Desirability in Predicting Suicidal Behavior: A Study of Prison Inmates." *Journal of Consulting and Clinical Psychology* 59:394–99.

Jobes, D., A. Berman, and A. Josselson. 1987. "Improving the Validity and Reliability of Medical-Legal Certifications of Suicide." *Suicide and Life-Threatening Behavior* 17:310–25.

Kallman, F., J. Deporte, E. Deporte, and L. Feingold. 1949. "Suicide in Twins and Only Children." *American Journal of Human Genetics* 1:113–26.

Kessler, R., G. Downey, H. Stipp, and R. Milavsky. 1989. "Network Television Story News About Suicide and Short-Term Changes in Total U.S. Suicide." *Journal of Nervous and Mental Disorders* 177(Supplement 9):551–55.

Kizer, K. W., M. Green, C. I. Perkins, G. Doebbert, and M. J. Hughes. 1988. "AIDS and Suicide in California." *Journal of American Medical Association* 260:1881.

Kreitmann, N. 1977. *Parasuicide.* London: Wiley.

Kreitmann, N., P. Smith, and E. Tan. 1970. "Attempted Suicide As a Language: An Empirical Study." *British Journal of Psychiatry* 116(534):465–73.

Kutchins, H. and S. A. Kirk. 1986. "The Reliability of DSM-III: A Critical Review." *Social Work Research Abstracts* 22(4):3–12.

Leenaars, A. 1992. "Suicide Notes, Communication and Ideation." In R. Maris, A. Berman, J. Maltsberger, and R. Yufit, eds., *Assessment and Prediction of Suicide,* pp. 337–61. New York: Guilford.

Lettieri, D. 1974a. "Research Issues in Developing Prediction Scales." In C. Neuringer, ed., *Psychological Assessment of Suicidal Risk,* pp. 43–73. Springfield, Ill.: Charles C Thomas.

———. 1974b. "Suicidal Death Prediction Scales." In A. Beck, H. Resnick, and D. Lettieri, eds., *The Prediction of Suicide,* pp. 163–92. Bowie, Md.: Charles Press.

Levenson, M. and C. Neuringer. 1971. "Problem-Solving Behavior in Suicidal Adolescents." *Journal of Consulting and Clinical Psychology* 37(3):433–36.

Levi, D., D. Fales, M. Skin, and V. Sharp. 1966. "Separation and Attempted Suicide." *Archives of General Psychiatry* 15:158–64.

Linehan, M. 1981. "A Socio-Behavioral Analysis of Suicide and Parasuicide: Implications for Clinical Assessment and Treatment." In H. Glazer and J. Clarkin, eds., *Depression: Behavioral and Directive Intervention Strategies,* pp. 147–69. New York: Garland.

———. 1986. "Suicidal People. Psychobiology of Suicidal Behavior." *Annals of the New York Academy of Sciences* 487:16–33.

———. 1988. "Dialectical Behavior Therapy: A Treatment for the Chronic Parasuicidal Client." *Journal of Personality Disorders* 1(4):328–33.

———. 1993a. *Cognitive Behavioral Treatment of Borderline Personality Disorder.* New York: Guilford Press.

———. 1993b. *Skills Training Manual for Treating Borderline Personality Disorder.* New York: Guilford Press.

Linehan, M., P. Camper, J. Chiles, K. Strosahl, and E. Shehann. 1987. "Interpersonal Problem Solving and Parasuicide." *Cognitive Therapy and Research Therapy* 11(1):1–12.

Mann, J. and D. Stoff. 1997. "A Synthesis of Current Findings Regarding Neurobiological Correlates and Treatment of Suicidal Behavior." *Annals of the New York Academy of Science* 836:352–63.

Maris, R., A. Berman, J. Maltsberger, and R. Yufit. 1992. *Assessment and Prediction of Suicide.* New York: Guilford Press.

Martunnen, M., M. Hillevi, M. Henriksson, and J. Lonnqvist. 1991. "Mental Disorders in Adolescent Suicide: DSM-III-R Axes I and II Diagnoses in Suicides Among 13- to 19-year-olds in Finland." *Archives of General Psychiatry* 48:834–39.

McCutcheon, S. 1985. *Understanding Attempted Suicide: A Decision Theory Approach.* Seattle: University of Washington Press.

Menninger, K. 1938. *Man Against Himself.* New York: Harcourt Brace.

Mintz, R. 1968. "Psychotherapy of the Suicidal Patient." In H. L. P. Resnik, ed., *Suicidal Behaviors: Diagnosis and Management,* pp. 271–96. Boston: Little, Brown.

Monk, M. 1987. "Epidemiology of Suicide." *Epidemiological Reviews* 9:51–69.

Moscicki, E. 1995. "Epidemiology of Suicidal Behavior." *Epidemiological Reviews* 25: 22–35.

Motto, J. 1986. "Clinical Consideration of Biological Correlates of Suicide." *Suicide and Life-Threatening Behavior* 16(2):83–102.

National Center for Health Statistics. 1998. *National Vital Statistics Report.* Hyattsville, Md.: Author.

O'Carroll, P. 1989. "A Consideration of the Validity and Reliability of Suicide Mortality Idea." *Suicide and Life-Threatening Behavior* 19:1–16.

Olin, H. 1976. "Psychotherapy of the Chronically Suicidal Patient." *American Journal of Psychotherapy* 30:570–75.

Overholser, J., D. Adams, K. Lehnert, and D. Brinkman. 1995. "Self-Esteem Deficits and Suicidal Tendencies Among Adolescents." *Journal of the American Academy of Child and Adolescent Psychiatry* 34(7):919–28.

Patsiokas, A., G. Clum, and R. Luscomb. 1979. "Cognitive Characteristics of Suicide Attempters." *Journal of Consulting and Clinical Psychology* 47(2):478–84.

Paykel, E. 1979. "Life Stress." In L. Hankoff and B. Einsidler, eds., *Suicide: Theory and Clinical Aspects,* pp. 225–34. Littleton, Mass.: PSG.

Paykel, E. and M. Dienelt. 1971. "Suicide Attempts Following Acute Depression." *Journal of Nervous and Mental Disease* 153:234–43.

Phillips, D. 1974. "The Influence of Suggestions on Suicide: Substantive and Theoretical Implications of the Werther Effect." *American Sociological Review* 39:340–54.

Pomeranz, D. and M. Goldfried. 1970. "An Intake Report Outline for Modification." *Psychological Reports* 26:447–50.

Poussaint, A. 1975. "Black Suicide." In R. Williams, ed., *Textbook of Black Related Diseases,* pp. 707–13. New York: McGraw-Hill.

Rich, C., D. Young, and M. Fowler. 1986. "San Diego Suicide Study, I: Young vs Old Subject." *Archives of General Psychiatry* 45:577–82.

Roberts, A. 1990. *Crisis Intervention Handbook.* Belmont, Calif.: Wadsworth.

Robins, E., G. Murphy, R. Wilkinson, S. Gassner, and J. Kayes. 1959. "Some Clinical Considerations in the Prevention of Suicide Based on a Study of 134 Successful Suicides." *American Journal of Public Health* 49:888–99.

Rosenbaum, M. and J. Richman. 1970. "Suicide: The Role of Hostility and Death Wishes from the Family and Significant Others." *American Journal of Psychiatry* 126:1652–55.

Rotheram-Borus, M. and P. Trautman. 1988. "Hopelessness, Depression, and Suicidal Intent Among Adolescent Suicide Attempters." *Journal of the American Academy of Child and Adolescent Psychiatry* 27(6):700–704.

Roy, A. and M. Linnoila. 1986. "Alcoholism and Suicide." *Suicide and Life-Threatening Behavior* 16(2):244–73.

Rubenstein, R., R. Moses, and T. Lidz. 1958. "On Attempted Suicide." *American Medical Association Archives of Neurology and Psychiatry* 79:103–12.

Shaffer, D. 1974. "Suicide in Childhood and Early Adolescence." *Journal of Child Psychology and Psychiatry and Allied Diciplines.* 15(4):275–91.

Shaffer, D., A. Bacon, P. Fisher, and A. Garland. 1987. "Review of Youth Suicide Prevention Programs." In *Youth Suicide Prevention: A Final Report of the Governor's Youth Suicide Prevention Council,* pp. 1–51. Albany: Office of the Governor of the State of New York.

Shaffer, D. and L. Craft. 1999. "Methods of Adolescent Suicide Prevention." *Journal of Clinical Psychiatry* 60(Supplement 2):70–74.

Shaffer, D., A. Garland, M. Gould, P. Fisher, and P. Trautman. 1988. "Preventing Teenage Suicide: A Critical View." *Journal of the American Academy of Child and Adolescent Psychiatry* 27(6):675–87.

Shaffer, D. and M. Gould. 1987. "Study of Completed and Attempted Suicides in Adolescents." Unpublished progress report, National Institute of Mental Health.

Shaffer, D., M. Gould, P. Fisher, P. Trautman, D. Moreau, M. Kleinman, and M. Flory. 1996. "Psychiatric Diagnosis in Child and Adolescent Suicide." *Archives of General Psychiatry* 53:339–48.

Shaffer, D. and C. Pfeffer. In review. "Practice Guidelines: Practice Parameters for the Assessment and Treatment of Children and Adolescents with Suicidal Behavior." *American Academy of Child and Adolescent Psychiatry.*

Shneidman, E. 1976. "The Components of Suicide." *Psychiatric Annals* 6:51–66.

Shneidman, E., N. Farberow, and R. Litman. 1970. *The Psychology of Suicide.* New York: Science House.

Slaby, A. 1998. "Outpatient Management of Suicidal Patients." In B. Bongar, A. Berman, R. Maris, E. Harris, and W. Packman, eds., *Risk Management with Suicidal Patients,* pp. 187–203. New York: Guilford Press.

Stengel, E. 1964. *Suicide and Attempted Suicide.* Baltimore: Penguin.

Swenson, C., C. Sanderson, and M. Linehan. 1996. "Applying Dialectical Behavior Therapy on Inpatient Units." Unpublished manuscript, University of Washington, Seattle, Washington.

Szasz, T. 1986. "The Case Against Suicide Prevention." *American Psychologist* 41(7): 806–12.

Teicher, J. and J. Jacobs. 1966. "Adolescents Who Attempt Suicide: Preliminary Findings." *American Journal of Psychiatry* 122:1248–57.

Tuckman, J. and F. Youngman. 1968. "Assessment of Suicide Risk in Attempted Suicides." In H. L. P. Resnik, ed., *Suicidal Behaviors: Diagnosis and Management,* pp. 190–97. Boston: Little, Brown.

Vaillant, G. E. and S. J. Blumenthal. 1990. "Introduction—Suicide Over the Life Cycle: Risk Factors and Life-Span Development." In S. J. Blumenthal and D. J. Kupfer, eds., *Suicide Over the Life Cycle: Risk Factors, Assessment, and Treatment of Suicidal Patients,* pp. 1–16. Washington, D.C.: American Psychiatry Press.

Velting, D. and M. Gould. 1997. "Suicide Contagion." In R. Maris, S. Canetto, and M. Silverman, eds., *Annual Review of Suicidology,* pp. 96–136. New York: Guilford Press.

Wallace, J., A. Calhoun, K. Powell, J. O'Neil, and S. James. 1996. *Homicide and Suicide Among Native Americans, 1979–1992.* Violence Surveillance Series, vol. 2. Atlanta, Ga.: Centers for Disease Control and Prevention, National Center for Injury Prevention and Control.

Wandrei, K. 1985. "Identifying Potential Suicides Among High-Risk Women." *Social Work* 30(6):511–17.

Wasserman, I. 1984. "Imitation and Suicide: A Reexamination of the Werther Effect." *American Sociological Review* 49:427–36.

Wetzel, R. 1976. "Semantic Differential Ratings of Concepts and Suicide Intent." *Journal of Clinical Psychology* 32:11–12.

Wexler, L., M. Weissman, and S. Kasl. 1978. "Suicide Attempts 1970–75: Updating a United States Study and Comparisons with International Trends." *British Journal of Psychiatry* 132:180–85.

Zilboorg, G. 1936. "Suicide Among Civilized and Primitive Races." *American Journal of Psychiatry* 92:1347–69.

28

Women of Color

Edith Lewis
Lorraine Gutiérrez
Izumi Sakamoto

Trainers working on organizational racism and sexism issues often use an exercise entitled "What do you know about . . . ?" The workshop or seminar participants are asked to brainstorm all the ideas used to describe or understand a particular group of people. Trainers capture these ideas on newsprint and provide opportunities for the participants to review them periodically during the training session. The goal of the exercise is to elicit common cultural stereotypes about a particular group so that they can be replaced with more accurate information. Often, when the focus of this exercise is on communities of color, many well-worn stereotypes of women of color will emerge. These stereotypes include such terms as *emasculators, prostitutes, welfare queens, unwed mothers, fighters, docile, subservient, low-income, illiterate,* or *sensuous.* Seldom does the exercise elicit words such as *resilient, powerful, capacity builders, employees, leaders, mothers, students,* or *professionals.* Yet the last group of adjectives are likely to be truer of women of color than the first. The lack of recognition of how these more accurate descriptors have influenced the lives of their families, communities, and societies limits the resources available to all women of color in times of difficulty.

This chapter focuses on retelling stories of the experiences of women of color so that we have more information about the role these women have played in the development of their own communities as well as our country. In presenting case examples, we are using a form of storytelling and narrative that is traditional and familiar in many communities of color. These stories about the experiences of women of color expand our knowledge base about the development of the country and inform us of effective strategies for dealing with contemporary social problems. They highlight types of resilience within and among women of color rather than sources of vulnerability. They also focus on strategies used by women of color historically that have relevance for current work. From these stories we identify a set of five practice principles that can foster the resilience of women of color.

DEFINING AND EXPLAINING WOMEN OF COLOR

Although we use the term "women of color" in our work (Gutiérrez and Lewis 1999), we do not intend to mask or deny the rich sources of diversity within and between each group that the term represents. The use of "umbrella" terms such as "Latinas" "Asian Americans," "African Americans," or "lesbians" can create difficulties for effective social work because they may inadvertently imply that members of these groups are homogeneous and differ on few dimensions. Yet we chose to use the term "women of color" to refer to African American, Asian American, Latina, and Native American women because research and practice suggest that women who are members of these groups are likely to share experiences related to identity, culture, and inequality. It is a political term that recognizes the ways in which similar historical, social, and political forces have influenced our experiences in the United States (Nagel 1994). From our perspective, using the term is a way of "naming our collective selves." The social stigma attached to our ethnic groups, the political actions we have taken in our neighborhoods, and the historical denigration of ourselves as women have all been among the common experiences making our ethnic groups more vulnerable to negative economic, social, and political forces. Within these experiences, however, many examples of our resilience in the face of great adversity can also be found. In this chapter we discuss these similarities but also "unpack" some of these identities to consider their complexity and intersectionality (Comas-Díaz and Greene 1994).

Social workers must recognize the ways in which women of color differ from white women and from men of color. We have most often recognized the impact of powerlessness on women of color from the perspective of institutional racism while overlooking the role of gender inequity in influencing the life chances of women of color. We make an equally grave error when we group all women's experience together without looking at ways in which women of color are impacted by racism and ethnocentrism (Baca-Zinn and Dill 1994; Comas-Díaz and Greene 1994; Kirk and Okasawa-Rey 1998). These perspectives also have overlooked the strengths and resources developed by women of color within their own communities. To understand women of color in our society, a multidimensional perspective must be used that takes into account the impact of multiple social identities and how that has shaped the worldviews, life chances, and survival strategies of the individual woman (Comas-Díaz and Greene 1994; Gutiérrez and Lewis 1999).

Despite these similarities, we must also remember the ways in which the umbrella terms of African American, Asian American, Native (Indian) American, and Latina mask our diversities. For all women of color, the diversities include economic situation, sexual orientation, physical and/or emotional ability or status, geographic birthplace, age, and national origin. For example, the African American umbrella can include women from the United States, Cuba, Jamaica, the Bahamas, or Canada. The term Latina encompasses Mexican, Puerto Rican, Cuban, and Central or South American women. More than thirty-six ethnic groups are often placed under the single umbrella term of Asian American, but their experiences are quite distinct in terms of a number of variables, such as modes of entrance into the United States and interaction with U.S. immigration policy. Native American Indian women are often "invisible" in the social policy development of the United States; however, they have been a part of the forces that have influenced its development (Allen 1986; Medicine 1988).

DEMOGRAPHIC PATTERNS

Although the specific ethnic and racial groups encompassed by the term "women of color" differ in many respects, together we share similarities in terms of our strengths, low social status, and power. Women of color experience unequal access to power and resources in our society due to the effects of racism, sexism, and often classism. We are consequently hampered by average earnings lower than that of white women, by overrepresentation in low status occupations, and by a low average level of education (Baca-Zinn and Dill 1994).

Women of color in all umbrella categories make up approximately half of their respective groups across age groups; however, the age distribution differs within these categories and the differential distributions may have direct effects on the lives of these women. Among Latinas, for example, the number of men to women is relatively equal from birth until ages 40 to 44 when women in each age group begin to outnumber their male counterparts. The same can be said for Native American groups, except the distributions begin to favor women at ages 30 to 34 rather than 40 to 44. For Asian Americans, the disparity in the number of women relative to men is evident as early as the age range of 25 to 29 and includes prime childbearing and employment years for these women. This disparity becomes most alarming for African Americans where women begin to outnumber men in the 20- to 24-year-old age range (U.S. Bureau of the Census 1992). For heterosexual women this disparity can influence marital or long-term commitments, childrearing, childbearing, and employment opportunities for mothers.

The poverty rate of women of color is two to three times that of white women: 36.5 percent of all black women and 31.2 percent of all Latinas live below the poverty line, in contrast to 12.7 percent of all white women (U.S. Bureau of the Census 1992). The economic challenges faced by women of color who are unmarried while raising minor children is also well established in the literature. The 1998 national indicators of well-being report on children and families identifies the prevalence of poverty among families of color (Federal Interagency Forum on Child and Family Statistics 1998:10):

> This contrast by family structure is especially pronounced among certain racial and ethnic minorities. For example, in 1996, 14 percent of Black children in married-couple families lived in poverty, compared to 58 percent of Black children in female-householder families. Twenty-nine percent of Hispanic children in married couples lived in poverty, compared to 67 percent in female-householder families. Most children in poverty are white and non-Hispanic. However, the proportion of Black and Hispanic children in poverty

is much higher than the proportion for white, non-Hispanic children. In 1996, 8 percent of all children lived in families with incomes less than half the poverty level, or $8,018 for a family of four, while 31 percent of children lived in families with incomes less than 150 percent of the poverty level or $24,054 a year for a family of four.

There are some hopeful demographic signs, however. Analyses of census data from 1994 and 1998 indicate that 16 percent of African American and 38 percent of Asian American women are employed in managerial and professional positions (U.S. Bureau of the Census 1992). Table 28.1 indicates how various groups of women of color differ in respect to educational attainment (by the level of completion of high school diplomas and college degrees).

SOCIETAL CONTEXT

Racism, sexism, ethnocentrism, and often classism impact women of color directly and indirectly. However, our scholarship on persons of color often fails to take gender or sex into consideration when identifying the experiences of ethnic groups of color in the United States (Medicine 1988). The confusion is exacerbated in the feminist scholarship about women, because the unique historical, social, and political experiences of women of color are not highlighted. Thus, much of our literature to date uses terms such as "women and people of color," where the word *women* is reserved for women of European American descent, and the potentially different experiences of women of color are often lost (Comas-Díaz and Greene 1994; Hurtado 1996; Johnsrud and Sadao 1998; Pyant and Yanico 1991).

In her work on black empowerment, Solomon (1976) identified how the powerlessness related to the experiences of racism, sexism, and other forms of societal inequality can lead to the denial of valued identities, social roles, and social resources available to individuals. She describes indirect and direct power blocks as the primary social mechanisms in this process. One form of indirect power blocks is the negative valuation, or stigma, that indicates to members of oppressed groups that they are deficient in some way. As negative valuations are incorporated into the development

TABLE 28.1. Percentage of Women of Color Completing High School and College Credentials

Group	High School Completion	College Degree Completion
African Americans	88	15
Asian American/Pacific Islanders	82	42
Latinas	50	16
Native Americans	63	2.1

Sources: U.S. Bureau of the Census, Table 3: Educational Attainment of Persons 25 Years and Over, by Sex, Region, and Race: March 1997; U.S. Bureau of the Census, Table 1: Highest Degree Earned, by Sex, Race, Hispanic Origin and Age: Spring, 1993; Bureau of the Census Statistical Brief, The Nation's Asian and Pacific Islander Population 1994, *www.census.gov/aspd/www/statbrief/sb95/24/pdf.*

of the individual, they can interfere with the development of adequate interpersonal, technical, and social skills. Direct power blocks, such as the provision of inadequate health services to the poor, also affect individuals in more concrete ways (Solomon 1976).

Therefore, women of color are disproportionately affected by the direct and indirect **power blocks** associated with low status and limited access to economic resources (Parsons 1991; Solomon 1976). Direct power blocks refer to access to material resources. Because they are disproportionately affected by poverty, women of color are more likely than white women to suffer from conditions of poor or no housing, insufficient food and clothing, inadequate access to health and mental health services, and to be located within low-income and physically deteriorating communities (Kirk and Okasawa-Rey 1998; Ortiz 1994). Indirect power blocks, which are reflected in the adjectives and stereotypes we discussed at the beginning of our article, can limit self-determination and engender a sense of dependency by undermining individuals' self-esteem and feelings of competence. These conditions perpetuate the problems of women of color and their position at the bottom of our social structure (Baca-Zinn and Dill 1994; Comas-Díaz and Greene 1994).

VULNERABILITIES AND RISK FACTORS

Earlier we identified the likelihood that social workers will be problem focused when discussing the lives of women of color. Although we have taken a strengths perspective in this essay, we do not overlook the challenges facing women of color across the country. Indeed, the demographic data and discussion of the societal context have identified ways in which women of color should be understood as a population at risk. As our discussion of the conditions faced by women of color have identified issues such as poverty, un- and underemployment, and access to education, our focus here is on health care risks. However, social workers must continue to be aware of the ways in which the material conditions that we have outlined are directly related to these risk factors.

Many women of color face a range of **health** challenges because of living in conditions of inequality. These may include differences in the rates of hypertension, osteoporosis, stomach cancer, diabetes, and cervical cancer (Cooper, Rotimi, and Ward 1999; Derrick 1997; National Journal Group 1999a, 1999b). It is unwise to generalize, however, that these health challenges occur with the same probability for all women of color or for all groups that might be included in the same umbrella group. For women from the African Diaspora, for example, Nigerians in West Africa had the lowest rates of hypertension, followed by Jamaicans, and, last, urban African Americans (Cooper et al. 1999). Derrick's (1997) review of recent literature on African American women and hypertension suggests that those individuals who confront racism and externalize it when they encounter it are more likely to have lower blood pressure readings than those who do not address it. The rate of cervical cancer among Vietnamese women is also alarming to medical researchers (National Journal Group 1999a), but that alarm does not appear to be generalizable to all women of Asian descent.

Concerns about the health status of women of color extend to their children. The percentage of women from the ethnic groups included in the U.S. Vital Statistics

Reports who had low-birth-weight infants in 1990 was higher than the national average of 7.0 percent for Puerto Ricans (9.0 percent), Filipinos (7.3 percent), Hawaiians (7.2 percent), and African Americans (13.3 percent) (U.S. Bureau of the Census 1992). During the last decade, in addition, women of color from African American, American Indian, Hawaiian, Mexican, Puerto Rican, and Central and South American backgrounds exceeded by at least two percentage points the percentage of mothers beginning prenatal care in their third trimester (U.S. Bureau of the Census 1992). While the average percentage of women failing to receive prenatal care until their last trimester of pregnancy was 6.0 in 1990, at least 10 percent of Puerto Rican, Mexican, American Indian, and African-American women had this experience (U.S. Bureau of the Census 1992).

Even for women who are not poor, social marginalization can contribute to poor **mental health** outcomes. Women, poor people, and members of ethnic and racial minority groups have on average much higher rates of mental illness than do men, whites, and the more affluent (Moos and Billings 1982). Most researchers who have studied this connection have focused on the stressful life circumstances of these groups and the resulting strain on their coping capacity (Gutiérrez 1994). This relationship can also be analyzed from the perspective of power and the effect marginalization has on reducing the ability to exercise personal control, on the development of negative stereotypes toward women of color, and on access to necessary social and material resources.

RESILIENCIES AND PROTECTIVE FACTORS

Social work can be distinguished from other helping professions in its ability to conceptualize individuals as parts of families, communities, and societies, using interactionist, ecological, and/or feminist models. These frameworks also can be used to understand women of color as well (Comas-Díaz and Greene 1994; Johnsrud and Sadao 1998). We propose that women of color use their **communities of color** (identified by the women) as buffers in their interactions with the wider societies. While these communities of color are likely to change over the developmental and experiential lives of women of color (in terms of race, ethnicity, geographic location, economic status, sexual orientation, or education) the buffer zone of the community of color is a space in which women of color develop and strengthen the biculturalism that allows the population to be resilient in this society.

Critical analyses of the community of color's utility as a source of key network supports or barriers has become a part of the social work practice literature on working with community of color (Congress 1997; Lum 1996). Social networks do not remain static, and it is imperative that those social workers who attempt to understand women of color's use of the networks identify the specific networks to which the women belong (Lewis and Ford 1990). The extent to which social work practitioners can incorporate the bicultural community of color as a focus of the intervention is one method of ensuring the appropriateness of the intervention (Reppucci, Woolard, and Fried 1999).

Evidence regarding how the inclusion of a focus on a woman of color's community (whether geographic, demographic, or philosophical) affects intervention outcomes can be drawn from the fields of public health. Winkler and Fontanarosa's study

(1998) of the relationship of social group memberships indicated that both societal and individual factors influence the health status of women of color. Their study of more than five thousand white, African American, and Mexican American women identifies some of the ways in which activities related to particular populations of color have differentially affected those populations. Shain et al.'s, study (1999) of the role of giving specific attention to the community of color in an intervention hoping to reduce the risk of sexually transmitted diseases among African American and Mexican American women noted that the rates of infection were significantly lower among women of color in treatment groups.

How does a community of color strengthen the resilience of women of color? Hurtado (1996) identifies these communities as places where women can practice using and developing **their voice** by telling stories and, as they age, serve as the oral historians for the communities. Reppucci et al.'s (1999) review of the literature on prevention and intervention programs at the individual and family level suggests that the most effective of these are grounded in an understanding of the unique cultural backgrounds of the communities of color, as well as demographic differences. The authors noted, "Programs focused solely on the individual seem destined to failure if they do not take into account community context" (Reppucci et al. 1999:18).

Social policy in the United States has been focused on social problems and has often missed the ways in which women of color in particular have built programs and communities in the midst of limited resources (Gutiérrez and Lewis 1999). As our public assistance for families programs have changed from an aid (e.g., Aid to Families with Dependent Children) to a personal responsibility model, researchers in Louisiana have lamented the punitive consequences facing older women of color with limited employment backgrounds (Monroe, Tiller, and Garand 1999). At the same time, however, women of color in their home communities are demonstrating their resilience in the creation and maintenance of self-help programs that provide avenues for the securing of job skills (Safran 1993). Another example of the resilience of women of color in addressing the concerns of their communities is the 1997 Summit on Asian American Women and Breast Cancer. This program focused on increasing outreach to the Asian American communities on the East and West Coasts of the United States. Social workers filled a large number of seats in the Summit Planning Committee. The Summit is an illustration of the use of the umbrella term Asian Americans as a way of building community within a set of ethnic groups with different historical, social, and political backgrounds (Nagel 1994). Programs for incarcerated mothers such as Sons and Daughters of the Incarcerated, based in Ann Arbor, Michigan, and developed by a social worker, have also addressed the needs of many women of color who are disproportionately represented in the prison population.

Reppucci et al. (1999) note the importance of multilevel interventions that consider the unique needs of populations. They state: "Focusing on diversity also suggests that alleviating a particular problem (e.g., preventing HIV transmission) may require multiple interventions targeted in ways that can be utilized by different groups. In other words, identical packaging of an intervention may be inappropriate and therefore ineffective for all groups. By being alert to diversity, interventions on the same problem can be tailored for various age, gender, ethnic and other groups . . ." (Reppucci et al. 1999:19).

Women of color also share other similarities in terms of strengths and coping strategies. Within our own communities we have highlighted values and developed behaviors that have allowed us to survive in the face of oppression. Economic necessity has led women of color traditionally to **participate in the labor market** at higher rates than European American women. Although this role has not always been voluntary, it has helped us to develop ties and a sense of self outside of the family and has reduced our economic dependency on men (Darity and Myers 1984; Hunter 1993). Women of color are also considered to have strong family and community ties, which we use for concrete and emotional support. Our informal and formal ties can be a form of strength. This history of coping and surviving within a hostile world has led many women of color to perceive themselves as strong and capable of dealing with adversity.

One important dimension in the lives of many women of color is **spirituality.** The health and mental health fields in the United States have been slow to incorporate the concept of spirituality into practice. In fact, in the United States many of the helping professions have traditionally associated spirituality with religion, and religion was viewed as an unhealthy defense mechanism (Gutiérrez and Lewis 1999). Professionals were trained to work "around" rather than "with" the spiritual realities of their clients and to view client spirituality as a crutch others leaned on. Practitioners were expected to split off their own spiritual or religious convictions, experiences, and instruction in order to provide quality service.

Incorporation of the spiritual acts of meditation, fasting, writing, dance, music, prayer, discernment, and service have been important for the survival of women of color in a hostile world (Adair and Howell 1994; Boyd-Franklin 1989; Mattis 1995; Starhawk 1992). For some women of color, these spiritual acts are combined with religious affiliations, but the lack of a formal affiliation with a recognized religious body does not automatically mean the lack of a spiritual base in the lives of women of color. Some of the membership in formal religious institutions has fostered women of color's ability to participate in, mobilize around, and monitor social change activities, as in the case of the role of African American women in the civil rights era of the 1950s and 1960s (Robnett 1997). Another example of the role of religion in helping women of color to influence change in their communities and the society at large is how researchers have built their study design and data collection efforts around the local mosques of the Southeast Dearborn, Michigan, community, which has the largest population of individuals from the Middle East in the United States (Aswad and Bilge 1996). The importance of spiritual belief as a way of coping with HIV/AIDS is also documented in the social work literature by Marcenko and Samost (1999).

The development of a **critical consciousness** can also be a source of resilience and strength (Gutiérrez 1994). An essential building block for critical consciousness is the recognition of one's social identities and how they relate to specific communities. These social identities can be shared with others with similar social, historical, or political backgrounds. Thus, there is a potential for ethnic identities, class identities, survivor identities, age identities, and parental identities. There are also many other potential identities for women of color far too numerous to describe here. Accompanying the numerous identities is a vast social science literature on identity development, much of which is beyond the scope of this chapter.

Mapping the ethnic and cultural identities of women of color can provide the service consumer with a visual record of the way women of color have integrated their interactions within their families, communities, and the wider society. This mapping exercise can include spatial (e.g., where the individual was in terms of geographic location or birth order) or temporal (e.g., the age of the individual or the activities occurring on a local or global scale when critical events were taking place in the individual's life) elements as well. Having the individual woman of color give meaning to how her life events have influenced her current decisions can further solidify what may be a new identity formation.

Of utmost importance to this discussion is the importance of naming our identities as women of color while simultaneously recognizing the impact of the ways others would name us. Earlier we discussed the use of umbrella terms as convenient but not universally accepted within our ethnic populations. Recognizing the identities important to women of color is one mechanism for building the relationship between social worker and service consumer. We might recognize, for example, that certain umbrella terms like American Indian or Native American are considered "colonized identities," that is, constructions of identity made by forces unfamiliar with or uncaring about the real social, historical, and political lives of the First Nations communities they supposedly encompass (Yellowbird 1999). We could also recognize that the most salient identities for women of color are those related to social group memberships other than race or ethnicity, even if the two constructs play a supporting role in the primary reason for entering a social work practice situation. It is possible, for example, to recognize the identity of a physical assault "survivor" as primary in a practice situation, while simultaneously recognizing that this identity may be uniquely grounded in contexts of the perpetrator's ethnicity and the woman's age. An older woman of color who has been assaulted in her home by an individual from her own ethnic group in a predominantly ethnic community may need to work through a different set of identities and potential outcomes than a younger woman of color who has been assaulted in her workplace by a perpetrator from another ethnic or racial group. The response rates of law enforcement officials may differ, as might the ability to prosecute the perpetrator, or the subsequent portrayals of the women in question in their own communities.

PROGRAMS AND SOCIAL WORK CONTRIBUTIONS

Social work practice with women of color can build on sources of strength and resilience to address areas of vulnerability. The material conditions of many women of color lead to increased risk for serious health and mental health problems. Sources of strength and resilience that exist in the identities, communities, and traditions of women of color can, however, be harnessed to directly address these risks. An empowerment approach that engages women actively in the change process is one method that can be used to assist individual women and their families while making changes in their material conditions through changes in communities, organizations, and policies. In this section we utilize our narrative traditions to describe this practice approach in two separate settings with women of color. The first example is a composite based on our previous practice experiences; the second is a program that is currently being implemented by two of the authors. In both of these examples we identify specific suggestions for assessment and intervention with women of color.

ILLUSTRATION AND DISCUSSION

The **Community Partners Project** (CPP), a citywide effort to combat forms of violence against low-income communities, began in an individual intake session between Dawn, a woman from a large western city and Pauline, a social worker who had been working in a community-based health and mental health organization for several years. Dawn had come to the center at the beginning of the year seeking assistance with familial concerns surrounding a daughter who had been sexually abused by a relative. Dawn initially felt helpless and hopeless about this situation but, with Pauline's assistance, had developed a plan to address the needs of her daughter and help to resolve the impact of this experience on the family unit. Specifically, she identified ways of getting counseling assistance for her daughter with a practitioner skilled in child sexual abuse, and she joined (with her husband) a support group for parents of abused children originally facilitated by Pauline but now meeting independently. Ten months after the first meeting with Pauline, Dawn stopped by the community-based organization to discuss her progress.

Empowering practitioners' work often begins on the individual, family, or group level. It differs in two respects from nonempowering forms of intervention, however. First, empowering practitioners have as a goal the **linkage** of individual and family to group methods to normalize and externalize the presenting target issues and to provide alternative models for change for the person(s) seeking assistance. Women of color, given the social and demographic restraints faced daily, often simply need to know that all of the difficulties they face *are not their individual fault.* Empowering practice models also attempt to have the social worker serve as a cofacilitator of the intervention process, not its director. Women of color seeking assistance are viewed as the most knowledgeable about their situation. Their resilience in the face of economic, social, or psychological barriers is also recognized.

While Dawn was pleased by the gains her own family had made during the period, she felt that her work had not been completed. Dawn had determined, through her discussions with other women in the family support group, that the issue of violence was much larger than that perpetrated on individual families and included the responses of the criminal justice system to child sexual abuse and spousal abuse, the solicitation of poor young women for prostitution by men from outside of the community, and the lack of a restitution system for women who had experienced violence in its varied forms. She had come to meet with Pauline that day to report her findings and dissatisfaction with current methods for addressing these issues.

Pauline, cognizant that Dawn's individual and family work had now expanded to community and societal issues, discussed the utility of taking the same problem-solving strategy they had used in their early individual sessions and expanding it to address these larger issues. They immediately began to work to determine who in the self-help parents' group might be interested in these concerns. After generating a list of potential participants, Dawn began to contact community residents about their interest in either beginning a new self-help group or expanding the scope of the existing family violence group. It became clear after four telephone calls that participants wanted to expand the scope of the group to include community violence and include as many more families as were interested in participating in such a venture.

The development of **critical consciousness** occurs when individual problems can be linked to their corollaries at the group, community, and societal levels. Developing a critical consciousness about an issue sometimes takes a great deal of time, however. Social workers must think about these linkages throughout the intervention period. Even when consumers are not initially interested in expanding their targets for action beyond their individual or family situation, empowering social workers can be involved in political and social action projects to address policies and programs contributing to the disease of individuals and families with whom they work.

The expanded group, with fourteen families represented, began to meet in the fall of the year. As they shared their stories, these were recorded and transcribed by Pauline, and the group spent time during each session identifying the major concerns and strategies for resolution discussed the previous session. The network charged itself with being concerned not only about problems but those avenues in and outside of their community that could serve as targets for action or resources for change. Before long, the group had identified needs and resources across the human service infrastructure of their city.

By the beginning of the next year after Dawn and Pauline had first met, the group, now calling itself The Community Partners Project (CPP), organized a conference on community violence. They generated a list of occupied housing in the community, divided the list among members, and individually visited each household on the list to invite them to the community conference, which was held in space donated by the community-based organization. CPP members also invited members of the city council, the police department, community-based social service and health organizations, and the county Department of Public Health to attend, and each of these units sent at least one representative. Again, CPP members reported their preliminary findings about areas of community violence and some of the solutions they had identified for alleviating it. It became clear at the end of the conference that one major system had been omitted from their list, the criminal justice system. Some of the community residents who had not been active with the CPP before had access to information about how the criminal justice system worked in their locality and state, and they agreed to be part of a task force targeting this system. Before the conference ended, task forces were established to work on all major targets of concern and charged with reporting their deliberations and findings back to the CPP central group quarterly. The CPP divided itself among the task groups and worked with each of them to develop an action plan for including resources both in and outside of the community, and to engage key personnel to activate their change strategies. The CPP continued to meet monthly at the community-based organization, which by now had donated a small office and telephone to serve as the CPP headquarters.

Social workers utilizing empowerment strategies serve as facilitators, rather than directors, of social change movements within communities. They take an active role in facilitating agency change so that the needs of individuals, families, and groups can be met. In this case, Pauline's role was to help Dawn develop a strategy toward the establishment of **procedural justice** for the community. Given her ties to the professional community, Pauline may also have identified some actors from other organizations who could be invited to the conference. Pauline also needed to support the creation of a procedural justice perspective within her own organization so that a new program, led and determined by community residents, could be housed in and supported by the physical plant of her agency.

When community change agents are given the opportunities to actually direct their efforts, they can successfully identify **key personnel** within their communities who can affect change. Leadership for the original conference was vested in the CPP, not the community based organization in which it was housed. The agency could take credit only as a supporter of this effort, but that did not preclude it from contributing space, refreshments, and transportation for the conference.

The CPP conference became an annual event. Because of the work of its task forces, the police department began a neighborhood-policing project, which gave residents the ability to target those nonresidents driving through the community to solicit prostitution from the young women. The license plates of the drivers were recorded and called into the new community policing office, and the individuals were stopped before they could leave the scene, arrested, and had their automobiles confiscated. A second outcome of the CPP's work was that the state's list of sex offenders was regularly checked to determine whether there were individuals in the community with prior offenses. When those people were identified, community health workers (neighbors from the community who had been trained to enhance the emotional, physical, and spiritual health of residents) visited them regularly and let them know that the community would be watching them to ensure the well-being of neighborhood children, as well as linking them to formal and informal community resources. One task force continued to facilitate the parents' group for those whose children had experienced violence, but another group was formed for women who had experienced violence at the hands of their intimate partners. Both groups were cofacilitated by CPP members. The task group charged with addressing needs in the criminal justice system began a letter-writing campaign in newspapers statewide until the state legislature held hearings on the issue, and members drafted a bill to develop a statewide restitution program for children and women who had experienced violence.

Institutionalizing a single social change strategy through collective action does not occur overnight. Institutionalizing a series of such strategies is extremely labor and time intensive. The CPP needed to have a plan that included the support of its members through the long period of **reactance** to social change experienced when new initiatives come up against old institutions and perspectives on social justice. In continuing to support the original self-help group for parents whose children had experienced violence, and expanding their work to women experiencing violence in intimate relationships, the CPP provided this support for its members as well as a mechanism to recruit new members whose individual critical consciousness would expand over time to larger community and societal issues.

Other forms of reactance, from the reluctance of the municipalities' police department to the community policing program conceived by the residents, to the state legislature's reluctance to support a bill of placing information about sexual offenders in the public domain, required the connection among CPP members and affiliates as well. The task forces inspired confidence in the CPP members by expanding their skills in developing letter-writing campaigns, effectively using the audio and visual media, and learning how to lobby at the state level for a bill. When reactance is anticipated, empowering practice can address it proactively rather than reactively, and determine the skills needed to overcome it.

Within three years, the CPP had gone from an individual's (i.e., Dawn's) recognition of the systemic connections among forms of violence to a network of individuals, families, and professionals who served as a prototype for other empowerment-based programs across the country. At the end of its third year of operation, Dawn was selected to receive the city's Volunteer of the Year Award. She insisted on accepting it jointly with Pauline, telling the story of her initial visit to the community-based organization and the subsequent birth of the CPP.

In a society where the focus is on identifying problems rather than solutions, it is critical for empowering social workers working with women of color to capture and share the **stories of success.** It is only in doing so, both within and outside of the community of color, that future programs and projects can benefit from the wisdom generated by these communities. Recording the stories also adds to the body of knowledge about the ways in which women of color have designed and implemented successful change strategies within their communities. The social worker's ability to work with the community of color to record the stories provides potential access to these stories internationally rather than simply locally. This can be done through formal methods of investigation including single case and survey research, through the completion of case narratives, and through the employment of the oral tradition to tell the stories to youth and other community members.

The International Families Outreach Project (IFOP) is a community development project active in the University of Michigan Family Housing, serving families of international students and scholars. The University of Michigan has one of the largest international student enrollments in the United States (Institute of International Education 1998). One in six graduate students attending the University of Michigan during the 1996–97 academic year were from another country (University of Michigan International Center 1997). Many international graduate students and scholars bring their families along. More than half of the University's fifteen hundred Family Housing units are leased to residents from other countries, the majority of them from East Asia (University of Michigan Family Housing 1997–1998). Other families come from Southeast Asia, South Asia, and Latin America. A small number of families also come from Africa, Russia, and other European countries. IFOP was initiated in 1996 by one of the authors (Sakamoto), who was herself an international woman graduate student, with the support of another one of the authors (Gutiérrez) and an advisory board comprised of staff and faculty members representing various units across the university.

International women spouses often face many challenges. Chief among them is the language. Our **needs assessment survey** with the international Family Housing residents was conducted from 1997 to 1998. Participants in community education events, in English language classes, and at a community health fair were invited to complete the survey questionnaire. One hundred forty-three residents from other countries responded to the survey questionnaire (108 women, 31 men, 4 did not identify a gender; mean age = 33.5). This survey was conducted in five languages: English, Japanese, Chinese, Korean, and Spanish. The respondents had been at the University of Michigan for an average of sixteen months and had an average of nineteen more months to remain in the United States. Most of the female respondents were in the United States due to their husband's job or education; almost all of the male respondents were either students or visiting scholars. This roughly reflects the characteristics of the target population. The questionnaire was developed from findings of focus groups conducted in the community with additional items, such as the Daily Hassles Scale (Kanner et al. 1981). To complement the survey data, informal needs assessments and exit interviews were conducted with several program participants.

The needs assessment findings suggested that the majority of women believed that language posed a real difficulty in their daily lives. Although not all the international women had difficulties with speaking English in our university environment (most, if not all, of the South Asians and Southeast Asians, and many of the Europeans and Africans are fluent in English), the needs assessment found that many international women believed it difficult to communicate with others in English.

Moreover, concerns about "language" were not just about fluency issues, but also about overall communication comprehension in different cultural, legal, and social contexts than what the international spouses were familiar with. For example, several Korean women expressed their distress when police officers came to their apartments when their children were crying loudly. Many said that they did not know what to say to the officers, partly due to the language difficulty, but also due to a shock of just seeing a police officer in their apartment and being suspected of child abuse. A Japanese mother experienced a conflict with child care providers and security officers when her child sustained a minor injury on his head while at the child care provider's. University security officers did not respond to the mother until twenty minutes after the emergency call was placed. After they arrived, the security officers refused to transport the child since they did not have the child car seats required by law, and the mother had to take her son to the clinic by herself. This mother was further frustrated when she felt that the child care providers did not attempt to support her and advocate for her with the security officers. This mother felt that the language and culture were the fundamental barriers between her and service providers, and she felt angry and powerless.

Financial and other material challenges also constrain the lives of these international women. The needs assessment findings indicated that half of the international women who came here as spouses had worked in their home countries, but almost all of them were currently unemployed, because dependents of student visa holders cannot work for money in the United States. Thus, international spouses, who are more often women than men, tend to be more confined in the United States, especially when they have difficulties with the language, have children, and cannot work in the United States. Since many international families are on limited budgets and child care is very expensive in the United States, many international women with children become homebound. This may make it even more difficult for these women to be connected to each other.

General cultural differences, including food availability and external support for religious practices, are also challenges for many. One Korean woman said that "different food is [one of the most difficult things about living in the United States]. It was hard to get authentic Korean food." Muslim residents often share their frustration when maintenance and police personnel do not take off their shoes inside their apartments. Keeping floors very clean is important to Muslims, as they pray on the floor five times a day. Unfamiliarity with and extreme sensitivity to child abuse laws sometimes leave international mothers vulnerable. Some mothers worry that even if they yell at their own children at home, their neighbors, suspecting child abuse, may report to the police. A Korean mother shared that she could only go to the laundry facilities located a few doors down from her own residence at midnight when her newborn, older children, and husband were asleep and she finally had time to leave home alone. She wanted to do it during the day, but without child care, she felt that she could not leave her children at home for fear of being reported to the police. Another Korean woman was also afraid of being reported as a child abuser ever since she was mistakenly reported to the police for child abuse right after she and her family came to the United States. She described her life:

> I was forced to come here [to the United States] by my husband. He thinks I need to be more active. The reason for my becoming more and more inactive is because of my two children. Moving around itself is hard. We can't even leave our children in automobiles (laughs), they cry when they are told to go to sleep.

Some international women find the transition of becoming a minority from a majority challenging. For those who come from racially or ethnically homogeneous environments, being visually different all the time could itself be a draining experience, especially when the experience was new for the woman. Some women who come from countries where hiring of domestic workers is common among the middle class may find it very challenging to have to learn and take care of all the housekeeping work on their own. The exchange rate for dollars is often unfavorable with regard to other currencies, and barely having enough to live on in a foreign country itself is a challenging task for those who were affluent in other countries. More generally, many find the experience of "becoming nobody" in a foreign country and being disconnected from familiar people and places difficult.

Other findings from the needs assessment had to do with the desire of international families and women to build a community within their geographic locations. In building that community, however, some women realized that old prejudices against members of other ethnic groups might be evoked during community-building activities. For example, social workers had to help IFOP participants use their problem-solving skills to determine whether conflicts were the result of cultural differences based on national boundaries or whether they were personality styles. Although women were interested in getting to know women from other countries, they still believed that it would be difficult to approach people from countries other than their own country of origin. To resolve this issue, the women wanted initially to meet and get to know women from their own countries who were living in Family Housing.

IFOP organizers took into consideration the results of the needs assessment in building the elements of the initial program. They demonstrated that simple tools can create comprehensive and useful interventions when adhering to the practice guidelines of identifying and addressing key supports and barriers and having the women tell their stories. (See table 28.2 for a summary of the practice guidelines.)

Situated in the transient student family communities with naturally high turnover rates, IFOP's major efforts have primarily been on outreach, increasing participation of the residents, and identifying resources, all leading toward **community building**. After three years of organizing, active involvement of community members in system change is now beginning.

Most of the work conducted by IFOP involves community workers, who are also spouses of students or scholars who are from other countries (Korea, Brazil, Trinidad, and Tobago). They live in the Family Housing with their

TABLE 28.2. Practice Guidelines

1. Resilience can be supported by externalizing rather than internalizing the presenting issue and placing women of color in leadership positions within the interventions serving them.
2. Resilience can be fostered through the development of women's critical consciousness.
3. Resilience can be facilitated through addressing key supports and barriers for women of color community change agents.
4. Resilience can be facilitated by normalizing the reactance of the host community and its institutions.
5. Resilience can be facilitated by "telling the stories."

husbands and children, and their work illustrates the second practice guideline of looking for and employing women of color who can take leadership positions in their own communities. The staff's peer status to the residents we work with makes it easier for us to develop helping relationships that are egalitarian and participatory. For example, during drop-in hours in the IFOP's shared office space, five to fifteen women usually stop by and stay for one to three hours. A core group of mothers drop by every week with their children. Over various kinds of international teas and snacks, the conversation ranges from cultural sharing about child-rearing practices, living in the United States in general, and previous careers and jobs to frustration about parenting and role sharing in households. Newcomers often generate excitement, which brightens up the entire group of people in the room. The synergy produced among those who are willing to make friends and do something is quite invigorating to the staff members and becomes the source of energy. In short, drop-in hours, an illustration of practice guideline 3 of identifying supports as well as barriers, are opportunities where community residents can meet their neighbors and IFOP staff in an informal setting, make friends, and sometimes vent their emotions and ask for advice from their peers. In this latter activity of sharing information and asking for advice, the women again utilized practice guideline 1 of externalizing their situation and practice guideline 4 of normalizing the reactance of institutions in the host culture.

The staff, when appropriate, often share their stories as mothers, wives, women, and being different, in response to the stories that the community members tell. The positioning of ourselves as peer helpers and facilitators as opposed to distanced professional helpers has been very effective in developing the power of residents, because being peers are not stigmatizing and the roles of the residents are not fixed as "clients," although there are times some do actively seek help. In fact, some of the "regulars" became the active volunteers who are now an integral part of our project. A Korean woman, who said that she only knew one Korean person in the community when she first came to IFOP, has been participating in the program for four months and has been introduced to many other Koreans partly through the informal contacts made through drop-in hours. Now she would like to teach Korean children in the area in an informal Saturday school that we cosponsor.

Another Korean woman initiated a "Walking Group" during the drop-in hours, called all of her friends from her ESL class, and pulled off a very successful activity that has been attracting five to twelve women every week for the past three months. She also volunteers as an editor of our monthly newsletter. This development of the critical consciousness, as in the case of Dawn discussed in the previous section of this paper, illustrates practice guideline 2. In her article about the Walking Group, the Korean woman collected the following voices of the participants of this group:

> I think the "Walking Group" is a really good idea. We always have a lot of fun and can practice our English amongst each other. We also learn more about different cultures from different countries. (An Indonesian woman)

This editor wrote the following about her experience as a volunteer, leader, and community builder in this newsletter: "As a volunteer, I am learning a lot of things. IFOP is important to me." Another volunteer editor from Japan also shared that "I am happy to meet other residents of Family Housing and feel that I am a part of the community."

This last comment about feeling a part of the community is significant, because not all the women from other countries may feel this way. This is largely because these international women in the university community are mostly temporary residents, thus not necessarily committed to the local community or to U.S. society in general. Some people who are in the United States for one to two years may feel that they are guests and that their stay is like a long vacation in the United States. This does not mean that they do not experience daily difficulties living in a foreign land. Rather, when they are not going to be living in the United States for a long time, feelings of marginalization may even reinforce the lack of a sense of responsibility as members of the community. Women's critical consciousness can be fostered by coplanning and participating in a diversity seminar for service providers' participation in a community-building project, as indicated by another IFOP volunteer:

> I think being in America for me is not only about a getting a degree. I represent a voice not only my own voice but also a voice as a woman, a voice from Turkey, a voice of a Muslim person. And I appreciate the effort for providing this opportunity to me and to the other panelists.

These women bring many strengths and skills to the community and IFOP program. First, after several months of staying in the Family Housing communities, the women become very knowledgeable of various cultural and inexpensive resources available in the area. Second, they are typically very eager to network with each other and bring in high energy to IFOP meetings and activities. Third, the international women are often very modest in learning about new cultural environments. In addition, their enthusiasm about learning is contagious. They often ask questions of each other about their cultural heritages and are impressed by what they have learned. This is another illustration of expression of the development of critical consciousness through storytelling as described by practice guidelines 2 and 5 in table 28.2.

Some of the IFOP participants are very eager to do something in the community. They often have new ideas for programs as seen in the development of the Walking Group. Many women are current or expectant mothers. Experiences in parenting and knowledge of its difficulties and rewards are definitely a strength they have. For example, when one German woman who was due to give birth in a couple weeks stopped by for the first time during the drop-in hours, she shared some of her anxieties about the childbirth. A few other women from various countries in the room volunteered their childbirth experiences, which were very moving to others who were present and left positive feelings about childbirth and being women in general. Last, about half of the women involved with IFOP have worked in their home country. Therefore, many of them have special skills and interesting backgrounds. One woman from China was a mechanical engineer. A Korean woman mentioned earlier was a math major. The Japanese woman who volunteers with us worked in a business firm on a career track. A woman from Nigeria was a community development worker. Most of them, unfortunately, cannot work due to the kind of visa that they have. This does not mean, however, that they do not have strong leadership skills and backgrounds. Thus volunteer experience also becomes valuable in a reciprocal manner, benefiting both the women of color and the IFOP program. Our job as social workers helping to facilitate IFOP's expanded role in the lives of these women and the Family Housing community is to match their talents, skills, and interests to existing and new volunteer opportunities. Even if they do not take on a concrete "job," being an active participant of the events and offering mutual support to other community members are very valuable assets for both Family Housing and the international women's community located therein.

These two examples identify how an understanding of the structural experience of women of color can be used in macro- and microlevel practice. In both of these cases, we utilize practice methods that are focused on identifying and building upon sources of resilience and strength that are within communities. The practice guidelines we identify (see table 28.2) can be used by any social workers interested in fostering the resilience of women of color and may be incorporated into the design and evaluation of their interventions.

CONCLUSION

In this chapter we have identified ways in which women of color can be a group considered to be a "population at risk" for health, mental health, poverty, and other serious problems. These problems most often originate in conditions of inequality that result from the interlocking oppressions of racism and sexism that affect the opportunity structures, resources, and experiences of women of color. However, women of color have not been passive in their experiences of inequality. Individual women and groups of women have developed strategies and resources within their communities that are sources of resilience and strength.

Effective social work practice with women of color will recognize and understand how societal conditions have impacted on the experience of women of color. This practice also requires a multidimensional perspective involving multiple levels of practice and skills for working with individuals, groups, families, and communities. Understanding women of color will focus specifically on how individual women have been affected by forces such as racism, ethnocentrism, and sexism and on ways in which social structures might be challenged. However, because women of color are at the bottom of our social hierarchy in terms of political power, we must also emphasize the interpersonal and political levels of change. As illustrated in our examples, practice with women of color must engage sources of resilience and strength to ameliorate systems on all levels.

Note

Special thanks to Virginia Gonzales, who assisted with the development of this chapter.

References

Adair, M. and S. Howell. 1994. *Breaking Old Patterns, Weaving New Ties: Alliance Building.* San Francisco: Tools for Change.

Allen, P. Gunn. 1986. *The Sacred Hoop: Recovering the Feminine in American Indian Traditions.* Boston: Beacon Press.

Aswad, B. and B. Bilge. 1996. *Family and Gender Among American Muslims: Issues Facing Middle Eastern Immigrants and Their Descendants.* Philadelphia, Pa.: Temple University Press.

Baca-Zinn, M. and B. Dill. 1994. *Women of Color in U.S. Society.* Philadelphia, Pa.: Temple University Press.

Boyd-Franklin, N. 1989. *Black Families in Therapy: A Multisystems Approach.* New York: Guilford.

Comas-Díaz, L. and B. Greene. 1994. *Women of Color: Integrating Ethnic and Gender Identities in Psychotherapy.* New York: Guilford.

Congress, E. 1997. *Multicultural Perspectives for Working with Families.* New York: Springer.

Cooper, R. S., C. N. Rotimi, and R. Ward. 1999. "The Puzzle of Hypertension in African-Americans." *Scientific American,* February, pp. 56–63.

Darity, W. A., Jr. and S. L. Myers. 1984. "Does Welfare Dependency Cause Female Headship? The Case of the Black Family." *Journal of Marriage and the Family* 46(4):765–80.

Derrick, R. C. 1997. "Healing the Wounds of Racism." *Essence,* March, p. 37.

Federal Interagency Forum on Child and Family Statistics. 1998. *America's Children: Key National Indicators of Well-Being, 1998.* Washington, D.C.: U.S. Government Printing Office.

Gutiérrez, L. 1994. "Beyond Coping: An Empowerment Perspective on Stressful Life Events." *Journal of Sociology and Social Welfare* 21(3):201–20.

Gutiérrez, L. and E. Lewis. 1999. *Empowering Women of Color.* New York: Columbia University Press.

Hunter, A. 1993. "Making a Way: Strategies of Southern Urban African American Families, 1900 and 1936." *Journal of Family History* 18:231–48.

Hurtado, A. 1996. *The Color of Privilege: Three Blasphemies on Race and Feminism.* Ann Arbor: University of Michigan Press.

Institute of International Education. 1998. *Open Doors 1997/1998.* New York: Author.

Johnsrud, L. K. and K. C. Sadao. 1998. "The Common Experience of 'Otherness': Ethnic and Racial Minority Faculty." *Review of Higher Education,* 21, no. 4 (Summer):315–42.

Kanner, A. D., J. C. Coyne, C. Schaefer, and R. S. Lazarus. 1981. "Comparison of Two Modes of Stress Measurement: Daily Hassles, Uplifts and Major Life Events to Health Status." *Journal of Behavioral Medicine* 4:1–39.

Kirk, G. and M. Okasawa-Rey. 1998. *Women's Lives: Multicultural Perspectives.* Mountain View, Calif.: Mayfield Press.

Lewis, E. A. and B. Ford. 1990. "The Network Utilization Project: Incorporating Traditional Strengths of African-American Families into Group Work Practice." *Social Work with Groups* 13(3):7–22.

Lum, D. 1996. *Social Work Practice and People of Color: A Process Stage Approach,* 3d ed. Pacific Grove, Calif.: Brooks/Cole.

Marcenko, M. and L. Samost. 1999. "Living with HIV/AIDS: The Voices of HIV Positive Mothers." *Social Work* 44(1):36–45.

Mattis, J. S. 1995. "Workings of the Spirit: Spirituality, Meaning Construction and Coping in the Lives of Black Women." Ph.D. diss., University of Michigan, Ann Arbor, Michigan.

Medicine, B. 1988. "Native American (Indian) Women." *Anthropology and Education Quarterly* 19:86–92.

Monroe, P. A., V. V. Tiller, and J. C. Garand. 1999. "Later Life as Welfare Resilient Woman." Paper presented at the Groves Conference on Marriage and the Family, Tampa, Florida, April 18.

Moos, R. and A. Billings. 1982. "Conceptualizing and Measuring Coping Resources and Processes." In C. Goldberger and S. Breznitz, eds., *Handbook of Stress: Theoretical and Clinical Aspects.* New York: Free Press.

Nagel, J. 1994. "Constructing Ethnicity: Creating and Recreating Ethnic Identity and Culture." *Social Problems* 41, no. 1(February):152–76.

National Journal Group. 1999a. "Minority Health: UPenn Receives $1.5M to Study Elderly." http://web.lexis-nexis.com/universe/docum 5a3&__md5 = 7a7ed8718fd92197 a026a44e2283c42 (26 January 1999).

——. 1999b. "Osteoporosis: Risk Higher Among Some Minority Women." http.//web .lexis-nexis.com/universe/docum 5a3&__md5 = 5a67ec59b174703082eddf5977f43d63 (5 January 1999).

Ortiz, V. 1994."Women of Color: A Demographic Overview." In M. Baca-Zinn and B. Dill, eds., *Women of Color in U.S. Society,* pp. 13–40. Philadelphia, Pa.: Temple University Press.

Parsons, R. 1991. "Empowerment: Purposes and Practice in Social Work." *Social Work with Groups* 14(2):7–22.

Pyant, C. T. and J. Yanico. 1991. "Relationship of Racial Identity and Gender-Role Attitudes to Black Women's Psychological Well-being." *Journal of Counseling Psychology* 38(3):315–22.

Reppucci, N. D., J. L. Woolard, and C. S. Fried. 1999. "Social, Community and Preventive Interventions." Annual Review of *Psychology.* http://web.lexis-nexis.com/universes/ docum 5a3&__md5 = aeb2c01ccaIa4fe408e667af381acf (1 January, 1999).

Robnett, B. 1997. *How Long? How Long? African American Women in the Struggle for Civil Rights.* New York: Oxford University Press.

Safran, C. 1993. "The Women Who Helped Themselves." *Good Housekeeping,* May, pp. 41–47.

Shain, R., J. Piper, E. Newton, S. Perdue, R. Ramos, J. Champion, and F. Guerra. 1999. "A Randomized, Controlled Trial of a Behavioral Intervention to Prevent Sexually Transmitted Disease Among Minority Women." *New England Journal of Medicine* 340(2): 93–100.

Solomon, B. 1976. *Black Empowerment.* New York: Columbia University Press.

Starhawk. 1992. *Truth or Dare.* New York: Harper & Row.

U.S. Bureau of the Census. 1992. *1990 Census of the Population.* Washington, D.C.: U.S. Department of Commerce.

U.S. National Center for Health Statistics. 1998. "Vital Statistics of the United States, Monthly Vital Statistics Report." U.S. Census Bureau, The Official Statistics. *Statistical Abstract of the United States.* (17 September 1998).

University of Michigan Family Housing. 1997–1998. *Family Housing: Living at Michigan.* Ann Arbor, Mich.: Author.

University of Michigan International Center. 1997. *Foreign Student and Staff Statistics: September 1995.* Ann Arbor, MI: Author.

Winkler, M. and P. Fontanarosa. 1998. "Ethnic and Socioeconomic Factors As Determinants of Health Status." *Journal of the American Medical Association* 280(23):1989–90.

Yellowbird, M. 1999. "Radical, Skewed, Benign and Calculated: Reflections on Teaching Diversity." *Reflections: Narratives on Professional Helping* 5(2):13–22.

29

Work and Job Jeopardy

Sheila H. Akabas
Lori Bikson

Think about the word *work,* and an endless stream of descriptors crosses one's mind. Included might be *financial support, social contacts, a means of organizing one's day, a source of status, a sense of accomplishment,* or alternatively *demanding, dirty, dull, unhealthy, unsafe, stressful* and *lacking in fulfillment* to list just a few. As a society we are ambivalent about work. Work is seen as a panacea that can remedy problems and a plague that precipitates them, as a cause of pernicious stress and a source of self-actualization. Yet work or the search for it is an activity that commands the majority of waking hours of approximately 140 million Americans on a daily basis (Folbre 1995). Most others under the age of 65 are engaged in activities designed to prepare them to work effectively. It is not surprising that anything gaining so much attention is a much debated phenomena. The reality probably lies between the extremes. Freud saw the ability to work as one of two hallmarks of adult functioning, the other being the ability to love (1930). Teenagers see work as the route to independence, or at least to ownership of a car, the unsurpassed symbol of American independence. Children have great curiosity about work, and their pretend activities often fantasize work roles. Aging persons ponder the right time to leave work, while employers frequently make that decision for their employees, aged and otherwise. Those outside the workplace often look longingly at work. Seventy-five percent of persons with disabilities who are not employed, for example, report a great desire to work (Stoddard et al. 1998). We are a society that holds work supreme as some societies do religion and others age or other personal characteristics (Ozawa 1982). For adults, to not work is to be outside the mainstream, almost less than human (Wagner 1994). As Tice (1994) has noted, "Employment can mark the difference between social skill development and social isolation, self-sufficiency and dependency, and a productive routine and boredom" (734).

Given the importance of work in people's lives, both for individual fulfillment and now, because of policy mandates, for sustenance, consideration of the conditions under which labor force participants have difficulty finding work, or are placed in jeopardy of not being able to manage job retention, and what social work and social workers can do about it, is in order. A wide variety of conditions place individuals in a vulnerable position in relation to entry into employment and job retention. For instance, it has been understood for a long time that there are workplaces known for their culture of drinking or drug abuse (Fine, Akabas, and Bellinger 1982), and much has been written about the impact of substance abuse on job retention (DiNitto 1988). The Drug Free Workplace Act of 1988 (PL 100–690) has made it a matter of public policy to require employers who hold federal contracts or receive federal grants to "police" their employees and certify that they are drug free. Other federal laws and regulations attend to the importance of control of substance use for those who hold safety-sensitive jobs in the transportation industry. Yet it is estimated that 90 percent of all substance abusers are active members of the workforce who endanger their continuity at work by their substance use. Well accepted, however, is the significant opportunity that threat of job jeopardy can offer in helping abusers, especially those who use excessive alcohol, to seek treatment and even spontaneously to cease the abuse (Hanson 1993). Because of the potentially costly impact of substance abuse on contractual obligations with the government and on actual productivity, Employee and Membership Assistance Programs (EAPs and MAPs) have gained widespread attention, resources, and managerial support for their role in using constructive confrontation (Trice and Sonnenstuhl 1985) and other forms of intervention (Walsh and Gust 1986) to reduce the numbers who risk their employment attachment by the use and abuse of alcohol and drugs at the workplace. Work, or job maintenance, is a crucial and desired treatment outcome for most programs that serve persons with addiction problems, and one to which EAPs and MAPs lay claim. A measure of their success is the reduced attention to this issue recently.

A condition of even greater pain typically faced by participants in the world of work is the circumstance of unemployment itself. Unemployment has been reported as arousing fear and despair, has been compared with experiencing rape, and has been linked with physical illness, child and spouse abuse, substance use, and premature death. Yet loss of a job at some time in one's adult life is almost a certainty in this era of fast-changing economies (Root 1993). Although unemployment insurance payments and severance pay may mitigate the immediate financial burden of separation, analysis by Sales (1995) shows that workers unemployed for more than six months experience a worsening financial plight. The trauma to personal and family health and well-being that results from an individual being laid off or fired has defied accurate estimation (Jones 1990; Liebow 1967). Such trauma becomes a community experience when a whole plant is closed (Vosler 1994). In this latter circumstance, public policy has sought to reduce the impact through the Worker Adjustment and Retraining Notification Act of 1988 (PL 100–379). It is an interesting historical note that when George Bush was vice-president, he urged President Reagan to sign this bill because he believed he could not face the electorate successfully without having responded to the widespread anger in the Midwest precipitated by the wave of plant closings. As Root (1993:343) has noted, "Requiring advance notification of intended plant closings, for example, appears to be a significant factor in improving employment opportunities for workers who are affected." It is obvious that there is a huge agenda appropriate to social workers who seek involvement in workplace issues, on all levels of practice, policy, and research.

Many other conditions place individuals in job jeopardy with its accompanying disturbances. Regardless of method, specialization, population focus or agency setting, every social worker deals with work or its absence on a daily basis (Akabas 1997). The remainder of this chapter will partialize; that is, it will deal with two of the many circumstances that account for job insecurity and unemployment and explore the potential for policy and practice responses. The particular issues to be reviewed are the condition of conflict between work and family demands and the impact of the onset or worsening of disability. For each, we attempt to define the risks and vulnerabilities as well as the coping mechanisms and protective factors that help individuals resolve these problems and the organizational policies and other strategies that can contribute to the remedies.

At first glance the loss or lack of work may seem relatively inconsequential when compared with some of the other conditions, circumstances, and events described in this volume. But for workers struggling unsuccessfully with work-family balance and workers who have a disability, their condition may result in oppression, poverty, and mental health problems not just for themselves but often for their families as well (Akabas 1988; Waldfogel 1997; Wetzel 1978). Lest the reader fall into the minimalist mind-set, we quote from a woman who has been fired, who describes the situation, "The feelings were so elemental, and so strong, just overpowering. Betrayal. Depression. Shock. . . . It has to have a lot of kinship with death. . . . It's the brutality. It may be more like rape than death. Being brutalized, violated, and being helpless" (Mauer 1981:20–21).

DEFINING AND EXPLAINING WORK AND WORK JEOPARDY

Work is both an individual experience and the basis for national policy. As we enter the new century, there is a conservative agenda at bay to make individuals solely responsible for their own economic welfare. Social policy is geared to move into the world of work as many of those able to work as the economy can employ, in effect making working a primary expectation for all adult Americans. In search of the elusive goal of full employment, a bevy of laws support the concept, if not the reality, of an equal playing field for those in the labor market. Discrimination in employment is illegal under Title VII of the Civil Rights Act of 1964 (PL 88–352), and its amendment in the Pregnancy Discrimination Act of 1978, the Age Discrimination in Employment Act of 1967 (ADEA PL 90–202), the Equal Pay Act of 1963 (PL 88–38), the Immigration Control and Reform Act of 1986 (IRCA PL 99–603), the Americans with Disabilities Act of 1990 (ADA PL 101–336), and even the Family Medical Leave Act of 1993 (FLMA PL 103–3), among others. With both a welfare to work program directed largely at mothers of young children, and a work incentive initiative for persons with disabilities, being available and ready to work is now a requirement rather than a choice for any adult who would apply for a social welfare benefit.

What is the environment in which this march to work occurs? The reality diverges sharply from policy expectations. The American workplace is in great flux. The superiority of U.S. industrial might has been challenged by global competition. Low skill and unskilled jobs have all but disappeared from our economy (Kahne 1994). Instead, even high school graduation is problematic in this knowledge revolution that makes jobs in the fastest-growing employment sectors dependent on understanding computers and medical technology (Judy and D'Amico 1997). Women have joined the labor force in record numbers, many of them the mothers of children under the age of 6, making conflict between work and family a given for a significant number, particularly due to the lack of any public availability of child care. Downsizing, right-sizing, and other euphemisms have translated into job insecurity for most, suggesting not only that the vast majority of us will occupy at least three different career tracks during our working lives but that periods of unemployment will threaten our mental health (Brenner 1973). Unions have found it difficult to organize and maintain their power in the collective bargaining situation, leaving more and more workers without the protection of representation. As the number of workers in our economy increases, the proportion of those represented by trade unions has steadily declined from approximately 24 percent in 1982 to 15 percent in 1994 (Mishel, Bernstein, and Schmitt 1997:199). With the disappearance of good jobs, most families have made economic progress only when two adult members of the family unit are working. This phenomena has increased the disparity between rich and poor, leading to the greatest inequity in income distribution the United States has ever known (Mishel et al. 1997), and greater than any other of the major industrial countries. Despite, or perhaps because of these trends, employment is at an all-time high, new jobs are being created at a pace that outstrips any previous experience, and unemployment is sufficiently low that concern is expressed about labor shortages. Common wisdom holds that prosperity, for most Americans, is no longer just around the corner. It is here, making job jeopardy or actual loss of employment all the more aberrant and painful.

DEMOGRAPHIC PATTERNS

Americans come in all shapes, sizes, ages, races, educational levels, religions, and both genders, and most of them are active workers. At the end of 1997, the labor force participation rate, the proportion of all Americans who work, was at the highest level ever, a startling 67.1 percent of noninstitutionalized persons between the ages of 16 and 65, up from 65.6 percent some ten years earlier, and accounting for 136,300,000 persons. With an unemployment rate at 4.9 percent, the lowest in almost thirty years, 129,500,000 Americans are working by latest count. This increasing participation holds for almost all groups regardless of characteristics of age, sex, race, geographic distribution, or class (Crawley 1992). There are exceptions, however. One of the outcomes of work is financial support. Not surprisingly, then, the poorer the group, the smaller the proportion employed. Increased participation is most apparent among women of childbearing and child-rearing age. In 1980, those in the age grouping of 20 to 24 had a participation rate of 68.9 percent, while those both in the 25 to 34 and 35 to 44 age groups had a rate of 65.5 percent. By 1997, those rates were 72.2 percent, 76.0 percent, and 77.7 percent, respectively, and the projections suggest that by the year 2006, they will be 71.8 percent, 77.6 percent, and 80.2 percent (U.S. Bureau of the Census 1998:403). (It is interesting to note that while rates for women are rising, those for men are declining, though very slightly in the younger age groups.) Figures by cohort for married men ages 25 to 34 were 97.5 percent in 1980 and 96.1 percent in 1997; for ages 35 to 44 they were 97.2 percent in 1980 and 95.7 percent in 1997. Though the figures are slightly different by race, they are all in the same direction (U.S. Bureau of the Census 1998:398–445).

Education is intimately related to employment. In 1997, for the same 16- to 65-year-old cohort, 88.5 percent of college graduates are working, compared with 83.7 percent of those with some college, 62.5 percent of high school graduates, and only 61.7 percent of those with less than a high school education. Although the percentages may vary by sex and race, the direction of the education connection is constant. Nonetheless, even controlling for education, unemployment hits harder for black and Hispanic Americans, and most severely for persons with disabilities.

> Among adults with disabilities of working age (18 to 64), three out of ten (29%) **work full or part-time,** compared to eight out of ten (79%) of those without disabilities, a gap of **fifty percentage points.** The proportion of working-age adults with disabilities who are employed has actually declined since 1986, when one in three (34%) were working. . . . Among those with disabilities age 16–64 who are not employed, seven out of ten (72%) say they would prefer to be working. (National Organization on Disability 1998:7)

The economic status of American workers has not improved over the last two decades. In constant 1982 dollars, the average hourly earnings in 1980 were $7.78; weekly, $275.00. In 1997, the comparable figures were $7.55 on an hourly basis and $261.00 weekly (U.S. Bureau of the Census 1998). Particular groups experience hardship beyond the problem of economic immobility. Factor in the circumstance that 3.9 million workers experienced disabling injuries at work in 1996 alone. Furthermore, among workers over the age of 20, with more than three years of job tenure, 4.1 million lost their jobs from January 1993 to December 1995 because plants closed or moved, positions were abolished, or work was slack (U.S. Bureau of the Census 1998:416) The obvious question arises, "Is it any wonder that a higher and higher proportion of the population is participating in the labor force?" As the safety net disappears, earnings in real dollars decline, and long-term jobs disappear, more work is the only answer to maintaining a household's standard of living. The stresses and pressures of the world of work are not a myth, but a reality for most American families, often causing a condition Michael Lerner (1980) tabbed "surplus powerlessness." Such conditions are not conducive to mental health and family well-being.

SOCIETAL CONTEXT

We may ask what happens to the individual who is not participating successfully in the American workplace. He or she is faced with a major life crisis, one that threatens all aspects of personal and family well-being. Self-blame shares the spotlight with blaming the victim. Based largely on societal expectations, individuals who find themselves in danger of unemployment seek reason for their condition in their own actions and are often able to convince themselves of fault or at least "contributory" negligence. If they should be so bold as to blame forces within the workplace or in the community, thereby escaping self-blame, they are likely to encounter the Horatio Alger myth: "If you try you can always find work, and if you labor hard enough at it, you can succeed." By this means the parties that have power to determine the opportunities for most of us are let off scot-free. It is not management's fault that your disabling accident occurred at the workplace. You should have been more careful. It is not the employer's problem if your absenteeism results from the fact that your child gets sick frequently and cannot go to day care. You should have some kind of backup service available. The employer is certainly not at fault if your heart condition has worsened and you cannot stand at the open hearth furnace for eight hours a day, winter and summer. The reasonable accommodation protection of the ADA is hard to apply in such circumstances. Nor can the employer bear responsibility for making your job secure when your parent requires attention at home because of a recent stroke and you, due to a lack of financial resources, must provide care that requires you to take more leave than the thirteen weeks that FLMA provides with its guarantee of return to the same or a similar job. The culture views these as private matters that should be solved privately. In these and many other ways the workplace is an unforgiving place where the golden rule is, "Produce or get out." Out to where, and to what safety net, is never specified.

Clearly, however, these are not individual cases but rather classes of problems, the causes for which reside often in the organizational nature of the workplace or the rules of society. And therein resides as well the potential to resolve these circumstances. First, work can serve as a respite from many of the problems discussed elsewhere in this volume. Then too, laws, like the Civil Rights Act of 1964 and the ADA, have helped to establish support for the requirement that the workplace respond to the diverse needs among labor force participants. For perhaps no other negative life circumstance is there greater potential resource availability than those involving job jeopardy. The functional community of work subsumes the power and the capacity within labor and management to offer economic support and alternative options. Solutions at that level, furthermore, keep the problem from becoming stigmatized (Googins and Davidson 1993). When a world of work auspice provides services, it means that the condition is viewed as a normative event. It calls forth a preventive response from employers, the parties most damaged by its occurrence. Employees are placed at risk not because of some individual failure, but because of the incompatibility between their realistic needs and the ways in which the work world is organized. How can we expect to raise and care for families if excessive overtime, and its more insidious partner "facetime," keep families apart when they need to be together (Hochschild 1997)? How can we continue to be productive when the normal difficulties of aging and disease create functional gaps in our capacity that are not accommodated by formal policy? How can we help someone suffering from substance abuse if we cannot use the incentive of a return to work as the reward for the struggle toward improvement? The solutions to the problems posed by these questions lie, for the most part, within the purview of labor, management, and government.

VULNERABILITIES AND RISK FACTORS

The question of how to achieve a balance between family and work weighs heavily on the minds of many American workers—most particularly, but not exclusively, women—who face a day-to-day struggle to meet the demands of both their workplaces and their families (Akabas 1988: Lechner 1993a, 1993b). Those who work in low-skilled, low-paying jobs have inadequate resources to pay individually for child care assistance. Subsidized child care is frequently unavailable (Meyers and Heintze 1999). Attempts to carve out additional space for family concerns, as a practical matter, are inhibited by the fear that one can be easily replaced by another worker prepared to subordinate family concerns more completely. This balancing problem, furthermore, is one that cuts across class lines. In professions of great prestige and demand, the hardship of creating a balance between family and work has stunted career advancement and has limited life choices. For example, a 1999 assessment of the state of medical practice found that:

> By all rights, this should be the perfect time to be a woman in medicine. . . . [Women now account for roughly 45 percent of all medical students and [women doctors] are in high demand. But despite these gains, the top tiers of medicine have remained inaccessible to many women, largely, experts say, because they are unwilling or unable to find a balance between the years of study those specialties require and a life outside of medicine . . . doctors looking for more balanced lives, experts say, has created an increasing "pink collar" level of medicine – in which more women are concentrated in the lowest paying, least prestigious specialties. (Steinhauer 1999:A1)

The number of parents working while raising children grows each year. The proportion of children under 6 with mothers in the workforce in 1990 was 44.1 percent for single mothers, 45.1 percent for married mothers, and 60.3 percent for mothers who were widowed, separated, or divorced. By 1997 these proportions had *increased* to 65.1 percent, 63.6 percent, and 74.2 percent, respectively, while for those with children between 6 and 17, the figures were 74 percent, 77.6 percent, and 81.1 percent in 1997 (U.S. Bureau of the Census 1998). The labor force is replete with mothers (Piechowski 1992). Projections suggest, furthermore, that 85 percent of employed women can expect to become pregnant at some point during their work life. Men, who are increasingly partnered with women who are lifetime labor force participants, are also beginning to feel the tensions between the demands of work and family (Brayfield 1995). Finally, as American society ages, more and more workers, again particularly women who are estimated to provide 90 percent of all family care for the aged, are called upon to offer care to aging parents (Kola and Dunkle 1988).

The problem of providing and paying for child care, and increasingly the problem of providing and paying for elder care, remain largely without response on a governmental policy level. Early legislation reflected the belief that the proper role of women was that of child bearer and at-home mother. Conservative groups continue to argue that providing funds for the construction of child care facilities and tax allowances to working families for child care expenses encourage women to leave home for work. This mantra of child care policy as "antifamily" stymies realistic legislation aimed at providing and monitoring high quality yet affordable child care.

Lacking legislation, family policies have been developed on an ad hoc basis by employers. Yet many employers still cling to the concept of the traditional family (father breadwinner, stay-at-home mom as caretaker) as a way to set boundaries at work and ignore the connections between work and family (Googins and Burden 1987). Those, on the other hand, who have established family policy have been credited, in both the popular and scholarly literature, under the assumption that their purpose is to help workers achieve a better balance between their work and family roles. It is unclear, however, whether family policies that do exist actually serve that function or are geared to enabling an employee with family responsibilities to adjust family life to conform to work requirements (Lambert 1993). Family policy has traditionally been seen by business as needing to have a direct payoff in terms of production and profitability. This hardly reflects the social policy perspective that would ask whether family policies are accessible, fairly distributed, and actually promote the welfare of workers and their families. Unions that might be the natural spokesgroup for family (and disability) policy have become too weak to bring this issue effectively to the bargaining table. This leaves families to solve their own problems, often at the cost of great personal stress, inadequate caregiving, and limited career options. As Coulton (1996) notes, "To respond to the challenges of the new era, social workers need a greater understanding of how to enhance employment opportunities. . . . Social workers will need new skills and knowledge to help large numbers of individuals move into the labor market and to enable communities to foster and sustain employment opportunities" (510).

Another curious phenomena concerns disability among workers. Although social policy appears deeply invested in ensuring that we all pull our own weight by working, neither the employer sector nor the government has done much to make that possible for persons experiencing physical, emotional, or sensory problems that may interfere. People with disabilities represent the largest minority group in the United States, comprising an estimated 43 million persons (Gliedman and Roth 1980). Disability is also a high cost item in most employers' benefit packages (Akabas, Gates, and Warren 1996), and persons with disabilities constitute a major constituency for government welfare payments (Stoddard et al. 1998:34, 41).

Leaving aside those who are already disabled when they reach an age appropriate for labor force participation, there are many millions of adults who experience the onset or worsening of disability while at work, or for whom an existing disability becomes more difficult to accommodate at the workplace because of changes in technology. (A startling example of this latter circumstance was evident when computers changed from DOS to Microsoft Windows, making the use of computers a more elusive aid for those with serious visual impairments and blindness.) Despite the fact that disability represents a high cost item to employers, whose motivation in most other circumstances is profit focused, few in the workplace other than workers with disabilities seem engaged with these causes of job jeopardy. Consider the usual experience of a worker facing the circumstance of disability sufficiently debilitating to cause lost time from work. If the cause was an accident or illness resulting from employment, Workers' Compensation payments are likely to begin within a week of onset. If the lost time results from causes not related to work, short-term disability payments might be provided. Rarely does the workplace contact such an employee to discern what could be helpful to return the person to work. There is a pervasive claim in the employment sector, on the one hand, that such a contact might be intrusive, and on the other hand, despite the requirements of the ADA, that one has to be "100 percent" to manage the demands of competitive employment. Lack of education, information, and understanding immobilizes everyone involved when a worker experiences job jeopardy because of disability.

The rational response of the former worker is to covet benefits. Along with the determination to overcome the problem are fear, anger, deterioration of self-image, sense of loss and vulnerability, and a host of other negatives. Questions arise, "Will the people at work care? Will I ever be able to work again? Will I be rewarded for my years of loyal service by accommodation? How am I going to make if financially? How will I best protect myself and my family?" The longer the time between the occurrence and contact from the workplace, the greater the likelihood that a productive worker will turn into an unemployed person with a disability seeking significant financial coverage. The scenario imagined is, "They do not want me back to work. They are paying me to stay home. I better get the message—hold on to these payments since they are the only thing between me and financial ruin." Thus is created the "disability mind-set" in which the person who, just days before, was a valued worker becomes, through fiscogenic policy, a disabled person unable to work. This happens despite systems that can be put in place that have the potential for fulfilling human needs, meeting legislative mandates, containing costs, and increasing productivity (Akabas and Gates 1995; Akabas, Gates, and Galvin 1992).

RESILIENCIES AND PROTECTIVE FACTORS

As already indicated, many conditions interfere with being able to secure and/or retain employment. Not working, however, is neither desired nor desirable (Gullotta 1984). Both by personal desire and by understanding the public message, most adults are likely to view employment as the essential goal. Research has shown that unemployment is usually followed in a lagged relationship, by illness, depression, and social disintegration (Brenner 1973; Weissman 1973). It even has been shown that work brings greater fulfillment than any other activity, including family involvement (Hochschild 1997). So the struggle is posed, "How can job jeopardy be overcome?" Since so much of the disruption of employment resulting from poor work/family balance or disability onset is caused by the inhospitable social policy, the parties might hope to look to the environment for a remedy. Government policy might be one avenue. Title VII of the Civil Rights Act of 1964 protects family needs under its gender protection provisions. The ADA protects persons with disabilities under its provisions requiring reasonable accommodation for otherwise qualified workers. Employees with disabilities, by virtue of employment, have provided prima facie evidence of being qualified to do the job. But inadequate financing of the Equal Employment Opportunity Commission (EEOC) and, hence, spotty enforcement have minimized the contribution of these laws to the achievement of equality in the workplace. Some research, furthermore, has suggested, in any event, that the affirmative action label involved with promoting one's rights under law has negative consequences for evaluation of one's competencies at work (Heilman, Block, and Stathatos 1997).

Another source of protective factors might be business policy. A business may utilize a range of policies as family and/or disability policy. In search of excellence in firms, measured by profitability, market share, low worker turnover, and other positive characteristics, researchers Peters and Waterman (1983) found that a factor that distinguished excellent firms was their high regard for the importance of their employees and their policies reflecting that regard. But here, too, the reality is disappointing. Currently what seems to lead a business to create family policy are particular characteristics of the organization (Glass and Estes 1997:298–99). These characteristics include size—large firms are much more likely to offer some work/family policies—how formalized the personnel and administrative function in a particular business is, the size of the skilled labor force (employees with more skills have more bargaining power with their employers), and finally, how many women are employed by the firm (family policy still being considered a "women's" issue) (Glass and Estes 1997). The fact that the conflict between work and family remains defined as a women's problem and that employers remain tied to outmoded job structures are fundamental structural problems in the area of family policy (Lambert 1993). The huge demand placed on women to cope with the responsibilities of work and family are highlighted in research conducted by Googins and Burden (1987). They write: "Having a spouse at home to share responsibilities did not reduce the workload of married women parents compared with single women parents" (298). For men, however, they found: "Having an employed wife is a particular advantage because it significantly increases family income without creating any increase in the amount of time men spend on home chores and child care" (298).

The policies in greatest use in the United States are policies that either provide workplace social supports for parents, such as on-site child care, child care referral services, or on-site counseling services, or policies that give the employee some flexibility to schedule their hours or the location of their work. Even these, however, are not organized to achieve fair distribution or distribution to the most in need. For example, only 27.6 percent of all workers had flexible schedules in 1997, and those were slightly more likely to be men than women (28.7 percent to 26.2 percent) and much more likely to be executives than semiskilled workers (42.4 percent to 14.6 percent) (U.S. Bureau of the Census 1998:413). Policies which reduce work hours such as part time or job sharing are far less common (Glass and Estes 1997).

Another arena where the traditional policy is detrimental to all interests is with regard to disability among workers. Although disability is a significant cost item, few employing organizations can place a figure on the amount it represents because there are many disparate cost pockets, for example, risk management, short-term disability, workers' compensation, long-term disability, and medical benefits, which rarely talk with each other. Employers continue to pay employees to stay home while they decry the cost of lost time from workers' compensation claimants and others who lose time because of illness or accidents that are not connected with workplace causes. This contradictory behavior does not make for the development of job maintenance policy efforts at the workplace (Gates, Taler, and Akabas 1989). It leaves individual workers with disabilities responsible for finding their own answers to job jeopardy problems.

In both these arenas, of work/family balance and of disability, the most vulnerable drop out of the labor force, starting the spiral of low income, loss of health care, declining saleable skills, loss of self-esteem, depression, somaticized illness, reduction of options, and poverty (Keefe 1984). But others find ways of challenging that cycle by strategies that range from acceptance to advocacy and activism. Some work part-time, work less demanding jobs, put their careers on halt, or recognize that not working has some advantages, too (Redcliff and Bogan 1988). This last solution is most welcomed by those with benefit entitlements. Others assume an activist stance. They join a union and force the policy issue onto the bargaining agenda. Some bring a lawsuit that both empowers them and serves to change the law. A recent suit, brought under the FMLA and a similar Maryland law, illustrates this remedy. In that case a father, employed as a Maryland state trooper, attempted to take a job-protected leave, as guaranteed in FLMA, to care for his wife who was hospitalized with a difficult pregnancy and then for their newborn child. As reported by Lewin (1999), the trooper was told by a personnel manager that "God made women to have babies and unless I could have babies, I could not be a primary care giver unless your wife is in a coma or dead." The personnel manager also told him that he could not use the Maryland state law provisions because those provisions were that "only women could be primary providers because only women can breast feed." (This law has since been amended to eliminate a distinction between primary and secondary care providers.) By his pursuit of justice the trooper did more than gain a substantial financial settlement. He reframed the embedded stereotype that calls forth reflexive discrimination against a father as the primary caregiver.

The same strategy would be available under ADA to an employed person with a disability, as noted earlier. The definition in the ADA seems most important. A person is classified as disabled for the protection of the Act if he or she has a limitation in a major life activity, is perceived of as having such a limitation, or has a history of such a limitation. Work is certainly a major life activity (Perlman 1968), as is mobility, seeing, hearing, speaking, thinking, as well as dressing, feeding, and toileting one's self. Limitations in any of these functions throw many persons into job jeopardy. For such persons who are qualified to do the work, the employer is obligated to provide reasonable accommodation so long as doing so does not cause undue hardship (usually defined as exorbitant financial expense) (Gates, Akabas, and Oran-Sabia 1998). Violations of these conditions by the employer allow the employee to bring a case before the EEOC. The EEOC has been used heavily and effectively by working persons who are protecting themselves against job loss due to disability.

Further effective coping has involved arranging support groups within the world of work. Such specialty caucuses serve to alert management to the needs of particular groups, provide a chance to exchange information and problem-solve, offer opportunities to gain mentoring support, and establish a base from which power can accrue to the members allowing them to achieve influence beyond their own numbers. Gummer (1998) has pointed out that diversity enriches an organization not by its hiring someone "different" to become like everyone else, but when those with a difference are hired to inform and influence the management and the structure in how to accommodate to the difference. It is the activist struggling to reduce the risk factors in work/family balance, or from disability, who can help that happen. Activists among people with disabilities, for example, would argue that these issues should not even arise. They view disability as a social construct resulting from an inhospitable environment that does not consider the differences in functional capacity among different people. If we had universal curb cuts, visual and verbal cues everywhere, and social attitudes and behavior that did not reflect stigma, people now viewed as disabled would not fall into that category. In the workplace, a strengths perspective offers considerable guidance. It has been said often that disability is a strength that teaches one how to accomplish the same things others do, but in new ways, ways that the workplace should not only accept but from which it should learn (Hockenberry 1995). The parallels for workers dealing with family/work balance are obvious.

PROGRAMS AND SOCIAL WORK CONTRIBUTIONS

Social workers may encounter problems of workers in job jeopardy in many locations

- as counselors in in-house (on-site) EAPs or MAPs
- as social workers at consulting or service organizations under contract with a workplace setting
- as social workers in a social agency or in private practice where one of a client's presenting problems is work connected

Roles and activities differ depending on the location of the social worker but the options are rich and varied (Mudrick 1991). Strategies can range from micro to macro. The first step in effective intervention is to recognize the potential in the world of work. Nowhere does the model of person in environment have greater application. The functional community of work provides an environment in which it is possible to gather reality information, negotiate among the parties, and influence the system. Advocacy for a particular person, for a specific organizational change, or for a major sociopolitical policy evolution are all appropriate avenues of social work response to the issues faced by those in job jeopardy. Helping a person sort out his or her choices and select an option that works for the individual is extraordinarily supportive under certain circumstances (Vigilante 1993). Operating from an internal position, the professional may be privy to information on the system, its structure and obstacles, that may provide the necessary data to influence the organization in behalf of the individual. The achievement of job security offers an individual support and restores his or her sense of power and self-efficacy.

But these opportunities to serve individuals pale beside the possibility of influencing the system in behalf of the many. The need for a more benign workplace policy has been a theme throughout this chapter. Using a force field analysis to identify forces promoting and restraining change, the social worker can develop a strategy that allows entry upstream from where the problem of job jeopardy arises to change the environment for all labor force participants. True prevention can be accomplished with the organization and the work culture as the target of intervention. Interdisciplinary collaboration with a whole new set of actors—union shop stewards and business agents, human resource managers and legal counsel—is available. Using knowledge of how individuals, groups, and organizations function, the social work professional in the world of work, or in a position related to that world, can use his or her expertise to achieve a more responsive work environment (Raber 1996). The remainder of this chapter focuses on how that can be helped to come about.

ASSESSMENT AND INTERVENTIONS

To understand the impact of paying attention to family needs that may interfere with work routines when one is a worker, to respond appropriately to having a disability that may result in a gap in task performance when one is a worker, and to perceive the problems of relationships with co-worker or supervisor under either of these conditions, one must consider the idea of stigma. Conceptually, stigma is a negative evaluation of differences. In the workplace, the differences enumerated are stigmatized and result, in the individuals experiencing them, in low self-esteem, poor self-image, self-doubt, insecurity, and interference in developing relationships that are essential for success on the job (Levy 1993). The combined effect is job jeopardy. A recent example of how difference, stigma, and job jeopardy are interrelated is informative. An African American attorney working for a large corporation became aware that he was never assigned to cases that would take him into court. He realized that without the high visibility such encounters allowed, he would never gain the support necessary for career advancement. When he raised the issue with his supervisor he was told, "Do you think I would send you before a judge with that exaggerated Afro hair-comb of yours?"

Job jeopardy is not costly to the employee alone. A high cost in turnover, loss of productivity, lack of commitment, and reduced creativity are experienced by the employer as well (Kamerman and Kahn 1987). Stigma can lose its significance, however, when differences are accepted. This speaks to the importance of societal definitions and the culture of the workplace. In a sense, the Civil Rights Act of 1964, the Americans with Disabilities Act of 1990, and other legislation "punish" people and systems that stigmatize those concerned with family needs or those dealing with disability. Observation, however, confirms that these legal mandates have been less than effective.

But knowing that a high cost is involved for the employer is sufficient to create the condition under which an enlightened management would want to find some means of accommodating workers. In an economic sense, it is just good business for an organization to be able to subsume differences. Arguments bearing on the value of including persons who reflect diversity can reinforce the inclination to action (Orlin 1995). Achieving a more protective environment for persons with disabilities or those with competing family/work demands requires influencing the social and physical environment. But no change of policy will be effective if the corporate culture of a particular organization stigmatizes the use of policy (Glass and Estes 1997:299). Otherwise, opting for benefits is a logical and protective response to the responsibility workers have to provide financial support for themselves and their families. The choice is in the hands of the employer. Creating a culture that everyone identifies can be counted on to respond humanistically to problems is possible, but it often requires significant changes from current practices. Social workers are well equipped to promote such change (Mudrick 1991).

ILLUSTRATION AND DISCUSSION

Consider an organization experiencing high costs of disability with many workers staying home and becoming increasingly debilitated, not from their disabling condition but from the aftermath of enforced idleness. An array of responses are possible. The social worker can assess those who make contact with her and provide them with case management services. Or she can ask her clients what would help get them back to work, identify that supervisors are a bottleneck, and suggest training of supervisors in accommodation. But these responses represent the proverbial Band-Aid. Each might make some difference, but organizational change is really required to achieve system improvement. A model of intervention to manage disability that has been developed by the Columbia University Center for Social Policy and Practice in the Workplace out of practice experience in system intervention seems relevant (Akabas and Gates 1995).

In the initiating stage, the social worker serves as a catalyst for arousing attention to the issue. *The first step in taking action is bringing the players together to identify their mutual interests.* If that group undertakes a needs assessment, gathering data including cost information, program needs will become apparent and the social worker can raise institutional awareness sufficiently to inspire a second step of constituting the group into a *coordinating committee to oversee a disability management initiative.* Included should be those who are interested in promoting an initiative and those who may act as restraining forces, for example, representatives from human resources, risk management, medical, benefits, EEOC, comptroller, and legal counsel as well as a union representative if the workplace is organized. A third step would be for the professional to facilitate the group process so that it is able to analyze the situation, identify gaps in policy that lie behind cost, and *formulate and issue a policy statement that establishes the organizational commitment to meeting the needs of employees with disabilities while regarding cost containment as a key criteria for action.* The special facilitating and advocacy skills of the social worker, whether EAP personnel or from an outside consultant under contract, would delineate him or her as a prime professional for fostering such an effort.

It is in the implementation stage, which calls on program development ability as well as clinical skills of engagement, assessment, contracting, problem solving, resource identification, and referral and case management, where social work involvement is even more essential. For at least a decade, we have known that early identification and intervention are essential in effective disability management (Akabas et al. 1992). Often the social worker is the first to know; that is, an employee comes to a social worker for advice or assistance in coping with personal or family disability problems. Implementation requires *identifying all the locations within the system that are likely to have early knowledge of individuals with disability problems.* A means must be established to collect this information and to develop a mechanism for contacting those who are likely to lose time from work because of the interaction between the demands of their jobs and their health condition. This contact involves sensitively reaching out to confirm that the person is valued by the workplace and that there are policy provisions *for transitional employment and accommodation at the workplace* to ease job retention or return to work. An assessment based on a biopsychosocial evaluation must be made to determine how the gaps in functional performance affect the tasks, routines, and relationships involved in the job. The social worker can carry out this assessment in situations involved with mental health problems but may need to serve as *case manager* when physical disability is involved.

The remaining steps call on the social worker's administrative skill coupled with research ability to build a database for project management and to analyze the data for feedback and program refinement. At this stage the activities are organized to help to ensure ongoing capacity within the organization to maintain the disability management initiative. First it is necessary to *communicate the program to the workforce and train those who have new responsibilities under the program (particularly the supervisors).* New tasks are involved in any policy change, and without training, organizational effectiveness is likely to be compromised. Because it is necessary to demonstrate that a program is accomplishing its goal, if it is to last beyond the interest of those involved in its introduction, the next step is to *implement a monitoring and evaluation system.* Equally important is the need to make use of the data from such a system to *develop a prevention strategy.* This feedback loop is a final step in achieving organizational change that will be lasting. It should be apparent to the reader that a full range of social work skills is involved in such a disability management program development effort. It should be apparent, as well, that a similar initiative would help resolve the problems of job jeopardy experienced by those trying to achieve a satisfactory balance between work and family demands.

Organizational intervention not only sets systems in place but also influences direct service significantly. Consider the following situation.

Maria Santini is a 35-year-old supervisor in the housekeeping department of a large hotel. Maria has been working for the hotel since she dropped out of high school at the age of 16, with short respites out for the birth of each of her children, now 10 and 7, respectively. Maria is a valued employee who has always been viewed as an intelligent and conscientious worker and has been urged to undertake additional education so that she might be eligible for promotion to a higher level of administrative work. She had acquired a GED at one point, but never seemed interested in going beyond that. Divorced for the past five years, Maria has been the sole support of the family, which includes her mother who is 75 years old and has been the prime caretaker for the two little girls, allowing Maria to maintain an unblemished record of attendance and performance.

Recently, Maria's situation has begun to fall apart. Her mother had a stroke and has not only been unable to function as a caretaker, but now requires considerable care herself, which has burdened Maria. Then, last week, Maria herself was in a serious automobile accident, breaking her hip and shoulder. Currently she is on disability benefits and her doctor has indicated that it is difficult to estimate how long, if ever, before she will be 100 percent—before she will be able to manage the lifting and other heavy work involved in housekeeping.

This mix of family/work problems and onset of disability might be totally overwhelming to someone like Maria. Paid to stay home, she might begin to find it an answer to her current situation, but the modest disability payment does not go far enough in covering the costs with which she is faced, and within six months her health insurance will terminate, placing her and her family in severe financial and personal jeopardy. Furthermore, having worked for nineteen years, Maria sees herself as a worker and does not know how she will feel about any extended period without employment. Such a situation could coincide with a downward spiral of depression, helplessness, hopelessness, and job loss were Maria's employer the typical workplace. But Maria was fortunate to work in a company with an extensive disability management initiative.

Within days of her accident, Maria's supervisor contacted her to determine what could be done to bring her back to work (early intervention). On report of her inability to carry out her usual duties, the EAP social worker was contacted. Her home visit confirmed Maria's fear of disability and her sense that her world was out of control. Her modest savings were being depleted since she needed attendant care for her mother and housekeeping assistance for herself. With permanent physical limitations a possibility, she deeply regretted not having pursued academic study. She was anxious to protect her health benefits and to explore alternative work options at least temporarily. It was in the employer's interest to return her to work as soon as possible since the company was self-insured for disability benefits (it had to pay the full cost out of its own funds while paying a full wage to a replacement employee), and it did not wish to lose the attachment of such a longstanding, effective, and reliable worker. The social worker was able to negotiate full pay on a transitional job in charge of ordering supplies and equipment for the housekeeping department. This was work for which Maria was extremely well qualified having spent almost twenty years in housekeeping. Her placement was to be preceded by computer training. Maria's accident was used as an opportunity to upgrade her position within the company and realize a promotion for which she had long been capable. It is improbable that she will ever return to her job as a supervisor in housekeeping, but her valuable services will not be lost to the company nor will she incur any great expense to the benefit system. Furthermore she will not have to face disruption of her employment or health care or the depression that could develop pursuant to such a circumstance. A win-win solution results from marshaling the system to respond to the personal crisis experienced by a valued employee.

The hoped-for outcome of such activity is to develop, among employees, a sense of community, defined as mutual commitment between workers and their employing organization (Lambert and Hopkins 1995). Ever since the Hawthorne experiments of the 1920s, we have known that paying attention to workers and their needs brings great rewards to employing organizations. Workers need a variety of supports—informational, instrumental, appraisal, and emotional—to maximize their contribution at work (House 1981). Supervisors are a key element in creating the conditions of support for workers. But it is management that must convince workers that management means what they say about an inclusive workplace. It is management that must sanction the change in workplace culture and encourage its fruition. And it is management that will reap the rewards of such a policy change. But there are rewards that accrue to communities as well. A humanist approach at the workplace allows for positive relationships with supervisors and co-workers (Seck et al. 1993), which in turn reduce stress and encourage positive coping not only at work, but in other aspects of the lives of individuals. Reduction of job jeopardy has far-reaching consequences.

CONCLUSION

We should not be sanguine, however, about the ease or likelihood of accomplishment of this paradigm just because it makes good sense. As Hopkins (1997) points out in reviewing supervisory behavior, "Embracing the supportive model was particularly difficult for supervisors because a supportive role was in conflict with the more formal production-oriented roles supervisors were also encouraged to play" (1220). There is an ongoing need to take into account organizational influences, cultural history, and productivity demands. Revisiting issues around family policy, we can note that the traditional male model of the ideal employee as a worker who manages all personal responsibilities in a way that does not interfere with any aspect of work performance (particularly long hours) has continuing credence. It rests on the theory that intense and sustained involvement in work ensures the employer both high productivity and profitability (Lambert 1993).

There is much to overcome in "selling" an alternative option to the world of work, (Weiner, Akabas, and Sommer 1973). The traditional business generated policy stands on a belief that job requirements need not be altered, and a worker's personal condition and responsibilities need not be accommodated because it is a worker's responsibility to bring and maintain total involvement in work. That the result of this belief system has been downward mobility for many workers, limits on their occupational attainment, and a disintegration of the individuals and their families is of interest to management only to the extent that it can be connected with profitability. Although this connection has been proven time and again, it remains for social workers to carry the message forth convincingly to the powers in the world of work and beyond. The profession must make these policy issues an ongoing part of the social policy agenda. Employers alone cannot be relied on to develop policies that actually meet the needs of workers and are distributed equally among employees of all skill levels, socioeconomic classes, and racial and ethnic groups. These work-related issues have lagged far behind social work's support for other social accomplishments for too long. Government, business, trade unions, and the social work profession must address work policy directly as part of a social policy and social service agenda.

References

Akabas, S. 1988. "Women, Work and Mental Health: Room for Improvement." *Journal of Primary Prevention* 9(1/2):130–39.

——. 1997. "Occupational Social Work." In R. L. Edwards, ed., *Encyclopedia of Social Work*, 19th ed., pp. 1779–86. Washington, D.C.: National Association of Social Workers Press.

Akabas, S. and L. Gates. 1995. *Planning for Disability Management: An Approach to Controling Costs While Caring for Employees.* Scottsdale, Ariz.: American Compensation Association.

Akabas, S., L. Gates, and D. Galvin. 1992. *Disability Management: A Complete System to Reduce Costs, Increase Productivity, Meet Employee Needs and Ensure Legal Compliance.* New York: AMACOM.

Akabas, S., L. Gates, and B. Warren. 1996. *College and University Disability Management: A Guide for Developing and Implementing Successful Programs.* Horsham, Pa.: LRP Publications.

Brayfield, A. 1995. "Juggling Jobs and Kids: The Impact of Employment Schedules on Fathers' Caring for Children." *Journal of Marriage and the Family* 57(2):321–32.

Brenner, M. 1973. *Mental Illness and the Economy.* Cambridge, Mass.: Harvard University Press.

Coulton, C. 1996. "Poverty, Work and Community: A Research Agenda for an Era of Diminished Federal Responsibility." *Social Work* 41(5):509–19.

Crawley, B. 1992. "The Transformation of the American Labor Force: Elder African-Americans and Occupational Social Work." *Social Work* 37(1):41–45.

DiNitto, D. 1988. "Drunk, Drugged, and on the Job." In G. Gould and M. Smith, eds., *Social Work in the Workplace: Practice and Principles,* pp. 75–95. New York: Springer.

Fine, M., S. Akabas, and S. Bellinger. 1982. "Cultures of Drinking: A Workplace Perspective." *Social Work* 27(5):436–40.

Folbre, N. 1995. *The New Field Guide to the U.S. Economy.* New York: New Press.

Freud, S. 1930. *Civilization and Its Discontents.* New York: W. W. Norton.

Gates, L., S. Akabas, and V. Oran-Sabia. 1998. "Relationship Accommodations Involving the Work Group: Improving Work Prognosis for Persons with Mental Health Conditions." *Psychiatric Rehabilitation Journal* 21(3):264–72.

Gates, L., Y. Taler, and S. Akabas. 1989. "Optimizing Return to Work Among Newly Disabled Workers." *Benefits Quarterly* 5(2):19–27.

Glass, J. and S. Estes. 1997. "The Family Responsive Workplace." *Annual Review of Sociology* 23:289–313.

Gliedman, J. and W. Roth. 1980. *The Unexpected Minority.* New York: Harcourt Brace Jovanovich.

Googins, B. and D. Burden. 1987. "Vulnerability of Working Parents: Balancing Work and Home Roles." *Social Work* 32(4):295–300.

Googins, B. and B. Davidson. 1993. "The Organization As Client: Broadening the Concept of Employee Assistance Programs." *Social Work* 38(4):477–84.

Gullotta, T. 1984. "Comment: Unemployment and Mental Health." *Journal of Primary Prevention* 4(1):3–4.

Gummer, B. 1998. "Current Perspectives on Diversity in the Workforce: How Diverse Is Diverse?" *Administration in Social Work* 22(1):83–111.

Hanson, M. 1993. "Serving the Substance Abuser in the Workplace." In P. Kurzman and S. Akabas, eds., *Work and Well-Being: The Occupational Social Work Advantage,* pp. 218–38. Washington, D.C.: National Association of Social Workers Press.

Heilman, M., C. Block, and P. Stathatos. 1997. "The Affirmative Action Stigma of Incompetence: Effects of Performance Information Ambiguity." *Academy of Management Journal* 40(3):603–25.

Hochschild, A. 1997. *The Time Bind: When Work Becomes Home and Home Becomes Work.* New York: Metropolitan Books.

Hockenberry, J. 1995. *Moving Violations: A Memoir—War Zones, Wheelchairs and Declarations of Independence.* New York: Hyperion.

Hopkins, K. 1997. "Supervisor Intervention with Troubled Workers: A Social Identity Perspective." *Human Relations* 50(10):1215–38.

House, J. 1981. *Work Stress and Social Support.* Reading, Mass.: Addison-Wesley.

Jones, L. 1990. "Unemployment and Child Abuse." *Families in Society: The Journal of Contemporary Human Services* 71(10):579–88.

Judy, R. and C. D'Amico. 1997. *Workforce 2020.* Indianapolis, Ind.: Hudson Institute.

Kahne, H. 1994. "Part-time Work: A Reassessment for a Changing Economy." *Social Service Review* 68(3):417–36.

Kamerman, S. and A. Kahn. 1987. *The Responsive Workplace.* New York: Columbia University Press.

Keefe, T. 1984. "The Stress of Unemployment." *Social Work* 29(3):264–68.

Kola, L. and R. Dunkle. 1988. "Eldercare in the Workplace." *Social Casework* 51(10): 569–74.

Lambert, S. 1993. "Workplace Policies As Social Policy." *Social Service Review* 67(2): 237–60.

Lambert, S. and K. Hopkins. 1995. "Occupational Conditions and Workers' Sense of Community: Variations by Gender and Race." *American Journal of Community Psychology* 23(2):151–79.

Lechner, V. 1993a. "Social Support and Stress Reduction Among Workers Caring for Dependent Parents." *Social Work* 38(4):461–69.

———. 1993b. "Racial Group Responses to Work and Parent Care." *Families in Society: The Journal of Contemporary Human Services* 74(2):93–103.

Lerner, M. 1980. "Stress at the Work Place: The Approach of the Institute for Labor and Mental Health." *Catalyst* 8:75–82.

Levy, A. 1993. "Stigma Management: A New Clinical Service." *Families in Society: The Journal of Contemporary Human Services* 73(4):226–31.

Lewin, T. 1999. "Father Awarded $375,000 in a Paternal Leave Case." *New York Times,* February 3, p. A9.

Liebow, E. 1967. *Tally's Corner: A Study of Negro Street Corner Men.* Boston: Little Brown.

Mauer, H. 1981. *Not Working.* New York: New American Library.

Meyers, M. and T. Heintze. 1999. "The Performance of the Child Care Subsidy System." *Social Service Review* 73(1):37–64.

Mishel, L., J. Bernstein, and J. Schmitt. 1997. *The State of Working America 1996–97.* Armonk, N.Y.: M. E. Sharpe.

Mudrick, N. 1991. "An Underdeveloped Role for Occupational Social Work: Facilitating the Employment of People with Disabilities." *Social Work* 36(6):490–95.

National Organization on Disability. 1998. *The 1998 N.O.D./Harris Survey of Americans with Disabilities.* New York: Louis Harris & Associates.

Orlin, M. 1995. "The Americans with Disabilities Act: Implications for Social Services." *Social Work* 40(2):233–39.

Ozawa, M. 1982. "Work and Social Policy." In P. Kurzman and S. Akabas, eds., *Work and Well-Being: The Occupational Social Work Advantage,* pp. 32–60. Washington, D.C.: National Association of Social Workers Press.

Perlman, H. H. 1968. *Persona—Social Role and Personality.* Chicago: University of Chicago.

Peters, T. J. and R. H. Waterman, Jr. 1982. *In Search of Excellence: Lessons from America's Best-Run Companies.* New York: Harper & Row.

Peters, T. J. and R. H. Waterman, Jr. 1983. *In Search of Excellence: Lessons from America's Best Run Companies.* New York: Harper & Row.

Piechowski L. 1992. "Mental Health and Women's Multiple Roles." *Families in Society: The Journal of Contemporary Human Services* 73(3):131–39.

Raber, M. 1996. "Downsizing of the Nation's Labor Force and a Needed Social Work Response." *Administration in Social Work* 20(1):47–58.

Redcliff, K. and J. Bogan. 1988. "Unemployed Women: When 'Social' Is Not Supportive." *Social Problems* 35(1):54–63.

Root, L. 1993. "Unemployment and Underemployment: A Policy and Program-Development Perspective." In P. Kurzman and S. Akabas, eds., *Work and Well-Being: The Occupational Social Work Advantage,* pp. 332–49. Washington, D.C.: National Association of Social Workers Press.

Sales, E. 1995. "Surviving Unemployment: Economic Resources and Job Loss Duration in Blue-Collar Households." *Social Work* 40(4):483–94.

Seck, E., W. Finch Jr., M. Mor-Baran, and L. Poverty. 1993. "Managing a Diverse Workforce." *Administration in Social Work* 17(2):67–79.

Steinhauer, J. 1999. "For Women in Medicine, a Road to Compromise, Not Perks." *New York Times,* March 1, p. A1.

Stoddard, S., L. Jans, J. Ripple, and L. Kraus. 1998. *Chartbook on Work and Disability in the United States, 1998.* An InfoUse Report. Washington, D.C.: U.S. National Institute on Disability and Rehabilitation Research.

Tice, C. 1994. "A Community's Response to Supported Employment: Implications for Social Work Practice." *Social Work* 39(6):728–48.

Trice, H. and W. Sonnenstuhl. 1985. "Constructive Confrontation and Counseling." *EAP Digest* 5(3):31–36.

U.S. Bureau of the Census. 1998. *Statistical Abstract of the United States: 1998,* 118th ed., Washington, D.C.: U.S. Government Printing Office.

Vigilante, F. 1993. "Work: Its Use in Assessment and Intervention with Clients in the Workplace." In P. Kurzman and S. Akabas, eds., *Work and Well-Being: The Occupational Social Work Advantage,* pp. 179–99. Washington, D.C.: National Association of Social Workers Press.

Vosler, N. 1994. "Displaced Manufacturing Workers and Their Families: A Research-Based Practice Model." *Families in Society: The Journal of Contemporary Human Services* 75(2):105–17.

Wagner, D. 1994. "Beyond the Pathologizing of Nonwork: Alternative Activities in a Street Community." *Social Work* 39:718–27.

Waldfogel, J. 1997. "Understanding the 'Family Gap' in Pay for Women with Children." *Journal of Economic Perspectives* 12(1):137–56.

Walsh, J. and S. Gust. 1986. *Consensus Summary: Interdisciplinary Approaches to the Problem of Drug Abuse in the Workplace.* Rockville, Md.: National Institute on Drug Abuse.

Weissman, M. 1973. "The Educated Housewife: Mild Depression and the Search for Work." *American Journal of Orthopsychiatry* 43(4):565–73.

Weiner, H., S. Akabas, and J. Sommer. 1973. *Mental Health Care in the World of Work.* New York: Association Press.

Wetzel, J. 1978. "The Work Environment and Depression: Implication for Intervention." In J. Hanks, ed., *Toward Human Dignity: Social Work in Practice,* pp. 236–45. Washington, D.C.: National Association of Social Workers Press.

AUTHOR INDEX